FOURTH EDITION

THE STRATEGY PROCESS

Concepts, Contexts, Cases

Henry Mintzberg
McGill University

Joseph Lampel
City University, London

James Brian Quinn
Dartmouth College

Sumantra Ghoshal
London Business School

Prentice
Hall

Upper Saddle River, New Jersey 07458

Library of Congress Cataloging-in-Publication Data

The strategy process: concepts, contexts, cases / Henry Mintzberg . . . [et al.].—4th ed.
    p. cm.
    Rev. ed. of: The strategy process / Henry Mintzberg, James Brian Quinn. 3rd ed. ©1996.
    Includes bibliographical references and index.
    ISBN 0-13-047913-6
    1. Strategic planning. 2. Strategic planning—Case studies. I. Mintzberg, Henry. II.
Mintzberg, Henry. Strategy process.

HD30.28 .Q53 2002
658.4′012—dc21
2002025120

VP/Editor-in-Chief:	Jeff Shelstad
Sr. Managing Editor (Editorial):	Jennifer Glennon
Assistant Editor:	Melanie Olsen
Editorial Assistant:	Kevin Glynn
Media Project Manager:	Michele Faranda
Sr. Marketing Manager:	Shannon Moore
Marketing Assistant:	Christine Genneken
Managing Editor (Production):	Judy Leale
Production Editor:	Theresa Festa
Permissions Coordinator:	Suzanne Grappi
Associate Director, Manufacturing:	Vincent Scelta
Production Manager:	Arnold Vila
Manufacturing Buyer:	Michelle Klein
Designer:	Blair Brown
Interior Design:	Karen Quigley
Cover Design:	Blair Brown
Illustrator (Interior):	UG / GGS Information Services, Inc.
Manager, Print Production:	Christy Mahon
Composition:	UG / GGS Information Services, Inc.
Full-Service Project Management:	UG / GGS Information Services, Inc.

Credits and acknowledgments borrowed from other sources and reproduced, with permission, in this textbook appear on appropriate page within text.

Pearson Education LTD.
Pearson Education Australia PTY, Limited
Pearson Education Singapore, Pte. Ltd
Pearson Education North Asia Ltd
Pearson Education, Canada, Ltd
Pearson Educación de Mexico, S.A. de C.V.
Pearson Education—Japan
Pearson Education Malaysia, Pte. Ltd

10 9 8 7 6 5 4 3 2 1
ISBN 0-13-047913-6

CONTENTS

Acknowledgments   viii
Introduction   ix

SECTION I   STRATEGY   1

CHAPTER 1   Strategies   2

1.1   Five Ps for Strategy   3
1.2   Strategies for Change   10
1.3   What Is Strategy?   16
1.4   Reflecting on the Strategy Process   22

CHAPTER 2   Strategists   30

2.1   The Manager's Job   32
2.2   Artists, Craftsmen, and Technocrats   46
2.3   Good Managers Don't Make Policy Decisions   52
2.4   The Leader's New Work: Building Learning Organizations   57
2.5   In Praise of Middle Managers   66

CHAPTER 3   Formulating Strategy   70

3.1   The Concept of Corporate Strategy   72
3.2   Evaluating Business Strategy   80
3.3   Strategic Intent   88

CHAPTER 4 Analyzing Strategy 92

4.1 How Competitive Forces Shape Strategy 94
4.2 Looking Inside for Competitive Advantage 102
4.3 Sustaining Superior Performance: Commitments and Capabilities 105
4.4 Competitive Maneuvering 112
4.5 Generic Strategies 115
4.6 A Guide to Strategic Positioning 127

CHAPTER 5 Strategy Formation 139

5.1 Crafting Strategy 141
5.2 Strategy as Strategic Decision Making 149
5.3 The Honda Effect 152
5.4 Honda Mythology and the Strategy Industry 160

CHAPTER 6 Strategic Change 166

6.1 Transforming Organizations 168
6.2 Convergence and Upheaval: Managing the Unsteady Pace of Organizational Evolution 176
6.3 Logical Incrementalism: Managing Strategy Formation 183
6.4 The Crescendo Model of Rejuvenation 189

SECTION II FORCES 199

CHAPTER 7 Cognition 200

7.1 The Dangers of Objectivity 201
7.2 Strategy as Cognition 203

CHAPTER 8 Organization 207

8.1 The Structuring of Organizations 209
8.2 Strategy and Organization Planning 226
8.3 The Design of New Organizational Forms 234

CHAPTER 9 Technology 242

9.1 Customizing Customization 243
9.2 Avoiding the Pitfalls of Emerging Technologies 248

CHAPTER 10   Collaboration   256

10.1   Collaborating to Compete   257
10.2   Why Create Alliances   261
10.3   Creating Knowledge Through Collaboration   267

CHAPTER 11   Globalization   272

11.1   Managing Across Borders: New Organizational Responses   273
11.2   Global Strategy . . . in a World of Nations   280
11.3   Seven Myths Regarding Global Strategy   289

CHAPTER 12   Values   294

12.1   New Values, Morality, and Strategic Ethics   295
12.2   Leadership in Administration   300
12.3   A New Manifesto for Management   303

SECTION III   CONTEXTS   311

CHAPTER 13   Managing Start-Ups   312

13.1   The Entrepreneurial Organization   315
13.2   Competitive Strategy in Emerging Industries   323
13.3   How Entrepreneurs Craft Strategies that Work   326

CHAPTER 14   Managing Maturity   334

14.1   The Machine Organization   336
14.2   Cost Dynamics: Scale and Experience Effects   350
14.3   Innovation in Bureaucracy   356
14.4   Challenges to Organizations and Information Technology   361

CHAPTER 15   Managing Experts   370

15.1   The Professional Organization   372
15.2   Managing Intellect   383
15.3   Balancing the Professional Service Firm   390
15.4   Covert Leadership: Notes on Managing Professionals   398

CHAPTER 16   Managing Innovation   403

     16.1   The Innovative Organization   405
     16.2   Managing in the Whitespace   419
     16.3   Anticipating the Cellular Form   423
     16.4   The Core Competencies of Project-Based Firms   426

CHAPTER 17   Managing Diversity   432

     17.1   The Diversified Organization   434
     17.2   Managing Large Groups in the East and West   445
     17.3   From Competitive Advantage to Corporate Strategy   451

CHAPTER 18   Managing Otherwise   460

     18.1   Beyond Configuration   462
     18.2   Organizational Adaptation   468
     18.3   Strategy Innovation and the Quest for Value   471
     18.4   How We Went Digital Without a Strategy   475
     18.5   Managing Quietly   479

Bibliography for Readings   484
Name Index   487
Subject Index   489

CASES 1

1 Robin Hood 3

2 Astral Records, Ltd., North America 5

3 MacArthur and the Philippines 27

4 Rudi Gassner and the Executive Committee of BMG International (A) 40

5 Arista Records 53

6 Algodonera del Plata 57

7 HBO 62

8 IMPSAT 66

9 Canon: Competing on Capabilities 75

10 MP3.com 88

11 WFNX-101.7FM and Boston's Radio Wars 93

12 Beijing Mirror Corp. 109

13 Lufthansa 2000: Maintaining the Change Momentum 124

14 The London Free Press (A)—A Strategic Change 146

15 NBC 156

16 LVMH: Taking the Western *Art de Vivre* to the World 160

17 Kami Corporation 171

18 Strategic Planning at the New York Botanical Garden (A) 176

19 Napoleon Bonaparte: Victim of an Inferior Strategy? 190

20 Honda Motor Company 1994 200

21 The Acer Group: Building an Asian Multinational 217

22 AmBev: The Making of a Brazilian Giant 229

23 Wipro Corporation: Balancing the Future 234

24 TV Asahi Theatrical Productions, Inc. 254

25 Selkirk Group in Asia 263

26 Sportsmake: A Crisis of Succession 273

27 S.A. Chupa Chups 276

28 Mountbatten and India 290

29 Saatchi & Saatchi: Worldwide: Globalization and Diversification 309

30 McKinsey & Company: Managing Knowledge and Learning 319

31 Sony: Regeneration (A) 333

32 Reorganization at Axion Consulting (A) 348

33 Reorganization at Axion Consulting (B) 350

34 Empire Plastics 352

35 Kao Corporation 355

36 Unipart Group of Companies: Uniting Stateholders to Build a World-Class Enterprise 370

37 Workbrain Corporation 382

38 Warner Brothers 390

39 Intel Corporation 394

40 The National Bicycle Industrial Company: Implementing a Strategy of Mass-Customization 411

41 NovaCare, Inc. 423

42 Lechabile: IT as a People Business 435

43 Phil Chan 447

44 Natura: The Magic Behind Brazil's Most Admired Company 455

45 Restaurant with a Difference 474

Case Notes 476

Name Index 481

Subject Index 484

ACKNOWLEDGMENTS

This book was originally brought together by James Brian Quinn and Henry Mintzberg, in the belief that the field of strategy badly needed a new kind of textbook. We wanted one that looked at process as well as analysis; that was built around dynamic strategy concepts and contexts instead of the overworked dichotomy of formulation and implementation; and that accomplished these aims in an intelligent, eclectic, and lively style. We sought to combine theory with practice, as well as description with prescription, in new ways that offered insights none could achieve alone. All of these goals remain exactly the same in this fourth edition.

This edition adds Joseph Lampel and Sumantra Ghoshal to the authorship. As Brian Quinn has retired from his long and impressive career at the Tuck School at Dartmouth, not least with the generation of so many impressive cases, Joseph Lampel of London's City University has taken over responsibility for the case portion of the book, as well as providing help on the selection of the readings. We have kept a number of Brian Quinn's most popular cases, and we have added many new cases of an especially international variety (probably unmatched in this regard by any other business textbook). Sumantra Ghoshal of the London Business School has contributed a number of these cases, as well as several articles. Henry Mintzberg of McGill University has retained responsibility for the readings, which have undergone the greatest revision since the inception of this book. We have kept earlier ones that worked in the belief that good readings do not go out of date; rather they age like good wine. But we have also found many good new readings, amounting to about half of all of those published in this edition compared with the previous one.

We wish to express our warmest appreciation to a number of people who have been helpful, especially Santa Balanca-Rodrigues, Chahrazed Abdallah, Pushkar Jha, and Daniel Ronen, and at Prentice Hall Jennifer Glennon, Theresa Festa, David Scheffer, and Geraldine Lyons.

A special thanks must also be offered to those who worked with the book in its early stages: the many classes of "guinea pig" McGill and Tuck M.B.A. students and our many professional and academic colleagues who made useful suggestions, taught from the book on an experimental basis, and thoughtfully commented on how to improve it. In particular, we thank Bill Joyce, Rich D'Aveni, Philip Anderson, and Sydney Finkelstein at Tuck; John Voyer at University of Southern Maine; Bill Davidson at the University of Southern California; Pierre Brunet and Bill Taylor at Concordia University in Montreal; Fritz Reiger at the University of Windsor; Jan Jorgensen, Cynthia Hardy, and Tom Powell at McGill; Robert Burgelman at Stanford; and Franz Lohrke and Gary Castrogiovanni at Louisiana State University.

One last word: This book is not finished. Like the subject of so much of its content, our text is an ongoing process, not a static statement. There are all kinds of opportunities for improvement. Please write to any of us with your suggestions on how to improve the readings, the cases, and the organization of the book at large and its presentation. Strategy making, we believe, is a learning process; we are also engaged in a learning process. Thank you and enjoy what follows.

Henry Mintzberg
Joseph Lampel
James Brian Quinn
Sumantra Ghoshal

INTRODUCTION

In our first edition, we set out to produce a different kind of textbook in the field of strategy, or general management.

We tried to provide the reader with a richness of theory, a richness of practice, and a strong basis for linkage between the two. We rejected the strictly case study approach, which leaves theory out altogether, or soft-pedals it, and thereby denies the accumulated benefits of many years of careful research and thought about management processes. We also rejected an alternate approach that forces on readers a highly rationalistic model of how the strategy process *should* function. We collaborated on this book because we believe that in this complex world of organizations a range of concepts is needed to cut through and illuminate particular aspects of that complexity.

There is no "one best way" to create strategy, nor is there "one best form" of organization. Quite different forms work well in particular contexts. We believe that exploring a fuller variety systematically will create a deeper and more useful appreciation of the strategy process. In this revised edition, we remain loyal to these beliefs and objectives, while making major changes in the readings and cases. We kept some of the classic readings, but there are many new ones.

A host of new cases provide rich vehicles for discussing the value and limits of new management approaches and the dimensions of new management issues. There is a conscious balance among small, medium, and large-scale companies. They are entrepreneurial, innovative, rapidly growing, or slowly maturing; and they run the gamut from consumer goods to high technology. We have made an effort to select cases from new areas of the economy, such as microelectronics, digital technology, software, personal computers, as well as areas that have been around for a while but are increasingly important, including media, entertainment, pharmaceuticals, and management consulting. Companies such as Sony, Acer, LVMH, Kami Corporation, S.A. Chupa Chups, and National Bicycle Industrial Company represent some of the most exciting experiments in products and services, and management itself, today. We have also set out to offer the most international set of cases available. Glance down the list of cases included in this book and you realize how widely we have covered the globe.

This text, unlike most others, is therefore eclectic. Presenting published articles and portions of other books in their original form, rather than filtered through our minds and pens, is one way to reinforce this variety. Each author has his or her ideas and his or her own best way of expressing them (ourselves included!). Summarized by us, these readings would lose a good deal of their richness.

We do not apologize for contradictions among the ideas of leading thinkers. The world is full of contradictions. The real danger lies in using pat solutions to a nuanced reality, not in opening perspectives up to different interpretations. The effective strategist is one who can live with contradictions, learn to appreciate their causes and effects, and reconcile them sufficiently for effective action. The readings have, nonetheless, been ordered by chapter to suggest some ways in which reconciliation can be considered. Our own chapter introductions are also intended to assist in this task and to help place the readings in perspective.

ON THEORY

A word on theory is in order. We do not consider theory a dirty word, nor do we apologize for making it a major component of this book. To some people, to be theoretical is to be detached and impractical. But a bright social scientist once said, "There is nothing so practical as a good theory." And every successful doctor, engineer, and physicist would have to agree: They would be unable to practice their modern work without theories. Theories are useful because they shortcut the need to store masses of data. It is easier to remember a simple framework about some phenomenon than it is to consider every small detail you ever observed. In a sense theories are a bit like cataloging systems in libraries: The world would be impossibly confusing without them. They enable you to store and conveniently access your own experiences as well as those of others.

One can, however, suffer not just from an absence of theories but also from being dominated by them without realizing it. To paraphrase the words of John Maynard Keynes, most "practical men" are the slaves of some defunct theory. Whether we realize it or not, our behavior is guided by the systems of ideas that we have internalized over the years. Much can be learned by bringing these out in the open, examining them more carefully, and comparing them with alternative ways to view the world—including ones based on systematic study (that is, research). One of our prime intentions in this book is to expose the limitations of conventional theories and to offer alternate explanations that can be superior guides for understanding and taking action in specific contexts.

PRESCRIPTIVE THEORY VERSUS DESCRIPTIVE THEORY

Unlike many textbooks in this field, this one tries to explain the world as it is rather than as someone thinks it is *supposed* to be. Although there has sometimes been a tendency to disdain such *descriptive* theories, *prescriptive* (or normative) ones have often been the problem, rather than the solution, in the field of management. There is no one best way in management; no prescription works for all organizations. Even when a prescription seems effective in some context, it requires a sophisticated understanding of exactly what that context is and how it functions. In other words, one cannot decide reliably what should be done in a system as complicated as a contemporary organization without a genuine understanding of how that organization really works. In engineering, no student ever questions having to learn physics, in medicine, having to learn anatomy. Imagine an engineering student's hand shooting up in physics class: "Listen, prof, it's fine to tell us how the atom does work. But what we really want to know is how the atom *should* work." Why should a management student's similar demand in the realm of strategy or structure be considered any more appropriate? How can people manage complex systems they do not understand?

Nevertheless, we have not ignored prescriptive theory when it appears useful. A number of prescriptive techniques (industry analysis, experience curves, and so on) are discussed. But these are associated both with other readings and with cases that will help you understand the context and limitations of their usefulness. Both readings and cases offer opportunities to pursue the full complexity of strategic situations. You will find a wide range of issues and perspectives addressed. One of our main goals is to integrate a variety of views, rather than allow strategy to be fragmented into just "human issues" and "economics issues." The text and cases provide a basis for treating the full complexity of strategic management.

ON SOURCES

How were the readings selected and edited? Some textbooks boast about how new all their readings are. We make no such claim; indeed we would like to make a different boast; many of our readings have been around quite a while, long enough to mature, like fine wine. Our criterion for inclusion was not the newness of the article so much as the quality of its insight—that is, its ability to explain some aspect of the strategy process better than any other article. Time does not age the really good articles. Quite the opposite—it distinguishes their quality. So look here for classics from the 1950s still fully relevant alongside the latest thinking in this new millennium.

We are, of course, not biased toward old articles—just toward good ones. Hence, the materials in this book range from the classics to some published just before our final selection was made (as well as a few hitherto unpublished pieces). You will find articles from the most serious academic journals, the best practitioner magazines, books, and some very obscure sources. The best can sometimes be found in strange places.

We have tried to include many shorter readings rather than fewer longer ones, and we have tried to present as wide a variety of good ideas as possible while maintaining clarity. To do so we often had to cut within readings. We have, in fact, put a great deal of effort into the cutting in order to extract the key messages of each reading in as brief, concise, and clear a manner as possible. Unfortunately, our cutting sometimes forced us to eliminate interesting examples and side issues. (In the readings, as well as some of the case materials from published sources, dots . . . signify portions that have been deleted from the original, while square brackets [ ] signify our own insertions of minor clarifications into the original text). We apologize to you, the reader, as well as to the authors, for having done this, but hope that the overall result has rendered these changes worthwhile.

We have also included a number of our own works. Perhaps we are biased, having less objective standards by which to judge what we have written. But we have messages to convey, too, and our own writings do examine the basic themes that we feel are important in policy and strategy courses today.

ON CASES

A major danger of studying the strategy process—probably the most enticing subject in the management curriculum, and at the pinnacle of organizational processes—is that students and professors can become detached from the basics of the enterprise. The "Don't bore me with the operating details; I'm here to tackle the really big issues?" syndrome has been the death of many strategy courses (not to mention managerial practices!). Effective strategy processes always come down to specifics. For this reason, cases are the most convenient way to introduce practice into the classroom, to cap a wide variety of experiences, and to involve students actively in analysis and decision making.

Cases are the pedagogical approach of choice when it comes to studying strategy, but it is an approach with potential pitfalls and blind alleys. It is easy to lose sight of the fact that cases are selective narratives. In this respect, short and tightly focused cases can be better than long and highly detailed cases: They are less likely to mislead one into seeing the narrative as recreation of reality, as opposed to representation of reality, and a partial one at that.

Though cases are partial representation of reality, they can be revealing if used wisely. Most cases pose a dilemma or a problem. They irresistibly draw us toward prescription. An invitation to pronounce is appealing: how many can resist being the CEO of IBM or Microsoft for a day? However, this is false empowerment. It is not only based on incomplete information (made worse by the illusion of comprehensive description), it also lacks the pressure and nuance that are indispensable to decision making.

Cases are positive when they are used to illustrate and stimulate. They illustrate situations and dilemmas. They stimulate thinking by focusing minds on crucial issues, forcing the student to struggle with questions without the comfort of pretending that questions posed in the classroom can be settled in the classroom.

Our cases consciously contain both descriptive and prescriptive aspects of strategy, and as authors of this text, we have different views on which to use—description only, or description with prescription. On the one hand, the cases provide the data and background for making a major decision. Students can appraise the situation in its full context, suggest what future directions would be best for the organization in question, and discuss how their solutions can realistically be implemented. On the other hand, each case is also an opportunity to understand the dynamics of an organization—the historical context of the problems it faces, the influence of its technology, values, relationship to other organizations, its probable reactions to varying solutions, and so on. Unlike many cases which focus on only the analytical aspects of a decision, ours constantly force you to consider the messy realities of arriving at decisions in organizations and obtaining a desired response to any decision. In these respects, case study can involve a good deal of descriptive *and* prescriptive analysis.

LINKING CASES AND READINGS

The cases in this book are not intended to emphasize any particular theories, any more than the theoretical materials are included because they explain particular cases. Each case presents a slice of some specific reality, each reading a conceptual interpretation of some phenomenon. The readings are placed in particular groupings because they approach some common aspects or issues in theory.

We have provided some general guidelines for relating particular cases to sets of readings. But do not push this too far: study each case for its own sake. Cases are intrinsically richer than readings. Each contains a wide variety of issues—many awfully messy—in no particular order. The readings, in contrast, are usually neat and tidy, professing one or a few basic conceptual ideas, and providing some specific vocabulary. When the two connect—sometimes through direct effort, more often indirectly as conceptual ideas are recalled in the situation of a particular case— some powerful learning can take place in the form of clarification and, we hope, revelation.

Try to see how particular theories can help you to understand some of the issues in the cases and provide useful frameworks for drawing conclusions. Perhaps the great military theorist, Von Clausewitz, said it best almost two centuries ago:

> All that theory can do is give the artist or soldier points of reference, and standards of evaluation, with the ultimate purpose not of telling him how to act but of developing his judgment. (1976:15)

In relating theory to cases bear in mind that sound judgment depends on knowing the limitations of the former and the incompleteness of the latter. Theories compartmentalize reality. You should not take this compartmentalization as a given. Go beyond it when preparing each case. Use whatever concepts you find helpful both from chapters of the book and from your personal knowledge. Likewise, bear in mind that cases never tell the whole story (how could they!). This is rather evident in ones that deal with real people and real companies. Because they leave out so much, it is worthwhile to reach out to newspapers, Websites, Who's Who, or any other reference that comes to mind. Some of our cases, however, present imaginary situations, but should not for this reason be considered unreal. Their intent is to enhance awareness of key issues by avoiding the bias that comes with our accidental knowledge of actual companies and events.

CASE DISCUSSION

Management cases provide a concrete information base for students to analyze and share as they discuss management issues. Without this focus, discussions of theory can become quite confusing. You may have in mind an image of an organization or a situation that is very different from that of other discussants. As a result, what appears to be a difference in theory will—after much argument—often turn out to be simply a difference in perception of the realities surrounding these examples.

In this text we try to provide three levels of learning: first, a chance to share the generalized insights of leading theoreticians (in the readings); second, an opportunity to test the applicability and limits of these theories in specific (case) situations; third, the capacity to develop one's own special amalgam of insights based upon empirical observations and inductive reasoning (from case analyses). All are useful approaches; some students and professors will find one mix more productive for their special level of experience or mindset. Another will prefer a quite different mix. Hence, we include a wide selection of cases and readings.

The cases are not intended as examples of either weak or exceptionally good management practices. Nor, as we noted, do they provide examples of the concepts of a particular reading. They are discussion vehicles for probing the benefits and limits of various approaches. And they are analytical vehicles for applying and testing concepts and tools developed in your education and experience. Cases can have marketing, operations, accounting, financial, human relations, planning and control, external environmental, ethical, political, and quantitative dimensions. Each dimension should be addressed in preparations and classroom discussions, although some aspects will inevitably emerge as more important in one situation than another.

In each case you should look for several sets of issues. First, you should understand what went on in that situation. Why did it happen this way? What are the strong or weak features of what happened? What could have been changed to advantage? How? Why? Second, there are always issues of what should be done next. What are the key issues to be resolved? What are the major alternatives available? What outcomes could the organization expect from each? Which alternative should it select? Why? Third, there will almost always be "hard" quantitative data and "soft" qualitative impressions about each situation. Both deserve attention.

But remember, no realistic strategy situation is just an organization behavior problem or just a financial or economic analytical one. Both sets of information should be considered, and an integrated solution developed. Our cases are consciously constructed for this. Given their complexity we have tried to keep the cases as short as possible. And we have tried to capture some of the flavour of the real organization. Moreover, we have sought to mix product and services cases, technological and "non-tech" cases, entrepreneurial, small company, and large enterprise situations. In this cross section, we have tried to capture some of the most important and exciting issues, concepts, and products of our times. We believe management is fun and important. The cases try to convey this.

There is no "correct" answer to any case. There may be several "good" answers and many poor ones. The purpose of a strategy course should be to help you understand the nature of these "better" answers, what to look for, how to analyze alternatives, and how to see through the complexities of reaching solutions and implanting them in real organizations. A strategy course can only improve your probability of success, not ensure it. The total number of variables in a real strategy situation is typically beyond the control of any one person or group. Hence another caveat; do not rely excessively on performance as a criteria for evaluating the effectiveness of a strategy. A company may have succeeded or failed not because of its specific decisions, but because of luck, an outstanding personality, the bizarre action of an opponent, international actions over which it had no control, and so on. One of the products of a successful strategy course should be a little humility.

CASE STUDY GUIDES

In our last edition we posed a few questions at the end of each case. In this edition we decided to drop the questions. A crucial part of reflection and analysis in the classroom, as in the real world, is coming up with the question that really matters. Asking the right question in strategy is analogous to an explorer's finding his or her bearing before starting the journey. There is no standard methodology for coming up with questions: intuition and experience play far too important a role in the process.

The cases provide a rich soil for investigating strategic realities. Their complexities always extend well below the surface. Each layer peeled back can reveal new insights and rewards. Like any good mystery story, a case provides many clues, never all, but, surprisingly, sometimes more than managers might have had time to absorb in the real situation.

Believing that no "canned approach" is viable for *all* strategic situations, we have selected cases that cut across a variety of issues and theoretical constructs. Almost any of these cases contains sufficient richness and complexity that it can be positioned at a number of different spots in a good strategy course. We leave the final case selection to the style and wisdom of the professor and his or her students.

THIS BOOK'S STRUCTURE

NOT FORMULATION, THEN IMPLEMENTATION

The first edition of this text offered a chapter format that was new to the strategy field. Unlike most others, it had no specific chapter or section devoted to "implementation" per se. The assumption in other texts is that strategy is formulated and then implemented, with organizational structures, control systems, and the like following obediently behind strategy. In this text, as in reality, formulation and implementation are intertwined as complex interactive processes in which politics, values, organizational culture, and management styles determine or constrain particular strategic decisions. And strategy, structure, and systems mix together in complicated ways to influence outcomes. While strategy formulation and implementation may be separated in some situations—perhaps in crises, in some totally new ventures, as well as in organizations facing predictable futures—these events are far from typical. We certainly do not believe in building a whole book (let alone a whole field) around this conceptual distinction.

BUT CONCEPTS, THEN CONTEXTS

The readings are divided roughly into two different parts. The first deals with *concepts,* the second with *contexts.* We introduce concepts early in the text as equal partners in the complex web of ideas that make up what we call "the strategy process." In the second half of the text we weave these concepts together in a number of distinct situations, which we call *contexts.*

Our theme diagram illustrates this. Concepts, shown on top, are divided into two groups—strategy and forces—

to represent the first two sections of the book. Contexts draw all these concepts together, in a variety of situations—covered in the third section—which we consider the key ones in the field of strategy today (though hardly the only ones). The outline of the text, chapter by chapter, proceeds as follows:

Section I: Strategy

The first section is called *Strategy;* it comprises six chapters, two introductory in nature and four on the processes by which strategy making takes place. Chapter 1 introduces strategies themselves and probes the meaning of this important word to broaden your view of it. Here the pattern is set of challenging you to question conventional views, especially when these act to narrow perspectives. The themes introduced in this chapter carry throughout the book and are worth care in understanding.

Chapter 2 introduces a very important set of actors in this book, the *strategists*—all those people who play key roles in the strategy process. In examining the work of the general manager and other strategists, we shall perhaps upset a number of widely accepted notions. We do this to help you understand the very real complexities and difficulties of making strategy and managing in contemporary organizations.

Chapters 3 to 5 take up a theme that is treated extensively in the text—to the point of being reflected in its title: the development of an understanding of the *processes* by which strategies are made. Chapter 3 looks at *formulating strategy,* specifically at some widely accepted prescriptive models for how organizations should go about developing their strategies. Chapter 4 extends these ideas to more formal ways of *analyzing strategy* and considering what, if any, "generic" forms a strategy can take. While readings in later chapters will challenge some of these precepts, what will not be questioned is the importance of having to understand them. They are fundamental to appreciating the strategy process today.

Chapter 5 switches from a prescriptive to a descriptive approach. Concerned with understanding *strategy formation,* it considers how strategies actually *do* form in organizations (not necessarily by being formulated) and *why* different processes may be effective in specific circumstances. This text takes an unconventional stand by viewing planning and other formal approaches as not the only—and often indeed not even the most desirable—ways to make strategy. You will find our emphasis on the descriptive process—as an equal partner with the more traditional concerns for technical and analytical issues—to be one of the unifying themes of this book. Chapter 6 then turns attention to the nature of *strategic change,* and how this can come about.

STRATEGY PROCESS THEME DIAGRAM

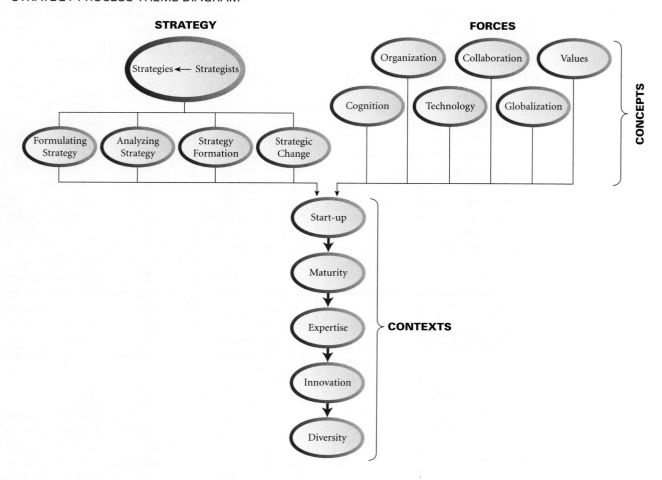

STRATEGY

Strategies ← Strategists

Formulating Strategy

Analyzing Strategy

Strategy Formation

Strategic Change

FORCES

Organization

Collaboration

Values

Cognition

Technology

Globalization

CONCEPTS

Start-up

Maturity

Expertise

Innovation

Diversity

CONTEXTS

Section II: Forces

In Section I, the readings introduced strategy, the strategist, and various ways in which strategy might be formulated and does in fact form. In Section II, entitled *Forces,* we introduce six additional concepts that constitute part of the strategy process.

In Chapter 7, the influence of *cognition* is discussed. Strategy is fundamentally a concept in people's minds, and so how we think about it—our cognitive process—must be understood. Chapter 8 looks at *organization,* how we put together and design those institutions for which strategies are created. Chapter 9 takes up another key force in the process, namely *technology.* We turn in Chapter 10 to the nature of *collaboration* as it influences the strategy process, from collaboration among individuals to alliances among corporations. Chapter 11 looks at *globalization,* that very popular yet over-hyped notion about which most of us need much more careful understanding. Last in this section, but

certainly not least, is consideration of the *values* that drive us all. Together, these six forces must be understood if modern day processes of strategy making are to be appreciated.

Section III: Contents

Section III is called *Contexts.* We consider how all of the elements introduced so far—strategies, the processes by which they are formulated and get formed, the strategists, cognition, organization, technology, collaboration, globalization and values—combine to suit particular contexts, five in all.

Chapter 13 deals with *managing start-up,* where often rather simple organizations come under the close control of strong leaders, or "entrepreneurs," frequently people with vision. Chapter 14 examines *managing maturity,* a context common to many large business and government organizations involved in the mass production and/or distribution of goods and services.

Chapters 14 and 15 consider *managing experts* and *managing innovation,* two contexts involving organizations of high expertise. In the first, experts work relatively independently in rather stable conditions, while in the innovation context, they combine in project teams under more dynamic conditions. What these two contexts have in common, however, is that they act in ways that upset many of the widely accepted notions about how organizations should be structured and make strategy.

Chapter 17 considers *managing diversity,* and deals with organizations that have diversified their product or service line and usually divisionalized their structures to deal with the greater varieties of environments they face. Finally, Chapter 18, called *Managing Otherwise,* closes the book by considering some rather unconventional views of the strategy process and of organizations that work despite being so different—and upsetting cherished beliefs. You don't have to be unusual to succeed, but you do have to be tolerant of the unusual to be a successful manager.

In considering each of these widely different contexts we seek to discuss the situation in which each is most likely to be found, the structures most suited to it, the kinds of strategies that tend to be pursued, the processes by which these strategies tend to be formed and might be formulated, and the social issues associated with the context.

Instructors' Supplements

The fourth edition of *The Strategy Process* is accompanied by a comprehensive Instructor's Manual and a Companion Website. The Instructor's Manual includes detailed summaries of all readings and discussion questions for each chapter, as well as Teaching Notes for the cases in each section. The accompanying Website features the materials included in the Instructor's Manual in an electronic format.

Well, there you have it. We worked hard on this book, in both the original and revised editions, to get it right. We have tried to think things through from the basics, with a resulting text that in style, format, and content is unusual for the field of strategy. Our product may not be perfect, but we believe it is good. Now it's your turn to find out if you agree. Enjoy yourself along the way.

Henry Mintzberg
Joseph Lampel
James Brian Quinn
Sumantra Ghoshal

ABOUT THE AUTHORS

HENRY MINTZBERG

Henry Mintzberg is Cleghorn Professor of Management Studies at McGill University in Montreal, Canada. His research has dealt with issues of general management and organizations, focusing on the nature of managerial work, forms of organizing, and the strategy formation process. Currently, he is completing a book about *Developing Managers, not MBAs,* and a pamphlet entitled *Getting Past Smith and Marx . . . Towards a Balanced Society.* He is also promoting the development of a family of masters programs for practicing managers. His own teaching activities focus on ad hoc seminars for managers and work with doctoral students.

He received his doctorate and master of science degrees from the M.I.T. Sloan School of Management and his mechanical engineering degree from McGill, working in between in operational research for the Canadian National Railways. He has recently been named an Officer of the Order of Canada and of l'Ordre Nationale du Quebec and holds honorary degrees from thirteen universities. He also served as President of the Strategic Management Society from 1988 to 1991, and is an elected Fellow of the Royal Society of Canada (the first from a management faculty), the Academy of Management, and the International Academy of Management. He was named Distinguished Scholar for the year 2000 by the Academy of Management.

JOSEPH LAMPEL

Joseph Lampel is Professor of Strategy at City University Business School, London. He received his doctorate in Strategic Management from McGill University in 1990, and was awarded Best Dissertation Award from the Administrative Science Association of Canada. Following his graduate studies Professor Lampel taught for seven years at the Stern School of Business, New York University. He subsequently moved to the United Kingdom where he held positions at University of St. Andrews and the University of Nottingham. Professor Lampel is the coauthor of *The Strategy Safari* with Henry Mintzberg and Bruce Ahalstrand. He has published extensively on strategy in management journals, and his articles have also appeared in the *Financial Times* and *Fortune Magazine.*

JAMES BRIAN QUINN

Professor Quinn is a recognized authority in the fields of strategic planning, management of technological change, entrepreneurial innovation, and management of intellect and technology in the services sector. He has received both the Academy of Management's prestigious Outstanding Educator Award and its Book of the Year award (for *Intelligent Enterprise*).

SUMANTRA GHOSHAL

Sumantra Ghoshal is Professor of Strategic and International Management at the London Business School. He also serves as the Founding Dean of the Indian School of Business in Hyderabad, of which LBS is a partner, and as a member of The Committee of Overseers of the Harvard Business School. *Managing Across Borders: The Transnational Solution,* a book he coauthored with Christopher Bartlett, has been listed in the *Financial Times* as one of the 50 most influential management books and has been translated into nine languages. *The Differentiated Network: Organizing the Multinational Corporation for Value Creation,* a book he coauthored with Nitin Nohria, won the George Terry Book Award in 1997. *The Individualized Corporation,* coauthored with Christopher Bartlett, won the Igor Ansoff Award in 1997, and has been translated into seven languages. His last book, *Managing Radical Change,* won the Management Book of the Year award in India. With doctoral degrees from both the MIT School of Management and the Harvard Business School, Sumantra serves on the editorial boards of several academic journals and has been nominated to the Fellowships at the Academy of Management, the Academy of International Business, and the World Economic Forum.

SECTION I

Strategy

CHAPTER 1

Strategies

We open this text on its focal point: strategy. The first section is called "Strategy," the first chapter, "Strategies." Later chapters in this section describe the role of strategists and consider the processes by which strategies develop from three perspectives: deliberate formulation, systematic analysis, and emergent formation. A last chapter looks at strategic change. But in this opening chapter, we consider the central concept—strategies themselves.

What is strategy? There is no single, universally accepted definition. Various authors and managers use the term differently; for example, some include goals and objectives as part of strategy whereas others make firm distinctions between them. Our intention in including the following readings is not to promote any one view of strategy but rather to suggest a number of views that seem useful. As will be evident throughout this text, our wish is not to narrow perspectives but to broaden them by trying to clarify issues. In pursuing these readings, it will be helpful to think about the meaning of strategy, to try to understand how different people have used the term, and later to see if certain definitions hold up better in particular contexts.

The first reading, by coauthor Henry Mintzberg of McGill University in Montreal, serves to open up the concept of strategy to a variety of views, some very different from traditional writings. Mintzberg focuses on various distinct definitions of strategy as plan (as well as ploy), pattern, position, and perspective. He uses the first two of these definitions to take us beyond deliberate strategy—beyond the traditional view of the term—to the notion of *emergent* strategy. This introduces the idea that strategies can form in an organization without being consciously intended, that is, without being *formulated*. This may seem to run counter to the whole thrust of the strategy literature, but Mintzberg argues that many people implicitly use the term this way even though they would not so define it.

The reading that follows, an award-winning article by Michael Porter of the Harvard Business School, takes us to a different place. Here Porter, probably the best-known writer in the field of strategy, focuses on strategy as a tightly integrated, clearly cohesive, and highly deliberate concept that positions a firm for competitive advantage. Porter suggests that excessive concern with operational effectiveness has displaced attention to strategy. Competitive strategy is about being different from one's rivals. This consists of tailoring a set of activities to support a strategic position. Defending this position, however, depends on crafting trade-offs that competitors will find very hard to imitate.

Our third reading in this chapter, by coauthors Mintzberg and Joseph Lampel of London's City University, "reflects" on the strategy process, specifically by introducing ten perspectives, or schools of thought, that describe the field today. Strategy is an elephant, they argue, and we are all the proverbial blind men grabbing at its different parts and pretending to understand the whole. These schools—and, more importantly, their interrelationships—reappear continually throughout this book so that, in a sense, this reading helps to introduce the book, too.

Upon completion of these readings, we hope that you will be less sure of the use of the word *strategy* but more ready to tackle the study of the strategy process with a broadened perspective and an open mind. There are no universally right answers in this field (any more than there are in most other fields), but there are interesting and constructive perspectives.

USING THE CASE STUDIES

Explicit and intuitive understanding is essential for understanding strategy. Sometimes, however, the issue of what strategy is to begin with is very much at the forefront of such understanding. The Robin Hood case strongly illustrates the multiple facets of strategy. One can argue with Porter in the reading "What Is Strategy?" that Robin Hood begins to have a strategy only when he starts to ask serious questions about what he is doing and where he is going. Or one can take Mintzberg's view in "Five Ps for Strategy" and argue that Robin Hood's actions, at different times, conform to different definitions of strategy.

Porter's insistence on a single definition of strategy works best in cases such as Apple Computer 1999, Selkirk, Acer, Inc., Sony, and Warner Brothers, where managers are asking hard questions about the future direction of the company. However, when one looks at cases such as Honda Motor Company, LVMH, and AmBev, which take the long view, it is possible to argue with Mintzberg and Lampel in "Reflecting on the Strategy Process" that there is no single school of strategy but rather different schools depending on assumptions and perspectives.

READING 1.1

FIVE Ps FOR STRATEGY*

BY HENRY MINTZBERG

■ Human nature insists on a definition for every concept. But the word *strategy* has long been used implicitly in different ways even if it has traditionally been defined in only one. Explicit recognition of multiple definitions can help people to maneuver through this difficult field. Accordingly, five definitions of strategy are presented here—as plan, ploy, pattern, position, and perspective—and some of their interrelationships are then considered.

*Originally published in the *California Management Review* (Fall 1987), © 1987 by the Regents of the University of California. Reprinted with deletions by permission of the *California Management Review*.

CHAPTER 1 STRATEGIES **3**

STRATEGY AS PLAN

To almost anyone you care to ask, **strategy is a plan**—some sort of *consciously intended* course of action, a guideline (or set of guidelines) to deal with a situation. A kid has a "strategy" to get over a fence, a corporation has one to capture a market. By this definition, strategies have two essential characteristics: they are made in advance of the actions to which they apply, and they are developed consciously and purposefully. A host of definitions in a variety of fields reinforce this view. For example:

- in the military: Strategy is concerned with "draft[ing] the plan of war . . . shap[ing] the individual campaigns and within these, decid[ing] on the individual engagements" (Von Clausewitz, 1976:177).
- in game theory: Strategy is "a complete plan: a plan which specifies what choices [the player] will make in every possible situation" (von Newman and Morgenstern, 1944:79).
- in management: "Strategy is a unified, comprehensive, and integrated plan . . . designed to ensure that the basic objectives of the enterprise are achieved" (Glueck, 1980:9).

As plans, strategies may be general or they can be specific. There is one use of the word in the specific sense that should be identified here. As plan, a **strategy can be a ploy**, too, really just a specific "maneuver" intended to outwit an opponent or competitor. The kid may use the fence as a ploy to draw a bully into his yard, where his Doberman pinscher awaits intruders. Likewise, a corporation may threaten to expand plant capacity to discourage a competitor from building a new plant. Here the real strategy (as plan, that is, the real intention) is the threat, not the expansion itself, and as such is a ploy.

In fact, there is a growing literature in the field of strategic management, as well as on the general process of bargaining, that views strategy in this way and so focuses attention on its most dynamic and competitive aspects. For example, in his popular book, *Competitive Strategy*, Porter (1980) devotes one chapter to "Market Signals" (including discussion of the effects of announcing moves, the use of "the fighting brand," and the use of threats of private antitrust suits) and another to "Competitive Moves" (including actions to preempt competitive response). And Schelling (1980) devotes much of his famous book, *The Strategy of Conflict*, to the topic of ploys to outwit rivals in a competitive or bargaining situation.

STRATEGY AS PATTERN

But if strategies can be intended (whether as general plans or specific ploys), surely they can also be realized. In other words, defining strategy as a plan is not sufficient; we also need a definition that encompasses the resulting behavior. Thus, a third definition is proposed: **strategy is a pattern**—specifically, a pattern in a stream of actions (Mintzberg and Waters, 1985). By this definition, when Picasso painted blue for a time, that was a strategy, just as was the behavior of the Ford Motor Company when Henry Ford offered his Model T only in black. In other words, by this definition, strategy is *consistency* in behavior, *whether or not* intended.

This may sound like a strange definition for a word that has been so bound up with free will ("strategos" in Greek, the art of the army general [Evered 1983]). But the fact of the matter is that while hardly anyone defines strategy in this way, many people seem at one time or another to so use it. Consider this quotation from a business executive: "Gradually the successful approaches merge into a pattern of action that becomes our strategy. We certainly don't have an overall strategy on this" (quoted in Quinn, 1980:35). This comment is inconsistent only if we restrict ourselves to one definition of strategy: what this man seems to be saying is that his firm has strategy as pattern, but not as plan. Or consider this comment in *Business Week* on a joint venture between General Motors and Toyota:

> The tentative Toyota deal may be most significant because it is another example of how GM's strategy boils down to doing a little bit of everything until the market decides where it is going. (*Business Week*, October 31, 1983)

A journalist has inferred a pattern in the behavior of a corporation and labeled it strategy.

The point is that every time a journalist imputes a strategy to a corporation or to a government, and every time a manager does the same thing to a competitor or even to the senior management of his own firm, they are implicitly defining strategy as pattern in action—that is, inferring consistently in behavior and labeling it strategy. They may, of course, go further and impute intention to that consistency—that is, assume there is a plan behind the pattern. But that is an assumption, which may prove false.

Thus, the definitions of strategy as plan and pattern can be quite independent of each other: plans may go unrealized, while patterns may appear without preconception. To paraphrase Hume, strategies may result from human actions but not human designs (see Majone, 1976–77). If we label the first definition *intended* strategy and the second *realized* strategy, as shown in Figure 1, then we can distinguish *deliberate* strategies, where intentions that existed previously were realized, from *emergent* strategies, where patterns developed in the absence of intentions, or despite them (which went *unrealized*).

For a strategy to be truly deliberate—that is, for a pattern to have been intended *exactly* as realized—would seem to be a tall order. Precise intentions would have had to be stated in advance by the leadership of the organization; these would have had to be accepted as is by everyone else, and then realized with no interference by market, technological, or political forces and so on. Likewise, a truly emergent strategy is again a tall order, requiring consistency in action without any hint of intention. (No consistency means *no* strategy, or at least unrealized strategy.) Yet some strategies do come close enough to either form, while others—probably most—sit on the continuum that exists between the two, reflecting deliberate as well as emergent aspects. Table 1 lists various kinds of strategies along this continuum.

STRATEGIES ABOUT WHAT?

Labeling strategies as plans or patterns still begs one basic question: *strategies about what?* Many writers respond by discussing the deployment of resources, but the question remains: which resources and for what purposes? An army may plan to reduce the number of nails in its shoes, or a corporation may realize a pattern of marketing only products painted black, but these hardly meet the lofty label "strategy." Or do they?

As the word has been handed down from the military, "strategy" refers to the important things, "tactics" to the details (more formally, "tactics teaches the use of armed forces in the engagement, strategy the use of engagements for the object of the war" [von Clausewitz, 1976:128]). Nails in shoes, colors of cars; these are certainly details. The problem is that in retrospect details can sometimes prove "strategic." Even in the military: "For want of a Nail, the Shoe was lost; for want of a Shoe the Horse was lost . . . ," and so on through the rider and general to the battle, "all for want of Care about a Horseshoe Nail" (Franklin, 1977: 280).

FIGURE 1
DELIBERATE AND
EMERGENT
STRATEGIES

TABLE 1
VARIOUS KINDS OF
STRATEGIES, FROM
RATHER DELIBERATE
TO MOSTLY
EMERGENT*

Planned Strategy: Precise intentions are formulated and articulated by a central leadership, and backed up by formal controls to ensure their surprise-free implementation in an environment that is benign, controllable, or predictable (to ensure no distortion of intentions); these strategies are highly deliberate.

Entrepreneurial Strategy: Intentions exist as the personal, unarticulated vision of a single leader, and so are adaptable to new opportunities; the organization is under the personal control of the leader and located in a protected niche in its environment; these strategies are relatively deliberate but can emerge too.

Ideological Strategy: Intentions exist as the collective vision of all the members of the organization, controlled through strong shared norms; the organization is often proactive vis-à-vis its environment; these strategies are rather deliberate.

Umbrella Strategy: A leadership in partial control of organizational actions defines strategic targets or boundaries within which others must act (for example, that all new products be high priced and at the technological cutting edge, although what these actual products are to be is left to emerge); as a result, strategies are partly deliberate (the boundaries) and partly emergent (the patterns within them); this strategy can also be called deliberately emergent, in that the leadership purposefully allows others the flexibility to maneuver and form patterns within the boundaries.

Process Strategy: The leadership controls the process aspects of strategy (who gets hired and so gets a chance to influence strategy, what structures they work within, etc.), leaving the actual content of strategy to others; strategies are again partly deliberate (concerning process) and partly emergent (concerning content), and deliberately emergent.

Disconnected Strategy: Members or subunits loosely coupled to the rest of the organization produce patterns in the streams of their own actions in the absence of, or in direct contradiction to the central or common intentions of the organization at large; the strategies can be deliberate for those who make them.

Consensus Strategy: Through mutual adjustment, various members converge on patterns that pervade the organization in the absence of central or common intentions; these strategies are rather emergent in nature.

Imposed Strategy: The external environment dictates patterns in actions, either through direct imposition (say, by an outside owner or by a strong customer) or through implicitly preempting or bounding organizational choice (as in a large airline that must fly jumbo jets to remain viable); these strategies are organizationally emergent, although they may be internalized and made deliberate.

*Adapted from Mintzberg and Waters (1985:270).

Indeed one of the reasons Henry Ford lost his war with General Motors was that he refused to paint his cars anything but black.

Rumelt (1980) notes that "one person's strategies are another's tactics—that what is strategic depends on where you sit." It also depends on *when* you sit; what seems tactical today may prove strategic tomorrow. The point is that labels should not be used to imply that some issues are *inevitably* more important than others. There are times when it pays to manage the details and let the strategies emerge for themselves. Thus, there is good reason to refer to issues as more or less "strategic," in other words, more or less "important" in some context, whether as intended before acting or as realized after it. Accordingly, the answer to the question, strategy about what, is: potentially about anything. About products and processes, customers and citizens, social responsibilities and self-interests, control and color.

Two aspects of the content of strategies must, however, be singled out because they are of particular importance.

STRATEGY AS POSITION

The fourth definition is that **strategy is a position**—specifically, a means of locating an organization in what organization theorists like to call an "environment." By this definition, strategy becomes the mediating force—or "match," according to Hofer and Schendel (1978:4)—between organization and environment, that is, between the internal and the external context. In ecological terms, strategy becomes a "niche"; in economic terms, a place that generates "rent" (that is, "returns to [being] in a 'unique' place" [Bowman, 1974:47]); in management terms, formally, a product-market "domain" (Thompson, 1967), the place in the environment where resources are concentrated.

Note that this definition of strategy can be compatible with either (or all) of the preceding ones; a position can be preselected and aspired to through a plan (or ploy) and/or it can be reached, perhaps even found, through a pattern of behavior.

In military and game theory views of strategy, it is generally used in the context of what is called a "two-person game," better known in business as head-on competition (where ploys are especially common). The definition of strategy as position, however, implicitly allows us to open up the concept, to so-called n-person games (that is, many players), and beyond. In other words, while position can always be defined with respect to a single competitor (literally so in the military, where position becomes the site of battle), it can also be considered in the context of a number of competitors or simply with respect to markets or an environment at large. But strategy as position can extend beyond competition too, economic and otherwise. Indeed, what is the meaning of the word "niche" but a position that is occupied to *avoid* competition. Thus, we can move from the definition employed by General Ulysses Grant in the 1860s, "Strategy [is] the deployment of one's resources in a manner which is most likely to defeat the enemy," to that of Professor Richard Rumelt in the 1980s, "Strategy is creating situations for economic rents and finding ways to sustain them" (Rumelt, 1982), that is, any viable position, whether or not directly competitive.

Astley and Fombrun (1983), in fact, take the next logical step by introducing the notion of "collective" strategy, that is, strategy pursued to promote cooperation between organizations, even would-be competitors (equivalent in biology to animals herding together for protection). Such strategies can range "from informal arrangements and discussions to formal devices such as interlocking directorates, joint ventures, and mergers." In fact, considered from a slightly different angle, these can sometimes be described as *political* strategies, that is, strategies to subvert the legitimate forces of competition.

STRATEGY AS PERSPECTIVE

While the fourth definition of strategy looks out, seeking to locate the organization in the external environment, and down to concrete positions, the fifth looks inside the organization, indeed inside the heads of the collective strategist, but up to a broader view. Here, **strategy is a perspective**, its content consisting not just of a chosen position, but of an ingrained way of perceiving the world. There are organizations that favor marketing and build a whole ideology around that (an IBM); Hewlett-Packard has developed the "H-P way," based on its engineering culture, while McDonald's has become famous for its emphasis on quality, service, and cleanliness.

Strategy in this respect is to the organization what personality is to the individual. Indeed, one of the earliest and most influential writers on strategy (at least as his ideas have been reflected in more popular writings) was Philip Selznick (1957:47), who wrote about the "character" of an organization—distinct and integrated "commitments to ways of acting and responding" that are built right into it. A variety of concepts from other fields also capture this notion; anthropologists refer to the "culture" of a society and sociologists to its "ideology"; military theorists write of the "grand strategy" of armies; while management theorists have used terms such as the "theory of the business" and its "driving force" (Drucker, 1974; Tregoe and Zimmerman, 1980); and Germans perhaps capture it best with their word "Weltanschauung," literally "world view," meaning collective intuition about how the world works.

This fifth definition suggests above all that strategy is a *concept*. This has one important implication, namely, that all strategies are abstractions which exist only in the minds of interested parties. It is important to remember that no one has ever seen a strategy or touched one; every strategy is an invention, a figment of someone's imagination, whether conceived of as intentions to regulate behavior before it takes place or inferred as patterns to describe behavior that has already occurred.

What is of key importance about this fifth definition, however, is that the perspective is *shared*. As implied in the words *Weltanschauung, culture,* and *ideology* (with respect to a society), but not the word *personality*, strategy is a perspective shared by the members of an organization, through their intentions and/or by their actions. In effect, when we are talking of strategy in this context, we are entering the realm of the *collective mind*—individuals united by common thinking and/or behavior. A major issue in the study of strategy formation becomes, therefore, how to read that collective mind—to understand how intentions diffuse through the system called organization to become shared and how actions come to be exercised on a collective yet consistent basis.

INTERRELATING THE Ps

As suggested above, strategy as both position and perspective can be compatible with strategy as plan and/or pattern. But, in fact, the relationships between these different definitions can be more involved than that. For example, while some consider perspective to *be* a plan (Lapierre, 1980, writes of strategies as "dreams in search of reality"), others describe it as *giving rise to* plans (for example, as positions and/or patterns in some kind of implicit hierarchy). But the concept of emergent strategy is that a pattern can emerge and be recognized so that it gives rise to a formal plan, perhaps within an overall perspective.

We may ask how perspective arises in the first place. Probably through earlier experiences: the organization tried various things in its formative years and gradually consolidated a perspective around what worked. In other words, organizations would appear to develop "character" much as people develop personality—by interacting with the world as they find it through the use of their innate skills and natural propensities. Thus pattern can give rise to perspective too. And so can position. Witness Perrow's (1970:161) discussion of the "wool men" and "silk men" of the textile trade, people who developed an almost religious dedication to the fibers they produced.

No matter how they appear, however, there is reason to believe that while plans and positions may be dispensable, perspectives are immutable (Brunsson, 1982). In other words, once they are established, perspectives become difficult to change. Indeed, a perspective may become so deeply ingrained in the behavior of an organization that the associated beliefs can become subconscious in the minds of its members. When that happens, perspective can come to look more like pattern than like plan—in other words, it can be found more in the consistency of behaviors than in the articulation of intentions.

Of course, if perspective is immutable, then change in plan and position within perspective is easy compared to change of perspective. In this regard, it is interesting to take up the case of Egg McMuffin. Was this product when new—the American breakfast in a bun—a strategic change for the McDonald's fast-food chain? Posed in MBA classes, this earth-shattering (or at least stomach-shattering) question inevitably evokes heated debate. Proponents (usually people sympathetic to fast food) argue that of course it was: it brought McDonald's into a new market, the breakfast one, extending the use of existing facilities. Opponents retort that this is nonsense; nothing changed but a few ingredients: this was the same old pap in a new package. Both sides are, of course, right—and wrong. It simply depends on how you define strategy. Position changed; perspective remained the same. Indeed—and this is the point—the position could be changed easily because it was compatible with the existing perspective. Egg McMuffin is pure McDonald's, not only in product and package, but also in production and propagation. But imagine a change of position at McDonald's that would require a change of perspective—say, to introduce candlelight dining with personal service (your McDuckling à l'Orange cooked to order) to capture the late evening market. We needn't say more, except perhaps to label this the "Egg McMuffin syndrome."

THE NEED FOR ECLECTICISM IN DEFINITION

While various relationships exist among the different definitions, no one relationship, nor any single definition for that matter, takes precedence over the others. In some ways, these definitions compete (in that they can substitute for each other), but in perhaps more important ways, they complement. Not all plans become patterns nor are all patterns that develop planned; some ploys are less than positions, while other strategies are more than positions yet less than perspectives. Each definition adds important elements to our understanding of strategy, indeed encourages us to address fundamental questions about organizations in general.

As plan, strategy deals with how leaders try to establish direction for organizations, to set them on predetermined courses of action. Strategy as plan also raises the fundamental issue of cognition—how intentions are conceived in the human brain in the first place, indeed, what intentions really mean. The road to hell in this field can be paved with those who take all stated intentions at face value. In studying strategy as plan, we must somehow get into the mind of the strategist, to find out what is really intended.

As ploy, strategy takes us into the realm of direct competition, where threats and feints and various other maneuvers are employed to gain advantage. This places the process of strategy formation in its most dynamic setting, with moves provoking countermoves and so on. Yet ironically, strategy itself is a concept rooted not in change but in stability—in set plans and established patterns. How then to reconcile the dynamic notions of strategy as ploy with the static ones of strategy as pattern and other forms of plan?

As pattern, strategy focuses on action, reminding us that the concept is an empty one if it does not take behavior into account. Strategy as pattern also introduces the notion of convergence, the achievement of consistency in an organization's behavior. How does this consistency form, where does it come from? Realized strategy, when considered alongside intended strategy, encourages us to consider the notion that strategies can emerge as well as be deliberately imposed.

As position, strategy encourages us to look at organizations in their competitive environments—how they find their positions and protect them in order to meet competition, avoid it, or subvert it. This enables us to think of organizations in ecological terms, as organisms in niches that struggle for survival in a world of hostility and uncertainty as well as symbiosis.

And finally as perspective, strategy raises intriguing questions about intention and behavior in a collective context. If we define organization as collective action in the pursuit of common mission (a fancy way of saying that a group of people under a common label—whether a General Motors or a Luigi's Body Shop—somehow finds the means to cooperate in the production of specific goods and services), then strategy as perspective raises the issue of how intentions diffuse through a group of people to become shared as norms and values, and how patterns of behavior become deeply ingrained in the group.

Thus, strategy is not just a notion of how to deal with an enemy or a set of competitors or a market, as it is treated in so much of the literature and its popular usage. It also draws us into some of the most fundamental issues about organizations as instruments for collective perception and action.

To conclude, a good deal of the confusion in this field stems from contradictory and ill-defined uses of the term strategy. By explicating and using various definitions, we may be able to avoid some of this confusion, and thereby enrich our ability to understand and manage the processes by which strategies form.

READING 1.2

**BY JAMES BRIAN
QUINN**

**SOME USEFUL
DEFINITIONS**

Because the words *strategy, objectives, goals, policy,* and *programs* have different meanings to individual readers or to various organizational cultures, I [try] to use certain definitions consistently. . . . For clarity—not pedantry—these are set forth as follows:

A **strategy** is the *pattern* or *plan* that *integrates* an organization's *major* goals, policies, and action sequences into a *cohesive* whole. A well-formulated strategy helps to *marshal* and *allocate* an organization's resources into a *unique and viable posture* based on its relative *internal competencies* and *shortcomings*, anticipated *changes in the environment*, and contingent moves by *intelligent opponents*.

Goals (or **objectives**) state *what* is to be achieved and *when* results are to be accomplished, but they do not state *how* the results are to be achieved. All organizations have multiple goals existing in a complex hierarchy (Simon, 1964): from value objectives, which express the broad value premises toward which the company is to strive; through overall organizational objectives, which establish the intended *nature* of the enterprise and the *directions* in which it should move; to a series of less permanent goals that define targets for each organizational unit, its subunits, and finally all major program activities within each subunit. Major goals—those that affect the entity's overall direction and viability—are called *strategic goals.*

Policies are rules or guidelines that express the *limits* within which action should occur. These rules often take the form of contingent decisions for resolving conflicts among specific objectives. For example: "Don't exceed three months' inventory in any item without corporate approval." Like the objectives they support, policies exist in a hierarchy throughout the organization. Major policies—those that guide the entity's overall direction and posture or determine its viability—are called *strategic policies.*

Programs specify the *step-by-step sequence of actions* necessary to achieve major objectives. They express *how* objectives will be achieved within the limits set by policy. They ensure that resources are committed to achieve goals, and they provide the dynamic track against which progress can be measured. Those major programs that determine the entity's overall thrust and viability are called *strategic programs.*

Strategic decisions are those that determine the overall direction of an enterprise and its ultimate viability in light of the predictable, the unpredictable, and the unknowable changes that may occur in its most important surrounding environments. They intimately shape the true goals of the enterprise. They help delineate the broad limits within which the enterprise operates. They dictate both the resources the enterprise will have accessible for its tasks and the principal patterns in which these resources will be allocated. And they determine the effectiveness of the enterprise—whether its major thrusts are in the right directions given its resource potentials—rather than whether individual tasks are performed efficiently. Management for efficiency, along with the myriad decisions necessary to maintain the daily life and services of the enterprise, is the domain of operations.

---

*Excerpted from James Brian Quinn, *Strategies for Change: Logical Incrementalism* (copyright © Richard D. Irwin, Inc. 1980), Chaps. 1 and 5; reprinted by permission of the publisher.

STRATEGIES VERSUS TACTICS

Strategies normally exist at many different levels in any large organization. For example, in government there are world trade, national economic, treasury department, military spending, investment, fiscal, monetary supply, banking, regional development, and local reemployment strategies—all related to each other somewhat hierarchically yet each having imperatives of its own. Similarly, businesses have numerous strategies from corporate levels to department levels within divisions. Yet if strategies exist at all these levels, how do strategies and tactics differ? Often the primary difference lies in the scale of action or the perspective of the leader. What appears to be a "tactic" to the chief executive officer (or general) may be a "strategy" to the marketing head (or lieutenant) if it determines the ultimate success and viability of his or her organization. In a more precise sense, tactics can occur at either level. They are the short-duration, adaptive, action-interaction realignments that opposing forces use to accomplish limited goals after their initial contact. Strategy defines a continuing basis for ordering these adaptations toward more broadly conceived purposes.

A genuine strategy is always needed when the potential actions or responses of intelligent opponents can seriously affect the endeavor's desired outcome—regardless of that endeavor's organizational level in the total enterprise. This condition almost always pertains to the important actions taken at the top level of competitive organizations. However, game theorists quickly point out that some important top-level actions—for example, sending a peacetime fleet across the Atlantic—merely require elaborate coordinative plans and programs (Von Neumann and Morgenstern, 1944; Shubik, 1975; McDonald, 1950). A whole new set of concepts, a true strategy, is needed if some people or nations decide to oppose the fleet's purposes. And it is these concepts that in large part distinguish strategic formulation from simpler programmatic planning.

Strategies may be looked at as either a priori statements to guide action or a posteriori results of actual decision behavior. In most complex organizations . . . one would be hard pressed to find a complete a priori statement of a total strategy that actually is followed. Yet often the existence of a strategy (or strategy change) may be clear to an objective observer, although it is not yet apparent to the executives making critical decisions. One, therefore, must look at the actual emerging *pattern* of the enterprise's operant goals, policies, and major programs to see what its true strategy is (Mintzberg, 1972). Whether it is consciously set forth in advance or is simply a widely held understanding resulting from a stream of decisions, this pattern becomes the real strategy of the enterprise. And it is changes in this pattern—regardless of what any formal strategic documents may say—that either analysts or strategic decision makers must address if they wish to comprehend or alter the concern's strategic posture. . . .

THE CLASSICAL APPROACH TO STRATEGY	Military-diplomatic strategies have existed since prehistoric times. In fact, one function of the earliest historians and poets was to collect the accumulated lore of these successful and unsuccessful life-and-death strategies and convert them into wisdom and guidance for the future. As societies grew larger and conflicts more complex, generals, statesmen, and captains studied, codified, and tested essential strategic concepts until a coherent body of principles seemed to emerge. In various forms these were ultimately distilled into the maxims of Sun Tzu (1963), Machiavelli (1950), Napoleon (1940), Von Clausewitz (1976), Foch (1970), Lenin (1927), Hart (1954), Montgomery (1958), or Mao Tse-Tung (1967). Yet with a few exceptions—largely introduced by modern technology—the most basic principles of strategy were in place and recorded long before the Christian era. More modern institutions primarily adapted and modified these to their own special environments.

Although one could choose any number of classical military-diplomatic strategies as examples, Philip and Alexander's actions at Chaeronea (in 338 B.C.) contain many currently relevant concepts (Varner and Alger, 1978; Green, 1970). . . .

A Classical Strategy

A Grand Strategy

Philip and his young son, Alexander, had very *clear goals*. They sought to rid Macedonia of influence by the Greek city-states and to *establish dominance* over what was then essentially northern Greece. They also wanted Athens to join a coalition with them against Persia on their eastern flank. *Assessing their resources*, they *decided* to avoid the overwhelming superiority of the Athenian fleet and *chose to forego* attack on the powerful walled cities of Athens and Thebes where their superbly trained phalanxes and cavalry would not *have distinct advantages*.

Philip and Alexander *used an indirect approach* when an invitation by the Amphictyonic Council brought their army south to punish Amphissa. In a *planned sequence of actions and deceptive maneuvers*, they cut away from a direct line of march to Amphissa, *bypassed the enemy*, and *fortified a key base*, Elatea. They then took steps to *weaken their opponents politically and morally* by pressing restoration of the Phoenician communities earlier dispersed by the Thebans and by having Philip declared a champion of the Delphic gods. Then *using misleading messages* to make the enemy believe they had moved north to Thrace and also *using developed intelligence sources*, the Macedonians in a *surprise attack* annihilated the Greeks' positions near Amphissa. This *lured their opponents away from their defensive positions* in the nearby mountain passes to *consolidate their forces* near the town of Chaeronea.

There, *assessing the relative strengths* of their opponents, the Macedonians first *attempted to negotiate* to achieve their goals. When this was unsuccessful they had a *well-developed contingency plan* on how to *attack and overwhelm* the Greeks. Prior to this time, of course, the Macedonians had *organized* their troops into the famed phalanxes, and had *developed the full logistics* needed for their field support including a longer spear, which helped the Macedonian phalanxes penetrate the solid shield wall of the heavily massed Greek formations. *Using the natural advantages* of their terrain, the Macedonians had developed cavalry support for their phalanxes' movements far beyond the Greek capability. Finally, using a *relative advantage*—the *command structure* their hierarchical *social system* allowed—against the more democratic Greeks, the Macedonian nobles had *trained their personnel* into one of the most *disciplined and highly motivated forces* in the world.

The Battle Strategy

Supporting this was the battle strategy at Chaeronea, which emerged as follows. Philip and Alexander first *analyzed their specific strengths and weaknesses and their opponents' current alignments and probable moves*. The Macedonian strength lay in their new spear technology, the *mobility* of their superbly disciplined phalanxes, and the powerful cavalry units led by Alexander. Their weaknesses were that they were badly outnumbered and faced—in the Athenians and the Theban Band—some of the finest foot troops in the world. However, their opponents had two weak points. One was the Greek left flank with lightly armed local troops placed near the Chaeronean Acropolis and next to some more heavily armed—but hastily assembled—hoplites bridging to the strong center held by the Athenians. The famed Theban Band anchored the Greek right wing near a swamp on the Cephissus River. [See Figure 1.]

Philip and Alexander *organized their leadership to command key positions*, Philip took over the right wing and Alexander the cavalry. They *aligned their forces* into a *unique posture* which *used their strengths* and *offset their weaknesses*. They decided on those spots at which they would *concentrate their forces*, what *positions to concede*, and what *key points* they *must take and hold*. Starting with their units angled back from the Greek lines (see map), they developed a *focused major thrust* against the Greek left wing and *attacked their opponents' weaknesses*—the troops near Chaeronea—with the most disciplined of the Macedonian units, the guards' brigade. After building up pressure and stretching the Greek line to its left, the guards' brigade abruptly began a *planned withdrawal*. This *feint* caused the Greek left to break ranks and rush forward, believing the Macedonians to be in full retreat. This *stretched the opponents' resources* as the Greek center moved left to *maintain contact* with its flank and to attack the "fleeing" Macedonians.

Then *with predetermined timing*, Alexander's cavalry *attacked the exposure* of the stretched line at the same moment Philip's phalanxes *re-formed as planned* on the high ground at the edge of the Heamon River. Alexander *broke through* and *formed a bridgehead* behind the Greeks. He *refocused his forces against a segment* of the opponents' line; his cavalry *surrounded and destroyed* the Theban Band as the *overwhelming power* of the phalanxes poured through the gap he had created. From its *secured position*, the Macedonian left flank then turned and *attacked the flank* of the Athenians. With the help of Philip's *planned counterattack*, the Macedonians *expanded their dominance and overwhelmed the critical target*, i.e., the Greek center. . . .

FIGURE 1
THE BATTLE OF
CHAERONEA
Source: Modified with permission from P. Green, *Alexander the Great*, Praeger Publishers, New York (1970).

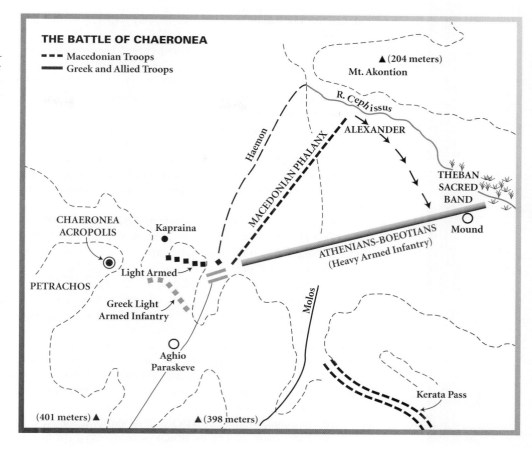

THE BATTLE OF CHAERONEA
- - - Macedonian Troops
—— Greek and Allied Troops

▲ (204 meters)
Mt. Akontion

R. Cephissus

ALEXANDER

MACEDONIAN PHALANX

THEBAN SACRED BAND

CHAERONEA ACROPOLIS

Kapraina

Mound

Light Armed

PETRACHOS

ATHENIANS-BOEOTIANS (Heavy Armed Infantry)

Greek Light Armed Infantry

Molos

Aghio Paraskeve

Kerata Pass

(401 meters) ▲

▲ (398 meters)

MODERN ANALOGIES

Similar concepts have continued to dominate the modern era of formal strategic thought. As this period begins, Scharnhorst still points to the need to *analyze social forces and structures* as a basis for *understanding effective command styles* and *motivational stimuli* (Von Clausewitz, 1976:8). Frederick the Great proved this point in the field. Presumably based on such analyses, he adopted *training, discipline,* and *fast maneuvers* as the central concepts for a tightly disciplined German culture that had to be constantly ready to fight on two fronts (Phillips, 1940). Von Bülow (1806) continued to emphasize the dominant strategic roles of *geographical positioning* and *logistical support systems* in strategy. Both Jomini (1971) and Von Bülow (1806) stressed the concepts of *concentration, points of domination,* and *rapidity of movement* as central strategic themes and even tried to develop them into mathematically precise principles for their time.

Still later Von Clausewitz expounded on the paramountcy of *clear major objectives* in war and on developing war strategies as a component of the nation's *broader goals* with *time horizons* extending beyond the war itself. Within this context he postulated that an effective strategy should be focused around a relatively *few central principles* which can *create, guide,* and *maintain dominance* despite the enormous frictions that occur as one tries to position or maneuver large forces in war. Among these he included many of the concepts operant in Macedonian times: *spirit or morale, surprise, cunning, concentration in space, dominance of selected positions, use of strategic reserves, unification over time, tension and release,* and so on. He showed how these broad principles applied to a number of specific attack, defense, flanking, and retreat situations; but he always stressed the intangible of *leadership.* His basic positioning and organizational principles were to be mixed with boldness, perseverance, and genius. He constantly emphasized—as did Napoleon—the need for *planned flexibility* once the battle was joined.

Later strategic analysts adapted these classic themes for larger-scale conflicts. Von Schlieffen linked together the huge numerical and production *strengths* of Germany and the vast *maneuvering capabilities* of Flanders fields to pull the nation's might together conceptually behind a *unique alignment of forces* ("a giant hayrake"), which would "outflank" his French opponents, *attack weaknesses* (their supply lines and rear), capture and *hold key political centers* of France, and *dominate or destroy* its weakened army in the field (Tuchman, 1962). On the other side, Foch and Grandmaison saw *morale* ("élan"), *nerve* ("cran"), and continuous *concentrated attack* ("attaque à outrance") as *matching the values* of a volatile, recently defeated, and vengeful French nation, which had decided (for both moral and *coalition* reasons) to *set important limits* on its own actions in World War I—that is, not to attack first or through Belgium.

As these two strategies lost shape and became the head-on slaughter of trench warfare, Hart (1954) revitalized the *indirect approach*, and this became a central theme of British strategic thinking between the wars. Later in the United States, Matloff and Snell (1953) began to stress planning for *large-scale coalitions* as the giant forces of World War II developed. The Enigma group *moved secretly to develop the intelligence network* that was so crucial in the war's outcome (Stevenson, 1976). But once engaged in war, George Marshall still saw the only hope for Allied victory in *concentrating overwhelming forces* against one enemy (Germany) first, then after *conceding early losses* in the Pacific, *refocusing Allied forces* in a gigantic *sequential coordinated movement* against Japan. In the eastern theater, MacArthur first *fell back, consolidated a base* for operations, *built up his logistics, avoided his opponent's strengths, bypassed* Japan's established defensive positions, and in a *gigantic flanking maneuver* was ready to invade Japan after *softening its political and psychological will* through saturation bombing (James, 1970).

All these modern thinkers and practitioners utilized classical principles of strategy dating back to the Greek era, but perhaps the most startling analogies of World War II lay in Patton's and Rommel's battle strategies, which were almost carbon copies of the Macedonians' concepts of planned concentration, rapid breakthrough, encirclement, and attack on the enemy's rear (Essame, 1974; Farago, 1964; Irving, 1977; Young, 1974).

Similar concepts still pervade well-conceived strategies—whether they are government, diplomatic, military, sports, or business strategies. What could be more direct than the parallel between Chaeronea and a well-developed business strategy that first probes and withdraws to determine opponents' strengths, forces opponents to stretch their commitments, then concentrates resources, attacks a clear exposure, overwhelms a selected market segment, builds a bridgehead in that market, and then regroups and expands from that base to dominate a wider field? Many companies have followed just such strategies with great success. . . .

DIMENSIONS OF STRATEGY

Analysis of military-diplomatic strategies and similar analogies in other fields provides some essential insights into the basic dimensions, nature, and design of formal strategies.

First, effective formal strategies contain three essential elements: (1) the most important *goals* (or objectives) to be achieved, (2) the most significant *policies* guiding or limiting action, and (3) the major *action sequences* (or programs) that are to accomplish the defined goals within the limits set. Since strategy determines the overall direction and action focus of the organization, its formulation cannot be regarded as the mere generation and alignment of programs to meet predetermined goals. Goal development is an integral part of strategy formulation. . . .

Second, effective strategies develop around a *few key concepts and thrusts*, which give them cohesion, balance, and focus. Some thrusts are temporary; others are carried through to the end of the strategy. Some cost more per unit gain than others. Yet resources must be *allocated in patterns* that provide sufficient resources for each thrust to succeed regardless of its relative cost/gain ratio. And organizational units must be coordinated and actions controlled to support the intended thrust pattern or else the total strategy will. . . .

Third, strategy deals not just with the unpredictable but also with the *unknowable.* For major enterprise strategies, no analyst could predict the precise ways in which all impinging forces could interact with each other, be distorted by nature or human emotions, or be modified by the imaginations and purposeful counteractions of intelligent opponents (Braybrooke and Lindblom, 1963). Many have noted how large-scale systems can respond quite counterintuitively (Forrester, 1971) to apparently rational actions or how a seemingly bizarre series of events can conspire to prevent or assist success (White, 1978; Lindblom, 1959). . . .

Consequently, the essence of strategy—whether military, diplomatic, business, sports, (or) political . . .—is to *build a posture* that is so strong (and potentially flexible) in selective ways that the organization can achieve its goals despite the unforeseeable ways external forces may actually interact when the time comes.

Fourth, just as military organizations have multiple echelons of grand, theater, area, battle, infantry, and artillery strategies, so should other complex organizations have a number of hierarchically related and mutually supporting strategies (Vancil and Lorange, 1975; Vancil, 1976). Each such strategy must be more or less complete in itself, congruent with the level of decentralization intended. Yet each must be shaped as a cohesive element of higher-level strategies. Although, for reasons cited, achieving total cohesion among all of a major organization's strategies would be a superhuman task for any chief executive officer, it is important that there be a systematic means for testing each component strategy and seeing that it fulfills the major tenets of a well-formed strategy.

The criteria derived from military-diplomatic strategies provide an excellent framework for this, yet too often one sees purported formal strategies at all organizational levels that are not strategies at all. Because they ignore or violate even the most basic strategic principles, they are little more than aggregates of philosophies or agglomerations of programs. They lack the cohesiveness, flexibility, thrust, sense of positioning against intelligent opposition, and other criteria that historical analysis suggests effective strategies must contain. Whether formally or incrementally derived, strategies should be at least intellectually tested against the proper criteria.

CRITERIA FOR EFFECTIVE STRATEGY

In devising a strategy to deal with the unknowable, what factors should one consider? Although each strategic situation is unique, are there some common criteria that tend to define a good strategy? The fact that a strategy worked in retrospect is not a sufficient criterion for judging any strategy. Was Grant really a greater strategist than Lee? Was Foch's strategy better than Von Schlieffen's? Was Xerxes's strategy superior to that of Leonidas? Was it the Russians' strategy that allowed them to roll over the Czechoslovaks in 1968? Clearly other factors than strategy—including luck, overwhelming resources, superb or stupid implementation, and enemy errors—help determine ultimate results. Besides, at the time one formulates a strategy, one cannot use the criterion of ultimate success because the outcome is still in doubt. Yet one clearly needs some guidelines to define an effective strategic structure.

A few studies have suggested some initial criteria for evaluating a strategy (Tilles, 1963; Christensen et al., 1978). These include its clarity, motivational impact, internal consistency, compatibility with the environment, appropriateness in light of resources, degree of risk, match to the personal values of key figures, time horizon, and workability. . . . In addition, historical examples—from both business and military-diplomatic settings—suggest that effective strategies should at a minimum encompass certain other critical factors and structural elements. . . .

■ *Clear, decisive objectives:* Are all efforts directed toward clearly understood, decisive, and attainable overall goals? Specific goals of subordinate units may change in the heat of campaigns or competition, but the overriding goals of the strategy for all units must remain clear enough to provide continuity and cohesion for tactical choices during the time horizon of the strategy. All goals need not be written down or numerically precise, but they must be understood and be decisive—that is, if they are achieved they should ensure the continued viability and vitality of the entity vis-à-vis its opponents.

- *Maintaining the initiative:* Does the strategy preserve freedom of action and enhance commitment? Does it set the pace and determine the course of events rather than reacting to them? A prolonged reactive posture breeds unrest, lowers morale, and surrenders the advantage of timing and intangibles to opponents. Ultimately such a posture increases costs, decreases the number of options available, and lowers the probability of achieving sufficient success to ensure independence and continuity.

- *Concentration:* Does the strategy concentrate superior power at the place and time likely to be decisive? Has the strategy defined precisely what will make the enterprise superior in power—that is, "best" in critical dimensions—in relation to its opponents. A distinctive competency yields greater success with fewer resources and is the essential basis for higher gains (or profits) than competitors. . . .

- *Flexibility:* Has the strategy purposely built in resource buffers and dimensions for flexibility and maneuver? Reserved capabilities, planned maneuverability, and repositioning allow one to use minimum resources while keeping opponents at a relative disadvantage. As corollaries of concentration and concession, they permit the strategist to reuse the same forces to overwhelm selected positions at different times. They also force less flexible opponents to use more resources to hold predetermined positions, while simultaneously requiring minimum fixed commitment of one's own resources for defensive purposes.

- *Coordinated and committed leadership:* Does the strategy provide responsible, committed leadership for each of its major goals? . . . [Leaders] must be so chosen and motivated that their own interests and values match the needs of their roles. Successful strategies require commitment, not just acceptance.

- *Surprise:* Has the strategy made use of speed, secrecy, and intelligence to attack exposed or unprepared opponents at unexpected times? With surprise and correct timing, success can be achieved out of all proportion to the energy exerted and can decisively change strategic positions. . . .

- *Security:* Does the strategy secure resource bases and all vital operating points for the enterprise? Does it develop an effective intelligence system sufficient to prevent surprises by opponents? Does it develop the full logistics to support each of its major thrusts? Does it use coalitions effectively to extend the resource base and zones of friendly acceptance for the enterprise? . . .

These are critical elements of strategy, whether in business, government, or warfare.

READING 1.3

BY MICHAEL E. PORTER

I. OPERATIONAL EFFECTIVENESS IS NOT STRATEGY

For almost two decades, managers have been learning to play by a new set of rules. Companies must be flexible to respond rapidly to competitive and market changes. They must benchmark continuously to achieve best practice. They must outsource aggressively to gain efficiencies. And they must nurture a few core competencies in the race to stay ahead of rivals.

---

*Excerpted from "What Is Strategy?" Michael E. Porter, *Harvard Business Review* (November–December 1996).

Positioning—once the heart of strategy—is rejected as too static for today's dynamic markets and changing technologies. According to the new dogma, rivals can quickly copy any market position, and competitive advantage is, at best, temporary.

But those beliefs are dangerous half-truths, and they are leading more and more companies down the path of mutually destructive competition. True, some barriers to competition are falling as regulation eases and markets become global. True, companies have properly invested energy in becoming leaner and more nimble. In many industries, however, what some call *hypercompetition* is a self-inflicted wound, not the inevitable outcome of a changing paradigm of competition.

The root of the problem is the failure to distinguish between operational effectiveness and strategy. The quest for productivity, quality, and speed has spawned a remarkable number of management tools and techniques: total quality management, benchmarking, time-based competition, outsourcing, partnering, reengineering, change management. Although the resulting operational improvements have often been dramatic, many companies have been frustrated by their inability to translate those gains into sustainable profitability. And bit by bit, almost imperceptibly, management tools have taken the place of strategy. As managers push to improve on all fronts, they move farther away from viable competitive positions.

OPERATIONAL EFFECTIVENESS: NECESSARY BUT NOT SUFFICIENT

Operational effectiveness and strategy are both essential to superior performance, which, after all, is the primary goal of any enterprise. But they work in very different ways.

A company can outperform rivals only if it can establish a difference that it can preserve. It must deliver greater value to customers or create comparable value at a lower cost, or do both. The arithmetic of superior profitability then follows: delivering greater value allows a company to charge higher average unit prices; greater efficiency results in lower average unit costs.

Ultimately, all differences between companies in cost or price derive from the hundreds of activities required to create, produce, sell, and deliver their products or services, such as calling on customers, assembling final products, and training employees. Cost is generated by performing activities, and cost advantage arises from performing particular activities more efficiently than competitors. Similarly, differentiation arises from both the choice of activities and how they are performed. Activities, then, are the basic units of competitive advantage. Overall advantage or disadvantage results from all a company's activities, not only a few.

Operational effectiveness (OE) means performing similar activities *better* than rivals perform them. Operational effectiveness includes but is not limited to efficiency. It refers to any number of practices that allow a company to better utilize its inputs by, for example, reducing defects in products or developing better products faster. In contrast, strategic positioning means performing *different* activities from rivals or performing similar activities in *different ways*.

Differences in operational effectiveness among companies are pervasive. Some companies are able to get more out of their inputs than others because they eliminate wasted effort, employ more advanced technology, motivate employees better, or have greater insight into managing particular activities or sets of activities. Such differences in operational effectiveness are an important source of differences in profitability among competitors because they directly affect relative cost positions and levels of differentiation. . . .

Imagine for a moment a *productivity frontier* that constitutes the sum of all existing best practices at any given time. Think of it as the maximum value that a company delivering a particular product or service can create at a given cost, using the best available technologies, skills, management techniques, and purchased inputs. The productivity frontier can apply to individual activities, to groups of linked activities such as order processing and manufacturing, and to an entire company's activities. When a company improves its operational effectiveness, it moves toward the frontier. Doing so may require capital investment, different personnel, or simply new ways of managing.

The productivity frontier is constantly shifting outward as new technologies and management approaches are developed and as new inputs become available. . . .

OE competition shifts the productivity frontier outward, effectively raising the bar for everyone. But although such competition produces absolute improvement in operational effectiveness, it leads to relative improvement for no one. Consider the $5 billion-plus U.S. commercial-printing industry. The major players—R.R. Donnelley & Sons Company, Quebecor, World Color Press, and Big Flower Press—are competing head to head, serving all types of customers, offering the same array of printing technologies (gravure and web offset), investing heavily in the same new equipment, running their presses faster, and reducing crew sizes. But the resulting major productivity gains are being captured by customers and equipment suppliers, not retained in superior profitability. . . .

The second reason that improved operational effectiveness is insufficient—competitive convergence—is more subtle and insidious. The more benchmarking companies do, the more they look alike. The more that rivals outsource activities to efficient third parties, often the same ones, the more generic those activities become. As rivals imitate one another's improvements in quality, cycle times, or supplier partnerships, strategies converge and competition becomes a series of races down identical paths that no one can win. Competition based on operational effectiveness alone is mutually destructive, leading to wars of attrition that can be arrested only by limiting competition.

The recent wave of industry consolidation through mergers makes sense in the context of OE competition. Driven by performance pressures but lacking strategic vision, company after company has had no better idea than to buy up its rivals. The competitors left standing are often those that outlasted others, not companies with real advantage.

II. STRATEGY RESTS ON UNIQUE ACTIVITIES

Competitive strategy is about being different. It means deliberately choosing a different set of activities to deliver a unique mix of value.

Southwest Airlines Company, for example, offers short-haul, low-cost, point-to-point service between midsize cities and secondary airports in large cities. Southwest avoids large airports and does not fly great distances. . . .

IKEA, the global furniture retailer based in Sweden, also has a clear strategic positioning. IKEA targets young furniture buyers who want style at low cost. What turns this marketing concept into a strategic positioning is the tailored set of activities that make it work. Like Southwest, IKEA has chosen to perform activities differently from its rivals. . . .

THE ORIGINS OF STRATEGIC POSITIONS

Strategic positions emerge from three distinct sources, which are not mutually exclusive and often overlap. First, positioning can be based on producing a subset of an industry's products or services. I call this *variety-based positioning* because it is based on the choice of product or service varieties rather than customer segments. Variety-based positioning makes economic sense when a company can best produce particular products or services using distinctive sets of activities.

Jiffy Lube International, for instance, specializes in automotive lubricants and does not offer other car repair or maintenance services. Its value chain produces faster service at a lower cost than broader line repair shops, a combination so attractive that many customers subdivide their purchases, buying oil changes from the focused competitor, Jiffy Lube, and going to rivals for other services. . . .

A second basis for positioning is that of serving most or all the needs of a particular group of customers. I call this *needs-based positioning*, which comes closer to traditional thinking about targeting a segment of customers. It arises when there are groups of customers with differing needs, and when a tailored set of activities can serve those needs best. Some groups of customers are more price sensitive than others, demand different product features, and need varying amounts of information, support, and services. IKEA's customers are a good example of such a group. IKEA seeks to meet all the home furnishing needs of its target customers, not just a subset of them. . . .

It is intuitive for most managers to conceive of their business in terms of the customers' needs they are meeting. But a critical element of needs-based positioning is not at all intuitive and is often overlooked. Differences in needs will not translate into meaningful positions unless the best set of activities to satisfy them *also* differs. If that were not the case, every competitor could meet those same needs, and there would be nothing unique or valuable about the positioning. . . .

The third basis for positioning is that of segmenting customers who are accessible in different ways. Although their needs are similar to those of other customers, the best configuration of activities reach them is different. I call this *access-based positioning*. Access can be a function of customer geography or customer scale—or of anything that requires a different set of activities to reach customers in the best way. . . .

Rural versus urban-based customers are one example of access driving differences in activities. Serving small rather than large customers or densely rather than sparsely situated customers are other examples in which the best way to configure marketing, order processing, logistics, and after-sale service activities to meet the similar needs of distinct groups will often differ. . . .

Having defined positioning, we can now begin to answer the question, "What is strategy?" Strategy is the creation of a unique and valuable position, involving a different set of activities. If there were only one ideal position, there would be no need for strategy. Companies would face a simple imperative—win the race to discover and preempt it. The essence of strategic positioning is to choose activities that are different from rivals'. If the same set of activities were best to produce all varieties, meet all needs, and access all customers, companies could easily shift among them and operational effectiveness would determine performance.

III. A SUSTAINABLE STRATEGIC POSITION REQUIRES TRADE-OFFS

Choosing a unique position, however, is not enough to guarantee a sustainable advantage. A valuable position will attract imitation by incumbents, who are likely to copy it in one of two ways.

First, a competitor can reposition itself to match the superior performer. . . . A second and far more common type of imitation is straddling. The straddler seeks to match the benefits of a successful position while maintaining its existing position. It grafts new features, services, or technologies onto the activities it already performs.

For those who argue that competitors can copy any market position, the airline industry is a perfect test case. It would seem that nearly any competitor could imitate any other airline's activities. Any airline can buy the same planes, lease the gates, and match the menus and ticketing and baggage handling services offered by other airlines.

Continental Airlines saw how well Southwest was doing and decided to straddle. While maintaining its position as a full-service airline, Continental also set out to match Southwest on a number of point-to-point routes. The airline dubbed the new service Continental Lite. It eliminated meals and first-class service, increased departure frequency, lowered fares, and shortened turnaround time at the gate. Because Continental remained a full-service airline on other routes, it continued to use travel agents and its mixed fleet of planes and to provide baggage checking and seat assignments.

But a strategic position is not sustainable unless there are trade-offs with other positions. Trade-offs occur when activities are incompatible. Simply put, a trade-off means that more of one thing necessitates less of another. An airline can choose to serve meals—adding cost and slowing turnaround time at the gate—or it can choose not to, but it cannot do both without bearing major inefficiencies. . . .

Trade-offs arise for three reasons. The first is inconsistencies in image or reputation. A company known for delivering one kind of value may lack credibility and confuse customers—or even undermine its reputation—if it delivers another kind of value or attempts to deliver two inconsistent things at the same time. . . .

Second, and more important, trade-offs arise from activities themselves. Different positions (with their tailored activities) require different product configurations, different equipment, different employee behavior, different skills, and different management systems. Many trade-offs reflect inflexibilities in machinery, people, or systems. The more IKEA has configured its activities to lower costs by having its customers do their own assembly and delivery, the less able it is to satisfy customers who require higher levels of service. . . .

Finally, trade-offs arise from limits on internal coordination and control. By clearly choosing to compete in one way and not another, senior management makes organizational priorities clear. Companies that try to be all things to all customers, in contrast, risk confusion in the trenches as employees attempt to make day-to-day operating decisions without a clear framework.

Positioning trade-offs are pervasive in competition and essential to strategy. They create the need for choice and purposefully limit what a company offers. They deter straddling or repositioning, because competitors that engage in those approaches undermine their strategies and degrade the value of their existing activities.

Trade-offs ultimately grounded Continental Lite. The airline lost hundreds of millions of dollars, and the CEO lost his job. Its planes were delayed leaving congested hub cities or slowed at the gate by baggage transfers. . . .

Continental tried to compete in two ways at once. In trying to be low cost on some routes and full service on others, Continental paid an enormous straddling penalty. . . .

For the past decade, as managers have improved operational effectiveness greatly, they have internalized the idea that eliminating trade-offs is a good thing. But if there are not trade-offs companies will never achieve a sustainable advantage. They will have to run faster and faster just to stay in place.

As we return to the question, What is strategy?, we see that trade-offs add a new dimension to the answer. Strategy is making trade-offs in competing. The essence of strategy is choosing what *not* to do. Without trade-offs, there would be no need for choice and thus no need for strategy. Any good idea could and would be quickly imitated. Again, performance would once again depend wholly on operational effectiveness.

IV. FIT DRIVES BOTH COMPETITIVE ADVANTAGE AND SUSTAINABILITY

Positioning choices determine not only which activities a company will perform and how it will configure individual activities but also how activities relate to one another. While operational effectiveness is about achieving excellence in individual activities, or functions, strategy is about *combining* activities. . . .

What is Southwest's core competence? Its key success factors? The correct answer is that everything matters. Southwest's strategy involves a whole system of activities, not a collection of parts. Its competitive advantage comes from the way its activities fit and reinforce one another.

Fit locks out imitators by creating a chain that is as strong as its *strongest* link. As in most companies with good strategies, Southwest's activities complement one another in ways that create real economic value. One activity's cost, for example, is lowered because of the way other activities are performed. Similarly, one activity's value to customers can be enhanced by a company's other activities. That is the way strategic fit creates competitive advantage and superior profitability.

TYPES OF FIT

The importance of fit among functional policies is one of the oldest ideas in strategy. Gradually, however, it has been supplanted on the management agenda. Rather than seeing the company as a whole, managers have turned to "core" competencies, "critical" resources, and "key" success factors. In fact, fit is a far more central component of competitive advantage than most realize. . . .

There are three types of fit, although they are not mutually exclusive. First-order fit is *simple consistency* between each activity (function) and the overall strategy. . . .

Consistency ensures that the competitive advantages of activities cumulate and do not erode or cancel themselves out. It makes the strategy easier to communicate to customers, employees, and shareholders, and improves implementation through single-mindedness in the corporation.

Second-order fit occurs when *activities are reinforcing*. . . . Bic Corporation sells a narrow line of standard, low-priced pens to virtually all major customer markets (retail, commercial, promotional, and giveaway) through virtually all available channels. As with any variety-based positioning serving a broad group of customers, Bic emphasizes a common need (low price for an acceptable pen) and uses marketing approaches with a broad reach (a large sales force and heavy television advertising). . . .

Third-order fit goes beyond activity reinforcement to what I call *optimization of effort*. The Gap, a retailer of casual clothes, considers product availability in its stores a critical element of its strategy. The Gap could keep products either by holding store inventory or by restocking from warehouses. The Gap has optimized its effort across these activities by restocking its selection of basic clothing almost daily out of three warehouses, thereby minimizing the need to carry large in-store inventories. The emphasis is on restocking because the Gap's merchandising strategy sticks to basic items in relatively few colors. . . .

In all three types of fit, the whole matters more than any individual part. Competitive advantage grows out of the *entire system* of activities. The fit among activities substantially reduces cost or increases differentiation. Beyond that, the competitive value of individual activities—or the associated skills, competencies, or resources—cannot be decoupled from the system or the strategy. Thus, in competitive companies it can be misleading to explain success by specifying individual strengths, core competencies, or critical resources. The list of strengths cuts across many functions, and one strength blends into others. It is more useful to think in terms of themes that pervade many activities, such as low cost, a particular notion of customer service, or a particular conception of the value delivered. These themes are embodied in nests of tightly linked activities.

FIT AND SUSTAINABILITY

Strategic fit among many activities is fundamental not only to competitive advantage but also to the sustainability of that advantage. It is harder for a rival to match an array of interlocked activities than it is merely to imitate a particular sales-force approach, match a process technology, or replicate a set of product features. Positions built on systems of activities are far more sustainable than those built on individual activities. . . .

The more a company's positioning rests on activity systems with second- and third-order fit, the more sustainable its advantage will be. Such systems, by their very nature, are usually difficult to untangle from outside the company and therefore hard to imitate. And even if rivals can identify the relevant interconnections, they will have difficulty replicating them. Achieving fit is difficult because it requires the integration of decisions and actions across many independent subunits. . . .

The most viable positions are those whose activity systems are incompatible because of trade-offs. Strategic positioning sets the trade-off rules that define how individual activities will be configured and integrated. Seeing strategy in terms of activity systems only makes it clearer why organizational structure, systems, and processes need to be strategy-specific. Tailoring organization to strategy, in turn, makes complementarities more achievable and contributes to sustainability.

One implication is that strategic positions should have a horizon of a decade or more, not of a single planning cycle. Frequent shifts in positioning are costly. Not only must a company reconfigure individual activities, but it must also realign entire systems. Some activities may never catch up to the vacillating strategy. The inevitable result of frequent shifts in strategy, or of failure to choose a distinct position in the first place, is "me-too" or hedged activity configurations, inconsistencies across functions, and organizational dissonance.

What is strategy? We can now complete the answer to this question. Strategy is creating fit among a company's activities. The success of a strategy depends on doing many things well—not just a few—and integrating among them. If there is no fit among activities, there is no distinctive strategy and little sustainability. Management reverts to the simpler task of overseeing independent functions, and operational effectiveness determines an organization's relative performance.

READING 1.4

BY HENRY MINTZBERG AND JOSEPH LAMPEL

■ We are the blind people and strategy formation is our elephant. Each of us, in trying to cope with the mysteries of the beast, grabs hold of some part or other, and, in the words of John Godfrey Saxe's poem of the last century:

> Rail on in utter ignorance
> of what each other mean,
> And prate about an Elephant,
> Not one of [us] has seen!

Consultants have been like big game hunters embarking on their safaris for tusks and trophies, while academics have preferred photo safaris—keeping a safe distance from the animals they pretend to observe.

Managers are encouraged to take one narrow perspective or another—the glories of planning or the wonders of learning, the demands of external competitive analyses or the imperatives of an internal "resource-based" view. Much of this writing and advising has been decidedly dysfunctional, simply because managers have no choice but to cope with the entire beast.

In the first part of this article, we review briefly the evolution of the field in terms of ten "schools" (based on Mintzberg, Ahlstrand, and Lampel, *Strategy Safari*, 1998). We ask whether these perspectives represent fundamentally different processes of strategy making or different *parts* of the same process. In both cases, our answer is yes. We seek to show how some recent work tends to cut across these historical perspectives—in a sense, how cross-fertilization has occurred. Our historical survey of strategy literature suggests that it had been characterized by ten major schools since its inception in the 1960s— three *prescriptive* (or "ought") and seven *descriptive* (or "is").

---

*Reprinted with deletions from "Reflecting on the Strategy Process," Henry Mintzberg and Joseph Lampel, *Sloan Management Review*, Vol. 40 (3), 1999, 21–30.

DESIGN SCHOOL: A PROCESS OF CONCEPTION

The original perspective—dating back to Selznick (1957) followed by Chandler (1962) and given sharper definition by Andrews (in Learned et al., 1965)—sees strategy formation as achieving the essential fit between internal strengths and weaknesses and external threats and opportunities. Senior management formulates clear, simple, and unique strategies in a deliberate process of conscious thought—which is neither formally analytical nor informally intuitive—so that everyone can implement the strategies. This was the dominant view of the strategy process, at least into the 1970s, and, some might argue, to the present day, given its implicit influence on most teaching and practice. The design school did not develop, however, in the sense of giving rise to variants within its own context. Rather, it combined with other views in rather different contexts.

PLANNING SCHOOL: A FORMAL PROCESS

The planning school grew in parallel with the design school—indeed H. Igor Ansoff's book appeared in 1965, as did the initial Andrews text. But, in sheer volume of publication, the planning school predominated by the mid-1970s, faltered in the 1980s, yet continues to be an important branch of the literature today. Ansoff's book reflects most of the design school's assumptions except a rather significant one: that the process is not just cerebral but formal, decomposable into distinct steps, delineated by checklists, and supported by techniques (especially with regard to objectives, budgets, programs, and operating plans). This means that staff planners replaced senior managers, de facto, as the key players in the process.

POSITIONING SCHOOL: AN ANALYTICAL PROCESS

The third of the prescriptive schools, commonly labeled positioning, was the dominant view of strategy formation in the 1980s. It was given impetus especially by Michael Porter in 1980, following earlier work on strategic positioning in academe (notably by Hatten and Schendel) and in consulting by the Boston Consulting Group and the PIMS project—all preceded by a long literature on military strategy, dating back to Sun Tzu in 400 B.C. (See Sun Tzu, 1971.) In this view, strategy reduces to generic positions selected through formalized analyses of industry situations. Hence, the planners become analysts. This proved especially lucrative to consultants and academics alike, who could sink their teeth into hard data and promote their "scientific truths" to journals and companies. This literature grew in all directions to include strategic groups, value chains, game theories, and other ideas—but always with this analytical bent.

ENTREPRENEURIAL SCHOOL: A VISIONARY PROCESS

Meanwhile, on other fronts, mostly in trickles and streams rather than waves, wholly different approaches to strategy formation arose. Much like the design school, the entrepreneurial school centered the process on the chief executive; but unlike the design school and opposite from the planning school, it rooted that process in the mysteries of intuition. That shifted strategies from precise designs, plans, or positions to vague *visions* or broad perspectives, to be seen, in a sense, often through metaphor. This focused the process on particular contexts—start-up, niche, or private ownership, as well as "turnaround" by the forceful leader—although the case was certainly put forth that every organization needs the vision of a creative leader. In this view, however, the leader maintains such close control over *implementing* his or her *formulated* vision that the distinction central to the three prescriptive schools begins to break down.

COGNITIVE SCHOOL: A MENTAL PROCESS

On the academic front, the origin of strategies generated considerable interest. If strategies developed in people's minds as frames, models, maps, concepts, or schemas, what could be

TABLE 1 DIMENSIONS OF THE TEN SCHOOLS, PART A

	DESIGN	PLANNING	POSITIONING	ENTREPRENEURIAL	COGNITIVE
Sources	P. Selznick (and perhaps earlier work, for example, by W.H. Newman), then K.R. Andrews.[a]	H.I. Ansoft.[b]	Purdue University work (D.E. Schendel, K.J. Hatten), then notably M.E. Porter.[c]	J.A. Schumpeter, A.H. Cole, and others in economics.[d]	H.A. Simon and J.G. March.[e]
Base Discipline	None (architecture as metaphor).	Some links to urban planning, systems theory, and cybernetics.	Economics (industrial organization) and military history.	None (although early writings come from economists).	Psychology (cognitive).
Champions	Case study teachers (especially at or from Harvard University), leadership aficionados—especially in the United States.	"Professional" managers, MBAs, staff experts (especially in finance), consultants, and government controllers—especially in France and the United States.	As in planning school, particularly analytical staff types, consulting "boutiques," and military writers—especially in the United States.	Popular business press, individualists, small business people everywhere, but most decidedly in Latin America and among overseas Chinese.	Those with a psychological bent—pessimists in one wing, optimists in the other.
Intended Message	Fit.	Formalize.	Analyze.	Envision.	Cope or create.
Realized Message	Think (strategy making as case study).	Program (rather than formulate).	Calculate (rather than create or commit).	Centralize (then hope).	Worry (being unable to cope in either case).
School Category	Prescriptive.	Prescriptive.	Prescriptive.	Descriptive (some prescriptive).	Descriptive.
Associated Homily	"Look before you leap."	"A stitch in time saves nine."	"Nothin' but the facts, ma'am."	"Take us to your leader."	"I'll see it when I believe it."

understood about those mental processes? Particularly in the 1980s and continuing today, research has grown steadily on cognitive biases in strategy making and on cognition as information processing, knowledge structure mapping, and concept attainment—the latter important for strategy formation, yet on which progress has been minimal. Meanwhile, another, newer branch of this school adopted a more subjective *interpretative* or *constructivist* view of the strategy process: that cognition is used to construct strategies as creative interpretations, rather than simply to map reality in some more or less objective way, however distorted.

LEARNING SCHOOL: AN EMERGENT PROCESS

Of all the *descriptive* schools, the learning school grew into a veritable wave and challenged the always dominant prescriptive schools. Dating back to Lindblom's early work on disjointed incrementalism (Braybrooke and Lindblom, 1963) and running through Quinn's (1980) logical incrementalism, Bower's (1970) and Burgelman's notions of venturing, Mintzberg et al.'s ideas about emergent strategy, and Weick's (1979) notion of retrospective sense making, a model of strategy making as learning developed that differed from the earlier schools. In this view, strategies are emergent, strategists can be found throughout the organization, and so-called formulation and implementation intertwine.

TABLE 1 DIMENSIONS OF THE TEN SCHOOLS, PART B

	LEARNING	POWER	CULTURAL	ENVIRONMENTAL	CONFIGURATION
Sources	C.E Lindblom, R.M. Cyert and J.G. March, K.E. Weick, J.B. Quinn, and C.K. Prahalad and G. Hamel.[f]	G.T. Allison (micro), J. Pfeffer and G.R. Salancik, and W.G. Astley (macro).[g]	E. Rhenman and R. Normann in Sweden. No obvious source elsewhere.[h]	M.T. Hannan and J. Freeman. Contingency theorists (e.g., D.S. Pugh et al.).[i]	A.D. Chandler, McGill University group (H. Mintzberg, D. Miller, and others), R.E. Miles and C.C. Snow.[j]
Base Discipline	None (perhaps some peripheral links to learning theory in psychology and education). Chaos theory in mathematics.	Political science.	Anthropology.	Biology.	History.
Champions	People inclined to experimentation, ambiguity, adaptability—especially in Japan and Scandinavia.	People who like power, politics, and conspiracy—especially in France.	People who like the social, the spiritual, the collective—especially in Scandinavia and Japan.	Population ecologists, some organization theorists, splitters, and positivists in general—especially in the Anglo-Saxon countries.	Lumpers and integrators in general, as well as change agents. Configuration perhaps most popular in the Netherlands. Transformation most popular in the United States.
Intended Message	Learn.	Promote.	Coalesce.	React.	Integrate, transform.
Realized Message	Play (rather than pursue).	Hoard (rather than share).	Perpetuate (rather than change).	Capitulate (rather than confront).	Lump (rather than split, adapt).
School Category	Descriptive.	Descriptive.	Descriptive.	Descriptive.	Descriptive and prescriptive.
Associated Homily	"If at first you don't succeed, try, try again."	"Look out for number one."	"An apple never falls far from the tree."	"It all depends."	"To everything there is a season. . . ."

POWER SCHOOL: A PROCESS OF NEGOTIATION

A thin, but quite different stream in the literature has focused on strategy making rooted in power. Two separate orientations seem to exist. *Micro* power sees the development of strategies *within* the organization as essentially political—a process involving bargaining, persuasion, and confrontation among actors who divide the power. *Macro* power views the organization as an entity that uses its power over others and among its partners in alliances, joint ventures, and other network relationships to negotiate "collective" strategies in its interest.

CULTURAL SCHOOL: A SOCIAL PROCESS

Hold power up to a mirror and its reverse image is culture. Whereas the former focuses on self-interest and fragmentation, the latter focuses on common interest and intergration—strategy formation as a social process rooted in culture. Again, we find a thin stream of literature, focused particularly on the influence of culture in discouraging significant strategic change. Culture became a big issue in the U.S. literature after the impact of Japanese management was fully realized in the 1980s; later, some attention to the implications for strategy formation followed. However, interesting research developed in Sweden in the 1970s with culture as a central, although hardly exclusive, theme, stimulated by the early work of Rhenman and Normann, and carried out by people such as Hedberg and Jonsson, and others.

ENVIRONMENTAL SCHOOL: A REACTIVE PROCESS

Perhaps not strictly strategic management, if one defines the term as being concerned with how organizations use degrees of freedom to maneuver through their environments, the environmental school nevertheless deserves some attention for illuminating the demands of environment. In this category, we include so-called "contingency theory" that considers which responses are expected of organizations facing particular environmental conditions and "population ecology" writings that claim severe limits to strategic choice. "Institutional theory," which is concerned with the institutional pressures faced by organizations, is perhaps a hybrid of the power and cognitive schools.

CONFIGURATION SCHOOL: A PROCESS OF TRANSFORMATION

Finally, we come to a more extensive and integrative literature and practice. One side of this school, more academic and descriptive, sees organization as configuration—coherent clusters of characteristics and behaviors—and integrates the claims of the other schools—each configuration, in effect, in its own place. Planning, for example, prevails in machine-type organizations under conditions of relative stability, while entrepreneurship can be found under more dynamic configurations of start-up and turnaround. But if organizations can be described by such *states*, change must be described as rather dramatic *transformation*—the leap from one state to another. And so, a literature and practice of transformation—more prescriptive and practitioner oriented (and consultant promoted)—developed. These two different literatures and practices nevertheless complement one another and so, in our opinion, belong to the same school.

PRATING ABOUT STRATEGIC MANAGEMENT

During the nineteenth century, numerous explorers went in search of the source of the Nile. In time, it became increasingly evident that the source was not definitive. This was not something the expedition backers or the public wanted to hear. After some debate, the explorers announced their discovery: the source of the Nile was Lake Victoria! This is a verdict generally rejected by contemporary geographers, who may come up with other answers in the future. The source of a river, after all, is a matter of interpretation, not a fact waiting to be discovered.

Strategic management has suffered from the problem that bedeviled the Victorian explorers. We, too, are a community of explorers, competing for discoveries, with backers eager for results and a public that demands answers.

Some explorers searching for the source of strategy have found "first principles" that explain the nature of the process. These have usually been rooted in basic disciplines, such as economics, sociology, or biology. Others have invoked a central concept, such as organization culture, to explain why some strategies succeed and others do not. The consequence has been to grasp one part of the strategic management elephant and prate about it as though none other exists. Of course, in the affairs of writing and consulting, to succeed and to sell, champions must defend their positions, erecting borders around their views while dismissing or denying others. Or, to return to our metaphor, like butchers (we include ourselves in this group), they chop up reality for their own convenience, just as poachers grab the tusks of the elephant and leave the carcass to rot.

To repeat a key issue, such behavior ultimately does not serve the practicing manager. These people, as noted, have to deal with the entire beast of strategy formation, not only to keep it alive but to help sustain some real life energy. True, they can use it in various ways—

TABLE 2
BLENDING OF THE
STRATEGY FORMATION
SCHOOLS

APPROACH	SCHOOLS
Dynamic capabilities	Design, Learning
Resource-based theory	Cultural, Learning
Soft techniques (e.g., scenario analysis and stakeholder analysis)	Planning, Learning or Power
Constructionism	Cognitive, Cultural
Chaos and evolutionary theory	Learning, Environmental
Institutional theory	Environmental, Power or Cognitive
Intrapreneurship (venturing)	Environmental, Entrepreneurial
Revolutionary change	Configuration, Entrepreneurial
Negotiated strategy	Power, Positioning
Strategic maneuvering	Positioning, Power

just as an elephant can be a beast of burden or a symbol of ceremony—but only if it remains intact as a living being. The greatest failings of strategic management have occurred when managers took one point of view too seriously. This field had its obsession with planning, then generic positions based on careful calculations, and now learning.

Hence, we take pleasure in noting that some of the more recent approaches to strategy formation cut across these ten schools in eclectic and interesting ways. This suggests a broadening of the literature. (See Table 2 for a list of these across-school approaches.) For example, research on stakeholder analysis links the planning and positioning schools, whereas the work of Porter and others on what can be called strategic maneuvering (first-mover advantage, use of feints, etc.) connect the positioning to the power school. And chaos theory, as applied to strategic management, might be seen as a hybrid of the learning and environmental schools. Perhaps best known is the "dynamic capabilities" approach of Prahalad and Hamel. We see their notions of core competence, strategic intent, and stretch—reminiscent of Itami's earlier work—as a hybrid of the learning and design schools: strong leadership to encourage continuous strategic learning.

ONE PROCESS OR DIFFERENT APPROACHES

Do these schools represent different processes of strategy formation, or different parts of the same process? We find either answer too constraining.

Some of the schools clearly are stages or aspects of the strategy formation process (see Figure 1):

- The cognitive school resides in the mind of the strategist located at the *center*.
- The positioning school looks *behind* at established data that is analyzed and fed into the black box of strategy making.
- The planning school looks slightly *ahead*, to program the strategies created in other ways.
- The design school looks farther *ahead* to a strategic perspective.
- The entrepreneurial school looks *beyond* to a unique vision of the future.
- The learning and power schools look *below,* enmeshed in details. Learning looks into the grass roots, whereas power looks under the rocks—to places that organizations may not want to expose.
- The cultural school looks *down,* enshrouded in clouds of beliefs.
- Above the cultural school, the environmental school looks *on,* so to speak.
- The configuration school looks *at* the process, or, we might say, *all around* it, in contrast to the cognitive school that tries to look *inside* the process.

FIGURE 1 STRATEGY FORMATION AS A SINGLE PROCESS

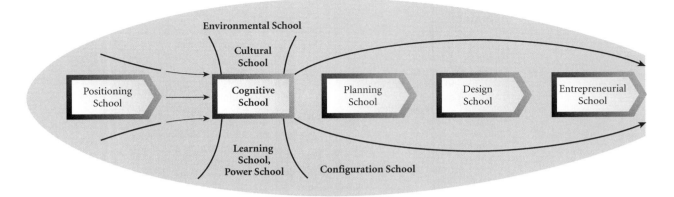

Dealing with all this complexity in one process may seem overwhelming. But that is the nature of the beast. Strategy formation *is* judgmental designing, intuitive visioning, and emergent learning; it is about transformation as well as perpetuation; it must involve individual cognition and social interaction, cooperative as well as conflictive; it has to include analyzing before and programming after as well as negotiating during; and all this must be in response to what may be a demanding environment. Try to omit any of this, and watch what happens!

Yet, just as clearly, the process can tilt toward the attributes of one school or another: toward the entrepreneurial school during start-up or when there is the need for a dramatic turnaround, toward the learning school under dynamic conditions when prediction is well nigh impossible, and so on. Sometimes the process has to be more individually cognitive than socially interactive (in small business, for example). Some strategies seem to be more rationally deliberate (especially in mature mass-production industries and government), whereas others tend to be more adaptively emergent (as in dynamic, high-technology industries). The environment can sometimes be highly demanding (during social upheaval), yet at other times (or even at the same times) entrepreneurial leaders are able to maneuver through it with ease. There are, after all, identifiable stages and periods in strategy making, not in any absolute sense but as recognizable tendencies.

Figure 2 plots the schools as different processes along two dimensions: states of the internal process and states of the external world. In this view, practitioners can pick and choose

FIGURE 2
STRATEGY FORMATION
AS MANY PROCESSES

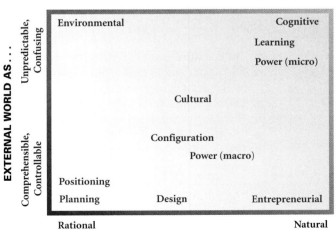

TABLE 3
GOING OVER THE
EDGE IN STRATEGY
FORMATION

SCHOOL	ILLOGICAL EXTREME
Design	Fixation
Planning	Ritual
Positioning	Fortification
Entrepreneurial	Idolatry
Cognitive	Fantasy
Learning	Drift
Power	Intrigue
Cultural	Eccentricity
Environmental	Conformity
Configuration	Degeneration

among the various processes (or combine them when appropriate)—as long as any one is not pushed to its illogical extreme (see Table 3).

IN SEARCH OF STRATEGIC MANAGEMENT

Scholars and consultants should certainly continue to probe the important elements of each school. But, more importantly, we have to get beyond the narrowness of each school: we need to know how strategy formation, which combines all these schools and more, really works.

We need to ask better questions and generate fewer hypotheses—to allow ourselves to be pulled by real-life concerns rather than being pushed by reified concepts. We need better practice, not neater theory. So we must concern ourselves with process and content, statics and dynamics, constraint and inspiration, the cognitive and the collective, the planned and the learned, the economic and the political. In other words, we must give more attention to the entire elephant—to strategy formation as a whole. We may never see it fully, but we can certainly see it better.

CHAPTER 2

Strategists

Every conventional strategy or policy textbook focuses on the job of the general manager as a main ingredient in understanding the process of strategy formation. The discussion of emergent strategy in the last chapter suggests that we do not take such a narrow view of the strategist. Anyone in the organization who happens to control key or precedent-setting actions can be a strategist; the strategist can be a collection of people as well. Managers are obviously prime candidates for such a role because their perspective is generally broader than any of the people who report to them and because so much power naturally resides with them. But they are not alone.

We present five readings that describe the work of the manager. The one by Mintzberg challenges the conventional view of the manager. The image presented in this article is a job characterized by pressure, interruption, orientation to action, oral rather than written communication, and working with outsiders and colleagues as much as with so-called subordinates. The reading then goes on to describe the content of managerial work, arguing that it takes place on three levels—a rather abstract information level, an in-between people level, and a concrete action level. The roles the manager performs can be seen to fit into these levels, but, as emphasized, all managers must ultimately deal with all levels in an integrated fashion, although most will favor one level or another.

The second reading brings some of these aspects of managing to life in different styles of managing. By Patricia Pitcher of Montreal's Ecole des Hautes Etudes Commerciales, it contrasts the three styles of artists, craftsmen, and technocrats—if you like, creative visionaries, sympathetic leaders, and systematic analysts. Pitcher is no friend of the technocrats, as you shall see, believing that artists and craftsmen have to take the lead in today's organizations.

One evident and important conclusion of this reading is that managers do not always function as the strategists they are supposed to be—as leaders directing their organizations the way conductors direct their orchestras (at least the way it looks on the podium, a point we shall develop further in Chapter 15). The article by Edward Wrapp of the University of Chicago illustrates how this happens in large organizations. He depicts managers as somewhat political animals, providing broad guidance but facilitating or pushing through their strategies, bit by bit, in rather unexpected ways. They rarely state specific goals. They practice "the art of imprecision," trying to "avoid policy strait-jackets," while concentrating on only a few really significant issues. They move whenever possible through "corridors of comparative indifference" to avoid undue opposition, at the same time that they are trying to ensure cohesive direction for their organizations.

The next article, by Peter Senge of the MIT Sloan School of Management and based on his highly successful book, *The Fifth Discipline,* characterizes the "leader's new work" as building the "learning organization." Senge views the ability to learn as the primary source of a company's competitive advantage and argues that facilitating organizational learning is the principal task of the strategist. Senge sees a long-term vision as the key source of tension in the organization and, therefore, of energy in the learning process. The manager must be the designer, the teacher, and the steward of the learning organization and, to play these roles, he or she must develop a new set of skills, which Senge describes in the article. Above all, the manager must promote systems thinking. On balance, Senge's new leader may well be Pitcher's craftsman (see especially the quote he uses to end his discussion—hardly the technocrat or even the artist), in which case this reading fleshes out that style in an interesting way.

Finally, there is a recent article by Quy Huy of INSEAD, the lead article in the September–October 2001 issue of the *Harvard Business Review.* Middle managers have received a bum rap, Quy believes, and so he set out to write "In Praise of Middle Managers." His point is an important one, long overdue, which helps to promote the fact that middle managers are critical components of every organization, *especially* those that wish to engage in effective processes of strategic change.

How do we reconcile these different views of the strategist? At one level, perhaps, we do not need a grand theory that integrates across all of them. There are different kinds of managers and different beliefs and styles, as well as different kinds of authors: Different lenses capture different aspects of managerial work. You may also observe similarities in the roles and tasks of the strategists described in these readings, despite the very different languages the authors use. Think, for example, about how the styles of Pitcher relate to the managerial roles Mintzberg describes.

USING THE CASE STUDIES

It is no accident that strategy was originally defined as the "art of the strategist." And, indeed, there is no shortage of fascinating strategists in our cases. General MacArthur and the Philippines shows how a deeply felt experience can dramatically affect strategic goals. The case on Napoleon Bonaparte shows how personal ambition creatively shaped strategy at the beginning of this general's career but distorted it as he gained more power and control. The Sportsmake case, on the other hand, deals with the impact of personality and the vision of a strategist on the organization after his untimely death. The board is faced with a decision of whom they should appoint as successor, and this raises the issue of whether such replacement should herald change or emphasize continuity.

The career and approach to work of Sarah Conner in Astral Records show how strategic decisions are woven into daily reality, a point that is forcefully argued by Mintzberg in "The Manager's Job." Her story and the story of Ian Jones in Empire Plastics illustrate the crucial role that middle managers play in strategy. "In Praise of Middle Managers" by Quy argues that companies ignore this role at their peril.

Rudi Gassner and the Executive Committee of BMG recounts the frustration of a new CEO in the face of top-management inertia, a situation perceptively analyzed by Wrapp in his "Good Managers Do Not Make Policy Decisions." Bernard Arnault, by contrast, rarely has problems with organizational inertia because he single-handedly crafts the strategy of LVMH. His approach is well described by Senge in "The Leader's New Work." It is a mixture of strong vision and fast learning. However, as Pitcher notes in her "Artists, Craftsmen, and Technocracts," both Rudi Gassner and Bernard Arnault, not to mention many of the other managers who play a prominent role in this book, practice strategy with a particular style. Rudi Gassner is clearly the craftsman, and Bernard Arnault is the artist. As to which of our cases describes the strategist as technocract, we leave you with the task of finding this out.

READING 2.1

BY HENRY MINTZBERG

■ Tom Peters tells us that good managers are doers. (Wall Street says they "do deals.") Michael Porter suggests that they are thinkers. Not so, argue Abraham Zaleznik and Warren Bennis: good managers are really leaders. Yet, for the better part of this century, the classical writers—Henri Fayol and Lyndell Urwick, among others—keep telling us that good managers are essentially controllers.

It is a curiosity of the management literature that its best-known writers all seem to emphasize one particular part of the manager's job to the exclusion of the others. Together, perhaps, they cover all the parts, but even that does not describe the whole job of managing.

Moreover, the image left by all of this of the manager's job is that it is a highly systematic, carefully controlled job. That is the folklore. The facts are quite different.

We shall begin by reviewing some of the early research findings on the *characteristics* of the manager's job, comparing that folklore with the facts, as I observed them in my first study of managerial work (published in the 1970s), reinforced by other research. Then we shall present a new framework to think about the *content* of the job—what managers really do—based on some recent observations I have made of managers in very different situations.

SOME FOLKLORE AND FACTS ABOUT MANAGERIAL WORK

There are four myths about the manager's job that do not bear up under careful scrutiny of the facts.

Folklore: The manager is a reflective, systematic planner. The evidence on this issue is overwhelming, but not a shred of it supports this statement.

Fact: Study after study has shown that managers work at an unrelenting pace, that their activities are characterized by brevity, variety, and discontinuity, and that they are strongly oriented to action and dislike reflective activities. Consider this evidence:

■ Half the activities engaged in by the five [American] chief executives [that I studied in my own research (Mintzberg, 1973a)] lasted less than nine minutes, and only 10% exceeded

*This paper combines excerpts from "The Manager's Job: Folklore and Fact," which appeared in the *Harvard Business Review* (July–August 1975) on the characteristics of the job, with the framework of the context of the job, which was published as "Rounding Out the Manager's Job" in the *Sloan Management Review* (Fall 1994).

one hour. A study of 56 U.S. foremen found that they averaged 583 activities per eight-hour shift, an average of 1 every 48 seconds (Guest, 1956:478). The work pace for both chief executives and foremen was unrelenting. The chief executives met a steady stream of callers and mail from the moment they arrived in the morning until they left in the evening. Coffee breaks and lunches were inevitably work related, and ever-present subordinates seemed to usurp any free moment.

- A diary study of 160 British middle and top managers found that they worked for a half hour or more without interruption only about once every two days (Stewart, 1967).

- Of the verbal contacts of the chief executives in my study, 93% were arranged on an ad hoc basis. Only 1% of the executives' time was spent in open-ended observational tours. Only 1 out of 368 verbal contacts was unrelated to a specific issue and could be called general planning. Another researcher finds that "in *not one single case* did a manager report the obtaining of important external information from a general conversation or other undirected personal communication" (Aguilar, 1967:102).

- No study has found important patterns in the way managers schedule their time. They seem to jump from issue to issue, continually responding to the needs of the moment.

Is this the planner that the classical view describes? Hardly. How, then, can we explain this behavior? The manager is simply responding to the pressures of the job. I found that my chief executives terminated many of their own activities, often leaving meetings before the end and interrupted their desk work to call in subordinates. One president not only placed his desk so that he could look down a long hallway but also left his door open when he was alone—an invitation for subordinates to come in and interrupt him.

Clearly, these managers wanted to encourage the flow of current information. But more significantly, they seemed to be conditioned by their own work loads. They appreciated the opportunity cost of their own time, and they were continually aware of their ever-present obligations—mail to be answered, callers to attend to, and so on. It seems that no matter what he or she is doing, the manager is plagued by the possibilities of what he or she might do and must do.

When the manager must plan, he or she seems to do so implicitly in the context of daily actions, not in some abstract process reserved for two weeks in the organization's mountain retreat. The plans of the chief executives I studied seemed to exist only in their heads—as flexible, but often specific, intentions. The traditional literature notwithstanding, the job of managing does not breed reflective planners; the manager is a real-time responder to stimuli, an individual who is conditioned by his or her job to prefer live to delayed action.

Folklore: The effective manager has no regular duties to perform. Managers are constantly being told to spend more time planning and delegating, and less time on operating details. These are not, after all, the true tasks of the manager. To use the popular analogy, the good manager, like the good conductor, carefully orchestrates everything in advance, then sits back to enjoy the fruits of his or her labor, responding occasionally to an unforeseeable exception. . . .

Fact: In addition to handling exceptions, managerial work involves performing a number of regular duties, including ritual and ceremony, negotiations, and processing of soft information that links the organization with its environment. Consider some evidence from the early research studies:

- A study of the work of the presidents of small companies found that they engaged in routine activities because their companies could not afford staff specialists and were so thin on operating personnel that a single absence often required the president to substitute (Choran in Mintzberg, 1973a).

- One study of field sales managers and another of chief executives suggest that it is a natural part of both jobs to see important customers, assuming the managers wish to keep those customers (Davis, 1957; Copeman, 1963).

- Someone, only half in jest, once described the manager as that person who sees visitors so that everyone else can get his or her work done. In my study, I found that certain ceremonial duties—meeting visiting dignitaries, giving out gold watches, presiding at Christmas dinners—were an intrinsic part of the chief executive's job.
- Studies of managers' information flow suggest that managers play a key role in securing "soft" external information (much of it available only to them because of their status) and in passing it along to their subordinates.

Folklore: The senior manager needs aggregated information, which a formal management information system best provides. In keeping with the classical view of the manager as that individual perched on the apex of a regulated, hierarchical system, the literature's manager was to receive all important information from a giant, comprehensive MIS.

But this never proved true at all. A look at how managers actually process information makes the reason quite clear. Managers have five media at their command—documents, telephone calls, scheduled and unscheduled meetings, and observational tours.

Fact: Managers strongly favor the verbal media—namely, telephone calls and meetings. The evidence comes from every one of the early studies of managerial work: Consider the following:

- In two British studies, managers spent an average 66% and 80% of their time in verbal (oral) communication (Stewart, 1967; Burns, 1954). In my study of five American chief executives, the figure was 78%.
- These five chief executives treated mail processing as a burden to be dispensed with. One came in Saturday morning to process 142 pieces of mail in just over three hours, to "get rid of all the stuff." This same manager looked at the first piece of "hard" mail he had received all week, a standard cost report, and put it aside with the comment, "I never look at this."
- These same five chief executives responded immediately to 2 of the 40 routine reports they received during the five weeks of my study and to four items in the 104 periodicals. They skimmed most of the periodicals in seconds, almost ritualistically. In all, these chief executives of good-sized organizations initiated on their own—that is, not in response to something else—a grand total of 25 pieces of mail during the 25 days I observed them.

An analysis of the mail the executives received reveals an interesting picture—only 13% was of specific and immediate use. So now we have another piece of the puzzle: not much of the mail provides live, current information—the action of a competitor, the mood of a government legislator, or the rating of last night's television show. Yet this is the information that drove the managers, interrupting their meetings and rescheduling their workdays.

Consider another interesting finding. Managers seem to cherish "soft" information, especially gossip, hearsay, and speculation. Why? The reason is its timeliness; today's gossip may be tomorrow's fact. The manager who is not accessible for the telephone call informing him or her that the firm's biggest customer was seen golfing with its main competitor may read about a dramatic drop in sales in the next quarterly report. But then it's too late.

Consider the words of Richard Neustadt, who studied the information-collecting habits of Presidents Roosevelt, Truman, and Eisenhower.

> It is not information of a general sort that helps a President see personal stakes; not summaries, not surveys, not the *bland amalgams*. Rather . . . it is the odds and ends of *tangible detail* that pieced together in his mind illuminate the underside of issues put before him. To help himself he must reach out as widely as he can for every scrap of fact, opinion, gossip, bearing on his interests and relationships as President. He must become his own director of his own central intelligence (1960:153–154: italics added).

The manager's emphasis on the verbal media raises two important points:

First, verbal information is stored in the brains of people. Only when people write this information down can it be stored in the files of the organization—whether in metal cabinets or computer memory—and managers apparently do not write down much of what they hear.

Thus, the strategic data bank of the organization is not in the memory of its computers but in the minds of its managers.

Second, the managers' extensive use of verbal media helps to explain why they are reluctant to delegate tasks. When we note that most of the managers' important information comes in verbal form and is stored in their heads, we can well appreciate their reluctance. It is not as if they can hand a dossier over to someone; they must take the time to "dump memory"—to tell that someone all they know about the subject. But this could take so long that the managers find it easier to do the task themselves. Thus the managers are damned by their own information systems to a "dilemma of delegation"—to do too much themselves or to delegate to their subordinates with inadequate briefing.

Folklore: Management is, or at least is quickly becoming, a science and a profession. By almost any definitions of *science* and *profession*, this statement is false. Brief observation of any manager will quickly lay to rest the notion that managers practice a science. A science involves the enaction of systematic, analytically determined procedures or programs. If we do not even know what procedures managers use, how can we prescribe them by scientific analysis? And how can we call management a profession if we cannot specify what managers are to learn?

Fact: The managers' programs—to schedule time, process information, make decisions, and so on—remain locked deep inside their brains. Thus, to describe these programs, we rely on words like judgment and intuition, seldom stopping to realize that they are merely labels for our ignorance.

I was struck during my study by the fact that the executives I was observing—all very competent by any standard—are fundamentally indistinguishable from their counterparts of a hundred years ago (or a thousand years ago, for that matter). The information they need differs, but they seek it in the same way—by word of mouth. Their decisions concern modern technology, but the procedures they use to make them are the same as the procedures of the nineteenth-century manager. In fact, the manager is in a kind of loop, with increasingly heavy work pressures but no aid forthcoming from management science.

Considering the facts about managerial work, we can see that the manager's job is enormously complicated and difficult. The manager is overburdened with obligations; yet he or she cannot easily delegate tasks. As a result, he or she is driven to overwork and is forced to do many tasks superficially. Brevity, fragmentation, and verbal communication characterize the work. Yet these are the very characteristics of managerial work that have impeded scientific attempts to improve it. As a result, the management scientists have concentrated their efforts on the specialized functions of the organization, where they could more easily analyze the procedure and quantify the relevant information. Thus, the first step in providing managers with some help is to find out what their job really is.

TOWARD A BASIC DESCRIPTION OF MANAGERIAL WORK

Now let us try to put some of the pieces of this puzzle together. The manager can be defined as that person in charge of an organization or one of its units. Besides chief executive officers, this definition would include vice presidents, head nurses, hockey coaches, and prime ministers. Can all of these people have anything in common? Indeed, they can. Our description takes the form of a model, building the image of the manager's job from the inside out, beginning at the center with the person and his or her frame and working out from there, layer by layer.

THE PERSON IN THE JOB

We begin at the center, with the person who comes to the job. People are not neutral when they take on a new managerial job, mere putty to be molded into the required shape. Figure 1 shows that an individual comes to a managerial job with a set of *values*, by this stage in life

FIGURE 1
THE PERSON
IN THE JOB

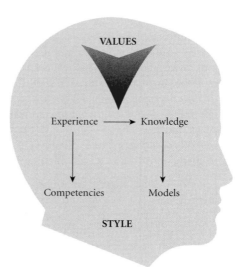

probably rather firmly set, also a body of *experience* that, on the one hand, has forged a set of skills or *competencies*, perhaps honed by training, and, on the other, has provided a base of *knowledge*. That knowledge is of course, used directly, but it is also converted into a set of *mental models*, key means by which managers interpret the world around them—for example, how the head nurse on a hospital ward perceives the behavior of the surgeons with whom she must work. Together, all these characteristics greatly determine how any manager approaches a given job—his or her *style* of managing. Style will come to life as we begin to see *how* a manager carries out *what* his or her job requires.

THE FRAME OF THE JOB

Embed the person depicted in a given managerial job and you get managerial work. At the core of it is some kind of *frame* for the job, the mental set the incumbent assumes to carry it out. Frame is strategy, to be sure, possibly even vision, but it is more than that. It is purpose, whether to create something in the first place, maintain something that has already been created or adapt it to changes, or else re-create something. Frame is also *perspective*—the broad view of the organization and its mission—and *positions*—concerning specific products, services, and markets.

Alain Noël, who studied the relationship between the frames and the work of the chief executives of three small companies, has said that managers have "occupations" and they have "preoccupations" (Noël, 1989). Frame describes the preoccupations, while roles (discussed below) describe the occupations. But frame does give rise to a first role in this model as well, which I call **conceiving**, namely thinking through the purpose, perspective, and positions of a particular unit to be managed over a particular period of time.

THE AGENDA OF THE WORK

Given a person in a particular managerial job with a particular frame, the question arises of how this is manifested in the form of specific activities. That happens through the *agenda* to carry out the work, and the associated role of **scheduling**, which has received considerable attention in the literature of management. Agenda is considered in two respects here. First, the frame gets manifested as a set of current *issues*, in effect, whatever is of concern to the manager, broken down into manageable units—what Tom Peters likes to call "chunks." Ask any manager about his or her work, and the almost inevitable first reply will be about the "issues" of central concern, those things "on the plate," as the saying goes. Or take a look at the agendas of meetings and you will likewise see a list of issues (rather than decisions). These, in effect, operationalize the frame (as well as change it, of course, by feeding in new concerns).

The sharper the frame, the more integrated the issues. The more realizable they may be as well, since it is a vague frame that gives rise to that all-too-common phenomenon of the unattainable "wishlist" in an organization. Sometimes a frame can be so sharp, and the issues therefore so tightly integrated, that they all reduce to what Noël has called one "magnificent obsession" (Noël, 1989). In effect, all the concerns of the manager revolve around one central issue, for example, making a new merger work.

Second, the frame and the issues get manifested in the more tangible *schedule*, the specific allocations of managerial time on a day-to-day basis. Also included here, however implicitly, is the setting of priorities among the issues. The scheduling of time and the prioritization of issues are obviously of great concern to all managers, and, in fact, are themselves significant consumers of managerial time. Accordingly, a great deal of attention has been devoted to these concerns, including numerous courses on "time management."

THE CORE IN CONTEXT

If we label the person in the job with a frame manifested by an agenda, the central *core* of the manager's job (shown by the concentric circles in Figure 2), then we turn next to the context in which this core is embedded, the milieu in which the work is practiced.

The context of the job is depicted in Figure 2 by the lines that surround the core. Context can be split into three areas, labeled inside, within, and outside on Figure 2.

Inside refers to the unit being managed, shown below the manager to represent his or her formal authority over its people and activities—the hospital ward in the case of the head nurse, for example. *Within*, shown to the right, refers to the rest of the organization—other members and other units with which the manager must work but over which he or she has no formal authority, for example, the doctors, the kitchen, the physiotherapists in the rest of the hospital, to continue with the same example. (Of course, in the case of the chief executive, there is no inside separate from within: that person has authority over the entire organization.) And *outside* refers to the rest of the context not formally part of the organization with which the manager must work—in this example, patients' relatives, long-term care institutions to which some of the unit's patients are discharged, nursing associations, and so on. The importance of this distinction (for convenience, we shall mostly refer to inside versus outside) is that much of managerial work is clearly directed either to the unit itself, for which the manager has official responsibility, or at its various boundary contexts, through which the manager must act without that responsibility.

FIGURE 2
THE CORE IN CONTEXT

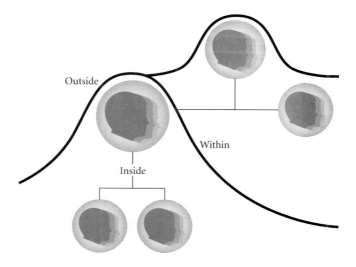

Outside

Within

Inside

MANAGING ON THREE LEVELS

We are now ready to address the actual behaviors that managers engage in to do their jobs. The essence of the model, designed to enable us to "see" managerial work comprehensively, in one figure, is that these roles are carried out on three successive levels, each inside and outside the unit. This is depicted by concentric circles of increasing specificity, shown in Figure 3.

From the outside (or most tangible level) in, managers can manage *action* directly, they can manage *people* to encourage them to take the necessary actions, and they can manage *information* to influence the people in turn to take their necessary actions. In other words, the ultimate objective of managerial work, and of the functioning of any organizational unit, the taking of action, can be managed directly, indirectly through people, or even more indirectly by information through people. The manager can thus choose to intervene at any of the three levels, but once done, he or she must work through the remaining ones. Later we shall see that the level a given manager favors becomes an important determinant of his or her managerial style, especially distinguishing so-called "doers" who prefer direct action, "leaders" who prefer working through people, and "administrators" who prefer to work by information.

MANAGING BY INFORMATION

To manage by information is to sit two steps removed from the purpose of managerial work. The manager processes information to drive other people who, in turn, are supposed to ensure that necessary actions are taken. In other words, here the managers' own activities focus neither on people nor on actions per se, but rather on information as an indirect way to make things happen. Ironically, while this was the classic perception of managerial work for the first half of this century, in recent years it has also become a newly popular, in some quarters almost obsessional, view, epitomized by the so-called "bottom line" approach to management.

The manager's various informational behaviors may be grouped into two broad roles, here labeled communicating and controlling, shown in Figure 4.

FIGURE 3
THREE LEVELS OF
EVOKING ACTIONS

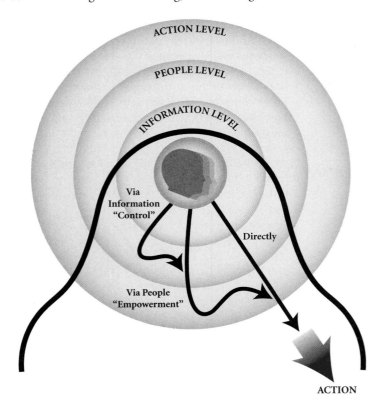

FIGURE 4
THE INFORMATION
ROLES

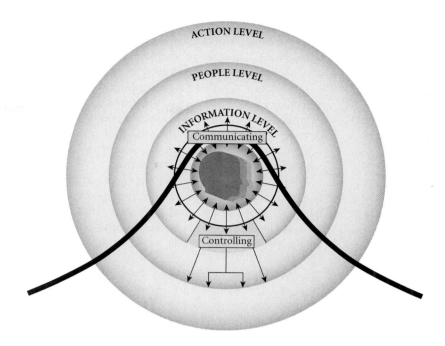

Communicating refers to the collection and dissemination of information. In Figure 4, communicating is shown by double arrows to indicate that managers devote a great deal of effort to the two-way flow of information with the people all around them—employees inside their own units, others in the rest of the organization, and especially, as the empirical evidence makes abundantly clear, a great number of outsiders with whom they maintain regular contact. Thus the head of one regional division of the national police force spent a good part of the day I observed him passing information back and forth between the central headquarters and the people on his staff.

Managers "scan" their environments, they monitor their own units, and they share with and disseminate to others considerable amounts of the information they pick up. Managers can be described as "nerve centers" of their units, who use their status of office to gain access to a wide variety of informational sources. Inside the unit, everyone else is a specialist who generally knows more about his or her specialty than the manager. But, because the manager is connected to all those specialists, he or she should have the broadest base of knowledge about the unit in general. This should apply to the head of a huge health care system, with regard to broad policy issues, no less than to the clinical director of one of its hospital units, with regard to the service rendered there. And externally, by virtue of their status, managers have access to other managers who are themselves nerve centers of their own units. And so they tend to be exposed to powerful sources of external information and thus emerge as external nerve centers as well. The health care chief executive can thus talk to people running health care systems in other countries and so gain access to an array of information perhaps inaccessible even to his most influential reports.

The result of all this is that a considerable amount of the manager's information turns out to be privileged, especially when we consider how much of it is oral and nonverbal. Accordingly, to function effectively with the people around them, managers have to spend considerable time sharing their information, both with outsiders (in a kind of spokesperson role) and with insiders (in a kind of disseminator role).

I found in my initial study of chief executives that perhaps 40 percent of their time was devoted almost exclusively to the communicating role—just to gaining and sharing information—leaving aside the information processing aspects of all the other roles. In other words, the job of managing is fundamentally one of processing information, notably by talking and especially listening. Thus Figure 4 shows the inner core (the person in the job, conceiving and scheduling) connected to the outer rings (the more tangible roles of managing people and action) through what can be called the membrane of information processing all around the job.

What can be called the **controlling** role describes the managers' efforts, not just to gain and share information, but to use it in a directive way inside their units: to evoke or provoke general action by the people who report to them. They do this in three broad ways: they develop systems, they design structures, and they impose directives. Each of these seeks to control how other people work, especially with regard to the allocation of resources, and so what actions they are inclined to take.

First, developing systems is the most general of these three, and the closest to conceiving. It uses information to control peoples' behaviors. Managers often take charge of establishing and even running such systems in their units, including those of planning and performance control (such as budgeting). Robert Simons has noted how chief executives tend to select one such system and make it key to their exercise of control, in a manner he calls "interactive" (Simons, 1990, 1991).

Second, managers exercise control through designing the structures of their units. By establishing responsibilities and defining hierarchical authority, they again exercise control rather passively, through the processing of information. People are informed of their duties, which in turn is expected to drive them to carry out the appropriate actions.

Third is imposing directives, which is the most direct of the three, closest to the people and action, although still informational in nature. Managers pronounce: they make specific choices and give specific orders, usually in the process of "delegating" particular responsibilities and "authorizing" particular requests. In effect, managers manage by transmitting information to people so that they can act.

If a full decision-making process can be considered in the three stages of diagnosing, designing, and deciding—in other words, identifying issues, working out possible solutions, and selecting one—then here we are dealing with a restricted view of decision making. Delegating means mostly diagnosing ("Would you please handle this problem in this context"), while authorizing means mostly deciding ("OK, you can proceed"). Either way, the richest part of the process, the stage of designing possible solutions, resides with the person being controlled rather than with the manager him or herself, whose own behavior remains rather passive. Thus, the manager as controller seems less an *actor* with sleeves rolled up, digging in, than a *reviewer* who sits back in the office and passes judgment. That is why this role is characterized as informational: I will describe a richer approach to decision making in the section on action roles.

The controlling role is shown in Figure 4 propelling down into the manager's own unit, since that is where formal authority is exercised. The single-headed arrows represent the imposed directives, while the pitchfork shape symbolizes both the design of structure and the development of systems. The proximity of the controlling role in Figure 4 to the manager's agenda reflects the fact that informational control is the most direct way to operationalize the agenda, for example, by using budgets to impose priorities or delegation to assign responsibilities. The controlling role is, of course, what people have in mind when they refer to the "administrative" aspect of managerial work.

MANAGING THROUGH PEOPLE

To manage through people, instead of by information, is to move one step closer to action, but still to remain removed from it. That is because here the focus of managerial attention becomes affect instead of effect. Other people become the means to get things done, not the manager him or herself, or even the substance of the manager's thoughts.

If the information roles (and controlling in particular) dominated our early thinking about managerial work, then after that, people entered the scene, or at least they entered the textbooks, as entities to be "motivated" and later "empowered." Influencing began to replace informing, and commitment began to vie with calculation for the attention of the manager. Indeed, in the 1960s and 1970s especially, the management of people, quite independent of content—of the strategies to be realized, the information to be processed, even the actions to be taken—became a virtual obsession of the literature, whether by the label of "human relations," "Theory Y," or "participative management" (and later "quality of work life," to be replaced by "total quality management").

For a long time, however, these people remained "subordinates" in more ways than one. "Participation" kept them subordinate, for this was always considered to be granted at the behest of the managers still fully in control. So does the currently popular term "empowerment," which implies that power is being granted, thanks to the managers. (Hospital directors do not "empower" physicians!) People also remained subordinates because the whole focus was on those inside the unit, not outside it. Not until serious research on managerial work began did it become evident how important to managers were contacts with individuals outside their units. Virtually every single study of how all kinds of managers spent their time has indicated that outsiders, of an enormously wide variety, generally take as much of the managers' attention as so-called "subordinates." We shall thus describe two people roles here, shown in Figure 5, one internal, called leading, and one external, called linking.

The **leading** role has probably received more attention in the literature of management than all other roles combined. And so we need not dwell on it here. But neither can we ignore it: managers certainly do much more than lead the people in their own units, and leading certainly infuses much else of what managers do (as, in fact, do all the roles, as we have already noted about communicating). But their work just as certainly cannot be understood without this dimension. We can describe the role of leading on three levels, as indicated in Figure 5.

First, managers lead on the *individual* level, "one on one," as the expression goes. They encourage and drive the people of their units—motivate them, inspire them, coach them, nurture them, push them, mentor them, and so on. All the managers I observed, from the chief executive of a major police force to the front-country manager in a mountain park, stopped to chat with their people informally during the day to encourage them in their work. Second, managers lead on the *group* level, especially by building and managing teams, an effort that has received considerable attention in recent years. Again, team meetings, including team

FIGURE 5
THE PEOPLE ROLES

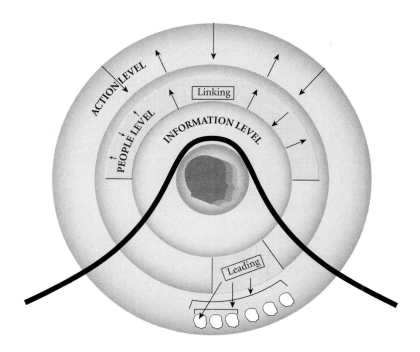

building, figured in many of my observations; for example, the head of a London film company who brought film-making teams together for both effective and affective purposes. And third, they lead on the *unit* level, especially with regard to the creation and maintenance of culture, another subject of increasing attention in recent years (thanks especially to the Japanese). Managers, for example, engage in many acts of symbolic nature ("figurehead" duties) to sustain culture, as when the head of the national police force visited its officer training institute (as he did frequently) to imbue the force's norms and attitudes in its graduating class.

All managers seem to spend time on all three levels of leadership, although, again, styles do vary according to context and personality. If the communicating role describes the manager as the nerve center of the unit, then the leading role must characterize him or her as its "energy center," a concept perhaps best captured in Maeterlinck's wonderful description of the "spirit of the hive" (Maeterlinck, 1918). Given the right managerial "chemistry" (in the case of Maeterlinck's queen bee, quite literally!), it may be the manager's mere presence that somehow draws things together. By exuding that mystical substance, the leader unites his or her people, galvanizing them into action to accomplish the unit's mission and adapt it to a changing world.

The excess attention to the role of leading has probably been matched by the inadequate attention to the role of **linking**. For, in their sheer allocation of time, managers have been shown to be external linkers as much as they are internal leaders, in study after study. Yet, still the point seems hardly appreciated. Indeed, now more than ever, it must be understood, given the great growth of joint ventures and other collaborating and networking relationships between organizations, as well as the gradual reconception of the "captive" employee as an autonomous "agent" who supplies labor.

Figure 5 suggests a small model of the linking role. The arrows go in and out to indicate that the manager is both an advocate of its influence outside the unit and, in turn, a recipient of much of the influence exerted on it from the outside. In the middle are two parallel lines to represent the buffering aspect of this role—that managers must regulate the receipt of external influence to protect their units. To use a popular term, they are the "gatekeepers" of influence. Or, to add a metaphor, the manager acts as a kind of valve between the unit and its environment. Nowhere was this clearer than in my observation of three levels of management in a national park system—a regional director, the head of one mountain park, and the front-country manager of that park. They sit in an immensely complex array of forces—developers who want to enhance their business opportunities, environmentalists who want to preserve the natural habitat, tourists who want to enjoy the beauty, truckers who want to drive through the park unimpeded, politicians who want to avoid negative publicity, etc. It is a delicate balancing, or buffering, act indeed!

All managers appear to spend a great deal of time "networking"—building vast arrays of contacts and intricate coalitions of supporters beyond their own units, whether within the rest of the organization or outside, in the world at large. To all these contacts, the manager represents the unit externally, promotes its needs, and lobbies for its causes. In response, these people are expected to provide a steady inflow of information to the unit as well as various means of support and specific favors for it. This networking was most evident in the case of the film company managing director I observed, who exhibited an impressive network of contacts in order to negotiate her complex contracts with various media in different countries.

In turn, people intent on influencing the behavior of an organization or one of its subunits will often exercise pressure directly on its manager, expecting that person to transmit the influence inside, as was most pointedly clear in the work of the parks manager. Here, then, the managerial job becomes one of delicate balance, a tricky act of mediation. Those managers who let external influence pass inside too freely—who act like sieves—are apt to drive their people crazy. (Of course, those who act like sponges and absorb all the influence personally are apt to drive themselves crazy!) And those who block out all influence—who act like lead to x-rays—are apt to detach their units from reality (and so dry up the sources of external support). Thus, what influence to pass on and how, bearing in mind the quid pro quo that influence exerted out is likely to be mirrored by influence coming back in, becomes another key aspect of managerial style, worthy of greatly increased attention in both the study of the job and the training of its occupants.

MANAGING ACTION

If managers manage passively by information and affectively through people, then they also manage actively and instrumentally by their own direct involvement in action. Indeed, this has been a long-established view of managerial work, although the excess attention in this century, first to controlling and then to leading, and more recently to conceiving (of planned strategy), has obscured its importance. Leonard Sayles, however, has long and steadily insisted on this, beginning with his 1964 book and culminating in *The Working Leader* (published in 1993), in which he makes his strongest statement yet, insisting that managers must be the focal points for action in and by their units (Sayles, 1964, 1993). Their direct involvement must, in his view, take precedence over the pulling force of leadership and the pushing force of controllership.

I shall refer to this involvement as the **doing** role. But, in using this label—a popular one in the managerial vernacular ("Mary Ann's a doer")—it is necessary to point out that managers, in fact, hardly ever "do" anything. Many barely even dial their own telephones! Watch a manager and you will see someone whose work consists almost exclusively of talking and listening, alongside, of course, watching and "feeling." (That, incidentally, is why I show the manager at the core of the model as a head and not a full body!)

What "doing" presumably means, therefore, is getting closer to the action, ultimately being just one step removed from it. Managers as doers manage the carrying out of action directly, instead of indirectly through managing people or by processing information. In effect, a "doer" is really someone who gets it done (or, as the French put it with their expression *faire faire*, to "make" something "get made"). And the managerial vernacular is, in fact, full of expressions that reflect just this: "doing deals," "championing change," "fighting fires," "juggling projects." In the terms of decision making introduced earlier, here the manager diagnoses and designs as well as decides: he or she gets deeply and fully involved in the management of particular activities. Thus, in the day I spent with the head of the small retail chain, I saw a steady stream of all sorts of people coming and going, most involved with some aspect of store development or store operations, and there to get specific instructions on how to proceed next. He was not delegating or authorizing, but very clearly managing specific development projects step by step.

Just as they communicate all around the circle, so too do managers "do" all around it, as shown in Figure 6. *Doing inside* involves projects and problems. In other words, much "doing" has to do with changing the unit itself, both proactively and reactively. Managers champion change to exploit opportunities for their units, and they handle its problems and resolve its crises, often with "hands on" involvement. Indeed, the president I observed of a large French systems company spent part of his day in a meeting on a very specific customer contract. Asked why he attended, he said it was a leading-edge project that could well change his company. He was being informed, to be sure, but also "doing" (more than controlling): he was an active member of the team. Here, then, the manager becomes a true designer (or, in the example above, a partner in the design), not of abstract strategies or of generalized structures, but of tangible projects of change. And the evidence, in fact, is that managers at all levels typically juggle many such projects concurrently, perhaps several dozen in the case of chief executives. Hence the popularity of the term "project management."

Some managers continue to do regular work after they have become managers as well. For example, a head nurse might see a patient, just as the Pope leads prayers, or a dean might teach a class. Done for its own sake, this might be considered separate from managerial work. But such things are often done for very managerial reasons as well. This may be an effective way of "keeping in touch" with the unit's work and finding out about its problems, in which case it falls under the role of communicating. Or it may be done to demonstrate involvement and commitment with others in the unit, in which case it falls under the role of culture building in the role of leading.

FIGURE 6
THE ACTION ROLES

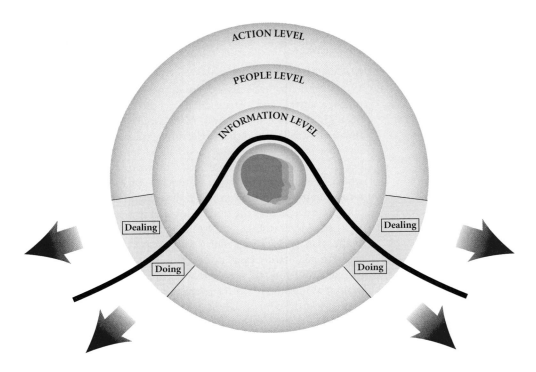

Doing outside, or *dealing*, takes place in terms of deals and negotiations. Again, there is no shortage of evidence on the importance of negotiating as well as dealing in managerial work. Most evident in my observations was the managing director of the film company, who was working on one intricate deal after another. This was a small company, and making deals was a key part of her job. But even in larger organizations, senior managers have to spend considerable time on negotiations themselves, especially when critical moments arise. After all, they are the ones who have the authority to commit the resources of their unit, and it is they who are the nerve centers of its information as well as the energy centers of its activity, not to mention the conceptual centers of its strategy. All around the circles, therefore, action connects to people who connect to information, which connects to the frame.

THE WELL-ROUNDED JOB OF MANAGING

I opened this article by noting that the best-known writers of management all seem to emphasize one aspect of the job—in the terms we now have, "doing" for Tom Peters, "conceiving" for Michael Porter, "leading" for Abraham Zaleznik and Warren Bennis, "controlling" for the classical writers. Now it can be appreciated why all may well be wrong: heeding the advice of any one of them must lead to the lopsided practice of managerial work. Like an unbalanced wheel at resonant frequency, the job risks flying out of control. That is why it is important to show all of the components of managerial work on a single integrated diagram, as in Figure 7, to remind people, at a glance, that these components form one job and cannot be separated.

Acceptance of Tom Peters's urgings—" 'Don't think, do' is the phrase I favor"—could lead to the centrifugal explosion of the job, as it flies off in all directions, free of a strong frame anchoring it at the core. But acceptance of the spirit of Michael Porter's opposite writings—that what matters most is conception of the frame, especially of strategic positions—could produce a result no better: centripetal implosion, as the job closes in on itself cerebrally, free of the tangible connection to its outer actions. Thinking is heavy and can wear down the incumbent, while acting is light and cannot keep him or her in place. Only together do they provide the balance that seems so characteristic of effective management.

FIGURE 7
MANAGERIAL WORK
ROUNDED OUT

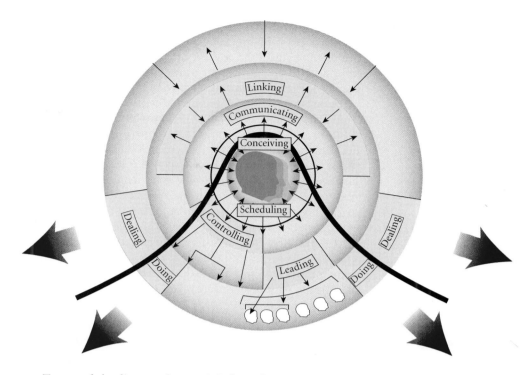

Too much leading produces a job free of content—aimless, frameless, and actionless—while too much linking produces a job detached from its internal roots—public relations instead of public service. The manager who only communicates or only conceives never gets anything done, while the manager who only "does" ends up doing it all alone. And, of course, we all know that happens to managers who believe their job is merely to control. A bad pun may thus make for good practice: the manager must practice a well-rounded job.

In fact, while we may be able to separate the components of this job conceptually, I maintain that they cannot be separated behaviorally. In other words, it may be useful, even necessary, to delineate the parts for purposes of design, selection, training, and support. But this job cannot be practiced as a set of independent parts. The core is a kind of magnet that holds the rest together, while the communication ring acts as a membrane that allows the flow of information between inner thinking and outer behaviors, which themselves tie people to action.

Indeed, the most interesting aspects of this job may well fall on the edges, between the component parts. For example, Andrew Grove, president of Intel, likes to describe what he does as "nudging," a perfect blend of controlling, leading, and doing (Grove, 1983). This can mean pushing people, tangibly but not aggressively, as might happen with pure doing, and not coldly, as with pure controlling, but with a sense of leading. There are similar edges between the inside and the outside, thinking and behaving, and communicating and controlling, as we shall see.

Managers who try to "deal" outside without "doing" inside inevitably get themselves into trouble. Just consider all those chief executives who "did the deal," acquired the company or whatever, and then dropped it into the laps of others for execution. Likewise, it makes no more sense to conceive and then fail to lead and do (as has been the tendency in so called "strategic planning," where controlling has often been considered sufficient for "implementation") than it makes sense to do or to lead without thinking through the frame in which to embed these activities. A single managerial job may be carried out by a small team, but only if its members are so tightly knitted together —especially by that ring of communication—that they act as a single entity. This is not to argue, of course, that different managers do not emphasize different roles or different aspects of the job. For example, we can distinguish a *conceptual* style of management, which focuses on the development of the frame, an *administrative* style, which concerns itself primarily with controlling, an *interpersonal* style, which favors leading on the inside or linking on the outside, and an *action* style, which is concerned mainly with tangible doing and dealing. And as we move out in this order, the overall style of managing can be described as less *opaque*, and more *visible*.

A final aspect of managerial style has to do with the interrelationships among the various components of managerial work. For example, an important distinction can be made between *deductive* and *inductive* approaches to managerial work. The former proceeds from the core out, as the conceived frame is implemented through scheduling that uses information to drive people to get action done. We can call this a *cerebral* style of managing—highly deliberate. But there is an alternate, emergent view of the management process as well, which proceeds inductively, from the outer surface to the inner core. We might label it an *insightful* style. As Karl Weick puts it, managers act in order to think. They try things to gain experience, retain what works, and then, by interpreting the results, gradually evolve their frames (Weick, 1979).

Clearly, there is an infinity of possible contexts within which management can be practiced. But just as clearly, perhaps, a model such as the one presented here can help to order them and so come to grips with the difficult requirements of designing managerial jobs, selecting the right people to fill them, and training people accordingly.

READING 2.2

ARTISTS, CRAFTSMEN, AND TECHNOCRATS*

BY PATRICIA PITCHER

■ . . . If you want to change corporate North America, you have to change its managers—not the culture, not the structure, but the people. All else is abstraction.

In my 20 years as an executive, a board member of multi-billion dollar corporations and, recently, an academic, one lesson stands out. Give a technocrat ultimate authority and he or she will drive out everything else: vision and its carriers—artists—will be replaced; experience and its carriers—craftsmen—will follow. Dissent will be driven from the board. The organization will ossify, turn inward and short-term. . . .

HOW TO IDENTIFY A TECHNOCRAT

Technocrats are never at a loss for words, charts, or graphs. They always have a plan of action in three parts. They rarely laugh out loud, except maybe at baseball games; never at work. When they explain to you why Jim or George had to be let go, they use expressions like, "He just wasn't tough, professional, modern, rigorous, serious, hard-working enough." If they go on to mention "too emotional," watch out! You have a technocrat on your hands. This person will be described by peers and colleagues as controlled, conservative, serious, analytical, no-nonsense, intense, determined, cerebral, methodical, and meticulous. Individually, any of these words might be a compliment; together, they represent a syndrome. Here is an example of how a technocrat thinks:

> Mirroring a world-wide trend . . . , we initiated in 1989 and continued in 1990 an extensive program under which operations were regrouped, assets sold, and activities rationalized. New chief executives have been appointed and our strategy is profitability.

*Reprinted with deletions from the article originally titled "Balancing Personality Types at the Top" with permission of *Business Quarterly* (Winter 1993) published by the Western Business School, University of Western Ontario, London, Canada.

In this one paragraph from an annual report, we notice three things. First, the technocrat loves conventional wisdom and thus the first phase, "Mirroring a world-wide trend"; if everyone else is doing it, it must be right. Second, we see the word "rationalized"; this is the watchword. Third, we are told that all the bad guys have been fired and replaced by serious folk. When things go wrong it is always the fault of someone else.

RECOGNIZING AN ARTIST

How do you recognize artists? Well, pretty much by the opposite. What is your strategic plan for the future? Answer: "to get big," "to hit $5 billion in sales," "to beat the pants off the competition," "to be a world leader by 2020." Artists may be a little short on the details, on the how. Board presentations are sometimes a little loose—unless they are done by the chief financial officer. The artist CEO might get overtly angry or euphoric at board meetings. How does the artist CEO talk? Listen to one.

> What is strategy anyway? Grand plan? No. You try to instill a vision you have and get people to buy in. The strategy comes from astrology; quirks, dreams, love affairs, science fiction, perception of society, some madness probably, ability to guess. It is clear but fluid. Action brings precision. Very vague, but becomes clear in the act of transformation. Creation is the storm.

When CEOs like this talk to their boards about "astrology; quirks, dreams," boards have a tendency to get a little uneasy. This person's peers and colleagues describe him or her as bold, daring, exciting, volatile, intuitive, entrepreneurial, inspiring, imaginative, unpredictable, and funny. Technocrats will apply labels like "star-trekky," or more simply, nuts. The artist makes both fast friends and abiding enemies. Very few have a neutral reaction. The organization as a whole is an exciting place to be; confusing maybe, dizzying maybe, but exciting nonetheless.

AND NOW, THE CRAFTSMAN

Rosabeth Moss Kanter insists, and I think she is dead right, that people take the long view when they perceive their leaders as trustworthy, and that the sacrifices they are called upon to make are genuinely for the collective future and not to line someone else's pockets today. The organizational craftsmen embody these values. People trust them. They see the organization as an enduring institution, one that has a life of its own, a past and a future, one of which he or she is but a custodian. They tend to stay in one organization and are therefore intimately familiar with its past and infinitely careful about preserving its identity in the midst of change. The craftsman provides continuity and organizational glue, and stimulates loyalty and commitment.

Craft is fundamentally conservative, rooted in tradition. Samuel Johnson, the great British satirist, wrote, "You cannot with all the talk in the world, enable a man to make a shoe." Experience and practice are essential to judgment. What happens if you do not have experience in the firm, in the industry, in the organization? As one CEO once said, referring to a famous bright, young, professional, "He'll get hit by every blue-suede shoes man in the country." What he meant was that this brilliant young man would fall prey to idea salesmen peddling old ideas in new packages, and he would buy because he has no experience. He could not possibly know that the idea had been tried—and rejected—20 years ago. Craft demands submission to authority. Apprenticeship is long, frustrating and sometimes arduous. There are not short cuts. Polanyi argues:

> To learn by example is to submit to authority. You follow your master because you trust his manner of doing things even when you cannot analyze or account in detail for its effectiveness. A society which wants to preserve a kind of personal knowledge must submit to tradition.

Imagine the frustration of a brilliant young executive when his or her craftsman boss cannot answer the question, "Why?" Craft is inarticulate. The answer to the young manager's question is locked away in the tricks of the trade, in tacit knowledge. So, he or she thinks the boss a fool. If he or she is the boss, the employee is condemned as an old-fashioned fool and fired.

What does this tell us about craftsmen? First of all, craftsmen are patient, both with themselves and with others; they know that it took them a long time to acquire their skills and that it will be true for others. They regularly exhibit that much-sought-after commodity, judgment; judgment flows out of long experience. Young people rarely exhibit it. Their colleagues will describe them as wise, amiable, humane, honest, straightforward, responsible, trustworthy, reasonable, open-minded, and realistic. Here is a craftsman speaking about technocrats:

> Even if they had a vision, how would they get it done? There's no managerial continuity. At this year's planning meeting, there were four out of 14 people left over from two years ago. Every two years there's a new chief executive. There's no opportunity to fail, so there's no continuity. They focus directly on profit but they'll never get it because profit comes from the vision and the people and they won't invest in people. If you look after the people, the profit follows. You can't drive at it directly. Twelve and a half percent ROI is a joke; we'll be dead [in five years]. They refuse to see this. You can't correct a problem unless you see it exists. It's like me. I look in the mirror and I see a young fullback, not a balding, middle-aged man with his chest on his belly. You have to see reality to change it.

Craftsmen believe that technocrats do not have vision, and even if they did it would not do any good because they "won't invest in people." The craftsman speaking above objects to trend-line projections; "Twelve and a half percent ROI is a joke; we'll be dead [in five years]." His credo is, "If you look after the people, the profit follows." . . . (See Figure 1 for a summary of these types of managerial stereotypes.)

TEAMWORK AND THE TYPES

When serious looks at funny what does it see? Red. It sees cavalier; it sees irresponsible; it sees childish. When analytical looks at intuitive, it sees dreamer, head-in-the-clouds. When wise stares at cerebral, it sees a head without a heart, it sees brilliance devoid of judgment. And so on down the list. In short, the three types of people cannot communicate. They live in differ-

FIGURE 1
MANAGERIAL
STEROTYPES

THE ARTIST	THE CRAFTSMAN	THE TECHNOCRAT
Bold	Responsible	Conservative
Daring	Wise	Methodical
Exciting	Humane	No-nonsense
Volatile	Straightforward	Controlled
Intuitive	Open-minded	Cerebral
Entrepreneurial	Realistic	Analytical
Inspiring	Trustworthy	Determined
Imaginative	Reasonable	Meticulous
Unpredictable	Honest	Intense
Funny	Amiable	Serious

ent worlds, with different values and different goals. They frame different questions and different answers to all issues confronting the corporation. They believe that their conflicts center on ideas, whereas, in fact, they center on character.

For example, recently, a major international corporation experienced pronounced difficulty with its stock price. No matter what it did, its stock traded at a 50% discount from book value. Why? Listen in on the dialogue of the deaf that goes on between senior officers and the CEO inside that corporation. They are all talking about the same subject, but you would not know it.

An *artist:* "Of course the stock price is low! (He always talks with exclamation points.) We're not doing anything to create interest, magic! We haven't bought anything, launched anything, dreamt up anything in months! Nobody believes we have an exciting future ahead of us! The stock will go up when people believe in our dream!"

A *technocrat* (firmly): "It's all the so-called dreams which have turned into cost-nightmares. We haven't showed consistent quarterly earnings over the last three years. For two quarters, our earnings have reflected some marginal improvement. As soon as the street begins to have some faith in our capacity to control costs they'll turn into believers and start to recommend our stock."

A *craftsman:* "The people on the street are not stupid. They know that we've had so much managerial turnover that we have no continuity. They know we've fallen out of touch with our traditional markets. The guy brought in to run our main widgets division wouldn't know a widget if he fell over one. The whole sales force is disillusioned. What we need is to get back in touch with what we do best."

Sticking to your knitting is not some new theoretical concept to craftsmen; it is their life. They have always done it. It comes as naturally as breathing. The cost-cutting program inevitably proposed by the technocrat strikes at the core of what the craftsman considers to be the answer to the problem. The technocrat wants to cut out the fat: inflated marketing budgets, sales training conferences, and staff development expenses. The craftsman sees the profitability problem as a symptom, a reflection of the demotivation of staff, as a diminished sense of loyalty and therefore of effort—a legacy of the last round of staff cuts and the replacement of leaders that they trusted. The technocrat is dangerous because, to the craftsman, he or she is too theoretical, "too distant from the coalface" to understand the real issues. . . .

In a major multinational I have studied for the last 10 years, the technocrats have truly triumphed. Figure 2 shows the 10-year evolution of the management team. Beginning with a healthy mix of artists, craftsmen and technocrats, by 1990 the structure had tilted irrevocably to the technocrat. Two remaining craftsmen were in the power structure only nominally; both were looking for jobs.

FIGURE 2
THE TECHNOCRATIC
TRANSFORMATION

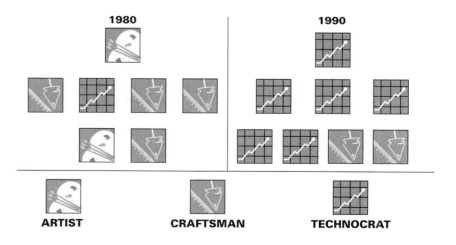

The result of this shift has been parallel changes in strategy and in structure. Under the aegis of the artist, the corporation had been outward-looking, increasingly internationally oriented. Fueled both by internal growth and acquisitions, assets climbed. Subsidiaries were left pretty much on their own—the power structure was decentralized—and the atmosphere, prevailing ethic, or culture if you will, was of teamwork, growth and excitement. Out of insecurity or a simple error in judgment, the artist chose as his successor his opposite. Promoted into the number one spot, the technocrat began to install others and to rationalize, organize and control. The by-product of rationalization, systematization and control was centralization. The by-product of centralization was demoralization. The strategy became, in the words of the annual reports, profitability. Profitability was not and is not a strategy and it can certainly not inspire anyone as an ultimate goal: "What do you do for a living?" "I make profit." Losing the artists, the company lost vision. Losing the craftsmen, it lost its humanity. Although profitability became the watchword, profits did not go up. Nor did share prices. The group was eventually absorbed by a more ambitious rival.

THE TRIUMPH OF THE TECHNOCRAT

. . . Technocrats have a way of making us feel secure. With their ready answers, their charts and their graphs, they give us the feeling that everything will be all right if we just follow the rules: the rules of logic, the rules of good business practice, matrix management, participatory management, total quality management and the new rules of globalization and strategic alliances. They make everything sound so straightforward, so rational, so comforting, so reassuring—sort of like Betty Crocker.

. . . What does a manager look like, I ask my students. "He's calm, rational, well-balanced, measured, analytical, methodological, skilled, trained, serious," they say. It occurs to me that I am listening to a liturgy—a liturgy from the gospel of the technocratic school. The person they describe is one kind of manager, and he or she is now firmly anchored as the only kind. It has become definitional.

THE LEARNING ORGANIZATION

If we concede for a moment the narcissistic presumption that ours is an age of discontinuity, then the old ways of doing things no longer work. Organizations need to learn—rapidly and continuously. How does learning take place? At the turn of the century, American philosopher George Santayana wrote, "Man's progress has a poetic phase in which he imagines the world, then a scientific phase in which he sifts and tests what he has imagined." Culturally, we have always relied on our visionaries to point us toward the new way. In science, we call a visionary a genius; in letters, a poet; in politics, a statesman; in business, a leader; generically, an artist. What all these labels have in common is the idea of someone who breaks radically with conventional wisdom, someone who sees what others do not, someone who imagines a new order. This is discontinuous learning. We call it imaginative.

Then, there is continuous learning, daily learning. What is found in art comes into use and is transformed, concretized, shaped and sculpted by experience. A great idea, usually quite vague, is refined by practice over time. The bugs are worked out. Flesh is added to the skeleton. The slow accumulation of talent in its application is the domain of craft. We call its carrier, skilled.

Finally, there is a third form of learning. It comes from the codification of old knowledge; it comes from books and scientific papers. It comes from studying and diligence, and requires neither insight nor practice to make it our own. We call the person who possesses it knowledgeable, and if he or she possesses it to a very fine degree, brilliant.

With our religion we have eliminated both the poetic and the craft phase of learning, and tried to reduce everything to the scientific. (We are sons and daughters of the Enlightenment, after all.) We have come to believe that managers who have an MBA, can read a balance sheet and can talk knowledgeably about strategic alliances must make good CEOs. This is nonsense.

If they have no imagination, they will only mimic the competition—strategy as paint-by-numbers art. If they have no skill, they will not understand their markets. If they have no wisdom, they will tear at the fabric of the organization.

VISION, CONTINUITY AND CONTROL

There are three ways of learning, each equally necessary. Leadership consists of knowing how to put the package together and make it work. It consists of integrating vision, continuity and control in the managerial team.

The first step is obviously diagnostic. What does my organization look like currently? How many artists, craftsmen and technocrats do I have, and how are they functionally distributed? What is the balance of power among them? What is the dominant ethic? Is there the freedom to fail, which is indispensable to the possibility to succeed? Is there sufficient pride of place given to emotion, to skill, to brilliance? This diagnosis is of course easier proposed than accomplished, and this for three main reasons:

1. Artists, craftsmen and technocrats rarely exist as such; they are archetypes. Real people come in more complex packages. We may see artists, for example, with an admixture of craft. We may see conservative, cerebral craftsmen and we may see emotionally hot technocrats, or highly analytical and determined artists. Rarely do we see someone who combines all three—although we all think we do.

2. The task is made more difficult by masquerades. Faced with an artistic type, we are rarely fooled. And, with their straightforwardness and frankness, craftsmen usually give themselves away. But the technocrat, particularly of the brilliant variety, is hard to see. Technocrats revere conventional wisdom—not wisdom of a traditional sort, but new wisdom. For example, I recently had the pleasure of listening to a discourse on total quality management and empowerment from an archetypal technocratic CEO. He had systematically eliminated all artists and craftsmen from his organization. Experimentation and loyalty were dead because one false step meant being fired. Now he wanted to graft onto this moribund organization new energies of empowerment. And, what is worse, he was sincere. He really could not know that these managerial recipes, conceived procedurally, will not work. The graft will not take. But, to his board and to other observers, this man was saying all the right things. He was masquerading as a craftsman. Others, again of the brilliant variety, will masquerade as artists; knowledgeable and well-read in a superficial sort of way, they will seem to know the future. Here, we can be radically misled.

3. Finally, there is a third reason why the diagnosis is so fraught with uncertainty. It is us. What we see depends on where we sit. If I am a technocrat, I will have a tendency to see other, more brilliant technocrats as artists. I will think of them as visionary and entrepreneurial, far-sighted and bold. If I am a pure craftsman, I will have no use for any technocrats. As one craftsman CEO put it to me recently, "They make good consultants." To him, a brilliant technocrat is dangerous as a manager because he or she is intellectually disconnected from reality. And artists, too, have their blind spots, not so much about people as about suitable objects of attention. Built into the diagnostic process, therefore, must be an element of collective judgment—judgment that does not rely too exclusively on the point of view of one or another of the archetypes. . . .

Growing frustration with formal managerial models coupled with increasing recognition of the difficulty of planning in a turbulent world, has led to the call for charismatic leadership, as though the presence of a charismatic leader could somehow take all the hard work out of managing a business. Certainly, the artists described here are charismatic and their presence is vital for success. But, they are not alone. You need artists, craftsmen and technocrats in the right dose and in the right places. You need someone with vision, but you also need someone who can develop the people, the structures and the systems to make the dream a reality. If you have the right people, they will do the job that comes naturally to them; you do not have to teach a fish how to swim. [The] key managerial task [of the CEO] is not to know everything but to build an executive team that can get the whole job done.

READING 2.3 GOOD MANAGERS DON'T MAKE POLICY DECISIONS*

BY H. EDWARD WRAPP

■ The upper reaches of management are a land of mystery and intrigue. Very few people have ever been there, and the present inhabitants frequently send back messages that are incoherent both to other levels of management and to the world in general. This may account for the myths, illusions, and caricatures that permeate the literature of management—for example, such widely held notions as these:

■ Life gets less complicated as a manager reaches the top of the pyramid.
■ The manager at the top level knows everything that's going on in the organization, can command whatever resources he may need, and therefore can be more decisive.
■ The general manager's day is taken up with making broad policy decisions and formulating precise objectives.
■ The top executive's primary activity is conceptualizing long-range plans.
■ In a large company, the top executive may be seen meditating about the role of his organization in society.

I suggest that none of these versions alone, or in combination, is an accurate portrayal of what a general manager does. Perhaps students of the management process have been overly eager to develop a theory and a discipline. As one executive I know puts it, "I guess I do some of the things described in the books and articles, but the descriptions are lifeless, and my job isn't."

What common characteristics, then, do successful executives exhibit *in reality?* I shall identify five skills or talents which, in my experience, seem especially significant. . . .

KEEPING WELL INFORMED

First, each of my heroes has a special talent for keeping himself informed about a wide range of operating decisions being made at different levels in the company. As he moves up the ladder, he develops a network of information sources in many different departments. He cultivates these sources and keeps them open no matter how high he climbs in the organization. When the need arises, he bypasses the lines on the organization chart to seek more than one version of a situation.

In some instances, especially when they suspect he would not be in total agreement with their decision, his subordinates will elect to inform him in advance, before they announce a decision. In these circumstances, he is in a position to defer the decision, or redirect it, or even block further action. However, he does not insist on this procedure. Ordinarily he leaves it up to the members of his organization to decide at what stage they inform him.

Top-level managers are frequently criticized by writers, consultants, and lower levels of management for continuing to enmesh themselves in operating problems, after promotion to

*Originally published in the *Harvard Business Review* (September–October 1967) and winner of the McKinsey prize for the best article in the *Review* in 1967. Copyright © 1967 by the President and Fellows of Harvard College; all rights reserved. Reprinted with deletions by permission of the *Harvard Business Review*.

the top, rather than withdrawing to the "big picture." Without any doubt, some managers do get lost in a welter of detail and insist on making too many decisions. Superficially, the good manager may seem to make the same mistake—but his purposes are different. He knows that only by keeping well informed about the decisions being made can he avoid the sterility so often found in those who isolate themselves from operations. If he follows the advice to free himself from operations, he may soon find himself subsisting on a diet of abstractions, leaving the choice of what he eats in the hands of his subordinates. As Kenneth Boulding puts it, "The very purpose of a hierarchy is to prevent information from reaching higher layers. It operates as an information filter, and there are little wastebaskets all along the way" (in *Business Week*, February 18, 1967:202). . . .

FOCUSING TIME AND ENERGY

The second skill of the good manager is that he knows how to save his energy and hours for those few particular issues, decisions, or problems to which he should give his personal attention. He knows the fine and subtle distinction between keeping fully informed about operating decisions and allowing the organization to force him into participating in these decisions, or, even worse, making them. Recognizing that he can bring his special talents to bear on only a limited number of matters, he chooses those issues which he believes will have the greatest long-term impact on the company, and on which his special abilities can be most productive. Under ordinary circumstances he will limit himself to three or four major objectives during any single period of sustained activity.

What about the situations he elects *not* to become involved in as a decision maker? He makes sure (using the skill first mentioned) that the organization keeps him informed about them at various stages; he does not want to be accused of indifference to such issues. He trains his subordinates not to bring the matters to him for a decision. The communication to him from below is essentially one of, "Here is our sizeup, and here's what we propose to do." Reserving his hearty encouragement for those projects which hold superior promise of a contribution to total corporate strategy, he simply acknowledges receipt of information on other matters. When he sees a problem where the organization needs his help, he finds a way to transmit his know-how short of giving orders—usually by asking perceptive questions.

PLAYING THE POWER GAME

To what extent do successful top executives push their ideas and proposals through the organization? The rather common notion that the "prime mover" continually creates and forces through new programs, like a powerful majority leader in a liberal Congress, is in my opinion very misleading.

The successful manager is sensitive to the power structure in the organization. In considering any major current proposal, he can plot the position of the various individuals and units in the organization on a scale ranging from complete, outspoken support down to determined, sometimes bitter, and oftentimes well cloaked opposition. In the middle of the scale is an area of comparative indifference. Usually, several aspects of a proposal will fall into this area, and *here is where he knows he can operate*. He assesses the depth and nature of the blocs in the organization. His perception permits him to move through what I call *corridors* of comparative indifference. He seldom challenges when a corridor is blocked, preferring to pause until it has opened up.

Related to this particular skill is his ability to recognize the need for a few trial-balloon launchers in the organization. He knows that the organization will tolerate only a certain number of proposals which emanate from the apex of the pyramid. No matter how sorely he may be tempted to stimulate the organization with a flow of his own ideas, he knows he must work through idea men in different parts of the organization. As he studies the reactions of key individuals and groups to the trial balloons these men send up, he is able to make a better assessment of how to limit the emasculation of the various proposals. For seldom does he find a proposal which is supported by all quarters of the organization. The emergence of strong support in certain quarters is almost sure to evoke strong opposition in others.

VALUE OF SENSE OF TIMING

Circumstances like these mean that a good sense of timing is a priceless asset for a top executive. . . . As a good manager stands at a point in time, he can identify a set of goals he is interested in, albeit the outline of them may be pretty hazy. His timetable, which is also pretty hazy, suggests that some must be accomplished sooner than others, and that some may be safely postponed for several months or years. He has a still hazier notion of how he can reach these goals. He assesses key individuals and groups. He knows that each has its own set of goals, some of which he understands rather thoroughly and others about which he can only speculate. He knows also that these individuals and groups represent blocks to certain programs or projects, and that these points of opposition must be taken into account. As the day-to-day operating decisions are made, and as proposals are responded to both by individuals and by groups, he perceives more clearly where the corridors of comparative indifference are. He takes action accordingly.

THE ART OF IMPRECISION

The fourth skill of the successful manager is knowing how to satisfy the organization that it has a sense of direction *without ever actually getting himself committed to a specific set of objectives.* This is not to say that he does not have objectives—personal and corporate, long-term and short-term. They are significant guides to his thinking, and he modifies them continually as he better understands the resources he is working with, the competition, and the changing market demands. But as the organization clamors for statements of objectives, these are samples of what they get back from him:

> "Our company aims to be number one in its industry."
> "Our objective is growth with profit."
> "We seek the maximum return on investment."
> "Management's goal is to meet its responsibilities to stockholders, employees, and the public."

In my opinion, statements such as these provide almost no guidance to the various levels of management. Yet they are quite readily accepted as objectives by large numbers of intelligent people.

MAINTAINING VIABILITY

Why does the good manager shy away from precise statements of his objectives for the organization? The main reason is that he finds it impossible to set down specific objectives which will be relevant for any reasonable period into the future. Conditions in business change continually and rapidly, and corporate strategy must be revised to take the changes into account. The more explicit the statement of strategy, the more difficult it becomes to persuade the organization to turn to different goals when needs and conditions shift.

The public and the stockholders, to be sure, must perceive the organization as having a well-defined set of objectives and clear sense of direction. But in reality the good top manager is seldom so certain of the direction which should be taken. Better than anyone else, he senses the many, many threats to his company—threats which lie in the economy, in the actions of competitors, and, not least, within his own organization.

He also knows that it is impossible to state objectives clearly enough so that everyone in the organization understands what they mean. Objectives get communicated only over time by a consistency or pattern in operating decisions. Such decisions are more meaningful than words. In instances where precise objectives are spelled out, the organization tends to interpret them so they fit its own needs.

Subordinates who keep pressing for more precise objectives are in truth working against their own best interests. Each time the objectives are stated more specifically, a subordinate's range of possibilities for operating are reduced. The narrower field means less room to roam and to accommodate the flow of ideas coming up from his part of the organization.

AVOIDING POLICY STRAITJACKETS

The successful manager's reluctance to be precise extends into the area of policy decisions. He seldom makes a forthright statement of policy. He may be aware that in some companies there are executives who spend more time in arbitrating disputes caused by stated policies than in moving the company forward. The management textbooks contend that well-defined policies are the sine qua non of a well-managed company. My research does not bear out this contention. For example,

> The president of one company with which I am familiar deliberately leaves the assignments of his top officers vague and refuses to define policies for them. He passes out new assignments with seemingly no pattern in mind and consciously sets up competitive ventures among his subordinates. His methods, though they would never be sanctioned by a classical organization planner, are deliberate—and, incidentally, quite effective.

Since able managers do not make policy decisions, does this mean that well-managed companies operate without policies? Certainly not. But the policies are those which evolve over time from an indescribable mix of operating decisions. From any single operating decision might have come a very minor dimension of the policy as the organization understands it; from a series of decisions comes a pattern of guidelines for various levels of the organization.

The skillful manager resists the urge to write a company creed or to compile a policy manual. Preoccupation with detailed statements of corporate objectives and departmental goals and with comprehensive organization charts and job descriptions is often the first symptom of an organization which is in the early stages of atrophy.

The "management by objectives" school, so widely heralded in recent years, suggests that detailed objectives be spelled out at all levels in the corporation. This method is feasible at lower levels of management, but it becomes unworkable at the upper levels. The top manager must think out objectives in detail, but ordinarily some of the objectives must be withheld, or at least communicated to the organization in modest doses. A conditioning process which may stretch over months or years is necessary in order to prepare the organization for radical departures from what it is currently striving to attain.

Suppose, for example, that a president is convinced his company must phase out of the principal business it has been in for 35 years. Although making this change of course is one of his objectives, he may well feel that he cannot disclose the idea even to his vice presidents, whose total know-how is in the present business. A blunt announcement that the company is changing horses would be too great a shock for most of them to bear. And so he begins moving toward this goal but without a full disclosure to his management group.

A detailed spelling out of objectives may only complicate the task of reaching them. Specific, detailed statements give the opposition an opportunity to organize its defenses.

MUDDLING WITH A PURPOSE

The fifth, and most important, skill I shall describe bears little relation to the doctrine that management is (or should be) a comprehensive, systematic, logical, well-programmed science. Of all the heresies set forth here, this should strike doctrinaires as the rankest of all!

The successful manager, in my observation, recognizes the futility of trying to push total packages or programs through the organization. He is willing to take less than total acceptance in order to achieve modest progress toward his goals. Avoiding debates on principles, he tries to piece together particles that may appear to be incidentals into a program that moves at least part of the way toward his objectives. His attitude is based on optimism and persistence. Over and over he says to himself, "There must be some parts of this proposal on which we can capitalize."

Whenever he identifies relationships among the different proposals before him, he knows that they present opportunities for combination and restructuring. It follows that he is a man of wide-ranging interests and curiosity. The more things he knows about, the more opportunities he will have to discover parts which are related. This process does not require great intellectual brilliance or unusual creativity. The wider ranging his interests, the more likely that he will be able to tie together several unrelated proposals. He is skilled as an analyst, but even more talented as a conceptualizer.

If the manager has built or inherited a solid organization, it will be difficult for him to come up with an idea which no one in the company has ever thought of before. His most significant contribution may be that he can see relationships which no one else has seen. . . .

CONTRASTING PICTURES

It is interesting to note, in the writings of several students of management, the emergence of the concept that, rather than making decisions, the leader's principal task is maintaining operating conditions which permit the various decision-making systems to function effectively. The supporters of this theory, it seems to me, overlook the subtle turns of direction which the leader can provide. He cannot add purpose and structure to the balanced judgments of subordinates if he simply rubberstamps their decisions. He must weigh the issues and reach his own decision. . . .

Many of the articles about successful executives picture them as great thinkers who sit at their desks drafting master blueprints for their companies. The successful top executives I have seen at work do no operate this way. Rather than produce a full-grown decision tree, they start with a twig, help it grow, and ease themselves out on the limbs only after they have tested to see how much weight the limbs can stand.

In my picture, the general manager sits in the midst of a continuous stream of operating problems. His organization presents him with a flow of proposals to deal with the problems. Some of these proposals are contained in voluminous, well-documented, formal reports; some are as fleeting as the walk-in visit from a subordinate whose latest inspiration came during the morning's coffee break. Knowing how meaningless it is to say, "This is a finance problem," or, "That is a communications problem," the manager feels no compulsion to classify his problems. He is, in fact, undismayed by a problem that defies classification. As the late Gary Steiner, in one of his speeches, put it, "He has a high tolerance for ambiguity."

In considering each proposal, the general manager tests it against at least three criteria:

1. Will the total proposal—or, more often, will some parts of the proposal—move the organization toward the objectives which he has in mind?
2. How will the whole or parts of the proposal be received by the various groups and subgroups in the organization? Where will the strongest opposition come from, which group will furnish the strongest support, and which group will be neutral or indifferent?
3. How does the proposal relate to programs already in process or currently proposed? Can some parts of the proposal under consideration be added on to a program already under way, or can they be combined with all or parts of other proposals in a package which can be steered through the organization? . . .

CONCLUSION

To recapitulate, the general manager possesses five important skills. He knows how to:

1. *Keep open many pipelines of information*—No one will quarrel with the desirability of an early warning system which provides varied viewpoints on an issue. However, very few managers know how to practice this skill, and the books on management add precious little to our understanding of the techniques which make it practicable.

2. *Concentrate on a limited number of significant issues*—No matter how skillful the manager is in focusing his energies and talents, he is inevitably caught up in a number of inconsequential duties. Active leadership of an organization demands a high level of personal involvement, and personal involvement brings with it many time-consuming activities which have an infinitesimal impact on corporate strategy. Hence this second skill, while perhaps the most logical of the five, is by no means the easiest to apply.

3. *Identify the corridors of comparative indifference*—Are there inferences here that the good manager has no ideas of his own, that he stands by until his organization proposes solutions, that he never uses his authority to force a proposal through the organization? Such inferences are not intended. The message is that a good organization will tolerate only so much direction from the top; the good manager therefore is adept at sensing how hard he can push.

4. *Give the organization a sense of direction with open-ended objectives*—In assessing this skill, keep in mind that I am talking about top levels of management. At lower levels, the manager should be encouraged to write down his objectives, if for no other reason than to ascertain if they are consistent with corporate strategy.

5. *Spot opportunities and relationships in the stream of operating problems and decisions*—Lest it be concluded from the description of this skill that the good manager is more an improviser than a planner, let me emphasize that he is a planner and encourages planning by his subordinates. Interestingly, though, professional planners may be irritated by a good general manager. Most of them complain about his lack of vision. They devise a master plan, but the president (or other operating executive) seems to ignore it, or to give it minimum acknowledgment by borrowing bits and pieces for implementation. They seem to feel that the power of a good master plan will be obvious to everyone, and its implementation automatic. But the general manager knows that even if the plan is sound and imaginative, the job has only begun. The long, painful task of implementation will depend on his skill, not that of the planner. . . .

READING 2.4

THE LEADER'S NEW WORK: BUILDING LEARNING ORGANIZATIONS*

BY PETER M. SENGE

■ Human beings are designed for learning. No one has to teach an infant to walk, or talk, or master the spatial relationships needed to stack eight building blocks that don't topple. Children come fully equipped with an insatiable drive to explore and experiment. Unfortunately, the primary institutions of our society are oriented predominantly toward controlling rather than learning, rewarding individuals for performing for others rather than for cultivating their natural curiosity and impulse to learn. The young child entering school discovers quickly that the name of the game is getting the right answer and avoiding mistakes—a mandate no less compelling to the aspiring manager.

---

*Reprinted from the *Sloan Management Review* (Fall 1990), pp. 7–23; by permission of the publisher. Copyright © 1990 by the *Sloan Management Review*. All rights reserved.

"Our prevailing system of management has destroyed our people," writes W. Edwards Deming, leader in the quality movement (Senge, 1990). "People are born with intrinsic motivation, self-esteem, dignity, curiosity to learn, joy in learning. The forces of destruction begin with toddlers—a prize for the best Halloween costume, grades in school, gold stars, and on up through the university. On the job, people, teams, divisions are ranked—reward for the one at the top, punishment at the bottom. MBO, quotas, incentive pay, business plans, put together separately, division by division, cause further loss, unknown and unknowable."

Ironically, by focusing on performing for someone else's approval, corporations create the very conditions that predestine them to mediocre performance. Over the long run, superior performance depends on superior learning. A Shell study showed . . . that "the key to the long term survival of the large industrial enterprise was the ability to run 'experiments in the margin,' to continually explore new business and organizational opportunities that create potential new sources of growth" (de Gues, 1988, pp. 70–74).

If anything, the need for understanding how organizations learn and accelerating that learning is greater today than ever before. The old days when a Henry Ford, Alfred Sloan, or Tom Watson *learned for the organization* are gone. In an increasingly dynamic, interdependent, and unpredictable world, it is simply no longer possible for anyone to "figure it all out at the top." The old model, "the top thinks and the local acts," must now give way to integrative thinking and acting at all levels. . . .

ADAPTIVE LEARNING AND GENERATIVE LEARNING

The prevailing view of learning organizations emphasizes increased adaptability. . . . But increasing adaptiveness is only the first stage in moving toward learning organizations. The impulse to learn in children goes deeper than desires to respond and adapt more effectively to environmental change. The impulse to learn, at its heart, is an impulse to be generative, to expand our capability. This is why leading corporations are focusing on *generative* learning, which is about creating, as well as *adaptive* learning, which is about coping. . . .

Generative learning, unlike adaptive learning, requires new ways of looking at the world, whether in understanding customers or in understanding how to better manage a business. For years, U.S. manufacturers sought competitive advantage in aggressive controls on inventories, incentives against overproduction, and rigid adherence to production forecasts. Despite these incentives, their performance was eventually eclipsed by Japanese firms who saw the challenges of manufacturing differently. They realized that eliminating delays in the production process was the key to reducing instability and improving cost, productivity, and service. They worked to build networks of relationships with trusted suppliers and to redesign physical production processes so as to reduce delays in materials procurement, production set up, and in-process inventory—a much higher-leverage approach to improving both cost and customer loyalty.

As Boston Consulting Group's George Stalk has observed, the Japanese saw the significance of delays because they saw the process of order entry, production scheduling, materials procurement, production, and distribution *as an integrated system.* "What distorts the system so badly is time," observed Stalk—the multiple delays between events and responses. "These distortions reverberate throughout the system, producing disruptions, waste, and inefficiency" (Stalk, 1988 pp. 41–51). Generative learning requires seeing the systems that control events. When we fail to grasp the systemic source of problems, we are left to "push on" symptoms rather than eliminate underlying causes. The best we can ever do is adaptive learning.

THE LEADER'S NEW WORK

. . . Our traditional view of leaders—as special people who set the direction, make the key decisions, and energize the troops—is deeply rooted in an individualistic and nonsystemic worldview. Especially in the West, leaders are *heroes*—great men (and occasionally women) who rise to the fore in times of crisis. So long as such myths prevail, they reinforce a focus on short-term events and charismatic heroes rather than on systemic forces and collective learning.

Leadership in learning organizations centers on subtler and ultimately more important work. In a learning organization, leaders' roles differ dramatically from that of the charismatic decision maker. Leaders are designers, teachers, and stewards. These roles require new skills: the ability to build shared vision, to bring to the surface and challenge prevailing mental models, and to foster more systemic patterns of thinking. In short, leaders in learning organizations are responsible for *building organizations* where people are continually expanding their capabilities to shape their future—that is, leaders are responsible for learning.

CREATIVE TENSION: THE INTEGRATING PRINCIPLE

Leadership in a learning organization starts with the principle of creative tension (Fritz, 1989, 1990). Creative tension comes from seeing clearly where we want to be, our "vision," and telling the truth about where we are, our "current reality." The gap between the two generates a natural tension. . . .

Creative tension can be resolved in two basic ways: by raising current reality toward the vision, or by lowering the vision toward current reality. Individuals, groups, and organizations who learn how to work with creative tension learn how to use the energy it generates to move reality more reliably toward their visions. . . .

Without vision there is no creative tension. Creative tension cannot be generated from current reality alone. All the analysis in the world will never generate a vision. Many who are otherwise qualified to lead fail to do so because they try to substitute analysis for vision. They believe that, if only people understood current reality, they would surely feel the motivation to change. They are then disappointed to discover that people "resist" the personal and organizational changes that must be made to alter reality. What they never grasp is that the natural energy for changing reality comes from holding a picture of what might be that is more important to people than what is.

But creative tension cannot be generated from vision alone; it demands an accurate picture of current reality as well. Just as Martin Luther King had a dream, so too did he continually strive to "dramatize the shameful conditions" of racism and prejudice so that they could no longer be ignored. Vision without an understanding of current reality will more likely foster cynicism than creativity. The principle of creative tension teaches that *an accurate picture of current reality is just as important as a compelling picture of a desired future.*

Leading through creative tension is different than solving problems. In problem solving, the energy for change comes from attempting to get away from an aspect of current reality that is undesirable. With creative tension, the energy for change comes from the vision, from what we want to create, juxtaposed with current reality. While the distinction may seem small, the consequences are not. Many people and organizations find themselves motivated to change only when their problems are bad enough to cause them to change. This works for a while, but the change process runs out of steam as soon as the problems driving the change become less pressing. With problem solving, the motivation for change is extrinsic. With creative tension, the motivation is intrinsic. This distinction mirrors the distinction between adaptive and generative learning.

NEW ROLES

The traditional authoritarian image of the leader as "the boss calling the shots" has been recognized as oversimplified and inadequate for some time. According to Edgar Schein (1985), "Leadership is intertwined with culture formation." Building an organization's culture and shaping its evolution is the "unique and essential function" of leadership. In a learning organization, the critical roles of leadership—designer, teacher, and steward—have antecedents in the ways leaders have contributed to building organizations in the past. But each role takes on new meaning in the learning organization and, as will be seen in the following sections, demands new skills and tools.

LEADER AS DESIGNER

Imagine that your organization is an ocean liner and that you are "the leader." What is your role?

I have asked this question of groups of managers many times. The most common answer, not surprisingly, is "the captain." Others say, "The navigator, setting the direction." Still others say, "The helmsman, actually controlling the direction," or "The engineer down there stoking the fire, providing energy," or "The social direction, making sure everybody's enrolled, involved, and communicating." While these are legitimate leadership roles, there is another which, in many ways, eclipses them all in importance. Yet rarely does anyone mention it.

The neglected leadership role is the *designer* of the ship. No one has a more sweeping influence than the designer. What good does it do for the captain to say, "Turn starboard 30 degrees," when the designer has built a rudder that will only turn to port, or which takes six hours to turn to starboard? It's fruitless to be the leader in an organization that is poorly designed.

The functions of design, or what some have called "social architecture," are rarely visible; they take place behind the scenes. The consequences that appear today are the result of work done long in the past, and work today will show its benefits far in the future. Those who aspire to lead out of a desire to control, or gain fame, or simply to be at the center of the action, will find little to attract them to the quiet design work of leadership.

But what, specifically, is involved in organizational design? "Organizational design is widely misconstrued as moving around boxes and lines," says Hanover Insurance Company's CEO William O'Brien. "The first task of organization design concerns designing the governing ideas of purpose, vision, and core values by which people will live." Few acts of leadership have a more enduring impact on an organization than building a foundation of purpose and core values....

If governing ideas constitute the first design task of leadership, the second design task involves the policies, strategies, and structures that translate guiding ideas into business decisions. Leadership theorist Philip Selznick (1957) calls policy and structure the "institutional embodiment of purpose." "Policy making (the rules that guide decisions) ought to be separated from decision making," says Jay Forrester (1965, pp. 5–17). "Otherwise, short-term pressures will usurp time from policy creation."

Traditionally, writers like Selznick and Forrester have tended to see policy making and implementation as the work of a small number of senior managers. But that view is changing. Both the dynamic business environment and the mandate of the learning organization to engage people at all levels now make it clear that this second design task is more subtle. Henry Mintzberg has argued that strategy is less a rational plan arrived at in the abstract and implemented throughout the organization than an "emergent phenomenon." Successful organizations "craft strategy" according to Mintzberg (1987, pp. 66–75) as they continually learn about shifting business conditions and balance what is desired and what is possible. The key is not getting the right strategy but fostering strategic thinking. "The choice of individual action is only part of . . . the policymaker's need," according to Mason and Mitroff (1981, p. 16). "More important is the need to achieve insight into the nature of the complexity and to formulate concepts and world views for coping with it."

Behind appropriate policies, strategies, and structures are effective learning processes: their creation is the third key design responsibility in learning organizations. This does not absolve senior managers of their strategic responsibilities. Actually, it deepens and extends those responsibilities. Now, they are not only responsible for ensuring that an organization has well-developed strategies and policies, but also for ensuring that processes exist whereby these are continually improved.

In the early 1970s, Shell was the weakest of the big seven oil companies. Today, Shell and Exxon are arguably the strongest, both in size and financial health. Shell's ascendance began with frustration. Around 1971 members of Shell's "Group Planning" in London began to foresee dramatic change and unpredictability in world oil markets. However, it proved impossible to persuade managers that the stable world of steady growth in oil demand and supply they had known for twenty years was about to change. Despite brilliant analysis and artful presentation, Shell's planners realized, in the words of Pierre Wack (1985, pp. 73–89), that they "had failed to change behavior in much of the Shell organization." Progress would probably have ended there, had the frustration not given way to a radically new view of corporate thinking.

As they pondered this failure, the planners' view of their basic task shifted: "We no longer saw our task as producing a documented view of the future business environment five or ten years ahead. Our real target was the microcosm (the 'mental model') of our decision makers." Only when the planners reconceptualized their basic task as fostering learning rather than devising plans did their insights begin to have impact. The initial tool used was "scenario analysis," through which planners encouraged operating managers to think through how they would manage in the future under different possible scenarios. It mattered not that the managers believed the planners' scenarios absolutely, only that they became engaged in ferreting out the implications. In this way, Shell's planners conditioned managers to be mentally prepared for a shift from low prices to high prices and from stability to instability. The results were significant. When OPEC became a reality, Shell quickly responded by increasing local operating company control (to enhance maneuverability in the new political environment), building buffer stocks, and accelerating development of non-OPEC sources—actions that its competitors took much more slowly or not at all.

Somewhat inadvertently, Shell planners had discovered the leverage of designing institutional learning processes, whereby, in the words of former planning director de Geus (1988), "Management teams change their shared mental models of their company, their markets, and their competitors." Since then, "planning as learning" has become a byword at Shell, and Group Planning has continually sought out new learning tools that can be integrated into the planning process. Some of these are described below.

LEADER AS TEACHER

"The first responsibility of a leader," writes retired Herman Miller CEO Max de Pree (1989, p. 9), "is to define reality." Much of the leverage leaders can actually exert lies in helping people achieve more accurate, more insightful, and more *empowering* views of reality.

Leader as teacher does *not* mean leader as authoritarian expert whose job it is to teach people the "correct" view of reality. Rather, it is about helping everyone in the organization, oneself included, to gain more insightful views of current reality. This is in line with a popular emerging view of leaders as coaches, guides, or facilitators. . . . In learning organizations, this teaching role is developed further by virtue of explicit attention to people's mental models and by the influence of the systems perspective.

The role of leader as teacher starts with bringing to the surface people's mental models of important issues. No one carries an organization, a market, or a state of technology in his or her head. What we carry in our heads are assumptions. These mental pictures of how the world works have a significant influence on how we perceive problems and opportunities, identify courses of action, and make choices.

One reason that mental models are so deeply entrenched is that they are largely tacit. Ian Mitroff, in his study of General Motors, argues that an assumption that prevailed for years was that, in the Unites States, "Cars are status symbols. Styling is therefore more important than quality" (Mitroff, 1988, pp. 66–67). The Detroit automakers didn't say, "We have a *mental model* that all people care about is styling." Few actual managers would even say publicly that all people care about is styling. So long as the view remained unexpressed, there was little possibility of challenging its validity or forming more accurate assumptions.

But working with mental models goes beyond revealing hidden assumptions. "Reality," as perceived by most people in most organizations, means pressures that must be borne, crises that must be reacted to, and limitations that must be accepted. Leaders as teachers help people *restructure their views of reality* to see beyond the superficial conditions and events into the underlying causes of problems—and therefore to see new possibilities for shaping the future.

Specifically, leaders can influence people to view reality at three distinct levels: events, patterns of behavior, and systemic structure.

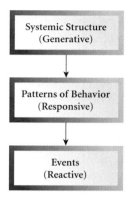

The key question becomes *where do leaders predominantly focus their own and their organization's attention?*

Contemporary society focuses predominantly on events. The media reinforces this perspective, with almost exclusive attention to short-term, dramatic events. This focus leads naturally to explaining what happens in terms of those events: "The Dow Jones average went up sixteen points because high fourth-quarter profits were announced yesterday."

Pattern-of-behavior explanations are rarer, in contemporary culture, than event explanations, but they do occur. "Trend analysis" is an example of seeing patterns of behavior. A good editorial that interprets a set of current events in the context of long-term historical changes is another example. Systemic, structural explanations go even further by addressing the question, "What causes the patterns of behavior?"

In some sense, all three levels of explanation are equally true. But their usefulness is quite different. Event explanations—who did what to whom—doom their holders to a reactive stance toward change. Pattern-of-behavior explanations focus on identifying long-term trends and assessing their implications. They at least suggest how, over time, we can respond to shifting conditions. Structural explanations are the most powerful. Only they address the underlying causes of behavior at a level such that patterns of behavior can be changed.

By and large, leaders of our current institutions focus their attention on events and patterns of behavior, and, under their influence, their organizations do likewise. That is why contemporary organizations are predominantly reactive, or at best responsive—rarely generative. On the other hand, leaders in learning organizations pay attention to all three levels, but focus especially on systemic structure; largely by example, they teach people throughout the organization to do likewise.

LEADER AS STEWARD

This is the subtlest role of leadership. Unlike the roles of designer and teacher, it is almost solely a matter of attitude. It is an attitude critical to learning organizations.

While stewardship has long been recognized as an aspect of leadership, its source is still not widely understood. I believe Robert Greenleaf (1977) came closest to explaining real stewardship, in his seminal book *Servant Leadership*. There, Greenleaf argues that "The servant leader *is* servant first. . . . It begins with the natural feeling that one wants to serve, to serve *first*. This conscious choice brings one to aspire to lead. That person is sharply different from one who is leader first, perhaps because of the need to assuage an unusual power drive or to acquire material possessions."

Leaders' sense of stewardship operates on two levels: stewardship for the people they lead and stewardship for the larger purpose or mission that underlies the enterprise. The first type arises from a keen appreciation of the impact one's leadership can have on others. People can suffer economically, emotionally, and spiritually under inept leadership. If anything, people in a learning organization are more vulnerable because of their commitment and sense of shared ownership. Appreciating this naturally instills a sense of responsibility in leaders. The second type of stewardship arises from a leader's sense of personal purpose and commitment to the organization's larger mission. People's natural impulse to learn is unleashed when they are engaged in an endeavor they consider worthy of their fullest commitment. Or, as Lawrence Miller (1984) puts it, "Achieving return on equity does not, as a goal, mobilize the most noble forces of our soul."

Leaders engaged in building learning organizations naturally feel part of a larger purpose that goes beyond their organization. They are part of changing the way businesses operate, not from a vague philanthropic urge, but from a conviction that their efforts will produce more productive organizations, capable of achieving higher levels of organizational success and personal satisfaction than more traditional organizations. . . .

NEW SKILLS

New leadership roles require new leadership skills. These skills can only be developed, in my judgment, through a lifelong commitment. It is not enough for one or two individuals to develop these skills. They must be distributed widely throughout the organization. This is one reason that understanding the *disciplines* of a learning organization is so important. These disciplines embody the principles and practice that can widely foster leadership development.

Three critical areas of skills (disciplines) are building shared vision, surfacing and challenging mental models, and engaging in systems thinking.*

BUILDING SHARED VISION

How do individual visions come together to create shared visions? A useful metaphor is the hologram, the three-dimensional image created by interacting light sources.

If you cut a photograph in half, each half shows only part of the whole image. But if you divide a hologram, each part, no matter how small, shows the whole image intact. Likewise, when a group of people come to share a vision for an organization, each person sees an individual picture of the organization at its best. Each shares responsibility for the whole, not just for one piece. But the component pieces of the holograms are not identical. Each represents the whole image from a different point of view. It's something like poking holes in a window shade; each hole offers a unique angle for viewing the whole image. So, too, is each individual's vision unique.

When you add up the pieces of a hologram, something interesting happens. The image becomes more intense, more lifelike. When more people come to share a vision, the vision becomes more real in the sense of a mental reality that people can truly imagine achieving. They now have partners, co-creators; the vision no longer rests on their shoulders alone. Early on, when they are nurturing an individual vision, people may say it is "my vision." But, as the shared vision develops, it becomes both "my vision" and "our vision."

The skills involved in building shared vision include the following:

■ *Encouraging Personal Vision.* Shared visions emerge from personal visions. It is not that people only care about their own self-interest—in fact, people's values usually include dimensions that concern family, organization, community, and even the world. Rather, it is that people's capacity for caring is *personal.*

---

*These points are condensed from the practices of the five disciplines examined in Senge (1990).

- *Communicating and Asking for Support.* Leaders must be willing to continually share their own vision, rather than being the official representative of the corporate vision. They also must be prepared to ask, "Is this vision worthy of your commitment?" This can be difficult for a person used to setting goals and presuming compliance.
- *Visioning as an Ongoing Process.* Building shared vision is a never-ending process. At any one point there will be a particular image of the future that is predominant, but that image will evolve. Today, too many managers want to dispense with the "vision business" by going off and writing the Official Vision Statement. Such statements almost always lack the vitality, freshness, and excitement of a genuine vision that comes from people asking, "What do we really want to achieve?"
- *Blending Extrinsic and Intrinsic Visions.* Many energizing visions are extrinsic—that it, they focus on achieving something relative to an outsider, such as a competitor. But a goal that is limited to defeating an opponent can, once the vision is achieved, easily become a defensive posture. In contrast, intrinsic goals like creating a new type of product, taking an established product to a new level, or setting a new standard for customer satisfaction can call forth a new level of creativity and innovation. Intrinsic and extrinsic visions need to coexist; a vision solely predicated on defeating an adversary will eventually weaken an organization.
- *Distinguishing Positive from Negative Visions.* Many organizations only truly pull together when their survival is threatened. Similarly, most social movements aim at eliminating what people don't want: for example, anti-drugs, anti-smoking, or anti-nuclear arms movements. Negative visions carry a subtle message of powerlessness: people will only pull together when there is sufficient threat. Negative visions also tend to be short term. Two fundamental sources of energy can motivate organizations: fear and aspiration. Fear, the energy source behind negative visions, can produce extraordinary changes in shorter periods, but aspiration endures as a continuing source of learning and growth.

SURFACING AND TESTING MENTAL MODELS

Many of the best ideas in organizations never get put into practice. One reason is that new insights and initiatives often conflict with established mental models. The leadership task of challenging assumptions without invoking defensiveness requires reflection and inquiry skills possessed by few leaders in traditional controlling organizations.*

- *Seeing Leaps of Abstraction.* Our minds literally move at lightning speed. Ironically, this often slows our learning, because we leap to generalizations so quickly that we never think to test them. We then confuse our generalizations with the observable data upon which they are based, treating the generalizations *as if they were data.* . . .
- *Balancing Inquiry and Advocacy.* Most managers are skilled at articulating their views and presenting them persuasively. While important, advocacy skills can become counterproductive as managers rise in responsibility and confront increasingly complex issues that require collaborative learning among different, equally knowledgeable people. Leaders in learning organizations need to have both inquiry *and* advocacy skills. . . .
- *Distinguished Espoused Theory from Theory in Use.* We all like to think that we hold certain views, but often our actions reveal deeper views. For example, I may proclaim that people are trustworthy, but never lend friends money and jealously guard my possessions. Obviously, my deeper mental model (my theory in use) differs from my espoused theory. Recognizing gaps between espoused views and theories in use (which often requires the help of others) can be pivotal to deeper learning.

---

*The ideas below are based to considerable extent on the work of Chris Argyris, Donald Schon, and their Action Science colleagues. C. Argyris and D. Schon, *Organizational Learning: A Theory-in-Action Perspective* (1978); C. Argyris, R. Putman, and D. Smith, *Action Science* (1985); C. Argyris, *Strategy, Change, and Defensive Routines* (1985); and C. Argyris, *Overcoming Organizational Defenses* (1990).

■ *Recognizing and Defusing Defensive Routines.* As one CEO in our research program puts it, "Nobody ever talks about an issue at the 8:00 business meeting exactly the same way they talk about it at home that evening or over drinks at the end of the day." The reason is what Chris Argyris calls "defensive routines," entrenched habits used to protect ourselves from the embarrassment and threat that come with exposing our thinking. For most of us, such defenses began to build early in life in response to pressures to have the right answers in school or at home. Organizations add new levels of performance anxiety and thereby amplify and exacerbate this defensiveness. Ironically, this makes it even more difficult to expose hidden mental models, and thereby lessens learning.

The first challenge is to recognize defensive routines, then to inquire into their operation. Those who are best at revealing and defusing defensive routines operate with a high degree of self-disclosure regarding their own defensiveness (e.g., I notice that I am feeling uneasy about how this conversation is going. Perhaps I don't understand it or it is threatening to me in ways I don't yet see. Can you help me see this better?).

SYSTEMS THINKING

We all know that leaders should help people see the big picture. But the actual skills whereby leaders are supposed to achieve this are not well understood. In my experience, successful leaders often are "systems thinkers" to a considerable extent. They focus less on day-to-day events and more on underlying trends and forces of change. But they do this almost completely intuitively. The consequence is that they are often unable to explain their intuitions to others and feel frustrated that others cannot see the world the way they do.

One of the most significant developments in management science today is the gradual coalescence of managerial systems thinking as a field study and practice. This field suggests some key skills for future leaders:

■ *Seeing Interrelationships, Not Things, and Processes, Not Snapshots.* Most of us have been conditioned throughout our lives to focus on things and to see the world in static images. This leads us to linear explanations of systemic phenomenon. For instance, in an arms race each party is convinced that the other is *the cause* of problems. They react to each new move as an isolated event, not as part of a process. So long as they fail to see the interrelationships of these actions, they are trapped.

■ *Moving Beyond Blame.* We tend to blame each other or outside circumstances for our problems. But it is poorly designed systems, not incompetent or unmotivated individuals, that cause most organizational problems. Systems thinking shows us that there is no outside—that you and the cause of your problems are part of a single system.

■ *Distinguishing Detail Complexity from Dynamic Complexity.* Some types of complexity are more important strategically than others. Detail complexity arises when there are many variables. Dynamic complexity arises when cause and effect are distant in time and space, and when the consequences over time of interventions are subtle and not obvious to many participants in the system. The leverage in most management situations lies in understanding dynamic complexity, not detail complexity.

■ *Focusing on Areas of High Leverage.* Some have called systems thinking the "new dismal science" because it teaches that most obvious solutions don't work—at best, they improve matters in the short run, only to make things worse in the long run. But there is another side to the story. Systems thinking also shows that small, well-focused actions can produce significant, enduring improvements, if they are in the right place. Systems thinkers refer to this idea as the principle of "leverage." Tackling a difficult problem is often a matter of seeing where the high leverage lies, where a change—with a minimum of effort—would lead to lasting, significant improvement.

■ *Avoiding Symptomatic Solutions.* The pressures to intervene in management systems that are going awry can be overwhelming. Unfortunately, given the linear thinking that predominates in most organizations, interventions usually focus on symptomatic fixes, not underlying causes. This results in only temporary relief, and it tends to create still more pressures later on for further, low-leverage intervention. If leaders acquiesce to these pressures, they can be sucked into an endless spiral of increasing intervention. Sometimes the most difficult leadership acts are to refrain from intervening through popular quick fixes and to keep the pressure on everyone to identify more enduring solutions.

While leaders who can articulate systemic explanations are not rare, those who *can* will leave their stamp on an organization. . . . The consequence of leaders who lack systems thinking skills can be devastating. Many charismatic leaders manage almost exclusively at the level of events. They deal in visions and in crises, and little in between. Under their leadership, an organization hurtles from crisis to crisis. Eventually, the worldview of people in the organization becomes dominated by events and reactiveness. Many, especially those who are deeply committed, become burned out. Eventually, cynicism comes to pervade the organization. People have no control over their time, let alone their destiny.

Similar problems arise with the "visionary strategist," the leader with vision who sees both patterns of change and events. This leader is better prepared to manage change. He or she can explain strategies in terms of emerging trends, and thereby fosters a climate that is less reactive. But such leaders impart a responsive orientation rather than a generative one.

Many talented leaders have rich, highly systemic intuitions but cannot explain those intuitions to others. Ironically, they often end up being authoritarian leaders, even if they don't want to, because only they see the decisions that need to be made. They are unable to conceptualize their strategic insights so that these can become public knowledge, open to challenge and further improvement. . . .

I believe that [a] new sort of management development will focus on the roles, skills, and tools for leadership in learning organizations. Undoubtedly, the ideas offered above are only a rough approximation of this new territory. The sooner we begin seriously exploring the territory, the sooner the initial map can be improved—and the sooner we will realize an age-old vision of leadership:

> The wicked leader is he who the people despise.
> The good leader is he who the people revere.
> The great leader is he who the people say, "We did it ourselves."

> —*Lao Tsu*

READING 2.5

BY QUY NGUYEN HUY

■ The very phrase "middle manager" evokes mediocrity: a person who stubbornly defends the status quo because he's too unimaginative to dream up anything better—or, worse, someone who sabotages others' attempts to change the organization for the better.

The popular press and a couple generations' worth of change-management consultants have reinforced this stereotype. Introducing a major change initiative? Watch out for the middle managers—that's where you'll find the most resistance. Reengineering your business processes? Start by sweeping out the middle managers—they're just intermediaries; they don't

---

*Excerpted from "In Praise of Middle Managers," Quy Nguyen Huy, *Harvard Business Review* (September–October 2001).

add value. Until very recently, anyone who spent time reading about management practices, as opposed to watching real managers at work, might have concluded that middle managers are doomed to extinction or should be.

But don't pull out the pink slips just yet. Middle managers, it turns out, make valuable contributions to the realization of radical change at a company—contributions that go largely unrecognized by most senior executives. These contributions occur in four major areas. First, middle managers often have value-adding entrepreneurial ideas that they are able and willing to realize—if only they can get a hearing. Second, they're far better than most senior executives are at leveraging the informal networks at a company that make substantive, lasting change possible. Third, they stay attuned to employees' moods and emotional needs, thereby ensuring that the change initiative's momentum is maintained. And finally, they manage the tension between continuity and change—they keep the organization from falling into extreme inertia, on the one hand, or extreme chaos, on the other.

Of course, not every middle manager in every organization is a paragon of entrepreneurial vigor and energy. But I would argue that if senior managers dismiss the role that middle managers play—and carelessly reduce their ranks—they will drastically diminish their chances of realizing radical change. Indeed, middle managers may be corner-office executives' most effective allies when it's time to make a major change in a business. Let's take a closer look at their underestimated strengths.

THE ENTREPRENEUR

When it comes to envisioning and implementing change, middle managers stand in a unique organizational position. They're close to day-to-day operations, customers, and frontline employees—closer than senior managers are—so they know better than anyone where the problems are. But they're also far enough away from frontline work that they can see the big picture, which allows them to see new possibilities, both for solving problems and for encouraging growth. Taken as a group, middle managers are more diverse than their senior counterparts are in, for instance, functional area, work experience, geography, gender, and ethnic background. As a result, their insights are more diverse. Middle management is thus fertile ground for creative ideas about how to grow and change a business. In fact, middle managers' ideas are often better than their bosses' ideas.

Consider a large telecommunications company that I studied. When it initiated a radical change program a few years ago, 117 separate projects were funded. Of the projects that senior executives had proposed, 80% fell short of expectations or failed outright. Meanwhile, 80% of the projects that middle managers had initiated succeeded, bringing in at least $300 million in annual profits.

Middle managers were equally successful at spurring innovation at other companies I studied. It was, for example, a middle-management team that developed Super Dry Beer, an innovative product that allowed Japanese brewer Asahi to capture new market share. That success set the stage for the struggling company's turnaround.

The more closely I looked at companies, the more examples I saw of senior executives failing to listen to their middle managers. Good ideas routinely died before they ever saw the light of day.

Not getting credit is [another] pervasive problem. When the telecom company I studied embraced its radical change program, it had a new leadership team. The top managers very sensibly pushed the task of generating new ideas down to a group of long-standing middle managers, whose ideas turned out to be more grounded and profitable than the senior managers' ideas. But that's not how the outside world saw it. Shareholders and the media perceived that the new team had come in, cleaned up, and turned the company around. In a sense they had, but they hadn't done it alone, and they hadn't done it by cleaning house.

THE COMMUNICATOR

Aside from being an important source of entrepreneurial ideas, middle managers are also uniquely suited to communicating proposed changes across an organization. Change initiatives have two stages, conception and implementation, and it's widely understood that failure most often occurs at the second stage. What's less understood is the central role that middle managers play during this stage. Successful implementation requires clear and compelling communication throughout the organization. Middle managers can spread the word and get people on board because they usually have the best social networks in the company. Many of them start their careers as operations workers or technical specialists. Over time and through various job rotations at the same company, they build webs of relationships that are both broad and deep. They know who really knows what and how to get things done. Typically their networks include unwritten obligations and favors traded, giving effective middle managers a significant amount of informal leverage.

Senior managers have their own networks, of course, but these tend to be less powerful because many of these executives have been at their companies for shorter periods of time. . . .

If the middle managers with the best networks—and the most credibility—genuinely buy into the change program, they'll sell it to the rest of the organization in subtle and nonthreatening ways. And they'll know which groups or individuals most need to be on board and how to customize the message for different audiences.

Sometimes senior executives themselves can be barriers to change, and it requires tactful communication by middle managers to keep the company on track. For instance, a middle manager at a large airline I studied realized that most of the senior executives barely know how to use a PC. Few of them understood the capabilities or limitations of the Web well enough to make complex strategic decisions about the company's use of the Internet and e-commerce. To educate them, the middle manager developed a reverse-mentoring program: Younger employees would teach experienced executives about the Internet. In turn, the executives would expose their young mentors to more senior-level business issues, decisions, and practices. Each member of the pair was separated by several hierarchical levels, and each came from different business units. The middle manager correctly assumed that this degree of separation would make the executives more comfortable about admitting their weaknesses with computers. The program was a success; eventually, hundreds of executives at the airline became more technology literate and less fearful of change. . . .

THE THERAPIST

Radical changes in the workplace can stir up high levels of fear among employees. Uncertainty about change can deflate morale and trigger anxiety that, unchecked, can degenerate into depression and paralysis. Once people are depressed, they stop learning, adapting, or helping to move the group forward. Senior managers can't do much to alleviate this pain; they're too removed from most workers to help, and they're also focused externally more than internally.

Middle managers, though, have no choice but to address their employees' emotional well-being during times of radical change. If they ignore it, most useful work will come to a grinding halt as people either leave the company or become afraid to act. Even as they privately deplore the lack of attention from their own bosses, many middle managers make sure that their own sense of alienation doesn't seep down to their subordinates. They do a host of things to create a psychologically safe work environment. They're able to do this, once again, because of their position within the organization. They know the people who report to them—as well as those reports' direct reports—and they can communicate directly and personally, rather than in vague corporate-speak. They can also tailor individual conversations to individual needs. Some employees will have big concerns about whether a new strategic direction is right for the organization; others will be far more interested in whether they're going to be forced to move or to give up a flexible schedule. . . .

THE TIGHTROPE ARTIST

Successful organizational change requires attention not only to employee morale but also to the balance between change and continuity. If too much change happens too fast, chaos ensues. If too little change happens too slowly, it results in organizational inertia. Both extremes can lead to severe underperformance. Even during normal times, middle managers allot considerable energy to finding the right mix of the two. When radical change is being imposed from the top, this balancing act becomes even more important—and far more difficult.

Middle managers, like the people who report to them, are overburdened and stressed out during periods of profound change—but I noticed that they found personal and professional fulfillment by taking on this particular balancing act. They're problem solvers, typically, and they find relief in rolling up their sleeves and figuring out how to make the whole messy thing work. They don't all do it the same way, of course—and, from a senior-management point of view, that's a good thing. Some middle managers pay more attention to the continuity side of the equation, and some tend more to the change side.

We've already looked at what middle managers do to ensure continuity. They "keep the company working," as one of them said to me with some pride. At the telecom company I studied, middle managers' focus on continuity contributed to a relatively smooth downsizing of 13,000 positions. By showing flexibility and fairness, and by working closely with union representatives, managers defused resentment and avoided a strike. Their concern for employees kept anxiety at manageable levels. Their loyalty to the organization probably slowed turnover rates. And as a result to the middle managers' actions, the telecom company was able to generate revenues at decent levels during an extraordinarily difficult time, thus providing needed cash for the multitude of change projects. Other middle managers are more interested in promoting change. They champion projects, putting intense pressure on the people who control resources and equally intense pressure on their own people.

The challenge [today] is figuring out how to hold on to core values and capabilities while simultaneously changing how work gets done and shifting the organization in new strategic directions. This simply won't happen unless people throughout the organization help make it happen. Middle managers understand—in a deep way—those core values and competencies. They're the ones who can translate and synthesize; who can implement strategy because they know how to get things done; who can keep work groups from spinning into alienated, paralyzed chaos; and who can be persuaded to put their credibility on the line to turn vision into reality.

The senior executive who learns to recognize, respect, and deal fairly with the most influential middle managers in an organization will gain trusted allies—and improve the odds of realizing a complex but necessary organizational change.

CHAPTER 3

Formulating Strategy

Most of what has been published on the strategy process deals with how strategy *should* be designed or consciously *formulated*. On how this works, there has been a good deal of consensus, although, as we shall see later, this is now eroding. Perhaps we should more properly conclude that there have been two waves of consensus. The first, which developed in the 1960s, is presented in this chapter; the second, which began in the 1980s, did not challenge the first so much as build on it. This is presented in Chapter 4. Both are very much alive—we should say, still dominant.

Ken Andrews of the Harvard Business School is the person most commonly associated with the first wave, although Bill Newman of Columbia wrote on some of these issues much earlier, and Igor Ansoff simultaneously outlined very similar views while he was at Carnegie-Mellon. But the Andrews text became the best known, in part because it was so simply and clearly written, in part because it was embodied in a popular textbook (with cases) emanating from the Harvard Business School.

We reproduce parts of the Andrews text (as revised in its own publication in 1980 but based on the original 1965 edition). These serve to introduce the basic point that strategy ultimately requires the achievement of fit between the external situation (opportunities and threats) and internal capability (strengths and weaknesses). As you read the Andrews text, a number of basic premises will quickly become evident. Among these are the clear distinction made between strategy formulation and strategy implementation (in effect, between thinking and action); the belief that strategy (or at least intended strategy) should be made explicit; the notion that structure should follow strategy (in other words, be designed in accordance with it); and the assumption that strategy emanates from the formal leadership of the organization. Similar premises underlie most of the prescriptive literature of strategic management.

This "model" (if we can call it that) has proven very useful in many circumstances as a broad way to analyze a strategic situation and to think about making strategy. A careful strategist should certainly touch all the bases suggested in this approach. But in many circumstances the model cannot or should not be followed to the letter, as shall be discussed in Chapter 5 and later.

The Rumelt reading elaborates on one element in this traditional model—the evaluation of strategies. Although the Andrews text contains a similar discussion, Rumelt, a graduate of the Harvard Business School and strategy professor at UCLA, develops it in a particularly elegant way.

The third reading is by Gary Hamel, who has built up quite a reputation in the strategy field as a consultant, author, and academic, and C. K. Prahalad, equally well known and associated with the University of Michigan. They make the case for "strategic intent," their take on vision, in a sense. The challenge of leadership is to create "an obsession with winning" that will energize the collection action of all employees. Managers have to build such an ambition, they believe, in order to help people develop faith in their own ability to deliver on tough goals, to motivate them to do so, and to channel their energies into a step-by-step progression that they compare with "running a marathon in 400-meter sprints." The traditional view of the strategy formulation is that it requires an accurate idea of the future and a plan for achieving this future. Andrews outlines a systematic process for carrying this out. Rumelt provides a methodology for judging whether this can be done. In practice, however, unfolding events tend to frustrate the most carefully formulated strategies. For some, this suggests that strategies should be allowed to evolve. Others, however, insist that strategy requires direction. Hamel and Prahalad argue that strategy formulation should consist of general goals that capture the essence of what the organization is trying to do. Correctly formulated and properly invested with energy and commitment, the resulting "strategic intent" challenges the organization to push boundaries and constraints beyond current limits.

Whereas traditional strategy formulation entails direction from the top, strategic intent entails empowerment. The goals are sufficiently general to allow members of the organization to infuse their own perspective into implementation.

USING THE CASE STUDIES

In one sense, companies are always formulating (or reformulating) their strategy. Formulating strategy, however, comes to the surface and becomes explicit when companies are at a crossroads, facing new threats or attractive opportunities. The Unipart Group case describes a company that has undergone an explicit formulation and reformulation of its strategy. The Lufthansa case deals with a company that overcame the threat of bankruptcy, in part by pursuing an alliance strategy. How will it go about formulating strategy jointly with other airlines? In the reading "The Concept of Corporate Strategy" Andrews lays out an orderly process that Lufthansa could follow for best results. In the Beijing Mirror case, Mr. Tian does a strength/weaknesses analysis, very much as Andrews would suggest.

The Sportsmake case, however, suggests that many corporations do not see strategy as an orderly process. They move from opportunity to opportunity, usually driven by the vision and personality of their CEO. And when this CEO unexpectedly departs from the scene, as he does in this case, the choice of a successor raises issues of strategic direction that are not easily addressed using the standard planning process. The same can be said of

Michael Robertson in the MP3.com case. Robertson's bold pioneering was shaking up the music business and was succeeding beyond expectations until the courts ruled that MP3.com violated copyright law. Faced with a $250 million fine and the prospects of being driven out of business, Robertson must come up with a new strategy. This is strategy formulation under pressure.

Rumelt's "Evaluating Business Strategy" puts forward criteria by which this strategy (or any other) can be judged. Mrs. Lee's agreement with Aiwa, which is a division of Sony, is an object lesson in the importance of making such an evaluation. The agreement is at the heart of the Kami Corporation case and a big challenge for Mr. Olano, the new general manager who has to implement it.

Gregory Long, president of the New York Botanical Gardens, would like to pursue an orderly formulation process, but he is buffeted by the contradictory pressures of stakeholders in this New York City institution. He would have the sympathies of Hamel and Prahalad, who argue that orderly formulation is more an ideal than a reality. They suggest that managers focus on the creation of "strategic intent" as a way of energizing strategic thinking. As CEO of the Acer Group, Stan Shih's slogan, "Global Brand, Local Touch," is a good example of strategic intent. And so is the LVMH drive to spread the "Western Art de Vivre."

READING 3.1

THE CONCEPT OF CORPORATE STRATEGY*

BY KENNETH R. ANDREWS

THE STRATEGY CONCEPT

WHAT STRATEGY IS

Corporate strategy is the pattern of decisions in a company that determines and reveals its objectives, purposes, or goals, produces the principal policies and plans for achieving those goals, and defines the range of business the company is to pursue, the kind of economic and human organization it is or intends to be, and the nature of the economic and noneconomic contribution it intends to make to its shareholders, employees, customers, and communities. . . .

The strategic decision contributing to this pattern is one that is effective over long periods of time, affects the company in many different ways, and focuses and commits a significant portion of its resources to the expected outcomes. The pattern resulting from a series of such decisions will probably define the central character and image of a company, the individuality it has for its members and various publics, and the position it will occupy in its industry and markets. It will permit the specification of particular objectives to be attained through a timed sequence investment and implementation decisions and will govern directly the deployment or redeployment of resources to make these decisions effective.

Some aspects of such a pattern of decision may be in an established corporation unchanging over long periods of time, like a commitment to quality, or high technology, or certain raw materials or good labor relations. Other aspects of strategy must change as or before the world

*Excerpted from Kenneth R. Andrews, *The Concept of Corporate Strategy,* rev. ed. (copyright © by Richard D. Irwin, Inc., 1980), Chaps. 2 and 3; reprinted by permission of the publisher.

changes, such as product line, manufacturing process, or merchandising and styling practices. The basic determinants of company character, if purposefully institutionalized, are likely to persist through and shape the nature of substantial changes in product-market choices and allocation of resources. . . .

It is important, however, not to take the idea apart in another way, that is, to separate goals from the policies designed to achieve those goals. The essence of the definition of strategy I have just recorded is *pattern*. The interdependence of purposes, policies, and organized action is crucial to the particularity of an individual strategy and its opportunity to identify competitive advantage. It is the unity, coherence, and internal consistency of a company's strategic decisions that position the company in its environment and give the firm its identity, its power to mobilize its strengths, and its likelihood of success in the marketplace. It is the interrelationship of a set of goals and policies that crystallizes from the formless reality of a company's environment a set of problems an organization can seize upon and solve.

What you are doing, in short, is never meaningful unless you can say or imply what you are doing it for: the quality of administrative action and the motivation lending it power cannot be appraised without knowing its relationship to purpose. Breaking up the system of corporate goals and the character-determining major policies for attainment leads to narrow and mechanical conceptions of strategic management and endless logic chopping. . . .

SUMMARY STATEMENTS OF STRATEGY

Before we proceed to clarification of this concept by application, we should specify the terms in which strategy is usually expressed. A summary statement of strategy will characterize the product line and services offered or planned by the company, the markets and market segments for which products and services are now or will be designed, and the channels through which these markets will be reached. The means by which the operation is to be financed will be specified, as will the profit objectives and the emphasis to be placed on the safety of capital versus level of return. Major policy in central functions such as marketing, manufacturing, procurement, research and development, labor relations, and personnel will be stated where they distinguish the company from others, and usually the intended size, form, and climate of the organization will be included.

Each company, if it were to construct a summary strategy from what it understands itself to be aiming at, would have a different statement with different categories of decision emphasized to indicate what it wanted to be or do. . . .

FORMULATION OF STRATEGY

Corporate strategy is an organization process, in many ways inseparable from the structure, behavior, and culture of the company in which it takes place. Nevertheless, we may abstract from the process two important aspects, interrelated in real life but separable for the purposes of analysis. The first of these we may call *formulation*, the second *implementation*. Deciding what strategy should be may be approached as a rational undertaking, even if in life emotional attachments . . . may complicate choice among future alternatives. . . .

The principal subactivities of strategy formulation as a logical activity include identifying opportunities and threats in the company's environment and attaching some estimate or risk to the discernible alternatives. Before a choice can be made, the company's strengths and weaknesses should be appraised together with the resources on hand and available. Its actual or potential capacity to take advantage of perceived market needs or to cope with attendant risks should be estimated as objectively as possible. The strategic alternative which results from matching opportunity and corporate capability at an acceptable level of risk is what we may call an *economic strategy*.

The process described thus far assumes that strategists are analytically objective in estimating the relative capacity of their company and the opportunity they see or anticipate in developing markets. The extent to which they wish to undertake low or high risk presumably depends on their profit objectives. The higher they set the latter, the more willing they must be to assume a correspondingly high risk that the market opportunity they see will not develop or that the corporate competence required to excel competition will not be forthcoming.

So far we have described the intellectual processes of ascertaining what a company *might do* in terms of environmental opportunity, of deciding what it can *do* in terms of ability and power, and of bringing these two considerations together in optimal equilibrium. The determination of strategy also requires consideration of what alternatives are preferred by the chief executive and perhaps by his or her immediate associates as well, quite apart from economic considerations. Personal values, aspirations, and ideals do, and in our judgment quite properly should, influence the final choice of purposes. Thus, what the executives of a company *want to do* must be brought into the strategic decision.

Finally strategic choice has an ethical aspect—a fact much more dramatically illustrated in some industries than in others. Just as alternatives may be ordered in terms of the degree of risk that they entail, so may they be examined against the standards of responsiveness to the expectations of society that the strategist elects. Some alternatives may seem to the executive considering them more attractive than others when the public good or service to society is considered. What a company *should do* thus appears as a fourth element of the strategic decision. . . .

THE IMPLEMENTATION OF STRATEGY

Since effective implementation can make a sound strategic decision ineffective or a debatable choice successful, it is as important to examine the processes of implementation as to weigh the advantages of available strategic alternatives. The implementation of strategy is comprised of a series of subactivities which are primarily administrative. If purpose is determined, then the resources of a company can be mobilized to accomplish it. An organizational structure appropriate for the efficient performance of the required tasks must be made effective by information systems and relationships permitting coordination of subdivided activities. The organizational processes of performance measurement, compensation, management development—all of them enmeshed in systems of incentives and controls—must be directed toward the kind of behavior required by organizational purpose. The role of personal leadership is important and sometimes decisive in the accomplishment of strategy. Although we know that organization structure and processes of compensation, incentives, control, and management development influence and constrain the formulation of strategy, we should look first at the logical proposition that structure should follow strategy in order to cope later with the organizational reality that strategy also follows structure. When we have examined both tendencies, we will understand and some extent be prepared to deal with the interdependence of the formulation and implementation of corporate purpose. Figure 1 may be useful in understanding the analysis of strategy as a pattern of interrelated decisions. . . .

RELATING OPPORTUNITIES TO RESOURCES	Determination of a suitable strategy for a company begins in identifying the opportunities and risks in its environment. This [discussion] is concerned with the identification of a range of strategic alternatives, the narrowing of this range by recognizing the constraints imposed by corporate capability, and the determination of one or more economic strategies at acceptable levels of risk. . . .

THE NATURE OF THE COMPANY'S ENVIRONMENT

The environment of an organization in business, like that of any other organic entity, is the pattern of all the external conditions and influences that affect its life and development. The environmental influences relevant to strategic decision operate in a company's industry, the total business community, its city, its country, and the world. They are technological, eco-

FIGURE 1

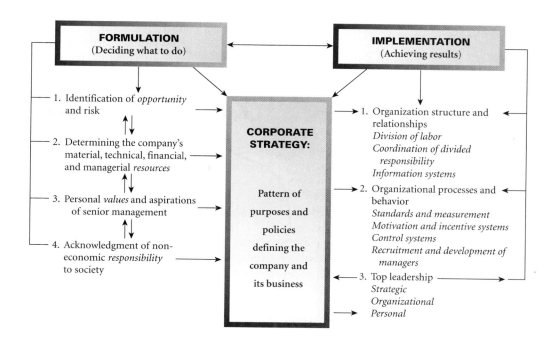

nomic, physical, social, and political in kind. The corporate strategist is usually at least intuitively aware of these features of the current environment. But in all these categories change is taking place at varying rates—fastest in technology, less rapidly in politics. Change in the environment of business necessitates continuous monitoring of a company's definition of its business, lest it falter, blur, or become obsolete. Since by definition the formulation of strategy is performed with the future in mind, executives who take part in the strategic planning process must be aware of those aspects of their company's environment especially susceptible to the kind of change that will affect their company's future.

Technology

From the point of view of the corporate strategist, technological developments are not only the fastest unfolding but the most far-reaching in extending or contracting opportunity for an established company. They include the discoveries of science, the impact of related product development, the less dramatic machinery and process improvements, and the progress of automation and data processing. . . .

Ecology

It used to be possible to take for granted the physical characteristics of the environment and find them favorable to industrial development. Plant sites were chosen using criteria like availability of process and cooling water, accessibility to various forms of transportation, and stability of soil conditions. With the increase in sensitivity to the impact on the physical environment of all industrial activity, it becomes essential, often to comply with law, to consider how planned expansion and even continued operation under changing standards will affect and be perceived to affect the air, water, traffic density, and quality of life generally of any area which a company would like to enter. . . .

Economics

Because business is more accustomed to monitoring economic trends than those in other spheres, it is less likely to be taken by surprise by such massive developments as the internationalization of competition, the return of China and Russia to trade with the West, the slower than projected development of the Third World countries, the Americanization of demand

and culture in the developing countries and the resulting backlash of nationalism, the increased importance of the large multinational corporations and the consequences of host-country hostility, the recurrence of recession, and the persistence of inflation in all phases of the business cycle. The consequences of world economic trends need to be monitored in much greater detail for any one industry or company.

Industry

Although the industry environment is the one most company strategists believe they know most about, the opportunities and risks that reside there are often blurred by familiarity and the uncritical acceptance of the established relative position of competitors. . . .

Society

Social developments of which strategists keep aware include such influential forces as the quest for equality for minority groups, the demand of women for opportunity and recognition, the changing patterns of work and leisure, the effects of urbanization upon the individual, family, and neighborhood, the rise of crime, the decline of conventional morality, and the changing composition of world population.

Politics

The political forces important to the business firm are similarly extensive and complex—the changing relations between communist and noncommunist countries (East and West) and between prosperous and poor countries (North and South), the relation between private enterprise and government, between workers and management, the impact of national planning on corporate planning, and the rise of what George Lodge (1975) calls the communitarian ideology. . . .

Although it is not possible to know or spell out here the significance of such technical, economic, social, and political trends, and possibilities for the strategist of a given business or company, some simple things are clear. Changing values will lead to different expectations of the role business should perform. Business will be expected to perform its mission not only with economy in the use of energy but with sensitivity to the ecological environment. Organizations in all walks of life will be called upon to be more explicit about their goals and to meet the needs and aspirations (for example, for education) of their membership.

In any case, change threatens all established strategies. We know that a thriving company—itself a living system—is bound up in a variety of interrelationships with larger systems comprising its technological, economic, ecological, social, and political environment. If environmental developments are destroying and creating business opportunities, advance notice of specific instances relevant to a single company is essential to intelligent planning. Risk and opportunity in the last quarter of the twentieth century require of executives a keen interest in what is going on outside their companies. More than that, a practical means of tracking developments promising good or ill, and profit or loss, needs to be devised. . . .

For the firm that has not determined what its strategy dictates it needs to know or has not embarked upon the systematic surveillance of environmental change, a few simple questions kept constantly in mind will highlight changing opportunity and risk. In examining your own company or one you are interested in, these questions should lead to an estimate of opportunity and danger in the present and predicted company setting.

1. What are the essential economic, technical, and physical characteristics of the industry in which the company participates? . . .
2. What trends suggesting future change in economic and technical characteristics are apparent? . . .
3. What is the nature of competition both within the industry and across industries? . . .

4. What are the requirements for success in competition in the company's industry? . . .

5. Given the technical, economic, social, and political developments that most directly apply, what is the range of strategy available to any company in this industry? . . .

IDENTIFYING CORPORATE COMPETENCE AND RESOURCES

The first step in validating a tentative choice among several opportunities is to determine whether the organization has the capacity to prosecute it successfully. The capability of an organization is its demonstrated and potential ability to accomplish, against the opposition of circumstance or competition, whatever it sets out to do. Every organization has actual and potential strengths and weaknesses. Since it is prudent in formulating strategy to extend or maximize the one and contain or minimize the other, it is important to try to determine what they are and to distinguish one from the other.

It is just as possible, though much more difficult, for a company to know its own strengths and limitations as it is to maintain a workable surveillance of its changing environment. Subjectivity, lack of confidence, and unwillingness to face reality may make it hard for organizations as well as for individuals to know themselves. But just as it is essential, though difficult, that a maturing person achieve reasonable self-awareness, so an organization can identify approximately its central strength and critical vulnerability. . . .

To make an effective contribution to strategic planning, the key attributes to be appraised should be identified and consistent criteria established for judging them. If attention is directed to strategies, policy commitments, and past practices in the context of discrepancy between organization goals and attainment, an outcome useful to an individual manager's strategic planning is possible. The assessment of strengths and weaknesses associated with the attainment of specific objectives becomes in Stevenson's (1976) words a "key link in a feedback loop" which allows managers to learn from the success or failures of the policies they institute.

Although [a] study by Stevenson did not find or establish a systematic way of developing or using such knowledge, members of organizations develop judgments about what the company can do particularly well—its core of competence. If consensus can be reached about this capability, no matter how subjectively arrived at, its application to identified opportunity can be estimated.

Sources of Capabilities

The powers of a company constituting a resource for growth and diversification accrue primarily from experience in making and marketing a product line or providing a service. They inhere as well in (1) the developing strengths and weaknesses of the individuals comprising the organization, (2) the degree to which individual capability is effectively applied to the common task, and (3) the quality of coordination of individual and group effort.

The experience gained through successful execution of a strategy centered upon one goal may unexpectedly develop capabilities which could be applied to different ends. Whether they should be so applied is another question. For example, a manufacturer of salt can strengthen his competitive position by offering his customers salt-dispensing equipment. If, in the course of making engineering improvements in this equipment, a new solenoid principle is perfected that has application to many industrial switching problems, should this patentable and marketable innovation be exploited? The answer would turn not only on whether economic analysis of the opportunity shows this to be a durable and profitable possibility, but also on whether the organization can muster the financial, manufacturing, and marketing strength to exploit the discovery and live with its success. The former question is likely to have a more positive answer than the latter. In this connection, it seems important to remember that individual and unsupported flashes of strength are not as dependable as the gradually accumulated product and market-related fruits of experience.

Even where competence to exploit an opportunity is nurtured by experience in related fields, the level of that competence may be too low for any great reliance to be placed upon it. Thus a chain of children's clothing stores might well acquire the administrative, merchandising, buying, and selling skills that would permit it to add departments in women's wear. Similarly, a sales force effective in distributing typewriters might gain proficiency in selling office machinery and supplies. But even here it would be well to ask what *distinctive* ability these companies could bring to the retailing of soft goods or office equipment to attract customers away from a plethora of competitors.

Identifying Strengths

The distinctive competence of an organization is more than what it can do; it is what it can do particularly well. To identify the less obvious or by-product strengths of an organization that may well be transferable to some more profitable new opportunity, one might well begin by examining the organization's current product line and by defining the functions it serves in its markets. Almost any important consumer product has functions which are related to others into which a qualified company might move. The typewriter, for example, is more than the simple machine for mechanizing handwriting that it once appeared to be when looked at only from the point of view of its designer and manufacturer. Closely analyzed from the point of view of the potential user, the typewriter is found to contribute to a broad range of information processing functions. Any one of these might have suggested an area to be exploited by a typewriter manufacturer. Tacitly defining a typewriter as a replacement for a fountain pen as a writing instrument rather than as an input-output device for word processing is the explanation provided by hindsight for the failure of the old-line typewriter companies to develop before IBM did the electric typewriter and the computer-related input-output devices it made possible. The definition of product which would lead to identification of transferable skills must be expressed in terms of the market needs it may fill rather than the engineering specifications to which it conforms.

Besides looking at the uses or functions to which present products contribute, the would-be diversifier might profitably identify the skills that underlie whatever success has been achieved. The qualifications of an organization efficient at performing its long-accustomed tasks come to be taken for granted and considered humdrum, like the steady provision of first-class service. The insight required to identify the essential strength justifying new ventures does not come naturally. Its cultivation can probably be helped by recognition of the need for analysis. In any case, we should look beyond the company's capacity to invent new products. Product leadership is not possible for a majority of companies, so it is fortunate that patentable new products are not the only major highway to new opportunities. Other avenues include new marketing services, new methods of distribution, new values in quality-price combinations, and creative merchandising. The effort to find or to create a competence that is truly distinctive may hold the real key to a company's success or even to its future development. For example, the ability of a cement manufacturer to run a truck fleet more effectively than its competitors may constitute one of its principal competitive strengths in selling an undifferentiated product.

Matching Opportunity and Competence

The way to narrow the range of alternatives, made extensive by imaginative identification of new possibilities, is to match opportunity to competence, once each has been accurately identified and its future significance estimated. It is this combination which establishes a company's economic mission and its position in its environment. The combination is designed to minimize organizational weakness and to maximize strength. In every case, risk attends it. And when opportunity seems to outrun present distinctive competence, the willingness to gamble that the latter can be built up to the required level is almost indispensable to a strategy that challenges the organization and the people in it. Figure 2 diagrams the matching of opportunity and resources that results in an economic strategy.

Before we leave the creative act of putting together a company's unique internal capability and opportunity evolving in the external world, we should note that—aside from distinctive

FIGURE 2

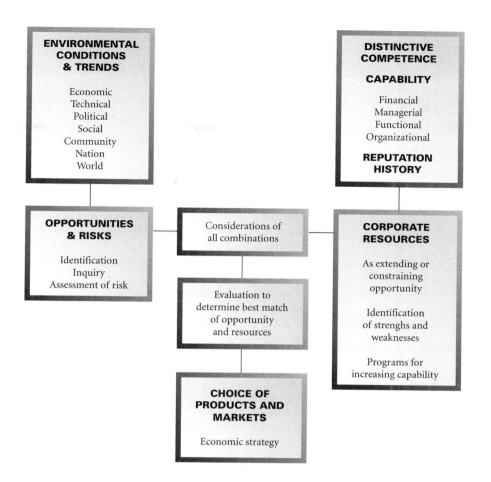

competence—the principal resources found in any company are money and people—technical and managerial people. At an advanced stage of economic development, money seems less a problem than technical competence, and the latter less critical than managerial ability. Do not assume that managerial capacity can rise to any occasion. The diversification of American industry is marked by hundreds of instances in which a company strong in one endeavor lacked the ability to manage an enterprise requiring different skills. The right to make handsome profits over a long period must be earned. Opportunism without competence is a path to fairyland.

Besides equating an appraisal of market opportunity and organizational capability, the decision to make and market a particular product or service should be accompanied by an identification of the nature of the business and the kind of company its management desires. Such a guiding concept is a product of many considerations, including the managers' personal values. . . .

Uniqueness of Strategy

In each company, the way in which distinctive competence, organizational resources, and organizational values are combined is or should be unique. Differences among companies are as numerous as differences among individuals. The combinations of opportunity to which distinctive competencies, resources, and values may be applied are equally extensive. Generalizing about how to make an effective match is less rewarding than working at it. The effort is a highly stimulating and challenging exercise. The outcome will be unique for each company and each situation.

BY RICHARD R. RUMELT

■ Strategy can neither be formulated nor adjusted to changing circumstances without a process of strategy evaluation. Whether performed by an individual or as part of an organizational review procedure, strategy evaluation forms an essential step in the process of guiding an enterprise.

For many executives strategy evaluation is simply an appraisal of how well a business performs. Has it grown? Is the profit rate normal or better? If the answers to these questions are affirmative, it is argued that the firm's strategy must be sound. Despite its unassailable simplicity, this line of reasoning misses the whole point of strategy—that the critical factors determining the quality of current results are often not directly observable or simply measured, and that by the time strategic opportunities or threats do directly affect operating results, it may well be too late for an effective response. Thus, strategy evaluation is an attempt to look beyond the obvious facts regarding the short-term health of a business and appraise instead those more fundamental factors and trends that govern success in the chosen field of endeavor.

THE CHALLENGE OF EVALUATION

However it is accomplished, the products of a business strategy evaluation are answers to these three questions:

■ Are the objectives of the business appropriate?
■ Are the major policies and plans appropriate?
■ Do the results obtained to date confirm or refute critical assumptions on which the strategy rests?

Devising adequate answers to these questions is neither simple nor straightforward. It requires a reasonable store of situation-based knowledge and more than the usual degree of insight. In particular, the major issues which make evaluation difficult and with which the analyst must come to grips are these:

■ Each business strategy is unique. For example, one paper manufacturer might rely on its vast timber holdings to weather almost any storm while another might place primary reliance in modern machinery and an extensive distribution system. Neither strategy is "wrong" nor "right" in any absolute sense; both may be right or wrong for the firms in question. Strategy evaluation must, then, rest on a type of situational logic that does not focus on "one best way" but which can be tailored to each problem as it is faced.
■ Strategy is centrally concerned with this selection of goals and objectives. Many people, including seasoned executives, find it much easier to set or try to achieve goals than to evaluate them. In part this is a consequence of training in problem solving rather than in problem structuring. It also arises out of a tendency to confuse values, which are fundamental expressions of human personality, with objectives, which are devices for lending coherence to action.
■ Formal systems of strategic review, while appealing in principal, can create explosive conflict situations. Not only are there serious questions as to who is qualified to give an objective evaluation, the whole idea of strategy evaluation implies management by "much more than results" and runs counter to much of currently popular management philosophy.

*This paper is a revised and updated version for this book. "The Evaluation of Business Strategy" was originally published in W. F. Glueck, *Strategic Management and Business Policy* (New York: McGraw-Hill, 1980). New version printed here by permission of the author.

The term "strategy" has been so widely used for different purposes that it has lost any clearly defined meaning. For our purposes a strategy is a set of objectives, policies, and plans that, taken together, define the scope of the enterprise and its approach to survival and success. Alternatively, we could say that the particular policies, plans, and objectives of a business express its strategy for coping with a complex competitive environment.

One of the fundamental tenets of science is that a theory can never be proven to be absolutely true. A theory can, however, be declared absolutely false if it fails to stand up to testing. Similarly, it is impossible to demonstrate conclusively that a particular business strategy is optimal or even to guarantee that it will work. One can, nevertheless, test it for critical flaws. Of the many tests which could be justifiably applied to a business strategy, most will fit within one of these broad criteria:

- *Consistency:* The strategy must not present mutually inconsistent goals and policies.
- *Consonance:* The strategy must represent an adaptive response to the external environment and to the critical changes occurring within it.
- *Advantage:* The strategy must provide for the creation and/or maintenance of a competitive advantage in the selected area of activity.
- *Feasibility:* The strategy must neither overtax available resources nor create unsolvable sub problems.

A strategy that fails to meet one or more of these criteria is strongly suspect. It fails to perform at least one of the key functions that are necessary for the survival of the business. Experience within a particular industry or other setting will permit the analyst to sharpen these criteria and add others that are appropriate to the situation at hand.

CONSISTENCY

Gross inconsistency within a strategy seems unlikely until it is realized that many strategies have not been explicitly formulated but have evolved over time in an ad hoc fashion. Even strategies that are the result of formal procedures may easily contain compromise arrangements between opposing power groups.

Inconsistency in strategy is not simply a flaw in logic. A key function of strategy is to provide coherence to organizational action. A clear and explicit concept of strategy can foster a climate of tacit coordination that is more efficient than most administrative mechanisms. Many high-technology firms, for example, face a basic strategic choice between offering high-cost products with high custom-engineering content and lower-cost products that are more standardized and sold at higher volume. If senior management does not enunciate a clear consistent sense of where the corporation stands on these issues, there will be continuing conflict between sales, design, engineering, and manufacturing people. A clear consistent strategy, by contrast, allows a sales engineer to negotiate a contract with a minimum of coordination—the trade-offs are an explicit part of the firm's posture.

Organizational conflict and interdepartmental bickering are often symptoms of a managerial disorder but may also indicate problems of strategic inconsistency. Here are some indicators that can help sort out these two different problems:

- If problems in coordination and planning continue despite changes in personnel and tend to be issue- rather than people-based, they are probably due to inconsistencies in strategy.
- If success for one organizational department means, or its interpreted to mean, failure for another department, either the basic objective structure is inconsistent or the organizational structure is wastefully duplicative.
- If, despite attempts to delegate authority, operating problems continue to be brought to the top for the resolution of policy issues, the basic strategy is probably inconsistent.

A final type of consistency that must be sought in strategy is between organizational objectives and the values of the management group. Inconsistency in this area is more of a problem in strategy formulation than in the evaluation of a strategy that has already been implemented. It can still arise, however, if the future direction of the business requires changes that conflict with managerial values. The most frequent source of such conflict is growth. As a business expands beyond the scale that allows an easy informal method of operation, many executives experience a sharp sense of loss. While growth can of course be curtailed, it often will require special attention to a firm's competitive position if survival without growth is desired. The same basic issues arise when other types of personal or social values come into conflict with existing or apparently necessary policies: the resolution of the conflict will normally require an adjustment in the competitive strategy.

CONSONANCE

The way in which a business relates to its environment has two aspects: the business must both match and be adapted to its environment and it must at the same time compete with other firms that are also trying to adapt. This dual character of the relationship between the firm and its environment has its analog in two different aspects of strategic choice and two different methods of strategy evaluation.

The first aspect of fit deals with the basic mission or scope of the business and the second with its special competitive position or "edge." Analysis of the first is normally done by looking at changing economic and social conditions over time. Analysis of the second, by contrast, typically focuses on the differences across firms at a given time. We call the first the *generic* aspect of strategy and the second *competitive* strategy. Generic strategy deals with the creation of social value—with the question of whether the products and services being created are worth more than their cost. Competitive strategy, by contrast, deals with the firm's need to capture some of the social value as profit. Exhibit 1 summarizes the differences between these concepts.

The notion of consonance, or matching, therefore, invites a focus on generic strategy. The role of the evaluator in this case is to examine the basic pattern of economic relationships that characterize the business and determine whether or not sufficient value is being created to sustain the strategy. Most macroanalysis of changing economic conditions is oriented toward the formulation or evaluation of generic strategies. For example, a planning department forecasts that within six years flat-panel liquid crystal displays will replace CRT-based video displays in computers. The basic message here to makers of CRT-based video displays is that their generic strategies are becoming obsolete. Note that the threat in this case is not to a particular firm, competitive position, or individual approach to the marketplace but to the basic generic mission.

EXHIBIT 1
GENERIC VERSUS
COMPETITIVE
STRATEGY

	GENERIC STRATEGY	COMPETITIVE STRATEGY
Value Issue	Social value	Corporate value
Value Constraint	Customer value > Cost	Price > Cost
Success Indicator	Sales growth	Increased corporate worth
Basic Strategic Task	Adapting to change	Innovating, impeding imitation, deterring rivals
How Strategy Is Expressed	Product-market definition	Advantage, position, and policies supporting them
Basic Approach to Analysis	Study of an industry over time	Comparison across rivals

One major difficulty in evaluating consonance is that most of the critical threats to a business are those which come from without, threatening an entire group of firms. Management, however, is often so engrossed in competitive thinking that such threats are only recognized after the damage has reached considerable proportions.

Another difficulty in appraising the fit between a firm's mission and the environment is that trend analysis does not normally reveal the most critical changes—they are the result of interactions among trends. The supermarket, for example, comes into being only when home refrigeration and the widespread use of automobiles allow shoppers to buy in significantly larger volumes. The supermarket, the automobile, and the move to suburbia together form the nexus which gives rise to shopping centers. These, in turn, change the nature of retailing and, together with the decline of urban centers, create new forms of enterprise, such as the suburban film theater with four screens. Thus, while gross economic or demographic trends might appear steady for many years, there are waves of change going on at the institutional level.

The key to evaluating consonance is an understanding of why the business, as it currently stands, exists at all and how it assumed its current pattern. Once the analyst obtains a good grasp of the basic economic foundation that supports and defines the business, it is possible to study the consequences of key trends and changes. Without such an understanding, there is no good way of deciding what kinds of changes are most crucial and the analyst can be quickly overwhelmed with data.

ADVANTAGE

It is no exaggeration to say that competitive strategy is the art of creating or exploiting those advantages that are most telling, enduring, and most difficult to duplicate.

Competitive strategy, in contrast with generic strategy, focuses on the differences among firms rather than their common missions. The problem it addresses is not so much "how can this function be performed" but "how can we perform it either better than, or at least instead of, our rivals?" The chain supermarket, for example, represents a successful generic strategy. As a way of doing business, of organizing economic transactions, it has replaced almost all the smaller owner-managed food shops of an earlier era. Yet a potential or actual participant in the retail food business must go beyond this generic strategy and find a way of competing in this business. As another illustration, IBM's early success in the PC industry was generic—other firms soon copied the basic product concept. Once this happened, IBM had to try to either forge a strong competitive strategy in this area or seek a different type of competitive arena.

Competitive advantages can normally be traced to one of the three roots:

- Superior skills
- Superior resources
- Superior position

In examining a potential advantage, the critical question is "What sustains this advantage, keeping competitors from imitating or replicating it?" A firm's skills can be a source of advantage if they are based on its own history of learning-by-doing and if they are rooted in the coordinated behavior of many people. By contrast, skills that are based on generally understood scientific principles, on training that can be purchased by competitors, or which can be analyzed and replicated by others are not sources of sustained advantage.

The *skills* which compose advantages are usually organizational, rather than individual, skills. They involve the adept coordination or collaboration of individual specialists and are built through the interplay of investment, work, and learning. Unlike physical assets, skills are enhanced by their use. Skills that are not continually used and improved will atrophy.

Resources include patents, trademark rights, specialized physical assets, and the firm's working relationships with suppliers and distribution channels. In addition, a firm's reputation with its employees, suppliers, and customers is a resource. Resources that constitute advantages are specialized to the firm, are built up slowly over time through the accumulated exercise of superior skills, or are obtained through being an insightful first mover, or by just plain luck. For example, Nucor's special skills in mini-mill construction are embodied in superior physical plants. Goldman Sachs's reputation as the premier U.S. investment banking house has been built up over many years and is now a major resource in its own right.

A firm's *position* consists of the products or services it provides, the market segments it sells to, and the degree to which it is isolated from direct competition. In general, the best positions involve supplying very uniquely valuable products to price insensitive buyers, whereas poor positions involve being one of many firms supplying marginally valuable products to very well informed, price sensitive buyers.

Positional advantage can be gained by foresight, superior skill and/or resources, or just plain luck. Once gained, a good position is defensible. This means that it (1) returns enough value to warrant its continued maintenance and (2) would be so costly to capture that rivals are deterred from full-scale attacks on the core of the business. Position, it must be noted, tends to be self-sustaining as long as the basic environmental factors that underlie it remain stable. Thus, entrenched firms can be almost impossible to unseat, even if their raw skill levels are only average. And when a shifting environment allows position to be gained by a new entrant or innovator, the results can be spectacular.

Positional advantages are of two types: (1) first mover advantages and (2) reinforcers. The most basic *first mover advantage* occurs when the minimum scale to be efficient requires a large (sunk) investment relative to the market. Thus, the first firm to open a large discount retail store in a rural area precludes, through its relative scale, close followers. More subtle first mover advantages occur when standardization effects "lock-in" customers to the first mover's product (e.g., Lotus 1-2-3). Buyer learning and related phenomena can increase the buyer's switching costs, protecting an incumbent's customer base from attack. Frequent flyer programs are aimed in this direction. First movers may also gain advantages in building distribution channels, in tying up specialized suppliers, or in gaining the attention of customers. The first product of a class to engage in mass advertising, for example, tends to impress itself more deeply in people's minds than the second, third, or fourth. In a careful study of frequently purchased consumer products, Urban et al. (1986) found that (other things being equal) the first entrant will have a market share that is $\sqrt{n}$ times as large as that of the nth entrant.

Reinforcers are policies or practices acting to strengthen or preserve a strong market position and which are easier to carry out because of the position. The idea that certain arrangements of one's resources can enhance their combined effectiveness, and perhaps even put rival forces in a state of disarray, is at the heart of the traditional notion of strategy. It is reinforcers which provide positional advantage, the strategic quality familiar to military theorists, chess players, and diplomats.

A firm with a larger market share, due to being an early mover or to having a technological lead, can typically build a more efficient production and distribution system. Competitors with less demand simply cannot cover the fixed costs of the larger more efficient facilities, so for them larger facilities are not an economic choice. In this case, scale economies are a reinforcer of market position, not the cause of market position. The firm that has a strong brand can use it as a reinforcer in the introduction of related brands. A company that sells a specialty coating to a broader variety of users may have better data on how to adapt the coating to special conditions than a competitor with more limited sales—properly used, this information is a reinforcer. A famous brand will appear on TV and in films because it is famous, another reinforcer. An example given by Porter (1985: 145) is that of Steinway and Sons, the premier U.S. maker of fine pianos. Steinway maintains a dispersed inventory of grand pianos that approved pianists are permitted to use for concerts at very low rental rates. The policy is less expensive for a leader than for a follower and helps maintain leadership.

The positive feedback provided by reinforcers is the source of the power of position-based advantages—the policies that act to enhance position may not require unusual skills; they simply work most effectively for those who are already in the position in the first place.

While it is not true that larger businesses always have the advantages, it is true that larger businesses will tend to operate in markets and use procedures that turn their size to advantage. Large national consumer-products firms, for example, will normally have an advantage over smaller regional firms in the efficient use of mass advertising, especially network TV. The larger firm will, then, tend to deal in those products where the marginal effect of advertising is most potent, while the smaller firms will seek product/market positions that exploit other types of advantage.

Other position-based advantages follow from such factors as:

- The ownership of special raw material sources or advantageous long-term supply contracts
- Being geographically located near key customers in a business involving significant fixed investment and high transport costs
- Being a leader in a service field that permits or requires the building of a unique experience base while serving clients.
- Being a full-line producer in a market with heavy trade-up phenomena
- Having a wide reputation for providing a needed product or service trait reliably and dependably

In each case, the position permits competitive policies to be adopted that can serve to reinforce the position. Whenever this type of positive-feedback phenomena is encountered, the particular policy mix that creates it will be found to be a defensible business position. The key factors that sparked industrial success stories such as IBM and Eastman Kodak were the early and rapid domination of strong positions opened up by new technologies.

FEASIBILITY

The final broad test of strategy is its feasibility. Can the strategy be attempted within the physical, human, and financial resources available? The financial resources of a business are the easiest to quantify and are normally the first limitations against which strategy is tested. It is sometimes forgotten, however, that innovative approaches to financing expansion can both stretch the ultimate limitations and provide a competitive advantage, even if it is only temporary. Devices such as captive finance subsidiaries, sale-leaseback arrangements, and tying plant mortgages to long-term contracts have all been used effectively to help win key positions in suddenly expanding industries.

The less quantifiable but actually more rigid limitation on strategic choice is that imposed by the individual and organization capabilities that are available.

In assessing the organization's ability to carry out a strategy, it is helpful to ask three separate questions:

1. Has the organization demonstrated that it possesses the problem-solving abilities and/or special competencies required by the strategy? A strategy, as such, does not and cannot specify in detail each action that must be carried out. Its purpose is to provide structure to the general issue of the business's goals and approaches to coping with its environment. It is up to the members and departments of the organization to carry out the tasks defined by strategy. A strategy that requires tasks to be accomplished which fall outside the realm of available or easily obtainable skill and knowledge cannot be accepted. It is either unfeasible or incomplete.

2. Has the organization demonstrated the degree of coordinative and integrative skill necessary to carry out the strategy? The key tasks required of a strategy not only require specialized skill, but often make considerable demands on the organization's ability to inte-

grate disparate activities. A manufacturer of standard office furniture may find, for example, that its primary difficulty in entering the new market for modular office systems is a lack of sophisticated interaction between its field sales offices and its manufacturing plant. Firms that hope to span national boundaries with integrated worldwide systems of production and marketing may also find that organizational process, rather than functional skill per se or isolated competitive strength, becomes the weak link in the strategic posture.

3. Does the strategy challenge and motivate key personnel and is it acceptable to those who must lend their support? The purpose of strategy is to effectively deploy the unique and distinctive resources of an enterprise. If key managers are unmoved by a strategy, not excited by its goals or methods, or strongly support an alternative, it fails in a major way.

THE PROCESS OF STRATEGY EVALUATION

Strategy evaluation can take place as an abstract analytic task, perhaps performed by consultants. But most often it is an integral part of an organization's process of planning, review, and control. In some organizations, evaluation is informal, only occasional, brief and cursory. Others have created elaborate systems containing formal periodic strategy review sessions. In either case, the quality of strategy evaluation, and ultimately, the quality of corporate performance, will be determined more by the organization's capacity for self-appraisal and learning than by the particular analytic technique employed.

In their study of organizational learning, Argyris and Schon distinguish between single-loop and double-loop learning. They argue that normal organizational learning is of the feedback-control type—deviations between expected and actual performance lead to problem solving which brings the system back under control. They note that

[Single-loop learning] is concerned primarily with effectiveness—that is, with how best to achieve existing goals and objectives and how best to keep organizational performance within the range specified by existing norms. In some cases, however, error correction requires a learning cycle in which organizational norms themselves are modified. . . . We call this sort of learning "double-loop." There is . . . a double feedback loop which connects the detection of error not only to strategies and assumptions for effective performance but to the very norms which define effective performance [1978: 20]

These ideas parallel those of Ashby, a cyberneticist. Ashby (1954) has argued that all feedback systems require more than single-loop error control for stability; they also need a way of monitoring certain critical variables and changing the system "goals" when old control methods are no longer working.

These viewpoints help to remind us that the real strategic processes in any organization are not found by looking at those things that happen to be labeled "strategic" or "long range." Rather, the real components of the strategic process are, by definition, those activities which most strongly affect the selection and modification of objectives and which influence the irreversible commitment of important resources. They also suggest that appropriate methods of strategy evaluation cannot be specified in abstract terms. Instead, an organization's approach to evaluation must fit its strategic posture and work in conjunction with its methods of planning and control.

In most firms comprehensive strategy evaluation is infrequent and, if it occurs, is normally triggered by a change in leadership or financial performance. The fact that comprehensive strategy evaluation is neither a regular event nor part of a formal system tends to be deplored by some theorists, but there are several good reasons for this state of affairs. Most obviously, any activity that becomes an annual procedure is bound to become more automatic. While evaluating strategy on an annual basis might lead to some sorts of efficiencies in data collection and analysis, it would also tend to strongly channel the types of questions asked and inhibit broad-ranging reflection.

Second, a good strategy does not need constant reformulation. It is a framework for continuing problem solving, not the problem solving itself. One senior executive expressed it this way: "If you play from strength you don't always need to be rethinking the whole plan; you can concentrate on details. So when you see us talking about slight changes in tooling, it isn't because we forgot the big picture, it's because we took care of it."

Strategy also represents a political alignment within the firm and embodies the past convictions and commitments of key executives. Comprehensive strategy evaluation is not just an analytical exercise, it calls into question this basic pattern of commitments and policies. Most organizations would be hurt rather than helped to have their mission's validity called into question on a regular basis. Zero-base budgeting, for example, was an attempt to get agencies to re-justify their existence each time a new budget is drawn up. If this were literally true, there would be little time or energy remaining for any but political activity.

Finally, there are competitive reasons for not reviewing the validity of a strategy too freely! There are a wide range of rivalrous confrontations in which it is crucial to be able to convince others that one's position, or strategy, is fixed and unshakable. Schelling's (1963) analysis of bargaining and conflict shows that a great deal of what is involved in negotiating is finding ways to bind or commit oneself convincingly. This is the principle underlying the concept of deterrence and what lies behind the union leader's tactic of claiming that while he would go along with management's desire for moderation, he cannot control the members if the less moderate demands are not met. In business strategy, such situations occur in classic oligopoly, plant-capacity duels, new-product conflicts, and other situations in which the winner may be the party whose policies are most credibly unswayable. Japanese electronics firms, for example, have gained such strong reputations as low-cost committed players that their very entry into a market has come to induce rivals to give up. If such firms had instead the reputation of continually reviewing the advisability of continuing each product, they would be much less threatening, and thus less effective, competitors. . . .

CONCLUSIONS

Strategy evaluation is the appraisal of plans and the results of plans that centrally concern or affect the basic mission of an enterprise. Its special focus is the separation between obvious current operating results and those factors which underlie success or failure in the chosen domain of activity. Its result is the rejection, modification, or ratification of existing strategies and plans. . . .

In most medium- to large-size firms, strategy evaluation is not a purely intellectual task. The issues involved are too important and too closely associated with the distribution of power and authority for either strategy formulation or evaluation to take place in an ivory tower environment. In fact, most firms rarely engage in explicit formal strategy evaluation. Rather, the evaluation of current strategy is a continuing process and one that is difficult to separate from the normal planning, reporting, control, and reward systems of the firm. From this point of view, strategy evaluation is not so much an intellectual task as it is an organizational process.

Ultimately, a firm's ability to maintain its competitive position in a world of rivalry and change may be best served by managers who can maintain a dual view of strategy and strategy evaluation—they must be willing and able to perceive the strategy within the welter of daily activity and to build and maintain structures and systems that make strategic factors the object of current activity.

**BY GARY HAMEL
AND C. K.
PRAHALAD**

■ Today managers in many industries are working hard to match the competitive advantages of their new global rivals. They are moving manufacturing offshore in search of low labor costs, rationalizing product lines to capture global scale economics, instituting quality circles and just-in-time production, and adopting Japanese human resource practices. When competitiveness still seems out of reach, they form strategic alliances, often with the very companies that upset the competitive balance in the first place.

Important as these initiatives are, few of them go beyond mere imitation. . . . For these executives and their companies, regaining competitiveness will mean rethinking many of the basic concepts of strategy. . . . The new global competitors approach strategy from a perspective that is fundamentally different from that which underpins Western management thought. . . .

Companies that have risen to global leadership over the past 20 years invariably began with ambitions that were out of all proportion to their resources and capabilities. But they created an obsession with winning at all levels of the organization and then sustained that obsession over the 10- to 20-year quest for global leadership. We term this obsession "strategic intent."

On the one hand, strategic intent envisions a desired leadership position and establishes the criteria the organization will use to chart its progress. Komatsu set out to "Encircle Caterpillar." Canon sought to "Beat Xerox." Honda strove to become a second Ford—an automotive pioneer. All are expressions of strategic intent.

At the same time, strategic intent is more than simply unfettered ambition. (Many companies possess an ambitious strategic intent yet fall short of their goals.) The concept also encompasses an active management process that includes: focusing the organization's attention on the essence of winning; motivating people by communicating the value of the target; leaving room for individual and team contributions; sustaining enthusiasm by providing new operations definitions as circumstances change; and using intent consistently to guide resource allocations.

Strategic intent captures the essence of winning. The Apollo program—landing a man on the moon ahead of the Soviets—was as competitively focused as Komatsu's drive against Caterpillar. The space program became the scorecard for America's technology race with the USSR. . . . For Coca-Cola, strategic intent has been to put Coke within "arm's reach" of every consumer in the world.

Strategic intent is stable over time. In battles for global leadership, one of the most critical tasks is to lengthen the organization's attention span. Strategic intent provides consistency to short-term action, while leaving room for reinterpretation as new opportunities emerge. . . .

Strategic intent sets a target that deserves personal effort and commitment. Ask the chairmen of many American corporations how they measure their contributions to their companies' success and you're likely to get an answer expressed in terms of shareholder wealth. In a company that possesses a strategic intent, top management is more likely to talk in terms of global market leadership. Market share leadership typically yields shareholder wealth, to be sure. But the two goals do not have the same motivational impact. It is hard to imagine middle managers, let alone blue-collar employees, waking up each day with the sole thought of creating more shareholder wealth. But mightn't they feel different given the challenge to "Beat Benz"— the rallying cry at one Japanese auto producer? Strategic intent gives employees the only goal that is worthy of commitment: to unseat the best or remain the best, worldwide. . . .

Just as you cannot plan a 10- to 20-year quest for global leadership, the chance of falling into a leadership position by accident is also remote. We don't believe that global leadership

---

comes from an undirected process of intrapreneurship. Nor is it the product of a skunkworks or other techniques for internal venturing. Behind such programs lies a nihilistic assumption: the organization is so hide-bound, so orthodox ridden that the only way to innovate is to put a few bright people in a dark room, pour in some money, and hope that something wonderful will happen. In the "Silicon Valley" approach to innovation, the only role for top managers is to retrofit their corporate strategy to the entrepreneurial successes that emerge from below. Here the value added of top management is low indeed. . . .

In companies that overcame resource constraints to build leadership positions, we see a different relationship between means and ends. While strategic intent is clear about ends, it is flexible as to means—it leaves room for improvisation. Achieving strategic intent requires enormous creativity with respect to means. . . . But this creativity comes in the service of a clearly prescribed end. Creativity is unbridled, but not uncorraled, because top management establishes the criterion against which employees can pretest the logic of their initiatives. Middle managers must do more than deliver on promised financial targets; they must also deliver on the broad direction implicit in their organization's strategic intent.

Strategic intent implies a sizable stretch for an organization. Current capabilities and resources will not suffice. This forces the organization to be more inventive, to make the most of limited resources. Whereas the traditional view of strategy focuses on the degree of fit between existing resources and current opportunities, strategic intent creates an extreme misfit between resources and ambitions. Top management then challenges the organization to close the gap by systematically building new advantages. For Canon this meant first understanding Xerox's patents, then licensing technology to create a product that would yield early market experience, then gearing up internal R&D efforts, then licensing its own technology to other manufacturers to fund further R&D, then entering marketing segments in Japan and Europe where Xerox was weak, and so on.

In this respect, strategic intent is like a marathon run in 400-meter sprints. No one knows what the terrain will look like at mile 26, so the role of top management is to focus the organization's attention on the ground to be covered in the next 400 meters. In several companies, management did this by presenting the organization with a series of corporate challenges, each specifying the next hill in the race to achieve strategic intent. One year the challenge might be quality, the next total customer care, the next entry into new markets, the next a rejuvenated product line. As this example indicates, corporate challenges are a way to stage the acquisition of new competitive advantages, a way to identify the focal point for employees' efforts in the near to medium term. As with strategic intent, top management is specific about the ends (reducing product development times by 75%, for example) but less prescriptive about the means.

Like strategic intent, challenges stretch the organization. To preempt Xerox in the personal copier business, Canon set its engineers a target price of $1,000 for a home copier. At the time, Canon's least expensive copier sold for several thousand dollars. . . . Canon engineers were challenged to reinvent the copier—a challenge they met by substituting a disposable cartridge for the complex image-transfer mechanism used in other copiers. . . .

For a challenge to be effective, individuals and teams throughout the organization must understand it and see its implications for their own jobs. Companies that set corporate challenges to create new competitive advantages (as Ford and IBM did with quality improvement) quickly discover that engaging the entire organization requires top management to:

Create a sense of urgency, or quasi crisis, by amplifying weak signals in the environment that point up the need to improve, instead of allowing inaction to precipitate a real crisis. . . .

Develop a competitor focus at every level though widespread use of competitive intelligence. Every employee should be able to benchmark his or her efforts against best-in-class competitors so that the challenge becomes personal. . . .

Provide employees with the skills they need to work effectively—training in statistical tools, problem solving, value engineering, and team building, for example.

Give the organization time to digest one challenge before launching another. When competing initiatives overload the organization, middle managers often try to protect their people from the whipsaw of shifting priorities. But this "wait and see if they're serious this time" attitude ultimately destroys the credibility of corporate challenges.

Establish clear milestones and review mechanisms to track progress and ensure that internal recognition and rewards reinforce desired behavior. The goal is to make the challenge inescapable for everyone in the company. . . .

Reciprocal responsibility means shared gain and shared pain . . . at Nissan when the yen strengthened: top management took a big pay cut and then asked middle managers and line employees to sacrifice relatively less. In too many companies, the pain of revitalization falls almost exclusively on the employees least responsible for the enterprise's decline. . . . This one-sided approach to regaining competitiveness keeps many companies from harnessing the intellectual horsepower of their employees.

Creating a sense of reciprocal responsibility is crucial because competitiveness ultimately depends on the pace at which a company embeds new advantages deep within its organization, not on its stock of advantages at any given time. Thus we need to expand the concept of competitive advantage beyond the scorecard many managers now use: Are my costs lower? Will my product command a price premium?

Few competitive advantages are long lasting. Uncovering a new competitive advantage is a bit like getting a hot tip on a stock: the first person to act on the insight makes more money than the last. . . .

Keeping score of existing advantages is not the same as building new advantages. The essence of strategy lies in creating tomorrow's competitive advantages faster than competitors mimic the ones you possess today. In the 1960s, Japanese producers relied on labor and capital cost advantages. As Western manufacturers began to move production offshore, Japanese companies accelerated their investment in process technology and created scale and quality advantages. Then as their U.S. and European competitors rationalized manufacturing, they added another string to their bow by accelerating the rate of product development. Then they built global brands. Then they deskilled competitors through alliances and outsourcing deals. The moral? An organization's capacity to improve existing skills and learn new ones is the most defensible competitive advantage of all.

To achieve strategic intent, a company must usually take on larger, better financed competitors. That means carefully managing competitive engagements so that scarce resources are conserved. Managers cannot do that simply by playing the same game better—making marginal improvement to competitor's technology and business practices. Instead, they must fundamentally change the game in ways that disadvantage incumbents—designing novel approaches to market entry, advantage building, and competitive warfare. For smart competitors, the goal is not competitive imitation but competitive innovation, the art of containing competitive risks within manageable proportions.

Four approaches to competitive innovation are evident in the global expansion of Japanese companies. These are: building layers of advantage, searching for loose bricks, changing the terms of engagement, and competing through collaboration.

The wider a company's portfolio of advantages, the less risk it faces in competitive battles. New global competitors have built such portfolios by steadily expanding their arsenals of competitive weapons. They have moved inexorably from less defensible advantages such as low wage costs to more defensible advantages like global brands. . . .

Business schools have perpetuated the notion that a manager with new present value calculations in one hand and portfolio planning in the other can manage any business anywhere.

In many diversified companies, top management evaluates line managers on numbers alone because no other basis for dialogue exists. Managers move so many times as part of their "career development" that they often do not understand the nuances of the businesses they are managing. At GE, for example, one fast-track manager heading an important new venture had moved across five businesses in five years. His series of quick successes finally came to an end when he confronted a Japanese competitor whose managers had been plodding along in the same business for more than a decade.

Regardless of ability and effort, fast-track managers are unlikely to develop the deep business knowledge they need to discuss technology options, competitors' strategies, and global opportunities substantively. Invariably, therefore, discussions gravitate to "the numbers," while the value added of managers is limited to the financial and planning savvy they carry from job to job. Knowledge of the company's internal planning and accounting systems substitutes for substantive knowledge of the business, making competitive innovation unlikely.

When managers know that their assignments have a two- to three-year time frame, they feel great pressure to create a good track record fast. This pressure often takes on one of two forms. Either the manager does not commit to goals whose time line extends beyond his or her expected tenure. Or ambitious goals are adopted and squeezed into an unrealistically short time frame. Aiming to be number one in a business is the essence of strategic intent; but imposing a three- to four-year horizon on that effort simply invites disaster. Acquisitions are made with little attention to the problems of integration. The organization becomes overloaded with initiatives. Collaborative ventures are formed without adequate attention to competitive consequences.

Almost every strategic management theory and nearly every corporate planning system is premised on a strategy hierarchy in which corporate goals guide business unit strategies and business unit strategies guide functional tactics. In this hierarchy, senior management makes strategy and low levels execute it. The dichotomy between formulation and implementation is familiar and widely accepted. But the strategy hierarchy undermines competitiveness by fostering an elitist view of management that tends to disenfranchise most of the organization. Employees fail to identify with corporate goals or involve themselves deeply in the work of becoming more competitive.

The strategy hierarchy isn't the only explanation for an elitist view of management, of course. The myths that grow up around successful top managers . . . perpetuate it. So does the turbulent business environment. Middle managers buffeted by circumstances that seem to be beyond their control desperately want to believe that top management has all the answers. And top management, in turn, hesitates to admit it does not for fear of demoralizing lower level employees. . . .

Unfortunately, a threat that everyone perceives but no one talks about creates more anxiety than a threat that has been clearly identified and made the focal point for the problem-solving efforts of the entire company. That is one reason honesty and humility on the part of top management may be the first prerequisite of revitalization. Another reason is the need to make participation more than a buzzword.

Programs such as quality circles and total customer service often fall short of expectations because management does not recognize that successful implementation requires more than administrative structures. Difficulties in embedding new capabilities are typically put down to "communication" problems, with the unstated assumption that if only downward communication were more effective—"if only middle management would get the message straight"— the new program would quickly take root. The need for upward communication is often ignored, or assumed to mean nothing more than feedback. In contrast, Japanese companies win, not because they have smarter managers, but because they have developed ways to harness the "wisdom of the anthill." They realize the top managers are a bit like the astronauts who circle the earth in the space shuttle. It may be the astronauts who get all the glory, but everyone knows that the real intelligence behind the mission is located firmly on the ground. . . .

Developing faith in the organization's ability to deliver on tough goals, motivating it to do so, focusing its attention long enough to internalize new capabilities—this is the real challenge for top management. Only by rising to this challenge will senior managers gain the courage they need to commit themselves and their companies to global leadership.

CHAPTER 4

Analyzing Strategy

As noted in the introduction to Chapter 3, a second prescriptive view of how strategy should be formulated developed in the 1980s. Its contribution is less as a new conceptual model—in fact, it embraces most of the assumptions of the traditional model—and more as a careful structuring of the kinds of formal analyses that should be undertaken to develop a successful strategy. One outcome of this more formal approach is that many of its adherents came to see strategies as fitting certain "generic" classifications—not being created individually so much as being selected from a limited set of options. This approach has proved to be powerful and useful in specific situations.

Michael Porter became the leader of this school after studying at the doctoral level in Harvard's economics department. By building intellectual bridges between the fields of management policy and industrial organization—the latter a branch of economics concerned with the performance of industries as a function of their competitive characteristics—Porter elaborated on the earlier views of Andrews, Ansoff, Newman, and others.

We open this chapter with Porter's basic model of competitive and industry analysis, probably his best-known work in the area of strategy analysis. As presented in this award-winning *Harvard Business Review* article, it proposes a framework of five forces that in his view defines the basic posture of competition in an industry—the bargaining power of existing suppliers and buyers, the threat of substitutes and new entrants, and the intensity of existing rivalry. The model is a powerful one, as you shall see in references to it in subsequent readings as well as in applications of it in the case studies.

The next two articles, by Jay Barney of Ohio State University and Pankaj Ghemawat and Gary Pisano of Harvard Business School, take this analytical perspective further into new aspects that developed since Porter wrote his path-breathing books of the 1980s. Sustainable competitive advantage is the holy grail of what we like to call the "content" approach to strategy. It is, however, a surprisingly elusive goal. Porter's five-forces model suggests that sustainable competitive advantage can be discovered by proper industry analysis. The only problem with his model is that the same analysis often applies equally well to more than one company (hence, the notion of "strategic groups"). Barney's article takes up the challenge, putting forward what has come to be known as the resource-based view of the firm. This argues that sustainable competitive advantage is not the product of correct position in the external environment but is derived from the firm's internal resources. More specifically, resources must meet four criteria to confer sustainable competitive advantage. They must be valuable, inimitable, rare, and nonsubstitutable.

In "Sustaining Superior Performance: Commitments and Capabilities" Ghemawat and Pisano maintain that Barney's criteria are not sufficient for assuring sustainable advantage. Sustainability must address other conditions—in particular the need to prevent other firms from imitating and appropriating resources, and the need to ensure that employees (or other agents of the organization) refrain from abusing their position through underperformance or by covertly appropriating resources. Large-scale investments in the right resources can help companies meet these conditions, but in addition to these discrete actions, companies should make regular small-scale investments that build their capabilities.

Porter is also known for a number of other concepts: "generic strategies," of which he argues there are three in particular—cost leadership, differentiation, and focus (or scope); the "value chain," as a way of decomposing the activities of a business to apply strategy analyses of various kinds; strategic groups, where firms with like sets of strategies compete in subsegments of an industry; and "generic industry environments," such as "fragmented" and "mature," which reflect similar characteristics.

We shall hear from Porter again on the last of these in our third section. But his three generic strategies as well as his value chain concept are summarized in the next reading in this chapter. Here Mintzberg seeks to present a more comprehensive picture of the various generic strategies that firms commonly pursue. These generic strategies are described at four levels as strategies concerned with locating the core business, with distinguishing the core business by means of "differentiation" and scope," with elaborating the core business, and with extending the core business.

The fourth reading of the chapter looks at strategic analysis quite differently, in a kind of political way. You may recall one of the definitions of strategy introduced in Chapter 1 that has not been heard from since—that of ploy. In this reading, ploy comes to life in the form of "competitive maneuvering" and the various means strategists use to outwit competitors. This reading is based on two short articles entitled "Brinkmanship in Business" and "The Nonlogical Strategy" by Bruce Henderson, drawn from his book, *Henderson on Corporate Strategy,* which is a collection of short, pithy, and rather opinionated views. Henderson founded the Boston Consulting Group and built it into a major international force in management consulting.

The literature of strategic analysis, or "positioning" as it is sometimes called, tends like analysis itself to be rather decomposed in that it is more concerned with probing into parts than combining into wholes. Accordingly, the concepts tend to come and go at a frantic pace, confusing reader and writer alike. Thus, Mintzberg has prepared for this book an integrative piece called "A Guide to Strategic Positioning," which sets out to place these many concepts into a single framework. To do so, he uses the metaphor of a launching vehicle that projects its products and services into the terrain of markets. You should have some fun with this new contribution to the strategic management literature.

USING THE CASE STUDIES

Porter's five-forces model is arguably the most influential analytical model in strategy. In principle, it can be applied to most of the cases in this book. In practice, it is best applied to cases in which strategic decision making is tightly coupled to industry conditions. This is very much in evidence in the cases of Impsat and telecommunications, WFNX-101.7FM and radio, the London Free Press and newspaper publishing, NBC and television broadcasting, AmBev and the beer industry, TV Asahi and musical theater, and Intel and semiconductors.

Porter's emphasis on the importance of external context is balanced by Barney's insistence that sustainable advantage depends as much or more on the internal resources of the firm. These resources are fairly easy to identify in the case of Intel but much harder to pinpoint when we turn to companies such as Lufthansa, LVMH, the London Free Press, and the New York Botanical Gardens. (Try it; it can be an interesting exercise.) Ghemawat and Pisano, of course, would argue that capabilities, not resources, are the key to sustainability. The Canon case has often been used to explore this view. However, capabilities, like resources, are a difficult analytical construct. It is often best approached when trying to explain the success of a company such as HBO, which seemingly violates every rule in its industry.

Effective strategic analysis may rely less on "grand" theories, such as those of Porter or Barney, and more on finding the right framework for identifying moves and positions. Henderson's "Competitive Maneuvering" brings Porter's model down to earth. Cases such as Impsat, NBC, Lufthansa, and the Acer Group show how companies focus on their competitors. In "Generic Business Strategies" and "A Guide to Strategic Positioning," Mintzberg opens up Porter's typology to new kinds of business strategies. This may be valuable for the top managers of WFNX-101.7FM, the Acer Group, and London Free Press, who are pondering where to position their companies.

READING 4.1   HOW COMPETITIVE FORCES SHAPE STRATEGY*

BY MICHAEL E. PORTER

■ The essence of strategy formulation is copying with competition. Yet it is easy to view competition too narrowly and too pessimistically. While one sometimes hears executives complaining to the contrary, intense competition in an industry is neither coincidence nor bad luck.

Moreover, in the fight for market share, competition is not manifested only in the other players. Rather, competition in an industry is rooted in its underlying economics, and competitive forces exist that go well beyond the established combatants in a particular industry. Customers, suppliers, potential entrants, and substitute products are all competitors that may be more or less prominent or active depending on the industry.

The state of competition in an industry depends on five basic forces, which are diagrammed in Figure 1. The collective strength of these forces determines the ultimate profit potential of an industry. It ranges from *intense* in industries like tires, metal cans, and steel, where no company earns spectacular returns on investment, to *mild* in industries like oil field services and equipment, soft drinks, and toiletries, where there is room for quite high returns.

---

*Originally published in the *Harvard Business Review* (March–April 1979) and winner of the McKinsey prize for the best article in the *Review* in 1979. Copyright © 1979 by the President and Fellows of Harvard College; all rights reserved. Reprinted with deletions by permission of the *Harvard Business Review*.

FIGURE 1 ELEMENTS OF INDUSTRY STRUCTURE

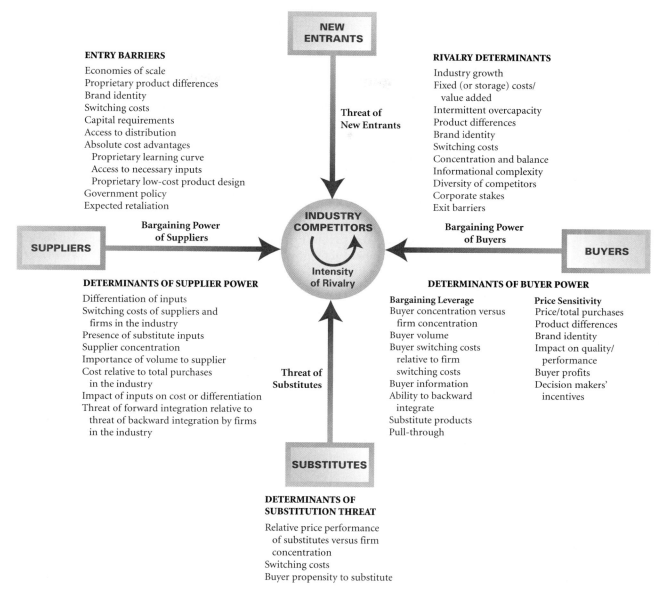

Used with permission of The Free Press, a Division of Macmillan, Inc., from *Competitive Strategy: Techniques for Analyzing Industries and Competitors* by Michael E. Porter. Copyright © 1960 by The Free Press. [Used in place of article's Figure 1 as it contains more detail.]

In the economists' "perfectly competitive" industry, jockeying for position is unbridled and entry to the industry very easy. This kind of industry structure, of course, offers the worst prospect for long-run profitability. The weaker the forces collectively, however, the greater the opportunity for superior performance.

Whatever their collective strength, the corporate strategist's goal is to find a position in the industry where his or her company can best defend itself against these forces or can influence them in its favor. The collective strength of the forces may be painfully apparent to all the antagonists; but to cope with them, the strategist must delve below the surface and analyze the sources of each. For example, what makes the industry vulnerable to entry? What determines the bargaining powers of suppliers?

Knowledge of these underlying sources of competitive pressure provides the groundwork for a strategic agenda of action. They highlight the critical strengths and weaknesses of the company, animate the positioning of the company in its industry, clarify the areas where strategic changes may yield the greatest payoff, and highlight the places where industry trends promise to hold the greatest significance as either opportunities or threats. Understanding these sources also proves to be of help in considering areas for diversification.

CONTENDING FORCES

The strongest competitive force or forces determine the profitability of an industry and so are of greatest importance in strategy formulation. For example, even a company with a strong position in an industry unthreatened by potential entrants will earn low returns if it faces a superior or lower-cost substitute product—as the leading manufacturers of vacuum tubes and coffee percolators have learned to their sorrow. In such a situation, coping with the substitute product becomes the number one strategy priority.

Different forces take on prominence, of course, in shaping competition in each industry. In the oceangoing tanker industry the key force is probably the buyers (the major oil companies), while in tires it is powerful OEM buyers coupled with tough competitors. In the steel industry the key forces are foreign competitors and substitute materials.

Every industry has an underlying structure, or a set of fundamental economic and technical characteristics, that gives rise to these competitive forces. The strategist, wanting to position his company to cope best with its industry environment or to influence the environment in the company's favor, must learn what makes the environment tick.

This view of competition pertains equally to industries dealing in services and to those selling products. To avoid monotony in this article, I refer to both products and services as "products." The same general principles apply to all types of business.

A few characteristics are critical to the strength of each competitive force. I shall discuss them in this section.

THREAT OF ENTRY

New entrants to an industry bring new capacity, the desire to gain market share, and often substantial resources. Companies diversifying through acquisition into the industry from other markets often leverage their resources to cause a shakeup, as Philip Morris did with Miller beer.

The seriousness of the threat of entry depends on the barriers present and on the reaction from existing competitors that the entrant can expect. If barriers to entry are high and a newcomer can expect sharp retaliation from the entrenched competitors, obviously he will not pose a serious threat of entering.

There are six major sources of barriers to entry:

1. *Economies of scale*—These economies deter entry by forcing the aspirant either to come in on a large scale or to accept a cost disadvantage. Scale economies in production, research, marketing, and service are probably the key barriers to entry in the mainframe computer industry, as Xerox and GE sadly discovered. Economies of scale can also act as hurdles in distribution, utilization of the sales force, financing, and nearly any other part of a business.

2. *Product differentiation*—Brand identification creates a barrier by forcing entrants to spend heavily to overcome customer loyalty. Advertising, customer service, being first in the industry, and product differences are among the factors fostering brand identification. It is perhaps the most important entry barrier in soft drinks, over-the-counter drugs, cosmetics, investment banking, and public accounting. To create high fences around their businesses, brewers couple brand identification with economies of scale in production, distribution, and marketing.

3. *Capital requirements*—The need to invest large financial resources in order to compete creates a barrier to entry, particularly if the capital is required for unrecoverable expenditures in up-front advertising or R&D. Capital is necessary not only for fixed facilities but also for customer credit, inventories, and absorbing start-up losses. While major corporations have the financial resources to invade almost any industry, the huge capital requirements in certain fields, such as computer manufacturing and mineral extraction, limit the pool of likely entrants.

4. *Cost disadvantages independent of size*—Entrenched companies may have cost advantages not available to potential rivals, no matter what their size and attainable economies of scale. These advantages can stem from the effects of the learning curve (and of its first cousin, the experience curve), proprietary technology, access to the best raw materials sources, assets purchased at preinflation prices, government subsidies, or favorable locations. Sometimes cost advantages are legally enforceable, as they are through patents. . . .

5. *Access to distribution channels*—The new boy on the block must, of course, secure distribution of his product or service. A new food product, for example, must displace others from the supermarket shelf via price breaks, promotions, intense selling efforts, or some other means. The more limited the wholesale or retail channels are and the more that existing competitors have these tied up, obviously the tougher that entry into the industry will be. Sometimes this barrier is so high that, to surmount it, a new contestant must create its own distribution channels, as Timex did in the watch industry in the 1950s.

6. *Government policy*—The government can limit or even foreclose industries with such controls as license requirements and limits on access to raw materials. Regulated industries like trucking, liquor retailing, and freight forwarding are noticeable examples; more subtle government restrictions operate in fields like ski-area development and coal mining. The government also can play a major indirect role by affecting entry barriers through controls such as air and water pollution standards and safety regulations.

The potential rival's expectations about the reaction of existing competitors also will influence its decision on whether to enter. The company is likely to have second thoughts if incumbents have previously lashed out at new entrants or if:

- The incumbents possess substantial resources to fight back, including excess cash and unused borrowing power, productive capacity, or clout with distribution channels and customers.
- The incumbents seem likely to cut prices because of a desire to keep market shares or because of industrywide excess capacity.
- Industry growth is slow, affecting its ability to absorb the new arrival and probably causing the financial performance of all the parties involved to decline.

Changing Conditions

From a strategic standpoint there are two important additional points to note about the threat of entry.

First, it changes, of course, as these conditions change. The expiration of Polaroid's basic patents on instant photography, for instance, greatly reduced its absolute cost entry barrier built by proprietary technology. It is not surprising that Kodak plunged into the market. Product differentiation in printing has all but disappeared. Conversely, in the auto industry economics of scale increased enormously with post–World War II automation and vertical integration—virtually stopping successful new entry.

Second, strategic decisions involving a large segment of an industry can have a major impact on the conditions determining the threat of entry. For example, the actions of many U.S. wine producers in the 1960s to step up product introductions, raise advertising levels, and expand distribution nationally surely strengthened the entry roadblocks by raising economies of scale and making access to distribution channels more difficult. Similarly, decisions by members of the recreational vehicle industry to vertically integrate in order to lower costs have greatly increased the economies of scale and raised the capital cost barriers.

POWERFUL SUPPLIERS AND BUYERS

Suppliers can exert bargaining power on participants in an industry by raising prices or reducing the quality of purchased goods and services. Powerful suppliers can thereby squeeze profitability out of an industry unable to recover cost increases in its own prices. By raising their prices, soft drink concentrate producers have contributed to the erosion of profitability of bottling companies because the bottlers, facing intense competition from powdered mixes, fruit drinks, and other beverages, have limited freedom to raise *their* prices accordingly. Customers likewise can force down prices, demand higher quality or more service, and play competitors off against each other—all at the expense of industry profits.

The power of each important supplier or buyer group depends on a number of characteristics of its market situation and on the relative importance of its sales or purchases to the industry compared with its overall business.

A *supplier* group is powerful if:

■ It is dominated by a few companies and is more concentrated than the industry it sells to.
■ Its product is unique or at least differentiated, or if it has built up switching costs. Switching costs are fixed costs buyers face in changing suppliers. These arise because, among other things, a buyer's product specifications tie it to particular suppliers, it has invested heavily in specialized ancillary equipment or in learning how to operate a supplier's equipment (as in computer software), or its production lines are connected to the supplier's manufacturing facilities (as in some manufacture of beverage containers).
■ It is not obliged to contend with other products for sale to the industry. For instance, the competition between the steel companies and the aluminum companies to sell to the can industry checks the power of each supplier.
■ It poses a credible threat of integrating forward into the industry's business. This provides a check against the industry's ability to improve the terms on which it purchases.
■ The industry is not an important customer of the supplier group. If the industry *is* an important customer, suppliers' fortunes will be closely tied to the industry, and they will want to protect the industry through reasonable pricing and assistance in activities like R&D and lobbying.

A *buyer* group is powerful if:

■ It is concentrated or purchases in large volumes. Large-volume buyers are particularly potent forces if heavy fixed costs characterize the industry—as they do in mental containers, corn refining, and bulk chemicals, for example— which raise the stakes to keep capacity filled.
■ The products it purchases from the industry are standard or undifferentiated. The buyers, sure that they can always find alternative suppliers, may play one company against another, as they do in aluminum extrusion.
■ The products it purchases from the industry form a component of its product and represent a significant fraction of its cost. The buyers are likely to shop for a favorable price and purchase selectively. Where the product sold by the industry in question is a small fraction of buyers' costs, buyers are usually much less price sensitive.
■ It earns low profits, which create great incentive to lower it purchasing costs. Highly profitable buyers, however, are generally less price sensitive (that is, of course, if the item does not represent a large fraction of their costs).
■ The industry's product is unimportant to the quality of the buyers' products or services. Where the quality of the buyers' products is very much affected by the industry's product,

buyers are generally less price sensitive. Industries in which this situation includes oil field equipment, where a malfunction can lead to large losses, and enclosures for electronic medical and test instruments, where the quality of the enclosure can influence the user's impression about the quality of the equipment inside.

- The industry's product does not save the buyer money. Where the industry's product or service can pay for itself many times over, the buyer is rarely price sensitive; rather, he is interested in quality. This is true in services like investment banking and public accounting, where errors in judgment can be costly and embarrassing, and in businesses like the logging of oil wells, where an accurate survey can save thousands of dollars in drilling costs.
- The buyers pose a credible threat of integrating backward to make the industry's product. The Big Three auto producers and major buyers of cars have often used the threat of self-manufacture as a bargaining lever. But sometimes an industry engenders a threat to buyers that its members may integrate forward.

Most of these sources of buyer power can be attributed to consumers as a group as well as to industrial and commercial buyers; only a modification of the frame of reference is necessary. Consumers tend to be more price sensitive if they are purchasing products that are undifferentiated, expensive relative to their incomes, and of a sort where quality is not particularly important.

The buying power of retailers is determined by the same rules, with one important addition. Retailers can gain significant bargaining power over manufacturers when they can influence consumers' purchasing decisions, as they do in audio components, jewelry, appliances, sporting goods, and other goods.

Strategic Action

A company's choice of suppliers to buy from or buyer groups to sell to should be viewed as crucial strategic decision. A company can improve its strategic posture by finding suppliers or buyers who possess the least power to influence it adversely.

Most common is the situation of a company being able to choose whom it will sell to—in other words, buyer selection. Rarely do all the buyer groups a company sells to enjoy equal power. Even if a company sells to a single industry, segments usually exist within that industry that exercise less power (and that are therefore less price sensitive) than others. For example, the replacement market for most products is less price sensitive than the overall market.

As a rule, a company can sell to powerful buyers and still come away with above-average profitability only if it is a low-cost producer in its industry or if its product enjoys some unusual, if not unique, features. In supplying large customers with electric motors, Emerson Electric earns high returns because its low-cost position permits the company to meet or undercut competitors' prices.

If the company lacks a low-cost position or a unique product, selling to everyone is self-defeating because the more sales it achieves, the more vulnerable it becomes. The company may have to muster the courage to turn away business and sell only to less potent customers.

Buyer selection has been a key to the success of National Can and Crown Cork & Seal. They focus on the segments of the can industry where they can create product differentiation, minimize the threat of backward integration, and otherwise mitigate the awesome power of their customers. Of course, some industries do not enjoy the luxury of selecting "good" buyers.

As the factors creating supplier and buyer power change with time or as a result of a company's strategic decisions, naturally the power of these groups rises or declines. In the ready-to-wear clothing industry, as the buyers (department stores and clothing stores) have become more concentrated and control has passed to large chains, the industry has come under increasing pressure and suffered falling margins. The industry has been unable to differentiate its product or engender switching costs that lock in its buyers enough to neutralize these trends.

SUBSTITUTE PRODUCTS

By placing a ceiling on prices it can charge, substitute products or services limit the potential of an industry. Unless it can upgrade the quality of the product or differentiate it somehow (as via marketing), the industry will suffer in earnings and possibly in growth.

Manifestly, the more attractive the price-performance trade-off offered by substitute products, the firmer the lid placed on the industry's profit potential. Sugar producers confronted with the large-scale commercialization of high-fructose corn syrup, a sugar substitute, are learning this lesson today.

Substitutes not only limit profits in normal times; they also reduce the bonanza an industry can reap in boom times. In 1978 the producers of fiberglass insulation enjoyed unprecedented demand as a result of high energy costs and severe winter weather. But the industry's ability to raise prices were tempered by the plethora of insulation substitutes, including cellulose, rock wool, and styrofoam. These substitutes are bound to become an even stronger force once the current round of plant additions by fiberglass insulation producers has boosted capacity enough to meet demand (and then some).

Substitute products that deserve the most attention strategically are those that (1) are subject to trends improving their price-performance trade-off with the industry's product, or (2) are produced by industries earning high profits. Substitutes often come rapidly into play if some development increases competition in their industries and causes price reduction or performance improvement.

JOCKEYING FOR POSITION

Rivalry among existing competitors takes the familiar form of jockeying for position—using tactics like price competition, product introduction, and advertising slugfests. Intense rivalry is related to the presence of a number of factors:

- Competitors are numerous or are roughly equal in size and power. In many U.S. industries in recent years foreign contenders, of course, have become part of the competitive picture.
- Industry growth is slow, precipitating fights for market share that involve expansion-minded members.
- The product or service lacks differentiation or switching costs, which lock in buyers and protect one combatant from raids on its customers by another.
- Fixed costs are high or the product is perishable, creating strong temptation to cut prices. Many basic materials businesses, like paper and aluminum, suffer from this problem when demand slackens.
- Capacity is normally augmented in large increments. Such additions, as in the chlorine and vinyl chloride businesses, disrupt the industry's supply-demand balance and often lead to periods of overcapacity and price cutting.
- Exit barriers are high. Exit barriers, like very specialized assets or management's loyalty to a particular business, keep companies competing even though they may be earning low or even negative returns on investment. Excess capacity remains functioning, and the profitability of the healthy competitors suffers as the sick ones hang on. If the entire industry suffers from overcapacity, it may seek government help—particularly if foreign competition is present.
- The rivals are diverse in strategies, origins, and "personalities." They have different ideas about how to compete and continually run head on into each other in the process. . . .

While a company must live with many of these factors—because they are built into industry economics—it may have some latitude for improving matters through strategic shifts. For example, it may try to raise buyers' switching costs or increase product differentiation. A focus on selling efforts in the fastest-growing segments of the industry or on market areas with the lowest fixed costs can reduce the impact of industry rivalry. If it is feasible, a company can try to avoid confrontation with competitors having high exit barriers and can thus sidestep involvement in bitter price cutting.

<table>
<tr><td>FORMULATION
OF STRATEGY</td><td>Once the corporate strategist has assessed the forces affecting competition in his industry and their underlying causes, he can identify his company's strengths and weaknesses. The crucial strengths and weaknesses from a strategic standpoint are the company's posture vis-à-vis the underlying causes of each force. Where does it stand against substitutes? Against the sources of entry barriers?</td></tr>
</table>

Then the strategist can devise a plan of action that may include (1) positioning the company so that its capabilities provide the best defense against the competitive force; and/or (2) influencing the balance of the forces through strategic moves, thereby improving the company's position; and/or (3) anticipating shifts in the factors underlying the forces and responding to them, with the hope of exploiting change by choosing a strategy appropriate for the new competitive balance before opponents recognize it. I shall consider each strategic approach in turn.

POSITIONING THE COMPANY

The first approach takes the structure of the industry as given and matches the company's strengths and weaknesses to it. Strategy can be viewed as building defenses against the competitive forces or as finding positions in the industry where the forces are weakest.

Knowledge of the company's capabilities and of the causes of the competitive forces will highlight the areas where the company should confront competition and where avoid it. If the company is a low-cost producer, it may choose to confront powerful buyers while it takes care to sell them only products not vulnerable to competition from substitutes. . . .

INFLUENCING THE BALANCE

When dealing with the forces that drive industry competition, a company can devise a strategy that takes the offensive. This posture is designed to do more than merely cope with the forces themselves; it is meant to alter their causes.

Innovations in marketing can raise brand identification or otherwise differentiate the product. Capital investments in large-scale facilities or vertical integration affect entry barriers. The balance of forces is partly a result of external factors and partly in the company's control.

EXPLOITING INDUSTRY CHANGE

Industry evolution is important strategically because evolution, of course, brings with it changes in the sources of competition I have identified. In the familiar product life-cycle pattern, for example, growth rates change, product differentiation is said to decline as the business becomes more mature, and the companies tend to integrate vertically.

These trends are not so important in themselves; what is critical is whether they affect the sources of competition. . . .

Obviously, the trends carrying the highest priority from a strategic standpoint are those that affect the most important sources of competition in the industry and those that elevate new causes to the forefront. . . .

The framework for analyzing competition that I have described can also be used to predict the eventual profitability of an industry. In long-range planning the task is to examine each competitive force, forecast the magnitude of each underlying cause, and then construct a composite picture of the likely profit potential of the industry. . . .

The key to growth—even survival—is to stake out a position that is less vulnerable to attack from head-to-head opponents, whether established or new, and less vulnerable to erosion from the direction of buyers, suppliers, and substitute goods. Establishing such a position can take many forms—solidifying relationships with favorable customers, differentiating the product either substantively or psychologically through marketing, integrating forward or backward, establishing technological leadership.

READING 4.2   LOOKING INSIDE FOR COMPETITIVE ADVANTAGE*

BY JAY B. BARNEY

■ The history of strategic management research can be understood as an attempt to "fill in the blanks" created by the SWOT framework; i.e., to move beyond suggesting that strengths, weaknesses, opportunities, and threats are important for understanding competitive advantage to suggest models and frameworks that can be used to analyze and evaluate these phenomena. Michael Porter (1980, 1985) and his associates have developed a number of these models and frameworks for analyzing environmental opportunities and threats. Porter's work on the "five forces model," the relationship between industry structure and strategic opportunities, and strategic groups can all be understood as an effort to unpack the concepts of environmental opportunities and threats in a theoretically rigorous, yet highly applicable way.

However, the SWOT framework tells us that environmental analysis—no matter how rigorous—is only half the story. A complete understanding of sources of competitive advantage requires the analysis of a firm's internal strengths and weaknesses as well. The importance of integrating internal with environmental analyses can be seen when evaluating the sources of competitive advantage of many firms. Consider, for example,

■ WalMart, a firm that has, for the last twenty years, consistently earned a return on sales twice the average of its industry;
■ Southwest Airlines, a firm whose profits continued to increase, despite losses at other U.S. airlines that totaled almost $10 billion from 1990 to 1993; and
■ Nucor Steel, a firm whose stock price continued to soar through the 1980s and '90s, despite the fact that the market value of most steel companies has remained flat or fallen during the same time period.

These firms, and many others, have all gained competitive advantages—despite the unattractive, high threat, low opportunity environments within which they operate. Even the most careful and complete analysis of these firms' competitive environments cannot, by itself, explain their success. Such explanations must also include these firms' internal attributes—their strengths and weaknesses—as sources of competitive advantage. Following more recent practice, internal attributes will be referred to as *resources* and *capabilities* throughout the following discussion.

A firm's resources and capabilities include all of the financial, physical, human, and organizational assets used by a firm to develop, manufacture, and deliver products or services to its customers. Financial resources include debt, equity, retained earnings, and so forth. Physical resources include the machines, manufacturing facilities, and buildings firms use in their operations. Human resources include all the experience, knowledge, judgment, risk taking propensity, and wisdom of individuals associated with a firm. Organizational resources

---

*Reprinted with deletions from "Looking Inside for Competitive Advantage," Jay B. Barney, *Academy of Management Executive*, 1995, Vol. 9(4), 49–61.

include the history, relationships, trust, and organizational culture that are attributes of groups of individuals associated with a firm, along with a firm's formal reporting structure, explicit management control systems, and compensation policies.

In the process of filling in the "internal blanks" created by SWOT analysis, managers must address four important questions about their resources and capabilities: (1) the question of value, (2) the question of rareness, (3) the question of imitability, and (4) the question of organization.

THE QUESTION OF VALUE

To begin evaluating the competitive implications of a firm's resources and capabilities, managers must first answer the question of value: Do a firm's resources and capabilities add value by enabling it to exploit opportunities and/or neutralize threats?

The answer to this question, for some firms, has been yes. Sony, for example, has a great deal of experience in designing, manufacturing, and selling miniaturized electronic technology. Sony has used these resources to exploit numerous market opportunities, including portable tape players, portable disc players, portable televisions, and easy-to-hold 8mm video cameras. . . .

Unfortunately, for other firms, the answer to the question of value has been no. . . . Sears was unable to recognize or respond to changes in the retail market that had been created by WalMart and specialty retail stores. In a sense, Sears's historical success, along with a commitment to stick with a traditional way of doing things, led it to miss some significant market opportunities.

Although a firm's resources and capabilities may have added value in the past, changes in customer tastes, industry structure, or technology can render them less valuable in the future. General Electric's capabilities in transistor manufacturing became much less valuable when semiconductors were invented. . . .

Some environmental changes are so significant that few, if any, of a firm's resources remain valuable in any environmental context. However, this kind of radical environmental change is unusual. More commonly, changes in a firm's environment may reduce the value of a firm's resources in their current use, while leaving the value of those resources in other uses unchanged. . . .

Numerous firms have weathered these environmental shifts by finding new ways to apply their traditional strengths. AT&T had developed a reputation for providing high-quality long distance telephone service. It moved rapidly to exploit this reputation in the newly competitive long distance market by aggressively marketing its services against MCI, Sprint, and other carriers. . . .

By answering the question of value, managers link the analysis of internal resources and capabilities with the analysis of environmental opportunities and threats. Firm resources are not valuable in a vacuum, but rather are valuable only when they exploit opportunities and/or neutralize threats. The models developed by Porter and his associates can be used to isolate potential opportunities and threats that the resources a firm controls can exploit or neutralize. . . .

THE QUESTION OF RARENESS

That a firm's resources and capabilities are valuable is an important first consideration in understanding internal sources of competitive advantage. However, if a particular resource and capability is controlled by numerous competing firms, then that resource is unlikely to be a source of competitive advantage for any one of them. Instead, valuable but common (i.e., not rare) resources and capabilities are sources of competitive parity. For managers evaluating the competitive implications of their resources and capabilities, these observations lead to the second critical issue: How many competing firms already possess these valuable resources and capabilities? . . .

While resources and capabilities must be rare among competing firms in order to be a source of competitive advantage, this does not mean that common, but valuable, resources are not important. Indeed, such resources and capabilities may be essential for a firm's survival. On the other hand, if a firm's resources are valuable and rare, those resources may enable a firm to gain at least a temporary competitive advantage. WalMart's skills in developing and using point-of-purchase data collection to control inventory have given it a competitive advantage over K-Mart, a firm that until recently has not had access to this timely information. . . .

THE QUESTION OF IMITABILITY

A firm that possesses valuable and rare resources and capabilities can gain, at least, a temporary competitive advantage. If, in addition, competing firms face a cost disadvantage in imitating these resources and capabilities, firms with these special abilities can obtain a sustained competitive advantage. These observations lead to the questions of imitability: Do firms without a resource or capability face a cost disadvantage in obtaining it compared to firms that already possess it?

Obviously, imitation is critical to understanding the ability of resources and capabilities to generate sustained competitive advantages. Imitation can occur in at least two ways: duplication and substitution. Duplication occurs when an imitating firm builds the same kinds of resources as the firm it is imitating. If one firm has a competitive advantage because of its research and development skills, then a duplicating firm will try to imitate that resource by developing its own research and development skills. In addition, firms may be able to substitute some resources for other resources. If these substitute resources have the same strategic implications and are no more costly to develop, then imitation through substitution will lead to competitive parity in the long run. . . .

As firms evolve, they pick up skills, abilities, and resources that are unique to them, reflecting their particular path through history. These resources and capabilities reflect the unique personalities, experiences, and relationships that exist in only a single firm. . . .

[Consider] The Mailbox, Inc., a very successful firm in the bulk mailing business in the Dallas–Ft. Worth market. If there was ever a business where it seems unlikely that a firm would have a sustained competitive advantage, it is bulk mailing. Firms in this industry gather mail from customers, sort it by postal code, and then take it to the post office to be mailed. Where is the competitive advantage here? And yet, The Mailbox has enjoyed an enormous market share advantage in the Dallas–Ft. Worth area for several years. Why?

When asked, managers at The Mailbox have a difficult time describing the sources of their sustained advantages. Indeed, they can point to *no* "Big Decisions" they have made to generate this advantage. However, as these managers begin to discuss their firm, what becomes clear is that their success does not depend on doing a few big things right, but on doing lots of little things right. The way they manage accounting, finance, human resources, production, or other business functions, separately, is not exceptional. However, to manage all these functions so well, and so consistently over time is truly exceptional. Firms seeking to compete against The Mailbox will not have to imitate just a few internal attributes; they will have to imitate thousands, or even hundreds of thousands of such attributes—a daunting task indeed.

[Another] reason that firms may be at a cost disadvantage in imitating resources and capabilities is that these resources may be socially complex. Some physical resources (e.g., computers, robots, and other machines) controlled by firms are very complex. However, firms seeking to imitate these physical resources need only purchase them, take them apart, and duplicate the technology in question. With just a couple of exceptions (including the pharmaceutical and specialty chemicals industries), patents provide little protection from the imitation of a firm's physical resources. On the other hand, socially complex resources and capabilities—organizational phenomena like reputation, trust, friendship, teamwork and culture—while not patentable, are much more difficult to imitate. Imagine the difficulty of imitating Hewlett Packard's (HP) powerful and enabling culture. . . .

THE QUESTION OF ORGANIZATION

A firm's competitive advantage potential depends on the value, rareness, and imitability of its resources and capabilities. However, to fully realize this potential, a firm must also be organized to exploit its resources and capabilities. These observations lead to the question of organization: Is a firm organized to exploit the full competitive potential of its resources and capabilities?

Numerous components of a firm's organization are relevant when answering the question of organization, including its formal reporting structure, its explicit management control systems, and its compensation policies. These components are referred to as *complementary resources* because they have limited ability to generate competitive advantage in isolation. However, in combination with other resources and capabilities, they can enable a firm to realize its full competitive advantage.

. . . WalMart's continuing competitive advantage in the discount retailing industry can be attributed to its early entry into rural markets in the southern United States. However, to fully exploit this geographic advantage, WalMart needed to implement appropriate reporting structures, control systems, and compensation policies. We have already seen that one of these components of WalMart's organization—its point-of-purchase inventory control system—is being imitated by K-Mart, and thus, by itself, is not likely to be a source of sustained competitive advantage. However, this inventory control system has enabled WalMart to take full advantage of its rural locations by decreasing the probability of stock outs and by reducing inventory costs. . . .

THE MANAGEMENT CHALLENGE

In the end, this discussion reminds us that sustained competitive advantage cannot be created simply by evaluating environmental opportunities and threats, and then conducting business only in high-opportunity, low-threat environments. Rather, creating sustained competitive advantage depends on the unique resources and capabilities that a firm brings to competition in its environment. To discover these resources and capabilities, managers must look inside their firm for valuable, rare and costly-to-imitate resources, and then exploit these resources through their organization.

READING 4.3 — SUSTAINING SUPERIOR PERFORMANCE: COMMITMENTS AND CAPABILITIES*

BY PANKAS GHEMAWAT AND GARY PISANO

■ . . . A competitive advantage is generally necessary for sustained superior performance. But experience suggests that it is far from sufficient. . . .

THREATS TO SUSTAINABILITY

A superior product market position is likely to yield sustained superior performance to the extent that it satisfies two conditions: *scarcity* and *appropriability*. The importance of scarcity in this context can be highlighted with the air *versus* diamond example beloved by economists. Why is the air in your lungs worth less, at market prices, than the gemstone that may be on your finger? Part of the reason is that less cost is incurred in transforming the air in the atmosphere into something that you are willing to breathe than in transforming a diamond in the

---

*Reprinted with deletions from P. Ghemawat and G. Pisano, "Sustaining Superior Performance: Commitments and Capabilities," *Harvard Business School Note:* 9–798–008, July 31, 1997.

rough into something that you are willing to wear. But this cost differential is not the only element of the difference in prices. Differential scarcity also takes a hand. Breathable air is available in such abundant quantities that it has virtually no scarcity value in most locations. Gem-quality diamonds are clearly much scarcer. The implied difference in scarcity values accounts for most of the sustained difference in the prices that air and diamonds can command.

To test whether a strategic position or option offers sustainable scarcity value, it is useful to ask two kinds of questions. The first question is why scarcity won't induce competitors, actual or potential, to copy the superior position: this is the threat of *imitation*. The second question is whether competitors, even if they are unable to attack scarcity value directly, won't be able to find a way around it: this is the threat of *substitution*.

The second condition for sustainability, appropriability, is of distinct interest because even when an organization can count on sustained scarcity value, the ability of its owners to pocket that value cannot be taken for granted. Non-owners out to further their own interests may be able to siphon off some of that value: this is the threat of *holdup*. They, particularly employees, may also squander some of it: this is the threat of *slack*. In other words, holdup threatens to divert scarcity value and slack to dissipate it.

All four threats to sustainability—imitation, substitution, holdup and slack—have two things in common: the intensity of each tends to increase with the amount of (positioning) value generated, and each tends to take time to make its effects felt. They will be elaborated and illustrated in detail one at a time, beginning with threats external to the organization and working in.

IMITATION

Imitation is the most direct and obvious threat to sustainability. According to the cross-sectional evidence, imitation is endemic. In capacity-driven industries, an addition by one player usually triggers additions by others aimed at preserving their capacity shares. . . .

The most obvious way of analyzing the threat of imitation (as well as the other threats to sustainability discussed in this note) is to figure out which players will be most affected by the organization's strategic choice, assess their likely responses and, to the extent that those responses appear threatening, think about how they can be thwarted or blunted. . . .

When the number of competitors to be considered is [large], or when the analysis focuses on the long run, it makes . . . sense to look for impediments to imitation. . . . Such impediments are usually categorized as different types of *early-mover advantages*. There seem to be five principal forms of early-mover advantages [based on earlier work by Ghemawat and Teece (ed.), 1987].

Private Information One possible reason for moving early is better information. To the extent that this information can be kept private—to the extent that it is costly for would-be imitators to tap into it—imitation will be inhibited. Privacy is most likely obtained when information is tacit rather than specifiable (i.e., doesn't lend itself to blueprinting), and when no one party can carry it out of the organization.

Size Economies Size economies refer to the (possible) advantages of being large. They come in three different varieties: scale economies, which are the advantages of being large in a particular business at a particular point in time; learning economies, which are the advantages of being large in a particular business over time; and scope economies, which are the advantages of being large across interrelated businesses. If there are size economies, the early mover may be able to deter imitation by committing itself to exploiting them. That possibility depends on the would-be imitator's fear that if it tried to match the early mover's size, supply might exceed demand by enough to make it rue the effort.

Enforceable Contracts/Relationships Early movers may be able to enter contracts or establish relationships on better terms than those available to late movers. . . .

Threats of Retaliation There are a number of reasons . . . why early movers may be able to deter imitation by threatening massive retaliation. Talk of retaliation is, however, cheap. To be credible, it must be backed up by both the ability and the willingness to retaliate. Retaliatory moves that satisfy both conditions may either be directly profitable or reflect the early mover's demonstrated willingness to be tough with interlopers in spite of the immediate losses to itself.

Response Lags Even if information isn't impacted, size isn't a source of economies, contracts/relationships aren't enforceable, and retaliation isn't credible, imitation usually requires a minimum time lag. From the early mover's perspective, this can be described as a response lag. . . . The only sensible conclusion about early versus late timing is the one drawn long ago by Alfred P. Sloan: If you are late, you have to be better.

SUBSTITUTION

Scarcity value may be threatened by substitution as well as by imitation: capacity in place may be displaced by newer and better capacity, customer preferences changed in ways that erode established customer bases and existing know-how improved upon. While they blur into each other at the boundaries, there are two respects in which substitution is less direct a threat to scarcity value than is imitation. First, substitution threats are less likely to be confined to direct competitors. Second, successful substitution involves finding a way around scarcity, not carrying out a direct attack on it. . . .

Substitution threats depend on environmental changes that create enough of a mismatch between established positions and market opportunities to override early-mover advantages. While such changes can take a variety of forms, changes in technology, in demand and in the availability or prices of inputs seem, in that order, to be the most significant gateways to successful substitution. Note the implication that substitution threats are likely to be most frequent in technology-intensive, fashion-intensive and other *creative* industries in which the salient sticky factors have short half-lives (i.e. are obsolesced relatively rapidly). . . .

HOLDUP

Even if scarcity value can be preserved from imitation and substitution the ability of the organization to appropriate the proceeds cannot be taken for granted. The possibility of expropriation is a consequence of the gap between ownership and control: there typically is such a gap, and it typically leaves room for self-serving behavior by non-owners. Such behavior can reduce either the owners' share of total scarcity value (holdup) or the total amount of scarcity value available to be divided among them and non-owners (slack), or both. The diversionary threat of holdup will be discussed in this subsection, and the dissipative threat of slack in the next one.

Holdup is a problem in negotiation rather than competition, conventionally defined. Holdup is a threat whenever the perpetuation of a superior competitive position depends on the continued cooperation of complementors. . . .

An example will help make this description more concrete. It concerns the holdup of the owners of National Football League (NFL) franchises in the 1970s and 1980s*. The NFL consists of independently owned franchises that have managed, for the most part, to function as a cartel on the basis of selective antitrust exemptions. Since 1970, the NFL has weathered threats of imitation by the World Football League (WFL) and the United States Football League (USFL), each of which operated less than three seasons. It has withstood substitution threats to sustain much higher broadcast ratings than any other sport. As a result, it managed to sign lucrative multiyear contracts with the three TV networks in 1978 and in 1982, contracts that increased the total revenue available to the average NFL team by 77% in *real* terms between 1970 and 1984. In spite of this winning record, however, the average team's operating income fell by a third between those years. Why?

---

*The description that follows is based, in part, on Michael E. Porter, "The NFL vs. the USFL," HBS Case No. 9-386-168.

Holdup by NFL players seems to have been the principal reason for decrease. People of the size, skill, and recklessness necessary to play professional football are obviously specialized resources. The essential complementarity of their services to the scarcity value of football franchises has been evident from the inception of professional football: crowds of 70,000 people. . . .

Recognizing the resultant potential for holdup, the NFL evolved a number of practices to contain it. Players were signed to enforceable multiyear contracts . . . [there were] exclusive rights to draft rookies and restrictions on free agency by veterans [etc.].

SLACK

Slack is the final threat to sustainability that must be taken into account. Slack measures the extent to which the scarcity value realized by the organization falls short of the amount potentially available to it. The conceptual distinction between slack and holdup is that the former shrinks the total size of the pie available to owners and non-owners while the latter shrinks the owners' slice of that pie. . . .

Slack cannot, be definition, be less than zero. An upper bound on it is implicit in the condition that organizations cannot sustain losses indefinitely. As a result, particularly valuable product market positions can be expected to afford the most scope for slack. Or in plainer language, rich diets tend to lead to a hardening of organizational arteries. Estimates of the fraction of revenues dissipated, on average, in this fashion tend to range from 10% to 40% [see, for instance, Caves and Barton, 1990]. These estimates hint at both the significance of slack and the difficulty of measuring it precisely.

[Consider] Xerox's copier business in the 1970s and 1980s. The information assembled . . . indicates that the 1980s marked a period of substantial turnaround for the company. Its managers seem to have achieved these improvements in a number of ways. They . . . establish[ed] targets for improvement and incentives to achieve them. And they reinforced these incentives by trying to create an organizational culture that emphasized quality, responsiveness and other good things. Xerox's management deserves considerable credit for successful implementation of all these initiatives in the 1980s.

It is also clear, however, that Xerox could not have wrung such significant improvements out of its copier business in the 1980s unless it had accumulated stupendous amounts of slack there in the 1970s. Xerox's own statements about the savings achieved in the 1980s as well as other estimates suggest that by the late 1970s, slack was dissipating at least 20% of the company's sales revenues. . . . The suggestion that Xerox squandered much of its birthright in the 1970s is strongly borne out by what happened to its shareholders during the 1970s and early 1980s: the ratio of shareholder enrichment to retained earnings over the 1970s and early 1980s was −220% for Xerox. . . .

BUILDING SUSTAINABLE COMPETITIVE ADVANTAGES

Multiple, potent threats to sustainability imply that managers cannot afford to take the sustainability of an actual or targeted competitive advantage for granted. Much has been written recently about the roots of sustained superior performance. Most of these contributions can be classified in terms of the debate about whether sustainability is *really* rooted in resources or activities.

The resource-based view seems to have won more adherents in academia. Partly as a result, there is no single authoritative statement of the resource-based view of sustainability. But writers in this tradition tend to flag resources that are *intrinsically inimitable*—resources for which imitation is, in effect, infinitely costly—as companies' crown jewels. Examples include physically unique resources (e.g., the best retail location in town), resources whose imitation is legally infeasible (e.g., patents) and composite resources which may be impossible to imitate because of *causal ambiguity* (the inability to figure out what makes a successful firm tick) or *social complexity* which may place them "beyond the ability of firms to systematically manage and influence" (e.g., corporate culture) [Barnes, 1991].

The activity-based approach, in contrast, focuses on the activities that firms perform rather than the resources that they possess. While the activity-based approach has long been employed to analyze competitive positioning, fit among many discrete but interactive activities has recently been proposed as an explanation of sustainability as well, as in Porter's "What Is Strategy?" article [1991]. The basic idea here is that imitation may take longer, cost more and offer less certain prospects for success when a competitor must be matched along many dimensions rather than just one or two.

We think that both these approaches are useful, especially if they are seen as complementary. Based on the conventional definition of resources as factors that are fixed in the short run, a firm's resource endowment determines the activities that it can perform at any given point in time. Those activities, in turn, are important because it is only with reference to them that competitive advantage or disadvantage can be evaluated.

We also think, however, that both of these approaches—even if taken together—are incomplete, . . . resource-based theorists typically take the firm's resource endowment as given and focus on the short-run deployment of those fixed factors in the product market. And the activity-based approach, while insisting that it may take longer and cost more to match a competitor along many dimensions rather than just one or two, fails to explain, by itself, why strategic innovation, in the sense of constructing an activity system that fits together, is any easier or more profitable than strategic imitation.

Remedying this deficiency seems to require integration and generalization of the resource- and activity-based approaches. . . . Figure 1 provides a simple dynamic framework of this sort in which both history and management matter. The two feedback loops (the dashed lines in the figure) that run from right to left capture the ways in which the activities that a firm performs, and the resource commitments that it makes, affect its future resource endowment or opportunity set. The bold arrows running from left to right indicate that choices about what activities to perform and how to perform them are constrained by resources that can be varied only in the long run. And the first bold arrow that runs from resource endowments to resource commitments also serves as a reminder that the terms on which an organization can make resource commitments depend, in part, on the undepreciated residue of the choices that is has made in the past. . . .

MAKING COMMITMENTS

By commitments, we mean to refer to a few large, lumpy decisions—such as acquiring another company, launching a new product, engaging in a major capacity expansion, and so on—that will have significant and lasting effects on possible future courses of action. The irreversibility of such major decisions or, equivalently, the costs of changing one's mind about them, mandates a deep look into the future. . . .

Irreversibility, not the amount of money involved, is the correct measure of whether a particular decision is commitment-intensive or not. There are three economic indicators of such irreversibility: significant sunk costs, opportunity costs and time lags. Consider these indicators in turn.

FIGURE 1
A DYNAMIC VIEW OF THE FIRM
Adapted from Figure 3, Pankaj Ghemawat, "Resources and Strategy: An IO Perspective," Harvard Business School Working Paper (1991), p. 20.

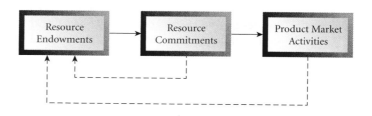

Sunk costs create irreversibility through *lock-in*. When a company sinks a lot of money into resources specialized to a particular course of action that cannot easily be sold off, there is a presumption in favor of continuing to use them. Otherwise, they would be valueless. Boeing's decision to develop the wide-bodied airframe for the 747 provides an example. At some point, the company's net investment in the project considerably exceeded its net worth. As a result, it was sunk unless it could make the plane fly. That meant Boeing was committed to the 747 once it was well into its development. . . .

Opportunity costs create irreversibility through *lock-out*, which is the mirror image of lock-in. Lock-out effects persist because of the difficulty of reactivating dormant resources, reacquiring discarded resources, or recreating lapsed opportunities to deploy particular resources in particular ways. Take, for example, the decision of Reynolds Metals to shut down its alumina refinery at Hurricane Creek, Arkansas, after years of unprofitable operations. This shutdown decision locked Reynolds out of ever using that refinery again—even if aluminum prices were to recover. . . .

The third economic indicator of irreversibility is the *time lag* in altering a firm's endowment of resources. For example, when Coors began to take its beer national in the late 1970s and early 1980s, everyone knew from the outset that the switch from a regional to a national position would require at least the better part of a decade. . . .

The Coors example also illustrates the point that choices of competitive position are themselves commitment-intensive (and therefore strategic) because they typically involve a host of hard-to-reverse commitments to performing particular activities in particular ways. If choices of positioning weren't hard to reverse, a firm could simply try out a particular position and, if it didn't work out, costlessly change it!

Having identified the factors that determine whether a particular decision represents a major commitment, it is time to turn to the ways in which commitments can lead to sustained superior performance. It is convenient to start with the two threats to scarcity, imitation and substitution. The way in which commitments can blunt the threat of imitation is fairly obvious: by staking out particular opportunities through commitments, a company may be able to create sustainable early-mover advantages for itself of the sort that were discussed in the previous section. . . .

The final threat to sustainability, slack, is the one that is the least tightly coupled to the kinds of commitments discussed in this section. While financial commitments (e.g., taking on debt) and other contractual mechanisms can sometimes help reduce slack, many other methods of improving organizational efficiency are hard to interpret in irreversibility-related terms. This is one reason why commitments need not always lead to superior performance: internal organization matters as well.

A second, even more important reason why commitments need not always lead to superior performance stems from uncertainty. In an uncertain world, many commitments fail, which is why commitments can lead to the persistence of inferior as well as superior performance. . . .

DEVELOPING CAPABILITIES

The previous section of this note highlighted how large-scale commitments to appropriate input factors can enable a company to build scarcity and maintain appropriability. Not all commitments, however, are "lumpy." In many cases, firms can build scarcity and maintain appropriability through a series of cumulative smaller-scale investments made over long periods of time. For instance, over many years and hundreds of individual product and process development projects, Intel has accumulated relatively unique knowledge about microprocessor design and manufacturing—knowledge that has proven to be a powerful and durable source of competitive advantage. How should one think about such "capabilities" that are developed incrementally over time?

One way to get a handle on the concept of organization capabilities is to reflect on what organizations do. At any given time, an organization—be it a bank, a biotech firm, or an academic institution—is engaged in a whole set of activities or processes (processing loans, researching drugs, teaching students, etc.) geared toward the development, production, and/or delivery of chosen sets of services and products. An organization's capabilities characterize what activities the organization can undertake within some predictable range of proficiency. . . .

Part of the reason [capabilities can be hard to imitate] seems to be related to private information . . . knowledge that capabilities are based on often seems to be tacit rather than specifiable . . . because it is rooted in detailed and complex organizational processes which, as a bonus, are often hard for competitors to observe. Cumulative learning, particularly localized learning-by-doing, and time lags also seem to play a prominent role in making capabilities hard to imitate. And finally, "metacapabilities" associated with integration, transformation and reconfiguration may also be subject to similar barriers to imitation, although our understanding of them is, at this point, woefully underdeveloped.*

Of course, imitation is just one of the threats to scarcity: scarcity value can also be eroded through substitution. As with imitation threats, substitution threats cannot be entirely blocked. They can be mitigated, however, through investments in "upstream" or "basic" capabilities that provide a foundation for shifting a firm's product market positions. . . .

Having said as much, we must add that the ability of firms to hedge substitution threats is limited: there is no such thing as an all-purpose capability that will give a firm competitive advantage under all circumstances. . . .

Finally, the competitive advantages afforded by superior capabilities must be resistant to threats of appropriability as well as scarcity if they are to afford a basis for sustained superior performance. Because capabilities are rooted in organizational processes that span many individuals and may link multiple firms, they are less subject to hold-up and, arguably, slack than some other types of assets. Where a competitive advantage rests on access to one person or a small group of people, or requires the services of one particular supplier, sustainability will be highly vulnerable to hold-up problems. . . .

Summing up across the various threats to sustainability, superior capabilities can indeed support sustained superior performance. But there are several challenges that have to be confronted in making this capability a reality. First of all, the competitive superiority of a capability must be demonstrable: the lack of an objective test along this dimension is likely to lead managers to designate anything the organization does that they care about as one of its core capabilities (or competencies). Unfortunately, many of the characteristics of capabilities that make them potential sources of sustainable competitive advantage also make them hard to benchmark competitively.

Second, given the incremental nature of capability development, firms that seek to develop superior capabilities as the basis of sustainable competitive advantages must prevent the overall coherence of their capability development efforts from being nibbled away, choice by choice, by drop-in-the-bucket biases and the like. Somewhat paradoxically, this makes the choice of which capabilities to develop, and how, a relatively lumpy choice. . . . The similarity becomes less paradoxical when one notes that a capability development thrust has the same lock-in, lock-out and lag effects associated with conventionally lumpy commitment decisions.

Third, the similarity with lumpy commitment decisions has some of the same awkward effects: specific capabilities also imply specific rigidities that can, in an uncertain world, result in inferior rather than superior performance [see Leonard-Barton, 1992]. In other words, neither capability development nor commitment affords foolproof recipes for success. Instead, careful thinking about strategy reveals what mathematicians call an impossibility theorem: no firm can hope to sustain a competitive advantage unless it has superior specialized

---

*For the original discussion that frames these and other issues concerning capabilities, see David J. Teece and Gary P. Pisano, "The Dynamic Capabilities of Firms: an Introduction," *Industrial and Corporate Change* (1994 No. 3), pp. 537–556.

resources or knowledge. Making commitments or developing firm-specific capabilities is therefore necessary for sustained success but may not be sufficient. This is a sobering note on which to end. Given the evidence on the extent of (un)sustainability, we think that that is appropriate.

READING 4.4

COMPETITIVE MANEUVERING*

BY BRUCE HENDERSON

BRINKMANSHIP IN BUSINESS

A businessman often convinces himself that he is completely logical in his behavior when in fact the critical factor is his emotional bias compared to the emotional bias of his opposition. Unfortunately, some businessmen and students perceive competition as some kind of impersonal, objective, colorless affair, with a company competing against the field as a golfer competes in medal play. A better case can be made that business competition is a major battle in which there are many contenders, each of whom must be dealt with individually. Victory, if achieved, is more often won in the mind of a competitor than in the economic arena.

I shall emphasize two points. The first is that the management of a company must persuade each competitor voluntarily to stop short of a maximum effort to acquire customers and profits. The second point is that persuasion depends on emotional and intuitive factors rather than on analysis or deduction.

The negotiator's skill lies in being as arbitrary as necessary to obtain the best possible compromise without actually destroying the basis for voluntary mutual cooperation of self-restraint. There are some commonsense rules for success in such an endeavor:

1. Be sure that your rival is fully aware of what he can gain if he cooperates and what it will cost him if he does not.
2. Avoid any action which will arouse your competitor's emotions, since it is essential that he behave in a logical, reasonable fashion.
3. Convince your opponent that you are emotionally dedicated to your position and are completely convinced that it is reasonable.

It is worth emphasizing that your competitor is under the maximum handicap if he acts in a completely rational, objective, and logical fashion. For then he will cooperate as long as he thinks he can benefit. In fact, if he is completely logical, he will not forgo the profit of cooperation as long as there is *any* net benefit.

FRIENDLY COMPETITORS

It may strike most businessmen as strange to talk about cooperation with competitors. But it is hard to visualize a situation in which it would be worthwhile to pursue competition to the utter destruction of a competitor. In every case there is a greater advantage to reducing the competition on the condition that the competitor does likewise. Such mutual restraint is cooperation, whether recognized as such or not.

---

*"Brinkmanship in Business" and "The Nonlogical Strategy," in *Henderson on Corporate Strategy* (Cambridge, MA: Abt Books, 1979), pp. 27–33, title selected for this book; section on "Rules for the Strategist" originally at the end of "Brinkmanship in Business" moved to the end of "The Nonlogical Strategy," reprinted by permission of publisher.

112 CHAPTER 4 ANALYZING STRATEGY

Without cooperation on the part of competitors, there can be no stability. We see this most clearly in international relationships during times of peace. There are constant encroachments and aggressive acts. And the eventual consequence is always either voluntarily imposed self-restraint or mutual destruction. Thus, international diplomacy has only one purpose: to stabilize cooperation between independent nations on the most favorable basis possible. Diplomacy can be described as the art of being stubborn, arbitrary, and unreasonable without arousing emotional responses.

Businessmen should notice the similarity between economic competition and the peacetime behavior of nations. The object in both cases is to achieve a voluntary, cooperative restraint on the part of otherwise aggressive competitors. Complete elimination of competition is almost inconceivable. The goal of the hottest economic war is an agreement for coexistence, not annihilation. The competition and mutual encroachment do not stop; they go on forever. But they do so under some measure of mutual restraint.

"COLD WAR" TACTICS

A breakdown in negotiations is inevitable if both parties persist in arbitrary positions which are incompatible. Yet there are major areas in business where some degree of arbitrary behavior is essential for protecting a company's self-interest. In effect, a type of brinkmanship is necessary. The term was coined to describe cold war international diplomacy, but it describes a normal pattern in business, too.

In a confrontation between parties who are in part competitors and in part cooperators, deciding what to accept is essentially emotional or arbitrary. Deciding what is attainable requires an evaluation of the other party's degree of intransigence. The purpose is to convince him that you are arbitrary and emotionally committed while trying to discover what he would really accept in settlement. The competitor known to be coldly logical is at a great disadvantage. Logically, he can afford to compromise until there is no advantage left in cooperation. If, instead, he is emotional, irrational, and arbitrary, he has a great advantage.

CONSEQUENCE

The heart of business strategy for a company is to promote attitudes on the part of its competitors that will cause them either to restrain themselves or to act in a fashion which management deems advantageous. In diplomacy and military strategy the key to success is very much the same.

The most easily recognized way of enforcing cooperation is to exhibit obvious willingness to use irresistible or overwhelming force. This requires little strategic skill, but there is the problem of convincing the competing organization that the force will be used without actually resorting to it (which would be expensive and inconvenient).

In industry, however, the available force is usually not overwhelming, although one company may be able to inflict major punishment on another. In the classic case, each party can inflict such punishment on the other. If there were open conflict, then both parties would lose. If they cooperate, both parties are better off, but not necessarily equally so—particularly if one is trying to change the status quo.

When each party can punish the other, the prospects of agreement depend on three things:

1. Each party's willingness to accept the risk of punishment
2. Each party's belief that the other party is willing to accept the risk of punishment
3. The degree of rationality in the behavior of each party

If these conclusions are correct, what can we deduce about how advantages are gained and lost in business competition?

First, management's unwillingness to accept the risk of punishment is almost certain to produce either the punishment or progressively more onerous conditions for cooperation—provided the competition recognized the attitude.

Second, beliefs about a competitor's future behavior or response are all that determine competitive cooperation. In other words, it is the judgment not of actual capability but of probable use of capability that counts.

Third, the less rational or less predictable the behavior of a competitor appears to be, the greater the advantage he possesses in establishing a favorable competitive balance. This advantage is limited only by his need to avoid forcing his competitors into an untenable position or creating an emotional antagonism that will lead them to be unreasonable and irrational (as he is).

THE NONLOGICAL STRATEGY

The goal of strategy in business, diplomacy, and war is to produce a stable relationship favorable to you with the consent of your competitors. By definition, restraint by a competitor is cooperation. Such cooperation from a competitor must seem to be profitable to him. *Any competition which does not eventually eliminate a competitor requires his cooperation to stabilize the situation.* The agreement is usually that of tacit nonaggression; the alternative is death for all but one competitor. A stable competitive situation requires an agreement between competing parties to maintain self-restrain. Such agreement cannot be arrived at by logic. It must be achieved by an emotional balance of forces. This is why it is necessary to appear irrational to competitors. For the same reason, you must seem unreasonable and arbitrary in negotiations with customers and suppliers.

Competition and cooperation go hand in hand in all real-life situations. Otherwise, conflict could only end in extermination of the competitor. There is a point in all situations of conflict where both parties gain more or lose less from peace than they can hope to gain from any foreseeable victory. Beyond that point cooperation is more profitable than conflict. But how will the benefits be shared?

In negotiated conflict situations, the participant who is coldly logical is at a great disadvantage. Logically, he can afford to compromise until there is no advantage left in cooperation. The negotiator/competitor whose behavior is irrational or arbitrary has a great advantage if he can depend upon his opponent being logical and unemotional. The arbitrary or irrational competitor can demand far more than a reasonable share and yet his logical opponent can still gain by compromise rather than breaking off the cooperation.

Absence of monopoly in business requires voluntary restraint of competition. At some point there must be a tactic agreement not to compete. Unless the restraint of trade were acceptable to all competitors, the resulting aggression would inevitably eliminate the less efficient competitors leaving only one. Antitrust laws represent a formal attempt to limit competition. All antimonopoly and fair trade laws constitute restraint of competition.

Utter destruction of a competitor is almost never profitable unless the competitor is unwilling to accept peace. In our daily social contracts, in our international affairs, and in our business affairs, we have far more ability to damage those around us than we ever dare use. Others have the same power to damage us. The implied agreement to restrain our potential aggression is all that stands between us and eventual elimination of one by the other. Both war and diplomacy are mechanisms for establishing or maintaining this self-imposed restrain on all competitors. The conflict continues, but within the implied area of cooperative agreement.

There is a definite limit to the range within which competitors can expect to achieve an equilibrium or negotiate a shift in equilibrium even by implication. Arbitrary, uncooperative, or aggressive attitudes will produce equally emotional reactions. These emotional reactions are in turn the basis for nonlogical and arbitrary responses. Thus, nonlogical behavior is self-limiting.

This is why the art of diplomacy can be described as the ability to be unreasonable without arousing resentment. It is worth remembering that the objective of diplomacy is to include cooperation on terms that are relatively more favorable to you than to your protagonist without actual force being used.

More business victories are won in the minds of competitors than in the laboratory, the factory or the marketplace. The competitor's conviction that you are emotional, dogmatic, or otherwise nonlogical in your business strategy can be a great asset. This conviction on his part can result in an acceptance of your actions without retaliation, which would otherwise be unthinkable. More important, the anticipation of nonlogical or unrestrained reactions on your part can inhibit his competitive aggression.

RULES FOR THE STRATEGIST

If I were asked to distill the conditions and forces described into advice for the business-strategist, I would suggest five rules:

1. You must know as accurately as possible just what your competition has at stake in his contact with you. It is not what you gain or lose, but what he gains or loses that sets the limit on his ability to compromise with you.
2. The less the competition knows about your stakes, the less advantage he has. Without a reference point, he does not even know whether you are being unreasonable.
3. It is absolutely essential to know the character, attitudes, motives, and habitual behavior of a competitor if you wish to have a negotiating advantage.
4. The more arbitrary your demands are, the better your relative competitive position—provided you do not arouse an emotional reaction.
5. The less arbitrary you seem, the more arbitrary you can in fact be.

These rules make up the art of business brinkmanship. They are guidelines for winning a strategic victory in the minds of competitors. Once this victory has been won, it can be converted into a competitive victory in terms of sales volume, costs, and profits.

READING 4.5

BY HENRY MINTZBERG

■ Almost every serious author concerned with "content" issues in strategic management, not to mention strategy consulting "boutiques," has his, her, or its own list of strategies commonly pursued by different organizations. The problem is that these lists almost always either focus narrowly on special types of strategies or else aggregate arbitrarily across all varieties of them with no real order.

In 1965, Igor Ansoff proposed a matrix of four strategies which became quite well known—market penetration, product development, market development, and diversification (1965: 109). But this was hardly comprehensive. Fifteen years later, Michael Porter (1980) introduced what became the best-known list of "generic strategies": cost leadership, differentiation, and focus. But the Porter list was also incomplete: while Ansoff focused on *extensions* of business strategy, Porter focused on *identifying* business strategy in the first place.

---

*Abbreviated version prepared for this book of an article by Henry Mintzberg, "Generic Strategies Toward a Comprehensive Framework," originally published in *Advances in Strategic Management*, Vol. 5 (Greenwich, CT: JAI Press, 1988) pp. 1–67.

We believe that families of strategies may be divided into five broad groupings. These are:

1. Locating the core business.

2. Distinguishing the core business.

3. Elaborating the core business.

4. Extending the core business.

5. Reconceiving the core business.

These five groupings of strategies are presented as a logical hierarchy, although it should be emphasized that strategies do not necessarily develop that way in organizations.

LOCATING THE CORE BUSINESS

A business can be thought to exist at a junction in a network of industries that take raw materials and through selling to and buying from each other produce various finished products (or services). Figure 1, for example, shows a hypothetical canoe business in such a network. Core location strategies can be described with respect to the stage of the business in the network and the particular industry in question.

STRATEGIES OF STAGE OF OPERATIONS

Traditionally, industries have been categorized as being in the primary (raw materials extraction and conversion), secondary (manufacturing) or tertiary (delivery or other service) stage of operations. More recently, however, state in the "stream" has been the favored form of description:

Upstream Business Strategy

Upstream businesses function close to the raw material. The flow of product tends to be divergent, from a basic material (wood, aluminum) to a variety of uses for it. Upstream business tends to be technology- and capital-intensive rather than people-intensive, and more inclined to search for advantage through low costs than through high margins and to favor sales push over market pull (Galbraith, 1983: 65–66).

Midstream Business Strategy

Here the organization sits at the neck of an hour-glass, drawing a variety of inputs into a single production process out of which flows the product to a variety of users, much as the canoe business is shown in Figure 1.

Downstream Business Strategy

Here a wide variety of inputs converge into a narrow funnel, as in the many products sold by a department store.

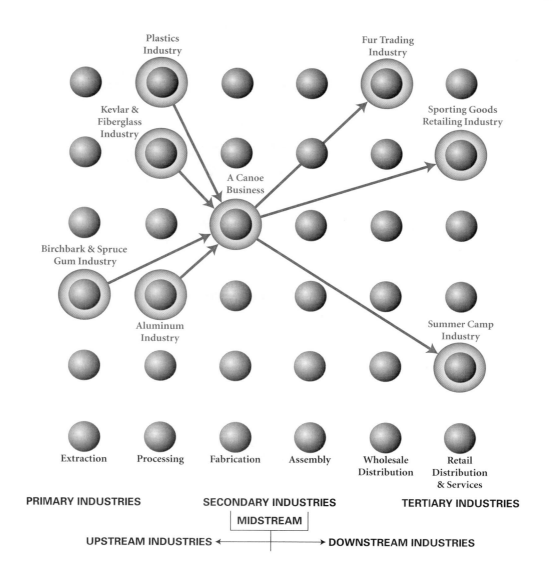

FIGURE 1
LOCATING A CORE
BUSINESS AS A
JUNCTION IN A
NETWORK OF
INDUSTRIES

Plastics
Industry

Fur Trading
Industry

Kevlar &
Fiberglass
Industry

Sporting Goods
Retailing Industry

A Canoe
Business

Birchbark & Spruce
Gum Industry

Aluminum
Industry

Summer Camp
Industry

| Extraction | Processing | Fabrication | Assembly | Wholesale Distribution | Retail Distribution & Services |

PRIMARY INDUSTRIES　　　　**SECONDARY INDUSTRIES**　　　　**TERTIARY INDUSTRIES**

MIDSTREAM

UPSTREAM INDUSTRIES ← → **DOWNSTREAM INDUSTRIES**

STRATEGIES OF INDUSTRY

Many factors are involved in the identification of an industry, so many that it would be difficult to develop a concise set of generic labels. Moreover, change continually renders the boundaries between "industries" arbitrary. Diverse products get bundled together so that two industries become one, while traditionally bundled products get separated so that one industry becomes two. Economists in government and elsewhere spend a great deal of time trying to pin these things down, via Standard Industrial Classification codes and the like. In effect, they try to fix what strategists try to change: competitive advantage often comes from reconceiving the definition of an industry.

DISTINGUISHING THE CORE BUSINESS

Having located the circle that identifies the core business, the next step is to open it up—to distinguish the characteristics that enable an organization to achieve competitive advantage and so to survive in its own context.

FIGURE 2 FUNCTIONAL AREAS IN SYSTEMS TERMS

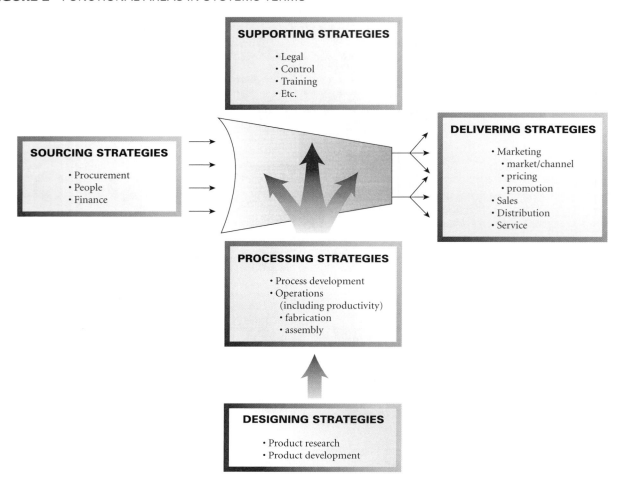

THE FUNCTIONAL AREAS

The second level of strategy can encompass a whole host of strategies in the various functional areas. As shown in Figure 2, they may include input "sourcing" strategies, throughput "processing" strategies, and output "delivery" strategies, all reinforced by a set of "supporting" strategies.

It has been popular to describe organizations in this way, especially since Michael Porter built his 1985 book around the "generic value chain," shown in Figure 3. Porter presents it as "a

FIGURE 3
THE GENERIC VALUE
CHAIN
Source: Porter (1983:3).

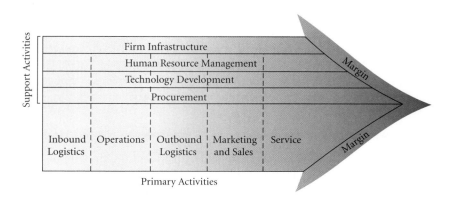

systematic way of examining all the activities a firm performs and how they interact . . . for analyzing the sources of competitive advantage" (1985: 33). Such a chain, and how it performs individual activities, reflects a firm's "history, its strategy, its approach to implementing its strategy, and the underlying economies of the activities themselves" (p. 36). According to Porter

> "the goal of any generic strategy" is to "create value for buyers" at a profit. Accordingly, the value chain displays total value, and consists of *value activities* and *margin*. Value activities are the physically and technologically distinct activities a firm performs. These are the building blocks by which a firm creates a product valuable to its buyers. Margin is the difference between total value and the collective cost of performing the value activities. . . .

Value activities can be divided into two broad types, *primary* activities and *support* activities. Primary activities, listed along the bottom of Figure 3, are the activities involved in the physical creation of the product and its sale and transfer to the buyer as well as after-sale assistance. In any firm, primary activities can be divided into the five generic categories shown in Figure 3. Support activities support the primary activities and each other by providing purchased inputs, technology, human resources, and various firmwide functions (p. 38). *

PORTER'S GENERIC STRATEGIES

Porter's framework of "generic strategies" has also become quite widely used. In our terms, these constitute strategies to distinguish the core business. Porter believes there are but two "basic types of competitive advantage a firm can possess: low costs or differentiation" (1985: 11). These combine with the "scope" of a firm's operation (the range of market segments targeted) to produce "three *generic strategies* for achieving above-average performance in an industry: cost leadership, differentiation, and focus" (namely, narrow scope), shown in Figure 4.

FIGURE 4
PORTER'S GENERIC
STRATEGIES
Source: Porter (1983:3).

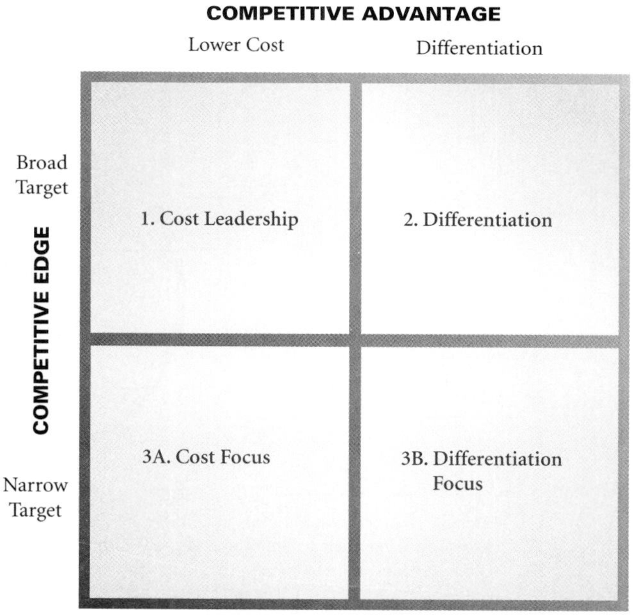

COMPETITIVE ADVANTAGE

	Lower Cost	Differentiation
Broad Target	1. Cost Leadership	2. Differentiation
Narrow Target	3A. Cost Focus	3B. Differentiation Focus

COMPETITIVE EDGE

---

*In other words, it is the differentiation of price that naturally drives the functional strategy of reducing costs just as it is the differentiation of product that naturally drives the functional strategies of enhancing quality or creating innovation. (To be consistent with the label of "cost leadership," Porter would have had to call his differentiation strategy "product leadership.") A company could, of course, cut costs while holding prices equivalent to competitors'. But often that means less service, lower quality, fewer features, etc., and so the customers would have to be attracted by lower prices. [See Mintzberg (1988: 14–17) for a fuller discussion of this point].

To Porter, firms that wish to gain competitive advantage must "make a choice" among these: "being 'all things to all people' is a recipe for strategic mediocrity and below-average performance" (p. 12). Or in the words that have become more controversial, "a firm that engages in each generic strategy but fails to achieve any of them is 'stuck in the middle' " (p. 16). Gilbert and Strebel (1992), however, have disagreed with this, arguing that highly successful companies, such as some of the Japanese automobile manufacturers, have adopted "outpacing strategies." First they use a low cost strategy to secure markets, and then, by "proactive" differentiation moves (say an increase in quality), they capture certain important market segments. Or else firms begin with value differentiation and follow that up with "preemptive" price cutting. In effect, the authors argue that companies can achieve both forms of Porter's competitive advantage simultaneously.

The strategies we describe in this section take their lead from Porter, but depart in some respects. We shall distinguish scope and differentiation, as Porter did in his 1980 book (focus being introduced as narrow scope in his later book), but we shall include cost leadership as a form of differentiation (namely, with regard to low price). If, as Porter argues, the intention of generic strategies is to seize and sustain competitive advantage, then it is not just taking leadership on cutting costs that matters so much as using that cost leadership to underprice competitors and so to attract buyers.*

Thus two types of strategy for distinguishing a core business are presented here. First is a set of increasingly extensive strategies of *differentiation*, shown on the face of the circle. These identify what is fundamentally distinct about a business in the marketplace, in effect as perceived by its customers. Second is a set of decreasingly extensive strategies of *scope*. These identify what markets the business is after, as perceived by itself.

STRATEGIES OF DIFFERENTIATION

As is generally agreed in the literature of strategic management, an organization distinguishes itself in a competitive marketplace by differentiating its offerings in some way—by acting to distinguish its product and services from those of its competitors. Hence, differentiation fills the face of the circle used to identify the core business. An organization can differentiate its offerings in six basic ways:

---

*Our figure differs from Porter's in certain ways. Because he places his major emphasis on the flow of physical materials (for example, referring to "inbound logistics" as encompassing materials handling, warehousing, inventory control, vehicle scheduling, and returns to suppliers), he shows procurement and human resource management as support activities, whereas by taking more of a general system orientation, our Figure 2 shows them as inputs, among the sourcing strategies. Likewise, he considers technology development as support whereas Figure 2 considers it as part of processing. (Among the reasons Porter gives for doing this is that such development can pertain to "outbound logistics" or delivery as well as processing. While true, it also seems true that far more technology development pertains to operations than to delivery, especially in the manufacturing firms that are the focus of Porter's attention. Likewise, Porter describes procurement as pertaining to any of the primary activities, or other support activities for that matter. But in our terms that does not make it any less an aspect of sourcing on the inbound side.) In fact, Porter's description would relegate engineering and product design (not to mention human resources and purchasing) to staff rather than line activities, a place that would certainly be disputed in many manufacturing firms (with product design, for example, being mentioned only peripherally in his text (p. 42) alongside other "technology development" activities such as media research and servicing procedures).

Price Differentiation Strategy

The most basic way to differentiate a product (or service) is simply to charge a lower price for it. All things being equal, or not too unequal, some people at least will always beat a path to the door of the cheaper product. Price differentiation may be used with a product undifferentiated in any other way—in effect, a standard design, perhaps a commodity. The producer simply absorbs the lost margin, or makes it up through a higher volume of sales. But other times, backing up price differentiation is a strategy of design intended to create a product that is intrinsically cheaper.

Image Differentiation Strategy

Marketing is sometimes used to feign differentiation where it does not otherwise exist—an image is created for the product. This can also include cosmetic differences to a product that do not enhance its performance in any serious way, for example, putting a fancier package around yogurt. (Of course, if it is the image that is for sale, in other words if the product is intrinsically cosmetic, as, say, in "designer" jeans, then cosmetic differences would have to be described in design differentiation.)

Support Differentiation Strategy

More substantial, yet still having no effect on the product itself, is to differentiate on the basis of something that goes alongside the product, some basis of support. This may have to do with selling the product (such as special credit or 24-hour delivery), servicing the product (such as exceptional after-sales service), or providing a related product or service alongside the basic one (paddling lessons with the canoe you buy). In an article entitled "Marketing Success Through Differentiation—of Anything," Theodore Levitt has argued the interesting point that "there is no such thing as a commodity" (1980: 8). His basic point is that no matter how difficult it may be to achieve differentiation by design, there is always a basis to achieve another substantial form of differentiation, especially by support.

Quality Differentiation Strategy

Quality differentiation has to do with features of the product that make it better—not fundamentally different, just better. The product performs with (1) greater initial reliability, (2) greater long-term durability, and/or (3) superior performance.

Design Differentiation Strategy

Last but certainly not least is differentiation on the basis of design—offering something that is truly different, that breaks away from the "dominant design" if there is one, to provide unique features. When everyone else was making cameras whose pictures could be seen next week, Edward Land made one whose pictures could be seen in the next minute.

Undifferentiation Strategy

To have no basis for differentiation is a strategy: indeed by all observation a common one, and in fact one that may be pursued deliberately. Hence there is a blank space in the circle. Given enough room in a market, and a management without the skill or the will to differentiate what it does, there can be a place for copycats.

SCOPE STRATEGIES

The second dimension to distinguish the core business is by the *scope* of the products and services offered, in effect the extent of the markets in which they are sold. Scope is essentially a demand-driven concept, taking its lead from the market for what exists out there. Differentiation, in contrast, is a supply-driven concern, rooted in the nature of the product itself—what is offered to the market (W. E. Smith, 1956). Differentiation, by concentrating on the product offered, adopts the perspective of the customer, existing only when that person perceives some characteristic of the product that adds value. And scope, by focusing on the market served, adopts the perspective of the producer, existing only in the collective mind of the organization—in terms of how it diffuses and disaggregates its markets (in other words, what marketing people call segmentation).

Unsegmentation Strategy

"One size fits all": the Ford Model T, table salt. In fact, it is difficult to think of any product today that is not segmented in some way. What the unsegmented strategy really means then is that the organization tries to capture a wide chunk of the market with a basic configuration of the product.

Segmentation Strategies

The possibilities for segmentation are limitless, as are the possible degrees. We can, however, distinguish a range of this, from a simple segmentation strategy (three basic sizes of paper clips) to a hyperfine segmentation strategy (as in designer lighting). Also, some organizations seek to be *comprehensive*, to serve all segments (department stores, large cereal manufacturers), others to be *selective*, targeting carefully only certain segments (e.g., "clean" mutual funds).

Niche Strategy

Niche strategies focus on a single segment. Just as the panda bear has found its biological niche in the consumption of bamboo shoots, so too is there the canoe company that has found its market niche in the fabrication of racing canoes, or the many firms which are distinguished only by the fact that they provide their highly standardized offerings in a unique place, a geographical niche—the corner grocery store, the regional cement producer, the national Red Cross office. All tend to follow "industry" recipes to the letter, providing them to their particular community. In a sense, all strategies are in some sense niche, characterized as much by what they exclude as by what they include. No organization can be all things to all people. The all-encompassing strategy is no strategy at all.

Customizing Strategies

Customization is the limiting case of segmentation: disaggregation of the market to the point where each customer constitutes a unique segment. *Pure* customization, in which the product is developed from scratch for each customer, is found in the architecturally designed house and the special purpose machine. It infiltrates the entire value chain: the product is not only delivered in a personalized way, not only assembled and even fabricated to order, but is also designed for the individual customer in the first place. Less ambitious but probably more common is *tailored* customization: a basic design is modified, usually in the fabrication stage, to the customer's needs or specifications (certain housing, prostheses modified to fit the bone joints of each consumer, and so on). *Standardized customization* means that final products are assembled to individual request for standard components—as in automobiles in which the customer is allowed to choose color, engine and various accessories. Advances in computer-aided design and manufacturing (CAD, CAM) have caused a proliferation of standardized customization, as well as tailored customization.

ELABORATING THE CORE BUSINESS

An organization can elaborate a business in a number of ways. It can develop its product offerings within that business, it can develop its market via new segments, new channels or new geographical areas, or it can simply push the same products more vigorously through the same markets. Back in 1965, Igor Ansoff showed these strategies as presented in Figure 5.

Penetration Strategies

Penetration strategies work from a base of existing products and existing markets, seeking to penetrate the market by increasing the organization's share of it. This may be done by straight *expansion* or by the *takeover* of existing competitors. Trying to expand sales with no fundamental change in product or market (buying market share through more promotion, etc.) is at one and the same time the most obvious thing to do and perhaps the most difficult to succeed at, because, at least in a relatively stable market, it means extracting market share from other firms, which logically leads to increased competition. Takeover, where possible, obviously avoids this, but perhaps at a high cost. The harvesting strategy, popularized in the 1970s by the Boston Consulting Group, in some ways represents the opposite of the penetration strategies. The way to deal with "cash cows"—businesses with high market shares but low growth potential—was to harvest them, cease investment and exploit whatever potential remained. The mixing of the metaphors may have been an indication of the dubiousness of the strategy since to harvest a cow is, of course, to kill it.

Market Development Strategies

A predominant strategy here is *market elaboration*, which means promoting existing products in new markets—in effect broadening the scope of the business by finding new market segments, perhaps served by new channels. Product substitution is a particular case of market elaboration, where uses for a product are promoted which enable it to substitute for other products. *Market consolidation* is the inverse of market elaboration, namely reducing the number of segments. But this is not just a strategy of failure. Given the common tendency to proliferate market segments, it makes sense for the healthy organization to rationalize them periodically, to purge the excesses.

Geographic Expansion Strategies

An important form of market development can be geographic expansion—carrying the existing product offering to new geographical areas, anywhere from the next block to across the world. When this also involves a strategy of geographic rationalization—locating different business functions in different places—it is sometimes referred to as a "global strategy." The IKEA furniture company, for example, designs in Scandinavia, sources in Eastern Europe among other places, and markets in Western Europe and North America.

Product Development Strategies

Here we can distinguish a simple *product extension* strategy from a more extensive *product line proliferation* strategy, and their counterparts, *product line rationalization*. Offering new or modified products in the same basic business is another obvious way to elaborate a core business—from cornflakes to bran flakes and rice crispies, eventually offering every permutation and combination of the edible grains. This may amount to differentiation by design, if the products are new and distinctive, or else to no more than increased scope through segmentation, if standardized products are added to the line. Product line proliferation means aiming at comprehensive product segmentation—the complete coverage of a given business. Rationalization means culling products and thinning the line to get rid of overlaps or unprofitable excesses. Again we might expect cycles of product extension and rationalization, at least in businesses (such as cosmetics and textiles) predisposed to proliferation in their product lines.

Next comes the question of what strategies of a generic nature are available to extend and reconceive that core business. These are approaches designed to answer the corporate-level question, "What business should we be in?"

Strategies designed to take organizations beyond their core business can be pursued in so-called vertical or horizontal ways, as well as combinations of the two. "Vertical" means backward or forward in the operating chain, the strategy being known formally as "vertical integration," although why this has been designated vertical is difficult to understand, especially since the flow of product and the chain itself are almost always drawn horizontally! Hence this will here be labeled chain integration. "Horizontal" diversification (its own geometry no more evident), which will be called here just plain diversification, refers to encompassing within the organization other, parallel businesses, not in the same chain of operations.

CHAIN INTEGRATION STRATEGIES

Organizations can extend their operating chains downstream or upstream, encompassing within their own operations the activities of their customers on the delivery end or their suppliers on the sourcing end. In effect, they choose to "make" rather than to "buy" or sell. *Impartation* (Barreyre, 1984; Barreyre and Carle, 1983) is a label that has been proposed to describe the opposite strategy, where the organization chooses to buy what it previously made (also called "outsourcing"), or sell what it previously transferred.

DIVERSIFICATION STRATEGIES

Diversification refers to the entry into some business not in the same chain of operation. It may be *related* to some distinctive competence or asset of the core business itself (also called *concentric* diversification); otherwise, it is referred to as *unrelated* or *conglomerate* diversification. In related diversification, there is evident potential synergy between the new business and the core one, based on a common facility, asset, channel, skill, even opportunity. Porter (1985: 323–4) makes the distinction here between "intangible" and "tangible" relatedness. The former is based on some functional or managerial skill considered common across the businesses, as in a Philip Morris using its marketing capabilities in Kraft. The latter refers to businesses that actually "share activities in the value chain" (p. 323), for example, different products sold by the same sales force. It should be emphasized here that no matter what its basis, every related diversification is also fundamentally an unrelated one, as many diversifying organizations have discovered to their regret. That is, no matter what is common between two different businesses, many other things are not.

STRATEGIES OF ENTRY AND CONTROL

Chain integration or diversification may be achieved by *internal development* or *acquisition*. In other words, an organization can enter a new business by developing it itself or by buying an organization already in business. Both internal development and acquisition involve complete ownership and formal control of the diversified business. But there are a host of other possible strategies, as follows:

STRATEGIES OF ENTRY AND CONTROL

Full ownership and control	• Internal development
	• Acquisition
Partial ownership and control	• Majority, minority
	• Partnership, including
	–Joint venture
	–Turnkey (temporary control)
Partial control without ownership	• Licensing
	• Franchising
	• Long-term contracting

COMBINED INTEGRATION-DIVERSIFICATION STRATEGIES

Among the most interesting are those strategies that combine chain integration with business diversification, sometimes leading organizations into whole networks of new businesses. *By-product diversification* involves selling off the by-products of the operating chain in separate markets, as when an airline offers its maintenance services to other carriers. The new activity amounts to a form of market development at some intermediate point in the operating chain. *Linked diversification* extends by-product diversification: one business simply leads to another, whether integrated "vertically" or diversified "horizontally." The organization pursues its operating chain upstream, downstream, sidestream; it exploits pre-products, end-products, and by-products of its core products as well as of each other, ending up with a network of businesses. *Crystalline diversification* pushes the previous strategy to the limit, so that it becomes difficult and perhaps irrelevant to distinguish integration from diversification, core activities from peripheral activities, closely related businesses from distantly related ones. What were once clear links in a few chains now metamorphose into what looks like a form of crystalline growth, as business after business gets added literally right and left as well as up and down. Here businesses tend to be related, at least initially, through internal development of core competencies, as in the "coating and bonding technologies" that are common to many of 3M's products.

WITHDRAWAL STRATEGIES

Finally there are strategies that reverse all those of diversification: organizations cut back on the businesses they are in. "Exit" has been one popular label for this, withdrawal is another. Sometimes organizations *shrink* their activities, canceling long-term licenses, ceasing to sell by-products, reducing their crystalline networks. Other times they abandon or *liquidate* businesses (the opposite of internal development), or else they *divest* them (the opposite of acquisition).

RECONCEIVING THE CORE BUSINESS(ES)

It may seem strange to end a discussion of strategies of ever more elaborate development of a business with ones involving reconception of the business. But in one important sense, there is a logic to this: after a core business has been identified, distinguished, elaborated and extended, there often follows the need not just to consolidate it but also to redefine it and reconfigure it—in essence, to reconceive it. As they develop, through all the waves of expansion, integration, diversification, and so on, some organizations lose a sense of themselves. Then reconception becomes the ultimate form of consolidation: rationalizing not just excesses in product offerings or markets segments or even new businesses, but all of these things together and more—the essence of the entire strategy itself. We can identify three basic reconception strategies.

BUSINESS REDEFINITION STRATEGY

A business, as Abell (1980) has pointed out, may be defined in a variety of ways—by the function it performs, the market it serves, the product it produces. All businesses have popular conceptions. Some are narrow and tangible, such as the canoe business, others broader and vague, such as the financial services business. All such definitions, no matter how tangible, are ultimately concepts that exist in the minds of actors and observers. It therefore becomes possible, with a little effort and imagination, to *redefine* a particular business—reconceive the "recipe" for how that business is conducted (Grinyer and Spender, 1979; Spender, 1989)—as Edwin Land did when he developed the Polaroid camera.*

BUSINESS RECOMBINATION STRATEGIES

As Porter notes, through the waves of diversification that swept American business in the 1960s and 1970s, "the concept of synergy has become widely regarded as passe"—a "nice idea" but "one that rarely occurred in practice" (1985: 317–18). Businesses were elements in a

---

*MacMillian refers to the business redefinition strategy as "reshaping the industry infrastructure" (1983:18), while Porter calls it "reconfiguration" (1985: 519–523), although his notion of product *substitution* (273–314) could sometimes also constitute a form of business redefinition.

portfolio to be bought and sold, or, at best, grown and harvested. Deploring that conclusion, Porter devoted three chapters of his 1985 book to "horizontal strategy," which we shall refer to here (given our problems with the geometry of this field) as *business recombination strategies*—efforts to recombine different businesses in some way, at the limit to reconceive various businesses as one. Businesses can be recombined tangibly or only conceptually. The latter was encouraged by Levitt's "Marketing Myopia" (1960) article. By a stroke of the pen, railroads could be in the transportation business, ball-bearing manufacturers in the friction reduction business. Realizing some practical change in behavior often proved much more difficult, however. But when some substantial basis exists for combining different activities, a strategy of business recombination can be very effective. There may never have been a transportation business, but 3M was able to draw on common technological capabilities to create a coating and bonding business.* Business recombination can also be more tangible, based on shared activities in the value chain, as in a strategy of *bundling*, where complementary products are sold together for a single price (e.g., automobile service with the new car). Of course, *unbundling* can be an equally viable strategy, such as selling "term" insurance free of any investment obligation. Carried to their logical extreme, the more tangible recombination strategies lead to a "systems view" of the business, where all products and services are conceived to be tightly interrelated.

CORE RELOCATION STRATEGIES

Finally we come full circle by closing the discussion where we began, on the location of the core business. An organization in addition to having one or more strategic positions in a marketplace, tends to have what Jay Galbraith (1983) calls a single "center of gravity," some conceptual place where is concentrated not only its core skills but also its cultural heart, as in a Procter & Gamble focusing its efforts on "branded consumer products," each "sold primarily by advertising to the homemaker and managed by a brand manager" (p. 13). But as changes in strategic position take place, shifts can also take place in this center of gravity, in

FIGURE 5
WAYS TO ELABORATE
A GIVEN BUSINESS
Source: Ansoff (1965:109) with minor modifications; see also Johnson and Jones (1957:52).

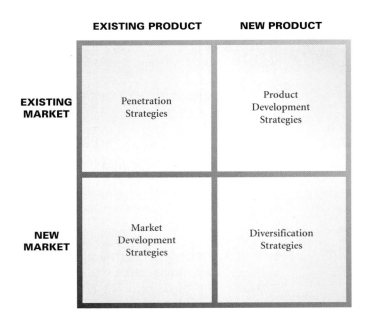

	EXISTING PRODUCT	**NEW PRODUCT**
EXISTING MARKET	Penetration Strategies	Product Development Strategies
NEW MARKET	Market Development Strategies	Diversification Strategies

---

*Our suspicion, we should note, is that such labels often emerge after the fact, as the organization seeks a way to rationalize the diversification that has already taken place. In effect, the strategy is emergent. (See Chapter 1 on "Five Ps for Strategy.")

various ways. First, the organization can move *along the operating chain*, upstream or downstream, as did General Mills "from a flour miller to a related diversified provider of products for the homemaker"; eventually the company sold off its flour milling operation altogether (p. 76). Second, there can be a shift *between dominant functions*, say from production to marketing. Third is the shift *to a new business*, whether or not at the same stage of the operating chain. Such shifts can be awfully demanding, simply because each industry is a culture with its own ways of thinking and acting. Finally is the shift *to a new core theme*, as in the reorientation from a single function or product to a broader concept, for example, when Procter & Gamble changed from being a soap company to being in the personal care business.

This brings us to the end of our discussion of generic strategies—our loop from locating a business to distinguishing it, elaborating it, extending it and finally reconceiving it.

We should close with a warning that while a framework of generic strategies may help to think about positioning an organization, use of it as a pat list may put that organization at a disadvantage against competitors that develop their strategies in more creative ways.

READING 4.6

**BY HENRY
MINTZBERG**

■ In the large literature of strategic management that deals with positioning, the concepts come and go at a frantic pace. There is thus a need to pin them down—to develop a framework to see them all, as well as to provide a "glossary" of what they are, even for experts who tend to beaver away in one area or another. There is woefully little synthesis in the world of analysis!

Thus, a little model is offered here. It is visual because, in a sense, all of this needs to be seen to be believed. The model is a metaphor of sorts, consisting of a **launching** devise, representing an organization, that sends **projectiles**, namely products and services, at a landscape of **targets**, meaning markets, faced with **rivals**, or competition, in the hope of attaining **fit**.

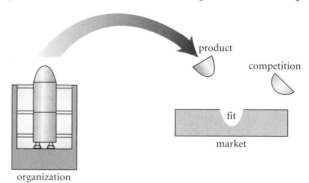

We should add that we have not chosen this metaphor casually: the hunting or military (or any other) implication very much reflects how writers of this school tend to see the world. We use the model to locate, explain, illustrate and especially link the various concepts that make up this school.

**THE VEHICLE
(ORGANIZATION)**

The organization is depicted as a launching device which develops, produces and distributes its products and services into markets. To do that, it performs a series of **business functions** that sequence themselves into what Michael Porter (1985) has labeled a **value chain**. As depicted in our figure, design (of product and process) and production are the basic platform, while supply and sourcing (including financing) form one tower, and administration and support (such as public relations and industrial relations) form the other. The launch vehicle has two booster rockets (which fall away during the product's voyage)—the first for sales and marketing, the second for physical distribution.

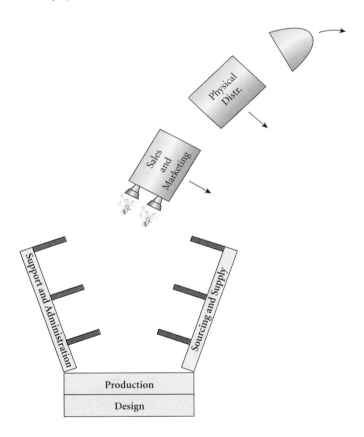

The business functions are executed by using a bundle of **competences** or **capabilities** of various kinds (such as the ability to do research or to produce products inexpensively) and supported by all sorts of **resources** or **assets** (including patents, machinery, and so on). Itami (1987) has referred to key competences as **invisible assets**, while Prahalad and Hamel (1990) have drawn attention to **core competences**, the ones that have developed deep within the organization over its history and explain its **comparative** and **competitive advantages** (as in the example of product venturing in 3M or quality design in Maytag). These can perhaps be distinguished from shallow or common competences, more tangible, codified and so **imitable** in nature (such as selling groceries in the corner shop). These are easily acquired and so easily lost too—more generic than genetic.

These core competences must be sustained and enhanced as the key to the organization's future. In part, this is done by accumulating **experience**, according to a theory popularized by the Boston Consulting Group in the 1970s (see Henderson, 1979): the more the organization produces, the more it engages in **learning**, and so the faster it reduces its costs.

Indeed, currently popular theory has it that the organization should shed as many of its non-core competences as it can, in order to become lean and flexible, and so be able to focus attention on doing what it does best. The rest should be bought from suppliers. Thus, the old strategy of **vertical integration**—encompassing your suppliers **upstream** as well as your intermediate customers **downstream** so that you can control their activities tightly—gets replaced by the new one of **outsourcing**, resulting in the **virtual organization**.

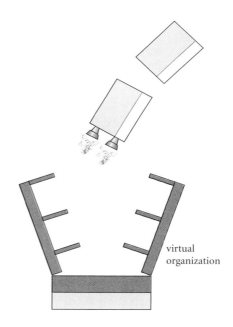

virtual organization

Competences can be combined in various ways, for example, through **joint ventures** or other forms of **alliances** with partners, **licensing** agreements, **franchising** relationships and **long-term contracts**, the extensive combinations of which result in **networks**. This can happen in parallel, as when an electronics firm combines its research capabilities with that of a mechanical products firm to develop new electromagnetic products together. Or it can happen sequentially, as when the design-capability of one firm is combined with the production-capability of another. These result in **synergy**, the 2 + 2 = 5 effect (Ansoff, 1965).

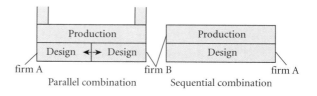

THE PROJECTILE (PRODUCTS AND SERVICES)

Proceeding along the value chain eventually creates a product (or service) which is launched at a target market. The ways in which this can be done are described, according to the positioning school, by a set of **generic strategies** (Porter, 1980). We can use our metaphor to describe a broad array of these (based on Mintzberg, 1988), according to the nature of the projectile (size, shape, surrounding, etc.) and the sequence of projectiles launched (frequency, direction, etc.). First are the generic strategies that characterize the product itself:

Low cost or **price differentiation strategy** (meaning high volume, commodity-type production)

Image differentiation strategy (e.g., nice packaging)

Support differentiation strategy (e.g., provision of after-sales service)

Quality differentiation strategy (e.g., more durable, more reliable, higher performance)

Design differentiation strategy (i.e., different in function)

Then there are the strategies that elaborate or extend the range of products offered:

Penetration strategy (targeting the same product more intensely at the same market, for example, through increased advertising)

Bundling strategy (selling two products together, such as computer software with hardware)

Market development strategy (targeting the same product at new markets)

Product development strategy (targeting new products at the same market)

Diversification strategy (targeting different products at different markets)

whether the different products are **unrelated** or **related**

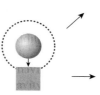

and whether this is done by the **acquisition** of other companies

or **internal development** of the new product/market

THE TARGET (MARKETS)

Again, the metaphor can be used for purposes of illustration, but here we show the generic characteristics of markets (the targeted place), first by size and divisibility, then by location, and finally by stage of evolution or change.

Mass market (large, homogeneous)

Fragmented market (many small niches)

Segmented market (differing demand segments)

Thin market (few, occasional buyers, as in nuclear reactors)

Geographic markets (looked at from the perspective of place)

local
regional
global

Emerging market (young, not yet clearly defined)

Established (mature) market (clearly defined)

Eroding market

Erupting market (undergoing destabilizing changes)

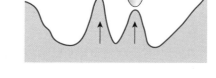

INDUSTRY AND GROUP

Where does one market end and another begin? In our discussion, we have spanned the concerns of various disciplines associated with strategy, from those of organization theory (the launching device) to strategic management (the projectile) and then to marketing (the target). Here, in further elaborating the target, or more exactly the nature of the targeted terrain, we move into the realm of economics, with its focus on "industry."

Economists spend a lot of time worrying about identifying industries (through the definition of SIC codes and the like). However, much of this is arbitrary, since they often no sooner find one than a strategist destroys it (because one job of the strategist is to break up the very industries that economists identify, as in the case of a CNN that took the news programme and turned it into a sub-industry, namely a television network, in its own right).

In our terms here, an industry can be defined as a landscape of associated markets, isolated from others by blockages in the terrain. In the literature of economics and strategic positioning, these are known as **barriers to entry**—for example, some kind of special know-how or close ties to the customers that keep potential new competitors out. Michael Porter (1980) elaborated on this with his notion of **strategic group**, really a kind of sub-industry, housing companies that pursue similar strategies (for example, national news magazines, as opposed to magazines targeted at specific audiences, such as amateur photographers). These are distinguished by **barriers to mobility**, in other words, difficulties of shifting into the group even though it is within the overall industry. These concepts map easily into our metaphor, with higher barriers shown for industries and lower ones for strategic groups, as follows:

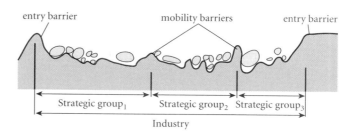

THE FIT (STRATEGIC POSITIONS)

When products and markets (projectiles and targets) come together, we reach the central concept of strategic management, namely **fit**, or the strategic position itself—how the product sits in the market. Fit is logically discussed, first in terms of the match between the breadth of the products offered and markets served (which Porter calls **scope**). After this, we shall turn to the quality of the fit and ways to improve it.

Commodity strategy targets a (perceived) mass market with a single, standardized product

Segmentation strategy targets a (perceived) segmented market with a range of products, geared to each of the different segments

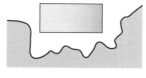

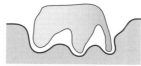

Niche strategy targets a small isolated market segment with a sharply delineated product

Customization strategy (the ultimate in both niching and segmentation) designs or tailors each specific product to one particular customer need (such as the architecturally designed home)

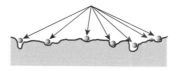

Once fit, or scope, is established, then attention turns to its strength, namely how secure it is—its durability, or **sustainability**. Here the concepts of the positioning school are less developed, so we use our metaphor to introduce some new ones that might prove useful.

First of all, we identify **natural fit**—where the product and market fit each other quite naturally, whether it was the product that created the market or the market that encouraged the development of the product. Natural fit is inherently sustainable (for example, because there is usually intrinsic customer loyalty, perhaps secured by high switching costs).

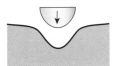
Natural fit: product push

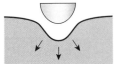
Natural fit: market pull

This can be distinguished from **forced fit**, as well as **vulnerable fit**, which is weak and so easily dislodged, whether by attack from competitors or loss of interest from customers.

Forced fit

Vulnerable fit

When fit is not perfect (as is always true in an imperfect world), and so not easily sustainable, attention has to be given to what can be called **reinforcing mechanisms**, to improve it, or **isolating mechanisms**, to protect it. Inspired by the metaphor itself, we suggest three types of these:

Burrowing strategy (driving into the market deeper, for example, by using advertising to strengthen brand loyalty—but this could prove costly)

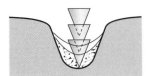

Packing strategy (tightening the fit by adding supporting elements, such as strong after-sales services, or the use of supporting brands—but the seller can get stuck too)

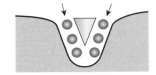

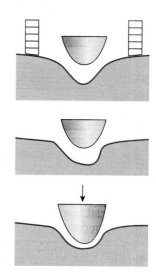

Fortifying strategy (building up barriers or **shelters** around the fit, such as seeking tariff or patent protection, or creating long-term contracts with customers—but these can topple, or else, in fact, blind the seller to changes occurring elsewhere)

There can also be a **learning strategy** to improve fit through adaptability, for example, by riding the **experience curve** to take advantage of the steady stream of learning that comes from producing more and more of the product, or simply by coming to know better the needs of the customers, or by taking advantage of the **complementarities** that come from different parts of a strategy that reinforce each other, such as franchising and mass preparation in fast food retailing.

Of course, if there can be natural fit and forced fit and vulnerable fit, then there can also be **misfit**. This concept has not been much developed in the literature, but we can at least offer a few ideas here:

Capacity misfit (what is offered exceeds what the market can take)

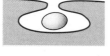

Competence misfit (the competences of the producer do not match the needs of the market)

Design misfit (the design is wrong for the market)

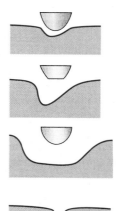

Sunk misfit (being stuck in a market due to **exit** barriers, as in **sunk costs** such as dedicated machinery that cannot be used elsewhere)

Myopic misfit (the producer cannot see the market—perhaps because of too long concentration on other markets)

Location misfit (the producer is in the wrong place, and cannot reach the market—perhaps because some barrier is too high)

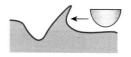

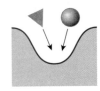

So far, almost all these relationships have been between a single seller and one or more target markets. But sellers are no more found alone than are buyers. There is **rivalry** in markets, consisting of **competitors**—capable of doing better or doing differently. So we return to economics to describe various competitive situations.

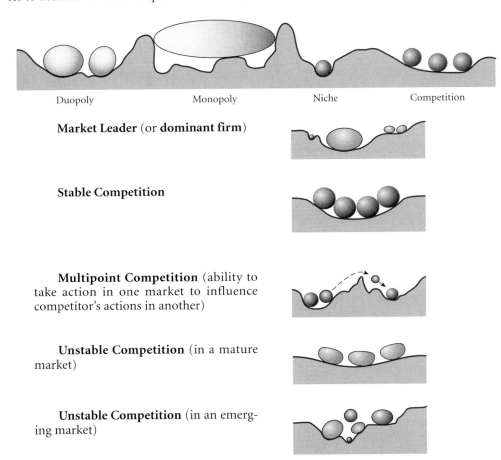

Duopoly Monopoly Niche Competition

Market Leader (or **dominant firm**)

Stable Competition

Multipoint Competition (ability to take action in one market to influence competitor's actions in another)

Unstable Competition (in a mature market)

Unstable Competition (in an emerging market)

CONTESTABILITY

Obviously, markets are **contestable**. New competitors can seek to drive themselves in. Here we draw especially on the literature of military strategy, adapted to business by such writers as Quinn (1980) and Porter (1980).

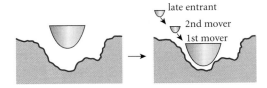

late entrant
2nd mover
1st mover

First movers seek to position themselves in new markets to keep rivals out. But **later entrants** (including **second movers**) come along and seek a share, if not to displace their rivals altogether. (**Strategic window** refers to the period of opportunity when an initial or later move becomes possible, for example, because the rival is having trouble, such as a strike in the factory, or because customers are suddenly vulnerable to a brand change.) Later entrants use various military-type strategies:

Frontal attack (by the **concentration of forces**, e.g., cost-cutting)

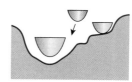

Lateral (or **indirect** or **flanking**) attack, perhaps by

— undermining (e.g., taking away the least loyal customers through lower prices)

— attacking a supporting brand (to dislodge the main one)

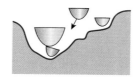

— attacking fortifications, through a **battering strategy** (e.g., lobbying for the elimination of tariff barriers)

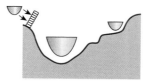

Guerrilla attack (series of small "hit and run" attacks, such as sudden moves of deep discounting)

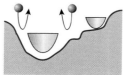

Market signalling by feint (giving the impression of doing something, such as pretending to expand plant to scare off potential competitor)

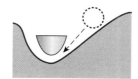

Later entrants may also seek to carve out small territories through niche strategies (sometimes called "picking up the crumbs").

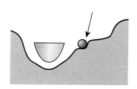

Finally, rivals may reach an accord with the existing players so that all settle down to a **collaborative strategy**, perhaps in a cozy price fixing or market allocating **cartel**.

The truly creative strategist, however, shuns all of these categories, or at least recombines them in innovative ways, to develop a **novel strategy**, for which there is no diagram, since no one can tell what it might look like!

CHAPTER 5

Strategy
Formation

The readings of the last two chapters describe how strategies are supposed to be made and thereby illustrate the prescriptive side of the field. This chapter presents readings that describe how strategies really do seem to be made, the *descriptive side*. We title this chapter "Strategy Formation" to emphasize the point introduced in Chapter 1 that strategies can form implicitly as well as be formulated explicitly.

The preceding chapters may seem to deal with an unattainable utopia and this one with an imperfect reality. But a better conclusion may be that prescription offers useful guidelines for thinking about ends and how to order physical resources efficiently to achieve them, whereas description provides a useful frame of reference for considering how these ends must be related to real-world patterns of behavior in organizations. Another way to say this is that although the analytical tools and models prescribed earlier are vital to thinking about strategy, they must also be rooted in a genuine understanding of the realities of organizations. Unfortunately, management writers have often been quick to prescribe without offering enough appreciation of why managers and organizations act in the ways they do.

We open with a reading by Henry Mintzberg called "Crafting Strategy." It suggests that managers mold strategies the way craftsmen mold clay. This reading also builds on Mintzberg's reading of Chapter 1 on the different forms of strategy, developing further the concept of emergent strategy.

Following this reading, Kathy Eisenhardt of Stanford University describes strategy as a process of decision making. Suited especially to more contemporary, dynamic conditions of many industries (which she calls "high velocity"), Eisenhardt sees the strategy process as a set of fast moves that uses collective intuition in an enterprise, stimulates conflict to improve thinking, and maintains a disciplined pace of decision making, while defusing wasteful political behavior.

In a chapter that challenges many of the accepted notions about how strategy should be made, the next reading may be the most upsetting of all. In it Richard Pascale, a well-known consultant, writer, and lecturer at Stanford Business School, challenges head-on not only the whole approach to strategy analysis (as represented in the last chapter), especially as practiced by the Boston Consulting Group (BCG), one of the better-known "strategy boutiques," but also the very concept of strategy formulation itself.

As his point of departure, Pascale describes a BCG study carried out for the British government to explain how manufacturers in that country lost the American motorcycle market to the Japanese and to Honda in particular. The analysis seems impeccable and eminently logical: The Japanese were simply more clever, by thinking through a brilliant strategy before they acted. But then Pascale flew to Japan and interviewed those clever executives who pulled off this coup. We shall save the story for Pascale, who tells it with a great deal of color, except to note here its basic message: An openness to learning and a fierce commitment to an organization and its markets may count for more in strategy making than all the brilliant analysis one can imagine. (Ask yourself while reading these accounts how the strategic behavior of the British motorcycle manufacturers who received the BCG report might have differed if they had instead received Pascale's story.) Pascale in effect takes the arguments for incrementalism and strategy making as a crafting and learning process to their natural conclusions.

No one who reads Pascale's account can ever feel quite so smug about rational strategy analysis again. We include this reading, however, not to encourage rejection of analysis or the very solid thinking that has gone into the works of Porter, Ansoff, and others. Rather, we wish to balance the message conveyed in so much of the strategy literature with the practical lessons from the field. The point is that successful strategies can no more rely exclusively on such analysis than they can do without it.

The next reading by Andrew Mair of Birkbeck College of the University of London, written especially for this edition, goes even further. Mair argues that many well-known authors in the strategy field have made use of Honda to promote their own angle on strategy to the exclusion of others (back to those ten schools and that elephant again). In his view, all these accounts are biased: They ignore crucial information and interpret the facts to make their own case. Their accounts may tell us more about the needs of academics and consultants than about the behavior of Honda. Mair offers a different and rather sobering interpretation of Honda's true behavior.

As we suggested in the introduction to this book, there is no truth, only closer approximations to the truth—by seeking to reconcile opposing perspectives, each with its own grain of truth. As Alfred North Whitehead remarked, "seek simplicity, and distrust it."

USING THE CASE STUDIES

Mintzberg's "Crafting Strategy" suggests that strategy formation is often strongly emergent. This is best seen when we take the long view as, for example, in the Acer Group and Lufthansa cases in which strategy evolves over a long period. But what about short periods? Surely, here there is not much scope for emergence.

As unlikely as it seems, the case on Napoleon Bonaparte suggests otherwise. In the popular mind Napoleon's approach to strategy is the antithesis of emergence. He is often portrayed as a masterful strategist who planned his way to victory. The case, however, suggests that Napoleon developed a strategy process that was oriented toward taking advantage of the unexpected rather than anticipating it.

The myth of Napoleon grew out of a tendency to attribute superior rationality to superior results. The Pascale and Mair readings debate whether the same holds true for explanations as to why the Japanese were so successful in entering and dominating the American motorcycle industry. The Honda Motor Company case clearly goes well with these readings.

Saatchi and Saatchi and McKinsey and Company suggest that in most instances strategy formation is both emergent and deliberate. Eisenhardt's more detailed picture of strategy formation goes with the Unipart Group case, which shows an organization that is intent on developing a strategy process that is open and inclusive.

READING 5.1

CRAFTING STRATEGY*

BY HENRY MINTZBERG

■ Imagine someone planning strategy. What likely springs to mind is an image of orderly thinking: a senior manager, or a group of them, sitting in an office formulating courses of action that everyone else will implement on schedule. The keynote is reason—rational control, the systematic analysis of competitors and markets, of company strengths and weaknesses, the combination of these analyses producing clear, explicit, full-blown strategies.

Now imagine someone *crafting* strategy. A wholly different image likely results, as different from planning as craft is from mechanization. Craft evokes traditional skill, dedication, perfection through the mastery of detail. What springs to mind is not so much thinking and reason as involvement, a feeling of intimacy and harmony with the materials at hand, developed through long experience and commitment. Formulation and implementation merge into a fluid process of learning through which creative strategies evolve.

My thesis is simple: the crafting image better captures the process by which effective strategies come to be. The planning image, long popular in the literature, distorts these processes and thereby misguides organizations that embrace it unreservedly.

In developing this thesis, I shall draw on the experiences of a single craftsman, a potter, and compare them with the results of a research project that tracked the strategies of a number of corporations across several decades. Because the two contexts are so obviously different, my metaphor, like my assertion, may seem far-fetched at first. Yet if we think of a craftsman as an organization of one, we can see that he or she must also resolve one of the great challenges the corporate strategist faces: knowing the organization's capabilities well enough to think deeply enough about its strategic direction. By considering strategy making from the perspective of one person, free of all the paraphernalia of what has been called the strategy industry, we can learn something about the formation of strategy in the corporation. For much as our potter has to manage her craft, so too managers have to craft their strategy.

At work, the potter sits before a lump of clay on the wheel. Her mind is on the clay, but she is also aware of sitting between her past experiences and her future prospects. She knows exactly what has and has not worked for her in the past. She has an intimate knowledge of her work, her capabilities, and her markets. As a craftsman, she senses rather than analyzes these things; her knowledge is "tacit." All these things are working in her mind as her hands are working the clay. The product that emerges on the wheel is likely to be in the tradition of her

*Originally published in the *Harvard Business Review* (July–August 1987) and winner of McKinsey prize for second best article in the *Review* 1987. Copyright © 1987 by the President and Fellows of Harvard College; all rights reserved. Reprinted with deletions by permission of the *Harvard Business Review*.

past work, but she may break away and embark on a new direction. Even so, the past is no less present, projecting itself into the future.

In my metaphor, managers are craftsmen and strategy is their clay. Like the potter, they sit between the past of corporate capabilities and a future of market opportunities. And if they are truly craftsmen, they bring to their work an equally intimate knowledge of the materials at hand. That is the essence of crafting strategy.

1. STRATEGIES ARE BOTH PLANS FOR THE FUTURE AND PATTERNS FROM THE PAST

Ask almost anyone what strategy is, and they will define it as a plan of some sort, an explicit guide to future behavior. Then ask them what strategy a competitor or a government or even they themselves have actually pursued. Chances are they will describe consistency in *past* behavior—a pattern in action over time. Strategy, it turns out, is one of those words that people define in one way and often use in another, without realizing the difference.

The reason for this is simple. Strategy's formal definition and its Greek military origins not withstanding, we need the word as much to explain past actions as to describe intended behavior. After all, if strategies can be planned and intended, they can also be pursued and realized (or not realized, as the case may be). And pattern in action, or what we call realized strategy, explains that pursuit. Moreover, just as a plan need not produce a pattern (some strategies that are intended are simply not realized), so too a pattern need not result from a plan. An organization can have a pattern (or realized strategy) without knowing it, let alone making it explicit.

Patterns, like beauty, are in the mind of the beholder, of course. But finding them in organizations is not very difficult. But what about intended strategies, those formal plans and pronouncements we think of when we use the term *strategy*? Ironically, here we run into all kinds of problems. Even with a single craftsman, how can we know what her intended strategies really were? If we could go back, would we find expressions of intention? And if we could, would we be able to trust them? We often fool ourselves, as well as others, by denying our subconscious motives. And remember that intentions are cheap, at least when compared with realizations.

READING THE ORGANIZATION'S MIND

If you believe all this has more to do with the Freudian recesses of a craftsman's mind than with the practical realities of producing automobiles, then think again. For who knows what the intended strategies of an organization really mean, let alone what they are? Can we simply assume in this collective context that the company's intended strategies are represented by its formal plans or by other statements emanating from the executive suite? Might these be just vain hopes or rationalizations or ploys to fool the competition? And even if expressed intentions do exist, to what extent do various people in the organization share them? How do we read the collective mind? Who is the strategist anyway?

The traditional view of strategic management resolves these problems quite simply, by what organizational theorists call attribution. You see it all the time in the business press. When General Motors acts, it's because its CEO has made a strategy. Given realization, there must have been intention, and that is automatically attributed to the chief.

In a short magazine article, this assumption is understandable. Journalists don't have a lot of time to uncover the origins of strategy, and GM is a large, complicated organization. But just consider all the complexity and confusion that gets tucked under this assumption—all the meetings and debates, the many people, the dead ends, the folding and unfolding of ideas. Now imagine trying to build a formal strategy-making system around that assumption. Is it any wonder that formal strategic planning is often such a resounding failure?

To unravel some of the confusion—and move away from the artificial complexity we have piled around the strategy-making process—we need to get back to some basic concepts. The most basic of all is the intimate connection between thought and action. That is the key to craft, and so also to the crafting of strategy.

2. STRATEGIES NEED NOT BE DELIBERATE— THEY CAN ALSO EMERGE, MORE OR LESS

Virtually everything that has been written about strategy making depicts it as a deliberate process. First we think, then we act. We formulate, then we implement. The progression seems so perfectly sensible. Why would anybody want to proceed differently?

Our potter is in the studio, rolling the clay to make a waferlike sculpture. The clay sticks to the rolling pin, and a round form appears. Why not make a cylindrical vase? One idea leads to another, until a new pattern forms. Action has driven thinking: a strategy has emerged.

Out in the field, a salesman visits a customer. The product isn't quite right, and together they work out some modifications. The salesman returns to his company and puts the changes through; after two or three more rounds, they finally get it right. A new product emerges, which eventually opens up a new market. The company has changed strategic course.

In fact, most salespeople are less fortunate than this one or than our craftsman. In an organization of one, the implementor is the formulator, so innovations can be incorporated into strategy quickly and easily. In a large organization, the innovator may be ten levels removed from the leader who is supposed to dictate strategy and may also have to sell the idea to dozens of peers doing the same job.

Some salespeople, of course, can proceed on their own, modifying products to suit their customers and convincing skunkworks in the factory to produce them. In effect, they pursue their own strategies. Maybe no one else notices or cares. Sometimes, however, their innovations do get noticed, perhaps years later, when the company's prevalent strategies have broken down and its leaders are groping for something new. Then the salesperson's strategy may be allowed to pervade the system, to become organizational.

Is this story farfetched? Certainly not. We've all heard stories like it. But since we tend to see only what we believe, if we believe that strategies have to be planned, we're unlikely to see the real meaning such stories hold.

Consider how the National Film Board of Canada (NFB) came to adopt a feature-film strategy. The NFB is a federal government agency, famous for its creativity and expert in the production of short documentaries. Some years back, it funded a filmmaker on a project that unexpectedly ran long. To distribute his film, the NFB turned to theaters and so inadvertently gained experience in marketing feature-length films. Other filmmakers caught onto the idea, and eventually the NFB found itself pursuing a feature-film strategy—a pattern of producing such films.

My point is simple, deceptively simple: strategies can *form* as well as be *formulated*. A realized strategy can emerge in response to an evolving situation, or it can be brought about deliberately, through a process of formulation followed by implementation. But when these planned intentions do not produce the desired actions, organizations are left with unrealized strategies.

Today we hear a great deal about unrealized strategies, almost always in concert with the claim that implementation has failed. Management has been lax, controls have been loose, people haven't been committed. Excuses abound. At times, indeed, they may be valid. But often these explanations prove too easy. So some people look beyond implementation to formulation. The strategists haven't been smart enough.

While it is certainly true that many intended strategies are ill conceived, I believe that the problem often lies one step beyond, in the distinction we make between formulation and implementation, the common assumption that thought must be independent of and precede action. Sure, people could be smarter—but not only by conceiving more clever strategies. Sometimes they can be smarter by allowing their strategies to develop gradually, through the organization's actions and experiences. Smart strategists appreciate that they cannot always be smart enough to think through everything in advance.

HANDS AND MINDS

No craftsman thinks some days and works others. The craftsman's mind is going constantly, in tandem with her hands. Yet large organizations try to separate the work of minds and hands. In so doing, they often sever the vital feedback linking between the two. The salesperson who finds a customer with an unmet need may possess the most strategic bit of information in the entire organization. But that information is useless if he or she cannot create a strategy in response to it or else convey the information to someone who can—because the channels are blocked or because the formulators have simply finished formulating. The notion that strategy is something that should happen way up there, far removed from the details of running an organization on a daily basis, is one of the great fallacies of conventional strategic management. And it explains a good many of the most dramatic failures in business and public policy today.

Strategies like the NFB's that appear without clear intentions— or in spite of them—can be called emergent. Actions simply converge into patterns. They may become deliberate, of course, if the pattern is recognized and then legitimated by senior management. But that's after the fact.

All this may sound rather strange, I know. Strategies that emerge? Managers who acknowledge strategies already formed? Over the years we have met with a good deal of resistance from people upset by what they perceive to be our passive definition of a word so bound up with proactive behavior and free will. After all, strategy means control—the ancient Greeks used it to describe the art of the army general.

STRATEGIC LEARNING

But we have persisted in this usage for one reason: learning. Purely deliberate strategy precludes learning once the strategy is formulated; emergent strategy fosters it. People take actions one by one and respond to them, so that patterns eventually form.

Our craftsman tries to make a freestanding sculptural form. It doesn't work, so she rounds it a bit here, flattens it a bit there. The result looks better, but still isn't quite right. She makes another and another and another. Eventually, after days or months or years, she finally has what she wants. She is off on a new strategy.

In practice, of course, all strategy making walks on two feet: one deliberate, the other emergent. For just as purely deliberate strategy making precludes learning, so purely emergent strategy making precludes control. Pushed to the limit, neither approach makes much sense. Learning must be coupled with control. That is why we use the word *strategy* for both emergent and deliberate behavior.

Likewise, there is no such thing as a purely deliberate strategy or a purely emergent one. No organization—not even the ones commanded by those ancient Greek generals—knows enough to work everything out in advance, to ignore learning en route. And no one—not even a solitary potter—can be flexible enough to leave everything to happenstance, to give up all control. Craft requires control just as it requires responsiveness to the material at hand. Thus deliberate and emergent strategy form the end points of a continuum along which the strategies that are crafted in the real world may be found. Some strategies may approach either end, but many more fall at intermediate points.

3. EFFECTIVE STRATEGIES DEVELOP IN ALL KINDS OF STRANGE WAYS

Effective strategies can show up in the strangest places and develop through the most unexpected means. There is no one best way to make strategy.

The form for a ceramic cat collapses on the wheel, and our potter sees a bull taking shape. Clay sticks to a rolling pin, and a line of cylinders results. Wafers come into being because of a shortage of clay and limited kiln space while visiting a studio in France. Thus errors become opportunities, and limitations stimulate creativity. The natural propensity to experiment, even boredom, likewise stimulates strategic change.

Organizations that craft their strategies have similar experiences. Recall the National Film Board with its inadvertently long film. Or consider its experiences with experimental films, which made special use of animation and sound. For 20 years, the NFB produced a bare but steady trickle of such films. In fact, every film but one in that trickle was produced by a single person, Norman McLaren, the NFB's most celebrated filmmaker. McLaren pursued a *personal strategy* of experimentation, deliberate for him perhaps (though who can know whether he had the whole stream in mind or simply planned one film at a time?) but not for the organization. Then 20 years later, others followed his lead and the trickle widened, his personal strategy becoming more broadly organizational.

While the NFB may seem like an extreme case, it highlights behavior that can be found, albeit in muted form, in all organizations. Those who doubt this might read Richard Pascale's account of how Honda stumbled into its enormous success in the American motorcycle market [the following article in this book].

GRASS-ROOTS STRATEGY MAKING

These strategies all reflect, in whole or part, what we like to call a grass-roots approach to strategic management. Strategies grow like weeds in a garden. They take root in all kinds of places, wherever people have the capacity to learn (because they are in touch with the situation) and the resources to support that capacity. These strategies become organizational when they become collective, that is, when they proliferate to guide the behavior of the organization at large.

Of course, this view is overstated. But it is no less extreme than the conventional view of strategic management, which might be labeled the hothouse approach. Neither is right. Reality falls between the two. Some of the most effective strategies we uncovered in our research combined deliberation and control with flexibility and organizational learning.

Consider first what we call the *umbrella strategy*. Here senior management sets out broad guidelines (say, to produce only high-margin products at the cutting edge of technology or to favor products using bonding technology) and leaves the specifics (such as what these products will be) to others lower down in the organization. This strategy is not only deliberate (in its guidelines) and emergent (in its specifics), but it is also deliberately emergent, in that the process is consciously managed to allow strategies to emerge en route. IBM used the umbrella strategy in the early 1960s with the impending 360 series, when its senior management approved a set of broad criteria for the design of a family of computers later developed in detail throughout the organization. [See the IBM case in this section.]

Deliberately emergent, too, is what we call the *process strategy*. Here management controls the process of strategy formation—concerning itself with the design of the structure, its staffing, procedures, and so on—while leaving the actual content to others.

Both process and umbrella strategies seem to be especially prevalent in businesses that require great expertise and creativity—a 3M, a Hewlett-Packard, a National Film Board. Such organizations can be effective only if their implementors are allowed to be formulators, because it is people way down in the hierarchy who are in touch with the situation at hand and have the requisite technical expertise. In a sense, these are organizations peopled with craftsmen, all of whom must be strategists.

---

4. STRATEGIC REORIENTATIONS HAPPEN IN BRIEF, QUANTUM LEAPS

The conventional view of strategic management, especially in the planning literature, claims that change must be continuous: the organization should be adapting all the time. Yet this view proves to be ironic because the very concept of strategy is rooted in stability, not change. As this same literature makes clear, organizations pursue strategies to set direction, to lay out courses of action, and to elicit cooperation from their members around common, established guidelines. By any definition, strategy imposes stability on an organization. No stability means no strategy (no course to the future, no pattern from the past). Indeed, the very fact of having a strategy, and especially of making it explicit (as the conventional literature implores managers to do), creates resistance to strategic change!

What the conventional view fails to come to grips with, then, is how and when to promote change. A fundamental dilemma of strategy making is the need to reconcile the forces for stability and for change—to focus efforts and gain operating efficiencies on the one hand, yet adapt and maintain currency with a changing external environment on the other.

QUANTUM LEAPS

Our own research and that of colleagues suggest that organizations resolve these opposing forces by attending first to one and then to the other. Clear periods of stability and change can usually be distinguished in any organization: while it is true that particular strategies may always be changing marginally, it seems equally true that major shifts in strategic orientation occur only rarely.

In our study of Steinberg, Inc., a large Quebec supermarket chain headquartered in Montreal, we found only two important reorientations in the 60 years from its founding to the mid-1970s: a shift to self-service in 1933 and the introduction of shopping centers and public financing in 1953. At Volkswagenwerk, we saw only one between the late 1940s and the 1970s, the tumultuous shift from the traditional Beetle to the Audi-type design. And at Air Canada, we found none over the airline's first four decades, following its initial positioning.

Our colleagues at McGill, Danny Miller and Peter Friesen (1984), found this pattern of change so common in their studies of large numbers of companies (especially the high-performance ones) that they built a theory around it, which they labeled the quantum theory of strategic change. Their basic point is that organizations adopt two distinctly different modes of behavior at different times.

Most of the time they pursue a given strategic orientation. Change may seem continuous, but it occurs in the context of that orientation (perfecting a given retailing formula, for example) and usually amounts to doing more of the same, perhaps better as well. Most organizations favor these periods of stability because they achieve success not by changing strategies but by exploiting the ones they have. They, like craftsmen, seek continuous improvement by using their distinctive competencies on established courses.

While this goes on, however, the world continues to change, sometimes slowly, occasionally in dramatic shifts. Thus gradually or suddenly, the organization's strategic orientation moves out of sync with its environment. Then what Miller and Friesen call a strategic revolution must take place. That long period of evolutionary change is suddenly punctuated by a brief bout of revolutionary turmoil in which the organization quickly alters many of its established patterns. In effect, it tries to leap to a new stability quickly to reestablish an integrated posture among a new set of strategies, structures, and culture.

But what about all those emergent strategies, growing like weeds around the organization? What the quantum theory suggests is that the really novel ones are generally held in check in some corner of the organization until a strategic revolution becomes necessary. Then, as an alternative to having to develop new strategies from scratch or having to import generic strategies from competitors, the organization can turn to its own emerging patterns to find its new orientation. As the old, established strategy disintegrates, the seeds of the new one begin to spread.

This quantum theory of change seems to apply particularly well to large established, mass-production companies, like a Volkswagenwerk. Because they are especially reliant on standardized procedures, their resistance to strategic reorientation tends to be especially fierce. So we find long periods of stability broken by short disruptive periods of revolutionary change. Strategic reorientations really are cultural revolutions.

In more creative organizations we see a somewhat different pattern of change and stability, one that is more balanced. Companies in the business of producing novel outputs apparently need to run off in all directions from time to time to sustain their creativity. Yet they also need to settle down after such periods to find some order in the resulting chaos—convergence following divergence.

Whether through quantum revolutions or cycles of convergence and divergence, however, organizations seem to need to separate in time the basic forces for change and stability, reconciling them by attending to each in turn. Many strategic failures can be attributed either to mixing the two or to an obsession with one of these forces at the expense of the other.

The problems are evident in the work of many craftsmen. On the one hand, there are those who seize on the perfection of a single theme and never change. Eventually the creativity disappears from their work and the world passes them by—much as it did Volkswagenwerk until the company was shocked into its strategic revolution. And then there are those who are always changing, who flit from one idea to another and never settle down. Because no theme or strategy ever emerges in their work, they cannot exploit or even develop any distinctive competence. And because their work lacks definition, identity crises are likely to develop, with neither the craftsmen nor their clientele knowing what to make of it. Miller and Friesen (1978: 921) found this behavior in conventional business too; they label it "the impulsive firm running blind." How often have we seen it in companies that go on acquisition sprees?

---

5. TO MANAGE STRATEGY, THEN, IS TO CRAFT THOUGHT AND ACTION, CONTROL AND LEARNING, STABILITY AND CHANGE

The popular view sees the strategist as a planner or as a visionary, someone sitting on a pedestal dictating brilliant strategies for everyone else to implement. While recognizing the importance of thinking ahead and especially of the need for creative vision in this pedantic world, I wish to propose an additional view of the strategist—as a pattern recognizer, a learner if you will—who manages a process in which strategies (and visions) can emerge as well as be deliberately conceived. I also wish to redefine that strategist, to extend that someone into the collective entity made up of the many actors whose interplay speaks an organization's mind. This strategist *finds* strategies no less than creates them, often in patterns that form inadvertently in his or her own behavior.

What, then, does it mean to craft strategy? Let us return to the words associated with craft: dedication, experience, involvement with the material, the personal touch, mastery of detail, a sense of harmony and integration. Managers who craft strategy do not spend much time in executive suites reading MIS reports or industry analyses. They are involved, responsive to their materials, learning about their organizations and industries through personal touch. They are also sensitive to experience, recognizing that while individual vision may be important, other factors must help determine strategy as well.

Manage Stability

Managing strategy is mostly managing stability, not change. Indeed, most of the time senior managers should not be formulating strategy at all; they should be getting on with making their organizations as effective as possible in pursuing the strategies they already have. Like distinguished craftsmen, organizations become distinguished because they master the details.

To manage strategy, then, at least in the first instance, is not so much to promote change as to know *when* to do so. Advocates of strategic planning often urge managers to plan for perpetual instability in the environment (for example, by rolling over five-year plans annually). But this obsession with change is dysfunctional. Organizations that reassess their strategies continuously are like individuals who reassess their jobs or their marriages continuously—in both cases, they will drive themselves crazy or else reduce themselves to inaction. The formal planning process repeats itself so often and so mechanically that it desensitizes the organization to real change, programs it more and more deeply into set patterns, and thereby encourages it to make only minor adaptations.

So-called strategic planning must be recognized for what it is: a means, not to create strategy, but to program a strategy already created—to work out its implications formally. It is essentially analytic in nature, based on decomposition, while strategy creation is essentially a process of synthesis. That is why trying to create strategies through formal planning most often leads to extrapolating existing ones or copying those of competitors.

This is not to say that planners have no role to play in strategy formation. In addition to programming strategies created by other means, they can feed ad hoc analyses into the strategy-making process at the front end to be sure that the hard data are taken into consideration. They can also stimulate others to think strategically. And of course people called planners can be strategists too, so long as they are creative thinkers who are in touch with what is relevant. But that has nothing to do with the technology of formal planning.

Detect Discontinuity

Environments don't change on any regular or orderly basis. And they seldom undergo continuous dramatic change, claims about our "age of discontinuity" and environmental "turbulence" notwithstanding. (Go tell people who lived through the Great Depression or survivors of the siege of Leningrad during World War II that ours are turbulent times.) Much of the time, change is minor and even temporary and requires no strategic response. Once in a while there is a truly significant discontinuity or, even less often, a gestalt shift in the environment, where everything important seems to change at once. But these events, while critical, are also easy to recognize.

The real challenge in crafting strategy lies in detecting the subtle discontinuities that may undermine a business in the future. And for that, there is no technique, no program, just a sharp mind in touch with the situation. Such discontinuities are unexpected and irregular, essentially unprecedented. They can be dealt with only by minds that are attuned to existing patterns yet able to perceive important breaks in them. Unfortunately, this form of strategic thinking tends to atrophy during the long periods of stability that most organizations experience. So the trick is to manage within a given strategic orientation most of the time yet be able to pick out the occasional discontinuity that really matters. The ability to make that kind of switch in thinking is the essence of strategic management. And it has more to do with vision and involvement than it does with analytic technique.

Know the Business

Note the kind of knowledge involved in strategic thinking: not intellectual knowledge, not analytical reports or abstracted facts and figures (though these can certainly help), but personal knowledge, intimate understanding, equivalent to the craftsman's feel for the clay. Facts are available to anyone; this kind of knowledge is not. Wisdom is the word that captures it best. But wisdom is a word that has been lost in the bureaucracies we have built for ourselves, systems designed to distance leaders from operating details. Show me managers who think they can rely on formal planning to create their strategies, and I'll show you managers who lack intimate knowledge of their businesses or the creativity to do something with it.

Craftsmen have to train themselves to see, to pick up things other people miss. The same holds true for managers of strategy. It is those with a kind of peripheral vision who are best able to detect and take advantage of events as they unfold.

Manage Patterns

Whether in an executive suite in Manhattan or a pottery studio in Montreal, a key to managing strategy is the ability to detect emerging patterns and help them take shape. The job of the manager is not just to preconceive specific strategies but also to recognize their emergence elsewhere in the organization and intervene when appropriate.

Like weeds that appear unexpectedly in a garden, some emergent strategies may need to be uprooted immediately. But management cannot be too quick to cut off the unexpected, for tomorrow's vision may grow out of today's aberration. (Europeans, after all, enjoy salads made from the leaves of the dandelion, America's most notorious weed.) Thus some patterns are worth watching until their effects have more clearly manifested themselves. Then those that prove useful can be made deliberate and be incorporated into the formal strategy, even if that means shifting the strategic umbrella to cover them.

To manage in this context, then, is to create the climate within which a wide variety of strategies can grow. In more complex organizations, this may mean building flexible structures, hiring creative people, defining broad umbrella strategies and watching for the patterns that emerge.

Reconcile Change and Continuity

Finally, managers considering radical departures need to keep the quantum theory of change in mind. As Ecclesiastes reminds us, there is a time to sow and a time to reap. Some new patterns must be held in check until the organization is ready for a strategic revolution, or at least a period of divergence. Managers who are obsessed with either change or stability are bound eventually to harm their organizations. As pattern recognizer, the manager has to be able to sense when to exploit an established crop of strategies and when to encourage new strains to displace the old.

While strategy is a word that is usually associated with the future, its link to the past is no less central. As Kierkegaard once observed, life is lived forward but understood backward. Managers may have to live strategy in the future, but they must understand it through the past.

Like potters at the wheel, organizations must make sense of the past if they hope to manage the future. Only by coming to understand the patterns that form in their own behavior do they get to know their capabilities and their potential. Thus crafting strategy, like managing craft, requires a natural synthesis of the future, present, and past.

READING 5.2   STRATEGY AS STRATEGIC DECISION MAKING*

BY KATHLEEN M. EISENHARDT

■ Many executives realize that to prosper in the coming decade, they need to turn to the fundamental issue of strategy. What is strategy? To use a simple yet powerful definition from *The Economist*, strategy answers two basic questions: "Where do you want to go?" and "How do you want to get there?"

Traditional approaches to strategy focus on the first question. They involve selecting an attractive market, choosing a defensible strategic position, or building core competencies. Only later, if at all, do executives address the second question. Yet in today's high-velocity, hotly competitive markets, these approaches are incomplete. They overemphasize executives' ability to analyze and predict which industries, competencies, or strategic positions will be viable and for how long, and they underemphasize the challenge of actually creating effective strategies.

Many managers of successful corporations have adopted a different perspective on strategy that Shona Brown and I call "competing on the edge." At the heart of this approach lies the recognition that strategy combines the questions of "where" and "how" to create a continuing flow of temporary and shifting competitive advantages. . . .

This article describes strategy as strategic decision making, especially in rapidly changing markets. Its underlying assumption is that "bet the company" decisions—those that change the firm's direction and generate new competitive advantages—arise much more often in these markets. Therefore, the ability to make fast, widely supported, and high-quality strategic decisions on a frequent basis is the cornerstone of effective strategy. To use the language of

*Excerpted from "Strategy as Strategic Decision Making" by Kathleen M. Eisenhardt, *MIT Sloan Management Review*, Spring 1999, pp. 65–72, by permission of the publisher. Copyright © 1999 by Massachusetts Institute of Technology. All rights reserved.

contemporary strategy thinking, strategic decision making is the fundamental dynamic capability in excellent firms. . . .

In both studies [done with colleagues], clear differences stood out between the strategic decision-making processes in the more and less effective firms. Strikingly, these differences counter commonly held beliefs that conflict slows down choice, politicking is typical, and fast decisions are autocratic. In other words, these findings challenge the assumption of trade-offs among speed, quality, and support. Instead, the most effective strategic decision makers made choices that were fast, high quality, and widely supported. How did they do it? Four approaches emerged from this research and my other work with executives. Effective decision makers create strategy by:

- Building collective intuition that enhances the ability of a top-management team to see threats and opportunities sooner and more accurately.
- Stimulating quick conflict to improve the quality of strategic thinking without sacrificing significant time.
- Maintaining a disciplined pace that drives the decision process to a timely conclusion.
- Defusing political behavior that creates unproductive conflict and wastes time.

BUILD COLLECTIVE INTUITION

One myth of strategic decision making in high-velocity markets is that there is no time for formal meetings and no place for the careful consideration of extensive information. Executives, the thinking goes, should consider limited, decision-specific data, concentrate on one or two alternatives, and make decisions on the fly.

Effective strategic decision makers do not follow that approach. They use as much as or more information than ineffective executives, and they are far more likely to hold regularly scheduled, "don't miss" meetings. They rely on extensive, real-time information about internal and external operations, which they discuss in intensive meetings. They avoid both accounting-based information because it tends to lag behind the realities of the business and predictions of the future because these are likely to be wrong. From extensive, real-time information, these executives build a collective intuition that allows them to move quickly and accurately as opportunities arise. . . .

Why do real-time information and "must attend" meetings lead to more effective strategic decision making? Intense interaction creates teams of managers who know each other well. Familiarity and friendship make frank conversation easier because people are less constrained by politeness and more willing to express diverse views. The strategic decision process then moves more quickly and benefits from high-quality information . . . when intense interaction focuses on the operating metrics of today's businesses, a deep intuition, or "gut feeling," is created, giving managers a superior grasp of changing competitive dynamics. Artificial intelligence research on championship chess players indicates how this intuition is formed. These players, for example, develop their so-called intuition through experience. Through frequent play, they gain the ability to recognize and process information in patterns or blocks that form the basis of intuition. This patterned processing (what we term "intuition") is faster and more accurate than processing single pieces of information. Consistent with this research, many effective decision makers were described by their colleagues as having "an immense instinctive feel," "a high quality of understanding," and "an intuitive sense of the business." This intuition gives managers a head start in recognizing and understanding strategic issues.

STIMULATE QUICK CONFLICT

In high-velocity markets, many executives are tempted to avoid conflict. They assume that conflict will bog down the decision-making process in endless debate and degenerate into personal attacks. They seek to move quickly toward a few alternatives, analyze the best ones, and make a quick choice that beats the competition to the punch.

Reality is different. In dynamic markets, conflict is a natural feature of high-stakes decision making because reasonable managers will often diverge in their views on how the marketplace will unfold. Furthermore, as research demonstrates, conflict stimulates innovative thinking, creates a fuller understanding of options, and improves decision effectiveness. Without conflict, decision makers commonly miss opportunities to question assumptions and overlook key elements of the decision. Given the value of conflict, effective strategic decision makers in rapidly changing markets not only tolerate conflict, they accelerate it.

One way that executives accelerate conflict is by assembling executive teams that are diverse in age, gender, functional background, and corporate experience. . . .

Another way that effective strategic decision makers accelerate conflict is by using "frame-breaking" tactics that create alternatives to obvious points of view. One technique is scenario planning: teams systematically consider strategic decisions in the light of several possible future states. Other techniques have executives advocate alternatives that they may or may not favor and perform role plays of competitors. The details of the techniques are not crucial. Rather, the point is to use and switch among them to prevent stale thinking. . . .

Perhaps the most powerful way to accelerate conflict is by creating multiple alternatives. The idea is to develop alternatives as quickly as possible so that the team can work with an array of possibilities simultaneously. As one executive . . . commented, "We play a larger set of options than most people." It is considered entirely appropriate for executives to advocate options that they may not prefer simply to encourage debate. . . .

Why do diverse teams, frame-breaking techniques, and multiple alternatives lead to faster conflict and ultimately more effective decisions? The rationale for diverse teams is clear: these teams come up with more varied viewpoints than homogeneous teams. The value of frame-breaking techniques is more subtle. In addition to the obvious benefit of generating many different perspectives, these techniques establish the norm that constructive conflict is an expected part of the strategic decision-making process. It is acceptable and even desirable to engage in conflict. Furthermore, frame-breaking techniques are intellectually engaging and even fun. They can motivate even apathetic executives to participate more actively in expansive strategic thinking.

The power of multiple alternatives comes from several sources. Clearly, pushing for multiple alternatives speeds up conflict by stimulating executives to develop divergent options. It also enables them to rapidly compare alternatives, helping them to better understand their own preferences. Furthermore, multiple alternatives provide executives with the confidence that they have not overlooked a superior option. That confidence is crucial in rapidly changing markets, where the blocks to effective decision making are emotional as much as cognitive. Finally, multiple alternatives defuse the interpersonal tension that can accompany conflict by giving team members room to maneuver and save face when they disagree. . . .

MAINTAIN THE PACE Less effective strategic decision makers face a dilemma. On the one hand, they believe that every strategic decision is unique. Each requires its own analytical approach, and each unfolds in its own way. On the other hand, these same decision makers believe that they must decide as quickly as possible. Yet making quick choices conflicts with making one-of-a-kind choices.

Effective strategic decision makers avoid this dilemma by focusing on maintaining decision pace, not pushing decision speed. They launch the decision-making process promptly, keep up the energy surrounding the process, and cut off debate at the appropriate moment. They drive strategic decision-making momentum. . . .

Effective strategic decision makers skillfully cut off debate, typically using a two-step method called "consensus with qualification" to bring decision making to a close. First, managers conduct the decision process itself with the goal of consensus in mind. If they reach consensus, the choice is made. If consensus does not emerge, they break the deadlock using a decision rule such as voting or, more commonly, allowing the manager with the largest stake in the outcome to make the decison. . . .

Decision-making rhythm helps managers plan their progress and forces them to recognize the familiar aspects of decision making that make the process more predictable. As significant, it emphasizes that hitting decision timing is more critical than forging consensus or developing massive data analyses. As one manager told us, "The worst decision is no decision at all." . . .

DEFUSE POLITICS

Some executives believe that politics are a natural part of strategic choice. They see strategic decision making as involving high stakes that compel managers to lobby one another, manipulate information, and form coalitions. The game quickly becomes a competition among ambitious managers.

More effective strategic decision makers take a negative view of politicking. Since politicking often involves managers using information to their own advantage, it distorts the information base, leading to a poor strategic decision-making process. Furthermore, these executives see political activity as wasting valuable time. Their perspective is collaborative, not competitive, setting limits on politics and, more generally, interpersonal conflict.

One way in which effective executives defuse politics is by creating common goals. These goals do not imply homogeneous thinking. Rather, they suggest that managers have a shared vision of where they want to be or who their external competitors are. Managers at Neptune, a successful multibusiness computing firm, are highly aware of their external competition. At their monthly meetings, they pay close attention to the moves of the competition and personalize that competition by referring to individual managers in competitor companies, particularly their direct counterparts. They have a clear collective goal for their own ranking and market-share position in the industry. It is to be number one. At Intel, managers typically contend that "only the paranoid survive." . . .

A more direct way to defuse politics is through a balanced power structure in which each key decision maker has a clear area of responsibility, but in which the leader is the most powerful decision maker. . . .

Humor defuses politics. Effective strategic decision makers often relieve tension by making business fun. They emphasize the excitement of fast-paced markets and the "rush" of competing in these settings. . . . Humor strengthens the collaborative outlook. It puts people into a positive mood. Research has shown that people whose frame of mind is positive have more accurate perceptions of each other's arguments and are more optimistic, creative in their problem solving, forgiving, and collaborative. Humor also allows managers to convey negative information in a less threatening way. Managers can say something as a joke that might otherwise be offensive.

READING 5.3

THE HONDA EFFECT*

BY RICHARD T. PASCALE

■ At face value, "strategy" is an innocent noun. Webster defines it as the large-scale planning and direction of operations. In the business context, it pertains to a process by which a firm searches and analyzes its environment and resources in order to (1) select opportunities defined in terms of markets to be served and products to serve them and (2) make discrete decisions to invest resources in order to achieve identified objectives. (Bower, 1970: 7–8).

But for a vast and influential population of executives, planners, academics, and consultants, strategy is more than a conventional English noun. It embodies an implicit model of how organizations should be guided and, consequently, preconfigures our way of thinking. Strategy formulation (1) is generally assumed to be driven by senior management whom we expect to set strategic direction, (2) has been extensively influenced by empirical models and concepts, and (3) is often associated with a laborious strategic planning process that, in some companies, has produced more paper than insight.

A $500-million-a-year "strategy" industry has emerged in the United States and Europe comprised of management consultants, strategic planning staffs, and business school academics. It caters to the unique emphasis that American and European companies place upon this particular aspect of managing and directing corporations.

Words often derive meaning from their cultural context. *Strategy* is one such word and nowhere is the contrast of meanings more pronounced than between Japan and the United States. The Japanese view the emphasis we place on "strategy" as we might regard their enthusiasm for Kabuki or sumo wrestling. They note our interests not with an intent of acquiring similar ones but for insight into our peculiarities. The Japanese are somewhat distrustful of a single "strategy" for in their view any idea that focuses attention does so at the expense of peripheral vision. They strongly believe that *peripheral vision* is essential to discerning changes in the customer, the technology or competition, and is the key to corporate survival over the long haul. They regard any propensity to be driven by a single-minded strategy as a weakness.

The Japanese have particular discomfort with strategic concepts. While they do not reject ideas such as the experience curve or portfolio theory outright they regard them as a stimulus to perception. They have often ferreted out the "formula" of their concept-driven American competitors and exploited their inflexibility. In musical instruments, for example (a mature industry facing stagnation as birthrates in the United States and Japan declined), Yamaha might have classified its products as "cash cows" and gone on to better things (as its chief U.S. competitor, Baldwin United, had done). Instead, beginning with a negligible share of the U.S. market, Yamaha plowed ahead and destroyed Baldwin's seemingly unchallengeable dominance. YKK's success in zippers against Talon (a Textron division) and Honda's outflanking of Harley-Davidson (a former AMF subsidiary) in the motorcycle field provide parallel illustrations. All three cases involved American conglomerates, wedded to the portfolio concept, that had classified pianos, zippers, and motorcycles as mature businesses to be harvested rather than nourished and defended. Of course, those who developed portfolio theory and other strategic concepts protest that they were never intended to be mindlessly applied in setting strategic direction. But most would also agree that there is a widespread tendency in American corporations to misapply concepts and to otherwise become strategically myopic—ignoring the marketplace, the customer, and the problems of execution. This tendency toward misapplication, being both pervasive and persistent over several decades, is a phenomenon that the literature has largely ignored [for exceptions, see Hayes and Abernathy, 1980: 67; Hayes and Garvin, 1982: 71]. There is a need to identify explicitly the factors that influence how we conceptualize strategy—and which foster its misuse.

| **HONDA: THE STRATEGY MODEL** | In 1975, Boston Consulting Group (BCG) presented the British government its final report: *Strategy Alternatives for the British Motorcycle Industry*. This 120-page document identified two key factors leading to the British demise in the world's motorcycle industry: |

- Market share loss and profitability declines
- Scale economy disadvantages in technology, distribution, and manufacturing

During the period 1959 to 1973, the British share of the U.S. motorcycle industry had dropped from 49% to 9%. Introducing BCG's recommended strategy (of targeting market segments where sufficient production volumes could be attained to be price competitive) the report states:

> The success of the Japanese manufacturers originated with the growth of their domestic market during the 1950s. As recently as 1960, only 4 percent of Japanese motorcycle production was exported. By this time, however, the Japanese had developed huge production volumes in small motorcycles in their domestic market, and volume-related cost reductions had followed. This resulted in a highly competitive cost position which the Japanese used as a springboard for penetration of world markets with small motorcycles in the early 1960s (BCG; 1975: xiv).

The BCG study was made public by the British government and rapidly disseminated in the United States. It exemplifies the necessary (and, I argue, insufficient) strategist's perspective of:

- examining competition primarily from an intercompany perspective,
- at a high level of abstraction,
- with heavy reliance on macroeconomic concepts (such as the experience curve).

Case writers at Harvard Business School, UCLA, and the University of Virginia quickly condensed the BCG report for classroom use in case discussions. It currently enjoys extensive use in first-term courses in business policy.

Of particular note in the BCG study, and in the subsequent Harvard Business School rendition, is the historical treatment of Honda.

> The mix of competitors in the U.S. motorcycle market underwent a major shift in the 1960s. Motorcycle registrations increased from 575,000 in 1960 to 1,382,000 in 1965. Prior to 1960 the U.S. market was served mainly by Harley-Davidson of U.S.A., BSA, Triumph and Norton of U.K. and Moto-Guzzi of Italy. Harley was the market leader with total 1959 sales of $16.6 million. After the second world war, motorcycles in the U.S.A. attracted a very limited group of people other than police and army personnel who used motorcycles on the job. While most motorcyclists were no doubt decent people, groups of rowdies who went around on motorcycles and called themselves by such names as "Hell's Angels," "Satan's Slaves" gave motorcycling a bad image. Even leather jackets which were worn by motorcyclists as a protective device acquired an unsavory image. A 1953 movie called "The Wild Ones" starring a 650cc Triumph, a black leather jacket and Marlon Brando gave the rowdy motorcyclists wide media coverage. The stereotype of the motorcyclist was a leather-jacketed, teenage troublemaker.
>
> Honda established an American subsidiary in 1959—American Honda Motor Company. This was in sharp contrast to other foreign producers who relied on distributors. Honda's marketing strategy was described in the 1963 annual report as "With its policy of selling, not primarily to confirmed motorcyclists but rather to members of the general public who had never before given a second thought to a motorcycle. . . . " Honda started its push in the U.S. market with the smallest, lightweight motorcycles. It had a three-speed transmission, an automatic clutch, five horsepower (the American cycle only had two and a half), an electric starter and step through frame for female riders. And it was easier to handle. The Honda machines sold for under $250 in retail compared with $1,000–$1,500 for the bigger American or British machines. Even at that early date Honda was probably superior to other competitors in productivity.
>
> By June 1960 Honda's Research and Development effort was staffed with 700 designers/engineers. This might be contrasted with 100 engineers/draftsmen employed by . . . (European and American competitors). In 1962 production per man-year was running at 159 units, (a figure not matched by Harley-Davidson until 1974). Honda's net fixed asset investment was $8170 per employee . . . (more than twice its European and American competitors). With 1959 sales of $55 million Honda was already the largest motorcycle producer in the world.
>
> Honda followed a policy of developing the market region by region. They started on the West Coast and moved eastward over a period of four–five years. Honda sold 2,500 machines in the U.S. in 1960. In 1961 they lined up 125 distributors and spent $150,000 on regional advertising. Their advertising was directed to the young families, their advertising theme was "You Meet the Nicest People on a Honda." This was a deliberate attempt to dissociate motorcycles from rowdy, Hell's Angels type people.
>
> Honda's success in creating demand for lightweight motorcycles was phenomenal. American Honda's sales went from $500,000 in 1960 to $77 million in 1965. By 1966 the market share data

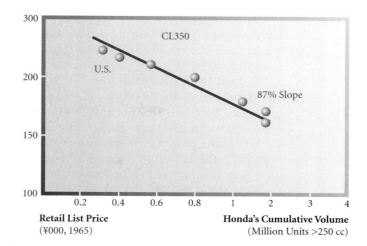

showed the ascendancy of Japanese producers and their success in selling lightweight motorcycles. [Honda had 63% of the market] . . . Starting from virtually nothing in 1960, the lightweight motorcycles had clearly established their lead (Purkayastha, 1981: 5, 10, 11, 12).

Quoting from the BCG report:
The Japanese motorcycle industry, and in particular Honda, the market leader, present a [consistent] picture. The basic philosophy of the Japanese manufacturers is that high volumes per model provide the potential for high productivity as a result of using capital intensive and highly automated techniques. Their marketing strategies are therefore directed towards developing these high model volumes, hence the careful attention that we have observed them giving to growth and market share.

    The overall result of this philosophy over time has been that the Japanese have now developed an entrenched and leading position in terms of technology and production methods. . . . The major factors which appear to account for the Japanese superiority in both these areas are . . . (specialized production systems, balancing engineering and market requirements, and the cost efficiency and reliability of suppliers) (BCG, 1975: 59, 40).

As evidence of Honda's strategy of taking position as low cost producer and exploiting economies of scale, other sources cite Honda's construction in 1959 of a plant to manufacture 30,000 motorcycles per month well ahead of existing demand at the time. (Up until then Honda's most popular models sold 2,000–3,000 units per month.) (Sakiya, 1982: 119)

    The overall picture as depicted by the quotes exemplifies the "strategy model." Honda is portrayed as a firm dedicated to being the low price producer, utilizing its dominant market position in Japan to force entry into the U.S. market, expanding that market by redefining a leisure class ("Nicest People") segment, and exploiting its comparative advantage via aggressive pricing and advertising. Richard Rumelt, writing the teaching note for the UCLA adaptation of the case states: "The fundamental contribution of BCG is not the experience curve per se but the ever-present assumption that differences in cost (or efficiency) are the fundamental components of strategy" (Rumelt, 1980: 2).

THE ORGANIZATIONAL PROCESS PERSPECTIVE

On September 10, 1982, the six Japanese executives responsible for Honda's entry into the U.S. motorcycle market in 1959 assembled in Honda's Tokyo headquarters. They had gathered at my request to describe in fine grain detail the sequence of events that had led to Honda's ultimate position of dominance in the U.S. market. All were in their sixties; three were retired. The story that unfolded, greatly abbreviated below, highlights miscalculation, serendipity, and organizational learning—counterpoints to the streamlined "strategy" version related earlier. . . .

Any account of Honda's successes must grasp at the outset the unusual character of its founder, Sochiro Honda, and his partner, Takeo Fujisawa. Honda was an inventive genius with a large ego and mercurial temperament, given to bouts of "philandering" (to use his expression) (Sakiya, 1979). . . .

Postwar Japan was in desperate need of transportation. Motorcycle manufacturers proliferated, producing clip-on engines that converted bicycles into makeshift "mopeds." Honda was among these but it was not until he teamed up with Fujisawa in 1949 that the elements of a successful enterprise began to take shape. Fujisawa provided money as well as financial and marketing strengths. In 1950 their first D-type motorcycle was introduced. They were, at that juncture, participating in a fragmented industry along with 247 other manufacturers. Other than its sturdy frame, this introductory product was unnoteworthy and did not enjoy great commercial success (Sakiya, 1979, 1982).

Honda embodied a rare combination of inventive ability and ultimate self-confidence. His motivation was not primarily commercial. Rather, the company served as a vehicle to give expression to his inventive abilities. A successful company would provide a resource base to pursue, in Fujisawa's words, his "grandiose dream." Fujisawa continues, "There was no end to his pursuit of technology" (Sakiya, 1982).

Fujisawa, in an effort to save the faltering company, pressed Honda to abandon their noisy two-stroke engine and pursue a four-stroke design. The quieter four-stroke engines were appearing on competitive motorcycles, therefore threatening Honda with extinction. Mr. Honda balked. But a year later, Honda stunned Fujisawa with a breakthrough design that doubled the horsepower of competitive four-stroke engines. With this innovation, the firm was off and putting, and by 1951 demand was brisk. There was no organization, however, and the plant was chaotic (Sakiya, 1982). Strong demand, however, required early investment in a simplified mass production process. As a result, *primarily* due to design advantages, and secondarily to production methods, Honda became one of the four or five industry leaders by 1954 with 15 percent market share (data provided by company). . . .

For Fujisawa, the engine innovation meant increased sales and easier access to financing. For Mr. Honda, the higher horsepower engine opened the possibility of pursuing one of his central ambitions in life—to race his motorcycle and win. . . .

Fujisawa, throughout the fifties, sought to turn Honda's attention from his enthusiasm with racing to the more mundane requirements of running an enterprise. By 1956, as the innovations gained from racing had begun to pay off in vastly more efficient engines, Fujisawa pressed Honda to adapt this technology for a commercial motorcycle (Sakiya, 1979, 1982). Fujisawa had a particular segment in mind. Most motorcyclists in Japan were male and the machines were used primarily as an alternative form of transportation to trains and buses. There were, however, a vast number of small commercial establishments in Japan that still delivered goods and ran errands on bicycles. Trains and buses were inconvenient for these activities. The pursestrings of these small enterprises were controlled by the Japanese wife—who resisted buying conventional motorcycles because they were expensive, dangerous, and hard to handle. Fujisawa challenged Honda: Can you use what you've learned from racing to come up with an inexpensive, safe-looking motorcycle that can be driven with one hand (to facilitate carrying packages).

In 1958, the Honda 50cc Supercub as introduced—with an automatic clutch, three-speed transmission, automatic starter, and the safe, friendly look of a bicycle (without the stigma of the outmoded mopeds). Owing almost entirely to its high horsepower but *lightweight 50cc engine* (not to production efficiencies), it was affordable. Overnight, the firm was overwhelmed with orders. Engulfed by demand, they sought financing to build a new plant with a 30,000 unit per month capacity. "It wasn't a speculative investment," recalls one executive. "We had the proprietary technology, we had the market and the demand was enormous." (The plant was completed in mid-1960.) Prior to its opening, demand was met through makeshift, high cost, company-owned assembly and farmed-out assembly through subcontractors. By the end of 1959, Honda had skyrocketed into first place among Japanese motorcycle manufacturers. Of its total sales that year of 285,000 units, 168,000 were Supercubs.

Fujisawa utilized the Supercub to restructure Honda's channels of distribution. For many years, Honda had rankled under the two-tier distribution system that prevailed in the industry. These problems had been exacerbated by the fact that Honda was a late entry and had been carried as secondary line by distributors whose loyalties lay with their older manufacturers. Further weakening Honda's leverage, all manufacturer sales were on a consignment basis.

Deftly, Fujisawa had characterized the Supercub to Honda's distributors as "something much more like a bicycle than a motorcycle." The traditional channels, to their later regret, agreed. Under amicable terms Fujisawa began selling the Supercub directly to retailers—and primarily through bicycle shops. Since these shops were small and numerous (approximately 12,000 in Japan), sales on consignment were unthinkable. A cash-on-delivery system was installed, giving Honda significantly more leverage over its dealerships than the other motorcycle manufacturers enjoyed.

The stage was now set for exploration of the U.S. market. Mr. Honda's racing conquests in the late 1950s had given substance to his convictions about his abilities. . . .

Two Honda executives—the soon-to-be-named president of American Honda, Kihachiro Kawashima, and his assistant—arrived in the United States in late 1958. Their itinerary: San Francisco, Los Angeles, Dallas, New York, and Columbus. Mr. Kawashima recounts his impressions:

> My first reaction after travelling across the United States was: how could we have been so stupid as to start a war with such a vast and wealthy country! My second reaction was discomfort. I spoke poor English. We dropped in on motorcycle dealers who treated us discourteously and in addition, gave the general impression of being motorcycle enthusiasts who, secondarily, were in business. There were only 3,000 motorcycle dealers in the United States at the time and only 1,000 of them were open five days a week. The remainder were open on nights and weekends. Inventory was poor, manufacturers sold motorcycles to dealers on consignment, the retailers provided consumer financing; after-sales service was poor. It was discouraging.
>
> My other impression was that everyone in the United States drove an automobile—making it doubtful that motorcycles could ever do very well in the market. However, with 450,000 motorcycle registrations in the U.S. and 60,000 motorcycles imported from Europe each year it didn't seem unreasonable to shoot for 10 percent of the import market. I returned to Japan with that report.
>
> In truth, we had no strategy other than the idea of seeing if we could sell something in the United States. It was a new frontier, a new challenge and it fit the "success against all odds" culture that Mr. Honda had cultivated. I reported my impressions to Fujisawa—including the seat-of-the-pants target of trying, over several years, to attain a 10 percent share of U.S. imports. He didn't probe that target quantitatively. We did not discuss profits or deadlines for breakeven. Fujisawa told me if anyone could succeed, I could and authorized $1 million for the venture.
>
> The next hurdle was to obtain a currency allocation from the Ministry of Finance. They were extraordinarily skeptical. Toyota had launched the Toyopet in the U.S. in 1958 and had failed miserably. "How could Honda succeed?" they asked. Months went by. We put the project on hold. Suddenly, five months after our application, we were given the go-ahead—but at only a fraction of our expected level of commitment. "You can invest $250,000 in the U.S. market," they said, "but only $110,000 in cash." The remainder of our assets had to be in parts and motorcycle inventory.
>
> We moved into frantic activity as the government, hoping we would give up on the idea, continued to hold us to the July 1959 start-up timetable. Our focus, as mentioned earlier, was to compete with the European exports. We knew our products at the time were good but not far superior. Mr. Honda was especially confident of the 250cc and 305cc machines. The shape of the handlebar on these larger machines looked like the eyebrow of Buddha, which he felt was a strong selling point. Thus, after some discussion and with no compelling criteria for selection, we configured our start-up inventory with 25 percent of each of our four products—the 50cc Supercub and the 125cc, 250cc, and 305cc machines. In dollar value terms, of course, the inventory was heavily weighted toward the larger bikes.
>
> The stringent monetary controls of the Japanese government together with the unfriendly reception we had received during our 1958 visit caused us to start small. We chose Los Angeles

where there was a large second and third generation Japanese community, a climate suitable for motorcycle use, and a growing population. We were so strapped for cash that the three of us shared a furnished apartment that rented for $80 per month. Two of us slept on the floor. We obtained a warehouse in a run-down section of the city and waited for the ship to arrive. Not daring to spare our funds for equipment, the three of us stacked the motorcycle crates three high—by hand, swept the floors, and built and maintained the parts bin.

We were entirely in the dark the first year. We were not aware the motorcycle business in the United States occurs during a seasonable April-to-August window—and our timing coincided with the closing of the 1959 season. Our hard-learned experiences with distributorships in Japan convinced us to try to go to the retailers direct. We ran ads in the motorcycle trade magazine for dealers. A few responded. By spring of 1960, we had forty dealers and some of our inventory in their stores—mostly larger bikes. A few of the 250cc and 305cc bikes began to sell. Then disaster struck.

By the first week of April 1960, reports were coming in that our machines were leaking oil and encountering clutch failure. This was our lowest moment. Honda's fragile reputation was being destroyed before it could be established. As it turned out, motorcycles in the United States are driven much farther and much faster than in Japan. We dug deeply into our precious cash reserves to air freight our motorcycles to the Honda testing lab in Japan. Through the dark month of April, Pan Am was the only enterprise in the U.S. that was nice to us. Our testing lab worked twenty-four-hour days bench testing the bikes to try to replicate the failure. Within a month, a redesigned head gasket and clutch spring solved the problem. But in the meantime, events had taken a surprising turn.

Throughout our first eight months, following Mr. Honda's and our own instincts, we had not attempted to move the 50cc Supercubs. While they were a smash success in Japan (and manufacturing couldn't keep up with demand there), they seemed wholly unsuitable for the U.S. market where everything was bigger and more luxurious. As a clincher, we had our sights on the import market—and the Europeans, like the American manufacturers, emphasized the larger machines.

We used the Honda 50s ourselves to ride around Los Angeles on errands. They attracted a lot of attention. One day we had a call from a Sears buyer. While persisting in our refusal to sell through an intermediary, we took note of Sears' interest. But we still hesitated to push the 50cc bikes out of fear they might harm our image in a heavily macho market. But when the larger bikes started breaking, we had no choice. We let the 50cc bikes move. And surprisingly, the retailers who wanted to sell them weren't motorcycle dealers, they were sporting goods stores.

The excitement created by the Honda Supercub began to gain momentum. Under restrictions from the Japanese government, we were still on a cash basis. Working with our initial cash and inventory, we sold machines, reinvested in inventory, and sunk the profits into additional inventory and advertising. Our advertising tried to straddle the market. While retailers continued to inform us that our Supercub customers were normal everyday Americans, we hesitated to target toward this segment out of fear of alienating the high margin end of our business—sold through the traditional motorcycle dealers to a more traditional "black leather jacket" customer.

Honda's phenomenal sales and share gains over the ensuing years have been previously reported. History has it that Honda "*redefined*" the U.S. motorcycle industry. In the view of American Honda's start-up team, this was an innovation they backed into—and reluctantly. It was certainly not the strategy they embarked on in 1959. As late as 1963, Honda was still working with its original Los Angeles advertising agency, its ad campaigns straddling all customers so as not to antagonize one market in pursuit of another.

In the spring of 1963, an undergraduate advertising major at UCLA submitted, in fulfillment of a routine course assignment, an ad campaign for Honda. Its theme: You Meet the Nicest People on a Honda. Encouraged by his instructor, the student passed his work on to a friend at Grey Advertising. Grey had been soliciting the Honda account—which with a $5 million a year budget was becoming an attractive potential client. Grey purchased the student's idea—on a tightly kept nondisclosure basis. Grey attempted to sell the idea to Honda.

Interestingly, the Honda management team, which by 1963 had grown to five Japanese executives, was badly split on this advertising decision. The president and treasurer favored another proposal from another agency. The director of sales, however, felt strongly that the Nicest People campaign was the right one—and his commitment eventually held sway. Thus, in 1963, through an inadvertent sequence of events, Honda came to adopt a strategy that directly identified and targeted that large untapped segment of the marketplace that has since become inseparable from the Honda legend.

The Nicest People campaign drove Honda's sales at an even greater rate. By 1964, nearly one out of every two motorcycles sold was a Honda. As a result of the influx of medium income leisure class consumers, banks and other consumer credit companies began to finance motorcycles—shifting away from dealer credit, which had been the traditional purchasing mechanism available. Honda, seizing the opportunity of soaring demand for its products, took a courageous and seemingly risky position. Late in 1964, they announced that thereafter, they would cease to ship on a consignment basis but would require cash on delivery. Honda braced itself for revolt. While nearly every dealer questioned, appealed, or complained, none relinquished his franchise. In one fell swoop, Honda shifted the power relationship from the dealer to the manufacturer. Within three years, this would become the pattern for the industry.

THE "HONDA EFFECT"

The preceding account of Honda's inroads in the U.S. motorcycle industry provides more than a second perspective on reality. It focuses our attention on different issues and raises different questions. What factors permitted two men as unlike one another as Honda and Fujisawa to function effectively as a team? What incentives and understandings permitted the Japanese executives at American Honda to respond to the market as it emerged rather than doggedly pursue the 250cc and 305cc strategy that Mr. Honda favored? What decision process permitted the relatively junior sales director to overturn the bosses' preferences and choose the Nicest People campaign? What values or commitment drove Honda to take the enormous risk of alienating its dealers in 1964 in shifting from a consignment to cash? In hindsight, these pivotal events all seem ho-hum common sense. But each day, as organizations live out their lives without the benefit of hindsight, few choose so well and so consistently.

The juxtaposed perspectives reveal what I shall call the "Honda Effect." Western consultants, academics, and executives express a preference for oversimplifications of reality and cognitively linear explanations of events. To be sure, they have always acknowledged that the "human factor" must be taken into account. But extensive reading of strategy cases at business schools, consultants' reports, strategic planning documents as well as the coverage of the popular press, reveals a widespread tendency to overlook the process through which organizations experiment, adapt, and learn. We tend to impute coherence and purposive rationality to events when the opposite may be closer to the truth. How an organization deals with miscalculation, mistakes, and serendipitous events *outside its field of vision is often crucial to success over time*. It is this realm that requires better understanding and further research if we are to enhance our ability to guide an organization's destiny. . . .

An earlier section has addressed the shortcomings of the narrowly defined macroeconomic strategy model. The Japanese avoid this pitfall by adopting a broader notion of "strategy." In our recent awe of things Japanese, most Americans forget that the original products of the Japanese automotive manufacturers badly missed the mark. Toyota's Toyopet was square, sexless, and mechanically defective. It failed miserably, as did Datsun's first several entries into the U.S. market. More recently, Mazda miscalculated badly with its first rotary engine and nearly went bankrupt. Contrary to myth, the Japanese did not from the onset embark on a strategy to seize the high-quality small-car market. They manufactured what they were accustomed to building in Japan and tried to sell it abroad. Their success, as any Japanese automotive executive will readily agree, did not result from a bold insight by a few big brains at the top. On the contrary, success was achieved by senior managers humble enough not to take their initial strategic positions too seriously. What saved Japan's near-failures was the cumulative impact of "little brains" in the form of salesmen and dealers and production workers, all contributing incrementally to the quality and market position these companies enjoy today. Middle and upper management saw their primary task as guiding and orchestrating this input from below rather than steering the organization from above along a predetermined strategic course.

The Japanese don't use the term "strategy" to describe a crisp business definition or competitive master plan. They think more in terms of "strategic accommodation," or "adaptive persistence," underscoring their belief that corporate direction evolves from an incremental adjustment to unfolding events. Rarely, in their view, does one leader (or a strategic planning group) produce a bold strategy that guides a firm unerringly. Far more frequently, the input is from below. It is this ability of an organization to move information and ideas from the bottom to the top and back again in continuous dialogue that the Japanese value above all things. As this dialogue is pursued, what in hindsight may be "strategy" evolves. In sum, "strategy" is defined as "all the things necessary for the successful functioning of organization as an adaptive mechanism." . . .

READING 5.4 HONDA MYTHOLOGY AND THE STRATEGY INDUSTRY*

BY ANDREW MAIR

■ Some years ago a professor at a well-known business school told me how much he liked Honda, "a lovely little company," that made an excellent strategy case study for MBA students. Similar opinions are shared widely among management educators. The Honda Motor Company has appeared in the strategic management literature so often over the past two decades that many academics, students, and practicing managers now feel a certain familiarity with the company, just as they might with other frequently cited companies like General Motors, 3M, or General Electric.

Yet a careful reading of the literature in the strategy field reveals that Honda's success story has been marshaled to support different, indeed opposing, positions in the discipline's central theoretical debates: the debate on strategy process paradigms between the analytical-planning school and the learning-adaptation school; the debate on strategy content paradigms between supporters of industry analysis/market positioning and resource-based approaches; and the debate within the last of these between proponents of core competencies and core capabilities. Supporters of different approaches have argued long and hard over the meaning of Honda (see the lengthy debate in the 1996 *California Management Review*, for instance). But how can evidence from the same firm be used to support diametrically opposed viewpoints? Does this tell us something about how the strategy industry's consultants and academics ply their trade?

THE MANY FACES OF HONDA

BOSTON CONSULTING GROUP'S EVOLVING ANALYSIS

Boston Consulting Group (1975) published its analysis of the motorcycle industry in 1975, at a time when Japanese motorcycle producers had displaced British companies in the North American market for medium and large motorcycles. BCG's study was grounded in traditional

*Revised by the author, with new material added, from "Learning from Honda," *Journal of Management Studies* 36.1, (1999) pp. 25–44.

industrial economics, and Honda furnished the majority of Japanese examples. The analysis focused on how Honda's large volumes permitted lower costs, through specialized production technology and an imputed "experience curve," the BCG analytical tool that proposed that costs declined with accumulated volumes. The British had helped Honda increase its sales volumes by steadily retreating from unprofitable market segments.

There was only brief discussion of how Honda had managed to enter the U.S. market in the first place, during the early 1960s. Honda was said to have used its huge sales and production volumes of small motorcycles in Japan as a springboard for penetrating world markets. At the same time, while Honda had changed the image of small bikes by advertising them as "fun" products, success depended on a sound and cheap product that really was fun.

Remarkably, by 1990 BCG had used Honda as a prominent example of three of the six core strategy concepts the group had developed: the experience curve (as above), debt-led growth/winner's competitive cycles, and product diversity/time-based competition (see Stalk and Hout, 1990). According to BCG consultants Abbeglen and Stalk (1985), successful Japanese companies incur substantial debt to establish a "winner's competitive cycle," a circle of larger production facilities, increased volume, decreased cost, increased profitability, and financial power, followed by reinvestment to fuel growth. They use the cycle both to topple market leaders and to defend strong competitive positions.

Honda provided case stories of dramatic incident to illustrate both roles. In the late 1950s, Honda overtook the domestic motorcycle market leader, Tohatsu, by borrowing heavily, increasing volumes and market share, and thereby reducing costs. Abbeglen and Stalk deduced from this that rate of growth, not market share, was the best indicator of future performance. In the early 1980s Honda fought off the challenge of Yamaha, which had invested in a large new factory, convinced that Honda was now more focused on its automobile markets. Honda defended its position in part through massive price cuts, promotions, and larger inventories for dealers but also used product variety as a competitive weapon, rapidly expanding its model range at a rate that Yamaha could not match. By 1990, Stalk and Hout were using the story of the "Honda Yamaha war" to illustrate the new BCG concept of "time-based competition," downplaying other aspects of Honda's defensive strategy.

PASCALE'S STRATEGIC LEARNING FROM HONDA

In a direct response to the 1975 BCG study, Pascale (1984) argued that Japanese firms actually view strategy quite differently from American and European firms and that they find Western (especially BCG) concepts, such as "portfolio theory" and the "experience curve," too formulaic and, indeed, too easy to read (and, therefore, to counter) in the behaviors of competitors. Pascale focused on Honda's early 1960s' entry into the American motorcycle market to illustrate the difference. He argued that BCG had imposed an inappropriately rationalist interpretation onto Honda's actual strategy. In contrast, Pascale emphasized the idiosyncratic characters and leadership of the company founders, product design over production process, and Honda's innovative U.S. distribution to big retail outlets instead of the traditional dealers. Pascale quoted one of the middle managers charged with exploring the U.S. market from 1958, concluding that the success of the small Super Cub motorcycle was a story of luck and learning from mistakes, of serendipity rather than planning.

QUINN'S IDIOSYNCRATIC HONDA

Quinn's (1991, 1996) strategy case study of Honda painted a similar picture of Honda to Pascale, this time for the whole of Honda's development as a company. In Quinn's interpretation, founder Soichiro Honda fostered an individualistic creative anarchy in his own image, with trial and error encouraged, and with innovative activity from middle managers and factory workers alike, in a quasi-democratic organisation.

MINTZBERG'S LUCK AND LEARNING FROM HONDA

Mintzberg has drawn on Pascale's Honda study on several occasions (1987, 1991, 1996a, 1996b) to support his own writing on strategy and to debate planning school proponent Igor Ansoff and BCG report author Goold, arguing that it is one of the few studies of real strategy making. Mintzberg portrayed Honda as a company whose market entry strategy may have looked brilliant in retrospect but had been flawed in every respect except for Honda's willingness to learn, grass-roots style, from its mistakes until it found a viable strategy: Sell small motorcycles, not the traditional U.S. large machines, through a new distribution network.

HAMEL AND PRAHALAD'S COMPETENCIES

BCG's interpretation of Honda strategy has also been challenged from the resource-based perspective, as Hamel and Prahalad (1994) have taken issue with BCG's traditional industrial economics version of how small companies can enter industries dominated by entrenched rivals. Indeed, Honda played a significant supporting role in Hamel and Prahalad's overall theory of strategy, exemplifying their concepts of stretched strategic ambitions, leverage of resources to maximum effect ("making a mockery" of the experience curve), and, above all, core competencies—in this case Honda's engine and powertrain technologies applied across a broad range of businesses. Honda was said to possess great foresight, exemplified by the Honda NSX, a high-technology sports car launched in 1990 with great success, that stood in stark contrast to rival Porsche, which had became too complacent in its product offerings and experienced a dramatic U.S. sales decline.

STALK, EVANS, AND SHULMAN'S CAPABILITIES

Our tour of strategy interpretations of Honda returns to BCG with Stalk, Evans, and Shulman's (1992) core capabilities version of the resource-based view to explain Honda's rise to challenge General Motors and Ford. In contrast to Hamel and Prahalad's concept of core technology and production competencies underlying diverse product lines, Stalk, Evans, and Shulman proposed core business process capabilities, arguing that Honda is actually distinguished by its expertise in dealer management and product development—capabilities Honda has replicated as it moved into new product areas. These capabilities were said to be more important than the competencies because they are more visible to the customer.

INSIGHT INTO THE STRATEGY INDUSTRY

The most striking impression of these pictures of Honda strategy is that they are often diametrically opposed in their explanations and implications. Moreover, when strategy writers debate the meaning of Honda, their positions become even more polarized. Hamel and Prahalad rejected the olive branch presented by Stalk, Evans, and Shulman, who proposed a unified competencies-capabilities theory, and insisted that core competencies were more significant to Honda than its capabilities. Mintzberg rejected BCG author Goold's (1996) peace proposal in the form of a synthesis or reconciliation between the design and learning schools of strategy formation to insist that learning plays a more important role than theoretical analysis, with the latter relegated to a subordinate role. Pascale (1996) agreed that the formalization of strategy only comes as post hoc rationalization. What are we to make of all this?

THE ONLY THING THAT MATTERS IS SUCCESS!

Readers of the strategy literature would be unaware of any significant strategic errors or crises at Honda, which is presented throughout as an unmitigated "small firm makes good" success story. Yet Honda has suffered four crises in its history so far—1954, 1966, 1969, and early 1990s—and their causes are illuminating (see Sakiya, 1987; Mair 1998a).

Honda's financial crisis in 1954 was largely the result of a debt-led "winner's competitive cycle" strategy, in the absence of competitive products. The key to success for a few years was the product; the 1958 Super Cub made the difference between near disaster and spectacular sales. The Super Cub boom in the United States was followed by a rapid decline in sales in 1966, blamed internally on complacency over the design of the Super Cub, unchanged since launch. The whole firm was almost bankrupted by foreign exchange problems. The recovery of U.S. motorcycle sales in the late 1960s was based on the larger motorcycles Honda had initially—and correctly—expected to sell well. Soon after Honda's move into mass automobile production in 1967, Soichiro Honda banned all work on the now standard water-cooled engines as he enlisted his engineers in the search for a masterpiece, powerful, air-cooled engine with which to crown his career—in line with the obsessive approach so admired by some. The outcome was a niche "sporty" car launched at precisely the moment, in 1969, when a mass-market car was needed to capitalize on the initial success. This car failed miserably in the market. Only after a major internal confrontation that left Mr. Honda isolated were the company's younger engineers permitted to develop water-cooled engines. Senior managers believed that Honda had committed a major blunder by missing the chance to offer a car like the hugely successful water-cooled 1972 Civic three years earlier.

Finally, in the early 1990s, with a worldwide recession and a sharp rise in the yen's value putting pressure on costs in Japan, Honda's long-standing product strategy problems came into the open. Commercial success had always rested on well-designed and well-made mass-market products: Super Cub (1958), Civic (1972), and Accord (1976) in particular. Financial difficulties brought the relationship between these mass products and the company's technology-driven niche products into sharp focus, as mass sales were no longer sufficient to support niche technology projects—such as the NSX high-technology sports car—that now lost considerable sums of money. Moreover, Honda R&D had defined the company's growth markets as sporty and luxury cars and had steadfastly refused to enter the rapidly expanding North American market for sports-utility vehicles and minivans in the 1980s, despite repeated calls for such products from the American dealership network. The outcome was an about-turn in Honda's product strategy, including the cancellation of sporty car projects and a belated move into the growth segments.

DON'T LET THE FACTS GET IN THE WAY OF A GOOD STORY!

In observing Honda, the strategy writers have seen only what they wanted to see. One-sided explanations are pervasive. Facts that don't fit are just left out.

The original 1975 BCG report focused entirely on structural economic factors to the neglect of the strategy formation process. Abbeglen and Stalk did not distinguish between two separate periods in the late 1950s: A period of cost reductions related to sales and volume increases (fits their theory) was preceded and permitted by a period of successful cost cutting at constant production volumes (doesn't fit their theory). They left out the Super Cub, the vital product that made the difference between success and failure, from their explanation of the "winner's competitive cycle" (doesn't fit their theory). Stalk and Hout themselves downplayed parts of the Honda–Yamaha story previously emphasized by Abbeglen and Stalk to make it fit their new "time-based" theory better (new products fit their new theory).

Pascale insisted that the Super Cub was inexpensive because its engine was small and lightweight—but the production costs of internal combustion engines do not vary so much by size. There is evidence that Honda did intend the Super Cub to be an important competitive weapon in the United States from the outset. Moreover, Pascale did not make clear just how un-innovative Honda's U.S. Super Cub strategy was. In Japan, Honda already made small machines in large numbers for one market, had already established a new type of distribution system through retail bicycle shops, which bypassed the traditional motorcycle distributors, and had already deliberately opened up a new market niche for small motorcycles based on ease of use while competitors focused on larger machines. Seen in this light, what Honda learned around 1960 was simply that the United States was more like Japan than initially anticipated—and receptive to the same strategy.

Finally, Pascale did not place Honda's U.S. entry in the context of the company's overall international strategy, a key element of which was already to "test its products against the best" (hence, Honda's early racing activities and very early exports). Senior management chose to focus Honda's meager foreign exchange on testing the U.S. market and imposed this strategy by overriding the strategy proposed (bottom-up, from the front line) by middle managers of concentrating internationalization on European and Asian markets. This context reduces the significance of "serendipity" and "bottom-up decision-making," confining them to specific, and not so remarkable, aspects of the strategy.

Quinn failed to distinguish the organization of basic research at Honda (fits his theory) from that of product development (doesn't fit). He dubiously asserted that Honda's production workers (rather than the specialist subsidiary set up for that purpose, Honda Engineering) designed production equipment. Quinn's application of the Pascale vision of Honda—bottom-up strategic learning—to all of Honda's processes left a firm renowned in the world of operations management for its original and tightly controlled operations and organization systems entirely devoid of these.

Mintzberg, like Pascale, dismissed all of Honda's systematic planning for U.S. market entry. He concluded that BCG's analysis had failed on the basis of statistics showing the respective success and failure of the Japanese and British motorcycle industries before and after publication of their report in 1975, thus committing the error of inferring causality from correlation with a single variable.

Hamel and Prahalad were still lauding the NSX supercar as an example of Honda's foresight some years after the car had turned out to be one of the company's late 1980s' Japanese "bubble economy" excesses. In fact, sales disintegrated with the collapse of the bubble economy in 1992, and output fell from 35 to 5 per day. And if Porsche's sales in the U.S. market did dip around 1990, the NSX's peak sales were only half of Porsche's lowest sales.

Hamel and Prahalad presented no evidence that Honda owed its success solely, or even largely, to stretch, leverage, and core competencies, offering only an implied correlation between Honda's focused form of corporate diversification and commercial success. Yet there has only been one strategically significant core competency diffusion at Honda to open new markets, the early 1960s' move into automobile production. Honda may sell an impressive list of other products powered by internal combustion engines, but the original motorcycles and automobiles account for over 90 percent of corporate turnover. Indeed, the actual significance of the core competency concept in Honda strategic thinking, as well as Honda's claimed closeness to its customers, is placed in considerable doubt by the company's conspicuous lateness in leveraging its competencies into the North American growth markets of the 1980s and 1990s (as above). Finally, it is impossible to draw valid inferences about the core competency theory by comparing Honda with Ford and General Motors, which differ from Honda on many other causally relevant dimensions, in particular their operations management systems. The appropriate stiff test would be to see how Honda has fared against the dominant player in the domestic Japanese market, especially Toyota, a company known to be very process—rather than product—driven. Honda has been restricted to a minor position in the domestic market, compared to Toyota's sustained 30 percent share.

KEEP IT SIMPLE . . . AND NEW!

Perhaps one cause of the continued opposing interpretations of Honda strategy, with facts selected to suit, is to be found in the binary divide between the root social science disciplines of strategic management thinking, with economics and sociology battling it out over Honda. Or explanation may extend more broadly to the essential "black or white" dualist philosophies that permeate much of Western culture. These factors may be relevant, but a more direct explanation of the doggedly dualist and contradictory presentations of Honda may be found closer to home, in the relationship between the strategy industry and its customers.

1. Buyers and sellers collude around "strategy bites."

   Some participants in the strategy industry seek relatively simple explanatory concepts to sell to their clients (clients are broadly defined, including not only organization leaders but students and practicing managers). Concepts need to be simple so that they can be more easily digested as strategy bites. Here there is collusion between the strategy thinkers and their clients to simplify and reduce explanations to one dimension.

2. Product differentiation encourages diametrically opposed strategy bites.

   The competitive process in the strategy industry, whether the direct competition of the strategy consultancy companies, or the less direct competition of the academics and other "gurus," requires continuous product innovation and differentiation. In the endeavor to differentiate strategy concepts as far as possible, in a manner consistent with Point 1, participants develop "revolutionary" ideas to overturn the ruling thinking. It makes strong sense to propose simple polar opposite approaches, which can be both revolutionary—to cure all ills—and no more difficult to grasp. Good advice to the budding business guru might, therefore, be to analyze the latest management fad, develop a theory based on its polar opposite, and launch this theory when growing dissatisfaction with the latest idea suggests that its short life cycle is waning.

3. Success stories endorse the strategy bites.

   "Success story" case studies are a vital vehicle for the communication—and commercialization—of the strategy bites. First, they embody and help communicate abstract new ideas, working as exemplars. Second, they legitimate and, indeed, endorse the quality of the new ideas if the latter can be said to explain the success (without too many unhelpful facts getting in the way). As Silbiger (1994: 340–341) notes, "History is often rewritten to suit the theories of strategic planners." Here it is rewritten to suit the new concepts the strategy industry has for sale.

   For the strategy industry, then, knowledge is about far more than a search for truth—it is a business, and a highly profitable one at that. The evolution of Honda mythology is the empirical evidence for some of the inner workings of the strategy industry in its frenetic search for new concepts that can guarantee success to the client.

HONDA'S LAST LAUGH?

There may be a final irony in the story of Honda and the strategy industry. There is considerable evidence to suggest that a significant characteristic of management thinking at Honda is a focus on the reconciliation of apparently contradictory conceptual dichotomies, and that this is a specific route to innovation. Novel solutions to management problems may be possible precisely by attempting to do what appears to some to be impossible. Elsewhere this capacity to manage apparently contradictory concepts and practices has been called Honda's "dichotomy-reconciling strategic capability" (Mair, 1998b). Strategic thinking at Honda may not be constrained by a dualist philosophy—or by strategy industry competition to sell concepts—that demands choice between learning or design, industry analysis or resource-based strategy, core capabilities or core competencies. It may, therefore, be high time to investigate the extent to which managers at Honda have been refining such a paradigm for many years—and thereby steering clear of, rather than endorsing, the ideas of some leading Western strategy writers. If this is the case, Honda executives will not have been losing sleep worrying that the strategy industry will divine and reveal to competitors the real recipe of Honda's success.

CHAPTER 6

Strategic Change

Strategy is technically about continuity rather than change: After all, it is concerned with imposing structured patterns of behavior on an organization, whether these take the form of intentions in advance that become deliberate strategies or actions after the fact that fall into the consistent patterns of emergent strategies. But to manage strategy today is frequently to manage change—to recognize when a shift of a strategic nature is possible, desirable, and necessary, and then to act—possibly putting into place mechanisms for continuous change.

Managing strategic change is generally far more difficult than it may at first appear. The need for reorientation occurs rather infrequently, and when it does, it means moving from a familiar domain into a less well-defined future where many of the old rules no longer apply. People must often abandon the roots of their past successes and develop entirely new skills and attitudes. This is clearly a demanding situation—and often, therefore, the most difficult challenge facing a manager.

The causes of such change also vary, from an ignored steady decline in performance, which ultimately demands a turnaround, to a sudden radical shift in a base technology that requires a reconceptualization of everything the organization does; from the gradual shift into the next stage of an organization's life cycle to the appearance of a new chief executive who wishes to put his or her particular stamp on the organization. The resulting strategic alignments may also take a variety of forms, from a shift of strategic position within the same industry to a whole new perspective in a new industry. Some changes require rapid transitions; others are accompanied by slower shifts. Each transition has its own management prerequisites and problems.

This chapter covers a number of these aspects of organizational change, presenting ideas on what evokes them in the first place, what forms they can take, and how they can and should be managed in differing situations.

We begin with an overview of the change process, excerpted from the Mintzberg, Ahlstrand, and Lampel book *Strategy Safari,* which was the basis for the "Reflections on the Strategy Process" readings about the ten schools in Chapter 1. Here, on strategy formation as a process of transformation, the authors provide a framework to think about the content of change (called the "change cube"), a map of the various popular techniques used to promote change in organizations, and a consideration of different programs that have been used to promote change in organizations, from rather "top down" to significantly "bottom up."

Our second reading on change considers the "Unsteady Pace of Organizational Evolution" in terms of distinct periods of convergence and upheaval. Related to the literature on organizational life cycles, its three authors, Michael Tushman, William Newman, and Elaine Romanelli, argue for what has also been referred to as a "quantum theory" of organizational change (Miller and Freisen, 1984). The essence of the argument is that organizations prefer to stay on course most of the time, accepting incremental changes to improve their strategies, processes, and structures. But periodically they must submit to dramatic shifts in these—"strategic revolutions" of a sort—to realign their overall orientation.

A very different perspective follows, from coauthor James Brian Quinn at the Dartmouth Tuck School and John Voyer of the University of Maine. Drawn from Quinn's book *Strategies for Change: Logical Incrementalism,* it develops a particular view of the strategy-making process based on intensive interviews in some of America's and Europe's best-known corporations. Planning does not capture the essence of strategy formation, according to Quinn and Voyer, although it does play an important role in developing new data and in confirming strategies derived in other ways. The traditional view of incrementalism does not fit observed behavior patterns either. The processes may seem randomly incremental on the surface, but a powerful logic underlies them. And, unlike the other incremental processes, these are not so much reactive as subtly proactive. Executives use incremental approaches to deal simultaneously with the informational, motivational, and political aspects of creating a strategy.

Above all, Quinn and Voyer depict strategy formation as a managed, interactive *learning* process in which the chief strategist gradually works out strategy in his or her own mind and orchestrates the organization's acceptance of it. In emphasizing the role of a central strategist—or small groups managing "subsystems" of strategy—Quinn and Voyer often seem close to Andrews's views. But the two differ markedly in other important respects. In their emphasis on the political and motivational dimensions of strategy, they may be closer to Wrapp, whose managers "don't make policy decisions." In fact, Quinn and Voyer attempt to integrate their views with the traditional one, noting that although the strategies themselves "emerge" from an incremental process, they have many of the characteristics of the highly deliberate ones of Andrews's strategists. This reading ends with practical advice on how to foster strategy making as an incremental process.

How do we reconcile this view of incrementalism with the previous view of quantum change, since both seem plausible? Perhaps they are not as contradictory as they may seem. Consider three dimensions: (1) the specific aspects of the strategy change process that each considers, (2) the time frames of the two viewpoints, and (3) the types of organizations involved. Quinn and Voyer's incrementalist view focuses on the processes going on in senior managers' minds as they think about new strategies. Because of the complexities involved, effective strategic thinking requires an incremental, interactive, learning process for all key players.

The quantum approach, in contrast, focuses not on the strategists' thinking as much as on the organization's actions—the strategies it actually pursues (referred to in Chapter 5 as the realized strategies of the organization). It is these that often seem to change in quantum fashion. It may be, therefore, that managers conceive and promote their intended strategies incrementally, but once that is accomplished they change their organizations in rapid, quantum fashion. But then again, each of these two approaches may also occur in its own situation. For example, quantum changes may more often take place in crisis situations, when external environments compress time frames often because of technological or regulatory shifts.

The last reading of the chapter, by Charles Baden-Fuller of the City University of London and John Stopford of the London Business School, presents a specific model of how a company can rejuvenate itself. The key challenge, these authors believe, lies in rebuilding corporate entrepreneurship, and they describe a four-step process of renewal, which starts with galvanizing the top team to create a commitment to change. In the next phase, the company must simplify both its businesses and its organization so as to create the base for the third step of building new skills, knowledge, and resources. Then, in the final step, the company can restart the growth engine by leveraging the new sources of advantage it has created. Over all, this model of change builds directly on the concept of core competencies and is quite consistent with Quinn and Voyer's views on strategies for change.

USING THE CASE STUDIES

The strategy process is more often than not about change rather than continuity. Thus, it would be difficult to single out a case in this book that is not about change. Nevertheless, some cases deal with change that is dramatic even by normal standards of strategy. Mountbatten and India focuses on the momentous change during the twilight of British rule in the Indian subcontinent. The politics of change so often evident in this case may be less visible but no less just as important in strategic change processes, as seen in the Agodonera del Plata case. The Sony and Lufthansa cases deal with strategic change faced repeatedly by two companies with global ambitions. Both the Tushman, Newman, and Romanelli reading and that by Baden-Fuller and Stopford are relevant to how these companies attempted to retain their vitality. And these readings are also relevant to the case of the London Free Press, a newspaper operating in a tradition-bound industry that must struggle to meet the challenge from new ways of distributing information. The Warner Brothers case describes a company that has fallen on hard times, in part because top managers developed a successful formula that outlived its usefulness. A comparison of these two companies should make for an interesting discussion, and the excerpt by Mintzberg, Ahlstrand, and Lampel from *Strategy Safari* describes frameworks that can be useful for doing this.

READING 6.1   TRANSFORMING ORGANIZATIONS*

BY HENRY MINTZBERG, BRUCE AHLSTRAND, AND JOSEPH LAMPEL

■ There is an enormous literature and consulting practice aimed at helping managers deal with major change in their organizations—turnaround, revitalization, downsizing, and the like. . . . Here, we seek to provide some overall structure for this work as well as some illustrations of it.

One word of caution before we begin. All of this is about "managed change." But a case can well be made. . . that this term is an oxymoron, that change should not be "managed," at least

---

*Reprinted with deletions from "Strategy Safari: A Guided Tour Through the Wilds of Strategic Management," Henry Mintzberg, Bruce Ahlstrand, and Joseph Lampel, New York: The Free Press, 1998.

when this word is used to mean forced, made to happen. Managers often claim that people in their organizations resist changing. True enough. But maybe that is because these people have for so long been *over*managed. The cure might actually prove to be just more of the cause. If so, then perhaps the best way to "manage" change is to allow for it to happen—to set up the conditions whereby people will follow their natural instincts to experiment and transform their behaviors. . . . "You deal with change by improving you. And then your time must come" (Clemmer, 1995).

CHANGING WHAT?

The first question is: *what* can be changed in an organization? One way to think of this is as a change cube, discussed in the accompanying box. It indicates what comprehensive change in an organization really means: it is about strategy and structure, ranging from the conceptual to the concrete and from highly formal behaviors to rather informal ones.

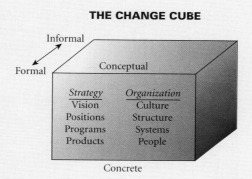

THE CHANGE CUBE

Change in organizations is greatly spoken about, yet all too often done in bits and pieces. We hear about turnaround, revitalization, cultural change, total quality management, venturing, new product development, and so on. Somehow all of this has to be put into perspective. The change cube is designed to do that.

The face of the cube shows two major dimensions of change. On the left side, change can be about *strategy*, the direction an organization is headed, and on the right, about *organization*, the state it is in. Both have to be considered when changing an organization.

Looking up and down the cube, both strategy and organization can range from the highly *conceptual*, or abstract, to the rather *concrete*, or tangible. On the strategy dimension, *vision* (or strategic perspective) is the most conceptual (rethinking, reconceiving), as is *culture* on the organization dimension (reenergizing, revitalizing). And going down the cube toward the more concrete, you can change, on the two sides, strategic *positions* (repositioning, reconfiguring) and organization *structure* (reorganizing, reducing), then *programs* and *systems* (reprogramming, reworking, reengineering), finally *products* and *people* (redesigning, retraining, replacing), which can also be thought of as changing *actions* on one side and *actors* on the other. Put differently, the broadest but most abstract things you can change in an organization are vision and culture, the most specific, actual products and real people (either by replacing the people who are there or by changing their behavior).

An organization can easily change a single product or an individual. But changing, say, a vision or a structure without changing anything else is silly, just an empty gesture. In other words, wherever you intervene on this cube, you have to change everything below. For example, it makes no sense to change structure without changing systems and people, or to change vision without rethinking strategic positions as well as redesigning programs and products.

Finally, all of this can range from the overt and formal, shown on the front face of the cube, to the rather more implicit and informal, shown on the back face. For example, a strategic position can be more deliberate (formal) or more emergent (informal), while people can be changed formally through education or informally through coaching and mentoring.

The point of this description is that serious change in organizations includes the entire cube: strategy and organization, from the most conceptual to the most concrete, informally as well as formally.

Now we can consider the methods of change. Needed here is some kind of *map*, to sort out and place into perspective the confusing array of approaches that have been developed over the years to change organizations. Figure 1 presents such a map, in which the methods of change are plotted on two dimensions. Along the top is a scale of the breadth of change, which runs from micro to macro. Micro change is focused within the organization: it might involve, for example, job redesign in a factory or the development of a new product. Macro change is aimed at the entire organization, for example, repositioning its place in the market or shifting all of its physical facilities.* David Hurst has expressed this in another way: "The *helmsman* manages change all the time. But the *navigator* changes course quite infrequently and then only as circumstances dictate. Changes in destination can be made by the *captain* even less frequently, for they require a total value change in the organization. And *discoverers* may find a new world only once in a lifetime" (unpublished material). . . .

On the horizontal scale of Figure 1, we suggest that there are three basic approaches to the process of change: planned change, driven change, and evolved change. *Planned* change is programmatic: there exists a system or set of procedures to be followed. These range from programs of quality improvement and training (micro) to ones of organizational development

FIGURE 1
MAP OF CHANGE
METHODS

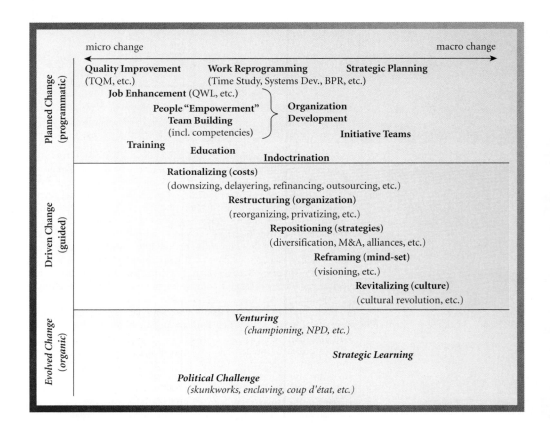

---

*Micro change tends to focus on the concrete level of the change cube, but it need not. One can change the vision of work design in a factory. Likewise macro change, while it often starts at the conceptual level, need not. The organization can shift all its physical facilities without any overarching vision, although that would hardly seem to be logical (which does not mean it never happens!).

and strategic planning (more macro). Consider, for example, this classic statement of organization development:

> Organizational development is an effort (1) *planned*, (2) *organization-wide*, and (3) *managed* from the *top*, to (4) increase organization *effectiveness* and *health* through (5) *planned interventions* in the organization's "processes" using *behavioral science* knowledge. (Beckhard, 1969: 9; italics in original)

Driven change is guided: a single individual or small group, usually in an influential position of authority, oversees the change and ensures that it happens. Here we find all the currently popular (mostly) "re" words, ranging from rationalization through restructuring to revitalizing. Doz and Thanheiser (1996) have referred to various among these as changing the strategic context, the organizational context, and the emotional context (culture). The sequence of these driven changes shown in the diagram, reading diagonally from more micro and closer to planned to more macro and closer to evolved, include changing operating costs, organizational structure, strategic positions, managerial mindset, and overall culture. . . .

Finally, *evolved* change is organic: it kind of happens, or at least is guided by people outside positions of significant authority, often in obscure places in the organization. Unlike the first two approaches, which are driven, or "managed" in some sense, whether more formally by procedures or less formally by managers, this third approach to change is neither managed nor even under the firm control of managers. More to the micro side, we show political challenge (which can, of course, be rather macro too, as in the coup d'état discussed in the power school), in the middle we see venturing, and on the more macro side, we find strategic learning (the last two discussed in the learning school). . . .

PROGRAMS OF COMPREHENSIVE CHANGE

A manager can simply pick something and try to change it: enhance the training of the sales force, for example, or reorganize the research laboratory. Most change is of this *piecemeal* type; it goes on all the time, here and there. Indeed Tom Peters has long been a fan of such change, which he has called "chunking." Don't get bogged down, he suggests, just grab something and change it.

The change cube suggests, however, that this probably works better at the more concrete (and micro) level than the conceptual (and macro) end. You can retrain a group of workers or reorganize one department, perhaps, but you cannot reposition strategy or change culture without making a lot of other associated changes. Indeed, "changing culture" alone is just a lot of empty words: as noted earlier, culture is not changed at all when nothing else changes.

So there has arisen a great deal of literature and consulting practice on massive programs of comprehensive change, namely *transformation*. These propose how to combine the various methods of change into logical sequences to "turn around" or "renew" an organization. (Turnaround implies quick, dramatic revolution; renewal, a slower building up of comprehensive change.) But this is a confusing body of work: just about every writer and consulting firm has his, her, or its own formula for success. There is no consensus at all as to what works best, although there are certainly periodic fads—galore. But all this seems to reveal mainly what *doesn't* work—namely last year's fad.

Here, then, as everywhere else, there are no magic formulas. Just as chunking can be suboptimal, so too can renewing be excessive. Despite all the current hype about change, not all organizations need to change everything all the time. The word for that is "anarchy." The trick is to balance change with continuity: to achieve change when and where necessary while maintaining order. Embracing the new while sweeping out the old may be the very modern thing to do, but it is generally a lot more effective—as well as difficult—to find ways to integrate the best of the new with most useful of the old. Too many organizations these days are subjected to too much ill-conceived change. Just because there is a new chief executive or some new fad does not mean that everything has to be thrown into turmoil.

Nevertheless, there are times when an organization has to be changed in a serious, comprehensive, way. Then the trick for management is to figure out where it can intervene, what it can change and leave others to change, when, how fast, and in what sequence. Start small and build up, or do something dramatic? Begin by replacing people, reconceiving vision, or redoing the chart? After that, concentrate on strategy, structure, culture, or shareholder value? Change everything at once or "chunk" along?

But might these questions set the wrong context: maybe management should just create the conditions for change and then let it happen? Perhaps it should lay off altogether. Maybe the best change begins on the ground, in the corner of some factory or a visit to some customers and then flows from there. Must change always end at the "bottom" after having been driven by the "top"? What about ending at the top after the people in touch with the customers have finally convinced the management of the problems? Or maybe the whole thing has to be driven organically from the outside?

It always seems so terribly confusing, especially when one considers all the evidence about resistance to change in organizations. Yet some do change. The French philosopher Alain provides hope with his comment that "All change seems impossible. But once accomplished, it is the state you are no longer in that seems impossible." When you do get there, "How did we ever tolerate that?" may be the reaction. With this in mind, let us sample some of the frameworks for comprehensive change.

In 1995, three McKinsey consultants, Dickhout, Denham, and Blackwell, published an interesting article on change, outlining six basic "strategies" used by the 25 companies studied:

- *Evolutionary/institution building:* a gradual reshaping of the "company's values, top-level structures and performance measures so that line managers could drive the change."
- *Jolt and refocus:* to "shake up a gridlocked power structure," leaders "in one fell swoop . . . delayered top management, defined new business units, and redesigned management processes."
- *Follow the leader:* for immediate results, leaders "initiated major changes from the top," for example, by selling off weak businesses, "while removing only the most critical organizational bottlenecks."
- *Multifront focus:* in this case, "change is driven by task teams whose targets are more wide ranging"—cost reduction, sales stimulation, etc.
- *Systematic redesign:* again task teams drive the process to boost performance, but "core process redesign and other organizational changes tend to be planned in parallel."
- *Unit-level mobilizing:* "change leaders empower task teams to tap into the pent-up ideas of middle managers and front-line employees." (102–104)

These describe mainly initial or focal activities. But a key question for many people working in this area is how the different activities should be sequenced over time to effect a major transformation. Let us consider first top-down change and then bottom-up.

TOP-DOWN CHANGE?

Perhaps most popular is the approach stimulated by the changes at General Electric under the leadership of Jack Welch over the past decade and a half. Tichy and Sherman (1993) have described these as a "three-act drama": *awakening, envisioning,* and *rearchitecturing,* as shown in Figure 2.

David Ulrich, who has also worked closely with Welch, in an article with Richard Beatty (1991) characterized this a bit differently. They describe a five-step process (which may occur simultaneously as well as in sequence), including both the "hardware" of the organization (strategy, structure, systems) and its "software" (employee behavior and mindset). Their description begins with *restructuring,* by which they mean downsizing and delayering, followed by *bureaucracy bashing,* to "get rid of unnecessary reports, approvals, meetings, measures," and the like. Then there is a stage of *employee empowerment,* which gives rise to one of

FIGURE 2
TRANSFORMATIONAL LEADERSHIP: A THREE-ACT DRAMA
Source: From Tichy and Sherman (1993: 305).

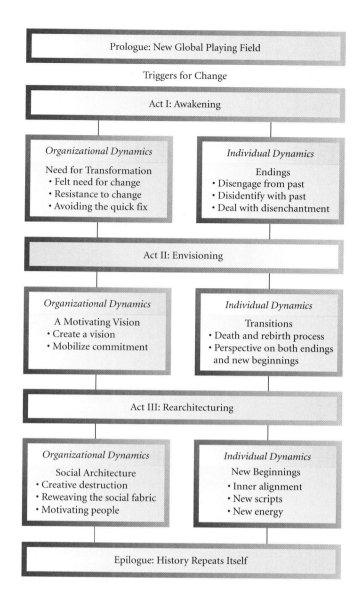

continuous improvement, before, as "an outgrowth of the other four," the culture is fundamentally changed (1991:22, 24 29). This is illustrated in Figure 3.

Baden-Fuller and Stopford's "crescendo model of rejuvenation" is similar:

1. Galvanize: create a top team dedicated to renewal.
2. Simplify: cut unnecessary and confusing complexity.
3. Build: develop new capabilities.
4. Leverage: maintain momentum and stretch the advantages. (1992)

Doz and Thanheiser (1996) noted in a survey of forty companies that almost all included in their transformational efforts portfolio restructuring, downsizing and outsourcing, benchmarking, and some sort of process improvement and quality management efforts. They found "periods of intense activity where high energy . . . [was] typically triggered by various 'turning points' [or 'crucible'] events such as retreats, workshops, or other employee-manager

FIGURE 3
A PROCESS FOR
REENGINEERING
MATURE
ORGANIZATIONS
Source: From Beatty and
Ulrich (1991: 25).

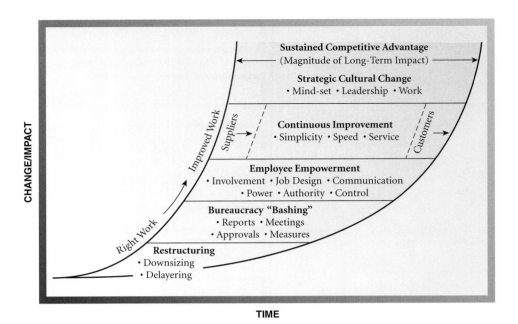

gatherings" (7), as in General Electric's "work out/team meetings." In the "more effective, longer term" transformations, they describe the following pattern:

- "from internal to external focus": first improve efficiency, then create new opportunities.
- "from top-down to delegated action": "the inertia breaking process was usually strongly driven from the top" even though "the transformation was sometimes piloted in a subunit . . . before being implemented in the whole company"; subsequent activities were often "at the initiative of subunits."
- "from emotion and intellect to organization": "in nearly all the cases . . . the initial transformation cycle was driven by a new strategic understanding that was brought into focus through an emotional process (part and parcel of 'crucible' events), then later reflected in more extensive, subtle, and multifaced changes in organizational context." (10–11)

In effect, the chief executive took some quick initial strategic actions, such as divesting some business or replacing key executives, but "winning the hearts" of others was key to the next step. These "changes in the emotional context permitted further, more subtle changes in strategic context," as well as in the organizational context, so that the chief executive could "let go" to allow for more "decentralized emergent initiatives."

In summary, over time the nature of the transformation process kept alternating from cycle to cycle between *bursts* of energy concentration and *periods* of energy diffusion, to smaller, less visible pulsations. Successful transformation processes shifted from corporate upheavals to ongoing learning and renewal. (11)

BOTTOM-UP CHANGE?

The above has been the view very much from strategic management: top-down, at least initially, leader-driven, and strategic. But, stemming from earlier work in "organizational development," others have described transformation as far more of a bottom-up process, in which small changes taken within pockets of the organization drive the overall change process. Change to these people is an exploratory journey rather than a predetermined trajectory, more of a learning process than a planned or driven one. Yet if it works, it can end up being significantly strategic.

This is the spirit of a 1990 article by Beer et al. in the *Harvard Business Review*, entitled "Why Change Programs Don't Produce Change." After discussing "the fallacy of programmatic change," they discuss the "more successful transformations" they studied that "usually

BOX 1

"Six Steps to Effective Change" for managers at the business unit or plant level

(from Beer, Eisenstat, and Spector, 1990: 161–164)

1. *Mobilize commitment to change through joint diagnosis of business problems.* . . . By helping people develop a shared diagnosis of what is wrong in an organization and what can and must be improved, a general manager [of a unit] mobilizes the initial commitment that is necessary to begin the change process. . . .

2. *Develop a shared vision of how to organize and manage for competitiveness.* Once a core group of people is committed to a particular analysis of the problem, the general manager can lead employees toward a task-aligned vision of the organization that defines new roles and responsibilities. . . .

3. *Foster consensus for the new vision, competence to enact it, and cohesion to move it along.* . . .

4. *Spread revitalization to all departments without pushing it from the top.* . . . The temptation to force newfound insights on the rest of the organization can be great, particularly when rapid change is needed, but it would be the same mistake that senior managers make when they try to push programmatic change throughout a company. It short-circuits the change process. It's better to let each department "reinvent the wheel"—that is, to find its own way to the new organization. . . .

5. *Institutionalize revitalization through formal policies, systems, and structures.* . . . The new approach has to become entrenched. . . .

6. *Monitor and adjust strategies in response to problems in the revitalization process.* The purpose of change is to create . . . a learning organization capable of adapting to a changing competitive environment. . . . Some might say that this is the general manager's responsibility. But monitoring the change process needs to be shared. . . .

BOX 2

TOP-DOWN TRANSFORMATION

"Eight Steps to Transforming Your Corporation" for its overall managers

(from Kotter, 1995: 61)

1. *Establishing a sense of urgency:* examining market and competitive realities; identifying and discussing crises, potential crises, or major opportunities.

2. *Forming a powerful guiding coalition:* assembling a group with enough power to lead the change effort; encouraging the group to work together as a team.

3. *Creating a vision:* creating a vision to help direct the change effort; developing strategies for achieving that vision.

4. *Commnicating the vision:* using every vehicle possible to communicate the new vision and strategies; teaching new behaviors by the example of the guiding coalition.

5. *Empowering others to act on the vision:* getting rid of obstacles to change; changing systems or structures that seriously undermine the vision; encouraging risk taking and nontraditional ideas, activities, and actions.

6. *Planning for and creating short-term wins:* planning for visible performance improvements; creating those improvements; recognizing and rewarding employees involved in the improvements.

7. *Consolidating improvements and producing still more changes:* using increased credibility to change systems, structures, and policies that don't fit the vision; hiring, promoting, and developing employees who can implement the vision; reinvigorating the process with new projects, themes, and change agents.

8. *Institutionalizing new approaches:* articulating the connections between the new behaviors and corporation success; developing the means to ensure leadership development and succession.

started at the periphery of the corporation in a few plants and divisions far from corporate headquarters" and were "led by the general managers of those units, not by the CEO or corporate staff people" (159). The best chief executives created "a market for change," but let others decide how to initiate changes and then used the most successfully revitalized units as models for the rest of the company. The accompanying box presents their "Six Steps to Effective Change" for the managers of such units.

Opposite this box we juxtapose another, from an article that appeared a few years later in the *Harvard Business Review*, with a remarkably similar title, "Leading Change: Why Transformation Efforts Fail." This was written by John Kotter, a colleague of Beer, in the same department at the Harvard Business School. But Kotter's "Eight Steps to Transforming Your Corporation" are very much top-down. "Change, by definition," Kotter wrote, "requires creating a new system, which in turn always demands leadership. [The start of] a renewal process typically goes nowhere until enough real leaders are promoted or hired into senior-level jobs" (1995:60).

So should the change process be top-down or bottom-up? If you are to believe the experts, then you will have to flip a coin. Or else try to understand what is broken in your own organization before you decide how to fix it. There is no formula for transforming any organization, and that includes the very notion that the organization needs transforming in the first place.

In fact, the McKinsey consultants, Dickhout and colleagues, whose set of change strategies were presented [earlier in] this discussion, are among the few in this literature who have made the welcome claim that which approach you use *depends* on your organization's goals, needs, and capabilities. In their study, "each transformation was a unique response to a specific set of problems and opportunities.... The leader appeared to have 'cracked a code' embedded within the organization ... [so that] energy was released and channeled to improve performance ... " (20). Wise words to end discussion of a literature and a practice that has not always been terribly wise.

READING 6.2 CONVERGENCE AND UPHEAVAL: MANAGING THE UNSTEADY PACE OF ORGANIZATIONAL EVOLUTION*

BY MICHAEL L. TUSHMAN, WILLIAM H. NEWMAN, AND ELAINE ROMANELLI

■ A snug fit of external opportunity, company strategy, and internal structure is a hallmark of successful companies. The real test of executive leadership, however, is in maintaining this alignment in the race of changing competitive conditions.

Consider the Polaroid or Caterpillar corporations. Both firms virtually dominated their respective industries for decades, only to be caught off guard by major environmental changes. The same strategic and organizational factors which were so effective for decades became the seeds of complacency and organization decline.

Recent studies of companies over long periods show that the most successful firms maintain a workable equilibrium for several years (or decades), but are also able to initiate and carry out sharp, widespread changes (referred to here as reorientations) when their environments shift. Such upheaval may bring renewed vigor to the enterprise. Less successful firms, on the other hand, get stuck in a particular pattern. The leaders of these firms either do not see the need for reorientation or they are unable to carry through the necessary frame-breaking changes. While not all reorientations succeed, those organizations which do not initiate reorientations as environments shift underperform.

*Copyright © 1986, by the Regents of the University of California. Excerpted from the *California Management Review*, Vol. 29, No. 1. By permission of the Regents.

This reading focuses on reasons why for long periods most companies make only incremental changes, and why they then need to make painful, discontinuous, system-wide shifts. We are particularly concerned with the role of executive leadership in managing this pattern of convergence punctuated by upheaval. . . .

The task of managing incremental change, or convergence, differs sharply from managing frame-breaking change. Incremental change is compatible with the existing structure of a company and is reinforced over a period of years. In contrast, frame-breaking change is abrupt, painful to participants, and often resisted by the old guard. Forging these new strategy-structure-people-process consistencies and laying the basis for the next period of incremental change calls for distinctive skills.

Because the future health, and even survival, of a company or business unit is at stake, we need to take a closer look at the nature and consequences of convergent change and of differences imposed by frame-breaking change. We need to explore when and why these painful and risky revolutions interrupt previously successful patterns, and whether these discontinuities can be avoided and/or initiated prior to crisis. Finally, we need to examine what managers can and should do to guide their organizations through periods of convergence and upheaval over time. . . .

The following discussion is based on the history of companies in many different industries, different countries, both large and small organizations, and organizations in various stages of their product class's life-cycle. We are dealing with a widespread phenomenon—not just a few dramatic sequences. Our research strongly suggests that the convergence/upheaval pattern occurs within departments at the business-unit level . . . and at the corporate level of analysis. . . . The problem of managing both convergent periods and upheaval is not just for the CEO, but necessarily involves general managers as well as functional managers.

PATTERNS IN ORGANIZATIONAL EVOLUTION: CONVERGENCE AND UPHEAVAL

BUILDING ON STRENGTH: PERIODS OF CONVERGENCE

Successful companies wisely stick to what works well. . . .

. . . convergence starts out with an effective dovetailing of strategy, structure, people, and processes. . . . The formal system includes decisions about grouping and linking resources as well as planning and control systems, rewards and evaluation procedures, and human resource management systems. The informal system includes core values, beliefs, norms, communication patterns, and actual decision-making and conflict resolution patterns. It is the whole fabric of structure, systems, people, and processes which must be suited to company strategy (Nadler and Tushman, 1986).

As the fit between strategy, structure, people, and processes is never perfect, convergence is an ongoing process characterized by incremental change. Over time, in all companies studied, two types of converging changes were common: fine-tuning and incremental adaptations.

- *Converging change: Fine-tuning*—Even with good strategy-structure-process fits, well-run companies seek even better ways of exploiting (and defending) their missions. Such effort typically deals with one or more of the following:
  - *Refining* policies, methods, and procedures.
  - Creating *specialized units and linking mechanisms* to permit increased volume and increased attention to unit quality and cost.
  - *Developing personnel* especially suited to the present strategy—through improved selection and training, and tailoring reward systems to match strategic thrusts.
  - Fostering individual and group *commitments* to the company mission and to the excellence of one's own department.
  - Promoting *confidence* in the accepted norms, beliefs, and myths.
  - *Clarifying* established roles, power, status, dependencies, and allocation mechanism.

The fine-tuning fills out and elaborates the consistencies between strategy, structure, people, and processes. These incremental changes lead to an ever more interconnected (and therefore more stable) social system. Convergent periods fit the happy, stick-with-a-winner situations romanticized by Peters and Waterman (1982).

■ *Converging change: Incremental adjustments to environmental shifts*—In addition to fine-tuning changes, minor shifts in the environment will call for some organizational response. Even the most conservative of organizations expect, even welcome, small changes which do not make too many waves.

A popular expression is that almost any organization can tolerate a "ten percent change." At any one time, only a few changes are being made; but these changes are still compatible with the prevailing structures, systems, and processes. Examples of such adjustments are an expansion in sales territory, a shift in emphasis among products in the product line, or improved processing technology in production.

The usual process of making changes of this sort is well known: wide acceptance of the need for change, openness to possible alternatives, objective examination of the pros and cons of each plausible alternative, participation of those directly affected in the preceding analysis, a market test or pilot operation where feasible, time to learn the new activities, established role models, known rewards for positive success, evaluation, and refinement.

The role of executive leadership during convergent periods is to reemphasize mission and core values and to delegate incremental decisions to middle-level managers. Note that the uncertainty created for people affected by such changes is well within tolerable limits. Opportunity is provided to anticipate and learn what is new, while most features of the structure remain unchanged.

The overall system adapts, but it is not transformed.

Converging Change: Some Consequences

For those companies whose strategies fit environmental conditions, convergence brings about better and better effectiveness. Incremental change is relatively easy to implement and ever more optimizes the consistencies between strategy, structure, people, and processes. At AT&T, for example, the period between 1913 and 1980 was one of ever more incremental change to further bolster the "Ma Bell" culture, systems, and structure all in service of developing the telephone network.

Convergent periods are, however, a double-edged sword. As organizations grow and become more successful, they develop internal forces for stability. Organizational structures and systems become so interlinked that they only allow compatible changes. Further, over time, employees develop habits, patterned behaviors begin to take on values (e.g., "service is good"), and employees develop a sense of competence in knowing how to get work done within the system. These self-reinforcing patterns of behavior, norms, and values contribute to increased organizational momentum and complacency and, over time, to a sense of organizational history. This organizational history—epitomized by common stories, heroes, and standards—specifies "how we work here" and "what we hold important here."

This organizational momentum is profoundly functional as long as the organization's strategy is appropriate. The Ma Bell . . . culture, structure, and systems—and associated internal momentum—were critical to [the] organization's success. However, if (and when) strategy must change, this momentum cuts the other way. Organizational history is a source of tradition, precedent, and pride which are, in turn, anchors to the past. A proud history often restricts vigilant problem solving and may be a source of resistance to change.

When faced with environmental threat, organizations with strong momentum

■ may not register the threat due to organization complacency and/or stunted external vigilance (e.g., the automobile or steel industries), or

- if the threat is recognized, the response is frequently heightened conformity to the status quo and/or increased commitment to "what we do best."

For example, the response of dominant firms to technological threat is frequently increased commitment to the obsolete technology (e.g., telegraph/telephone; vacuum tube/transistor; core/semiconductor memory). A paradoxical result of long periods of success may be heightened organizational complacency, decreased organizational flexibility, and a stunted ability to learn.

Converging change is a double-edged sword. Those very social and technical consistencies which are key sources of success may also be the seeds of failure if environments change. The longer the convergent periods, the greater these internal forces for stability. This momentum seems to be particularly accentuated in those most successful firms in a product class . . . in historically regulated organizations . . . or in organizations that have been traditionally shielded from competition. . . .

ON FRAME-BREAKING CHANGE
Forces Leading to Frame-Breaking Change
What, then, leads to frame-breaking change? Why defy tradition? Simply stated, frame-breaking change occurs in response to or, better yet, in anticipation of major environmental changes—changes which require more than incremental adjustments. The need for discontinuous change springs from one or a combination of the following:

- *Industry discontinuities*—Sharp changes in legal, political, or technological conditions shift the basis of competition within industries. *Deregulation* has dramatically transformed the financial services and airlines industries. *Substitute product technologies* . . . or *substitute process technologies* . . . may transform the bases of competition within industries. Similarly, the emergence of industry standards, or *dominant designs* (such as the DC-3, IBM 360, or PDP-8) signal a shift in competition away from product innovation and towards increased process innovation. Finally, *major economic changes* (e.g., oil crises) and *legal shifts* (e.g., patent protection in biotechnology or trade/regulator barriers in pharmaceuticals or cigarettes) also directly affect bases of competition.
- *Product life-cycle shifts*—Over the course of a product class life cycle, different strategies are appropriate. In the emergence phase of a product class, competition is based on product innovation and performance, where in the maturity stage, competition centers on cost, volume, and efficiency. Shifts in patterns of demand alter key factors for success. For example, the demand and nature of competition for mini-computers, cellular telephones, wide-body aircraft, and bowling alley equipment was transformed as these products gained acceptance and their product classes evolved. Powerful international competition may compound these forces.
- *Internal company dynamics*—Entwined with these external forces are breaking points within the firm. Sheer size may require a basically new management design. For example, few inventor-entrepreneurs can tolerate the formality that is linked with large volume. . . . Key people die. Family investors may become more concerned with their inheritance taxes than with company development. Revised corporate portfolio strategy may sharply alter the role and resources assigned to business units or functional areas. Such pressures, especially when coupled with external changes, may trigger frame-breaking change.

Scope of Frame-Breaking Change
Frame-breaking change is driven by shifts in business strategy. As strategy shifts so too must structure, people, and organizational processes. Quite unlike convergent change, frame-breaking reforms involve discontinuous changes throughout the organization. These bursts of change do not reinforce the existing system and are implemented rapidly. . . . Frame-breaking changes are revolutionary changes *of* the system as opposed to incremental changes *in* the system.

The following features are usually involved in frame-breaking change:

- *Reformed mission and core values*—A strategy shift involves a new definition of company mission. Entering or withdrawing from an industry may be involved; at least the way the company expects to be outstanding is altered. . . .
- *Altered power and status*—Frame-breaking change always alters the distribution of power. Some groups lose in the shift while others gain. . . . These dramatically altered power distributions reflect shifts in bases of competition and resource allocation. A new strategy must be backed up with a shift in the balance of power and status.
- *Reorganization*—A new strategy requires a modification in structure, systems, and procedures. As strategic requirements shift, so too must the choice of organization form. A new direction calls for added activity in some areas and less in others. Changes in structure and systems are means to ensure that this reallocation of effort takes place. New structures and revised roles deliberately break business-as-usual behavior.
- *Revised interaction patterns*—The way people in the organization work together has to adapt during frame-breaking change. As strategy is different, new procedures, work flows, communication networks, and decision-making patterns must be established. With these changes in work flows and procedures must also come revised norms, informal decision-making/conflict-resolution procedures, and informal roles.
- *New executives*—Frame-breaking change also involves new executives, usually brought in from outside the organization (or business unit) and placed in key managerial positions. Commitment to the new mission, energy to overcome prevailing inertia, and freedom from prior obligations are all needed to refocus the organization. A few exceptional members of the old guard may attempt to make this shift, but habits and expectations of their associations are difficult to break. New executives are most likely to provide both the necessary drive and an enhanced set of skills more appropriate for the new strategy. While the overall number of executive changes is usually relatively small, these new executives have substantial symbolic and substantive effects on the organization. . . .

Why All at Once?

Frame-breaking change is revolutionary in that the shifts reshape the entire nature of the organization. Those more effective examples of frame-breaking change were implemented rapidly. . . . It appears that a piecemeal approach to frame-breaking changes gets bogged down in politics, individual resistance to change, and organizational inertia. . . . Frame-breaking change requires discontinuous shifts in strategy, structure, people, and processes concurrently—or at least in a short period of time. Reasons for rapid, simultaneous implementation include:

- *Synergy* within the new structure can be a powerful aid. New executives with a fresh mission, working in a redesigned organization with revised norms and values, backed up with power and status, provide strong reinforcement. The pieces of the revitalized organization pull together, as opposed to piecemeal change where one part of the new organization is out of synch with the old organization.
- *Pockets of resistance* have a chance to grow and develop when frame-breaking change is implemented slowly. The new mission, shifts in organization, and other frame-breaking changes upset the comfortable routines and precedent. Resistance to such fundamental change is natural. If frame-breaking change is implemented slowly, then individuals have a greater opportunity to undermine the changes and organizational inertia works to further stifle fundamental change.
- Typically, there is a *pent-up need for change*. During convergent periods, basic adjustments are postponed. Boat rocking is discouraged. Once constraints are relaxed, a variety of desirable improvements press for attention. The exhilaration and momentum of a fresh effort (and new team) make difficult moves more acceptable. Change is in fashion.

- Frame-breaking change is an inherently *risky and uncertain venture*. The longer the implementation period, the greater the period of uncertainty and instability. The most effective frame-breaking changes initiate the new strategy, structure, processes, and systems rapidly and begin the next period of stability and convergent change. The sooner fundamental uncertainty is removed, the better the chances of organizational survival and growth. While the pacing of change is important, the overall time to implement frame-breaking change will be contingent on the size and age of the organization.

Patterns in Organization Evolution

This historical approach to organization evolution focuses on convergent periods punctuated by reorientation—discontinuous, organizationwide upheavals. The most effective firms take advantage of relatively long convergent periods. These periods of incremental change build on and take advantage of organization inertia. Frame-breaking change is quite dysfunctional if the organization is successful and the environment is stable. If, however, the organization is performing poorly and/or if the environment changes substantially, frame-breaking change is the only way to realign the organization with its competitive environment. Not all reorientations will be successful. . . . However, inaction in the face of performance crisis and/or environmental shifts is a certain recipe for failure.

Because reorientations are so disruptive and fraught with uncertainty, the more rapidly they are implemented, the more quickly the organization can reap the benefits of the following convergent period. High-performing firms initiate reorientations when environmental conditions shift and implement these reorientations rapidly. . . . Low-performing organizations either do not reorient or reorient all the time as they root around to find an effective alignment with environmental conditions. . . .

EXECUTIVE LEADERSHIP AND ORGANIZATION EVOLUTION

Executive leadership plays a key role in reinforcing systemwide momentum during convergent periods and in initiating and implementing bursts of change that characterize strategic reorientations. The nature of the leadership task differs sharply during these contrasting periods of organization evolution.

During convergent periods, the executive team focuses on *maintaining* congruence and fit within the organization. Because strategy, structure, processes, and systems are fundamentally sound, the myriad of incremental substantive decisions can be delegated to middle-level management, where direct expertise and information resides. The key role for executive leadership during convergent periods is to reemphasize strategy, mission, and core values and to keep a vigilant eye on external opportunities and/or threats.

Frame-breaking change, however, requires direct executive involvement in all aspects of the change. Given the enormity of the change and inherent internal forces for stability, executive leadership must be involved in the specification of strategy, structure, people, and organizational processes *and* in the development of implementation plans. . . .

The most effective executives in our studies foresaw the need for major change. They recognized the external threats and opportunities, and took bold steps to deal with them. . . . Indeed, by acting before being forced to do so, they had more time to plan their transitions.

Such visionary executive teams are the exceptions. Most frame-breaking change is postponed until a financial crisis forces drastic action. The momentum, and frequently the success, of convergent periods breeds reluctance to change. . . .

. . . most frame-breaking upheavals are managed by executives brought in from outside the company. The Columbia research program finds that externally recruited executives are more than three times more likely to initiate frame-breaking change than existing executive teams. Frame-breaking change was coupled with CEO succession in more than 80% of the cases. . . .

There are several reasons why a fresh set of executives is typically used in company transformations. The new executive team brings different skills and a fresh perspective. Often they arrive with a strong belief in the new mission. Moreover, they are unfettered by prior commitments linked to the status quo; instead, this new top team symbolizes the need for change. Excitement of a new challenge adds to the energy devoted to it.

We should note that many of the executives who could not, or would not, implement frame-breaking change went on to be quite successful in other organizations. . . . The stimulation of a fresh start and of jobs matched to personal competence applies to individuals as well as to organizations.

Although typical patterns for the when and who of frame-breaking change are clear—wait for a financial crisis and then bring in an outsider, along with a revised executive team, to revamp the company—this is clearly less than satisfactory for a particular organization. Clearly, some companies benefit from transforming themselves before a crisis forces them to do so, and a few exceptional executives have the vision and drive to reorient a business which they nurtured during its preceding period of convergence. The vital tasks are to manage incremental change during convergent periods; to have the vision to initiate and implement frame-breaking change prior to the competition; and to mobilize an executive team which can initiate and implement both kinds of change.

CONCLUSION

. . . Managers should anticipate that when environments change sharply:

- Frame-breaking change cannot be avoided. These discontinuous organizational changes will either be made proactively or initiated under crisis/turnaround conditions.
- Discontinuous changes need to be made in strategy, structure, people, and processes concurrently. Tentative change runs the risk of being smothered by individual, group, and organizational inertia.
- Frame-breaking change requires direct executive involvement in all aspects of the change, usually bolstered with new executives from outside the organization.
- There are no patterns in the sequence of frame-breaking changes, and not all strategies will be effective. Strategy and, in turn, structure, systems, and processes must meet industry-specific competitive issues.

Finally, our historical analysis of organizations highlights the following issues for executive leadership:

- Need to manage for balance, consistency, or fit during convergent period.
- Need to be vigilant for environmental shifts in order to anticipate the need for frame-breaking change.
- Need to manage effectively incremental as well as frame-breaking change.
- Need to build (or rebuild) a top team to help initiate and implement frame-breaking change.
- Need to develop core values which can be used as an anchor as organizations evolve through frame-breaking changes (e.g., IBM, Hewlett-Packard).
- Need to develop and use organizational history as a way to infuse pride in an organization's past and for its future.
- Need to bolster technical, social, and conceptual skills with visionary skills. Visionary skills add energy, direction, and excitement so critical during frame-breaking change. . . .

Effective organizations seem to do both, but that raises a major problem in the strategy process: the middle managers may get caught in the middle, between these two. How can one reconcile the two opposing pressures? The Andersen Consulting (Europe), The Transformation of AT&T, Microsoft Corporation (B), SAS and the European Airline Industry, and Nintendo of America cases give some indication of the issues and how managers may deal with them. In the Sayles reading of Chapter 8, we shall return to this important issue.

BY JAMES BRIAN QUINN AND JOHN VOYER

THE LOGIC OF LOGICAL INCREMENTALISM

Strategy change processes in well-managed major organizations rarely resemble the rational-analytical systems touted in the literature. Instead, strategic change processes are typically fragmented, evolutionary, and intuitive. Real strategy *evolves* as internal decisions and external events flow together to create a new, widely shared consensus for action.

THE FORMAL SYSTEMS PLANNING APPROACH

There is a strong literature stating which actors *should* be included in a systematically planned strategy. This systems-planning approach focuses on quantitative factors, and underemphasizes qualitative, organizational, and power factors. Systems planning *can* make a contribution, but it should be just one building block in the continuous stream of events that creates organizational strategy.

THE POWER-BEHAVIORAL APPROACH

Another body of literature has enhanced our understanding of *multiple goal structures*, the *politics* of strategic decisions, *bargaining* and *negotiation* processes, *satisficing* in decision making, the role of *coalitions*, and the practice of *"muddling"* in public sector management. The shortcomings of this body of literature are that it has typically been far-removed from strategy making, it has ignored the contributions of useful analytical approaches, and it has offered few practical recommendations for the strategist.

SUMMARY FINDINGS FROM STUDY OF ACTUAL CHANGE PROCESSES

Recognizing the strengths and weaknesses of each of these approaches, the change processes in ten major organizations were documented. Several important findings emerged from these investigations.

- Neither approach above adequately describes strategy processes.
- Effective strategies tend to emerge incrementally and opportunistically, as subsystems of organizational activity (e.g., acquisitions, divestitures, major reorganizations, even formal plans) are blended into a coherent pattern.

---

*Originally published in the collegiate edition of *The Strategy Process*, Prentice Hall, 1994. Based on James Brian Quinn, "Strategic Change: Logical Incrementalism," *Sloan Management Review,* Fall 1978, pp. 1–21, and James Brian Quinn, "Managing Strategies Incrementally," O*mega: The International Journal of Management Science,* 1982, drawn from his book *Strategies for Change: Logical Incrementalism* (Irwin, 1980).

- The logic behind this process is so powerful that it may be the best approach to recommend for strategy formation in large companies.
- Because of cognitive and process limits, this approach must be managed and linked together in a way best described as "logical incrementalism."
- Such incrementalism is not "muddling." It is a purposeful, effective, active management technique for improving and integrating *both* the analytical and behavioral aspects of strategy formation.

CRITICAL STRATEGIC ISSUES

Though "hard data" decisions dominate the literature, there are various "soft" kinds of changes that affect strategy:

- The design of an organization's structure
- The characteristic management style in the firm
- A firm's external (especially government) relations
- Acquisitions, divestitures, or divisional control issues
- A firm's international posture and relationships
- An organization's innovative capabilities
- The effects of an organization's growth on the motivation of its personnel
- Value and expectation changes, and their effects on worker and professional relationships in the organization
- Technological changes that affect the organization

Top executives made several important points about these kinds of changes. Few of these issues lend themselves to quantitative modeling or financial analysis. Most firms use different subsystems to handle different types of strategic changes, yet the subsystems were similar across firms. Lastly, no single formal analytical process could handle all strategic variables simultaneously using a planning approach.

Precipitating Events and Incremental Logic

Executives reported that various events often resulted in interim decisions that shaped the company's future strategy. This was evident in the decisions forced on General Motors by the 1973–74 oil crisis, in the shift in posture pressed upon Exxon by the Prince William Sound oil spill, or in the dramatic opportunities allowed for Haloid Corporation and Pilkington Brothers by the unexpected inventions of xerography and float glass. No organization—no matter how brilliant, rational, or imaginative—could possibly have foreseen the timing, severity, or even the nature of all such precipitating events.

Recognizing this, top executives tried to respond incrementally. They kept early commitments broadly formative, tentative, and subject to later review. Future implications were too hard to understand, so parties wanted to test assumptions and have an opportunity to learn. Also, top executives were sensitive to social and political structures in the organization; they tried to handle things in a way that would make the change process a good one.

The Diversification Subsystem

Strategies for diversification provide excellent examples of the value of proceeding incrementally. Incremental processes aid both the formal aspects of diversification (price and strategic fit, for example), and the psychological and political aspects. Most important among the latter are generating a genuine, top-level psychological commitment to diversification, consciously preparing the firm to move opportunistically, building a "comfort factor" for risk taking, and developing a new ethos based on the success of new divisions.

The Major Reorganization Subsystem

Large-scale organizational moves may have negative effects on organizational politics and social structure. Logical incrementalism makes it easier to avoid those negative effects. As the organization proceeds incrementally, it can assess the new roles, capabilities, and individual reactions of those involved in the restructuring. It allows new people to be trained and tested, perhaps for extended periods. Logical incrementalism allows organizational actors to modify the idea behind the reorganization as more is learned. It also gives executives the luxury of making final commitments as late as possible. Executives may move opportunistically, step-by-step, selectively moving people as developments warrant (events seldom come together at one convenient time). They may also articulate the broad organizational concept in detail only when the last pieces fit together. Lastly, logical incrementalism works well in large-scale reorganization because it allows for testing, flexibility, and feedback.

FORMAL PLANNING IN CORPORATE STRATEGY

Formal planning techniques do serve some essential functions. They discipline managers to look ahead, and to express goals and resource allocations. Long-term planning encourages longer time horizons, and eases the evaluation of short-term plans. Long-term plans create a psychological backdrop and an information framework about the future against which managers can calibrate short-term or interim decisions. Lastly, "special studies," like the white papers used at Pillsbury to inform the chicken-business divestiture decision, have a large effect at key junctures for specific decisions.

Planning may make incrementalism standard organizational practice, for two reasons. First, most planning is "bottom up," and the people at the bottom have an interest in their existing products and processes. Second, executives want most plans to be "living" or "ever green," intended to be only frameworks, providing guidance and consistency for incremental decisions. To do otherwise would be to deny that further information could have value. Thus, properly used formal planning can be part of incremental logic.

Total Posture Planning

Occasionally, managements did attempt very broad assessments of their companies' total posture. But these major product thrusts were usually unsuccessful. Actual strategies *evolved*, as each company overextended, consolidated, made errors, and rebalanced various thrusts over time. The executives thought that this was both logical and expected.

LOGICAL INCREMENTALISM

Strategic decisions cannot be aggregated into a single decision matrix, with factors treated simultaneously to achieve an optimum solution. There are cognitive limits, but also "process limits"—timing and sequencing requirements, the needs to create awareness, to build comfort levels, to develop consensus, to select and train people, and so forth.

A Strategy Emerges

Successful executives connect and sequentially arrange a series of strategic processes and decisions over a period of years. They attempt to build a resource base and posture that are strong enough to withstand all but the most devastating events. They constantly reconfigure corporate structure and strategy as new information suggests better—but never perfect—alignments. The process is dynamic, with no definite beginning or end.

CONCLUSIONS

Strategy deals with the unknowable, not the uncertain. It involves so many forces, most of which have great strength and the power to combine, that one cannot, in a probabilistic sense, predict events. Therefore, logic dictates that one proceed flexibly and experimentally from broad ideas toward specific commitments. Making the latter concrete as late as possible narrows the bands of uncertainty, and allows the firm to benefit from the best available information. This is the process of "logical incrementalism." It is not "muddling." Logical incrementalism is conscious, purposeful, active, good management. It allows executives to blend analysis, organizational politics, and individual needs into a cohesive new direction.

MANAGING INCREMENTALLY

How can one actively manage the logical incremental process? The study discussed here shows that executives tend to use similar incremental processes as they manage complex strategy shifts.

Being Ahead of the Formal Information System

The earliest signals for strategy change rarely come from formal company systems. Using multiple internal and external sources, managers "sense" the need for change before the formal systems do. T. Vincent Learson at IBM drove the company to develop the 360 series of computers based on his feeling that, despite its current success, IBM was heading toward market confusion. IBM's formal intelligence system did not pick up any market signals until three years after Learson launched the development process.

Building Organizational Awareness

This is essential when key players lack information or psychological stimulation to change. At early stages, management processes are broad, tentative, formative, information-seeking, and purposely avoid irreversible commitments. They also try to avoid provoking potential opponents of an idea.

Building Credibility/Changing Symbols

Symbols may help managers signal to the organization that certain types of changes are coming, even when specific solutions are not yet in hand. Highly visible symbolic actions can communicate effectively to large numbers of people. Grapevines can amplify signals of pending change. Symbolic moves often verify the intention of a new strategy, or give it credibility in its early stages. Without such actions, people may interpret even forceful verbiage as mere rhetoric and delay their commitment to new strategic ideas.

Legitimizing New Viewpoints

Planned delays allow the organization to debate the discuss threatening issues, work out implications of new solutions, or gain an improved information base. Sometimes, strategic ideas that are initially resisted can gain acceptance and commitment simply by the passage of time and open discussion of new information. Many top executives, planners and change agents consciously arrange such "gestation periods." For example, William Spoor at Pillsbury allowed more than a year of discussion and information-gathering before the company decided to divest its chicken business.

Tactical Shifts and Partial Solutions

These are typical steps in developing a new strategic posture, especially when early problem resolutions need to be partial, tentative or experimental. Tactical adjustments, or a series of small programs, typically encounter little opposition, while a broad strategic change could encounter much opposition. These approaches allow the continuation of ongoing strengths while shifting momentum at the margin. Experimentation can occur with minimized risk, leading to many different ways to succeed.

As events unfurl, the solutions to several problems, which may initially have seemed unrelated, tend to flow together into a new combination. When possible, strategic logic (risk minimization) dictates starting broad initiatives that can be flexibly guided in any of several possible desirable directions.

Broadening Political Support

This is an essential and consciously-active step in major strategy changes. Committees, task forces or retreats tend to be favored mechanisms. By selecting such groups' chairpersons, membership, timing, and agenda the guiding executives can largely influence and predict a desired outcome, yet nudge other executives toward a consensus. Interactive consensus building also improves the quality of decisions, and encourages positive and innovative help when things go wrong.

Overcoming Opposition

Unnecessary alienation of managers from an earlier era in the organization's history should be avoided; their talents may be needed. But overcoming opposition is usually necessary. Preferred methods are persuasion, co-optation, neutralization, or moving through zones of indifference (i.e., pushing those portions of a project that are non-controversial to most of the interested parties). To be sure, successful executives honor and even stimulate legitimate differences. Opponents sometimes thoughtfully shape new strategies into more effective directions; sometimes they even change their views. Occasionally, though, strong-minded executives may need to be moved to less-influential positions, or be stimulated to leave.

Consciously Structured Flexibility

Flexibility is essential in dealing with the many "unknowables" in the environment. Successful organizations actively create flexibility. This requires active horizon scanning, creating resource buffers, developing and positioning champions, and shortening decision lines. These are the keys to *real* contingency planning, not the usual pre-capsuled (and shelved) programs designed to respond to stimuli that never occur quite as expected.

Trial Balloons and Systematic Waiting

Strategists may have to wait patiently for the proper option to appear or precipitating event to occur. For example, although he wanted to divest Pillsbury's chicken business, William Spoor waited until his investment bankers found a buyer at a good price. Executives may also consciously launch trial ideas, like Spoor's "Super Box" at Pillsbury, to attract options and concrete proposals. Without making a commitment to any specific solution, the executive mobilizes the organization's creative abilities.

Creating Pockets of Commitment

Executives often need this tactic when they are trying to get organizations to adopt entirely new strategic directions. Small projects, deep within the organization, are used to test options, create skills, or build commitments for several possible options. The executive provides broad goals, proper climate, and flexible resource support, without public commitment. This avoids attention on, and identification with, any project. Yet executives can stimulate the good options, make life harder for the poorer options, or even kill the weakest ones.

Crystallizing the Focus

At some point, this becomes vital. Early commitments are necessarily vague, but once executives develop information or consensus on desirable ways to proceed, they may use their prestige or power to push or crystallize a particular formulation. This should not be done too early, as it might inadvertently centralize the organization or preempt interesting options. Focusing too early might also provide a common target for otherwise fragmented opposition, or cause the organization to undertake undesirable actions just to carry out a stated commitment. When to crystallize viewpoints and when to maintain open options is a true art of strategic management.

Formalizing Commitment

This is the final step in the logical incremental strategy formation process. It usually occurs after general acceptance exists, and when the timing is right. Typically, the decision is announced publicly, programs and budgets are formed, and control and reward systems are aligned to reflect intended strategic emphases.

Continuing the Dynamics and Mutating the Consensus

Advocates of the "new" strategy can become as strong a source of inflexible resistance to new ideas as were the advocates of the "old" strategy. Effective strategic managers immediately introduce new ideas and stimuli at the top, to maintain the adaptability of the strategic thrusts they have just solidified. This is a most difficult, but essential, psychological task.

Not a Linear Process

While generation of a strategy generally flows along the sequence presented above, the stages are usually not ordered or discrete. The process is more like fermentation in biochemistry, instead of being like an industrial assembly line. Segments of major strategies are likely to be at different stages of development. They are usually integrated in the minds of top executives, each of whom may nevertheless see things differently. Lastly, the process is so continuous that it may be hard to discern the particular point in time when specific clear-cut decisions are made.

An important point to remember is that the validity of a strategy lies not in its pristine clarity or rigorously maintained structure. Its value lies in its capacity to capture the initiative, to deal with unknowable events, and to redeploy and concentrate resources as new opportunities and thrusts emerge. This allows the organization to use resources most effectively toward selected goals.

INTEGRATING THE STRATEGY

The process described above may be incremental, but it is not piecemeal. Effective executives constantly reassess the total organization, its capacities, and its needs as related to the surrounding environment.

Concentrating on a Few Key Thrusts

Effective strategic managers constantly seek to distill a few (six to ten) "central themes" that draw the firm's actions together. These maintain focus and consistency in the strategy. They make it easier to discuss and monitor intended directions. By contrast, formal models, designed to keep track of divisional progress toward realizing strategy, tend to become bound up in red tape, procedure, and rigid bureaucracy.

Coalition Management

The heart of all controlled strategy development is coalition management. Top managers act at the confluence of pressures from all stakeholders. These stakeholders will form coalitions, so managers must be active in forming their own. People selection and coalition management are the ultimate controls top executives have in guiding and coordinating their companies' strategies.

CONCLUSIONS

Many recent attempts to devise strategy using approaches that emphasize formal planning have failed because of poor implementation. This results from the classic trap of thinking about strategy formulation and implementation as separate and sequential processes. Successful managers who operate logically and actively, in an *incremental* mode, build the seeds of understanding, identity and commitment into the very processes that create their strategies. Strategy "formulation" and strategy "implementation" interact in the organization's continuing stream of events.

BY CHARLES BADEN-FULLER AND JOHN M. STOPFORD

■ Is rejuvenation really possible? How does a business paralyzed by years of turmoil and failure and constrained by limited resources create a vibrant organization committed to entrepreneurship? Unless the organization is frugal and produces some short-term results, it risks losing support from its many stakeholders. But short-term results alone are not enough; longer-term survival must be sought. A start must be made to initiate a form of entrepreneurial behavior that increases the chances of durable recovery. As one chairman said, "We have put in new controls and financial disciplines that have stanched the hemorrhaging, cut costs, and returned us, temporarily, to profit. That's the easy part. Getting some momentum going is much harder." . . .

THE CRESCENDO MODEL

We regard building corporate entrepreneurship as the essential ingredient for lasting rejuvenation. . . . The task is difficult and often subtle. To ensure that all the attributes of entrepreneurship are diffused throughout an organization, the business must avoid the "quick fixes" so beloved by many. . . . Massive capital investment programs, aggressive but shallow attempts to force total quality management, or reengineering, or "cultural immersion" are usually ineffective if undertaken with insufficient attention to the issues we raised. The quick fix rarely delivers any long-term sustainable reward for, like the Tower of Babel, it falls if its foundations are insecure. The way forward must carry the whole organization to be self-sustaining.

Rebuilding a mature organization takes time; it cannot be done with a leap. It is, for example, seldom clear at the outset, because of information gaps, just where the business should be headed. Even when the direction has become clear, the details of the twists and turns in the road ahead can remain fogbound. Experimentation is necessary to test the feasibility of ideas. Too early commitment to a new direction can be unduly risky. A way has to be found to build consistently and to link newfound strengths before real and lasting transformation can be achieved.

While there are many routes mature businesses might take, the experience of firms can be distilled to identify one path that we feel is more sure than many others. It is a four-stage renewal process, an orchestrated crescendo. Crescendo is a musical term meaning "a gradual increase in volume." Our renewal process is also gradual, requiring many steps over many years. The crescendo has to be managed and momentum for change established to allow businesses to reach for ever more challenging targets.

. . . We address the question of how businesses can get started and shrug off the stasis that has plagued so may mature firms. To place that start in context and show where we are headed, we begin with a brief summary of the overall model. . . .

BOX 1
FOUR STAGES FOR REJUVENATION

1. Galvanize: create a top team dedicated to renewal.
2. Simplify: cut unnecessary and confusing complexity.
3. Build: develop new capabilities.
4. Leverage: maintain momentum and stretch the advantages.

---

*Reprinted with deletions by permission of Harvard Business School Press. From "The Crescendo Model of Rejuvenation" from *Rejuvenating the Mature Business* by Baden-Fuller and Stopford. Boston, MA 1994. Copyright © 1994 by the Harvard Business School Publishing Corporation; All Rights Reserved.

GALVANIZE

Although it seems obvious to begin by creating a top team dedicated to renewal, this vital stage is often overlooked. Rejuvenation is not the fixing up of a few activities or functions that have gone awry; it is the process of changing every part of an organization and the way its functions, territories, and various groups interact. No individual, not even the chief executive, can alone achieve this magnitude of change, but at the start it requires leadership from the top team. Such commitment carries important positive messages to the whole organization, for without that commitment those who labor in the firm become demoralized or frustrated.

To galvanize the top team, the agenda for action needs to be drawn up carefully. At the start, detailed plans of action are neither necessary nor wise. Instead there must be a broad understanding of the issues and a belief that progress will be achieved only by many small steps. There is serious danger in the early stages that top management will either try to buy its way out of difficulties with overgrandiose schemes, such as investing in expensive state-of-the-art technology that few in the organization understand, or spend too much time chasing culture change programs and not enough time initiating action.

SIMPLIFY

Simplifying the business helps change managers and workers' perceptions of what has been wrong and what new actions are required. Like clearing the rubbish from an overgrown garden, cutting some activities is a necessary precursor to building something new. Removing outdated control systems and incorrect data helps eliminate the causes of resistance to change. Simplifying the business concentrates scarce resources on a smaller agenda and so increases the chances of gaining positive results in the short to medium term. Simplification also signals to outside stakeholders—owners, suppliers, customers, bankers, and employers alike—that something positive is being attempted.

Actions to simplify the task and provide focus for the effort are no more than temporary measures. They must be regarded as work to provide a "beachhead" in complex industry structures that can be defended while work to build new strengths can proceed.

BUILD

In the third stage, which overlaps the second, the organization must set about building new advantages for later deployment as the business breaks out of the beachhead. It is at this stage that corporate rather than individual entrepreneurship must be developed. Beginning with raised aspirations to do better and resolve old problems, in the course of time new challenges need to be articulated, which will help all to work to a common purpose. That purpose, expressed in terms of visions and a direction for progress, is typically phrased in terms that all can understand. Making progress along the chosen path requires managers to experiment and to discover what can work and what fails.

Experiments, of necessity, have to be small at the start: resources are limited, knowledge about possibilities uncertain, and the risks seem immense. As some experiments pay off, momentum should increase to the point where major investments in new technology for delivering the product or service may be required. Learning may also start slowly, though ordinarily some parts of the organization progress more quickly than others. Over time the organization must invest in deepening existing skills and acquiring new ones, developing new systems, data bases, and knowledge. Alongside these initiatives, teamwork must be developed, first on a small scale to deal with essential tasks but then growing across the whole organization and extending along the supply chain. The momentum created helps build the values that underpin the crucial ingredient of the will to win.

LEVERAGE

The final stage is leveraging advantages and maintaining momentum. As the organization grows in competitive strength, it can expand the sphere of its operations into new markets, new products, and new parts of the value chain. Leveraging capabilities can be by acquisition, alliances, or internal moves so that the business can extend its newfound advantages to a much wider sphere of activities. Pressures for expansion must be balanced against the danger of too much complexity slowing down the pace of innovation and forcing the organization to a standstill.

We label the rejuvenation process a *crescendo* to emphasize that the four stages are not discrete steps but rather activities which merge into each other as the magnitude of change increases over time. The reality of all organizations is messy, confusing, and complex. In the building of corporate entrepreneurship, activities in one department or at one level of the organization may proceed faster and more effectively than others. Moreover, organizations do not rejuvenate only once: they may need to do so repetitively. The challenges of one period may be resolved, but those of the next may again require organizational change.

The rejuvenation steps are summarized in Figure 1. The arrows are drawn as lines, though in practice progress is usually made in loops of learning. The dance to the crescendo of music is the samba. *One step back to take two steps forward* describes how organizations proceed—and it is exactly what happens with simplification and building. Let us use an analogy: renovators of old buildings know full well that the plaster has to come off the walls if a rotten structure is to be repaired. It is rarely possible to fix it without spoiling the decorations. . . .

We emphasize that in the early simplifying stage of renewal, cutting may have to be radical. The contraction can be tangible, for example, cutting out parts of the product range, geographic territory, or stages of the value chain; it can also be less tangible, for example, eliminating systems and procedures. Even profitable activities may have to be dropped if they distract attention and deflect resources from building the new "core."

In building, progress is best achieved by many small initiatives, because resources are limited. Small steps spread the risks and prevent the organization from betting everything on one initiative. As rejuvenation proceeds, the risks become better understood and progress more secure, allowing the steps to get bigger. Small steps also allow the organization to encourage initiatives from below and help build an entrepreneurial culture. Whereas instructions for surgery are imposed from the top, it is the bottom-up flow of ideas and actions that accelerates the convalescence and return to fighting fitness.

We stress that organizations need a long time to rejuvenate. It takes years to build a truly entrepreneurial company. Like builders of houses, who spend almost two-thirds of the cost

FIGURE 1
CRITICAL PATH FOR
CORPORATE RENEWAL

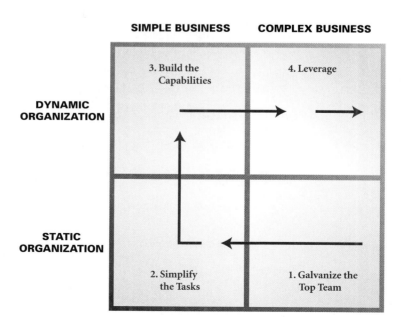

and time below ground digging foundations and preparing the site, effective organizations that aim to become entrepreneurial also have to sink deep foundations; rushing for the quick-fix solution is unlikely to result in long-term rewards. . . .

GALVANIZING THE TOP TEAM

Rejuvenating a mature organization is impossible without commitment from the top. As we pointed out, . . . many mature organizations show signs of life with innovative actions being taken in parts, and include many able individuals who are committed to change. Entrepreneurial individuals generally labor in isolated groups. They are unable to make the connections essential to altering the path of the organization, for that requires linkages across functions and territories, which cannot be achieved without the backing of top management.

Initial moves are often made by a new chief executive, and in all the firms we studied, the CEO played a vital and decisive role. The effective ones, however, did not act alone; they all realized the importance of teams. . . .

Building a top team dedicated to change provides continuity and reduces the risks that the process will falter if one person leaves. In several of our organizations the chief executive changed without loss of momentum. . . .

Effective top teams span all the key functions. Rejuvenation involves changing the way in which the functions work and the way in which they relate. An effective top team must have a real understanding of the functions so that it understands what is technically possible, what is required by customers, suppliers, the workforce, and other stakeholders. Without shared knowledge within the team, there can be no intuition, which is vital for the business.

The need to involve the key functions also ensures the involvement of the vital power brokers of the organization. Functional or territorial heads carry weight in getting things done. They can influence the perceptions and actions of their group, perhaps because of their position but often because of their background and skills. Unless they are involved in the early stages, the power brokers may sabotage or slow down the process through misunderstanding and lack of appreciation.

For rejuvenation, all members of the top team must share an understanding of the problem. An effective top team avoids vacillation, does not seek outsiders to resolve its problems (although they may help), does not look for a quick fix or shirk dealing with immediate issues. In short, many rocks and whirlpools have to be avoided. To sidestep these hazards, the team must believe that there is a crisis, that action has to be taken, and that the action must extend throughout the organization. Only where there is real common acceptance of these three priorities does the top team feel empowered to start the process of rejuvenation. Achieving consensus is not easy, so we examine the issues. (See Table 1.)

TABLE 1
GALVANIZING THE TOP TEAM

LIMITING PERCEPTIONS	GALVANIZING PERCEPTIONS
The problem we face is temporary.	There is a crisis and the issues are major and fundamental.
We must move slowly to avoid upsetting the existing order.	There is a sense of urgency. Change must be set into motion even if we do not know exactly where we are going.
It is someone else's fault that we are in trouble.	We must understand why we are in the mess, so that we, the top team, can lead the way forward.
The problems lie in specific areas of the organization; they are not widespread.	Firmwide change is needed across functions, territories, and hierarchy.
The financial figures tell us what is wrong.	We have to look behind the figures to find out where the markets are going and the needed capabilities.

SENSING THE NEED TO START

What triggers actions that can lead to rejuvenation? Why is correct sensing so critical to generating a sense of urgency? Earlier we discussed the difficulty of recognizing crises in a form that can lead to action and the even more serious problem of using the recognition of an opportunity as a way of focusing energies to change behavior. It is one thing to bring together a top team, quite another to have it share, collectively, a sense that change is imperative. We use the word *sense* advisedly, because at the earliest stages only rarely does hard data indicate a clear direction; information by itself seldom "proves" or "disproves" any action.

Consider what can happen when managers sense the signals for change. They may seem so vague that they are effectively ignored. They may point to solutions that are beyond current capabilities, they can provoke responses of general concern, but the actions are little more than tinkering with the symptoms. More precise signals can also be ignored, even when the solutions are within capabilities, because the team has yet to share a common will to respond. The issue of the urgency is also embodied in the message. Managers may feel that they have plenty of time and allow other agendas to preoccupy them. Alternatively, an urgent message may seem to be so complex that appropriate responses are hard to calculate.

We found that all the top teams of rejuvenating firms had experienced many of these difficulties before they could commit themselves to collective internal action. Often, we found top teams working to exhaust all the "obvious" actions before they could perceive the need to consider more radical approaches to transform the business as a whole. Rational calculations of partial response to complex challenges can be used, perhaps unwittingly, to perpetuate the inertia of maturity. The problem is exacerbated when the agenda is so complex that team members cannot agree on priorities. . . .

It is important to appreciate that the data in signals for change need to be interpreted for others, particularly when they are weak. Consider the assessment of competitors, so commonly undertaken by top management. Measures of competition may cover profitability, productivity, reliability, or customer acceptance. Generally, a few competitors are doing better on some if not all the measures, but many may be similar to a given organization and some may be doing worse. Should this fact be seen as a trigger for action or a signal for complacency? Unless someone has high aspirations and a sense of danger, complacency prevails. . . . There are always those who believe that poor performance, be it in profits or some other measure, can be excused: "It is not our fault." Worse yet, competitor benchmarking studies can be used to justify the status quo. One mature firm that later went out of business went so far as to reject a study that indicated the need for a fundamental change of approach. In the words of one director, it was "obviously fallacious. If this was possible, we would be doing it already."

There are many other reasons why managers may fail to react to changing circumstance. Mature organizations can become trapped in an illusion bred of undue focus on accounting profits. Of necessity, accounting figures can register only what has happened, not what is about to happen; when confronted by "satisfactory" profits, many top groups ignored other signals indicating declining competitiveness. . . .

Only a few of our rejuvenators did the obvious thing at the start, that is, establish measures that heighten the sense of urgency to deal with emergent problems before they become serious. Wise and successful organizations broaden their measures of performance to include specific indicators of relative achievement of financial and nonfinancial goals. A broader and more balanced scorecard helps top teams in general, and chief executives in particular, to anticipate where trouble might strike. It amplifies the weak signals that forewarn of danger and diminishes those signals which encourage complacency. If the top team does not anticipate it, the organization may be submerged and unable to retrieve itself when the real crisis arrives.

TRIGGERS FOR ACTION

Sensing impending doom is not always sufficient to induce action. Although it comes late in the day, falling profitability seems to be the most common trigger for inducing a sufficient enough sense of urgency and crisis that actions to cure the roots of the problem can be instituted. . . .

Must firms wait for a financial crisis before top managers do more than tinker with some of the parts? Though harder to do, it is possible for individuals to anticipate a looming crisis and initiate corrective action before it is too late or too expensive to try. It is relatively easier for that to happen when an individual has the power to act. The awareness may come first to shareholders, who appoint a new chief executive to carry the message, or the chief executive may be prescient. It is more difficult when the messages come from outside and are heard by individual managers without power. Dealings with suppliers, customers, bankers, and innumerable others can highlight the problem and stir up action within isolated groups. But when that happens, action to change business fundamentally usually has to wait until . . . there is a chief executive who listens and buys into the possibilities.

. . . It is possible to anticipate a real crisis. Those who have done so have been able to take positive action at less cost than would have been incurred had they procrastinated. In such instances, hindsight seems to show repetitively that the actions taken were less risky than a policy of standing still. But before the event, the risks may have appeared large.

EMPOWERING MANAGEMENT

Bringing together a top team and making its members realize that there is a crisis is not enough to start rejuvenation: the team must believe that it has the power and the responsibility to do something. It is necessary that certain aspects of the problem are appreciated by the top team: that the problem is not limited to a single part of the organization, that the quick fix does not work. The top team must also appreciate that it does not have to know all the answers before it can act. Its job is to chart the direction ahead and enlist the aid of others in finding durable solutions. It is tempting to suggest that the realization comes quickly, but the truth is that appreciation comes gradually.

. . . Managers of mature organizations are often keen to fasten blame on others. Sometimes they blame the environment, poor demand, overfussy customers, adverse exchange rates, even the weather. Sometimes they blame the decisions of previous top management and sometimes the failure of current middle management to implement decisions made by the top team. While an element of blame may rightly be attached to these groups, in all cases top management showed insufficient appreciation of the issues at stake. Progress can take place only when team members appreciate the extent of a problem and realize that they, and only they, are ultimately responsible for [their] organization's failures. More important, only the top team can lead the organization out of its mess.

It is also common for senior managers to perceive that the problems (and hence the solutions) lie in a single function or part of their organization. Blaming particular functions, territories, or groups is often unhelpful, as the crisis reflects failures of the whole organization. For example, when high-cost products are also poor quality, the production department is usually blamed. Such finger-pointing is naive, for rarely is production alone to blame for poor quality. It may be that production, not being told by the service department which failures occur most frequently, is trying to improve the wrong elements. Distribution may be at fault, damaging goods in transit. Purchasing may be paying insufficient attention to ensuring that suppliers provide quality components, and marketing may insist on designs that are difficult and expensive to produce. Quality at low cost can be achieved only when all functions work closely together. . . .

The dawning realization that the problems are serious and that the causes extend beyond a single function to all parts of the organization is one step on the road toward taking necessary corrective actions. But before effective action can be initiated, hard choices among many alternatives must be made. Here the chief executive has the central role of holding the ring as people test their intuition against always imperfect data. Lacking hard evidence, a top team always has members with competing senses of priority. And lacking anything more than a common will to be positive, the debates can all too readily become unproductive without firm leadership.

<table>
<tr><td>

**CHOOSING
EFFECTIVE ACTION**

</td><td>

Some top teams choose to manage their way forward by exhaustive analysis of the alternatives they can perceive at the time of crisis. Others feel their way by trying solutions and discovering what does and does not work. Still others examine the experience of other organizations. And often all these approaches are combined. However choices are made, there are many false paths and blind alleys, which can seduce and lull management into thinking that it is effectively dealing with the issues at hand.

</td></tr>
</table>

The steps that we suggest mark out the most effective path of action are in stark contrast to other actions we observed. Simplification involves cutting to conserve resources, revealing a new core, and pointing the way forward. The subsequent building, later described in detail, lays new foundations for the entrepreneurial organization and requires an extended time perspective. These measured steps contrast with the following alternatives, which many have taken and which fail to address key issues effectively: scrapping everything and starting afresh—rather than saving what is of value, looking to outsiders to alleviate a problem—as a substitute for internal action; vacillation among extreme directives issued by top management—paralyzed uncomprehending top management; large-scale investments in state-of-the art technology and systems at the initial stages—quick fix or big hit; and culture change programs without parallel actions—denying that there is an immediate crisis. These issues . . . are discussed more fully below.

SCRAP EVERYTHING AND START AFRESH

Consider first the problem of those Cassandras who argue that it is hopeless to try to rejuvenate—better to give up without a struggle and go elsewhere. Their pessimistic views can be justified if *all* the alternatives are more costly and more risky. Only if all else fails must an organization be extinguished.

One U.S. company considered seeking the rejuvenation of an existing operation a waste of time. Instead of tackling the deep-seated problems in its Midwest plants, it moved the whole operation to the South, leaving its past behind. In so doing, the company abandoned many skilled and loyal workers who might have been capable of adapting to new working methods faster than it took to train a brand new workforce and at less cost. The Japanese experience of buying U.S. facilities and doubling or trebling productivity within less than a year illustrates that the possibility of rejuvenation often exists. Their experience also confirms that faster returns may come from renewal rather than greenfield initiatives, a point often overlooked by those in a hurry to "'get something going."*

Sometimes, to be sure, troubled organizations do not have the option of a clean start elsewhere. Even though they might wish to walk away, the owners may not be able to afford the exit costs. They may also face severe union opposition and the resistance of politicians and local government officials. In such cases, management is obliged to try to find a middle way, regardless of how many Cassandras argue that the effort will be in vain.

SEEKING OUTSIDE SUPPORT

For years, many major European chemical companies, particularly the Italian giants, the French and Belgians, and even the British ICI, perceived the problems of their industry as being caused by government's failure to manage demand in the economy and allowing the Middle Eastern countries power over oil prices. In these firms, top management consistently lobbied governments for support to resolve their problems and failed to take internal initiatives. ICI, one of the

---

*The West German approach to rebuilding East Germany also had the appearance of trying to start afresh: old factories were demolished, workers dismissed, and the new owners acted as if they were setting up greenfield sites. For an academic view of when it is best to start afresh, see M. T. Hannan and J. Freeman, "Structural Inertia and Organizational Change," in K. S. Cameron, R. I. Sutton, and D. A. Whetten, eds., *Readings in Organizational Decline* (Cambridge, MA: Ballinger, 1988).

bigger culprits, was also one of the first to break out of the vicious circle and realize that internal action was necessary. A galvanized top management led the way, and ten years later, in better shape than many of its European counterparts, it is still trying to pull its organization around. . . .

Lest we be accused of ignoring politics and reality, we fully recognize that all organizations have a role to lobby and put their case to government, and all need to watch and influence events. However, we draw a distinction between this approach and those failing organizations which do nothing for themselves while waiting to be rescued by the white knight of outside support. The first puts the role of public policy in perspective, while the second fails in the duties of management.

TOP-DOWN DIRECTIVES THAT ADDRESS SYMPTOMS, NOT CAUSES

Many top managers seem to believe that issuing orders from the top and expecting immediate responses is the best way to start things going. . . . This is unlikely to instill corporate entrepreneurship. As a sense of crisis looms, if statements from the top become hysterical, they can be met by inaction or lack of results from below. Vacillation is usually another sign that top management is not really in control and does not understand either the causes of a problem or how to respond effectively. Seldom can top-down directives do more than preserve yesterday's "formula." . . .

GOING FOR THE BIG HIT

The recognition that an organization is far behind in its capabilities can drive top management to seek a quick fix. At the beginning of the renewal process there is a temptation to spend money on modern capital by buying state-of-the-art factories, service delivery systems, or other forms of technology. Typically, consultants or other outsiders have suggested that such investments permit a firm to catch up with its industry leaders. Usually the investments are large, take several years to build, and commit the organization to a single unchangeable route for the future. There is often an absence of understanding in the organization of how the new technology works, and certainly a lack of appreciation for all the issues it involves. At the early stages of rejuvenation, big programs are dangerous, not least because most of the organization's resources are bet on a single course.

For the mature organization in crisis, the arrival of massive amounts of new capital, new computers, or new systems without a corresponding building of a skill base risks disasters. All our rejuvenators discovered, if they did not already know, that skills have to be built in tandem with investment in hardware. Without the proper skills and awareness throughout the whole organization, the investments are misused or underused. Little progress is made in delivering either financial results or building a competitive edge. Worse, the spirit of entrepreneurial enthusiasm with its characteristics of learning and experimentation may be repressed.

We should make it clear that large investment programs can pay off handsomely when undertaken by firms that have gained entrepreneurial capabilities. When organizations have built their internal skills and processes, they can leverage new investments effectively.

CULTURE CHANGE PROGRAMS WITHOUT CORRESPONDING ACTION

If the big hit is dangerous because it squanders resources, takes unnecessary risks, and does not build a new organization, the culture change program goes to the opposite extreme. It is certainly true that mature organizations need to change their culture if they are to become entrepreneurial, but many mistakenly believe that the culture has to be changed before actions for improvement can be taken, or that culture change is sufficient in itself. A culture change program without action is very risky because it denies the existence of a crisis and takes the organization's attention away from the necessity for immediate action. Moreover, it fails to appreciate the most obvious fact that organizations change only through actions because actions reflect and alter beliefs.

Our finding echoes the observations of Tom Peters and Robert Waterman (1982), who noted that effective organizations had a bias for action. Their point was that unless action is taken, progress cannot be made. Their message is highly appropriate for rejuvenating organizations. We found a surprising number of firms investing heavily in changing the culture of their organizations without ensuring that deliberate progress was made in the specification of the actual tasks. . . .

Rejuvenating a business does require a culture change, but change must be linked to action. Our research suggests that effective culture change requires managers to deal with tasks. Thus, abolishing the executive dining room at one firm did help, but only because it reinforced other important initiatives dealing with productivity and quality. In many organizations, quality circles and the like are introduced, and it seems that those which work well are those which have short-term tangible goals as well as long-term ones. Grand schemes for change without action seldom work. . . .

THE QUICK FIX: TQM OR PROCESS REENGINEERING

All our rejuvenators subscribed in one way or another to aspects of total quality management (TQM) and all have reengineered their processes, occasionally several times over. But what they did . . . bore little relation to those peddlers of snake oil who claim instant results.

A few less careful proponents of TQM or process engineering (or the equivalent) portray complex philosophies as quick-fix solutions. They understate the investment in the time, energy, and effort required to yield results. In their desire for speed, they fail to stress the need to teach the organization the skills to ensure that the process can be continued and typically do not build a proper foundation for lasting success. Not surprisingly, recent surveys of organizations that took up the TQM fad in the 1980s show that many have been disappointed and stopped earlier initiatives.* To be sure, there have been successes, but we suggest that they have probably been organizations which were either far down the rejuvenation road or, like our mature firms, patient and persistent ones. We forecast the same for process reengineering.

Claims by consultants that process reengineering can deliver a ten-fold improvement come as no surprise. . . . But boasts that such progress is achieved quickly do not ring true. Long before the recent fad, we observed mature firms attempting such rapid engineering without preparation and failing. . . .

THE WAY FORWARD

To go forward, the mature firm aspiring to rejuvenate must galvanize and build a top team committed to action. Crucial choices need to be made about the scope of the firm and how and where it will compete. In addition, action must be taken to start the building of entrepreneurship, which we assert is necessary for renewal and any higher aspirations. Some businesses have found that outside stakeholders can play a role. One such group is the top team of a business that is part of a holding company or parent organization. . . .

There may be a gap in cultural perceptions on these matters about what is and is not effective. Where many U.S. managers espouse the value of directives from the very top and point to the benefits of the resulting focus and speed of change, many we spoke to across Europe adopted a different perspective. Those whose job it was to look after a whole portfolio often preferred to work on encouraging managers to embrace the values of creativity, innovation, and challenge to conventions without specifying the actions or processes. Many set challenging targets, but some who regarded their approach as slower and harder to control, bet that the end results would be much more durable.

---

*See, for instance, the studies by Arthur D. Little in the United States and A. T. Kearney in the United Kingdom as reported in *The Economist*, April 18, 1992.

There is no way we know to resolve the issue of which is the superior approach. Both have good and bad points and both are dependent on the climate of attitudes into which such initiatives are introduced. The difference of opinion, however, serves to reinforce the point we made at the start: . . . real transformation of a business cannot begin in earnest without the recognition by its top managers that a new direction must be found.

SECTION II

Forces

CHAPTER 7

Cognition

The first section of this book has taken us through strategy in its various aspects. Now we turn to the *forces* that drive the strategy process, including human cognition, organization, technology, collaboration, globalization, and values.

We begin here with cognition, to get inside the head of the strategists. No one has ever seen a strategy or touched one. Strategies don't exist in any concrete form; they are nothing more than concepts in people's heads. So cognition—namely, how people think about, conceive, and perceive strategy—has to figure importantly in any book about the strategy process.

We include two readings here. The first by David Hurst, long a business executive and now a management writer and consultant in Toronto, picks up where the previous chapter on change left off. Hurst suggests that successful change processes may not benefit but instead be harmed by too much rationality. Hurst discusses the changes of objectivity: "When it comes to real change, too much objectivity may be fatal to the process." We need to step outside our frameworks and beliefs to assess them. In the final analysis, "there can be no final analysis." So managers have to be "ingredients" instead of cooks and be deeply involved themselves.

The second reading draws on the cognitive school chapter of the Mintzberg, Ahlstrand, and Lampel *Strategy Safari* book to review various views of "Strategy as Cognition": for example, the limitations of cognition and the mistakes people make when faced with strategic complexity; cognition as the processing of information; cognition as "mapping" through the use of mental models; and the currently popular view of cognition as "construction"— that we don't *see* our world of strategy out there so much as *create* it inside our brains.

USING THE CASE STUDIES

David Hurst's argument that what appears "hard" to managers as socially and subjectively constructed is illustrated by the luxury goods producer LVMH: The profits and market share are "objective" enough, but the reputation on which they are based is the result of complex cognitive and social processes.

The "objective" character that products often take during strategic planning tends to dissolve when we get close to the people who use these products. The WFNX-101.7FM case describes a radio station caught between its belief in the enduring appeal of alternative programming and market research that suggests that it is fighting against the trend. The crowd of 100,000 that turned up for a concert organized by WFNX points to a large pool of loyal listeners, but the ratings suggest otherwise. Which should form the basis of the station's strategy? Mintzberg, Ahlstrand, and Lampel suggest in "Strategy as Cognition" that the way that you process information can have an important bearing on the strategy that eventually develops. The Honda case, in particular the debates over Honda's entry into the U.S. market, suggest that information is susceptible to radically different interpretations depending on your frame of reference.

READING 7.1

THE DANGERS OF OBJECTIVITY*

BY DAVID K. HURST

■ Enthusiasm for reengineering may be fading, but it will not be the last management formula offered to us. It is the objectivity that frameworks such as reengineering give their users that undermines the social dynamics leading to fundamental change. Indeed, the intellectual detachment of the designers and managers of change from the process itself should be identified as a leading cause of the failure of such change efforts. Perhaps the frameworks should come with a warning label: *When it comes to real change, too much objectivity may be fatal to the process.*

Managerial objectivity is the power to stand outside of a situation, to map it onto a logical framework and initiate the action it suggests. Usually these frameworks are abstracted from the experiences of other prominent organizations, and their plausibility depends upon the cause-effect relationships that they explain. These explanations usually take the form of likely stories about how successful companies became successful or how failing companies turned themselves around. . . . The assumption implicit in each story is that the logic is context-free. The implication is that "you, too" can use these techniques to achieve similar results. The assumption these likely stories share is that managers can behave rationally in the achievement of desirable organizational goals. That is, they can think before they take action, identify cause-effect relationships, start organizational processes, and monitor progress toward these goals.

This assumption is flawed. While nobody suggests that managers can never be instrumentally rational (as this form of rationality is known), the unasked question is whether they can or should be rational in this way *at all times, especially during periods of radical change.* There are two reasons why managers cannot and should not try to behave in this way at such times: the first is intellectual, the second is social.

The intellectual problem is that business realities do not exist independently of their observers. Economies, markets, organizations, and strategies are constructed rather than natural objects. Thus, objectivity is never absolute—it is always relative to some frame of reference

---

*Excerpted from an article originally published as "When it comes to real change, too much objectivity may be fatal to the process," by David K. Hurst, *Strategy and Leadership*, March/April 1997, pp. 6–12.

developed from the past. Because real change means that the frames themselves have to be altered, a rigid objectivity freezes this process, preventing the examination of the assumptions that support the framework. Some explicit assumptions can be examined, but most assumptions are tacit—they are the answers to the questions we never asked. *They can be tested only from outside the framework of logic in use.* And that takes action—experience. We can't just rethink our way into a better way of thinking.

Take the trade-off between cost and quality for example. For years, everyone in North America who had ever taken Economics 101 knew that there was a negative relationship between the two—the more quality one put into a product, the more it would cost. The power of this model is probably the single most important reason why North American business academics were so comprehensively surprised by the quality revolution. It took the success of the lean Japanese automobile manufacturing system to show us that quality could be systemically improved without adding costs. In fact, costs might drop if the production system was changed. The assumptions of manufacturing economics made it impossible for us to conceive of an alternative to mass manufacturing—until we saw one. Thus, the systems logic that supports "lean-flow" principles was developed after the practical results had been confirmed. As a result, all the books on quality have been rewritten.

The second reason why an excess of objectivity is a hindrance to change is demonstrated by the senior executive . . . [who sees him- or herself] outside the change process, diagnosing the condition of those within it. The implication [is] that *they* [have to change. He or she does] not. For much of the time in every change initiative, the situation demands that *everyone* in the organization be seen and felt to share a common fate. Suggestions that the change process is entirely objective and rational introduce a fatal distance between managers and the managed. This distance is lethal to the change effort, for it leads to cynicism in the workers, arouses their suspicion that they are being manipulated, and increases their resistance—not to change itself, but to *being changed*. Instead of feeling empowered, workers feel exhausted and drained by the change process. A typical response: "Why should I change the system if it's going to cost me my job?" (O'Neill and Lenn, 1995).

SELF-SEALING BELIEFS

. . . Reengineering . . . developed [a] self-sealing quality to its rhetoric. Managers were warned to expect resistance, to anticipate where it would come from, and to motivate and involve people. Communication had to "anticipate what people will want to know at every stage," and so on. But this meant that senior managers had to know more about the direction of the change process than those within it. They were on the outside, manipulating those within. Anticipating this, the gurus even warned management to expect feelings of disaster midway through the change process and of the need to stay the course. The implication was that there was nothing wrong with the process or the assumptions that underpinned it; all one had to do was apply them properly. Without any feedback loops, many organizations set out upon a series of escalating commitments to a doomed course of action. Cyberneticists call this condition "systems runaway."

. . . the essence of empowerment [is] that people genuinely feel that the future is up to them to invent, not someone else's plan that they have to implement. And they will get this feeling only if the senior managers behave in a way that expresses these open, egalitarian values. . . .

SENIOR MANAGERS AREN'T COOKS, THEY'RE INGREDIENTS

In the final analysis, when it comes to fundamental change in organizations, there can be no *final analysis*. For it is the very frameworks of analysis that need to be changed. In fundamental organizational change, *it takes behavior to change behavior: change cannot be managed, it can only be led.* Thus, managers of change are not just cooks preparing a meal by following a recipe, they are also key ingredients. Senior managers are powerful role models, and their key contribution to the process of change is to lead by modeling the new behaviors that they expect of their people. They can plan and orchestrate the arrangements only up to a point. Then they have to throw themselves into the mixture with everyone else and trust that their behavior will be copied by others. . . .

Our Western bias is to believe that we can think our way into a better way of *acting*. Experience with real change suggests that just the opposite is true—we have to *act* our way into a better way of *thinking*. As managers, the only behavior we can hope to change directly is our own.

READING 7.2

BY HENRY MINTZBERG, BRUCE AHLSTRAND, AND JOSEPH LAMPEL

"I'll see it when I believe it"

—*Anonymous*

If we are really serious about understanding strategic vision as well as how strategies form under other circumstances, then we had better probe into the mind of the strategist . . . to get at what this process means in the sphere of human cognition, drawing especially on the field of cognitive psychology.

. . . strategists are largely self-taught: they develop their knowledge structures and thinking processes mainly through direct experience. That experience shapes what they know, which in turn shapes what they do, thereby shaping their subsequent experience. This duality plays a central role in [cognition], giving rise to two rather different wings.

One wing, more positivistic, treats the processing and structuring of knowledge as an effort to produce some kind of *objective* motion picture of the world. The mind's eye is thus seen as a kind of camera: it scans the world, zooming in and out in response to its owner's will, although the pictures it takes are considered in this school to be rather distorted.

The other wing sees all of this as *subjective*: strategy is some kind of *interpretation* of the world. Here the mind's eye turns inward, on how the mind does its "take" on what it sees out there—the events, the symbols, the behavior of customers, and so on. So while the other wing seeks to understand cognition as some kind of *re-creation* of the world, this wing drops the prefix and instead believes that cognition *creates* the world. . . .

COGNITION AS CONFUSION

Scholars have long been fascinated by the peculiarities of how individuals process information to make decisions, especially the biases and distortions that they exhibit. Management researchers have been especially stimulated by the brilliant work of Herbert Simon (1947, 1957; see also March and Simon, 1958) . . . [who] popularized the notion that the world is large and complex, while human brains and their information-processing capacities are highly limited in comparison. Decision making thus becomes not so much rational as a vain effort to be rational.

A large research literature on judgmental biases followed . . . some of the results of which [are] reproduced in the accompanying table. All have obvious consequences for strategy

---

*Excerpted from "Strategy as Cognition" by H. Mintzberg, B. Ahlstrand, and J. Lampel in *Strategy Safari*, New York: The Free Press, 1998.

making. These include the search for evidence that supports rather than denies beliefs, the favoring of more easily remembered recent information over earlier information, the tendency to see a causal effect between two variables that may simply be correlated, the power of wishful thinking, and so on.

BIASES IN DECISION MAKING	
TYPE OF BIAS	**DESCRIPTION OF BIAS**
Search for supportive evidence	Willingness to gather facts which lead toward certain conclusions and to disregard other facts which threaten them
Inconsistency	Inability to apply the same decision criteria in similar situations
Conservatism	Failure to change (or changing slowly) one's own mind in light of new information/evidence
Recency	The most recent events dominate those in the less recent past, which are downgraded or ignored
Availability	Reliance upon specific events easily recalled from memory, to the exclusion of other pertinent information
Anchoring	Predictions are unduly influenced by initial information which is given more weight in the forecasting process
Illusory correlations	Belief that patterns are evident and/or two variables are causally related when they are not
Selective perception	People tend to see problems in terms of their own background and experience
Regression effects	Persistent increases [in some phenomenon] might be due to random reasons which, if true, would [raise] the chance of a [subsequent] decrease. Alternatively, persistent decreases might [raise] the chances of [subsequent] increases
Attribution of success and failure	Success is attributed to one's skills while failure to bad luck, or someone else's error. This inhibits learning as it does not allow recognition of one's mistakes
Optimism, wishful thinking	People's preferences for future outcomes affect their forecasts of such outcomes
Underestimating uncertainty	Excessive optimism, illusory correlation, and the need to reduce anxiety result in underestimating future uncertainty

Source: From Makridakas (1990: 36–37).

COGNITION AS INFORMATION PROCESSING

Beyond the biases in individual cognition are the effects of working in the collective system for processing information that is called an organization. Managers are information workers. They serve their own needs for information as well as that of their colleagues and of the managers who supervise them. In large organizations especially, this creates all sorts of well-known problems. Senior managers have limited time to oversee vast arrays of activities. Hence much of the information they receive has to be aggregated, which can pile distortions upon distortions. If the original inputs have been subjected to all the biases discussed above, then think about what happens when all of this gets combined and presented to the "boss." No wonder so many senior managers become the captives of their information-processing organizations.

COGNITION AS MAPPING

. . . on one point there is widespread agreement: an essential prerequisite for strategic cognition is the existence of mental structures to organize knowledge. These are the "frames" referred to above, although a host of other labels have been used over the years, including schema, concept, script, plan, mental model, and map.

Map is a currently popular label, perhaps because of its metaphoric value. It implies the navigation through confusing terrain with some kind of representative model. . . .

All experienced managers carry around in their heads all kinds of . . . *causal maps*, or *mental models* as they are sometimes called. And their impact on behavior can be profound. For example, Barr, Stimpert, and Huff (1992) compared two railroads, Rock Island and C&NW, over a twenty-five-year period (1949–1973). They were similar to begin with, but one eventually went bankrupt while the other survived. The researchers attributed this to their managers' causal maps about the environment. Initially, both firms ascribed poor performance to bad weather, government programs, and regulations. Then one firm's maps shifted to a focus on the relationships between costs, productivity, and management style, and that provoked the necessary changes.

COGNITION AS CONCEPT ATTAINMENT

Managers are, of course, map makers as well as map users. How they create their cognitive maps is key to our understanding of strategy formation. Indeed, in the most fundamental sense, this *is* strategy formation. A strategy is a *concept*, and so, to draw on an old term from cognitive psychology, strategy making is "concept attainment."

["Insight" and "intuition" may be key here]. In reference to the Japanese executive, Shimizu (1980) has referred to insight as "intuitive sensibility," and "ability to grasp instantly an understanding of the whole structure of new information." He mentioned the "sixth sense or *kan*" which, in contrast to the "sequential steps of logical thinking," entails the "fitting together of memory fragments that had until then been mere accumulation of various connected information" (23). *In*-sight, seeing inside, seems to come to the decision maker when he or she can see beyond given facts to understand the deeper meaning of an issue. "If the soldier's lot is months of boredom interrupted by moments of terror, to cite an old adage, then the lot of organizations may likewise be described as years of routine reconfigured by flashes of insight. . . ." (Langley et al., 1995: 268). . . . We need to understand, therefore, how it is that strategists are sometimes able to synthesize vast arrays of soft information into new perspectives. Perhaps this will require less study of words and other "recognizable chunks" and more recognition of images. . . . The work of Roger Sperry (1974), who won a Nobel Prize in physiology for his work on split brain research, at least suggests the existence of two very different sets of processes operating within the human brain. One, accessible to verbalization, is usually associated with the left hemisphere, while the other, more spatial, is apparently often found in the mute right hemisphere. Have we, therefore, focused too much of our research and technique of strategic management on the wrong side of the human brain? . . .

COGNITION AS CONSTRUCTION

There is another side to the cognitive school (at least as we interpret it), very different and potentially, perhaps, more fruitful. . . . This views strategy as interpretation, based on cognition as construction.

To proponents of this view, the world "out there" does not simply drive behavior "in here," even if through the filters of distortion, bias, and simplification. There is more to cognition than some kind of effort to mirror reality—to be out there with the best map of the market. . . . These people ask: What about those strategies that change the world? Where do they come from?

For the *interpretative* or *constructionist* view, what is inside the human mind is not a reproduction of the external world. All that information flowing in through those filters, supposedly to be decoded by those cognitive maps, in fact interacts with cognition and is shaped by it. The mind, in other words, imposes some interpretation on the environment—it constructs its world. In a sense, the mind has a mind of its own—it marches to its own cognitive dynamics. Or perhaps we might better say *they* march, because there is a collective dimension to this too: people interact to create their mental worlds. . . .

One obvious conclusion is that . . . managers need a rich repertoire of frames—alternate views of their world, so as not to be imprisoned by any one. Hence the success of books such as Gareth Morgan's *Images of Organizations* (1986), which offers chapters on seeing organizations as machines, as organisms, as brains, and so on. Bolman and Deal's *Reframing Organizations* (1997) suggests that managerial insight hinges on a willingness to use multiple lenses or vantage points, which they too present. . . .

The problem, of course, is that the practice of management requires focus, sometimes . . . even obsession. "On the one hand, on the other hand" is hardly the best route to decisive action. On the other hand, opening up perspectives is also critical for effective management.

IS THE "ENVIRONMENT" CONSTRUCTED?

The social constructionist view begins with a strong premise: no one in an organization "sees" the environment. Instead, organizations construct it from rich and ambiguous information in which even such basic categories as "inside" and "outside" can be very fuzzy. While this premise is strongly supported by evidence, what the social constructionists do with it is more controversial. They argue that since environments are constructed within the organization, they are little more than the product of managerial beliefs. Harking back to the Andrews reading, we now find that the big box on the SWOT chart—the one that deals with environment and of which Michael Porter has made so much—suddenly gets relegated to a minor role. . . . And in its place appears that most obscure box on the chart—the beliefs of the managers.

Many people balk at this conclusion. Surely, they say, there is an environment out there. Markets are, after all, littered with the debris of companies that got them wrong, regardless (or some would say because) of what their managers believed. To which social constructionists reply: this objection itself represents a simplistic assumption about the meaning of "environment." Is it "objective," "perceived," or "enacted?" (Smircich and Stubbart, 1985).

Under this constructionist perspective, strategy formation takes on a whole new color. Metaphors become important, as do symbolic actions and communications . . . all based on the manager's total life experience. . . . And vision emerges as more than an instrument for guidance: it becomes the leader's interpretation of the world made into a collective reality. . . .

CHAPTER 8

Organization

Organization is a major force in society today: We are born in organizations called hospitals and buried by organizations called funeral homes; most everything that happens in between involves formal organizations in one way or another. So we had better understand them by appreciating the strategy process.

Organizational structure, in our view, no more follows strategy than the left foot follows the right in walking. The two exist interdependently, each influencing the other. There are certainly times when a structure is redesigned to carry out a new strategy. But the choice of any new strategy is likewise influenced by the realities and potentials of the existing structure. Indeed, the classical model of strategy formulation (discussed in Chapter 3) implicitly recognizes this by showing the strengths and weaknesses of the organization as an input to the creation of strategies. Surely, these strengths and weaknesses are deeply rooted within the existing structure, indeed often part and parcel of it. Hence, we introduce here organization and the associated structures that make it work as essential factors to consider in the strategy process. Later we present the various contexts within which strategy and structure interact.

We begin with a reading, excerpted originally from Mintzberg's book *The Structuring of Organizations*, that probes comprehensively the design of organizations. It seeks to do two things: first to delineate the basic dimensions of organizations, and then to combine these to identify various basic types of organizations, called "configurations." The dimensions introduced include mechanisms used to coordinate work in organizations, parameters to consider in designing structures, and situational factors that influence choices among these design parameters. This reading also introduces a somewhat novel diagram to depict organizations—not as the usual organizational chart or cybernetic flow process but as a visual combination of the key parts of an organization. This reading then clusters all these dimensions into a set of configurations, each introduced briefly here and discussed at length in the later chapters on context. In fact, the choice of the chapters on context was really based on these types, so this reading will introduce you to Section III.

In his article "Strategy and Organization Planning," Jay Galbraith, who worked as an independent management consultant for several years and now teaches at the University of Southern California, also views structure broadly, as encompassing support systems of various kinds. Building on concepts such as "driving force" and "center of gravity," Galbraith links various strategies (of vertical integration and diversification) to forms of structure, ranging from the functional to the increasingly diversified. Galbraith covers a wide body of important literature and uses visual imagery to make his points. The result is one of the best articles in print on the relationship between the strategy of diversification and the structure of divisionalization.

In "The Design of New Organizational Forms," authors Herber from Goldman Sachs and Singh and Useem from the Wharton School faculty describe a number of interesting new forms of organization to deal with changing environments. These include the virtual organization, network organization (external and internal), spin-out organization, ambidextrous organization, front-back organization, and sense-and-respond organization.

USING THE CASE STUDIES

The relationship between strategy and organization is explored in many of the cases. In several, however, the organization or, more specifically, organizational structure plays a central role in the strategy process. Structure is a key issue for Nobuyuki Idei in Sony Regeneration (A). Corporate restructuring plays an important role in Lufthansa's return to profitability. The regional structure of BMG International strongly influences strategic planning. "The Structuring of Organizations" by Mintzberg provides a general framework for analyzing the relationship between strategy and organization in these cases. "Strategy and Organization Planning" by Galbraith focuses on organizational structure in diversified corporations. It is especially relevant to Rudi Gassner and the Executive Committee of BMG International and also to Wipro Corporation, Selkirk Group in Asia, and Saatchi and Saatchi.

The last 20 years have been a period of extraordinary organizational experimentation and innovation. Singh, Herber, and Useem examine many of the new organizational forms that have emerged. Their analysis relates to several cases of companies involved in organizational experimentation. In the Unipart Group of Companies we see an organization experimenting with new organizational practices as a way of breaking the mold. Kao Corporation shows a company that is consciously pursuing new organizational forms. McKinsey and Company deals with a major consulting company coming to terms with its key business activity, managing knowledge, and takes this further into a search for an organizational structure that will facilitate knowledge management.

**BY HENRY
MINTZBERG**

■ The "one best way" approach has dominated our thinking about organizational structure since the turn of the century. There is a right way and a wrong way to design an organization. A variety of failures, however, has made it clear that organizations differ, that, for example, long-range planning systems or organizational development programs are good for some but not others. And so recent management theory has moved away from the "one best way" approach, toward an "it all depends" approach, formally known as "contingency theory." Structure should reflect the organization's situation—for example, its age, size, type of production system, the extent to which its environment is complex and dynamic.

This reading argues that the "it all depends" approach does not go far enough, that structures are rightfully designed on the basis of a third approach, which might be called the "getting it all together" or "configuration" approach. Spans of control, types of formalization and decentralization, planning systems, and matrix structures should not be picked and chosen independently, the way a shopper picks vegetables at the market. Rather, these and other elements of organizational design should logically configure into internally consistent groupings.

When the enormous amount of research that has been done on organizational structure is looked at in the light of this conclusion, much of its confusion falls away, and a convergence is evident around several configurations, which are distinct in their structural designs, in the situations in which they are found, and even in the periods of history in which they first developed.

To understand these configurations, we must first understand each of the elements that make them up. Accordingly, the first four sections of this reading discuss the basic parts of organizations, the mechanisms by which organizations coordinate their activities, the parameters they use to design their structures, and their contingency, or situational, factors. The final section introduces the structural configurations, each of which will be discussed at length in Section III of this text.

**SIX BASIC PARTS OF
THE ORGANIZATION**

At the base of any organization can be found its operators, those people who perform the basic work of producing the products and rendering the services. They form the *operating core*. All but the simplest organizations also require at least one full-time manager who occupies what we shall call the *strategic apex*, where the whole system is overseen. And as the organization grows, more managers are needed—not only managers of operators but also managers of managers. A *middle line* is created, a hierarchy of authority between the operating core and the strategic apex.

As the organization becomes still more complex, it generally requires another group of people, whom we shall call the analysts. They, too, perform administrative duties—to plan and control formally the work of others—but of a different nature, often labeled "staff." These analysts form what we shall call the *technostructure*, outside the hierarchy of line authority. Most organizations also add staff units of a different kind, to provide various internal services, from a cafeteria or mailroom to a legal counsel or public relations office. We shall call these units and the part of the organization they form the *support staff*.

Finally, every active organization has a sixth part, which we call its *ideology* (by which is meant a strong "culture"). Ideology encompasses the traditions and beliefs of an organization

---

*Excerpted originally from *The Structuring of Organizations* (Prentice Hall, 1979), with added sections from *Power in and Around Organizations* (Prentice Hall, 1983). This chapter was rewritten for this edition of the text, based on two other excerpts: "A Typology of Organizational Structure," published as Chapter 3 in Danny Miller and Peter Friesen, *Organizations: A Quantum View* (Prentice Hall, 1984) and "Deriving Configurations," Chapter 6 in *Mintzberg on Management: Inside Our Strange World of Organizations* (Free Press, 1989).

FIGURE 1
THE SIX BASIC PARTS
OF THE
ORGANIZATION

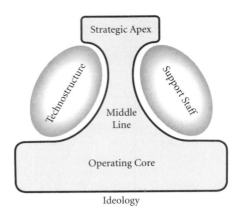

that distinguish it from other organizations and infuse a certain life into the skeleton of its structure.

This gives us six basic parts of an organization. As shown in Figure 1, we have a small strategic apex connected by a flaring middle line to a large, flat operating core at the base. These three parts of the organization are drawn in one uninterrupted sequence to indicate that they are typically connected through a single chain of formal authority. The technostructure and the support staff are shown off to either side to indicate that they are spearate from this main line of authority, influencing the operating core only indirectly. The ideology is shown as a kind of halo that surrounds the entire system.

These people, all of whom work inside the organization to make its decisions and take its actions—full-time employees or, in some cases, committed volunteers—may be thought of as *influencers* who form a kind of internal coalition. By this term, we mean a system within which people vie among themselves to determine the distribution of power.

In addition, various outside people also try to exert influence on the organization, seeking to affect the decisions and actions taken inside. These external influencers, who create a field of forces around the organization, can include owners, unions and other employee associations, suppliers, clients, partners, competitors, and all kinds of publics, in the form of governments, special interest groups, and so forth. Together they can all be thought to form an *external coalition.*

Sometimes the external coalition is relatively *passive* (as in the typical behavior of the shareholders of a widely held corporation or the members of a large union). Other times it is *dominated* by one active influencer or some group of them acting in concert (such as an outside owner of a business firm or a community intent on imposing a certain philosophy on its school system). And in still other cases, the external coalition may be *divided*, as different groups seek to impose contradictory pressures on the organization (as in a prison buffeted between two community groups, one favoring custody, the other rehabilitation).

SIX BASIC COORDINATING MECHANISMS

Every organized human activity—from the making of pottery to the placing of a man on the moon—gives rise to two fundamental and opposing requirements: the *division of labor* into various tasks to be performed and the *coordination* of those tasks to accomplish the activity. The structure of an organization can be defined simply as the total of the ways in which its labor is divided into distinct tasks and then its coordination achieved among those tasks.

1. *Mutual adjustment* achieves coordination of work by the simple process of informal communication. The people who do the work interact with one another to coordinate, much as two canoeists in the rapids adjust to one another's actions. Figure 2a shows mutual adjustment in terms of an arrow between two operators. Mutual adjustment is obviously

FIGURE 2
THE BASIC
MECHANISMS OF
COORDINATION

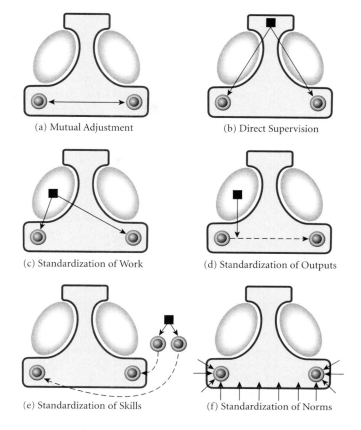

(a) Mutual Adjustment

(b) Direct Supervision

(c) Standardization of Work

(d) Standardization of Outputs

(e) Standardization of Skills

(f) Standardization of Norms

used in the simplest of organizations—it is the most obvious way to coordinate. But, paradoxically, it is also used in the most complex, because it is the only means that can be relied upon under extremely difficult circumstances, such as trying to figure out how to put a man on the moon for the first time.

2. *Direct supervision* in which one person coordinates by giving orders to others, tends to come into play after a certain number of people must work together. Thus, fifteen people in a war canoe cannot coordinate by mutual adjustment; they need a leader who, by virtue of instructions, coordinates their work, much as a football team requires a quarterback to call the plays. Figure 2b shows the leader as a manager with the instructions as arrows to the operators.

Coordination can also be achieved by *standardization*—in effect, automatically, by virtue of standards that predetermine what people do and so ensure that their work is coordinated. We can consider four forms—the standardization of the work processes themselves, of the outputs of the work, of the knowledge and skills that serve as inputs to the work, or of the norms that more generally guide the work.

3. *Standardization of work processes* means the specification—that is, the programming—of the content of the work directly, the procedures to be followed, as in the case of the assembly instructions that come with many children's toys. As shown in Figure 2c, it is typically the job of the analysts to so program the work of different people in order to coordinate it tightly.

4. *Standardization of outputs* means the specification not of what is to be done but of its results. In that way, the interfaces between jobs is predetermined, as when a machinist is told to drill holes in a certain place on a fender so that they will fit the bolts being welded by someone else, or a division manager is told to achieve a sales growth of 10% so that the corporation can meet some overall sales target. Again, such standards generally emanate from the analysts, as shown in Figure 2d.

5. *Standardization of skills*, as well as knowledge, is another, though looser way to achieve coordination. Here, it is the worker rather than the work or the outputs that is standardized. He or she is taught a body of knowledge and a set of skills which are subsequently applied to the work. Such standardization typically takes place outside the organization—for example, in a professional school of a university before the worker takes his or her first job—indicated in Figure 2e. In effect, the standards do not come from the analyst; they are internalized by the operator as inputs to the job he or she takes. Coordination is then achieved by virtue of various operators' having learned what to expect of each other. When an anesthetist and a surgeon meet in the operating room to remove an appendix, they need hardly communicate (that is, use mutual adjustment, let alone direct supervision); each knows exactly wha the other will do and can coordinate accordingly.

6. *Standardization of norms* means that the workers share a common set of beliefs and can achieve coordination based on it, as implied in Figure 2f. For example, if every member of a religious order shares a belief in the importance of attracting converts, then all will work together to achieve this aim.

These coordinating mechanisms can be considered the most basic elements of structure, the glue that holds organizations together. They seem to fall into a rough order. As organizational work becomes more complicated, the favored means of coordination seems to shift from mutual adjustment (the simplest mechanism) to direct supervision, then to standardization, preferably of work processes or norms, otherwise of outputs or of skills, finally reverting back to mutual adjustment. But no organization can rely on a single one of those mechanisms; all will typically be found in every reasonably developed organization.

Still, the important point for us here is that many organizations do favor one mechanism over the others, at least at certain stages of their lives. In fact, organizations that favor none seem most prone to becoming politicized, simply because of the conflicts that naturally arise when people have to vie for influence in a relative vacuum of power.

THE ESSENTIAL PARAMETERS OF DESIGN

The essence of organizational design is the manipulation of a series of parameters that determine the division of labor and the achievement of coordination. Some of these concern the design of individual positons, others the design of the superstructure (the overall network of subunits, reflected in the organizational chart), some the design of lateral linkages to flesh out that superstructure, and a final group concerns the design of the decision-making system of the organization. Listed as follows are the main parameters of structural design, with links to the coordinating mechanisms.

- **Job specialization** refers to the number of tasks in a given job and the workers' control over these tasks. A job is *horizontally* specialized to the extent that it encompasses a few narrowly defined tasks, *vertically* specialized to the extent that the worker lacks control of the tasks performed. *Unskilled* jobs are typically highly specialized in both dimensions; skilled or *professional* jobs are typically specialized horizontally but not vertically. "Job enrichment" refers to the enlargement of jobs in both the vertical and horizontal dimension.

- **Behavior formalization** refers to the standardization of work processes by the imposition of operating instructions, job descriptions, rules, regulations, and the like. Structures that rely on any form of standardization for coordination may be defined as *bureaucratic*, those that do not as *organic*.

- **Training** refers to the use of formal instructional programs to establish and standardize in people the requisite skills and knowledge to do particular jobs in organizations. Training is a key design parameter in all work we call professional. Training and formalization are basically substitutes for achieving the standardization (in effect, the bureaucratization) of behavior. In one, the standards are learned as skills, in the other they are imposed on the job as rules.

- **Indoctrination** refers to programs and techniques by which the norms of the members of an organization are standardized, so that they become responsive to its ideological needs and can thereby be trusted to make its decisions and take its actions. Indoctrination too is a substitute for formalization, as well as for skill training, in this case the standards being internalized as deeply rooted beliefs.

- **Unit grouping** refers to the choice of the bases by which positions are grouped together into units, and those units into higher-order units (typically shown on the organization chart). Grouping encourages coordination by putting different jobs under common supervision, by requiring them to share common resources and achieve common measures of performance, and by using proximity to facilitate mutual adjustment among them. The various bases for grouping—by work process, product, client, place, and so on—can be reduced to two fundamental ones—the *function* performed and the *market* served. The former (illustrated in Fig. 3) refers to means, that is to a single link in the chain of processes by which products or services are produced; the latter (in Fig. 4) to ends, that is, the whole chain for specific end products, services, or markets. On what criteria should the choice of a basis for grouping be made? First, there is the consideration of workflow linkages, or "interdependencies." Obviously, the more tightly linked are positions or units in the workflow, the more desirable that they be grouped together to facilitate their coordination. Second is the consideration of process interdependencies—for example, across people doing the same kind of work but in different workflows (such as maintenance men working on different machines). It sometimes makes sense to group them together to facilitate their sharing of equipment or ideas, to encourage the improvement of their skills, and so on. Third is the question of scale interdependencies. For example, all maintenance people in a factory may have to be grouped together because no single department has enough maintenance work for one person. Finally, there are the social interdependencies, the need to group people together for social reasons, as in coal mines where mutual support under dangerous working conditions can be a factor in deciding how to group people. Clearly, grouping by function is favored by process and scale interdependencies, and to a lesser extent by social interdependencies (in the sense that people who do the same kind of job often tend to get along better). Grouping by function also encourages specialization, for example, by allowing specialists to come together under the supervision of one of their own kind. The problem with functional grouping, however, is that it narrows perspectives, encouraging a focus on means instead of ends—the way to do the job instead of the reason for doing the job in the first place. Thus grouping by market is used to favor coordination in the workflow at the expense of process and scale specializaiton. In general, market grouping reduces the ability to do specialized or repetitive tasks well and is more wasteful, being less able to take advantage of economies of scale and often requiring the duplication of resources. But it enables the organization to accomplish a wider variety of tasks and to

FIGURE 3
GROUPING
BY FUNCTION:
A CULTURAL CENTER

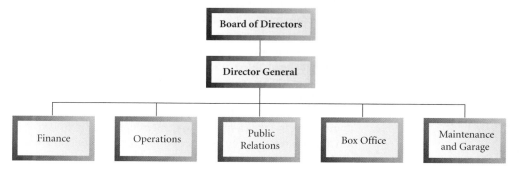

FIGURE 4
GROUPING BY MARKET:
THE CANADIAN POST OFFICE*

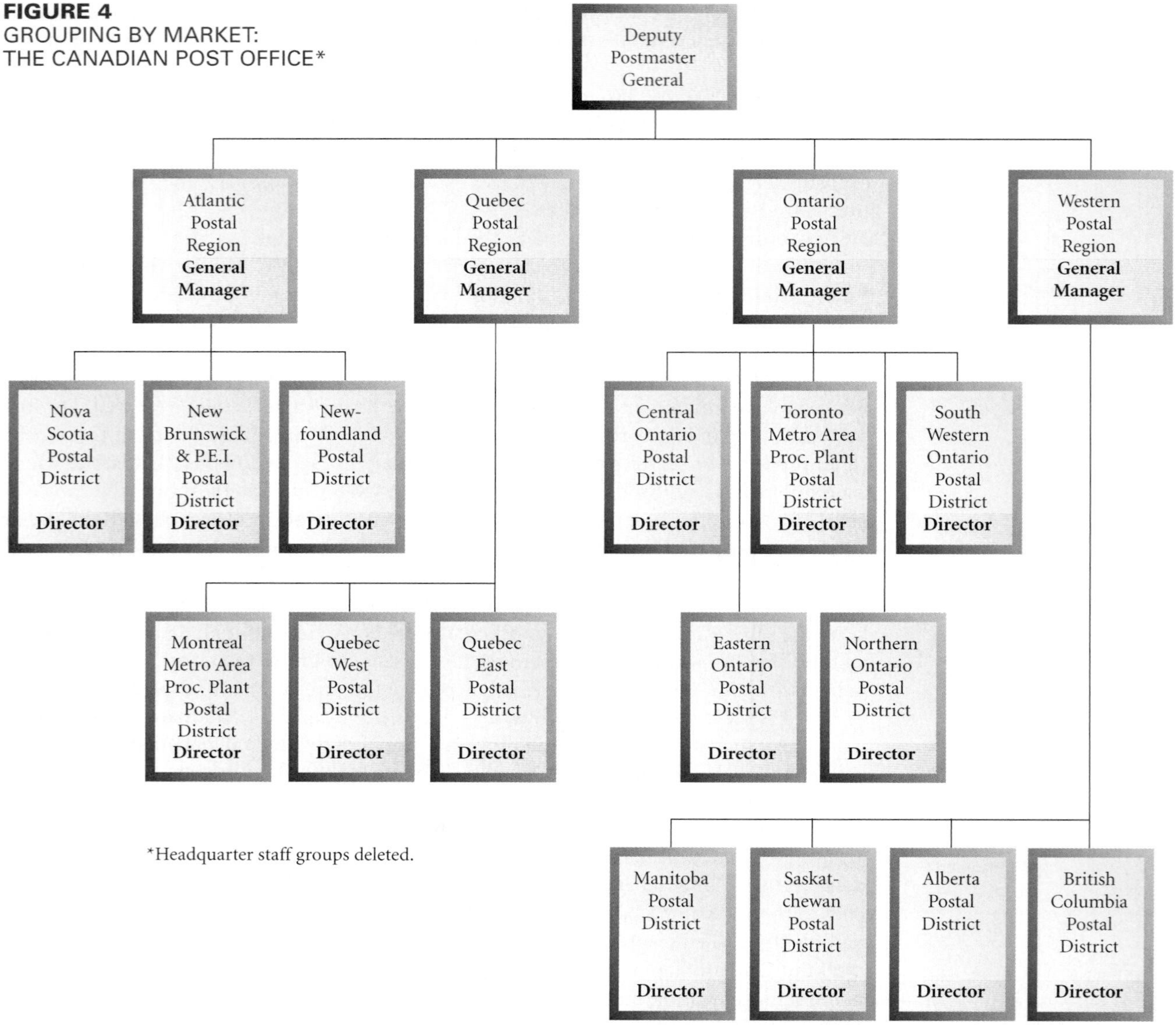

```
                          Deputy
                          Postmaster
                          General
```

| Atlantic Postal Region **General Manager** | Quebec Postal Region **General Manager** | Ontario Postal Region **General Manager** | Western Postal Region **General Manager** |

Atlantic Postal Region:
- Nova Scotia Postal District **Director**
- New Brunswick & P.E.I. Postal District **Director**
- New-foundland Postal District **Director**

Quebec Postal Region:
- Montreal Metro Area Proc. Plant Postal District **Director**
- Quebec West Postal District **Director**
- Quebec East Postal District **Director**

Ontario Postal Region:
- Central Ontario Postal District **Director**
- Toronto Metro Area Proc. Plant Postal District **Director**
- South Western Ontario Postal District **Director**
- Eastern Ontario Postal District **Director**
- Northern Ontario Postal District **Director**

Western Postal Region:
- Manitoba Postal District **Director**
- Saskatchewan Postal District **Director**
- Alberta Postal District **Director**
- British Columbia Postal District **Director**

*Headquarter staff groups deleted.

change its tasks more easily to serve the organization's end markets. And so if the workflow interdependencies are the important ones and if the organization cannot easily handle them by standardization, then it will tend to favor the market bases for grouping in order to encourage mutual adjustment and direct supervision. But if the workflow is irregular (as in a "job shop"), if standardization can easily contain the important workflow interdependencies, or if the process or scale interdependencies are the important ones, then the organization will be inclined to seek the advantages of specialization and group on the basis of function instead. Of course in all but the smallest organizations, the question is not so much *which* basis of grouping, but in what *order*. Much as fires are built by stacking logs first one way and then the other, so too are organizations built by varying the different bases for grouping to take care of various interdependencies.

■ **Unit size** refers to the number of positions (or units) contained in a single unit. The equivalent term, *span of control*, is not used here, because sometimes units are kept small despite an absence of close supervisory control. For example, when experts coordinate extensively by mutual adjustment, as in an engineering team in a space agency, they will form into small units. In this case, unit size is small and span of control is low despite a relative absence of direct supervision. In contrast, when work is highly standardized (because of either formalization or training), unit size can be very large, because there is little need for direct supervision. One foreman can supervise dozens of assemblers, because they work according to very tight instructions.

- **Planning and control systems** are used to standardize outputs. They may be divided into two types: *action planning* sytems, which specify the results of specific actions before they are taken (for example, that holes should be drilled with diameters of 3 centimeters); and *performance control* systems, which specify the desired results of whole ranges of actions after the fact (for example, that sales of a division should grow by 10% in a given year).

- **Liaison devices** refer to a whole series of mechanisms used to encourage mutual adjustment within and between units. Four are of particular importance:
  - *Liaison positions* are jobs created to coordinate the work of two units directly, without having to pass through managerial channels, for example, the purchasing engineer who sits between purchasing and engineering or the sales liaison person who mediates between the sales force and the factory. These positions carry no formal authority per se; rather, those who serve in them must use their powers of persuasion, negotiation, and so on to bring the two sides together.
  - *Task forces and standing committees* are institutionalized forms of meetings which bring members of a number of different units together on a more intensive basis, in the first case to deal with a temporary issue, in the second, in a more permanent and regular way to discuss issues of common interest.
  - *Integrating managers*—essentially liaison personnel with formal authority—provide for stronger coordination. These "managers" are given authority not over the units they link, but over something important to those units, for example, their budgets. One example is the brand manager in a consumer goods firm who is responsible for a certain product but who must negotiate its production and marketing with different functional departments.
  - *Matrix structure* carries liaison it its natural conclusion. No matter what the bases of grouping at one level in an organization, some interdependencies always remain. Figure 5 suggests various ways to deal with these "residual interdependencies": a different type of grouping can be used at the next level in the hierarchy; staff units can be formed next to line units to advise on the problems; or one of the liaison devices already discussed

FIGURE 5
STRUCTURES TO DEAL
WITH RESIDUAL
INTERDEPENDENCIES

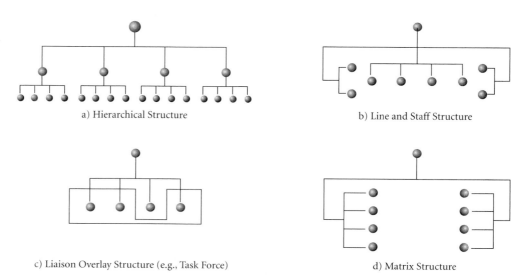

a) Hierarchical Structure

b) Line and Staff Structure

c) Liaison Overlay Structure (e.g., Task Force)

d) Matrix Structure

can be overlaid on the grouping. But in each case, one basis of grouping is favored over the others. The concept of matrix structure is balance between two (or more) bases of grouping, for example functional with market (or for that matter, one kind of market with another—say, regional with product). This is done by the creation of a dual authority structure—two (or more) managers, units, or individuals are made jointly and equally responsible for the same decisions. We can distinguish a *permanent* form of matrix structure, where the units and the people in them remain more or less in place, as shown in the example of a whimsical multinational firm in Figure 6, and a *shifting* form, suited to project work, where the units and the people in them move around frequently. Shifting matrix structures are common in high-technology industries, which group specialists in functional departments for housekeeping purposes (process interdependencies, etc.) but deploy them from various departments in project teams to do the work, as shown for NASA in Figure 7.

■ **Decentralization** refers to the diffusion of decision-making power. When all the power rests at a single point in an organization, we call its structure centralized; to the extent that the power is dispersed among many individuals, we call it relatively decentralized. We can distinguish *vertical decentralization*—the delegation of formal power down the hierarchy to line managers—from *horizontal decentralization*—the extent to which formal or informal power is dispersed out of the line hierarchy to nonmanagers (operators, analysts, and support staffers). We can also distinguish *selective* decentralization—the dispersal of power over different decisions to different places in the organization—from *parallel* decentralization—where the power over various kinds of decisions is delegated to the same place. Six forms of decentralization may thus be described: (1) vertical and horizontal centralization, where all the power rests at the strategic apex; (2) limited horizontal decentralization (selective), where the strategic apex shares some power with the technostructure that standardizes everybody else's work; (3) limited vertical decentralization (parallel), where managers of market-based units are delegated the power to control most of the decisions concerning their line units; (4) vertical and horizontal decentralization, where most of the power rests in the operating core, at the bottom of the structure; (5) selective vertical and horizontal decentralization, where the power over different decisions is dispersed to various places in the organization, among managers, staff experts, and operators who work in teams at various levels in the hierarchy; and (6) pure decentralization, where power is shared more or less equally by all members of the organization.

FIGURE 6
A PERMANENT
MATRIX STRUCTURE
IN AN INTERNATIONAL
FIRM

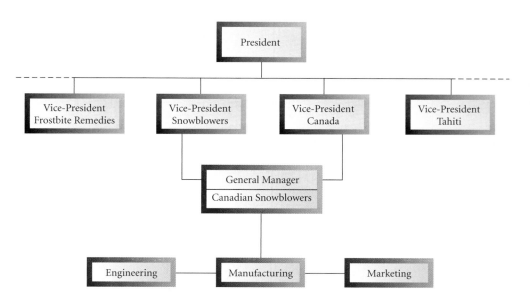

FIGURE 7
SHIFTING MATRIX
STRUCTURE IN THE
NASA WEATHER
SATELLITE PROGRAM
Source: Modified from
Delbecq and Filley (1974: 16).

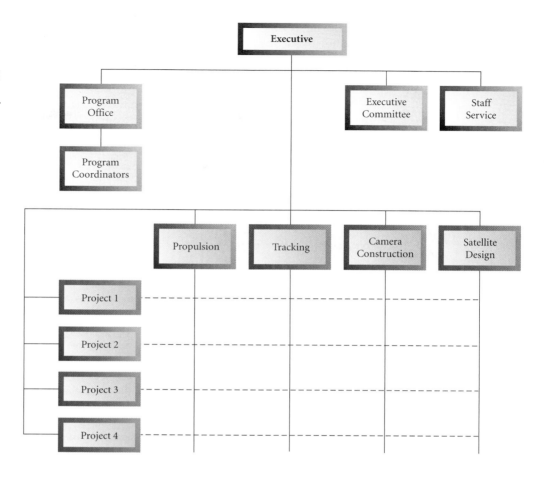

THE SITUATIONAL FACTORS

A number of "contingency" or "situational" factors influence the choice of these design parameters, and vice versa. They include the age and size of the organization; its technical system of production; various characteristics of its environment, such as stability and complexity; and its power system, for example, whether or not it is tightly controlled by outside influencers. Some of the effects of these factors, as found in an extensive body of research literature, are summarized below as hypotheses.

AGE AND SIZE

- **The older an organization, the more formalized its behavior.** What we have here is the "we've-seen-it-all-before" syndrome. As organizations age, they tend to repeat their behaviors: as a result, these become more predictable and so more amenable to formalization.
- **The larger an organization, the more formalized its behavior.** Just as the older organization formalizes what it has seen before, so the larger organization formalizes what it sees often. ("Listen mister, I've heard that story at least five times today. Just fill in the form like it says.")
- **The larger an organization, the more elaborate its structure; that is, the more specialized its jobs and units and the more developed its administrative components.** As organizations grow in size, they are able to specialize their jobs more finely. (The big barbershop can afford a specialist to cut children's hair; the small one cannot.) As a result, they can also specialize—or "differentiate"—the work of their units more extensively. This requires more effort at coordination. And so the larger organization tends also to enlarge its hierarchy to

effect direct supervision and to make greater use of its technostructure to achieve coordination by standardization, or else to encourage more coordination by mutual adjustment.

- **The larger the organization, the larger the size of its average unit.** This finding relates to the previous two, the size of units growing larger as organizations themselves grow larger because (1) as behavior becomes more formalized, and (2) as the work of each unit becomes more homogeneous, managers are able to supervise more employees.
- **Structure reflects the age of the industry from its founding.** This is a curious finding, but one that we shall see holds up remarkably well. An organization's structure seems to reflect the age of the industry in which it operates, no matter what its own age. Industries that predate the industrial revolution seem to favor one kind of structure, those of the age of the early railroads another, and so on. We should obviously expect different structures in different periods; the surprising thing is that these structures seem to carry through to new periods, old industries remaining relatively true to earlier structures.

TECHNICAL SYSTEM

Technical system refers to the instruments used in the operating core to produce the outputs. (This should be distinguished from "technology," which refers to the knowledge base of an organization.)

- **The more regulating the technical system—that is, the more it controls the work of the operators—the more formalized the operating work and the more bureaucratic the structure of the operating core.** Technical systems that regulate the work of the operators—for example, mass production assembly lines—render that work highly routine and predictable, and so encourage its specialization and formalization, which in turn create the conditions for bureaucracy in the operating core.
- **The more complex the technical system, the more elaborate and professional the support staff.** Essentially, if an organization is to use complex machinery, it must hire staff experts who can understand that machinery—who have the capability to design, select, and modify it. And then it must give them considerable power to make decisions concerning that machinery, and encourage them to use the liaison devices to ensure mutual adjustment among them.
- **The automation of the operating core forms a bureaucratic administrative structure into an organic one.** When unskilled work is coordinated by the standardization of work processes, we tend to get bureaucratic structure throughout the organization, because a control mentality pervades the whole system. But when the work of the operating core becomes automated, social relationships tend to change. Now it is machines, not people, that are regulated. So the obsession with control tends to disappear—machines do not need to be watched over—and with it go many of the managers and analysts who were needed to control the operators. In their place come the support specialists to look after the machinery, coordinating their own work by mutual adjustment. Thus, automation reduces line authority in favor of staff expertise and reduces the tendency to rely on standardization for coordination.

ENVIRONMENT

Environment refers to various characteristics of the organization's outside context, related to markets, political climate, economic conditions, and so on.

- **The more dynamic an organization's environment, the more organic its structure.** It stands to reason that in a stable environment—where nothing changes—an organization can predict its future conditions and so, all other things being equal, can easily rely on standardization for coordination. But when conditions become dynamic—when the need for product change is frequent, labor turnover is high, and political conditions are unstable—the organization cannot standardize but must instead remain flexible through the use of direct supervision or mutual adjustment for coordination, and so it must use a more organic structure. Thus, for example, armies, which tend to be highly bureaucratic institutions in peacetime, can become rather organic when engaged in highly dynamic, guerilla-type warfare.

- **The more complex an organization's environment, the more decentralized its structure.** The prime reason to decentralize a structure is that all the information needed to make decisions cannot be comprehended in one head. Thus, when the operations of an organization are based on a complex body of knowledge, there is usually a need to decentralize decision-making power. Note that a simple environment can be stable or dynamic (the manufacturer of dresses faces a simple environment yet cannot predict style from one season to another), as can a complex one (the specialist in perfected open heart surgery faces a complex task, yet knows what to expect).

- **The more diversified an organization's markets, the greater the propensity to split it into market-based units, or divisions, given favorable economies of scale.** When an organization can identify distinct markets—geographical regions, clients, but especially products and services—it will be predisposed to split itself into high level units on that basis, and to give each a good deal of control over its own operations (that is, to use what we called "limited vertical decentralization"). In simple terms, diversification breeds divisionalization. Each unit can be given all the functions associated with its own markets. But this assumes favorable economies of scale: If the operating core cannot be divided, as in the case of an aluminum smelter, also if some critical function must be centrally coordinated, as in purchasing in a retail chain, then full divisionalization may not be possible.

- **Extreme hostility in its environment drives any organization to centralize its structure temporarily.** When threatened by extreme hostility in its environment, the tendency for an organization is to centralize power, in other words, to fall back on its tightest coordinating mechanism, direct supervision. Here a single leader can ensure fast and tightly coordinated response to the threat (at least temporarily).

POWER

- **The greater the external control of an organization, the more centralized and formalized its structure**. This important hypothesis claims that to the extent that an organization is controlled externally—for example by a parent firm or a government that dominates its external coalition—it tends to centralize power at the strategic apex and to formalize its behavior. The reason is that the two most effective ways to control an organization from the outside are to hold its chief executive officer responsible for its actions and to impose clearly defined standards on it. Moreover, external control forces the organization to be especially careful about its actions.

- **A divided external coalition will tend to give rise to a politicized internal coalition, and vice versa.** In effect, conflict in one of the coalitions tends to spill over to the other, as one set of influencers seeks to enlist the support of the others.

- **Fashion favors the structure of the day (and the culture), sometimes even when inappropriate.** Ideally, the design parameters are chosen according to the dictates of age, size, technical system, and environment. In fact, however, fashion seems to play a role too, encouraging many organizations to adopt currently popular design parameters that are inappropriate for themselves. Paris has its salons of haute couture; likewise New York has its offices of "haute structure," the consulting firms that sometimes tend to oversell the latest in structural fashion.

THE CONFIGURATIONS

We have now introduced various attributes of organizations—parts, coordinating mechanisms, design parameters, situational factors. How do they all combine?

We proceed here on the assumption that a limited number of configurations can help explain much of what is observed in organizations. We have introduced in our discussion six basic parts of the organization, six basic mechanisms of coordination, as well as six basic types

FIGURE 8
BASIC PULLS
ON THE
ORGANIZATION

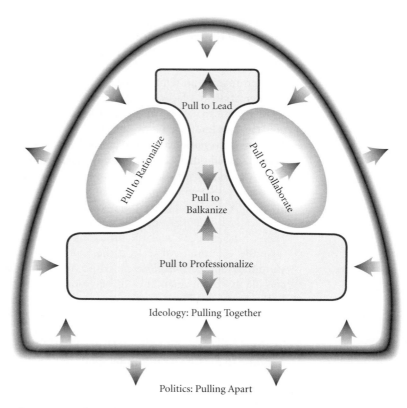

of decentralization. In fact, there seems to be a fundamental correspondence between all of these sixes, which can be explained by a set of pulls exerted on the organization by each of its six parts, as shown in Figure 8. When conditions favor one of these pulls, the associated part of the organization becomes key, the coordinating mechanism appropriate to itself becomes prime, and the form of decentralization that passes power to itself emerges. The organization is thus drawn to design itself as a particular configuration. We list here (see Table 1) and then introduce briefly the six resulting configurations, together with a seventh that tends to appear when no one pull or part dominates.

THE ENTREPRENEURIAL ORGANIZATION

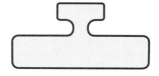

The name tells it all. And the figure above shows it all. The structure is simple, not much more than one large unit consisting of one or a few top managers, one of whom dominates by the pull to lead, and a group of operators who do the basic work. Little of the behavior in the organization is formalized and minimal use is made of planning, training, or the liaison devices. The absence of standardization means that the structure is organic and has little need for staff analysts. Likewise there are few middle line managers because so much of the coordination is handled at the top. Even the support staff is minimized, in order to keep the structure lean, the organization flexible.

The organization must be flexible because it operates in a dynamic environment, often by choice since that is the only place where it can outsmart the bureaucracies. But that environment must be simple, as must the production system, or else the chief executive could not for

TABLE 1

CONFIGURATION	PRIME COORDINATING MECHANISM	KEY PART OF ORGANIZATION	TYPE OF DECENTRALIZATION
Entrepreneurial organization	Direct supervision	Strategic apex	Vertical and horizontal centralization
Machine organization	Standardization of work processes	Technostructure	Limited horizontal decentralization
Professional organization	Standardization of skills	Operating core	Horizontal decentralization
Diversified organization	Standardization of outputs	Middle line	Limited vertical decentralization
Innovative organization	Mutual adjustment	Support staff	Selected decentralization
Missionary organization	Standardization of norms	Ideology	Decentralization
Political organization	None	None	Varies

long hold on to the lion's share of the power. The organization is often young, in part because time drives it toward bureaucracy, in part because the vulnerability of its simple structure often causes it to fail. And many of these organizations are often small, since size too drives the structure toward bureaucracy. Not infrequently the chief executive purposely keeps the organization small in order to retain his or her personal control.

The classic case is of course the small entrepreneurial firm, controlled tightly and personally by its owner. Sometimes, however, under the control of a strong leader the organization can grow to large. Likewise, entrepreneurial organizations can be found in other sectors too, like government, where strong leaders personally control particular agencies, often ones they have founded. Sometimes under crisis conditions, large organizations also revert temporarily to the entrepreneurial form to allow forceful leaders to try to save them.

THE MACHINE ORGANIZATION

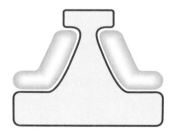

The machine organization is the offspring of the Industrial Revolution, when jobs became highly specialized and work became highly standardized. As can be seen in the figure above, in contrast to entrepreneurial organizations, the machine one elaborates its administration. First, it requires a large technostructure to design and maintain its systems of standardization, notably those formalize its behaviors and plan its actions. And by virtue of the organization's dependence on these systems, the technostructure gains a good deal of informal power, resulting in a limited amount of horizontal decentralization reflecting the pull to rationalize. A large hierarchy of middle-line managers emerges to control the highly specialized work of the operating core. But the middle line hierarchy is usually structured on a functional basis all the way up to the top, where the real power of coordination lies. So the structure tends to be rather centralized in the vertical sense.

To enable the top managers to maintain centralized control, both the environment and the production system of the machine organization must be fairly simple, the latter regulating the work of the operators but not itself automated. In fact, machine organizations fit most naturally with mass production. Indeed it is interesting that this structure is most prevalent in industries that date back to the period from the Industrial Revolution to the early part of this century.

THE PROFESSIONAL ORGANIZATION

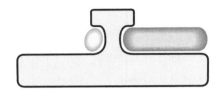

There is another bureaucratic configuration, but because this one relies on the standardization of skills rather than of work processes or outputs for its coordination, it emerges as dramatically different from the machine one. Here the pull to professionalize dominates. In having to rely on trained professionals—people highly specialized, but with considerable control over their work, as in hospitals or universities—to do its operating tasks, the organization surrenders a good deal of its power not only to the professionals themselves but also to the associations and institutions that select and train them in the first place. So the structure emerges as highly decentralized horizontally; power over many decisions, both operating and strategic, flows all the way down the hierarchy, to the professionals of the operating core.

Above the operating core we find a rather unique structure. There is little need for a technostructure, since the main standardization occurs as a result of training that takes place outside the organization. Because the professionals work so independently, the size of operating units can be very large, and few first line managers are needed. The support staff is typically very large too, in order to back up the high-priced professionals.

The professional organization is called for whenever an organization finds itself in an environment that is stable yet complex. Complexity requires decentralization to highly trained individuals, and stability enables them to apply standardized skills and so to work with a good deal of autonomy. To ensure that autonomy, the production system must be neither highly regulating, complex, nor automated.

THE DIVERSIFIED ORGANIZATION

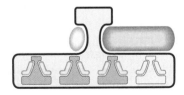

Like the professional organization, the diversified one is not so much an integrated organization as a set of rather independent entities coupled together by a loose administrative structure. But whereas those entities of the professional organization are individuals, in the diversified one they are units in the middle line, generally called "divisions," exerting a dominant pull to Balkanize. This configuration differs from the others in one major respect: it is not a complete structure, but a partial one superimposed on the others. Each division has its own structure.

An organization divisionalizes for one reason above all, because its product lines are diversified. And that tends to happen most often in the largest and most mature organizations, the ones that have run out of opportunities—or have become bored—in their traditional markets. Such diversification encourages the organization to replace functional by market-based units, one for each distinct product line (as shown in the diversified organization figure), and to grant considerable autonomy to each to run its own business. The result is a limited form of decentralization down the chain of command.

How does the central headquarters maintain a semblance of control over the divisions? Some direction supervision is used. But too much of that interferes with the necessary divisional autonomy. So the headquarters relies on performance control systems, in other words, the standardization of outputs. To design these control systems, headquarters creates a small technostructure. This is shown in the figure, across from the small central support staff that headquarters sets up to provide certain services common to the divisions such as legal counsel and public relations. And because headquarters' control constitutes external control, as discussed in the first hypothesis on power, the structure of the divisions tend to be drawn toward the machine form.

THE INNOVATIVE ORGANIZATION

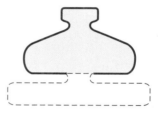

None of the structures so far discussed suits the industries of our age, industries such as aerospace, petrochemicals, think-tank consulting, and film making. These organizations need above all to innovate in very complex ways. The bureaucratic structures are too inflexible, and the entrepreneurial one too centralized. These industries require "project structures," ones that can fuse experts drawn from different specialties into smoothly functioning creative teams. That is the role of our fifth configuration, the innovative organization, which we shall also call "adhocracy," dominated by the experts' pull to collaborate.

Adhocracy is an organic structure that relies for coordination on mutual adjustment among its highly trained and highly specialized experts, which it encourages by the extensive use of the liaison devices—integrating managers, standing committees, and above all task forces and matrix structure. Typically the experts are grouped in functional units for housekeeping purposes but deployed in small market based project teams to do their work. To these teams, located all over the structure in accordance with the decisions to be made, is delegated power over different kinds of decisions. So the structure becomes decentralized selectively in the vertical and horizontal dimensions, that is, power is distributed unevenly, all over the structure, according to expertise and need.

All the distinctions of conventional structure disappear in the innovative organization, as can be seen in the figure above. With power based on expertise, the line-staff distinction evaporates. With power distributed throughout the structure, the distinction between the strategic apex and the rest of the structure blurs.

These organizations are found in environments that are both complex and dynamic, because those are the ones that require sophisticated innovation, the type that calls for the cooperative efforts of many different kinds of experts. One type of adhocracy is often associated with a production system that is very complex, sometimes automated, and so requires a highly skilled and influential support staff to design and maintain the technical system of the operating core. (The dashed lines of the figure designate the separation of the operating core from the adhocratic administrative structure.) Here the projects take place in the administration to bring new operating facilities on line (as when a new complex is designed in a petrochemicals firm). Another type of adhocracy produces its projects directly for its clients (as in a think tank consulting firm or manufacturer of engineering prototypes). Here, as a result, the operators also take part in the projects, bringing their expertise to bear on them; hence the operating core blends into the administrative structure (as indicated in the figure above the dashed line). This second type of adhocracy tends to be young on average, because with no standard products or services, many tend to fail while others escape their vulnerability by standardizing some products or services and so converting themselves to a form of bureaucracy.*

THE MISSIONARY ORGANIZATION

Our sixth configuration forms another rather distinct combination of the elements we have been discussing. When an organization is dominated by its ideology, its members are encouraged to pull together, and so there tends to be a loose division of labor, little job specialization, as well as a reduction of the various forms of differentiation found in the other configurations—of the strategic apex from the rest, of staff from line or administration from operations, between operators, between divisions, and so on.

What holds the missionary together—that is, provides for its coordination—is the standardization of norms, the sharing of values and beliefs among all its members. And the key to ensuring this is their socialization, effected through the design parameter of indoctrination. Once the new member has been indoctrinated into the organization—once he or she identifies strongly with the common beliefs—then he or she can be given considerable freedom to make decisions. Thus the result of effective indoctrination is the most complete form of decentralization. And because other forms of coordination need not be relied upon, the missionary organization formalizes little of its behavior as such and makes minimal use of planning and control systems. As a result, it has little technostructure. Likewise, external professional training is not relied upon, because that would force the organization to surrender a certain control to external agencies.

Hence, the missionary organization ends up as an amorphous mass of members, with little specialization as to job, differentiation as to part, division as to status.

---

*We shall clarify in a later reading these two basic types of adhocracies. Toffler employed the term *adhocracy* in his popular book *Future Shock*, but it can be found in print at least as far back as 1964

Missionaries tend not to be very young organizations—it takes time for a set of beliefs to become institutionalized as an ideology. Many missionaries do not get a chance to grow very old either (with notable exceptions, such as certain long standing religious orders). Missionary organizations cannot grow very large per se—they rely on personal contacts among their members—although some tend to spin off other enclaves in the form of relatively independent units sharing the same ideology. Neither the environment nor the technical system of the missionary organization can be very complex, because that would require the use of highly skilled specialists, who would hold a certain power and status over others and thereby serve to differentiate the structure. Thus we would expect to find the simplest technical systems in these organizations, usually hardly any at all, as in religious orders or in the primitive farm cooperatives.

THE POLITICAL ORGANIZATION

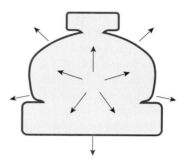

Finally, we come to a form of organization characterized, structurally at least, by what it lacks. When an organization has no dominate part, no dominant mechanism of coordination, and no stable form of centralization or decentralization, it may have difficulty tempering the conflicts within its midst, and a form of organization called the *political* may result. What characterizes its behavior is the pulling apart of its different parts, as shown in the figure above.

Political organizations can take on different forms. Some are temporary, reflecting difficult transitions in strategy or structure that evoke conflict. Others are more permanent, perhaps because the organization must face competing internal forces (say, between necessarily strong marketing and production departments), perhaps because a kind of political rot has set in but the organization is sufficiently entrenched to support it (being, for example, a monopoly or a protected government unit).

Together, all these configurations seem to encompass and integrate a good deal of what we know about organizations. It should be emphasized, however, that as presented, each configuration is idealized—a simplification, really a caricature of reality. No real organization is ever exactly like any one of them, although some do come remarkably close, while others seem to reflect combinations of them, sometimes in transition from one to another.

The first five represent what seem to be the most common forms of organizations; thus these will form the basis for the "context" section of this book—labeled entrepreneurial, mature, diversified, innovation, and professional. There, a reading in each chapter will be devoted to each of these configurations, describing its structure, functioning, conditions, strategy-making process, and the issues that surround it. Other readings in these chapters will look at specific strategies in each of these contexts, industry conditions, strategy techniques, and so on.

The other two configurations—the missionary and the political—seem to be less common, represented more by the forces of culture and conflict that exist in all organizations than by distinct forms as such. Hence they will not be discussed further as such. But because all these configurations themselves must not be taken as hard and fast, a reading in the final chapter, called "Beyond Configuration: Forces and Forms in Effective Organizations," has been included to broaden this view of organizations.

BY JAY R. GALBRAITH

■ ... There has been a great deal of progress in the knowledge base supporting organization planning in the last twenty-five years. Modern research on corporate structures probably started with Chandler's *Strategy and Structure*. Subsequent research has been aimed at expanding the number of attributes of an organization beyond that of just structure. I have used the model shown in Figure 1 to indicate that organization consists of structure, processes that cut the structural lines like budgeting, planning, teams, and so on, reward systems like promotions and compensation, and finally people practices like selection and development (Galbraith, 1977). The trend ... is to expand to more attributes like the 7-Ss (Waterman, 1980) comprising structure, strategy, systems, skills, style, staff, and superordinate goals and to "softer" attributes like culture.

All of these models are intended to convey the same ideas. First, organization is more than just structure. And, second, all of the elements must "fit" to be in "harmony" with each other. The effective organization is one that has blended its structure, management practices, rewards, and people into a package that in turn fits with its strategy. However, strategies change and therefore the organization must change.

The research of the past few years is creating some evidence by which organizations and strategies are matched. Some of the strategies are proving more successful than others. One

*Originally published in *Human Resource Management* (Spring–Summer 1983). Copyright © 1983 John Wiley & Sons, Inc. Reprinted with deletions by permission of John Wiley & Sons, Inc.

FIGURE 1
MODEL OF
ORGANIZATION
STRUCTURE

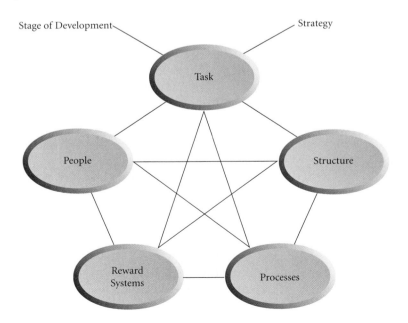

of the explanations is organizational in nature. Also the evidence shows that for any strategy, the high performers are those who have achieved a fit between their strategy and their organization.

These findings give organization planning a base from which to work. The organization planner should become a member of the strategic team in order to guide management to choose the appropriate strategies for which the organization is developed or to choose the appropriate organization for the new strategy.

In the sections that follow, the strategic changes that are made by organizations are described. Then the strategy and organization evidence is presented. Finally the data on economic performance and fit is discussed.

STRATEGY AND ORGANIZATION

There has been a good deal of recent attention given to the match between strategy and organization. Much of this work consists of empirical tests of Chandler's ideas presented in *Strategy and Structure* (1962). Most of this material is reviewed elsewhere (Galbraith and Nathanson, 1978). However, some recent work and ideas hold out considerable potential for understanding how different patterns of strategic change lead to different organization structures, management systems, and company cultures. In addition, some good relationships with economic performance are also attained.

The ideas rest on the concept of an organization having a center of gravity or driving force (Tregoe and Zimmerman, 1980). This center of gravity arises from the firm's initial success in the industry in which it grew up. Let us first explore the concept of center of gravity, then the patterns of strategic change that have been followed by American enterprises.

The center of gravity of a company depends on where in the industry supply chain the company started. In order to explain the concept, manufacturing industries will be used. Figure 2 depicts the stages of supply in an industry chain. Six stages are shown here. Each industry may have more or fewer stages. Service industries typically have fewer stages.

The chain begins with a raw material extraction stage which supplies crude oil, iron ore, logs, or bauxite to the second stage of primary manufacturing. The second stage is a variety-reducing stage to produce a standardized output (petrochemicals, steel, paper pulp, or aluminum ingots). The next stage fabricates commodity products from this primary material. Fabricators produce polyethylene, cans, sheet steel, cardboard cartons, and semiconductor components. The next stage is the product producers who add value, usually through product development, patents, and proprietary products. The next stage is the marketer and distributors. These are the consumer branded product manufacturers and various distributors. Finally, there are the retailers who have the direct contact with the ultimate consumer.

The line splitting the chain into two segments divides the industry into upstream and downstream halves. While there are differences between each of the stages, the differences between the upstream and downstream stages are striking. The upstream stages add value by reducing the variety of raw materials found on the earth's surface to a few standard commodities. The purpose is to produce flexible, predictable raw materials and intermediate products from which an increasing variety of downstream products are made. The downstream stages add value through producing a variety of products to meet varying customer needs. The downstream value is added through advertising, product positioning, marketing channels,

FIGURE 2
SUPPLY STAGES IN AN
INDUSTRY CHAIN

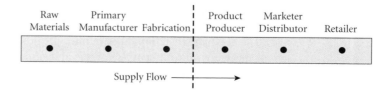

and R&D. Thus, the upstream and downstream companies face very different business problems and tasks.

The reason for distinguishing between upstream and downstream companies is that the factors for success, the lessons learned by managers, and the organizations used are fundamentally different. The successful, experienced manager has been shaped and formed in fundamentally different ways in the different stages. The management processes are different, as are the dominant functions. In short, the company's culture is shaped by where it began in the industry chain. Listed are some fundamental differences that illustrate the contrast:

UPSTREAM	DOWNSTREAM
Standardize/homogenize	Customize/segment
Low-cost producer	High margins/proprietary positions
Process innovation	Product innovation
Capital budget	R&D/advertising budget
Technology/capital intensive	People intensive
Supply/trader/engineering	R&D/marketing dominated
Line driven	Line/staff
Maximize end users	Target end users
.	.
.	.
.	.
Sales push	Market pull

The mind-set of the upstream manager is geared toward standardization and efficiency. They are the producers of standardized commodity products. In contrast, downstream managers try to customize and tailor output to diverse customer needs. They segment markets and target individual users. The upstream company wants to standardize in order to maximize the number of end users and get volume to lower costs. The downstream company wants to target particular sets of end users. Therefore, the upstreamers have a divergent view of the world based on their commodity. For example, the cover of the 1981 annual report of Intel (a fabricator of commodity semiconductors) is a listing of the 10,000 uses to which microprocessors have been put. The downstreamers have a convergent view of the world based on customer needs and will select whatever commodity will best serve that need. In the electronics industry there is always a conflict between the upstream component types and the downstream systems types because of this contrast in mind sets.

The basis of competition is different in the two stages. Commodities compete on price since the products are the same. Therefore, it is essential that the successful upstreamer be the low-cost producer. Their organizations are the lean and mean ones with a minimum of overheads. Low cost is also important for the downstreamer, but it is proprietary features that generate high margins. That feature may be a brand image, such as Maxwell House, a patented technology, an endorsement (such as the American Dental Association's endorsement of Crest toothpaste), customer service policy, and so on. Competition revolves around product features and product positioning and less on price. This means that marketing and product management sets prices. Products move by marketing pull. In contrast, the upstream company pushes the product through a strong sales force. Often salespeople negotiate prices within limits set by top management.

The organizations are different as well. The upstream companies are functional and line driven. They seek a minimum of staff, and even those staffs that are used are in supporting roles. The downstream company with multiple products and multiple markets learns to manage diversity early. Profit centers emerge and resources need to be allocated across products and markets. Larger staffs arise to assist top management in priority setting across competing product/market advocates. Higher margins permit the overhead to exist.

Both upstream and downstream companies use research and development. However, the upstream company invests in process development in order to lower costs. The downstream company invests primarily in product development in order to achieve proprietary positions.

The key managerial processes also vary. The upstream companies are driven by the capital budget and have various capital appropriations controls. The downstream companies also have a capital budget but are driven by the R&D budget (product producers) or the advertising budget (marketers). Further downstream it is working capital that becomes paramount. Managers learn to control the business by managing the turnover of inventory and accounts receivable. Thus, the upstream company is capital intensive and technological "know-how" is critical. Downstream companies are more people intensive. Therefore, the critical skills revolve around human resources management.

The dominant functions also vary with stages. The raw material processor is dominated by geologists, petroleum engineers, and traders. The supply and distribution function which searches for the most economical end use is powerful. The manufacturers of commodities are dominated by engineers who come up through manufacturing. The downstream companies are dominated first by technologists in research and product development. Farther downstream, it is marketing and then merchandising that emerge as the power centers. The line of succession to the CEO usually runs through this dominant function.

In summary, the upstream and downstream companies are very different entities. The differences, a bit exaggerated here because of the dichotomy, lead to differences in organization structure, management processes, dominant functions, succession paths, management beliefs and values or, in short, the management way of life. Thus, companies can be in the same industry but be very different because they developed from a beginning at a particular stage of the industry. This beginning, and the initial successes, teaches management the lessons of that stage. The firm develops an integrated organization (structure, processes, rewards, and people) which is peculiar to that stage and forms the center of gravity.

STRATEGIC CHANGE   The first strategic change that an organization makes is to vertically integrate within its industry. At a certain size, the organization can move backward to prior stages to guarantee sources of supply and secure bargaining leverage on vendors. And/or it can move forward to guarantee markets and volume for capital investments and become a customer to feed back data for new products. This initial strategic move does not change the center of gravity because the prior and subsequent stages are usually operated for the benefit of the center-of-gravity stage.

The paper industry is used to illustrate the concepts of center of gravity and vertical integration. Figure 3 depicts five paper companies which operate from different centers of gravity. The first is Weyerhauser. Its center of gravity is at the land and timber stage of the industry. Weyerhauser seeks the highest return use for a log. They make pulp and paper rolls. They make containers and milk cartons. But they are a timber company. If the returns are better in lumber, the pulp mills get fed with sawdust and chips. International Paper (the name of the company tells it all), by contrast, is a primary manufacturer of paper. It also has timber lands, container plants, and works on new products around aseptic packaging. However, if the pulp mills ran out of logs, the manager of the woodlands used to be fired. The raw material stage is to supply the manufacturing stage, not seek the highest return for its timber. The Container Corporation (again, the name describes the company) is the example of the fabricator. It also has woodlands and pulp mills, but they are to supply the container making operations. The product producer is Appleton. It makes specialty paper products. For example, Appleton produces a paper with globules of ink inbedded in it. The globules burst and form a letter or number when struck with an impact printer.

FIGURE 3
EXAMPLES OF FIVE
PAPER COMPANIES
OPERATING AT
DIFFERENT CENTERS
OF GRAVITY

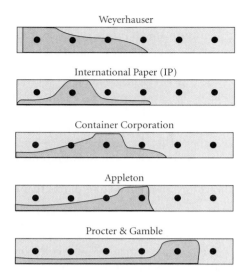

The last company is Procter & Gamble. P&G is a consumer products company. And, like the other companies, it operates pulp mills and owns timber lands. However, it is driven by the advertising or marketing function. If one wanted to be CEO of P&G, one would not run a pulp mill or the woodlands. The path to CEO is through the brand manager for Charmin or Pampers.

Thus, each of these companies is in the paper industry. Each operates at a number of stages in the industry. Yet each is a very different company because it has its center of gravity at a different stage. The center of gravity establishes a base from which subsequent strategic changes take place. That is, as a company's industry matures, the company feels a need to change its center of gravity in order to move to a place in the industry where better returns can be obtained, or move to a new industry but use its same center of gravity and skills in that industry, or make some combination of industry and center of gravity change. These options lead to different patterns of corporate developments.

BY-PRODUCTS DIVERSIFICATION

One of the first diversification moves that a vertically integrated company makes is to sell by-products from points along the industry chain. Figure 4 depicts this strategy. These companies appear to be diversified if one attributes revenue to the various industries in which the company operates. But the company has changed neither its industry nor its center of gravity. The company is behaving intelligently by seeking additional sources of revenue and profit. However, it is still psychologically committed to its center of gravity and to its industry. Alcoa is such a firm. Even though they operate in several industries, their output varies directly with the aluminum cycle. They have not reduced their dependence on a single industry, as one would with real diversification.

RELATED DIVERSIFICATION

Another strategic change is the diversification into new industries but at the same center of gravity. This is called "related diversification." The firm diversifies into new businesses, but they are all related. The relationship revolves around the company's center of gravity. Figure 5

FIGURE 4
BY-PRODUCT
DIVERSIFICATION

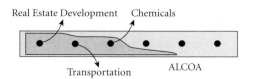

FIGURE 5
RELATED
DIVERSIFICATION

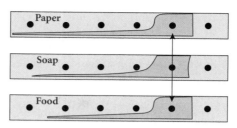

Procter & Gamble

depicts the diversification moves of Proctor & Gamble. After beginning in the soap industry, P&G vertically integrated back into doing its own chemical processing (fatty acids) and seed crushing. Then, in order to pursue new growth opportunities, it has been diversifying into paper, food, beverages, pharmaceuticals, coffee, and so on. But each move into a new industry is made at the company's center of gravity. The new businesses are all consumer products which are driven out of advertising by brand managers. The 3M Company also follows a related diversification strategy, but theirs is based on technology. They have 40,000 different products which are produced by some seventy divisions. However, 95% of the products are based on coating and bonding technologies. Its center of gravity is a product producer, and it adds value through R&D.

LINKED DIVERSIFICATION

A third type of diversification involves moving into new industries and operating at different centers of gravity in those new industries. However, there is a linkage of some type among various businesses. Figure 6 depicts Union Camp as following this pattern of corporate development. Union Camp is a primary producer of paper products. As such, it vertically integrated backwards to own woodlands. From there, it moved downstream within the wood products industry by running sawmills and fabricating plants. However, they recently purchased a retail lumber business.

They also moved into the chemical business by selling by-products from the pulping process. This business was successful and expanded. Recently, Union Camp was bidding for a flavors and fragrances (F&F) company. The F&F company is a product producer which adds value through creating flavors and fragrances for mostly consumer products companies.

Thus, Union Camp is an upstream company that is acquiring downstream companies. However, these new companies are in industries in which the company already diversified from its upstream center of gravity. But these new acquisitions are not operated for the benefit of the center of gravity but are stand-alone profit centers.

UNRELATED DIVERSIFICATION

The final type of strategic change is to diversify into unrelated businesses. Like the linked diversifiers, unrelated diversifiers move into new industries often at a different centers of gravity. They almost always use acquisition, while related and linked companies will use some acquisitions but

FIGURE 6
LINKED
DIVERSIFICATION

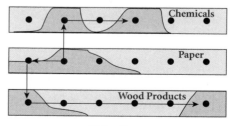

Union Camp

rely heavily on internal development. There is often very little relation between the industries into which the unrelated company diversifies. Textron and Teledyne have been the paradigm examples. They operate in industrial equipment, aerospace, consumer products, insurance, and so on. Others have spread into retailing, services, and entertainment. The purpose is to insulate the company's earnings from the uncertainties of any one industry, or from the business cycle.

CENTER OF GRAVITY CHANGE

Another possibility is for an organization to stay in the same industry but change its center of gravity in that industry. Recent articles describe the attempts of chemical companies to move downstream into higher margin, proprietary products. They want to move away from the overcapacity/undercapacity cycles of commodity businesses with their low margins and high capital intensity. In aerospace, some of the system integration houses are moving backward into making electronic components. For example, there are going to be fewer airplanes and more effort on the avionics, radars, weapons, and so on that go into airplanes. In either case, it means a shift in the center of gravity of the company.

In summary, several patterns of strategic change can occur in a company. These involve changes to the company's industry of origination, changes to the center of gravity of the company, or some combination of the two. For some of the strategic changes there are appropriate organizations and measures of their economic performance.

STRATEGY, ORGANIZATION, AND PERFORMANCE

For a number of years now, studies have been made of strategy and structure of the *Fortune* 500. Most of these were conducted by the Harvard Business School. These studies were reviewed in previous work (Galbraith and Nathanson, 1978). The current view is illustrated in Table 1. If one samples the *Fortune* 500 and categorizes them by strategy and structure, the following relationships hold.

One can still find organizations staying in their same original business. Such a single business is Wrigley Chewing Gum. These organizations are run by centralized functional organizations. The next strategic type is the vertically integrated by-product seller. Again, these companies have some diversification but remain committed to their industry and center of gravity. The companies are also functional, but the sequential stages are often operated as profit and loss divisions. The companies are usually quite centralized and run by collegial management groups. The profit centers are not true ones in being independent to run their own businesses. These are almost all upstream companies.

The related businesses are those that move into new industries at their center of gravity. Usually these are downstream companies. They adopt the decentralized profit center divisions. However, the divisions are not completely decentralized. There are usually strong corporate staffs and some centralized marketing, manufacturing, and R&D. There may be several thousand people on the corporate payroll.

TABLE 1

STRATEGY	STRUCTURE
Single business	Functional
Vertical by-products	Functional with P&Ls
Related businesses	Divisional
Linked businesses	Mixed structures
Unrelated businesses	Holding company

The clearest contrast to the related diversifier is the unrelated business company. These companies enter a variety of businesses at several centers of gravity. The organization they adopt is the very decentralized holding company. Their outstanding feature is the small corporate staff. Depending on their size, the numbers range between fifty and two hundred. Usually these are support staffs. All of the marketing, manufacturing, and R&D is decentralized to the divisions. Group executives have no staffs and are generally corporate oriented.

The linked companies are neither of these extremes. Often linked forms are transitory. The organizations that they utilize are usually mixed forms that are not easily classified. Some divisions are autonomous, while others are managed out of the corporate HQ. Still others have strong group executives with group staffs. Some work has been done on classifying these structures (Allen, 1978).

There has been virtually no work done on center of gravity changes and their changes in structure. Likewise, there has been nothing done on comparisons for economic performance. But for the other categories and structures, there is emerging some good data on relative economic performance.

The studies of economic performance have compared the various strategic patterns and the concept of fit between strategy and organization. Both sets of results have organization design implications. The economic studies use return on equity as the performance measure. If one compares the strategic categories listed in Table 1, there are distinct performance differences. The high performers are consistently the related diversifiers (Rumelt, 1974; Galbraith and Nathanson, 1978; Nathanson and Cassano, 1982; Bettis, 1981; Rumelt, 1982). There are several explanations for this performance difference. One explanation is that the related diversifiers are all downstream companies in businesses with high R&D and advertising expenditures. These businesses have higher margins and returns than other businesses. Thus, it may not be the strategy but the businesses the relateds happen to be in. However, if the unrelateds are good acquirers, why do they not enter the high-return businesses?

The other explanation is that the relateds learn a set of core skills and design an organization to perform at a particular center of gravity. Then, when they diversify, they take on the task of learning a new business, but at the same center of gravity. Therefore, they get a diversified portfolio of businesses but each with a system of management and an organization that is understood by everyone. The management understands the business and is not spread thin.

The unrelateds, however, have to learn new industries and also how to operate to a different center of gravity. This latter change is the most difficult to accomplish. One upstream company diversified via acquisition into downstream companies. It consistently encountered control troubles. It instituted a capital appropriation process for each investment of $50,000 or more. It still had problems, however. The retail division opened a couple of stores with leases for $40,000. It didn't use the capital process. The company got blindsided because the stores required $40 million in working capital for inventory and receivables. Thus, the management systems did not fit the new downstream business. It appears that organizational fit makes a difference. . . .

One additional piece of evidence results from the studies of economic performance. This result is that the poorest performer of the strategic categories is the vertically integrated by-product seller. Recall these companies are all upstream, raw material, and primary manufacturers. They make up a good portion of "Smokestack America." In some respects, these companies made their money early in the century, and their value added is shifting to lesser developed countries in the natural course of industrial development. However, what is significant here is their inability to change. It is no secret to anyone that they have been underperformers, yet they have continued to put money back into the same business.

My explanation revolves around the center of gravity. These previously successful companies put together an organization that fit their industry and stage. When the industry declined, they were unable to change as well as the downstream companies. The reason is that upstream companies were functional organizations with few general managers. Their resource allocation was within a single business, not across multiple products. The management skill is partly technological know-how. This technology does not transfer across industries at the primary manufacturing center of gravity. The knowledge of paper making does not help very much in glass making. Yet both might be combined in a package company. Also, the capital intensity of these industries limits the diversification. Usually one industry must be chosen and capital invested to be the low-cost producer. So there are a number of reasons why these companies have been notoriously poor diversifiers.

In addition, it appears to be very difficult to change centers of gravity no matter where an organization is along the industry chain. The reason is that a center of gravity shift requires a dismantling of the current power structure, rejection of parts of the old culture, and establishing all new management systems. The related diversification works for exactly the opposite reasons. They can move into new businesses with minimal change to the power structure and accepted ways of doing things. Changes in the center of gravity usually occur by new start-ups at a new center of gravity rather than a shift in the center of established firms. . . .

There are some exceptions that prove the rule. Some organizations have shifted from upstream commodity producers to downstream product producers and consumer product firms. General Mills moved from a flour miller to a related diversified provider of products for the homemaker. Over a long period of time they shifted downstream into consumer food products from their cake mix product beginnings. From there, they diversified into related areas after selling off the milling operations, the old core of the company. . . . [In these cases], however, new management was brought in and acquisition and divestment used to make the transition. So, even though vestiges of the old name remain, these are substantially different companies. . . .

The vast majority of our research has examined one kind of strategic change—diversification. The far more difficult one, the change in center of gravity, has received far less [attention]. For the most part, the concept is difficult to measure and not publicly reported like the number of industries in which a company operates. Case studies will have to be used. But there is a need for more systematic knowledge around this kind of strategic change.

READING 8.3 THE DESIGN OF NEW ORGANIZATIONAL FORMS*

BY JENNIFER HERBER, JITENDRA V. SINGH, AND MICHAEL USEEM

■ . . . One of the more hallowed management truisms is that organizations should adapt to changing environmental conditions. But successful organizations frequently have trouble responding to discontinuous, competence-destroying change such as the advent of the Internet. Dominant players often fail to adapt because it means dismantling the very organizations that have led to their success. They had mastered current technologies and customer needs, but by virtue of having established that expertise and focus they had also become ill prepared to face innovative technologies and new customers. Past adaptations become inertial constraints, leading to a kind of "competency trap." The organizational architectures that companies have built to propel their success can become as outmoded as feudal kingdoms in an age of democracy.

Yet we have entered an era of intense experimentation with new organizational forms, as innovative technologies have created radically different opportunities for doing business. As a result, company architectures are changing, reporting relations are flattening, work designs are

*Excerpted from Jennifer Herber, Jitendra V. Singh, and Michael Useem, "The Design of New Organizational Forms" in *Wharton on Managing Emerging Technologies*, 2000, pp. 376–392.

empowering, and markets are opening. We examine new organizational forms that are emerging in response to the discontinuous technological breaks of recent years. We seek to understand what makes these organizational forms distinctive and how they provide competitive advantage. . . .

Experimenting managers have generally designed these new forms to capture two capabilities viewed as critical for success in environments of discontinuous technological change. The first capability is an effective balancing [of] exploration and exploitation. When a company focuses entirely on the exploitation of its current competitive advantages, it certainly becomes better at what it is doing well, but at the same time it becomes vulnerable to abrupt changes that negate the value of what it does best. On the other hand, if a firm focuses solely on exploration of future capabilities, it risks near-term failure for lack of tangible results. A balance, then, of both building the future and exploiting the past is seen as essential. The second capability is a recombination of established competencies. Organizations that take what they already do well and create fresh blends can capitalize on existing competencies without being locked into them.

Distinctive organizational forms are defined by unique reconfigurations of six elements:

1. *Organizational goals* are the firm's broad objectives and performance-related outcomes ranging from market share and customer satisfaction to total shareholder return. They implicitly contain time frames for measuring the extent to which they are achieved. A company goal, for instance, might be to establish the dominant market share in an emerging area over the next three years, much as Amazon.com has achieved in online bookselling.
2. *Strategies* concern intended and emergent patterns of long-term methods for achieving goals at both the firm and business unit levels.
3. *Authority relations* include organizational architecture and reporting structures.
4. *Technologies* refer to information, communication, and production methods.
5. *Markets* include relationships with customers, suppliers, partners, and competitors.
6. *Processes* refer to dynamic links among these elements, such as recruitment, budgeting, compensation, and performance evaluation.

. . . Among the emerging forms, we see six relatively different and potentially enduring organizational models. They are not necessarily mutually exclusive, with some companies simultaneously building two or more at the same time. Nor are the boundaries between them precisely defined. Still, they are coming to represent relatively distinct responses to emerging technologies of production, communication, and distribution. The six new organizational forms are (1) virtual organization, (2) network organization, (3) spinout organization, (4) ambidextrous organization, (5) front-back organization, and (6) sense-and-respond organization.

VIRTUAL ORGANIZATION

The virtual form is an organization in which employees, suppliers, and customers are geographically dispersed but united by technology. A network of distributed organizational units and individuals act in concert to serve widely scattered customers. New information technologies have driven the rise of this form, as customers and companies come to utilize high-speed, broadband communication systems to buy and sell products and services anywhere rather than at a point of direct contact in a store or office. These technologies have also created mechanisms for inexpensively weaving together far-flung organizations and operations. The virtual organization is largely boundary-less, with tasks performed, suppliers accessed, and products delivered in hundreds if not thousands of widely strewn physical locations. Headquarters may be little more than the chief executive's home computer and an internet connection.

The virtual form minimizes asset commitments, resulting in greater flexibility, lower costs, and consequentially, faster growth. Its application and value can be well seen in the experience of Dell Computer Corporation. Founded in 1984, Dell seized on emergent technologies and information management to integrate supplier partnership, mass customization, and just-in-time manufacturing for fast and precise responsiveness to fast-evolving customer demand. It introduced virtual organizational forms across the entire value chain, from suppliers to manufacturers to customers.

The backbone of Dell's exceptional productivity, efficiency, and mass customization has been its company-wide coordination across businesses, customers, and suppliers. In maintaining real-time links with its suppliers, for instance, Dell could provide the kind of detailed data that would allow them to reduce inventory, enhance speed, and improve logistics. The sharing of information with the suppliers enhanced their incentives to collaborate. And Dell's use of electronic logs rather than written forms reduced the cost for many functions ranging from order taking to quality inspection. The technology thus enabled Dell to benefit from a de facto vertical integration without the liabilities and inflexibilities of owning the supply chain.

Dell Computer's virtual linkage with customers via Internet and voice channels also permitted Dell to circumvent traditional dealership channels and thereby create a sustainable competitive advantage of lower selling cost and higher customer responsiveness. By the late 1990s, Dell had become the world's second largest computer maker, with 30,000 employees, annual revenues of $21 billion, and $30 million in daily Internet sales.

Electronic technologies have been used by other companies to push the limits of virtual relationships. In such relationships, products never appear in showrooms, customers never meet salespeople, and dollars never physically change hands. Amazon.com, CDNow, and thousands of kindred e-commerce start-ups have mastered the use of cyber catalogs in place of storefronts, credit cards instead of cash, and e-mail confirmations in place of paper receipts.

Virtual companies have also learned to exploit the unique potential of the two-way medium through which they both sell and learn. They have created more enduring and more customized relations with individual customers and they have constructed communities among customers. . . .

Yet this flexibility of the virtual organizational form created its own new set of challenges, especially in the area of authority relations. The ties of communication technologies were strong enough that it no longer mattered if employees sat next to each other or even nearby. They could as well work from home offices miles away or even business offices a continent removed. They need not work full-time or from 9 to 5 either. But in that lessening of physical proximity and contact frequency, the traditional role of supervisors would change from overseeing work processes to job outcomes, from exercising authority over tasks to delegating responsibility for results. Supervisors would also no longer stand at the center of communication and coordination since the increasing horizontal collaboration negated the necessity of going up the organization to obtain downward cooperation in other operations. An enduring by-product has been for bosses to become less central in giving feedback and appraising performance—and peers to become more central. Vertical organization gives way to lateral relations. . . .

The virtual organizational form brings many advantages to companies that are themselves building and marketing emerging technologies. This form serves as a magnet for attracting creative and energetic employees who eschew bureaucracy and favor sovereignty. This advantage can turn to disadvantage, however, when pushing the emerging technologies to their next stage of development depends on a critical mass of creative people working intensively together. The need for geographic proximity partially explains why even the most technologically advanced industries—which would seemingly lend themselves best to virtual forms—are often geographically concentrated, as seen in computer making in Silicon Valley and telecommunication services in Northern Virginia.

| NETWORK ORGANIZATION | The network form is based on an organized set of relationships among autonomous or semi-autonomous work units for delivering a complete product or service to a customer. Network forms are found both inside companies and across sets of companies. |

EXTERNAL NETWORK FORM

External networks among companies can be viewed as outsourcing in the extreme. At the core are organizations that have chosen to concentrate on a particular competence or specific slice of the value chain. The central organizations create symbiotic ties among a host of legally independent entities to aggregate the necessary skills, assembly, and services. They rely on other entities from suppliers and distributors to complete the value chain in the delivery of a complete product or service.

Some external networks can be described as *federated* in that a set of loosely affiliated firms work relatively autonomously but nonetheless engage in mutual monitoring and control of one another. Other external networks can be viewed more as evanescent *organizational webs* in which constellations of players coalesce around an emerging business opportunity and dissipate just as rapidly once it runs its course. Still another subspecies is the *strategic partnership* in which companies form cooperative deals, often across continents, with suppliers to achieve lowest cost manufacturing, or collaborate with research companies worldwide to acquire highest quality innovation.

External networks are stitched together with a variety of methods, ranging from joint ventures and formal partnerships to franchising systems and research consortia. Whatever the specific type of external network, they transform the competitive fray to one of rivalries between constellations of collaborating enterprises.

The textile industry in Prato, Italy, during the 1980s exemplifies the external network. Here, tiny firms came to specialize in a particular niche of the industry in response to customer demand for lower prices and greater variety. No single company dominated, and independent master brokers—*impannatores*—served as the customer interface, taking orders that far exceeded the capacity of any one producer. They divided and dispatched the orders to hundreds of producers over which they held no formal authority. The region's 15,000 independent firms, with an average of just five employees each, collectively produced what would ordinarily have only been available from a few massive companies. Though these miniature producers competed vigorously against one another, they also established strong cooperatives for tasks where economies of scale and joint practices proved . . . lucrative. . . .

The external network organizational form brings distinctive authority and market relations, relying on lateral communication instead of vertical clout to achieve coordination. . . .

INTERNAL NETWORK FORM

The internal network structure builds on much the same premise that undergirds the external network—aligned but loose relations among a set of operations can often beat a hierarchy of control among the operations—but here the premise is applied inside the firm. Strategic business units, microenterprises, and autonomous work teams are the building blocks, and their work is coordinated and disciplined but rarely directed by the top of the pyramid. Headquarters sets global strategy, allocates assets, and monitors results, but is otherwise little concerned with daily operations. Top executives establish a cultural esprit and common mindset across the operating units and teams, and then the upper echelon leaves it almost entirely to each of the operations to devise its own methods for making and selling.

An exemplary case is the Zurich-based ABB, Asea Brown Boveri, which has networked its many fully owned subsidiaries and business units to an extreme. This engineering and technology company employed 200,000 people in more than 100 countries during the late 1990s, and in 1998 it earned $2 billion on $31 billion in revenue. Yet its home office housed fewer than 100 managers, and virtually all of its decisions were centered in 1,300 operating units and 5,000 profit centers around the world. Described as "obsessively decentralized," the ABB pyramid is about as flat as they come, with a single layer of management between top executives and field managers. The field managers as a result have the autonomy to do what they want so long as their decisions are aligned with the firm's goals. . . .

Both external and internal network organization forms benefit from the adaptive flexibility that comes with their built-in modularity. Whether inside a company or across a lattice of companies, units can be opened, moved, or closed, and each is far closer to its respective customers than anybody else in the operation. . . .

This organizational form may be particularly useful in industries with fast-moving technological change and rapidly emergent new ways of producing and selling. When uncertainty is high, risk is great, and time is punishing, the modularity of the network form provides for quick response. The customer focus of the network form provides for nuanced response. And the local autonomy of the network form provides for a creative response.

SPIN-OUT ORGANIZATION

The spin-out organizational form is built when companies establish fresh entities inside from new business concepts and then send them off at least partially on their own. The parent organization, sometimes resembling a holding company, serves as venture capitalist, protective incubator, and proud mentor, but the successful units are sooner or later pushed out of the nest. The parent may relinquish all ownership and control, or it may choose to retain a 20, 50, or 70 percent stake. Whatever the lingering tether, the spin-out is left largely to its own devices to sink or swim.

During the spin-out process, authority relations between the company and business unit evolve from parental control to adult independence. The goals of the spin-out will diverge from the parent's objectives once the offspring is legally separate. Still, gentle parental advice is frequently continued, and some offspring continue to make good use of the parent's accounting, legal, and investment functions.

. . . Thermo Electron has long served as an "innovation incubator" for thermodynamic, medical, and technology related products for well-defined market niches. . . . Founded in 1956, the company in 1982 began "spinning out" promising technologies and services by offering minority shares in newly created subsidiaries to the public. To ensure that its managers of the spin-outs continued to produce great returns even when they could no longer be required to do so, Thermo Electron created highly leveraged incentive packages. Given a chance to behave like an entrepreneur and be rewarded for doing so, and with a proven product in hand from the incubation period, spin-out managers have often outperformed the market. So, too, has Thermo Electron, which by 1999 had grown into a $4 billion enterprise with 26,000 employees worldwide. . . .

Spin-outs can . . . constitute an excellent vehicle for not only developing but also commercializing expensive and risky emerging technologies. Because they become legally separate from the corporate parent, they can pursue variant growth strategies, financing objectives, and performance goals, permitting greater responsiveness to fast-changing market conditions and emerging possibilities. They can use stock-options to attract and retain talent who might otherwise exit the parent firm for the lack of real wealth incentives. And once the spin-outs are on their own in the market, the joint forces of demanding investors and aggressive competitors impose a financial discipline with an intensity rarely felt inside a large parent.

AMBIDEXTROUS ORGANIZATION

If the spin-out form is designed to take a new venture out of the sometimes inhospitable environment of a large organization, the ambidextrous organizational form creates an environment in which both established and emerging businesses flourish side by side. Some parts of the organization are working on incremental improvements in technologies, others are looking for breakthroughs. The ambidextrous form overcomes the "innovator's dilemma," the conundrum of listening so well to current customers that the company never anticipates radically new technologies that customers have not yet come to appreciate but will eventually demand. This organizational scheme is designed to ensure simultaneous dexterity in both continuous improvement and discontinuous innovation.

With 125,000 employees and sales of $47 billion in 1998, Hewlett-Packard was concerned that the success of existing products would dampen new products because champions of the latter would not have the political clout to obtain funding and attention. The firm thus created an internal consulting group to help its autonomous business units do two things at once. As characterized by Stu Winby, its director of Strategic Change Services, the objective is to improve a business unit's sale of today's technologies, with a focus on raising volumes and lowering costs. But a concurrent objective is to organize part of the same business unit around future technologies, with an emphasis on entrepreneurship and speed to market. The latter's products sometimes compete head-on with existing products or even threaten to cannibalize them entirely, and managers of well-established product lines are predictably wary. Still, Hewlett-Packard's experience confirms that ways can be found to keep both agendas successfully working under the same roof.

The ambidextrous form can be especially useful for fostering emerging technologies without abandoning the old. Doing both at the same time runs the risk of sowing conflict, but when well orchestrated, this form helps reconcile otherwise opposed agendas. A critical feature is limiting their separation: Those responsible for traditional products are brought into active dialogue with those at the forefront of new ideas. Lateral linkages rather than segregated operations become important here for mutual stimulation. And when well incentivized to share rather than hoard knowledge, to communicate rather than isolate, both sides contribute more to the company's ultimate objectives and devote less energy to thwarting the other party.

FRONT-BACK ORGANIZATION

The front-back organizational form is organized around customers in the front, with all company functions placed at the back to serve the front. The purpose is to provide customers with fast, responsive and customized solutions.

One type of front-back form is an inverted organization in which all line executives, systems, and support staff in effect work for the front-line person, allowing him or her to concentrate the company's capabilities on satisfying the customer. With the firm's systems and procedures so focused, the front-line person commands the resources to respond swiftly and precisely to evolving customer needs. The organization chart is turned upside down, with customers on top, customer-contact people next, and the rest below.

The front-back form can be seen in many health maintenance organizations. They still divide medical practices into specialties such as radiology, anesthesiology, and cardiology, but many now also designate a primary care provider to coordinate the back-end functions to deliver a complete health package to the patient.

A second variant of the front-back form is a hybrid of vertical and horizontal process teams. Here, companies are divided into units with vertical reporting lines, but they also establish formal means for transcending vertical barriers when they get in the way. Sometimes front-back companies are focused on products, in other cases on geography or distribution channels. However configured, they come to resemble a "centerless corporation" in which resources are directed at whatever part is most in frontal contact with customers.

The hybrid model with horizontal work that transects vertical reporting lines can be found in many management-consulting firms. Partners and associates at McKinsey & Company, Andersen Consulting, and kindred companies are organized into specialized practices, such as strategy, information, and change, but they also create temporary client teams drawn from several of the practices. Team leaders have command over the resources of the specialized practices for the duration of the engagement to ensure that their clients receive the right combination of technical expertise to solve the problems they face. . . .

Front-back organizations differ from traditional forms most starkly in their reconfigured authority relations. Health maintenance organizations, for example, realign incentives to foster cooperation instead of adversarial relationships among physicians, health workers, and medical plans. . . .

SENSE-AND-RESPOND ORGANIZATION

The sense-and-respond organizational form is focused even more intensely on identifying emerging customer needs. While the front-back form develops a distinctive relationship with customers, the sense-and-respond form orients the entire organization around meeting ever-changing customer demands. The working premise is that unpredictable change is inevitable in the marketplace, and the challenge is to ready the organization to capitalize on whatever discontinuity confronts it.

Adaptability is among the foremost capacities of sense-and-respond firms. They tend to plan from the bottom up with few predetermined long-term plans, reacting almost daily to market movements. They occupy a middle ground between a strategy of "control your own destiny" and a strategy of "let your destiny happen to you." One variation of this form is what has been termed a "MegaStrategic Business Entity," found among giant, diversified companies that continuously change to stay with their same customers for years.

Westpac Banking Corporation, an Australian-based firm with 31,000 employees and $6 billion in revenue in 1998, illustrates the sense-and-respond form. For a decade it has worked as a collection of capabilities and assets managed to adapt to customer requests. It is not especially efficient at processing, but its modularity ensures that it gathers detailed information from customers and responds with precisely what each needs. It sets as its main objective continuously responding to customers and anticipating their coming needs. Authority relations necessarily are more fluid to ensure flexible response to customer requests. . . .

CONCLUSIONS

. . . For managers asking which of the six organizational forms holds greatest promise for their firm, the choice is a contingent one. As summarized in Table 1, the selection depends on the unique configuration of a company's goals and authority relations on the one hand, and the nature of its changing technologies and markets on the other. When a firm's technologies and markets are relatively fresh but its goals and authority relationships are not, the ambidextrous form may be most appropriate. When an enterprise's goals and authority relations are new but its technologies and markets are less so, the spin-out form may be most suited. When a company is facing change in both areas, the sense-and-respond form may well be more appropriate.

TABLE 1
ORGANIZATIONAL FORMS AND CHANGING ENVIRONMENTS

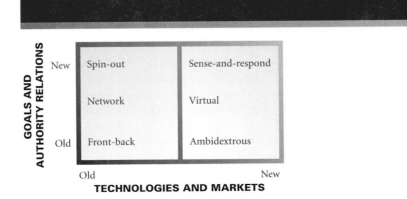

Organizations must look carefully at their competitive environments and internal capacities in selecting the right organizational form. The six forms described here represent distinctive models, but hybrids can be found among each and some companies have simultaneously adopted two or more at the same time. The six forms can best be seen as a starting point for thinking about a form that is uniquely tailored to meet the specific challenges facing a company. Because those challenges are so varied, we are likely to see a host of organizational forms that borrow no model intact and custom-build what will be needed to develop, manage, use, and sell emerging technologies during the years ahead.

CHAPTER 9

Technology

Technology is a key factor in almost any conceivable strategy process today. So, in a sense, the choice of readings to include was vast. We settled on two to give a flavor of some of the newer ideas (and, it should be noted, various readings in other chapters return to technology themes).

Lampel and Mintzberg are critical of a popular issue in technology today, namely, customization. After laying out a framework to think about what customization really means, they conclude that most of what is called customization, and especially so-called "mass customization," actually sits at a midpoint between pure customization and pure standardization. They call it standardized customization.

The second reading, by George Day and Paul Schoemaker of the Wharton School of Business, lays out the pitfalls to be avoided in emerging technologies. They examine what may be called the "rational conservatism" of most firms in the face of new technologies. It is rational to stick to what you know best and wait for the new technology to be proven in the marketplace. It is rational to commit to a technology if it is promising, but only up to a point. And it is rational to throw in the towel if the technology fails to live up to its early promise. These are precisely the reasons why so many established and ostensibly well-managed companies lose their business to new technologies. The remedy, these authors suggest, is for companies to be mindful of the paradoxical nature of new technologies and to pay attention to information from the periphery of one's business, to challenge deep-rooted assumptions, to experiment and learn, and to remain flexible in the face of new technological options.

USING THE CASE STUDIES

Strategy is often focused on pioneering technologically innovative products. MP3.com describes the strategy of a company created and later sent into crisis by a new technology. The company's fluctuating fortunes and the fortunes of many high-technology firms are discussed by Day and Schoemaker in their reading, "Avoiding the Pitfalls of Emerging Technologies." The Acer Group case deals with a personal computer company that comes to the new industry as a late mover. The Intel case, on the other hand, describes a high-technology pioneer that has successfully avoided the pitfalls of emerging technology.

New products operate on one side of the high-technology coin. On the other side we have technology shaping strategy by shaping the way that organizations design, produce, and distribute products. The National Bicycle Industry Company case deals with the impact of new technologies on the production process. In particular, we see how the flexibility of new production technologies allows these companies to pursue a strategy of "mass customization" related to the Mintzberg and Lampel reading.

READING 9.1
CUSTOMIZING CUSTOMIZATION*

**BY JOSEPH LAMPEL
AND HENRY
MINTZBERG**

■ The history of U.S. business during the past 100 years has been a story of mass production and mass distribution of standardized goods. Scholars and practitioners who examined the economic landscape have generally been drawn to large corporations that built their fortunes by transforming fragmented and heterogeneous markets into unified industries. At the heart of this transformation were strategies based on standardization: standardization of taste that allowed for standardized design, standardization of design that allowed for mechanized mass production, and a resulting standardization of products that allowed for mass distribution.

Recently, a growing number of economists and management scholars have declared that this era is over. Numerous books and articles have posited that we are witnessing the dawn of a new age of customization, an age in which new technologies, increased competition, and more assertive customers are leading firms toward customization of their products and services. Not surprisingly, firms that have adopted customization strategies have attracted considerable attention as models of what is expected to become commonplace in the near future.

We begin by describing these two logics. We then argue that this conceptual polarization, which took firm root in the theory and practice of management, led management thinkers to ignore strategies that combine these logics. Put simply, this view itself represents an inappropriate standardization of management theory—or, more exactly, continuation of the standardization mentality that has long pervaded such theory. Since the days of Frederick Taylor, the notion that managers should single-mindedly pursue the "one best way" has led management writers to seize on one solution or another (or, more often, one solution and *then* another) as the best practice. Indeed, the enthusiasm for customization today was paralleled by an even greater enthusiasm for standardization many years ago.

What has been ignored in all this is that customization and standardization do not define alternative models of strategic action but, rather, poles of a continuum of real-world strategies. By promoting customization as the answer to what ails many organizations, we may be replacing

*Excerpted from "Customizing Customization," Joseph Lampel and Henry Mintzberg, *Sloan Management Review*, Fall 1996, Vol. 38(1), 21–30.

one extreme with another. Managers need to locate their strategies along the continuum, and the role of management writers is to provide the conceptual tools to make this easier.

It is not an accident of history that customization is now promoted with the same enthusiasm with which standardization was promoted almost a century ago. Today's customization movement is a reaction to significant economic and technological forces, much as the standardization movement was in its time. But these developments must be viewed with a clear perspective. Therefore, we begin by reviewing how the standardization and customization distinction emerged in the first place.

THE LOGIC OF AGGREGATION

Economic theory takes a bird's-eye view of markets. It strips them of their complexity and variability, aggregating firms and individuals into two groups: buyers and sellers. In contrast, management theory, especially in strategy, starts with the relationships of specific firms to their environments. Sellers are therefore disaggregated. Customers, however, continue to be viewed collectively as a group (or a set of segmented groups) that shares common characteristics. This has led managers and researchers alike to emphasize the advantage of economies of scale in every part of the value chain, from development to production to distribution, which in turn has promoted a focus on industries in which customers' shared characteristics are easily established. Thus, in his 1980 book, Porter draws on 196 industries to illustrate his ideas. By our count, 176 of these have been dominated by the logic of aggregation, while only 20 can be considered to have tilted toward that of disaggregation.

The following maxims capture the basic imperative of the logic of aggregation: (1) reduce the impact of customers' variability on internal operations, (2) do so by identifying general product and customer categories, and then (3) simplify and streamline interactions with the customer. Over time, these coalesced into a well-defined set of strategies that promoted the advantages of scale economies and standardization with particular success.

By 1929, a survey of eighty-four product classes showed a reduction in variety at times amounting to 98 percent of its 1921 level. For example, the number of bed blanket sizes dropped from seventy-eight to twelve; hospital beds that had come in thirty-three different sizes were all standardized to a single size by 1929. . . . As one manager explained, "Over a period of years of experience with builders and architects, as well as homeowners, we have found that the five-foot tub is on the average an adequate size bathtub for the average size person."

The practical lessons learned during this period were subsequently incorporated into the mind-set of the newly emerging management "profession." When the study of business became a scholarly pursuit at the turn of the century, the mass production and mass distribution firm was singled out as the most rational approach to gaining competitive advantage. Management thinkers counseled against the proliferation of products, and even such an influential writer as Lyndall Urwick warned that the temptation to respond to customers' demands could be ruinous: "To allow the individual idiosyncrasies of a wide range of customers to drive administration away from the principles on which it can manufacture most economically is suicidal—the kind of good intention with which the road to hell or bankruptcy is proverbially paved."

In the mid-1950s, there began a gradual move away from the extreme forms of aggregation, under the label of "market segmentation." Encouraged by automation in manufacturing as well as the shift from rail to road in transportation and changes in the mass media, companies began to target specific groups of consumers. Nevertheless, the logic remained the same, for this was not a movement toward serious customization so much as toward the aggregation of the submarket or the market class. Indeed, the mass market in many industries had reached such a large scale that segmentation posed few real dangers to efficiency in production if not strictly in distribution.

THE LOGIC OF INDIVIDUALIZATION

Although the logic of aggregation became dominant in many industries, there remained areas of economic activity where it failed to take over. Obvious examples are certain traditional crafts, such as personal tailoring, fine jewelry making, fine restaurant cooking, and grinding prescription eyeglass lenses. More significant, perhaps, is the capital goods sector, where products continue to be designed to customer specifications and manufactured in job-shop facilities. In industries such as pulp and paper machinery, steam turbines, commercial aircraft, flight simulators, and construction, the individual customer can be deeply involved in every aspect of the transaction and expects key product decisions to be negotiated jointly.

More recently, of course, there has been a move to greater customization in a wide variety of industries, including services. In some cases, the change has been highly visible. The standard telephone service of the past has given way to a varied menu of features from which customers may select their own preferred combination.

In industries where the logic of individualization is pervasive, different forms of marketing, production, and product development dominate. In marketing, firms seek to develop a direct relationship with the individual customer. In production, products can be "made to order" or "tailor made." And since products can be designed for particular customers, research and design can lose much of their isolation from the marketplace. In effect, the orientation is toward the management of each transaction. But, as we shall see, there are industries where product, process, and transaction vary markedly in their degree of customization.

BETWEEN AGGREGATION AND INDIVIDUALIZATION: A CONTINUUM OF STRATEGIES

Although pure aggregation and pure individualization are perceived as opposing logics, this influence has not led to the emergence of two distinct groups of strategies. Instead, we find a continuum of strategies, depending on which functions lean to standardization and which to customization. In the manufacturing firm, to take a common example, production managers often see aggregation as the best way to increase efficiency, whereas sales managers often consider individualization as the surest approach to increase sales. It is perhaps not a coincidence that the term *customer* looms large in sales managers' vocabularies, while production managers prefer to speak of outputs and schedules.

But the best solution is not necessarily a compromise. In just the operating processes, some firms tilt one way or the other because of the needs of the customers they choose to serve, while others favor intermediate positions. The latter reflect an organization's ability to customize partway back in its value chain, while retaining standardization for the rest. Since the cost of customization tends to increase in proportion to the number of product changes, it makes sense to customize the downstream functions first. Firms may offer customers special delivery services or individualized financing, while refusing to allow changes in production. Or, beyond this, they may be prepared to assemble on demand, according to customers' requests, while refusing to modify a product's core design and the standardized fabrication of its parts.

Thus value chain customization begins with the downstream activities, closest to the marketplace, and may then spread upstream. Standardization, in contrast, begins upstream, with fundamental design, and then progressively embraces fabrication, assembly, and distribution. These two approaches give rise to the continuum of strategies based on standardization and customization that we introduce here.

We develop this continuum for a manufacturing firm with four stages in its value chain: design, fabrication, assembly, and distribution. These refer, respectively, to the extent to which the firm conceives the product initially with regard to a single customer's needs, constructs and then assembles the product with regard to those needs, and distributes it individually to the single customer (as opposed to selling it generically, as in "over the counter"). Stepping customization back one notch at a time along this chain gives rise to five different strategies (see Figure 1):

FIGURE 1 A CONTINUUM OF STRATEGIES

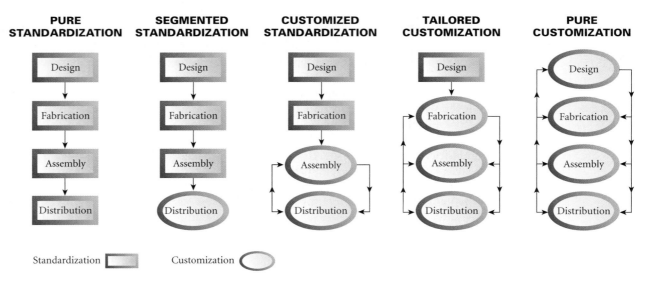

- **Pure Standardization.** Ford Motor Company's strategy during the era of the Model T was the quintessential example of pure standardization—any color so long as it was black. This strategy is based on a "dominant design" targeted to the broadest possible group of buyers, produced on as large a scale as possible, and then distributed commonly to all. Under such a strategy of pure standardization, there are no distinctions between different customers. The buyer has to adapt or else switch to another product. He or she has no direct influence over design, production, or even distribution decisions. The entire organization is geared to pushing the product from one stage to the next, beginning with design and ending in the marketplace.

- **Segmented Standardization.** The proliferation of cereal brands and the variety of automobiles that followed the Model T are examples of segmented standardization. Firms respond to the needs of different clusters of buyers, but each cluster remains aggregated. Thus the products offered are standardized within a narrow range of features. A basic design is modified and multiplied to cover various product dimensions but not at the request of individual buyers. Individual choice is thus anticipated but not directly catered to. A segmented standardization strategy therefore increases the choices available to customers without increasing their direct influence over design or production decisions. At most, there may be a somewhat greater tendency to customize the distribution process, for example, in the delivery schedules of major appliances. When pushed to the limit, the segmented standardization strategy results in hyperfine distribution—as in the market for designer lamps, which offers almost limitless variety, but not at the customer's request.

- **Customized Standardization.** Automobile companies that offer the buyer the option of selecting his or her own set of components engage in customized standardization, as do hamburger chains that allow customers to specify their preferences for mustard, ketchup, mayonnaise, tomatoes, and so on. In other words, products are made to order from standardized components. The assembly is thus customized, while the fabrication is not, hence our label of customized standardization, although we might also call this standardized customization, "modularization," or "configuration." Basic design is not customized, and the components are all mass produced for the aggregate market. Each customer thus gets his or her own configuration but constrained by the range of available components. This is sometimes constructed around a central standard core, such as a hamburger or an automobile body.

- **Tailored Customization.** A tailored suit, a rug woven to order, or a birthday cake with your name on it are examples of tailored customization. The company presents a product prototype to a potential buyer and then adapts or tailors it to the individual's wishes or needs. Here customization works backward to the fabrication stage but not to the design stage. Thus the traditional men's tailor will show the client standard fabrics and cuts that he can adapt to the client—for example, wider lapels than normal or adjustments to accommodate an unusual physique. The client will later come back for a fitting and more tailoring. A good deal of traditional business is conducted this way; for example, in home construction, the builder will modify a standard design for particular customer wishes.
- **Pure Customization.** Individualization reaches its logical conclusion when the customer's wishes penetrate deeply into the design process itself, where the product is truly made to order. Artisans who do this are well known, for example, a jeweler or a residential architect who designs to customer specifications. Of greater impact, perhaps, is the pure customization of major products and services, including large-scale production machinery, industrial instrumentation, and much construction work. So-called "megaprojects," such as NASA's Apollo project or the Olympic Games, represent major instances of pure customization. Here, all stages—design, fabrication, assembly, and distribution—are largely customized. The traditional polarization between buyers and sellers is transformed into a genuine partnership in which both sides are deeply involved in each other's decision making.

| TOWARD THE CUSTOMIZATION OF PERSPECTIVES | A flood of recent publications attests to the widespread belief that we are in the midst of a fundamental technological change in manufacturing, communications, distribution, and retailing—a virtual renaissance of customization. |

TOWARD THE CUSTOMIZATION OF PERSPECTIVES

A flood of recent publications attests to the widespread belief that we are in the midst of a fundamental technological change in manufacturing, communications, distribution, and retailing—a virtual renaissance of customization.

The initial impetus is generally considered to have come from new information, engineering, and manufacturing technologies that have blurred the traditional barriers between batch and mass production, have opened the way to the restoration of individualization in business areas hitherto dominated by the logic of aggregation, and have served to uncouple formerly tight relationships between manufacturing and design. In our opinion, however, these new technologies have not had the effects accorded them, specifically the dramatic shift to customization. Rather, all sorts of situations continue to exist. Indeed, if there is one dominant trend—which, we repeat, must coexist with all kinds of countertrends—it is from both ends of our strategy continuum toward the middle, namely toward the strategy of customized standardization, as a number of our examples show.

The shift from pure or segmented standardization to customized standardization has certainly been most obvious. The effects of computer-aided design and manufacturing have produced striking examples of previously standardized products that can now be customized.

Yet the shift from the other end of the continuum—from pure or tailored customization to that same middle position of customized standardization—while less publicized, may in fact be equally noteworthy and, in fact, driven by the same technologies. The high-rise building that was once uniquely designed may today look like a combination of rather standardized components.

An important consequence of this trend is that, as consumers, we lose flexibility in one area while gaining it in another. And, ironically, we lose individuality as we settle in the middle, on customized standardization. The right to specify mayonnaise on a hamburger or a bigger engine in an automobile, may give some individuals more choice, to be sure, but can hardly be described as constituting great freedom, in the marketplace or the body politic. In a sense, we lose choice as we all become categories of generic consumers in an assembly operation.

Our new theory may be about customization, but our thinking remains standardized. Our temptation to standardize concepts is ultimately rooted in the wish to simplify the world and make our frameworks as general as possible. Yet one secret of successful management today, as at the turn of the century, is to customize standard concepts to fit specific applications. After a century in which management writing has been dominated by the search for the standardized solution, isn't it time to customize our concepts too?

READING 9.2   AVOIDING THE PITFALLS OF EMERGING TECHNOLOGIES*

BY GEORGE S. DAY AND PAUL J. H. SCHOEMAKER

■ Emerging technologies**—such as gene therapy, interactivity and electronic commerce, intelligent sensors, digital imaging, micro-machines, or super conductivity—have the potential to remake entire industries and obsolete established strategies. This is exhilarating for the attackers who can write—and exploit—the new rules of competition, especially if they are not encumbered by an existing business.

For incumbents, however, emerging technologies are often traumatic. Most of these firms feel they must participate in the markets that emerge. Their first reason is defensive, driven by the belief that the newcomers are plotting to use the new functionalities to attack their core markets. Home banking via the Internet is already happening, although no one knows how widely it will be adopted. Yet many bankers are filled with trepidation that the banking industry will be profoundly reshaped (see Bowers and Singer, 1996.) Their second reason is the converse of the first: if the emerging technology realizes its potential, it will be too attractive to ignore. However, the odds of large, established incumbents prevailing in these emerging markets are generally poor. . . . In this article, we address the questions of *why* these incumbents have so much difficulty with disruptive technologies, and *how* they can anticipate and overcome their handicaps. . . .

PITFALLS FOR ESTABLISHED FIRMS

The emergence of a challenging technology such as interactive computing or electronic commerce is seldom a surprise. Most managers attend industry conferences, read the trade press, buy consulting studies, talk with customers, and generally monitor developments in their field. The problem is that each of these sources tends to offer conflicting opinions that are reflected in divergent views within the firm. The inherent ambiguity of an emerging technology, and the new markets it creates, coupled with the dominance of traditional thinking frameworks, make established firms vulnerable to four related sequential pitfalls: delayed participation; sticking with the known technology; reluctance to commit fully; and lack of persistence.

---

*Reprinted with deletions from "Avoiding the Pittfalls of Emerging Technologies," George S. Day and Paul J. H. Schoemaker, *California Management Review*, Vol. 42(2), Winter 2000, 8–33.
**We define emerging technologies as science-based innovations that have potential to create a new industry or transform an existing one. They include discontinuous innovations derived from radical innovations (e.g., micro-robots) as well as more evolutionary technologies formed by the convergence of previously separate research streams (e.g., the fax machine or the Internet).

PITFALL ONE: DELAYED PARTICIPATION

When faced with high uncertainty, it is tempting and perhaps rational to just "watch and wait." A watching brief may be assigned to a development group or to a consulting team commissioned to study the implications. Whether there is any organizational energy behind these probes depends critically on whether there is a credible champion for the emerging technology within the firm, who offers an alternative paradigm for encoding the weak external signals.

Managers use mental models to simplify and impose order on ambiguous and volatile situations in order to reduce uncertainty to manageable levels. These are sensible adaptations to what the managers have learned from their past experience. (Supporting evidence can be found in Day and Nedungadi, 1994.) Managers see what they are prepared to see and either filter out or distort what does not fit their mental maps.

The mental models of established firms are helpful for incremental innovations within familiar settings, but they become myopic and dysfunctional when applied to unfamiliar situations such as emerging technologies. Using the lens of the familiar may lead to an inappropriate framing of the opportunity. When IBM considered adding the Haloid-Xerox 914 copier in 1958, the main concern was whether the existing electric typewriter sales force could handle the product. The focus was on spreading the selling cost of this division over two product lines, rather than viewing it as an entirely new business for IBM. Since copiers did not look attractive within this narrow frame, the opportunity was rejected.*

Emerging technologies are often framed as suitable only for narrow applications that are not demanded by existing customers, who often favor the current features. It is easy to dismiss such unproven technologies on the grounds that their small markets will not solve the growth needs of large firms. Of course, all large markets were once in an embryonic state with their origins in limited applications. IBM at first did not see the great opportunity in PCs. They were deemed to be entry systems from which buyers would eventually move to mainframes.

Managers tend to compare the first imperfect and costly versions of the emerging technology against the refined versions of the established technology. Of course, pictures from electronic cameras initially lacked the resolution of chemical emulsion film . . . the first electronic watches were bulky and unattractive. . . . This makes it easy to dismiss or underestimate the long-run possibilities.

PITFALL TWO: STICKING WITH THE FAMILIAR

The choice of technology path is inherently difficult because of doubts about whether the technical hurdles can be overcome and which standard or architecture will prevail as the dominant design. The problem is most acute with emerging technologies derived from radical innovations. . . .

The most demanding technology choices are those where there are competing and multiple versions vying to be the dominant design, as occurred historically with the light bulb and more recently with VCRs, modems, and digital wireless telephones. A design dominates when it commands allegiance of the market, so that competitors and suppliers are forced to adopt it if they want to participate in the market. This represents a milestone in the emergence of a technology for it enforces standardization that enables product or network economics to be realized, and it removes a major inhibitor to the wide adoption of the technology.

Often there is fierce competition among firms to set the industry standard around their approach in hopes of gaining an enduring advantage. . . . The stakes may be very large, for if another design or standard prevails, the losers are trapped. Witness the struggle to set standards for HDTV, which encompasses the display technology to be used for television receivers

---

*See Vincent Barabba (1995), *Meeting of the Minds: Creating the Market-Based Enterprise.* IBM's study of the potential for copiers also overlooked the huge demand for the copying of copies, beyond simply copying originals.

as well as standards for delivery, transmission, and emission of images. (See Hariharan and Prahalad, 1994.)

The odds of picking the familiar but wrong technology path go up when:

- Past success reinforces certain ways of problem solving. Previous choices about appropriate technology solutions may lead the firm to search in areas that are closely related to their current skills and technologies. Thus, their capabilities limit what they can perceive and develop effectively.
- The firm lacks in-house capability to appraise the emerging technology fully. Thus, it may be underestimated or feared. Running a branch banking network is very different from electronic commerce, for example. Consequently, banks may at first shy away from offering electronic services.
- A proprietary mind-set gets in the way. The instinct of a large company with a proprietary position in its core market is to find a comparable proprietary position with the new technology that will lock in customers. Such a move makes customers suspicious, however, especially in today's open system environment.

Pitfalls one and two are both rooted in two familiar decision-making biases. First, most people have an aversion to ambiguity and risk (Hogarth and Kunreuther, 1989; also Schoemaker, 1991) such that a relatively known prospect usually is preferred over an unknown prospect of equal expected value (Kahneman and Tversky, 1979). Second, a deep-seated preference for the status quo puts the burden of proof on those wanting change. This status quo bias is partly due to our greater sensitivity to losses than to comparable gains (Kahneman et al., 1990).

PITFALL THREE: RELUCTANCE TO FULLY COMMIT

When firms from an established industry attempt to adopt a threatening technology, such as mechanical typewriter firms making electric typewriters or steam locomotive firms making diesel locomotives, they often enter reluctantly with token or staged commitments. One study of 27 established firms found that only four entered aggressively while three didn't participate at all in the threatening technology (Smith and Cooper, 1994). The remaining 20 made a modest initial commitment which gave the entrants from outside the established industry enough time to secure a strong market position. Why are leading firms repeatedly unable or unwilling to make aggressive commitments to an emerging technology once they decide to participate? Five plausible explanations or causes have been proposed.

The first is that managers are rightfully concerned about the possibility of cannibalizing existing profitable products or about resistance from channel partners, and thus they hold back their full support. . . .

Second, there is a paradox in managerial risk taking in that managers tend toward *bold* forecasts on the one hand and toward *timid* choices on the other (Kahneman and Lovallo, 1993). Bold forecasts can stem from overconfidence in general or, more specifically, a limited ability to see arguments contrary to the prediction. Timid choices reflect an inclination toward risk-aversion and a tendency to look at choices in isolation (rather than from a portfolio perspective) (Kahneman and Tversky, 1979). So, even if strong beliefs exist about the potential of a new technology, the corresponding actions may be inadequate—as evidenced today by most newspapers' weak responses to the threats and opportunities of the Internet.

Third, when the profit prospects are unclear and appear less attractive than the current business, investments are difficult to justify under strict ROI criteria. The customary decision processes and choice criteria are biased against risky, long-term investments . . . For emerging technologies, the payouts are often staged, with further investments being contingent on reaching key milestones or resolving key uncertainties. . . .

Furthermore, the projected returns from an emerging technology are often worse than those from established or new technologies that address the predictable performance needs of current customers. . . .

A fourth explanation is that the attention of managers is primarily focused on their current customers. Thus, they dismiss or overlook new technologies that seem mostly applicable to smaller market segments they do not serve or don't understand (Christensen and Rosenbloom, 1995). This makes them vulnerable to unexpected attacks by outsiders who use the emerging technology as their entry platform. For example, the large copying centers that were the core of Xerox and Kodak's traditional market failed to appreciate the value of small, slow tabletop copiers. This oversight opened the way for Canon. . . .

Finally, successful organizations are not naturally ambidextrous. They encounter numerous, debilitating problems in balancing the familiar demands of competing in markets presently served with the unfamiliar requirements of an emerging and potentially threatening technology. Within the core business there is usually close alignment among the strategy, capabilities, structure, and culture, which in turn is supported by well-established processes and routines for keeping these elements in balance. This gives the organization a great deal of stability, which must be overcome before the new routines and capabilities needed to compete with the emerging technology can be developed (Tushman and O'Reilly, 1997). Indeed, the more successful the firm, the more closely the elements of strategy, capabilities, structure, and culture will be aligned and the more difficult and time-consuming discontinuous changes become.

These five explanations are not independent; instead they commingle and reinforce each other to impair decision making, erode the necessary enthusiasm of the advocates, and cause firms to hesitate or hedge before making major commitments. These afflictions do not inhibit the new entrants who often sense the opportunity earlier, better comprehend or believe in the benefits of the new technology, and do not have any misleading history or culture to contend with.

PITFALL FOUR: LACK OF PERSISTENCE

Suppose, however, that an established firm has managed to avoid the first three pitfalls and has made significant investments in a newly emerging technology. Will it have the fortitude to stay the course? Large companies typically have little patience for continuing adverse results. Yet, missed forecasts and dashed hopes are commonly experienced during the gestation of new technologies that eventually do succeed. Market demand may not materialize as soon as expected, too many competitors might crowd into the market, or the technology may veer off in a new and unexpected direction. In time, the initial enthusiasm may be replaced with skepticism about when—if ever—the new technology will become a profitable business reality. This trap of weak commitment is the flip side of another well-known trap—the sunk cost fallacy. The irony is that the very firms that are overly committed to their core business (the sunk cost trap) are often too quick to pull the plug on investments in emerging technologies.

Those who truly appreciate the possibilities of the emerging technology and feel enthusiasm for any given new project are often deep in the organization and may have little influence on high-level strategic thinking. Thus, if a company's core business begins to struggle and senior managers are looking for ways to cut costs or reduce assets, the new venture is an easy target. . . . The established firms that do prevail follow a more aggressive path that balances flexibility of posture with sustained commitment and follow through. This path entails four approaches: widening peripheral vision, creating a learning culture, staying flexible in strategic ways, and providing organizational autonomy. . . .

ATTENDING TO SIGNALS FROM THE PERIPHERY

Emerging technologies signal their arrival long before they bloom into full-fledged commercial successes. However, the signal-to-noise ratio is initially low so one has to work hard to appreciate the early indicators. This means looking past the disappointing results, limited functionality, and modest initial applications to anticipate the possibilities. Many signals are available to those who look: other signals can only be seen by the prepared mind. As the philosopher Kant noted, we can only see what we are prepared to see. The winners are those who hear the weak signals and can anticipate and imagine future possibilities faster than the competition. . . .

The weak signals to be captured usually come from the periphery, where new competitors are making inroads, unfamiliar customers are participating in early applications, and unfamiliar technology or business paradigms are used. However, the periphery is very noisy, with many possible emerging technologies that might be relevant. . . .

BUILDING A LEARNING CAPACITY

The diverse sources of information flowing from the periphery create a lot of noise. There will be confusion and immobility rather than insight and action unless this information is absorbed, communicated widely, and discussed intensively so that the full implications are understood. This requires a learning capacity that is characterized by:

- an openness to a diversity of viewpoints within and across organizational units,
- a willingness to challenge deep-seated assumptions of entrenched mental models while facilitating the forgetting of outmoded approaches, and
- continuous experimentation in an organizational climate that encourages and rewards "well-intentioned" failure.

Encouraging Openness to Diverse Viewpoints

The uncertainties surrounding disruptive emerging technologies require thorough debate. The early emphasis should be on encouraging *divergent* opinions about technological solutions, market opportunities, and strategies for participating. As learning evolves, one or multiple views may emerge as a basis for *convergence* toward a few commercializable solutions that can be tested. The tone of this extended debate should be set by senior management through their willingness to bring in outsiders with non-traditional backgrounds, to immerse themselves in the stream of data, and to ask challenging questions. They must be outside their office, having conversations with informed insiders, outside experts, and customers. They must study competitive moves and analogous situations, float ideas, and seek collaborations. This can be done in diverse forums, including team meetings, outside conferences, and electronic bulletin boards. Top-down involvement will only be productive if there is active bottom-up participation. Employees from different levels bring different points-of-view and expertise, and they are typically closer to market and technology realities. . . . Organizations need a mechanism for coalescing and focusing the on-going dialogue while reducing the various uncertainties to manageable chunks. Scenario analysis achieves this through a process of collectively envisioning a limited set of plausible futures that are internally consistent and detailed. Each scenario can be used to generate strategic options, evaluate prospective investments, and assess their robustness (Schoemaker, 1991).

Challenge the Prevailing Mind-Set

Diverse viewpoints will not have an impact on the prevailing mind-set if the organization prevents it from absorbing these insights. Expansive thinking about the future is readily subverted by the rigidities and restrictions of the prevailing mental models, industry success formulas, conventional wisdom, and false analogies from the past. The limiting and simplifying operation of deeply embedded mental models raises serious questions about whether even scenario approaches can deal with profoundly disruptive and discontinuous change. The concern is that the scenario-building process anchors on the present—as shaped by the prevailing mind-set—and then projects forward to what *might* happen. By contrast, firms that successfully exploit discontinuities may have to separate their thinking from current beliefs and realities to envision what *could be* and then work back to what must be done to ensure this aspired future will be realized. . . .

Experiment Continually

Successful adaptation to the vagaries of emerging technologies requires a willingness to experiment and an openness to learn from the inevitable failures and set-backs. There are several facets to the call for continual experimentation. Sometimes it means a willingness to create a diverse portfolio of technological solutions by endorsing parallel development activities. . . .

Continually experimenting and improvising with a new technology produces insights about the possibilities and limits of the technology, the responses of diverse market segments, and the competitive options that customers consider. Once important uncertainties are resolved, such learning organizations are ready to act. . . .

Experimentation requires a tolerance for failure. The trial-and-error learning that relies on experimentation is quickly subverted if there is a fear-of-failure syndrome. Organizations that reward those who play it safe and blame risk takers for "well-intentioned" failures will quickly discourage learning. The path of learning is marked by serendipity and the knowledge gleaned from careful diagnoses of the possible reasons for failure. . . . It takes concerted leadership to create a more open climate that rewards improvisation and makes learning from failures possible. . . .

MAINTAINING FLEXIBILITY: BALANCING COMMITMENT AND OPTIONS

Investments in emerging technologies present a dilemma. On one hand there is compelling evidence that long-run winners are often early movers who committed quickly and unequivocally to a technology path. Andy Grove (1996) of Intel argues that it takes all the energy of an organization to pursue one clear and simple strategic aim—especially in the face of aggressive and focused competitors—and that hedging by exploring a number of alternative directions is expensive and dilutes commitment. . . .

On the other hand, there are persuasive arguments that investments in emerging technologies should be viewed as creating a portfolio of options where the commitment of additional resources is subject to attaining defined milestones and resolving key uncertainties. These options are investments that give the investor the right but not the obligation to make further investments. Additional funds are provided only if the project continues to appear promising. . . .

At first glance, commitment seems to be the opposite of flexibility and you may not be able to have it both ways (Ghemawat, 1991). However, only if the commitment is *irreversible* does it directly contravene flexibility. For instance, if you make a commitment to make a cruise voyage and pay the full amount up-front, it may seem that your flexibility has been diminished. However, if you also purchase cancellation insurance (in case of illness or a death in the family) you preserve considerable flexibility to change course when needed. This is the art of options management: it involves creativity, hedging, and an ability to imagine diverse scenarios. The only downside of creating flexibility is that it may reduce the strategic signaling value of making a commitment, which truly requires irreversibility to be credible. . . .

Managing Real Options

The basic issue is when to make an aggressive commitment that does not have a high risk of failure. Best practice suggests it is desirable in the early stages of exploration of an emerging technology to keep a number of options open by only committing investments in stages, following multiple technology paths, and delaying some projects. Once uncertainty has been reduced to a tolerable level and there is a widespread consensus within the organization on an appropriate technology path that can utilize the firm's internal development capabilities—as in the case with Intel's choice of personal computer over television as the preferred information appliance—then full-scale internal development can begin.

However, what if there are many plausible technology paths, the risks of pursuing one to the exclusion of others are unacceptable, and the firm lacks the necessary internal capabilities? . . . Ultimately, the optimal approach (ranging from betting the farm to watch-and-wait) depends on the choice set a company and its competitors face. Only careful analysis can sort out the best path for any one company guided by its long-term vision.

ORGANIZATIONAL SEPARATION

The culture, mind-set, risk-avoidance tendencies, and controls of an existing organization are usually stifling to an embryonic initiative based on an emerging technology. This is why large companies are counseled to set up separate organizations dedicated to pursuing a new endeavor (such as GM's Saturn division, IBM's PC unit, or Roche's Genentech investment). The objective of "cocooning" the new business is to create a boundary that enables the new group to do things differently while still permitting the sharing of resources and ideas with the parent. This also permits separate objectives, tolerance for long development cycles, and continuing cash drains, as well as differentiated measurement criteria so that the performance of managers in the rest of the organization is not jeopardized. Above all, it creates flexibility. . . . (See Homa Bahrami, "The Emerging Flexible Organization: Perspectives from Silicon Valley," *California Management Review*, 3414 (Summer 1992), pp. 33–52.)

How Much Independence Is Optimal?

This depends on the magnitude of the technological discontinuity and whether it threatens to erode or obsolete the competencies of the core business, the extent to which the activities and customers of the two businesses are different, and the difference in profitability. The greater the differences, the more important it is that the new business not be evaluated using the lens of the old. For completely new and disruptive technologies both *physical* and *structural* separation may be necessary and involve setting up a separate division that reports to senior management. Even when such a full degree of separation is not warranted, it is still desirable to have separate *funding* and *accounting*, so losses from the new projects are not carried by an established business unit.

The new venture also needs distinct *policies* that match the realities of building a new business. The new venture must be able to attract the best personnel and it must have the latitude to do fast prototyping and probe ill-defined markets while keeping restrictive controls and burdensome overhead to a minimum. They must be exempted from much of the routine planning and budgeting required of their more mature siblings. Above all, the new unit should be allowed and indeed encouraged to cannibalize the established business. . . .

What About "Synergy"?

When should the two structures cooperate? One view is that internal competition and some redundancy should always be encouraged, with different business units championing different models (based on Chandy and Tellis, 1999). A more nuanced view is that the separated venture should be able to leverage the parent's strengths while avoiding absorption or subservience. It is ironic and instructive that IBM, in its quest to develop a truly new personal computer, set up a separate and geographically removed unit in 1980 that failed to tap into any of IBM's formidable technological capabilities. The IBM PC was an assembled product without any proprietary systems or semiconductors, and it quickly attracted clones. . . .

CONCLUSIONS

How can established firms compete, survive, and succeed in industries that are being created or transformed by emerging technologies? Success requires continuing support from senior management, separation of the new venture from continuing activities, and a willingness to take risks and learn from experiments. Investments should be treated as options to position the company to make informed investments at some later time—if and when the uncertainties are reduced. There should be a diversity of viewpoints that can challenge prevailing mind-sets, misleading precedents, and potentially myopic views of new ventures. The best innovators seem to be able to think broadly and to entertain a wide range of possibilities before they converge on any one solution.

These prescriptions appear directionally correct, but need tailoring to the distinctive character of each emerging technology and the particular organization involved. The design challenge is to create a high commitment organization that can cope with the tensions of high uncertainty of results while achieving alignment of all levels and functions in support of the strategic choices made. The main point is that managing emerging technologies constitutes a different game for established firms, with its own pitfalls and solutions.

CHAPTER 10

Collaboration

It all used to be so easy. You developed a strategy, negotiated arrangements with suppliers (better still, bought them up, to become "vertically integrated"), and off you went. Today's world of partnerships and alliances and outsourcing makes the strategy process much more complicated. In place of a good deal of competition, collaboration has become king.

Our first reading, called "Collaborating to Compete," reviews alliances. This article is adapted from the recent book of that title by two McKinsey and Company consultants, Joel Bleeke and David Ernst, who sought to capture the company's experiences with such activities. The old style of competition is out, they argue, replaced by a more collaborative style. And to succeed at it, companies must arbitrage their skills and gain access to market and capital, and they must see this as a flexible sequence of actions.

The second reading by Stephen Preece of Wilfred Laurier University in Canada explains why firms create alliances in the first place—for learning, for leaving, for leveraging, for linking, for leaping, and for locking out. Very colorful! Very relevant!

The third reading by Andrew Inkpen of Thunderbird, The American Graduate School of International Management, looks inside collaborative arrangements to describe how knowledge, both tacit and explicit, is created: by technology sharing, by interactions with parent firms or joint ventures, by the movement of personnel across cooperating units, and by the linkage between parent strategies and alliance strategies. All of this requires flexible learning objectives, a committed leadership, a climate of trust alongside a tolerance for redundancy, and some good old-fashioned creative chaos.

USING THE CASE STUDIES

To understand joint ventures and alliances, we need to appreciate the forces leading to their formation and examine their management. In practice, as many of the cases show, the two are closely related. The Lufthansa case examines the formation and management of the Star Alliance. By banding together, airlines changed the structure of their industry, thereby increasing pressure on other airlines to join forces. The case can be used in conjunction with Bleeke and Ernst's "Collaborating to Compete," which deals with the motives and pressures that lead firms to seek joint ventures and alliances. The Kami Corporation case deals with the consequences of a close alliance between Mega Corporation, Kami's parent firm, and Sony. Preece's "Why Create Alliances" is especially relevant to this case. It is also relevant to S.A. Chupa Chups, which describes the reliance of this Spanish firm on joint ventures to enter the Russian and Chinese markets.

In his "Creating Knowledge Through Collaboration," Inkpen argues that ultimately the most enduring payoff from collaboration is acquisition of knowledge. Acer Group describes the use of joint ventures as a strategy of capturing local knowledge. In the Unipart case, however, knowledge acquisition through joint venture is central to the turn-around strategy of the company.

READING 10.1

COLLABORATING TO COMPETE*

BY JOEL BLEEKE AND DAVID ERNST

■ For most global businesses, the days of flat-out, predatory competition are over. The traditional drive to pit one company against the rest of an industry, to pit supplier against supplier, distributor against distributor, on and on through every aspect of a business no longer guarantees the lowest cost, best products or services, or highest profits for winners of this Darwinian game. In businesses as diverse as pharmaceuticals, jet engines, banking, and computers, managers have learned that fighting long, head-to-head battles leaves their companies financially exhausted, intellectually depleted, and vulnerable to the next wave of competition and innovation.

In place of predation, many multinational companies are learning that they must collaborate to compete. Multinationals can create highest value for customers and stakeholders by selectively sharing and trading control, costs, capital, access to markets, information, and technology with competitors and suppliers alike. Competition does not vanish. The computer and commercial aircraft markets are still brutally competitive.

Instead of competing blindly, companies should increasingly compete only in those precise areas where they have a durable advantage or where participation is necessary to preserve industry power or capture value. In packaged goods, that power comes from controlling distribution; in pharmaceuticals, having blockbuster drugs and access to doctors. Managers are beginning to see that many necessary elements of a global business are so costly (like R&D in semiconductors), so generic (like assembly), or so impenetrable (like some of the Asian markets) that it makes no sense to have a traditional competitive stance. The best approach is to find partners that already have the cash, scale, skills, or access you seek.

When a company reaches across borders, its ability and willingness to collaborate is the best predictor of success. The more equal the partnership, the brighter its future. This means

*Excerpted from "Collaborating to Compete," *Directors and Boards* (Winter 1994); used with the permission of McKinsey & Company.

that both partners must be strong financially and in the product or function that they bring to the venture. Of 49 alliances that we examined in detail, two thirds of those between equally matched strong partners succeeded, while about 60% of those involving unequal partners failed. So, too, with ownership. Fifty-fifty partnerships had the highest rate of success of any deal structure that we have examined.

THREE THEMES   The need for better understanding of cross-border alliances and acquisitions is increasingly clear. Cross-border linkages are booming, driven by globalization, Europe 1992, the opening of Eastern European and Asian markets, and an increased need for foreign sales to cover the large fixed costs of playing in high-technology businesses. Go-it-alone strategies often take too long, cost too much, or fail to provide insider access to markets. Yet, large numbers of strategic alliances and cross-border acquisitions are failing. When we examined the cross-border alliances and acquisitions of the largest 150 companies in the United States, Europe, and Japan, we found that only half of these linkages succeed. The average life expectancy for most alliances is approximately seven years. Common lessons from the wide experience of many companies in cross-border strategies are beginning to emerge.

In general, three themes emerge from our studies of alliances:

- First, as we have mentioned, companies are learning that they must collaborate to compete. This requires different measurements of "success" from those used for traditional competition.
- Second, alliances between companies that are potential competitors represent an arbitrage of skills, market access, and capital between the companies. Maintaining a fair balance in this arbitrage is essential for success.
- Third, it is important for managers to develop a vision of international strategy and to see cross-border acquisitions and alliances as a flexible sequence of actions—not one-off deals driven by temporary competitive or financial benefit. The remainder of this article discusses each of these three themes in more detail. . . .

Old measures such as financial hurdles and strategic goals only have meaning in the new context of collaboration. As markets become increasingly competitive, managers are beginning to measure success based on the scarcest resources, including skills and access, not only capital. In the global marketplace, maximizing the value of skills and access can often be achieved only if managers are willing to share ownership with and learn from companies much *different* from their own. Success increasingly comes in proportion to a company's willingness to accept differences.

Successful collaboration also requires flexibility. Most alliances that endure are redefined in terms of geographic or product scope. The success rate for alliances that have changed their scope over time is more than twice that of alliances where the scope has not evolved. Alliances with legal or financial structures that do not permit change are nearly certain to fail. (See Figure 1, which gives Kenichi Ohmae's Tips for Collaboration.)

ALLIANCES AS ARBITRAGE

If all markets were equally accessible, all management equally skilled, all information readily available, and all balance sheets equally solid, there would be little need for collaboration among competitors. But they are not, so companies increasingly benefit by trading these "chips" across borders.

The global arbitrage reflected in cross-border alliances and acquisitions takes place at a slower pace than in capital markets, but the mechanism is similar. Each player uses the quirks, irrational differences, and inefficiencies in the marketplace as well as each company's advantages to mutual benefit. This concept applies mostly to alliances, but cross-border acquisitions can also be viewed as an extreme example of arbitrage: all cash or shares from the buyer, for all the skills, products, and access of the other company. . . .

FIGURE 1
KENICHI OHMAE'S TIPS
FOR COLLABORATION

1. Treat the collaboration as a personal commitment. Its' people that make partnerships work.
2. Anticipate that it will take up management time. If you can't spare the time, don't start it.
3. Mutual respect and trust are essential. If you don't trust the people you are negotiating with, forget it.
4. Remember that both partners must get something out of it (money, eventually). Mutual benefit is vital. This will probably mean you've got to give something up. Recognize this from the outset.
5. Make sure you tie up a tight legal contract. Don't put off resolving unpleasant or contentious issues until "later." Once signed, however, the contract should be put away. If you refer to it, something is wrong with the relationship.
6. Recognize that during the course of a collaboration, circumstances and markets change. Recognize your partner's problems and be flexible.
7. Make sure that you and your partner have mutual expectations of the collaboration and its time scale. One happy and one unhappy partner is a formula for failure.
8. Get to know your opposite numbers at all levels socially. Friends take longer to fall out.
9. Appreciate that cultures— both geographic and corporate—are different. Don't expect a partner to act or respond identically to you. Find out the true reason for a particular response.
10. Recognize your partner's interests and independence.
11. Even if the arrangement is tactical in your eyes, make sure you have corporate approval. Your tactical activity may be a key piece in an overall strategic jigsaw puzzle. With corporate commitment to the partnership, you can act with the positive authority needed in these relationships.
12. Celebrate achievement together. It's a shared elation, and you'll have earned it!

Postscript

Two further things to bear in mind:

1. If you're negotiating a product original equipment manufacturer (OEM) deal, look for a quid pro quo. Remember that another product may offer more in return.
2. Joint development agreements must include joint marketing arrangements. You need the largest market possible to recover development costs and to get volume/margin benefits.
   —*Kenichi Ohmae*
   Kenichi Ohmae is Chairman of McKinsey & Co.'s offices in Japan.

Successful alliance partners follow several patterns in handling the inherent tensions of arbitrating with potential competitors. To begin with, they approach the negotiation phase with a win-win situation. As one executive said, "Do not sit down to negotiate a deal—build links between the companies."

Successful partners also build in conflict-resolution mechanisms such as powerful boards of directors (for joint ventures) and frequent communication between top management of the parent companies and the alliance. The CEOs of the parent companies need to be absolutely clear on where cooperation is expected and where the "old rules" of competition will apply.

In approaching alliances as arbitrage, managers should recognize that the value of "chips" is likely to change over time. The key is to maximize your bargaining power—that is, the value of your company's contribution to the alliance—while also being ready to renegotiate the alliance as necessary. Some of the best alliances have had built-in timetables for assessing partner contributions and clear rules for valuing the contributions going forward.

A SEQUENCE OF ACTIONS

Beyond the themes of collaboration and arbitrage involved in individual deals, cross-border alliances and acquisitions need to be viewed as a *sequence* of actions in the context of overall international strategy—not as one-off transactions. Companies that take a purely financial, deal-driven approach to cross-border alliances and acquisitions usually wind up in trouble.

Looking at cross-border M&A [mergers and acquisitions], the most successful companies make a series of acquisitions that build presence in core businesses over time in the target country. One consumer goods company, for example, made an "anchor" acquisition of a leading brand to establish a solid presence in an important European market, then used its enhanced distribution clout to ensure the acceptance of several brands that were subsequently acquired.

In our study of the cross-border acquisition programs of the largest Triad companies [Asia, Europe, North America], successful acquirers had nearly twice the average and median number of purchases as unsuccessful companies. Through initial acquisitions, the acquirer refines M&A skills and becomes more comfortable with, and proficient at, using M&A for international expansion. And by completing a sequence of transactions, particularly in the same geography, it is possible to gain economies through integrating operations and eliminating overlapping functions.

WILLINGNESS TO RETHINK

It is important to think about cross-border alliances, as well as acquisitions, as a part of a sequence of actions. Most alliances evolve over time, so the initial charter and contract often are not meaningful within a few years. Since trouble is the rule, not the exception, and since two thirds of all cross-border alliances run into management trouble during the first few years, alliances require a willingness by partners to rethink their situation on a constant basis—and renegotiate as necessary.

Alliances should usually be considered as an intermediate strategic device that needs other transactions surrounding it. Approximately half of all cross-border alliances terminate within seven years, so it is critical that managers have a point of view early on of "what's next?"

Most terminating alliances are purchased by one of the partners, and termination need not mean failure. But the high rate of termination suggests that both parties should think hard early on about likely roles as a buyer or seller—the probabilities are high that alliance partners eventually will be one or the other.

The companies that can bring the largest short-term synergies to an alliance are often those companies that will most likely be direct competitors in the long term. So, if the desired sequence of management action does not include selling the business, a different, more complementary partner may need to be found at the outset. Understanding the probable sequence of transactions is therefore important in selecting even early alliance of acquisition partners. As our colleagues in Japan remind us, nothing is worse in cross-border alliances or acquisitions than to have "partners in the same bed with different dreams."

POSTSCRIPT: A LOOK AHEAD

Global corporations of the future will be rather like amoebas. The single-celled aquatic animal is among the most ancient life-forms on earth. It gets all its nourishment directly from its environment through its permeable outer walls. These walls define the creature as distinct from its environment, but allow much of what is inside to flow out and much of what is outside to come in. The amoeba is always changing shape, taking and giving with the surroundings, yet it always retains its integrity and identity as a unique creature.

To be truly global and not merely "big," organizations of the future must hold this permeability as one of their highest values. When managers enter a new market, they should first ask these questions: "How is business here different? What do I need to learn?" They have to seek partners that can share costs and swap skills and access to markets. In the fluid global marketplace, it is no longer possible or desirable for single organizations to be entirely self-sufficient. Collaboration is the value of the future. Alliances are the structure of the future.

This has enormous impact on corporate strategy. It makes the world very complex, because there is no single valid rule book for all markets. As our studies have demonstrated, alliances are based on arbitrating the unique differences between markets and partners. And so it is impossible to standardize an approach to the topic. Managers at the corporate center must be able to tolerate and in fact encourage variation: 10 different markets, 10 different partners, 10 different organization charts, 10 reporting systems, and so on. Policies and procedures must be fluid. The word *schizophrenia* has negative connotations, but it captures this idea that truly global organization must entertain two seemingly contradictory aspects—a strong identity, along with an openness to different ways of doing business, to the values of different cultures and localities.

This duality is going to be very difficult for many of the "global" companies of today. Companies with a sales-based culture, where senior executives all come from a sales background, will have a particularly hard time adapting to this new collaborative world. Such companies see the world as "us and them." They reject ideas from the outside world, even if the concept is helpful. They find it hard to live without standardization. They find it hard to collaborate with partners. Deep down, they are trying to convert everyone to their own way of doing things.

This makes them inflexible and confrontational. They don't know how to communicate and work with the outside world on its own terms. They cannot be like the amoeba, with its permeable walls and changing shape, its openness to take from every environment. These companies may survive because they are large and powerful, but they will cease to be leaders.

READING 10.2

WHY CREATE ALLIANCES*

BY STEPHEN B.
PREECE

■ In response to global competitive forces, business leaders are increasingly turning to cooperative arrangements to advance their competitive edge internationally.

The rise of ISA (International Strategic Alliances) formation has brought about both euphoria over the potential of such arrangements to meet the intensifying demands of global competition, as well as disappointment over the challenges inherent in their implementation. Important to the success of these arrangements is that managers be clear about their overall strategic purpose. Alliances are often spoken of in terms of specific functions

---

*Excerpted from "Why Create Alliances" from "Incorporating International Strategic Alliances into Overall Firm Strategy" by S. Preece found in *The International Executive*, Vol. 37 (3), May/June 1995, pp. 261–277. Copyright © 1995 by John Wiley & Sons, Inc. Used by permission of John Wiley & Sons, Inc.

performed (i.e., market extension, technology sharing). However, the decision to engage a company in a major alliance often represents a substantive strategic alternative having wide-ranging implications for overall firm competitiveness, both positive and negative. The way in which an ISA is incorporated into the overall firm strategy, the long-run strategic objective assumed by management, is critical to the effectiveness of this competitive tool. This article suggests that there are multiple objectives managers can take regarding the integration of ISAs into the strategic management of the organization, with varying consequences.

The three ways to conceptualize ISAs are: structures, functions, and objectives (see Table 1). Perhaps the most common way of thinking about ISAs focuses on alliance organizational structures. The most prevalent organizational structure is the joint venture, where two firms contribute equity in order to create a new and separate entity; some have described this new organization as the "child" with contributing firms assuming the role of "parents" (Harrigan and Newman, 1990). A variation on the joint venture is the minority-equity investment, where one firm takes a minority-equity position in another ongoing firm. Nonequity cooperative arrangements are also possible where firms agree to share efforts, assets, and profits without engaging in equity ties. The extent of collaborative intensity is not necessarily obvious when comparing equity with nonequity arrangements, despite the obvious tangible effect equity provides. . . .

Other efforts to analyze the structure of alliances have focused on issues such as the impact of varying levels of partnership equity on performance . . . small versus large firm alliances . . . specific industry sectors . . . and nationality issues. . . . The prevailing message of this literature is that certain structural arrangements are to be avoided or pursued in the formation and implementation of ISAs.

A second conceptualization of ISAs relates to the various functions of alliances. The primary areas targeted for alliance formation are often collapsed into four primary categories: technology, finance, markets, and production. . . . Technology-driven alliances include such activities as technology development, commercialization, sharing, or licensing. Finance-driven alliances focus on gaining access to financial markets at least cost and the sharing of risk where the product gestation period is long. Market-driven alliances emphasize the penetration of new foreign markets, sharing distribution channels, or extending a brand name. Production-driven alliances include the sharing of production facilities, rationalizing manufacturing, or integrating supplier relationships. A large amount of literature focuses on the functions relevant to technology, finance, markets, and production, and although the term "international strategic alliances" assumes a strategic activity, the actual link to overall firm strategy is not always clear.

Although the structure and functional conceptualizations address important elements of collaborative activity, it is the third category, ISA strategic objectives, that will potentially have the greatest impact on the overall strategic direction and future organizational capabilities of the firm. The variety of options available to managers in approaching strategic alliance objectives and their consequences has not been well developed in the literature. This article presents a typology defining six cooperative objectives [see Table 2], in hopes that it will assist managers in assessing their own vision of strategic alliances and contribute to the understanding of how such relationships can work to their advantage both cooperatively and competitively. . . . It is important to emphasize that both structural and functional issues are important, and

TABLE 1
ISA STRUCTURES, FUNCTIONS, AND OBJECTIVES

Structures	The organizational form chosen for the collaboration. May include joint venture, minority-equity, licensing, nonequity contractual, etc.
Functions	The specific activities to be performed by the alliance. May include market access, technology development, production sharing, financial access, risk sharing, etc.
Objectives	The overall contribution the alliance is intended to have on the strategic direction and capabilities of the firm, i.e., its long-run significance.

TABLE 2
SIX ISA OBJECTIVES

OBJECTIVE	DESCRIPTION	POSITIVE ASPECTS	NEGATIVE ASPECTS
Learning	Acquire needed know-how (markets, technology, managment)	Inexpensive and efficient acquisition	Partner opportunism, organizational challenges
Leaning	Replace value-chain activities, fill in missing firm infrastructure	Specialization advantages	Partner dependency
Leveraging	Fully integrate firm operations with partner	Entirely new portfolio of resources	Decision paralysis, evolving environment
Linking	Closer links with suppliers and customers	Closer coordination of vertical activities	Greater inflexibility in vertical relations
Leaping	Pursue radically new area of endeavor	Expanding universe of market opportunity	Cultural incompatibility
Locking out	Reduce competitive pressure from non-partners	Temporary competitive hiatus	Static strategic position, ephemeral advantage

inextricably linked, to the various strategic objectives that will be discussed. It is also evident that while one alliance objective will likely dominate, others may play secondary roles.

LEARNING

The first strategic objective is *learning*. In this case the firm enters into the alliance with the intention of acquiring needed know-how from the partner through the learning process. Learning becomes attractive when a firm is incapable of performing certain value-chain activities that have the potential to make it either more powerful or more profitable. Two important assumptions linked to this objective are: there is an advantage to maintaining the function/technology within the firm hierarchy; and the function/technology is embedded within the firm, making an arm's-length (market) transaction difficult.

It is unlikely that the learning alliance will actually be described by the participants in these terms. The stated rationale will be defined as an agreement to combine R&D efforts, jointly manufacture a product, and/or share distribution outlets (all functional arrangements). However, one or both sides may aggressively use the alliance to acquire valuable know-how, gradually becoming independent of the "teaching" partner once the learning process is complete.

The positive elements of pursuing alliances as a learning vehicle are speed, efficiency, and cost. Rather than developing a new capability (process, market, or technology) by trial and error through internal development, the alliance provides immediate access to the desired skill. An alternative to alliance learning would be to acquire a firm that carries the needed know-how. However, this strategy can prove to be confrontational and ultimately result in losing the desired skills by way of workplace disruptions, distrust, and defections. Licensing can also serve as an alternative for developing needed know-how; however, some of the most valuable technologies (management, process, and product) are often so embedded in the organizational framework that they are difficult to separate and transfer effectively to a new organization. In short, the strategic alliance relationship with learning as a primary intent has many advantages over the alternatives—acquisition, in-house development, or licensing.

The negative elements of learning alliances primarily accrue to the nonlearner. If an alliance partner does not have a learning motive, it may view partner learning efforts to be predatory or in bad faith, resulting in conflict or even dissolution. Further, the learning alliance assumes an organizational ability to learn and a willingness of the partner to allow learning to take place. . . . The potential for learning in alliances to dramatically impact the competitive dynamics among competing firms makes it an alliance objective that must be seriously considered and appropriately grappled with.

LEANING

The second objective in ISA relationships is *leaning*. In this case the alliance is entered with the intention of having the partner replace an element of the firm's value-chain activities that was previously performed internally. An important assumption is that by ceding out certain operational segments, firms will be able to focus on what they do best, placing an emphasis on their core competence. The firm picking up the value-chain activity is assumed to have its own core competence in that particular area. Leaning objectives, to the extent that the firm is moving away from unattractive value-chain activities, may be considered to be the opposite of the learning objective that seeks to take on particular activities and competencies.

A natural opportunity for leaning in ISAs occurs through cooperative relationships with firms located in countries that provide a comparative advantage in specific value-added activities.

The advantage of such a strategy can result in substantial short-term gains in a production cost structure. Both parties benefit through specialization in the functions that are most amenable to their environments or organizations. The risk in a leaning strategy is in determining which activities are not critical to the core competence of the firm. If a firm mistakenly cedes out crucial activities it can severely cripple its long-term strategy.

A central problem to this alliance objective is functional impotence resulting from a loss of skills. When a set of operations is removed from the "vocabulary" of the firm, the organization may forget how to use it and end up losing it forever. This can lead to a dependency relationship where the original firm can no longer perform production or other functions internally without incurring substantial costs.

Another problem with the leaning strategy is associated with the geographic and organizational separation of value-chain functions. Performing design and research functions in one country while production takes place on the other side of the world can lead to inefficiencies and slower response times. In addition, important feedback and interactive development and production processes are noticeably absent.

Finally, the risk of creating a competitor is great. The number of industries that have relied on cooperative relationships to substitute internal processes only to be later overtaken by the partners are numerous.

LEVERAGING

The third strategic objective to be addressed in ISA relationships is *leveraging*. In this case the alliance represents a major integration of firm functions between partners in order to benefit from size and/or scope advantages. The competitive structure of numerous global industries often requires a critical mass in areas such as market reach, R&D dollars, and product offerings to compete with other dominant global players. While the costs of amassing the necessary size or scope may be prohibitive for an individual firm, two or more smaller firms can enter into an ISA to achieve similar results. The outcome is the leveraging of individual firm strengths with those of a partner for size and/or scope advantages.

In early 1991 Sterling Drug (US) and Sanoñ S.A. (France) joined their pharmaceutical operations in what could be considered a leveraging alliance. The arrangement, which involved no equity exchange, enabled Sanoñ to market its products through the extensive Sterling distribution system in both North and Latin America, while Sterling gained access to the extensive Sanoñ distribution system throughout Europe (Ansberry, 1991). In addition to market sharing arrangements, the alliance included a significant R&D component.

. . . Two medium-sized pharmaceutical companies with complementary markets, product capabilities, and research budgets, combined efforts to become a powerhouse in a global industry. The extensiveness of this relationship was such that the two companies had to coordinate activities on virtually every level of business practice. The obvious advantage of this kind of alliance objective is the opportunity to expand assets, resources, capabilities, and opportunities significantly in a very short time frame. . . .

Two negative elements stand out in the leveraging strategy. Organizational inertia and bureaucratic stagnation is possible when any organization reaches the point of having multiple management layers and departments . . . combining two large bureaucracies increases complexity and the potential for decision hang-ups. Procedural issues as well as trust, reciprocity, and monitoring issues affect the commitment and durability of the relationship. . . .

The other negative aspect of this strategy is the problem of a changing world. The top management of two major companies may see eye-to-eye regarding industry and competitive factors that make such an alliance favorable today. However, the question becomes, will this consensus in "world view" exist 1, 2, or 5 years from now? Extensive research suggests that industry evolution and the shifting of the competitive landscape are major contributors to alliance instability. . . .

LINKING

The fourth ISA objective considered in this analysis is *linking*. This particular relationship approach is most frequently associated with vertical relationships (as opposed to horizontal) and are often singular in their functional scope. Strategic supplier and customer relationships are becoming much more prevalent as a specific example of this relationship type. . . .

The traditional model in the United States has been to maintain multiple suppliers for any given component and then to foster an environment that makes them compete against one another. Annual or biannual bidding arrangements would lead to constant competitive pressure through low-price seeking and the willingness to shift suppliers with virtually interchangeable component parts. A changing trend, however, is for manufacturers to seek tighter links with supplier companies, based on the belief that closer cooperation and coordination will lead to a more effective relationship, because the sharing of information, specifications, and expertise over time will result in shorter lead times, higher quality, and greater control in the manufacturing process.

The advantage to the linking strategic objective is that it brings about opportunities for greater coordination and a tighter relationship between partners than would be available in an arm's-length supplier relationship.

The major negative element of this strategy is inflexibility. When a traditional supplier relationship is reevaluated annually or biannually, there is little problem in severing a relationship when it becomes necessary; with an alliance relationship it becomes much more difficult. As the relationship deepens and intensifies over time, specific assets and personnel are exclusively devoted to the relationship. If the firm encounters a downturn in business or a reduction in customer orders, it is much more difficult to sever the relationship with the one supplier with which the firm has developed an involved relationship than it would be otherwise, and the damage to both may be severe.

LEAPING

The fifth alliance objective is *leaping*. In this case a company benefits from the expertise of another firm whose core competency is substantially different, thereby allowing the former to expand into largely disparate but potentially viable areas in which it would otherwise not venture. This objective is called leaping because the areas of expertise sought for in the partner enable the firm to explore product or market opportunities, leaping over otherwise formidable entry barriers, that would be difficult to exploit internally due to a lack of specific firm capabilities.

An example of leaping is the strategic alliance between Sony and ESPN to develop and jointly market a new line of sports video games. In this case Sony had an established expertise in consumer electronics applications in many areas. ESPN, through its sports cable broadcasting, had established a solid reputation with, and understanding of, sports fans.

. . . leaping may represent cultural or geographic expansions necessary to access foreign markets. In many cases companies may have products that are appropriate for a particular country or market, but may have little expertise in the cultural practices of the residents. This is particularly true of less-developed countries, and may explain why culturally sensitive sectors such as retailing involve alliances.

Leaping differs from learning in that the leaping firm is not likely to have the desire to internalize the expertise of its partner. The technological infrastructure is so different that this would be a far too onerous task. In the Sony example, Sony is unlikely to have the interest or capacity to develop the sports knowledge and understanding of ESPN; likewise ESPN is unlikely to digress into consumer electronics. Leaping differs from leveraging in that the leaping segment of the firm typically does not represent the core technological thrust and integration that the leveraging relationship would encompass.

The negatives associated with leaping alliances are primarily those of cultural incompatibility. Any ISA arrangement presents challenges to the successful integration of management styles as well as bridging the cultural gap between nations. However, efforts to cooperate between companies that occupy *radically* different industry and technological capabilities can prove to be particularly difficult to manage due to organizational cultural differences. Organizational traditions in such areas as decision-making processes, risk preferences, and managerial styles can represent enormous invisible barriers to the successful implementation of desired alliance objectives.

LOCKING OUT

The sixth ISA strategic objective to be considered is *locking out*. In this scenario two or more partners come together in order to thwart competition and benefit from the combined market power or structural relationship of the cooperating firms. The intention is not particularly to advance a new technology, innovation, or market, but rather to protect existing advantages from potential competition.

Examples of such alliances may include large manufacturers consolidating supplier networks to make it more difficult for competing firms to gain access.

The primary negative element of locking-out alliances is their ephemeral nature. The antitrust issues related to strategic alliances are often complex and untested in many countries. As potential competitors fall to unfair market obstructions and as customers complain about the lack of competition, governments may quickly disallow an alliance and threaten a competitive advantage stronghold. Additionally, alliances used to neutralize competition may make the involved firms enjoy a false sense of competitive advantage, ultimately making them vulnerable to more innovative and nimble competitors.

CONCLUSION

In conclusion, there are three important steps in developing appropriate ISA arrangements. The first is to conceive of and adequately define a primary objective for the alliance arrangement. This article has argued that several alliance objectives are possible and can have significantly differing implications for the firm. The next step is to ensure that such an objective is appropriate given the firm's broader strategies and objectives. If there is a good alliance/strategy fit, then the final step is to ensure that the partner's alliance objects are compatible. Such strategic planning activities are likely to reduce conflictual foundations for ISAs and increase the possibility that they will ultimately contribute to firm competitive advantages as planned.

BY ANDREW C. INKPEN

■ Increasingly, the creation of new organizational knowledge is becoming a managerial priority. New knowledge provides the basis for organizational renewal and sustainable competitive advantage (Quinn, 1992). By examining knowledge creation through alliance strategies, this article provides insights into how firms manage knowledge.

In the past five years, the number of domestic and international alliances has grown by more than 25 percent annually (Bleeke and Ernst, 1995). Peter Drucker (1995) has suggested that the greatest change in the way business is being conducted is in the accelerating growth of relationships based not on ownership but on partnership. Many firms have now realized that self-sufficiency is becoming increasingly difficult in a business environment that demands strategic focus, flexibility, and innovation. Alliances provide firms with a unique opportunity to leverage their strengths with the help of partners.

Many firms enter into alliances with specific learning objectives. Although learning through alliances can and does occur successfully, it is a difficult, frustrating, and often misunderstood process. The primary obstacle to success is a failure to execute the specific organizational processes necessary to access, assimilate, and disseminate alliance knowledge. Successful firms exploit learning opportunities by acquiring knowledge through "grafting," a process of internalizing knowledge not previously available within the organization. . . .**

This research study examined two main questions: Do alliance parents recognize and seek to exploit alliance learning opportunities? and What organizational conditions facilitate effective or ineffective learning? The sample of alliance organizations for the research consisted of 40 American-Japanese joint ventures (JVs) located in North America and involved interviews with their managers. All of the JVs were suppliers to the automotive industry and, with two exceptions, all were startup or greenfield organizations. In terms of ownership, 17 ventures were 50-50, in 15 ventures the Japanese partners had majority equity, and in eight ventures the American partners had majority equity. Five cases from the initial study were selected for further study.

EXPLOTING COLLABORATIVE KNOWLEDGE

There are four critical knowledge management processes used by firms to access and transform knowledge from an alliance context to a partner context: technology sharing; JV-parent interactions; personnel movement; and linkages between parent and alliance strategies. These processes create connections for individual managers through which they can communicate their alliance experiences to others and form the foundation for the integration of knowledge into the parent's collective knowledge base.

**Huber (1991) has explored the various ways by which organizations are exposed to new knowledge: congenital learning, experiential learning, vicarious learning, searching, and grafting. Of specific interest in this study is grafting knowledge from outside the organization's boundaries; for example, through mergers, acquisitions.

TABLE 1
KNOWLEDGE
MANAGEMENT
PROCESSES AND
TYPES OF KNOWLEDGE

KNOWLEDGE MANAGEMENT PROCESSES	TYPES OF KNOWLEDGE	EXAMPLES OF KNOWLEDGE POTENTIALLY USEFUL TO AMERICAN JV PARENTS
Technology Sharing	Explicit	• quality control processes • product designs • scheduling systems
JV–Parent Interactions	Explicit Tacit	• specific human resource practices • expectations of Japanese customers
Personnel Movement	Tacit	• continuous improvement objectives • commitment to customer satisfaction
Linkages Between Parent and Alliance Strategies	Explicit Tacit	• market intelligence • visions for the future • partner's keiretsu relationships

TACIT AND EXPLICIT KNOWLEDGE

Organizational knowledge creation involves a continuous interplay between tacit and explicit knowledge (Nonaka and Takeuchi, 1995). Tacit knowledge is hard to formalize, making it difficult to communicate or share with others. Tacit knowledge involves intangible factors embedded in personal beliefs, experiences, and values. Explicit knowledge is systematic and easily communicated in the form of hard data or codified procedures. Often there will be a strong tacit dimension associated with how to use and implement explicit knowledge. Table 1 shows the four knowledge management processes and the primary types of knowledge associated with each process.

TECHNOLOGY SHARING

In the cases studied, parent firms had put into place various mechanisms to gain access to JV manufacturing process and product technology. The most common approach was also the most straightforward—meetings between JV and parent managers. In once case, monthly meetings were held, with the location alternating between the JV and one of the American parent plants. In attendance at the meetings were plant managers, heads of quality control, R&D managers, the VP of manufacturing at the American parent head office, and several senior JV managers. In addition, quarterly R&D meetings were held involving the JV and American parent.

Access to partner technology skills also occurred through direct linkages between Japanese and American partners. In two cases, there were regular visits by American parent personnel to Japanese parent facilities.

In another case, the partners signed a very broad global technology agreement. Both partners agreed to be completely open in sharing both product and manufacturing technology.

Not all American parents were interested in access to Japanese partner technology. In one case, a Japanese partner offered to share its manufacturing technology with its American partner. The Japanese partner had developed some proprietary process technology and was willing to share it at no cost. The technology was used in the JV and was very visible to American partner managers. The offer was communicated in a written memo from a JV manager to the American partner president. The American firm never followed up on the offer. Why was the offer refused? One JV manager's opinion was that "the people from the American parent do not want to learn because they see the JV as an upstart."

JV–PARENT INTERACTIONS

The JV–parent relationship plays a key role in knowledge management. In addition to the technology-sharing initiatives discussed above, other JV–parent interactions can create the social context necessary to bring JV knowledge into a wider arena. JV–parent interactions can provide the basis for what have been referred to as "communities of practice" (Brown and Duguid, 1991). A community of practice is a group of individuals that is not necessarily recognizable within strict organizational boundaries. The members share community knowledge and may be willing to challenge the organization's conventional wisdom. Communities emerge not when the members absorb abstract knowledge, but when the members become "insiders" and acquire the particular community's subjective viewpoint and learn to speak its language.

Visits and tours of JV facilities were an effective means for parent managers to learn about their JVs. JV managers were generally convinced that differences embodied in the JV were visible and parent managers would appreciate the differences if they spent more time in the JV.

Customer–supplier relationships between the JV and the American parent also created a basis for extensive JV–parent interaction. In one case, the American parent substantially increased its quality because of pressure from the JV customer, which in turn was under pressure from its Japanese transplant supplier. Until the JV was formed, the American parent had not had any extensive interactions with Japanese customers. In supplying the JV, and indirectly becoming a transplant supplier, the American parent was forced to evaluate some of its manufacturing operations.

PERSONNEL MOVEMENT

The rotation of personnel between the alliance and the parent can be a very effective means of "mobilizing" personal knowledge. Rotation helps members of an organization understand the business from a multiplicity of perspectives, which in turn makes knowledge more fluid and easier to put into practice. In this study, the rotation of interest was a two-way movement of personnel between the JV and parent. If there is only one-way movement, such as from the parent to the JV, this was not considered rotation.

The attitude of the Japanese parent sometimes constrained rotation. In one case, the Japanese parent preferred that JV personnel not move to the American parent. The Japanese parent saw the JV as distinct and separate from the American parent. Despite this concern, the American parent has moved personnel from the JV to the parent. In another case, personnel were willing to move from the parent to the JV but less willing to return to the American parent. This prompted the American parent to ask its JV not to "poach" any more personnel from the parent.

LINKAGES BETWEEN PARENT AND ALLIANCE STRATEGIES

The degree to which the parent and alliance strategies are linked plays an important role in the management of alliance knowledge. A JV perceived as peripheral to the parent organization's strategy will likely yield few opportunities for the transfer of alliance knowledge to the parent. A JV viewed as important may receive more attention from the parent organization, leading to substantial parent–JV interaction and a greater commitment of resources to the management of the collaboration.

Through strategic linkages between the JV and the parent, the partners can gain important insights into each other's businesses. For example, an American parent won a contract to supply a part but was unable to meet the target cost. The parent decided to use its JV to produce the parts because of the JV's superior process technology. This type of linkage indicates that the American parent has internalized the differences between the parent and JV. It also opens the door for more knowledge sharing and cooperation in the future.

FACILITATING FACTORS

Why do some firms actively seek to leverage alliance knowledge while others make only a minimal effort? Why are some firms more effective at leveraging alliance knowledge? There are six factors that facilitate effective knowledge management: flexible learning objectives; leadership commitment; a climate of trust; a tolerance for redundancy; creative chaos; and an absence of performance myopia.

FLEXIBLE LEARNING OBJECTIVES

The collaborative objectives of the JV partners are a key element in alliance knowledge creation. However, it is not enough to enter a JV with a learning objective. Initial learning objectives may have little impact on the effectiveness of knowledge creation efforts. This is not to suggest that learning objectives are unimportant. If learning objectives are associated with the formation of a JV, a parent firm may enter more actively into the search for knowledge. However, if the initial learning objective is not correctly focused and management is unwilling or unable to adjust the objective, knowledge management efforts may be ineffective. For example, in one case the American partner had a very explicit technology learning objective. However, this firm's knowledge management efforts were weak and inconsistent because the firm did not have a clear understanding of its partner's skills. . . .

In another JV, the situation was almost the reverse. The American parent was interested in forming a JV primarily to gain access to the Japanese transplant market. When negotiations to form the JV were started, American parent management made it clear that they were only willing to be involved if they managed the JV. According to the JV president, "we have a quality reputation which we should be able to carry over to the JV." But, after working together for several years, American parent management realized that alliance knowledge could be important to their firm and greater effort was made to gain access to the JV operations and JV partner knowledge. . . .

LEADERSHIP COMMITMENT

Top management's role in managing knowledge should be one of architect and catalyst. While multiple advocates are important, there must be at least one strong champion of knowledge creation in a leadership position. The leader's role is especially important in initiating linkages between parent and alliance strategies. In one JV, the primary impetus for this close relationship came from the president of the American parent. The president had a long-standing personal relationship with the chairman of the Japanese partner. The president was committed to building the JV relationship and leveraging the JV experience to strengthen the American parent business. Through the president's efforts, both explicit knowledge management efforts designed to transfer specific technologies were initiated as well as more exploratory exchanges of personnel and ideas. . . .

CLIMATE OF TRUST

A climate of trust between both the JV partners and between the JV and parent organizations is critical to the free exchange of information. Trust between the partners appeared to be both a function of top management involvement in the relationship and a history of cooperation prior to the formation of the JV. . . .

TOLERANCE FOR REDUNDANCY

Redundancy means the conscious overlapping of company information, activities, and management responsibilities. Redundancy encourages frequent dialogue and, as Peter Senge (1990) argues, dialogue is a key element of collective learning. In a dialogue, complex issues are explored with the objective of collectively achieving common meaning. Dialogue involves conversations and connections between people at different organization levels. Inevitably, as issues are debated and assumptions questioned, dialogue will lead to some redundancy in information. Without a tolerance for redundancy, sharing of ideas and effective dialogue will be difficult. . . .

CREATIVE CHAOS

Chaos is created naturally when an organization faces a crisis, such as a rapid decline in performance. Chaos can also occur when differences or discrepancies disrupt normal routines. Chaos increases tension within the organization and focuses attention on forming and solving new problems. The job of managers in the knowledge creating company is to orient the chaos toward knowledge creation by providing managers with a conceptual framework that can be used to interpret experience (Nonaka, 1991).

PERFORMANCE MYOPIA

Managers seeking to create knowledge must cope with confusing experiences. One such "experience" for JV parents was the assessment of JV performance. Several managers in the American parent companies pointed to the poor financial performance of the JVs as evidence that learning was not occurring, or could not occur. More generally, a myopic preoccupation with short-term issues was a common characteristic of the American partners. Although it is too simplistic to describe Japanese management as long-term oriented and American management as short-term oriented, the Japanese partner firms in this study appeared to focus on customer satisfaction and product quality rather than on profit-based performance. Consistent with other studies (for example, Abbeglen and Stalk, 1995), the Japanese firms seemed less constrained by issues of share price and by impatient boards of directors than their American counterparts. While North Americans focused on the bottom line, the Japanese focused on improving productivity, quality, and delivery.

When a firm is heavily focused on financial performance issues, learning will often be a secondary and less tangible concern. In the poorly performing JVs, American managers found it difficult to conceive that learning could be occurring in the face of poor performance. . . .

CONCLUSION

Knowledge creation is a dynamic process involving interactions at various organizational levels and it encompasses a community of individuals that enlarge, amplify, and disseminate their knowledge. It can be haphazard and idiosyncratic and should be viewed as a continuous process, rather than one with identifiable input-output phases. It may occur unintentionally and it may occur even if success cannot be assessed in terms of objective outcomes. Given its haphazard and idiosyncratic nature, firms may view resources committed to knowledge creation as extravagant and wasteful. The view here is that the ability to create knowledge and move it from one part of the organization to another is the basis for competitive advantage. While not all knowledge creation efforts will be successful, some will yield surprisingly important results. Also, not all knowledge creation efforts will have immediate performance payoffs. However, over the long term, successful knowledge creation should strengthen and reinforce a firm's competitive strategy.

CHAPTER 11

Globalization

The attention to the international dimension in this book is hardly casual or cosmetic. A glance at the list of cases reveals just how international this book is. Here we turn to the conceptual side under the label of globalization, which is certainly a major force in business today.

Operating in an international rather than a domestic arena presents managers with many new opportunities. Having worldwide operations not only gives a company access to new markets and specialized resources, but it also opens up new sources of information to stimulate future product development. And it broadens the options of strategic moves and countermoves the company might make in competing with its domestic or more narrowly international rivals. However, with all these new opportunities comes the challenge of managing strategy, organization, and operations that are innately more complex, diverse, and uncertain. We include three readings here to help consider this.

The first, by Christopher Bartlett of the Harvard Business School and coauthor Sumantra Ghoshal of the London Business School, deals with the organizational aspects of managing in the international context. To operate effectively on a worldwide basis, Bartlett and Ghoshal suggest, companies must learn to differentiate how they manage different businesses, countries, and functions; create interdependence among units instead of either dependence or independence; and focus on coordination and co-option rather than control. The key to such organizational capability lies in shared vision and values.

The second reading by George Yip, who is at the London Business School, focuses on the strategic aspects of managing in an international context. Yip's views on global strategy reflect the same orientation of industrial organization economies that influenced

Porters' work: In deciding on markets in which to participate, products and services to offer, and location of specific activities and tasks, managers must analyze the "globalization drivers" in their industries and find the right strategic fit.

Finally, Subramanian Rangan of INSEAD offers "seven myths" about global strategy, another set of warnings that *globalism* is not as simple as the word implies. This kind of sobering advice is central in a world perhaps a little too casual about terms like *globalization*.

USING THE CASE STUDIES

There is a distinction to be made between going global and operating as a global company. Many of the cases describe companies that have long been global. Cases such as BMG International, Lufthansa, and McKinsey and Company deal with the problems of running organizations that span the globe. Ghoshal's reading, "Managing Across Borders," considers how global companies can deal with this challenge. By contrast, cases such as AmBev consider the pitfalls of going global. It is a good illustration of Rangan's warning in "Seven Myths Regarding Global Strategies" that going global may be fashionable, but doing it right is more important. Yip's argument in "Going Global . . . in a World of Nations" is useful for analyzing the globalization of companies such as the Selkirk Group and S.A. Chupa Chups that seem to get it right.

Of course, it should be remembered that one does not have to be global or go global to face the challenge of globalization. Beijing Mirror Corporation, Wipro Corporation, TV Asahi Theatrical Productions, and AmBev are cases that deal with the consequences of globalization for firms that are rooted in their local environment. Yip examines the dilemma of going global. It is useful for analyzing companies such as the Selkirk Group and S.A. Chupa Chups that began as local and then went global, but it is also useful for analyzing companies that have to deal with the consequences of globalization without going global themselves.

READING 11.1

MANAGING ACROSS BORDERS: NEW ORGANIZATIONAL RESPONSES*

BY CHRISTOPHER A. BARTLETT AND SUMANTRA GHOSHAL

■ . . . Recent changes in the international operating environment have forced companies to optimize *efficiency, responsiveness* and *learning* simultaneously in their worldwide operations. To companies that previously concentrated on developing and managing one of these capabilities, this new challenge implie[s] not only a total strategic reorientation but a major change in organizational capability as well.

Implementing such a complex, three-pronged strategic objective would be difficult under any circumstances, but in a worldwide company the task is complicated even further. The very act of "going international" multiplies a company's organizational complexity. Typically, doing so requires adding a third dimension to the existing business- and function-oriented management structure. It is difficult enough balancing product divisions that bring efficiency and focus to domestic product market strategies with corporate staffs whose functional expertise allows them to play an important counterbalance and control role. The thought of adding

---

*Originally published in *Sloan Management Review* 43 (Autumn 1987). Reprinted with deletions by permission of the *Review*.

capable, geographically oriented management—and maintaining a three-way balance of organizational perspectives and capabilities among product, function and area—is intimidating to most managers. The difficulty is increased because the resolution of tensions among product, function and area managers must be accomplished in an organization whose operating units are often divided by distance and time, and whose key members are separated by culture and language.

FROM UNIDIMENSIONAL TO MULTIDIMENSIONAL CAPABILITIES	Faced with the task of building multiple strategic capabilities in highly complex organizations, managers in almost every company we studied* made the simplifying assumption that they were faced with a series of dichotomous choices. They discussed the relative merits of pursuing a strategy of national responsiveness as opposed to one based on global integration; they considered whether key assets and resources should be centralized or decentralized; and they debated the need for strong central control versus greater subsidiary autonomy. How a company resolved these dilemmas typically reflected influences exerted and choices made during its historical development. In telecommunications, ITT's need to develop an organization responsive to national political demands and local specification differences was as important to its survival in the pre– and post–World War II era as was NEC's need to build its highly centralized technological manufacturing and marketing skills and resources in order to expand abroad in the same industry in the 1960s and 1970s.

When new competitive challenges emerged, however, such unidimensional biases became strategically limiting. As ITT demonstrated by its outstanding historic success and NEC showed by its more delayed international expansion, strong *geographic management* is essential for development of dispersed responsiveness. Geographic management allows worldwide companies to sense, analyze and respond to the needs of different national markets.

Effective competitors also need to build strong *business management* with global product responsibilities if they are to achieve global efficiency and integration. These managers act as champions of manufacturing rationalization, product standardization and low-cost global sourcing. (As the telecommunications switching industry globalized, NEC's organizational capability in this area gave it a major competitive advantage.) Unencumbered by either territorial or functional loyalties, central product groups remain sensitive to overall competitive issues and become agents to facilitate changes that, though painful, are necessary for competitive viability.

Finally, a strong, worldwide *functional management* allows an organization to build and transfer its core competencies—a capability vital to worldwide learning. Links between functional managers allow the company to accumulate specialized knowledge and skills and to apply them wherever they are required in the worldwide operations. Functional management acts as the repository of organizational learning and as the prime mover for its consolidation and circulation within the company. It was for want of a strongly linked research and technical function across subsidiaries that ITT failed in its attempt to coordinate the development and diffusion of its System 12 digital switch.

Thus, to respond to the needs for efficiency, responsiveness and learning *simultaneously*, the company must develop a multidimensional organization in which the effectiveness of each management group is maintained *and* in which each group is prevented from dominating the others. As we saw in company after company, the most difficult challenge for managers trying to respond to broad, emerging strategic demands was to develop the new elements of multidimensional organization without eroding the effectiveness of their current unidimensional capability.

---

*The findings presented in this article are based on a three-year research project on the organization and management of multinational corporations. Extensive discussions were held with 250 managers in nine of the world's largest multinational companies, in the United States, Europe and Japan. Complete findings are presented in *Managing across Borders: The transnational solution* (Boston: Harvard Business School Press, 1988).

OVERCOMING SIMPLIFYING ASSUMPTIONS

For all nine companies at the core of our study, the challenge of breaking down biases and building a truly multidimensional organization proved difficult. Behind the pervasive either/or mentality that led to the development of unidimensional capabilities, we identified three simplifying assumptions that blocked the necessary organizational development. The need to reduce organizational and strategic complexity has made these assumptions almost universal in worldwide companies, regardless of industry, national origin or management culture.

- There is a widespread, often implicit assumption that roles of different organizational units are uniform and symmetrical; different businesses should be managed in the same way, as should different functions and national operations.
- Most companies, some consciously, most unconsciously, create internal inter-unit relationships on clear patterns of dependence or independence, on the assumption that such relationships *should* be clear and unambiguous.
- Finally, there is the assumption that one of corporate management's principal tasks is to institutionalize clearly understood mechanisms for decision making and to implement simple means of exercising control.

Those companies most successful in developing truly multidimensional organizations were the ones that challenged these assumptions and replaced them with some very different attitudes and norms. Instead of treating different businesses, functions and subsidiaries similarly, they systematically *differentiated* tasks and responsibilities. Instead of seeking organizational clarity by basing relationships on dependence or independence, they built and managed *interdependence* among the different units of the companies. And instead of considering control their key task, corporate managers searched for complex mechanisms to *coordinate and coopt* the differentiated and interdependent organizational units into sharing a vision of the company's strategic tasks. These are the central organizational characteristics of what we described in the earlier article as transnational corporations—those most effective in managing across borders in today's environment of intense competition and rapid, often discontinuous change.

FROM SYMMETRY TO DIFFERENTIATION

. . . Just as they saw the need to change symmetrical structures and homogeneous processes imposed on different businesses and functions, most companies we observed eventually recognized the importance of differentiating the management of diverse geographic operations. Despite the fact that various national subsidiaries operated with very different external environments and internal constraints, they all traditionally reported through the same channels, operated under similar planning and control systems and worked under a set of common and generalized mandates.

Increasingly, however, managers recognized that such symmetrical treatment can constrain strategic capabilities. At Unilever, for example, it became clear that Europe's highly competitive markets and closely linked economies meant that its operating companies in that region required more coordination and control than those in, say, Latin America. Little by little, management increased the product coordination groups' role in Europe until they had direct line responsibility for all operating companies in their businesses. Elsewhere, however, national management maintained its historic line management role, and product coordinators acted only as advisors. Unilever has thus moved in sequence from a symmetrical organization to a much more differentiated one: differentiating by product, then by function and finally by geography. . . .

But Unilever is far from unique. In all of the companies we studied, senior management was working to differentiate its organizational structure and processes in increasingly sophisticated ways. For example, . . . Proctor & Gamble is differentiating the roles of it subsidiaries by giving some of them responsibilities as "lead countries" in product strategy development, then rotating that leadership role from product to product. . . . Thus, instead of deciding the overall roles of product, functional and geographic management on the basis of simplistic dichotomies such as global versus domestic businesses or centralized versus decentralized organizations, many companies are creating different levels of influence for different groups as they perform different activities. Doing this allows the relatively underdeveloped management perspectives to be built in a gradual, complementary manner rather than in the sudden, adversarial environment often associated with either/or choices. Internal heterogeneity has made the change from unidimensional to multidimensional organization easier by breaking the problem up into many small, differentiated parts and by allowing for a step-by-step process of organizational change.

FROM DEPENDENCE OR INDEPENDENCE TO INTERDEPENDENCE

. . . New strategic demands make organizational models of simple inter-unit dependence *or* independence inappropriate. The reality of today's worldwide competitive environment demands collaborative information-sharing and problem-solving, cooperative support and resource-sharing, and collective action and implementation. Independent units risk being picked off one-by-one by competitors whose coordinated global approach gives them two important strategic advantages—the ability to integrate research, manufacturing and other scale-efficient operations, and the opportunity to cross-subsidize the losses from battles in one market with funds generated by profitable operations in home markets or protected environments. . . .

On the other hand, foreign operations totally dependent on a central unit must deal with problems reaching beyond the loss of local market responsiveness. . . . They also risk being unable to respond effectively to strong national competitors or to sense potentially important local market or technical intelligence. This was the problem Proctor & Gamble's Japan subsidiary faced in an environment where local competitors began challenging P&G's previously secure position with successive, innovative product changes and novel market strategies, particularly in the disposable nappies business. After suffering major losses in market share, management recognized that a local operation focused primarily on implementing the company's classic marketing strategy was no longer sufficient; the Japanese subsidiary needed the freedom and incentive to be more innovative. Not only to ensure the viability of the Japanese subsidiary, but also to protect its global strategic position, P&G realized it had to expand the role of the local unit and change its relationship with the parent company to enhance two-way learning and mutual support.

But it is not easy to change relationships of dependence or independence that have been built up over a long history. Many companies have tried to address the increasing need for inter-unit collaboration by adding layer upon layer of administrative mechanisms to foster greater cooperation. Top managers have extolled the virtues of teamwork and have even created special departments to audit management response to this need. In most cases these efforts to obtain cooperation by fiat or by administrative mechanisms have been disappointing. The independent units have feigned compliance while fiercely protecting their independence. The dependent units have found that the new cooperative spirit implies little more than the right to agree with those on whom they depend.

Yet some companies have gradually developed the capability to achieve such cooperation and to build what Rosabeth Kanter (1983) calls an "integrative organization." Of the companies we studied, the most successful did so not by creating new units, but by changing the basis of the relationships among product, functional, and geographic management groups. From relations based on dependence or independence, they moved to relations based on formidable levels of explicit, genuine interdependence. In essence, they made integration and collaboration self-enforcing by making it necessary for each group to cooperate in order to achieve its own interests. . . .

Proctor & Gamble . . . in Europe, for example, [has] formed a number of Eurobrand teams for developing product-market strategies for different product lines.* Each team is headed by the general manager of a subsidiary that has a particularly well-developed competence in that business. It also includes the appropriate product and advertising managers from the other subsidiaries and relevant functional managers from the company's European headquarters. . . .

In observing many such examples of companies building and extending interdependence among units, we were able to identify three important flows, which seem to be at the centre of the emerging organizational relationships. Most fundamental was the product interdependence which most companies were building as they specialized and integrated their worldwide manufacturing operations to achieve greater efficiency, while retaining sourcing flexibility and sensitivity to host country interests. The resulting *flow of parts, components and finished goods* increased the interdependence of the worldwide operations in an obvious and fundamental manner.

We also observed companies developing a resource interdependence that often contrasted sharply with earlier policies that had either encouraged local self-sufficiency or required the centralization of all surplus resources. . . .

Finally, the worldwide diffusion of technology, the development of international markets and the globalization of competitive strategies have meant that vital strategic information now exists in many different locations worldwide. Furthermore, the growing dispersion of assets and delegation of responsibilities to foreign operations have resulted in the development of local knowledge and expertise that has implications for the broader organization. With these changes, the need to manage the *flow of intelligence, ideas and knowledge* has become central to the learning process and has reinforced the growing interdependence of worldwide operations, as P&G's Eurobrand teams illustrate.

It is important to emphasize that the relationships we are highlighting are different from the interdependencies commonly observed in multi-unit organizations. Traditionally, MNC managers have attempted to highlight what has been called "pooled interdependence" to make subunit managers responsive to global rather than local interests. (Before the Euroteam approach, for instance, P&G's European vice-president often tried to convince independent-minded subsidiary managers to transfer surplus generated funds to other, more needy subsidiaries, in the overall corporate interest, arguing that, "Someday when you're in need they might be able to fund a major product launch for you.")

As the example illustrates, pooled interdependence is often too broad and amorphous to affect day-to-day management behaviour. The interdependencies we described earlier are more clearly reciprocal, and each unit's ability to achieve its goals is made conditional upon its willingness to help other units achieve their own goals. Such interdependencies more effectively promote the organization's ability to share the perspectives and link the resources of different components, and thereby to expand its organizational capabilities.**

FROM CONTROL TO COORDINATION AND COOPTION

The simplifying assumptions of organizational symmetry and dependence (or independence) had allowed the management processes in many companies to be dominated by simple controls—tight operational controls in subsidiaries dependent on the centre, and a looser system of administrative or financial controls in decentralized units. When companies began to challenge the assumptions underlying organizational relationships, however, they found they also had to adapt their management processes. The growing interdependence of organizational units strained the simple control-dominated systems and underlined the need to supplement existing

---

*For a full description of the development of Eurobrand in P&G, see C. A. Bartlett, "Proctor & Gamble Europe: Vizir launch" (Boston: Harvard Business School, Case Services #9-384-139).
**The distinction among sequential, reciprocal and pooled interdependencies has been made in J. D. Thompson, *Organizations in Action* (New York: McGraw-Hill, 1967).

processes with more sophisticated ones. Furthermore, the differentiation of organizational tasks and roles amplified the diversity of management perspectives and capabilities and forced management to differentiate management processes.

As organizations became, at the same time, more diverse and more interdependent, there was an explosion in the number of issues that had to be linked, reconciled, or integrated. The rapidly increasing flows of goods, resources and information among organizational units increased the need for *coordination* as a central management function. But the costs of coordination are high, both in financial and human terms, and coordinating capabilities are always limited. Most companies, though, tended to concentrate on a primary means of coordination and control—the company's way of doing things. . . .

In a number of companies, we saw a . . . broadening of administrative processes as managers learned to operate with previously underutilized means of coordination. Unilever's heavy reliance on the socialization of managers to provide the coordination "glue" was supplemented by the growing role of the central product coordination departments. In contrast, NEC reduced central management's coordination role by developing formal systems and social processes in a way that created a more robust and flexible coordinative capability.

Having developed diverse new means of coordination, management's main task is carefully to ration their usage and application. . . . it is important to distinguish where tasks can be formalized and managed through systems, where social linkages can be fostered to encourage informal agreements and cooperation, and where the coordination task is so vital or sensitive that it must use the scarce resource of central management arbitration. . . .

We have described briefly how companies began to . . . differentiat[e] roles and responsibilities within the organization. Depending on their internal capabilities and on the strategic importance of their external environments, organizational units might be asked to take on roles ranging from that of strategic leader with primary corporate-wide responsibility for a particular business or function, to simple implementer responsible only for executing strategies and decisions developed elsewhere.

Clearly, these roles must be managed in quite different ways. The unit with strategic leadership responsibility must be given freedom to develop responsibility in an entrepreneurial fashion, yet must also be strongly supported by headquarters. For this unit, operating controls may be light and quite routine, but coordination of information and resource flows to and from the unit will probably require intensive involvement from senior management. In contrast, units with implementation responsibility might be managed through tight operating controls, with standardized systems used to handle much of the coordination—primarily of goods flows. Because the tasks are more routine, the use of scarce coordinating resources could be minimized.

Differentiating organizational roles and management processes can have a fragmenting and sometimes demotivating effect, however. Nowhere was this more clearly illustrated than in the many companies that unquestioningly assigned units the "dog" and "cash cow" roles defined by the Boston Consulting Group's growth-share matrix in the 1970s. (See Haspeslagh, 1982.) Their experience showed that there is another equally important corporate management task, which complements and facilitates coordination effectiveness. We call this task *cooption:* the process of uniting the organization with a common understanding of, identification with, and commitment to the corporation's objectives, priorities and values.

A clear example of the importance of cooption was provided by the contrast between ITT and NEC managers. At ITT, corporate objectives were communicated more in financial than in strategic terms, and the company's national entities identified almost exclusively with their local environment. When corporate management tried to superimpose a more unified and integrated global strategy, its local subsidiaries neither understood nor accepted the need to do so. For years they resisted giving up their autonomy, and management was unable to replace the interunit rivalry with a more cooperative and collaborative process.

In contrast, NEC developed an explicitly defined and clearly communicated global strategy enshrined in the company's "C&C" motto—a corporate-wide dedication to building business and basing competitive strategy on the strong link between computers and communications. For over a decade, the C&C philosophy was constantly interpreted, refined, elaborated and eventually institutionalized in organizational units dedicated to various C&C missions (e.g., the C&C Systems Research Laboratories, the C&C Corporate Planning Committee and eventually the C&C Systems Division). Top management recognized that one of its major tasks was to inculcate the worldwide organization with an understanding of the C&C strategy and philosophy and to raise managers' consciousness about the global implications of competing in these converging businesses. By the mid-1980s, the company was confident that every NEC employee in every operating unit had a clear understanding of NEC's global strategy as well as of his or her role in it. Indeed, it was this homogeneity that allowed the company to begin the successful decentralization of its management processes.

Thus the management process that distinguished transnational organizations from simpler unidimensional forms was one in which control was made less dominant by the increased importance of interunit integration and collaboration. These new processes required corporate management to supplement its control role with the more subtle tasks of coordination and cooption, giving rise to a much more complex and sophisticated management process.

SUSTAINING A DYNAMIC BALANCE: ROLE OF THE "MIND MATRIX"

Developing multidimensional perspectives and capabilities does not mean that product, functional and geographic management must have the same level of influence on all key decisions. Quite the contrary. It means that the organization must possess a differentiated influence structure—one in which different groups have different roles for different activities. These roles cannot be fixed but must change continually to respond to new environmental demands and evolving industry characteristics. Not only is it necessary to prevent any one perspective from dominating the others, it is equally important not to be locked into a mode of operation that prevents reassignment of responsibilities, realignment of relationships and rebalancing of power distribution. This ability to manage the multidimensional organization capability in a flexible manner is the hallmark of a transnational company.

In the change processes we have described, managers were clearly employing some powerful organizational tools to create and control the desired flexible management process. They used the classic tool of formal structure to strengthen, weaken or shift roles and responsibilities over time, and they employed management systems effectively to redirect corporate resources and to channel information in a way that shifted the balance of power. By controlling the ebb and flow of responsibilities, and by rebalancing power relationships, they were able to prevent any of the multidimensional perspectives from atrophying. Simultaneously, they prevented the establishment of entrenched power bases.

But the most successful companies had an additional element at the core of their management processes. We were always conscious that a substantial amount of senior management attention focused on the *individual* members of the organization. NEC's continual efforts to inculcate all corporate members with a common vision of goals and priorities; P&G's careful assignment of managers to teams and task forces to broaden their perspectives; Philips's frequent use of conferences and meetings as forums to reconcile differences; and Unilever's extensive use of training as a powerful socialization process and its well-planned career path management that provided diverse experience across businesses, functions, and geographic locations—all are examples of companies trying to develop multidimensional perspectives and flexible approaches at the level of the individual manager.

What is critical, then, is not just the structure, but also the mentality of those who constitute the structure. The common thread that holds together the diverse tasks we have described is a managerial mindset that understands the need for multiple strategic capabilities, that is able to view problems from both local and global perspectives, and that accepts the importance of a flexible approach. This pattern suggests that managers should resist the temptation to view their task in the traditional terms of building a formal global matrix structure—an organizational form that in practice has proved extraordinarily difficult to manage in the international environment. They might be better guided by the perspective of one top manager who described the challenge as "creating a matrix in the minds of managers."

Our study has led us to conclude that a company's ability to develop transnational organizational capability and management mentality will be the key factor that separates the winners from the mere survivors in the emerging international environment.

READING 11.2   GLOBAL STRATEGY . . . IN A WORLD OF NATIONS*

BY GEORGE S. YIP

■ Whether to globalize, and how to globalize, have become two of the most burning strategy issues for managers around the world. Many forces are driving companies around the world to globalize by expanding their participation in foreign markets. Almost every product market in the major world economies—computers, fast food, nuts and bolts—has foreign competitors. Trade barriers are also falling; the recent United States/Canada trade agreement and the impending 1992 harmonization in the European Community are the two most dramatic examples. Japan is gradually opening up its long barricaded markets. Maturity in domestic markets is also driving companies to seek international expansion. This is particularly true of U.S. companies that, nourished by the huge domestic market, have typically lagged behind their European and Japanese rivals in internationalization.

Companies are also seeking to globalize by integrating their worldwide strategy. Such global integration contrasts with the multinational approach whereby companies set up country subsidiaries that design, produce, and market products or services tailored to local needs. This multinational model (also described as a "multidomestic strategy") is now in question (Hout et al., 1982). Several changes seem to increase the likelihood that, in some industries, a global strategy will be more successful than a multidomestic one. One of these changes, as argues forcefully and controversially by Levitt (1983) is the growing similarity of what citizens of different countries want to buy. Other changes include the reduction of tariff and nontariff barriers, technology investments that are becoming too expensive to amortize in one market only, and competitors that are globalizing the rules of the game.

FIGURE 1
TOTAL GLOBAL
STRATEGY

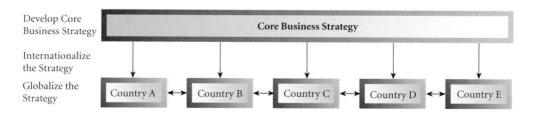

Develop Core Business Strategy — Core Business Strategy

Internationalize the Strategy

Globalize the Strategy — Country A ↔ Country B ↔ Country C ↔ Country D ↔ Country E

*My framework, developed in this article, is based in part on M. E. Porter's (1986) pioneering work on global strategy. Bartlett and Ghoshal (1987) define a "transnational industry" that is somewhat similar to Porter's "global industry." Originally published in the *Sloan Management Review* (Fall 1989). Copyright © *Sloan Management Review* Association 1989; all rights reserved; reprinted with deletions by permission of the publisher.

FIGURE 2
FRAMEWORK OF
GLOBAL STRATEGY
FORCES

Companies want to know how to globalize—in other words, expand market participation—and how to develop an integrated worldwide strategy. As depicted in Figure 1, three steps are essential in developing a total worldwide strategy:

- Developing the core strategy—the basis of sustainable competitive advantage. It is usually developed for the home country first.
- Internationalizing the core strategy through international expansion of activities and through adaptation.
- Globalizing the international strategy by integrating the strategy across countries.

Multinational companies know the first two steps well. They know the third step less well since globalization runs counter to the accepted wisdom of tailoring for national markets (Douglas and Wind, 1987).

This article makes a case for how a global strategy might work and directs managers toward opportunities to exploit globalization. It also presents the drawbacks and costs of globalization. Figure 2 lays out a framework for thinking through globalization issues.

Industry globalization drivers (underlying market, cost, and other industry conditions) are externally determined, while global strategy levers are choices available to the worldwide business. Drivers create the potential for a multinational business to achieve the benefits of global strategy. To achieve these benefits, a multinational business needs to set its *global strategy levers* (e.g., use of product standardization) appropriately to industry drivers, and to the position and resources of the business and its parent company. The organization's ability to implement the strategy affects how well the benefits can be achieved.

WHAT IS GLOBAL STRATEGY?

Setting strategy for a worldwide business requires making choices along a number of strategic dimensions. Table 1 lists five such dimensions or "global strategy levels" and their respective positions under a pure multidomestic strategy and a pure global strategy. Intermediate positions are, of course, feasible. For each dimension, a multidomestic strategy seeks to maximize worldwide performance by maximizing local competitive advantage, revenues, or profits; a global strategy seeks to maximize worldwide performance through sharing and integration.

MARKET PARTICIPATION

In a multidomestic strategy, countries are selected on the basis of their stand-alone potential for revenues and profits. In a global strategy, countries need to be selected for their potential contribution to globalization benefits. This may mean entering a market that is unattractive in

TABLE 1
GLOBALIZATION
DIMENSIONS/GLOBAL
STRATEGY LEVERS

DIMENSION	SETTING FOR PURE MULTIDOMESTIC STRATEGY	SETTING FOR PURE GLOBAL STRATEGY
Market Participation	No particular pattern	Significant share in major markets
Product Offering	Fully customized in each country	Fully standardized worldwide
Location of Value-Added Activities	All activities in each country	Concentrated—one activity in each (different) country
Marketing Approach	Local	Uniform worldwide
Competitive Moves	Stand-alone by country	Integrated across countries

its own right, but has global strategic significance, such as the home market of a global competitor. Or it may mean building share in a limited number of key markets rather than undertaking more widespread coverage. . . . The Electrolux Group, the Swedish appliance giant, is pursing a strategy of building significant share in major world markets. The company aims to be the first global appliance maker. . . .

PRODUCT OFFERING

In a multidomestic strategy, the products offered in each country are tailored to local needs. In a global strategy, the ideal is a standardized core product that requires minimal local adaptation. Cost reduction is usually the most important benefit of product standardization. . . . Differing worldwide needs can be met by adapting a standardized core product. In the early 1970s, sales of the Boeing 737 began to level off. Boeing turned to developing countries as an attractive new market, but found initially that its product did not fit the new environments. Because of the shortness of runways, their greater softness, and the lower technical expertise of their pilots, the planes tended to bounce a great deal. When the planes bounced on landing, the brakes failed. To fix this problem, Boeing modified the design by adding thrust to the engines, redesigning the wings and landing gear, and installing tires with lower pressure. These adaptations to a standardized core product enabled the 737 to become the best selling plane in history.

LOCATION OF VALUE ADDED ACTIVITIES

In a multidomestic strategy, all or most of the value chain is reproduced in every country. In another type of international strategy—exporting—most of the value chain is kept in one country. In a global strategy, costs are reduced by breaking up the value chain so each activity may be conducted in a different country. . . .

MARKETING APPROACH

In a multidomestic strategy, marketing is fully tailored for each country, being developed locally. In a global strategy, a uniform marketing approach is applied around the world, although not all elements of the marketing mix need be uniform. Unilever achieved great success with a fabric softener that used a globally common positioning, advertising theme, and symbol (a teddy bear), but a brand name that varied by country. Similarly, a product that serves a common need can be geographically expanded with a uniform marketing program, despite differences in marketing environments.

COMPETITIVE MOVES

In a multidomestic strategy, the managers in each country make competitive moves without regard for what happens in other countries. In a global strategy, competitive moves are integrated across countries at the same time or in a systematic sequence: a competitor is attacked in one country in order to drain its resources for another country, or a competitive attack in one country is countered in a different country. Perhaps the best example is the counterattack in a competitor's home market as a parry to an attack on one's own home market. Integration of competitive strategy is rarely practiced, except perhaps by some Japanese companies.

Bridgestone Corporation, the Japanese tire manufacturer, tried to integrate its competitive moves in response to global consolidation by its major competitors. . . . These competitive actions forced Bridgestone to establish a presence in the major U.S. market in order to maintain its position in the world tire market. To this end, Bridgestone formed a joint venture to own and manage Firestone Corporation's worldwide tire business. This joint venture also allowed Bridgestone to gain access to Firestone's European plants.

BENEFITS OF A GLOBAL STRATEGY

Companies that use global strategy levels can achieve one or more of these benefits. . . .

- cost reductions
- improved quality of products and programs
- enhanced customer preference
- increased competitive leverage

COST REDUCTIONS

An integrated global strategy can reduce worldwide costs in several ways. A company can increase the benefits from economies of scale by *pooling production or other activities* for two or more countries. Understanding the potential benefit of these economies of scale, Sony Corporation has concentrated its compact disc production in Terre Haute, Indiana, and Salzburg, Austria.

A second way to cut costs is by *exploiting lower factor costs* by moving manufacturing or other activities to low-cost countries. This approach has, of course, motivated the recent surge of offshore manufacturing, particularly by U.S. firms. For example, the Mexican side of the U.S.-Mexico border is now crowded with "maquiladoras"—manufacturing plants set up and run by U.S. companies using Mexican labor.

Global strategy can also cut costs by *exploiting flexibility*. A company with manufacturing locations in several countries can move production from location to location on short notice to take advantage of the lowest costs at a given time. Dow Chemical takes this approach to minimize the cost of producing chemicals. Dow uses a linear programming model that takes account of international differences in exchange rates, tax rates, and transportation and labor costs. The model comes up with the best mix of production volume by location for each planning period.

An integrated global strategy can also reduce costs by *enhancing bargaining power*. A company whose strategy allows for switching production among different countries greatly increases its bargaining power with suppliers, workers, and host governments. . . .

IMPROVED QUALITY OF PRODUCTS AND PROGRAMS

Under a global strategy, companies focus on a smaller number of products and programs than under a multidomestic strategy. This concentration can improve both product and program quality. Global focus is one reason for Japanese success in automobiles. Toyota markets a far smaller number of models around the world than does General Motors, even allowing for its unit sales being half that of General Motors. . . .

ENHANCED CUSTOMER PREFERENCE

Global availability, serviceability, and recognition can enhance customer preference through reinforcement. Soft drink and fast food companies are, of course, leading exponents of this strategy. Many suppliers of financial services, such as credit cards, must have a global presence because their service is travel related. . . .

INCREASED COMPETITIVE LEVERAGE

A global strategy provides more points from which to attack and counterattack competitors. In an effort to prevent the Japanese from becoming a competitive nuisance in disposable syringes, Becton Dickinson, a major U.S. medical products company, decided to enter three markets in Japan's backyard. Becton entered the Hong Kong, Singapore, and Philippine markets to prevent further Japanese expansion (Var, 1986).

DRAWBACKS OF GLOBAL STRATEGY

Globalization can incur significant management costs through increased coordination, reporting requirements, and even added staff. It can also reduce the firm's effectiveness in individual countries if overcentralization hurts local motivation and morale. In addition, each global strategy lever has particular drawbacks.

A global strategy approach to *market participation* can incur an earlier or greater commitment to a market than is warranted on its own merits. Many American companies, such as Motorola, are struggling to penetrate Japanese markets, more in order to enhance their global competitive position than to make money in Japan for its own sake.

Product standardization can result in a product that does not entirely satisfy *any* customers. When companies first internationalize, they often offer their standard domestic product without adapting it for other countries, and suffer the consequences. . . .

A globally standardized product is designed for the global market but can seldom satisfy all needs in all countries. For instance, Canon, a Japanese company, sacrificed the ability to copy certain Japanese paper sizes when it first designed a photocopier for the global market.

Activity concentration distances customers and can result in lower responsiveness and flexibility. It also increases currency risk by incurring costs and revenues in different countries. Recently volatile exchange rates have required companies that concentrate their production to hedge their currency exposure.

Uniform marketing can reduce adaptation to local customer behavior. For example, the head office of British Airways mandated that every country use the "Manhattan Landing" television commercial developed by advertising agency Saatchi and Saatchi. While the commercial did win many awards, it has been criticized for using a visual image (New York City) that was not widely recognized in many countries.

Integrated competitive moves can mean sacrificing revenues, profits, or competitive position in individual countries, particularly when the subsidiary in one country is asked to attack a global competitor in order to send a signal or to divert that competitor's resources from another country.

FINDING THE BALANCE

The most successful worldwide strategies find a balance between overglobalizing and underglobalizing. The ideal strategy matches the level of strategy globalization to the globalization potential of the industry. . . .

INDUSTRY GLOBALIZATION DRIVERS

To achieve the benefits of globalization, the managers of a worldwide business need to recognize when industry globalization drivers (industry conditions) provide the opportunity to use global strategy levers. These drivers can be grouped in four categories: market, cost, governmental, and competitive. Each industry globalization driver affects the potential use of global strategy levers. . . .

MARKET DRIVERS

Market globalization drivers depend on customer behavior and the structure of distribution channels. These drivers affect the use of all five global strategy levers.

Homogeneous Customer Needs

When customers in different countries want essentially the same type of product or service (or can be so persuaded), opportunities arise to market a standardized product. Understanding which aspects of the product can be standardized and which should be customized is key. In addition, homogeneous needs make participation in a large number of markets easier because fewer different product offerings need to be developed and supported.

Global Customers

Global customers buy on a centralized or coordinated basis for decentralized use. The existence of global customers both allows and requires a uniform marketing program. There are two types of global customers: national and multinational. A national global customer searches the world for suppliers but uses the purchased product or service in one country. National defense agencies are a good example. A multinational global customer also searches the world for suppliers, but uses the purchased product or service in many countries. The World Health Organization's purchase of medical products is an example. Multinational global customers are particularly challenging to serve and often require a global account management program. . . .

Global Channels

Analogous to global customers, channels of distribution may buy on a global or at least a regional basis. Global channels or middlemen are also important in exploiting differences in prices by buying at a lower price in one country and selling at a higher price in another country. Their presence makes it more necessary for a business to rationalize its worldwide pricing. Global channels are rare, but regionwide channels are increasing in number, particularly in European grocery distribution and retailing.

Transferable Marketing

The buying decision may be such that marketing elements, such as brand names and advertising, require little local adaptation. Such transferability enables firms to use uniform marketing strategies and facilitates expanded participation in markets. A worldwide business can also adapt its brand names and advertising campaigns to make them more transferable, or, even better, design global ones to start with. Offsetting risks include the blandness of uniformly acceptable brand names or advertising, and the vulnerability of relying on a single brand franchise.

COST DRIVERS

Cost drivers depend on the economics of the business; they particularly affect activity concentration.

Economies of Scale and Scope

A single-country market may not be large enough for the local business to achieve all possible economies of scale or scope. Scale at a given location can be increased through participation in multiple markets combined with product standardization or concentration of selected value activities. Corresponding risks include rigidity and vulnerability to disruption. . . .

Learning and Experience

Even if economies of scope and scale are exhausted, expanded market participation and activity concentration can accelerate the accumulation of learning and experience. The steeper the learning and experience curves, the greater the potential benefit will be. Managers should beware, though, of the usual danger in pursuing experience curve strategies—overaggressive pricing that destroyed not just the competition but the market as well. Prices get so low that profit is insufficient to sustain any competitor.

Sourcing Efficiencies
Centralized purchasing of new materials can significantly lower costs. . . .

Favorable Logistics
A favorable ratio of sales value to transportation cost enhances the company's ability to concentrate production. Other logistical factors include nonperishability, the absence of time urgency, and little need for location close to customer facilities. . . .

Differences in Country Costs and Skills
Factor costs generally vary across countries; this is particularly true in certain industries. The availability of particular skills also varies. Concentration of activities in low-cost or high-skill countries can increase productivity and reduce costs, but managers need to anticipate the danger of training future offshore competitors. . . .

Product Development Costs
Product development costs can be reduced by developing a few global or regional products rather than many national products. The automobile industry is characterized by long product development periods and high product development costs. One reason for the high costs is duplication of effort across countries. The Ford Motor Company's "Centers of Excellence" program aims to reduce these duplicating efforts and to exploit the differing expertise of Ford specialists worldwide. As part of the concentrated effort, Ford of Europe is designing a common platform for all compacts, while Ford of North America is developing platforms for the replacement of the mid-sized Taurus and Sable. This concentration of design is estimated to save "hundreds of millions of dollars per model by eliminating duplicative efforts and saving on retooling factories" (*Business Week*, 1987).

GOVERNMENTAL DRIVERS
Government globalization drivers depend on the rules set by national governments and affect the use of all global strategy levers.

Favorable Trade Policies
Host governments affect globalization potential through import tariffs and quotas, nontariff barriers, export subsidies, local content requirements, currency and capital flow restrictions, and requirements on technology transfer. Host government policies can make it difficult to use the global levers of major market participation, product standardization, activity concentration, and uniform marketing; they also affect the integrated-competitive moves lever. . . .

Compatible Technical Standards
Differences in technical standards, especially government-imposed standards, limit the extent to which products can be standardized. Often, standards are set with protectionism in mind. Motorola found that many of their electronics products were excluded from the Japanese market because these products operated at a higher frequency than was permitted in Japan.

Common Marketing Regulations
The marketing environment of individual countries affects the extent to which uniform global marketing approaches can be used. Certain types of media may be prohibited or restricted.

For example, the United States is far more liberal than Europe about the kinds of advertising claims that can be made on television. The British authorities even veto the depiction of socially undesirable behavior. For example, British television authorities do not allow scenes of children pestering their parents to buy a product. . . .

COMPETITIVE DRIVERS

Market, cost, and governmental globalization drivers are essentially fixed for an industry at any given time. Competitors can play only a limited role in affecting these factors (although a sustained effort can bring about change, particularly in the case of consumer preferences). In contrast, competitive drivers are entirely in the realm of competitor choice. Competitors can raise the globalization potential of their industry and spur the need for a response on the global strategy levers.

Interdependence of Countries

A competitor may create competitive interdependence among countries by pursuing a global strategy. The basic mechanism is through sharing of activities. When activities such as production are shared among countries, a competitor's market share in one country affects its scale and overall cost position in the shared activities. Changes in that scale and cost will affect its competitive position in all countries dependent on the shared activities. Less directly, customers may view market position in a lead country as an indicator of overall quality. Companies frequently promote a product as, for example, "the leading brand in the United States." Other competitors then need to respond via increased market participation, uniform marketing, or integrated competitive strategy to avoid a downward spiral of sequentially weakened positions in individual countries.

In the automobile industry, where economies of scale are significant and where sharing activities can lower costs, markets have significant competitive interdependence. As companies like Ford and Volkswagen concentrate production and become more cost competitive with the Japanese manufacturers, the Japanese are pressured to enter more markets so that increased production volume will lower costs. Whether conscious of this or not, Toyota has begun a concentrated effort to penetrate the German market: between 1984 and 1987, Toyota doubled the number of cars produced for the German market.

Globalized Competitors

More specifically, matching or preempting individual competitor moves may be necessary. These moves include expanding into or within major markets, being the first to introduce a standardized product, or being the first to use a uniform marketing program.

The need to preempt a global competitor can spur increased market participation. In 1986, Unilever, the European consumer products company, sought to increase its participation in the U.S. market by launching a hostile takeover bid for Richardson-Vicks Inc. Unilever's global archrival, Proctor & Gamble, saw the threat to its home turf and outbid Unilever to capture Richardson-Vicks. With Richardson-Vicks European system, P&G was able to greatly strengthen its European positioning. So Unilever's attempt to expand participation in a rival's home market backfired to allow the rival to expand participation in Unilever's home markets.

In summary, industry globalization drivers provide opportunities to use global strategy levers in many ways. Some industries, such as civil aircraft, can score high on most dimensions of globalization (Yoshino, 1986). Others, such as the cement industry, seem to be inherently local. But more and more industries are developing globalization potential. Even the food industry in Europe, renowned for its diversity of taste, is now a globalization target for major food multinationals.

CHANGES OVER TIME

Finally, industry evolution plays a role. As each of the industry globalization drivers changes over time, so too will the appropriate global strategy change. For example, in the European major appliance industry, globalization forces seem to have reversed. In the late 1960s and early 1970s, a regional standardization strategy was successful for some key competitors (Levitt, 1983). But in the 1980s the situation appears to have turned around, and the most successful strategies seem to be national (Baden-Fuller et al., 1987).

In some cases, the actions of individual competitors can affect the direction and pace of change; competitors positioned to take advantage of globalization forces will want to hasten them. . . .

MORE THAN ONE STRATEGY IS VIABLE

Although they are powerful, industry globalization drivers do not dictate one formula for success. More than one type of international strategy can be viable in a given industry.

Industries Vary Across Drivers

No industry is high on every one of the many globalization drivers. A particular competitor may be in a strong position to exploit a driver that scores low on globalization. . . . The hotel industry provides examples both of successful global and successful local competitors.

Global Effects Are Incremental

Globalization drivers are not deterministic for a second reason: the appropriate use of strategy levers adds competitive advantage to existing sources. These other sources may allow individual competitors to thrive with international strategies that are mismatched with industry globalization drivers. For example, superior technology is a major source of competitive advantage in most industries, but can be quite independent of globalization drivers. A competitor with sufficiently superior technology can use it to offset globalization disadvantages.

Business and Parent Company Position and Resources Are Crucial

The third reason that drivers are not deterministic is related to resources. A worldwide business may face industry drivers that strongly favor a global strategy. But global strategies are typically expensive to implement initially even though great cost savings and revenue gains should follow. High initial investments may be needed to expand within or into major markets, to develop standardized products, to relocate value activities, to create global brands, to create new organization units or coordination processes, and to implement other aspects of a global strategy. The strategic position of the business is also relevant. Even though a global strategy may improve the business's long-term strategic position, its immediate position may be so weak that resources should be devoted to short-term, country-by-country improvements. Despite the automobile industry's very strong globalization drivers, Chrysler Corporation had to deglobalize by selling off most of its international automotive businesses to avoid bankruptcy. Lastly, investing in nonglobal sources of competitive advantage, such as superior technology, may yield greater returns than global ones, such as centralized manufacturing.

Organizations Have Limitations

Finally, factors such as organization structure, management processes, people, and culture affect how well a desired global strategy can be implemented. Organizational differences among companies in the same industry can, or should, constrain the companies' pursuit of the same global strategy. . . .

BY SUBRAMANIAN RANGAN

■ Companies of all shapes and sizes are pondering global strategies. While there are many useful ideas and opinions on this topic, there are also unfortunately a number of myths. In this article I will highlight seven common ones and discuss them briefly below.

1. ANY COMPANY WITH MONEY CAN GO GLOBAL

The flaw with this is that going global and going global successfully are not the same thing. The Paris department store Galéries Lafayette went global with much fanfare, setting up shop in New York some years ago. However, success proved elusive and the store folded its operations after sustained losses, returning to its home base a wiser company. Expansion into Europe by Whirlpool, the US home appliances manufacturer, has not exactly been smooth either.

The reasons are rooted in an idea known as "the liability of foreignness." A company attempting to sell into a foreign market tends to face an inherent handicap relative to local rivals. Customer needs and tastes in the foreign market are likely to be different; obstacles may abound, from identifying good local suppliers to dealing with skeptical host authorities; and the very model of business may be different. Crucially, on all these fronts, local rivals are likely to have the home advantage. If a company is to succeed abroad, it must possess some valuable intangible asset that will enable it to meet and beat local rivals in their own home market. This could be advanced technology (as with Canon, the copier and camera maker); an appreciably superior value proposition (such as that developed by IKEA, the Swedish furniture group); a well-known brand name (e.g., Coca-Cola); low unit costs deriving from scale or process knowhow (e.g., Dell in PCs, or South African Breweries in beer); or some combination of the above (e.g., Toyota, L'Oréal and Citibank).

When Galéries Lafayette went to New York, it faced established rivals as diverse as Macy's and Bloomingdale's, as well as Saks Fifth Avenue, and it did not have any valuable intangible asset that would set it apart. Whirlpool faces similar challenges in Europe.

Implications: If the urge to expand internationally should strike your company, first study local rivals abroad and look for concrete evidence that you can beat them. A track record of solid and growing exports into the target market can be a credible sign that you can deliver value that local rivals either do not or cannot deliver themselves. This is why companies tend to export before they set up shop abroad. Also, ensure that you dominate your home market. As the foreign market poses inherent handicaps, you may not be ready for global expansion if you are not a domestic leader (if you are not, in other words, a Samsung, a Telefónica, or a Cemex). The broader point is that a global strategy is no substitute for a good business strategy. Also, remember that low growth at home is neither a necessary nor sufficient condition for global expansion. So, if your company does not possess valuable intangible assets, then, no matter how deep its pockets, expansion abroad is unlikely to be profitable (and hence should be postponed).

2. INTERNATIONAL-IZATION IN SERVICES IS DIFFERENT

Companies in the services sector are indeed, in many important ways, different from companies in the manufacturing and primary sectors. Services tend to be less transportable (and, hence, less tradable), less storable, more regulated. But, when it comes to internationalization, services are no different. From hotels to healthcare, retail to real estate, financial services to fast

---

*Reprinted from S. Rangan, "Seven myths regarding global strategy," in *Financial Times Mastering Strategy: The Complete MBA Companion in Strategy*. Harlow: Pearson Education Limited: Financial Times Prentice Hall, 2000.

food, service-sector companies are subject to the viability test stated above. That is, if a service company does not possess a valuable intangible asset, internationalization is not going to be profitable.

Before embarking on international expansion, service companies, as much as manufacturers, must also respond affirmatively to two other questions. First, is there sufficient and steady demand abroad (backed by purchasing power) for the service offered? French cuisine, Spanish bullfighting, and US football might not meet this test. Second, is the service experience replicable abroad? Disney may (with some difficulty) be able to re-create its theme parks in Japan and France, and Club Med can offer its convivial holiday village atmosphere not only in southern Europe but also in North Africa—but Virgin Airways, Toys "R" Us, and Indian diamond cutters may be less able to replicate their value proposition abroad. Reasons include regulatory hurdles, costly access to key inputs, and the difficulty of transferring competences abroad.

Implications: Internationalization in services is no different from that in manufacturing. A service company can internationalize successfully as long as it meets the intangible asset test, the effective demand test, and the replicability test. Companies as diverse as Blockbuster Video, the US video rental operator, Sodehxo Alliance, the French in-house catering company, and Goldman Sachs, the US investment bank, have met these tests and expanded abroad profitably. But fail one or more of the three, and expansion abroad is unlikely to be profitable.

3. DISTANCE AND NATIONAL BORDERS MATTER NO MORE

Spurred by developments like the internet, some observers have proclaimed the demise of distance. Others, perhaps persuaded by the omnipresence (from Mexico to Malaysia, from Iceland to New Zealand) of the US-based broadcaster CNN and of McDonald's fast-food outlets, believe that national cultures have converged and can be safely disregarded when it comes to global business. In the latter view, the only culture that matters now is corporate culture; national borders are passé.

There may sometimes be some truth in these assertions, but they should, at least for now, be treated with skepticism. Indeed, besides being exaggerated they are plainly incorrect as generalizations. Take distance. In books and CDs, software and remote diagnostics, new technologies continue to shrink physical distance; but in most spheres of economic activity transport and telecommunication costs, small though they may have become, are still positive and still increase with distance.

Moreover, as every executive knows, reliable information is the lifeblood of economic decisions. And, even in this day and age, reliable information is acquired more readily and more reliably locally than from afar. This is partly why companies tend to cluster close to others in their industry—part of the explanation perhaps for the "home bias" that economists have documented in trade and investment. It is also why, even after controlling for transport costs, distance has a significant (and negative) influence on economic exchange.

National culture and borders are also still significant. National cultures shape national institutions and influence economic values and ethos. Although patterns are changing, economic organization in Japan still seems to favor business above labor and consumers; in parts of Europe labor comes first, followed by producers and consumers; in the US consumers tend to rank ahead of producers and labor.

Cultural values aid interpretation and are an input in business decisions. The relationship of a company to its customers, national and local governments, rivals, shareholders, financial institutions, and the local community, all tend to be influenced by national culture. From language to labor policy, punctuality to property rights, taxation to transfer pricing, accounting rules to supplier relationships, business still operates differently across nations and regions. As a result, companies that cross national borders tend to face sharp discontinuities, and those that disregard or fail to anticipate the latter are likely to see successful home-grown strategies meet a poor reception abroad (just ask Lincoln Electric Holdings, the welding systems equipment maker, or Otis, the lifts and elevators manufacturer).

National borders represent the combined forces of national history, institutions, and conditioning, and give potent meaning to the terms insiders and outsiders. Even the seemingly innocuous US–Canada border appears to operate in this way. Empirically, language and national borders show up as significant and large determinants of international trade and investment. Even in our increasingly digital and anglicized global economy, national language and cultural affinity are still a crucial determinant of trade and investment decisions. US companies still head for Canada first, Portuguese companies for Brazil, Spanish companies for Latin America, Japanese companies for other parts of Asia.

Implications: In view of the above, it continues to make sense to expand regionally before entering more distant markets: to head for familiar markets before unfamiliar ones. Companies that respect national borders and cultures are more likely to win back respect from employees, suppliers, customers, and national authorities. This hardly means forsaking "globality;" it just means placing added emphasis on being both local and global. Indeed, companies that embrace this ambiguity will more likely be rewarded with profitable growth.

4. DEVELOPING COUNTRIES ARE WHERE THE ACTION IS

In much public discourse on globalization, there is a view that the big markets are in the large developing countries (such as Mexico, Brazil, China, and India). In fact, globalization is still very much a concentrated, rich country game. Of the 100 largest multinationals, only two are from developing countries. In terms of international trade and inward and outward foreign direct investment, ten nations—Canada, the US, the UK, Germany, France, the Netherlands, Sweden, Switzerland, Japan, and Australia—account for 50, 70, and 90 percent of respective world totals. Their purchasing power is till unrivaled despite recent economic convergence.

Implications: No company that wants to be counted as world class can afford to ignore developed country markets. Indeed, as Japan restructures its economy and recovers from a prolonged slump, it should not be surprising to see the US–European cross-border merger mania being followed by a similar Europe–Japan and US–Japan company-driven integration. The 1999 Renault–Nissan deal may only be a harbinger of things to come.

5. MANUFACTURE WHERE LABOR COSTS ARE CHEAPEST

During the debate on the North American Free Trade Agreement or NAFTA, the "sucking sound" hypothesis—that multinationals will shift their operations to nations where labor costs are lowest—was elevated to new heights. In reality, of course, the only sounds that low wages should stir are loud yawns. As every business executive knows, what matters first off is delivered unit costs and not just wage costs. Materials are typically a big chunk of total costs and by levying import duties and such, developing countries (that boast low wages) often make local manufacturing expensive. Second, where wages are low, productivity tends to be low too. Consequently, hourly wage costs may appear ridiculously low, but unit costs tend to be high. Lastly, it is generally optimal to manufactors in (or the least near) the big markets. Not only does such a strategy minimize tariffs, transport costs, and logistical problems; it also creates a structural hedge against unfavorable changes in real exchange rates. If, for instance, Mercedes had opened its plants in Mexico rather than in the US, it would have traded off its deutschmark–dollar currency exposure for peso–dollar exposure.

Implications: As a generalization (but not as a rule), make where you sell. For large companies that sell in the triad (Europe, Japan, the United States), this means operating in that triad. Young European managers might care to concentrate on learning Japanese; as European consumers warm to Japanese products, Japanese companies will continue to raise their presence in Europe significantly. For similar reasons, young Japanese managers should brush up on their English; foreign investment into Japan is likely to rise significantly as well. Envy the British and the Americans; when it comes to foreign tongues, the default status of English as the language of international business offers them a free ride.

6. GLOBALIZATION IS HERE TO STAY

A sentiment that is often part of the hype surrounding the "new economy" is that globalization, like a genie, is out of the bottle and cannot be pushed back in. Here again, there is some truth to the claim, but serious skepticism is also warranted. To see why, consider the key developments that have enabled globalization.

First and most familiar are technology changes. It would appear that these are unlikely to be reversed. Second is the phenomenon referred to as economic convergence. As per capita incomes converge across nations, demand patterns tend to converge (people in more and more nations want fast food, cars, and JVCs), and capabilities converge as well (people in more and more nations can now write software, make new medicines, and build fancy products). This convergence process might suffer interruptions (witness the recent Asian crisis), but it appears unlikely to be arrested for long, let alone reversed.

The most important driver of globalization, though, is the spread of economic liberalism. The recent and widespread change in ideology—from state socialism to market capitalism—has unleashed much internal deregulation and external liberalization, from France to the former Soviet Union. The embrace of openness that took hold during the late 1980s and early 1990s trailed a half-century of economic growth and global peace. Take away either of the latter two conditions and liberalization might become a potential casualty. Globalization has been willed into existence due to the changed beliefs and acts of national governments. Bring serious war or sustained high unemployment into the picture and governments may start to act in ways that could reverse globalizing trends. Even at the end of 1999, with just 5 percent unemployment and a seemingly unstoppable economy, the US sometimes appeared to be ambiguous on globalization. What would the attitude be if it faced Europe's double-digit unemployment?

Implications: Economic growth is key if globalization is to continue apace. In a "winner takes all" economy, we are building a shaky enterprise and a fragile society if all cannot (sooner or later) be winners. Companies need to explore issues such as unemployment, employee retraining, and equality of opportunity, if not incomes. If business does not become more sensitive to this possibility, expect to see much more resistance to the structural adjustment that globalization tends to bring, and expect to see governments reasserting themselves.

7. GOVERNMENTS DON'T MATTER ANYMORE

Beneath a headline saying that 1998 sales by the world's 100 largest multinational enterprises were one-and-a-half times the gross domestic product (GDP) of France, a cartoon in *Le Monde* newspaper showed executives (atop skyscrapers) clasping their stomachs and roaring with laughter at a remark by Prime Minister Lionel Jospin, "L'état ne peut pas tout" (roughly, "the state cannot do everything"). The cartoon's implicit message: multinationals are the masters of today's world, governments are powerless. Move over Lionel Jospin, make way for Bill Gates.

Those who fail to treat this as an exaggerated claim are likely to be in for some unpleasant surprises. As long as people attach value to a collective national identity and as long as they value local representation in decision making, governments will continue to matter greatly. The reality is that people are not very mobile across national borders; we tend to become part of the local and national communities where we are born. In this kind of society, concepts such as local and national interests have real meaning, and local and national governments have evolved to be the key institutions that promise to advance those interests with any constancy. After all, companies come and companies go (take Digital Equipment in Massachusetts); their identities may change through acquisitions (as in DaimlerChrysler or Renault–Nissan). To the extent that corporate interests align with those of the local community this may be welcome, but it is no longer to be counted on (just ask the community living in Clermont-Ferrand, home town of the French tyre maker Michelin).

In a world where people no longer expect companies to give primacy to local interests, local and national governments will be viewed as a necessary counterweight. Governments know this and will willingly serve that function. Of course, to do so credibly, from time to time governments will push their weight around. They may break up large firms, prevent foreign investment in so-called culture industries, and tie up the hands of companies in other ways. All this is easier to do when the companies are foreign and the voters local. As Raymond Vernon warned in his book *In the Hurricane's Eye*, multinationals and governments—both legitimate entities—will confront one another again; when this happens, it will be seen that power has not slipped away from sovereign nations.

Equally importantly, a working global economy needs global rules. There are too many countries (with perhaps as many interests) and they can't all be invited to make those rules. Global rules are therefore still the prerogative of governments, and so long as rules matter (and, in the future, they are likely to matter more not less), governments will continue to matter.

Implications: Companies should resist the temptation to write off governments as ineffective anachronisms. Rather, they should recognize governments as important and legitimate institutions in the world economy. Indeed, if companies are to benefit from globalization and wish to encourage its spread, they should work with governments to establish how local and global can evolve in an acceptably balanced manner. Jobs and profits might be traded off in the short but not the long run. Managers must recognize this. In the twentieth century, prime responsibility for jobs fell on governments, while that for profits fell on companies. If we are to rest on the tremendous economic gains made in that century, this division of labor might work well. Without engagement and imaginative coordination among private enterprises and governments, neither the concept of the market nor that of democracy is likely to deliver its full promise. To avoid that outcome should be the goal of all economic entities.

CHAPTER 12

Values

Right from the early days, when Kenneth Andrews wrote about strategy in the mid-1960s, values were included as an integral part of the process. In a way, that has been forgotten with all the attention to strategic analysis. It should not have been, and we include three rather interesting readings here to put the spotlight on values in this chapter.

First is a paper by Claes Gustafssan of Abo Akademi University in Finland. "Why strategy?" he asks, and what does an "ethical strategy" mean? He then goes on to consider the moral responsibility of managers—necessary words, perhaps, in a world obsessed with shareholder value. This launches Gustafssan into a general discussion of ethics in today's world—and tomorrow's. A most unusual and welcome paper!

In "A New Manifesto for Management," Sumantra Ghoshal and Chris Bartlett team up with Ghoshal's colleague at the London Business School, Peter Moran, to present this unusual "manifesto." We need to rethink our very basis of managing, they argue, to move away from tight controls and narrow theories to a new philosophy that recognizes companies as value creators that reclaim their legitimacy by engaging their people.

Our third reading on values actually predates Andrews's early writings on strategy and, in fact, can be seen as a predecessor to it. From a book published in 1957 by sociologist Philip Selznick of the Berkeley campus of the University of California entitled *Leadership in Administration*, this excerpt introduces the wonderful ideas of organizations as sustained "institutions" and of managers as people who "infuse" them with value. That is leadership! This reading, almost 50 years old, is perfectly contemporary; indeed, it contains messages that we need to heed perhaps now more than ever.

USING THE CASE STUDIES

Values can be a driving force and a stabilizing influence in strategy. In the Acer Group, the values of Stan Shih shape Acer's strategy. Gregory Long, president of the New York Botanical Gardens, must change this century-old institution but at the same time keep the values that made it a leader in its field. In the Reorganization at Axion Consulting case, Matt Walsh, a member of the executive committee, must decide whether advancing his career should take precedence over loyalty to the values and mission of his organization. In all these instances, what we see in action is consistent with Selznick's argument in "Leadership in Administration," namely that values provide the "backbone" for strategy formation during times of considerable change. Ghoshal, Bartlett, and Moran expand on this argument in "A New Manifesto for Management." The Natura case, which deals with a Brazilian consumer goods company that puts ethics and honesty at the center of its strategy, is a good illustration of the basic thesis. And if Gustafsson's argument in "New Values, Morality, and Strategic Ethics" is to be believed, companies such as Natura and Kao are harbingers of a future trend.

READING 12.1   NEW VALUES, MORALITY, AND STRATEGIC ETHICS*

BY CLAES GUSTAFSSON

1. WHY STRATEGY?

The idea of an ethical strategy is, you might say, a contradiction of moral logic. You should behave ethically, we could say, out of personal conviction and of moral feeling, not out of sheer strategic calculation of self interest. Ethics should not be an instrument for furthering possibly un-ethical aims. Or, put in another way, ethics is a question of values and goals, not of methods. . . .

. . . we can choose to study the morality of the actors in the "business game"—"are managers ethical and what are their values?"—or of the organizations as such, provided, of course, that we believe "organizations" can have a morality apart from that of its members. On the other hand, we can direct our interest to the specific ethical position of, e.g., business firms. What are the norms or norm structures important for economic action, where are the moral traps and fallacies, what should the firm—or rather the managers—do in order to avoid these traps? What is good and right in connection with the business world, and what kinds of difficulties can we expect to meet?

Into this perspective I want to put the question of an "ethical strategy." For many reasons the modern corporation is doomed to stumble into all kinds of moral conflicts, even insoluble paradoxical ones. There are several reasons for this. On the one hand, you could say that the modern corporation lives at the crossroads of many legitimate groups of stakeholders, with rightful and legitimate interests. On the other hand, corporate activities are large-scale, highly efficient, and often have long-range effects. A single individual can usually only commit small sins; a large firm can commit grandiose ones. The latter capacity was earlier a prerogative of the state—for good or bad. As it is now, we do not know for sure which one has the greater potential for doing good or evil, the large firm or the state.

---

*Claes Gustafsson, "New Values, Morality, and Strategic Ethics," working paper; reprinted with deletions by permission of the author.

If you are doing something wrong, and somebody points this out to you, then, being a good person, you change your ways of acting. That is the simple logic of being a morally "good" person. It is always possible to make mistakes, but you try to avoid them and to correct yourself whenever you find that you have been wrong. Of course, it is better to know in advance what to do—a really good person knows that. But you should, in any case, try your best.

For the modern corporation the question of doing right is, however, not so easy. Doing the wrong thing may, as such, be expensive, and doing it on a large scale multiplies the damage. Doing something on a large scale usually implies doing it far into the future. Large-scale organized action is usually planned years in advance and is slow to change. It is, in other words, not always so easy to change your ways when told that you are wrong. Or you can do it only at great cost. The problem is further aggravated by the obvious fact that conceptions regarding good and bad change over time. Thus it is possible, at least in theory, that a certain act or state is considered "good" or at least acceptable when it is planned and put into action, but that it has changed to be "bad" or unacceptable, when it is about to be implemented.

All this makes talk about an ethical strategy legitimate. As a good man tries to act in the right way and to search for knowledge about good and bad in order to be able to act accordingly, so does a good corporation. The good man needs to know what is good and bad **just now**. The good corporation, however, needs to know what is good and bad not only just now, but also within the action-relevant future.

2. IS THERE A MORAL RESPONSIBILITY?

You might, of course, argue that the corporation—or its managers—have no moral responsibility outside that given by the law. You might add, like Milton Friedman (1962), that the managers of the firm have no moral responsibility except for taking care of the interests of the owners. In that perspective the question of an ethical strategy will not even arise.

This view is, however, simplistic and misleading. Regarding the moral responsibility of the firm as such, we can note that it is not and never has acted in a vacuum. Every business activity means taking part in a grand social play, where the acceptance of the surrounding social network is a **conditio sine qua non**. Ordered economic activity—leaving robbery and some other marginally extreme, economically directed activities aside—is always a question of legitimation and institutionalization. If the surrounding social network—society—does not accept your behavior, it will react quickly and harshly. There has never been a society where business activities have been exempt from social regulations and moral demands. Moral responsibility is not only something you decide yourselves; it is determined by the moral demands of the environment. Immoral action or gross neglect of moral responsibilities may, thus, become costly. This means that even for a subjectively amoral person, morality exists as a question of cost/benefit.

There is, however, another aspect of corporate ethics, too. No firm exists as a technical and economic unit only—it lives and works in the form of human decisions and choices. On a trivial level of conceptual definition we can see that everybody has some kind of moral conceptions—even the mafia or the robber on the street. Any social grouping rests on some set of generalized normative expectations regarding the actions of others. Human reasoning, moreover, seems to be based, at least partly, on moral-like normative conceptions.

On the other hand, business as such is strongly moralistic. Textbooks in business administration are probably among the most moralistic found, constantly stressing the importance of loyalty, credibility, diligence, and effective management of whatever activity you are supposed to be in charge of. It is in this case interesting to note that, whereas the mythology of business mostly stresses speculative greed and the possibility of enriching yourselves, corporate logic, both in theory and in practice, as stubbornly tells us about how professional managers take care of somebody else's interests. The modern corporation does not depend on the unrestricted personal greed of a set of free agents, but instead, and very much so, on highly restricted personal interests, on loyal cooperation, reliable mutual expectations and skillful management. Even those few who, perhaps for romantic reasons, maintain that they are in business "just for the money," at the same time demand extreme loyalty of their subordinates.

The truth is, of course, that even if street robbery might be possible for a totally immoral loner, highly organized cooperation is impossible without strong moral ties. This is found to be the fact empirically, too. The most constant characteristic you will find when interviewing managers is that they all have strong moralistic conceptions regarding business activities.

There are, in other words, two arguments for the concern regarding ethical strategy: firstly, the fact that most managers, at least within certain limits, personally would not like to be caught with the hand in the till. There are things, for all of us, that we would not like to be part of, and there are things that we do not want our children to accuse us of. Secondly, stumbling into moral pitfalls may be extremely expensive—even in the way that rather small sins can lead to excessive losses.

---

3. STRUCTURES OF ETHICAL REASONING

When discussing business ethics, it might be a good idea first to point out certain traits that are specifically manifest in business firms. The private corporation is a child of the "invisible hand." Its basic existential assumption is that of free and unregulated action. The corporation is expected to pursue its own internal interests in ways it sees fit, as long as it does not break the laws of the land. The manager, forming the will of the firm, is supposed to choose the best ways of action available, considering the specific resources and interests of the corporation. In this way, as a matter of principle, the horizon of action is open to the private firm—only the sky is the limit.

Business firms are highly instrumental social constructs. They are social structures and meeting places where people converge under the common tacit assumption of rationally planned and effective action. The basic idea of the firm is premeditated action, not spontaneous socializing, it is goal-directed and goal-attaining action. . . .

If you study the moral—more or less moral—argumentation of business managers, you are bound to find, rather quickly, that "rationality," "efficiency" and "the will to work" (diligence) form dominant structures of moralizing norms in economic action. The same is true, to a very high degree, of textbooks in management and business administration. Behind the normatively instrumental discussion, we find a strong moralistic tone, stressing the unavoidable importance of rationality, efficiency and hard work. . . .*

There are other moral values to be found in business firms, of course. Loyalty and trustworthiness—to tell the truth and not to tell lies, to keep your word and your promises—form a large and important ethical structure of argument. . . .

Instrumentality and cooperation, thus, form the bases for the moral backbone of managerial logic. Add to this all other "normal" moral considerations from the culture of the surrounding society—humanity, integrity, equality, justice, altruism, environmental concerns, and so on. Even if these do not necessarily derive from the logic of large-scale organized instrumental action, everybody working in the corporation accepts them.

---

*The work ethic, which in fact has become a household word in day-to-day moralizing discussions, is eminently handled in Weber's (1978) famous treatise on the relation between the Protestant ethic and the spirit of Western capitalism.

4. PREDICTING CHANGES IN VALUE PATTERNS

Moral values change over time. Some change slowly, over centuries, at a pace which is not detectable in ordinary life. Some change more quickly, needing only decades. Sometimes they change abruptly, usually in connection with some socially catastrophic event like natural disasters—not, perhaps, earthquakes, but rather epidemic diseases—war, genocide, and the like. Studying the history of ideas you lose the belief that any moral value will hold for ever. . . . The astonishing 180 degree turn in "Western" culture, from the social altruism of the late sixties, to the neo-liberal egoism of the late eighties, is an example of [rapid] change. . . .

5. WHAT CAN WE EXPECT IN THE NEAR FUTURE?

What, then, can we expect in the near future? Where are the ethical minefields to be found? That we do not know; as noted above, we cannot know for sure. We can, however, try to develop some reasonable expectations. These expectations concern, for obvious reasons, the action-relevant future of ten to fifteen years.

Even if moral values seem to change unpredictably, there is usually a pattern to be found. Morality is an aspect of culture, in the sense that different cultures have different moral systems—or, turning the question around, that cultural differences to a great degree consist of moral differences. If we want to know how moral values change, we have to look at the dynamics of cultural change.

Culture is as such a complex and elusive phenomenon, a kind of generalized space of values, ideas, habits, expectations, traditions, artifacts and techniques. Culture forms behavioral regularities and patterns which are not genetically determined. . . .

Predicting changes in moral values is always a question of guessing. I shall make two guesses regarding social and cultural changes which could lead to ethical problems in the future, and which, in my opinion, are questions of strategic concern. They concern the effects of our rapid technological development, and, possibly more destructive, the cultural effects of environmental changes.

The fact of technological development is nothing new. Especially in the field of computerization and robotization technological innovations come at an increasing pace. The cultural effects, however, are yet to be seen. During the coming decade or two we can expect not only new technology, but also the first generations of a working force that has been born and grown up in the computerized world. We have, thus, a two-sided change: on the one side, a technological breakthrough which must be expected to have immense cultural side effects, and on the other side, a population which, being tuned to that technology, is more able than ever to use and develop that technology further. Several areas of concern may arise out of this. There is a strong risk of techniques and practices leading to infringement of the personal integrity of almost anybody coming into contact with the modern corporation. This concerns not only employees, but customers, the general public, competitors, etc. On the other hand, the fast pace of action made possible may lead to ethical concerns just because there is no time left for reflection, and because of new possibilities for a quick unethical rip-off. The virulent ethical problems connected with the stock exchange might partly derive from these kinds of processes. Legitimate business practices, which as a whole determine much of what is morally right in business, depend on accumulated experience from a relatively stable world. The faster the pace of change in that world, the weaker the moral agreement.

In the relatively short time of about thirty years, i.e., since Rachel Carson published her book *The Silent Spring* in the beginning of the sixties, the question of disturbing refuse and dirty swimming water has turned into a problem for the twenty-first century. It has at the same time formed a new class of knowledge—"environmental pollution" and, connected with it, a new category of moral concern.

A closer look at what might be called "environmental ethics" shows that there is a common base forming something like a "future-directed morality." There is, deeply embedded in human reasoning, a tendency to transcendental empathy, i.e., a tendency to feel empathy and responsibility for coming generations, for humanity as such. . . .

6. ETHICAL STRATEGY FOR THE FUTURE?

I shall finish by asking what can be done in a strategic perspective to meet possible dramatic ethical conflicts. As always, when discussing strategy, the answers seem somewhat elusive. On the other hand, it would seem that some kind of preparedness is better than just waiting for it all to happen.

There is always a reason for some kind of ethical strategic concern, as long as there is reason to assume that moral values change. The forms of change, however, are unclear. What we need, then, is some kind of ethic sensitivity in the corporation. This can be organized, to some degree. Some firms do it by establishing **ethical committees**. The important thing to remember, in the case of ethical committees, is that they should aim not just at handling hot potatoes and exploding ethical conflicts. Rather they ought to establish some kind of routine for probing into the general ethical climate of the firm.

The ethical problems are to be found partly inside the organization, when the **ethical climate** begins to deviate too sharply from that of the surrounding culture. An internal organization culture heavily dominated by greed, for example, can be expected to produce behavior leading to ethical conflicts over a broad spectrum from insider crimes to embezzlement, both on the individual level and on the level of organizational action. This might be important especially in banking and finance, and among stockbrokers. It is important to remember that moral values constitute a truth-forming logic of action. In a culture of greed, its members really "believe" that economic egoism is good and virtuous—not exclusively, but to a high degree. Their activities are then formed according to that logic. This does not mean that everybody instantly starts breaking laws or acting unethically, but rather that the probability of ethical transgressions increases.

It is not enough, of course, to acknowledge the problem. Something ought to be done, too. One central question regarding business ethics concerns the possibilities of influencing the ethical climate in the corporation. I shall here limit myself to some superficial comments.

Codes of conduct, in use in many places, may have some positive effect—not in the form, however, of some kind of local organizational law, linked to control systems and sanctions. The logical structure of norms quickly neutralizes this approach, because strict rules lead to all kinds of dysfunctional behavior in the form of cheating, hypocrisy and evasion. On the other hand, codes of conduct, especially if management visibly supports and emphasizes them, often have a good educating effect. In a way they form a **statement of corporate vision**. A clear and consistent show of personal corporate vision and moral conviction may have strong unifying cultural effects in the organization. On the other hand, it should never take too heavy a "preaching" form.

By consistently trying to strengthen the moral base in a firm, you may give it the intellectual power to handle coming ethical conflicts and to evade the most critical pitfalls.

The other side of an ethical strategy concerns predicting and preparing for the future. This is not easy, as is known. The two fields of value change depicted above, however, seem to have such a high probability, even if the patterns are not clear, as to warrant closer scrutiny. Detecting the pattern of change in advance, perhaps by some kind of scenario technique, by forming discussion groups in the tradition of early operations analysis, may be one way. The question is not so much about meteological, climatological and technical knowledge, but more about the knowledge given by historians, sociologists, cultural anthropologists, philosophers, and their likes.

BY PHILIP SELZNICK

■ The nature and quality of leadership, in the sense of statesmanship, is an elusive but persistent theme in the history of ideas. Most writers have centered their attention on *political* statesmen, leaders of whole communities who sit in the high places where great issues are joined and settled. In our time, there is no abatement of the need to continue the great discussion, to learn how to reconcile idealism with expediency, freedom with organization

But an additional emphasis is necessary. Ours is a pluralist society made up of many large, influential, relatively autonomous groups. The U.S. government itself consists of independently powerful agencies which do a great deal on their own initiative and are largely self-governing. These, and the institutions of industry, politics, education, and other fields, often command large resources; their leaders are inevitably responsible for the material and psychological well-being of numerous constituents; and they have become increasingly *public* in nature, attached to such interests and dealing with such problems as affect the welfare of the entire community. In our society the need for statesmanship is widely diffused and beset by special problems. An understanding of leadership in both public and private organizations must have a high place on the agenda of social inquiry. . . .

The argument of this essay is quite simply stated: *The executive becomes a statesman as he makes the transition from administrative management to institutional leadership.* This shift entails a reassessment of his own tasks and of the needs of the enterprise. It is marked by a concern for the evolution of the organization as a whole, including its changing aims and capabilities. In a word, it means viewing the organization as an institution. To understand the nature of institutional leadership, we must have some notion of the meaning and significance of the term "institution" itself.

ORGANIZATIONS AND INSTITUTIONS

The most striking and obvious thing about an administrative organization is its formal system of rules and objectives. Here tasks, powers, and procedures are set out according to some officially approved pattern. This pattern purports to say how the work of the organization is to be carried on, whether it be producing steel, winning votes, teaching children, or saving souls. The organization thus designed is a technical instrument for mobilizing human energies and directing them toward set aims. We allocate tasks, delegate authority, channel communication, and find some way of coordinating all that has been divided up and parceled out. All this is conceived as an exercise in engineering; it is governed by the related ideals of rationality and discipline.

The term "organization" thus suggests a certain bareness, a lean, no-nonsense system of consciously coordinated activities (Barnard, 1938: 73). It refers to an *expendable tool*, a rational instrument engineered to do a job. An "institution," on the other hand, is more nearly a natural product of social needs and pressures—a responsive, adaptive organism. This distinction is a matter of analysis, not of direct description. It does not mean that any given enterprise must be either one or the other. While an extreme case may closely approach either an "ideal" organization or an "ideal" institution, most living associations resist so easy a classification. They are complex mixtures of both designed and responsive behavior. . . .

In what is perhaps its most significant meaning, "to institutionalize" is to *infuse with value* beyond the technical requirements of the task at hand. The prizing of social machinery beyond its technical role is largely a reflection of the unique way in which it fulfills personal or group needs. Whenever individuals become attached to an organization or a way of doing

*Excerpted from *Leadership in Administration*, by Philip Selznick, New York: Harper and Row, 1957.

things as persons rather than as technicians, the result is a prizing of the device for its own sake. From the standpoint of the committed person, the organization is changed from an expendable tool into a valued source of personal satisfaction. Some manifestations of this process are quite obvious; others are less easily recognized. It is commonplace that administrative changes are difficult when individuals have become habituated to and identified with long-established procedures. For example, the shifting of personnel is inhibited when business relations become personal ones and there is resistance to any change that threatens rewarding ties. A great deal of energy in organizations is expended in a continuous effort to preserve the rational, technical, impersonal system against such counterpressures. . . .

The test of infusion with value is *expendability*. If an organization is merely an instrument, it will be readily altered or cast aside when a more efficient tool becomes available. Most organizations are thus expendable. When value infusion takes place, however, there is a resistance to change. People feel a sense of personal loss; the "identity" of the group or community seems somehow to be violated; they bow to economic or technological considerations only reluctantly, with regret. A case in point is the perennial effort to save San Francisco's cable cars from replacement by more economical forms of transportation. The Marine Corps has this institutional halo, and it resists administrative measures that would submerge its identity. . . .

To summarize: organizations are technical instruments, designed as means to definite goals. They are judged on engineering premises; they are expendable. Institutions, whether conceived as groups or practices, may be partly engineered, but they have also a "natural" dimension. They are products of interaction and adaptation; they become the receptacles of group idealism; they are less readily expendable. . . .

THE DEFAULT OF LEADERSHIP

When institutional leadership fails, it is perhaps more often by default than by positive error or sin. Leadership is lacking when it is needed; and the institution drifts, exposed to vagrant pressures, readily influenced by short-run opportunistic trends. This default is partly a failure of nerve, partly a failure of understanding. It takes nerve to hold a course; it takes understanding to recognize and deal with the basic sources of institutional vulnerability.

One type of default is the failure to set goals. Once an organization becomes a "going concern," with many forces working to keep it alive, the people who run it can readily escape the task of defining its purposes. This evasion stems partly from the hard intellectual labor involved, a labor that often seems but to increase the burden of already onerous daily operations. In part, also, there is the wish to avoid conflicts with those in and out of the organization who would be threatened by a sharp definition of purpose, with its attendant claims and responsibilities. Even business firms find it easy to fall back on conventional phrases, such as that "our goal is to make profit," phrases which offer little guidance in the formulation of policy.

A critique of leadership, we shall argue, must include this emphasis on the leader's responsibility to define the mission of the enterprise. This view is not new. It is important because so much of administrative analysis takes the goal of the organization as given, whereas in many crucial instances this is precisely what is problematic. We shall also suggest that the analysis of goals is itself dependent on an understanding of the organization's social structure. In other words, the purposes we have or can have depend on what we are or what we can be. In statesmanship no less than in the search for personal wisdom, the Socratic dictum—know thyself—provides the ultimate guide.

Another type of default occurs when goals, however neatly formulated, enjoy only a superficial acceptance and do not genuinely influence the total structure of the enterprise. Truly accepted values must infuse the organization at many levels, affecting the perspectives and attitudes of personnel, the relative importance of staff activities, the distribution of authority, relations with outside groups, and many other matters. Thus if a large corporation asserts a wish to change its role in the community from a narrow emphasis on profit making to a larger social responsibility (even though the ultimate goal remains some combination of survival and profit-making ability), it must explore the implications of such a change for decision making in a wide variety of organizational activities. We shall stress that the task of building special values and a distinctive competence into the organization is a prime function of leadership. . . .

Finally, the role of the institutional leader should be clearly distinguished from that of the "interpersonal" leader. The latter's task is to smooth the path of human interaction, ease communication, evoke personal devotion, and allay anxiety. His expertness has relatively little to do with content; he is more concerned with persons than with policies. His main contribution is to the efficiency of the enterprise. The institutional leader, on the other hand, *is primarily an expert in the promotion and protection of values*. The interpretation that follows takes this idea as a starting point, exploring its meaning and implications. . . .

It is in the realm of policy—including the areas where policy formation and organization building meet—that the distinctive quality of institutional leadership is found. Ultimately, this is the quality of statesmanship which deals with current issues, not for themselves alone but according to their long-run implications for the role and meaning of the group. Group leadership is far more than the capacity to mobilize personal support; it is more than the maintenance of equilibrium through the routine solution of everyday problems; it is the function of the leader-statesman—whether of a nation or a private association—to define the ends of group existence, to design an enterprise distinctively adapted to these ends, and to see that that design becomes a living reality. These tasks are not routine; they call for continuous self-appraisal on the part of the leaders; and they may require only a few critical decisions over a long period of time. "Mere speed, frequency, and vigor in coming to decisions may have little relevance at the top executive level, where a man's basic contribution to the enterprise may turn on his making two or three significant decisions a year" (Learned, Ulricnh, and Booz, 1951: 57). This basic contribution is not always aided by the traits often associated with psychological leadership, such as aggressive self-confidence, intuitive sureness, ability to inspire. . . .

| CHARACTER AS DISTINCTIVE COMPETENCE | In studying character we are interested in the *distinctive competence or inadequacy* that an organization has acquired. In doing so, we look beyond the formal aspects to examine the commitments that have been accepted in the course of adaptation to internal and external pressures. . . . Commitments to ways of acting and responding are built into the organization. When integrated, these commitments define the "character" of the organization. . . . |

| THE FUNCTIONS OF INSTITUTIONAL LEADERSHIP | We have argued that policy and administration are interdependent in the special sense that certain areas of organizational activity are peculiarly sensitive to policy matters. Because these areas exist, creative men are needed—more in some circumstances than in others—who know how to transform a neutral body of men into a committed polity. These men are called leaders; their profession is politics. . . . |

Leadership sets goals, but in doing so takes account of the conditions that have already determined what the organization can do and to some extent what it must do. Leadership creates and molds an organization embodying—in thought and feeling and habit—the value premises of policy. Leadership reconciles internal strivings and environmental pressures, paying close attention to the way adaptive behavior brings about changes in organizational character. When an organization lacks leadership, these tasks are inadequately fulfilled, however expert the flow of paper and however smooth the channels of communication and command. And this fulfillment requires a continuous scrutiny of how the changing social structure affects the evolution of policy.

The relation of leadership to organizational character may be more closely explored if we examine some of the key tasks leaders are called on to perform:

1. *The definition of institutional mission and role.* The setting of goals is a creative task. It entails a self-assessment to discover the true commitments of the organization, as set by effective internal and external demands. The failure to set aims in the light of these commitments is a major source of irresponsibility in leadership.

2. *The institutional embodiment of purpose.* The task of leadership is not only to make policy but to build it into the organization's social structure. This, too, is a creative task. It means shaping the "character" of the organization, sensitizing it to ways of thinking and responding, so that increased reliability in the execution and elaboration of policy will be achieved according to its spirit as well as its letter.

3. *The defense of institutional integrity.* The leadership of any polity fails when it concentrates on sheer survival: institutional survival, properly understood, is a matter of maintaining values and distinctive identity. This is at once one of the most important and least understood functions of leadership. This area (like that of defining institutional mission) is a place where the intuitively knowledgeable leader and the administrative analyst often part company, because the latter has no tools to deal with it. The fallacy of combining agencies on the basis of "logical" association of functions is a characteristic result of the failure to take account of institutional integrity.

4. *The ordering of internal conflict.* Internal interest groups form naturally in large-scale organizations, since the total enterprise is in one sense a polity composed of a number of suborganizations. The struggle among competing interests always has a high claim on the attention of leadership. This is so because the direction of the enterprise as a whole may be seriously influenced by changes in the internal balance of power. In exercising control, leadership has a dual task. It must win the consent of constituent units, in order to maximize voluntary cooperation, and therefore must permit emergent interest blocs a wide degree of representation. At the same time, in order to hold the helm, it must see that a balance of power appropriate to the fulfillment of key commitments will be maintained.

READING 12.3

A NEW MANIFESTO FOR MANAGEMENT*

BY SUMANTRA GHOSHAL, CHRISTOPHER A. BARTLETT, AND PETER MORAN

■ Why do corporations elicit such powerful love-hate responses? On the one hand, amid the decay of influence and legitimacy of other institutions—such as states, political parties, churches, monarchies, or even families—the corporation has emerged as perhaps the most powerful social and economic institution of modern society. Versatile and creative, the corporation is a prodigious amplifier of human effort across national and cultural boundaries. Corporations, not abstract economic forces or governments, create and distribute most of an economy's wealth, innovate, trade, and raise living standards. Historically, they have served as a pervasive force for civilization, promoting honesty, trust, and respect for contracts. As the market sphere has grown to annex areas such as health and sports, companies loom even larger in the lives of individuals. People look to them for community and identity as well as economic well-being.

---

*Reprinted with deletions from "A New Manifesto for Management," S. Ghoshal, C. A. Bartlett, and P. Moran, *Sloan Management Review*, Spring 1999, 9–20.

Yet, in the closing year of the century, corporations and managers suffer from a profound social ambivalence. Hero-worshipped by the few, they are deeply distrusted by the many. In popular mythology, the corporate manager is Gordon Gecko, the financier who preaches the gospel of greed in Hollywood's *Wall Street*. Corporations are "job killers."

There is so much uncertainty about what companies represent that Bill Clinton in the United States and Tony Blair in the United Kingdom set up reviews of companies' roles. Big business arouses big suspicion in France, Korea, and Germany. Even in the United States, executive salaries have caused a public furor, while the equally astronomical remuneration of entertainers, entrepreneurs, and bond traders raises scarcely an eyebrow. When asked by pollsters to rank professionals by ethical standing, people consistently rate managers the lowest of the low—below even politicians and journalists.

People are *right* in their intuition that something is wrong. But this is not because large corporations or management are inherently harmful or evil. It is because of the deeply unrealistic, pessimistic assumptions about the nature of individuals and corporations that underlie current management doctrine and that, in practice, cause managers to undermine their own worth. . . . It is time to expose the old, disabling assumptions and replace them with a different, more realistic set that calls on managers to act out a positive role that can release the vast potential still trapped in the old model. The new role for management breaks from the narrow economic assumptions of the past to recognize that:

■ Modern societies are not market economies, they are organizational economies in which companies are the chief actors in creating value and advancing economic progress.
■ The growth of firms and, therefore, economies is primarily dependent on the quality of their management.
■ The foundation of a firm's activity is a new "moral contract" with employees and society, replacing paternalistic exploitation and value appropriation with employability and value creation in a relationship of shared destiny.

BETWEEN A ROCK AND A HARD PLACE

To understand why rethinking is necessary, start by looking at what happened to the corporate world in the 1980s. Driven by vociferous shareholders and global competition, managers have concentrated on enhancing competitiveness by improving their operating efficiencies. Managers have enlisted an array of techniques such as total quality, continuous improvement, and process reengineering to this end. Firms have cut costs, eliminated waste, focused, outsourced, downsized, let go, and generally pared themselves to the bone. The result has been victory—of a sort. Shareholder returns (and senior executives' pay) have, in many cases, soared. Value has been extracted, but at what price?

Explicit or implicit past contracts with both employees and suppliers were broken. Employee loyalty and commitment have been shattered. So has management confidence in its ability to create instead of cut; witness the vogue of high-growth companies like Reuters handing back cash to shareholders via share buybacks and special dividends instead of investing it to pursue emerging opportunities. Michael Porter (1996) expressed alarm that the obsession with operating efficiencies was "leading more and more companies down the path of mutually destructive competition." Stephen Roach (1998), chief economist of Morgan Stanley, reversed his previous enthusiasm for downsizing and warned that if cutting labor costs and hollowing companies were all there was to the productivity-led recovery, "the nation could well be on a path toward industrial extinction." . . .

GENEEN'S MONKEY

The top jaw of the pincer is the doctrine by which managers run their companies.

Two generations of top managers have learned to frame their task through the viewfinder of the three Ss: crafting *strategy*, designing the *structure* to fit, and locking both in place with supporting *systems*. In its time, the strategy-structure-systems trilogy was a revolutionary discovery. Invented in the 1920s by Alfred Sloan and others as a technology to support their pioneering strategy of diversification, it served companies well for decades. It supported vertical and horizontal integration, the wave of conglomerate diversification in the 1960s, and the start of globalization in the 1970s and 1980s. But then it began to break down. However sophisticated their structure and systems, the great companies that had been bidding fair to inherit the earth—a French intellectual warned in the early 1980s that IBM had everything it needed to become a world power—were suddenly transformed into stumbling giants. The decline of excellence is well known. So what went wrong?

What happened was the "real world" changed. The strength—and fundamental weakness—of the classic strategy-structure-systems model was the primacy it gave to control. As Frederick Taylor had made complex assembly repeatable by breaking it down to its simplest component tasks, so the new doctrine, the managerial equivalent of Taylorism, aimed to make the management of complex corporations systematic and predictable. Once strategy had been set at the top, structures and systems would banish troublesome human idiosyncrasy, enabling large, diversified companies to be run in the same machine-like ways. Like the workers on Henry Ford's assembly lines, all employees were replaceable parts. Harold Geneen, the accountant who ran the quintessential 1970s conglomerate ITT, used to boast that he was building a system that "a monkey will be able to run when I'm gone."

Famous last words. In the world that today's companies operate in—a world of converging technologies and markets, swirling competition, and innovation that can outdate established industry structures overnight—machine-like systems of control aren't helpful. In a situation where the most important corporate resources are not the financial funds in the hands of top management but the knowledge and expertise of the people on the front lines, they are downright unhelpful. To say that they stifle initiative, creativity, and diversity is true—but that was their point. They were designed for an organization man who has turned out to be an evolutionary dead end.

THE TYRANNY OF THEORY

The second jaw of the pincer in which companies are gripped is theory. Instead of providing remedies, academic prescriptions mostly have tightened the squeeze on managers and companies. They are part of the problem. Consider two strands of theory that have dominated managerial discourse, both academic and practical, for the past decade.

The first is Michael Porter's theory of strategy, grounded in industrial organization economics. Crudely, under Porter's theory, the essence of strategy is competition to appropriate value. Companies strive to seize and keep for themselves as much as they can of the value embodied in the products and services they deal with, while allowing as little of this value as possible to fall into the hands of others. Employees, customers, suppliers, and direct or potential competitors are all trying to do the same thing. In short, strategy is positioning to grab all you can, while preventing anyone else from eating your lunch.

The difficulty is that, in this view, the interests of the company are incompatible with those of society. For society, the freer the competition among companies the better. But for individual firms, the purpose of strategy is precisely to restrict the play of competition to get as much as possible for themselves. To do their jobs, managers must prevent free competition, at the cost of social welfare. The destruction of social welfare is not just a coincidental by-product of strategy; it is the fundamental objective of profit-seeking firms and, therefore, of their managers.

The second influential strand of theory addresses a very basic question. Why do companies exist? The answer provided by most economists is so straightforward that it appears compelling; companies exist simply because markets fail. Accept this and it's only a short step toward the dangerously misleading belief that markets represent some sort of ideal way to organize all economic activities. According to "transaction-cost economics," the dominant branch of theorizing on this subject, a company is an inferior substitute for markets. Oliver

Williamson (1985), a key contributor to one strand of this theory, refers to companies as the organizing means of "last resort, to be employed when all else fails." Markets fail, Williamson presumes, because people are weak. It is only because we, as humans, are limited in our ability to act rationally and because at least some of us are prone to acting "opportunistically" that we need organizations to save us from ourselves. In some of our dealings with others, particularly those requiring complex coordination of tasks, our opportunity to behave strategically is too great for markets to restrain. In these cases, companies are necessary because managers, with their hierarchical authority and their power to monitor and control, can keep the opportunism of employees in check.

Unfortunately, the practical consequence of these two theories is to make managers not architects but wreckers of their own corporations. What they have in common, apart from their narrow, instrumental, and largely pessimistic view of human enterprise, is an emphasis on static rather than dynamic efficiencies. Static efficiency is about exploiting available economic options as efficiently as possible—making the economy more efficient by shifting existing resources to their highest valued use. Dynamic efficiency comes from the innovations that create new options and new resources—moving the economy to a different level. Porter's theory is static in that it focuses strategic think-firms into the market logic of static efficiency. Fit the pieces together and we can see why this unholy alliance of theory and practice should have destructive consequences. In its constant struggle for appropriating value, the company is pitted against its own employees as well as business rivals and the rest of society. The economic challenge for society is to keep human discretion in check. This is accomplished in markets through a focus on individualism and the power of sharp incentives and, within the firm, through hierarchical control. In other words, as Williamson wrote, and Geneen practiced, companies must act as if they were "a continuation of market relations, by other means." Caught as it is, between the sound logic of efficiency and the harsh reality of human frailties and pathologies, it is no wonder that dominant doctrine focuses managers' attention almost exclusively on concerns of appropriation and control. The resulting pathological economic role for companies and individuals should also be no surprise. It follows naturally from the premise that "markets rule" that any and all failures to heed the market's corrective discipline are likely to be futile for firms and individuals and inefficient for society.

When in a hole, the first thing to do is to stop digging. The outlines are beginning to take shape of a different management model, based on a better understanding of both individual and corporate motivation. If downsizing, cost-cutting, and "getting lean and mean" were the mantras of the past decade, the desire for growth and renewal will be the major concern of the next.

A NEW MANAGEMENT PHILOSOPHY

Start by turning the conventional justification for the existence of the company around: markets begin where firms leave off. As Nobel laureate Herbert Simon (1957) has put it, "modern societies are not primarily market but *organizational economies*." That is, most of their value is created not by individuals transacting individually in the market, as in the economists' ideal, but by organizations involving people acting collectively, with their motives empowered and their actions coordinated by their companies' purpose. Far from destroying social welfare, the rise of the corporation over the past century has coincided with a sustained and unprecedented improvement in living standards, fueled by the ability of companies to enhance productivity and create new products and services. Indeed, the clearest evidence for Simon's contention lies in a strong positive correlation between the relative prosperity of an economy and its quotient of large, healthy companies. Growing, efficient companies help create growing, efficient economies. Not only is the premise of a fundamental conflict between corporate well-being and social welfare wrong; the reality is exactly the reverse.

In terms of static efficiency, much of what happens inside a company *is* inefficient. That's its point. It exists precisely to provide a haven and (temporary) respite from the laws of the market in which humans can combine to do something that markets aren't very good at: innovating. From a static viewpoint, the 15 percent of their time that 3M encourages its employees to spend on their own projects is wasted. And, indeed, a lot of it is. But the company willingly makes this sacrifice, banking that out of their efforts will come products that alter the bounds of the existing market. Sony and Intel duplicate development teams for the same purpose. Companies create fresh value for society by developing new products and services and finding better ways for providing existing ones. Markets relentlessly force the same companies eventually to "hand off" most of the newly created value to others, increasing, not diminishing, social welfare. In this symbiotic coexistence, they jointly drive the process of "creative destruction" that the Austrian economist Joseph Schumpeter identified sixty years ago as the engine of economic progress.

Reversing the logic pries companies from the crushing hold of the pincer, with liberating effect for their managers and employees. The difference between old and new is not just economic but also philosophical. In an organizational economy in which the essence of the company is value creation, the corporation and society are no longer in conflict. They are interdependent, and the starting point is a new moral contract between them. In this framework, management too wins back its legitimacy: not only is the "destroy it to save it" nightmare banished, but the success of the company and the economy as a whole can be seen to depend on how well management does its job. Far from being villainous or exploitative, management as a profession can be seen for what it is—the primary engine of social and economic progress. Individual inventors and entrepreneurs develop new products and, sometimes, new businesses. A vast majority of new products and new businesses, however, are created by established organizations. Managers build organizations, the embodiments of an economy's social capital—a factor that is beginning to be recognized as perhaps the key driver of economic growth.

COMPANIES AS VALUE CREATORS

The contrast between these two views of a company comes sharply into focus if we compare the management approaches of Norton and 3M, or of Westinghouse and ABB. As we have described elsewhere, managers at Norton and Westinghouse lived in the zero-sum, dog-eat-dog world of traditional management theory. When they found a company that had created an attractive new product or business, they bought it. When they found the market for a product to be too competitive for them to dictate terms to their buyers and suppliers, they sold those businesses. Their primary management focus was on value appropriation—not only vis-à-vis their customers and suppliers, but also vis-à-vis their own employees.

At 3M and ABB, in contrast, a very different management philosophy was at work. While Norton tried to develop increasingly sophisticated strategic resource allocation models, 3M's entire strategy was based on the value-creating logic of continuous innovation. The same power equipment business that Westinghouse abandoned as unattractive (that is, not enough opportunity for value appropriation), ABB rejuvenated, in part by its own investments in productivity and in new technologies to enhance products' functionality or their appropriateness for new markets.

Norton and Westinghouse managers thought of their companies in market terms: they bought and sold businesses, created internal markets whenever they could, and dealt with their people with market rules. Through the power of sharp, marketlike incentives, they got what they wanted. People began to behave as they would in a market—acting alone as independent agents with an atomistic concern only for their self-interest.

By thinking of their companies in market terms, Norton and Westinghouse became the victims of the very logic that both companies sought to live by—a market logic that left little choice but to squeeze out more efficiency in everything that was attempted. Their strategy focused entirely on productivity improvement and cost cutting. Their structures for controlling behavior rewarded autonomy, while their elaborate systems for monitoring performance were finely tuned to eliminate even the smallest pools of waste. Yet, they could not create any value that was new. . . . people [were] unable to cooperate among themselves or to pool their resources and capabilities in order to create new combinations—particularly, new combinations of knowledge and expertise—that most innovations require.

Visions like ABB's purpose "to make economic growth and improved living standards a reality for all nations throughout the world," values such as Kao Corporation's espoused belief that "we are, first of all, an educational institution," and norms like 3M's acceptance that "products belong to divisions but technologies belong to the company" all emphasize the non-marketlike nature of a company, encouraging people to work collectively toward shared goals and values rather than more restrictively, within their narrow self-interests. They can share resources, including knowledge, without having to be certain of how precisely each of them will benefit personally—as long as they believe that the company overall will benefit, to their collective gain. . . .

The manager's primary task is redefined from institutionalizing control to embedding trust, from maintaining the status quo to leading change. As opposed to being the designers of strategy, managers take on the role of establishing a sense of *purpose* within the company. Defined in terms of how the company will create value for society, purpose allows strategy to emerge from within the organization, from the energy and alignment created by that sense of purpose. As opposed to playing with the boxes and lines that represent the company's formal structure, managers focus on building the core organizational processes that would release the entrepreneurs held hostage in the front-line units of that structure; integrate the resources and capabilities across those units to create new combinations of resources and knowledge; and create the stretch that would drive the whole organization into continuously striving for new value creation. And, from being the builders of systems, managers transform into the developers of people, helping each individual in the company become the best he or she can be. The three Ss of strategy, structure, and systems that were at the core of the managerial role give way to the three Ps: purpose, process, and people.

CREATING VALUE FOR PEOPLE

This kind of management also demands a qualitatively different employment relationship from that of the past. The contrast is perhaps the clearest statement of the new management philosophy in action. In a value-appropriating, cost-cutting mode, part of the firm's advantage comes from its monopoly power over people's capabilities. In return, it takes on, or was understood to take on, responsibility for the employees' careers. Counterintuitively, the offer of job security has allowed companies to extract the maximum value from their people in the past.

Unlike machines, people cannot be owned. Yet, like machines, the way people become most valuable to a company is by becoming specialized to the company's businesses and activities. The more specific the employee's knowledge and skills are to a company's unique set of customers, technologies, equipment, and so on, the more productive they become and the more efficient the company becomes in all that is does. Without employment security, employees hesitate to invest their time and energy to acquire such specialized knowledge and skills that may be very useful to the company, but may have limited value outside of it. Without any assurance of a long-term association, companies too lack the incentive to commit resources to help employees develop such company-specific expertise. Employment security provides a viable basis for both to make such investments. . . .*

But even if they wanted to, companies can no longer meaningfully give the kind of job security that was their side of the bargain. One reason is the hyper-competition they have brought on themselves. In any case, security could hardly survive in an unstable world in which competitive advantage in one period becomes competitive disadvantage in another. . . .

---

*This is a core argument of the theory of internal labor markets. See P. B. Doeringer and M. J. Piore, *Internal Labor Markets and Manpower Analysis* (Lexington, MA: D. C. Heath, 1971).

At the same time, a free-market hire-and-fire regime is no alternative, as many companies have come to recognize. Paradoxically, the same forces of ferocious competition and turbulent change that make job security impossible also increase the need for trust and teamwork. These can't be fostered in an affection-free environment of reciprocal opportunism and continuous spot contracting. On the contrary, firms such as Intel and 3M have intuited that value creation demands something much more inspiring than individual self-interest: a community of purpose in which individuals can share resources, including knowledge, without knowing precisely how they will benefit, but confident of collective gain. In other words, innovation depends on a company acting as a social and an economic institution, in which individuals can behave accordingly.

This requirement is embodied in a new moral contract with employees to anchor the similar contract with society. In the new contract, employees take responsibility for the competitiveness of both themselves and the part of the company to which they belong. In return, the company offers not the dependence of employment security but the independence of employability—a guarantee that they fulfill through continuous education and development. Says GE's Welch: "The new psychological contract . . . is that jobs at GE are the best in the world for people who are willing to compete. We have the best in training and development resources, and an environment committed to providing opportunities for personal and professional growth." . . .

Few companies take their commitment to employability of people more seriously than Motorola. In a context of radical decentralization of resources and decisions to the divisional level, employee education is one activity that Motorola manages at the corporate level, through the large and well-funded Motorola University that has branches all over the world. Each employee, including the chief executive, has to undertake a minimum of forty hours of formal coursework each year. Courses span a wide range of topics—from state-of-the-art coverage of new technologies to broad general management topics and issues, so as to allow Motorola employees around the world to update knowledge and skills in their chosen areas. It is this commitment to adding value to people that allowed Motorola to launch and implement its much-imitated "Six Sigma" total quality initiative. At the same time, the reputation of Motorola University increasingly has become a key source of the company's competitive advantage in recruiting and retaining the best graduates from leading schools in every country in which it operates.

More recently, Motorola has further upped the ante on its commitment employability by launching the "Individual Dignity Entitlement" (or IDE) program. The program requires all supervisors to discuss, on a quarterly basis, six questions with everyone whose work they supervise. A negative response from any employee to any one of these questions is treated as a quality failure, to be redressed in accordance with the principles of total quality management. Yet even Motorola, a company that has invested more in its people than most and that has long been an adherent of employability, was surprised to learn that some of its units reported failures in excess of 70 percent the first time that IDE was implemented. Beginning in 1995, the company began addressing the negatives systematically by identifying and then eliminating their root causes. This is the hard edge of the new moral contract on management's side—the commitment to help people become the best they can be—that counterbalances the new demands on people which the "employability for competitiveness" contract creates.

WHAT THE NEW CONTRACT IS NOT

It is important to emphasize that this new moral contract is not a catchy new slogan to free managers from a sense of responsibility to protect the jobs of their staff. At Intel, Andy Grove could make the kind of demands he did because his own past actions had established, beyond any doubt, the extent to which he was willing to go to protect the interests of his employees. During the memory-products blood bath in the early 1980s, when every other semiconductor company in the United States immediately laid off many people, Grove adopted the 90 percent rule, with everyone, from the chairman down, accepting a 10 percent pay cut, to avoid layoffs. Then, to tide the company over the bad period without losing people he had nurtured for years, Grove sold 20 percent of the company to IBM for $350 million in cash. When cost pressures continued to mount, he implemented the 125 percent rule by asking everyone to work an extra ten hours a week with no pay increase, again to avoid cutbacks. Only after all these efforts proved insufficient did he finally close some operations, with the attending job losses. This kind of proven commitment to people makes a contract based on employability credible, and its hard-edged demands on people acceptable. . . .

. . . the contract based on employability is not some program that can be installed by a company's HR department. Rather, it must be inculcated as a very different philosophy—one that requires management at every level to work hard, on an ongoing basis, to create an exciting and invigorating work environment, a place of enormous pride and satisfaction that bonds people to the company even more tightly than any bond of dependency that employment security could create. The combination of a moral contract based on employability and a management commitment to empowerment leads, as a consequence, to the durable long-term and mutually satisfying relationship between the individual and the organization that the traditional employment contract abandoned. But, by building the new company-employee relationship on a platform of mutual value-adding and continuous choice, rather than on a self-degrading acceptance of one-way dependence, the new contract is not just functional. It is also moral. . . .

A MANIFESTO FOR RECLAIMING MANAGERIAL LEGITIMACY

Institutions decline when they lose their source of legitimacy. This happened to the monarchy, to organized religion, and to the state. This will happen to companies unless managers accord the same priority to the collective task of rebuilding the credibility and legitimacy of their institutions as they do to the individual task of enhancing their company's economic performance.

Ideas matter. In a practical discipline like management, the normative influence of ideas can be powerful, as they can manifest themselves as uniquely beneficial or uniquely dangerous. Bad theory and a philosophical vacuum have caused managers to subvert their own practice, trapping them in a vicious circle. But there is a choice. Management can continue down the well-worn path to illegitimacy or begin to chart a new course by laying claim to a higher purpose. When the solution to a recurring problem is always "try harder," there is usually something wrong with the terms, not the execution. Get out of the pincer's grip. Throw out the old paradigm while you still can, before the growing gap between companies' economic power and their social legitimacy proves it right. Take responsibility before management is held to blame for stunting the growth potential of individuals, companies, and society.

SECTION III

Contexts

CHAPTER 13

Managing Start-Ups

The text of this book really divides into two basic parts, although there are three sections. The first, encompassing Chapters 1 through 12 and Sections I and II, introduces a variety of important concepts of organizations—strategy, strategist, process, organization, values, and so on. The second, beginning here with Section III and Chapter 13, considers how these concepts combine to form major contexts of organizations. In effect, a context is a type of situation wherein can be found particular strategies, structures, and processes.

Traditionally, policy and strategy textbooks are divided into two very different parts—a first part on the formulation of strategy and a second part on its implementation (including discussion of structure, systems, culture, etc.). As some of the readings of Chapter 5 have already made clear, we believe this is often a false dichotomy: In many situations (i.e., contexts), formulation and implementation can be so intertwined that it makes no sense to separate them. To build a textbook around a questionable dichotomy likewise makes no sense to us, and so we have instead proceeded by introducing all the concepts related to the strategy process first and then considering the various ways in which they might interact in specific situations.

There is no "one best way" to manage the strategy process. The notion that there are several possible "good ways," however—various contexts appropriate to strategic management—was first developed in the Mintzberg reading in Chapter 8. In fact, his *configurations* of organization serve as the basis for determining the set of contexts we include here. These are as follows.

We start in Chapter 13 with what seems to be the simplest context, certainly one that has had much good press in America since Horatio Alger first went into business—that of the *start-up*. Here a single leader usually takes personal charge in a highly dynamic situation, as in a new firm or a small one operating in a growing market, or even sometimes in a large organization facing turnaround.

We next consider in Chapter 14 a contrasting context that often dominates large business as well as big government. We label it the *mature* context, although it might equally be referred to as the stable context or the mass-production or mass-service context. Here rather formal structures combine with strategy processes that are heavily analytical.

Our third and fourth contexts are those of organizations largely dependent on specialists and experts. These contexts are called *expert* when the environment is stable, *innovation* when it is dynamic. Here responsibility for strategy making tends to diffuse throughout the organization, sometimes even lodging itself at the bottom of the hierarchy. The strategy process tends to become rather emergent in nature.

Fifth, we consider the context of the *diversified* organization, which became increasingly important as waves of mergers swept across various Western economies. Because product-market strategies are diversified, the structures tend to get divisionalized, and the focus of strategy shifts to two levels: the corporate or portfolio level and the divisional or business level.

In the chapter on each context, our intention is to include material that describes all the basic concepts as they take shape in that context. We wish to describe the form of organization and of strategic leadership found there, the nature of the strategy-making process, including its favored forms of strategic analysis and its most appropriate types of strategies (generic and otherwise) and social issues that surround it. Unfortunately, appropriate readings on all these aspects are not available—in part we do not yet know all that we must about each context.

Before beginning, we should warn you of one danger in focusing this discussion on contexts such as these: It may make the world of organizations appear to be more pat and ordered than it really is. Many organizations certainly seem to fit one context or another, as numerous examples will make clear. But none ever does so quite perfectly—the world is too nuanced for that. And then there are the organizations that do not fit a single context. We believe and have included arguments in a concluding chapter to this section that, in fact, the whole set of contexts forms a framework by which to understand better all kinds of organizations. But until we get to this, you should bear in mind that much of this material caricatures reality as much as it mirrors it.

Of course, such caricaturing is a necessary part of formal learning and of acting. Managers, for example, would never get anything done if they could not use simplified frameworks to comprehend their experiences in order to act on them. As Miller and Mintzberg have argued in a paper called "The Case for Configuration," managers are attracted to a particular, well-defined context because that allows them to achieve a certain consistency and coherence in the design of their organization and so to facilitate its effective performance. Each context, as you will see, has its own logic—its own integrated way of dealing with its part of the world—that makes things more manageable.

This chapter of Section III discusses managing the start-up. At least in its traditional form, this encompasses situations in which a single individual, typically with a clear and distinct vision of purpose, directs an organization that is structured to be as responsive as possible to his or her personal wishes. Strategy making, thus, revolves around a single brain, unconstrained by forces of bureaucratic momentum.

Such entrepreneurship is commonly found in young organizations, especially ones in new or emerging industries, where vision may be essential because of long delays between the conception of an idea and its commercial success. But in crisis situations, a similar type of strong and visionary leadership may offer the best hope for successful turn-around. And it can thrive as well in highly fragmented industries, where small, flexible organizations can move quickly into and out of specialized market niches and so outmaneuver the big bureaucracies.

The word *entrepreneurship* has also been associated with change and innovation inside larger, more bureaucratic organizations—sometimes under the label *intrapreneurship*. In these situations, it is often not the boss but someone in an odd corner of the organization—a champion for some technology or strategic issue—who takes on the entrepreneurial role. We believe, however, for reasons that will become evident that intrapreneurship better fits into our chapter on the innovation context.

To describe the structure that seems to be most logically associated with start-ups and entrepreneurship in general, we open with material on the entrepreneurial form of organization from Mintzberg's book, *The Structuring of Organizations*. Combined with this is a discussion of strategy making in the entrepreneurial context, especially with regard to strategic vision, based on research carried out at McGill University. In one, strategies of visionary leadership were studied through biographies and autobiographies; in the other, the strategies of entrepreneurial firms were tracked across several decades of their histories.

Then to investigate the external situation that seems to be most commonly (although not exclusively) associated with this context, we present excerpts from a chapter on emerging industries from Michael Porter's book *Competitive Strategy*.

The final reading of this chapter by Amar Bhide of the Harvard Business School tells how entrepreneurs go about crafting their strategies, based on his and associates' research. Entrepreneurs select carefully but are also careful not to be too analytical (recall Pitcher's artists versus the technocrats of Chapter 2), and they maintain their ability to maneuver and to "hustle." Action must be integrated with analysis.

USING THE CASE STUDIES

Many of the cases recount the early histories of what are now large, established companies. In this respect, cases such as Honda, Sony, and the Selkirk Group can be regarded as start-up cases. However, cases such as MP3.com and Workbrain deal with start-ups before the outcome is known. The approach to managing start-ups described in these cases is relevant to the analysis presented by Mintzberg's reading "The Entrepreneurial Organization." But Workbrain, which deals with an e-business pioneer, is particularly relevant to Porter's discussion of "Competitive Strategy in Emerging Industries." Arguably, however, the Robin Hood case deals with a start-up, albeit not in the usual sense of the term. Bhide's advice to entrepreneurial start-ups would have been surprisingly useful to Robin, as it is for more conventional entrepreneurs.

BY HENRY MINTZBERG

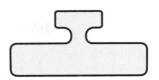

Consider an automobile dealership with a flamboyant owner, a brand-new government department, a corporation or even a nation run by an autocratic leader, or a school system in a state of crisis. In many respects, those are vastly different organizations. But the evidence suggests that they share a number of basic characteristics. They form a configuration we shall call the *entrepreneurial organization*.

THE BASIC STRUCTURE

The structure of the entrepreneurial organization is often very simple, characterized above all by what it is not: elaborated. As shown in the opening figure, typically it has little or no staff, a loose division of labor, and a small managerial hierarchy. Little of its activity is formalized, and it makes minimal use of planning procedures or training routines. In a sense, it is nonstructure; in my "structuring" book, I called it *simple structure*.

Power tends to focus on the chief executive, who exercises a high personal profile. Formal controls are discouraged as a threat to the chief's flexibility. He or she drives the organization by sheer force of personality or by more direct interventions. Under the leader's watchful eye, politics cannot easily arise. Should outsiders, such as particular customers or suppliers, seek to exert influence, such leaders are as likely as not to take the organizations to a less exposed niche in the marketplace.

Thus, it is not uncommon in small entrepreneurial organizations for everyone to report to the chief. Even in ones not so small, communication flows informally, much of it between the chief executive and others. As one group of McGill MBA students commented in their study of a small manufacturer of pumps: "It is not unusual to see the president of the company engaged in casual conversation with a machine shop mechanic. [That way he is] informed of a machine breakdown even before the shop superintendent is advised."

Decision making is likewise flexible, with a highly centralized power system allowing for rapid response. The creation of strategy is, of course, the responsibility of the chief executive, the process tending to be highly intuitive, often oriented to the aggressive search for opportunities. It is not surprising, therefore, that the resulting strategy tends to reflect the chief executive's implicit vision of the world, often an extrapolation of his or her own personality.

Handling disturbances and innovating in an entrepreneurial way are perhaps the most important aspects of the chief executive's work. In contrast, the more formal aspects of managerial work—figurehead duties, for example—receive less attention, as does the need to disseminate information and allocate resources internally, since knowledge and power remain at the top.

---

*Adapted from *The Structuring of Organizations* (Prentice Hall, 1979, Chap. 17 on "The Simple Structure"), *Power In and Around Organizations* (Prentice Hall, 1983, Chap. 20 on "The Autocracy"), and the material on strategy formation from "Visionary Leadership and Strategic Management," *Strategic Management Journal* (1989), coauthored with Frances Westley; see also, "Tracking Strategy in an Entrepreneurial Firm," *Academy of Management Journal* (1982), and "Researching the Formation of Strategies: The History of a Canadian Lady, 1939–1976," in R. B. Lamb, ed., *Competitive Strategic Management* (Prentice Hall, 1984), the last two coauthored with James A. Waters. A chapter similar to this appeared in *Mintzberg on Management: Inside Our Strange World of Organizations* (Free Press, 1989).

CONDITIONS OF THE ENTREPRENEURIAL ORGANIZATION

A centrist entrepreneurial configuration is fostered by an external context that is both simple and dynamic. Simpler environments (say, retailing food as opposed to designing computer systems) enable one person at the top to retain so much influence, while it is a dynamic environment that requires flexible structure, which in turn enables the organization to outmaneuver the bureaucracies. Entrepreneurial leaders are naturally attracted to such conditions.

The classic case of this is, of course, the entrepreneurial firm, where the leader is the owner. Entrepreneurs often found their own firms to escape the procedures and control of the bureaucracies where they previously worked. At the helm of their own enterprises, they continue to loathe the ways of bureaucracy, and the staff analysts that accompany them, and so they keep their organizations lean and flexible. Figure 1 shows the organigram for Steinberg's, a supermarket chain we shall be discussing shortly, during its most classically entrepreneurial years. Notice the identification of people above positions, the simplicity of the structure (the firm's sales by this time were on the order of $27 million), and the focus on the chief executive (not to mention the obvious family connections).

Entrepreneurial firms are often young and aggressive, continually searching for the risky markets that scare off the bigger bureaucracies. But they are also careful to avoid the complex markets, preferring to remain in niches that their leaders can comprehend. Their small size and focused strategies allow their structures to remain simple, so that the leaders can retain tight control and maneuver flexibly. Moreover, business entrepreneurs are often visionary, sometimes charismatic or autocratic as well (sometimes both, in sequence!). Of course, not all "entrepreneurs" are so aggressive or visionary; many settle down to pursue common strategies in small geographic niches. Labeled the *local producers*, these firms can include the corner restaurant, the town bakery, the regional supermarket chain.

But an organization need not be owned by an entrepreneur, indeed need not even operate in the profit sector, to adopt the configuration we call entrepreneurial. In fact, most new organizations seem to adopt this configuration, whatever their sector, because they generally have to rely on personalized leadership to get themselves going—to establish their basic direction, or *strategic vision*, to hire their first people and set up their initial procedures. Of course, strong leaders are likewise attracted to new organizations, where they can put their own stamp on things. Thus, we can conclude that most organizations in business, government, and not-for-profit areas pass through the entrepreneurial configuration in their formative years, during *start-up*.

Moreover, while new organizations that quickly grow large or that require specialized forms of expertise may make a relatively quick transition to another configuration, many

FIGURE 1
ORGANIZATION OF STEINBERG'S, AN ENTREPRENEURIAL FIRM (CIRCA 1948)

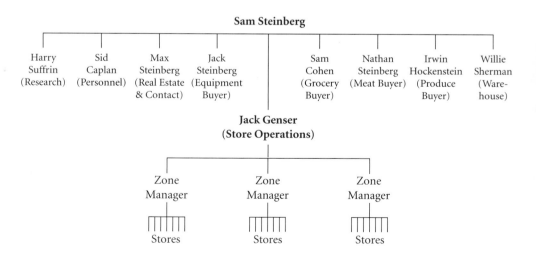

others seem to remain in the entrepreneurial form, more or less, as long as their founding leaders remain in office. This reflects the fact that the structure has often been built around the personal needs and orientation of the leader and has been staffed with people loyal to him or her.

This last comment suggests that the personal power needs of a leader can also, by themselves, give rise to this configuration in an existing organization. When a chief executive hoards power and avoids or destroys the formalization of activity as an infringement on his or her right to rule by fiat, then an autocratic form of the entrepreneurial organization will tend to appear. This can be seen in the cult of personality of the leader, in business (the last days of Henry Ford) no less than in government (the leadership of Stalin in the Soviet Union). Charisma can have a similar effect, though different consequences, when the leader gains personal power not because he or she hoards it but because the followers lavish it on the leader.

The entrepreneurial configuration also tends to arise in any other type of organization that faces severe crisis. Backed up against a wall, with its survival at stake, an organization will typically turn to a strong leader for salvation. The structure thus becomes effectively (if not formally) simple, as the normal powers of existing groups—whether staff analysts, line managers, or professional operators, and so on, with their perhaps more standardized forms of control—are suspended to allow the chief to impose a new integrated vision through his or her personalized control. The leader may cut costs and expenses in an attempt to effect what is known in the strategic management literature as an *operating turnaround*, or else reconceive the basic product and service orientation, to achieve *strategic turnaround*. Of course, once the turnaround is realized, the organization may revert to its traditional operations, and, in the bargain, spew out its entrepreneurial leader, now viewed as an impediment to its smooth functioning.

STRATEGY FORMATION IN THE ENTREPRENEURIAL ORGANIZATION

How does strategy develop in the entrepreneurial organization? And what role does that mysterious concept known as "strategic vision" play? We know something of the entrepreneurial mode of strategy making, but less of strategic vision itself, since it is locked in the head of the individual. But some studies we have done at McGill do shed some light on both these questions. Let us consider strategic vision first.

VISIONARY LEADERSHIP

In a paper she coauthored with me, my McGill colleague Frances Westley contrasted two views of visionary leadership. One she likened to a hypodermic needle, in which the active ingredient (vision) is loaded into a syringe (words) which is injected into the employees to stimulate all kinds of energy. There is surely some truth to this, but Frances prefers another image, that of drama. Drawing from a book on theater by Peter Brook (1968), the legendary director of the Royal Shakespeare Company, she conceives strategic vision, like drama, as becoming magical in that moment when fiction and life blend together. In drama, this moment is the result of endless "rehearsal," the "performance" itself, and the "attendance" of the audience. But Brook prefers the more dynamic equivalent words in French, all of which have English meanings—"repetition," "representation," and "assistance." Frances likewise applies these words to strategic vision.

"Repetition" suggests that success comes from deep knowledge of the subject at hand. Just as Sir Laurence Olivier would repeat his lines again and again until he had trained his tongue muscles to say them effortlessly (Brook, p. 154), so too Lee Iacocca "grew up" in the automobile business, going to Chrysler after Ford because cars were "in his blood" (Iacocca, 1984: 141). The visionary's inspiration stems not from luck, although chance encounters can play a role, but from endless experience in a particular context.

"Representation" means not just to perform but to make the past live again, giving it immediacy, vitality. To the strategist, that is vision articulated, in words and actions. What distinguishes visionary leaders is their profound ability with language, often in symbolic form, as metaphor. It is not just that they "see" things from a new perspective but that they get others to so see them.

Edwin Land, who built a great company around the Polaroid camera he invented, has written of the duty of "the inventor to build a new gestalt for the old one in the framework of society" (1975: 50). He himself described photography as helping "to focus some aspect of [your] life"; as you look through the viewfinder, "it's not merely the camera you are focusing: you are focusing yourself . . . when you touch the button, what is inside of you comes out. It's the most basic form of creativity. Part of you is now permanent" (*Time*, 1972: 84). Lofty words for 50 tourists filing out of a bus to record some pat scene, but powerful imagery for someone trying to build an organization to promote a novel camera. Steve Jobs, visionary (for a time) in his promotion, if not invention, of the personal computer, placed a grand piano and a BMW in Apple's central foyer, with the claim that "I believe people get great ideas from seeing great products" (in Wise, 1984: 146).

"Assistance" means that the audience for drama, whether in the theater or in the organization, empowers the actor no less than the actor empowers the audience. Leaders become visionary because they appeal powerfully to specific constituencies at specific periods of time. That is why leaders once perceived as visionary can fall so dramatically from grace—a Steve Jobs, a Winston Churchill. Or to take a more dramatic example, here is how Albert Speer, arriving skeptical, reacted to the first lecture he heard by his future leader: "Hitler no longer seemed to be speaking to convince; rather, he seemed to feel that he was experiencing what the audience, by now transformed into a single mass, expected of him" (1970: 16).

Of course, management is not theater; the leader who becomes a stage actor, playing a part he or she does not live, is destined to fall from grace. It is integrity—a genuine feeling behind what the leader says and does—that makes leadership truly visionary, and that is what makes impossible the transition of such leadership into any formula.

This visionary leadership is style and strategy, coupled together. It is drama, but not play-acting. The strategic visionary is born and made, the product of a historical moment. Brook closes his book with the following quotation:

In everyday life, "if" is a fiction, in the theatre "if" is an experiment.
In everyday life, "if" is an evasion, in the theatre "if" is the truth.
When we are persuaded to believe in this truth, then the theatre and life are one.
This is a high aim. It sounds like hard work.
To play needs much work. But when we experience the work as play, then it is not work anymore.
A play is play. (p. 157)

In the entrepreneurial organization, at best, "theater," namely strategic vision, becomes one with "life," namely organization. That way leadership creates drama; it turns work into play.

Let us now consider the entrepreneurial approach to strategy formation in terms of two specific studies we have done, one of a supermarket chain, the other of a manufacturer of women's undergarments.

THE ENTREPRENEURIAL APPROACH TO STRATEGY FORMATION IN A SUPERMARKET CHAIN

Steinberg's is a Canadian retail chain that began with a tiny food store in Montreal in 1917 and grew to sales in the billion-dollar range during the almost 60-year reign of its leader. Most of that growth came from supermarket operations. In many ways, Steinberg's fits the entrepreneurial model rather well. Sam Steinberg, who joined his mother in the first store at the age of 11 and personally made a quick decision to expand it 2 years later, maintained complete formal control of the firm (including every single voting share) to the day of his death in 1978. He also exercised close managerial control over all its major decisions, at least until the firm began to diversify after 1960, primarily into other forms of retailing.

It has been popular to describe the "bold stroke" of the entrepreneur (Cole, 1959). In Steinberg's we saw only two major reorientations of strategy in the sixty years, moves into self-service in the 1930s and into the shopping center business in the 1950s. But the stroke was not bold so much as tested. The story of the move into self-service is indicative. In 1933 one of the company's eight stores "struck it bad," in the chief executive's words, incurring "unacceptable" losses ($125 a week). Sam Steinberg closed the store one Friday evening, converted it to self-service, changed its name from "Steinberg's Service Stores" to "Wholesale Groceteria," slashed its prices by 15–20%, printed handbills, stuffed them into neighborhood mailboxes, and reopened on Monday morning. That's strategic change! But only once these changes proved successful did he convert the other stores. Then, in his words, "We grew like Topsy."

This anecdote tells us something about the bold stroke of the entrepreneur—"controlled boldness" is a better expression. The ideas were bold, the execution careful. Sam Steinberg could have simply closed the one unprofitable store. Instead he used it to create a new vision, but he tested that vision, however ambitiously, before leaping into it. Notice the interplay here of problems and opportunities. Steinberg took what most businessmen would probably have perceived as a *problem* (how to cut the losses in one store) and by treating it as a *crisis* (what is wrong with our *general* operation that produces these losses) turned it into an *opportunity* (we can grow more effectively with a new concept of retailing). That was how he got energy behind actions and kept ahead of his competitors. He "oversolved" his problem and thereby remade his company, a characteristic of some of the most effective forms of entrepreneurship.

But absolutely central to this form of entrepreneurship is intimate, detailed knowledge of the business or of analogous business situations, the "repetition" discussed earlier. The leader as conventional strategic "planner"—the so-called architect of strategy—sits on a pedestal and is fed aggregate data that he or she uses to "formulate" strategies that are "implemented" by others. But the history of Steinberg's belies that image. It suggests that clear, imaginative, integrated strategic vision depends on an involvement with detail, an intimate knowledge of specifics. And by closely controlling "implementation" personally, the leader is able to reformulate en route, to adapt the evolving vision through his or her own process of learning. That is why Steinberg tried his new ideas in one store first. And that is why, in discussing his firm's competitive advantage, he told us: "Nobody knew the grocery business like we did. Everything has to do with your knowledge." He added: "I knew merchandise, I knew cost. I knew selling, I knew customers. I knew everything . . . and I passed on all my knowledge; I kept teaching my people. That's the advantage we had. They couldn't touch us."

Such knowledge can be incredibly effective when concentrated in one individual who is fully in charge (having no need to convince others, not subordinates below, not superiors at some distant headquarters, nor market analysts looking for superficial pronouncements) and who retains a strong, long-term commitment to the organization. So long as the business is simple and focused enough to be comprehended in one brain, the entrepreneurial approach is powerful, indeed unexcelled. Nothing else can provide so clear and complete a vision, yet also allow the flexibility to elaborate and rework that vision when necessary. The conception of a new strategy is an exercise in synthesis, which is typically best carried out in a single, informed brain. That is why the entrepreneurial approach is at the center of the most glorious corporate success.

But in its strength lies entrepreneurship's weakness. Bear in mind that strategy for the entrepreneurial leader is not a formal, detailed plan on paper. It is a personal vision, a concept of the business, locked in a single brain. It may need to get "represented," in words and metaphors, but that must remain general if the leader is to maintain the richness and flexibility of his or her concept. But success breeds a large organization, public financing, and the need for formal planning. The vision must be articulated to drive others and gain their support, and that threatens the personal nature of the vision. At the limit, as we shall see later in the case of Steinberg's, the leader can get captured by his or her very successes.

In Steinberg's, moreover, when success in the traditional business encouraged diversification into new ones (new regions, new forms of retailing, new industries), the organization moved beyond the realm of its leader's personal comprehension, and the entrepreneurial mode of strategy formation lost its viability. Strategy making became more decentralized, more analytic, in some ways more careful, but at the same time less visionary, less integrated, less flexible, and ironically, less deliberate.

CONCEIVING A NEW VISION IN A GARMENT FIRM

The genius of an entrepreneur like Sam Steinberg was his ability to pursue one vision (self-service and everything that entailed) faithfully for decades and then, based on a weak signal in the environment (the building of the first small shopping center in Montreal), to realize the need to shift that vision. The planning literature makes a big issue of forecasting such discontinuities, but as far as I know there are no formal techniques to do so effectively (claims about "scenario analysis" notwithstanding). The ability to perceive a sudden shift in an established pattern and then to conceive a new vision to deal with it appears to remain largely in the realm of informed intuition, generally the purview of the wise, experienced, and energetic leader. Again, the literature is largely silent on this. But another of our studies, also concerning entrepreneurship, did reveal some aspects of this process.

Canadelle produces women's undergarments, primarily brassieres. It was a highly successful organization, although not on the same scale as Steinberg's. Things were going well for the company in the late 1960s, under the personal leadership of Larry Nadler, the son of its founder, when suddenly everything changed. A sexual revolution of sorts was accompanying broader social manifestations, with bra burning a symbol of its resistance. For a manufacturer of brassieres the threat was obvious. For many other women the miniskirt had come to dominate the fashion scene, obsoleting the girdle and giving rise to pantyhose. As the executives of Canadelle put it, "the bottom fell out of the girdle business." The whole environment—long so receptive to the company's strategies—seemed to turn on it all at once.

At the time, a French company had entered the Quebec market with a light, sexy, molded garment called "Huit," using the theme, "just like not wearing a bra." Their target market was 15–20-year-olds. Though the product was expensive when it landed in Quebec and did not fit well in Nadler's opinion, it sold well. Nadler flew to France in an attempt to license the product for manufacture in Canada. The French firm refused, but, in Nadler's words, what he learned in "that one hour in their offices made the trip worthwhile." He realized that what women wanted was a more natural look, not no bra but less bra. Another trip shortly afterward, to a sister American firm, convinced him of the importance of market segmentation by age and life-style. That led him to the realization that the firm had two markets, one for the more mature customer, for whom the brassiere was a cosmetic to look and feel more attractive, and another for the younger customer who wanted to look and feel more natural.

Those two events led to a major shift in strategic vision. The CEO described it as sudden, the confluence of different ideas to create a new mental set. In his words, "all of a sudden the idea forms." Canadelle reconfirmed its commitment to the brassiere business, seeking greater market share while its competitors were cutting back. It introduced a new line of more natural brassieres for the younger customers, for which the firm had to work out the molding technology as well as a new approach to promotion.

We can draw on Kurt Lewin's (1951) three-stage model of unfreezing, changing and refreezing to explain such a gestalt shift in vision. The process of *unfreezing* is essentially one of overcoming the natural defense mechanisms, the established "mental set" of how an industry is supposed to operate, to realize that things have changed fundamentally. The old assumptions no longer hold. Effective managers, especially effective strategic managers, are supposed to scan their environments continually, looking for such changes. But doing so continuously, or worse, trying to use technique to do so, may have exactly the opposite effect. So much attention may be given to strategic monitoring when nothing important is happening that when something really does, it may not even be noticed. The trick, of course, is to pick out the discontinuities that matter, and as noted earlier that seems to have more to do with informed intuition than anything else.

A second step in unfreezing is the willingness to step into the void, so to speak, for the leader to shed his or her conventional notions of how a business is supposed to function. The leader must above all avoid premature closure—seizing on a new thrust before it has become clear what its signals really mean. That takes a special kind of management, one able to live with a good deal of uncertainty and discomfort. "There is a period of confusion," Nadler told us, "you sleep on it . . . start looking for patterns . . . become an information hound, searching for [explanations] everywhere."

Strategic *change* of this magnitude seems to require a shift in mind-set before a new strategy can be conceived. And the thinking is fundamentally conceptual and inductive, probably stimulated (as in this case) by just one or two key insights. Continuous bombardment of facts, opinions, problems, and so on may prepare the mind for the shift, but it is the sudden *insight* that is likely to drive the synthesis—to bring all the disparate elements together in one "eureka"-type flash.

Once the strategist's mind is set, assuming he or she has read the new situation correctly and has not closed prematurely, then the *refreezing* process begins. Here the object is not to read the situation, at least not in a global sense, but in effect to block it out. It is a time to work out the consequences of the new strategic vision.

It has been claimed that obsession is an ingredient in effective organizations (Peters, 1980). Only for the period of refreezing would we agree, when the organization must focus on the pursuit of the new orientation—the new mind-set—with full vigor. A management that was open and divergent in its thinking must now become closed and convergent. But that means that the uncomfortable period of uncertainty has passed, and people can now get down to the exciting task of accomplishing something new. Now the organization knows where it is going; the object of the exercise is to get there using all the skills at its command, many of them formal and analytic. Of course, not everyone accepts the new vision. For those steeped in old strategies, *this* is the period of discomfort, and they can put up considerable resistance, forcing the leader to make greater use of his or her formal powers and political skills. Thus, refreezing of the leader's mind-set often involves the unfreezing, changing, and refreezing of the organization itself! But when the structure is simple, as it is in the entrepreneurial organization, that problem is relatively minor.

LEADERSHIP TAKING PRECEDENCE IN THE ENTREPRENEURIAL CONFIGURATION

To conclude, entrepreneurship is very much tied up with the creation of strategic vision, often with the attainment of a new concept. Strategies can be characterized as largely deliberate, since they reside in the intentions of a single leader. But being largely personal as well, the details of those strategies can emerge as they develop. In fact, the vision can change too. The leader can adapt en route, can learn, which means new visions can emerge too, sometimes, as we have seen, rather quickly.

In the entrepreneurial organization, as shown in Figure 2, the focus of attention is on the leader. The organization is malleable and responsive to that person's initiatives, while the environment remains benign for the most part, the result of the leader's selecting (or "enacting") the correct niche for his or her organization. The environment can, of course, flare up occasionally to challenge the organization, and then the leader must adapt, perhaps seeking out a new and more appropriate niche in which to operate.

SOME ISSUES ASSOCIATED WITH THE ENTREPRENEURIAL ORGANIZATION

We conclude briefly with some broad issues associated with the entrepreneurial organization. In this configuration, decisions concerning both strategy and operations tend to be centralized in the office of the chief executive. This centralization has the important advantage of rooting strategic response in deep knowledge of the operations. It also allows for flexibility and adaptability: Only one person need act. But this same executive can get so enmeshed in operating problems that he or she loses sight of strategy; alternatively, he or she may become so enthusiastic about strategic opportunities that the more routine operations can wither for lack of attention and eventually pull down the whole organization. Both are frequent occurrences in entrepreneurial organizations.

This is also the riskiest of organizations, hinging on the activities of one individual. One heart attack can literally wipe out the organization's prime means of coordination. Even a leader in place can be risky. When change becomes necessary, everything hinges on the chief's response to it. If he or she resists, as is not uncommon where that person developed the existing strategy in the first place, then the organization may have no means to adapt. Then the great strength of the entrepreneurial organization—the vision of its leader plus its capacity to respond quickly—becomes its chief liability.

Another great advantage of the entrepreneurial organization is its sense of mission. Many people enjoy working in a small, intimate organization where the leader—often charismatic—knows where he or she is taking it. As a result, the organization tends to grow rapidly, with great enthusiasm. Employees can develop a solid identification with such an organization.

But other people perceive this configuration as highly restrictive. Because one person calls all the shots, they feel not like the participants on an exciting journey, but like cattle being led to market for someone else's benefit. In fact, the broadening of democratic norms into the sphere of organizations has rendered the entrepreneurial organization unfashionable in some quarters of contemporary society. It has been described as paternalistic and sometimes autocratic, and accused of concentrating too much power at the top. Certainly, without countervailing powers in the organization the chief executive can easily abuse his or her authority.

Perhaps the entrepreneurial organization is an anachronism in societies that call themselves democratic. Yet there have always been such organizations, and there always will be. This was probably the only structure known to those who first discovered the benefits of coordinating their activities in some formal way. And it probably reached its heyday in the era of the great American trusts of the late nineteenth century, when powerful entrepreneurs personally controlled huge empires. Since then, at least in Western society, the entrepreneurial organization has been on the decline. Nonetheless, it remains a prevalent and important configuration, and will continue to be so as long as society faces the conditions that require it: the prizing of entrepreneurial initiative and the resultant encouragement of new organizations, the need for small and informal organizations in some spheres and of strong personalized leadership despite larger size in others, and the need periodically to turn around ailing organizations of all types.

BY MICHAEL E. PORTER

■ Emerging industries are newly formed or reformed industries that have been created by technological innovations, shifts in relative cost relationships, emergence of new consumer needs, or other economic and sociological changes that elevate a new product or service to the level of a potentially viable business opportunity. . . .

The essential characteristic of an emerging industry from the viewpoint of formulating strategy is that there are no rules of the game. The competitive problem in an emerging industry is that all the rules must be established such that the firm can cope with and prosper under them.

THE STRUCTURAL ENVIRONMENT

Although emerging industries can differ a great deal in their structures, there are some common structural factors that seem to characterize many industries in this stage of their development. Most of them relate either to the absence of established bases for competition or other rules of the game or to the initial small size and newness of the industry.

COMMON STRUCTURAL CHARACTERISTICS
Technological Uncertainty
There is usually a great deal of uncertainty about the technology in an emerging industry: What product configuration will ultimately prove to be the best? Which production technology will prove to be the most efficient? . . .

Strategic Uncertainty
. . . No "right" strategy has been clearly identified, and different firms are groping with different approaches to product/market positioning, marketing, servicing, and so on, as well as betting on different product configurations or production technologies. . . . Closely related to this problem, firms often have poor information about competitors, characteristics of customers, and industry conditions in the emerging phase. No one knows who all the competitors are, and reliable industry sales and market share data are often simply unavailable, for example.

High Initial Costs but Steep Cost Reduction
Small production volume and newness usually combine to produce high costs in the emerging industry relative to those the industry can potentially achieve. . . . Ideas come rapidly in terms of improved procedures, plant layout, and so on, and employees achieve major gains in productivity as job familiarity increases. Increasing sales make major additions to the scale and total accumulated volume of output produced by firms. . . .

Embryonic Companies and Spin-Offs
The emerging phase of the industry is usually accompanied by the presence of the greatest proportion of newly formed companies (to be contrasted with newly formed units of established firms) that the industry will ever experience. . . .

First-Time Buyers

Buyers of the emerging industry's product or service are inherently first-time buyers. The marketing task is thus one of inducing substitution, or getting the buyer to purchase the new product or service instead of something else. . . .

Short Time Horizon

In many emerging industries the pressure to develop customers or produce products to meet demand is so great that bottlenecks and problems are dealt with expediently rather than as a result of an analysis of future conditions. At the same time, industry conventions are often born out of pure chance. . . .

Subsidy

In many emerging industries, especially those with radical new technology or that address areas of societal concern, there may be subsidization of early entrants. Subsidy may come from a variety of government and nongovernment sources. . . . Subsidies often add a great degree of instability to an industry, which is made dependent on political decisions that can be quickly reversed or modified. . . .

EARLY MOBILITY BARRIERS

In an emerging industry, the configuration of mobility barriers is often predictably different from that which will characterize the industry later in its development. Common early barriers are the following:

- proprietary technology
- access to distribution channels
- access to raw materials and other inputs (skilled labor) of appropriate cost and quality
- cost advantages due to experience, made more significant by the technological and competitive uncertainties
- risk, which raises the effective opportunity cost of capital and thereby effective capital barriers.

. . . The nature of the early barriers is a key reason why we observe newly created companies in emerging industries. The typical early barriers stem less from the need to command massive resources than from the ability to bear risk, be creative technologically, and make forward-looking decisions to garner input supplies and distribution channels. . . . There may be some advantages to late entry, however. . . .

STRATEGIC CHOICES

Formulation of strategy in emerging industries must cope with the uncertainty and risk of this period of an industry's development. The rules of the competitive game are largely undefined, the structure of the industry unsettled and probably changing, and competitors hard to diagnose. Yet all these factors have another side—the emerging phase of an industry's development is probably the period when the strategic degrees of freedom are the greatest and when the leverage from good strategic choices is the highest in determining performance.

Shaping Industry Structure

The overriding strategic issue in emerging industries is the ability of the firm to shape industry structure. Through its choices, the firm can try to set the rules of the game in areas like product policy, marketing approach, and pricing strategy. . . .

Externalities in Industry Development

In an emerging industry, a key strategic issue is the balance the firm strikes between industry advocacy and pursuing its own narrow self-interest. Because of potential problems with industry image, credibility, and confusion of buyers . . . in the emerging phase the firm is in part dependent on others in the industry for its own success. The overriding problem for the industry is inducing substitution and attracting first-time buyers, and it is usually in the firm's interest during this phase to help promote standardization, police substandard quality and fly-by-night producers, and present a consistent front to suppliers, customers, government, and the financial community. . . .

It is probably a valid generalization that the balance between industry outlook and firm outlook must shift in the direction of the firm as the industry begins to achieve significant penetration. Sometimes firms who have taken very high profiles as industry spokespersons, much to their and the industry's benefit, fail to recognize that they must shift their orientation. As a result, they can be left behind as the industry matures. . . .

Changing Role of Suppliers and Channels

Strategically, the firm in an emerging industry must be prepared for a possible shift in the orientation of its suppliers and distribution channels as the industry grows in size and proves itself. Suppliers may become increasingly willing (or can be forced) to respond to the industry's special needs in terms of varieties, service, and delivery. Similarly, distribution channels may become more receptive to investing in facilities, advertising, and so forth in partnership with the firms. Early exploitation of these changes in orientation can give the firm strategic leverage.

Shifting Mobility Barriers

As outlined earlier . . . the early mobility barriers may erode quickly in an emerging industry, often to be replaced by very different ones as the industry grows in size and as the technology matures. This factor has a number of implications. The most obvious is that the firm must be prepared to find new ways to defend its position and must not rely solely on things like proprietary technology and a unique product variety on which it has succeeded in the past. Responding to shifting mobility barriers may involve commitments of capital that far exceed those that have been necessary in the early phases.

Another implication is that the *nature of entrants* into the industry may shift to more established firms attracted to the larger and increasingly proven (less risky) industry, often competing on the basis of the newer forms of mobility barriers, like scale and marketing clout. . . .

TIMING ENTRY

A crucial strategic choice for competing in emerging industries is the appropriate timing of entry. Early entry (or pioneering) involves high risk but may involve otherwise low entry barriers and can offer a large return. Early entry is appropriate when the following general circumstances hold:

- Image and reputation of the firm are important to the buyer, and the firm can develop an enhanced reputation by being a pioneer.
- Early entry can initiate the learning process in a business in which the learning curve is important, experience is difficult to imitate, and it will not be nullified by successive technological generations.
- Customer loyalty will be great, so that benefits will accrue to the firm that sells to the customer first.
- Absolute cost advantages can be gained by early commitment to supplies of raw materials, distribution channels, and so on. . . .

Tactical Moves

The problems limiting development of an emerging industry suggest some tactical moves that may improve the firm's strategic position:

- Early commitments to suppliers of raw materials will yield favorable priorities in times of shortages.
- Financing can be timed to take advantage of a Wall Street love affair with the industry if it happens, even if financing is ahead of actual needs. This step lowers the firm's cost of capital. . . .

The choice of which emerging industry to enter is dependent on the outcome of a predictive exercise such as the one described above. An emerging industry is attractive if its ultimate structure (not its *initial* structure) is one that is consistent with above-average returns and if the firm can create a defendable position in the industry in the long run. The latter will depend on its resources relative to the mobility barriers that will evolve.

Too often firms enter emerging industries because they are growing rapidly, because incumbents are currently very profitable, or because ultimate industry size promises to be large. These may be contributing reasons, but the decision to enter must ultimately depend on a structural analysis. . . .

READING 13.3   HOW ENTREPRENEURS CRAFT STRATEGIES THAT WORK*

BY AMAR BHIDE

- However popular it may be in the corporate world, a comprehensive analytical approach to planning doesn't suit most start-ups. Entrepreneurs typically lack the time and money to interview a representative cross section of potential customers, let alone analyze substitutes, reconstruct competitors' cost structures, or project alternative technology scenarios. In fact, too much analysis can be harmful; by the time an opportunity is investigated fully, it may no longer exist. A city map and restaurant guide on a CD may be a winner in January but worthless if delayed until December.

Interviews with the founders of 100 companies on the 1989 *Inc.* "500" list of the fastest growing private companies in the United States and recent research on more than 100 other thriving ventures by my MBA students suggest that many successful entrepreneurs spend little time researching and analyzing. . . . And those who do often have to scrap their strategies and start over. Furthermore, a 1990 National Federation of Independent Business study of 2,994 start-ups showed that founders who spent a long time in study, reflection, and planning were no more likely to survive their first three years than people who seized opportunities without planning. In fact, many corporations that revere comprehensive analysis develop a refined incapacity for seizing opportunities. Analysis can delay entry until it's too late or kill ideas by identifying numerous problems.

Yet all ventures merit some analysis and planning. Appearances to the contrary, successful entrepreneurs don't take risks blindly. Rather, they use a quick, cheap approach that represents a middle ground between planning paralysis and no planning at all. They don't expect perfection—even the most astute entrepreneurs have their share of false starts. Compared to typical corporate practice, however, the entrepreneurial approach is more economical and timely.

*Originally published as "How Entrepreneurs Craft Strategies that Work," in the *Harvard Business Review*, March–April 1994, pp. 150–161. Copyright © 1994 by the President and Fellows of Harvard College; all rights reserved. Reprinted with deletions by permission of the *Harvard Business Review*.

What are the critical elements of winning entrepreneurial approaches? Our evidence suggests three general guidelines for aspiring founders:

1. Screen opportunities quickly to weed out unpromising ventures.
2. Analyze ideas parsimoniously. Focus on a few important ideas.
3. Integrate action and analysis. Don't wait for all the answers, and be ready to change course.

SCREENING OUT LOSERS

Individuals who seek entrepreneurial opportunities usually generate lots of ideas. Quickly discarding those that have low potential frees aspirants to concentrate on the few ideas that merit refinement and study.

Screening out unpromising ventures requires judgment and reflection, not new data. The entrepreneur should already be familiar with the facts needed to determine whether an idea has prima facie merit. Our evidence suggests that new ventures are usually started to solve problems the founders have grappled with personally as customers or employees. . . . Companies like Federal Express, which grew out of a paper its founder wrote in college, are rare.

Profitable survival requires an edge derived from some combination of a creative idea and a superior capacity for execution. . . . The entrepreneur's creativity may involve an innovative product or a process that changes the existing order. Or the entrepreneur may have a unique insight about the course or consequence of an external change: the California gold rush, for example, made paupers of the thousands caught in the frenzy, but Levi Strauss started a company—and a legend—by recognizing the opportunity to supply rugged canvas and later denim trousers to prospectors.

But entrepreneurs cannot rely on just inventing new products or anticipating a trend. They must also execute well, especially if their concepts can be copied easily. For example, if an innovation cannot be patented or kept secret, entrepreneurs must acquire and manage the resource needed to build a brand name or other barrier that will deter imitators. Superior execution can also compensate for a me-too concept in emerging or rapidly growing industries where doing it quickly and doing it right are more important than brilliant strategy.

Ventures that obviously lack a creative concept or any special capacity to execute—the ex-consultant's scheme to exploit grandmother's cookie recipe, for instance—can be discarded without much thought. In other cases, entrepreneurs must reflect on the adequacy of their ideas and their capacities to execute them.

Successful start-ups don't need an edge on every front. The creativity of successful entrepreneurs varies considerably. Some implement a radical idea, some modify, and some show no originality. Capacity for execution also varies among entrepreneurs. Selling an industrial niche product doesn't call for the charisma that's required to pitch trinkets through infomercials. Our evidence suggests that there is no ideal entrepreneurial profile either: successful founders can be gregarious or taciturn, analytical or intuitive, good or terrible with details, risk averse or thrill seeking. They can be delegators or control freaks, pillars of the community or outsiders. In assessing the viability of a potential venture, therefore, each aspiring entrepreneur should consider three interacting factors:

1. Objectives of the Venture

Is the entrepreneur's goal to build a large, enduring enterprise, carve out a niche, or merely turn a quick profit? Ambitious goals require great creativity. Building a large enterprise quickly, either by seizing a significant share of an existing market or by creating a large new market, usually calls for a revolutionary idea. . . .

Requirements for execution are also stiff. Big ideas often necessitate big money and strong organizations. Successful entrepreneurs, therefore, require an evangelical ability to attract, retain, and balance the interests of investors, customers, employees, and suppliers for a seemingly outlandish vision, as well as the organizational and leadership skills to build a large, complex company quickly. In addition, the entrepreneur may require considerable technical know-how in deal making, strategic planning, managing overhead, and other business skills. The revolutionary entrepreneur, in other words, would appear to require almost superhuman qualities: ordinary mortals need not apply.

Consider Federal Express founder Fred Smith. His creativity lay in recognizing that customers would pay a significant premium for reliable overnight delivery and in figuring out a way to provide the service for them. Smith ruled out using existing commercial flights, whose schedules were designed to serve passenger traffic. Instead, he had the audacious idea of acquiring a dedicated fleet of jets and shipping all packages through a central hub that was located in Memphis.

As with most big ideas, the concept was difficult to execute. Smith, 28 years old at the time, had to raise $91 million in venture funding. The jets, the hub, operations in 25 states, and several hundred trained employees had to be in place before the company could open for business. And Smith needed great fortitude and skill to prevent the fledgling enterprise from going under: Federal Express lost over $40 million in its first three years. Some investors tried to remove Smith, and creditors tried to seize assets. Yet Smith somehow preserved morale and mollified investors and lenders while the company expanded its operations and launched national advertising and direct-mail campaigns to build market share.

In contrast, ventures that seek to capture a market niche, not transform or create an industry, don't need extraordinary ideas. Some ingenuity is necessary to design a product that will draw customers away from mainstream offerings and overcome the cost penalty of serving a small market. But features that are too novel can be a hindrance; a niche market will rarely justify the investment required to educate customers and distributors about the benefits of a radically new product. Similarly, a niche venture cannot support too much production or distribution innovation; unlike Federal Express, the Cape Cod Potato Company, for example, must work within the limits of its distributors and truckers.

And since niche markets cannot support much investment or overhead, entrepreneurs do not need the revolutionary's ability to raise capital and build large organizations. Rather, the entrepreneur must be able to secure others' resources on favorable terms and make do with less, building brand awareness through guerilla marketing and word of mouth instead of national advertising, for example.

Jay Boberg and Miles Copeland, who launched International Record Syndicate (IRS) in 1979, used a niche strategy, my students Elisabeth Bentel and Victoria Hackett found, to create one of the most successful new music labels in North America. Lacking the funds or a great innovation to compete against the major labels, Boberg and Miles promoted "alternative" music—undiscovered British groups like the buzzcocks and Skafish—which the major labels were ignoring because their potential sales were too small. And IRS used low-cost, alternative marketing methods to promote their alternative music. At the time, the major record labels had not yet realized that music videos on television could be used effectively to promote their products. Boberg, however, jumped at the opportunity to produce a rock show, "The Cutting Edge," for MTV. The show proved to be a hit with fans and an effective promotional tool for IRS. Before "The Cutting Edge," Boberg had to plead with radio stations to play his songs. Afterward, the MTV audience demanded that disc jockeys play the songs they had heard on the show.

2. Leverage Provided by External Change

Exploiting opportunities in a new or changing industry is generally easier than making waves in a mature industry. Enormous creativity, experience, and contacts are needed to take business away from competitors in a mature industry, where market forces have long shaken out weak technologies, strategies, and organizations.

But new markets are different. There start-ups often face rough-around-the-edges rivals, customers who tolerate inexperienced vendors and imperfect products, and opportunities to profit from shortages. Small insights and marginal innovations, a little skill or expertise (in the land of the blind, the one-eyed person is king), and the willingness to act quickly can go a long way. In fact, with great external uncertainty, customers and investors may be hesitant to back a radical product and technology until the environment settles down. Strategic choices in a new industry are often very limited; entrepreneurs have to adhere to the emerging standards for product features, components, or distribution channels.

The leverage provided by external change is illustrated by the success of numerous start-ups in hardware, software, training, retailing, and systems integration that emerged from the personal computer revolution of the 1980s. Installing or fixing a computer system is probably easier than repairing a car; but because people with the initiative or foresight to acquire the skill were scarce, entrepreneurs like Bohdan's Peter Zacharkiw built successful dealerships by providing what customers saw as exceptional service. . . . As one midwestern dealer told me, "We have a joke slogan around here: We aren't as incompetent as our competitors!"

Bill Gates turned Microsoft into a multibillion-dollar company without a breakthrough product by showing up in the industry early and capitalizing on the opportunities that came his way. Gates, then 19, and his partner Paul Allen, 21, launched Microsoft in 1975 to sell software they had created. By 1979, Microsoft had grown to 25 employees and $2.5 million in sales. Then in November 1980, IBM chose Microsoft to provide an operating system for its personal computer. Microsoft thereupon bought an operating system from Seattle Computer Products, which it modified into the now ubiquitous MS-DOS. The IBM name and the huge success of the 1-2-3 spreadsheet, which only ran on DOS computers, soon helped make Microsoft the dominant supplier of operating systems.

3. Basis of Competition: Proprietary Assets Versus Hustle

In some industries, such as pharmaceuticals, luxury hotels, and consumer goods, a company's profitability depends significantly on the assets it owns or controls—patents, location, or brands, for example. Good management practices like listening to customers, maintaining quality, and paying attention to costs, which can improve the profits of a going business, cannot propel a start-up over such structural barriers. Here a creative new technology, product, or strategy is a must.

Companies in fragmented service industries, such as investment management, investment banking, head hunting, or consulting cannot establish proprietary advantages easily but can nonetheless enjoy high profits by involving exceptional service tailored to client demands. Start-ups in those fields rely mainly on their hustle (Bhide, 1986). Successful entrepreneurs depend on personal selling skills, contacts, their reputations for expertise, and their ability to convince clients of the value of the services rendered. They also have the capacity for institution building—skills such as recruiting and motivating stellar professionals and articulating and reinforcing company values. Where there are few natural economies of scale, an entrepreneur cannot create a going concern out of a one-man-band or ad hoc ensemble without a lot of expertise in organizational development. . . .

GAUGING ATTRACTIVENESS

Entrepreneurs should also screen potential ventures for their attractiveness—their risks and rewards—compared to other opportunities. Several factors should be considered. Capital requirements, for example, matter to the entrepreneur who lacks easy access to financial markets. An unexpected need for cash because, say, one large customer is unable to make a timely payment may shut down a venture or force a fire sale of the founder's equity. Therefore, entrepreneurs should favor ventures that aren't capital intensive and have the profit margins to sustain rapid growth with internally generated funds. In a similar fashion, entrepreneurs should look for a high margin for error, ventures with simple operations and low fixed costs that are less likely to face a cash crunch because of factors such as technical delays, cost overruns, and slow buildup of sales.

Other criteria reflect the typical entrepreneur's inability to undertake multiple projects: an attractive venture should provide a substantial enough reward to compensate the entrepreneur's exclusive commitment to it. Shut-down costs should be low: the payback should be quick, or failure soon recognized so that the venture can be terminated without a significant loss of time, money, or reputation. And the entrepreneur should have the option to cash in, for example, by selling all or part of the equity. An entrepreneur locked into an illiquid business cannot easily pursue other opportunities and risks fatigue and burnout. . . .

Ventures must also fit what the individual entrepreneur values and wants to do. Surviving the inevitable disappointments and near disasters one encounters on the rough road to success requires a passion for the chosen business. . . .

Surprisingly, small endeavors often hold more financial promise then large ones. Often the founders can keep a larger share of the profits because they don't dilute their equity interest through multiple rounds of financings. But entrepreneurs must be willing to prosper in a backwater; dominating a neglected market segment is sometimes more profitable than intellectually stimulating or glamorous. Niche enterprises can also enter the "land of the living dead" because their market is too small for the business to thrive but the entrepreneur has invested too much effort to be willing to quit. . . .

PARSIMONIOUS PLANNING AND ANALYSIS

To conserve time and money, successful entrepreneurs minimize the resources they devote to researching their ideas. Unlike the corporate world, where foil mastery and completed staff work can make a career, the entrepreneur only does as much planning and analysis as seems useful and makes subjective judgment calls when necessary. . . .

In setting their analytical priorities, entrepreneurs must recognize that some critical uncertainties cannot be resolved through more research. For example, focus groups and surveys often have little value in predicting demand for products that are truly novel. At first, consumers had dismissed the need for copiers, for instance, and told researchers they were satisfied with using carbon paper. With issues like this, entrepreneurs have to resist the temptation of endless investigation and trust their judgment. . . .

Revenues are notoriously difficult to predict. At best, entrepreneurs may satisfy themselves that their novel product or service delivers considerably greater value than current offerings do; how quickly the product catches on is a blind guess. Leverage may be obtained, however, from analyzing how customers might buy and use the product or service. Understanding the purchase can help identify the right decision makers for the new offering. With Federal Express, for instance, it was important to go beyond the mailroom managers who traditionally bought delivery services. Understanding how products are used can also help by revealing obstacles that must be overcome before consumers can benefit from a new offering.

Visionary entrepreneurs must guard against making competitors rich from their work. Many concepts are difficult to prove but, once proven, easy to imitate. Unless the pioneer is protected by sustainable barriers to entry, the benefits of a hard-fought revolution can become a public good rather than a boon to the innovator. . . .

Entrepreneurs who hope to secure a niche face different problems: they often fail because the costs of serving a specialized segment exceed the benefits to customers. Entrepreneurs should therefore analyze carefully the incremental costs of serving a niche and take into account their lack of scale and the difficulty of marketing to a small, diffused segment. And especially if the cost disadvantage is significant, entrepreneurs should determine whether their offering provides a significant performance benefit. Whereas established companies can vie for share through line extensions or marginal tailoring of their products and services, the start-up must really wow its target customers. A marginally tastier cereal won't knock Kellogg's Cornflakes off supermarket shelves.

Inadequate payoffs also pose a risk for ventures that address small markets. For example, a niche venture that can't support a direct sales force may not generate enough commissions to attract an independent broker or manufacturer's rep. Entrepreneurs will eventually lose interest too if the rewards aren't commensurate with their efforts. Therefore, the entrepreneur should make sure that everyone who contributes can expect a high, quick, or sustainable return even if the venture's total profits are small.

Entrepreneurs who seek to leverage factors like changing technologies, customer preferences, or regulations should avoid extensive analysis. Research conducted under conditions of such turbulence isn't reliable, and the importance of a quick response precludes spending the time to make sure every detail is covered. . . .

Analyzing whether or not the rewards for winning are commensurate with the risks, however, can be a more feasible and worthwhile exercise. In some technology races, success is predictably short-lived. In the disk-drive industry, for example, companies that succeed with one generation of products are often leap-frogged when the next generation arrives. In engineering workstations, however, Sun enjoyed long-term gains from its early success because it established a durable architectural standard. If success is unlikely to be sustained, entrepreneurs should have a plan for making a good return while it lasts. . . .

INTEGRATING ACTION AND ANALYSIS

Standard operating procedure in large corporations usually makes a clear distinction between analysis and execution. In contemplating a new venture, managers in established companies face issues about its fit with ongoing activities. Does the proposed venture leverage corporate strengths? Will the resources and attention it requires reduce the company's ability to build customer loyalty and improve quality in core markets? These concerns dictate a deliberate, "trustee" approach: before they can launch a venture, managers must investigate an opportunity extensively, seek the counsel of people higher up, submit a formal plan, respond to criticisms by bosses and corporate staff, and secure a headcount and capital allocation.

Entrepreneurs who start with a clean slate, however, don't have to know all the answers before they act. In fact, they often can't easily separate action and analysis. The attractiveness of a new restaurant, for example, many depend on the terms of the lease; low rents can change the venture from a mediocre proposition into a money machine. But an entrepreneur's ability to negotiate a good lease cannot be easily determined from a general prior analysis; he or she must enter into a serious negotiation with a specific landlord for a specific property.

Acting before an opportunity is fully analyzed has many benefits. Doing something concrete builds confidence in oneself and in others. Key employees and investors will often follow the individual who has committed to action, for instance, by quitting a job, incorporating, or signing a lease. By taking a personal risk, the entrepreneur convinces other people that the venture *will* proceed, and they may believe that if they don't sign up, they could be left behind.

Early action can generate more robust, better informed strategies too. Extensive surveys and focus-group research about a concept can produce misleading evidence: slippage can arise between research and reality because the potential customers interviewed are not representative of the market, their enthusiasm for the concept wanes when they see the actual product, or they lack the authority to sign purchase orders. More robust strategies may be developed by first building a working prototype and asking customers to use it before conducting extensive market research.

The ability of individual entrepreneurs to execute quickly will naturally vary. Trial and error is less feasible with large-scale, capital-intensive ventures like Orbital Sciences, which had to raise over $50 million to build rockets for NASA, than with a consulting firm start-up. Nevertheless, some characteristics are common to an approach that integrates action and analysis:

Handling Analytical Tasks in Stages

Rather than resolve all issues at once, the entrepreneur does only enough research to justify the next action or investment. For example, an individual who has developed a new medical technology may first obtain crude estimates of market demand to determine whether it's worth seeing a patent lawyer. If the estimates and lawyer are encouraging, the individual may do more analysis to investigate the wisdom of spending money to obtain a patent. Several more iterations of analysis and action will follow before the entrepreneur prepares and circulates a formal business plan to venture capitalists.

Plugging Holes Quickly

As soon as any problems or risks show up, the entrepreneur begins looking for solutions. For example, suppose that an entrepreneur sees it will be difficult to raise capital. Rather than kill the idea, he or she thinks creatively about solving the problem. Perhaps the investment can be reduced by modifying technology to use more standard equipment that can be rented instead of bought. Or under the right terms, a customer might underwrite the risk by providing a large initial order. Or expectations and goals for growth might be scaled down, and a niche market could be tackled first. Except with obviously unviable ideas that can be ruled out through elementary logic, the purpose of analysis is not to find fault with new ventures or find reasons for abandoning them. Analysis is an exercise in what to do next more than what not to do.

Evangelical Investigation

Entrepreneurs often blur the line between research and selling. As one founder recalls, "My market research consisted of taking a prototype to a trade show and seeing if I could write orders." Software industry "beta sites" provide another example of simultaneous research and selling; customers actually pay to help vendors test early versions of their software and will often place larger orders if they are satisfied with the product.

From the beginning, entrepreneurs don't just seek opinions and information, they also look for commitment from other people. Entrepreneurs treat everyone whom they talk to as a potential customer, investor, employee, or supplier, or at least as a possible source of leads down the road. Even if they don't actually ask for an order, they take the time to build enough interest and rapport so they can come back later. This simultaneous listening and selling approach may not produce truly objective market research and statistically significant results. But the resource-constrained entrepreneur doesn't have much choice in the matter. Besides, in the initial stages, the deep knowledge and support of a few is often more valuable then broad, impersonal data.

Smart Arrogance

An entrepreneur's willingness to act on sketchy plans and inconclusive data is often sustained by an almost arrogant self-confidence. One successful high-tech entrepreneur likens his kind to "gamblers in a casino who know they are good at craps and are therefore likely to win. They believe: 'I'm smarter, more creative, and harder working than most people. With my unique and rare skills, I'm doing investors a favor by taking their money.' " Moreover, the entrepreneur's arrogance must stand the test of adversity. Entrepreneurs must have great confidence in their talent and ideas to persevere as customers stay away in droves, the product doesn't work, or the business runs out of cash.

But entrepreneurs who believe they are more capable or venturesome than others must also have the smarts to recognize their mistakes and to change their strategies as events unfold. Successful ventures don't always proceed in the direction on which they initially set out. A significant proportion develop entirely new markets, products, and sources of competitive advantage. Therefore, although perseverance and tenacity are valuable entrepreneurial traits, they must be complemented with flexibility and a willingness to learn. If prospects who were expected to place orders don't, the entrepreneur should consider reworking the concept. Similarly, the entrepreneur should also be prepared to exploit opportunities that didn't figure in the initial plan. . . .

The apparently sketchy planning and haphazard evolution of many successful ventures . . . doesn't mean that entrepreneurs should follow a ready-fire-aim approach. Despite appearances, astute entrepreneurs do analyze and strategize extensively. They realize, however that businesses cannot be launched like space shuttles, with every detail of the mission planned in advance. Initial analyses only provide plausible hypotheses, which must be tested and modified. Entrepreneurs should play with and explore ideas, letting their strategies evolve through a seamless process of guesswork, analysis, and action.

CHAPTER 14

Managing Maturity

In this chapter, we focus on what has historically been one of the more common contexts for organizations. Whether we refer to this by its form of operations (usually mass production or the mass provision of services), by the form of structure adopted (machine-like bureaucracy), by the type of environment it prefers (a stable one in a mature industry), or by the specific generic strategy often found there (low cost), the context tends to give rise to a certain relatively well-defined configuration.

Although this context has received bad press lately, don't think that it has gone away. Amidst all the talk of change, turbulence, and hypercompetition, this context remains common, indeed quite possibly still the most likely that a manager will encounter. Bureaucracy is alive, if not always well, we assure you!

The readings on what we shall refer to as the mature context cover these different aspects and examine some of the problems and opportunities of functioning in this realm. The first reading on the machine organization from Mintzberg's work describes the organization for this context as well as the environment in which it tends to be found and also investigates some of the social issues surrounding this particular form of organization. This reading also probes the nature of the strategy-making process in this context. Here we can see what happens when large organizations accustomed to stability suddenly have to change their strategies dramatically. The careful formal planning, on which they tend to rely so heavily in stable times, seems ill-suited to dealing with changes that may require virtual revolutions in their functioning. A section of this reading, thus, considers what the role of planners can be when their formal procedures fail to come to grips with the needs of strategy making.

A particular technique designed for use with this strategy and the mature context in general is the subject of the second reading. Called "Cost Dynamics: Scale and Experience Effects" and written by Derek Abell and John Hammond for a marketing textbook, it probes the "experience curve." Developed by the Boston Consulting Group some years ago, this technique became quite popular in the 1970s. Although its limitations are now widely recognized, it still has certain applications to firms operating in the mature context.

When machine-like, mature organizations do have to change, the next two readings explain how this can be done. James Q. Wilson of the Andreson School at University of California at Los Angeles has written a widely respected book entitled *Bureaucracy*. Here we reprint excerpts from the chapter on innovation. The book is about government, but as will become evident, the reading applies no less obviously to business or to mature organizations in any other sphere of activity. Wilson points out that the main reason that people in bureaucracy resist change is because they are supposed to: These organizations are designed for stability. But entrepreneurs do bring about changes by acting on the periphery, at least initially. Wilson also points out in this sophisticated piece that changes can be bad as well as good, and he discusses most insightfully what role executives can play in effective change processes.

Andrew Boynton of IMD in Switzerland, Bart Victor of the Own Graduate School of Management in Vanderbilt University, and Joseph B. Pine, founder of Ohio-based Strategic Horizons LLP, in a sense pick up where Wilson leaves off by probing more specifically into how stable, mature organizations faced with changes in products or process adapt. Although some may shift their whole approach radically to structures of more perpetual innovation (the subject of Chapter 16), this article describes ones that adapt less radically and so really remain in this context. They move either to mass customization or to continuous process improvement, although the best ones, the authors argue, move to a combination of the two.

USING THE CASE STUDIES

Many of the cases struggle with the consequences of longevity, both in terms of absolute age and also in terms of product and industry maturity. Lufthansa and NBC examine how companies of approximately the same age deal with the need to regain their vitality. In a sense they both struggle against what Mr. Kawamoto calls in the Honda case "the big company disease." All these organizations are to some extent an example of Mintzberg's "Machine Organization." Firms such as Intel, however, although perhaps more in the context of innovation, still have to manage maturity, which involves attaining efficiency through the use of scale and experience effects, as described in the reading by Abell and Hamond. At the same time, Intel has had to reconcile scale efficiencies with the need to manage technological discontinuities. Wilson's discussion of "Innovation in Bureaucracy" and Boynton, Victor, and Pine's analysis go a long way toward explaining how Intel addresses this problem.

**BY HENRY
MINTZBERG**

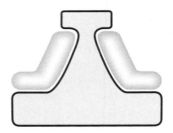

A national post office, a custodial prison, an airline, a giant automobile company, even a small security agency—all these organizations appear to have a number of characteristics in common. Above all, their operating work is routine, the greatest part of it rather simple and repetitive; as a result, their work processes are highly standardized. These characteristics give rise to the machine organizations of our society, structures fine-tuned to run as integrated, regulated, highly bureaucratic machines.

**THE BASIC
STRUCTURE**

A clear configuration of the attributes has appeared consistently in the research: highly specialized, routine operating tasks; very formalized communication throughout the organization; large-size operating units; reliance on the functional basis for grouping tasks; relatively centralized power for decision making; and an elaborate administrative structure with a sharp distinction between line and staff.

THE OPERATING CORE AND ADMINISTRATION

The obvious starting point is the operating core, with its highly rationalized work flow. This means that the operating tasks are made simple and repetitive, generally requiring a minimum of skill and training, the latter often taking only hours, seldom more than a few weeks, and usually in-house. This in turn results in narrowly defined jobs and an emphasis on the standardization of work processes for coordination, with activities highly formalized. The workers are left with little discretion, as are their supervisors, who can therefore handle very large spans of control.

To achieve such high regulation of the operating work, the organization has need for an elaborate administrative structure—fully developed middle-line hierarchy and technostructure—but the two clearly distinguished.

The managers of the middle line have three prime tasks. One is to handle the disturbances that arise in the operating core. The work is so standardized that when things fall through the cracks, conflict flares, because the problems cannot be worked out informally. So it falls to managers to resolve them by direct supervision. Indeed, many problems get bumped up suc-

---

*Adapted from *The Structure of Organizations* (Prentice Hall, 1979), Chap. 18 on "The Machine Bureaucracy"; also *Power In and Around Organizations* (Prentice Hall, 1983), Chaps. 18 and 19 on "The Instrument" and "The Closed System"; the material on strategy formation from "Patterns in Strategy Formation," *Management Science* (1978); "Does Planning Impede Strategic Thinking? Tracking the Strategies of Air Canada, from 1937–1976" (coauthored with Pierre Brunet and Jim Waters), in R. B. Lamb and P. Shrivastava, eds., *Advances in Strategic Management*, Volume IV (JAI press, 1986); and "The Mind of the Strategist(s)" (coauthored with Jim Waters), in S. Srivastva, ed., *The Executive Mind* (Jossey-Bass, 1983); the section on the role of planning, plans, and planners is drawn from a book in progress on strategic planning. A chapter similar to this appeared in *Mintzberg on Management: Inside Our Strange World of Organizations* (Free Press, 1989).

cessive steps in the hierarchy until they reach a level of common supervision where they can be resolved by authority (as with a dispute in a company between manufacturing and marketing that may have to be resolved by the chief executive). A second task of the middle-line managers is to work with the staff analysts to incorporate their standards down into the operating units. And a third task is to support the vertical flows in the organization—the elaboration of action plans flowing down the hierarchy and the communication of feedback information back up.

The technostructure must also be highly elaborated. In fact this structure was first identified with the rise of technocratic personnel in early-nineteenth-century industries such as textiles and banking. Because the machine organization depends primarily on the standardization of its operating work for coordination, the technostructure—which houses the staff analysts who do the standardizing—emerges as the key part of the structure. To the line managers may be delegated the formal authority for the operating units, but without the standardizers—the cadre of work-study analysts, schedulers, quality control engineers, planners, budgeters, accountants, operations researchers, and many more—these structures simply could not function. Hence, despite their lack of formal authority, considerable informal power rests with these staff analysts, who standardize everyone else's work. Rules and regulations permeate the entire system: The emphasis on standardization extends well beyond the operating core of the machine organization, and with it follows the analysts' influence.

A further reflection of this formalization of behavior are the sharp divisions of labor all over the machine organization. Job specialization in the operating core and the pronounced formal distinction between line and staff have already been mentioned. In addition, the administrative structure is clearly distinguished from the operating core; unlike the entrepreneurial organization, here managers seldom work alongside operators. And they themselves tend to be organized along functional lines, meaning that each runs a unit that performs a single function in the chain that produces the final outputs. Figure 1 shows this, for example, in the organigram of a large steel company, traditionally machinelike in structure.

All this suggests that the machine organization is a structure with an obsession—namely, control. A control mentality pervades it from top to bottom. At the bottom, consider how a Ford Assembly Division general foreman described his work:

> I refer to my watch all the time. I check different items. About every hour I tour my line. About six thirty, I'll tour labor relations to find out who is absent. At seven, I hit the end of the line. I'll check paint, check my scratches and damage. Around ten I'll start talking to all the foremen. I make sure they're all awake. We can't have no holes, no nothing.

And at the top, consider the words of a chief executive:

> When I was president of this big corporation, we lived in a small Ohio town, where the main plant was located. The corporation specified who you could socialize with, and on what level. (His wife interjects: "Who were the wives you could play bridge with.") In a small town they didn't have to keep check on you. Everybody knew. There are certain sets of rules. (Terkel, 1972: 186, 406)

The obsession with control reflects two central facts about these organizations. First, attempts are made to eliminate all possible uncertainty, so that the bureaucratic machine can run smoothly, without interruption, the operating core perfectly sealed off from external influence. Second, these are structures ridden with conflict; the control systems are required to contain it. The problem in the machine organization is not to develop an open atmosphere where people can talk the conflicts out, but to enforce a closed, tightly controlled one where the work can get done despite them.

The obsession with control also helps to explain the frequent proliferation of support staff in these organizations. Many of the staff services could be purchased from outside suppliers. But that would expose the machine organization to the uncertainties of the open market. So it "makes" rather than "buys," that is, it envelops as many of the support services as it can within its own structure in order to control them, everything from the cafeteria in the factory to the law office at headquarters.

FIGURE 1 ORGANIGRAM OF A LARGE STEEL COMPANY

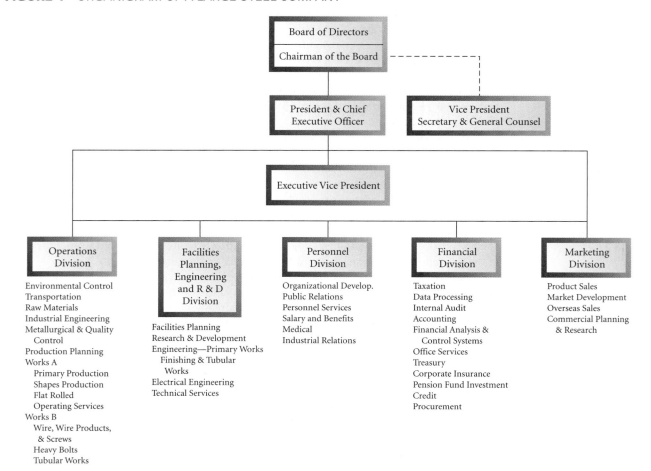

THE STRATEGIC APEX

The managers at the strategic apex of these organizations are concerned in large part with the fine-tuning of their bureaucratic machines. Theirs is a perpetual search for more efficient ways to produce the given outputs.

But not all is strictly improvement of performance. Just keeping the structure together in the face of its conflicts also consumes a good deal of the energy of top management. As noted, conflict is not resolved in the machine organization; rather it is bottled up so that the work can get done. And as in the case of a bottle, the cork is applied at the top: Ultimately, it is the top managers who must keep the lid on the conflicts through their role of handling disturbances. Moreover, the managers of the strategic apex must intervene frequently in the activities of the middle line to ensure that coordination is achieved there. The top managers are the only generalists in the structure, the only managers with a perspective broad enough to see all the functions.

All this leads us to the conclusion that considerable power in the machine organization rests with the managers of the strategic apex. These are, in other words, rather centralized structures: The formal power clearly rests at the top; hierarchy and chain of authority are paramount concepts. But so also does much of the informal power, since that resides in knowledge, and only at the top of the hierarchy does the formally segmented knowledge of the organization come together.

Thus, our introductory figure shows the machine organization with a fully elaborated administrative and support structure—both parts of the staff component being focused on the operating core—together with large units in the operating core but narrower ones in the middle line to reflect the tall hierarchy of authority.

CONDITIONS OF THE MACHINE ORGANIZATION

Work of a machine bureaucratic nature is found, above all, in environments that are simple and stable. The work associated with complex environments cannot be rationalized into simple tasks, and that associated with dynamic environments cannot be predicted, made repetitive, and so standardized.

In addition, the machine configuration is typically found in mature organizations, large enough to have the volume of operating work needed for repetition and standardization, and old enough to have been able to settle on the standards they wish to use. These are the organizations that have seen it all before and have established standard procedures to deal with it. Likewise, machine organizations tend to be identified with technical systems that regulate the operating work, so that it can easily be programmed. Such technical systems cannot be very sophisticated or automated (for reasons that will be discussed later).

Mass production firms are perhaps the best-known machine organizations. Their operating work flows through an integrated chain, open at one end to accept raw materials, and after that functioning as a sealed system that processes them through sequences of standardized operations. Thus, the environment may be stable because the organization has acted aggressively to stabilize it. Giant firms in such industries as transportation, tobacco, and metals are well known for their attempts to influence the forces of supply and demand by the use of advertising, the development of long-term supply contacts, sometimes the establishment of cartels. They also tend to adopt strategies of "vertical integration," that is, extend their production chains at both ends, becoming both their own suppliers and their own customers. In that way they can bring some of the forces of supply and demand within their own planning processes.

Of course, the machine organization is not restricted to large, or manufacturing, or even private enterprise organizations. Small manufacturers—for example, producers of discount furniture or paper products—may sometimes prefer this structure because their operating work is simple and repetitive. Many service firms use it for the same reason, such as banks or insurance companies in their retailing activities. Another condition often found with machine organizations is external control. Many government departments, such as post offices and tax collection agencies, are machine bureaucratic not only because their operating work is routine but also because they must be accountable to the public for their actions. Everything they do—treating clients, hiring employees, and so on—must be seen to be fair, and so they proliferate regulations.

Since control is the forte of the machine bureaucracy, it stands to reason that organizations in the business of control—regulatory agencies, custodial prisons, police forces—are drawn to this configuration, sometimes in spite of contradictory conditions. The same is true for the special need for safety. Organizations that fly airplanes or put out fires must minimize the risks they take. Hence they formalize their procedures extensively to ensure that they are carried out to the letter. A fire crew cannot arrive at a burning house and then turn to the chief for orders or discuss informally who will connect the hose and who will go up the ladder.

MACHINE ORGANIZATIONS AS INSTRUMENTS AND CLOSED SYSTEMS

Control raises another issue about machine organizations. Being so pervasively regulated, they themselves can easily be controlled externally, as the *instruments* of outside influencers. In contrast, however, their obsession with control runs not only up the hierarchy but beyond, to control of their own environments, so that they can become *closed systems* immune to external influence. From the perspective of power, the instrument and the closed system constitute two main types of machine organizations.

In our terms, the instrument form of machine organization is dominated by one external influencer or by a group of them acting in concert. In the "closely held" corporation, the dominant influencer is the outside owner; in some prisons, it is a community concerned with the custody rather than the rehabilitation of prisoners.

Outside influencers render an organization their instrument by appointing the chief executive, charging that person with the pursuit of clear goals (ideally quantifiable, such as return on investment or prisoner escape measures), and then holding the chief responsible for performance. That way outsiders can control an organization without actually having to manage it. And such control, by virtue of the power put in the hands of the chief executive and the numerical nature of the goals, acts to centralize and bureaucratize the internal structure, in other words, to drive it to the machine form.

In contrast to this, Charles Perrow, the colorful and outspoken organizational sociologist, does not quite see the machine organization as anyone's instrument:

> Society is adaptive to organizations, to the large, powerful organizations controlled by a few, often overlapping, leaders. To see these organizations as adaptive to a "turbulent," dynamic, very changing environment is to indulge in fantasy. The environment of most powerful organizations is well controlled by them, quite stable, and made up of other organizations with similar interests, or ones they control. (1972: 199).

Perrow is, of course, describing the closed system form of machine organization, the one that uses its bureaucratic procedures to seal itself off from external control and control others instead. It controls not only its own people but its environment as well: perhaps its suppliers, customers, competitors, even government and owners too.

Of course, autonomy can be achieved not only by controlling others (for example, buying up customers and suppliers in so-called vertical integration) but simply by avoiding the control of others. Thus, for example, closed system organizations sometimes form cartels with ostensible competitors or, less blatantly, diversify markets to avoid dependence on particular customers, finance internally to avoid dependence on particular financial groups, and even buy back their own shares to weaken the influence of their own owners. Key to being a closed system is to ensure wide dispersal, and therefore pacification, of all groups of potential external influence.

What goals does the closed system organization pursue? Remember that to sustain centralized bureaucracy the goals should be operational, ideally quantifiable. What operational goals enable an organization to serve itself, as a system closed to external influence? The most obvious answer is growth. Survival may be an indispensable goal and efficiency a necessary one, but beyond those what really matters here is making the system larger. Growth serves the system by providing greater rewards for its insiders—bigger empires for managers to run or fancier private jets to fly, greater programs for analysts to design, even more power for unions to wield by virtue of having more members. (The unions may be external influencers, but the management can keep them passive by allowing them more of the spoils of the closed system.) Thus the classic closed system machine organization, the large, widely held industrial corporation, has long been described as oriented far more to growth than to the maximization of profit per se (Galbraith, 1967).

Of course, the closed system form of machine organization can exist outside the private sector too, for example in the fundraising agency that, relatively free to external control, becomes increasingly charitable to itself (as indicated by the plushness of its managers' offices), the agricultural or retail cooperative that ignores those who collectively own it, even government that becomes more intent on serving itself than the citizens for which it supposedly exists.

The communist state, at least up until very recently, seemed to fit all the characteristics of the closed system bureaucracy. It had no dominant external influencer (at least in the case of the Soviet Union, if not the other East European states, which were its "instruments"). And the population to which it is ostensibly responsible had to respond to its own plethora of rules and regulations. Its election procedures, traditionally offering a choice of one, were similar to those for the directors of the "widely held" Western corporation. The government's own structure was heavily bureaucratic, with a single hierarchy of authority and a very elaborate technostructure, ranging from state planners to KGB agents. (As James Worthy [1959: 77] noted, Frederick Taylor's "Scientific Management had its fullest flowering not in America but in Soviet Russia.") All significant resources were the property of the state—the collective system—not the individual. And, as in other closed systems, the administrators tend to take the lion's share of the benefits.

SOME ISSUES ASSOCIATED WITH THE MACHINE ORGANIZATION

No structure has evoked more heated debate than the machine organization. As Michel Crozier, one of its most eminent students, has noted,

> On the one hand, most authors consider the bureaucratic organization to be the embodiment of rationality in the modern world, and, as such, to be intrinsically superior to all other possible forms of organizations. On the other hand, many authors—often the same ones—consider it a sort of Leviathan, preparing the enslavement of the human race. (1964: 176)

Max Weber, who first wrote about this form of organization, emphasized its rationality; in fact, the word *machine* comes directly from his writings (see Gerth and Mills 1958). A machine is certainly precise; it is also reliable and easy to control; and it is efficient—at least when restricted to the job it has been designed to do. Those are the reasons many organizations are structured as machine bureaucracies. When an integrated set of simple, repetitive tasks must be performed precisely and consistently by human beings, this is the most efficient structure—indeed, the only conceivable one.

But in these same advantages of machinelike efficiency lie all the disadvantages of this configuration. Machines consist of mechanical parts; organizational structures also include human beings—and that is where the analogy breaks down.

HUMAN PROBLEMS IN THE OPERATING CORE

James Worthy, when he was an executive of Sears, wrote a penetrating and scathing criticism of the machine organization in his book *Big Business and Free Men*. Worthy traced the root of the human problems in these structures to the "scientific management" movement led by Frederick Taylor that swept America early in this century. Worthy acknowledged Taylor's contribution to efficiency, narrowly defined. Worker initiative did not, however, enter into his efficiency equation. Taylor's pleas to remove "all possible brain work" from the shop floor also removed all possible initiative from the people who worked there: the "machine has no will of its own. Its parts have no urge to independent action. Thinking, direction—even purpose—must be provided from outside or above." This had the "consequence of destroying the meaning of work itself," which has been "fantastically wasteful for industry and society," resulting in excessive absenteeism, high worker turnover, sloppy workmanship, costly strikes, and even outright sabotage (1959: 67, 79, 70). Of course, there are people who like to work in highly structured situations. But increasing numbers do not, at least not *that* highly structured.

Taylor was fond of saying, "In the past the man has been first; in the future the system must be first" (in Worthy 1959: 73). Prophetic words, indeed. Modern man seems to exist for his systems; many of the organizations he created to serve him have come to enslave him. The result is that several of what Victor Thompson (1961) has called "bureaupathologies"—dysfunctional behaviors of these structures—reinforce each other to form a vicious circle in the machine organization. The concentration on means at the expense of ends, the mistreatment of clients, the various manifestations of worker alienation—all lead to the tightening of controls on behavior. The implicit motto of the machine organization seems to be, "When in doubt, control." All problems have to be solved by the turning of the technocratic screws. But since that is what caused the bureaupathologies in the first place, increasing the controls serves only to magnify the problems, leading to the imposition of further controls, and so on.

COORDINATION PROBLEMS IN THE ADMINISTRATIVE CENTER

Since the operating core of the machine organization is not designed to handle conflict, many of the human problems that arise there spill up and over, into the administrative structure.

It is one of the ironies of the machine configuration that to achieve the control it requires, it must mirror the narrow specialization of its operating core in its administrative structure (for example, differentiating marketing managers from manufacturing managers, much as salesmen are differentiated from factory workers). This, in turn, means problems of communication and coordination. The fact is that the administrative structure of the machine organization is also ill suited to the resolution of problems through mutual adjustment. All the communication barriers in these structures—horizontal, vertical, status, line/staff—impede informal communication among managers and with staff people. "Each unit becomes jealous of its own prerogatives and finds ways to protect itself against the pressure or encroachments of others" (Worthy 1950: 176). Thus narrow functionalism not only impedes coordination; it also encourages the building of private empires, which tends to produce top-heavy organizations that can be more concerned with the political games to be won than with the clients to be served.

ADAPTATION PROBLEMS IN THE STRATEGIC APEX

But if mutual adjustment does not work in the administrative center—generating more political heat than cooperative light—how does the machine organization resolve its coordination problems? Instinctively, it tries standardization, for example, by tightening job descriptions or proliferating rules. But standardization is not suited to handling the nonroutine problems of the administrative center. Indeed, it only aggravates them, undermining the influence of the line managers and increasing the conflict. So to reconcile these coordination problems, the machine organization is left with only one coordinating mechanism, direct supervision from above. Specifically, nonroutine coordination problems between units are "bumped" up the line hierarchy until they reach a common level of supervision, often at the top of the structure. The result can be excessive centralization of power, which in turn produces a host of other problems. In effect, just as the human problems in the operating core become coordination problems in the administrative center, so too do the coordination problems in the administrative center become adaptation problems at the strategic apex. Let us take a closer look at these by concluding with a discussion of strategic change in the machine configuration.

STRATEGY FORMATION IN THE MACHINE ORGANIZATION	Strategy in the machine organization is supposed to emanate from the top of the hierarchy, where the perspective is broadest and the power most focused. All the relevant information is to be sent up the hierarchy, in aggregated, MIS-type form, there to be formulated into integrated strategy (with the aid of the technostructure). Implementation then follows, with the intended strategies sent down the hierarchy to be turned into successively more elaborated programs and action plans. Notice the clear division of labor assumed between the formulators at the top and the implementers down below, based on the assumption of perfectly deliberate strategy produced through a process of planning. That is the theory. The practice has been shown to be another matter. Drawing on our strategy research at McGill University, we shall consider first what planning really proved to be in one machinelike organization, how it may in fact have impeded strategic thinking in a sec-

ond, and how a third really did change its strategy. From there we shall consider the problems of strategic change in machine organizations and their possible resolution.

PLANNING AS PROGRAMMING IN A SUPERMARKET CHAIN

What really is the role of formal planning? Does it produce original strategies? Let us return to the case of Steinberg's in the later years of its founder, as large size drove this retailing chain toward the machine form, and as is common in that form, toward a planning mode of management at the expense of entrepreneurship.

One event in particular encouraged the start of planning at Steinberg's: the company's entry into capital markets in 1953. Months before it floated its first bond issue (stock, always nonvoting, came later), Sam Steinberg boasted to a newspaper reporter that "not a cent of any money outside the family is invested in the company." And asked about future plans, he replied: "Who knows? We will try to go everywhere there seems to be a need for us." A few months later he announced a $5 million debt issue and with it a $15 million five-year expansion program, one new store every two months for a total of thirty, the doubling of sales, new stores to average double the size of existing ones.

What happened in those ensuing months was Sam Steinberg's realization, after the opening of Montreal's first shopping center, that he needed to enter the shopping center business himself to protect his supermarket chain and that he could not do so with the company's traditional methods of short-term and internal financing. And, of course, no company is allowed to go to capital markets without a plan. You can't just say: "I'm Sam Steinberg and I'm good," though that was really the issue. In a "rational" society, you have to plan (or at least appear to do so).

But what exactly was that planning? One thing for certain: It did not formulate a strategy. Sam Steinberg already had that. What planning did was justify, elaborate, and articulate the strategy that already existed in Sam Steinberg's mind. Planning operationalized his strategic vision, programmed it. It gave order to that vision, imposing form on it to comply with the needs of the organization and its environment. Thus, planning followed the strategy-making process, which had been essentially entrepreneurial.

But its effect on that process was not incidental. By specifying and articulating the vision, planning constrained it and rendered it less flexible. Sam Steinberg retained formal control of the company to the day of his death. But his control over strategy did not remain so absolute. The entrepreneur, by keeping his vision personal, is able to adapt it at will to a changing environment. But by being forced to program it, the leader loses that flexibility. The danger, ultimately, is that the planning mode forces out the entrepreneurial one; procedure replaces vision. As its structure became more machinelike, Steinberg's required planning in the form of strategic programming. But that planning also accelerated the firm's transition toward the machine form of organization.

Is there, then, such a thing as "strategic planning"? I suspect not. To be more explicit, I do not find that major new strategies are formulated through any formal procedure. Organizations that rely on formal planning procedures to formulate strategies seem to extrapolate existing strategies, perhaps with marginal changes in them, or else copy the strategies of other organizations. This came out most clearly in another of our McGill studies.

PLANNING AS AN IMPEDIMENT TO STRATEGIC THINKING IN AN AIRLINE

From about the mid-1950s, Air Canada engaged heavily in planning. Once the airline was established, particularly once it developed its basic route structure, a number of factors drove it strongly to the planning mode. Above all was the need for coordination, both of flight schedules with aircraft, crews, and maintenance, and of the purchase of expensive aircraft with the structure of the route system. (Imagine someone calling out in the hangar: "Hey, Fred, this guy says he has two 747s for us; do you know who ordered them?") Safety was another factor.

The intense need for safety in the air breeds a mentality of being very careful about what the organization does on the ground, too. This is the airlines' obsession with control. Other factors included the lead times inherent in key decisions, such as ordering new airplanes or introducing new routes, the sheer cost of the capital equipment, and the size of the organization. You don't run an intricate system like an airline, necessarily very machinelike, without a great deal of formal planning.

But what we found to be the consequence of planning at Air Canada was the absence of a major reorientation of strategy during our study period (up to the mid-1970s). Aircraft certainly changed—they became larger and faster—but the basic route system did not, nor did markets. Air Canada gave only marginal attention, for example, to cargo, charter, and shuttle operations. Formal planning, in our view, impeded strategic thinking.

The problem is that planning, too, proceeds from the machine perspective, much as an assembly line or a conventional machine produces a product. It all depends on the decomposition of analysis: You split the process into a series of steps or components parts, specify each, and then by following the specifications in sequence you get the desired product. There is a fallacy in this, however. Assembly lines and conventional machines produce standardized products, while planning is supposed to produce a novel strategy. It is as if the machine is supposed to design the machine; the planning machine is expected to create the original blueprint—the strategy. To put this another way, planning is analysis oriented to decomposition, while strategy making depends on synthesis oriented to integration. That is why the term "strategic planning" has proved to be an oxymoron.

ROLES OF PLANNING, PLANS, PLANNERS

If planning does not create strategy, then what purpose does it serve? We have suggested a role above, which has to do with the programming of strategies already created in other ways. This is shown in Figure 2, coming out of a box labeled strategy formation—meant to represent what is to planning a mysterious "black box." But if planning is restricted to programming strategy, plans and planners nonetheless have other roles in play, shown in Figure 2 and discussed alongside that of planning itself.

Role of Planning

Why do organizations engage in formal planning? The answer seems to be: not to create strategies, but to program the strategies they already have, that is, to elaborate and operationalize the consequences of those strategies formally. We should really say that *effective* organizations so engage in planning, at least when they require the formalized implementation of their strategies. Thus strategy is not the *consequence* of planning but its starting point. Planning helps to translate the intended strategy into realized ones, taking the first step that leads ultimately to implementation.

This *strategic programming*, as it might properly be labeled, can be considered to involve a series of steps, namely the *codification* of given strategy, including its clarification and articulation, the *elaboration* of that strategy into substrategies, ad hoc action programs, and plans of

FIGURE 2
SPECIFIC ROLLS
OF PLANNERS

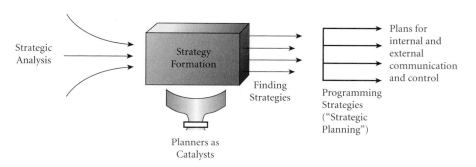

various kinds, and the *translation* of those substrategies, programs, and plans into routine budgets and objectives. In these steps, we see planning as an analytical process that takes over after the synthesis of strategic formation is completed.

Thus formal planning properly belongs in the *implementation* of strategy, not in its formulation. But it should be emphasized that strategic programming makes sense when viable intended strategies are available, in other words when the world is expected to hold still while these strategies unfold, so that formulation can logically precede implementation, and when the organization that does the implementing in fact requires clearly codified and elaborated strategies. In other circumstances, strategic programming can do organizations harm by preempting the flexibility that managers and others may need to respond to changes in the environment, or to their own internal processes of learning.

Roles of Plans

If planning is programming, then plans clearly serve two roles. They are a medium for communication and a device for control. Both roles draw on the analytical character of plans, namely, that they represent strategies in decomposed and articulated form, if not quantified then often at least quantifiable.

Why program strategy? Most obviously for coordination, to ensure that everyone in the organization pulls in the same direction, a direction that may have to be specified as precisely as possible. In Air Canada, to use our earlier example, that means linking the acquisition of new aircraft with the particular routes that are to be flown, and scheduling crews and planes to show up when the flights are to take off, and so on. Plans, as they emerge from strategic programming as programs, schedules, budgets, and so on, can be prime media to communicate not just strategic intention but also the role each individual must play to realize it.

Plans, as communication media, inform people of intended strategy and its consequences. But as control devices they can go further, specifying what role departments and individuals must play in helping to realize strategy and then comparing that with performance in order to feed control information back into the strategy-making process.

Plans can help to effect control in a number of ways. The most obvious is control of the strategy itself. Indeed what has long paraded under the label of "strategy planning" has probably had more to do with "strategic control" than many people may realize. Strategic control has to do with keeping organizations on their strategic tracks: to ensure the realization of intended strategy, its implementation as expected, with resources appropriately allocated. But there is more to strategic control than this. Another aspect includes the assessment of the realization of strategies in the first place, namely, whether the patterns realized corresponded to the intentions specified beforehand. In other words, strategic control must assess behavior as well as performance. Then the more routine and traditional form of control can come in to consider whether the strategies that were in fact realized proved effective.

Roles of Planners

Planners, of course, play key roles in planning (namely, strategic programming), and in using the resulting plans for purposes of communication and control. But many of the most important things planners do have little to do with planning or even plans per se. Three roles seem key here.

First, planners can play a role in finding strategies. This may seem curious, but if strategies really do emerge in organizations, the planners can help to identify the patterns that are becoming strategies, so that consideration can be given to formalizing them, that is, making them deliberate. Of course, finding the strategies of competitors—for assessment and possible modified adoption—is also important here.

Second, planners play the roles of analysts, carrying out ad hoc studies to feed into the black box of strategy making. Indeed, one could argue that this is precisely what Michael Porter proposes with his emphasis on industry and competitive analysis. The ad hoc nature of such studies should, however, be emphasized because they feed into a strategy-making process that is itself irregular, proceeding on no schedule and following no standard sequence of steps. Indeed, regularity in the planning process can interfere with strategic thinking, which must be flexible, responsive, and creative.

The third role of the planner is as a catalyst. This refers not to the traditional role long promoted in the literature of selling formal planning as some kind of religion, but to encourage strategic *thinking* throughout the organization. Here the planner encourages *informal* strategy making, trying to get others to think about the future in a creative way. He or she does not enter the black box of strategy making so much as ensure that the box is occupied with active line managers.

A Planner for Each Side of the Brain

We have discussed various roles for planning, plans, and planners, summarized around the black box of strategy formation in Figure 2. These roles suggest two different orientations for planners.

On one hand (so to speak), the planner must be a highly analytic, convergent type of thinker, dedicated to bringing order to the organization. Above all, this planner programs intended strategies and sees to it that they are communicated clearly and used for purposes of control. He or she also carries out studies to ensure that the managers concerned with strategy formation take into account the necessary hard data that they may be inclined to miss and that the strategies they formulate are carefully and systematically evaluated before they are implemented.

On the other hand, there is another type of planner, less conventional a creative, divergent thinker, rather intuitive, who seeks to open up the strategy-making process. As a "soft analyst," he or she tends to conduct "quick and dirty" studies, to find strategies in strange places, and to encourage others to think strategically. This planner is inclined toward the intuitive process identified with the brain's right hemisphere. We might call him or her a *left-handed planner*. Some organizations need to emphasize one type of planner, others the other type. But most complex organizations probably need some of both.

STRATEGIC CHANGE IN AN AUTOMOBILE FIRM

Given planning itself is not strategic, how does the planning-oriented machine bureaucracy change its strategy when it has to? Volkswagenwerk was an organization that had to. We interpreted its history from 1934 to 1974 as one long cycle of a single strategic perspective. The original "people's car," the famous "Beetle," was conceived by Ferdinand Porsche: the factory to produce it was built just before the war but did not go into civilian automobile production until after. In 1948, a man named Heinrich Nordhoff was given control of the devastated plant and began the rebuilding of it, as well as of the organization and the strategy itself, rounding out Porsche's original conception. The firm's success was dramatic.

By the late 1950s, however, problems began to appear. Demand in Germany was moving away from the Beetle. The typically machine-bureaucratic response was not to rethink the basic strategy—"it's okay" was the reaction—but rather to graft another piece onto it. A new automobile model was added, larger than the Beetle but with a similar no-nonsense approach to motoring, again air-cooled with the engine in the back. Volkswagenwerk added position but did not change perspective.

But that did not solve the basic problem, and by the mid-1960s the company was in crisis. Nordhoff, who had resisted strategic change, died in office and was replaced by a lawyer from outside the business. The company then underwent a frantic search for new models, designing, developing, or acquiring a whole host of them with engines in the front, middle, and rear; air and water cooled; front- and rear-wheel drive. To paraphrase the humorist Stephen

Leacock, Volkswagenwerk leaped onto its strategic horse and rode off in all directions. Only when another leader came in, a man steeped in the company and the automobile business, did the firm consolidate itself around a new strategic perspective, based on the stylish front-wheel drive, water-cooled designs of one of its acquired firms, and thereby turn its fortunes around.

What this story suggests, first of all, is the great force of bureaucratic momentum in the machine organization. Even leaving planning aside, the immense effort of producing and marketing a new line of automobiles locks a company into a certain posture. But here the momentum was psychological, too. Nordhoff, who had been the driving force behind the great success of the organization, became a major liability when the environment demanded change. Over the years, he too had been captured by bureaucratic momentum. Moreover, the uniqueness and tight integration of Volkswagenwerk's strategy—we labeled it *gestalt*—impeded strategic change. Change an element of a tightly integrated gestalt and it *dis*integrates. Thus does success eventually breed failure.

BOTTLENECK AT THE TOP

Why the great difficulty in changing strategy in the machine organization? Here we take up that question and show how changes generally have to be achieved in a different configuration, if at all.

As discussed earlier, unanticipated problems in the machine organization tend to get bumped up the hierarchy. When these are few, which mean conditions are relatively stable, things work smoothly enough. But in times of rapid change, just when new strategies are called for, the number of such problems magnifies, resulting in a bottleneck at the top, where senior managers get overloaded. And that tends either to impede strategic change or else to render it ill considered.

A major part of the problem is information. Senior managers face an organization decomposed into parts, like a machine itself. Marketing information comes up one channel, manufacturing information up another, and so on. Somehow it is the senior managers themselves who must integrate all that information. But the very machine bureaucratic premise of separating the administration of work from the doing of it means that the top managers often lack the intimate, detailed knowledge of issues necessary to effect such an integration. In essence, the necessary power is at the top of the structure, but the necessary knowledge is often at the bottom.

Of course, there is a machinelike solution to that problem too—not surprisingly in the form of a system. It is called a management information system, or MIS, and what it does is combine all the necessary information and package it neatly so that top managers can be informed about what is going on—the perfect solution for the overloaded executive. At least in theory.

Unfortunately, a number of real-world problems arise in the MIS. For one thing, in the tall administrative hierarchy of the machine organization, information must pass through many levels before it reaches the top. Losses take place at each one. Good news gets highlighted while bad news gets blocked on the way up. And "soft" information, so necessary for strategy information, cannot easily pass through, while much of the hard MIS-type information arrives only slowly. In a stable environment, the manager may be able to wait; in a rapidly changing one, he or she cannot. The president wants to be told right away that the firm's most important customer was seen playing golf yesterday with a main competitor, not to find out six months later in the form of a drop in a sales report. Gossip, hearsay, speculation—the softest kinds of information—warn the manager of impeding problems; the MIS all too often records for posterity ones that have already been felt. The manager who depends on an MIS in a changing environment generally finds himself or herself out of touch.

The obvious solution for top managers is to bypass the MIS and set up their own informal information systems, networks of contacts that bring them the rich, tangible, instant information they need. But that violates the machine organization's presuppositions of formality and respect for the chain of authority. Also, that takes the managers' time, the lack of which caused the bottleneck in the first place. So a fundamental dilemma faces the top managers of the machine organization as a result of its very own design: in times of change, when they most need the time to inform themselves, the system overburdens them with other pressures. They are thus reduced to acting superficially, with inadequate, abstract information.

THE FORMULATION/IMPLEMENTATION DICHOTOMY

The essential problem lies in one of the chief tenets of the machine organization, that strategy formation must be sharply separated from strategy implementation. One is thought out at the top, the other then acted out lower down. For this to work assume two conditions: first, that the formulator has full and sufficient information, and second, that the world will hold still, or at least change in predictable ways, during the implementation, so that there is no need for *re*formulation.

Now consider why the organization needs a new strategy in the first place. It is because its world has changed in an unpredictable way, indeed may continue to do so. We have just seen how the machine bureaucratic structure tends to violate the first condition—it misinforms the senior manager during such times of change. And when change continues in an unpredictable way (or at least the world unfolds in a way not yet predicted by an ill-informed management), then the second condition is violated too—it hardly makes sense to lock in by implementation a strategy that does not reflect changes in the world around it.

What all this amounts to is a need to collapse the formulation/implementation dichotomy precisely when the strategy of machine bureaucracy must be changed. This can be done in one of two ways.

In one case, the formulator implements. In other words, power is concentrated at the top, not only for creating the strategy but also for implementing it, step by step, in a personalized way. The strategist is put in close personal touch with the situation at hand (more commonly a strategist is appointed who has or can develop that touch) so that he or she can, on one hand, be properly informed and, on the other, control the implementation en route in order to reformulate when necessary. This, of course describes the entrepreneurial configuration, at least at the strategic apex.

In the other case, the implementers formulate. In other words, power is concentrated lower down, where the necessary information resides. As people who are naturally in touch with the specific situations at hand take individual actions—approach new customers, develop new products, et cetera—patterns form, in other words, strategies emerge. And this describes the innovative configuration, where strategic initiatives often originate in the grass roots of the organization, and then are championed by managers at middle levels who integrate them with one another or with existing strategies in order to gain their acceptance by senior management.

We conclude, therefore, that the machine configuration is ill suited to change its fundamental strategy, that the organization must in effect change configuration temporarily in order to change strategy. Either it reverts to the entrepreneurial form, to allow a single leader to develop vision (or proceed with one developed earlier), or else it overlays an innovative form on its conventional structure (for example, creates an informed network of lateral teams and task forces) so that the necessary strategies can emerge. The former can obviously function faster than the latter; that is why it tends to be used for drastic *turnaround*, while the latter tends to proceed by the slower process of *revitalization*. (Of course, quick turnaround may be necessary because there has been no slow revitalization.) In any event, both are characterized by a capacity to *learn*—that is the essence of the entrepreneurial and innovative configurations, in one case learning centralized for the simpler context, in the other, decentralized for the more complex one. The machine configuration is not so characterized.

This, however, should come as no surprise. After all, machines are specialized instruments, designed for productivity, not for adaptation. In Hunt's (1970) words, machine bureaucracies are performance systems, not problem-solving ones. Efficiency is their forte, not innovation. An organization cannot put blinders on its personnel and then expect peripheral vision. Managers here are rewarded for cutting costs and improving standards, not for taking risks and ignoring procedures. Change makes a mess of the operating systems: change one link in a carefully coupled system, and the whole chain must be reconceived. Why, then, should we be surprised when our bureaucratic machines fail to adapt?

Of course, it is fair to ask why we spend so much time trying to make them adapt. After all, when an ordinary machine becomes redundant, we simply scrap it, happy that it served us for as long and as well as it did. Converting it to another use generally proves more expensive than simply starting over. I suspect the same is often true for bureaucratic machines. But here, of course, the context is social and political. Mechanical parts don't protest, nor do displaced raw materials. Workers, suppliers, and customers do, however, protest the scrapping of organizations, for obvious reasons. But that the cost of this is awfully high in a society of giant machine organizations will be the subject of the final chapter of this book.

STRATEGIC REVOLUTIONS IN MACHINE ORGANIZATIONS

Machine organizations do sometimes change, however, at times effectively but more often it would seem at great cost and pain. The lucky ones are able to overlay an innovative structure for periodic revitalization, while many of the other survivors somehow manage to get turned around in entrepreneurial fashion.

Overall, the machine organizations seem to follow what my colleagues Danny Miller and Peter Friesen (1984) call a "quantum theory" of organization change. They pursue their set strategies through long periods of stability (naturally occurring or created by themselves as closed systems), using planning and other procedures to do so efficiently. Periodically these are interrupted by short bursts of change, which Miller and Friesen characterize as "strategic revolutions" (although another colleague, Mihaela Firsirotu [1985], perhaps better labels it "strategic turnaround as cultural revolution").

ORGANIZATION TAKING PRECEDENCE IN THE MACHINE ORGANIZATION

To conclude, as shown in Figure 3, it is organization—with its systems and procedures, its planning and its bureaucratic momentum—that takes precedence over leadership and environment in the machine configuration. Environment fits organization, either because the organization has slotted itself into a context that matches its procedures, or else because it has forced the environment to do so. And leadership generally falls into place too, supporting the organization, indeed often becoming part of its bureaucratic momentum.

This generally works effectively, though hardly nonproblematically, at least in times of stability. But in times of change, efficiency becomes ineffective and the organization will falter unless it can find a different way to organize for adaptation.

All of this is another way of saying that the machine organization is a configuration, a species, like the others, suited to its own context but ill suited to others. But unlike the others, it is the dominant configuration in our specialized societies. As long as we demand inexpensive and so necessarily standardized goods and services, and as long as people continue to be more efficient than real machines at providing them, and remain willing to do so, then the machine organization will remain with us—and so will all its problems.

FIGURE 3
ORGANIZATION TAKES
PRECEDENCE

Environment ← Leadership → ORGANIZATION

BY DEREK F. ABELL AND JOHN S. HAMMOND

■ Market share is one of the primary determinants of business profitability; other things being equal, businesses with a larger share of a market are more profitable than their smaller-share competitors. For instance, a study by the PIMS Program (Buzzell, Gale and Sultan, 1975) . . . found that, on average, a difference of 10 percentage points in market share is accompanied by a difference of about 5 points in pretax ROI ("pretax operating profits" divided by "long-term debt plus equity"). Additional evidence is that companies having large market shares in their primary product markets—such as General Motors, IBM, Gillette, Eastman Kodak, and Xerox—tend to be highly profitable.

An important reason for the increase in profitability with market share is that large-share firms usually have *lower costs*. The lower costs are due in part to economies of scale; for instance, very large plants cost less per unit of production to build and are often more efficient than smaller plants. Lower costs are also due in part to the so-called *experience effect*, whereby the cost of many (if not most) products declines by 10–30 percent each time a company's experience at producing and selling them doubles. In this context *experience* has a precise meaning: it is the cumulative number of units produced to date. Since at any point in time, businesses with large market shares typically (but not always) have more experience than their smaller-share competitors, they would be expected to have lower cost. . . .

This [reading] considers how costs decline due to scale and to experience, practical problems in analyzing the experience effect, strategic implications of scale and experience, and limitations of strategies based on cost reduction. . . .

SCALE EFFECT

As mentioned earlier, scale effect refers to the fact that large businesses have the potential to operate at lower unit costs than their smaller counterparts. The increased efficiency due to size is often referred to as "economy of scale"; it could equally be called "economy of size."

Most people think of economy of scale as a manufacturing phenomenon because large manufacturing facilities can be constructed at a lower cost per unit of capacity and can be operated more efficiently than smaller ones. . . .

Just as they cost less to build, large-scale plants have lower *operating* costs per unit of output. . . . While substantial in manufacturing, scale effect is also significant in other cost elements, such as marketing, sales, distribution, administration, R&D, and service. For instance, a chain with 30 supermarkets in a metropolitan area needs much less than three times as much advertising as a chain of 10 stores. . . . Economies of scale are also achieved with purchased items such as raw material and shipping. . . .

Although scale economies potentially exist in all cost elements of a business in both the short and long run, large size alone doesn't assure the benefits of scale. It is evident from the above illustrations that size provides an *opportunity* for scale economies; to achieve them requires strategies and actions consciously designed to seize the opportunity, especially with operating costs. . . .

EXPERIENCE EFFECT

The experience effect, whereby costs fall with cumulative production, is measurable and predictable; it has been observed in a wide range of products including automobiles, semiconductors, petrochemicals, long-distance telephone calls, synthetic fibers, airline transportation,

*Originally published in *Strategic Market Planning: Problems and Analytical Approaches* (Prentice Hall, 1979), Chap. 3. Copyright © Prentice Hall, 1979; reprinted with deletions by permission of the publisher.

FIGURE 1
A TYPICAL
EXPERIENCE CURVE
[85%]

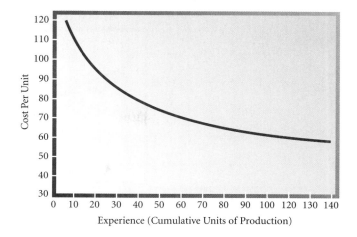

the cost of administering life insurance, and crushed limestone, to mention a few. Note that this list ranges from high technology to low technology products, service to manufacturing industries, consumer to industrial products, new to mature products, and process to assembly oriented products, indicating the wide range of applicability. . . .

. . . it is only comparatively recently that this phenomenon has been carefully measured and quantified; at first it was thought to apply only to the labor portion of *manufacturing* costs. . . . In the 1960s evidence mounted that the phenomenon was broader. Personnel from the Boston Consulting Group and others showed that each time cumulative volume of a product doubled, total value added costs—including administration, sales, marketing, distribution, and so on in addition to manufacturing—fell by a constant and predictable percentage. In addition, the costs of purchased items usually fell as suppliers reduced prices as their costs fell, due also to the experience effect. The relationship between costs and experience was called the *experience curve* (Boston Consulting Group, 1972).

An experience curve is plotted with the cumulative units produced on the horizontal axis, and cost per unit on the vertical axis. An "85%" experience curve is shown in Figure 1. The "85%" means that every time experience doubles, costs per unit drop to 85% of the original level. It is known as the *learning rate*. Stated differently, costs per unit decrease 15 percent for every doubling of cumulative production. For example, the cost of the 20th unit produced is about 85% of the cost of the 10th unit. . . .

An experience curve appears as a straight line when plotted on a double log paper (logarithmic scale for both the horizontal and vertical axes). Figure 2 shows the "85 percent" expe-

FIGURE 2
AN 85% EXPERIENCE
CURVE DISPLAYED ON
LOG-LOG SCALES

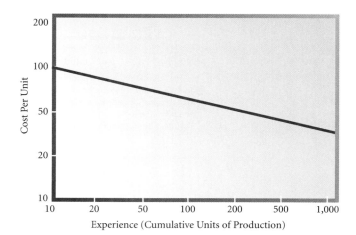

FIGURE 3
SOME SAMPLE
EXPERIENCE CURVES

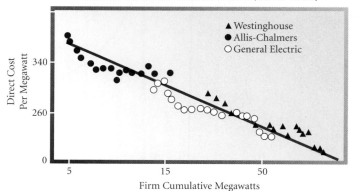

STEAM TURBINE GENERATORS (1946–1963)

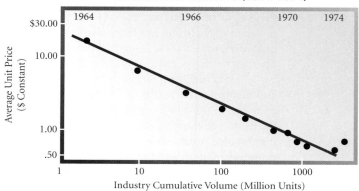

INTEGRATED CIRCUITS (1964–1974)

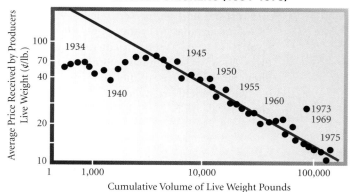

BROILER CHICKENS (1934–1975)

Note: Technically an experience curve shows the relationship between cost and experience. However, cost figures are seldom publicly available: therefore most of the above experience curves show industry price (in constant dollars) vs. experience.
Source: The Boston Consulting Group

rience curve from Figure 1 on the double logarithmic scale. . . . Figure 3 provides illustrations for [some specific] products.

SOURCES OF THE EXPERIENCE EFFECT

The experience effect has a variety of sources; to capitalize on it requires knowledge of why it occurs. Sources of the experience effect are outlines as follows:

1. *Labor efficiency.* . . . As workers repeat a particular production task, they become more dexterous and learn improvements and shortcuts which increase their collective efficiency. The greater the number of worker-paced operations, the greater the amount of learning which can accrue with experience. . . .
2. *Work specialization and methods improvements.* Specialization increases worker proficiency at a given task. . . .
3. *New production processes.* Process innovations and improvements can be an important source of cost reductions, especially in capital intensive industries. . . .
4. *Getting better performance from production equipment.* When first designed, a piece of production equipment may have a conservatively rated output. Experience may reveal innovative ways of increasing its output. . . .
5. *Changes in the resource mix.* As experience accumulates, a producer can often incorporate different or less expensive resources in the operation. . . .
6. *Product standardization.* Standardization allows the replication of tasks necessary for worker learning. Production of the Ford Model T, for example, followed a strategy of deliberate standardization; as a result, from 1909 to 1923 its price was repeatedly reduced, following an 85 percent experience curve (Abernathy and Wayne, 1974). . . .
7. *Product redesign.* As experience is gained with a product, both the manufacturer and customers gain a clearer understanding of its performance requirements. This understanding allows the product to be redesigned to conserve material, allows greater efficiency in manufacture, and substitutes less costly materials and resources, while at the same time improving performance on relevant dimensions. . . .

The foregoing list of sources dramatizes the observation that cost reductions due to experience don't occur by natural inclination; they are the result of substantial, concerted effort and pressure to lower costs. In fact, left unmanaged, costs rise. Thus, experience does not cause reductions but rather provides an opportunity that alert managements can exploit. . . .

The list of reasons for the experience effect raises perplexing questions on the difference between experience and scale effects. For instance, isn't it true that work specialization and project standardization, mentioned in the experience list, become possible because of the *size* of an operation? Therefore, aren't they each really scale effects? The answer is that they are probably both.

The confusion arises because growth in experience usually coincides with growth in size of an operation. We consider the experience effect to arise primarily due to ingenuity, cleverness, skill, and dexterity derived from experience as embodied in the adages "practice makes perfect" and "experience is the best teacher." On the other hand, scale effect comes from capitalizing on the size of an operation. . . .

Usually the overlap between the two effects is so great that it is difficult (and not too important) to separate them. This is the practice we will adopt from here on. . . .

PRICES AND EXPERIENCE

In stable competitive markets, one would expect that as costs decrease due to experience, prices will decrease similarly. (The price-experience curves in Figure 3 are examples of prices falling with experience.) If profit margins remain at a constant percentage of price, average

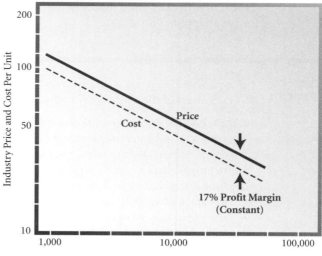

industry costs and prices should follow identically sloped experience curves (on double loga-rithmic scales). The constant gap separating them will equal the profit margin percentage; Figure 4 illustrates such an idealized situation.

In many cases, however, prices and costs exhibit a relationship similar to the one shown in Figure 5, where prices start briefly below cost, then cost reductions exceed price reductions until prices suddenly tumble. Ultimately the price and cost curves parallel, as they do in Figure 4. Specifically, in the development phase, new product prices are below average industry costs due to pricing based on anticipated costs. In the price umbrella phase, when demand exceeds supply, prices remain firm under a price umbrella supported by the market leader. This is unstable. At some point a shakeout phase starts; one producer will almost certainly reduce prices to gain share. If this does not precipitate a price decline, the high profit margins will attract enough new entrants to produce temporary overcapacity, causing prices to tumble faster than costs, and marginal producers to be forced out of the market. The stability phase starts when profit margins return to normal levels and prices begin to follow industry costs down the experience curve. . . .

FIGURE 5
TYPICAL PRICE-COST
RELATIONSHIP
Source: Adapted from
Perspectives on Experience
(Boston: The Boston Consulting
Group, 1972), p. 21

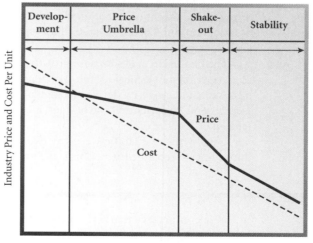

STRATEGIC IMPLICATIONS

In industries where a significant portion of total cost can be reduced due to scale or experience, important cost advantages can usually be achieved by pursuing a strategy geared to accumulating experience faster than competitors. (Such a strategy will ultimately require that the firm acquire the largest market share relative to competition.)

The dominant producer can greatly influence industry profitability. The rate of decline of competitors' costs must at least keep pace with the leader if they are to maintain profitability. If their costs decrease more slowly, either because they are pursuing cost reductions less aggressively or are growing more slowly than the leader, then their profits will eventually disappear, thus eliminating them from the market.

. . . the advantage of being the leader is obvious. Leadership is usually best seized at the start when experience doubles quickly (e.g., experience increases tenfold as you move from the 20th to the 2,000th unit, but only doubles as you move from the 2,000th to the 4,000th unit). Then a firm can build an unassailable cost advantage and at the same time gain price leadership. The best course of action for a product depends on a number of factors, one of the most important being the market growth rate. In fast-growing markets, experience can be gained by taking a disproportionate share of new sales, thereby avoiding taking sales away from competitors (which would be vigorously resisted). Therefore, with high rates of growth, aggressive action may be called for. But share-gaining tactics are usually costly in the short run, due to reduced margins from lower prices, added advertising and marketing expense, new product development costs, and the like. This means that if it lacks the resources (product, financial, and other) for leadership and in particular if it is opposed by a very aggressive competitor, a firm may find it wise to abandon the market entirely or focus on a segment it can dominate. On the other hand, in no-growth or slowly growing markets it is hard to take share from competitors and the time it takes to acquire superior experience is usually too long and the cost too great to favor aggressive strategies.

In stable competitive markets, usually the firm with the largest share of market has the greatest experience and it is often the case that each firm's experience is roughly proportional to market share. A notable exception occurs when a late entrant to a market quickly obtains a commanding market share. It may have less experience than some early entrants. . . .

EFFICIENCY VERSUS EFFECTIVENESS: LIMITATIONS TO STRATEGIES BASED ON EXPERIENCE OR SCALE

The selection of a competitive strategy based on cost reduction due to experience or scale often involves a fundamental choice. It is the selection of cost-price *efficiency* over noncost-price marketing *effectiveness*. However, when the market is more concerned with product and service features and up-to-date technology, a firm pursuing efficiency can find itself offering a low-priced product that few customers want. Thus two basic questions arise: (1) when to use an efficiency strategy and (2) if used, how far to push it before running into dangers of losing effectiveness. . . .

Whether to pursue an efficiency strategy depends on answers to questions such as,

1. Does the industry offer significant cost advantages from experience or scale (as in semiconductors or chemicals)?
2. Are there significant market segments that will reward competitors with low prices?
3. Is the firm well equipped (financially, managerially, technologically, etc.) for or already geared up for strategies relying heavily on having the lowest cost. . . . ?

If the answer is "yes" to all these questions, then "efficiency" strategies should probably be pursued.

Once it decided to pursue an "efficiency" strategy a firm must guard against going so far that it loses effectiveness, primarily through inability to respond to changes. For instance, experience-based strategies frequently require a highly specialized work force, facilities and organization, making it difficult to respond to changes in consumer demand, to respond to competitors' innovations, or to initiate them. In addition, large-scale plants are vulnerable to changes in process technology, and the heavy cost of operation below capacity.

For example, Ford's Model T automobile ultimately suffered the consequences of inflexibility due to overemphasizing "efficiency" (Abernathy and Wayne, 1974). Ford followed a classic experience-based strategy; over time it slashed its product line to a single model (the Model T), built modern plants, pushed division of labor, introduced the continuous assembly line, obtained economies in purchased parts through high volume, backward integrated, increased mechanization, and cut prices as costs fell. The lower prices increased Ford's share of a growing market to a high of 55.4% by 1921.

In the meantime, consumer demand began shifting to heavier, closed-body cars and to more comfort. Ford's chief rival, General Motors, had the flexibility to respond quickly with new designs. Ford responded by adding features to its existing standard design. While the features softened the inroads of GM, the basic Model T design, upon which Ford's "efficiency" strategy was based, inadequately met the market's new performance standards. To make matters worse, the turmoil in production due to constant design changes slowed experience-based efficiency gains. Finally Ford was forced, at enormous cost, to close for a whole year beginning May 1927 while it retooled to introduce its Model A. Hence experience or scale-based *efficiency* was carried too far and thus it ultimately limited *effectiveness* to meet consumer needs, to innovate, and to respond.

Thus the challenge is to decide when to emphasize efficiency and when to emphasize effectiveness, and further to design efficiency strategies that maintain effectiveness and vice versa. . . .

READING 14.3   INNOVATION IN BUREAUCRACY*

BY JAMES Q. WILSON

■ . . . At one level, the history of the United States Army since World War II provides little support for the common view that bureaucracies never change. At the level of doctrine, and to some degree of organization, there has been little *but* change since 1945. . . .

But at a deeper level, very little changed. As Kevin Sheehan makes clear . . . the army limited its innovations to thinking about better ways to counter a Soviet invasion of Western Europe. Every alteration in doctrine and structure was based on the assumption that the war for which the army should prepare itself was a conventional war on the plains of Germany. But during this period there was no such war. Instead the army found itself fighting in Korea, Vietnam, the Dominican Republic, and Grenada, and threatened with the prospect of having to fight in the Middle East and Central America. None of these *actual* or *likely* wars produced the same degree of rethinking and experimentation that was induced by the *possibility* of a war in Europe. As a result, changes in the army were essentially limited to trying to find ways to take advantage of new technological developments in the kind of weaponry that either it or its adversary might employ in Bavaria.

INNOVATION AND TASKS

We ought not to be surprised that organizations resist innovation. They are supposed to resist it. The reason an organization is created is in large part to replace the uncertain expectations and haphazard activities of voluntary endeavors with the stability and routine of organized

*Reprinted with deletions from *Bureaucracy: What Government Agencies Do and Why They Do It*, James Q. Wilson, 1989, Basic Books.

relationships. The standard operating procedure (SOP) is not the enemy of organization; it is the essence of organization. . . .

For the purposes of this discussion what I mean by innovation is not any new program or technology, but only those that involve the performance of new tasks or a significant alteration in the way in which existing tasks are performed. Organizations will readily accept (or at least not bitterly resist) inventions that facilitate the performance of existing tasks in a way consistent with existing managerial arrangements. Armies did not resist substituting trucks for horse-drawn carts. It is striking, however, how many technical inventions whose value seems self-evident to an outsider are resisted to varying degrees because their use changes operator tasks and managerial controls. When breech-loading rifles and machine guns became available, they dramatically increased the firepower of armies. But the improved firepower forced commanders either to disperse their infantry on the battlefield or to hide them in trenches and bunkers. The former response required decentralizing the command system, the latter permitted command to remain centralized. . . .

This bias toward maintaining existing task definitions often leads bureaucracies to adopt new technologies without understanding their significance. The tank made its appearance in World War I. Armies did not ignore this machine, they purchased it in large numbers—but as a more efficient way of performing a traditional task, that of cavalry scouting. The true innovation occurred when some armies (but not most) saw that the tank was not a mechanical horse but the means for a wholly new way of conducting battles. . . . Similarly, many navies purchased airplanes before World War II but most viewed them simply as an improved means of reconnaissance. Thus, the first naval planes were launched by catapults from battleships in order to extend the vision of the battleship's captain. The organizational innovation occurred when aviation was recognized as a new form of naval warfare and the aircraft were massed on carriers deployed in fast-moving task forces.

Changes that are consistent with existing task definitions will be accepted; those that require a redefinition of those tasks will be resisted. . . .

The tendency to resist innovations that alter tasks is not limited to the military or even to government agencies. Take the computer. Its use spread quickly in some firms and was resisted in others. Without a close understanding of the core tasks of these organizations it is impossible to explain why some bought early and others late. When the core task was writing, filing, or calculating, the computer was seen as faster and more efficient, and so it was adopted. It was an improvement rather than an innovation (as the word is used here). For example, department stores were quick to acquire computers to make their accounting programs more efficient, but slow to make extensive use of computers for inventory control. The reason, as Harvey Sapolsky has shown, is that inventory control touches on the core task in a department store, that of the buyer: the person in charge of a line of goods (sportswear, budget dresses, men's furnishings) who in exchange for a share of the profits takes responsibility for buying, displaying, and selling that line. The use of a computer to manage inventory threatened to alter the role of buyer by taking decisions (over what and how much to buy) out of the hands of the buyer, who traditionally was a nearly autonomous businessperson, and placing them in the hands of central managers and staff officers. In time the computer advocates won out and the power of the buyers was diminished. . . .

Government agencies change all the time, but the most common changes are add-ons: a new program is added on to existing tasks without changing the core tasks or altering the organizational culture. The State Department accepted the job of improving security in American embassies by adding on a unit designed to do this; . . . the add-on did not significantly change the way foreign service officers behaved (and thus did not do much to improve embassy security). . . .

Real innovations are those that alter core tasks; most changes add to or alter peripheral tasks. These peripheral changes often are a response to a demand in the agency's environment. Many observers have noted that most educational changes (they always seem to be called "reforms" without regard to whether in fact they make things better) were forced on the schools by the political system. Many important changes in the military also were reactions to political demands: Some key air force generals were at first reluctant to develop the intercontinental missile; the navy for a long time was unsure about the desirability of a submarine-launched missile program; the army bowed to presidential demands for a counterinsurgency unit. Outside forces—academic scientists, industrial engineers, civilian theorists, members of Congress, and presidential aides—all helped induce the military to embrace programs that initially seemed irrelevant to (or at odds with) their core tasks.

Sometimes entrepreneurs within an agency bring about the peripheral changes. In many cases their success depends on their ability to persuade others that the changes *are* peripheral and threaten no core interests. Despite the myths about General Billy Mitchell shaming the navy into acknowledging the military potential of the airplane, the navy had taken a keen interest in aviation from the very first. At issue was the role the airplane was to play. The organizational culture of the navy—the black-shoe, battleship navy—was very much inclined to view the airplane as a scout. The first chief of the Bureau of Aeronautics, Rear Admiral William Moffett, took pains not to contradict this view. As a former battleship commander he had the credentials that line naval officers would respect. He endorsed the idea of the airplane as a scout for the battleship, suggesting only that this scouting function might be served more efficiently if the planes were on aircraft carriers that would accompany the battleship. But quietly, if not secretly, Moffett was promoting the idea of naval aviation as a separate striking force operating independently of battleships. He did this in confidential memos, by getting contracts for high-speed carriers approved, and by intervening in the promotion process to insure that a lot of aviators rose in rank. (By 1926 there were already four admirals, two captains, and sixty-three commanders who were aviators.) So successful was he that a full year before Pearl Harbor ten fast carriers were under construction.

Had it not been for Pearl Harbor, however, the carrier task force might never have become the core of the surface navy. But after December 7, 1941, there was no alternative; five American battleships were sunk or put out of action. To fight a war in the Pacific it now would be carriers or nothing. . . .

| EXECUTIVES AND INNOVATION | Whether changes are core or peripheral, externally imposed or internally generated, understanding why they occur at all requires one to understand the behavior of the agency executive. As persons responsible for maintaining the organization it is executives who identify the external pressures to which the agency must react. As individuals who must balance competing interests inside the agency it is they who must decide whether to protect or to ignore managers who wish to promote changes. Almost every important study of bureaucratic innovation points to the great importance of executives in explaining change. For example, Jerald Hage and Robert Dewar studied changes that occurred in sixteen social welfare agencies in a midwestern city and found that the beliefs of the top executives were better predictors of the change than any structural features of the organizations. If John Russell had not been commandant of the Marine Corps or William Moffett had not been chief of the Bureau of Aeronautics, the Fleet Marine Force and carrier-based naval aviation would not have emerged when and as they did. |

It is for this reason, I think, that little progress has been made in developing theories of innovation. Not only do innovations differ so greatly in character that trying to find one theory to explain them all is like trying to find one medical theory to explain all diseases, but innovations are so heavily dependent on executive interests and beliefs as to make the chance appearance of a change-oriented personality enormously important in explaining change. It is not easy to build a useful social science theory out of "chance appearances."

In this regard the study of innovation in government agencies is not very different from its study in business firms. In a purely competitive marketplace there would never be any entrepreneurship because anybody producing a better product would immediately attract competitors who would drive the price down (and thus the entrepreneur's profits), possibly to the point where the entrepreneur's earnings from his or her new venture would be zero. Yet new firms and new products are created. The people who create them are willing to run greater than ordinary risks. Predicting who they will be is not easy; so far as it has turned out to be impossible.

Executives are important but also can be perverse. Innovation is not inevitably good; there are at least as many bad changes as good. And government agencies are especially vulnerable to bad changes because, absent a market that would impose a fitness test on any organizational change, a changed public bureaucracy can persist in doing the wrong thing for years. The Ford Motor Company should not have made the Edsel, but if the government had owned Ford it would still be making Edsels. . . .

Uncertainty, as Jonathan Bendor has written, is to organizations what original sin is to individuals—they are born into it. Government organizations are steeped in uncertainty because it is so hard to know what might produce success or even what constitutes success. Executives and higher-level managers have an understandable urge to reduce that uncertainty. They also have a less understandable belief that more information means less uncertainty. That may be true if what they obtain by sophisticated communications and computation equipment is actually information—that is, a full, accurate, and properly nuanced body of knowledge about important matters. Often what they get is instead a torrent of incomplete facts, opinions, guesses, and self-serving statements about distant events.

The reason is not simply the limitations in information-gathering and -transmitting processes. It is also that the very creation of such processes alters the incentives operating on subordinates. These include the following:

1. If higher authority can be sent a message about a decision, then higher authority will be sent a message asking it to make the decision.
2. If higher authority can hear a lot, then higher authority will be told what it wants to hear.
3. Since processing information requires the creation of specialized bureaus, then these units will demand more and more information as a way of justifying their existence.

A good example of all of these incentives at work can be found in the consequences for some armies of the invention of the railroad and the telegraph. Now troop movement could be centrally planned (only headquarters could coordinate all the complex railroad timetables). Now army commanders could spend more time communicating with headquarters (because the telegraph and telephone lines running to the rear were likely to be intact) than with the troops at the front (where communication lines were often broken). As a result, commanders found it easier to yield to the temptation to adopt a headquarters perspective on the battle (which often was hopelessly distorted) than to take a fighting-front view of the battle. The reliance on railroads and telegraphs enhanced the power of engineering units at headquarters; soon the direction of the war itself came to be seen as an engineering matter only. Creveld quotes an Austrian officer who wrote in 1861 that as a result of better communications a commander now "has two enemies to defeat, one in front and another in the rear." . . .

It is not simply that some innovations are perverse; it is also the case that any top-down change is risky. When government executives are the source of a change, they are likely to overestimate its benefits and underestimate its costs. This is true not only because executives lack the detailed and specialized knowledge possessed by operators and lower-level managers, but also because of the incentives operating on the executives. Often they are drawn from outside the agency to serve for a brief period. Their rewards come not from the agency but from what outsiders (peers, the media, Congress) think of them. A "go-getter" who "makes a difference" and does not "go native" usually wins more praise than someone who is cautious and slow-moving. . . .

Sometimes being bold about top-down innovations is desirable, since operators not only have detailed knowledge, they have cultural and mission-oriented biases. Had they been listened to, battleship admirals might well have blocked the creation of a carrier navy until it was too late. . . .

Moreover, there are kinds of innovations that almost no subordinate will support. If an executive sees that an agency ought to be abolished, he or she is not likely to find many supporters among the rank and file, even though in this case *how* it is abolished or drastically reduced in size ought to be guided by the knowledge that only operators possess. . . .

When should executives defer to subordinates and when should they overrule them? If this were a book about how to run an agency, the answer would be: "It all depends. Use good judgment." Not very helpful comments. Moreover, the organizational arrangements that encourage members to propose an innovation often are different from those that make it easy to implement one, once proposed. An agency that wants its managers and operators to suggest new ways of doing their tasks will be open, collegial, and supportive; an agency that wishes to implement an innovation over the opposition of some of its members often needs to concentrate power in the hands of the boss sufficient to permit him or her to ignore (or even dismiss) opponents. . . .

However authority is distributed, the executive who wishes to make changes has to create incentives for subordinates to think about, propose, and help refine such changes, and this means convincing them that if they join the innovative efforts of a (usually) short-term executive, their careers will not be blighted if the innovation fails or the executive departs before it is implemented. Admiral Moffett did this in the navy. . . .

To implement a proposed change often requires either creating a specialized subunit that will take on the new tasks (such as the Bureau of Aeronautics in the navy) or if the task cannot be confined to a subunit, retraining or replacing subordinates who oppose the change. Caspar Weinberger did this at the Federal Trade Commission where, in order to instill a new sense of vigor and commitment to consumer protection, he replaced eighteen of the thirty-one top staff members and about two hundred of the nearly six hundred staff attorneys. Weinberger and his successors as FTC chairman brought in new people specially recruited because they supported a new way of defining the agency's core tasks (namely, to attack deceptive advertising and monopolistic structures rather than to prosecute small-scale price-fixing cases). . . .

None of this implies that agency members always oppose innovations and therefore must be bypassed, dismissed, or re-educated. The reaction of operators to a proposed change will be governed by the incentives to which they respond; in government agencies that are limited in their ability to use money as a reward, one important set of incentives is that derived from the way tasks are defined. Tasks that are familiar, easy, professionally rewarded, or well adapted to the circumstances in which operators find themselves will be preferred because performing them is less costly than undertaking tasks that are new, difficult, or professionally unrewarded or that place the operator in conflict with his or her environment. . . .

The longer an agency exists the more likely that its core tasks will be defined in ways that minimize the costs to the operators performing them, and thus in ways that maximize the costs of changing them. The most dramatic and revealing stories of bureaucratic innovation are therefore found in organizations . . . that have acquired settled habits and comfortable routines. Innovation in these cases require an exercise of judgment, personal skill, and misdirection, qualities that are rare among government executives. And so innovation is rare.

**BY A. C. BOYNTON,
B. VICTOR, AND
B. J. PINE II**

■ How to succeed in today's rapidly changing competitive environment is a question weighing heavily on many a manager's mind. Everything seems to be changing—markets, customer demands, technologies, global boundaries, products, and processes. In the midst of this seemingly overwhelming change, managers are being asked to make critical competitive decisions that will affect not only the present position of their firm (the legal or competitive entity), but also its future success.

Much to their dismay, however, many managers are finding out, sometimes the hard way, that it is a different game, and the old rules do not apply anymore. To compete in today's rapidly changing competitive environment, new strategic responses are required that most managers may have never thought possible. In addition, managers must understand that at the heart of these new strategic responses is innovative management through advanced information technologies. . . .

Through three years of in-depth field research of a number of leading organizations . . . we have witnessed a wide variety of firms from many different industries responding to the competitive environment of today by turning to new strategic responses that are based on innovative I/T systems and solutions.** On the one hand, some firms are choosing a strategy of low-cost product or service customization and invention. We call this strategy *mass customization.* . . . This strategy seeks to build a stable set of core I/T process capabilities that are stable in the long term, but that are flexible, generic, and modular.

On the other hand, there are firms that appear to be pursuing a strategy of continually innovating process capabilities. At the same time these firms compete on price with standardized products in large, mature markets. We call this strategy *continuous improvement.* . . . The objective here is to pursue constant innovation within its I/T process platform and at the same time create the most efficient, highest-quality operations in the world. . . .

**PRODUCT-PROCESS
CHANGE MATRIX:
A LENS OF
UNDERSTANDING**

. . . change in the present competitive environment may be understood best by means of what we call the *product-process change matrix.*

As its name implies, there are two broad categories of change in this matrix. *Product change* involves the demands for new products or services. The changes firms face in their markets because of competitor moves, shifting customer preferences, or entering new geographical or national markets are categorized as product changes. *Process change* involves the procedures and technologies used to produce or deliver products or services. The term *process,* as it is used here, refers broadly to all the organizational capabilities resulting from people, systems, technologies, and procedures that are used to develop, produce, market, and deliver products or services.

These two types of change can be either stable or dynamic. *Stable change* is slow, evolutionary, and generally predictable. *Dynamic change* is rapid, revolutionary, and generally

*Reprinted with deletions from an article originally printed as "New Competitive Strategies: Challenges to Organizations and Information Technology," A. C. Boynton, B. Victor, and B. J. Pine II, *IBM Systems Journal,* Vol. 32(1), 1993, 40–65.
**This paper is based on an ongoing research project sponsored by the IBM Advanced Business Institute and the Darden Graduate School of Business Administration at the University of Virginia. The authors have met with over 120 managers from 18 firms based in six countries on five continents. The firms are from various industries, including health care, consumer products, industrial products, telecommunications, financial services, and industrial manufacturing.

FIGURE 1
PRODUCT-PROCESS
CHANGE MATRIX

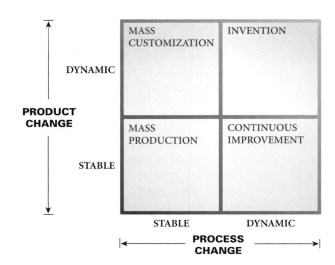

unpredictable.* Taken together, these types of change provide the following four possible combinations of change conditions that can confront an organization, as illustrated in Figure 1:

- Stable product and process change
- Dynamic product and process change
- Stable product and dynamic process change
- Dynamic product and dynamic process change

THE OLD COMPETITIVE STRATEGIES: MASS PRODUCTION AND INVENTION

We turn now to an in-depth look at each of the four quadrants on the product-process change matrix. We begin with the two quadrants *mass production* and *invention*, which represent what we call the old competitive strategy.

MASS PRODUCTION: STABLE PRODUCT AND PROCESS CHANGE

Throughout this century most large companies have competed under conditions of *stable product* and *stable process change.* Under these conditions, product specifications and demand are relatively stable and predictable. This permits a firm to standardize products, centralize decision making, routinize work and reward, develop and enforce standard rules and procedures, and allocate work to dedicated, specialized jobs. These are the elements of the mass production of goods and services (Blau and Schoenherr, 1971; Thompson, 1967).

The mass-production design is often a large, hierarchical, vertically integrated organization. Information systems in this case, tend to resemble the rest of the firm. People have used the metaphor of vertical stovepipes and silos for these information systems. They are efficient for the long term but are not very flexible (Galbraith, 1973). Strategy and command are isolated from the work itself in management control units (Taylor, 1911). Maximum efficiency is achieved by dedicating the capital and human assets of the firm to the production of stan-

---

*This idea, known as industrial dualism, can be found in M. J. Piore (1980).

dardized goods or services (Piore and Sabel, 1984). Competitive advantage and profitability are founded on reduction of unit costs.

Change in either process or product works against the mass-production formula. Changes in product make machinery obsolete, force costly changeovers, and reduce managerial control. Changes in process complicate individual jobs, raise waste and error, and increase unit costs. Thus a mass-production organization is intended to respond to and initiate as little change as possible. This design for stability requires limiting product variety as illustrated by Ford's promise to deliver a car painted any color the customer desired, as long as it was black. Mass production also requires limiting process innovation. For example, E. I. Du Pont de Nemours & Co. (Du Pont) managers used to classify production lines into those that had been standardized, and those yet to be standardized.

The role of information technology in mass production is relatively well understood. In the mass-production design, *I/T alignment* means the building and running of information systems that efficiently perform routine tasks. By substituting for previously manual processes, I/T has lowered costs, increased reliability, and reduced waste.

For nearly a century, the mass-production organization has clearly demonstrated its effectiveness under conditions where change is limited. However, mass production has never been able to eliminate completely the need for change. Shifting markets, intensifying competition, and advancing technologies have always forced it (Chandler, 1962). A distinct organizational design fills this need.

INVENTION: DYNAMIC PRODUCT AND PROCESS CHANGE

Another organizational design in our matrix is labeled invention, but is also known as organic or job-shop design. This design arose to take advantage of conditions involving both dynamic process and product change. Consider the basic characteristics of the invention design. In contrast to the large scale and stability of a mass-production organization, the invention design creates small volumes of new products, while constantly innovating the processes required to develop and produce them (Miller, 1986). To take advantage of the possibilities of change, workers in invention organizations are assumed to require a wide degree of latitude in the exploration of new ideas, highly skilled jobs, and little responsibility for the costs of production. These organizations often are separate research and development units within mass-production organizations. Indeed, the prototypical invention design organization is a research organization. . . .

Unlike the mass-production design that seeks stability, the invention design is inherently organized for change. The reason is that product specifications and work processes are unpredictable and constantly shifting. To compete under invention conditions, firms decentralize decision making, define jobs broadly, develop few rules or procedures, and evaluate performance subjectively. Information technology and systems are often distributed throughout the organization, perhaps in a loosely coupled structure, but flexible and adaptable to differing and changing requirements. The role of I/T in an invention-oriented organization is to provide specialized and independent information-processing capabilities to support the creative process.*

In keeping with their organic designs, the innovative firms are generally smaller in size to ensure focus on product variety and process innovation. In such an environment, investments in product-specific process capabilities are high risk because dynamic change renders structures, systems, and know-how rapidly obsolete. . . .

---

*It is easy to see that the problem of information technology alignment in the either/or environment of mass production and invention is simply a matter of making the choice between (1) a centralized, efficient, routine information-processing capability, or (2) a distributed, specialized, flexible collection of systems, both of which can be readily managed with the planning and resource evaluation tools currently available.

SYNERGY BETWEEN MASS PRODUCTION AND INVENTION

The product-process change matrix shows that the mass-production and invention designs and conditions are at opposite ends of the spectrum with respect to product and process change. In particular, mass production focuses on building an organization capable of competing under conditions of stable product and process change, whereas the world of invention is characterized by innovative processes and a widening demand for product variety. Even with these differences, a critical synergy grows between the mass-production design and the invention design. Their synergy has roots in the nineteenth century Industrial Revolution. . . .*

Although the mass-production firm is designed to respond to and initiate as little change as possible, occasionally it needs to retool completely new processes for completely new products. However, not only is the mass-production organizational design incapable of creating new and specialized products and processes, it is also seen as undesirable to use the mass-production organizational design even to try to create change. Thus it falls to the invention design to supply new products and processes for the mass producer. In effect, the mass production design creates a demand for highly specialized and innovative process capabilities that only research and development organizations, specialized machinery makers, and other invention designs can fill.

This working synergy between the two types of designs is based on the unique capabilities of each type. Such a synergy also requires an effective allocation of the product market and product life cycle. Invention designs reap premiums for their innovativeness during the emergence and early growth stages of the product life cycle. However, once a dominant product design has emerged and a market of sufficient size has developed, the mass producer takes over. The entry of the mass producer signals the beginning of the end of the competitive advantage of the invention design. If it is competing on innovativeness and variety, but not cost, the invention firm is eventually priced out of the market (Abernathy and Utterback, 1978). . . .

THE NEW COMPETITIVE STRATEGIES: MASS CUSTOMIZATION AND CONTINUOUS IMPROVEMENT

Although mass production and invention have been the predominant forms of competition during the 20th century, we see this beginning to change. Many firms are facing neither simultaneous dynamic-dynamic change (in which high costs of process innovation are supported because premium prices are available from the continuous product innovation), nor simultaneous stable-stable change (where the focus is on building stable, efficient processes in response to predictable product demands). Instead, these designs are facing a whole new and different set of . . . conditions, marked by different characteristics and qualities of change: stable product and dynamic process change, or dynamic product and stable process change. . . .

What is emerging is not a single new organizational design, however, but two new designs, each of which is adapting to different rates of process and product change conditions. Each design brings with it competitive advantage through that adaptation. Our research has found that information technology is often the driving force that leads to competitive advantage for these new organizational designs. Just as a synergy existed between the mass-production and invention designs, a new synergy is developing between the new designs. This synergy may become the defining basis of competition into the next century.

---

*This idea, known as industrial dualism, can be found in M. J. Piore, "Dualism as a Response to Flux and Uncertainty," and "The Technological Foundations of Dualism and Discontinuity," *Dualism and Discontinuity in Industrial Societies*, S. Berger and M. J. Piore, Editors, Cambridge University Press, New York (1980).

MASS CUSTOMIZATION: DYNAMIC PRODUCT CHANGE, STABLE PROCESS CHANGE

The first of these new designs competes under *dynamic product change* and *stable process change*. On the one hand, organizations across a variety of industries agree that customers are increasingly making unique and unpredictable product demands. Customers want the product or service that is right for them, and they want it now. As new competitors arrive and customer preferences change, predicting customer demand and articulating product specifications is becoming more difficult than ever. These are clearly conditions of dynamic product change.

On the other hand, these organizations also report that the basic processes their companies are instituting to meet these demands are more, not less, stable. The rapid and unpredictable process technology changes that the organization first experiences soon evolve into recognizable patterns. These patterns allow the organization to build stable but flexible platforms of process capabilities or know-how over time. As a result, organizations are able to improve process capabilities and know-how incrementally on a continuing basis. This increases the organization's base of knowledge, while continuing to increase process efficiencies. These are clearly conditions of stable process change.

If this scenario of dynamic product and stable process change, as noted on the product-process change matrix, is one of the realities of today's competitive environment (and our research tells us many leading organizations believe it is), many of today's companies need to be organized and managed not for mass production or invention, but for *mass customization*. Mass customization is the ability to serve a wide range of customers and meet changing product demands through service or product variety and innovation. Simultaneously, mass customization builds on existing long-term process experience and knowledge. The result is increased efficiencies. . . .

Characteristics of the Mass-Customization Design

We now take a closer look at the organizational design required to provide firms with mass-customization capabilities. The major distinguishing characteristics of the mass-customization design is its capacity to produce product variety rapidly and inexpensively. In direct contradiction of the assumption that cost and variety are trade-offs, mass customizers organize for efficient flexibility. A number of fundamental elements of these trade-offs can also be identified, including process structure, decision-making structure, and organization of labor. . . .

One of the keys to mass customization is what might be labeled the network structure. The network structure in the mass-customization organization is a system of material or information flows between generic, reusable, flexible, modular units. It is important to understand that these units can be people, teams, software components, or manufacturing devices, depending on the critical resources employed by the firm. Whatever the combination of units, they must be loosely coupled. That is, they are not pre-engineered or prealigned for some known end product. The network structure, when implemented, permits a unique combination of processing steps for any customer order. By engineering the flexibility of the processing units and coordinating the flow of materials or service needs between units, the mass customizer can produce virtually an infinite variety of products at costs competitive with the mass producer. . . .

Compare this network structure with the design requirements for mass production. Mass producers assume that change in product specifications introduces higher costs. They assume that change requires resetting production processes, relearning production tasks, and coordinating fluctuations in supply and processing requirements. I/T is used for single products and services that are designed to last for the long run. People are trained and specialized in known and long-term product or service needs. Today's mass customizer defies this old logic by organizing and engineering both the processes and the connections between processes for low-cost flexibility (Teece, 1980). Instead of building a single-product, large-volume focused production process, the mass customizer builds a dynamic network of potentially infinite numbers of interchangeable and intercompatible individual unit production processes. Thus, the challenge of alignment in the dynamic network environment of the mass-customization design is to make the unpredictable combinations of processing units function both seamlessly and efficiently. . . .

It is important to understand that in some ways the mass-customization organizational design resembles the mass producer. There is a high degree of centralization in both designs. In the case of the mass customizer, coordination and control are centralized in the hub of a web of loosely linked processing units.* The central decision-making function allocates the work necessary to produce the customer's product or service order. . . .

Unlike the mass producer, the mass customizer organizes labor to work effectively in a dynamic network of relationships, and to respond to work requirements as defined by customer needs. Whereas labor in the mass-production design was organized to perform specialized tasks according to a unitary set of rules and commands, the mass customizer organizes labor to routinely respond to a changing set of rules and commands. This requires that the setup time be greatly reduced to change from one set of inputs to be processed into a corresponding set of outputs, to a new set of inputs. Reducing setup times in the mass-customization organization involves three things: eliminating tasks that do not need to be done, streamlining all remaining tasks so that cycle time equals value-added time, and performing as many of those tasks in parallel with the preceding process operation as possible. This reduction applies to the plant floor, the back office, and the front office. . . .

In summary, the mass customizer combines the product variety of the invention design with the production efficiency of the mass producer. To accomplish this, the mass customizer employs a new organizational design based on the network rather than the assembly line. Although this organization is designed to compete under conditions under which product change is highly variable, it does so by maintaining an evolutionary level of stable change in processes.

CONTINUOUS IMPROVEMENT: STABLE PRODUCT AND DYNAMIC PROCESS CHANGE

Although mass-customization conditions of dynamic product change characterize a number of markets, they do not represent all of them. In some markets, the nature of product demand is still relatively mature, stable, large, and homogeneous. These markets, however, are not necessarily havens for the traditional mass producer that achieves efficiencies through stability and avoiding change.

We now consider the kinds of designs that are effectively competing in these environments and how they are competing. As the product-process change matrix describes, in these environments winning organizations are competing on *dynamic process* terms. That is, they are achieving constant advances in process quality, speed, and cost, which are providing them with real competitive advantage. The quality revolution and increasingly severe cost and time competition in such industries as automobiles, financial services, machine tools, and retailing are being led by a new kind of competitor, one that we call the *continuous improvement* design.

---

*The value-chain activities for a mass customizer or for any other design do not have to be owned by the company in a vertically integrated fashion. For many companies, value-chain activities are acquired from other firms, thus extending the boundaries of the organization. This has given rise to the *disaggregated-value-chain* concept or the *networked organization design*. Becoming a firm that relies extensively on external companies for value-chain activities is a critical strategic choice. Given the importance of maintaining tightly connected, flexible, and highly responsive process capabilities for mass customization, the decision to rely on externally owned value-chain process requirements should be made with extreme caution. This topic deserves more extensive discussion than this paper allows. For an excellent discussion of networks composed of multiple companies, see C. Snow, R. Miles, and H. Coleman (1992).

The continuous improvement design is the second of the new designs we have observed. This type of organization competes under conditions of *stable product change* and *dynamic process change*. We term such designs continuous improvement designs because the organization manages rapid innovation and use of new process capabilities. They also strive constantly to improve their response to large, stable product requirements. In general, organizations facing a continuous improvement environment require systems and structures that facilitate long-term organizational learning about products, but at the same time achieve rapid and radical changes in the processes employed to meet stable product demands. . . .

Characteristics of the Continuous Improvement Design

. . . the distinguishing characteristic of the continuous improvement design is its ongoing capacity to improve the operating performance of its processes and products rapidly and inexpensively. . . . low-cost advantage can be achieved while investing in changing process capabilities that anticipate future market needs in service and quality. In direct contradiction to the old assumption that cost and process or product change are trade-offs and that choices must be made between the two, continuous improvement designs organize for efficient process innovation. These designs also allow firms to achieve efficiency, quality, and ongoing product improvements simultaneously (Womack et al., 1990; Quinn and Paquette, 1990).

The key to the continuous improvement design is a team-based structure. The team structure is an integrated and ongoing collaboration among process specialists. The characteristic that distinguishes the team structure from the network is the collaborative nature of the work. Teams are intensive forums through which process change is pursued and implemented. The hand-off between operating units of a network stands in stark contrast with the codevelopment work of teams. The team structure permits the organization to make complex, value-adding transformations of its business processes. By integrating the specialized work of functional units and managing the rapid and effective refocusing of these functional units, the continuous improvement design pursues process innovation while remaining cost competitive with the mass producer.

The importance of team-based structures for both product and process innovation has only recently been recognized in management literature. The classic prescription in mass production has been to isolate process and product innovation from production. The purpose is to buffer production from the disruptions of the developers and to free the developers from the short-term concerns of production. More recent research and practice have muddied this picture by demonstrating that the interdependence among functional units, i.e., production, product development, information systems, and marketing, is intensely reciprocal. . . . While the mass producer achieves efficiency by isolating innovation from the concerns of the workforce, the continuous improvement design achieves efficiency by making innovation everyone's concern. For example, when asked how many process engineers he had, the plant manager at NUMMI (New United Motor Manufacturing, Inc.), a Toyota-General Motors joint venture in Fremont, California, pointed to his production floor of 2100 workers and said, "2100." Indeed, the prototypical continuous improvement design users have been such Japanese manufacturers as Toyota. This design has produced relatively standard products through constant enhancement of the processes of these manufacturers to achieve higher quality, lower costs, faster cycle time, less inventory, and greater innovation.

To make innovation efficient, the continuous improvement design manages an ongoing sequence of what we call *microtransformations*. Innovation is pursued by cross-functional teams that collaborate to improve operating processes or plan for product enhancement. The members of these teams then turn to their function-specific work and execute the rules they just developed, accomplishing a microtransformation. In this sense the teams of the continuous improvement design are intended to be as process-innovative as the invention design, and as process-efficient as the mass-production design.

The microtransformations created through the team-based structure have changed the role of supervision in these organizations. In the mass-production design, doers' jobs are designed for maximum efficiency. All work is allocated based on specialized functional capabilities and dedicated to the execution of standardized, product-defined tasks. The design of the jobs and the selection and evaluation of work processes are reserved for the managerial role. These thinkers are expected to preplan all doer roles and to evaluate and correct all doer task work. The difference in the continuous improvement design lies in the fact that the rules are generated by the same team that is expected to execute them. Thus, the continuous improvement designs are taking advantage of breakthroughs in information-technology architecture that bring modularity, flexibility, and reusability to design systems to support microtransformations. For many, such systems are the key to enabling the organization to improve coordination, integration, and control of core capabilities and know-how across a variety of functional areas. In many cases, new I/T systems not only improve speed to market but also increase the efficiency and effectiveness of important process activities.

A NEW SYNERGY BETWEEN MASS CUSTOMIZATION AND CONTINUOUS IMPROVEMENT: DYNAMIC STABILITY

Just as there is a symbiotic relationship between the mass-production design and the invention design, there exists a vital relationship between mass customization and continuous improvement. As we briefly mentioned earlier, this new synergy may well define the basis of competition into the next century.

We refer to this synergy as *dynamic stability*, which defines organizational designs that combine the best of mass customization and continuous improvement. These organizations can respond to rapidly changing and unpredictable product or service markets (dynamic) from an efficient, long-term (stable), flexible, and adaptive base of process capabilities. Such stable process capabilities are the key to mass customizers and enable them to respond to dynamic product change. However, these process capabilities cannot be developed once for all time. Instead, they must be developed in a continuous-improvement stage. They are applied to competitive advantage as a mass customizer. They are continuously enhanced, using continuous improvements design characteristics to ensure that the organization maintains world-class process capabilities. . . .

The synergy that exists between mass customization and continuous improvement revolves primarily around the need to adopt the invention and innovation of vital processes from the continuous improvement design. This can occur in three basic ways.

One way is that the mass-customization design may borrow process innovation from an entirely separate continuous improvement design. That is especially true when that process innovation results in low-cost, highly flexible process capabilities. By another mode, both the mass-customization design and the continuous improvement design coexist within the same organization, sharing process innovations within the organization. Third, . . . companies attempting to move from mass production to mass customization must pursue a path through a stage of process re-engineering and development (continuous improvement) before they can apply those processes to mass customizing products or services. We refer to this path as the *right path*.

There are also examples of organizations that can and must balance and move between the continuous improvement and mass-customization designs. This is critical because, for long-term success, part of a mass customizer must attend to process innovation to increase its ability to pursue a strategy of efficient product variety. Mass customizers, while achieving a low-cost, product-variety strategic position, must be formidable competitors in many related industries. Thus they must continuously enhance their process capabilities that are the key to success. . . .

What we have observed is a vital new synergy between the continuous improvement design and the mass-customization design. . . . It is no longer an either-or choice. Firms must choose a vision that includes both decentralization and centralization, global and local, fast and efficient, innovative and low cost. . . .

TAKING THE RIGHT PATH TO MASS CUSTOMIZATION

. . . the path to dynamic stability requires that the organization undergo significant process development or redevelopment effort aimed specifically at building process or knowledge capabilities. Any attempt to move to dynamic stability from the old competitive strategies without significant process transformation does not work. Using the product-process change matrix to illustrate the point, firms with process capabilities designed to manage change that characterizes mass production cannot take those capabilities and apply them to the change that characterizes the new competitive strategy. This is the wrong path to transformation. . . .

Understanding that transformation to mass customization must follow a carefully thought-out right path is a critical step to success for firms in attempting to position themselves on the new competitive strategies. [Firms that have done this are] investing in and carefully designing information architectures that are stable and efficient platforms. These systems simultaneously provide flexible, general-purpose, information-processing capabilities. The firms themselves did not try to leapfrog existing capabilities without thinking through organizational design issues and consequent information challenges required for dynamic stability. In each case, careful engineering or re-engineering of process capabilities positioned the firms and their managers to meet the dual competitive challenges of product differentiation and low cost made possible by mass customization.

CHAPTER 15

Managing
Experts

Although most large organizations draw on a variety of experts to get their jobs done, there has been a growing interest in recent years in those organizations whose work, because it is highly complex, is organized primarily around experts. These range from hospitals, universities, and research centers to consulting firms, space agencies, and biomedical companies.

This context is a rather unusual one, at least when judged against the more traditional contexts discussed in previous chapters. Both its processes and its structures tend to take on forms quite different from those presented earlier. Organizations of experts, in fact, seem to divide into two somewhat different contexts. In one, the experts work in rapidly changing situations that demand a good deal of collaborative innovation (as in biotechnology) whereas in the other, experts work more or less alone in more stable situations involving slower-changing bodies of skill or knowledge (as in law, university teaching, and accounting). This chapter takes up the latter with regard to managing experts (since the focus is on them, not their processes). The next chapter discusses the context of innovation and managing experts when they have to work together.

We open this chapter with a description of the type of organization that seems best suited to the context of the more stable application of expertise. Drawn from Mintzberg's work, primarily his original description of "professional bureaucracy," it looks at the structure of the professional organization, including its important characteristic of "pigeonhol-ing" work. The chapter also looks at the management of professionals and the unusual nature of strategy in such organizations (drawing from a paper Mintzberg coauthored with Cynthia Hardy, Ann Langley, and Janet Rose) and at some issues associated with these organizations.

In "Managing Intellect," the second reading, Quinn, Anderson, and Finkelstein, all from the Tuck School at Dartmouth College in New Hampshire, address the question of managing experts head-on. After describing the characteristics of intellect—for example, its pursuit of perfection rather than creativity (which puts this reading squarely in this chapter, not the next)—they suggest various interesting new forms by which companies can manage intellect: the "infinitely flat" organization, the inverted organization, the star-burst, and the "spider's web."

The third reading in this chapter, written by consultant David Maister and originally pub-lished in the *Sloan Management Review,* focuses on one particular instance of the profes-sional context that has become an increasingly important career option for management stu-dents: the professional service firm. Maister describes how companies in businesses such as consulting, investment banking, accounting, architecture, and law manage the interactions among revenue generation, compensation, and staffing to ensure long-term balanced growth.

Finally, in "Covert Leadership: Notes on Managing Professionals," Mintzberg turns around the old metaphor of the manager as orchestra conductor to see how the orchestra conductor really manages. What comes out is not the image of the leader on a pedestal in absolute control but one perhaps akin to what it really means to lead an organization of professional experts.

Over all, these readings suggest that the traditional concepts of managing and organi-zation simply do not work as we move away from conventional mass production—which has long served as the model for "one best way" concepts in management. Whether it be highly expert work in general or service work subjected to new technologies and skills in particular, our thinking has to be opened up to some very different needs. In a widely dis-cussed article ("The Coming of the New Organization," *Harvard Business Review*, January–February 1988), Peter Drucker has argued that work in general is becoming more skilled and so structures of organizations in general are moving toward what we would call the professional form. Although we would *not* go that far—we maintain our contin-gency view of different needs for different contexts—we do believe this is becoming a much more important form of organization.

USING THE CASE STUDIES

Managing experts and expertise is a crucial issue in many organizations where knowledge is central to strategy. The management of experts, however, acquires special significance when the experts have strong professional identity. In the London Free Press case Phil McLeod seeks to implement organizational change in the face of resistance from his reporters. Mintzberg's "The Professional Organization" is a good reading for analyzing his approach to strategy making. The McKinsey and Company case and the Lechabile case shift the problem to managing expertise rather than managing professional identity per se. Quinn, Andrews, and Finkelstein's "Managing Intellect" provides a useful framework for evaluating McKinsey's attempts to integrate its consultants into a knowledge-based learning organization and Lechabile's struggle to sustain its culture of empowerment.

Novacare examines the management of expert medical staff. The case deals at some length with the needs to resolve the inevitable tension between individual professional identities and to integrate professionals into a cohesive organization. Maister's "Balancing the Professional Service Firm" deals with this dilemma and, hence, is relevant. Mintzberg's "Covert Leadership" opens up the wider issue of how professionals can be managed with-out suppressing their initiative.

**BY HENRY
MINTZBERG**

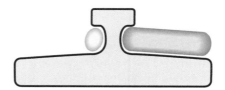

**THE BASIC
STRUCTURE**

An organization can be bureaucratic without being centralized. This happens when its work is complex, requiring that it be carried out and controlled by professionals, yet at the same time remains stable, so that the skills of those professionals can be perfected through standardized operating programs. The structure takes on the form of professional bureaucracy, which is common in universities, general hospitals, public accounting firms, social work agencies, and firms doing fairly routine engineering or craft work. All rely on the skills and knowledge of their operating professionals to function; all produce standardized products or services.

THE WORK OF THE PROFESSIONAL OPERATORS

Here again we have a tightly knit configuration of the attributes of structure. Most important, the professional organization relies for coordination on the standardization of skills, which is achieved primarily through formal training. It hires duly trained specialists—professionals—for the operating core, then gives them considerable control over their own work.

Control over their work means that professionals work relatively independently of their colleagues but closely with the clients they serve—doctors treating their own patients and accountants who maintain personal contact with the companies whose books they audit. Most of the necessary coordination among the operating professionals is then handled automatically by their set skills and knowledge—in effect, by what they have learned to expect from each other. During an operation as long and as complex as open-heart surgery, "very little needs to be said [between the anesthesiologist and the surgeon] preceding chest opening and during the procedure on the heart itself . . . [most of the operation is] performed in absolute silence" (Gosselin, 1978). The point is perhaps best made in reverse by the cartoon that shows six surgeons standing around a patient on an operating table with one saying, "Who opens?"

Just how standardized the complex work of professionals can be is illustrated in a paper read by Spencer before a meeting of the International Cardiovascular Society. Spencer notes that an important feature of surgical training is "repetitive practice" to evoke "an automatic reflex." So automatic, in fact, that this doctor keeps a series of surgical "cookbooks" in which he lists, even for "complex" operations, the essential steps as chains of thirty to forty symbols on a single sheet, to "be reviewed mentally in sixty to 120 seconds at some time during the day preceding the operation" (1976: 1179, 1182).

*Adapted from *The Structuring of Organizations* (Prentice Hall, 1979), Chap. 19 on "The Professional Bureaucracy"; also *Power In and Around Organizations* (Prentice Hall, 1983), Chap. 22 on "The Meritocracy"; the material on strategy formation from "Strategy Formation in the University Setting," coauthored with Cynthia Hardy, Ann Langley, and Janet Rose, in J. L. Bess (ed.),*College and University Organization* (New York University Press, 1984). A chapter similar to this one appeared in *Mintzberg on Management: Inside Our Strange World of Organizations* (Free Press, 1989).

But no matter how standardized the knowledge and skills, their complexity ensures that considerable discretion remains in their application. No two professionals—no two surgeons or engineers or social workers—ever apply them in exactly the same way. Many judgments are required.

Training, reinforced by indoctrination, is a complicated affair in the professional organization. The initial training typically takes place over a period of years in a university or special institution, during which the skills and knowledge of the profession are formally programmed into the students. There typically follows a long period of on-the-job training, such as internship in medicine or articling in accounting, where the formal knowledge is applied and the practice of skills perfected. On-the-job training also completes the process of indoctrination, which began during the formal education. As new knowledge is generated and new skills develop, of course (so it is hoped) the professional upgrades his or her expertise.

All that training is geared to one goal, the internalization of the set procedures, which is what makes the structure technically bureaucratic (structure defined earlier as relying on standardization for coordination). But the professional bureaucracy differs markedly from the machine bureaucracy. Whereas the latter generates its own standards—through its technostructure, enforced by its line managers—many of the standards of the professional bureaucracy originate outside its own structure, in the self-governing associations its professionals belong to with their colleagues from other institutions. These associations set universal standards, which they ensure are taught by the universities and are used by all the organizations practicing the profession. So whereas the machine bureaucracy relies on authority of a hierarchical nature—the power of office—the professional bureaucracy emphasizes authority of a professional nature—the power of expertise.

Other forms of standardization are, in fact, difficult to rely on in the professional organization. The work processes themselves are too complex to be standardized directly by analysts. One need only try to imagine a work-study analyst following a cardiologist on rounds or timing the activities of a teacher in a classroom. Similarly, the outputs of professional work cannot easily be measured and so do not lend themselves to standardization. Imagine a planner trying to define a cure in psychiatry, the amount of learning that takes place in a classroom, or the quality of an accountant's audit. Likewise, direct supervision and mutual adjustment cannot be relied upon for coordination, for both impede professional autonomy.

THE PIGEONHOLING PROCESS

To understand how the professional organization functions at the operating level, it is helpful to think of it as a set of standard programs—in effect, the repertoire of skills the professionals stand ready to use—that are applied to known situations, called contingencies, also standardized. As Weick notes of one case in point, "schools are in the business of building and maintaining categories" (1976: 8). The process is sometimes known as *pigeonholing*. In this regard, the professional has two basic tasks: (1) to categorize, or "diagnose," the client's need in terms of one of the contingencies, which indicates which standard program to apply, and (2) to apply, or execute, that program. For example, the management consultant carries a bag of standard acronymic tricks: MBO, MIS, LRP, OD. The client with information needs gets MIS; the one with managerial conflicts, OD. Such pigeonholing, of course, simplifies matters enormously; it is also what enables each professional to work in a relatively autonomous manner.

It is in the pigeonholing process that the fundamental differences among the machine organization, the professional organization, and the innovative organization (to be discussed next) can best be seen. The machine organization is a single-purpose structure. Presented with a stimulus, it executes its one standard sequence of programs, just as we kick when tapped on the knee. No diagnosis is involved. In the professional organization, diagnosis is a fundamental task, but one highly circumscribed. The organization seeks to match a predetermined contingency to a standardized program. Fully open-ended diagnosis—that which seeks a creative solution to a unique problem—requires the innovative form of organization. No standard contingencies or programs can be relied upon there.

THE ADMINISTRATIVE STRUCTURE

Everything we have discussed so far suggests that the operating core is the key part of the professional organization. The only other part that is fully elaborated is the support staff, but that is focused very much on serving the activities of the operating core. Given the high cost of the professionals, it makes sense to back them up with as much support as possible. Thus, universities have printing facilities, faculty clubs, alma mater funds, publishing houses, archives, libraries, computer facilities, and many, many other support units.

The technostructure and middle-line management are not highly elaborated in the professional organization. They can do little to coordinate the professional work. Moreover, with so little need for direct supervision of, or mutual adjustment among, the professionals, the operating units can be very large. For example, the McGill Faculty of Management functions effectively with 50 professors under a single manager, its dean, and the rest of the university's academic hierarchy is likewise thin.

Thus, the diagram at the beginning of this chapter shows the professional organization, in terms of our logo, as a flat structure with a thin middle line, a tiny technostructure, but a fully elaborated support staff. All these characteristics are reflected in the organigram of a university hospital, shown in Figure 1.

Coordination within the administrative structure is another matter, however. Because these configurations are so decentralized, the professionals not only control their own work but they also gain much collective control over the administrative decisions that affect them—decisions, for example, to hire colleagues, to promote them, and to distribute resources. This they do partly by doing some of the administrative work themselves (most university professors, for example, sit on various administrative committees) and partly by ensuring that important administrative posts are staffed by professionals or at least sympathetic people appointed with the professionals' blessing. What emerges, therefore, is a rather democratic administrative structure. But because the administrative work requires mutual adjustment for coordination among the various people involved, task forces and especially standing committees abound at this level, as is in fact suggested in Figure 1

Because of the power of their professional operators, these organizations are sometimes described as inverse pyramids, with the professional operators on top and the administrators down below to serve them—to ensure that the surgical facilities are kept clean and the classrooms well supplied with chalk. Such a description slights the power of the administrators of professional work, however, although it may be an accurate description of those who manage the support units. For the support staff—often more numerous than the professional staff, but generally less skilled—there is no democracy in the professional organization, only the oligarchy of the professionals. Such support units as housekeeping in the hospital or printing in the university are likely to be managed tightly from the top, in effect as machinelike enclaves within the professional configuration. Thus, what frequently emerges in the professional organization are parallel and separate administrative hierarchies, one democratic and bottom-up for the professionals, a second machinelike and top-down for the support staff.

THE ROLES OF THE ADMINISTRATORS OF PROFESSIONAL WORK

Where does all this leave the administrators of the professional hierarchy, the executive directors and chiefs of the hospitals and the presidents and deans of the universities? Are they powerless? Compared with their counterparts in the entrepreneurial and machine organizations, they certainly lack a good deal of power. But that is far from the whole story. The administrator of professional work may not be able to control the professionals directly, but he or she does perform a series of roles that can provide considerable indirect power.

FIGURE 1 ORGANIZATION OF A UNIVERSITY HOSPITAL

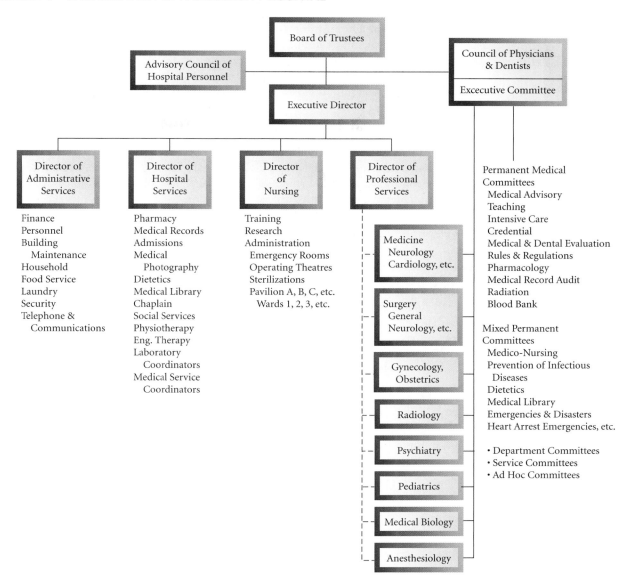

First, this administrator spends much time handling disturbances in the structure. The pigeonholing process is an imperfect one at best, leading to all kinds of jurisdictional disputes between the professionals. Who should perform mastectomies in the hospitals, surgeons who look after cutting or gynecologists who look after women? Seldom, however, can one administrator impose a solution on the professionals involved in a dispute. Rather, various administrators must often sit down together and negotiate a solution on behalf of their constituencies.

Second, the administrators of professional work—especially those at higher levels—serve in key roles at the boundary of the organization, between the professionals inside and the influencers outside: governments, client associations, benefactors, and so on. On the one hand, the administrators are expected to protect the professionals' autonomy, to "buffer" them from external pressures. On the other hand, they are expected to woo those outsiders to support the organization, both morally and financially. And that often leads the outsiders to expect these administrators, in turn, to control the professionals, in machine bureaucratic ways. Thus, the external roles of the manager—maintaining liaison contacts, acting as figurehead and spokesman in a public relations capacity, negotiating with outside agencies—emerge as primary ones in the administration of professional work.

Some view the roles these administrators are called upon to perform as signs of weakness. They see these people as the errand boys of the professionals, or else as pawns caught in various tugs of war—between one professional and another, between support staffer and professional, between outsider and professional. In fact, however, these roles are the very sources of administrators' power. Power is, after all, gained at the locus of uncertainty, and that is exactly where the administrators of professionals sit. The administrator who succeeds in raising extra funds for his or her organization gains a say in how they are distributed; the one who can reconcile conflicts in favor of his or her unit or who can effectively buffer the professionals from external influence becomes a valued, and therefore powerful, member of the organization.

We can conclude that power in these structures does flow to those professionals who care to devote effort to doing administrative instead of professional work, so long as they do it well. But that, it should be stressed, is not laissez-faire power; the professional administrator maintains power only as long as the professionals perceive him or her to be serving their interests effectively.

CONDITIONS OF THE PROFESSIONAL ORGANIZATION

The professional form of organization appears wherever the operating work of an organization is dominated by skilled workers who use procedures that are difficult to learn yet are well defined. This means a situation that is both complex and stable—complex enough to require procedures that can be learned only through extensive training yet stable enough so that their use can become standardized.

Note that an elaborate technical system can work against this configuration. If highly regulating or automated, the professionals' skills might be amenable to rationalization, in other words, to be divided into simple, highly programmed steps that would destroy the basis for professional autonomy and thereby drive the structure to the machine form. And if highly complicated, the technical system would reduce the professionals' autonomy by forcing them to work in multidisciplinary teams, thereby driving the organization toward the innovative form. Thus the surgeon uses a scalpel, and the accountant a pencil. Both must be sharp, but both are otherwise simple and commonplace instruments. Yet both allow their users to perform independently what can be exceedingly complex functions.

The prime example of the professional configuration is the personal-service organization, at least the one with complex, stable work not reliant on a fancy technical system. Schools and universities, consulting firms, law and accounting offices, and social work agencies all rely on this form of organization, more or less, so long as they concentrate not on innovating in the solution of new problems but on applying standard programs to well-defined ones. The same seems to be true of hospitals, at least to the extent that their technical systems are simple. (In those areas that call for more sophisticated equipment—apparently a growing number, especially in teaching institutions—the hospital is driven toward a hybrid structure, with characteristics of the innovative form. But this tendency is mitigated by the hospital's overriding concern with safety. Only the tried and true can be relied upon, which produces a natural aversion to the looser innovative configuration.)

So far, our examples have come from the service sector. But the professional form can be found in manufacturing too, where the above conditions hold up. Such is the case of the craft enterprise, for example, the factory using skilled workers to produce ceramic products. The very term *craftsman* implies a kind of professional who learns traditional skills through long apprentice training and then is allowed to practice them free of direct supervision. Craft enterprises seem typically to have few administrators, who tend to work, in any event, alongside the operating personnel. The same would seem to be true for engineering work oriented not to creative design so much as to modification of existing dominant designs.

STRATEGY FORMATION IN THE PROFESSIONAL ORGANIZATION

It is commonly assumed that strategies are formulated before they are implemented, that planning is the central process of formulation, and that structures must be designed to implement these strategies. At least this is what one reads in the conventional literature of strategic management. In the professional organization, these imperatives stand almost totally at odds with what really happens, leading to the conclusion either that such organizations are confused about how to make strategy, or else that the strategy writers are confused about how professional organizations must function. I subscribe to the latter explanation.

Using the definition of strategy as pattern in action, strategy formation in the professional organization takes on a new meaning. Rather than simply throwing up our hands at its resistance to formal strategic planning, or, at the other extreme, dismissing professional organizations as "organized anarchies" with strategy-making processes as mere "garbage cans" (March and Olsen, 1976) we can focus on how decisions and actions in such organizations order themselves into patterns over time.

Taking strategy as pattern in action, the obvious question becomes, which actions? The key area of strategy making in most organizations concerns the elaboration of the basic mission (the products or services offered to the public); in professional organizations, we shall argue, this is significantly controlled by individual professionals. Other important areas of strategy here include the inputs to the system (notably the choice of professional staff, the determination of clients, and the raising of external funds), the means to perform the mission (the construction of buildings and facilities, the purchase of research equipment, and so on), the structure and forms of governance (design of the committee system, the hierarchies, and so on), and the various means to support the mission.

Were professional organizations to formulate strategies in the conventional ways, central administrators would develop detailed and integrated plans about these issues. This sometimes happens, but in a very limited number of cases. Many strategic issues come under the direct control of individual professionals, while others can be decided neither by individual professionals nor by central administrators, but instead require the participation of a variety of people in a complex collective process. As illustrated in Figure 2, we examine

FIGURE 2
THREE LEVELS OF DECISION MAKING IN THE PROFESSIONAL ORGANIZATION

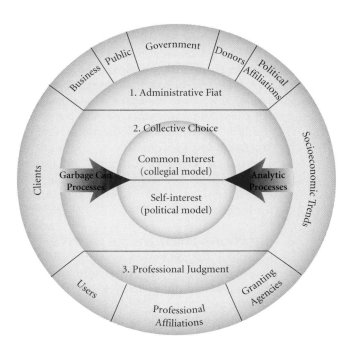

in turn the decisions controlled by individual professionals, by central administrators, and by the collectivity.

DECISIONS MADE BY PROFESSIONAL JUDGMENT

Professional organizations are distinguished by the fact that the determination of the basic mission—the specific services to be offered and to whom—is in good part left to the judgment of professionals as individuals. In the university, for example, each professor has a good deal of control over what is taught and how, as well as what is researched and how. Thus the overall product-market strategy of McGill University must be seen as the composite of the individual teaching and research postures of its 1,200 professors.

That, however, does not quite constitute full autonomy, because there is a subtle but not insignificant constraint on that power. Professionals are left to decide on their own only because years of training have ensured that they will decide in ways generally accepted in their professions. Thus professors choose course contents and adopt teaching methods highly regarded by their colleagues, sometimes even formally sanctioned by their disciplines; they research subjects that will be funded by the granting agencies (which usually come under professional controls); and they publish articles acceptable to the journals refereed by their peers. Pushed to the limit, then, individual freedom becomes professional control. It may be explicit freedom from administrators, even from peers in other disciplines, but it is not implicit freedom from colleagues in their own discipline. Thus we use the label "professional judgment" to imply that while judgment may be the mode of choice, it is informed judgment, mightily influenced by professional training and affiliation.

DECISIONS MADE BY ADMINISTRATIVE FIAT

Professional expertise and autonomy, reinforced by the pigeonholing process, sharply circumscribe the capacity of central administrators to manage the professionals in the ways of conventional bureaucracy—through direct supervision and the designation of internal standards (rules, job descriptions, policies). Even the designation of standards of output or performance is discouraged by the intractable problem of operationalizing the goals of professional work.

Certain types of decisions, less related to the professional work per se, do however fall into the realm of what can be called administrative fiat, in other words, become the exclusive prerogative of the administrators. They include some financial decisions, for example, to buy and sell property and embark on fund-raising campaigns. Because many of the support services are organized in a conventional top-down hierarchy, they too tend to fall under the control of the central administration. Support services more critical to professional matters, however, such as libraries or computers in the universities, tend to fall into the realm of collective decision making, where the central administrators join the professionals in the making of choices.

Central administrators may also play a prominent role in determining the procedures by which the collective process functions: what committees exist, who gets nominated to them, and so on. It is the administrators, after all, who have the time to devote to administration. This role can give skillful administrators considerable influence, however indirect, over the decisions made by others. In addition, in times of crisis administrators may acquire more extensive powers, as the professionals become more inclined to defer to leadership to resolve the issues.

DECISIONS MADE BY COLLECTIVE CHOICE

Many decisions are, however, determined neither by administrators nor by individual professionals. Instead they are handled in interactive processes that combine professionals with administrators from a variety of levels and units. Among the most important of these decisions seem to be ones related to the definition, creation, design, and discontinuation of the pigeonholes, that is, the programs and departments of various kinds. Other important decisions here include the hiring and promotion of professionals and, in some cases, budgeting and the establishment and design of the interactive procedures themselves (if they do not fall under administrative fiat).

Decision making may be considered to involve the three phases of *identification* of the need for decision, *development* of solutions, and *selection* of one of them. Identification seems to depend largely on individual initiative. Given the complexities of professional work and the rigidities of pigeonholing, change in this configuration is difficult to imagine without an initiating "sponsor" or "champion." Development may involve the same individual but often requires the efforts of collective task forces as well. And selection tends to be a fully interactive process, involving several layers of standing committees composed of professionals and administrators, and sometimes outsiders as well (such as government representatives). It is in this last phase that we find the full impact and complexity of mutual adjustment in the administration of professional organizations.

MODELS OF COLLECTIVE CHOICE

How do these interactive processes in fact work? Some writers have traditionally associated professional organizations with a *collegial* model, where decisions are made by a "community of individuals and groups, all of whom may have different roles and specialties, but who share common goals and objectives for the organization" (Taylor, 1983: 18). *Common interest* is the guiding force, and decision making is therefore by consensus. Other writers instead propose a political model, in which the differences of interest groups are irreconcilable. Participants thus seek to serve their *self-interest*, and political factors become instrumental in determining outcomes.

Clearly, neither common interest nor self-interest will dominate decision processes all the time; some combination is naturally to be expected. Professionals may agree on goals yet conflict over how they should be achieved; alternatively, consensus can sometimes be achieved even where goals differ—Democrats do, after all, sometimes vote with Republicans in the U. S. Congress. In fact, we need to consider motivation, not just behavior, in order to distinguish collegiality from politics. Political success sometimes requires a collegial posture—one must cloak self-interest in the mantle of the common good. Likewise, collegial ends sometimes require political means. Thus, we should take as collegial any behavior that is *motivated* by a genuine concern for the good of the institution, and politics as any behavior driven fundamentally by self-interest (of the individual or his or her unit).

A third model that has been used to explain decision making in universities is the *garbage can*. Here decision making is characterized by "collections of choices looking for problems, issues and feelings looking for decision situations in which they may be aired, solutions looking for issues to which they might be an answer, and decision makers looking for work" (Cohen and Olsen, 1972: 1). Behavior is, in other words, nonpurposeful and often random, because goals are unclear and the means to achieve them problematic. Furthermore, participation is fluid because of the cost of time and energy. Thus, in place of the common interest of the collegial model and the self-interest of the political model, the garbage can model suggests a kind of *disinterest*.

The important question is not whether garbage can processes exist—we have all experienced them—but whether they matter. Do they apply to key issues or only to incidental ones? Of course, decisions that are not significant to anyone may well end up in the garbage can, so to speak. There is always someone with free time willing to challenge a proposal for the sake of so doing. But I have difficulty accepting that individuals to whom decisions are important do not invest the effort necessary to influence them. Thus, like common interest and self-interest, I conclude that disinterest neither dominates decision processes nor is absent from them.

Finally, *analysis* may be considered a fourth model of decision making. Here calculation is used, if not to select the best alternative, then at least to assess the acceptability of different ones. Such an approach seems consistent with the machine configuration, where a technostructure stands ready to calculate the costs and benefits of every proposal. But, in fact, analysis figures prominently in the professional configuration too, but here carried out mostly by professional operators themselves. Rational analysis structures arguments for communication and debate and enables champions and their opponents to support their respective positions. In fact, as each side seeks to pick holes in the position of the other, the real issues are more likely to emerge.

Thus, as indicated in Figure 2, the important collective decisions of the professional organization seem to be most influenced by collegial and political processes, with garbage can pressures encouraging a kind of haphazardness on one side (especially for less important decisions) and analytical interventions on the other side encouraging a certain rationality (serving as an invisible hand to keep the lid on the garbage can, so to speak!).

STRATEGIES IN THE PROFESSIONAL ORGANIZATION

Thus, we find here a very different process of strategy making, and very different resulting strategies, compared with conventional (especially machine) organizations. While it may seem difficult to create strategies in these organizations, due to the fragmentation of activity, the politics, and the garbage can phenomenon, in fact the professional organization is inundated with strategies (meaning patterning in its actions). The standardization of skills encourages patterning, as do the pigeonholing process and the professional affiliations. Collegiality promotes consistency of behavior; even politics works to resist changing existing patterns. As for the garbage can model, perhaps it just represents the unexplained variance in the system; that is, whatever is not understood looks to the outside observer like organized anarchy.

Many different people get involved in the strategy-making process here, including administrators and the various professionals, individually and collectively, so that the resulting strategies can be very fragmented (at the limit, each professional pursues his or her own product-market strategy). There are, of course, forces that encourage some overall cohesion in strategy too: the common forces of administrative fiat, the broad negotiations that take place in the collective process (for example, on new tenure regulations in a university), even the forces of habit and tradition, at the limit ideology, that can pervade a professional organization (such as hiring certain kinds of people or favoring certain styles of teaching or of surgery).

Over all, the strategies of the professional organization tend to exhibit a remarkable degree of stability. Major reorientations in strategy—"strategic revolutions"—are discouraged by the fragmentation of activity and the influence of the individual professionals and their outside associates. But at a narrower level, change is ubiquitous. Inside tiny pigeonholes, services are continually being altered, procedure redesigned, and clientele shifted, while in the collective process, pigeonholes are constantly being added and rearranged. Thus, the professional organization is, paradoxically, extremely stable at the broadest level and in a state of perpetual change at the narrowest one.

SOME ISSUES ASSOCIATED WITH THE PROFESSIONAL ORGANIZATION

The professional organization is unique among the different configurations in answering two of the paramount needs of contemporary men and women. It is democratic, disseminating its power directly to its workers (at least those lucky enough to be professional). And it provides them with extensive autonomy, freeing them even from the need to coordinate closely with their colleagues. Thus, the professional has the best of both worlds. He or she is attached to an organization yet is free to serve clients in his or her own way constrained only by the established standards of the profession.

The result is that professionals tend to emerge as highly motivated individuals, dedicated to their work and to the clients they serve. Unlike the machine organization, which places barriers between the operator and the client, this configuration removes them, allowing a personal relationship to develop. Moreover, autonomy enables the professionals to perfect their skills free of interference, as they repeat the same complex programs time after time.

But in these same characteristics, democracy and autonomy, lie the chief problems of the professional organization. For there is no evident way to control the work, outside of that exercised by the profession itself, no way, to correct deficiencies that the professionals choose to overlook. What they tend to overlook are the problems of coordination, of discretion, and of innovation that arise in these configurations.

PROBLEMS OF COORDINATION

The professional organization can coordinate effectively in its operating core only by relying on the standardization of skills. But that is a loose coordinating mechanism at best; it fails to cope with many of the needs that arise in these organizations. One need is to coordinate the work of professionals with that of support staffers. The professionals want to give the orders. But that can catch the support staffers between the vertical power of line authority and the horizontal power of professional expertise. Another need is to achieve overriding coordination among the professionals themselves. Professional organizations, at the limit, may be viewed as collections of independent individuals who come together only to draw on common resources and support services. Though the pigeonholing process facilitates this, some things inevitably fall through the cracks between the pigeonholes. But because the professional organization lacks any obvious coordinating mechanism to deal with these, they inevitably provoke a great deal of conflict. Much political blood is spilled in the continual reassessment of contingencies and programs that are either imperfectly conceived or artificially distinguished.

PROBLEMS OF DISCRETION

Pigeonholing raises another serious problem. It focuses most of the discretion in the hands of single professionals, whose complex skills, no matter how standardized, require the exercise of considerable judgment. Such discretion works fine when professionals are competent and conscientious. But it plays havoc when they are not. Inevitably, some professionals are simply lazy or incompetent. Others confuse the needs of their clients with the skills of their trade. They thus concentrate on a favored program to the exclusion of all others (like the psychiatrist who thinks that all patients, indeed all people, need psychoanalysis). Clients incorrectly sent their way get mistreated (in both senses of that word).

Various factors confound efforts to deal with this inversion of means and ends. One is that professionals are notoriously reluctant to act against their own, for example, to censure irresponsible behavior through their professional associations. Another (which perhaps helps to explain the first) is the intrinsic difficulty of measuring the outputs of professional work. When psychiatrists cannot even define the word *cure* or *healthy*, how are they to prove that psychoanalysis is better for schizophrenics than is chemical therapy?

Discretion allows professionals to ignore not only the needs of their clients but also those of the organization itself. Many professionals focus their loyalty on their profession, not on the place where they happen to practice it. But professional organizations have needs for loyalty too—to support their overall strategies, to staff their administrative committees, to see them through conflicts with the professional associations. Cooperation is crucial to the functioning of the administrative structure, yet many professionals resist it furiously.

PROBLEMS OF INNOVATION

In the professional organization, major innovation also depends on cooperation. Existing programs may be perfected by the single professional, but new ones usually cut across the established specialties—in essence, they require a rearrangement of the pigeonholes—and so call for collective action. As a result, the reluctance of the professionals to cooperate with each other and the complexity of the collective processes can produce resistance to innovation.

These are, after all, professional *bureaucracies,* in essence, performance structures designed to perfect given programs in stable environments, not problem-solving structures to create new programs for unanticipated needs.

The problems of innovation in the professional organization find their roots in convergent thinking, in the deductive reasoning of the professional who sees the specific situation in terms of the general concept. That means new problems are forced into old pigeonholes, as is excellently illustrated in Spencer's comments: "All patients developing significant complications or death among our three hospitals . . . are reported to a central office with a narrative description of the sequence of events, with reports varying in length from a third to an entire page." And six to eight of these cases are discussed in the one-hour weekly "mortality-morbidity" conferences, including presentation of it by the surgeon and "questions and comments" by the audience (1978: 118). An "entire" page and ten minutes of discussion for a case with "significant complications"! Maybe that is enough to list the symptoms and slot them into pigeonholes. But it is hardly enough even to begin to think about creative solutions. As Lucy once told Charlie Brown, great art cannot be done in half an hour; it takes at least 45 minutes!

The fact is that great art and innovative problem solving require *inductive* reasoning—that is, inference of the new general solution from the particular experience. And that kind of thinking is *divergent*; it breaks away from old routines or standards rather than perfecting existing ones. And that flies in the face of everything the professional organization is designed to do.

PUBLIC RESPONSES TO THESE PROBLEMS

What responses do the problems of coordination, discretion, and innovation evoke? Most commonly, those outside the profession see the problems as resulting from a lack of external control of the professional and the profession. So they do the obvious: try to control the work through other, more traditional means. One is direct supervision, which typically means imposing an intermediate level of supervision to watch over the professionals. But we already discussed why this cannot work for jobs that are complex. Another is to try to standardize the work or its outputs. But we also discussed why complex work cannot be formalized by rules, regulations, or measures of performance. All these types of controls really do, by transferring the responsibility for the service from the professional to the administrative structure, is destroy the effectiveness of the work. It is not the government that educates the student, not even the school system or the school itself; it is not the hospital that delivers the baby. These things are done by the individual professional. If that professional is incompetent, no plan or rule fashioned in the technostructure, no order from any administrator or government official, can ever make him or her competent. But such plans, rules, and orders can impede the competent professional from providing his or her service effectively.

Are there then no solutions for a society concerned about the performance of its professional organizations? Financial control of them and legislation against irresponsible professional behavior are obviously in order. But beyond that solutions must grow from a recognition of professional work for what it is. Change in the professional organization does not *sweep* in from new administrators taking office to announce wide reforms, or from government officials intent on bringing the professionals under technocratic control. Rather, change *seeps* in through the slow process of changing the professionals—changing who enters the profession in the first place, what they learn in its professional schools (norms as well as skills and knowledge), and thereafter how they upgrade their skills. Where desired changes are resisted, society may be best off to call on its professionals' sense of public responsibility or, failing that, to bring pressure on the professional associations rather than on the professional bureaucracies.

BY JAMES BRIAN QUINN, PHILIP ANDERSON, AND SYDNEY FINKELSTEIN

■ With rare exceptions, the economic and producing power of a modern corporation or nation lies more in its intellectual and systems capabilities than in its hard assets—raw materials, land, plant, and equipment. Intellectual and information processes create most of the value added for firms in the large service industries—like software, medical care, communications, education, entertainment, accounting, law, publishing, consulting, advertising, retailing, wholesaling, and transportation—which provide 79 percent of all jobs and 76 percent of all U.S. GNP. In manufacturing as well, intellectual activities—like R&D, process design, product design, logistics, marketing, marketing research, systems management, or technological innovation—generate the preponderance of value added. . . .

The capacity to manage intellect and to convert it into useful outputs has become the critical executive skill of the era. Yet few managements have systematic answers to even these basic questions:

■ What is intellect? Where does it reside? How do we capture it? Leverage it?
■ What special skills are needed to manage professional vs. creative intellect? How can a firm measure the value of its intellect? How can managers leverage their firm's intellectual resources to the maximum?

WHAT IS INTELLECT?

Webster's Dictionary defines intellect as "knowing or understanding: the capacity for knowledge, for rational or highly developed use of intelligence." The intellect of an organization—in order of increasing importance—includes: (1) *cognitive knowledge* (or know what); (2) *advanced skills* (know how); (3) *system understanding* and *trained intuition* (know why); and (4) *self-motivated creativity* (care why). Intellect clearly resides inside the firm's human brains. The first three levels can also exist in the organization's systems, databases, or operating technologies. If properly nurtured, intellect in each form is both highly leverageable and protectable. *Cognitive knowledge* is essential, but usually far from sufficient for success. Many may know the rules for performance—on a football field, piano, or accounting ledger—but lack the higher skills necessary to make money at it in competition.

Similarly, some possess advanced skills but lack system understanding: they can perform selected tasks well, but often do not fully understand how their actions affect other elements of the organization or how to improve the total entity's effectiveness. Similarly, some people may possess both the knowledge to perform a task and the *advanced skills* to compete, but lack the will, motivation, or adaptability for success. Highly *motivated* and *creative* groups often outperform others with greater physical or fiscal endowments.

The value of a firm's intellect increases markedly as one moves up the intellectual scale from cognitive knowledge toward motivated creativity. Yet, in a strange and costly anomaly, most enterprises reverse this priority in their training and systems development expenditures, focusing virtually all their attention on basic (rather than advanced) skills development and little or none on systems, motivational, or creative skills. . . .

CHARACTERISTICS OF INTELLECT

The best managed companies avoid this by exploiting certain critical characteristics of intellect at both the strategic and operational levels.

---

*Reprinted with deletions from "Managing Expertise," J. B. Quinn, P. Anderson, and S. Finkelstein, *Academy of Management Executive*, Vol. 10 (3), 1996, 7–27.

EXPONENTIALITY

Properly stimulated, knowledge and intellect grow exponentially. All learning and experience curves have this characteristic. As knowledge is captured or internalized, the available knowledge base itself becomes higher. . . . The effect accelerates as higher levels of knowledge allow the organization to attack more complex problems and to interrelate with other knowledge sources it earlier could not access. . . .

The strategic consequences of exploiting exponentiality are profound. Once a firm obtains a knowledge-based competitive edge, it becomes ever easier to maintain its lead and harder for competitors to catch up. The most serious threat is that through complacency intellectual leaders may lose their knowledge advantage. . . . This is why the highest level of intellect, self-motivated creativity, is so vital. Firms that nurture "care why" are able to thrive on today's rapid changes. . . .

SHARING

Another important characteristic is that knowledge is one of the few assets that grows most—also usually exponentially—when shared. . . . The core intellectual competency of many financial firms . . . lies in the human experts and the systems software that collect and analyze the data surrounding their investment specialties. Access to the internals of these centralized software systems is tightly limited to a few specialists working at headquarters. Here they share and leverage their own specialized analytical skills through close interactions with other financial specialists, "rocket scientist" modelers, and the unique access the firm has to massive transactions data. . . .

EXPANDABILITY

Unlike physical assets, intellect: (a) increases in value with use; (b) tends to have much under-utilized capacity; (c) can be self-organizing; and (d) is greatly expandable under pressure. How can a company exploit these characteristics? . . . The processes they use resemble successful coaching more than anything else. The critical activities are: (1) recruiting the right people; (2) stimulating them to internalize the information knowledge, skills, and attitudes needed for success; (3) creating systematic technological and organizational structures to capture, focus, and leverage intellect to the greatest possible extent; and (4) demanding and rewarding top performance from all players. . . .

There are important differences between managing professional versus creative intellect. Although much attention has been given to managing creativity, little has been written about managing professionals. Yet professionals are the most important source of intellect for most organizations. For every truly creative organization, there are probably twenty to 100 professional groups creating high value deep within integrated firms or directly for customers. What characterizes such professionals?

PERFECTION, NOT CREATIVITY

While no precise delineation applies in all cases, most (90 to 98 percent) of a typical professional's activity is directed at perfection, not creativity (Schön, 1983). The true professional commands a complete body of knowledge—a discipline—and updates that knowledge constantly. In most cases, the customer wants the knowledge delivered reliably with the most advanced skill available. Although there is an occasional call for creativity, the preponderance of work in actuarial units, dentistry, hospitals, accounting units, opera companies, universities, law firms, aircraft operations, equipment maintenance, etc. requires the repeated use of highly developed skills on relatively similar, though complex, problems. People rarely want their surgeons, accountants, airline pilots, maintenance personnel, or nuclear plant operators to be very creative, except in emergencies. . . . Finding and developing extraordinary talent is thus the first critical managerial prerequisite. McKinsey long focused on only the top 1 percent of graduates from the top five business schools and screened heavily from these. . . .

Intense Training, Mentoring, and Peer Pressure

These factors literally force professionals to the top of their knowledge ziggurat. The best students go to the most demanding schools. The top graduate schools—whether in law, business, engineering, science, or medicine—further reselect and drive these students with greater challenges and with 100-hour work weeks. Then upon graduation the best of the survivors go back to even more intense "boot camps" in medical internships, law associate programs, or other outrageously demanding training situations as pilots, consultants, or technical specialists. The result is to drive the best professionals up a learning curve that is steeper than anyone else's. . . . The keys are forcing professional trainees' growth with constantly heightened (preferably customer-induced) complexity, thoroughly planned mentoring, high rewards for performance, and strong stimuli to understand, systematize, and advance their professional disciplines. . . .

Constantly Increasing Challenges

Intellect grows most when challenged. Hence, heavy internal competition and constant performance appraisal are common. . . . The best organizations constantly push their professionals beyond the comfort of their catalogued book knowledge, simulation models, and controlled laboratories. They relentlessly drive associates to deal with the more complex intellectual realms of live customers, real operating systems, and highly differentiated external environments and cultural differences. They insist on and actively support mentoring by those nearest the top of their fields. And they reward associates for their competencies. Mediocre organizations do not.

Managing an Elite

Each profession tends to regard itself as an elite. Members look to their profession and to their peers to determine codes for behavior and acceptable performance standards. They often disdain the values and evaluations of those "outside their discipline." This is the source of many professional organizations' problems. Professionals tend to surround themselves with people having similar backgrounds and values. Unless consciously fractured, these discipline-based cocoons quickly become inward-looking bureaucracies, resistant to change, and detached from customers. Because professionals' knowledge is their power base, many are reluctant to share it with others unless there are powerful inducements. . . .

Because they have unique knowledge and have been trained as an elite, professionals tend to regard their judgment in all realms as sacrosanct. Professionals hesitate to subordinate themselves to others to support organizational goals not completely congruent with their special viewpoint. This is why most professional firms operate as partnerships and not hierarchies, and why it is so hard for them to adopt a distinctive strategy. . . .

FEW SCALE ECONOMIES?

Yet many enterprises seem to overlook or violate all these critical characteristics in developing, leveraging, and measuring professionals' capabilities. One reason: conventional wisdom has long held that there are few scale economies—which allow leverages—in professional activities. A pilot can only handle one aircraft; a great chef can cook only so many different dishes at once; a top researcher can conduct only so many unique experiments; a doctor can only diagnose one patient's illness at a time; and so on. In such situations, adding professionals at a minimum multiplies costs at the same rates as outputs. In fact, most often, growth brought *diseconomies* of scale as the bureaucracies coordinating, monitoring, or supporting the professionals actually expanded faster than the professional base. . . .

But new technologies and management approaches now enable firms to develop, capture, and leverage intellectual resources to much higher levels. The keys are: (1) to design organizations and technology systems around *intellectual flows* rather than command and control concepts; (2) to develop performance measurements and incentive systems that reward managers for developing intellectual assets and customer value—and not just for producing current profits and using physical assets more efficiently. . . .

The crux of leveraging intellect is to focus one's own resources on those things—important to customers—where the company can create uniquely high value for its customers. Conceptually, this means disaggregating both corporate staff activities and the value chain into manageable intellectual clusters. . . . Such activities can either be performed internally or outsourced depending on one's own relative costs and competencies. For maximum effectiveness, a company should concentrate its own resources and executive time on those few activities where it performs at "best-in-world" levels. . . .

ORGANIZING AROUND INTELLECT

Exploiting these new intellectually based strategies often calls for new organization concepts. . . . we expect much greater use of four [of these] basic organizational forms that leverage professional intellect uniquely well. These are the infinitely flat, inverted, starburst, and spider's web forms. . . .

All the forms tend to push responsibility outward to the point at which the company contacts the customer. All tend to flatten the organization and remove layers of hierarchy. All seek faster, more responsive action to deal with the customization and personalization an affluent and complex marketplace demands. All require breaking away from traditional thinking about: lines of command, one person–one boss structures, the center as a directing force, and management of physical assets as the key to success. But each differs substantially in its purpose and management. . . .

"INFINITELY FLAT" ORGANIZATIONS

[The] infinitely flat organizations [are] so called because there is no inherent limit to their span. . . . Single centers in such organizations presently can coordinate anywhere from 20 to 18,000 individual nodes. Common examples include highly dispersed fast-food, brokerage, shipping, mail order, or airline flight operations.

Several other characteristics are also important. The nodes themselves rarely communicate with each other, operating quite independently. The center rarely needs to give direct orders to the line organization. Instead, it is primarily an information source, a communications coordinator, and a reference desk for unusual inquiries. Lower organizational levels generally connect into the center to obtain information to improve their performances, rather than for instructions or specific guidance. Most operating rules are programmed into the system and changed automatically by software. . . . For example, Merrill Lynch's 480 domestic brokerage offices each connect directly into the parent's central information office to satisfy the bulk of their information and analytic needs. . . .

Infinitely flat organizations present certain inherent management problems. Lower level personnel wonder how to advance in a career path when there is no "up." Those at the center require totally different skills from those at the nodes. Traditional job evaluation systems break down, and new compensation systems based on professional capability, individual performance, and customer satisfaction become imperative. . . . the essence of . . . management is capturing, analyzing, and disseminating the most detailed possible level of customer-relevant information from the center to the contact nodes.

FIGURE 1
THE INVERTED
ORGANIZATION

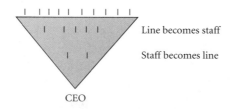

THE INVERTED ORGANIZATION

In the inverted form, the major locus of *both* knowledge and the conversion of knowledge into solutions is at the point of contact with customers, not at the center. Hospitals or medical clinics, therapeutic care-giving units, or consulting-engineering firms provide typical examples. These "nodes" tend to be highly professional and self-sufficient. Accordingly, there is no need for direct linkage between the nodes. When critical knowledge about operations diffuses, it usually does so informally from node to node—or formally from node to center—the opposite of the infinitely flat organization. . . .

In inverted organizations, the former line hierarchy becomes a "support" structure, only intervening in extreme emergencies—as might the CEO of a hospital or the chief pilot of an airline (see Figure 1). The function of "line" managers becomes bottleneck breaking, culture development, communication of values, developing special studies, consulting on request, expediting resource movements, and providing service economies of scale. . . . Generally . . . what was "line" (order giving) management now performs essentially "staff" (analytical or support) activities.

A well-known example is NovaCare, the largest provider of rehabilitation care in the United States and one of the fastest growing health care companies of the last decade. With its central resource—well-trained physical, occupational, and speech therapists in short supply—NovaCare provides the business infrastructure for over 4,000 therapists, arranging and merging contracts with nursing homes and chains, handling accounting and credit activities, providing training updates, and stabilizing and enhancing therapists' earnings. However, the key to performance is the therapists' knowledge and their capability to deliver this individually to patients. . . .

The inverted organization poses certain unique challenges. The apparent loss of formal authority can be very traumatic for former "line managers." Given acknowledged formal power, contact people may tend to act ever more like specialists with strictly "professional" outlooks, and to resist any set of organization rules or business norms. Given their predilections, contact people often don't stay current with details about the firm's own complex internal systems. And their empowerment without adequate information and controls (embedded in the firm's technology systems) can be extremely dangerous. A classic example is the rapid decline of People Express, which enjoyed highly empowered and motivated point people, but lacked the systems or computer infrastructures to enable them to self-coordinate as the organization grew. . . .

THE STARBURST

Another highly leverageable form, the starburst, serves well when there is highly specialized and valuable intellect at *both* the nodes and the center. Starbursts are common in creative organizations that constantly peel off more permanent, but separate, units like shooting stars from their core competencies (see Figure 2). These spin-offs remain partially or wholly owned by the parent, usually can raise external resources independently, and are controlled primarily by market mechanisms. Some common examples . . . include: movie studios, mutual fund groups or venture capitalists. . . .

Unlike holding companies, starbursts contain some central core of intellectual competency. They are not merely banks or portfolio managers. The nodes—essentially separate

FIGURE 2
THE STARBURST
ORGANIZATION

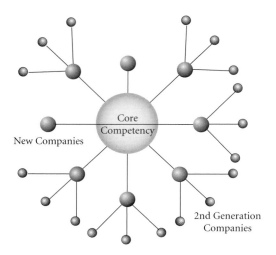

permanent business units, not individuals or temporary clusters—have continuing relationships with given marketplaces and are the locus of important, specialized, market, or production knowledge. The nodes may in time spin out further enterprises from their core. . . .

Starburst organizations work well when the core embodies an expensive or complex set of competencies and houses a few knowledgeable risk takers who realize they cannot micromanage the diverse entities at the nodes. . . . Usually they occur in environments where entrepreneurship—not merely flexible response—is critical. . . . In addition to maintaining the core competency, the corporate center generally manages the culture, sets broad priorities, selects key people, and raises resources more efficiently than could the nodes. Unlike conglomerates, starbursts maintain some cohesive, constantly renewed, and critical intellectual competencies at their center.

The classic problem of this organizational form is that managements often lose faith in their freestanding "shooting stars." After some time they try to consolidate functions in the name of efficiency or economies of scale—as some movie studios, HP, TI, and 3M did to their regret—and only recover by reversing such policies.

THE "SPIDER'S WEB"

The spider's web form is a true network. (The term "spider's web" avoids confusion with other "network-like" forms, particularly those that are more akin to holding company or matrix organizations.) In the spider's web there is often *no* intervening hierarchy or order-giving center among the nodes. In fact it may be hard to define where the center is. The locus of intellect is highly dispersed, residing largely at the contact nodes (as in the inverted organization). However, solutions are developed around a project or problem that requires the nodes to interact intimately or to seek others who happen to have the knowledge or special capabilities that a particular problem requires.

The purest example of a spider's web is the Internet, which is managed by no one. Other common examples include most open markets, securities exchanges, library consortia, diagnostic teams, research, or political action groups.

Individual nodes may operate quite independently, when it is not essential to tap the knowledge of other sources to solve a problem efficiently. On a given project there may or may not be a single authority center. Often decisions will merely occur through informal processes if the parties agree. . . . This form of organizing releases the imaginations of many different

FIGURE 3
SPIDER'S WEB
ORGANIZATIONS

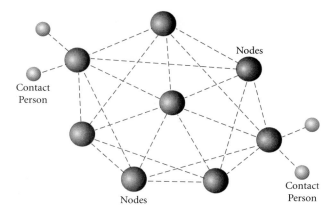

searchers in diverse locations, multiplies the numbers of possible opportunity encounters, and encourages the formation of entirely new solutions from a variety of disciplines.

While they are usually effective for problem finding and analysis, spider's webs present important challenges when used for decision making. Dawdling is common, as nodes work on refining their specialist solutions instead of solving the complete problem together. Assigning credit for intellectual contributions is difficult, and cross-competition among nodes can inhibit the sharing on which such networks depend (see Figure 3).

Each organization form performs best for a specific set of intellectual tasks. Hence most large enterprises will require a mixture of these basic building blocks, combined with more traditional hierarchical structures (see Figure 4).

FIGURE 4
HOW DIFFERENT
ORGANIZING FORMS
DEVELOP INTELLECT

TYPE OF INTELLECT	INFINITELY FLAT	INVERTED	STARBURST	SPIDER'S WEB
Cognitive (Know-what)	Deep knowledge and information at center	Primary intellect at nodes, support services from center	Depth at center (technical) and (markets) at the nodes	Dispersed, brought together for projects
Advanced Skill (Know-how)	Programmed into systems	Professionalized skills informally transferred node to node	Transferred from center to node, then node to node via the core	Latent until a project assembles a skill collection
Systems Knowledge (Know-why)	Systems experts at the center. Customer knowledge at the nodes	Systems and customer expertise at the nodes	Split: between central technical competency at the core, systematic market knowledge at nodes	Discovered in interaction or created via search enabled by the network
Motivated Creativity (Care-why)	Frees employees from routine for more skilled work	Great professional autonomy	Entrepreneurial incentives	Personal interest, leveraged through active interdependence stimulation

BY DAVID H. MAISTER

■ The topic of managing professional service firms (PSF) (including law, consulting, investment banking, accountancy, architecture, engineering, and others) has been relatively neglected by management researchers. . . . Yet in recent years large (if not giant) PSFs have emerged in most of the professional service industries. . . .

The professional service firm is the ultimate embodiment of that familiar phrase "Our assets are our people." Frequently, a PSF tends to sell to its clients the services of particular individuals (or a team of such individuals) more than the services of the firm. Professional services usually involve a high degree of interaction with the client, together with a high degree of customization. Both of these characteristics demand that the firm attract (and retain) highly skilled individuals. The PSF, therefore, competes in two markets simultaneously: the "output" market for its services and the "input" market for its productive resources—the professional workforce. It is the need to balance the often conflicting demands and constraints imposed by these two markets that consitutes the special challenge for managers of the professional service firm.

This article explores the interaction of these forces inside the professional service firm, and examines some of the major variables that firm management can attempt to manipulate in order to bring these forces into balance. The framework employed for this examination is shown in Figure 1, which illustrates the proposition that balancing the demands of the two markets is accomplished through the firm's economic and organizational structures. All four of these elements—the two markets and the two structures—are tightly interrelated. By examining each in turn, we shall attempt to identify the major variables which form the links shown in Figure 1. First, the article will examine the typical organizational structure of the firm; second, it

FIGURE 1
FRAMEWORK FOR
ANALYZING THE PSF

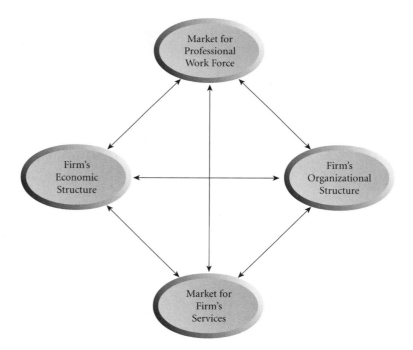

will explore the economic structure and its relation to other elements. It shall then consider the market for professional labor, and finally discuss the market for the firm's services. As we shall see, successful PSF management is a question of balance among the four elements of Figure 1.

THE ORGANIZATIONAL STRUCTURE OF THE PSF

The archetypal structure of the professional service firm is an organization containing three professional levels which serve as a normal or expected career path. In a consulting organization, these levels might be labeled junior consultant, manager, and vice-president. In a CPA firm they might be referred to as staff accountant, manager, and partner. Law firms tend to have only two levels, associate and partner, although there is an increasing tendency in large law firms to formally recognize what has long been an informal distinction between junior and senior partners. Whatever the precise structure, nearly all PSFs have the pyramid form shown in Figure 2.

There is nothing magical about the common occurrence of three levels (a greater or lesser number may be found), but it is instructive to consider other organizations that have this pattern. One example is the university which has assistant professors, associate professors, and full professors. These ranks may be signs of status as well as function (reminding us of another three-level status structure: the common people, the peerage, and royalty). Another analogy is found in the organization of the medieval craftsman's shop which had apprentices, journeymen, and master craftsmen. Indeed, the early years of an individual's association with a PSF are usually viewed as an apprenticeship: the senior craftsmen repay the hard work and assistance of the juniors by teaching them their craft.

PROJECT TEAM STRUCTURE

What determines the shape or architecture of the organization—the relative mix of juniors, managers, and seniors that the organization requires? Fundamentally, this depends on the nature of the professional services that the firm provides, and how these services are delivered. Because of their customized nature, most professional activities are organized on a project basis: the professional service firms are the job shops of the service sector. The project nature of the work means that there are basically three major activities in the delivery of professional services: client relations, project management, and the performance of the detailed professional tasks.

In most PSFs, primary responsibility for these three tasks is allocated to the three levels of the organization: seniors (partners or vice-presidents) are responsible for client relations; managers, for the day-to-day supervision and coordination of projects; and juniors, for the many

FIGURE 2
THE PROFESSIONAL
PYRAMID

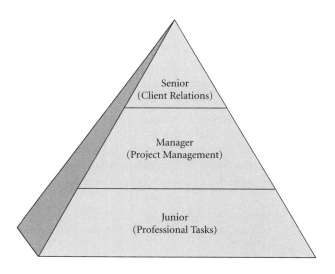

technical tasks necessary to complete the study. In the vernacular, the three levels are "the finders, the minders and the grinders" of the business.* Naturally, such an allocation of tasks need not (indeed, should not) be as rigid as this suggests. In a well-run PSF, juniors are increasingly given "manager" tasks to perform (in order to test their competence and worthiness to be promoted to the manager level), and managers are gradually given tasks that enable them to develop client-relations skills to prepare for promotion to the senior level. Nevertheless, it is still meaningful to talk of "senior tasks," "manager tasks," and "junior tasks."

CAPACITY PLANNING

The required shape of the PSF is thus primarily influenced by the mix of client relations, project management, and professional tasks involved in the firm's projects. If the PSF is a job shop, then its professional staff members are its "machines" (productive resources). As with any job shop, a balance must be established between the types of work performed and the number of different types of "machines" (people) that are required. The PSF is a "factory," and the firm must plan its capacity. . . .

THE ECONOMICS OF THE PSF

Most professional service firms are partnerships; some are corporations. Regardless of the precise form, however, certain regularities in the economic structure are observable. For example, since most PSFs have few fixed assets, they only require capital to fund accounts receivable and other working capital items. Consequently, the vast majority of revenues are disbursed in the form of salaries, bonuses, and net partnership profits. A typical division of revenues might be 33 percent for professional salaries, 33 percent for support staff and overhead, and 33 percent for senior (or shareholder) salary compensation. However, in some PSFs, partnership salary and profits might rise to 50 percent or more, usually corresponding to lower support staff and overhead costs.

GENERATING REVENUES

If revenues are typically disbursed in this way, how are they generated? . . . The relevant variable is, of course, the billing rate—the hourly charge to clients for the services of individuals at different levels of the hierarchy. The ratio between the lowest and highest rates in some firms can exceed 3 or 4 to 1. The "rewards of partnership" come only in part from the high rates that top professionals can charge their clients. Partners' rewards are also derived, in large part, from the firm's ability, through its project team structure, to *leverage* the professional skills of the seniors with the efforts of juniors. As the managing senior of a top consulting firm observed, "How is it that a young MBA, straight from graduate school, can give advice to top corporate officers?" The answer lies in the synergy of the PSF's project team. Acting independently, the juniors could not "bill out" the results of their efforts at the rates that can be charged by the PSF. The firm can obtain higher rates for the juniors' efforts because they are combined with the expertise and guidance of the seniors. . . .

The Billing Multiple

It is also instructive to compare the net weighted billing rate to compensation levels within the firm. This (conventional) calculation is known as the billing multiple, and is calculated (for either the firm or an individual) as the billing rate per hour divided by the total compensation per hour. . . . The average multiple for most firms is between 2.5 and 4.

---

*This characteristic is, of course, simplified. Additional "levels" or functions can be identified at both the top and the bottom of the pyramid. To the top we can add those individuals responsible for managing the *firm* (rather than managing projects). At the bottom of the pyramid lie both "nonprofessional" support staff and trainees.

The appropriate billing multiple that the firm can achieve will, of course, be influenced by the added value that the firm provides and by the relative supply and demand conditions for the firm's services. The market for the firm's services will determine the fees it can command for a given project. The firm's costs will be determined by its ability to deliver the service with a "profitable" mix of junior, manager, and senior time. If the firm . . . can find a way to deliver the service with a higher proportion of juniors to seniors, it will be able to achieve lower costs and hence a higher multiple. The project team structure of the firm is, therefore, an important component of firm profitability.

The billing multiple is intimately related to the breakeven economics of the firm. If total professional salaries are taken as an amount $Y, and support staff and overhead cost approximate, say, an equivalent amount $Y, then breakeven will be attained when the firm bills $2Y. This could be attained by charging clients a multiple of 2 for professional services, but only if all available time was billed out. If the firm wishes to break even at 50 percent target utilization (a common figure in many PSFs), then the required net billing multiple will be 4. . . .

THE PSF AND THE MARKET FOR PROFESSIONAL LABOR

One of the key characteristics of the PSF is that the three levels (junior, manager, senior) constitute a well-defined career path. Individuals joining the organization normally begin at the bottom, with strong expectations of progressing through the organization at some pace agreed to (explicitly or implicitly) in advance. While this pace may not be a rigid one ("up or out in the X years"), both the individual and the organization usually share strong expectations about what constitutes a reasonable period of time. Individuals that are not promoted within this period will seek greener pastures elsewhere, either by their own choice or career ambitions or at the strong suggestion of those who do not consider them promotable. Intermediate levels in the hierarchy are not considered by the individual or the organization as career positions. It is this characteristic, perhaps more than any other, that distinguishes the PSF from other types of organizations.

Promotion Policy

While there are many considerations that attract young professionals to a particular firm, career opportunities within the firm usually play a large role. Two dimensions of this rate of progress are important: the normal amount of time spent at each level before being considered for promotion and the "odds of making it" (the proportion promoted). These promotion policy variables perform an important screening function. Not all young professionals are able to develop the managerial and client-relations skills required at the higher levels. While good recruiting procedures may reduce the degree of screening required through the promotion process, they can rarely eliminate the need for the promotion process to serve this important function. The "risk of not making it" also serves the firm by placing pressure on junior personnel to work hard and succeed. This pressure can be an important motivating tool in light of the discretion which many PSF professionals have over their working schedules. . . .

Accommodating Rapid Growth

. . . What adjustments can be made to allow faster growth? Basically, there are four strategies. First, the firm can devote more attention and resources to its hiring process so that a higher proportion of juniors can be routinely promoted to managers. (In effect, this shifts the quality-of-personnel screen from the promotion system to the hiring system, where it is often more difficult and speculative.) Second, the firm can attempt to hasten the "apprenticeship" process through more formal training and professional development programs, rather than the " learn by example" and mentoring relationships commonly found in smaller firms and those growing at a more leisurely pace. In fact, it is the rate of growth, rather than the size of the firm, which necessitates formal development programs. . . .*

The third mechanism that the firm can adopt to accelerate its target growth rate is to make use of "lateral hires": bringing in experienced professionals at other than the junior level. In most PSFs, this strategy is avoided because of its adverse effect upon the morale of junior personnel, who tend to view such actions as reducing their own chances for promotion. Even if these have been accelerated by the fast growth rate, juniors will still tend to feel that they have been less than fairly dealt with.

Modifying the project team structure is the final strategy for accommodating rapid growth without throwing out of balance the relationships between organizational structure, promotion incentives, and economic structure. In effect, the firm would alter the mix of senior, manager, and junior time devoted to a project. This strategy will be discussed in a later section.

Turnover

. . . In most PSF industries, one or more firms can be identified that have a high target rate of turnover (or alternatively, choose to grow at less than their optimal rate). Yet individuals routinely join these organizations knowing that the odds of "making it" are very low. Such "churning" strategies have some clear disadvantages *and* benefits for the PSF itself. One of the benefits is that the firm's partners (or shareholders) can routinely earn the surplus value of the juniors without having to repay them in the form of promotion. The high turnover rate also allows a significant degree of screening so that only the "best" stay in the organization. Not surprisingly, firms following this strategy tend to be among the most prestigious in their industry.

This last comment gives us a clue as to why such firms are able to maintain this strategy over time. For many recruits, the experience, training, and association with a prestigious firm compensate for poor promotion opportunities. Young professionals view a short period of time at such a firm as a form of " post-postgraduate" degree, and often leave for prime positions they could not have achieved (as quickly) by another route. Indeed, most of the prestigious PSFs following this strategy not only encourage this, but also provide active "outplacement" assistance. Apart from the beneficial effects that such activities provide in recruiting the next generation of juniors, such "alumni/ae" are often the source of future business for the PSF when they recommend that their corporate employers hire their old firm (which they know and understand) over other competitors. The ability to place ex-staff in prestigious positions is one of the prerequisites of a successful churning strategy. . . .

THE MARKET FOR THE FIRM'S SERVICES

The final element in our model is the market for the firm's services. We have already explored some of the ways in which this market is linked to the firm's economic structure (through the billing rates the firm charges) and to the organizational structure (through the project team structure and target growth rate).

We must add to our model one of the most basic linkages in the dynamics of the PSF: the direct link between the market for professional labor and the market for the firm's services. The key variable that links these two markets is the quality of professional labor that the firm

---

*Speeding the development of individuals so that the firm can grow faster is, of course, not the only role for formal training programs. They can also be a device to allow the firm to hire less (initially) qualified and hence lower wage individuals, thereby reducing its costs for juniors.

requires and can attract. Earlier, when we considered the factors that attract professionals to a given PSF, we omitted a major variable that often enters into the decision process: the types of projects undertaken by the firm. Top professionals are likely to be attracted to the firm that engages in exciting or challenging projects, or that provides opportunities for professional fulfillment and development. In turn, firms engaged in such projects *need* to attract the best professionals. It is, therefore, necessary to consider different types of professional service activity.

Project Types

While there are many dimensions which may distinguish one type of professional service activity from another, one in particular is crucial: the degree of customization required in the delivery of the service. To explore this, we will characterize professional service projects into three types: "Brains," "Grey Hair," and "Procedure."

In the first type (Brains), the client's problem is likely to be extremely complex, perhaps at the forefront of professional or technical knowledge. The PSF that targets this market will be attempting to sell its services on the basis of the high professional craft of its staff. In essence, this firm's appeal to its market is "hire us because we're smart." The key elements of this type of professional service are creativity, innovation, and the pioneering of new approaches, concepts, or techniques—in effect, new solutions to new problems. [See next chapter on the innovative context.]

Grey Hair projects may require highly customized "output," but they usually involve a lesser degree of innovation and creativity than a Brains' project. The general nature of the problem is familiar, and the activities necessary to complete the project may be similar to those performed on other projects. Clients with Grey Hair problems seek out PSFs with experience in their particular type of problem. The PSF sells it knowledge, its experience, and its judgment. In effect, it is saying: "Hire us because we have been through this before. We have practice in solving this type of problem."

The third type of project (Procedure) usually involves a well-recognized and familiar type of problem, at least within the professional community. While some customization is still required, the steps necessary to accomplish this are somewhat programmatic. Although clients may have the ability and resources to perform the work themselves, they may turn to the PSF because it can perform the service more efficiently; because it is an outsider; or because the clients' staff capabilities may be employed better elsewhere. In essence, the PSF is selling its procedures, its efficiency, and its availability: "Hire us because we know how to do this and can deliver it effectively."

Project Team Structure

One of the most significant differences between the three types of projects is the project team structure required to deliver the firm's services. Brains projects are usually denoted by an extreme job-shop operation, involving highly skilled and highly paid professionals. Few procedures are routinizable: each project is a "one-off." Accordingly, the opportunities for leveraging the top professionals with juniors are relatively limited. Even though such projects may involve significant data collection and analysis (usually done by juniors), even these activities cannot be clearly specified in advance and require the involvement of at least middle-level (project management) professionals on a continuous basis. Consequently, the ratio of junior time to middle-level and senior time on Brains projects tends to be low. The project team structure of a firm with a high proportion of Brains projects will tend to have a relatively low emphasis on juniors, with a corresponding impact on the shape of the organization.

Since the problems to be addressed in Grey Hair projects are somewhat familiar, some of the tasks to be performed (particularly the early ones) are known in advance and can be specified and delegated. More juniors can be employed to accomplish these tasks, which are then assembled and jointly evaluated at some middle stage of the process. Unlike the "pure job-shop" nature of Brains projects, the appropriate process to create and deliver a Grey Hair project more closely resembles a disconnected assembly line.

Procedure projects usually involve the highest proportion of junior time relative to senior time, and hence imply a different organizational shape for firms that specialize in such projects. The problems to be addressed in such projects, and the steps necessary to complete the analysis, diagnosis, and conclusions, are usually sufficiently well established so that they can be easily delegated to junior staff (with supervision). Whereas in Grey Hair projects senior or middle-level staff must evaluate the results of one stage of the project before deciding how to proceed, in Procedure projects the range of possible outcomes for some steps may be so well known that the appropriate responses can be "programmed." The operating procedure takes on even more of the characteristics of an assembly line.

While the three categories described are only points along a spectrum of project types, it is a simple task in any PSF industry to identify types of problems that fit these categories. The choice that the firm makes in its mix of project types is one of the most important variables available to balance the firm. As we have shown, this choice determines the firm's project team structure, thereby influencing significantly the economic and organizational structures of the firm.

CONCLUSIONS: BALANCING THE PROFESSIONAL SERVICE FIRM

Figure 3 summarizes our review of the four major elements involved in balancing the PSF and the major variables linking these elements. What may we conclude from this review? Our discussion has shown that the four elements are, indeed, tightly linked. The firm cannot change one element without making corresponding changes in one or more of the other three. . . .

In performing these balance analyses, the firm must distinguish between the "levers" (variables that it controls) and the "rocks" (variables substantially constrained by the forces of the market). . . .

FIGURE 3
BALANCING THE PSF

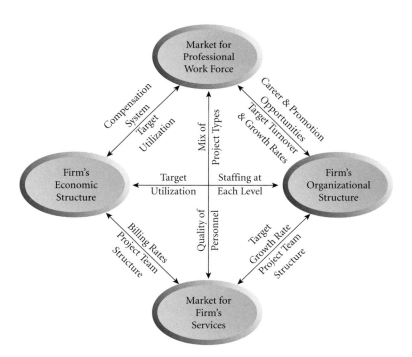

Perhaps the most significant management variable is the mix of projects undertaken and the implications this has for the project team structure. This variable is a significant force in influencing the economics of the firm, its organizational structure, and both markets. The project team structure as defined in this article (i.e., the *average* or typical proportion of time required from professionals at different levels) has not been a variable that is routinely monitored by PSF management. However, as we have shown, its role in balancing the firm is critical.

It is possible, and not uncommon, for the firm's project team structure to change over time. If it is possible to deliver the firm's services with a greater proportion of juniors, this will reduce the costs of the project. Competition in the market will, over time, require the firm to seek lower costs for projects, thus creating opportunities for more juniors to be used on projects that required a high proportion of senior time in the past. Projects that, in the past, had Brains or Grey Hair characteristics may be accomplished as Procedure projects in future years.*

When considering new projects to undertake, it is usually more profitable for the firm to engage in a project similar to one recently performed for a previous client. The knowledge, expertise, and basic approaches to the problem that were developed (often through significant personal and financial investment) can be capitalized upon by applying them to a similar or related problem. Frequently, the second project can be billed out to the client at a similar (or only slightly lower) rate, since the client perceives (and receives) something equally custom-tailored: the solution to his or her problem. However, the savings in PSF costs in delivering this customization are not all shared with the client (if, indeed, any are). The firm thus makes its most money by "leading the market": selling a service with reproducible, standardizable elements as a fully customized service at a fully customized price.

Unfortunately, even before the market catches up and refuses to bear the fully customized price, the firm may encounter an internal behavior problem. While it is in the best interest of the *firm* to undertake similar or repetitive engagements, often this does not coincide with the desires of the *individuals* involved. Apart from any reasons of status, financial rewards, or fulfillment derived from serving the clients' needs, most individuals join PSFs to experience the professional challenge and variety and to avoid routine repetition. While individuals may be content to undertake a similar project for the second or third time, they will not be for the fourth, sixth, or eighth. Yet it is in the interest of the firm (particularly if the market has not yet caught up) to take advantage of the experience and expertise that it has acquired. One solution, of course, is to convert the past experience and expertise of the individual into the expertise of the firm by accepting a similar project, but utilizing a greater proportion of juniors on it. Besides requiring a lesser commitment of time from the experienced seniors, this device serves to train the juniors.

For all these reasons, we might suspect that the proportion of juniors to seniors required by the firm *in a particular practice area* will tend to increase over time. If this is allowed to proceed without corresponding adjustments in the range of practice areas, the project team structure of the firms will be altered, causing significant impacts on the economics and organization of the firm. The dangers of failing to monitor the project team structure are thus clearly revealed. Examples of this failure abound in many PSF industries. One consulting firm that learned how to increasingly utilize junior professionals began to aggressively hire new junior staff. After a reasonable period of time for the promotion decision, the firm realized that, at its current growth rate, it could not promote its "normal" proportion of promotion candidates: it did not need as many partners and managers in relation to the number of juniors it now had. Morale and productivity in the junior ranks suffered. . . . Successful PSF management is a question of balance.

---

*This argument suggests that there is a "life-cycle" to professional "products" in the same way that such cycles exist for tangible products.

BY HENRY MINTZBERG

■ Bramwell Tovey, artistic director and conductor of the Winnipeg Symphony Orchestra, may not seem like your typical manager. Indeed, in comparison with, say, the usual *New Yorker* cartoon of the nicely manicured executive surrounded by performance charts sitting in a corner office, orchestra conducting may seem like a rather quirky form of management. Yet as knowledge work has grown in importance—and as more and more work is done by trained and trusted professionals—the way Bramwell leads his orchestra may illustrate a good deal of what today's managing is all about.

I have been studying the work of managers on and off throughout my career, more recently spending days with a wide variety of managers. Because the metaphor of the orchestra leader is so often used to represent what business leaders do, I thought that spending time with a conductor might prove instructive. The day with Bramwell was intended to explore, and perhaps explode, the myth of the manager as the great conductor at the podium—the leader in complete control.

When you reflect on it, the symphony orchestra is like many other professional organizations—for example, consulting firms and hospitals—in that it is structured around the work of highly trained individuals who know what they have to do and just do it. Such professionals hardly need in-house procedures or time-study analysts to tell them how to do their jobs. That fundamental reality challenges many preconceptions that we have about management and leadership. Indeed, in such environments, *covert leadership* may matter more than overt leadership.

WHO CONTROLS?

When the maestro walks up to the podium and raises his baton, the musicians respond in unison. Another motion, and they all stop. It's the image of absolute control—management captured perfectly in caricature. And yet it is all a great myth.

What does Bramwell Tovey really control? What choices does he really have? Bramwell says his job consists of selecting the program, determining how the pieces are played, choosing guest artists, staffing the orchestra, and managing some external relations. (Conductors apparently vary in their propensity to engage in external work. Bramwell enjoys it.) The administrative and finance side of the orchestra is handled by an executive director—at the time, Max Tapper, who comanaged the orchestra with Bramwell.

So much of the classic literature on management has been about the need for *controlling*, which is about designing systems, creating structures, and making choices. There are systems galore in symphony orchestras, all meant to control the work. But they are systems inherent to the profession, not to management. Bramwell inherited them all. The same can be said about structures; in fact, even more so. Just look at how everyone sits, in prearranged rows, according to a very strict and externally imposed pecking order; how they tune their instruments before playing and stomp their feet after a good solo rehearsal. These rituals imply a high degree of structure, and yet they all come with the job.

The profession itself, not the manager, supplies much of the structure and coordination. While the work of some experts takes place in small teams and task forces with a great deal of informal communication, professional work here consists of applying standard operating routines: the composer started work with a blank sheet of paper, but the musicians start with the composer's score. The object is to play it well—interpreting it but hardly inventing something new. Indeed, the work, the workers, their tools—almost everything in a symphony is highly standardized. . . .

---

*Reprinted with deletions from "Covert Leadership: Notes on Managing Professionals," *Harvard Business Review*, November–December 1998, 140–147.

In organizations where standard operating routines are applied, the experts work largely on their own, free of the need to coordinate with their colleagues. This happens almost automatically. . . . They were able to coordinate their efforts because of the standardization of their skills and by what they were trained to expect from each other. . . . in the orchestra, even though the musicians play together, each and every one of them plays alone. They each follow a score and know precisely when to contribute. The instrument not only identifies each player but also distinguishes him or her from the other musicians.

Most professional workers require little direct supervision from managers. . . . Surgeons [for example] hardly expect a medical chief or a hospital director to appear, let alone set the pace for one of their operations. That observation may not seem to hold for a symphony orchestra, where the conductor certainly sets the pace. But it is a lot more relevant than it might at first appear.

Along with *controlling* and *coordinating, directing* is one of the oldest and most common words used to describe managerial work. Among other things, directing means issuing directives, delegating tasks, and authorizing decisions. Yet despite his designation as orchestra director, Bramwell's actual "directing" is highly circumscribed. The day I was with him, he hardly ran around giving orders. Indeed, he explained that even comments made during rehearsals have to be aimed at sections rather than at individuals. . . . conducting has changed considerably, Bramwell points out, since the days of the great autocrats like Toscanini.

A great deal of the conventional manager's control is exercised through formal information. Such information plays a rather limited role for the orchestra conductor. When Bramwell reads or processes information on the job, it is more about scores than about budgets. For him, musical information provides a much more relevant and direct way of judging performance. Just by listening with a trained ear, the conductor knows immediately how well the orchestra has done. Nothing needs to be measured. How could it be? One is led to wonder how much of the music of more conventional managing gets drowned out by the numbers. Of course, there is a need to count here, too—for example, the number of seats occupied in the hall. But by making that the job of the executive director, Bramwell is left free to focus his attention on the real music of managing.

What, then, do conductors control? Although they choose the program and decide how the score should be played, they are constrained by the music that has been written, by the degree to which it can be interpreted, by the sounds the audience will be receptive to, and by the ability and willingness of the orchestra to produce the music. . . . On this particular day, Hindemith and Stravinsky were pulling the strings—of the conductor no less than of the violinists.

Leonard Sayles, who has written extensively on middle management, once reversed the myth of manager as magisterial conductor. In his book *Managerial Behavior: Administration in Complex Organizations* (McGraw-Hill, 1964), Sayles wrote, "[The manager] is like a symphony orchestra conductor, endeavoring to maintain a melodious performance . . . while the orchestra members are having various personal difficulties, stage hands are moving music stands, alternating excessive heat and cold are creating audience and instrument problems, and the sponsor of the concert is insisting on irrational changes in the program." When I read this to Bramwell, he laughed. All of this had happened to him. . . .

Taken together, the various constraints within which the orchestra conductor works describe a very common condition among managers—not being in absolute control of others nor being completely powerless, but functioning somewhere in between.

LEADING IS COVERT

When someone asked Indian-born Zubin Mehta about the difficulties of conducting the Israel Philharmonic, where everyone is said to consider him or herself a soloist, he reportedly replied, "I'm the only Indian; they're all the chiefs!" Leadership is clearly a tricky business in professional organizations. It was very much on Bramwell's mind in our discussions. He pointed out the qualifications of many of the players—some trained at Juilliard and Curtis, many of them with doctorates in music—and he expressed his discomfort in having to be a leader among ostensible equals. "I think of myself as a soccer coach who plays," he said, adding that "there are moments when I have to exert my authority in a fairly robust fashion. . . although it always puzzles me why I have to."

Watching Bramwell in a day of rehearsals, I saw a lot more *doing* than what we conventionally think of as *leading*. More like a first-line supervisor than a hands-off executive, Bramwell was taking direct and personal charge of what was getting done. Rehearsals themselves are about results—about pace, pattern, tempo, and about smoothing, harmonizing, perfecting. The preparation for a concert could itself be described as a project, with the conductor as a hands-on project manager. This, if you like, is orchestra *operating*, not orchestra *leading*, let alone *directing*.

In the course of my day with Bramwell, which involved many hours of rehearsal, I saw only one overt act of leadership. As the afternoon wore on, Bramwell was dissatisfied. "Come on guys—you're all asleep. You need to do this. It's not good enough." Later, he told me if he had to do that all the time, it would be intrusive. Fortunately, he does not. The fear of censure by the conductor is very powerful, he explained, because "instruments are the extensions of their souls!"

In conducting an orchestra, it seems that *covert leadership*—to use Bramwell's own phrase—may be far more important than overt leadership. Leadership infused everything Bramwell did, however invisibly. His "doing," in other words, was influenced by all the interpersonal concerns in the back of his mind: players' sensitivities, union contracts, and so on. Perhaps we need a greater appreciation in all managerial work of this kind of covert leadership: not leadership actions in and of themselves—motivating, coaching, and all that—but rather unobtrusive actions that infuse all the other things a manager does.

Bramwell, in fact, expressed discomfort with overt leadership. After all, the players are there because they are excellent performers—they all know the score, so to speak. Anyone who cannot play properly can be replaced. Rehearsals are not about enhancing skills but about coordinating the skills that are present.

Nevertheless, a symphony orchestra is not a jazz quartet any more than a racing scull is a canoe. With a large number of people, someone has to take the lead, set the pace, call the stroke. The Russians tried to achieve a leaderless orchestra in the heady days after the revolution, but all they succeeded in doing was relabelling the conductor. Given that all the musicians have to play in perfect harmony, the role of conductor emerges naturally. "I completely control the orchestra's timing—and timing is everything," Bramwell said, maybe because timing is one of the few things he can completely control.

Hence, a good symphony orchestra requires both highly trained professionals and clear personal leadership. And that has the potential to produce cleavage along the line where those two centers of power meet. If the players do not accept the conductor's authority or if the conductor does not accept the player's expertise, the whole system breaks down.

Bramwell's deepest concerns seem to focus precisely on this potential fault line. How can he remain true to his profession, which is music, while properly performing his job, which is management? He seems to find little comfort in that tension. Indeed, he appears most comfortable when he retreats back into the profession. Bramwell loves to play the piano by himself; he also composes music. Both of those activities, it should be noted, are pointedly free of the need to manage or be managed.

THE CULTURE IS IN THE SYSTEM

Leadership is generally exercised on three different levels. At the *individual* level, leaders mentor, coach, and motivate; at the *group* level, they build teams and resolve conflicts; at the *organizational* level, leaders build culture. In most organizations, these three levels are discrete and easily identifiable.

Not so in the symphony orchestra. Here we have a most curious phenomenon: one great big team with approximately 70 people and a single leader. (There are sections, but they have no levels of supervision). The members of this team sit together, in one space, to be heard at one time. How often do customers see the whole product being delivered by the entire operating core of the organization?

As already noted, leadership at the individual level is highly circumscribed. Empowerment is a silly notion here. Musicians hardly need to be empowered by conductors. Inspired maybe—infused with feeling and energy—but not empowered. Leaders energize people by treating them not as detachable "human resources" . . . but as respected members of a cohesive social system. When people are trusted, they do not have to be empowered.

Furthermore, in an orchestra, all these people come together for rehearsals and then disperse. How and where is the culture to be built up? The answers take us back to an earlier point: culture building, too, is covert, infused in everything the conductor does. Moreover, much of this culture is already built into the system. This is a culture of symphony orchestras—not just the Winnipeg Symphony Orchestra. A new player can to a large extent join days before a concert and still harmonize, socially as well as musically. This is not to deny the effects of the conductor's charisma or the effect that Bramwell Tovey can have on the culture of the Winnipeg Symphony Orchestra. It is only to argue that any conductor begins with several centuries of established cultural tradition.

This reality should make the job of leading at the cultural level that much easier. Culture does not have to be created so much as enhanced. People come together knowing what to expect and how they have to work. The leader has to use this culture to define the uniqueness of the group and its spirit in comparison with other orchestras. Indeed, maybe the culture, and not the personal chemistry, is the key to the ostensible "charisma" of all those famous conductors—and perhaps many other managers as well.

This point is reinforced by the fact that about half the time, symphony orchestras are not even led by their own conductors. An outsider comes in to perform the job—a so-called guest conductor. Imagine a "guest manager" almost anywhere else. Yet here it works—sometimes remarkably well—precisely because everything is so programmed by both the composer and the profession. That leaves the conductor free to inject his or her style and energy into the system.

MANAGING ALL AROUND

As noted above, Bramwell Tovey is a doer, right there on the floor. He doesn't read reports in some corner office. (Indeed, he took almost 18 months to give me feedback on my report.) He doesn't take his team off to some distant retreat to climb ropes so that they will come to trust one another. He simply ensures that a group of talented people come together to make beautiful music. In that sense, he is like a first-line supervisor, like a foreman in a factory or a head nurse of a hospital ward.

Yet at the end of our day together, Bramwell also turned around to maintain personal relationships with key stakeholders of the organization, the elite of the symphony's municipal society. In other words, the foreman acting on the factory floor by day becomes the statesman out networking in the Maestro's Circle—a group of the orchestra's most generous supporters—by night. The whole hierarchy gets compressed into the job of just one person.

Connecting to important outsiders—what is called *linking*—is an important aspect of all managerial work. There are always people to be convinced so that deals can be done. In Bramwell's case, this involves networking to represent the orchestra in the community to help it gain legitimacy and support. The other side of the linking role is serving as the conduit for social pressures on the organization. As we have seen, professionals require little direction and supervision. What they do require is protection and support. And so their managers have to pay a lot of attention to managing the boundary condition of the organization. In consulting firms, for example, it is top management that does the selling.

CODA

So what kind of organization is this in which one Indian has to put up with all those chiefs and someone like Bramwell Tovey can be so reticent about having to exercise leadership? More specifically, can we really call Bramwell a manager? Does he even want to be? Will the musicians let him be?

The answer has to be yes.

Uncomfortable as it may be to manage a group of such talented people, I believe Bramwell loves it. After all, he still gets to play often, and, when he does, no one is waving a baton at him. He is able to conduct the pieces he likes best, at least much of the time, and he experiences the extraordinary joy of seeing the work of the organization all come together at the wave of his hand—even if the composer is really pulling the strings. How many managers get this kind of satisfaction from their work?

And not only do the musicians let him do this, they actually encourage him, no matter how disagreeable some of them may find it. After all, they need him as much as he needs them. Bramwell commented, "I don't see myself as a manager. I consider myself more of a lion tamer." It is a good line, always likely to get a good laugh, and it echoes the popular description of managing professionals as "herding cats." But it hardly captures the image of 70 rather tame people sitting in neatly ordered rows ready to play together at the flick of a wand.

So even if he does not see his job as a manager, which I doubt, I certainly do. Get past the myth of the conductor in complete control and you may learn from this example what a good deal of today's managing is all about. Not obedience and harmony, but nuances and constraints. So maybe it is time for conventional managers to step down from their podiums, get rid of their budgeting batons, and see the conductor for who he or she really is. Only then can anyone appreciate the myth of the manager up there as well as the reality of the conductor down here. Perhaps that is how the manager and the organization can make beautiful music together.

CHAPTER 16

Managing
Innovation

Although often seen as a high-technology event involving inventor-entrepreneurs, innovation may, of course, occur in high- or low-technology, product or service, large or small organizational situations. Innovation may be thought of as the *first reduction to practice* of an idea in a culture. The more radical the idea, the more traumatic and profound its impact will tend to be. But there are no absolutes. Whatever is newest and most difficult to understand becomes the "high technology" of its age. As Jim Utterback of MIT is fond of pointing out, the delivery of ice was high technology at the turn of the twentieth century, and later it was the production of automobiles. By the same token, 50 years from now, electronics may be considered mundane.

Our focus here, however, is not on innovation per se but on the innovation *context*, that is, the situation in which steady or frequent innovation of a complex nature is an intrinsic part of the organization and the industry segment in which it chooses to operate. Such organizations depend not on a single entrepreneurial individual but on teams of experts molded together.

The innovation context is one in which the organization often must deal with complex technologies or systems under conditions of dynamic change. Typically, major innovations require that a variety of experts work toward a common goal, often led by a single champion or a small group of committed individuals. Much has been learned from research in recent years on such organizations. Although this knowledge may seem less structured than that of previous chapters, several dominant themes have emerged.

This chapter opens with a description of the fifth of Mintzberg's structures, here titled the innovative organization. This is the structure that, in a sense, achieves its effectiveness by being inefficient. This reading probes into the unusual ways in which strategies evolve in the context of work that is both highly complex and highly dynamic. Here we see the full flowering of the notion of emergent strategy, culminating in a description of a grass-roots model of the process. We also see here a strategic leadership less concerned with formulating and then implementing strategies and more with managing a process through which strategies almost seem to *form* by themselves.

When it is successful, intrapreneurship—implying the stimulation and diffusion of innovative capacity throughout a larger organization, with many champions of innovations—tends to follow most of Quinn's precepts. As such, it seems to belong more to this context than the entrepreneurial one, which focuses on organizations highly centralized around the initiatives of their single leaders, whether or not innovative.

From this description of the nature of the adhocratic organization, we move to articles on how organizations can manage in the context of innovation. Mark Maletz of Bobson College and Nitin Nohria of Harvard Business School write about "Managing in the Whitespace"—that unoccupied territory in every organization where everything is vague. The keys are to establish legitimacy, mobilize resources, build momentum—and have understanding managers!

The next reading, by Raymond E. Miles (University of California, Berkeley), Charles C. Snow (Smeal College of Business Administration, Pennsylvania State University), John A. Mathews (University of New South Wales), Grant Miles (University of North Texas), and Henry Coleman, Jr. (St. Mary's College of California), focuses on one particular form of organization well suited to a situation of demanding innovation. They call it the "cellular form." It combines entrepreneurship, self-organization, and a sense of member ownership.

The final reading of this chapter by Joseph Lampel considers the difficulties of having to innovate in a particularly interesting, contemporary environment: that of engineering-construction-procurement firms, whose massive projects can include the development of power plants, oil platforms, and toll roads. Lampel discusses their competencies—entrepreneurial, technical, evaluative, and relational—and then compares strategies of focusing on core competencies with those of pursuing far-flung opportunities. Lampel argues that the main challenge facing firms whose main business depends on projects is balancing efficiency and flexibility under conditions of diversity. Striking this balance takes place at the operating and strategic levels. At the operating level, project-based firms build core competencies that contain the tacit and codified knowledge needed to effectively execute projects. At the strategic level, project-based firms face trade-offs between pursuing opportunities and developing their competencies.

USING THE CASE STUDIES

Managing innovation is crucial for the vitality of established as well as new companies. The Workbrain case, which deals with e-business pioneering, is an example of the latter. Cases such as Canon, Sony, and Lechabile, deal with consistent efforts to manage innovation successfully. This often involves experimentation with organizational forms that facilitate innovation. The reading by Miles, Snow, Mathews, Miles, and Coleman, "Anticipating the Cellular Form," provides a framework for explaining the forces that drive such experimentation.

Innovations are often closely tied to projects. The Acer Group case deals with the implications of an innovative project developed in its American subsidiary. Stan Shih,

Acer's CEO, must consider whether he should exercise caution or run with this project. Sony's woes in the aftermath of its entry into the American motion picture industry, which are described in the Sony Regeneration case, suggest that managing innovation in industries where projects are central to strategy requires a different strategic approach. In the reading "The Core Competencies of Project-Based Firms," Lampel outlines a typology of key competencies that are needed to manage firms in project-based industries, such as motion pictures, consulting, pharmaceuticals, aircraft, and construction. The McKinsey and Company case and the Empire Plastics case go well with this reading.

READING 16.1

BY HENRY MINTZBERG

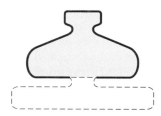

■ None of the organization forms so far discussed is capable of sophisticated innovation, the kind required of a high-technology research organization, an avant-garde film company, or a factory manufacturing complex prototypes. The entrepreneurial organization can certainly innovate, but only in relatively simple ways. The machine and professional organizations are performance, not problem-solving types, designed to perfect standardized programs, not to invent new ones. And although the diversified organization resolves some problem of strategic inflexibility found in the machine organization, as noted earlier it too is not a true innovator. A focus on control by standardizing outputs does not encourage innovation.

Sophisticated innovation requires a very different configuration, one that is able to fuse experts drawn from different disciplines into smoothly functioning ad hoc project teams. To borrow the word coined by Bennis and Slator in 1964 and later popularized in Alvin Toffler's *Future Shock* (1970), these are the *adhocracies* of our society.

THE BASIC STRUCTURE

Here again we have a distinct configuration of the attributes of design: highly organic structure, with little formalization of behavior; specialized jobs based on expert training; a tendency to group the specialists in functional units for housekeeping purposes but to deploy

---

*Adapted from *The Structuring of Organizations* (Prentice Hall, 1979), Chap. 21 on the adhocracy; on strategy formation from "Strategy Formation in an Adhocracy," coauthored with Alexandra McHugh, *Administrative Science Quarterly* (1985: 160–197), and "Strategy of Design: A Study of Architects in Co-Partnership," coauthored with Suzanne Otis, Jamal Shamsie, and James A. Waters, in J. Grant (ed.), *Strategic Management Frontiers* (JAI Press, 1988). A chapter similar to this one appeared in *Mintzberg on Management: Inside Our Strange World of Organizations* (Free Press, 1989).

them in small project teams to do their work; a reliance on teams, on task forces, and on integrating managers of various sorts in order to encourage mutual adjustment, the key mechanism of coordination, within and between these teams; and considerable decentralization to and within these teams, which are located at various places in the organization and involve various mixtures of line managers and staff and operating experts.

To innovate means to break away from established patterns. Thus the innovative organization cannot rely on any form of standardization for coordination. In other words, it must avoid all the trappings of bureaucratic structure, notably sharp divisions of labor, extensive unit differentiation, highly formalized behaviors, and an emphasis on planning and control systems. Above all, it must remain flexible. A search for organigrams to illustrate this description elicited the following response from one corporation thought to have an adhocracy structure: "[We] would prefer not to supply an organization chart, since it would change too quickly to serve any useful purpose." Of all the configurations, this one shows the least reverence for the classical principles of management, especially unity of command. Information and decision processes flow flexibly and informally, wherever they must, to promote innovation. And that means overriding the chain of authority if need be.

The entrepreneurial configuration also retains a flexible, organic structure, and so is likewise able to innovate. But that innovation is restricted to simple situations, ones easily comprehended by a single leader. Innovation of the sophisticated variety requires another kind of flexible structure, one that can draw together different forms of expertise. Thus the adhocracy must hire and give power to experts, people whose knowledge and skills have been highly developed in training programs. But unlike the professional organization, the adhocracy cannot rely on the standardized skills of its experts to achieve coordination, because that would discourage innovation. Rather, it must treat existing knowledge and skills as bases on which to combine and build new ones. Thus the adhocracy must break through the boundaries of conventional specialization and differentiation, which it does by assigning problems not to individual experts in preestablished pigeonholes but to multidisciplinary teams that merge their efforts. Each team forms around one specific project.

Despite organizing around market-based projects, the organization must still support and encourage particular types of specialized expertise. And so the adhocracy tends to use a matrix structure: Its experts are grouped in functional units for specialized housekeeping purposes—hiring, training, professional communication, and the like—but are then deployed in the project teams to carry out the basic work of innovation.

As for coordination in and between these project teams, as noted earlier standardization is precluded as a significant coordinating mechanism. The efforts must be innovative, not routine. So, too, is direct supervision precluded because of the complexity of the work: Coordination must be accomplished by those with the knowledge, namely the experts themselves, not those with just authority. That leaves just one of our coordinating mechanisms, mutual adjustment, which we consider foremost in adhocracy. And, to encourage this, the organization makes use of a whole set of liaison devices, liaison personnel and integrating managers of all kinds, in addition to the various teams and task forces.

The result is that managers abound in the adhocracy: functional managers, integrating managers, project managers. The last-named are particularly numerous, since the project teams must be small to encourage mutual adjustment among their members, and each, of course, needs a designated manager. The consequence is that "spans of control" found in adhocracy tend to be small. But the implication of this is misleading, because the term is suited to the machine, not the innovative configuration: The managers of adhocracy seldom "manage" in the usual sense of giving orders; instead, they spend a good deal of time acting in a liaison capacity, to coordinate the work laterally among the various teams and units.

With its reliance on highly trained experts the adhocracy emerges as highly decentralized, in the "selective" sense. That means power over its decisions and actions is distributed to various places and at various levels according to the needs of the particular issue. In effect, power flows to wherever the relevant expertise happens to reside—among managers or specialists (or teams of those) in the line structure, the staff units, and the operating core.

To proceed with our discussion and to elaborate on how the innovative organization makes decisions and forms strategies, we need to distinguish two basic forms that it takes.

THE OPERATING ADHOCRACY

The *operating adhocracy* innovates and solves problems directly on behalf of its clients. Its multidisciplinary teams of experts often work under contract, as in the think-tank consulting firm, creative advertising agency, or manufacturer of engineering prototypes.

In fact, for every operating adhocracy, there is a corresponding professional bureaucracy, one that does similar work but with a narrower orientation. Faced with a client problem, the operating adhocracy engages in creative efforts to find a novel solution; the professional bureaucracy pigeonholes it into a known contingency to which it can apply a standard program. One engages in divergent thinking aimed at innovation, the other in convergent thinking aimed at perfection. Thus, one theater company might seek our new avant-garde plays to perform, while another might perfect its performance of Shakespeare year after year.

A key feature of the operating adhocracy is that its administrative and operating work tend to blend into a single effort. That is, in ad hoc project work it is difficult to separate the planning and design of the work from its execution. Both require the same specialized skills, on a project-by-project basis. Thus it can be difficult to distinguish the middle levels of the organization from its operating core, since line managers and staff specialists may take their place alongside operating specialists on the project teams.

Figure 1 shows the organigram of the National Film Board of Canada, a classic operating adhocracy (even though it does produce a chart—one that changes frequently it might be added). The Board is an agency of the Canadian federal government and produces mostly short films, many of them documentaries. At the time of this organigram, the characteristics of adhocracy were particularly in evidence: It shows a large number of support units as well as liaison positions (for example, research, technical, and production coordinators), with the operating core containing loose concurrent functional and market groupings, the latter by region as well as by type of film produced and, as can be seen, some not even connected to the line hierarchy!

THE ADMINISTRATIVE ADHOCRACY

The second type of adhocracy also functions with project teams, but toward a different end. Whereas the operating adhocracy undertakes projects to serve its clients, the *administrative adhocracy* undertakes projects to serve itself, to bring new facilities or activities on line, as in the administrative structure of a highly automated company. And in sharp contrast to the operating adhocracy, the administrative adhocracy makes a clear distinction between its administrative component and its operating core. That core is *truncated*—cut right off from the rest of the organization—so that the administrative component that remains can be structured as an adhocracy.

This truncation may take place in a number of ways. First, when the operations have to be machinelike and so could impede innovation in the administration (because of the associated need for control), it may be established as an independent organization. Second, the operating core may be done away with altogether—in effect, contracted out to other organizations. That leaves the organization free to concentrate on the development work, as did NASA during the Apollo project. A third form of truncation arises when the operating core becomes automated. This enables it to run itself, largely independent of the need for direct controls from the administrative component, leaving the latter free to structure itself as an adhocracy to bring new facilities on line or to modify old ones.

FIGURE 1 THE NATIONAL FILM BOARD OF CANADA: AN OPERATING ADHOCRACY (CIRCA 1975; USED WITH PERMISSION)

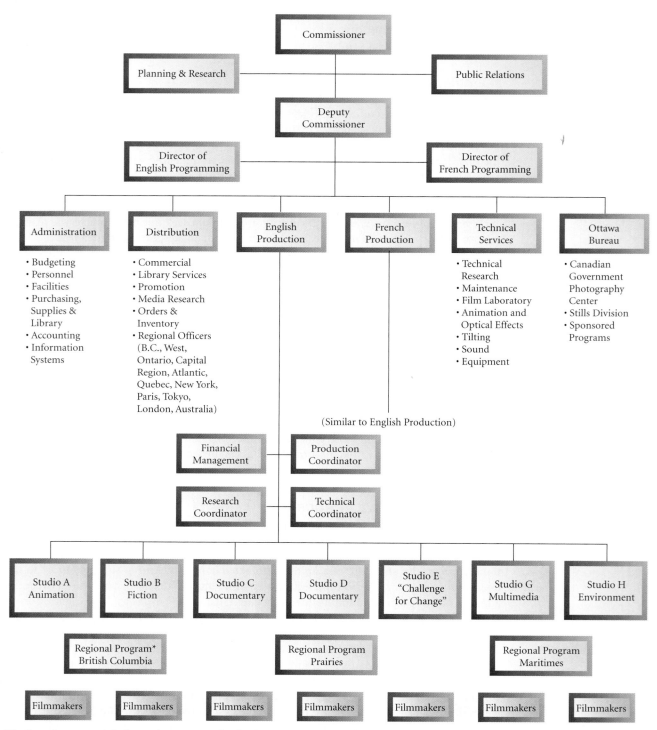

*No lines shown on original organigram connecting Regional Programs to Studios or Filmmakers.

Oil companies, because of the high degree of automation of their production process, are in part at least drawn toward administrative adhocracy. Figure 2 shows the organigram for one oil company, reproduced exactly as presented by the company (except for modifications to mask its identity, done at the company's request). Note the domination of "Administration and Services," shown at the bottom of the chart; the operating functions, particularly "Production," are lost by comparison. Note also the description of the strategic apex in terms of standing committees instead of individual executives.

FIGURE 2 ORGANIGRAM OF AN OIL COMPANY: AN ADMINISTRATIVE ADHOCRACY

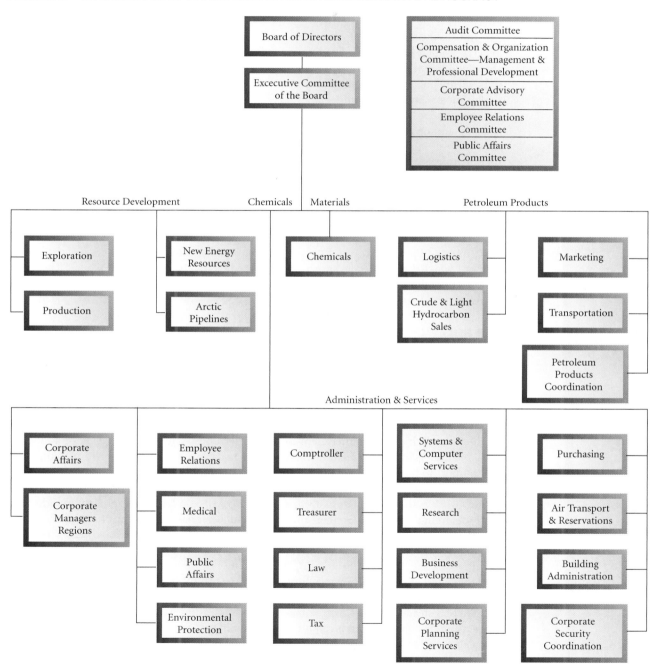

THE ADMINISTRATIVE COMPONENT OF THE ADHOCRACIES

The important conclusion to be drawn from this discussion is that in both types of adhocracy the relation between the operating core and the administrative component is unlike that in any other configuration. In the administrative adhocracy, the operating core is truncated and becomes a relatively unimportant part of the organization; in the operating adhocracy, the two merge into a single entity. Either way, the need for traditional direct supervision is diminished, so managers derive their influence more from their expertise and interpersonal skills than from formal position. And that means the distinction between line and staff blurs. It no longer makes sense to distinguish those who have the formal power to decide from those who have only the informal right to advise. Power over decision making in the adhocracy flows to anyone with the required expertise, regardless of position.

In fact, the support staff plays a key role in adhocracy, because that is where many of the experts reside (especially in administrative adhocracy). As suggested, however, that staff is not sharply differentiated from the other parts of the organization, not off to one side, to speak only when spoken to, as in the bureaucratic configurations. The other type of staff, however, the technostructure, is less important here, because the adhocracy does not rely for coordination on standards that it develops. Technostructure analysts may, of course, be used fro some action planning and other forms of analysis—marketing research and economic forecasting, for example—but these analysts are as likely to take their place alongside the other specialists on the project teams as to stand back and design systems to control them.

To summarize, the administrative component of the adhocracy emerges as an organic mass of line managers and staff experts, combined with operators in the operating adhocracy, working together in ever-shifting relationships on ad hoc projects. Our logo figure at the start of this chapter shows adhocracy with its parts mingled together in one amorphous mass in the middle. In the operating adhocracy, that mass includes the middle line, support staff, technostructure, and operating core. Of these, the administrative adhocracy excludes just the operating core, which is truncated, as shown by the dotted section below the central mass. The reader will also note that the strategic apex of the figure is shown partly merged into the central mass as well, for reasons we shall present in our discussion of strategy formation.

THE ROLES OF THE STRATEGIC APEX

The top managers of the strategic apex of this configuration do not spend much time formulating explicit strategies (as we shall see). But they must spend a good deal of their time in the battles that ensue over strategic choices and in handling the many other disturbances that arise all over these fluid structures. The innovative configuration combines fluid working arrangements with power based on expertise, not authority. Together those breed aggressiveness and conflict. But the job of the managers here, at all levels, is not to bottle up that aggression and conflict so much as to channel them to productive ends. Thus, the managers of adhocracy must be masters of human relations, able to use persuasion, negotiation, coalition, reputation, and rapport to fuse the individualistic experts into smoothly functioning teams.

Top managers must also devote a good deal of time to monitoring the projects. Innovative project work is notoriously difficult to control. No MIS can be relied upon to provide complete, unambiguous results. So there must be careful personal monitoring of projects to ensure that they are completed according to specifications, on schedule and within budget (or, more likely, not excessively late and not too far in excess of cost estimates).

Perhaps the most important single role of the top management of this configuration (especially the operating adhocracy form) is liaison with the external environment. The other configurations tend to focus their attention on clearly defined markets and so are more or less assured of a steady flow of work. Not so the operating adhocracy, which lives from project to project and disappears when it can find no more. Since each project is different, the organization can never be sure where the next one will come from. So the top managers must devote a great deal of their time to ensuring a steady and balanced stream of incoming projects. That means developing liaison contacts with potential customers and negotiating contracts with them. Nowhere is this more clearly illustrated than in the consulting business, particularly where the approach is innovative. When a consultant becomes a partner in one of these firms, he or she normally hangs up the calculator and becomes virtually a full-time salesperson. It is a distinguishing characteristic of many an operating adhocracy that the selling function literally takes place at the strategic apex.

Project work poses related problems in the administrative adhocracy. Reeser asked a group of managers in three aerospace companies, "What are some of the human problems of project management?" Among the common answers: "[M]embers of the organization who are displaced because of the phasing out of [their] work . . . may have to wait a long time before they get another assignment at as high a level of responsibility" and "the temporary nature of the organization often necessitates 'make work' assignments for [these] displaced members" (1969: 463). Thus senior managers must again concern themselves with a steady flow of projects, although in this case, internally generated.

CONDITIONS OF THE INNOVATIVE ORGANIZATION

This configuration is found in environments that are both dynamic and complex. A dynamic environment, being unpredictable, calls for organic structure; a complex one calls for decentralized structure. This configuration is the only type that provides both. Thus we tend to find the innovative organization wherever these conditions prevail, ranging from guerrilla warfare to space agencies. There appears to be no other way to fight a war in the jungle or to put the first man on the moon.

As we have noted for all the configurations, organizations that prefer particular structures also try to "choose" environments appropriate to them. This is especially clear in the case of the operating adhocracy. Advertising agencies and consulting firms that prefer to structure themselves as professional bureaucracies seek out stable environments; those that prefer the innovative form find environments that are dynamic, where the client needs are difficult and unpredictable.*

A number of organizations are drawn toward this configuration because of the dynamic conditions that result from very frequent product change. The extreme case is the unit producer, the manufacturing firm that custom-makes each of its products to order, as in the engineering company that produces prototypes or the fabricator of extremely expensive machinery. Because each customer order constitutes a new project, the organization is encouraged to structure itself as an operating adhocracy.

Some manufacturers of consumer goods operate in markets so competitive that they must be constantly changing their product offerings, even though each product may itself be mass produced. A company that records rock music would be a prime example, as would some cosmetic and pharmaceutical companies. Here again, dynamic conditions, when coupled with some complexity, drive the organization toward the innovative configuration, with the mass production operations truncated to allow for adhocracy in product development.

Youth is another condition often associated with this type of organization. That is because it is difficult to sustain any structure in a state of adhocracy for a long period—to keep behaviors from formalizing and thereby discouraging innovation. All kinds of forces drive the innovative configuration to bureaucratize itself as it ages. On the other hand, young organizations

---

*I like to tell a story of the hospital patient with an appendix about to burst who presents himself to a hospital organized as an adhocracy: "Who wants to do another appendectomy? We're into livers now," as they go about exploring new procedures. But the patient returning from a trip to the jungle with a rare tropical disease had better beware of the hospital organized as a professional bureaucracy. A student came up to me after I once said this and explained how hospital doctors puzzled by her bloated stomach and not knowing what to do took out her appendix. Luckily, her problem resolved itself, some time later. Another time, a surgeon told me that his hospital no longer does appendectomies!

prefer naturally organic structures, since they must find their own ways and tend to be eager to innovate. Unless they are entrepreneurial, they tend to become intrapreneurial.

The operating adhocracy is particularly prone to a short life, since it faces a risky market which can quickly destroy it. The loss of one major contract can literally close it down overnight. But if some operating adhocracies have short lives because they fail, others have short lives because they succeed. Success over time encourages metamorphosis, driving the organization toward a more stable environment and a more bureaucratic structure. As it ages, the successful organization develops a reputation for what it does best. That encourages it to repeat certain activities, which may suit the employees who, themselves aging, may welcome more stability in their work. So operating adhocracy is driven over time toward professional bureaucracy to perfect the activities it does best, perhaps even toward the machine bureaucracy to exploit a single invention. The organization survives, but the configuration dies.

Administrative adhocracies typically live longer. They, too, feel the pressures to bureaucratize as they age, which can lead them to stop innovating or else to innovate in stereotyped ways and thereby to adopt bureaucratic structure. But this will not work if the organization functions in an industry that requires sophisticated innovation from all its participants. Since many of the industries where administrative adhocracies are found do, organizations that survive in them tend to retain this configuration for long periods.

In recognition of the tendency for organizations to bureaucratize as they age, a variant of the innovative configuration has emerged—"the organizational equivalent of paper dresses or throw-away tissues" (Toffler, 1970: 133)—which might be called the "temporary adhocracy." It draws together specialists from various organizations to carry out a project, and then it disbands. Temporary adhocracies are becoming increasingly common in modern society: the production group that performs a single play, the election campaign committee that promotes a single candidate, the guerrilla group that overthrows a single government, the Olympic committee that plans a single game. Related is what can be called the "mammoth project adhocracy," a giant temporary adhocracy that draws on thousands of experts for a number of years to carry out a single major task, the Manhattan Project of World War II being one famous example.

Sophisticated and automated technical systems also tend to drive organizations toward the administrative adhocracy. When an organization's technical system is sophisticated, it requires an elaborate, highly trained support staff, working in teams, to design or purchase, modify, and maintain the equipment. In other words, complex machinery requires specialists who have the knowledge, power, and flexible working arrangements to cope with it, which generally requires the organization to structure itself as an adhocracy.

Automation of a technical system can evoke even stronger forces in the same direction. That is why a machine organization that succeeds in automating its operating core tends to undergo a dramatic metamorphosis. The problem of motivating bored workers disappears, and with it goes the control mentality that permeates the structure; the distinction between line and staff blurs (machines being indifferent to who turns their knobs), which leads to another important reduction in conflict; the technostructure loses its influence, since control is built into the machinery by its own designers rather than having to be imposed on workers by the standards of the analysts. Overall, then, the administrative structure becomes more decentralized and organic, emerging as an adhocracy. Of course, for automated organizations with simple technical systems (as in the production of hand creams), the entrepreneurial configuration may suffice instead of the innovative one.

Fashion is most decidedly another condition of the innovative configuration. Every one of its characteristics is very much in vogue today: emphasis on expertise, organic structure, project teams, task forces, decentralization of power, matrix structure, sophisticated technical systems, automation, and young organizations. Thus, if the entrepreneurial and machine forms were earlier configurations, and the professional and the diversified forms yesterday's, then the innovative is clearly today's. This is the configuration for a population growing ever better educated and more specialized, yet under constant encouragement to adopt the "systems" approach—to view the world as an integrated whole instead of a collection of loosely coupled parts. It is the configuration for environments that are becoming more complex and more insistent on innovation, and for technical systems that are growing more sophisticated and more highly automated. It is the only configuration among our types appropriate for those who believe organizations must become at the same time more democratic and less bureaucratic.

Yet despite our current infatuation with it, adhocracy is not the structure for all organizations. Like all the others, it too has its place. And that place, as our examples make clear, seems to be in the new industries of our age—aerospace, electronics, think-tank consulting, research, advertising, filmmaking, petrochemicals—virtually all of which experienced their greatest development since World War II. The innovative adhocracy appears to be the configuration for the industries of the last half of the twentieth century.

| **STRATEGY FORMATION IN THE INNOVATIVE ORGANIZATION** | The structure of the innovative organization may seem unconventional, but its strategy making is even more so, upsetting virtually everything we have been taught to believe about that process. |

The structure of the innovative organization may seem unconventional, but its strategy making is even more so, upsetting virtually everything we have been taught to believe about that process.

Because the innovative organization must respond continuously to a complex, unpredictable environment, it cannot rely on deliberate strategy. In other words, it cannot predetermine precise patterns in its activities and then impose them on its work through some kind of formal planning process. Rather, many of its actions must be decided upon individually, according to the needs of the moment. It proceeds incrementally; to use Charles Lindblom's words, it prefers "continual nibbling" to a "good bite" (1968: 25).

Here, then, the process is best thought of as strategy *formation*, because strategy is not formulated consciously in one place so much as formed implicitly by the specific actions taken in many places. That is why action planning cannot be extensively relied upon in these organizations: Any process that separates thinking from action—planning from execution, formalization from implementation—would impede the flexibility of the organization to respond creatively to its dynamic environment.

STRATEGY FORMATION IN THE OPERATING ADHOCRACY

In the operating adhocracy, a project organization never quite sure what it will do next, the strategy never really stabilizes totally but is responsive to new projects, which themselves involve the activities of a whole host of people. Take the example of the National Film Board. Among its most important strategies are those related to the content of the hundred or so mostly short, documentary-type films that it makes each year. Were the Board structured as a machine bureaucracy, the word on what films to make would come down from on high. Instead, when we studied it some years ago, proposals for new films were submitted to a standing committee, which included elected filmmakers, marketing people, and the heads of production and programming—in other words, operators, line managers, and staff specialists. The chief executive had to approve the committee's choices, and usually did, but the vast majority of the proposals were initiated by the filmmakers and the executive producers lower down. Strategies formed as themes developed among these individual proposals. The operating adhocracy's strategy thus evolves continuously as all kinds of such decisions are made, each leaving its imprint on the strategy by creating a precedent or reinforcing an existing one.

STRATEGY FORMATION IN THE ADMINISTRATIVE ADHOCRACY

Similar things can be said about the administrative adhocracy, although the strategy-making process is slightly neater there. That is because the organization tends to concentrate its attention on fewer projects, which involve more people. NASA's Apollo project, for example, involved most of its personnel for almost ten years.

Administrative adhocracies also need to give more attention to action planning, but of a loose kind—to specify perhaps the ends to be reached while leaving flexibility to work out the means en route. Again, therefore, it is only through the making of specific decisions—namely, those that determine which projects are undertaken and how these projects unfold—that strategies can evolve.

STRATEGIES NONETHELESS

With their activities so disjointed, one might wonder whether adhocracies (of either type) can form strategies (that is, patterns) at all. In fact, they do, at least at certain times.

At the Film Board, despite the little direction from the management, the content of films did converge on certain clear themes periodically and then diverge, in remarkably regular cycles. In the early 1940s, there was a focus on films related to the war effort. After the war, having lost that raison d'être as well as its founding leader, the Board's films went off in all directions. They converged again in the mid-1950s around series of films for television, but by the late 1950s were again diverging widely. And in the mid-1960s and again in the early 1970s (with a brief period of divergence in between), the Board again showed a certain degree of convergence, this time on the themes of social commentary and experimentation.

The habit of cycling in and out of focus is quite unlike what takes place in the other configurations. In the machine organization especially, and somewhat in the entrepreneurial one, convergence proves much stronger and much longer (recall Volkswagenwerk's concentration on the Beetle for twenty years), while divergence tends to be very brief. The machine organization, in particular, cannot tolerate the ambiguity of change and so tries to leap from one strategic orientation to another. The innovative organization, in contrast, seems not only able to function at times without strategic focus, but positively to thrive on it. Perhaps that is the way it keeps itself innovative—by periodically cleansing itself of some of its existing strategic baggage.

THE VARIED STRATEGIES OF ADHOCRACY

Where do the strategies of adhocracy come from? While some may be imposed deliberately by the central management (as in staff cuts at the Film Board), most seem to emerge in a variety of other ways.

In some cases, a single ad hoc decision sets a precedent which evokes a pattern. That is how the National Film Board got into making series of films for television. While a debate raged over the issue, with management hesitant, one filmmaker slipped out and made one such series, and when many of his colleagues quickly followed suit, the organization suddenly found itself deeply, if unintentionally, committed to a major new strategy. It was, in effect, a strategy of spontaneous but implicit consensus on the part of its operating employees. In another case, even the initial precedent-setting decision wasn't deliberate. One film inadvertently ran longer than expected, it had to be distributed as a feature, the first for the organization, and as some other filmmakers took advantage of the precedent, a feature film strategy emerged.

Sometimes a strategy will be pursued in a pocket of an organization (perhaps in a clandestine manner, in a so-called "skunkworks"), which then later becomes more broadly organizational when the organization, in need of change and casting about for new strategies, seizes upon it. Some salesman has been pursuing a new market, or some engineer has developed a new product, and is ignored until the organization has need for some fresh strategic thinking. Then it finds it, not in the vision of its leaders or the procedures of its planners, not elsewhere in its industry, but hidden in the bowels of its own operations, developed through the learning of its workers.

What then becomes the role of the leadership of the innovative configuration in making strategy? If it cannot impose deliberate strategies, what does it do? The answer is that it manages patterns, seeking partial control over strategies but otherwise attempting to influence what happens to those strategies that do emerge lower down.

These are the organizations in which trying to manage strategy is a little like trying to drive an automobile without having your hands on the steering wheel. You can accelerate and brake but cannot determine direction. But there do remain important forms of control. First the leaders can manage the *process* of strategy-making if not the content of strategy. In other words, they can set up the structures to encourage certain kinds of activities and hire the people who themselves will carry out these activities. Second, they can provide general guidelines for strategy—what we have called *umbrella* strategies—seeking to define certain boundaries outside of which the specific patterns developed below should not stray. Then they can watch the patterns that do emerge and use the umbrella to decide which to encourage and which to discourage, remembering, however, that the umbrella can be shifted too.

A GRASS-ROOTS MODEL OF STRATEGY FORMATION

We can summarize this discussion in terms of a "grass-roots" model of strategy formation, comprising six points.

1. *Strategies grow initially like weeds in a garden, they are not cultivated like tomatoes in a hothouse.* In other words, the process of strategy formation can be overmanaged; sometimes it is more important to let patterns emerge than to force an artificial consistency upon an organization prematurely. The hothouse, if needed, can come later.

2. *These strategies can take root in all kinds of places, virtually anywhere people have the capacity to learn and the resources to support that capacity.* Sometimes an individual or unit in touch with a particular opportunity creates his, her, or its own pattern. This may happen inadvertently, when an initial action sets a precedent. Even senior managers can fall into strategies by experimenting with ideas until they converge on something that works (though the final result may appear to the observer to have been deliberately designed). At other times, a variety of actions converge on a strategic theme through the mutual adjustment of various people, whether gradually or spontaneously. And then the external environment can impose a pattern on an unsuspecting organization. The point is that organizations cannot always plan where their strategies will emerge, let alone plan the strategies themselves.

3. *Such strategies become organizational when they become collective, that is, when the patterns proliferate to pervade the behavior of the organization at large.* Weeds can proliferate and encompass a whole garden; then the conventional plants may look out of place. Likewise, emergent strategies can sometimes displace the existing deliberate ones. But, of course, what is a weed but a plant that wasn't expected? With a change of perspective, the emergent strategy, like the weed, can become what is valued (just as Europeans enjoy salads of the leaves of America's most notorious weed, the dandelion!).

4. *The processes of proliferation may be conscious but need not be; likewise they may be managed but need not be.* The processes by which the initial patterns work their way through the organization need not be consciously intended, by formal leaders or even informal ones. Patterns may simply spread by collective action, much as plants proliferate themselves. Of course, once strategies are recognized as valuable, the processes by which they proliferate can be managed, just as plants can be selectively propagated.

5. *New strategies, which may be emerging continuously, tend to pervade the organization during periods of change, which punctuate periods of more integrated continuity.* Put more simply, organizations, like gardens, may accept the biblical maxim of a time to sow and a time

to reap (even though they can sometimes reap what they did not mean to sow). Periods of convergence, during which the organization exploits its prevalent, established strategies, tend to be interrupted periodically by periods of divergence, during which the organization experiments with and subsequently accepts new strategic themes. The blurring of the separation between these two types of periods may have the same effect on an organization that the blurring of the separation between sowing and reaping has on a garden—the destruction of the system's productive capacity.

6. *To manage this process is not to preconceive strategies but to recognize their emergence and intervene when appropriate.* A destructive weed, once noticed, is best uprooted immediately. But one that seems capable of bearing fruit is worth watching, indeed sometimes even worth building a hothouse around. To manage in this context is to create the climate within which a wide variety of strategies can grow (to establish flexible structures, develop appropriate processes, encourage supporting ideologies, and define guiding "umbrella" strategies) and then to watch what does in fact come up. The strategic initiatives that do come "up" may in fact originate anywhere, although often low down in the organization, where the detailed knowledge of products and markets resides. (In fact, to be successful in some organizations, these initiatives must be recognized by middle-level managers and "championed" by combining them with each other or with existing strategies before promoting them to the senior management.) In effect, the management encourages those initiatives that appear to have potential, otherwise it discourages them. But it must not be too quick to cut off the unexpected: Sometimes it is better to pretend not to notice an emerging pattern to allow it more time to unfold. Likewise, there are times when it makes sense to shift or enlarge an umbrella to encompass a new pattern—in other words, to let the organization adapt to the initiative rather than vice versa. Moreover, a management must know when to resist change for the sake of internal efficiency and when to promote it for the sake of external adaptation. In other words, it must sense when to exploit an established crop of strategies and when to encourage new strains to displace them. It is the excesses of either—failure to focus (running blind) or failure to change (bureaucratic momentum)—that most harms organizations.

I call this a "grass-roots" model because the strategies grow up from the base of the organization, rooted in the solid earth of its operations rather than the ethereal abstractions of its administration. (Even the strategic initiatives of the senior management itself are in this model rooted in its tangible involvement with the operations.)

Of course, the model is overstated. But no more so than the more widely accepted deliberate one, which we might call the "hothouse" model of strategy formulation. Management theory must encompass both, perhaps more broadly labeled the *learning* model and the *planning* model, as well as a third, the *visionary* model.

I have discussed the learning model under the innovative configuration, the planning model under the machine configuration, and the visionary model under the entrepreneurial configuration. But in truth, all organizations need to mix these approaches in various ways at different times in their development. For example, our discussion of strategic change in the machine organization concluded, in effect, that they had to revert to the learning model for revitalization and the visionary model for turnaround. Of course, the visionary leader must learn, as must the learning organization evolve a kind of strategic vision, and both sometimes need planning to program the strategies they develop. And over all, no organization can function with strategies that are always and purely emergent; that would amount to a complete abdication of will and leadership, not to mention conscious thought. But none can function either with strategies that are always and purely deliberate; that would amount to an unwillingness to learn, a blindness to whatever is unexpected.

FIGURE 3
ENVIRONMENT
TAKING THE
LEAD IN ADHOCRACY

ENVIRONMENT ← Leadership → Organization

ENVIRONMENT TAKING PRECEDENCE IN THE INNOVATIVE ORGANIZATION

To conclude our discussion of strategy formation, as shown in Figure 3 in the innovative con-figuration it is the environment that takes precedence. It drives the organization, which responds continuously and eclectically, but does nevertheless achieve convergence during cer-tain periods.* The formal leadership seeks somehow to influence both sides in this relation-ship, negotiating with the environment for support and attempting to impose some broad general (umbrella) guidelines on the organization.

If the strategist of the entrepreneurial organization is largely a concept attainer and that of the machine organization largely a planner, then the strategist of the innovative organiza-tion is largely a *pattern recognizer*, seeking to detect emerging patterns within and outside the strategic umbrella. Then strategies deemed unsuitable can be discouraged while those that seem appropriate can be encouraged, even if that means moving the umbrella. Here, then, we may find the curious situation of leadership changing its intentions to fit the realized behav-ior of its organization. But that is curious only in the perspective of traditional management theory.

SOME ISSUES ASSOCIATED WITH THE INNOVATIVE ORGANIZATION

Three issues associated with the innovative configuration merit attention here: its ambiguities and the reactions of people who must live with them, its inefficiencies, and its propensity to make inappropriate transitions to other configurations.

HUMAN REACTIONS TO AMBIGUITY

Many people, especially creative ones, dislike both structural rigidity and the concentration of power. That leaves them only one configuration, the innovative, which is both organic and decentralized. Thus they find it a great place to work. In essence, adhocracy is the only struc-ture for people who believe in more democracy with less bureaucracy.

But not everyone shares those values (not even everyone who professes to). Many people need order, and so prefer the machine or professional type of organization. They see adhoc-racy as a nice place to visit but no place to spend a career. Even dedicated members of adhoc-racies periodically get frustrated with this structure's fluidity, confusion, and ambiguity. "In these situations, all managers some of the time and many managers all the time yearn for more definition and structure" (Burns and Stalker, 1966: 122–123). The managers of innova-tive organizations report anxiety related to the eventual phaseout of projects; confusion as to who their boss is, whom to impress to get promoted; a lack of clarity in job definitions, authority relationships, and lines of communication; and intense competition for resources, recognition, and rewards (Reeser, 1969). This last point suggests another serious problem of ambiguity here, the politicization of these configurations. Combining its ambiguities with its interdependencies, the innovative form can emerge as a rather politicized and ruthless orga-nization—supportive of the fit, as long as they remain fit, but destructive of the weak.

---

*We might take this convergence as the expression of an "organization's mind"—the focusing on a strategic theme as a result of the mutual adjustments among its many actors.

PROBLEMS OF EFFICIENCY

No configuration is better suited to solving complex, ill-structured problems than this one. None can match it for sophisticated innovation. Or, unfortunately, for the costs of that innovation. This is simply not an efficient way to function. Although it is ideally suited for the one-of-a-kind project, the innovative configuration is not competent at doing *ordinary* things. It is designed for the *extra*ordinary. The bureaucracies are all mass producers; they gain efficiency through standardization. The adhocracy is a custom producer, unable to standardize and so be efficient. It gains its effectiveness (innovation) at the price of efficiency.

One source of inefficiency lies in the unbalanced workload, mentioned earlier. It is almost impossible to keep the personnel of a project structure—high-priced specialists, it should be noted—busy on a steady basis. In January they may be working overtime with no hope of completing the new project on time; by May they may be playing cards for want of work.

But the real root of inefficiency is the high cost of communication. People talk a lot in these organizations; that is how they combine their knowledge to develop new ideas. But that takes time, a great deal of time. Faced with the need to make a decision in the machine organization, someone up above gives an order and that is that. Not so in the innovative one, where everyone must get into the act—managers of all kinds (functional, project, liaison), as well as all the specialists who believe their point of view should be represented. A meeting is called, probably to schedule another meeting, eventually to decide who should participate in the decision. The problem then gets defined and redefined, ideas for its solution get generated and debated, alliances build and fall around different solutions, until eventually everyone settles down to the hard bargaining over which one to adopt. Finally a decision emerges—that in itself is an accomplishment—although it is typically late and will probably be modified later.

THE DANGERS OF INAPPROPRIATE TRANSITION

Of course, one solution to the problems of ambiguity and inefficiency is to change the configuration. Employees no longer able to tolerate the ambiguity and customers fed up with the inefficiency may try to drive the organization to a more stable, bureaucratic form.

That is relatively easily done in the operating adhocracy, as noted earlier. The organization simply selects the set of standard programs it does best, reverting to the professional configuration, or else innovates one last time to find a lucrative market niche in which to mass produce, and then becomes a machine configuration. But those transitions, however easily effected, are not always appropriate. The organization came into being to solve problems imaginatively, not to apply standards indiscriminately. In many spheres, society has more mass producers than it needs; what it lacks are true problem solvers—the consulting firm that can handle a unique problem instead of applying a pat solution, the advertising agency that can come up with a novel campaign instead of the common imitation, the research laboratory that can make the really serious breakthrough instead of just modifying an existing design. The television networks seem to be classic examples of bureaucracies that provide largely standardized fare when the creativity of adhocracy is called for (except, perhaps, for the newsrooms and the specials, where an ad hoc orientation encourages more creativity).

The administrative adhocracy can run into more serious difficulties when it succumbs to the pressures to bureaucratize. It exists to innovate for itself, in its own industry. Unlike the operating adhocracy, it often cannot change orientation while remaining in the same industry. And so its conversion to the machine configuration (the natural transition for administrative adhocracy tired of perpetual change), by destroying the organization's ability to innovate, can eventually destroy the organization itself.

**BY MARK C. MALETZ
AND NITIN NOHRIA**

■ The wisdom of the day is that your business is doomed to fail if you don't overturn the status quo. You have to think outside the box, start a revolution, break all the rules—pick your own overheated rhetoric. The assumption is that new value in a company can be created only when people shed their suits, don khakis and Hawaiian shirts, and think and act like the most passionate entrepreneurs. The problem is, they're rarely told when it makes sense to do those things—or how to do them.

We recently conducted a unique research project that tried to fill in those gaps. The project focused on what we call the whitespace: the large but mostly unoccupied territory in every company where rules are vague, authority is fuzzy, budgets are nonexistent, and strategy is unclear—and where, as a consequence, entrepreneurial activity that helps reinvent and renew an organization takes place. The project worked on two levels: trained ethnographers shadowed entrepreneurial managers who were actually operating in the whitespace, while a steering committee of senior organization specialists met with top managers about their efforts to oversee whitespace activities. . . .

Whitespace exists in all companies, and enterprising people are everywhere testing the waters with unofficial efforts to boost the bottom line. The managers who operate in these uncharted seas are often the ones most successful at driving innovation, incubating new businesses, and finding new markets. The task for senior managers is to avoid letting whitespace efforts "just happen." Instead, they should actively support and monitor these activities, even as they keep them separate from the organization's formal work. If companies leave this valuable territory to the scattershot whims and talents of individual managers, they are likely to miss out on many of the opportunities that come from exploring the next frontier.

**MOVING INTO
THE WHITESPACE**

The blackspace encompasses all the business opportunities that a company has formally targeted and organized itself to capture. The whitespace, then, contains all the opportunities that fall outside the scope of formal planning, budgeting, and management.

Whether you're an entrepreneurial middle manager or a senior executive trying to keep an eye on whitespace activities, the first challenge is knowing when it's appropriate to leave the blackspace. The simple truth is that most projects should be conceived, developed, and managed within the organization's formal structures: that's what they're there for. Managers, then, should consider shifting to the whitespace only if one or more of three conditions exists.

Great uncertainty over a recognizable business opportunity is the first condition. We don't mean the garden variety uncertainty that all managers grapple with; successful managers make a career of taking on tough problems, creating plans, building consensus, and moving forward through regular company channels. We're talking about the kind of uncertainty that surrounds, for example, e-commerce, where it's unclear who has the best idea, how it should be implemented, who should be in charge, which unit should house the opportunity—and if taking the time to figure all that out would mean the opportunity would vanish altogether.

The second condition has to do with organizational politics. Sometimes turf battles make it impossible to proceed in the blackspace. . . . other times, the problem stems from the need to get resources from several groups that are generally uncooperative. In those situations, it's

---

*Reprinted with deletions from "Managing in the Whitespace," M. C. Maletz and N. Nohria, *Harvard Business Review*, February 2001, 103–111.

certainly not worth reorganizing around a new opportunity until it's proven viable. An entrepreneurial manager working in the whitespace can often bootstrap resources from competing groups without their formal involvement—and often, even without their explicit approval.

The third condition, linked to the first two, is that the company's blackspace operations are performing extremely well and would likely be profoundly disrupted by the opportunity at hand. In those circumstances, it's too risky to interfere with the existing business by formally redirecting resources. Instead, it makes sense to place some bets on the new opportunity in the whitespace and see what emerges. . . .

Knowing when to leave the blackspace is an important first step, but the actual leap to whitespace can be hazardous. It's unfamiliar ground for most managers, and it requires a different way of thinking about how work gets completed, measured, and recognized. The next step is understanding the particular challenges of operating in the whitespace and how to meet them.

MANAGING IN THE WHITESPACE

Although navigating in the whitespace requires a new compass, the rewards from successful voyages can be great. Consider this example: An executive at a major global bank developed a virtual trust business that managed assets of more than $1 billion without even appearing on top management's (or financial control's) radar screen. She designed and assembled products and services that had been manufactured for her by the bank's asset management division and sold for her by the bank's retail-banking division. The bank's organization chart indicated that the executive was a bit player without P&L responsibility or staff. And yet she was responsible for the trust business's P&L, and more than 70 people throughout the bank looked to her as their informal leader. . . .

Through examples like [this] and many others, we have identified four challenges faced by managers operating in the whitespace: establishing legitimacy, mobilizing resources, building momentum, and measuring results. The first challenge is peculiar to the whitespace; the remaining three also play out in the blackspace but much differently.

ESTABLISHING LEGITIMACY

Blackspace projects begin with a formal launch, a process that confers automatic legitimacy on them. Whitespace activities don't have that benefit; their managers must work to actively establish their legitimacy at the start if they are to get off the ground. We observed managers using a variety of techniques to show others in the organization that they deserved support.

Some traded on their superior technical skills, which made them appear uniquely qualified to lead an informal project. . . .

Depending on how whitespace efforts emerge, managers have to walk a fine line in communicating their existence to the rest of the organization and the outside world. Invisibility can protect whitespace managers while they wrestle with how best to operate, but it also makes it more difficult to mobilize needed resources.

MOBILIZING RESOURCES

Possessing a degree of legitimacy—even if it is informal—allows whitespace managers to move on to the next task: gathering the resources they'll need to move projects forward. Managers in the blackspace have a clear sense of their budgets and other resources at their disposal; the whitespace managers in our study had to beg, borrow, and steal to get what they needed.

Like fund-raisers at college telethons or on National Public Radio, effective whitespace managers recognize that you can raise a fair amount of money by asking a lot of people for a little at a time. Once people have contributed a little and been embraced as co-owners, they're likely to give again. . . .

Managers can bootstrap resources in many ways, but several characteristics are necessary regardless of one's approach: persistence, creativity, and a willingness to work with what you can get rather than what you think you need.

BUILDING MOMENTUM

Even after a whitespace project has been able to attract some resources, its mangers must find ways to build momentum and prevent the initiative from fizzling out or getting mired in corporate politics. They constantly look for ways to rapidly prototype their ideas, run experiments, crate pilots, and so on. These visible products make it harder for others to kill whitespace efforts, although they also heighten the risk that blackspace managers might see such efforts as a competitive threat. . . .

Presenting visible products is one way to build momentum; another is to share any wealth generated by a project. Blackspace managers are often suspicious of whitespace efforts; they believe that whitespace managers are pursuing their personal agendas rather than organizational objectives. To win over people in the blackspace—and to ensure that their resources are not cut off—effective whitespace manages share credit for their successes with others. . . .

Once a whitespace project has been launched, the key is to show some clear returns from the initial investments of time, money, and people. Effective whitespace managers recognize that their best bet is to make converts of their blackspace counterparts by spreading the wealth.

MEASURING RESULTS

Clearly, wealth—revenue—is one marker of a whitespace effort's progress. In general, however, results in the whitespace are difficult to measure. A product prototype, while potentially valuable, may not bring in much money in its initial form. A rapidly increasing number of hits to a Web site may be valuable but not in ways that translate directly to the bottom line. Even revenue earned in the whitespace is tricky: when the organization doesn't officially recognize the costs or the benefits involved with a product or project, crunching the numbers can get complicated. . . .

When measuring whitespace results, creativity matters. Revenues, Web site hits, and the existence of prototypes are all important, but they won't lead to the clear answers about an initiative's success that one would expect to find with a blackspace project. This is just one of the areas where senior managers, with their bird's-eye view of the company, can help the process work.

SENIOR MANAGERS AND THE WHITESPACE

Individual whitespace efforts can succeed without help from senior executives, but their chances are much improved when high-level people do get involved—provided they understand that traditional blackspace levers (planning, organizing, and controlling) have limited utility in the whitespace. To reap the full benefit of whitespace activities for their companies, senior managers must learn to nurture these informal efforts in the following ways.

FRAME THE STRATEGY

In whitespace, strategic imperatives typically emerge over time. Thus rather than being prematurely precise, the trick is to frame the whitespace work as broadly as possible. . . .

PROVIDE SUPPORT

Whitespace initiatives shouldn't be starved of resources, but they shouldn't be overfed, either. When whitespace managers are forced to sell their ideas to the organization to obtain resources, only the most persuasive ideas, supported by the most credible managers, will take off. Keeping funding tight also makes it easier to halt whitespace activities that are clearly failing.

Senior managers can provide something more valuable than money to whitespace managers: organizational and moral support. . . .

BUILD ENTHUSIASM

Senior executives should not only support those working in the whitespace, they should also communicate whitespace achievements to others within and outside the organization. But they have to be careful about how much light they shine on whitespace efforts, particularly in the early stages. At times, delaying the release of information to allow the whitespace activity to gain more credibility will be the wisest course. On other occasions, it may be more helpful to quickly announce results so the activity can gain momentum. . . .

MONITOR PROGRESS

Senior managers must track whitespace activities and, more important, decide what constitutes success for the projects. Only they have the broad perspective necessary to make that kind of call.

We observed senior managers staying on top of whitespace activities by using monitors throughout the organization. In a large global bank, a senior manager created a loose network of respected opinion leaders who generally heard about whitespace activities early on. By remaining in regular contact with these individuals, the senior manager had a good sense of the progress of whitespace efforts over time.

Judging the success or failure of a project can be difficult. In some cases, a project that doesn't generate a lot of revenue by company standards will be considered a failure. In other cases, where the investment is low, simply picking up the money lying on the table may be enough. Or there may be other considerations: a whitespace effort that generates only $5 million at a bank may be considered paltry by the whitespace manager, and yet if that money comes through cross-selling and leads to higher customer retention rates, it may be considered extremely valuable by senior managers.

Once senior managers have judged that a whitespace effort is valuable, they'll face the final challenge: deciding whether to keep it in the whitespace or migrate it into the blackspace.

MOVING TO BLACKSPACE

If a whitespace effort becomes successful, it will likely end up migrating to the blackspace. Ideally, there should come a point when a whitespace manager voluntarily lets go. Senior managers usually have to step in, however, and make a conscious decision to move the activity into the blackspace, leave it in the whitespace, or kill it altogether.

If an activity has reached critical mass—meaning that it has significant value to the company and a high degree of organizational support and visibility—it should probably be moved. At that point, it's likely that the effort will require such large investments and affect such important clients that it will have passed out of the whitespace comfort zone. It's also true that as the effort scales up, a problem that seemed small at first (a channel conflict, for example) may become unmanageable and will require the control found in the blackspace.

Some efforts, however, have value only in the whitespace and should be kept there indefinitely. For example, an initiative at an investment bank that is valuable to customers—say, the introduction of estate planning services at a bank that didn't have a significant trust business—would be killed immediately in the blackspace unless it brought in revenue, even though it could contribute to higher revenues by boosting customer retention. It also makes sense to keep a project going in the whitespace if bringing it into the blackspace would require the forced reconciliation of warring organizations. In that case, better to just let the whitespace informally maintain connections between the two.

Some whitespace efforts add little value, and most of the failures will die a natural death because they won't be able to attract the resources needed for continued survival. But others survive simply because they don't appear to create any obvious harm or because they generate some positive results while quietly draining away resources that could be better deployed elsewhere. Senior managers have to be aggressive about killing off such efforts. Sometimes that's not easy to do; whitespace activities have a way of reappearing in different guises. The most effective way of preventing a failed effort from resurfacing may simply be to shift the people involved to a more interesting whitespace project.

Whether the decision is to migrate a project to the blackspace, keep it alive in the whitespace, or kill it off, the important thing is to avoid letting the whitespace drift, unmonitored and unnoticed.

In an era when speed and flexibility are the watchwords, opportunities in the whitespace are likely to emerge in great profusion in most industries and companies. Some entrepreneurial managers, through their own force of will and talent, will produce huge successes. Others will pursue personal agendas, waste resources, build private empires, and suck value from other parts of the company. Whether—and how—senior managers oversee the whitespace will be a significant factor in their companies' success. Those that leave it to the luck of the draw, hoping that their entrepreneurs hold aces, risk coming up empty. Those that carefully nurture the space won't always win, but they'll have a much better sense of which bets are likely to pay off.

READING 16.3 — ANTICIPATING THE CELLULAR FORM*

BY RAYMOND E. MILES, CHARLES C. SNOW, JOHN A. MATHEWS, GRANT MILES, AND HENRY J. COLEMAN, JR.

■ Since the Industrial Revolution, the United States economy has moved through the machine age into the information age and now stands at the threshold of the knowledge age. The locus of organizational exemplars has shifted from capital-intensive industries, such as steel and automobiles, to information-intensive industries, such as financial services and logistics, and now toward innovation-driven industries, such as computer software and biotechnology, where competitive advantage lies mostly in the effective use of human resources.

This evolution has been simultaneously powered and facilitated by the invention of a succession of new organizational forms—new approaches to accumulating and applying know-how to the key resources of the day. The contribution of each new form has been to allow firms to use their expanding know-how to adapt to market opportunities and demands, first for standardized goods and services, then to increasing levels of product and service customization, and presently toward the expectation of continuous innovation. . . .

THE TWENTY-FIRST CENTURY: ERA OF INNOVATION

In tomorrow's business world, some markets will still be supplied with standard products and services, while other markets will demand large amounts of customization. However, the continued pull of market forces, and the push of ever-increasing know-how honed through network partnering, is already moving some industries and companies toward what amounts to a continuous process of innovation. Beyond the customization of existing designs, product and service invention is becoming the centerpiece of value-adding activity in an increasing number of firms. So-called knowledge businesses—such as design and engineering services, advanced electronics and biotechnology, computer software design, health care, and consulting—not

---

*Reprinted with deletions from an article originally published as "Organizing in the Knowledge Age: Anticipating the Cellular Form," *Academy of Management Executive*, Vol. 11 (4), 1997, 7–19.

only feed the process of innovation but feed upon it in a continuous cycle that creates more, and more complex, markets and environments (Kauffman, 1995). Indeed, for companies in such businesses, both by choice and by the consequences of their choices, organizational inputs and outputs become highly unpredictable.

For example, according to the CEO of a biotechnology firm, the potential inputs to the firm are spread across hundreds and even thousands of scientists worldwide. Around each prominent researcher is a cluster of colleagues, and each cluster is a rich mix of talent held together by a set of connecting mechanisms, including shared interests, electronic mail systems, and technical conferences. Connecting devices are not coordinated by plan but rather are self-organizing, reflecting the knowledge needs and data-sharing opportunities recognized by members of the various clusters. The overall challenge of the biotechnology firm is to maintain close contact with as much of this continuously evolving knowledge field as it can. A similarly complex pattern is visible at the output interface of the firm, as myriad alliances and partnerships are formed to take partially developed products (and by-products) through the stages of final design, testing, and marketing. Clearly, a biotechnology firm that is rigidly structured will not be able to muster the internal flexibility required to match the complexity of its environment.

A NEW ORGANIZATIONAL FORM FOR A NEW ECONOMIC ERA

Similar elements of complexity are visible in a growing number of industries. In computer software, for example, there are few limits on potentially profitable product designs, and a vast array of independent designers move in and around software companies of every size. The choices firms face at both the input and output ends of their operation are thus large and constantly changing. Faced with these opportunities, and projecting the evolutionary trends discussed above, one would expect the twenty-first century organization to rely heavily on clusters of self-organizing components collaboratively investing the enterprise's know-how in product and service innovations for markets that they have helped create and develop.

Such firms can best be described as cellular.* The cellular metaphor suggests a living, adaptive organization. Cells in living organisms possess fundamental functions of life and can act alone to meet a particular need. However, by acting in concert, cells can perform more complex functions. Evolving characteristics, or learning, if shared across all cells, can create a higher-order organism. Similarly, a cellular organization is made up of cells (self-managing teams, autonomous business units, etc.) that can operate alone but that can interact with other cells to produce a more potent and competent business mechanism. It is this combination of independence and interdependence that allows the cellular organizational form to generate and share the know-how that produces continuous innovation.

BUILDING BLOCKS OF THE CELLULAR FORM

In the future, complete cellular firms will achieve a level of know-how well beyond that of earlier organizational forms by combining entrepreneurship, self-organization, and member ownership in mutually reinforcing ways. Each cell (team, strategic business unit, firm) will have an entrepreneurial responsibility to the large organization. The customers of a particular cell can be outside clients or other cells in the organization. In either case, the purpose is to spread an entrepreneurial mind-set throughout the organization so that every cell is concerned about improvement and growth. Indeed, giving each cell entrepreneurial responsibility is essential to the full utilization of the firm's constantly growing know-how. Of course, each cell must also have the entrepreneurial skills required to generate business for itself and the overall organization.

Each cell must be able to continually reorganize in order to make its expected contribution to the overall organization. Of particular value here are the technical skills needed to per-

---

*We did not invent the cellular label. The concept of cellular structures has been discussed at least since the 1960s. For a review, see J. A. Mathews (1996).

form its function, the collaborative skills necessary to make appropriate linkages with other organizational units and external partner firms, and the governance skills required to manage its own activities. Application of this cellular principle may require the company to strip away most of the bureaucracy that is currently in place and replace it with jointly defined protocols that guide internal and external collaboration.

Each cell must be rewarded for acting entrepreneurially and operating in a business-like manner. If the cellular units are teams or strategic business units instead of complete firms, psychological ownership can be achieved by organizing cells as profit centers, allowing them to participate in company stock-purchase plans, and so on. However, the ultimate cellular solution is probably actual member ownership of those cell assets and resources that they have created and that they voluntarily invest with the firm in expectation of a joint return. . . .

ADDING VALUE BY USING THE CELLULAR FORM

A close examination of cellularly structured firms . . . indicates that they also share some of the features of earlier organizational forms. Indeed, each new form . . . incorporates the major value-adding characteristics of the previous forms and adds new capabilities to them. Thus, the cellular form includes the dispersed entrepreneurship of the divisional form, customer responsiveness of the matrix form, and self-organizing knowledge and asset sharing of the network form.

The cellular organizational form, however, offers the potential to add value even beyond asset and know-how sharing. In its fully developed state, the cellular organization adds value through its unique ability to create and utilize knowledge. For example, knowledge sharing occurs in networks as a by-product of asset sharing rather than as a specific focus of such activity. Similarly, matrix and divisionalized firms recognize the value that may be added when knowledge is shared across projects or divisions, but they must create special-purpose mechanisms (e.g., task forces) in order to generate and share new knowledge. By contrast . . . the cellular form lends itself to sharing not only the explicit know-how that cells have accumulated and articulated, but also the tacit know-how that emerges when cells combine to design unique new customer solutions (Nonaka and Takeuchi, 1995). Such learning focuses not on the output of the innovation process, but on the innovation process itself: It is know-how that can be achieved and shared only by doing.

Beyond knowledge creation and sharing, the cellular form has the potential to add value through its related ability to keep the firm's total knowledge assets more fully invested than do the other organizational forms. Because each cell has entrepreneurial responsibility, and is empowered to draw on any of the firm's assets for each new business opportunity, high levels of knowledge utilization across cells should be expected. Network organizations aspire to high utilization of know-how and assets, but upstream firms are ultimately dependent on downstream partners to find new product or service uses. In the cellular firm, the product/service innovation process is continuous and fully shared. . . . The competence of organization members is no longer merely an option, it is an economic must.*

Given the required levels of investment, risk-taking, and member ownership, many companies will not—and need not—move completely to the cellular organizational form. Firms that produce standard products or services to forecast or order may still be most productive if arranged in at least shallow hierarchies. Groups of such firms may be linked into networks for greater speed and customization. The push toward cellular approaches . . . is appearing first in firms focused on rapid product and service innovation—unique and/or state-of-the-art offerings. However, while cellular firms are most easily associated with newer, rapidly evolving industries, the form lends itself to firms providing the design initiative in virtually any type of industry. Within a network of companies in a mature business, it is the cellularly structured firms that are likely to provide leadership in new product and service development.

---

* For an example of a firm that seriously and creatively attempted to calculate the value of its intellectual capital and other intangible assets, see L. Edvinsson and M. S. Malone, *Intellectual Capital: Realizing Your Company's True Value by Finding Its Hidden Brainpower*, New York, NY: Harper Business, 1997.

BY JOSEPH LAMPEL

■ "Project-based firms" focus on the design, development, and delivery of projects. Examples of such firms can be found in areas as disparate as motion pictures, software engineering, or satellite launching. Their challenge is to reconcile flexibility with efficiency: finding a workable balance between the demand of clients for customized and highly specific products, and the imperative of remaining commercially viable (Turner and Keegan, 1999).

The challenge is particularly acute for project-based firms whose primary business is designing, building, and supplying large projects such as power plants, oil platforms, mass transit systems, and toll roads. Collectively, project-based firms that specialize in this area are often known as EPC firms, or "engineering-procurement-construction" firms. Dealing with diversity stretches the resource base of EPC firms to the limit, principally because they are required to configure and reconfigure their resources on a project-by-project basis. Achieving the flexibility necessary for addressing project variation calls for a matrix structure, but this is at best a partial solution to the essential problem of diversity (Bartlett and Ghoshal, 1990). In this paper, we argue that EPC firms develop a more robust approach that is based on developing core competencies that support reconfiguration of resources in response to shifting design and market demands.

THE COMPETENCY BASE OF ENGINEERING-CONSTRUCTION FIRMS

Flexibility in this context means an ability to configure and reconfigure a bundle of resources according to the demands of a particular project. This ability is in turn an expression of what Prahalad and Hamel (1990) term the firm's "core competencies." For them, the key characteristics were the following:

a. Core competencies embody the collective learning of the organization: it is the tested and proven knowledge the firm acquires in the process of learning its business.

b. Core competencies embody coordinating skills: skills to coordinate diverse operations, skills to harmonize different technologies, and skills to coordinate relationships with a heterogeneous customer base.

c. Core competencies embody a shared understanding of customer needs, even before these become explicit to the customer.

d. Core competencies embody the deep understanding of the product and market possibilities that are inherent in the firm's technological knowledge base.

e. Core competencies embody intangibles such as culture and ideology that serve to bind the firm's various businesses together.

Strategy for diversified corporations, argue Prahalad and Hamel, is not based on static synergies or on finding the optimal portfolio of businesses, but on constantly renewing the firm's market position. Core competencies are the key to this renewal. Their relationship to the market is not, however, direct. Core competencies nourish core products and technologies. These core products and technologies in turn generate the products that are sold in the marketplace. In project-based service firms, however, where final products are defined by the unique requirements of individual consumers, there are no core products or core technologies to link final products with core competencies. Instead, what we have are core processes that describe the life cycle of most, if not all, large projects, from an exploratory phase involving formulation of the basic project concept—usually involving contacts with potential clients

---

*Adapted from "The Core Competencies of Project-Based Firms," *International Journal of Project Management*, 2001.

and sponsors—which leads to detailed technical studies and costing estimates, and then uses the analysis to prepare bids. Bids may be won directly, or they may form the basis for further negotiations with clients and sponsors. EPC firms that win contracts become part of the execution phase during which the project becomes a reality. The project comes to an end when the system is commissioned and put into operation.

Applying the Prahalad and Hamel (1990) framework to the EPC sector suggests that these core processes form an intermediate link between specific projects and core competencies. They structure activities and routines of projects but they do not account for the quality of outcome because they do not contain the full range of knowledge, both explicit and tacit, needed to tackle the key problems of project planning and execution. This knowledge is contained in the core competencies of EPC firms.

Our research on EPC firms in the United States, Canada, the United Kingdom, France, Malaysia, and Japan suggests that they base their operations on essentially four types of core competencies: entrepreneurial competencies, technical competencies, evaluative competencies, and relational competencies.

ENTREPRENEURIAL COMPETENCIES

Entrepreneurial competencies are by their nature experience based. Capturing contracts depends on detecting opportunities as they emerge, or even better, of stimulating the emergence of opportunities by bringing project ideas to the attention of potential clients. To do this well, EPC firms must be able to "sell" the idea to potential clients. Selling ideas is intrinsically difficult. Clients are naturally risk averse when it comes to large projects—large projects call for large investments with pay-offs that are many years in the future. They are even more risk averse when the projects do not originate from within their own organization, or from organizations and institutions with which they have a long-standing relationship.

Entrepreneurial competencies are the product of experience, but they also depend on intuition, which in turn makes them almost impossible to articulate and share. This makes it difficult for organizations to evaluate the quality of entrepreneurial decision making by individuals who are assumed to have these competencies. It is generally difficult in retrospect to isolate the reasons that led to the success or failure of particular projects. Much depends ultimately on the history of the organization. Some EPC firms begin their life highly entrepreneurial and gradually lose these competencies, becoming highly bureaucratic. Other EPC firms we interviewed were highly bureaucratic to begin with but subsequently made strenuous efforts to acquire entrepreneurial competencies (e.g., utilities that undertake projects overseas).

TECHNICAL COMPETENCIES

There is a curious paradox in the large project game: Owners and sponsors have the power to define the project broadly, but only the EPC firm has the knowledge to fill in the details. Bridging this gap is costly and time consuming for the owners and sponsors. They would like to place a limit on the number of bids they must evaluate, and they would also like to avoid costly evaluation of bids from EPC firms that lack the knowledge and experience needed to undertake the project in the first place. In order to achieve this aim owners and sponsors institute a qualifying process, which allows only a selected number of firms to participate in the competitive bidding. The key question this process seeks to answer is: Can this firm develop a technically proficient bid, and if it can, will it be able to execute the contract successfully?

The qualifying process highlights the technical competencies of the EPC firm. Engineering, procurement, construction, and operations are embedded and supported by a wide array of activities that are technical in both the narrow and broad sense of this term. Technical competencies relate first and foremost to the effective use of technological assets and engineering know-how.

Technical competencies target areas that are programmable. Programmable activities are activities that can be broken down, analyzed, and described in detail. They can be acquired via traditional education methods and are widely available in books, monographs, and manuals. The knowledge base of programmable competencies is, therefore, relatively accessible. In this respect it is relatively shallow, representing the minimum necessary for qualifying in bidding but in itself not sufficient for translating this into contracts. To do this, technical competencies must be able to identify crucial knowledge and move it to the place where it is needed in a timely fashion; it must be able to rapidly absorb knowledge from the wider environment; it must be able to learn from its own experience; and it must be able to innovate solutions for both old and new problems.

None of these activities is programmable in the strict sense of the term. They simply resist being broken down, analyzed, described, and codified. They are richly tacit precisely because they require a large amount of experience and sensitivity to context.

EVALUATIVE COMPETENCIES

It is not sufficient for EPC firms to transform opportunities into contracts, it must do so at a profit. A crucial stage in this process arrives when the EPC firm must move beyond exploration to commitment: what is it willing to do, and at what price? In the game of large projects, this overt declaration is crucial because EPC firms are stuck with their initial estimates of what they are willing to do and at what price. There is rarely much latitude for revision once the contract has been signed.

Given the complexity and uncertainty of projects these estimates are guesswork, but they are guesswork on which the welfare of the firm depends. A low cost estimate or an overly ambitious schedule may result in losses or may even bankrupt the company. A high cost estimate or an excessively cautious schedule may lose a promising contract to a competitor. The EPC firm must navigate between these two undesirable outcomes, and it must also do it in such a way as to make as much money as possible. Ultimately, this is a judgment of risks.

Every EPC firm that we surveyed had in place a system charged with this task. The system was invariably a mixture of formal analysis and informal organizational processes. With the advent of high-power information systems there have been determined efforts by many organizations to shift the process as far toward the formal as possible. However, even these organizations recognize that there are limits to how far this can be accomplished. Large projects are customized systems; they are intrinsically complex and almost always contain features that are unique to the particular project. Estimating the cost of large projects is ultimately an art, not a science; the task is simply not programmable. An assessment of the cost of a project in light of a given design and customer requirement must rely on the tacit expertise of experience of engineers and managers. But tapping this expertise requires an elaborate review system in which potential problems are identified and collectively discussed.

The review system is based on two elements: judgment and memory. Both have explicit and tacit elements, and the balance between the two varies, depending on the organizations. Almost every organization employs checklists and other formal methods to break down and weigh the elements of the project that may impact on cost, performance, or schedule. These methods, however, are supplemented and modified by managerial judgment. The process is social: managers and engineers discuss and debate their judgments. It is also often aided by specialist organizational units which deal with financial engineering and bid preparation.

The other aspect of the review system is memory. Evaluation always relies on what the organization has learned from other projects. This learning is embedded in human recollection: those who were involved in previous projects can provide information about the problems that were encountered in similar projects in the past. Memory, however, is also based on documentation. Many organizations systematically collect and analyze data about every project in which they have been involved. This data is often transformed into "work books" which are consulted when a new project is evaluated. Many organizations are also beginning to use information systems to create databases which can be consulted more efficiently and thoroughly.

RELATIONAL COMPETENCIES

Large projects are interdependent and evolving relational systems (Fonfara, 1989). They bring together a wide range of actors and institutions in different capacities, with different degree of involvement, and different amount of power to facilitate or hinder the development of the project. The interaction among these actors and institutions is unpredictable and prone to breakdowns. A manager in one of the firms we interviewed reflected on the fragility of the process in the following way: "A project is a life-organism that is subject to a lot of unexpected shocks and discontinuities. The attempt of all involved is to keep this organism moving forward. The unexpected is almost inevitable, and there is always a need for a lot of adjustment."

Getting all involved to adjust to unforeseen circumstances is essential in all projects. There are always unforeseen contingencies that call for improvisation and creative problem solving. In projects that are largely confined to a single organization, adjustment is greatly facilitated by the existence of centralized coordination. But large projects are normally a collaborative effort by a group of organizations in which none wields complete control. Adjustment in such a situation may unleash conflicts that can threaten the foundations of the collaborative process. The threat is present throughout the project but is particularly acute during the front-end part when many issues have yet to be resolved and final commitments have yet to be made.

Forestalling this threat, or dealing with it effectively when it arises, calls for a range of relational skills. The skills are an expression of relational competencies that combine both individual and organizational experiences. Their primary relevance is for managing the business interaction, but by having an impact on the interaction process, relational competencies have a substantial impact on its content as well.

Nowhere is this more important than in the interaction between EPC firms and their primary clients. The relationship is fraught with paradox. EPC firms and their clients begin with opposing interests. Each one wants to strike a deal that will maximize its own advantage, but each also knows that the relentless pursuit of advantage may undermine the very goal they are seeking, which is concluding a deal.

This transforming of an adversarial interaction into a cooperative relationship, and then making this relationship last through the vicissitudes of the project, is the basic challenge confronting EPC firms. Relational competencies are crucial to this process, but until recently these competencies were confined largely to the marketing and sales department of most EPC firms. It was their task to inform and persuade clients, and to act as liaison between the client and the rest of the organization when difficulties arise. The disadvantage of this approach is that it did not deal with adversarial attitude in the rest of the organization, in particular in the engineering and execution areas. This may result in organizational polarization to the point where, as one manager put it: "The salesman is Mr. Nice Guy, and the project manager is Mr. Nasty."

Submerging conflict during project development and contractual discussion, only to have it surface subsequently, can be costly and destructive. Otherwise, there is much recrimination. Since many projects do not end well, it is not surprising that the history of large projects is rife with bitter disputes between EPC firms and their clients. Playing Mr. Nice Guy at the beginning works when one side, or both, prefer to look the other way with the hope or intention of dealing with the downside of the agreement when it suits them. As one manager put it: "The clients like to perceive a 'cozy' relationship. In reality it is mayhem. We renegotiate all the time."

A new model is currently emerging which relies heavily on relational competencies: partnering. The essence of partnering is the joint exploration of scoping and design prior to agreement. Instead of negotiating the project from a zero-sum perspective, the firms involved explore options that maximize performance and reduce costs simultaneously. Teamwork is the operative intent. Let the professionals get together without the interfering presence of pure commercial and legal considerations, and they will come up with solutions that would not have emerged from an adversarial process.

THE STRATEGIES OF EPC FIRMS FROM A CORE COMPETENCE PERSPECTIVE

The notion of strategy revolves around creating a close relationship between actions and preferred outcomes. In most industries gaining and holding high market share is a preferred outcome. Failure to do this is seen as a sign that the company is either undertaking the wrong actions, or that the actions that it is undertaking have no impact on outcomes. This model cannot be applied to EPC firms. Large projects are too heterogeneous to allow for meaningful and stable market definition; and without market definition the concept of market share also has no meaning.

Our research suggests that when it comes to addressing this issue EPC firms are pulled in two opposing directions. On the one hand there is the pressure to remain close to what the EPC firm knows and does best; to leverage rather than stretch core competencies (Prahalad and Hamel 1993). On the other hand, there is the pressure to focus on the portfolio; to generate volume, build economies of scale, and reduce overall risk. Our study suggests that EPC firms respond to these forces by developing three generic strategies. The first, which we call "focusing strategy," is to target opportunities that are close to their existing competencies. The second, which we call "switching strategy," is at the opposite extreme of the spectrum. It involves targeting lucrative opportunities almost anywhere that they can be found, stretching existing competencies as far as they allow. Finally, a third strategy, which we call "combining strategy," attempts to find a balance between existing competencies and lucrative opportunities.

FOCUSING STRATEGY

A focusing strategy sees opportunities through the lens of competencies. The strategic cycle of EPC firms that pursue a focusing strategy begins with competencies and from there it leads to opportunities. Competencies should beget lucrative opportunities rather than the other way around. First, because a firm with strong competencies has a better chance when it comes to bidding. And, second, because having strong competencies not only improves quality and performance, but it also reduces costly errors.

But what are strong competencies? EPC firms that follow a focusing strategy see strong competencies as competencies that provide the greatest leverage. This inevitably leads to an emphasis on competency depth at the expense of breadth. Experience and knowledge are cultivated as much as possible along a narrow front, rather than seeking a broad coverage of many different types of projects.

SWITCHING STRATEGIES

EPC firms that follow a switching strategy fall on the other side of the competencies–opportunities spectrum. They are determinedly opportunity driven. This means seeking high-quality opportunities wherever they may be found; trying to capture these opportunities, and then turning their attention to transforming these opportunities into revenues.

The advantage of this strategy resides in the fact that it deals directly with the key uncertainty of the large project game: the difficulty of predicting the flow or composition of projects. A switching strategy seeks to avoid the perils of specializing in a particular region or type of projects by maintaining a flexible set of competencies. The intent is not so much to create a diversified project portfolio as it is to have the ability to track changes in the stream of projects. The key to switching strategy is the ability to stretch competencies to cover a multitude of contexts and requirements. By definition, this is easier to do when competencies are broad rather than deep.

COMBINING STRATEGY

Focusing strategy and switching strategy represent two poles of a continuum. For firms that wish neither to be dominated by their competencies nor to be driven by opportunities, the third choice is to find a middle ground. This middle ground is grounded in competencies but is on the whole still oriented toward opportunities. The main difference here, however, is that there is a systematic attempt to focus on related opportunities areas and then work backward to the competencies necessary to serve these areas.

If firms that follow a focusing strategy are specialists when it comes to their approach to competencies and opportunities, firms that follow a combining strategy are specialists when it comes to pursing opportunities, and generalists when it comes to competencies. Careful attention to organizational design helps to balance the inevitable tension that exists between these two opposing imperatives. There is no one way of achieving this goal; each organization evolves its own approach.

CONCLUSION

In this paper we argue that the life cycle of large projects can be described by core processes that structure activities and routines. The transition from one process to the next is often punctuated by key events during which the impact of core competencies becomes strongly evident. Perhaps the main event confronting EPC firms is the moment when they discover whether they have succeeded or failed in winning the contract. EPC firms use their competencies to accomplish this goal, but they are aware that they cannot craft their strategies with a view to winning specific projects. All they can do is craft their strategies to maximize their chances of winning certain projects on advantageous terms.

The key to doing this successfully is developing a positively reinforcing relationship among core competencies, project choice, and project portfolio. Crucial to achieving this virtuous cycle is acquiring, developing, and managing the correct mix of key competencies: technical, which contain basic know-how and ability to design and execute a particular project; entrepreneurial, that contain marketing and project opportunity know-how; relational, that contain skills and know-how for developing and negotiating projects; and evaluative, that contain routines designed to evaluate costs and measure risks.

EPC firms must cultivate all four competencies because each competency addresses problems that are intrinsic to the business they are in. They are also in principle insoluble: economic change, political turmoil, and technological innovations are constantly changing the nature of the problems facing EPC firms and, hence, reducing the effectiveness of proven practices and solutions. To maintain their strategic position EPC firms must, therefore, not only possess competencies that deal with current problems, they must also have the ability to reshape these competencies in the light of new circumstances.

How do EPC firms do this? To some extent competencies evolve indirectly as a result of the inevitable learning that takes place when EPC firms tackle new projects. Such evolution, however, is haphazard. It is contingent on organizational processes that are often poorly understood and mostly difficult to control. Factors such as top management thinking, team dynamics, and political rivalries can hinder as well as facilitate the development of competencies. Ultimately, however, strategy exercises an important influence on competence development, and EPC strategy, as noted earlier, is shaped by pervasive tension between the imperative of competencies and the lure of market opportunities.

CHAPTER 17

Managing Diversity

A good deal of evidence has accumulated on the relationship between diversification and divisionalization. Once organizations diversify their product or service lines, they tend to create distinct divisions to deal with each business. This relationship was perhaps first carefully documented in the classic historical study by Alfred D. Chandler, *Strategy and Structure: Chapters in the History of the Great American Enterprise*. Chandler traced the origins of diversification and divisionalization in Du Pont and General Motors in the 1920s, which were followed later by other major firms. A number of other studies elaborated on Chandler's conclusions, as discussed in the readings of this chapter.

The first reading, drawn from Mintzberg's work on structuring, probes the structure of divisionalization—how it works, what brings it about, what intermediate variations of it exist, and what problems it poses for organizations that use it and for society at large. It concludes on a rather pessimistic note about conglomerate diversification and about the purer forms of divisionalization.

Across the world, diversified corporations take many different forms. That is why we have included the next reading by Philippe Lasserre of INSEAD. Lasserre describes three forms that such organizations take in the West, which he labels industrial group, industrial holdings, and financial conglomerates. Then he describes three that are common in Asia, labeled entrepreneurial conglomerates, *keiretsus*, and national holdings. When he compares them, an interesting result emerges: Whereas organizations in the West tend to control impersonally (or analytically) and yet in some ways more loosely (or less synergistically), the Asians favor softer and more personalized forms of control but often achieve tighter connections. (Harking back to Pitcher's three styles of managing, the technocrats are more common in the West apparently, whereas the artists and craftsmen are easier to find in the East.) Lasserre warns, however, that you cannot just adopt an approach because it looks good: Beware of the limitations of your own culture!

Aspects of the diversified organization, particularly in its more conglomerate form, come in for some heavy criticism in this chapter and in the next reading, too. But it quickly turns to the more constructive question of how to use strategy to combine a cluster of different businesses into an effective corporate entity. This is Michael Porter's article entitled "From Competitive Advantage to Corporate Strategy." Porter discusses in a most insightful way various types of overall corporate strategies, including portfolio management, restructuring, transferring skills, and sharing activities (the last two are referred to in his 1985 book *Competitive Advantage* as "horizontal strategies"). The former deals with "intangible" whereas the latter deals with "tangible" interrelationships among business units and are conceived in terms of his value chain.

USING THE CASE STUDIES

The strategy process in diversified firms can be strongly influenced by the size and geographic reach of the firm in question. The Wipro Corporation case deals with a diversified Indian conglomerate. Selkirk Group in Asia, on the other hand, deals with a company focused primarily on the production of bricks, but one that is also involved in an ambitious program of geographic diversification. The challenge for both these companies is finding the right structure to manage diversity effectively. The article that examines the different structural options available to diversified corporations is relevant for analysis of these cases, as well as for Saatchi & Saatchi and LVMH, which also deal with geographic and product diversity. The reading by Phillip Lasserre, "Managing Large Groups in the East and West," suggests that different approaches to diversity are more likely to emerge in the East as opposed to Europe or North America. The book contains a number of cases that deal with diversified Asian corporations, for example, Wipro Corporation and Canon, and Western diversified corporations such as BMG, Saatchi & Saatchi, LVMH, and Selkirk. A number of these are expanding into Asia. It would be interesting to see if they shift structure in response to their new environment.

Porter's reading opens up the issue of managing diversity to wider consideration. Diversity is often a by-product of growth, but it is growth with potential pitfalls. Porter's analysis of the advantages and disadvantages of corporate diversification is relevant to cases such as Wipro Corporation. It can also be used to explain Sony's push into the personal computer market, the difficulties confronting Saatchi & Saatchi, and to evaluate if Howard Fisk, the head of Axion Consulting, is right to pursue a merger with a management consulting firm.

**BY HENRY
MINTZBERG**

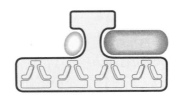

**THE BASIC
DIVISIONALIZED
STRUCTURE**

The diversified organization is not so much an integrated entity as a set of semiautonomous units coupled together by a central administrative structure. The units are generally called *divisions*, and the central administration, the *headquarters*. This is a widely used configuration in the private sector of the industrialized economy; the vast majority of the *Fortune* 500, America's largest corporations, use this structure or a variant of it. But, as we shall see, it is also found in other sectors as well.

In what is commonly called the "divisionalized" form of structure, units, called "divisions," are created to serve distinct markets and are given control over the operating functions necessary to do so, as shown in Figure 1. Each is therefore relatively free of direct control by headquarters or even of the need to coordinate activities with other divisions. Each, in other words, appears to be a self-standing business. Of course, none is. There *is* a headquarters, and it has a series of roles that distinguish this overall configuration from a collection of independent businesses providing the same set of products and services.

ROLES OF THE HEADQUARTERS

Above all, the headquarters exercises performance control. It sets standards of achievement, generally in quantitative terms (such as return on investment or growth in sales), and then monitors the results. Coordination between headquarters and the divisions thus reduces largely to the standardization of outputs. Of course, there is some direct supervision—headquarters' managers have to have personal contact with and knowledge of the divisions. But that is largely circumscribed by the key assumption in this configuration that if the division managers are to be responsible for the performance of their divisions, they must have considerable autonomy to manage them as they see fit. Hence there is extensive delegation of authority from headquarters to the level of division manager.

Certain important tasks do, however, remain for the headquarters. One is to develop the overall *corporate* strategy, meaning to establish the portfolio of businesses in which the organization will operate. The headquarters establishes, acquires, divests, and closes down divisions in order to change its portfolio. Popular in the 1970s in this regard was the Boston Consulting Group's "growth share matrix," where corporate managers were supposed to allocate funds to divisions on the basis of their falling into the categories of dogs, cash cows, wildcats, and stars. But enthusiasm for that technique waned, perhaps mindful of Pope's warning that a little learning can be a dangerous thing.

Second, the headquarters manages the movement of funds between the divisions, taking the excess profits of some to support the greater growth potential of others. Third, of course,

---

*Adapted from *The Structuring of Organizations* (Prentice Hall, 1979), Chap. 20 on "The Divisionalized Form." A chapter similar to this appeared in *Mintzberg on Management: Inside Our Strange World of Organizations* (Free Press, 1989).

FIGURE 1
TYPICAL ORGANIGRAM
FOR A DIVISIONALIZED
MANUFACTURING
FIRM

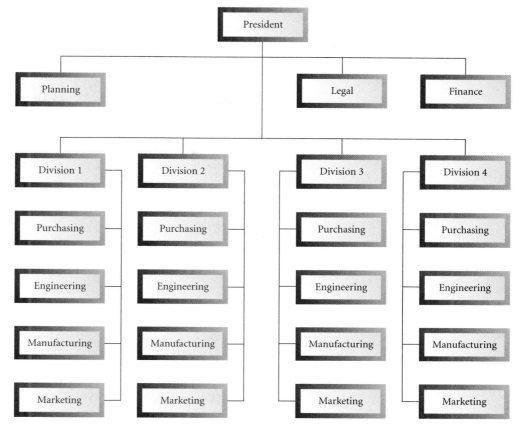

the headquarters, through its own technostructure, designs and operates the performance control system. Fourth, it appoints and therefore retains the right to replace the division managers. For a headquarters that does not directly manage any division, its most tangible power when the performance of a division lags—short of riding out an industry downturn or divesting the division—is to replace its leader. Finally, the headquarters provides certain support services that are common to all the divisions—a corporate public relations office or legal counsel, for example.

STRUCTURE OF THE DIVISIONS

It has been common to label divisionalized organizations "decentralized." That is a reflection of how *certain* of them came to be, most notably Du Pont early in this century. When organizations that were structured functionally (for example, in departments of marketing, manufacturing, and engineering, etc.) diversified, they found that coordination of their different product lines across the functions became increasingly complicated. The central managers had to spend great amounts of time intervening to resolve disputes. But once these corporations switched to a divisionalized form of structure, where all the functions for a given business could be contained in a single unit dedicated to that business, management became much simpler. In effect, their structures became *more* decentralized, power over distinct businesses being delegated to the division managers.

But more decentralized does not mean *decentralized.* That word refers to the dispersal of decision-making power in an organization, and in many of the diversified corporations much of the power tended to remain with the few managers who ran the businesses. Indeed, the most famous case of divisionalization was one of relative *centralization:* Alfred P. Sloan introduced the divisionalized structure to General Motors in the 1920s to *reduce* the power of its autonomous business units, to impose systems of financial controls on what had been a largely unmanaged agglomeration of different automobile businesses.

In fact, I would argue that it is the *centralization* of power within the divisions that is most compatible with the divisionalized form of structure. In other words, the effect of having a headquarters over the divisions is to drive them toward the machine configuration, namely a structure of centralized bureaucracy. That is the structure most compatible with headquarters control, in my opinion. If true, this would seem to be an important point, because it means that the proliferation of the diversified configuration in many spheres—business, government, and the rest—has the effect of driving many suborganizations toward machine bureaucracy, even where that configuration may be inappropriate (school systems, for example, or government departments charged with innovative project work).

The explanation for this lies in the standardization of outputs, the key to the functioning of the divisionalized structure. Bear in mind the headquarters' dilemma: to respect divisional autonomy while exercising control over performance. This it seeks to resolve by after-the-fact monitoring of divisional results, based on clearly defined performance standards. But two main assumptions underlie such standards.

First, each division must be treated as a single integrated system with a single, consistent set of goals. In other words, although the divisions may be loosely coupled with each other, the assumption is that each is tightly coupled internally.*

Second, these goals must be operational ones, in other words, lend themselves to quantitative measurement. But in the less formal configurations—entrepreneurial and innovative—which are less stable, such performance standards are difficult to establish, while in the professional configuration, the complexity of the work makes it difficult to establish such standards. Moreover, while the entrepreneurial configuration may lend itself to being integrated around a single set of goals, the innovative and professional configurations do not. Thus, only the machine configuration of the major types fits comfortably into the conventional divisionalized structure, by virtue of its integration and its operational goals.

In fact, when organizations with another configuration are drawn under the umbrella of a divisionalized structure, they tend to be forced toward the machine bureaucratic form, to make them conform with *its* needs. How often have we heard stories of entrepreneurial firms recently acquired by conglomerates being descended upon by hordes of headquarters technocrats bemoaning the loose controls, the absence of organigrams, the informality of the systems? In many cases, of course, the very purpose of the acquisition was to do just this, tighten up the organization so that its strategies can be pursued more pervasively and systematically. But other times, the effect is to destroy the organization's basic strengths, sometimes including its flexibility and responsiveness. Similarly, how many times have we heard tell of government administrators complaining about being unable to control public hospitals or universities through conventional (meaning machine bureaucratic) planning systems?

This conclusion is, in fact, a prime manifestation of the hypothesis that concentrated external control of an organization has the effect of formalizing and centralizing its structure, in other words, of driving it toward the machine configuration. Headquarters' control of divisions is, of course, concentrated; indeed, when the diversified organization is itself a *closed system*, as I shall argue later many tend to be, then it is a most concentrated form of control. And, the effect of that control is to render the divisions its *instruments*.

There is, in fact, an interesting irony in this, in that the less society controls the overall diversified organization, the more the organization itself controls its individual units. The

---

*Unless, of course, there is a second layer of divisionalization, which simply takes this conclusion down another level in the hierarchy.

result is increased autonomy for the largest organizations coupled with decreased autonomy for their many activities.

To conclude this discussion of the basic structure, the diversified configuration is represented in the opening figure, symbolically in terms of our logo, as follows. Headquarters has three parts: a small strategic apex of top managers, a small technostructure to the left concerned with the design and operation of the performance control system, and a slightly larger staff support group to the right to provide support services common to all the divisions. Each of the divisions is shown below the headquarters as a machine configuration.

CONDITIONS OF THE DIVERSIFIED ORGANIZATION

While the diversified configuration may arise from the federation of different organizations, which come together under a common headquarters umbrella, more often it appears to be the structural response to a machine organization that has diversified its range of product or service offerings. In either case, it is the diversity of markets above all that drives an organization to use this configuration. An organization faced with a single integrated market simply cannot split itself into autonomous divisions; the one with distinct markets, however, has an incentive to create a unit to deal with each.

There are three main kinds of market diversity—product and service, client, and region. In theory, all three can lead to divisionalization. But when diversification is based on variations in clients or regions as opposed to products or services, divisionalization often turns out to be incomplete. With identical products or services in each region or for each group of clients, the headquarters is encouraged to maintain central control of certain critical functions, to ensure common operating standards for all the divisions. And that seriously reduces divisional autonomy, and so leads to a less than complete form of divisionalization.

Thus, one study found that insurance companies concentrate at headquarters the critical function of investment, and retailers concentrate that of purchasing, also controlling product range, pricing, and volume (Channon, 1975). One need only look at the individual outlets of a typical retail chain to recognize the absence of divisional autonomy: usually they all look alike. The same conclusion tends to hold for other businesses organized by regions, such as bakeries, breweries, cement producers, and soft drink bottlers: Their "divisions," distinguished only by geographical location, lack the autonomy normally associated with ones that produce distinct products or services.

What about the conditions of size? Although large size itself does not bring on divisionalization, surely it is not coincidental that most of America's largest corporations use some variant of this configuration. The fact is that as organizations grow large, they become inclined to diversify and then to divisionalize. One reason is protection: large organizations tend to be risk averse—they have too much to lose—and diversification spreads the risk. Another is that as firms grow large, they come to dominate their traditional market, and so must often find growth opportunities elsewhere, through diversification. Moreover, diversification feeds on itself. It creates a cadre of aggressive general managers, each running his or her own division, who push for further diversification and further growth. Thus, most of the giant corporations—with the exception of the "heavies," those with enormously high fixed-cost operating systems, such as the oil or aluminum producers—not only were able to reach their status by diversifying but also feel great pressures to continue to do so.

Age is another factor associated with this configuration, much like size. In larger organizations, the management runs out of places to expand in its traditional markets; in older ones, the managers sometimes get bored with the traditional markets and find diversion through diversification. Also, time brings new competitors into old markets, forcing the management to look elsewhere for growth opportunities.

As governments grow large, they too tend to adopt a kind of divisionalized structure. The central administrators, unable to control all the agencies and departments directly, settle for granting their managers considerable autonomy and then trying to control their results through planning and performance controls. Indeed the "accountability" buzzword so often heard in governments these days reflects just this trend—to move closer to a divisionalized structure.

One can, in fact, view the entire government as a giant diversified configuration (admittedly an oversimplification, since all kinds of links exist among the departments), with its three main coordinating agencies corresponding to the three main forms of control used by the headquarters of the large corporation. The budgetary agency, technocratic in nature, concerns itself with performance control of the departments; the public service commission, also partly technocratic, concerns itself with the recruiting and training of government managers; and the executive office, top management in nature, reviews the principal proposals and initiatives of the departments.

In the preceding chapter, the communist state was described as a closed-system machine bureaucracy. But it may also be characterized as the ultimate closed system diversified configuration, with the various state enterprises and agencies its instruments, machine bureaucracies tightly regulated by the planning and control systems of the central government.

STAGES IN THE TRANSITION TO THE DIVERSIFIED ORGANIZATION

There has been a good deal of research on the transition of the corporation from the functional to the diversified form. Figure 2 and the discussion that follows borrow from this research to describe four stages in that transition.

At the top of Figure 2 is the pure *functional* structure, used by the corporation whose operating activities form one integrated, unbroken chain from purchasing through production to marketing and sales. Only the final output is sold to the customers.* Autonomy cannot, therefore, be granted to the units, so the organization tends to take on the form of one overall machine configuration.

As an integrated firm seeks wider markets, it may introduce a variety of new end products and so shift all the way to the pure diversified form. A less risky alternative, however, is to start by marketing its intermediate products on the open market. This introduces small breaks in its processing chain, which in turn calls for a measure of divisionalization in its structure, giving rise to the *by-product* form. But because the processing chain remains more or less intact, central coordination must largely remain. Organizations that fall into this category tend to be vertically integrated, basing their operations on a single raw material, such as wood, oil, or aluminum, which they process to a variety of consumable end products. The example of Alcoa is shown in Figure 3.

Some corporations further diversify their by-product markets, breaking down their processing chain until what the divisions sell on the open market becomes more important than what they supply to each other. The organization then moves to the *related-product* form. For example, a firm manufacturing washing machines may set up a division to produce the motors. When the motor division sells more motors to outside customers than to its own sister division, a more serious form of divisionalization is called for. What typically hold the divisions of these firms together is some common thread among their products, perhaps a core skill or technology, perhaps a central market theme, as in a corporation such as 3M that likes to describe itself as being in the coating and bonding business. A good deal of the control over the specific product-market strategies can now revert to the divisions, such as research and development.

As a related-product firm expands into new markets or acquires other firms with less regard to a central strategic theme, the organization moves to the *conglomerate* form and so adopts a pure diversified configuration, the one described at the beginning of this reading.

---

*It should be noted that this is in fact the definition of a functional structure: Each activity contributes just one step in a chain toward the creation of the final product. Thus, for example, engineering is a functionally organized unit in the firm that produces and markets its own designs, while it would be a market organized unit in a consulting firm that sells its design services, among other, directly to clients.

FIGURE 2
STAGES IN THE
TRANSITION TO THE
PURE DIVERSIFIED
FORM

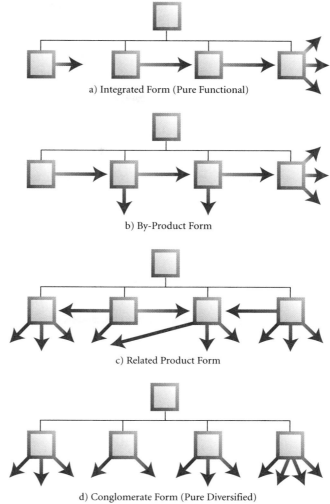

a) Integrated Form (Pure Functional)

b) By-Product Form

c) Related Product Form

d) Conglomerate Form (Pure Diversified)

Each division serves its own markets, producing products unrelated to those of the other divisions—chinaware in one, steam shovels in a second, and so on.* The result is that the headquarters planning and control system becomes simply a vehicle for regulating performance, and the headquarters staff can diminish to almost nothing—a few general and group managers supported by a few financial analysts with a minimum of support services.

SOME ISSUES ASSOCIATED WITH THE DIVERSIFIED ORGANIZATION

THE ECONOMIC ADVANTAGES OF DIVERSIFICATION?

It has been argued that the diversified configuration offers four basic advantages over the functional structure with integrated operations, namely an overall machine configuration. First, it encourages the efficient allocation of capital. Headquarters can choose where to put its

---

*I wrote this example here somewhat whimsically before I encountered a firm in Finland with divisions that actually produce, among other things, the world's largest icebreaker ships and fine pottery!

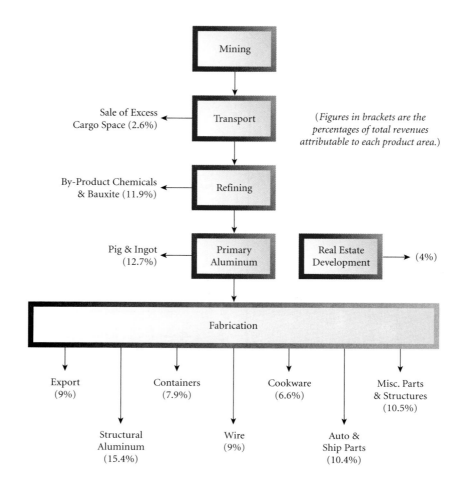

FIGURE 3
BY-PRODUCT AND
END-PRODUCT SALES
OF ALCOA
(from Rumelt, 1974: 21)
Note: Percentages for 1969
prepared by Richard Rumelt
from data in company's
annual reports.

money and so can concentrate on its strongest markets, milking the surpluses of some divisions to help others grow. Second, by opening up opportunities to run individual businesses, the diversified configuration helps to train general managers. Third, this configuration spreads its risk across different markets, whereas the focused machine bureaucracy has all its strategic eggs in one market basket, so to speak. Fourth, and perhaps most important, the diversified configuration is strategically responsive. The divisions can fine-tune their bureaucratic machines while the headquarters can concentrate on the strategic portfolio. It can acquire new businesses and divest itself of old, unproductive ones.

But is the single machine organization the correct basis of comparison? Is not the real alternative, at least from society's perspective, the taking of a further step along the same path, to the point of eliminating the headquarters altogether and allowing the divisions to function as independent organization? Beatrice Foods, described in a 1976 *Fortune* magazine article, had 397 different divisions (Martin, 1976). The issue is whether this arrangement was more efficient than 397 separate corporations.* In this regard, let us reconsider the four advantages discussed earlier.

---

*The example of Beatrice was first written as presented here in the 1970s, when the company was the subject of a good deal of attention and praise in the business press. At the time of our first revision, in 1988, the company was being disassembled. It seemed appropriate to leave the example as first presented, among other reasons to question the tendency to favor fashion over investigation in the business press.

In the diversified corporation, headquarters allocates the capital resources among the divisions. In the case of 397 independent corporations, the capital markets do that job instead. Which does it better? Studies suggest that the answer is not simple.

Some people, such as the economist Oliver Williamson (1975, 1985), have argued that the diversified organization may do a better job of allocating money because the capital markets are inefficient. Managers at headquarters who know their divisions can move the money around faster and more effectively. But others find that arrangement more costly and, in some ways, less flexible. Moyer (1970), for example, argued early on that conglomerates pay a premium above stock market prices to acquire businesses, whereas the independent investor need pay only small brokerage fees to diversify his or her own portfolio, and can do so easier and more flexibly. Moreover, that provides the investor with full information on all the businesses owned, whereas the diversified corporation provides only limited information to stockholders on the details inside its portfolio.

On the issue of management development, the question becomes whether the division managers receive better training and experience than they would as company presidents. The diversified organization is able to put on training courses and to rotate its managers to vary their experience; the independent firm is limited in those respects. But if, as the proponents of diversification claim, autonomy is the key to management development, then presumably the more autonomy the better. The division managers have a headquarters to lean on—and to be leaned on by. Company presidents, in contrast, are on their own to make their own mistakes and to learn from them.

On the third issue, risk, the argument from the diversified perspective is that the independent organization is vulnerable during periods of internal crisis or economic slump; conglomeration offers support to see individual businesses through such periods. The counterargument, however, is that diversification may conceal bankruptcies, that ailing divisions are sometimes supported longer than necessary, whereas the market bankrupts the independent firm and is done with it. Moreover, just as diversification spreads the risk, so too does it spread the consequences of that risk. A single division cannot go bankrupt; the whole organization is legally responsible for its debts. So a massive enough problem in one division can pull down the whole organization. Loose coupling may turn out to be riskier than no coupling!

Finally, there is the issue of strategic responsiveness. Loosely coupled divisions may be more responsive than tightly coupled functions. But how responsive do they really prove to be? The answer appears to be negative: this configuration appears to inhibit, not encourage, the taking of strategic initiatives. The problem seems to lie, again, in its control system. It is designed to keep the carrot just the right distance in front of the divisional managers, encouraging them to strive for better and better financial performance. At the same time, however, it seems to dampen their inclination to innovate. It is that famous "bottom line" that creates the problem, encouraging short-term thinking and shortsightedness; attention is focused on the carrot just in front instead of the fields of vegetables beyond. As Bower has noted,

> [T]he risk to the division manager of a major innovation can be considerable if he is measured on short-run, year-to-year, earnings performance. The result is a tendency to avoid big risk bets, and the concomitant phenomenon that major new developments are, with few exceptions, made outside the major firms in the industry. Those exceptions tend to be single-product companies whose top managements are committed to true product leadership. . . . Instead the diversified companies give us a steady diet of small incremental change. (1970: 194)

Innovation requires entrepreneurship, or intrapreneurship, and these, as we have already argued, do not thrive under the diversified configuration. The entrepreneur takes his or her own risks to earn his or her own rewards; the intrapreneur (as we shall see) functions best in the loose structure of the innovative adhocracy. Indeed, many diversified corporations depend on those configurations for their strategic responsiveness, since they diversify not by innovating themselves but by acquiring the innovative results of independent firms. Of course, that may be their role—to exploit rather than create those innovations—but we should not, as a result, justify diversification on the basis of its innovative capacity.

THE CONTRIBUTION OF HEADQUARTERS

To assess the effectiveness of conglomeration, it is necessary to assess what actual contribution the headquarters makes to the divisions. Since what the headquarters does in a diversified organization is otherwise performed by the various boards of directors of a set of independent firms, the question then becomes, what does a headquarters offer to the divisions that the independent board of directors of the autonomous organization does not?

One thing that neither can offer is the management of the individual business. Both are involved with it only on a part-time basis. The management is, therefore, logically left to the full-time managers, who have the required time and information. Among the functions a headquarters *does* perform, as noted earlier, are the establishment of objectives for the divisions, the monitoring of their performance in terms of these objectives, and the maintenance of limited personal contacts with division managers, for example to approve large capital expenditures. Interestingly, those are also the responsibilities of the directors of the individual firm, at least in theory.

In practice, however, many boards of directors—notably, those of widely held corporations—do those things rather ineffectively, leaving business managements carte blanche to do what they like. Here, then, we seem to have a major advantage to the diversified configuration. It exists as an administrative mechanism to overcome another prominent weakness of the free-market system, the ineffective board.

There is a catch in this argument, however, for diversification by enhancing an organization's size and expanding its number of markets, renders the corporation more difficult to understand and so to control by its board of part-time directors. Moreover, as Moyer has noted, one common effect of conglomerate acquisition is to increase the number of shareholders, and so to make the corporation more widely held, and therefore less amenable to director control. Thus, the diversified configuration in some sense resolves a problem of its own making—it offers the control that its own existence has rendered difficult. Had the corporation remained in one business, it might have been more narrowly held and easier to understand, and so its directors might have been able to perform their functions more effectively. Diversification thus helped to create the problem that divisionalization is said to solve. Indeed, it is ironic that many a diversified corporation that does such a vigorous job of monitoring the performance of its own divisions is itself so poorly monitored by its own board of directors!

All of this suggests that large diversified organizations tend to be classic closed systems, powerful enough to seal themselves off from much external influence while able to exercise a good deal of control over not only their own divisions, as instruments, but also their external environments. For example, one study of all 5,995 directors of the *Fortune* 500 found that only 1.6 percent of them represented major shareholder interests (Smith, 1978) while another survey of 855 corporations found that 84 percent of them did not even formally require their directors to hold any stock at all (Bacon, 1973: 40)!

What does happen when problems arise in a division? What can a headquarters do that various boards of directors cannot? The chairman of one major conglomerate told a meeting of the New York Society of Security Analysts, in reference to the headquarters vice presidents who oversee the divisions, that "it is not too difficult to coordinate five companies that are well run" (in Wrigley, 1970: V78). True enough. But what about five that are badly run? What could the small staff of administrators at a corporation's headquarters really do to correct problems in that firm's thirty operating divisions or in Beatrice's 397? The natural tendency to tighten the control screws does not usually help once the problem has manifested itself, nor does exercising close surveillance. As noted earlier, the headquarters managers cannot manage the divisions. Essentially, that leaves them with two choices. They can either replace the division manager, or they can divest the corporation of the division. Of course, a board of directors can also replace the management. Indeed, that seems to be its only real prerogative; the management does everything else.

On balance, then, the economic case for one headquarters versus a set of separate boards of directors appears to be mixed. It should, therefore, come as no surprise that one important study found that corporations with "controlled diversity" had better profits than those with conglomerate diversity (Rumelt, 1974). Overall, the pure diversified configuration (the conglomerate) may offer some advantages over a weak system of separate boards of directors and inefficient capital markets, but most of those advantages would probably disappear if certain problems in capital markets and boards of directors were rectified. And there is reason to argue, from a social no less than an economic standpoint, that society would be better off trying to correct fundamental inefficiencies in its economic system rather than encourage private administrative arrangements to circumvent them, as we shall now see.

THE SOCIAL PERFORMANCE OF THE PERFORMANCE CONTROL SYSTEM

This configuration requires that headquarters control the divisions primarily by quantitative performance criteria, and that typically means financial ones—profit, sales growth, return on investment, and the like. The problem is that these performance measures often become virtual obsessions in the diversified organization, driving out goals that cannot be measured—product quality, pride in work, customers well served. In effect, the economic goals drive out the social ones. As the chief of a famous conglomerate once remarked, "We, in Textron, worship the god of Net Worth" (in Wrigley, 1970: V86).

That would pose no problem if the social and economic consequences of decisions could easily be separated. Governments would look after the former, corporations the latter. But the fact is that the two are intertwined; every strategic decision of every large corporation involves both, largely inseparable. As a result, its control systems, by focusing on economic measures, drive the diversified organization to act in ways that are, at best, socially unresponsive, at worst, socially irresponsible. Forced to concentrate on the economic consequences of decisions, the division manager is driven to ignore their social consequences. (Indeed, that manager is also driven to ignore the intangible economic consequences as well, such as product quality or research effort, another manifestation of the problem of the short-term, bottom-line thinking mentioned earlier.) Thus, Bower found that "the best records in the race relations area are those of single-product companies whose strong top managements are deeply involved in the business" (1970: 193).

Robert Ackerman, in a study carried out at the Harvard Business School, investigated this point. He found that social benefits such as "a rosier public image . . . pride among managers . . . an attractive posture for recruiting on campus" could not easily be measured and so could not be plugged into the performance control system. The result was that

> . . . the financial reporting system may actually inhibit social responsiveness. By focusing on economic performance, even with appropriate safeguards to protect against sacrificing long-term benefits, such a system directs energy and resources to achieving results measured in financial terms. It is the only game in town, so to speak, at least the only one with an official scoreboard. (1975: 55, 56)

Headquarters managers who are concerned about legal liabilities or the public relations effects of decisions, or even ones personally interested in broader social issues, may be tempted to intervene directly in the divisions' decision-making process to ensure proper attention to social matters. But they are discouraged from doing so by this configuration's strict division of labor: divisional autonomy requires no meddling by the headquarters in specific business decisions.

As long as the screws of the performance control system are not turned too tight, the division managers may retain enough discretion to consider the social consequences of their actions, if they so choose. But when those screws are turned tight, as they often are in the diversified corporation with a bottom-line orientation, then the division managers wishing to keep their jobs may have no choice but to act socially unresponsively, if not actually irresponsibly. As Bower has noted of the General Electric price-fixing scandal of the 1960s, "a very severely managed system of reward and punishment that demanded yearly improvements in earnings, return and market share, applied indiscriminately to all divisions, yielded a situation which was—at the very least—conducive to collusion in the oligopolistic and mature electric equipment markets" (1970: 193).

THE DIVERSIFIED ORGANIZATION IN THE PUBLIC SPHERE

Ironically, for a government intent on dealing with these social problems, solutions are indicated in the very arguments used to support the diversified configuration. Or so it would appear.

For example, if the administrative arrangements are efficient while the capital markets are not, then why should a government hesitate to interfere with the capital markets? And why shouldn't it use those same administrative arrangements to deal with the problems? If Beatrice Foods really can control those 397 divisions, then what is to stop Washington from believing it can control 397 Beatrices? After all, the capital markets don't much matter. In his book on "countervailing power," John Kenneth Galbraith (1952) argued that bigness in one sector, such as business, promotes bigness in other sectors, such as unions and government. That has already happened. How long before government pursues that logical next step and exercises direct controls?

While such steps may prove irresistible to some governments, the fact is that they will not resolve the problems of power concentration and social irresponsibility but rather will aggravate them, but not just in the ways usually assumed in Western economics. All the existing problems would simply be bumped up to another level, and there increase. By making use of the diversified configuration, government would magnify the problems of size. Moreover, government, like the corporation, would be driven to favor measurable economic goals over intangible social ones, and that would add to the problems of social irresponsibility—a phenomenon of which we have already seen a good deal in the public sector.

In fact, these problems would be worse in government, because its sphere is social, and so its goals are largely ill suited to performance control systems. In other words, many of the goals most important for the public sector—and this applies to not-for-profit organizations in spheres such as health and education as well—simply do not lend themselves to measurement, no matter how long and how hard public officials continue to try. And without measurement, the conventional diversified configuration cannot work.

There are, of course, other problems with the application of this form of organization in the public sphere. For example, government cannot divest itself of subunits quite so easily as can corporations. And public service regulations on appointments and the like, as well as a host of other rules, preclude the degree of division manager autonomy available in the private sector. (It is, in fact, these central rules and regulations that make governments resemble integrated machine configurations as much as loosely coupled diversified ones, and that undermine their efforts at "accountability.")

Thus, we conclude that, appearances and even trends notwithstanding, the diversified configuration is generally not suited to the public and not-for-profit sectors of society. Governments and other public-type institutions that wish to divisionalize to avoid centralized machine bureaucracy may often find the imposition of performance standard an artificial exercise. They may thus be better off trying to exercise control of their units in a different way. For example, they can select unit managers who reflect their desired values, or indoctrinate them in those values, and then let them manage freely, the control in effect being normative rather than quantitative. But managing ideology, even creating it in the first place, is no simple matter, especially in a highly diversified organization.

IN CONCLUSION: A STRUCTURE ON THE EDGE OF A CLIFF

Our discussion has led to a "damned if you do, damned if you don't" conclusion. The pure (conglomerate) diversified configuration emerges as an organization perched symbolically on the edge of the cliff, at the end of a long path. Ahead, it is one step away from disintegration—breaking up into separate organizations on the rocks below. Behind it is the way back to a more stable integration, in the form of the machine configuration at the start of that path. And ever hovering above is the eagle, representing the broader social control of the state, attracted by the organization's position on the edge of the cliff and waiting for the chance to pull it up to a higher cliff, perhaps more dangerous still. The edge of the cliff is an uncomfortable place to be, perhaps even a temporary one that must inevitably lead to disintegration on the rocks below, a trip to that cliff above, or a return to a safer resting place somewhere on that path behind.

READING 17.2   MANAGING LARGE GROUPS IN THE EAST AND WEST*

BY PHILIPPE LASSERRE

■ ... there is no one single best method for managing groups of businesses, and the globalization of markets and competition has revealed the emergence of organizational forms of business, particularly in the Asia Pacific region, which differs significantly from the one adopted in Europe and North America. The purpose of this article is to underline some of the salient differences between corporations in Asia and in Europe, to analyze the basis of those differences and finally to draw some recommendations.

In the first and second parts one will identify some prominent types of corporations in Europe and in Asia Pacific. In a third part, their organizational forms and their corporate control styles will be compared. Finally, some recommendations ... will be proposed.

EUROPEAN CORPORATE ARCHTYPES

European groups can be broadly classified into three major types: industrial groups, industrial holdings, and financial conglomerates.

A first type of corporation is characterized by a portfolio of business activities which share a common set of competences and in which a high degree of synergy is achieved by managing key interdependencies at corporate level. Andrew Campbell and Michael Goold at the Ashridge Strategic Management Center in the UK, in their study of British corporations, have named this type "Strategic Planning" groups (Campbell and Goold, 1987), because of the strong input from corporate headquarters in those groups into the strategy formulation of business units. Here, those groups are identified as *industrial groups*. Examples of industrial groups in Europe are British Petroleum or Glaxo in the UK, Daimler Benz or Henkel in Germany, Philips in the Netherlands, or l'Air Liquide and Michelin in France.

Industrial holdings are corporations in which the business units are clustered into subgroups or sectors. In this type of corporate grouping, synergies are strong within subgroups and weak between subgroups. In industrial holdings, the task of value creation through synergies is delegated to the subgroup level of management, while the corporate role is to impose management discipline through the implementation of planning and control systems, to

*Originally published as 'The Management of Large Groups: Asia and Europe Compared," in *European Management Journal*, Vol. 10, No. 2, June 1992, 157–12. Reprinted with deletions with permission of the Journal, Elsevier Science Ltd., Pergamon Imprint, Oxford, England.

manage acquisitions and leverage and allocate human and financial resources. Campbell and Goold call these groups "Strategic Control" groups, because of their intensive use of planning and control systems to regulate the relationships between business units and corporate headquarters. Examples of industrial holdings are: ICI or Courtaulds in the UK, BSN or Alsthom-Alcatel in France, Siemens or BASF in Germany.

Financial conglomerates are characterized by a constellation of business units which do not necessarily share any common source of synergies and whose corporate value is essentially created by the imposition of management discipline, financial leverage, and the management of acquisitions and restructuring. Heavy reliance on financial control systems as the major mechanisms of corporate governance have led Campbell and Goold to call these "Financial Control" groups. Hanson Trust or BTR in the UK are examples of financial conglomerates. A more recent and extreme version of financial conglomerates has appeared in the USA under the form of what Professor Michael Jensen at the Harvard Business School has identified as "LBO Partnerships," in which value is extracted through corporate restructuring and financial discipline imposed on business units under the form of heavy debts, as in the case of Kolberg, Kravis and Roberts (Jensen, 1989).

In Europe one can find examples of the three types of groups in a variety of corporate ownership arrangements, whether private or government-owned. In France one can find in the public sector industrial groups such as Renault, SNECMA, or Aerospatiale or, in the private sector, Peugeot, Dassault, or Michelin. Similarly Rhone Poulenc, a government-owned group, is managed as an industrial holding like BSN, which is a privately-owned group. . . .

ASIAN CORPORATE ARCHETYPES

In the Asia Pacific region, where in the past three decades local corporations have emerged as strong competitors, one can possibly identify three major types: the entrepreneurial conglomerates, the Japanese Keiretsus, and the national holdings.

The *entrepreneurial conglomerate* is a prevailing form of corporate organization in South East Asia, Korea, Taiwan and Hong Kong. Entrepreneurial conglomerates are widely diversified into a large number of unrelated activities ranging from banking, trading, real estate, manufacturing, and services. These groups are usually under the leadership of a father figure who exercises control over the strategic decisions of business units and is the driving force behind any strategic move. Very little attempt is made in Asian entrepreneurial conglomerates to manage synergies. The major source of value in those groups emanates from the ability of the entrepreneur to leverage financial and human resources, to establish political connections, to conclude deals with governments and business partners, and to impose loyalty and discipline upon business units. One can distinguish three major types of entrepreneurial conglomerates in Asia: the large Korean groups or Chaebols such as Samsung, Daewoo, or Hyundai; the Overseas Chinese groups such as Liem Sioe Liong or Astra International in Indonesia, Formosa Plastics in Taiwan, Charoen Pokphand in Thailand or Li Ka Shing in Hong Kong; and the colonial "Hongs" such as Swire or Jardine Matheson in Hong Kong.

The *Keiretsus* are a unique feature of Japanese corporate organization. They constitute super groups, or clusters of groups in which businesses are either vertically integrated as in the case of Honda, NEC, Toyota, or Matsushita, or horizontally connected as in the case of Mitsubishi, Mitsui, or Sumitomo. Although some companies in the groups exercise greater "power" than others, Keiretsus are not hierarchically organized. They are like a club of organizations which share common interests. Linkages across companies are made through cross shareholdings, the regular meeting of a "Presidential council" in which chairmen of leading companies exchange views. Transfer of staff and, in some cases, long-term supplier-client relationships are also mechanisms used among the vertical Keiretsus. Value is added in Keiretsus through their ability to coordinate informally a certain number of key activities (R&D, export contracts), to transfer expertise through personnel rotation, and to build strong supplier-distributor chains.

The Asian *national holdings* groups have been formed more recently as an expression of industrial independence in order to capitalize on domestic markets and public endowment. Some of these are government-owned like Petronas in Malaysia, Singapore Airlines, Singapore Technology, Gresik in Indonesia, or private like Siam Cement in Thailand or San Miguel in the Philippines. Their business portfolios tend to be less diversified than the ones of the entrepreneurial conglomerates, and their value creation capabilities stem from their "nationality." . . .

GROUP MANAGEMENT: A COMPARISON

In order to proceed to a comparison of the ways groups organize themselves to control and coordinate their activities, one needs to define the key dimensions which capture the most significant differences. In the management literature, various parameters have been proposed to study organizational differences, and the objective of this article is not to review previous research, but to propose what seem to be the most salient measures of differences. Two dimensions are considered as the most important ones:

a. First, the way corporations organize the respective roles of headquarters, the "center," and business units, whether those are divisions or subsidiaries. This dimension is referred to as *Organizational Setting*.

b. Second, the way headquarters ensure that business units' performances and behavior are in line with corporate expectations. This is referred to as *Corporate Control*.

ORGANIZATIONAL SETTING

Corporations around the world appear to cluster themselves around four types of corporate organizational settings.

In the first type of organization, the center plays an important role in managing synergies. Strategic and operational integration and coordination of business units are considered to be the major sources of competitive advantage. Interdependencies are achieved through a variety of mechanisms, including centralized functions, top-down strategic plans, strong corporate identity and socialization of personnel. Given this high role assigned to the center of this form of organization, it can be qualified as a *federation*. This form prevails in the first type of European groups identified above: the industrial groups, and in certain of national holdings in the Asia Pacific region.

In a second type, the center functions as both resource allocator, guardian of the corporate identity, and source of strategic renewal. Business units enjoy a large degree of strategic autonomy provided that their strategies are "negotiated" and fit with the overall "corporate strategic framework" inspired by the center. Bottom-up planning, negotiated strategies, operational autonomy, and central mechanisms of financial and human resources allocation are key characteristics of this type of organizational setting. It differs from the federate organization by the more balanced power sharing between the center and the operating units; for that reason it is referred to, here, as a *confederation*. This form is most often characteristic of the European industrial holdings as well as Asian national holdings.

In a third category, one can find groups organized as a multitude of uncoordinated business units, each of them linked directly or indirectly to the center. The role of the center in those groups can be either "hands on," as in the case of Asian entrepreneurial conglomerates, or "hands off," as in the case of European financial conglomerates. What characterizes these groups is the fact that the relationships between business units and corporate headquarters are composed of a series of one to one "contractual" agreements. This form resembles a *constellation* and, as said earlier, is predominantly adopted by Asian and European conglomerates.

Finally, in a fourth type of organizational setting, one can find groups in which there is no center or, on the contrary, there are several centers. Some coordination mechanisms are loose, as in the case of informal meetings, while some are more tightly controlled, as in the case of long-term suppliers' contracts. Japanese Keiretsus are representative of this organizational type. Because it is structured as a network, it is called here the *connexion* type of organization.

CORPORATE CONTROL

Corporate control describes how groups ensure that business units' performances and behaviors are in line with corporate expectations. One can distinguish five major methods of exercising control: control by financial performance only, control by systems, control by strategy, direct subjective control of the persons, and control by ideology.

In groups which rely primarily on *financial controls*, headquarters assign financial goals based on financial standards (return on assets, shareholder value). Performances are monitored and evaluated according to achievement of these financial goals. Rewards and punishments of managers are based on those achievements and, for the group, the strategic value of businesses is assessed on their capacities to produce the "figures." This method of control prevails in European financial conglomerates.

The exercise of *control by systems* is based on the implementation of planning and control mechanisms such as interactive strategic planning sessions, investments decisions using capital budgeting techniques, control reviews, etc. Systems use financial as well as non-financial information (strategic, marketing). This mode of control predominates in the European industrial holdings and the European industrial groups.

In the *control by strategy* mode, the emphasis is neither on the financial measurement of performance nor on "systems," but on the appreciation of the strategic trajectory of business units and on their degree of fit with the whole corporation. This is done through task forces, corporate conferences, informal meetings, temporary assignments of key executives to business units, etc. European industrial groups and, to some extent, Japanese Keiretsus are practicing this form of control, whose purpose is not to measure or enforce, but to make sure that there is a coherent corporate strategic fit.

Personalized control is exercised through a direct interface between the group chairman and business units' key managers. Subjective, holistic forms of assessment are in use. Although some form of measurement and use of systems can be found in these groups, the main concern for unit managers is to behave according to the norms and beliefs of the chairman. Asian entrepreneurial conglomerates are practicing, nearly exclusively, this form of control.

Finally, with *ideological control* the focus is to make sure that managers have internalized the values of the group and are behaving accordingly. Systems, financial measurements, special relationships with the chairman, if used at all, do not play a dominant role here. What does matter is the development of strong beliefs, norms, values across the organization. Recruitments, socialization, training, rotation of staff are all kinds of process which build and maintain an ideology. This type of control prevails in the Asian national holdings in which strong national and corporate identities constitute the essential glue of group performance. Vertical Keiretsus are also well-known to use extensively this form of control.

COMPARING EUROPEAN AND ASIAN GROUPS

Those two dimensions combined give the opportunity to contrast the Asian groups with their European counterparts in the chart represented in Figure 1. As it appears in this figure, Asian and European large corporations live in a different organizational world. While they share some similarities in the way they control their operations, they differ in the way they design their organizational settings, and vice versa. What is interesting to observe in Figure 1 is that Asian corporations introduce, in any case, an interpersonal feature in their management system.

The Keiretsus are built around the ability of group members to connect to each other in one way or another through personal contacts. In the entrepreneurial conglomerate, the

FIGURE 1
ASIAN AND EUROPEAN
GROUPS

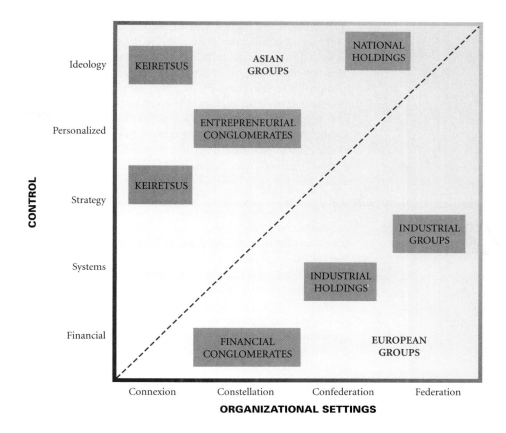

entrepreneur is in direct contact with business units and all relationships are personalized. In the case of national holdings, the personification of rapport is established through ideological means, sense of belonging, and nationalistic stand.

The European groups, by contrast, tend to prefer systematic or administrative features in their corporate management. Financial conglomerates are driven by "numbers," industrial holdings favor complex planning and control mechanisms, while industrial groups adopt structural and regulatory means of coordination. When confronted by a problem of change the typical reaction of a Western corporation will be to find a new "structure" or a new "system." . . .

Western corporate designers adopt an "engineering" approach to building and regulating organizational life. Although over the past 50 years behavioral sciences have brought an immense contribution to the art of management, this has been, most of the time, translated into practice with an instrumental perspective. Motivation theories have given birth to "management by objectives," experimental psychology using conditioning techniques has been used for the design of rewards and bonus systems, information theory is applied in the setting up of computer systems, etc. The rationale underlying this effort is probably the belief that human behavior can be influenced by the *manipulation* of organizational mechanisms. The main concern of Western managers confronted with a situation of strategic change is to install a new "organization" or a new "management system" which is supposed to align behavior with the new realities.

This instrumental engineering approach is challenged by Asian corporate architects who conceive enterprises as living entities where various individuals and groups obtain mutual benefit through cooperation. Organizations are not seen as independent of the people who compose them and, most of the time, enterprises are compared to "families." In 1984, Chairman Kim Woo Choong, founder of Daewoo, was participating in a session at the

Harvard Business School with a group of US senior executives. He was asked by one participant how he could coordinate some 40 subsidiaries without controlling them. Chairman Kim answered that coordination was achieved through "*spiritual linkages*"! (Aguilar, 1984.) That does not mean that Asian firms do not use systems for their management, but that personification of interrelationships are given priorities over formal systems. One major underlying assumption of Asian managers is that organizational mechanisms are not set up to "'manipulate" people but rather to give a structure to social interactions. In fact, most of the time, people are not rewarded for their performance, as measured in terms of results, but in terms of conformity to behavior. Organizations are not seen as machines (an engineering view) but as a set of "codified" relationships (a biological view).

DECODING ASIAN FIRMS

. . . When the competitive pressure from Asian firms becomes too intense, Western managers try to emulate them. One good example is provided by an article published in 1990 in the *Harvard Business Review* by Charles Ferguson (1990) in which the author proposes the creation of Western Keiretsus between US and European countries in the computer industry! This proposition reflects an engineering view of the organizational world: the machine "works" in Japan, why don't we import the machine? It is as if we asked US society to renounce individualism. What an ambition! Instead of trying to "import the machine," Western managers should be inspired to gain an understanding of the way the relationships function or don't function in these groups, what social roles do they play, in other terms to "decode" and not to "imitate" Asian organizations. This decoding ability requires three attitudes: (a) getting rid of *a priori* judgments, (b) making the necessary effort to study the social and cultural background of Asian societies, and (c) resisting the temptation of easy translations.

A. GET RID OF *A PRIORI* JUDGMENTS

More often than not, when presented with Asian cases, particularly successful ones, Western managers give ready-made explanations: Japan Inc. exploited manpower, "workaholism," nationalism, sacrificed generation, etc. Those views are meaningless because they are based on a simplistic engineering causality leading to defeatism or stubborn protectionism. Understanding the functionality of a social structure is the first necessary step in the analysis of organization, while the deciphering of causal links comes second. A rushed application of ready-made causal schemes based on superficial facts does not help to understand Asian partners and competitors.

B. INVEST IN THE STUDY OF CULTURES AND SOCIETIES

One of the dangers of "instrumental" thinking is that it bypasses what is not considered of immediate relevance. Cultural and social knowledge are all too frequently considered to be a waste of time or, at best, as subjects of "executive summaries." Organization and business behavior are part of an historical and cultural heritage which, in the case of Asian societies, is very rich, complex and heterogeneous. The manager who does not make the necessary efforts to enlighten him or herself with such knowledge is condemned to go from surprise to surprise if not from disillusion to disillusion.

C. RESIST THE TEMPTATION OF "EASY TRANSLATIONS"

Some managers fall into the trap of adopting, naively, a so-called "Asian" way of doing things. In the early 1980s, a European bank set up a regional office in Singapore, its first commitment in the region. The newly appointed general manager, a very enthusiastic person, decided that he would work "the Chinese way": handshakes, networking, personal trust, etc. He found himself trapped two years later with a portfolio of bad debts amounting to several million US$! Such horror stories can only fuel the resistance of corporate boards to commit resources for developing strategies in the Asia Pacific region. . . .

READING 17.3 FROM COMPETITIVE ADVANTAGE TO CORPORATE STRATEGY*

BY MICHAEL E. PORTER

■ Corporate strategy, the overall plan for a diversified company, is both the darling and the stepchild of contemporary management practice—the darling because CEOs have been obsessed with diversification since the early 1960s, the stepchild because almost no consensus exists about what corporate strategy is, much less about how a company should formulate it.

A diversified company has two levels of strategy: business unit (or competitive) strategy and corporate (or companywide) strategy. Competitive strategy concerns how to create competitive advantage in each of the businesses in which a company competes. Corporate strategy concerns two different questions: what businesses the corporation should be in and how the corporate office should manage the array of business units.

Corporate strategy is what makes the corporate whole add up to more than the sum of its business unit parts.

The track record of corporate strategies has been dismal. I studied the diversification records of 33 large, prestigious U.S. companies over the 1950–1986 period and found that most of them had divested many more acquisitions than they had kept. The corporate strategies of most companies have dissipated instead of created shareholder value.

The need to rethink corporate strategy could hardly be more urgent. By taking over companies and breaking them up, corporate raiders thrive on failed corporate strategy. Fueled by junk bond financing and growing acceptability, raiders can expose any company to takeover, no matter how large or blue chip. . . .

A SOBER PICTURE

. . . My study of 33 companies, many of which have reputations for good management, is a unique look at the track record of major corporations. . . . Each company entered an average of 80 new industries and 27 new fields. Just over 70% of the new entries were acquisitions, 22% were start-ups, and 8% were joint ventures. IBM, Exxon, Du Pont, and 3M, for example, focused on startups, while ALCO Standard, Beatrice, and Sara Lee diversified almost solely through acquisitions. . . .

My data paint a sobering picture of the success ratio of these moves. . . . I found that on average corporations divested more than half their acquisitions in new industries and more than 60% of their acquisitions in entirely new fields. Fourteen companies left more than 70% of all the acquisitions they had made in new fields. The track record in unrelated acquisitions

*Originally published in the *Harvard Business Review* (May–June 1987) and winner of the McKinsey Prize for the best in the *Review* in 1987. Copyright © 1987 by the President and Fellows of Harvard College; all rights reserved. Reprinted with deletions by permission of the *Harvard Business Review*.

is even worse—the average divestment rate is a startling 74%. Even a highly respected company like General Electric divested a very high percentage of its acquisitions, particularly those in new fields. . . . Some [companies] bear witness to the success of well-thought-out corporate strategies. Others, however, enjoy a lower rate simply because they have not faced up to their problem units and divested them. . . .

I would like to make one comment on the use of shareholder value to judge performance. Linking shareholder value quantitatively to diversification performance only works if you compare the shareholder value that is with the shareholder value that might have been without diversification. Because such a comparison is virtually impossible to make, my own measure of diversification success—the number of units retained by the company—seems to be as good an indicator as any of the contribution of diversification to corporate performance.

My data give a stark indication of the failure of corporate strategies.* Of the 33 companies, 6 had been taken over as my study was being completed. . . . Only the lawyers, investment bankers, and original sellers have prospered in most of these acquisitions, not the shareholders.

<table>
<tr><td>

PREMISES OF CORPORATE STRATEGY

</td><td>

Any successful corporate strategy builds on a number of premises. These are facts of life about diversification. They cannot be altered, and when ignored, they explain in part why so many corporate strategies fail.

Competition Occurs at the Business Unit Level

Diversified companies do not compete; only their business units do. Unless a corporate strategy places primary attention on nurturing the success of each unit, the strategy will fail, no matter how elegantly constructed. Successful corporate strategy must grow out of and reinforce competitive strategy.

Diversification Inevitably Adds Costs and Constraints to Business Units

Obvious costs such as the corporate overhead allocated to a unit may not be as important or subtle as the hidden costs and constraints. A business unit must explain its decisions to top management, spend time complying with planning and other corporate systems, live with parent company guidelines and personnel policies, and forgo the opportunity to motivate employees with direct equity ownership. These costs and constraints can be reduced but not entirely eliminated.

Shareholders Can Readily Diversify Themselves

Shareholders can diversify their own portfolios of stocks by selecting those that best match their preferences and risk profiles (Salter and Weinhold, 1979). Shareholders can often diversify more cheaply than a corporation because they can buy shares at the market price and avoid hefty acquisition premiums.

These premises mean that corporate strategy cannot succeed unless it truly adds value—to business units by providing tangible benefits that offset the inherent costs of lost independence and to shareholders by diversifying in a way they could not replicate.

</td></tr>
</table>

---

*Some recent evidence also supports the conclusion that acquired companies often suffer eroding performance after acquisition. See Frederick M. Scherer, "Mergers, Sell-Offs and Managerial Behavior," in *The Economics of Strategic Planning*, ed. Lacy Glenn Thomas (Lexington, MA: Lexington Books, 1986), p. 143, and David A. Ravenscraft and Frederick M. Scherer, "Mergers and Managerial Performance," paper presented at the Conference on Takeovers and Contests for Corporate Control, Columbia Law School, 1985.

To understand how to formulate corporate strategy, it is necessary to specify the conditions under which diversification will truly create shareholder value. These conditions can be summarized in three essential tests:

1. *The attractiveness test.* The industries chosen for diversification must be structurally attractive or capable of being made attractive.
2. *The cost-of-entry test.* The cost of entry must not capitalize all the future profits.
3. *The better-off test.* Either the new unit must gain competitive advantage from its link with the corporation or vice versa.

Of course, most companies will make certain that their proposed strategies pass some of these tests. But my study clearly shows that when companies ignored one or two of them, the strategic results were disastrous.

HOW ATTRACTIVE IS THE INDUSTRY?

In the long run, the rate of return available from competing in an industry is a function of its underlying structure [see Porter reading in Chapter 4]. An attractive industry with a high average return on investment will be difficult to enter because entry barriers are high, suppliers and buyers have only modest bargaining power, substitute products or services are few, and the rivalry among competitors is stable. An unattractive industry like steel will have structural flaws, including a plethora of substitute materials, powerful and price-sensitive buyers, and excessive rivalry caused by high fixed costs and a large group of competitors, many of whom are state supported.

Diversification cannot create shareholder value unless new industries have favorable structures that support returns exceeding the cost of capital. If the industry doesn't have such returns, the company must be able to restructure the industry or gain a sustainable competitive advantage that leads to returns well above the industry average. An industry need not be attractive before diversification. In fact, a company might benefit from entering before the industry shows its full potential. The diversification can then transform the industry's structure.

In my research, I often found companies had suspended the attractiveness test because they had a vague belief that the industry "fit" very closely with their own businesses. In the hope that the corporate "comfort" they felt would lead to a happy outcome, the companies ignored fundamentally poor industry structures. Unless the close fit allows substantial competitive advantage, however, such comfort will turn into pain when diversification results in poor returns. Royal Dutch Shell and other leading oil companies have had this unhappy experience in a number of chemicals businesses, where poor industry structures overcame the benefits of vertical integration and skills in process technology.

Another common reason for ignoring the attractiveness test is a low entry cost. Sometimes the buyer has an inside track or the owner is anxious to sell. Even if the price is actually low, however, a one-shot gain will not offset a perpetually poor business. Almost always, the company finds it must reinvest in the newly acquired unit, if only to replace fixed assets and fund working capital.

Diversifying companies are also prone to use rapid growth or other simple indicators as a proxy for a target industry's attractiveness. Many that rushed into fast-growing industries (personal computers, video games, and robotics, for example) were burned because they mistook early growth for long-term profit potential. Industries are profitable not because they are sexy or high tech; they are profitable only if their structures are attractive.

WHAT IS THE COST OF ENTRY?

Diversification cannot build shareholder value if the cost of entry into a new business eats up its expected returns. Strong market forces, however, are working to do just that. A company can enter new industries by acquisition or start-up. Acquisitions expose it to an increasingly efficient merger market. An acquirer beats the market if it pays a price not fully reflecting the prospects of the new unit. Yet multiple bidders are commonplace, information flows rapidly, and investment bankers and other intermediaries work aggressively to make the market as efficient as possible. In recent years, new financial instruments such as junk bonds have brought new buyers into the market and made even large companies vulnerable to takeover. Acquisition premiums are high and reflect the acquired company's future prospects—sometimes too well. Philip Morris paid more than four times book value for Seven-Up Company, for example. Simple arithmetic meant that profits had to more than quadruple to sustain the preacquisition ROI. Since there proved to be little Philip Morris could add in marketing prowess to the sophisticated marketing wars in the soft drink industry, the result was the unsatisfactory financial performance of Seven-Up and ultimately the decision to divest.

In a start-up, the company must overcome entry barriers. It's a real catch-22 situation, however, since attractive industries are attractive because their entry barriers are high. Bearing the full cost of the entry barriers might well dissipate any potential profits. Otherwise, other entrants to the industry would have already eroded its profitability.

In the excitement of finding an appealing new business, companies sometimes forget to apply the cost-of-entry test. The more attractive a new industry, the more expensive it is to get into.

WILL THE BUSINESS BE BETTER OFF?

A corporation must bring some significant competitive advantage to the new unit, or the new unit must offer potential for significant advantage to the corporation. Sometimes, the benefits to the new unit accrue only once, near the time of entry, when the parent instigates a major overhaul of its strategy or installs a first-rate management team. Other diversification yields ongoing competitive advantage if the new unit can market its product, through the well-developed distribution system of it sister units, for instance. This is one of the important underpinnings of the merger of Baxter Travenol and American Hospital Supply.

When the benefit to the new unit comes only once, the parent company has no rationale for holding the new unit in its portfolio over the long term. Once the results of the one-time improvement are clear, the diversified company no longer adds value to offset the inevitable costs imposed on the unit. It is best to sell the unit and free up corporate resources.

The better-off test does not imply that diversifying corporate risk creates shareholder value in and of itself. Doing something for shareholders that they can do themselves is not a basis for corporate strategy. (Only in the case of a privately held company, in which the company's and the shareholder's risk are the same, is diversification to reduce risk valuable for its own sake.) Diversification of risk should only be a by-product of corporate strategy, not a prime motivator.

Executives ignore the better-off test most of all or deal with it through arm waving or trumped-up logic rather than hard strategic analysis. One reason is that they confuse company size with shareholder value. In the drive to run a bigger company, they lose sight of their real job. They may justify the suspension of the better-off test by pointing to the way they manage diversity. By cutting corporate staff to the bone and giving business units nearly complete autonomy, they believe they avoid the pitfalls. Such thinking misses the whole point of diversification, which is to create shareholder value rather than to avoid destroying it.

CONCEPTS OF CORPORATE STRATEGY

The three tests for successful diversification set the standards that any corporate strategy must meet; meeting them is so difficult that most diversification fails. Many companies lack a clear concept of corporate strategy to guide their diversification or pursue a concept that does not address the tests. Others fail because they implement a strategy poorly.

My study has helped me identify four concepts of corporate strategy that have been put into practice—portfolio management, restructuring, transferring skills, and sharing activities. While the concepts are not always mutually exclusive, each rests on a different mechanism by which the corporation creates shareholder value and each requires the diversified company to manage and organize itself in a different way. The first two require no connections among business units; the second two depend on them. . . . While all four concepts of strategy have succeeded under the right circumstances, today some make more sense than others. Ignoring any of the concepts is perhaps the quickest road to failure.

PORTFOLIO MANAGEMENT

The concept of corporate strategy most in use is portfolio management, which is based primarily on diversification through acquisition. The corporation acquires sound, attractive companies with competent managers who agree to stay on. While acquired units do not have to be in the same industries as existing units, the best portfolio managers generally limit their range of businesses in some way, in part to limit the specific expertise needed by top management.

The acquired units are autonomous, and the teams that run them are compensated according to unit results. The corporation supplies capital and works with each to infuse it with professional management techniques. At the same time, top management provides objective and dispassionate review of business unit results. Portfolio managers categorize units by potential and regularly transfer resources from units that generate cash to those with high potential and cash needs. . . .

In most countries, the days when portfolio management was a valid concept of corporate strategy are past. In the face of increasingly well-developed capital markets, attractive companies with good managements show up on everyone's computer screen and attract top dollar in terms of acquisition premium. Simply contributing capital isn't contributing much. A sound strategy can easily be funded; small to medium-size companies don't need a munificent parent.

Other benefits have also eroded. Large companies no longer corner the market for professional management skills; in fact, more and more observers believe managers cannot necessarily run anything in the absence of industry-specific knowledge and experience. . . .

But it is the sheer complexity of the management task that has ultimately defeated even the best portfolio managers. As the size of the company grows, portfolio managers need to find more and more deals just to maintain growth. Supervising dozens or even hundreds of disparate units and under chain-letter pressures to add more, management begins to make mistakes. At the same time, the inevitable costs of being part of a diversified company take their toll and unit performance slides while the whole company's ROI turns downward. Eventually, a new management team is installed that initiates wholesale divestments and pares down the company to its core businesses. . . .

In developing countries, where large companies are few, capital markets are undeveloped, and professional management is scarce, portfolio management still works. But it is no longer a valid model for corporate strategy in advanced economies. . . . Portfolio management is no way to conduct corporate strategy.

RESTRUCTURING

Unlike its passive role as a portfolio manager, when it serves as banker and reviewer, a company that bases its strategy on restructuring becomes an active restructurer of business units. The new businesses are not necessarily related to existing units. All that is necessary is unrealized potential.

The restructuring strategy seeks out undeveloped, sick, or threatened organizations or industries on the threshold of significant change. The parent intervenes, frequently changing the unit management team, shifting strategy, or infusing the company with new technology. Then it may make follow-up acquisitions to build a critical mass and sell off unneeded or unconnected parts and thereby reduce the effective acquisition cost. The result is a strengthened company or a transformed industry. As a coda, the parent sells off the stronger unit once results are clear because the parent is no longer adding value, and top management decides that its attention should be directed elsewhere. . . .

When well implemented, the restructuring concept is sound, for it passes the three tests of successful diversification. The restructurer meets the cost-of-entry test through the types of company it acquires. It limits acquisition premiums by buying companies with problems and lackluster images or by buying into industries with as yet unforeseen potential. Intervention by the corporation clearly meets the better-off test. Provided that the target industries are structurally attractive, the restructuring model can create enormous shareholder value. . . . Ironically, many of today's restructurers are profiting from yesterday's portfolio management strategies.

To work, the restructuring strategy requires a corporate management team with the insight to spot undervalued companies or positions in industries ripe for transformation. The same insight is necessary to actually turn the units around even though they are in new and unfamiliar businesses. . . .

Perhaps the greatest pitfall . . . is that companies find it very hard to dispose of business units once they are restructured and performing well. . . .

TRANSFERRING SKILLS

The purpose of the first two concepts of corporate strategy is to create value through a company's relationship with each autonomous unit. The corporation's role is to be a selector, a banker, and an intervenor.

The last two concepts exploit the interrelationships between businesses. In articulating them, however, one comes face-to-face with the often ill-defined concept of synergy. If you believe the text of the countless corporate annual reports, just about anything is related to just about anything else! But imagined synergy is much more common than real synergy. GM's purchase of Hughes Aircraft simply because cars were going electronic and Hughes was an electronics concern demonstrates the folly of paper synergy. Such corporate relatedness is an ex post facto rationalization of a diversification undertaken for other reasons.

Even synergy that is clearly defined often fails to materialize. Instead of cooperating, business units often compete. A company that can define the synergies it is pursuing still faces significant organizational impediments in achieving them.

But the need to capture the benefits of relationships between businesses has never been more important. Technological and competitive developments already link many businesses and are creating new possibilities for competitive advantage. In such sectors as financial services, computing, office equipment, entertainment, and health care, interrelationships among previously distinct businesses are perhaps the central concern of strategy.

To understand the role of relatedness in corporate strategy, we must give new meaning to this often ill-defined idea. I have identified a good way to start—the value chain. [See Readings 4-1 and 4-2.] Every business unit is a collection of discrete activities ranging from sales to accounting that allow it to compete. I call them value activities. It is at this level, not in the company as a whole, that the unit achieves competitive advantage.

I group these activities in nine categories. *Primary* activities create the product or service, deliver and market it, and provide after-sale support. The categories of primary activities are inbound logistics, operations, outbound logistics, marketing and sales, and service. *Support* activities provide the input and infrastructure that allow the primary activities to take place. The categories are company infrastructure, human resource management, technology development, and procurement.

The value chain defines the two types of interrelationships that may create synergy. The first is a company's ability to transfer skills or expertise among similar value chains. The second is the ability to share activities. Two business units, for example, can share the same sales force or logistics network.

The value chain helps expose the last two (and most important) concepts of corporate strategy. The transfer of skills among business units in the diversified company is the basis for one concept. While each business unit has a separate value chain, knowledge about how to perform activities is transferred among the units. For example, a toiletries business unit, expert in the marketing of convenience products, transmits ideas on new positioning concepts, promotional techniques, and packaging possibilities to a newly acquired unit that sells cough syrup. Newly entered industries can benefit from the expertise of existing units, and vice versa.

These opportunities arise when business units have similar buyers or channels, similar value activities like government relations or procurement, similarities in the broad configuration of the value chain (for example, managing a multisite service organization), or the same strategic concept (for example, low cost). Even though the units operate separately, such similarities allow the sharing of knowledge. . . .

Transferring skills leads to competitive advantage only if the similarities among businesses meet three conditions:

1. The activities involved in the businesses are similar enough that sharing expertise is meaningful. Broad similarities (marketing intensiveness, for example, or a common core process technology such as bending metal) are not a sufficient basis for diversification. The resulting ability to transfer skills is likely to have little impact on competitive advantage.
2. The transfer of skills involves activities important to competitive advantage. Transferring skills in peripheral activities such as government relations or real estate in consumer goods units may be beneficial but is not a basis for diversification.
3. The skills transferred represent a significant source of competitive advantage for the receiving unit. The expertise or skills to be transferred are both advanced and proprietary enough to be beyond the capabilities of competitors. . . .

Transferring skills meets the tests of diversification if the company truly mobilizes proprietary expertise across units. This makes certain the company can offset the acquisition premium or lower the cost of overcoming entry barriers.

The industries the company chooses for diversification must pass the attractiveness test. Even a close fit that reflects opportunities to transfer skills may not overcome poor industry structure. Opportunities to transfer skills, however, may help the company transform the structures of newly entered industries and send them in favorable directions.

The transfer of skills can be one time or ongoing. If the company exhausts opportunities to infuse new expertise into a unit after the initial post-acquisition period, the unit should ultimately be sold. . . .

By using both acquisitions and internal development, companies can build a transfer-of-skills strategy. The presence of a strong base of skills sometimes creates the possibility for internal entry instead of the acquisition of a going concern. Successful diversifiers that employ the concept of skills transfer may, however, often acquire a company in the target industry as a beachhead and then build on it with their internal expertise. By doing so, they can reduce some of the risks of internal entry and speed up the process. Two companies that have diversified using the transfer-of-skills concept are 3M and PepsiCo.

SHARING ACTIVITIES

The fourth concept of corporate strategy is based on sharing activities in the value chains among business units. Procter & Gamble, for example, employs a common physical distribution system and sales force in both paper towels and disposable diapers. McKesson, a leading distribution company, will handle such diverse lines as pharmaceuticals and liquor through superwarehouses.

The ability to share activities is a potent basis for corporate strategy because sharing often enhances competitive advantage by lowering cost or raising differentiation. . . .

Sharing activities inevitably involves costs that the benefits must outweigh. One cost is the greater coordination required to manage a shared activity. More important is the need to compromise the design or performance of an activity so that it can be shared. A salesperson handling the products of two business units, for example, must operate in a way that is usually not what either unit would choose were it independent. And if compromise greatly erodes the unit's effectiveness, then sharing may reduce rather than enhance competitive advantage. . . .

Despite . . . pitfalls, opportunities to gain advantage from sharing activities have proliferated because of momentous developments in technology, deregulation, and competition. The infusion of electronics and information systems into many industries creates new opportunities to link businesses. . . .

Following the shared-activities model requires an organizational context in which business unit collaboration is encouraged and reinforced. Highly autonomous business units are inimical to such collaboration. The company must put into place a variety of what I call horizontal mechanisms—a strong sense of corporate identity, a clear corporate mission statement that emphasizes the importance of integrating business unit strategies, an incentive system that rewards more than just business unit results, cross-business-unit task forces, and other methods of integrating.

A corporate strategy based on shared activities clearly meets the better-off test because business units gain ongoing tangible advantages from others within the corporation. It also meets the cost-of-entry test by reducing the expense of surmounting the barriers to internal entry. Other bids for acquisitions that do not share opportunities will have lower reservation prices. Even widespread opportunities for sharing activities do not allow a company to suspend the attractiveness test, however. Many diversifiers have made the critical mistake of equating the close fit of a target industry with attractive diversification. Target industries must pass the strict requirement test of having an attractive structure as well as a close fit in opportunities if diversification is to ultimately succeed.

CHOOSING A CORPORATE STRATEGY

. . . Both the strategic logic and the experience of the companies I studied over the last decade suggest that a company will create shareholder value through diversification to a greater and greater extent as its strategy moves from portfolio management toward sharing activities. . . .

Each concept of corporate strategy is not mutually exclusive of those that come before, a potent advantage of the third and fourth concepts. A company can employ a restructuring strategy at the same time it transfers skills or shares activities. A strategy based on shared activities becomes more powerful if business units can also exchange skills. . . .

My study supports the soundness of basing a corporate strategy on the transfer of skills or shared activities. The data on the sample companies' diversification programs illustrate some important characteristics of successful diversifiers. They have made a disproportionately low percentage of unrelated acquisitions, *unrelated* being defined as having no clear opportunity to transfer skills or share important activities. . . . Even successful diversifiers such as 3M, IBM, and TRW have terrible records when they strayed into unrelated acquisitions. Successful acquirers diversify into fields, each of which is related to many others. Proctor & Gamble and IBM, for example, operate in 18 and 19 interrelated fields respectively and so enjoy numerous opportunities to transfer skills and share activities.

Companies with the best acquisition records tend to make heavier-than-average use of start-ups and joint ventures. Most companies shy away from modes of entry besides acquisition. My results cast doubt on the conventional wisdom regarding startups. . . . successful companies often have very good records with start-up units, as 3M, P&G, Johnson & Johnson,

IBM, and United Technologies illustrate. When a company has the internal strength to start up a unit, it can be safer and less costly to launch a company than to rely solely on an acquisition and then have to deal with the problem of integration. Japanese diversification histories support the soundness of start-up as an entry alternative.

My data also illustrate that none of the concepts of corporate strategy works when industry structure is poor or implementation is bad, no matter how related the industries are. Xerox acquired companies in related industries, but the business had poor structures and its skills were insufficient to provide enough competitive advantage to offset implementation problems.

AN ACTION PROGRAM

. . . A company can choose a corporate strategy by:

1. Identifying the interrelationships among already existing business units. . . .
2. Selecting the core businesses that will be the foundation of the corporate strategy. . . .
3. Creating horizontal organizational mechanisms to facilitate interrelationships among the core businesses and lay the groundwork for future related diversification. . . .
4. Pursuing diversification opportunities that allow shared activities. . . .
5. Pursuing diversification through the transfer of skills if opportunities for sharing activities are limited or exhausted. . . .
6. Pursuing a strategy of restructuring if this fits the skills of management or no good opportunities exist for forging corporate interrelationships. . . .
7. Paying dividends so that the shareholders can be the portfolio managers. . . .

CREATING A CORPORATE THEME

Defining a corporate theme is a good way to ensure that the corporation will create shareholder value. Having the right theme helps unite the efforts of business units and reinforces the ways they interrelate as well as guides the choice of new businesses to enter. NEC Corporation, with its "C&C" theme, provides a good example. NEC integrates its computer, semiconductor, telecommunications, and consumer electronics businesses by merging computers and communication.

It is all too easy to create a shallow corporate theme. CBS wants to be an "entertainment company," for example, and built a group of businesses related to leisure time. It entered such industries as toys, crafts, musical instruments, sports teams, and hi-fi retailing. While this corporate theme sounded good, close listening revealed its hollow ring. None of these businesses had any significant opportunity to share activities or transfer skills among themselves or with CBS's traditional broadcasting and record businesses. They were all sold, often at significant losses, except for a few of CBS's publishing-related units. Saddled with the worst acquisition record in my study, CBS has eroded the shareholder value created through its strong performance in broadcasting and records.

Moving from competitive strategy to corporate strategy is the business equivalent of passing through the Bermuda Triangle. The failure of corporate strategy reflects the fact that most diversified companies have failed to think in terms of how they really add value. A corporate strategy that truly enhances the competitive advantage of each business unit is the best defense against the corporate raider. With a sharper focus on the tests of diversification and the explicit choice of a clear concept of corporate strategy, companies' diversification track records from now on can look a lot different.

CHAPTER 18

Managing Otherwise

We close the readings of this book in the spirit we have tried to create throughout, only, perhaps, more so: to open up perspectives to new, unconventional ideas. Hence, we call this chapter "Managing Otherwise." It is a context onto itself.

The first reading takes us beyond the five forms of organizing introduced by Mintzberg at the beginning of the last five chapters. That was playing jigsaw puzzle—choosing the right structural form to fit in. But perhaps designing organizations has to be more like playing Lego: using the forms as forces to be combined in all sorts of creative ways. Here Mintzberg brings some closure to our discussion of the different configurations of this section. Called "Beyond Configuration," it is, in a sense, the final chapter of his book on structure, except that it was written more recently and edited down for this text. The reading seeks to do just what its title says: Make the point that although the different forms (configurations) of the last chapters can help us to make sense of and to manage in a complex world, there is also a need to go beyond configurations, to consider the nuanced linkages among these various forms. Mintzberg proposes that this be done by treating all the forms as a framework of forces that acts on every organization and whose contradictions need to be reconciled. By so doing, we can begin to see the weaknesses in each form as well as the times when an organization is better off to design itself as a combination of two or more forms. This reading also discusses how the forces of ideology (representing cooperation—pulling together) and of politics (representing competition—pulling apart) work both to promote change and also to impede it, and how the contradictions among these two must also be reconciled if an organization is to remain effective in the long run.

Next comes a colorful reading by James March of Stanford University about the difference between organizations that *exploit* existing situations and those that *explore* in the hope of creating new ones. March also addresses "the perils and glories of imagination."

Next comes a reading by Gary Hamel, who sets out to upset all that is sacred about strategy, including how it gets created. Indeed, conventional views of how that happens, in Hamel's opinion, get in the way of strategic innovation, which is what he believes really counts: how you break away from the pack rather than analyzing your way into the middle of it. Hamel suggests how this might happen, continuing to upset all the sacred cows of the field.

Ricardo Semco, head of the Brazilian firm by that name, has published a popular book called *Maverick* and a series of startling *Harvard Business Review* articles, the latest of which, "How We Went Digital Without a Strategy," is reproduced here. In the first sentence, he writes that he owns a $160,000,000 company "and I have no idea what business it's in." That is just Semler's opening shot! If Hamel seemed provocative, try Semler! This is not every company by a long shot, but it could be a part of every company that wants to move forward.

Finally, Mintzberg takes on in a similar vein the nature of managing itself. Enough of "loud" managing, he says—enough of the hype of "globalization" and "shareholder value" and "empowerment" and "change." Enough heroic leadership. Time for "managing quietly," by inspiring not empowering, caring not curing, infusing not intruding, initiating not imposing.

USING THE CASE STUDIES

New ideas in strategy usually come from managers who go against conventional wisdom. Several of the cases deal with managers who have developed new ways of doing strategy. The Natura case describes a Brazilian company where three presidents share equally the decision-making power. The Unipart Group of Companies case deals with a strategy that revolves around stakeholder management. In the Kao Corporation case, Yoshio Maruta pursues a philosophy of harmony and absolute equality. In "How We Went Digital Without a Strategy" Semler suggests that strategic experimentation need not be driven by this sort of overarching vision. In his reading, Hamel argues that innovation in strategy should focus on the "how" of the strategy process rather than the "what" of its content. It is significant in this respect that the Natura, Unipart, and Kao Corporation cases deal with industries and products that are not particularly glamorous. None of these companies stake their fortunes on finding lucrative niches or hot products.

The "Disposable Organization" by March explores the obstacles to strategic experimentation. On the other hand, the "Beyond Configuration" reading by Mintzberg suggests that escaping the intrinsic contradictions of organizing is the main impetus to strategic creativity. The previously mentioned three cases support Mintzberg's optimism, but cases such as Rudi Gassner and the Executive Committee of BMG International support March's pessimism.

Strategy innovation, however, can have modest beginnings. The case of A Restaurant with a Difference deals with a couple exploring a new business idea: a learning restaurant. What is contemplated is certainly far smaller in scale than the learning organization championed by Yoshio Maruta of the Kao Corporation. However, as Mintzberg points out in "Managing Quietly," original thinking in management often takes place away from the limelight. In fact, original thinking in strategy may not be revolutionary at all. It just has to be an idea that makes all the difference.

**BY HENRY
MINTZBERG**

■ "Lumpers" are people who categorize, who synthesize. "Splitters" are people who analyze, who see all the nuances. From the standpoint of organization, both are right and both are wrong. Without categories, it would be impossible to practice management. With only categories, it could not be practiced effectively.

The author was mostly a lumper until a colleague asked him if he wanted to play "jigsaw puzzle" or "LEGO" with his concepts. In other words, do all these concepts fit together in set ways and known images (puzzle), or were they to be used creatively to create new images? The remainder of this reading is presented in the spirit of playing "organizational LEGO." It tries to show how we can use splitting as well as lumping to understand what makes organizations effective as well as what causes many of their fundamental problems.

FORMS AND FORCES

The configurations described in the chapters of this section of the book are *forms*, and they are laid out at the nodes of a pentagon in Figure 1. Many organizations seem to fit naturally into one of the original five, but some do not fit, to the lumpers' chagrin. To respond to this, five *forces* have been added, each associated with one of the original forms:

■ *Direction* for the entrepreneurial form, for some sense of where the organization must go. This is often called "strategic vision." Without direction the various activities of an organization cannot easily work together to achieve common purpose.
■ *Efficiency* for the machine form. This ensures a viable ratio of benefits gained to costs incurred. Lack of concern for efficiency would cause all but the most protected organization to fade.
■ *Proficiency* for the professional form. Organizations need this to carry out tasks with high levels of knowledge and skill. The difficult work of organizations would otherwise simply not get done.
■ *Accountability* for the diversified form. If individual units in an organization are not accountable for their efforts in particular markets, it becomes almost impossible to manage a diversified organization.
■ *Learning* for the innovative or adhocracy form. Organizations need to be able to learn, to discover new things for their customers and themselves—to adapt and to innovate.

Two other forces exist that are not necessarily associated with a particular form:

■ *Cooperation*, represented by ideology. This is the force for pulling together.
■ *Competition*, represented by politics. This is the force for pulling apart.

For the lumpers we now have a *portfolio of forms*, and for the splitters we now have a *system of forces*. Both views are critical for the practice of management. One represents the most fundamental forces that act on organizations. All serious organizations experience all seven of them, at one time or another, if not all the time. The other represents the fundamental forms that organizations can take, which some of them do some of the time. Together, these forces and forms appear to constitute a powerful diagnostic framework by which to understand what goes on in organizations and to prescribe effective change in them.

When one force dominates an organization, it is drawn toward the associated *configuration*, but must deal with *contamination*. When no force dominates, the organization

---

*Adapted from a chapter of this title in *Mintzberg on Management: Inside Our Strange World of Organizations* (Free Press, 1989); an article similar to this chapter was published in the *Sloan Management Review*.

FIGURE 1 AN INTEGRATING PENTAGON OF FORCES AND FORMS

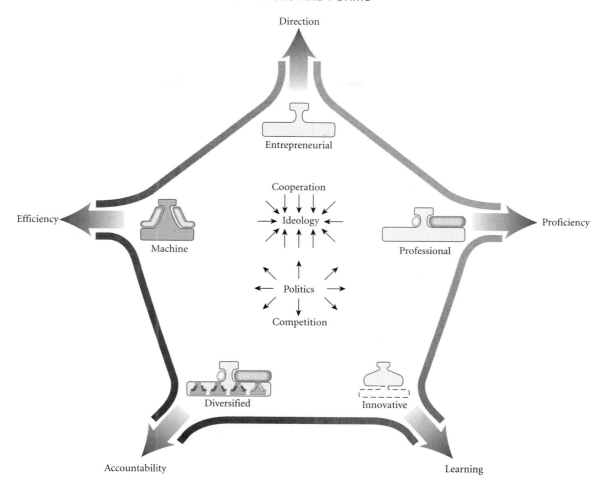

is a balanced *combination* of forces, including periods of *conversion* from one form to another. But then there is a problem of *cleavage*. Contamination and cleavage require the management of *contradiction*, which is where ideology and politics come in. We shall discuss each of these notions shortly.

Dominant forces drive an organization to one of the pure forms discussed earlier—entrepreneurial, machine, professional, diversified, innovative. These are not "real," but are abstract models designed to capture some reality. Some organizations *do* match the pure forms closely. If the form fits, the organization should wear it. Configuration has benefits: the organization achieves a sense of order, or integration. Configuration also helps outsiders understand an organization. The consistency of configuration keeps workers from being confused. For classification, for comprehension, for diagnosis, and for design, configuration seems to be effective. But only so long as everything holds still. Introduce the dynamics of evolutionary change and, sooner or later, configuration becomes ineffective.

CONTAMINATION BY CONFIGURATION

The harmony, consistency, and fit that is configuration's greatest strength is also its greatest weakness. The dominant force can become so strong that it drives out everything else. For example, control in machine organizations may contaminate the innovators in research. Machine organizations recognize this when they put their research and development facilities away from the head office, to avoid the contaminating effects of the central efficiency experts. The opposite case is also well known—the "looseness" in adhocracies may contaminate the efforts of the accountants concerned with efficiency. This contamination may be a small price to pay for being coherently organized, until things go out of control.

CONFIGURATION OUT OF CONTROL

When the need arises for change, the dominating forces may act to hold the organization in place. The other forces may have atrophied, and so the organization goes out of control. For instance, the machine organization in need of a new strategy may have no entrepreneurs and no innovators left to give it its new direction. Miller and Kets de Vries (1987) have developed five organizational "neuroses" that correspond roughly to what can happen in extreme cases of contamination in the five forms. Each is an example of a system that may once have been healthy but has run of control.

- *Dramatic:* the entrepreneur, freed from other forces, may take the organization on an ego trip. This can even occur in large diversified organizations that are dominated by strong CEOs.
- *Compulsive:* this happens when there is completeness of control in machine organizations. This is the classic overbearing bureaucracy.
- *Paranoid:* paranoia is often a collective tendency in some professional organizations like universities and hospitals. Professors and doctors are always suspicious that their peers, or worse, the "the administration," are planning to undermine their efforts.
- *Depressive:* this can be the result of an obsession with the bottom line in diversified organizations. Being a cash cow that is constantly being "milked" is very bad for morale.
- *Schizoid:* the need to innovate, and to get the commercial benefits from innovation, means that adhocracies can be in constant oscillation between divergent and convergent thinking.

In other words, behaviors that were once functional become dysfunctional when pursued to excess.

CONTAINMENT OF CONFIGURATION

Truly effective organizations thus do not exist in pure form. What keeps a configuration effective is not only the dominance of a single force but also the constraining effects of other forces. This is *containment*. To manage configuration effectively is to exploit one form but also to reconcile the different forces. Machine organizations must exploit their efficiency but must still allow for innovation. Innovative forms must exploit their power to create, but must find a way to remain somewhat efficient.

COMBINATION

Configuration is nice if you can have it. But some organizations all of the time, and all organizations some of the time, are unable to have it. They must instead balance competing forces. Organizations like this can be called *combinations*; instead of being a node in the pentagon, they are somewhere within it.

KINDS OF COMBINATIONS

When only two of the five forces meet in rough balance, that is a *hybrid*. A symphony orchestra is an example, being a rough balance of entrepreneurial and professional forms. Some organizations experience *multiple combinations*. Apple Computer in Canada was once described as a combination of adhocracy (a legacy of its founder, Steve Jobs), machine (for efficiency in production and distribution), entrepreneurial (in the person of a dynamic sales manager), and professional (in marketing and training).

CLEAVAGE IN COMBINATIONS

If configuration encourages contamination, sometimes combination encourages *cleavage*. Instead of one force dominating, two or more confront each other to the point of paralyzing the organization. A common example from business organizations is the innovative drive of R&D against the machine-like drive of production

Despite the problems created by having to balance forces, combination of one kind or another is probably necessary in most organizations. Effective organizations usually balance many forces. Configuration merely means a tilt toward one force; combination is more balanced.

CONVERSION

The preceding discussions of configuration and combination implied stability. But few organizations stay in one form or combination; they undergo *conversion* from one configuration or combination to another. Often these result from external changes. For example, an innovative organization decides to settle down as a machine to exploit an innovation. Or a suddenly unstable market makes a machine become more innovative. Conversions are often temporary, as in the machine organization that becomes an entrepreneurial organization during a crisis.

CYCLES OF CONVERSION

The forces that may destroy the organization may instead drive it to another, perhaps more viable, configuration. For example, the entrepreneurial form is inherently vulnerable, because of its reliance on a single leader. It may work well for the young organization, but with aging and growth a dominant need for direction may be displaced by that for efficiency. Then conversion to the machine form becomes necessary—the power of one leader must be replaced by that of administrators.

The implication is that organizations go through stages as they develop, sequenced into so-called life cycles. The most common life cycle is the one mentioned above. It begins with the entrepreneurial form and moves down along the left edge of the pentagon. Growth leads to the machine form, and even greater growth leads ultimately to the diversified form. Another life cycle, depicted along the right edge of the pentagon, occurs for firms dependent on expertise. They move from the entrepreneurial form to either the professional form (if they can standardize their services) or the innovative form (if their services are more creative). Another common conversion is when an innovative form decides to exploit and perfect the skills it has developed and settles into a professional form, a common conversion in consulting.

Ideology and politics play a role in conversion. Ideology is a more important form in young organizations. That is because cultures can develop more easily there, especially with charismatic leadership in the entrepreneurial stage. By comparison, it is extremely difficult to build a strong and lasting culture in a mature organization. Politics, by contrast, typically spreads as the energy of the young organization dissipates and its activities become more diffuse. As the organization becomes more formalized, its culture is blunted, and politics becomes a more important force.

CLEAVAGE IN CONVERSION

Some conversions are easy because they are so overdue. But most are more difficult and conflictual, requiring periods of transition, prolonged and agonizing. As the organization in transition sits between its old and new forms, it becomes a kind of combination. The forces that create the conversion also create the possibility of cleavage. How does the organization deal with these contradictions?

CONTRADICTION

Organizations that have to reconcile contradictory forces, especially in dealing with change, often turn to the cooperative force of ideology or the competitive force of politics. Indeed, these two forces themselves represent a contradiction that must be managed if an organization is not to run out of control.

While it is true that each can dominate an organization, and so draw it toward a missionary or political form, more commonly they act differently, as *catalysts*. Ideology tends to draw behavior inwards toward a common core; politics drives behavior away from any central place. One force is centripetal, the other centrifugal. Both can act to promote change or also to prevent it. Either way, they sometimes render an organization more effective, sometimes less.

COOPERATION THROUGH IDEOLOGY

Ideology (or strong culture) represents the force for cooperation in an organization, for collegiality and consensus. It encourages members to look inward, to take their lead from the imperatives of the organization's own vision. One important implication is that infusion of ideology renders any particular configuration more effective. People get fired up to pursue efficiency or proficiency or whatever else drives the organization. When this happens to a machine organization—as in a McDonald's, very responsive to its customers and very sensitive to its employees—we have a "snappy bureaucracy." Bureaucratic machines are not supposed to be snappy, but ideology changes the nature of their quest for efficiency.

Another implication is that ideology helps an organization manage contradiction and so to deal with change. The innovative machine and the tightly controlled innovative organization are inherent contradictions. These organizations handle their contradictions by having strong cultures. Such organizations can more easily reconcile their opposing forces because what matters to their people ultimately is the organization itself, more than any of its particular parts, like efficient manufacturing or innovative R&D. This is how Toyota gets efficiency and high quality at the same time.

LIMITS TO COOPERATION

Ideologies sound wonderful, but they are difficult to build and sustain. And established ideologies can get in the way of organizational effectiveness. They may discourage change by forcing everyone to work within the same set of beliefs. This has implications for strategy. Change *within* strategic perspective, to a new position, is facilitated by a strong ideology. But change *of* perspective—fundamental change—is discouraged by it.

COMPETITION THROUGH POLITICS

Politics represents the force for competition in an organization, for conflict and confrontation. It too can infuse any of the configurations or combinations, in this case aggravating contamination and cleavage. In a configuration, the representative of the dominant force "lord it" over others. This could lead to contamination. In a combination, representatives of the various forces relish opportunities to do battle with each other, aggravating the cleavage.

One problem facing strategic managers is that politics may be a more "natural" force than ideology. Left to themselves, organizations seem to pull apart rather easily. Keeping them together requires considerable and constant effort.

BENEFITS OF COMPETITION

If the pulling together of culture discourages people from addressing fundamental change, then the pulling apart of politics may become the only way to ensure that happens. Change requires challenging the status quo. Politics may facilitate this; if there are no entrepreneurial or innovative forces stimulating strategic change, it may be the *only* available force for change.

Both politics and ideology can promote organizational effectiveness as well as undermine it. Ideology can be a force for revitalization, energizing the organization and making its people more responsive. But it can also hinder fundamental change. Likewise, politics often impedes necessary change and wastes valuable resources. But it can also promote important change that may be available in no other way. It can enable those who realize the need for change to challenge those who do not.

COMBINING COOPERATION AND COMPETITION

The last remaining contradiction is the one between ideology and politics themselves. Ideology and politics themselves have to be reconciled. Pulling together ideologically infuses life; splitting apart politically challenges the status quo. Only be encouraging both can an organization sustain its viability. Ideology helps secondary forces to contain a dominant one; politics encourages them to challenge it.

The balance between ideology and politics should be a dynamic equilibrium. Most of the time ideology should be pulling things together, contained by healthy internal competition. When fundamental change becomes necessary, however, politics should help pull the organization apart temporarily.

COMPETENCE

What makes an organization effective? The "Peterian" view (named after Tom Peters of *In Search of Excellence* fame) is that organizations should be "hands on, value driven." The "Porterian" view (named after Michael Porter) says that organizations should use competitive analysis. To Porter, effectiveness resides in strategy, while to Peters it is the operations that count. One says do the right things, the other says do things right. But we need to understand what takes an organization to a viable strategy in the first place, what makes it excellent there, and how some organizations are able to sustain viability and excellence in the face of change

Here are five views to guide us in our search for organizational effectiveness:

Convergence

First is the *convergence* hypothesis. Its motto is that there is "one best way" to design an organization. This is usually associated with the machine form. A good structure is one with a rigid hierarchy of authority, with spans of control no greater than six, with heavy use of strategic planning, MIS, and whatever else happens to be in the current fashion of the rationalizers. In *In Search of Excellence*, by contrast, Peters and Waterman argued that ideology was the key to an organization's success. We cannot dismiss this hypothesis—sometimes there *are* proper things to do in most, perhaps all, organizations. But we must take issue with its general thrust. Society has paid an enormous price for "one best way" thinking over the course of this century, on the part of all its organizations that have been drawn into using what is fashionable rather than functional. We need to look beyond the obvious, beyond the convergence hypothesis.

Congruence

Beyond convergence is the *congruence* or "it all depends" approach. Introduced into organization theory in the 1960s, it suggests that running an organization is like choosing dinner from a buffet table—a little bit of this, a little bit of that, all selected according to specific needs. Organizational effectiveness thus becomes a question of matching a given set of internal attributes, treated as a kind of portfolio, with various situational factors. The congruence hypothesis has certainly been an improvement, but like a dinner plate stacked with an old assortment of foods, it has not been good enough.

Configuration

The motto of the *configuration* hypothesis is "getting it all together." Design your organization as you would a jigsaw puzzle, fitting the organizational pieces together to create a coherent, harmonious picture. There is reason to believe that organizations succeed in good part because they are consistent in what they do; they are certainly easier to manage that way. But, as we have seen, configuration has its limits, too.

Contradiction

While the lumpers may like the configuration hypothesis, splitters prefer the *contradiction* hypothesis. Their call is to manage the dynamic tension between contradictory forces. They point to the common occurrence of combinations and conversions, where organizations are forced to manage contradictory forces. This is an important hypothesis—together with that of configuration (which are in their own dynamic tension) it is an important clue to organizational effectiveness. But still it is not sufficient.

Creation

The truly great organization transcends all of the foregoing while building on it to achieve something more. It respects the *creation* hypothesis. Creativity is its forte, "understand your inner nature" is its motto, LEGO its image. The most interesting organizations live at the edges, far from the logic of conventional organizations, where as Raphael (1976: 5–6) has pointed out in biology (for example, between the sea and the land, or at the forest's edge), the richest, most varied, and most interesting forms of life can be found. This might be called the "Prahaladian" view (after C. K. Prahalad, and his ideas of "strategic intent" discussed in Chapter 3). Don't just do the right things right, but keep doing them! Such organizations keep inventing novel approaches that solve festering problems and so provide all of us with new ways to deal with our world of organizations.

READING 18.2 ORGANIZATIONAL ADAPTATION*

BY JAMES G. MARCH

■ . . . Almost every theory of organizations presumes a tendency for environmental change to be reflected in organizational change. Environments and history shape organizational forms and practices, although they do so inefficiently . . . and often jerkily. . . . As a result, specific changes in the world are seen as likely to lead to specific changes in organizations as they seek to survive and are selected by their competitive environments. For example, increases in global connectedness and uses of modern information technology are often seen as likely to lead to increased uses of non-hierarchical networks in coordinating activities, and increases in the importance of knowledge and in the rate of change in its content are often seen as likely to lead to a decreased emphasis on learning by doing and an increased emphasis on access to external sources of knowledge.

At a more general level, however, stories of rapid environmental change invite a prediction that future environments will favor organizations that are able to be flexible and to adapt quickly to change. Organizations that fail to adapt seem destined to expire as the world around

---

*Reprinted with deletions from an article originally entitled "The Future Disposable Organizations and the Rigidities of Management," *Organization*, November 1995.

them changes. This has led to considerable enthusiasm for designing organizations that are capable of learning, of adapting to the changes they face. . . .

Adaptiveness involves both the exploitation of what is known and the exploration of what might come to be known (March, 1991; 1994b). *Exploitation* refers to the short-term improvement, refinement, routinization, and elaboration of existing ideas, paradigms, technologies, strategies, and knowledge. It thrives on focused attention, precision, repetition, analysis, sanity, discipline, and control. Exploitation is served by knowledge, forms, and practices that facilitate an organization's well-being in the short run. It emphasizes improving existing capabilities and technologies. It profits from close attention, systematic reason, risk aversion, sharp focus, hard work, training, and refined detail. It includes locating and developing competencies and tying those competencies together to produce joint products. It includes managing the capabilities of an organization, facilitating communication and coordination, tightening slack. It includes defining and measuring performance and linking activities powerfully to performance measures.

Exploitation is also served by a pursuit of legitimacy. People in organizations and people with whom they deal are driven by understandings of appropriate behavior. They try to act appropriately and they expect others to do so also. Exhibiting proper organization forms and acting in an appropriate manner generate support and thereby aid survival. . . . As organizations seek technical efficiency and legitimacy, they focus energy on relatively short-run concerns. They refine capabilities, reduce costs, and adopt standard procedures. They mobilize efforts to achieve clearly defined, short-term objectives. Some modern terms are reengineering, downsizing, and total quality management.

Exploration refers to experimentation with new ideas, paradigms, technologies, strategies, and knowledge in hopes of finding alternatives that improve on old ones. It thrives on serendipity, risk taking, novelty, free association, madness, loose discipline, and relaxed control. The characteristic feature of exploration is that it is risky. Success is not assured, indeed is often not achieved. Even when exploration is successful, its rewards are often slow in coming and not necessarily realized by the parts of the organization that have paid the costs. Exploratory risk taking appears to be more likely when an organization is falling somewhat behind its target aspirations than when it is achieving them. It is stimulated by failure. It is sometimes also stimulated, largely unintentionally, by organizational slack and by illusions that organizational actors have about their abilities to overcome risks. . . .

Adaptiveness requires both exploitation and exploration. A system that specializes in exploitation will discover itself becoming better and better at an increasingly obsolescent technology. A system that specializes in exploration will never realize the advantages of its discoveries. . . .

The dynamics of learning tend to destroy the balance. . . . In general, returns to the exploitation of existing knowledge are systematically closer in time and space than are returns to the explorations of possible new knowledge. This produces two well-known "traps" of adaptive systems. The first is the "failure" trap. In the failure trap, an organization fails, tries a new direction, fails again, and tries still another direction, and so on. The process leads to an endless cycle of failure and exploration. The cycle is sustained by the fact that most new directions are bad ideas and that most new ideas that are good ideas usually require practice and time in order to realize their capabilities. In the short run, even good ideas fail and are rejected. The failure trap leads to impatience with a new course of action and an excess of exploration.

The second trap is a "success" trap. When an organization succeeds, it repeats actions that appear to have produced the success. As a result of repeating actions, it becomes more proficient at the technology involved. As a result of the greater proficiency, it is likely to be successful again, and so on. The process leads to an endless cycle of success, increased competence, and local efficiency. New good ideas or technologies are not tried, or if tried do not do as well as the existing technology (because of the disparity in competence with the two). The success trap leads to a failure to experiment adequately. . . .

Within this short story of organizational change can be seen a fundamental dilemma of organizations. Exploitation and exploration are linked in an enduring symbiosis. Each requires the other in order to contribute effectively to an organization's survival and prosperity. At the same time, however, each interferes with the other. Exploitation undermines exploration. It discourages the experimentation and variation that are essential to long-term survival. It results in sticking to one (currently effective) capability to such an extent that there is little exploration of others, or in failing to stick to one (currently ineffective) capability long enough to determine its true value. In a similar fashion, exploration undermines exploitation. Efforts to promote experimentation encourage impatience with new ideas, technologies, and strategies. They are likely to be abandoned before enough time has been devoted to developing the competence that would make them useful. The impatience of exploration results in unrealized dreams and unelaborated discoveries. As a result of the ways in which exploitation and exploration tend to extinguish each other, organizations persistently fail to maintain an effective balance between the two. . . .

THE PERILS AND GLORIES OF IMAGINATION

Enthusiasts for foretelling the future face a grim reality. Predictions about the future of organizations are predictably bad. Well-informed, careful analysts do not have a much better record than do consultants of tea leaves. This is not because tea leaf consultation has a good record but because analysis has a poor one. Even Marx, who was considerably smarter than most of us, didn't get it entirely right. Organizational futurology is a profession in which reputations are crafted from the excitements of novelty, fear, and hope. They are destroyed by the unfolding of experience.

Imaginations of possible organizations are justified not by their potential for predicting the future (which is almost certainly small) but by their potential for nurturing the uncritical commitment and persevering madness required for sustained organizational and individual rigidity in a selective environment. Many observers have noted the role of imagination in stimulating discoveries, but from this point of view its primary role is less in creating new ideas than in protecting them from disconfirmation. Imagination is unlikely to be more correct than convention, but it is more lucid, more autonomous, and more compelling.

Clarity of vision protects deviant imaginations from the disconfirmations of experience and knowledge. Attachment to a fantasy converts the ambiguities of history into confirmations of belief and a willingness to persist in a course of action. This self-sustaining character of imagination protects commitment from the importunities of reality. Soothsayers of the future create sheltered worlds of ignorance, ideology, and faith. Within the shell that they provide, craziness is protected long enough to elaborate its challenge to orthodoxy.

> I began to wonder whether anything truly existed, whether reality wasn't an unformed and gelatinous substance only half-captured by my senses. . . . I was consoled by the idea that I could take the gelatin and mold it to create anything I wanted, . . . a world of my own populated with living people, a world where I imposed the rules and could change them at will. In the motionless sands where my stories germinated, every birth, death, and happening depended on me. I could plant anything I wanted in those sands; I had only to speak the right word to give it life. At times I felt that the universe fabricated from the power of the imagination had stronger and more lasting contours than the blurred realm of the flesh-and-blood creatures around me. (Eva Luna in Allende, 1989, pp. 187–188)

The modern word is "vision," and its overtones of dreams are appropriate. Imaginations of the future are stronger and more lasting than the blurred realm of the flesh-and-blood creatures around us, and that power protects exploration from its enemies. . . .

As Eva Luna reminds us, intellectual passions for reasoned intelligence and constrained imagination have never entirely extinguished a human aesthetic based on fantasy. A commitment to arbitrarily imagined worlds has elements of simple beauty in it. . . . From this perspective, the occasional argument between those who imagine individual organizations as changing and enduring and those who imagine them as rigid and disposable is an argument not only about the truth but also about the beauty and justice of possible fantasies of human existence, thus perhaps worth taking seriously.

BY GARY HAMEL

■ . . . I believe that only those companies that are capable of reinventing themselves and their industry in a profound way will be around a decade hence. The question today is not whether you can reengineer your processes; the question is whether you can reinvent the entire industry model—as Amazon.com has been attempting to do in book selling. . . .

In industry after industry, it is the revolutionaries—usually newcomers—who are creating the new wealth. Of course, there are examples of incumbents like Coca-Cola and Procter & Gamble that are able to continually reinvent themselves and their industry, but all too often, industry incumbents fail to challenge their own orthodoxies and succumb to unconventional rivals.

The point seems incontestable: *in a discontinuous world, strategy innovation is the key to wealth creation.* Strategy innovation is the capacity to reconceive the existing industry model in ways that create new value for customers, wrong-foot competitors, and produce new wealth for all stakeholders. Strategy innovation is the only way for newcomers to succeed in the face of enormous resource disadvantages, and the only way for incumbents to renew their lease on success. And if one redefines the metric of corporate success as *share of new wealth creation* within some broad opportunity domain—e.g., energy, transportation, communication, computing, and so on— the innovation imperative becomes inescapable.

Today, many companies are worrying about EVA (economic value added), but EVA—earning more than your cost of capital—is just the starting point. The goal is not to earn more than your cost of capital; the goal is to capture a disproportionate share of industry wealth creation. There are many semiconductor companies that earn more than their cost of capital, but it is Intel that has created and captured much of the new value in the microprocessor industry during the past decade. Of course Intel earns its cost of capital, but it earns much more than that. . . .

Growth is the scoreboard, but it is definitely not the game. Focusing on growth, rather than on the game of strategy innovation, is likely to destroy wealth rather than create it. The reason is simple. There are as many stupid ways to grow as there are to cut: acquisitions that destroy value (Sony and Matsushita in Hollywood), market share battles that lower industry profitability (the airlines' perennial favorite), and megabucks blue-sky projects (think Apple and the Newton) are just a few examples that should illustrate the danger of go-for-broke growth strategies. Needless to say, companies pursuing value-destroying growth won't make it onto any list of star performers.

When we dig deeper, we find that . . . extraordinarily successful companies . . . grew by radically changing the basis for competition in their industries. They either invented totally new industries or dramatically reinvented existing ones. This is true for Home Depot, Amgen, Nike, Intel, Compaq, the Gap, and most of the other companies on the super-star list. They all developed nonlinear strategies.

---

*Reprinted with deletions from "Strategy Innovation and the Quest for Value," Gary Hamel, *Sloan Management Review*, Winter 1998, 7–14.

IS STRATEGY IRRELEVANT?

So if strategy innovation is key to creating new wealth, why is "strategy" no longer a "big idea" in most companies? Why does it seem to command so little of top management's time and attention? And why are planners an increasingly endangered species?

The competitive environment faced by companies today is far, far different from that which gave birth to the concept of strategy some thirty years ago. But, while the rapidly shifting strategy environment has partially devalued some traditional strategy concepts, such as industry structure analysis, it has also provided the impetus for much new thinking. Indeed, the changing context for strategy has provoked a huge amount of new thinking on the *content* of strategy. The new themes in the strategy world include: foresight, knowledge, competencies, coalitions, networks, extra-market competition, ecosystems, transformation, renewal. All these subjects are intensely contemporary.

So strategists certainly can't be accused of being ignorant of the new competitive realities. But as informed as they may be, impactful they are not. Why? Because managers simply do not know what to do with all the wonderful concepts, frameworks, and buzzwords that tumble from the pages of the *Harvard Business Review*, that jam the business aisles of bookstores, and that glisten in the slickly edited pages of business magazines.

Strategists may have a lot to say about the context and content of strategy, but, in recent years, they have had precious little to say about the *conduct* of strategy—that is, the task of strategy making. No one seems to know much about how to create strategy. Managers today know how to embed quality disciplines, how to reengineer processes, and how to reduce cycle times, but they don't know how to foster the development of innovative wealth-creating strategies.

So, while there has been enormous innovation around the content of strategy—management has an ever-expanding list of "strategic" issues to address—there has been no corresponding innovation around the conduct of strategy. Let's face it, the annual strategic planning process in most companies has changed hardly at all during the past decade or two.

It's ironic; never has a capacity for deep strategic thinking been so necessary as in today's turbulent times, and yet never, in the past two decades, has strategy's "share of voice" been lower in the corridors of corporate power. . . .

WHAT ARE THE SECRETS OF STRATEGY CREATION?

The strategy industry—all those consultants, business school professors, authors, and planners—has a dirty little secret. Everyone knows a strategy when they see one—be it Microsoft's, Nucor's, or Virgin Atlantic's. We all recognize a great strategy after the fact. In the case study method, professors hold strategies up to be admired, or ridiculed, by preternaturally wise MBA students. Their post hoc explanations of the competitive success and failure that ensue are stunningly beautiful. We are great at pinning down butterflies. But our case libraries and business magazines, with their stories of corporate success and failure, are museums filled with dead specimens. Simply put, we all know strategy as a "thing"—once someone else has bagged it and tagged it. We also understand planning as a "process." But the planning process doesn't produce strategy, it produces plans—a point that Henry Mintzberg has made on more than one occasion.

Anyone who claims to be a strategist should be intensely embarrassed by the fact that the strategy industry doesn't have a theory of strategy creation! It doesn't know where bold, new value-creating strategies come from. . . .

The questions we must address are these: How can we create a Cambrian explosion of innovative strategies inside the firm? What does it take to invent new strategy "S curves"? To answer these questions, we must have a theory of strategy innovation. Developing such a theory is a grand project. All I can do here is to offer a few starting propositions.

I agree with Mintzberg that strategy "emerges." But I don't believe the emergent nature of strategy creation prevents us from aiding and abetting the process of strategy innovation. We are not helpless. The reason I don't believe we're helpless is because strategy doesn't simply emerge—rather, it is *emergent*, in the same full-bodied sense that life itself is emergent. One of the things we're learning from complexity theorists is that by creating the right set of preconditions, one can provoke emergence. Stuart Kauffman, a pioneer in complexity theory, has suggested that life began with an "autocatalytic" system—a self-reinforcing set of chemical reactions. Whether you agree or disagree, the analogy may be useful. What, we must ask, would catalyze the emergence of new, viable strategies in a successful, though complacent, organization? My guess is that the answer, while perhaps subtle, will nevertheless be easier to come by than the mystery of life.

Once you start thinking of strategy as an emergent phenomenon, you realize that we have often attacked the wrong end of the problem. Strategists and senior executives have too often worked on "the strategy," rather than on the preconditions that could give rise to strategy innovation. In essence, they've been trying to design complex, multicell organisms, rather than trying to understand and create the conditions from which such organisms will emerge. . . .

Two great forces of nature seem to be counterposed. On one hand, there is the general trend toward entropy. When we convert fossil fuel into heat, to power our cars or heat our homes, we are turning highly ordered energy—complex carbon molecules—into "disordered" energy—heat, as well as a variety of pollutants. These things can never be "put back together." The second law of thermodynamics suggests that we are sliding inevitably toward chaos. Not only does the law characterize physical systems, it often seems to characterize human systems. Many organizations seem to be affected by a kind of "institutional entropy" in which energy, enthusiasm, and effectiveness slowly dissipate over time.

Yet we see order all around us: the New York Stock Exchange, Toyota's supplier network, a great university, or, most miraculous of all, ourselves. A human being is an almost infinitely more ordered thing, and a much, much more complex system, than a single-celled organism. Order seems to be the second great force in nature. And while entropy may be inevitable in physical systems, there is nothing to suggest that it is inevitable in biological or human systems. . . .

While a complex living system, and the order it possesses, is probably not the product of random variation, neither can it be designed top-down. The New York Stock Exchange couldn't be designed top-down. Neither could life on the Internet, nor a human being, nor a complex but internally consistent strategy. What is going on in all these cases is what Kauffman calls "order without careful crafting." "Order *without* careful crafting"—I'd like to suggest that this is the goal of strategizing.

Order arises from simple, deep rules. Craig Reynolds has shown that with three simple rules, one can richly simulate the behavior of a flock of birds in flight. So it's not that there is *no* crafting, *no* design, only that it works at the level of preconditions and broad parameters—not at the level of a detailed design. So while there was a simple architecture underlying the Internet, no one could have envisioned all the rich permutations of Net-based life that would emerge in the new on-line biosphere. . . .

Like all forms of complexity, strategy is poised on the border between perfect order and total chaos, between absolute efficiency and blind experimentation, between autocracy and complete *ad hocracy*. . . .

Let me ask a question of those who've ever sat through a business school case study: Have you ever gotten halfway through a brilliant exposition of a company's strategy and thought to yourself, "Did they really have this thing figured out ahead of time? Isn't this just luck? Isn't this 20/20 hindsight? What about all the failures?" Sure, you have. These impertinent questions lie at the heart of our search for a theory of strategy creation. Is a great strategy luck, or is it foresight? Of course, the answer is that it is both. Circumstance, cognition, data, and desire converge, and a strategy insight is born. The fact that strategy has a significant element of serendipity to it shouldn't cause us to despair. The alternatives are not the "big brain" design school of strategy, nor the "muddle along" process school. The question is, how can we increase the odds that new wealth-creating strategies emerge? How can we make serendipity happen? How can we prompt emergence?

HOW DOES STRATEGY EMERGE?

The most fundamental insight of complexity theory is that "complex behavior need not have complex roots," as Christopher Langton has so succinctly put it. So what are the simple roots of strategy creation? My experience, and that of my colleagues at Strategos, in helping companies improve their capacity for strategizing suggests that there are five preconditions for the emergence of strategy. . . .

1. **New voices.** Bringing new "genetic material" into the strategy process always serves to illuminate unconventional strategies. Top management must give up its monopoly on strategy creation, and previously underrepresented constituencies must be given a larger share of voice in the strategy creation process. Specifically, I believe that young people, newcomers, and those at the geographic periphery of the organization deserve a larger share of voice. It is in these constituencies where diversity lurks. So strategy creation must be a pluralistic process, a deeply participative undertaking.

2. **New conversations.** Creating a dialogue about strategy that cuts across all the usual organizational and industry boundaries substantially increases the odds that new strategy insights will emerge. All too often, in large organizations, conversations become hard-wired over time, with the same people talking to the same people about the same issues year after year. After a while, individuals have little left to learn from each other. Opportunities for new insights are created when one juxtaposes previously isolated knowledge in new ways.

3. **New passions.** Unleashing the deep sense of discovery that resides in almost every human being, and focusing that sense of discovery on the search for new wealth-creating strategies is another prerequisite. I believe the widespread assumption that individuals are against change is flat wrong. People are against change when it doesn't offer the prospect of new opportunity. There is much talk today about return on investment, but I like to think in terms of return on emotional investment. Individuals will not invest emotionally in a firm and its success unless they believe they will get a return on that investment. All my experience suggests that individuals will eagerly embrace change when given the chance to have a share of voice in inventing the future of their company. They will invest when there's a chance to create a unique and exciting future in which they can share.

4. **New perspectives.** New conceptual lenses that allow individuals to reconceive their industry, their company's capabilities, customer needs, and so on substantially aid the process of strategy innovation. To increase the probability of strategy innovation, managers must become the merchants of new perspective. They must search constantly for new lenses that help companies reconceive themselves, their customers, their competitors, and, thereby, their opportunities.

5. **New experiments.** Launching a series of small, risk-avoiding experiments in the market serves to maximize a company's rate of learning about just which new strategies will work and which won't. The insights that come from a broad-based strategy dialogue will never be perfect. While much traditional analysis can be done to refine those insights into viable strategies, there is much that can be learned only in the marketplace.

So where does this leave us? We should spend less time working on strategy as a "thing" and more time working to understand the preconditions that give rise to the "thing." Executives, consultants, and business school professors must rebalance the attention given to context, content, and conduct in favor of conduct.

In focusing on the conduct of strategy, not only are we trying to *discover* something—the hidden properties of strategy emergence—we are also trying to *invent* something. Like those long-ago Neanderthals trying to figure out the principles of cooking . . . we need to invent an oven—*a strategy oven.* . . .

READING 18.4

HOW WE WENT DIGITAL WITHOUT A STRATEGY*

BY RICARDO SEMLER

■ I own a $160 million South American company named Semco, and I have no idea what business it's in. I know what Semco does—we make things, we provide services, we host Internet communities—but I don't know what Semco is. Nor do I want to know. For the 20 years I've been with the company, I've steadfastly resisted any attempt to define its business. The reason is simple: once you say what business you're in, you put your employees into a mental straitjacket. You place boundaries around their thinking and, worst of all, you hand them a ready-made excuse for ignoring new opportunities: "We're not in that business." So rather than dictate Semco's identity from on high, I've let our employees shape it through their individual efforts, interests, and initiatives.

That rather unusual management philosophy has drawn a good deal of attention over the years. Nearly 2,000 executives from around the world have trekked to São Paulo to study our operations. Few, though, have tried to emulate us. The way we work—letting our employees choose what they do, where and when they do it, and even how they get paid—has seemed a little too radical for mainstream companies.

But recently a funny thing happened: the explosion in computing power and the rise of the Internet reshaped the business landscape, and the mainstream shifted. Today, companies are desperately looking for ways to increase their creativity and flexibility, spur their idea flow, and free their talent—to do, in other words, what Semco has been doing for 20 years.

I don't propose that Semco represents the model for the way businesses will operate in the future. Let's face it: we're a quirky company. But I do suggest that some of the principles that underlie the way we work will become increasingly common and even necessary in the new economy. In particular, I believe we have an organization that is able to transform itself continuously and organically—without formulating complicated mission statements and strategies, announcing a bunch of top-down directives, or bringing in an army of change-management consultants. As other companies seek to build adaptability into their organizations, they may be able to learn a thing or two from Semco's example.

TRANSFORMATION WITHOUT END

Over the last ten years, Semco has grown steadily, quadrupling its revenues and expanding from 450 to 1,300 employees. More important, we've extended our range dramatically. At the start of the '90s, Semco was a manufacturer, pure and simple. We made things like pumps, industrial mixers, and dishwashers. But over the course of the decade, we diversified successfully into higher-margin services. Last year, almost 75% of our business was in services. Now we're stretching out again—this time into e-business. We expect that more than a quarter of

*Reprinted with deletions from "How We Went Digital Without a Strategy," R. Semler, *Harvard Business Review*, September–October 2000, 51.

our revenues next year will come from Internet initiatives, up from nothing just one year ago. We never planned to go digital, but we're going digital nonetheless.

You may wonder how that's possible. How do you get a sizable organization to change without telling it—or even asking it—to change? It's actually easy—but only if you're willing to give up control. People, I've found, will act in their best interests, and by extension in their organizations' best interests, if they're given complete freedom. It's only when you rein them in, when you tell them what to do and how to think, that they become inflexible, bureaucratic, and stagnant. Forcing change is the surest way to frustrate change.

Enough lecturing. Let me give you a concrete example of how our transformation has played out. Ten years ago, one of the things we did was manufacture cooling towers for large commercial buildings. In talking with the property owners who bought these products, some of our salespeople began to hear a common refrain. The customers kept complaining about the high cost of maintaining the towers. So our salespeople came back to Semco and proposed starting a little business in managing cooling-tower maintenance. They said, "We'll charge our customers 20% of whatever savings we generate for them, and we'll give Semco 80% of those revenues and take the remaining 20% as our commission." We said, "Fine, give it a shot."

Well, the little business was successful. We reduced customers' costs and eliminated some of their hassles, and they were happy. In fact, they were so happy that they came back and asked if we'd look after their air-conditioning compressors as well. Even though we didn't manufacture the compressors, our people didn't hesitate. They said yes. And when the customers saw we were pretty good at maintaining compressors, they said, "You know, there are a lot of other annoying functions that we'd just as soon off-load, like cleaning, security, and general maintenance. Can you do any of those?"

At that point, our people saw that their little business might grow into quite a big business. They began looking for a partner who could help bolster and extend our capabilities. They ended up calling the Rockefeller Group's Cushman & Wakefield division, one of the largest real-estate and property-management companies in the United States, and proposing that we launch a 50–50 joint venture in Brazil. Cushman wasn't very keen on the idea at first. People there said, "Property management by itself isn't a very lucrative business. Why don't we talk about doing something that involves real estate? That's where the money is."

We spent some time thinking about going into the real-estate business. We didn't have any particular expertise there, but we were willing to give it a try. When we started asking around, though, we found that no one in the company had much interest in real estate. It just didn't get anyone excited. So we went back to the Cushman folks and said, "Real estate sounds like a great business, but it's not something we care about right now. Why don't we just start with property management and see what happens?" They agreed, though not with a lot of enthusiasm.

We ponied up an initial investment of $2,000 each, just enough to pay the lawyers to set up a charter. Then we set our people loose. In no time, we had our first contract, with a bank, and then more and more business came through the door. Today, about five years later, the joint venture is a $30 million business.

It's also the most profitable property-management business within Cushman & Wakefield. The reason it has been so successful is that our people came into it fresh, with no preconceived strategies, and they were willing to experiment wildly. Instead of charging customers in the traditional way—a flat fee based on a building's square footage—they tried a partnership model. We'd take on all of a property owner's noncore functions, run them like a business, and split the resulting savings. . . .

Most manufacturers would probably consider a shift from making cooling towers to managing buildings pretty radical. Before making such a leap, they'd do a lot of soul-searching about their core businesses and capabilities. They'd run a lot of numbers, hold a lot of meetings, do a lot of planning. We didn't bother with any of that. We just let our people follow their instincts and apply their common sense, and it worked out fine.

Our recent move into the digital space has proceeded in much the same way, with our people again taking the lead. In fact, some of the eight Internet ventures we've launched grew directly out of our earlier service initiatives. As our facility-management business expanded, for example, we extended it, through a joint venture with Johnson Controls, to managing retail facilities. As our people began to work closely with store managers, they began to notice the huge costs retailers incur from lost inventory. One employee came forward and asked for a paid leave to study opportunities in that area. We gave him a green light, and within a year he had helped us set up a joint venture with RGIS, the largest inventory-tracking company in the world. Less than two years later, the venture had become the biggest inventory-management business in South America. Now it is branching out into Web-enabled inventory control, helping on-line companies coordinate the fulfillment of electronic orders.

Our work in property management also brought us face to face with the disorganization and inefficiency of the construction business. Here, too, our people saw a big business opportunity, one that would build on the unique capabilities of the Internet. A number of the members of our joint ventures with Cushman & Wakefield and Johnson Controls banded together, with Semco's support, to set up an on-line exchange to facilitate the management of commercial construction projects. All the participants in a building project—architects, banks, construction companies, contractors, and project managers—can now use our exchange to send messages, hold real-time chats, issue proposals and send bids, and share documents and drawings. . . .

That business, which we're operating as a 50–50 joint venture with the U.S. Internet software company Bidcom, has itself become a springboard for further new initiatives. One of the most exciting is the creation of a South American Web portal for the entire building industry. . . . We make money by charging transaction fees on all the business that takes place through the portal. . . .

MANAGEMENT WITHOUT CONTROL

Semco's ongoing transformation is a product of a very simple business philosophy: give people the freedom to do what they want, and over the long haul their successes will far outnumber their failures. Operationalizing that philosophy has involved a lot of trial and error, of taking a few steps forward and a couple back. The company remains a work in progress—and I hope it stays that way forever.

As I reflect on our experience, though, I see that we've learned some important lessons about creating an adaptive, creative organization. I'll share six of those lessons with you. I won't be so presumptuous as to say they'll apply to your company, but at least they'll stir up your thinking.

FORGET ABOUT THE TOP LINE

The biggest myth in the corporate world is that every business needs to keep growing to be successful. That's baloney. The ultimate measure of a business's success, I believe, is not how big it gets, but how long it survives. Yes, some businesses are meant to be huge, but others are meant to be medium-sized and still others are meant to be small. At Semco, we never set revenue targets for our businesses. We let each one find its natural size—the size at which it can maintain profitability and keep customers happy. It's fine if a business's top line stays the same or even shrinks as long as its bottom line stays healthy. Rather than force our people to expand an existing business beyond its natural limits, we encourage them to start new businesses, to branch out instead of building up.

NEVER STOP BEING A START-UP

Every six months, we shut down Semco and start it up all over again. Through a rigorous budgeting and planning process, we force every one of our businesses to justify its continued existence. If this business didn't exist today, we ask, would we launch it? If we closed it down, would we alienate important customers? If the answers are no, then we move our money, resources, and talent elsewhere. We also take a fresh look at our entire organization, requiring that every employee—leaders included—resign (in theory) and ask to be rehired. All managers are evaluated anonymously by all workers who report to them, and the ratings are posted publicly. It has always struck me as odd that companies force new business ideas and new hires to go through rigorous evaluations but never do the same for existing businesses or employees.

DON'T BE A NANNY

Most companies suffer from what I call boarding-school syndrome. They treat their employees like children. They tell them where they have to be at what time, what they need to be doing, how they need to dress, whom they should talk to, and so on. But if you treat people like immature wards of the state, that's exactly how they'll behave. They'll never think for themselves or try new things or take chances. They'll just do what they're told, and they probably won't do it with much spirit.

At Semco, we have no set work hours, no assigned offices or desks, no dress codes. We have no employee manuals, no human resource rules and regulations. We don't even have an HR department. People go to work when they want and go home when they want. They decide when to take holidays and how much vacation they need. They even choose how they'll be compensated. . . . In other words, we treat our employees like adults. And we expect them to behave like adults. If they screw up, they take the blame. And since they have to be rehired every six months, they know their jobs are always at risk. Ultimately, all we care about is performance. An employee who spends two days a week at the beach but still produces real value for customers and coworkers is a better employee than one who works ten-hour days but creates little value.

LET TALENT FIND ITS PLACE

Companies tend to hire people for specific jobs and then keep them stuck in one career track. They also tend to choose which businesses people work in. The most talented people, for instance, may be assigned automatically to the business unit with the biggest growth prospects. The companies don't take into account what the individual really wants. The resulting disconnect between corporate needs and individual desires shows up in the high rates of talent churn that afflict most companies today.

We take a very different approach. We let people choose where they'll work and what they'll do (and even decide, as a team, who their leaders will be). All entry-level new hires participate in a program called Lost in Space. They spend six months to a year floating around the company, checking out businesses, meeting people, and trying out jobs. When a new hire finds a place that fits with his personality and goals, he stays there. Since our turnover rate in the last six years has been less than 1%—even though we've been targeted heavily by headhunters—we must be doing something right.

MAKE DECISIONS QUICKLY AND OPENLY

The best way for an organization to kill individual initiative is to force people to go through a complicated, bureaucratic review and approval process. We strive to make it as easy as possible for Semco employees to propose new business ideas, and we make sure they get fast and clear decisions. All proposals go through an executive board that includes representatives from our major business units. The board meetings are completely open. All employees are welcome to attend—in fact, we always reserve two seats on the board for the first two employees who arrive at a meeting. Proposals have to meet two simple criteria that govern all the businesses we launch. First, the business has to be a premium provider of its product or service. Second, the product or service has to be complex, requiring engineering skills and presenting high entry barriers. Well-considered proposals that meet those standards get launched within Semco. Even if a proposed business fails to meet both criteria, we'll often back it as a minority investor if its prospects look good.

PARTNER PROMISCUOUSLY

To explore and launch new businesses quickly and efficiently, you need help; it's pure arrogance to assume you can do everything on your own. I'm proud to say that we partner promiscuously at Semco. Indeed, I can't think of a single new business we've started without entering into some kind of alliance, whether to gain access to software, draw on a depth of experience, bring in new capabilities, or just share risk. Partnerships have provided the foundation for our experiments and our expansion over the years. Our partners are as much a part of our company as our employees.

STAYING FREE

I travel a lot in my job, and recently I've been spending time in Silicon Valley. I've been visiting Internet companies, talking with technology visionaries, and participating in panel discussions on the future of business. The new companies and their founders excite me. I see in them the same spirit we've nurtured at Semco—a respect for individuals and their ideas, a distrust of bureaucracy and hierarchy, a love for openness and experimentation.

But I'm beginning to see troubling signs that the traditional ways of doing business are reasserting their hegemony. Investors, I fear, are starting to force young start-ups into the molds of the past—molds that some thought had been broken forever. CEOs from old-line companies are being brought in to establish "discipline" and "focus." Entrepreneurs are settling into corner offices with secretaries and receptionists. HR departments are being formed to issue policies and to plot careers. Strategies are being written. The truly creative types are being caged up in service units and kept further and further from the decision makers.

It's sad and, I suppose, predictable. But it isn't necessary. If my 20 years at Semco have taught me anything, it's that successful businesses do not have to fit into one tight little mold. You can build a great company without fixed plans. You can have an efficient organization without rules and controls. You can be unbuttoned and creative without sacrificing profit. You can lead without wielding power. All it takes is faith in people.

READING 18.5   MANAGING QUIETLY*

BY HENRY MINTZBERG

■ A prominent business magazine hires a journalist to write about the chief executive of a major corporation. The man has been at the helm for several years and is considered highly effective. The journalist submits an excellent piece, capturing the very spirit of the man's managerial style. The magazine rejects it—not exciting enough, no hype. Yet the company has just broken profit records for its industry.

Not far away, another major corporation is undergoing dramatic transformation. Change is everywhere, the place is teeming with consultants, people are being released in huge numbers. The chief executive has been all over the business press. Suddenly he is fired: the board considers the turnaround a failure.

Go back five, ten, twenty or more years and read the business press—about John Scully at Apple, James Robinson at American Express, Robert McNamara at the Defense Department. Heroes of American management all . . . for a time. Then consider this proposition: maybe really good management is boring. Maybe the press is the problem, alongside the so-called gurus, since they are the ones who personalize success and deify the leaders (before they defile them). After

---

*Reprinted with deletions from "Managing Quietly," H. Mintzberg, *Leader to Leader* Spring 1999, 24–30.

all, corporations are large and complicated; it takes a lot of effort to find out what has really been going on. It is much easier to assume that the great one did it all. Makes for better stories too.

If you want to test this proposition, try Switzerland. It is a well-run country. No turn-arounds. Ask the next Swiss you meet the name of the head of state. Don't be surprised if he or she does not know: the seven people who run the country sit around a table, rotating that position on an annual basis.

MANAGEMENT BY BARKING AROUND

"Forget what you know about how business should work—most of it is wrong!" screams the cover of that book called *Reengineering the Corporation*. Just like that. "Business reengineering means putting aside much of the received wisdom of two hundred years of industrial management," say the authors. Never mind that Henry Ford and Frederick Taylor, to name just two, "reengineered" businesses nearly a century ago. The new brand of reengineering "is to the next revolution of business what the specialization of labor was to the last" (meaning the Industrial Revolution). Are we so numbed by the hype of management that we accept such overstatement as normal?

There is no shortage of noisy words in the field of management. A few favored standbys merit special comment.

- *Globalization:* The Red Cross Federation headquarters in Geneva, Switzerland, has managers from over fifty countries. The Secretary General is Canadian, the three Under Secretary Generals are British, Swedish, and Sudanese. (There used to be a Swiss manager, but he retired recently.) The closest I know to a global company is perhaps Royal Dutch Shell, most of whose senior management comes from two countries—twice as many as almost any other company I can think of. But still a long way from the Red Cross Federation. Global coverage does not mean a global mind-set.

  And is "globalization" new? Certainly the word is. They used to call it other things. At the turn of the century, the Singer Sewing Machine Company covered the globe (and that included some of the remotest parts of Africa) as few so-called global companies do today.

- *Shareholder value:* Is "shareholder value" new as well, or just another old way to sell the future cheap? Is this just an easy way for chief executives without ideas to squeeze money out of rich corporations? This mercenary model of management (greed is good, only numbers count, people are human "resources" who must be paid less so that executives can be paid more, and so on and on) is so antisocial that it will doom us if we don't doom it first.

- *Empowerment:* Organizations that have real empowerment don't talk about it. Those that make a lot of noise about it generally lack it: they have been spending too much of their past disempowering everybody. Then, suddenly, empowerment appears as a gift from the gods.

  In actual fact, real empowerment is a most natural state of affairs: people know what they have to do and simply get on with it, like the worker bees in a beehive. Maybe the really healthy organizations empower their leaders, who in turn listen to what is going on and so look good.

- *Change management:* This is the ultimate in managerial noise. Companies are being turned around left and right—all part of today's *managerial correctness*, which, in its mindlessness, puts political correctness to shame.

On March 2, 1998, *Fortune* put on display "America's Most Admired Corporations." But the accompanying article said hardly anything about these corporations. It was all about their leaders. After all, if the corporations succeeded, it must have been the bosses.

Lest that not have been enough, another article touted America's most admired CEOs. One was Merck's Raymond Gilmartin: "When Merck's directors tapped Gilmartin, 56, as CEO four years ago, they gave him a crucial mission: Create a new generation of blockbuster drugs to replace important products whose patents were soon to expire. Gilmartin has delivered."

You would think he had his hands full managing the company. Yet there he apparently was, in the labs, developing those drugs. And in just four years at that. From scratch.

"There is, believe it or not, some academic literature that suggests that leadership doesn't matter," we are told by the astonished *Fortune* writer. Well, this academic is no less astonished: there are, believe it or not, some business magazines so mesmerized with leadership that nothing else matters. "In four years Gerstner has added more than $40 billion to IBM's share value," this magazine proclaimed on April 14, 1997. Every penny of it! Nothing from the hundreds of thousands of other IBM employees. No role for the complex web of skills and relationships these people form. No contribution from luck. No help from a growing economy. Just Gerstner.

Years ago, Peter Drucker wrote that the administrator works within the constraints; the manager removes the constraints. Later, Abraham Zaleznik claimed that managers merely manage; real leaders lead. Now we seem to be moving beyond leaders who merely lead; today heroes save. Soon heroes will only save; then gods will redeem. We keep upping the ante as we drop ever deeper into the morass of our own parochialism.

THE PROBLEM IS THE PRESENT

Let's go back to that book on reengineering, the same page quoted earlier: "What matters in reengineering is how we want to organize work *today*, given the demands of *today's* market and the power of *today's* technologies. How people and companies did things yesterday doesn't matter to the business reengineer" (italics added).

Today, today, always *today.* This is the voice of the obsessively analytic mind, shouting into today's wind.

But if you want the imagination to see the future, then you'd better have the wisdom to appreciate the past. An obsession with the present—with what's "hot" and what's "in"—may be dazzling, but all that does is blind everyone to the reality. Show me a chief executive who ignores yesterday, who favors the new outsider over the experienced insider, the quick fix over steady progress, and I'll show you a chief executive who is destroying an organization.

To "turn around" is to end up facing the same way. Maybe that is the problem: all this turning around. Might not the white knight of management be the black hole of organizations? What good is the great leader if everything collapses when he or she leaves? Perhaps good companies don't need to be turned around at all because they are not constantly being thrust into crises by leaders who have to make their marks today. Maybe these companies are simply managed quietly.

MANAGING QUIETLY

What has been the greatest advance ever in health care? Not the dramatic discoveries of penicillin or insulin, it has been argued, but simply cleaning up the water supply. Perhaps, then, it is time to clean up our organizations, as well as our thinking. In this spirit I offer a few thoughts about some of the quiet words of managing.

- *Inspiring:* Quiet managers don't empower their people—"empowerment" is taken for granted. They *inspire* them. They create the conditions that foster openness and release energy. The queen bee, for example, does not make decisions; she just emits a chemical substance that holds the whole social system together. In human hives, that is called *culture.*

    Quiet managers strengthen the cultural bonds between people, not by treating them as detachable "human resources" (probably the most offensive term ever coined in management, at least until "human capital" came along), but as respected members of a cohesive social system. When people are trusted, they do not have to be empowered.

The queen bee does not take credit for the worker bees' doing their jobs effectively. She just does her job effectively, so that they can do theirs. There are no bonuses for the queen bee beyond what she needs.

Next time you hear a chief executive go on about teamwork, about how "we" did it by all pulling together, ask who among the "we" is getting what kind of bonus. When you hear that chief boasting about taking the long view, ask how those bonuses are calculated. If cooperation and foresight are so important, why have these few been cashing in on generous stock options? Do we take the money back when the price plummets? Isn't it time to recognize this kind of executive compensation for what it is: a form of corruption, not only of our institutions, but of our societies as democratic systems?

■ *Caring:* Quiet managers care for their organizations; they do not try to slice away problems as surgeons do. They spend more time preventing problems than fixing them, because they know enough to know when and how to intervene. In a sense, this is more like homeopathic medicine: the prescription of small doses to stimulate the system to fix itself. Better still, it is like the best of nursing: gentle care that, in itself, becomes cure.

■ *Infusing:* "If you want to know what problems we have encountered over the years," someone from a major airline once told me, "just look at our headquarters units. Every time we have a problem, we create a new unit to deal with it." That is management by intrusion. Stick in someone or something to fix it. Ignore everyone and everything else: that is the past. What can the newly arrived chief know about the past, anyway? Besides, the stock analysts and magazine reporters don't have the time to allow the new chief to find out.

Quiet managing is about *infusion*, change that seeps in slowly, steadily, profoundly. Rather than having change thrust upon them in dramatic, superficial episodes, everyone takes responsibility for making sure that serious changes take hold.

This does not mean changing everything all the time—which is just another way of saying anarchy. It means always changing some things while holding most others steady. Call this *natural* continuous improvement, if you like. The trick, of course, is to know what to change when. And to achieve that there is no substitute for a leadership with an intimate understanding of the organization working with a workforce that is respected and trusted. That way, when people leave, including the leaders, progress continues.

■ *Initiating:* Moses supplies our image of the strategy process: walking down the mountain carrying the word from on high to the waiting faithful. Redemption from the heavens. Of course, there are too many people to read the tablets, so the leaders have to shout these "formulations" to all these "implementors." All so very neat.

Except that life in the valleys below is rich and complicated. And that is what strategy has to be about—not the neat abstractions of the executive suite, but the messy patterns of daily life. So long as loud management stays up there disconnected, it can shout down all the strategies it likes: they will never work.

Quiet management is . . . about rolling up sleeves and finding out what is going on. And it is not parachuted down on the organization; it rises up from the base. But it never leaves that base. It functions "on the floor," where the knowledge for strategy making lies. Such management blends into the daily life of the corporation, so that all sorts of people with their feet planted firmly on the ground can pursue exciting initiatives. Then managers who are in touch with them can champion these initiatives and so stimulate the process by which strategies evolve.

Put differently, the manager is not the organization any more than [a painting of a pipe is a pipe]. . . . A healthy organization does not have to leap from one hero to another; it is a collective social system that naturally survives changes in leadership. If you want to judge the leader, look at the organization ten years later.

BEYOND QUIET

Quiet management is about thoughtfulness rooted in experience. Words like wisdom, trust, dedication, and judgment apply. Leadership works because it is legitimate, meaning that it is an integral part of the organization and so has the respect of everyone there. Tomorrow is appreciated because yesterday is honored. That makes today a pleasure.

Indeed, the best managing of all may well be silent. That way people can say, "We did it ourselves." Because we did.

BIBLIOGRAPHY FOR READINGS

Abbeglen, J. C., & G. Stalk, Jr., *Kaisha, The Japanese Corporation.* New York: Basic Books, 1985.

Abernathy, W. J., & K. Wayne, "Limits on the Learning Curve," *Harvard Business Review,* September–October 1974: 109–119.

Abernathy, W. J. & J. M. Utterback, "Patterns of Industrial Innovation," *Technology Review,* 1978: 40–47.

Ackerman, R. W., *The Social Challenge to Business.* Cambridge, MA: Harvard University Press, 1975.

Aguilar, F. J., *Scanning the Business Environment.* New York: Macmillan, 1967.

Allen, S. A., "Organizational Choices and General Management Influence Networks in Divisionalized Companies," *Academy of Management Journal,* 1978: 393–406.

Allende, I., *Eva Luna.* New York: Bantam Books, 1989.

Ansberry, C., "Kodak, Sanofi Plan Alliance in Drug Sector," *Wall Street Journal,* January 9, A3, 1991.

Bacon, J., *Corporate Directorship Practices: Membership and Committees of the Board.* Conference Board and American Society of Corporate Secretaries, Inc., 1973.

Baden-Fuller, C., et al., "National or Global? The Study of Company Strategies and the European Market for Major Appliances," London Business School Center for Business Strategy, *Working Paper Series No. 28* (June 1987).

Barnard, C. I., *The Functions of the Executive.* Cambridge, MA: Harvard University Press, 1938.

Barr, P. S., J. L. Stimpert, & A. S. Huff, "Cognitive Change, Strategic Action and Organizational Renewal," *Strategic Management Journal,* 1992: 15–36.

Bartlett, C. A., & S. Ghoshal, "Managing Across Borders: New Strategic Requirements," *Sloan Management Review,* Summer 1987: 7–17.

Bartlett, C. A., & S. Ghoshal, "Matrix Management: Not a Structure, a Frame of Mind," *Harvard Business Review,* July/August 1990, 68(4): 138–146.

Beckhard, R. *Organizational Development: Strategies and Models.* Reading, MA: Addison-Wesley, 1969.

Beer, M., R. A. Eisenstat, & B. Spector, "Why Change Programs Don't Produce Change," *Harvard Business Review,* 1990: 158–166.

Bettis, R. A., "Performances Differences in Related and Unrelated Diversified Firms," *Strategic Management Journal,* 1981: 379–394.

Bhide, A., "Hustle as Strategy," *Harvard Business Review,* September–October 1986.

Blau, P. M. & P. A. Schoenherr, *The Structure of Organizations,* New York: Basic Books, 1971.

Bleeke, J., & D. Ernst, "Is Your Strategic Alliance Really a Sale?" *Harvard Business Review,* 1995: 97–105.

Bolman, L. G., & T. Deal, *Reframing Organizations: Artistry, Choice, and Leadership,* 2nd edition. San Francisco: Jossey-Bass Publishers, 1997.

Boston Consulting Group, *Perspective on Experience.* Boston, 1972.

Boston Consulting Group, *Strategy Alternatives for the British Motorcycle Industry.* London: Her Majesty's Stationery Office, 1975.

Boston Consulting Group, *Strategy Alternatives for the British Motorcycle Industry.* London: HMSO, 1975.

Bower, J. L., "Planning Within the Firm," *The American Economic Review,* 1970: 186–194.

Bowers, T., & M. Singer, "Who Will Capture Value in On-Line Financial Services," *The McKinsey Quarterly,* 1996: 78–83.

Braybrook, D. & C. E. Lindblom, *A Strategy of Decision: Policy Evaluation as a Social Process.* New York: New York University Press, 1967.

Brook, P., *The Empty Space.* Hammondsworth, Middlesex: Penguin Books, 1968.

Brown, J. S., & P. Duguid, "Organizational Learning and Communities of Practice: Towards a Unified View of Working, Learning, and Organization," *Organization Science,* 1991: 40–57.

Burns, T., "The Directions of Activity and Communication in a Departmental Executive Group," *Human Relations,* 1954: 73–97.

Burns, T., "Micropolitics: Mechanisms of Institutional Change," *Administrative Science Quarterly,* 1961: 257–281.

Burns, T., & G. M. Stalker, *The Management of Innovation,* 2nd ed. London: Tavistock, 1966.

Business Week, "From the Halls of Ivy: Some Questions About Data and Organization in the Executive Suite," February 18, 1967:202.

Business Week, "Subcompacts: Detroit Is Giving Japan the Right of Way," October 31, 1983: 42–43.

Buzzell, R. D., B. T. Gale, & R. G. M. Sultan, "Market Share—A Key to Profitability," *Harvard Business Review,* January–February 1975: 97–106.

Campbell, A., & M. Goold, *Strategy and Style: The Role of the Centre in Managing Diversified Corporations.* Oxford: Basil Blackwell, 1987.

Chandler, A. D., *Strategy and Structure: Chapters in the History of the Industrial Enterprise.* Cambridge, MA: M.I.T. Press, 1962.

Chandler, A. D., Jr., *Strategy and Structure: Chapters in the History of the American Industrial Enterprise,* Cambridge, MA: The M.I.T. Press, 1962.

Chandy, R., & G. Tellis, in J. Useem, "Internet Defense Strategy: Cannibalize Yourself," *Fortune,* September 6, 1999: 121–134.

Channon, D. F., "The Strategy, Structure and Financial Performance of the Service Industries," Working Paper, Manchester Business School, 1975.

Christensen, C. M., & R. S. Rosenbloom, "Explaining the Attacker's Advantage: Technological Paradigms, Organizational Dynamics, and the Value Network," *Research Policy,* 1995: 233–257.

Clemmer, J. *Pathways to Performance: A Guide to Transforming Yourself, Your Team, and Your Organization.* Toronto: Macmillan Canada, 1995.

Cole, A. H., *Business Enterprise in Its Social Setting.* Cambridge, MA: Harvard University Press, 1959.

Coleman, J. S., *The Foundations of Social Theory.* Cambridge: Harvard University Press, 1990.

Crozier, M., *The Bureaucratic Phenomenon.* Chicago: University of Chicago Press, 1964.

Davis, S. M., *Future Perfect,* Reading, MA: Addison-Wesley Publishing Co., 1978.

Day, G. S., & P. Nedungadi, "Managerial Representations of Competitive Advantage," *Journal of Marketing,* 1994: 31–44.

Dickhout, R., M. Denham, & N. Blackwell, "Designing Change Programs That Won't Cost You Your Job," *The McKinsey Quarterly,* 1995: 101–116.

Doeringer, P. B. & M. J. Poire. *Internal Labor Markets and Manpower Analysis.* Lexington, MA: D.C. Heath, 1971.

Douglas, S. P., & Y. Wind, "The Myth of Globalization," *Columbia Journal of World Business,* Winter 1987: 19–29.

Doz, Y. L., & Thanheiser, H., "Embedding Transformational Capability," *ICEDR, October 1996 Forum Embedding Transformation Capabilities,* INSEAD, Fontainebleau, France, 1996.

Drucker, P., "The Network Society," *Wall Street Journal,* March 29, 1995: 12.

Evered, R., "So What Is Strategy?" *Long Range Planning,* Vol. 16(3), 1983: 57–73.

Fahey, L., & R. M. Randall, *Learning from the Future: Competitive Foresight Scenarios.* New York: John Wiley & Sons, 1998.

Ferguson, C., "Computers and the Coming of US Keiretsus," *Harvard Business Review,* July–August 1990.

Firsirotu, M. Y. S., "Strategic Turnaround as Cultural Revolution: The Case of Canadian National Express," Doctoral Dissertation, Faculty of Management, 1985.

Fonfara, K., "Relationships in the Complex Construction Venture Market," *Advances in International Marketing,* 1989: 235–247.

Friedman, M., *Capitalism and Freedom.* Chicago and London: The University of Chicago Press, 1962.

Galbraith, J. K., *American Capitalism: The Concept of Countervailing Power.* Boston: Houghton Mifflin, 1952.

Galbraith, J. K., *The New Industrial State.* Boston: Houghton Mifflin, 1967.

Galbraith, J. R., & D. Nathanson, *Strategy Implementation.* St. Paul, MN: West Publishing, 1978.

Galbraith, J. R., *Organization Design.* Reading, MA: Addison-Wesley, 1977.

Galbraith, J. R., *Designing Complex Organizations,* Reading, MA: Addison-Wesley Publishing Co., 1973.

Gerth, H. H., & C. Wright Mills, eds., *From Max Webber: Essays in Sociology.* New York: Oxford University Press, 1958.

Ghemawat, P., *Commitment: The Dynamic of Strategy*. New York: Free Press, 1991.

Gilbert, X., & P. Strebel, "Strategies for Outpacing the Competition," *The Journal of Business Strategy*, June 1987: 28.

Goold, M., "Learning, Planning, and Strategy: Extra Time," *California Management Review*, 1996: 100–102.

Gosselin, R., *A Study of the Interdependence of Medical Specialists in Quebec Teaching Hospitals*. Ph.D. thesis, McGill University, 1978.

Grove, A., *Only the Paranoid Survive*. New York: Doubleday, 1996.

Hamel, G., & C. K. Prahalad. *Competing for the Future*. Boston: Harvard Business School Press, 1994.

Hariharan, S., & C. K. Prahalad, "Strategic Windows in the Structuring of Industries: Compatibility Standards and Industry Evolution," in H. Thomas, D. O'Neal, R. White, & D. Hurst, *Building the Strategically Responsive Organization*. New York: John Wiley & Sons, 1994.

Harrigan, K., & W. Newman, "Bases of Interorganization Cooperation: Propensity, Power, Persistence," *Journal of Management Studies*, 1990: 417–434.

Haspeslagh, P., "Portfolio Planning: Uses and Limits," *Harvard Business Review*, 1982: 58–73.

Hayes, R. H., & D. A. Garvin, "Managing as If Tomorrow Mattered," *Harvard Business Review*, May–June 1982: 70–79.

Hayes, R. H., & W. J. Abernathy, "Managing Our Way to Economic Decline," *Harvard Business Review*, July–August 1980: 67–77.

Henderson, B. D. *Henderson on Corporate Strategy*. Cambridge, MA: Abt Books, 1979.

Hogarth, R., & H. Kunreuther, "Risk, Ambiguity and Insurance," *Journal of Risk and Uncertainty*, 1989: 5–35.

Hout, T. M., E. Porter, & E. Rudden, "How Global Companies Win Out," *Harvard Business Review*, September–October 1982: 98–108.

Hunt, R. G., "Technology and Organization," *Academy of Management Journal*, 1970: 235–252.

Iacocca, L., with W. Novack, *Iacocca: An Autobiography*. New York: Bantam Books, 1984.

Itami, H., & T. W. *Mobilizing Invisible Assets*. Cambridge, MA: Harvard University Press, 1987.

J. D. Thompson, *Organizations in Action*, New York: McGraw-Hill, 1967.

Jensen, M., "The Eclipse of the Public Corporation," *Harvard Business Review*, September–October 1989.

Kahneman, D., & A. Tversky, "Prospect Theory", *Econometrica*, 1979: 283–291.

Kahneman, D., & D. Lovallo, "Timid Choices and Bold Forecasts: A Cognitive Perspective on Risk Taking," *Management Science*, 1993: 17–31.

Kahneman, D., J. L. Knetsch, & R. Thaler, "Experimental Tests of the Endowment Effect and the Coase Theorem," *Journal of Political Economy*, 1990: 1325–1348.

Kanter, R. M., *The Change Masters*. New York: Simon & Schuster, 1983.

Kauffman, S., *At Home in the Universe*. New York: Oxford University Press, 1995.

Kotter, J. P., "Leading Change: Why Transformation Efforts Fail," *Harvard Business Review*, 1995: 59–67.

Land, E. "People Should Want More from Life . . . ," *Forbes*, June 1, 1975.

Langley, A., H. Mintzberg, P. Pitcher, E. Posada, & J. Saint-Macary, "Opening Up Decision Making: The View from the Black Stool," *Organization Science*, 1995.

Learned, E. P., D. N. Ulrich, & D. R. Booz, *Executive Action*. Boston: Harvard Business School, 1951.

Levitt, T., "The Globalization of Markets," *Harvard Business Review*, May–June 1983: 92–102.

Lewin, K., *Field Theory in Social Science*. New York: Harper & Row, 1951.

Lindblom, C. E., *The Policy-Making Process*. Englewood Cliffs, NJ: Prentice Hall, 1968.

Mair, A., "The Honda Motor Company, 1967–1995: Globalization of an Innovative Mass Production Model," in M. Freyssenet, A. Mair, K. Shimizu, & G. Volpato, eds., *One Best Way? Trajectories and Industrial Models of the World's Automobile Producers, 1970–1995*. Oxford: Oxford University Press, 1998a.

Mair, A., "Reconciling Managerial Dichotomies at Honda Motors" in R. de Wit and R. Meyer, Eds., *Strategy: Process, Content, Context*. London: International Thomson Business Press, 2nd edition, 1998b.

Makridakis, S., *Forecasting, Planning, and Strategy for the 21st Century*. New York: The Free Press, 1990.

Malone, M. S., *Intellectual Capital: Realizing Your Company's True Value by Finding Its Hidden Brainpower*. New York: HarperBusiness, 1997.

March, J. G., & J. P. Olsen, *Ambiguity and Choice in Organizations*. Bergen, Norway: Universitetsforlaget, 1976.

March, J. G., "Exploration and Exploitation in Organizational Learning," *Organization Science*, (2), 1991: 71–87.

March, J. G., *Three Lectures on Efficiency and Adaptiveness*. Helsinki: Swedish School of Economics and Business Administration, 1994b.

March, J. G., & H. A. Simon, *Organizations*. New York: John Wiley, 1958.

Martin, L. C., "How Beatrice Foods Sneaked Up on $5 Billion," *Fortune*, April 1976: 119–129.

Mason, R., & I. Mitroff, *Challenging Strategic Planning Assumptions*. New York: John Wiley, 1981.

Mathews, J. A., "Holonic Organizational Architectures," *Human Systems Management*, 1996: 1–29.

Miller, D., & M. Kets De Vries, *The Neurotic Organization*. San Francisco: Jossey-Bass, 1984.

Miller, D., & P. H. Friesen, "Archetypes of Strategy Formulation," *Management Science*, May 1978: 921–933.

Miller, D., & P. H. Friesen, *Organizations: A Quantum View*. Englewood Cliffs, NJ: Prentice Hall, 1984.

Miller, D., "Configurations of Strategy and Structure: Toward a Synthesis," *Strategic Management Journal*, 1986: 233–249.

Mintzberg, H., & J. A. Waters, "Tracking Strategy in an Entrepreneurial Firm," *Academy of Management Journal*, 1982: 465–499.

Mintzberg, H., "Crafting Strategy," *Harvard Business Review*, 1987: 66–75.

Mintzberg, H., "Introduction: CMR Forum: The 'Honda Effect' Revisited," *California Management Review*, 1996a: 78–79.

Mintzberg, H., "Learning 1, Planning 0: Reply to Igor Ansoff," *Strategic Management Journal*, 1991: 464–466.

Mintzberg, H., "Reply to Michael Goold," *California Management Review*, 1996b: 96–99.

Moran, P. & S. Ghoshal, "Value Creation by Firms," in J. B. Keys and N. Dosier, eds., *Academy of Management Best Paper Proceedings*, 1996.

Morgan, G. *Images of Organizations*. Beverly Hills, CA: Sage, 1986.

Moyer, R. C., "Berle and Means Revisited: The Conglomerate Merger," *Business and Society*, Spring 1970, 20–29.

Nadler, D., & M. L. Tushman, *Strategic Organization Design*. Homewood, IL: Scott Foresman, 1986.

Nahaplet, J. & S. Ghoshal, " Social Capital, Intellectual Capital, and the Organizational Advantage," *Academy of Management Review*, 1998: 242–266.

Nathanson, D., & J. Cassano, "Organization Diversity and Performance," *The Wharton Magazine*, Summer 1982: 18–26.

Nonaka, I., & H. Takeuchi, *The Knowledge-Creating Company: How Japanese Companies Create the Dynamics of Innovation*. New York: Oxford University Press, 1995.

O'Neill, H. M., & J. Lenn, "Voices of Survivors: Words That Downsizing CEOs Should Hear," *The Academy of Management Executives*, 1995 (9:4).

Ohmae, K., *The Mind of the Strategist*. New York: McGraw-Hill, 1982.

Pascale, R. T., "Perspectives on Strategy: The Real Story Behind Honda's Success," *California Management Review*, 1984: 47–72.

Pascale, R. T., "Reflections on Honda," *California Management Review*, 1996: 112–117.

Perrow, C., *Complex Organizations: A Critical Essay*. New York: Scott, Foresman, 1972.

Peters, T. J., & R. H. Waterman, *In Search of Excellence: Lessons from America's Best Run Companies*. New York: Harper & Row, 1982.

Piore, M. J., & C. F. Sabel, *The Second Industrial Divide: Possibilities for Prosperity*, New York: Basic Books, 1984.

Piore, M. J., "Dualism as a Response to Flux and Uncertainty," *Dualism and Discontinuity in Industrial Societies*, S. Berger and M. J. Piore, eds., New York: Cambridge University Press, 1980.

Porter, M. E., "Competition in Global Industries: A Conceptual Framework," in M. E. Porter, ed., *Competition in Global Industries*. Boston: Harvard Business School Press, 1986.

Porter, M. E., "What Is Strategy?" *Harvard Business Review*, 1996: 61–78.

Porter, M. E., *Competitive Strategies: Techniques for Analyzing Industries and Competitors*. New York: Free Press, 1980.

Prahalad, C., & G. Hamel, "Strategy as Stretch and Leverage," *Harvard Business Review*, March–April 1993.

Prahalad, C., & G. Hamel, "The Core Competence of the Organization," *Harvard Business Review*, March–April 1990, 68(3): 79–91.

Purkayastha, D., "Note on the Motorcycle Industry 1975." Copyrighted Case, Harvard Business School, 1981.

Quinn, J. B., & P. C. Paquette, "Technology in Services: Creating Organizational Revolutions," *Sloan Management Review*, 1990: 67–78.

Quinn, J. B., "Honda Motor Company 1994." In Mintzberg, H., & J. B. Quinn, *The Strategy Process: Concepts, Contexts, Cases*. 3rd ed. Upper Saddle River, NJ: Prentice Hall International, 1996: 849–863.

Quinn, J. B., "Honda Motor Company." In Mintzberg, H., & J. B. Quinn, *The Strategy Process: Concepts, Contexts, Cases*. 2nd ed. Upper Saddle River, NJ: Prentice Hall International, 1991: 284–299.

Quinn, J. B., *Strategies for Change: Logical Incrementalism*. Homewood, Ill.: Richard D. Irwin, 1980.

Quinn, J. B., *The Intelligent Enterprise*. New York: Free Press, 1992.

Raphael, R., *Edges*. New York: Alfred A. Knopf, 1976.

Reeser, C., "Some Potential Human Problems in the Project Form of Organization," *Academy of Management Journal*, 1969: 459–467.

Roach, S. S., "In Search of Productivity," *Harvard Business Review*, 1998: 153–159.

Rumelt, R. P., "A Teaching Plan for Strategy Alternatives for the British Motorcycle Industry," in *Japanese Business: Business Policy*. New York: The Japan Society, 1980.

Rumelt, R. P., "Diversification Strategy and Profitability," *Strategic Management Journal*, 1982: 359–370.

Rumelt, R. P., *Strategy, Structure and Economic Performance*. Boston: Harvard Business School Press, 1974.

Sakiya, T., "The Story of Honda's Founders," *Asahi Evening News*, June–August 1979.

Sakiya, T., *Honda Motor: The Men, the Management, the Machines*. 2nd ed. Tokyo: Kodansha International, 1981.

Sakiya, T., *Honda Motor: The Men, the Management, the Machines*. Tokyo, Japan: Kadonsha International, 1982.

Salter, M. S., & W. A. Weinhold, *Diversification Through Acquisition*. New York: Free Press, 1979.

Schelling, T. C., *The Strategy of Conflict*. Cambridge, MA: Harvard University Press, 1963.

Schoemaker, P. J. H., "Choices Involving Uncertain Probabilities: Test of Generalized Utility Models," *Journal of Economic Behavior and Organization*, 1991: 295–317.

Schoemaker, P. J. H., "When and How to Use Scenario Planning: A Heuristic Approach with Illustration," *Journal of Forecasting*, 1991: 549–564.

Schon, D., *The Reflective Practioner*, New York: Basic Books, 1983.

Senge, P. M. *The Fifth Discipline: The Art and Practice of the Learning Organization*. New York: Doubleday, 1990.

Shimizu, R. *The Growth of Firms in Japan*. Tokyo: Keio Tsushin, 1980.

Silbiger, S., *The 10-Day MBA*. London: Piatkus, 1994.

Simon, H. A., "The Architecture of Complexity," *Proceedings of the American Philosophical Society*, 1962: 122–137.

Simon, H. A., *Administrative Behavior*. New York: Macmillan, 1947 and 1957.

Smircich, L., & C. Stubbart, "Strategic Management in an Enacted World," *Academy of Management Review*, 1985: 724–736.

Smith, L., "The Boardroom Is Becoming a Different Scene," *Fortune*, May 8, 1978: 150–188.

Smith, C. G., & A. C. Cooper, "Entry into Threatening New Industries: Challenges and Pitfalls," in H. Thomas, D. O'Neal, R. White, & D. Hurst, eds., *Building the Strategically Responsive Organization*. New York: John Wiley & Sons, 1994.

Snow, C., R. Miles, and H. Coleman, "Managing the 21st Century Network Organizations," *Organizational Dynamics*, 1992: 5–20.

Spencer, F. C., "Deductive Reasoning in the Lifelong Continuing Education of a Cardiovascular Surgeon," *Archives of Surgery*, 1976: 1177–1183.

Sperry, R., "Message from the Laboratory," *Engineering and Science*, 1974: 29–32.

Stalk, G., & T. M. Hout, *Competing Against Time*. New York: The Free Press, 1990.

Stalk, G., P. Evans, & L. Shulman, "Competing on Capabilities: The New Rules of Corporate Strategy," *Harvard Business Review*, 1992: 57–69.

Taylor, F. W., *Scientific Management*. New York: Harper, 1911.

Taylor, W. H., "The Nature of Policy Making in Universities," *The Canadian Journal of Higher Education*, 1983: 17–32.

Teece, D. J., "Economies of Scope and Economies of the Enterprise," *Journal of Economic Behavior and Organization*, 1980: 223–247.

Terkel, S. *Working*. New York: Pantheon Books, 1972.

Thompson, V. A., *Modern Organizations*. New York: Alfred A. Knopf, 1961.

Tichy, N. M., & S. Sherman, *Control Your Destiny or Someone Else Will: How Jack Welch Is Making General Electric the World's Most Competitive Corporation*. New York: Doubleday, 1993.

Time, "The Most Basic Form of Creativity," June 26, 1972.

Toffler, A., *Future Shock*. New York: Bantam Books, 1970.

Tregoe, B., & I. Zimmerman, *Top Management Strategy*. New York: Simon & Schuster, 1980.

Turner, J. R., & A. Keegan, "The Versatile Project-Based Organization: Governance and Operational Control," *The European Management Journal*, 22(3), 1999: 296–309.

Tushman, M., & C. A. O'Reilly III, *Winning Through Innovation: A Practical Guide to Leading Organizational Change and Renewal*. Boston, MA: Harvard Business School Press, 1997.

Waterman, R. H., T. J. Peters, & J. R. Phillips, "Structure Is Not Organization," *Business Horizons*, June 1980: 14–26.

Weber, M., *The Protestant Ethic and the Spirit of Capitalism*. Upper Saddle River, NJ: Prentice Hall, 1977.

Weick, K. E., "Educational Organizations as Loosely Coupled Systems," *Administrative Science Quarterly*, 1976: 1–19.

Weick, K. E., *The Social Psychology of Organizing*. Reading, MA: Addison-Wesley, first edition 1969, second edition, 1979.

Williamson, O. E., "Comparative Economic Organization: The Analysis of Discrete Structural Alternatives," *Administrative Science Quarterly*, 1991: 269–276.

Williamson, O. E., *Markets and Hierarchies: Analysis and Antitrust Implications*. New York: Free Press, 1975.

Williamson, O. E., *The Economic Institutions of Capitalism*. New York: Free Press, 1985.

Wise, D., "Apple's New Crusade," *Business Week*, November 26, 1984.

Womack, J. P., D. T. Jones, and D. Roos, *The Machine That Changed the World*. New York: Rawson Associates, 1990.

Worthy, J. C., "Organizational Structure and Employee Morale," *American Sociological Review*, 1950: 169–179.

Worthy, J. C., *Big Business and Free Men*. New York: Harper & Row, 1959.

Wrigley, L., "Diversification and Divisional Autonomy," DBA dissertation, Graduate School of Business Administration, Harvard University, 1970.

Yoshino, M. Y., "Global Competition in a Salient Industry: The Case of Civil Aircraft," in M. E. Porter, ed., *Competition in Global Industries*. Boston: Harvard Business School Press, 1986.

NAME INDEX

Abbeglen, J. C., 161, 271
Abell, Derek F., 125, 335, 350
Abernathy, W. J., 153, 353, 356, 364
Ackerman, Robert, 443
Aguilar, F. J., 33
Ahlstrand, Bruce, 22, 167, 168, 200, 203
Alexander the Great, 11–12
Allen, S. A., 233
Allende, I., 470
Anderson, Philip, 371, 383, 383n
Andrews, K. R., 70–71, 72, 92, 167, 294, 371
Ansberry, C., 265
Ansoff, H. Igor, 23, 24, 92, 115, 122, 129, 162
Argyris, Chris, 64n, 65, 86
Arnault, Bernard, 32

Bacon, J., 442
Baden-Fuller, Charles, 168, 173, 189, 288
Barabba, Vincent, 249n
Barlett, C. A., 426
Barnard, C. I., 300
Barney, Jay B., 93, 102
Barr, P. S., 205
Bartlett, C. A., 272, 273, 277n, 280n, 294, 295, 303
Beatty, Richard, 172
Beckhard, R., 171
Beer, M., 174
Bendor, Jonathan, 359
Bennis, Warren, 32, 44, 404, 405
Bentel, Elisabeth, 328
Bettis, R. A., 233
Bhide, A., 314, 326, 329
Blackwell, N., 172, 176
Blair, Tony, 304
Blau, P. M., 362
Bleeke, Joel, 256, 257, 267
Boberg, Jay, 328
Bolman, L. G., 206
Bonaparte, Napoleon, 11, 31, 140–41
Booz, D. R., 23, 302
Boulding, Kenneth, 53
Bower, J. L., 153, 441, 443, 444
Bowers, T., 24, 248
Boynton, Andrew, 335, 361
Bramwell, 399, 400, 402
Brando, Marlon, 154
Braybrook, D., 15, 24
Brook, Peter, 317
Brown, Shona, 149
Brunet, Pierre, 336n
Burns, T., 34, 417
Buzzell, R. D., 350

Campbell, Andrew, 445
Carson, Rachel, 298
Cassano, J., 233
Chandler, A. D., 23, 226, 227, 363, 432
Chandy, R., 254
Channon, D. F., 437
Christensen, C. M., 15, 251
Churchill, Winston, 318
Clemmer, J., 169
Clinton, Bill, 304
Cole, A. H., 319
Coleman, H., 366n, 405, 423
Coleman, J. S., 33, 404
Conner, Sarah, 31
Cooper, A. C., 250
Copeland, Miles, 328
Crozier, Michel, 341

Davis, S. M., 33
Day, G. S., 242, 243, 248, 249
Deal, T., 206
Deming, W. Edwards, 58
Denham, M., 172, 176
de Pree, Max, 61
Dickhout, R., 172, 176
Doeringer, P. B., 308n
Douglas, S. P., 281

Doz, Y. L., 171, 173
Drucker, P., 7, 267, 371, 481

Eisenhardt, K., 140, 141, 149
Eisenhower, Dwight D., 34
Eisenstat, R. A., 174
Ernst, David, 256, 257, 267
Evans, P., 162
Evered, R., 4

Fayol, Henri, 32
Ferguson, Charles, 450
Finkelstein, S., 371, 383, 383n
Fisirotu, Mihaela, 349
Fisk, Howard, 433
Fonfara, K., 429
Ford, Henry, 4, 6, 58, 305, 317, 480
Forrester, J., 15, 60
Frederick the Great, 13
Friedman, Milton, 296
Friesen, P. H., 146, 147, 167, 349
Fujisawa, Takeo, 156–57

Galbraith, J. K., 126, 208, 226, 227, 340, 362, 444
Galbraith, J. R., 232, 233
Gale, B. T., 350
Garvin, D. A., 153
Gassner, Rudi, 32, 208, 461
Gates, Bill, 292, 329
Gecko, Gordon, 304
Geneen, Harold, 304–5, 306
Gerth, H. H., 341
Ghemawat, P., 93, 106, 253
Ghoshal, S., 272, 273, 280n, 294, 295, 303, 426
Gilbert, X., 120
Gilmartin, Raymond, 480–81
Godfrey, John, 22
Goold, Michael, 162, 445–46
Gosselin, R., 372, 372n
Grant, Ulysses, 7, 15
Greenleaf, Robert, 62
Grove, A., 45, 253, 309–10
Gustafsson, Claes, 294, 295

Hackett, Victoria, 328
Hamel, G., 27, 71, 72, 88, 128, 162, 164, 426, 427, 430, 461, 471
Hammond, John S., 335, 350
Hardy, Cynthia, 371, 372n
Hariharan, S., 250
Harrigan, K., 262
Haspeslaugh, P., 278
Hayes, R. H., 153
Henderson, B., 93, 112, 129
Herber, J., 208, 234
Hogarth, R., 250
Honda, Sochiro, 156, 161
Hout, T. M., 161, 163, 280
Huff, A. S., 205
Hunt, R. G., 348–49
Hurst, D., 170, 200, 201
Huy, Quy Nguyen, 31, 66

Iacocca, Lee, 317
Idei, Nobuyuki, 208
Inkpen, Andrew C., 256, 267
Itami, H., 128
Itami, T. W., 128

Jensen, Michael, 446
Jobs, Steve, 318, 464
Jones, D. T., 367
Jospin, Lionel, 292

Kahneman, D., 250
Kant, I., 252
Kanter, Rosabeth Moss, 47, 276
Kauffman, Stuart, 473
Kawashima, Kihachiro, 157
Keegan, A., 426
Kets de Vries, M., 464

Kierkegaard, S., 149
Kim Woo Choong, 449–50
King, Martin Luther, 59
Knetsch, J. L., 250
Kotter, John, 175, 176
Kunreuther, H., 250

Lampel, Joseph, 3, 22, 167, 168, 200, 203, 242, 243, 404, 426
Land, E., 121, 318
Langley, A., 205, 372n
Langton, Christopher, 474
Lao Tsu, 66
Lasserre, P., 432–33, 445
Leacock, Stephen, 346–47
Learned, E. P., 23, 302
Learson, T. Vincent, 186
Lee, Robert E., 15
Lenin, V., 11, 202
Levitt, Theodore, 121, 126, 280, 288
Lewin, Kurt, 320
Lindblom, C. E., 15, 24, 413
Lodge, George, 76
Long, Gregory, 72, 295
Lovallo, D., 250
Luna, Eva, 470

MacArthur, D., 14, 31
Machiavelli, N., 11
Mair, Andrew, 140, 141, 160, 162
Maister, David H., 371, 390
Maletz, M. C., 404, 419
Malone, M. S., 5
Mao Tse-Tung, 11
March, J. G., 203, 377, 461, 468–71
Marshall, George, 14
Martin, L. C., 440
Maruta, Yoshio, 461
Marx, K., 470
Mason, R., 60
Mathews, J. A., 404, 405, 423, 424n
McHugh, Alexandra, 405n
McLaren, Norman, 145
McNamara, Robert, 479
Mehta, Zubin, 399
Miles, Grant, 404, 423
Miles, R., 366n, 405, 423
Miller, D., 146, 147, 167, 313, 349, 363, 464
Miller, Herman, 61
Miller, Lawrence, 63
Mintzberg, H., 2–3, 3, 4, 6n, 11, 22, 24, 30, 32, 33, 60, 93, 115, 127, 130, 139, 140, 141, 162, 164, 167, 168, 200, 203, 205, 207–8, 209, 242, 243, 313, 314, 334, 335, 336, 370–71, 372, 398, 404, 405, 432, 434, 460–61, 462, 472, 473, 479
Mitchell, Billy, 358
Mitroff, I., 60, 61
Moffett, William, 358, 360
Moran, Peter, 294, 295, 303
Morgan, Gareth, 206
Moyer, R. C., 441, 442

Nadler, Larry, 177, 320
Nathanson, D., 227, 232, 233
Nedungadi, P., 94, 249
Neustadt, Richard, 34
Newman, W. H., 92, 167, 176, 262
Noël, Alain, 36, 37
Nohria, Nitin, 404, 419, 419n
Nonaka, I., 268, 271, 425
Nordhoff, Heinrich, 346–47

O'Brien, William, 60
Ohmae, Kenichi, 258
Oliver, Laurence, 317
Olsen, J. P., 377, 379
O'Neill, H. M., 202
O'Reilly, C. A., III, 167, 176, 177
Otis, Suzanne, 405n

Paquette, P. C., 367
Pascale, Richard T., 140, 141, 152, 161, 162, 163, 164

Perrow, Charles, 8, 340
Peters, T. J., 32, 36, 44, 178, 196, 321, 467
Philip of Macedonia, 11–12
Phillips, J. R., 13
Picasso, P., 4
Pine, B., II, 361
Pine, Joseph B., 335
Piore, M. J., 362n, 363
Pisano, Gary P., 93, 111n
Pitcher, P., 30–31, 46, 205
Poire, M. J., 308n
Porsche, Ferdinand, 346
Porter, E., 163, 280
Porter, Michael E., 3, 4, 16, 23, 27, 44, 84, 92, 93, 94, 102,
    115, 118–19, 120, 124, 125, 128, 130, 132, 136, 206,
    244, 280n, 304, 305, 306, 314, 323, 345–46, 433, 451
Posada, E., 205
Prahalad, C. K., 27, 71, 72, 88, 128, 162, 164, 250, 426,
    427, 430, 468
Preece, Stephen B., 256, 257, 261
Putman, R., 64n

Quinn, J. B., 4, 10, 10n, 24, 136, 161, 164, 167, 183, 267,
    367, 371, 383, 383n, 404

Rangan, Subramanian, 273, 289, 289n
Raphael, R., 468
Ravenscraft, David A., 452n
Reeser, C., 411, 417
Reynolds, Craig, 473
Roach, Stephen, 304
Robertson, Michael, 72
Robinson, James, 479
Romanelli, Elaine, 167, 176
Roos, D., 367
Roosevelt, Franklin D., 34
Rose, Janet, 372n
Rosenbloom, R. S., 15, 251
Rudden, E., 163, 280
Rumelt, R. P., 6, 7, 71, 72, 80, 155, 233, 443
Russell, John, 358

Sabel, C. F., 363
Saint-Macary, J., 205
Sakiya, T., 155, 156, 162
Salk, George, 58
Salter, M. S., 404, 405, 452
Santayana, George, 50
Sayles, Leonard, 43, 399
Schein, Edgar, 59
Schelling, T. C., 4, 87
Scherer, Frederick M., 452n

Schoemaker, P. J. H., 242, 243, 248, 250
Schoenherr, P. A., 362
Schön, Donald, 64n, 86, 385
Scully, John, 479
Selznick, Philip, 7, 23, 60, 294, 295, 299
Semler, Ricardo, 461, 475
Senge, Peter M., 31, 32, 57, 58, 63n, 270
Shamsie, Jamal, 405n
Sheehan, Kevin, 356
Shih, Stan, 72, 295, 405
Shimizu, R., 205
Shulman, L., 162
Silbiger, S., 165
Simon, H. A., 10, 203, 306
Simons, Robert, 40
Singer, M., 248
Singh, J. V., 208, 234
Sloan, Alfred P., 58, 305, 435–36
Smircich, L., 206
Smith, C. G., 250
Smith, D., 64n
Smith, Fred, 328
Smith, L., 442
Smith, W. E., 121
Snow, C., 366n, 404, 405, 423
Spector, B., 174
Speer, Albert, 318
Spencer, F. C., 125, 372, 381
Sperry, Roger, 205
Spoor, William, 186, 187
Stalin, J., 317
Stalk, G., 161, 162, 163, 271
Stalker, G. M., 417
Steinberg, Sam, 316, 320, 343
Steiner, Gary, 56
Stimpert, J. L., 205
Stopford, John M., 168, 173, 189
Strebel, P., 120
Stubbart, C., 206
Sultan, R. G. M., 350
Sun Tzu, 11, 23

Takeuchi, H., 268, 425
Tapper, Max, 398
Taylor, Frederick W., 243, 341, 480
Taylor, W. H., 362, 379
Teece, D. J., 106, 111n, 365
Tellis, G., 254
Terkel, S., 337
Thaler, R., 250
Thanheiser, H., 171, 173
Thompson, J. D., 277n

Thompson, V. A., 7, 341, 362
Toffler, Alvin, 404, 405, 412
Tovey, Bramwell, 398, 401
Tregoe, B., 7, 227
Truman, Harry S., 34
Turner, J. R., 426
Tushman, M., 14, 167, 176, 177
Tversky, A., 250

Ulrich, D. N., 23, 172, 302
Urwick, Lyndell, 32, 244
Useem, J., 208, 254
Useem, Michael, 234
Utterback, J. M., 364, 403

Vernon, Raymond, 293
Victor, Bart, 335, 361
Von Bülow, C., 13
Voyer, John, 167

Wack, Pierre, 61
Walsh, Matt, 295
Waterman, R. H., 178, 196, 226, 467
Waters, J. A., 4, 6n, 315n, 336n
Watson, Tom, 58
Wayne, K., 353, 356
Weber, Max, 297n, 341
Weick, K. E., 24, 45, 373
Weinberger, Caspar, 360
Weinhold, W. A., 452
Welch, Jack, 172, 309
Westley, Frances, 315n, 317
White, R., 15
Whitehead, Alfred North, 140
Williamson, O., 306, 441
Wilson, James Q., 335, 356
Winby, Stu, 239
Wind, Y., 281
Wise, D., 318
Womack, J. P., 367
Worthy, James, 341, 342
Wrapp, Edward, 31, 52
Wrigley, L., 442, 443

Xerxes, I, 15

Yip, George S., 272–73, 280
Yoshino, M. Y., 287

Zacharkiw, Peter, 329
Zaleznik, Abraham, 32, 44, 481
Zimmerman, I., 7, 227

SUBJECT INDEX

Accountability, 438, 444, 462
Accounting-based information, 150
Acer, Inc., 3, 405
Acer Group, 243
Acquisitions, 124, 131. *See also* Mergers
　cross-border, 258, 260
Action
　managing, 43–44
　planning, 215, 413, 414
Action planning systems, 215
Activity-based approach, 109
Activity concentration, 284
Adaptation, organizational, 468–71
Adaptive learning, 58
Adaptiveness, 469
Adaptive persistence, 160
Adhocracy, 223–24, 405, 406–7, 417, 464, 473
　administrative, 407, 409, 410, 412, 418
　innovative, 441
　operating, 407, 412, 418
　role of support staff in, 410
　strategy formation in operating, 413
　temporary, 412
　varied strategies of, 414–15
Administration, leadership in, 300–303
Administrative adhocracy, 407, 409, 410, 412, 418
　strategy formation in, 413–14
Administrative fiat, decisions made by, 378
Administrative structure, 374
Administrators, roles of, of professional work, 374–76
Advanced electronics and biotechnology, 423–24
Advanced skill intellect, 389
Adversarial interaction, transforming, into cooperative
　relationship, 429
Aerospatiale, 446
Age, divisionalization and, 437
Agenda of management, 36–37
Aggregation, logic of, 244
Air Canada, 146, 343–44, 345
Alcoa, 230, 440
ALCO Standard, 451
Alliances, 129, 257–67
　as arbitrage, 258–60
　average life expectancy for, 258
　cross-border, 258, 260
　finance-driven, 262
　growth in number of domestic and international,
　　267
　learning through, 267
　linkages between parent company and, 269
　market-driven, 262
　production-driven, 262
　reasons for creating, 261–67
　technology-driven, 262
　terminating, 260
Alsthom-Alcatel, 446
Alternatives, creating multiples, 151
Amazon.com, 236
AmBev, 3, 273
Ambidextrous organization, 208, 238–39
Ambiguity, human reactions to, 417
American Express, 479
American Hospital Supply, 454
American Telephone & Telegraph (AT&T) Company,
　183
Amgen, 471
Analytical priorities, setting, 330–31
Analytical tasks, handling, in stages, 331–32
Andersen Consulting, 182, 239
Apollo program, 88, 247, 407, 413–14
Apple Computer, 3, 318, 464, 471, 479
Apprenticeship, 393
Appropriability, 105
A priori statements, 11
Arbitrage
　alliances as, 258–60
　global, 258
Archetypes, 51
Arms-length supplier relationship, 265
Arms-length transaction, 263
Articling in accounting, 373
Artificial intelligence research, 150

Artists, 433
　identifying, 47
Asea Brown Boveri (ABB), 237, 307, 308
Asian corporate archetypes, 446–47
Asian firms, decoding, 450–51
Asian groups, comparing European groups with, 448–50
Assets, 128
　invisible, 128
　sharing, 425
Assistance, 318
Assumptions, overcoming simplifying, 275
Astra International, 446
Astral Records, 31
Attractiveness test, 453
Automobile firms, strategic change in, 346–47
Autonomy, diversification and, 441
Axion Consulting, 433

Baldwin United, 153
Bargaining power, maximizing, 259–60
Barriers to entry, 132
　sources of, 96–97
Barriers to mobility, 133
BASF, 446
Battering strategy, 137
Baxter Travenol, 454
Beatrice Foods, 440, 442, 444, 451
Becton Dickinson, 284
Behavior formalization, 212
Beijing Mirror Corporation, 273
Benchmarking, 17
Benefits of global strategy, 283–84
Better-off test, 454, 456
Bic Corporations, 21
Bidcom, 477
Big Flower Press, 18
Billing multiple, 392–93
Biotechnology, 370
Blackspace
　budgeting in, 420
　defined, 419
　knowing when to leave, 420
　moving, 422–23
　projects, 420
Blockbuster Video, 290
Bloomingdale's, 289
BMG International, 208, 273, 433, 461
BMW, 318
Boarding-school syndrome, 478
Boeing, 282
Boston Consulting Group (BCG), 23, 123, 129, 140,
　153–54, 155, 160–61, 162, 278, 351
　growth share matrix, 434
Bottom line approach to management, 38
Bottom-up change, 167, 174, 175, 176, 185
Bottom-up decision-making, 164
Brand identification, 96
Bridgestone Corporation, 283
Brinkmanship in business, 112–15
British Petroleum, 445
BSA, 154
BSN, 446
Budgetary agency, 438
Bundling strategy, 126, 130
Bureaucracy
　bashing, 172
　innovation in, 356–60
　machine, 373
　professional, 370, 372, 373, 382, 411
Bureaupathologies, 341
Burrowing strategy, 134
Business, brinkmanship in, 112–15
Business functions, 128
Business management, 274
Business strategies
　downstream, 116
　evaluating, 80–87
　generic, 115–27
　midstream, 116
　recombination, 125–26, 126
　redefinition, 125
　upstream, 116
Buyer group, power of, 98–99

By-product diversification, 124–25, 230
By-product firm, 438

Canadelle, 320
Canon, 88, 89, 251, 284, 289
Capabilities, 128
　developing, 110–12
　sources of, 77–78
Capacity misfit, 135
Capacity planning, 392
Cape Cod Potato Company, 328
Capital-intensive industries, 423
Capital markets, inefficiency of, 441
Captive finance subsidiaries, 85
Cartel, 138
Cash cows, 123, 153, 278
Caterpillar, 88, 176
Causal ambiguity, 108–9
CBS, 459
CD Now, 236
Cellular organization, 404, 423–31
　adding value by using, 425–27
　building blocks of, 424–25
Cemex, 289
Center of gravity, 208, 227
　change, 232
Central administrators, 378
Chain integration strategies, 124
Challenges, constantly increasing, 385
Change
　center of gravity, 232
　dynamic, 361–62
　mapping processes of, 170
　pent-up need for, 180
　quantum theory of, 146–47
　reconciling continuity and, 149
　in resource mix, 353
　stable, 361–62
　stable process, 362
　strategies for, 10–16
Change cube, 167, 169, 171
Change management, 17, 480
Channels, global, 285
Chaos, creative, 270–71
Chaos theory, 27
Character as distinctive competence, 302
Charisma, 317
Charoen Pokphand, 446
Chrysler Corporation, 288
Chunking, 171
S. A. Chupa Chups, 257, 273
Citibank, 289
Classical approach to strategy, 11–14
Cleavage
　in combinations, 465
　in conversion, 465
Climate of trust, 270
Closed systems, 339–41, 436, 442
Club Med, 290
CNN, 290
Coalition management, 188
Coca-Cola, 88, 289, 471
Codes of conduct, 299
Cognition, 200–206
　as concept attainment, 205
　as confusion, 203–4
　as construction, 205–6
　damages of objectivity, 200, 201–3
　as information processing, 204
　as mapping, 204–5
　strategy as, 200, 203–6
Cognitive intellect, 389
Cognitive knowledge, 383
Cognitive school, 23, 24, 27
Collaboration, 256–70
　alliances and, 257–67
　in creating knowledge, 267–71
　flexibility in successful, 258
　by multinationals, 257
　Ohmae's tips for, 259
Collaborative innovation, 370
Collaborative strategy, 138
Collective action, 381

Collective choice
  decisions made by, 378–79
  models of, 379–80
Collective intuition, 150
  building, in strategic decision making, 150
Collective strategy, 7
Collegiality, 380
Collegial model, 379
Combinations, 464
  cleavage in, 465
  kinds of, 464–65
Combining strategy for entrepreneurial competency
  firms, 431
Commitments
  balancing options and, 253–54
  making, 109–10
Commodity strategy, 133
Common interest, 379
Communicating role, 39–40
Communication, inefficiency and, 418
Communicator, middle managers as, 68
Companies
  downstream, 228, 229
  nature of environment, 74–77
  upstream, 228, 229
  as value creators, 307–8
Compaq, 471
Comparative advantages, 129
Competence, 128, 467–68
  matching opportunity and, 78–79
  relational, 429
Competence misfit, 135
Competencies-capabilities theory, 162
Competency base of engineering-construction firms,
  426–27
Competing on the edge, 149
Competition, 462
  benefits of, 466–67
  combining cooperation and, 467
  forces in shaping strategy, 94–102
  through politics, 466
Competitive advantage, 21, 83–85, 102–5, 120, 129, 149
  to corporate strategy, 451–59
  fit in driving, 20–22
  imitability and, 104
  organization and, 105
  rareness and, 103–4
  value and, 103
Competitive innovation, 90–91
Competitive maneuvering, 112–15
Competitive moves in global strategy, 282–83
Competitive strategy, 3, 83, 451
  in emerging industries, 323–26
Complementarities, 135
Comprehensive change, 169
Computer software design, 424
Conceiving, 36
Concept attainment, cognition as, 205
Conditio sine qua non, 296
Confederation, 447
Configuration, 207, 462, 468
  containment of, 464
  contamination by, 463–64
  of organization, 313
  out of control, 464
Configuration school, 26, 27
Conflict, stimulating quick, in strategic decision making,
  150–51
Conflict-resolution mechanisms, 259
Confusion, cognition as, 203–4
Conglomerate firm, 438–39
Congruence, 467
Connexion type of organization, 448
Consensus
  with qualification, 151–52
  strategy, 6
Conservatism, rational, 242
Consistency in strategy evaluation, 81–82
Consonance in strategy evaluation, 82–83
Constellation, 447
Construction, cognition as, 205–6
Construction-procurement firms, 404
Consulting, 424
Container Corporation, 229
Containment of configuration, 464
Contamination, 462
  by configuration, 463–64
Contestability, 136–37
Continental Airlines, 19, 20

Contingencies, 373
Contingency theory, 26, 209
Continuity, reconciling change and, 149
Continuous improvement, 146, 173, 304, 361, 366–68
  characteristics of design, 367–68
  synergy between mass customization and, 368
Continuous learning, 50
Continuous process of innovation, 423
Contracts/relationships, enforceable, 106
Contradiction, 466–67, 468
Control
  in covert leadership, 398–99
  by strategy, 448
  by systems, 448
Controlling role, 40
Convergence, 146–47, 177–79, 252, 467
Conversion, 465
  cleavage in, 465
  cycles of, 465
Cooperation, 297, 381, 462
  combining competition and, 467
  limits to, 466
  through ideology, 466
Cooperative relationships, transforming adversarial inter-
  action into, 429
Coordination, problems of, 381
Coors, 110
Core business
  distinguishing, 117–22
  elaborating, 122–25
  locating, 116–17
  reconceiving, 125–27
Core competences, 128
  of project-based firms, 426–31
    entrepreneurial, 427
    evaluative, 428–29
    relational, 429–30
    technical, 427–28
Core competency theory, 164
Core relocation strategies, 128–29
Corporate competence and resources, identifying, 77–79
Corporate ethics, 296
Corporate restructuring, 208
Corporate strategy, 72–79, 451
  choosing, 458–59
  competitive advantage to, 451–59
  concepts of, 454–58
  defined, 72–73
  formal planning in, 185
  formulation of, 73–74
  implementation of, 74
  premises of, 452
  summary statement of, 73
Corporate theme, creating, 459
Corporations, 392
  transition from functional to diversified, 438
  vertical integration, 438
Cost, trade-off between quality and, 202
Cost dynamics, 350–56
Cost of entry, 453–54
Cost reductions, 282
  in global strategy, 283
Countervailing power, 444
Courtaulds, 446
Covert leadership, 371, 398–402
  coda, 402
  control in, 398–99
  culture in system, 400–401
Craft enterprises, 376
Crafting image, 141
Crafting of strategy, 141–49
Craftsman, 376, 433
  identifying, 47–48
  potter as, 141–49
Creation, 468
Creative chaos, 270–71
Creative organizations, starburst organization in, 387–88
Creative tension, 59
  leading through, 59
Creativity in measuring whitespace results, 421
Crescendo model of rejuvenation, 189–97
Crest toothpaste, 228
Critical knowledge management processes, 267
Critical mass, 422
Critical strategic issues, 184–85
Cross-border acquisitions, 258, 260
Cross-border alliances, 258, 260
Cross-border linkages, 258
Cross-border mergers, 260

Crown Cork & Seal, 99
Crystalline diversification, 125
Cultural change, 169
  programs for, 196–97
Cultural school, 25–26, 27
Culture in system, 400–401
Cumulative learning, 111
Cushman & Wakefield, 476, 477
Customers
  global, 285
  homogeneous needs, 285
  preference of, in global strategy, 283–84
  rural versus urban-based, 19
Customization, 242
  customizing, 243–48
  mass, 243, 364–66, 368–69
  pure, 247
  standardized, 122
  strategies, 133
  tailored, 247
  value chain, 245
Customized standardization, 246
Customizing customization, 243–48
Customizing strategies, 122
Cybernetic flow process, 208

Daewoo, 449–50
Daimler Benz, 445
Daimler Chrysler, 293
Dassault, 446
Datsun, 159
Decentralization, 216, 374
  horizontal, 216
  parallel, 216
  vertical, 216
Decision making
  by administrative fiat, 378
  by collective choice, 378–79
  in entrepreneurial organization, 315
  by professional judgment, 378
  in professional organization, 377–80
  strategic, 72, 149–52
Default of leadership, 301–2
Defense Department, U.S., 479
Delayed participation, 249
Delegating, 40
Deliberate formulation, 2
Deliberate strategy, 2, 5
Dell Computer, 235–36, 289
Democrats, 379
Deregulation, 179
Design and engineering services, 423–24
Design differentiation strategy, 121, 130
Designer, leader as, 60–61
Design misfit, 135
Design school, 23, 24, 27
Dichotomy-reconciling strategic capability, 165
Differentiation, 121–22, 275–76
  strategies of, 120–21
Digital imaging, 248
Dimensions of strategy, 14–16
Directing, 399
Direction, 462
Direct supervision, 211, 382
Disconnected strategy, 6
Discontinuity, detecting, 148
Discontinuous learning, 50
Discretion, problems of, 381
Diseconomies of scale, 386
Disinterest, 379
Disney, 290
Divergence, 146–47
Divergent opinions, 252
Divergent thinking, 407
Diversification
  by-product, 230
  in creating shareholder value, 453
  crystalline, 125
  economic advantages of, 439–42
  linked, 125, 231
  related, 230–31
  relationship between divisionalization and, 432
  strategies, 124, 131
  subsystem, 184
  unrelated, 231–32
Diversified corporations, 432–33
Diversified forms, 463
Diversified organizations, 222–23, 313, 434–45
  basic divisionalized structure, 434–37

conditions of, 437–38
contribution of headquarters to, 442–43
issues associated with, 439–45
in public sphere, 444–45
roles of headquarters, 434–35
social performance of performance control system, 443–44
stages in transition to, 438–39
structure of divisions, 435–37
Diversity, managing, 432–59
from competitive advantage to cooperative strategy, 451–59
diversified organization in, 434–45
large groups in East and West, 445–51
Divisionalization, 432, 437
age and, 437
relationship between diversification and, 432
size and, 437
Divisionalized form of structure, 434
Dog, 278
Doing role, 43
Dominant designs, 179
Dominant firm, 136
R. R. Donnelley & Sons Company, 18
Don't Miss meetings, 150
Double-loop learning, 86
Dow Chemical, 283
Downsizing, 168, 173
Downstream business strategy, 116, 129
Downstream companies, 228, 229
Drawbacks of global strategy, 284
Driven change, 171
Driving force, 208, 227
DuPont, 432, 435, 451
Dynamic capabilities approach, 27
Dynamic change, 361–62
Dynamic efficiency, 306
Dynamic process, 366
change in, 366–68
Dynamic product, 363
change in, 364–66
Dynamic stability, 368

Early-mover advantages, 106
Eastman Kodak, 85, 97, 251, 350
Eclecticism, need for, 9
Ecology, 75
E-commerce, 419
Economics, 75–76
advantages of diversification, 439–42
of professional service firm, 392
transaction-cost, 305–6
Economic strategy, 73
Economic value added, 471
Economies, size, 106
Economies of scale, 96, 285
Economies of scope, 285
Effective manager, 33–34
Effectiveness, efficiency versus, 355–56
Efficiency, 462
effectiveness versus, 355–56
problems of, 418
Electrolux, 282
Electronic commerce, 248
Elite, managing, 385
Embryonic companies, 323
Emergent strategies, 2, 146, 148
Emerging industries, competitive strategy in, 323–26
Emerging market, 132
Emerging technologies, avoiding pitfalls of, 248–55
Empire Plastics, 31
Employee empowerment, 172–73
Empowerment, 480, 481
employee, 172–73
Engineering-construction firms, 426
competency base of, 426–27
Engineering-construction-procurement (EPC) firms, 426
interaction between primary clients and, 429
strategies of, from core competence perspective, 430–31
Enthusiasm, building, 422
Entrepreneurial approach to strategy formation in super-market chain, 318–22
Entrepreneurial competencies in project-based firms, 427
Entrepreneurial competency firms, strategies of, from core competence perspective, 430–31
Entrepreneurial configuration, 406, 436
Entrepreneurial conglomerates, 433, 446
Entrepreneurial forms, 463

Entrepreneurial one, 414
Entrepreneurial organization, 220–21, 315–22, 404, 405
autocratic form of, 317
basic structure, 315
conditions of, 316–17
decision making in, 315
issues associated with, 322
precedence of leadership in, 321–22
strategy formation in, 317–18
Entrepreneurial school, 23, 24, 27
Entrepreneurial strategy, 6
Entrepreneurs
crafting of successful strategies of, 326–33
middle managers as, 67
Entrepreneurship, 314, 441
starburst organizations and, 388
Entry and control, strategies of, 124
Environmental, taking precedence in innovative organization, 417
Environmental analysis, 102
Environmental ethics, 299
Environmental school, 26
Eroding market, 132
Erupting market, 132
ESPN, 266
Established (mature) market, 132
Ethical climate, 299
Ethical committees, 299
Ethical reasoning, structures of, 297
Ethical strategy, 294, 295–99
for the future, 299
Ethics
corporate, 296
environmental, 299
strategic, 295–99
European Community (1992), harmonization in, 280
European corporate archetypes, 445–46
European groups, comparing Asian groups with, 448–50
Evaluative competencies in project-based firms, 428–29
Evolutionary/institution building, 172
Evolved change, 171
Executive leadership
organization evolution and, 181–82
role of, during convergent periods, 178
Executive office, 438
Executives, innovation and, 358–60
Executive summaries, 450
Exit barriers, 135
Expandability, 384
Expendability, 301
Experience curve, 135, 153, 161, 351
Experience effect, 350–53
sources of, 353
Experimentation, 189
Experts, 313, 370–71
organizations of, 370–402
covert leadership, 371, 398–402
intellect, 371, 383–89
professional, 370–71, 372–82
professional service firms, 371, 390–97
Explicit knowledge, 268
Exploitation, 469
Exploration, 469
External change, leverage provided by, 328–29
External coalition, 210
Externalities in industry development, 325
External network form, 237
External roles of manager, 376
Exxon, 451

Fashion, 412
Feasibility in strategy evaluation, 85–86
Feature-film strategy, 143
Federal Express (FedEx), 327, 328
Federation, 447
Figurehead duties, 315
Finance-driven alliances, 262
Financial conglomerates, 432, 446
Financial controls, 446, 448
Fine-tuning, 177–78
Firestone Corporation, 283
First movers, 137
advantage, 84
First-order fit, 21
Fit, 133–35. See also Misfits
between firm's mission and environment, 83
first-order, 21
forced, 134
importance of, among functional policies, 21

second-order, 21
sustainability and, 21–22
third-order, 21
types of, 21
vulnerable, 134
Five forces model, 102
Flanking attack, 137
Flat structure, 374
Focusing strategy for EPC firms, 430
Follow the leader, 172
Forced fit, 134
Ford Motor Company, 4, 89, 162, 164, 246, 286, 287, 337, 356
Formal planning in corporate strategy, 185
Formal systems planning approach, 183
Formosa Plastics, 446
Formulation/implementation dichotomy, 348–49
Fortifying strategy, 135
Fragmented market, 131
Fragmented opposition, 187
Frame-breaking change, 181
forces leading to, 179
scope of, 179–80
Frame-breaking tactics, 151
Franchising, 129
Frontal attack, 137
Front-back organization, 208, 239–40
Functional areas, 118–19
Functional grouping, 213–14
Functional management, 274
Functional policies, importance of fit among, 21
Functional structure, 438

Galéries Lafayette, 289
Game theory, strategy in, 4
The Gap, 21, 471
Garbage can model, 379
Garbage can phenomenon, 380
General Electric, 160, 309, 452
price-fixing scandal of 1960s, 444
work out/team meetings, 174
General Mills, 127, 234
General Motors, 4, 6, 9, 61, 142, 160, 162, 164, 254, 283, 350, 356, 432, 436, 456
Generative learning, 58
Generic business strategies, 115–27
distinguishing core business, 117–22
elaborating core business, 122–25
locating core business, 116–17
reconceiving core business, 125–27
Generic strategy, 83
Generic value chain, 118–19
Gene therapy, 248
Geographic expansion strategies, 123
Geographic management, 274
Geographic markets, 132
Gillette, 350
Glaxo, 445
Global arbitrage, 258
Global channels, 285
Global customers, 285
Globalization, 272–93, 480
benefits of, 283–84
competitive moves, 282–83
drawbacks of, 284
drivers of, 284–88
location of value added activities, 282
managing across borders in and, 273–80
market participation in, 281–82
myths regarding, 289–93
product offering, 282
strategic aspects of, 280–88
Goals, 10
Goldman Sachs, 208, 290
Grass-roots strategy, 145, 415–17
Great Britain, motorcycle industry in, 153–54
Gresik, 447
Grey Advertising, 158
Group management
corporate control, 448
organizational setting in, 447–48
Groups, comparing European and Asian, 448–50
Guerrilla attack, 137

Hanover Insurance Company, 60
Harley-Davidson, 153, 154
Headquarters
contribution of, to diversified organizations, 442
role of, in diversified organization, 434–35

Health care, 424
Henkel, 445
Herding cats, 402
Heterogeneity, internal, 276
Hewlett-Packard, 7, 104, 145, 239
Holdup, 107–8
Home Depot, 471
Honda effect, 152–60
Honda Motor Company, 3, 140, 141, 314, 446
    in Britain, 153–54
    financial crisis in, 162–63
    historical treatment of, 154–56
    innovations offered by, 156–57
    in Japan, 156–57
    Nicest People advertising campaign, 158–59
    organizational process perspective, 156–59
    regional policy of, 154
    research and development in, 154, 163
    strategy industry and, 160–65
    systemic planning by, 164
    in United States market, 154–55, 157–59, 161
Horizontal decentralization, 216
Horizontal diversification, 124
Horizontal strategies, 433
Hothouse model of strategy formulation, 416
Hughes Aircraft, 456
Human reactions, to ambiguity, 417
Human relations, 41
Hybrid, 464
Hypercompetition, 17

IBM Corporation, 7, 85, 89, 179, 249, 254, 310, 329, 350, 451, 459, 481
ICI, 446
Ideological control, 448
Ideological strategy, 6
Ideology, 209–10
    cooperation through, 466
Ikea, 18, 19, 20, 123, 289
Image differentiation strategy, 121, 130
Imagination, perils and glories of, 470–71
Imitability, 104
Imitable, 129
Imitation, 106–7
Impannatores, 237
Impartation, 124
Imposed strategy, 6
Imprecision, 54–55
Incremental adaptations, 177, 178
Incremental change, 178
    managing, 177–79
Incrementalism, 167–68
Incremental logic, precipitating events and, 184
Indirect attack, 137
Individualization, logic of, 245
Indoctrination, 213, 373
Inductive reasoning, 381
Industrial dualism, 362n
Industrial groups, 432, 445
Industrial holdings, 432, 445–46
Industrial Revolution, 423
Industry, 76
    discontinuities, 179
    exploiting change, 101
    externalities in development, 325
    strategies of, 117
Inefficiency, sources of, 418
Infinitely flat organizations, 371, 386, 389
Influencers, 210
Information
    accounting-based, 150
    managing by, 38–40
    marketing, 347
    private, 106
    real-time, 150
Information age, 423
Information-intensive industries, 423
Information processing, cognition as, 204
Information technology, challenges to, 361–69
Innovation, 313, 403–31
    in bureaucracy, 356–60
    collaborative, 370
    executives and, 358–60
    problems of, 381–82
    Silicon Valley approach to, 89
    sophisticated, 404, 405
    tasks and, 356–58
    twenty-first century as era of, 423–25
Innovation context, 403–4

Innovation-driven industries, 423
Innovative adhocracy, 441
Innovative forms, 463
Innovative organization, 223–24, 373, 404, 405–18
    basic structure, 405–11
    conditions of, 411–13
    environment taking precedence in, 417
    issues associated with, 417–18
    strategy formation in, 413–17
INSEAD, 432
Insight, 205
Institutional leader
    distinguishing interpersonal leader from, 302
    functions of, 302–3
Instrumentality, 297
Integrated competitive moves, 284
Integrating action and analysis in large corporations, 331
Integrating managers, 215
Integrating principle, 59
Integration
    chain, 124
    vertical, 340
Integration-diversification strategies, combined, 124–25
Integrative organization, 276
Intel, 309, 471
Intellect, 371, 383–89
    characteristics of, 383
    defined, 383
    expandability of, 385
    exponentially, 384–86
    organizing around, 386–89
    perfection of, 384–85
    scale economies in, 385–86
    sharing of, 384
    value of firm's, 383
Intellectual flows, 386
Intelligent sensors, 248
Intended strategy, 5
Interactive computing, 248
Interactive learning, 167
Interactivity and electronic commerce, 248
Internal company dynamics, 179
Internal development, 124, 131
Internal heterogeneity, 276
Internalization of set procedures, 373
Internal network form, 237–38
Internationalization in services, 289–90
International Paper, 229
International Record Syndicate, 328
International Strategic Alliances (ISA), 261–67
    structures, functions, and objectives, 262
Internet, 388
Internship in medicine, 373
Interpersonal leader, distinguishing institutional leader from, 302
Intrapreneurship, 314, 404, 441
Intuition, 205
    building collective, 150
Invention, 363
    synergy between mass production and, 364
Inverse pyramids, 374
Inverted organization, 371, 387, 389
Invisible assets, 128
Irreversibility, 109–10, 110
Isolating mechanisms, 134
It all depends approach, 209
ITT, 274, 278

Japan, strategy in, 153
Jardine Matheson, 446
Jiffy Lube International, 18
Job enrichment, 212
Job evaluation systems, 386
Job specialization, 212
Johnson Controls, 477
Johnson & Johnson, 458
Joint ventures, 259, 262
    American-Japanese, 267
    climate of trust, 270
    flexible learning objectives, 270
    leadership commitment, 270
    parent interactions with, 268–69
    performance myopia and, 271
    personal movement in, 269
    technology sharing in, 268
Jolt and refocus, 172
Judgment in project-based firms, 428

Kai, 295
Kao Corporation, 208, 308, 461
Keiretsus, 433, 446–47, 448–49
K-Mart, 105
Knowledge. See also Learning
    age, 423
    base of programmable competencies, 428
    businesses, 423
    cognitive, 383
    creating, through collaboration, 267–71
    explicit, 268
    involved in strategic thinking, 148
    sharing, 425
    tacit, 141, 268
Kolberg, Kravis and Roberts, 446
Komatsu, 88

Labor efficiency, 353
L'Air Liquide, 445
Langley, Ann, 371
Large groups, managing, in the East and West, 445–51
Lateral attack, 137
Lateral hires, 394
Later entrants, 137
Launching devise, 127
LBO Partnerships, 446
Leaders
    in building learning organizations, 57–66
    as designer, 60–61
    as steward, 62–63
    as teacher, 61–62
    traditional view of, 58
Leadership
    in administration, 300–303
    commitment, 270
    covert, 398–402
    default of, 301–2
    overt, 400
    precedence of, in entrepreneurial organization, 321–22
    visionary, 317–18
Leading role, 41–42
Lean-flow principles, 202
Leaning in strategic objectives, 264
Leaping in strategic objectives, 265–66
Learning, 129, 462. See also Knowledge
    adaptive, 58
    building capacity, 252–53
    continuous, 50
    cumulative, 111
    discontinuous, 50
    double-loop, 86
    by example, 393
    flexible objectives in, 270
    generative, 58
    interactive, 167
    single-loop, 86
    strategic, 144, 161
    as strategic objective, 263–64
    strategy of, 135
    through alliances, 267
    trail-and-error, 253
Learning organizations, 50–51
    building, 57–66
    leadership in, 59
Learning rate, 351
Learning school, 24, 25
Learning schools, 27
Leather-jacketed, teenage troublemaker, 154
Left-handed planner, 346
Legitimacy, establishing, in whitespace, 420
Leverage
    increased competitive, 284
    provided by external change, 328–29
    in strategic objectives, 264–65
Liaison positions, 215
Licensing, 263
    agreements, 129
Liem Sioe Liong, 446
Life cycles, 465
Li Ka Shing, 446
Lincoln Electronic Holdings, 291
Linkages
    cross-border, 258
    between parent and alliance strategies, 269
Linked diversification, 125, 231
Linking, 401
    role, 42–43
    in strategic objectives, 265

Local producers, 316
Location
    of value added activities in global strategy, 282
Location misfit, 135
Lock-in, 110
Locking out in strategic objectives, 266
Logical incrementalism, 183–88
    logic of, 183–86
Logistics, favorable, 286
London Free Press, 371
Long-term contracts, 129
L'Oréal, 289
Low cost differentiation strategy, 130
Loyalty, 297
Lufthansa, 273
Luigi's Body Shop, 9
LVMH, 3, 433

Machine, 464
    bureaucracy, 373
    forms, 463
    professional organizations and, 405
Machine organizations, 221–22, 336–49, 373–74, 414,
    464
    basic structure, 336–39
    comparison of professional organization to, 373,
        380
    conditions of, 339
    as instruments and closed systems, 339–41
    issues associated with, 341–42
    organization taking precedence in, 349
    strategic revolutions in, 349
    strategy formation in, 342–49
    types of, 417
Macro change, 170
Macroeconomic strategy model, 159–60
Macro power, 25
Macy's, 289
Mailbox, Inc., 104
Managed change, 168–69
Management
    action, 43–44
    bottom line approach to, 38
    business, 274
    diversification and development, 441
    elite, 385
    empowering, 194
    functional, 274
    geographic, 274
    by information, 38–40
    new manifesto for, 303–10
    quiet, 479–83
    strategy in, 4
    through people, 40–43
    well-rounded job of, 44–46
    without control, 477–79
Management information system (MIS), 347–48
Managerial correctness, 480
Managerial legitimacy, reclaiming, 310
Managerial objectivity, 201
Managerial styles, teamwork and, 48–50
Managerial work
    basic description of, 35–46
    deductive and inductive approaches to, 46
    folklore and facts about, 32–35
Managers
    agenda of work, 36–37
    communicating role of, 39–40
    controlling role of, 40
    doing role of, 43
    effective, 33–34
    external roles of, 376
    in focusing time and energy, 53
    frame of job, 36
    job of, 32–46
    keeping well informed, 52–53
    leading role of, 41–42
    linking role of, 42–43
    middle, 66–69
    person in job of, 35–36
    in playing power game, 53–54
    policy decisions and, 52–57
    rules for, 16
    sense of timing in, 54
Managing maturity, 334–69
Manhattan Project, 412
Mapping, cognition as, 204–5
Maquiladoras, 283
Market consolidation, 123

Market demand, 251
Market development strategies, 123, 130
Market diversity, 437
Market-driven alliances, 262
Market elaboration, 123
Marketing
    common regulations, 286–87
    in global strategy, 282
    transferable, 285
Marketing information, 347
Market leader, 136
Market participation, 284
    in global strategy, 281–82
Market segmentation, 244
Market signaling by feint, 137
Mass customization, 243, 364–66
    characteristics of design, 365–66
    synergy between continuous improvement and,
        368
    taking right path to, 368–69
Mass markets, 131
Mass production, 362–63
    synergy between invention and, 364
Mass production firms, 339
Matrix structure, 215–16, 406
Matsushita, 446, 471
Mature context, 313
Mature organizations
    challenge to organizations and information
        technology, 361–69
    cost dynamics, 350–56
    machine organizations as, 336–49
Maturity, managing, 334–69
Maxwell House, 228
Maytag, 129
Mazda, 159
McDonald's, 7, 8–9, 290, 466
McKesson, 457–58
McKinsey & Company, 208, 239, 273, 371, 405
Medical internships, 385
Meetings
    don't miss, 150
    must attend, 150
Megaprojects, 247
MegaStrategic Business Entity, 240
Memory in project-based firms, 428–29
Mental models, surfacing and testing, 64–65
Mentoring, 385, 393
Merck, 480–81
Mergers. See also Acquisitions
    cross-border, 260
Merrill Lynch, 386
Methods improvements, 353
Michelin, 293, 445, 446
Micro change, 170
Micro-machines, 248
Micro power, 25
Microsoft Corporation, 183, 329, 472
Microtransformations, 367
Middle line, 209
Middle managers, 66–69, 374
    as communicator, 68
    as entrepreneurs, 67
    tasks of, 336–37
    as therapist, 68–69
    as tightrope artist, 69
Midstream business strategy, 116
Military, strategy in, 4
Military-diplomatic strategies, 11
Miller beer, 96
Minority-equity investment, 262
Misfits. See also Fit
    capacity, 135
    competence, 135
    design, 135
    location, 135
    myopic, 135
    sunk, 135
Missionary organization, 224–25
Mitsubishi, 446
Mitsui, 446
Mobility barriers, shifting, 325
Momentum, building, in whitespace, 421
Moral contract, 309–10
Moral responsibility, 296–97
Moral values
    changes in over time, 298
    expectations in near future, 298–99
Motivated creativity intellect, 389

Moto-Guzzi, 154
Motorola, 286, 309
MP3.com, 314
Multidimensional organization
    building truly, 275
    development of, 274
Multidomestic strategy, 280
Multifront focus, 172
Multinationals, collaboration by, 257
Multiple combinations, 464
Multipoint competition, 136
Must attend meetings, 150
Mutual adjustment, 210–11, 406
Myopia, performance, 271
Myopic misfits, 135

National Aeronautics and Space Administration (NASA),
    331, 407
    Apollo project of, 88, 247, 407, 413–14
National Bicycle Industry Company, 243
National Can, 99
National Film Board of Canada (NFB), 143, 144–45, 407,
    408, 413, 414
National Football League (NFL), 107
National holdings, 433, 447
National Public Radio, 420
Natura, 295, 461
Natural fit, 134
NEC Corporation, 274, 278, 279, 446, 459
Needs-based positioning, 18–19
Negotiations, breakdown, 113
Neptune, 152
Networking, 42, 401
Network organizations, 208, 236–38, 425
Network partnering, 423
Networks, 129
New product development, 169
Newton, 471
New United Motor Manufacturing, Inc. (NUMMI),
    367
Niche markets, 328
Niche strategy, 7, 122, 133, 330–31
Nike, 471
Nintendo, 183
Nonlogical strategy, 114–15
Norms, standardization of, 212
Norten (UK), 154
North American Free Trade Agreement (NAFTA), 291
Norton, 307
NovaCare, 387
Novel strategy, 138
N-person games, 7
Nucor Steel, 102, 472

Objectives, 10
    clear, decisive, 15–16
Objectivity, dangers of, 201–3
Olympic Games, 247
One-best approach, 209
One best way concepts in management, 371
On-the-job training, 373
Open-ended diagnosis, 373–74
Operating adhocracy, 407, 412, 418
Operating core, 209
Operating turnaround, 317
Operational effectiveness, 16–18
Opportunities
    matching, and competence, 78–79
    resources relating to, 74–77
Opportunity costs, 110
Optimization of effort, 21
Options, balancing commitment and, 253–54
Orbital Sciences, 331
Organigrams, 374, 406
Organizational adaptation, 468–71
Organizational awareness, building, 186
Organizational design, 60
Organizational economies, 306
Organizational evolution, patterns in, 177–81
Organizational forms, design of new, 234–41
Organizational politics, 419–20
Organizational process perspective, 155–59
Organizational separation, 254
Organizational structure, 207
Organization capabilities, 110–12
Organization evolution
    executive leadership and, 181–82
    patterns in, 181
Organization planning, strategy and, 226–34

Organizations, 105, 207–41, 373
  ambidextrous, 208, 238–39
  basic parts of, 209–10
  challenges to, 361–69
  configurations, 219–26
  coordinating mechanisms, 210–12
  diversified, 222–23
  entrepreneurial, 220–21, 405
  essential parameters of, 212–17
  front-back, 208, 239–40
  innovative, 223–24
  learning, 50–51
  machine, 221–22
  missionary, 224–25
  network, 208, 236–38
  political, 225–26
  professional, 222
  reading mind of, 142
  sense-and-respond, 208, 240
  situational factors, 217–19
    age and size, 217–18
    environment, 218–19
    power, 219
    technical system, 218
  spin-out, 208, 238
  structuring of, 209–26
  virtual, 208, 235–36
Otis Elevators, 291
Outputs, standardization of, 211–12
Outsourcing, 17, 129, 173
Overt leadership, 400

Pace, maintaining, in strategic decision making, 151–52
Packing strategy, 134
Parallel decentralization, 216
Parent company, linkages between alliances and, 269
Participative management, 41
Partnering, 17, 429–30
Partnerships, 392
Pattern
  recognizer, 417
  strategy, 4–6, 9
Patterning, 380
Pattern-of-behavior explanations, 62
Peer pressure, 385
Peer review, journals, 378
Penetration strategies, 123, 130
People, managing through, 40–43
People Express, 387
PepsiCo., 457
Perfection, 384–85
Performance
  sustaining superior, 105–12
Performance control system, 215
  social performance of, 443–44
Performance myopia, 271
Personalized control, 448
Personal-service organization, 376
Personal vision, encouraging, 63
Personnel, rotation of, between alliance and parent, 269
Perspective strategy, 7–8, 9
Petronas, 447
Peugeot, 446
Philip Morris, 96, 454
Philips, 445
Pigeonholing process, 373–74, 375, 380, 381
Pillsbury, 186, 187
PIMS project, 23
Planned change, 170–71
Planned strategy, 6
Planners, roles of, 345–46
Planning
  image, 141
  as impediment to strategic thinking in airline, 343–44
  as programming supermarket chain, 343
  role of, 344–45
  scenario, 151
Planning school, 23, 24, 27
Plans
  roles of, 345
  strategy, 4, 9
Ploy strategy, 9
Pockets of resistance, 180
Polaroid, 97, 176, 318
Policies, 10
Political organization, 225–26
Political strategies, 7

Politics, 76–77
  competition through, 466
  defusing, in strategic decision making, 152
Pooled interdependence, 277
Portfolio management, 433, 455
Portfolio of forms, 462
Portfolio restructuring, 173
Portfolio theory, 153, 161
Position
  strategy as, 6–7
Positional advantage, 84
Position-based advantages, 85
Positioning, 9, 17
  access-based, 19
  needs-based, 18–19
  strategic, 22, 127–38
  variety-based, 18
Positioning company, 101
Positioning school, 23, 24, 27
Positions
  liaison, 215
  sustainable strategic, 19–20
Potter as craftsman, 141–49
Power
  macro, 25
  micro, 25
  in professional organization, 376
Power-behavioral approach, 183
Power game, 53–54
Power school, 25
Power schools, 27
Price differentiation strategy, 121, 130
Price-experience curves, 353–54
Primary activities, 456
Primary clients, interaction between EPC firms and, 429
Private information, 106
Problems
  of coordination, 381
  of discretion, 381
  of innovation, 381–82
Process change, 361, 363
Process innovations and improvements, 353
Process reengineering, 197, 304
Process strategy, 6, 145
Procter & Gamble, 126, 230, 231, 276, 277, 279, 287, 457, 458–59, 471
Product change, 361
Product development
  costs, 286
  strategies, 123–24, 130
Production-driven alliances, 262
Productivity frontier, 17–18
Product life-cycle shifts, 179
Product line rationalization, 123
Product-process change matrix, 361–62
Products
  differentiation, 96, 165
  interdependence, 277
  offering in global strategy, 282
  prototype, 421
  redesign, 353
  standardization, 284, 353
  substitute, 100
Professional associations, 381
Professional bureaucracies, 370, 372, 373, 382, 411
Professional forms, 463
Professional judgment, decisions made by, 378
Professional labor, professional service firm and market for, 393–94
Professional operators, work of, 372–73
Professional organizations, 222, 372–82
  basic structure, 372–76
  change in, 382
  conditions of, 376
  issues associated with, 380–82
  power in, 376
  problems of innovation in, 381–82
  strategy formation in, 377–80
  three levels of decision making in, 377–80
  training in, 372–73
  types of, 417
Professional service firm, 371, 390–97
  balancing, 396–97
  capacity planning in, 392
  economics of, 392
  market for, 394–96
  market for professional labor and, 393–94
  organizational structure of, 391

project team structure in, 391–92
  revenue generation in, 392–93
Professional service projects, 395
Professional work, roles of administrators of, 374–76
Proficiency, 462
Programmable competencies, knowledge base of, 428
Programs, 10
Progress, monitoring, 422
Project-based firms, 404
  core competencies of, 426–31
    entrepreneurial, 427
    evaluative, 428–29
    relational, 429–30
    technical, 427–28
Projectiles, 127
Project team structure, 391–92, 394, 395–96
Project work, 411
Promotion policy, 393
Public responses, to problems, 382
Public service commission, 438
Public sphere, diversified organization in, 444–45
Pure customization, 247
Pure standardization, 246

Quality
  improved, in global strategy, 283
  trade-off between cost and, 202
Quality circles, 91
Quality differentiation strategy, 121, 130
Quality of work life, 41
Quantum approach, 168
Quantum theory of change, 146–47
Quebecor, 18
Quiet management, 479–83

Rareness, 103–4
Rational analysis, 379–80
Rational conservatism, 242
Rational control, 141
Realized strategy, 5
Real-time information, 150
Reasoning, inductive, 381
Reciprocal responsibility, 90
Red Cross, 122
Redundancy, tolerance for, 270
Reengineering, 17, 202
  enthusiasm for, 201
Refreezing, 321
Reinforcers, 84
Reinforcing mechanisms, 134
Rejuvenation, crescendo model of, 189–97
Related diversification, 230–31
Related-product firm, 438
Relational competencies in project-based firms, 429
Renault-Nissan, 291, 293, 446
Renewal, four-step process of, 168
Reorientations, 176
Repetition, 317
Representation, 317–18
Republicans, 379
Resource-based view, 108–9
Resources, 83–84, 128
  mobilizing in whitespace, 420–21
  relating opportunities to, 74–77
Response lags, 107
Responsibility, reciprocal, 90
Restructuring, 433, 455–56
Results, measuring, in whitespace, 421
Retaliation, threats of, 106–7
Revenues, generating, 392–93
Revitalization, 168, 169, 348
Reynolds Metals, 110
RGIS, 477
Rhone Poulenc, 446
Richardson-Vicks, 287
Risk, diversification and, 441
Rivals, 127
Roche, 254
Rose, Janet, 371

Saatchi & Saatchi, 284, 433
Saks Fifth Avenue, 289
Sale-leaseback arrangements, 85
Samsung, 289
San Miguel, 447
Sanoñ S. A., 264–65
Sara Lee, 451
SAS, 183

Scale economies, 385–86
Scale effect, 350
Scarcity, 105
Scenario planning, 151
Scheduling, 36
Scope strategies, 121–22, 133–35
Sears, 341
Seattle Computer Products, 329
Second movers, 137
Second-order fit, 21
Segmentation strategies, 122, 133
Segmented market, 132
Segmented standardization, 246
Self-interest, 379
Selkirk Group, 3, 273, 314, 433
Semco, 475–79
Senior managers, whitespace and, 421–22
Sense-and-respond organization, 208, 240
Separation, organizational, 254
Service industries, stages of, 227
Services, internationalization in, 289–90
Seven-Up Company, 454
Shared vision, building, 63–64
Shareholder value, 480
    diversification in creating, 453
Sharing, 384
    activities, 433, 457–58
Shell, 60–61
Shelters, 135
Siam Cement, 447
Siemens, 446
Silicon Valley approach, to innovation, 89
Simple structure, 315
Singapore Airlines, 447
Singer Sewing Machine, 480
Single-loop learning, 86
Six Sigma total quality initiative, 309
Size, divisionalization and, 437
Size economies, 106
Skills, 83
    standardization of, 212
Skunkworks, 414
Slack, 108, 110
SNECMA, 446
Social constructionist view, 206
Social performance of performance control system,
    443–44
Society, 76
Sodehxo Alliance, 290
Sony Corporation, 3, 266, 283, 314, 405, 433, 471
Sophisticated innovation, 404, 405
Sourcing efficiencies, 286
Southwest Airlines, 18, 19, 20, 102
Span of control, 214–15, 406
Spider web, 371, 388–89, 389
Spin-offs, 323
Spin-out organization, 208, 238
Stability, managing, 147–48
Stable change, 361–62
Stable competition, 136
Stable process change, 362, 364–66, 366–68
Stable product, 362
Standardization, 211, 243
    customized, 246
    forms of, 373
    of norms, 212
    of outputs, 211–12
    pure, 246
    segmented, 246
    of skills, 212
    of work processes, 211, 212
Standardized customization, 122
Standardize work, 382
Standard operating procedures (SOP), 357
Standing committees, 215
Starburst, 371, 387–88, 389
Start-up management, 312–33
Statement of corporate vision, 299
Static efficiency, 306–7
Steinberg, Inc., 146, 318–22
Steinway and Sons, 84
Sterling Drug, 264–65
Steward, leader as, 62–63
Straddling, 19
Strategic accommodation, 160
Strategic action, 99
Strategic analysis, effective, 94
Strategic apex, 209

Strategic change, 166–97, 229–32
    in automobile firm, 346–47
    causes of, 166–67
    convergence and upheaval, 176–83
    crescendo model of rejuvenation, 189–97
    logical incrementalism, 183–88
    managing, 166
    mapping processes of, 170–71
    programs of comprehensive, 171–76
    transforming organizations, 168–76
Strategic choices, 324–25
Strategic control groups, 446
Strategic decision making, 149–52
    building collective intuition, 150
    defuse politics, 152
    maintaining pace, 151–52
    myth of, 150
    stimulating quick conflict, 150–51
Strategic decisions, 10, 72
Strategic ethics, 295–99
Strategic failures, attributions of, 147
Strategic goals, 10
Strategic group, 132
Strategic implications, 355
Strategic intent, 88–91
Strategic learning, 144, 161
Strategic management, 147–49
    conventional view of, 145
    prating about, 26–29
    traditional view of, 142
Strategic objectives
    leaning in, 264
    leaping in, 265–66
    learning in, 263–64
    leveraging in, 264–65
    linking in, 265
    locking out in, 266
Strategic orientation, 146
Strategic partnership, 237
Strategic planning, 147
Strategic policies, 10
Strategic positioning, 22, 127–38
    origins of, 18–19
    products and services, 130–31
    rivalry competition, 136–38
    strategic positions, 133–35
    target markets, 131–33
    vehicle organization, 128–29
Strategic programming, 10, 344–45
Strategic reorientations, 145–47
Strategic responsiveness, diversification and, 441
Strategic revolutions, 146, 380
    in machine organizations, 349
Strategic thinking
    knowledge involved in, 148
    planning as impediment to, in airline, 343–44
Strategic turnaround, 317, 349
Strategic uncertainty, 323
Strategic vision, 314, 316, 317–18
Strategic window, 137
Strategies, 2–29
    in business context, 152–53
    for change, 10–16
    classical approach to, 11–14
    as cognition, 203–6
    collective, 7
    competitive, 3, 83
    competitive forces in shaping, 94–102
    consensus, 6
    corporate, 72–79
    crafting, 141–49
    crafting of successful, by entrepreneurs, 326–33
    criteria for effective, 15–16
    cultural context of, 153
    customizing, 122
    defined, 16–22, 152–53, 160
    deliberate, 2, 5
    as deliberate process, 143–44
    dimensions of, 14–16
    disconnected, 6
    economic, 73
    effective, 144–45
    emergent, 2
    entrepreneurial, 6
    generic, 83
    ideological, 6
    imposed, 6

    intended, 5
    Japanese view of, 153
    military-diplomatic, 11
    military origins of, 142
    need for eclecticism in, 9
    organization planning and, 226–34
    pattern, 9
    as pattern, 4–6
    perspective, 9
    as perspective, 7–8
    plan, 9
    as plan, 4
    planned, 6
    ploy, 9
    political, 7
    as position, 6–7, 9
    realized, 5, 143
    secrets of creation, 472–74
    tactics versus, 11
    traditional approaches to, 149
    umbrella, 6, 145
    uniqueness, 79
    unrealized, 5
Strategists, 30–69
    artists as, 47
    craftsmen as, 47–48
    learning organizations and, 50–51, 57–66
    in making policy decisions, 52–57
    manager's job as, 32–46
    middle managers as, 66–69
    rules for, 115
    teamwork and, 48–50
    technocrats as, 46–47, 50
    vision of, 51–52
Strategy analysis, 92–138
    competitive advantage in, 102–5
    competitive forces in, 94–102
    competitive maneuvering in, 112–15
    effective, 94
    generic business strategies in, 115–27
    strategic positioning and, 127–38
    in sustaining superior performance, 105–12
Strategy evaluation
    challenge of, 80
    competitive advantages, 83–85
    consistency in, 81–82
    consonance in, 82–83
    feasibility in, 85–86
    process of, 86–87
Strategy formation, 23, 139–65
    in administrative adhocracy, 413–14
    crafting strategy in, 141–49
    decision making in, 149–52
    entrepreneurial approach to, in supermarket chain,
        318–22
    essence of, 94
    grass-roots model of, 415–17
    Honda effect in, 152–65
    in innovative organization, 413–17
    in operating adhocracy, 413
    in professional organization, 377–80
Strategy formulation, 70–91
    corporate, 72–79
    evaluating business strategy in, 80–87
    intent in, 88–91
Strategy hierarchy, 91
Strategy industry, 141
    emergence of, 153
    Honda Motor Company and, 160–65
Strategy innovation, quest for value and, 471–75
Strategy process, 6, 145
    reflecting on, 22–29
Strengths, identifying, 78
Substitute products, 100, 179
Substitution, 107
Sumitomo, 446
Summary statement of strategy, 73
Sunk costs, 110, 135
    fallacy of, 251
Sunk misfit, 135
Super conductivity, 248
Supermarket chain
    entrepreneurial approach to strategy formation in,
        318–22
    planning as programming in, 343
Supplier group, power of, 98
Support activities, 119, 456
Support differentiation strategy, 121, 130

Support staff, 209, 374
Sustainability, 93, 134
    fit and, 21–22
    threats to, 105–8
Sustainable competitive advantage, 93
    building, 108–10
Sustainable strategic position, trade-offs for, 19–20
Sustaining superior performance, 105–12
Swire, 446
Switching strategies for EPC firms, 430
SWOT analysis, 102, 103, 206
Symmetry, 275–76
Synergy, 125, 129, 180, 254
    between mass customization and continuous
        improvement, 368
    between mass production and invention, 364
System, culture in, 400–401
Systematic redesign, 172
Systemic analysis, 2
Systems approach, 412–13
Systems knowledge intellect, 389
Systems thinking, 65–66

Tacit knowledge, 141, 268
Tactical adjustments, 186
Tactical moves, 326
Tactics, 5
    frame-breaking, 151
    strategies versus, 11
Tailored customization, 247
Takeover, 123
Talon, 153
Targets, 127
Task forces, 215
Tasks, innovation and, 356–58
Teacher, leader as, 61–62
Teamwork, 429–30
    managerial styles and, 48–50
Technical competencies in project-based firms, 427
Technical standards, compatible, 286
Technocrats, 433
    identifying, 46–47
    triumph of, 50
Technological uncertainty, 323
Technology, 75, 242–55
    customizing customization, 243–48
    sharing, 268
Technology-driven alliances, 262
Technostructure, 209, 374, 410
Teledyne, 232
Telefónica, 289
Temporary adhocracy, 412
Terminating alliances, 260
Textron, 232, 443
Theory Y, 41
Therapist, middle managers as, 68–69
Thermo Electron, 238
Thinking, divergent, 407
Thin market, 132
Third-order fit, 21
3M Company, 129, 145, 160, 231, 307, 308, 309, 438, 451,
    457, 458

Tightrope artist, middle managers as, 69
Time-based competition, 17, 161
Time-based theory, 163
Timing entry, 325–26
Tolerance for redundancy, 270
Top-down change, 167, 172–74, 175
Top-down hierarchy, 378
Total customer service, 91
Total quality management, 17, 41, 169, 197, 304
Toyota, 4, 159–60, 287, 289, 446, 466, 473
Toys "R" Us, 290
Trade-offs for sustainable strategic position, 19–20
Trade policies, favorable, 286
Training, 212–13
    in professional organization, 372–73
Transaction-cost economics, 305–6
Transferable marketing, 285
Transfer-of-skills concept, 433, 456–57, 457
Transformation, 26, 171
Transforming organizations, 168–76
Transition, dangers of inappropriate, 418
Trend analysis, 62
Trial-and-error learning, 253
Triumph, 154
Trust, climate of, 270
Trustworthiness, 297
TRW, 458
Turnaround, 168, 169, 171, 348
    operating, 317
    strategic, 317
Turnover, 394
TV Asahi Theatrical Productions, 273
Two-person game, 7

Umbrella strategies, 6, 145, 415, 416
Unbundling, 126
Uncertainty
    strategic, 323
    technological, 323
Undifferentiation strategy, 121
Unfreezing, 320–21
Uniform marketing, 284
Unilever, 275–76, 278, 282, 287
Union Camp, 231
Unipart Group of Companies, 461
United States Football League (USFL), 107
United Technologies, 459
Unit grouping, 213–14
Unit-level mobilizing, 172
Unit size, 214
Unity of command, 406
Unrealized strategies, 5
Unrelated diversification, 231–32
Unsegmentation strategy, 122
Unstable competition, 136
Upstream, 129
Upstream business strategy, 116
Upstream companies, 228, 229

Value-added activities, 423
    location of, 282

Value chain, 93, 128, 457
    customization, 245
    functions, 267
    generic, 118–19
Values, 103, 294–310
    activities, 119
    adding, by using cellular organization, 425–27
    creating, for people, 308–10
    strategy innovation and quest for, 471–75
Variety-based positioning, 18
Ventures
    gauging attractiveness of, 329–30
    screening out unpromising, 327–29
Venturing, 169
Vertical decentralization, 216
Vertical integration, 123–24, 129, 339, 340
Viability, maintaining, 54–55
Virgin Airways, 290
Virgin Atlantic, 472
Virtual organization, 129, 208, 235–36
Visionary leadership, 317–18
Volkswagenwerk, 146, 147, 287, 347, 414
Vulnerable fit, 134

WalMart, 102, 105
Warner Brothers, 3
Waters, James A., 405n
Westinghouse, 307
Westpac Banking Corporation, 240
Weyerhauser, 229
Whirlpool, 289
Whitespace, 419–23
    building enthusiasm in, 422
    building momentum in, 421
    defined, 419
    establishing legitimacy in, 420
    managing, 420–21
    measuring results in, 421
    mobilizing resources in, 420–21
    monitoring process in, 421
    moving into, 419–20
    moving to blackspace, 422–23
    providing support in, 421–22
    senior managers and, 421–22
    strategic imperatives in, 421
Winnipeg Symphony Orchestra, 398
Wipro Corporation, 208, 273, 433
Withdrawal strategies, 125
Work books, 428–29
Workbrain, 314
Work processes, standardization of, 211, 212
Work specialization, 353
World Color Press, 18
World Football League (WFL), 107
Wrigley Chewing Gum, 232

Xerox, 88, 89, 108, 251, 350

Yamaha, 153

Zero-based budgeting, 87
Zero-sum perspective, 429–30

CASES

1   Robin Hood   3
2   Astral Records, Ltd., North America   5
3   MacArthur and the Philippines   27
4   Rudi Gassner and the Executive Committee of BMG International (A)   40
5   Arista Records   53
6   Algodonera del Plata   57
7   HBO   62
8   IMPSAT   66
9   Canon: Competing on Capabilities   75
10 MP3.com   88
11 WFNX-101.7FM and Boston's Radio Wars   93
12 Beijing Mirror Corp.   109
13 Lufthansa 2000: Maintaining the Change Momentum   124
14 The London Free Press (A)— A Strategic Change   146
15 NBC   156
16 LVMH: Taking the Western *Art de Vivre* to the World   160
17 Kami Corporation   171
18 Strategic Planning at the New York Botanical Garden (A)   176
19 Napoleon Bonaparte: Victim of an Inferior Strategy?   190
20 Honda Motor Company 1994   200
21 The Acer Group: Building an Asian Multinational   217
22 AmBev: The Making of a Brazilian Giant   229
23 Wipro Corporation: Balancing the Future   234
24 TV Asahi Theatrical Productions, Inc.   254
25 Selkirk Group in Asia   263
26 Sportsmake: A Crisis of Succession   273
27 S.A. Chupa Chups   276
28 Mountbatten and India   290
29 Saatchi & Saatchi Worldwide: Globalization and Diversification   309
30 McKinsey & Company: Managing Knowledge and Learning   319

31   Sony: Regeneration (A)   333

32   Reorganization at Axion
     Consulting (A)   348

33   Reorganization at Axion
     Consulting (B)   350

34   Empire Plastics   352

35   Kao Corporation   355

36   Unipart Group of Companies:
     Uniting Stakeholders to Build a
     World-Class Enterprise   370

37   Workbrain Corporation   382

38   Warner Brothers   390

39   Intel Corporation   394

40   The National Bicycle Industrial
     Company: Implementing a
     Strategy of Mass-Customization
     411

41   NovaCare, Inc.   423

42   Lechabile: IT as a People Business
     435

43   Phil Chan   447

44   Natura: The Magic Behind Brazil's
     Most Admired Company   455

45   Restaurant with a Difference   474

Robin Hood

It was in the spring of the second year of his insurrection against the High Sheriff of Nottingham that Robin Hood took a walk in Sherwood forest. As he walked he pondered the progress of the campaign, the disposition of his forces, the Sheriff's recent moves and the options that confronted him.

The revolt against the Sheriff had begun as a personal crusade, it erupted out of Robin's conflict with the Sheriff and his administration. However, alone Robin Hood could do little. He therefore sought allies, men with grievances and a deep sense of injustice. Later he welcomed all who came, asking few questions and only demanding a willingness to serve. Strength, he believed, lay in numbers.

He spent the first year forging the group into a disciplined band, united in enmity against the Sheriff, and willing to live outside the law. The band's organization was simple. Robin ruled supreme, making all important decisions. He delegated specific tasks to his lieutenants. Will Scarlett was in charge of intelligence and scouting. His main job was to shadow the Sheriff and his men, always alert to their next move. He also collected information on the travel plans of rich merchants and tax collectors. Little John kept discipline among the men, and saw to it that their archery was at the high peak that their profession demanded. Scarlock took care of the finances, converting loot to cash, paying shares of the take and finding suitable hiding places for the surplus. Finally, Much the Miller's son had the difficult task of provisioning the ever-increasing band of Merrymen.

The increasing size of the band was a source of satisfaction for Robin, but also a source of concern. The fame of his Merrymen was spreading, and new recruits poured in from every corner of England. As the band grew larger, their small bivouac became a major encampment. Between raids the men milled about, talking and playing games. Vigilance was in decline, and discipline was becoming harder to enforce. 'Why?' Robin reflected, 'I don't know half the men I run into these days.'

The growing band was also beginning to exceed the food capacity of the forest. Game was becoming scarce, and supplies had to be obtained from outlying villages. The cost of buying food was beginning to drain the band's financial reserves at the very moment when revenues were in decline. Travelers, especially those with the most to lose, were now giving the forest a wide berth. This was costly and inconvenient to them, but it was preferable to having all their goods confiscated.

Robin believed that the time had come for the Merrymen to change their policy of outright confiscation of goods to one of a fixed transit tax. His lieutenants strongly resisted this idea. They were proud of the Merrymen's famous motto: 'Rob the rich and give to the poor.' 'The farmers and the townspeople', they argued, 'are our most important allies.' 'How can we tax them, and still hope for their help in our fight against the Sheriff?'

Prepared by Joseph Lampel, New York University.
Copyright Joseph Lampel © 1985, revised 1991.

Robin wondered how long the Merrymen could keep to the ways and methods of their early days. The Sheriff was growing stronger and better organized. He now had the money and the men, and was beginning to harass the band, probing for its weaknesses. The tide of events was beginning to turn against the Merrymen. Robin felt that the campaign must be decisively concluded before the Sheriff had a chance to deliver a mortal blow. 'But how', he wondered, 'could this be done?'

Robin had often entertained the possibility of killing the Sheriff, but the chances for this seemed increasingly remote. Besides, killing the Sheriff might satisfy his personal thirst for revenge, but it would not improve the situation. Robin had hoped that the perpetual state of unrest, and the Sheriff's failure to collect taxes, would lead to his removal from office. Instead, the Sheriff used his political connections to obtain reinforcement. He had powerful friends at court, and was well regarded by the regent, Prince John.

Prince John was vicious and volatile. He was consumed by his unpopularity among the people, who wanted the imprisoned King Richard back. He also lived in constant fear of the barons, who had first given him the regency, but were now beginning to dispute his claim to the throne. Several of these barons had set out to collect ransom that would release Richard the Lionheart from his jail in Austria. Robin was invited to join the conspiracy in return for future amnesty. It was a dangerous proposition. Provincial banditry was one thing, court intrigue another. Prince John's spies were everywhere. If the plan failed the pursuit would be relentless, and retribution swift.

The sound of the supper horn startled Robin from his thoughts. There was the smell of roasting venison in the air. Nothing was resolved or settled. Robin headed for camp promising himself that he would give these problems his utmost attention after tomorrow's raid.

CASE 2

Astral Records, Ltd., North America

The date was August 24, 1993, and Sarah Conner felt overwhelmed and more than a little disoriented. Only two days ago, she had rushed from her office at Bendini, Lambert & Locke (BLL), a well-known venture-capital firm, to board the company jet for Knoxville, Tennessee, where she would assume operating control of Astral Records, Ltd., North America (Astral N.A.). One week earlier, Astral N.A.'s president and chief executive officer, Sir Maxwell S. Hammer, had been killed in a tragic hunting accident. As the owner of 60 percent of the company, BLL had felt an immediate need to protect its investment. Accordingly, BLL's managing director, T.J. Lambert, had asked Conner to run the company while the firm planned its next moves. He had assured her that she would be in Pigeon Forge, Tennessee, for at least a year.

Conner was the obvious choice. After graduating from Wellesley College in 1982 with a degree in classical music, she had gone to work for Galaxy Records, first in marketing and later in production. In 1987 she was admitted to the Darden Graduate School of Business Administration, where she was president of the Entrepreneurs Club, a Shermet scholar, and, upon graduation, a recipient of the Faculty Award for academic excellence. Hoping to combine her love of music with her business acumen, she joined BLL as assistant manager of the entertainment portfolio. That BLL was acquiring new music-industry companies made it the perfect and first choice among her several job offers.

Conner had progressed quickly during her four years at BLL. Nevertheless, she was rather surprised at how quickly she had been asked to assume operating control of one of the fastest growing compact-disc (CD) manufacturers in the world. In two weeks she was scheduled to meet with BLL's principals. They wanted a status report, a set of recommendations, and an action plan for the next year. She knew that a number of important issues were likely to need attention in the wake of Sir Maxwell's death.

THE CD INDUSTRY

In principle, CD technology was an evolutionary refinement of records and tapes. Under the old technology, music and voice were converted into electronic impulses that were then embedded in a medium such as vinyl or magnetic tape. These impulses were then decoded and amplified to reproduce the original music. CDs, however, represented a huge technological leap forward. Sound was converted into digital code that could then be decoded by a laser to reproduce exactly the original digital information.

CDs were produced in two steps. First, a "master" was made. An extremely flat, glass master disc received an adhesive and a thin (0.12 micron) layer of light-sensitive photoresist on one side. The photoresist was then exposed to a 100-milliwatt laser beam that applied the sequence of

This case was prepared by Lynn A. Isabella, Associate Professor of Business Administration, and Ted Forbes. Copyright © 1993 by the University of Virginia Darden School Foundation, Charlottesville, VA. All rights reserved. Revised August 1994.

coded digits in real time to the photoresist. After an alkaline bath removed unwanted resist, a pattern of micropits was left. A nickel impression, known as the "father," was made from the glass master. The positive "mothers" that were produced from the negative father were used to make the stampers of the polycarbonate substrate.

Because the photoresist was damaged when it was developed, the exposed glass master could normally be put to use only once. Four or five nickel mothers were usually made from a single father. Another four or five stampers could be sputtered in metal from each mother, for a total of up to 25 stampers from the single master disc. The master could thus become the source of up to 10,000 discs per stamper, or 250,000 CDs.

In the second step, a mold received polycarbonate resin that was stamped to make the hard, transparent CD wafer. A vaporized metal layer, usually aluminum, was applied in a vacuum chamber as the surface that reflected the laser beam for player reading. Then came another hard, protective resin layer, the printed label, automatic inspection, and packaging.

CDs were first mass-produced in 1980. Since then, CD technology had seen mostly refinements rather than breakthroughs. For example, in 1989 CD-production cycle times were 13 seconds; now those times were less than 7 seconds, and leading-edge technology produced CDs in less than 5 seconds. The machinery was more efficient and less expensive than the old equipment, with the cost of a new small plant in the range of $8–$10 million.

Although industry dynamics had stabilized in recent years, predicting volume and designing appropriate capacity were as much art as science. "Correct capacity, either annually or monthly, is like an Indiana spring. It's only two or three days a year. You're either over or under capacity. If we weren't talking about being over capacity, we'd be talking about a shortage; it's never correct very long," stated Robert McGee, executive director of ComDisc, a trade association.

Quality had improved dramatically over the past 10 years. In most plants, quality control was completely automated. The implementation of statistical process controls had a tremendous impact. In 1986 industry reject rates were approximately 12 percent. By 1993 rates were as low as 1.5 percent. "The discs coming off the machines today are simply better quality. Because of our knowledge and machine consistency, inspection is made easy," said Billie Holliday, director of quality for Celestial Records.

As the technology matured, producers discovered that cover art was increasingly important in selling CDs. Many CD replicators now had 5-color capacity. Most CD producers used silk-screen printing, and the large operations used offset printing. Over the years, packaging was standardized around the "jewel box," a hard, plastic case used to hold both the CD and accompanying liner notes. Efforts to move toward "environmentally friendly" packaging had not succeeded.

Wholesale prices for finished product averaged $1.30. Packaging costs were approximately 23 cents per disc and the finished disc itself cost approximately 90 cents. Industry analysts asserted that price competition among disc replicators had come down to pennies and half pennies, as opposed to differences of 15–25 cents in the late 1980s. "When the business is soft and you establish a price, it's very difficult to establish a higher price once business picks up. The gross margins on CDs have eroded tremendously over the past five years. I don't see any more maneuvering left on the price," said Eleanor Rigby, record-industry analyst with Sergeant and Pepper Investments.

Record labels contracted with manufacturing facilities to produce the finished product. The labels then sold, either directly or through a distributor, to the retail outlets. Sales from label/distributor to retail outlets were on a consignment basis. Continued Rigby,

> Although quantity discounts are available, most labels are placing smaller orders and then reordering on a more frequent basis to keep inventory at manageable levels. There are only so many returns a label can take and still turn a profit, so we're seeing labels be a bit more cautious about their opening orders and then coming back for more in a shorter turnaround period than before.

Recent advances in laser technology had opened up the market in both the computer and video arenas. Because the technologies were essentially the same, audio CD manufacturers could easily produce CD-ROM discs for computers or laser discs for video. Sam Cooke, vice president of marketing and sales, Galaxy Records, asserted,

> Quality of the CD in the industry is fairly standard now. A disc we stamp is the same quality as any of the other major houses. What might set a company apart, though, is what we do in terms of fulfillment services, packaging and design, and drop shipping. Customer service has definitely become the buzzword among replicators for the 90s.

COMPANY HISTORY

Astral Records was founded by Count Francisco Smirnov, a Franco-Russian nobleman, in 1967 in Wollaston-on-Heath, England. Smirnov was a professional musician who had a vision of building a new kind of record company. Appalled by the quality of records at that time, Smirnov set out to construct a studio whose sole purpose would be to produce classical-music record masters of a quality greater than that of any other company in the world. The count had been disappointed to learn that the long-playing records made from his masters were little better in sound quality than most others on the market. Undaunted, he decided to move into manufacturing.

Smirnov's vision was of a utopian musical village, where classical musicians and company directors would reside in luxury and elegance. The count wanted nothing to impede the creative process: "Beautiful music can only happen in beautiful surroundings. If society continues to ignore the high arts, then society will be led into a barbarian condition."

In 1975 Astral purchased a 50-room Georgian mansion on 187 acres near the top of the Cynwyr valley not far from Wales. Each step in the production process would be carried out onsite. The ballroom was turned into one of the most elegant recording studios in the industry. The count and five of the seven managing directors continued to live the vision, residing in the exquisitely furnished headquarters and taking all their meals together. Key business decisions were often made casually over lunch and dinner. Recording musicians were invited to live on the grounds for as long as they needed to complete their projects.

Astral Records might well have continued to operate in this idyllic setting, but for a major technological breakthrough. The count was captivated by the emerging compact-disc technology. He immediately saw the medium's potential for producing virtually flawless recordings. The combination of pure digital sound and laser technology became the count's obsession, even though he would be going up against the industry giants.

Instead of simply licensing CD technology from the giants, the count and his researchers decided to develop their own process. In eight months they developed production capabilities that not only saved them millions in royalty fees, but also won them a Queen's Award for technological achievement. Astral Records was the first company in the United Kingdom to produce CDs, two years ahead of its major competitors. By the mid-1980s, more than 50 record labels were using Astral's facilities to record, produce, and manufacture CDs. Astral's own labels constituted a mere 10 percent of the company's sales.

Astral's bold, yet whimsical, business decisions had been wildly successful. In 1980 Astral Records, Ltd., U.K., employed 27 people and grossed 600,000 pounds. By 1992 the company had 500 employees and turned a pre-tax profit of £2.7 million on sales of £20 million.

ASTRAL RECORDS, LTD., NORTH AMERICA

In 1986 the count entered into negotiations with Bendini, Lambert & Locke to secure capital for a planned expansion into the U.S. market. The market for CDs was booming and the plant in England was struggling to keep pace with demand. One night Smirnov had a vision of the new facility: It would be nestled among mountains and streams surrounded by lush pastures. In 1987, in exchange for 60 percent ownership of the U.S. operation, BLL financed the construction of a $14 million plant on 265 acres in Pigeon Forge, Tennessee. The count chose Sir Maxwell S. Hammer, an English aristocrat and hunting partner, to run the U.S. operation. "I shall endeavor to carry the mission of Astral Records to the States," Sir Maxwell stated.

Astral Records, Ltd., N.A., was predominately a manufacturing facility, capable of pressing 100,000 CDs per day. Ninety percent of its business was producing CDs for a variety of other record labels. Diverging from the Astral, U.K., core business and classical tradition, Sir Maxwell had begun to explore recording and producing CDs beyond Astral's classical catalog, which contained 300 titles. Sir Maxwell's wide-ranging interests ran from classical to blues to rock and roll to new age to rap. Having seen the phenomenal sales of many of the artists whose CDs Astral manufactured under contract, Sir Maxwell entered into negotiations with a variety of country, world-music, and new-age artists to bring them under Astral's own labels.

Under Sir Maxwell's leadership, Astral Records quickly became known as the premier CD manufacturer in the United States. Astral's stringent quality-control standards were far higher than those set by its competitors. Within the industry, an Astral CD was widely believed to be playable without error on any CD player. "It's quality. I think if we lost that, then the company would be truly adrift. Music and all the arts are extremely fragile creations and it's quite simple to lose that very thing after which you are chasing," said Mr. Kite, Astral's celebrated music director.

Sir Maxwell built a reputation as an innovator in the industry. Astral invented multisonic recording, a method of capturing reverberated sounds from the rear of the orchestra. Astral also pioneered the use of new packaging systems that used recycled paper. The company's current research focused on creating the ability to compress feature-length motion pictures onto a standard 5-inch disc. In his last interview before his death, Sir Maxwell stated, "People no longer want to just hear music; they want to see it. Video is the future."

He had also embarked on a path of expansion in order to increase capacity in a growing market. In 1991 the company completed a $3-million capital project that increased capacity by 40 percent. Production lines were expanded from five to eight, and two new mastering systems were added. Astral represented the latest in CD-manufacturing systems.

Sir Maxwell ran the U.S. operation as though it were his own colonial outpost. "Sir Max," as his employees called him, affectionately referred to his top managers as "toppers." He quickly established a reputation as a demanding taskmaster, and he insisted on being involved in every aspect of the business. He oversaw every major decision.

Not surprisingly, the managers and employees at Astral were feeling adrift in the wake of Sir Maxwell's death.

SARAH CONNER TAKES CHARGE

At 8:00 A.M., Sarah Conner sat in the walnut-paneled conference room overlooking the Great Smokey Mountains. Sir Maxwell's office was elegant, but Conner did not feel comfortable in it yet. In front of her was an assortment of memos, phone messages, faxes, and other correspondence that had accumulated, mostly over the past week (see the exhibits that follow). Conner believed she needed to deal with all of these papers and also begin preparing the report for the upcoming meeting with the partners from BLL. The next couple of weeks promised to be interesting.

EXHIBIT 1

| ASTRAL RECORDS, Ltd. | *North America* | *Pigeon Forge, TN* | Tel. (615) 356-9889 |

TO: All Astral Toppers
FROM: Sir Maxwell S. Hammer
DATE: August 18, 1993
SUBJECT: Staff Meeting

Please join me for high tea in the boardroom on August 24th at 3:00 P.M.

EXHIBIT 2

| ASTRAL RECORDS, Ltd. | *North America* | *Pigeon Forge, TN* | Tel. (615) 356-9889 |

August 24, 1993

Sarah—

Welcome to Astral. We are all glad to have you with us.

I've gone ahead and told our toppers that you would want to meet them at 3 p.m. as was scheduled. It was so shocking about Sir Max!

I'm sure you'd appreciate some advice from an "old pro." (I've been Sir Max's right-hand man since the beginning.) Sir Max commanded respect and you should do the same. Make quick decisions. The E.P.A. can wait, for example, but that conflict in production needs your attention. I won't put too much stock in O'Reilly or Sandy either. I'll stop by around 2 p.m. to brief you on what Sir Max would have wanted.

Wallace Alexander

Wallace Alexander
Assistant to the President

EXHIBIT 3

To	Ms. Conner
Date	8/23 Time 10:03 ☒ AM ☐ PM

WHILE YOU WERE OUT

M   Prof. Calhoun

of   Univ. of Tennessee

Phone (_____) _____

    Area code   Number   Extension

TELEPHONED	✓	PLEASE CALL	✓
CALLED TO SEE YOU		WILL CALL AGAIN	
WANTS TO SEE YOU		URGENT	
RETURNED YOUR CALL			

Message   *Confirming student visits tomorrow @ 10am. Final count—50 MBA students for tour & mgmt. briefings. Look forward to continuing relationship with Astral.*

                                         Operator

EXHIBIT 4

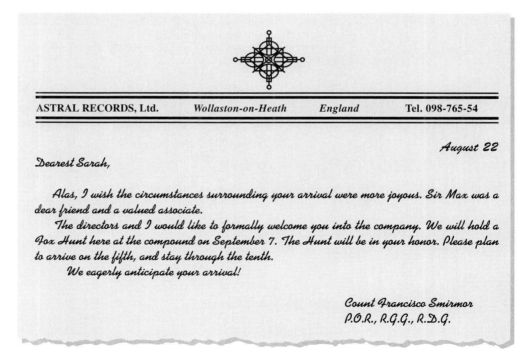

ASTRAL RECORDS, Ltd.   *Wollaston-on-Heath*   *England*   Tel. 098-765-54

August 22

Dearest Sarah,

    Alas, I wish the circumstances surrounding your arrival were more joyous. Sir Max was a dear friend and a valued associate.

    The directors and I would like to formally welcome you into the company. We will hold a Fox Hunt here at the compound on September 7. The Hunt will be in your honor. Please plan to arrive on the fifth, and stay through the tenth.

    We eagerly anticipate your arrival!

                                Count Francisco Smirmor
                                P.O.R., R.G.G., R.D.G.

EXHIBIT 5

ASTRAL RECORDS, Ltd.	*North America*	*Pigeon Forge, TN*	**Tel. (615) 356-9889**

August 20, 1993

TO: Bart O'Reilly
     Vice President, Operations
     Astral NA
CC: Sir Maxwell S. Hammer
FAX: 804-555-1234

FROM: Roberta Prospect
       District Sales Manager
FAX: 804-458-0000

URGENT ACTION REQUEST!!!!!!!

Purchasing personnel from Republic Music Distributors, Inc., are on their way to see us once again, and we need your help. Can you meet with me on Wednesday, August 25, to help us figure a way out of the current order backlog—particularly since Republic is my largest customer? Currently, we have a production run that is out-of-spec on color and electrical properties, but Republic is still willing to take it. Our plant manager is balking at shipping anything out-of-spec.

The new equipment still has problems. The plant manager and the staff have been working around the clock, it seems, to get the utilization promised by the equipment manufacturers. They have made great progress in stabilizing the production processes, particularly in view of the new technology in the NCC-1701A equipment, but there are still problems.

My issue at the moment is the plant's unwillingness to be a bit flexible in what it ships out to Republic. Here is the latest incident. This afternoon, I called our shipping department to verify that the Republic order would be picked up by Smith's Transfer. We had promised a ship date of Tuesday of this week, and I have been reassuring Republic's purchasing agent all week that this shipment would be made by the week's end.

When I found out the products were being scrapped, I really hit the ceiling. I felt like this action would be the last straw with Republic. We will lose all credibility if we don't get product to them by next Thursday. There is no way to meet their needs if we start a new production run. I was able to get the current run placed on hold by the Q.A. manager. The plant manager promises a new run from NCC-1701A by next Friday afternoon. Even if this run goes perfect, and we airship, the product will arrive too late for Republic to meet its customer ship date.

(continued on next page)

EXHIBIT 5
(continued)

2

I proposed to the plant manager and quality assurance manager that the plant work overtime on Monday and Tuesday, sorting the products on electrical properties conformance. The purchasing people at Republic said they would be willing to accept "sorted-product." Moreover for this *one order*, they would allow off-specification occurrences for the color schemes on the various outside graphics. (We will have to process all of the 8,000 units through the certifier to sort "good/bad" on electrical properties. There are nine critical electrical performance attributes that must meet specifications.) Then the color consistency must be checked visually by our people. This visual check is a manual process and will take a lot of labor, particularly since the visual check requires a tricky disassembly step to remove the protective shield covering the minted surface.

So, I can get the purchasing people at Republic off my back with this one-time stop gap sort, and yet the plant manager refuses to schedule the overtime. He says that my proposal and the plant's TQM initiative don't go hand-in-hand. Their TQM activities have been underway for eight months, so I don't see how the actions would impact his TQM implementation. We need to be more customer focused at Astral.

Please call me later today and give me some help on this one. Thanks.

EXHIBIT 6

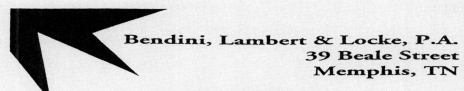

Bendini, Lambert & Locke, P.A.
39 Beale Street
Memphis, TN

FACSIMILE TRANSMISSION

TO: Sarah Conner   FROM: T.J. Lampert
       Astral Records, NA   Partner, BLL

DATE: August 24, 1993

MESSAGE:

Sarah.... Welcome to Astral. Hope your flight on the Lear was enjoyable. Just wanted to once again let you know that we are expecting great things from you. This Astral Records affair has cost us a great deal more money than we had anticipated. Arthur and I know that you will work your magic on Astral in short order. Let's get this company straightened out.

As we set up before you left, Arthur, Helen and I will be coming to Astral on September 7th to meet with you. Please arrange appropriate accommodations for us. You know what we like.

By the way, we have been unable to locate the financial model you built for the TechnoWiz deal. As I recall, this was an extremely complex spreadsheet. Celia, your former secretary, left unexpectedly last Friday and no one can find her files. Can you build it for us again by the end of this week as we hope to complete this deal immediately?

Look forward to seeing you in two weeks. Best of luck.

EXHIBIT 7

"WE COVER THE WORLD WITH CHEMICALS"

POLYCARBONATE SUBSTRATE INC.
R.D. #3
BOX 4788
KENNER, LOUISIANA

TO: Sir Maxwell S. Hammer
FROM: J. Cash
           Manager, Accounts Receivable
DATE: August 9, 1993
SUBJECT: Overdue Account

This is to notify you that Astral Records, North America, is more than 90 days overdue in its payment to us. You currently owe us $27,914.22.

If payment is not received by August 26, 1993, we will not deliver the next shipment of resins. Thank you for your prompt attention to this matter.

EXHIBIT 8

To _____ **Ms. Conner** _____

Date _____ **8/23** _____ Time _____ **1:43** _____   ☐ AM ☒ PM

WHILE YOU WERE OUT

M _____ **Bea Walters** _____
of _____ **Billboard Magazine** _____
Phone (_____) _____
        Area code   Number   Extension

TELEPHONED		PLEASE CALL	✓
CALLED TO SEE YOU		WILL CALL AGAIN	
WANTS TO SEE YOU		URGENT	
	RETURNED YOUR CALL		

Message _____
    _____ *Would like interview ASAP* _____
    _____ *regarding management* _____
    _____ *transition.* _____
    _____
    _____
    _____   Operator

EXHIBIT 9

ASTRAL RECORDS, Ltd.   *North America*   *Pigeon Forge, TN*   Tel. (615) 356-9889

TO: Sir Max
CC: Bart O'Reilly
          Vice President, Manufacturing
CC: Safety Committee
FROM: Mr. and Mrs. Richard Clark
          Shipping Department
DATE: August 16, 1993

As you may know, the September 1993 Safety Day plans are almost finished. We had a chance to see the last working document that was prepared by the Plant Safety Committee. We are really upset and want to see you ASAP. Can we schedule ourselves into one of your "open doors" later this week?

For the fourth year in a row, there will be a Safety Day exhibition on Home Safety. We applaud Home Safety as one of the key themes. However, this year's focus on "Construction of a Deer Stand: Safety and Safe Hunting" is offensive to many of us. First, it is a fact that 38% of our plant employees are female, and they have no interest in hunting, particularly shooting deer from a stand placed off the ground in the trees somewhere on the company's property. Certainly, you understand this point personally. Second, we think it is time to step up to the environmental issues and get our employees involved with recycling (newspapers, aluminum cans, plastic bottles, glass). Can't you order the Safety Committee to drop the "Deer Stand Construction" exhibition? After all, we think productivity/absenteeism and quality suffer at the opening of deer season every year. It is time, we think, to de-emphasize hunting and get people to stay focused on what they are paid to do.

EXHIBIT 10

ASTRAL RECORDS, Ltd.   *North America*   *Pigeon Forge, TN*   Tel. (615) 356-9889

TO: Sir Max
CC: G. Scott Herron
          Vice President, Marketing and Sales
FROM: Larry Taylor
          Account Manager
DATE: August 13, 1993
SUBJECT: Unauthorized Return of Merchandise

Harris' Sound Machine, the largest chain of retail music stores in New York City, has informed me they intend to return 1,252 CDs with the title, "Buddy Holly's Greatest Hits," and are asking for a full refund. They claim the CDs arrived damaged. The one they sent me looks like it was cut with a knife used to open the shipping cartons. Since this is a slow seller, I am somewhat doubtful about how the CDs were damaged. Please let me know what to do.

EXHIBIT 11

"SERVING PIGEON FORGE'S FAMILIES AND BUSINESSES SINCE 1929"
2300 MAIN STREET
PIGEON FORGE, TN

TO: Sir Maxwell S. Hammer
FROM: C. Hewitt Farmington
           Senior Relationship Manager
           YurBank
DATE: July 1, 1993
SUBJECT: Renewal of Revolving Credit Agreement

Sir Max, this is to remind you that your revolver with the bank is due for review and renewal at the end of this month. As it currently stands, the bank is committed to lend you up to $500,000 at LIBOR + 1% with a 0.5% fee on the unused portion of the commitment. In light of the growth of last year's sales and your expectation of future growth, I recommend that we increase the commitment to $600,000. I do not expect the pricing structure to change before the end of this month.

Our understanding is that the line is used for seasonal working capital needs and as such your company will be out of the bank loan for at least 45 days during the next 12 months. Part of the purpose of the review is to see if the financial condition of the company has changed substantially since last year. Historically, your peak loan needs have occurred from September through December. My back-of-the-envelope calculations show that increasing the revolver will not violate the debt-to-equity covenant of the term loan unless equity is unexpectedly low prior to or during your peak seasonal need.

Is the early part of next week too early for your people to get the financials prepared so we can discuss things? I'll check back with you in a day or so to confirm.

EXHIBIT 12

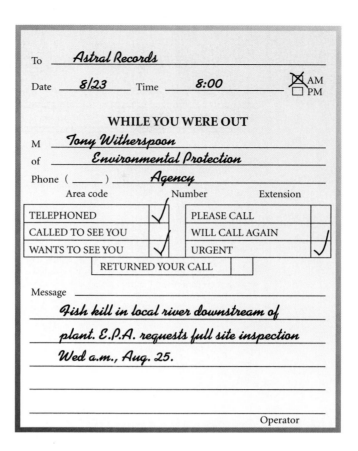

To **Astral Records**

Date **8/23** Time **8:00** ☒ AM ☐ PM

WHILE YOU WERE OUT

M **Tony Witherspoon**

of **Environmental Protection**

Phone (_____) **Agency**

Area code   Number   Extension

TELEPHONED	✓	PLEASE CALL	
CALLED TO SEE YOU	✓	WILL CALL AGAIN	✓
WANTS TO SEE YOU	✓	URGENT	✓
	RETURNED YOUR CALL		

Message

Fish kill in local river downstream of plant. E.P.A. requests full site inspection Wed a.m., Aug. 25.

Operator

EXHIBIT 13

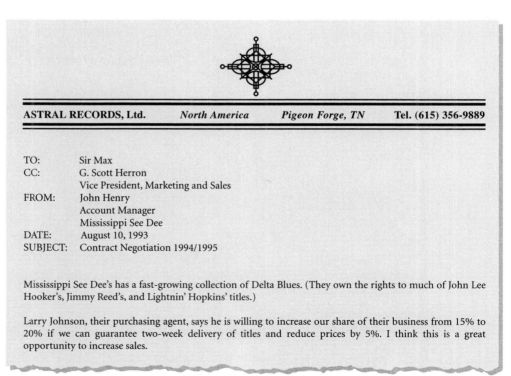

ASTRAL RECORDS, Ltd.   *North America*   *Pigeon Forge, TN*   Tel. (615) 356-9889

TO: Sir Max
CC: G. Scott Herron
        Vice President, Marketing and Sales
FROM: John Henry
        Account Manager
        Mississippi See Dee
DATE: August 10, 1993
SUBJECT: Contract Negotiation 1994/1995

Mississippi See Dee's has a fast-growing collection of Delta Blues. (They own the rights to much of John Lee Hooker's, Jimmy Reed's, and Lightnin' Hopkins' titles.)

Larry Johnson, their purchasing agent, says he is willing to increase our share of their business from 15% to 20% if we can guarantee two-week delivery of titles and reduce prices by 5%. I think this is a great opportunity to increase sales.

EXHIBIT 14

ASTRAL RECORDS, Ltd.   *North America*   *Pigeon Forge, TN*   **Tel. (615) 356-9889**

TO: Richard & Emma Clark
CC: Sir Max
           Bart O'Reilly, Vice President, Manufacturing
FROM: Maggie May
DATE: August 17, 1993

Will you get off it! Who do you think you are suggesting that women don't enjoy hunting? I'll have you know I've been hunting since I was six when my daddy let me load his gun. I won't miss deer season and, believe me, these safety reminders are important. Not all women want to join your sewing circle, Emma. So stop writing memos to the VP and accusing us of not doing our work. If you are writing memos, how can you two be doing your own jobs!

EXHIBIT 15

To _____ *Astral* _____

Date ____ *8/24* ____ Time ____ *10:06* ____ ☒ AM ☐ PM

WHILE YOU WERE OUT

M ____ *Tony Witherspoon* ____

of ____ *E.P.A.* ____

Phone (_____) _____
      Area code   Number   Extension

TELEPHONED	✓	PLEASE CALL	
CALLED TO SEE YOU		WILL CALL AGAIN	
WANTS TO SEE YOU		URGENT	
	RETURNED YOUR CALL		

Message _____
     Suggests Astral legal counsel be present
       during tomorrow's inspection.

_____
_____
_____
                                  Operator

EXHIBIT 16

| ASTRAL RECORDS, Ltd. | *North America* | *Pigeon Forge, TN* | Tel. (615) 356-9889 |

TO: Sir Max
CC: Bart O'Reilly, Vice President, Manufacturing
     G. Scott Herron, Vice President, Marketing and Sales
FROM: Phil Kreutzman
     Purchasing
DATE: August 11, 1993
SUBJECT: Proposal for New Plastic Packaging Material

As you know, our packaging costs are substantial. I have a new plastic supplier who can cut our total COGS by 20%. Eventually, costs might be even lower.

The advantage of this company's new formula is that it is *completely* biodegradable in 10 years. The disadvantage is that the package will no longer be serviceable after 3–5 years of normal usage. Should we pursue this project?

EXHIBIT 17

| ASTRAL RECORDS, Ltd. | *North America* | *Pigeon Forge, TN* | Tel. (615) 356-9889 |

TO: Sir Maxwell S. Hammer
FROM: Richard Cory
     Treasurer
DATE: July 3, 1993
SUBJECT: Approval of New Packaging Equipment

Below is a summary of the analysis we have been conducting on some new packaging equipment. Based on a discounted cash flow analysis, we estimate that the $1MM investment will increase firm value by $200,000. If we order by the end of this month, we should have the equipment installed and running in time for the increase in production that always occurs around October. The supplier will accept installment payments of $400,000, $300,000, and $300,000 over the next three months as payment. Since we are currently out of the bank, we could use the revolver line to make the $400,000 initial payment.

I hope the numbers on the attached sheet help show the merits of the new system. Frankly, Sir Max, it is rare that such a good opportunity comes around. The sooner we start using it, the better.

(continued on next page)

EXHIBIT 17
(continued)

ASTRAL RECORDS, Ltd.	*North America*	*Pigeon Forge, TN*	Tel. (615) 356-9889

2

Cash Flow Analysis
New Packaging Equipment

Initial investment: $1.0MM
Projected annual savings:[a] $160M
Corporate tax rate: 34%
Economic/depreciable life: 7 years

Cash flow summary ($000):

Year →	0		1	2	3	4	5	6	7
Investment	(1000)								
After-tax savings			106	106	106	106	106	106	106
+ Depreciation			143	143	143	143	143	143	143
Total after-tax cash flows	(1000)		248	248	248	248	248	248	248

Net present value = $209,000
Internal rate of return = 16.1%
Payback = 4 years

_____

[a]After depreciation, before taxes.

EXHIBIT 18

YURBANK

"SERVING PIGEON FORGE'S FAMILIES AND BUSINESSES SINCE 1929"
2300 MAIN STREET
PIGEON FORGE, TN

TO: Sir Maxwell S. Hammer

FROM: C. Hewitt Farmington
            Senior Relationship Manager
            YurBank

DATE: August 10, 1993

SUBJECT: Renewal of Revolving Credit Agreement

Things have changed. The credit review committee has put your company on its credit watch list because of our increasing exposure and the growth-induced strain on your balance sheet. They do not want to renew the revolver unless you can give us some sort of indication of how you are going to manage the growth of the firm going forward. Frankly, there is a general concern that your company is growing beyond its financial capabilities and that we might find ourselves with a bad term loan and very little usable collateral.

I spent the better part of an hour arguing with the credit committee, and I can tell you that these people are serious. This is all part of the tightened credit standards that were instituted following the S&L crisis. The only way I can see us doing business in the future is for you to strengthen the balance sheet with an equity infusion. The investment banking folks here would be very interested in helping you take the company public. I think you should consider it. The equity markets are very strong these days, and you may not be able to get a better price in the near future if this bull market turns bearish.

Sorry to catch you with this news with such little notice, but there was nothing I could do. I will meet anytime you are available. Obviously, time is of the essence.

EXHIBIT 19

ASTRAL RECORDS, Ltd.　　*North America*　　*Pigeon Forge, TN*　　Tel. (615) 356-9889

TO:　　　Sir Maxwell S. Hammer
FROM:　　Abby McDeere
　　　　　Chief Legal Counsel
DATE:　　July 17, 1993
SUBJECT:　Lawsuit against Astral

Please be advised that MasterVision Associates of Burbank, California, has filed suit in the Los Angeles Superior Court against us. They are a worldwide optical disc licensor. They charge that some of our CD manufacturing equipment infringes on their patents. They are seeking unspecified "substantial damages" and note that there is still litigation pending from 1988 when they accused us of two other optical disc patent violations.

The resolution of these charges is uncertain. I will keep you advised.

EXHIBIT 20

ASTRAL RECORDS, Ltd.　　*North America*　　*Pigeon Forge, TN*　　Tel. (615) 356-9889

TO:　　　Sir Max
FROM:　　Sandy Bien-Fait
　　　　　Human Resource Manager
DATE:　　August 16, 1993
SUBJECT:　Hiring

Sir Max—

We can't afford to lose any more time addressing the issue of hiring. The increase in production has strained the existing shift personnel. And, as I mentioned last week at our weekly tea, the surrounding area just doesn't have the numbers of workers we need. Either we have to pay more or get them from somewhere else. I need authorization to hire 20 shift workers immediately.

Also, Sir Max, I think it is time to eliminate playing a musical instrument as a hiring criterion. We have simply run out of musicians in the community.

EXHIBIT 21

ASTRAL RECORDS, Ltd.   *North America*   *Pigeon Forge, TN*   **Tel. (615) 356-9889**

TO: Sir Max
FROM: Margaret Lee
           Public Relations
CC: Bart O'Reilly
           Vice President, Operations
DATE: March 7, 1993
SUBJECT: CD Rot

There have been an increasing number of articles in the trade press describing a phenomenon known as "CD rot." If the CD rot stories are true, certain CDs may begin to self-destruct within 8–10 years because the ink used for labeling begins to eat into the protective lacquer coating. This in turn can oxidize the aluminum layer resulting in an unplayable CD.

Although we have not yet had any inquiries or returns due to "CD rot," we should nevertheless be prepared to respond to this possible crisis.

EXHIBIT 22

ASTRAL RECORDS, Ltd.   *North America*   *Pigeon Forge, TN*   **Tel. (615) 356-9889**

TO: Sir Max
FROM: Carl Christie, Ph.D.
           Research and Development
DATE: August 16, 1993
SUBJECT: Project FutureVision

We are at the breakthrough stage on Project FutureVision. Compression technologies are progressing at an acceptable rate, and we anticipate being able to place full-length motion pictures with Dolby Surround Sound tracks on a 5-inch disc within the next 6 months.

I don't need to tell you about the commercial possibilities. However, the lab is feeling the pinch financially right now. My people have estimated that we need another $3.5 million within the next month in order to complete our work. Since you have been so generous in the past, I know that we all can count on your continued support.

EXHIBIT 23

ASTRAL RECORDS, Ltd.   *North America*   *Pigeon Forge, TN*   **Tel. (615) 356-9889**

TO: Sir Maxwell S. Hammer
FROM: Abby McDeere
           Chief Legal Counsel
DATE: August 10, 1993
SUBJECT: Lawsuit against Astral

On August 7th, I met with Richard Milhous, Chief Legal Counsel for MasterVision. After protracted discussion and negotiation, they have offered a settlement for all litigation pending against us.

They have offered to settle for either a one-time cash payment of $5 million or a 4-cent-per-disc royalty over the next 10 years of production.

We must respond by the 24th of August. Please advise me of your decision.

EXHIBIT 24

ASTRAL RECORDS, Ltd.   *North America*   *Pigeon Forge, TN*   **Tel. (615) 356-9889**

TO: Sir Max
FROM: Bruce Park-Asbury
           Shift Supervisor
CC: Sandy Bien-Fait
           Human Resource Manager
DATE: August 17, 1993
SUBJECT: Employee Reprimand

This is the third time that I have had to reprimand Sonny Barger for being insubordinate. I am at my wits end with him and don't know what to do.

On February 7, Barger refused to clean up his work area, and I gave him a formal reprimand. On March 23, Barger was found taking an unauthorized cigarette break and was again reprimanded. On August 16, Barger left his station 15 minutes before quitting time to run to his car to turn on the air conditioning. I suppose so it would be cool when he got out. I wrote him up for this incident. He told me to watch out, he was going to get me and "the whole damn company."

I honestly believe that Barger is trying to undermine my authority as shift supervisor. If something doesn't change, I may have to leave Astral.

EXHIBIT 25

CROSBY, SELLS, CASH AND YOUNG

CERTIFIED PUBLIC ACCOUNTANTS   KNOXVILLE, TN

TO: Sarah Conner
FROM: Janet Young
SUBJECT: Audit Planning Meeting
DATE: August 23, 1993

I wanted to make sure that you were aware of the planning meeting to discuss our audit of Astral's financial statements for the fiscal year ended December 31, 1993, that is scheduled for 10:00 A.M. on Friday, September 10th. We hope to begin our preliminary audit work on Monday, September 27th.

Please be advised that we intend to continue our discussion about Astral's contingent environmental liabilities. We told Sir Max last year that the 1993 financial statements would likely contain at least footnote disclosure of environmental issues and, perhaps, even reflect actual environmental liabilities. Please be prepared to bring us up to date on all environmental matters.

Also, we just heard about the "CD rot" problem. This could have a material effect on Astral's financial statements. We are anxious to learn more about it from your production personnel. Finally, we will need current information about actual and pending litigation. What is happening regarding the MasterVision case?

I look forward to meeting you. If you need to reschedule our meeting, that's OK, but we don't have a lot of flexibility. Please let me know ASAP.

EXHIBIT 26

ASTRAL RECORDS, Ltd.   *North America*   *Pigeon Forge, TN*   **Tel. (615) 356-9889**

TO: Sir Max
FROM: Ed Heath
           Foreman, Waste Disposal Unit
SUBJECT: Equipment Maintenance
DATE: August 13, 1993

The PCB filtration actuators are breaking down regularly these days. We really need to replace these units. I know replacements are very expensive, but this stuff is really toxic and these units are almost to the end of their serviceable life. It won't take much to cause a major problem. In fact, just yesterday, one of our technicians knocked the master valve loose and it took us almost three hours to clean up the spill.

I've talked with the finance people a number of times about getting replacements, but I can't seem to get an answer. We need to move on this soon.

EXHIBIT 27

August 17, 1993

Sir Maxwell S. Hammer
President and CEO
Astral Records, N.A.
Pigeon Forge, TN

Sir Max:

DECEMBER is thrilled that Astral Records is interested in placing them under contract. Plans are well underway for the signing party and free concert in Pigeon Forge on the 26th.

I know this will be the begining of a successful relationship. Attached is our sketch for the cover art of our first CD.

Regards,

Matthew D. Booth

Matthew D. Booth
Business Manager, DECEMBER

Attachments: 1

EXHIBIT 27
(continued)

For the World Is Hollow and I Have Touched the Sky

DECEMBER is
Kevin Albers—Keyboards
Matt Booth—Bass Guitar
Michael King—Vocals
Bryce Smith—Drums

Lighting Techs:
George Ackert, Steven Harper

Road Crew:
Kevin Asherfeld, Dave Erickson

Recorded at: SRS Austin TX

Engineered by: Ben Blank

Send all correspondence to:

DECEMBER
P.O. Box 49188
Austin, TX 78765
(512) 472-8943

Thanks To:
Steven, George, Kevin, Dave, Jim,
Sharron, Tim, Matt, Jeanette W., Mark
P., and Liberty Lunch. Grace Wall,
Derek "Matt kicked me out of the
band" Brownlee, Jan Long, Mark A.,
Dave H., and especially Jill Isreal, and
Lisa McBride.

Back-up vocals on
Darkest Cave by:
Jill Isreal

Lyrics to *A Letter to Vernon Lee*
Inspired by the play *Madame X*
by Anne Ciccolella

EXHIBIT 28

ASTRAL RECORDS, Ltd.　　*North America*　　*Pigeon Forge, TN*　　Tel. (615) 356-9889

Sir Max,

　You should know that Roberta Prospect was seen leaving Arnold Smither's house yesterday morning at 6 a.m.! Smither is the purchasing manager at Republic Records. Aren't they one of our biggest customers? I think this is just scandalous.

Your faithful employee
(Sorry, but I can't sign my name.)

EXHIBIT 29

ASTRAL RECORDS, Ltd.　　*North America*　　*Pigeon Forge, TN*　　Tel. (615) 356-9889

TO:　　　Sarah Conner
FROM:　　Richard Cory
　　　　　Treasurer
DATE:　　August 24, 1993
SUBJECT:　Capital Structure Summary

In response to your request, I am summarizing Astral's current financial structure below. Note that the line of credit and 5-year term loan are with YurBank and that the 15-year subordinated debt is a loan obtained at a favorable rate from BLL in 1987. As you can see, we have just about reached our debt limit. We probably should discuss this at your convenience. However, the sooner the better.

CAPITAL STRUCTURE ($ MILLIONS)	
Line of credit	0.5
Term loan	3.0
Subordinated debt	10.0
Equity	6.5
Total	20.0

CASE 3

MacArthur and the Philippines

The Americans never came. *They never came.* Month after month the embattled garrison awaited a blow in vain. . . . Truk was being devastated by Nimitz's carrier planes, but the sky over Rabaul was serene, and sentinels posted to sound the alarm when Allied patrols approached overland from Cape Gloucester and Arawe stared out at a mocking green silence. All they wanted was an opportunity to sell their lives dearly before they were killed or eviscerated themselves in honorable seppuku. They believed that they were entitled to a Nipponese gotterdammerung. . . . MacArthur was denying them it, and they were experiencing a kind of psychological hernia.[1]

Here they were, commanding an army larger than Napoleon's at Waterloo or Lee's at Gettysburg—or Wellington's or Meade's for that matter—which was spoiling for a fight. Their sappers had thrown up ramparts, revetments, parapets, barbicans, and ravelins. Hull-down tanks were in position. Mines had been laid, Hotchkiss-type guns sited, Nambus cunningly camouflaged. Mortarmen had calculated precise ranges. Crack troops, designated to launch counterattacks, lurked in huge bunkers behind concertinas of barbwire. And there they remained, in an agony of frustration, for the rest of the war. . . .

"BYPASS" OR "ISLAND HOP?"

This phenomenon was not confined to Rabaul. . . . Exactly who first suggested the stratagem is unclear. MacArthur himself has been widely credited with it, largely on the basis of his own recollections and those of the men around him. In *Reminiscences* he writes:

> To push back the Japanese perimeter of conquest by direct pressure against the mass of enemy-occupied islands would be a long and costly effort. My staff worried about Rabaul and other strongpoints. . . . I intended to envelop them, incapacitate them, apply the "hit 'em where they ain't—let 'em die on the vine" philosophy. I explained that this was the very opposite of what was termed "island-hopping," which is the gradual pushing back of the enemy by direct frontal pressure, with the consequent heavy casualties which would certainly be involved. There would be no need for storming the mass of islands held by the enemy.

According to Huff, Willoughby, and Kenney, the General first unveiled this concept at a council of war attended by, among others, Halsey, Krueger, and Australia's Sir Thomas Blamey. Gesturing at the map, one of the conferees said, "I don't see how we can take these strongpoints with our limited forces." Tapping his cigarette on an ashtray, MacArthur said in a slow deliberate voice: "Well, let's just say that we don't take them. In fact, gentlemen, I don't want them." Turning to Kenney [head of Allied air forces in the area], he said: "You incapacitate them. . . . " He told the airman: "Starve Rabaul! The jungle! Starvation! They're my allies."[2]

But the notion that the isolation of Rabaul was the General's inspiration just won't wash. Apparently the first references to the possibility of such a bypass were made in March of 1943, during Washington talks which were attended by Sutherland, Kenney, and Stephen J. Chamberlain, the General's operations officer. If they mentioned it to MacArthur on their return, he was unimpressed. Eight months earlier the Joint Chiefs had instructed him to take Rabaul and Kavieng. He hadn't protested then, and he didn't now. Indeed, when the Chiefs sounded him out in June, informing him that some Pentagon officers thought that Rabaul could be cut off and left to rot, he objected. He needed "an adequate forward naval base" there, he said, to protect his right flank; without it, his westward drive along the back of New Guinea's plucked buzzard "would involve hazards rendering success doubtful."

"THE STRATEGY WE HATED MOST"

The issue was resolved in August, at the Quadrant conference in Quebec. Ironically, this boldest stratagem of the Pacific war was decided, not on its merits, but because the Anglo-American Combined Chiefs were searching for a compromise. The British wanted more U.S. troops and more landing craft in the European theater. They didn't see why the American offensive against Japan couldn't be mounted on a single front—Nimitz's, in the central Pacific—and U.S. admirals were inclined to agree with them. Roosevelt and his political advisers demurred, however. They had to reckon with MacArthur's popularity at home. . . . In the end FDR sided with MacArthur's strongest supporter at the conference—George Marshall. MacArthur never acknowledged Marshall's strong support at Quebec and elsewhere, and it is possible that he never knew of it. . . .

However, the fact remains that MacArthur transformed the bypass maneuver into the war's most momentous strategic concept. Here the most impressive testimony comes from the Japanese. After the war Colonel Matsuichi Juio, a senior intelligence officer who had been charged with deciphering the General's intentions, told an interrogator that MacArthur's swooping envelopment of Nipponese bastions was "the type of strategy we hated most." The General, he said, repeatedly, "with minimum losses, attacked and seized a relatively weak area, constructed airfields and then proceeded to cut the supply lines to [our] troops in that area. . . . Our strongpoints were gradually starved out. The Japanese Army preferred direct [frontal] assault, after the German fashion, but the Americans flowed into our weaker points and submerged us, just as water seeks the weakest entry to sink a ship. We respected this type of strategy . . . because it gained the most while losing the least."[3]

Yet, while GIs would proudly identify themselves as members of his army, they disparaged their commander in chief, or rather the image of himself he had created. Distrust of great commanders by their troops is nothing new; the British rank and file loathed Wellington, and during the American Revolution, as Gore Vidal has pointed out, "the private soldiers disliked Washington as much as he disdained them." In MacArthur's case it was ironical, however, for had his bitter men understood the consequences of the General's strategy they would have taken a very different view. For every Allied serviceman killed, the General killed ten Japanese. Never in history, John Gunther wrote, had there been a commander so economical in the expenditure of his men's blood. In this respect certain comparisons with European Theater Operations campaigns are staggering. During the single Battle of Anzio, 72,306 GIs fell. In the Battle of Normandy, Eisenhower lost 28,366. Between MacArthur's arrival in Australia and his return to Philippine waters over two years later, his troops suffered just 27,684 casualties.[4]

THE HAWAIIAN CONFERENCE

The one great Pacific issue confronting American strategists that summer [1944] was where to strike next. MacArthur wanted to reconquer the Philippines. Admiral King recommended bypassing the archipelago and invading Formosa instead; he saw no reason to risk becoming mired in the great land masses of the islands. The dispute had been almost a year in the making. The previous October Eichelberger [field Commander of American Forces] had heard in Hawaii that once MacArthur had reached the equator, the admirals wanted the war against Japan to be "their show and no one else's." The decision could be deferred no longer.[5]

They needed each other, and the President, the more flexible of the two, recognized that. Therefore he decided, after MacArthur had dropped out of the presidential race, to meet him in Hawaii. The Joint Chiefs—to their discomfiture—would be left in Washington. Nimitz would represent the navy. The three of them, as power brokers, would hammer out the wisest way to defeat the Japanese, who, despite the vicissitudes of quadrennial politics, were after all, the real enemy.[6]

Roosevelt's military advisers were sharply divided on the subject. MacArthur was at one end of the spectrum; King at the other. Field commanders of all services in the

Pacific tended to agree with the General, while George Marshall (chief of staff) and Hap Arnold leaned toward King, though individuals changed their minds from week to week. By the week of the Honolulu conference, Marshall was beginning to side with MacArthur. Hap Arnold, eager for B-29 bases on Formosa, continued to support King. Admiral Nimitz, wavering, instructed his staff to draw up plans for assaults on all possible objectives, including the Japanese homeland.

If Roosevelt was already familiar with the Pentagon's views, vacillating as they were, he knew those of MacArthur and Nimitz, too. . . . The blunt fact is that he was running for a fourth term, and being photographed with MacArthur and Nimitz would be more impressive to his constituents than pictures of him politicking at the Democratic National Convention.

A GREAT ENTRANCE

Roosevelt knew how to make a great entrance; a huge crowd of Hawaiians, who had been alerted to his approach, cheered as the *Baltimore* docked at 3:00 P.M. on Wednesday, July 26, and fifty high-ranking military officers, led by Nimitz and Lieutenant General Robert C. Richardson, the commander of Nimitz's ground forces, mounted the gangboard. But MacArthur could be dramatic, too. Though [MacArthur's] B-17 had landed an hour earlier, . . . , he would be the last officer to board the cruiser. . . . Roosevelt had just asked Nimitz if he knew the General's whereabouts when "a terrific automobile siren was heard, and there raced on to the dock and screeched to a stop a motorcycle escort and the longest open car I have ever seen. . . . The car traveled some distance around the open space and stopped at the gangplank. When the applause died down, the General strode rapidly to the gangplank all alone."[7]

[Later the President] led MacArthur, Nimitz, and Leahy into [a large] room, one wall of which was covered by a huge map of the Pacific. Picking up a long bamboo pointer, the President touched the islands with it and suddenly spun his wheelchair around to face the General. "Well, Douglas," he said challengingly, "Where do we go from here?" MacArthur shot back, "Mindanao, Mr. President, then Leyte—and then Luzon."[8]

He and Nimitz took turns at the map arguing their cases forcefully while the President listened intently, interrupting now and then to ask a question or suggest another line of reasoning. Leahy thought he was "at his best as he tactfully steered the discussion from one point to another and narrowed down the areas of disagreement between MacArthur and Nimitz." Despite his earlier misgivings, the General

found himself thoroughly enjoying the session. The President, he said afterward, had conducted himself as a "chairman," and had remained "entirely neutral," while Nimitz displayed a "fine sense of fair play." . . . [But Nimitz] lacked the General's eloquence. He was arguing King's case, not his own; under FDR's skillful questioning he conceded that Manila Bay would be useful to him, and admitted that an attack on Formosa, instead of Luzon, would succeed only if anchorages and fighter strips had been established in the central and southern Philippines. Finally, he was unprepared or unwilling to discuss the political problems which would arise if the archipelago were bypassed.[9]

Here MacArthur was his most trenchant. The Filipinos, he said, felt that they had been betrayed in 1942—he did not add that he had shared the feeling, but FDR knew it— and they would not forgive a second betrayal. "Promises must be kept," he said forcefully, meaning his own vow to return at the head of an army of liberation, a pledge which, he believed, had committed the United States. . . . In the postwar world all Asian eyes would be on the emerging Philippine republic. If its people thought they had been sold out, the reputation of the United States would be sullied with a stain that could never be removed.[10]

Again and again he used the words "ethical" and "unethical," "virtue" and "shame." As Barbey later wrote, "General MacArthur approached the matter from a different point of view" than the Joint Chiefs; "he felt it was as much a moral issue as a military one." In addition, however, "He did not think the military conquest of the Philippines would be as costly, lengthy, or difficult as the conquest of Formosa, and yet the same military purposes would be accomplished." . . .

THE GREATER PRIZE?

Luzon was a greater [strategic] prize than Formosa . . . the Filipinos, unlike the Formosans, would provide the Americans with powerful guerilla support. Last—and here Leahy thought he saw Nimitz nod—Luzon couldn't be enveloped. It was too big. Rabaul and Wewak could be bypassed because their land masses were smaller. Attempting to detour around Luzon would expose U.S. flanks to crippling attacks from the enemy's bomber bases there.[11]

Newspapers and even some correspondence of that summer support the premise that the issue had been resolved at Waikiki. After MacArthur had left Hickam Field, FDR told reporters that "we are going to get the Philippines back, and without question General MacArthur will take a part in it." There was more to it than that, however. Under the Constitution Roosevelt's power over the Pentagon was absolute, but in practice he couldn't act without the support of the military advisers who hadn't accompanied him to Hawaii. In effect, he, MacArthur, and Leahy had formed a coalition, the object of which was the conversion of the Joint Chiefs.

The Joint Chiefs continued the Luzon-or-Formosa debate through August and September. Leahy had briefed them on the Waikiki talks and told them that both he and Roosevelt were impressed by MacArthur's political and moral arguments. The Chiefs weren't. They insisted that the matter be decided wholly on the grounds of military merit. They agreed to a Leyte landing, but added that a "decision as to whether Luzon will be occupied before Formosa will be made later." King still wanted to land in southern Formosa, supported by American aircraft using Chaing Kai-shek's bases. . . . [Then over] the last weekend in September, Nimitz convinced him. The two admirals met in San Francisco, and Nimitz, pointing to recent Japanese successes against Chaing's troops, said the United States could no longer rely on his airdromes. An attack on Formosa, Nimitz said, would now be impossible unless Luzon were seized first. And back in Washington, King withdrew his objections to MacArthur's Philippine plans.

THE INVASION TIMETABLE

MacArthur, meanwhile, had been contemplating a continuation of his steady advance northward, with each amphibious thrust providing airfields for the next, so that Kenney could always fill the skies over the beaches with friendly fighters and bombers. Under this principle their schedule had called for vaults into Morotai (September 15), Mindanao (November 15), and Leyte (December 20). Then, in the waning days of summer, even before King's capitulation, Admiral Halsey gave the General a tremendous lift by proposing that the timetable be scrapped for a bolder leap.[12]

Halsey had been cruising off the Philippines, launching carrier strikes at Japanese bases. One of his pilots had been shot down over Leyte, the archipelago's midrib. Parachuting to safety and rescued by a submarine, he had reported that Leyte was held by far fewer Japanese troops than the Americans had thought. All week the admiral had noticed that his fleet was rarely challenged by land-based enemy aircraft. The rescued flier seemed to confirm his suspicion that, in his words, the central Philippines were "a hollow shell, with weak defense and skimpy facilities. In my opinion, this was the vulnerable belly of the imperial dragon." . . . Finally on Wednesday, September 13, 1944, he radioed Nimitz in Pearl Harbor, suggesting that assaults on the Talauds, Mindanao, and the Palaus be canceled. In their place he urged the swift seizure of Leyte.[13]

At that moment two U.S. invasion convoys were at sea. MacArthur, aboard the cruiser *Nashville*, was bound for Morotai, the northeasternmost island of the Molucas, which would be needed to launch any blow at the Philippines. . . . Halsey's proposals were forwarded to Quebec, where the Combined Chiefs were attending a formal dinner as guests of Prime Minister W. L. Mackenzie King. As Hap Arnold later wrote, "Admiral Leahy, General Marshall, Admiral King, and I excused ourselves, read the message, and had a staff officer prepare an answer which naturally was in the affirmative." There was one small difficulty. MacArthur's approval was needed, and he couldn't be reached; the *Nashville*, in enemy waters, was observing radio silence. Thus the momentous message from Canada was handed to Sutherland [MacArthur's chief of staff]. That normally impassive officer's hands trembled; he was, Kenney later recalled, "worried about what the General would say about using his name and making so important a decision without consulting him." After a long, tense pause, the chief of staff radioed back an endorsement in MacArthur's name.[14]

The General had gone ashore on Morotai after the first wave had hit the beach. His Higgins boat had grounded on a rock, and when he stepped off the ramp he found the water was chest deep, . . . [but] if his clothes were damp, his mood wasn't. The landing was unopposed; without losing a man, he had anchored his right flank for the next amphibious bound. By now he had evaded 220,000 enemy troops and was within three hundred miles of the Philippines. On hearing the news from Sutherland, he instantly approved.

THE PHILIPPINE INVASION

In the fall of 1944 the Philippines were inhabited by about 18,160,000 Filipinos, 80 percent of whom worshiped the Roman Catholic God, and some 400,000 Japanese soldiers, all of whom venerated their emperor and could imagine no greater honor than to die for him in battle. The twain seldom met. Except for chronic food shortages and the repressive regime, life in the thousand-mile chain of islands had for the most part been unaffected by enemy rule, now approaching the end of its third year. The hulk of [the giant island fortress of] Corregidor lay dead in the slate gray waters of Manila Bay. . . . An unwary stranger might have concluded that it was a land finished with fiery deeds, was now slumbering, indolent, indifferent. But the General knew better. He understood that the flames of ardor needed only a spark of hope to be rekindled. He had a better grasp of the Philippines than of the United States. It was his second homeland, and in some ways it was a metaphor of his intricate personality: dramatic, inconsistent, valiant, passionate, and primitive.[15]

No sparrow fell there but MacArthur knew of it; his files held everything from the transcripts of executive sessions in Malacanan to the guest lists of the Manila Hotel. His submarines brought the guerillas equipment, technicians, transmitters, and commando teams, and he personally interviewed each partisan who escaped into his lines. . . . The resistance grew and grew. . . . The strategic information the partisans sent southward was priceless. Their eagerness to provide it was an index of their enthusiasm for the U.S. cause and their devotion was translated into loyalty to two men, MacArthur and Quezon. When Quezon died of tuberculosis at Saranac, New York, the day after the General returned from his Hawaii conference with Roosevelt, MacArthur became their sole idol. He was, quite simply, the symbol of their hopes for a better postwar world. American GIs ridiculed him. Filipinos didn't. Carlos Romulo wrote: "To me he represents America."[16]

LEYTE—THE GIANT MOLAR

Leyte Gulf, the chief anchorage in the central islands, is approachable through only two major entrances. Surigao Strait to the southwest and San Bernardino Strait to the northwest. These tropical waters were about to become the scene of the greatest naval battle in history, for the Japanese were now desperate. If they were unable to prevent MacArthur from retaking the Philippine archipelago, they knew they would no longer have access to the Indies' oil, the lifeblood of their generals and admirals.[17]

Imperial Japanese headquarters in Tokyo had drawn up a do-or-die plan encoded "Sho-Go," or "Operation Victory." Everything would be thrown into an attempt to prevent the General from establishing a foothold in the islands. . . . There would be no sense in saving the fleet at the expense of the loss of the Philippines.

When word reached [the Japanese] that a seven-hundred-ship, hundred-mile-long American armada was steaming toward Surigao Strait between Dinagat and Homonhon islands, they brimmed with confidence. Lieutenant General Sosaku Suzuki, commander of the Thirty-fifth Army in the Visayan Islands, the central Philippines, told his staff: "We don't even need all the reinforcements they are sending us." His only worry, he said, was that the American leader might attempt to surrender just the troops participating in this operation: "We must demand the capitulation of MacArthur's entire forces, those in New Guinea and other places as well as the troops on Leyte."[18]

The most cheerful news, for many Japanese, was the identity of the new overall commander of Philippine defenses. He was Lieutenant General Tomoyuki Yamashita,

the legendary "Tiger of Malaya" of the war's opening weeks. Jealous of his fame, Tojo had shunted him off to minor posts, but now Tojo was out of office, and Koiso needed someone in Manila in whom the country had faith. Yamashita seemed to be just the man; his appointment as MacArthur's adversary meant that two gifted generals, each at the height of his powers, would be pitted against each other. . . .

GUNS AT LEYTE

Leyte at that moment was under the awesome guns of two U.S. fleets, Halsey's Third and Tom Kinkaid's Seventh. Kinkaid was subordinate to MacArthur, but Halsey—whose force was faster and far more powerful—was answerable only to Nimitz in Honolulu. The split command worried MacArthur. He repeatedly urged the Joint Chiefs to designate one commander in chief, and had even offered to step down if they thought that necessary. They didn't believe he was serious, and they were probably right. In any event, shunting a national idol aside in the middle of a presidential campaign was unthinkable, especially when he belonged to the party out of power. George Marshall wouldn't agree to an admiral as supreme commander, so the flawed command structure remained. Presently it would lead the Allied cause in the Pacific to the brink of disaster.[19]

[MacArthur] had perfected a battle plan which he considered his best yet. After the war Vincent Sheean agreed: "His operations towards the end . . . were extremely daring, more daring and far more complicated than those of Patton in Europe, because MacArthur used not infantry alone but also air and seapower in a concerted series of jabbing and jumping motions designed to outflank and bypass the Japanese all through the islands. The operation in which he jumped from Hollandia to Leyte will remain, I believe, the most brilliant strategic conception and tactical execution of the entire war."[20]

He knew that his reputation was as imperiled as the lives of his men. Kenney had pointed out one glaring flaw in the plan—until Japanese landing strips had been captured, they would be fighting five hundred miles beyond the range of their fighter cover. Kenney recalls: "He stopped pacing the floor and blurted out, 'I tell you I'm going back there this fall if I have to paddle a canoe with you flying cover for me with that B-17 of yours.' "[21]

At daybreak, the U.S. warships opened fire on the beach. The General stood on the bridge. The shore was dimly visible through an ominous, rising haze shot with yellow flashes; inland, white phosphorus crumps were bursting among the thick, ripe underbrush of the hills. The light of the rising sun spread rapidly across the smooth green water of the gulf. . . . Halsey had been misinformed; the enemy was nowhere as weak as the admiral had thought. Imperial General Headquarters had been holding back, waiting until MacArthur committed himself. Even more alarming, Kenney would discover before the day was out that because of the island's unstable soil, airfields there were unusable during the rainy season, which had just begun. U.S. air support would be limited to carrier planes through most of the coming engagement.[22]

After lunch the General reappeared on deck wearing a freshly pressed khaki uniform, sun glasses, and his inimitable cap. He stood, akimbo, watching the diving enemy planes zooming overhead; then he looked shoreward, where the sand pits, palms, thick underbrush, and tin grass-thatched huts were obscured by the burst of exploding shells and tall columns of black smoke.

In his *Reminiscences* he writes that he went in with the third assault wave. Actually the invasion was four hours old when he descended ladder to a barge; his staff and war correspondents followed him aboard. . . . Then, fifty yards from shore, they ran aground. . . . The General, impatient and annoyed, ordered the barge ramp lowered, stepped off into knee-deep brine, splashed forty wet strides to the beach, destroying the neat creases of his trousers. A news photographer snapped the famous picture of this.

His scowl, which millions of readers interpreted as a reflection of his steely determination, was actually a wrathful glare at the impertinent naval officer. When MacArthur saw a print of it, however, he instantly grasped its dramatic value, and the next day he deliberately waded ashore for cameramen on the 1st Calvary Division's White Beach. By then the shore was safe there, and troopers watching him assumed that he had waited until Japanese snipers had been cleared out. Later, seeing yesterday's photography, they condemned it as a phony. Another touch had been added to his antihero legend.[23]

"SIR, THERE ARE SNIPERS OVER THERE"

[But the facts were very different.] On Red Beach that first afternoon there were plenty of snipers, tied in trees or huddled in takotsubo—literally, "octopus traps," the Nipponese equivalent of foxholes. In his braided cap, pausing to relight his corncob from time to time, he once more made a conspicuous target. A Nambu opened up. He didn't even duck. As he strolled about, inspecting four damaged landing craft and looking for the 24th Division's command post, Kenney heard the General murmer to himself. "This is what I dreamed about." Kenney thought it was more like a nightmare. He could hear the taunts of enemy soldiers, speaking that broken English which was so familiar to soldiers and marines in the Pacific. . . .

The airman heard a GI crouched behind a coconut log gasp: "Hey, there's General MacArthur!" Without turning to look, the GI beside him drawled, "Oh yeah? And I suppose he's got Eleanor Roosevelt along with him." . . . Hearing heavy fire inland, he strolled in that direction, jovially asked an astonished fire team of the 24th, "How do you find the Nip?" and, seeing several fresh Japanese corpses, kicked them over with his wet toe to read their insignia. He said with deep satisfaction: "The Sixteenth Division. They're the ones that did the dirty work on Bataan."

Back at the shore, he sat on a coconut log by four wrecked Higgins boats, his back to the surf. A nervous lieutenant pointed toward a nearby grove and said, "Sir, there are snipers over there." The General seemed not to have heard him. He continued to stare entranced at the Leyte wilderness.

[Sitting there] MacArthur scrawled a letter to President Roosevelt.[24] Granting the Filipinos independence swiftly, he predicted, would "place American prestige in the Far East at the highest pinnacle of all times." On "the highest plane of statesmanship" the General urged "that this great ceremony be presided over by you in person": such a step would "electrify the world and rebound immeasurably to the credit and honor of the United States for a thousand years." . . .

[But] Roosevelt's failing health, his global command responsibilities, and his campaign for reelection prevented him from agreeing to broadcast an address to the Filipinos, so their first vivid recollection of their liberation was the two minute address which the General had edited on the *Nashville* and was now prepared to deliver.

"I HAVE RETURNED"

"People of the Philippines: I have returned," he said. His hands were shaking, and he had to pause to smooth out the wrinkles in his voice. He then continued, "By the grace of Almighty God, our forces stand again on Philippine soil—soil consecrated in the blood of our two peoples. . . . At my side is your President, Sergio Osmena, a worthy successor of that great patriot, Manuel Quezon. . . . The seat of your government is now, therefore, firmly reestablished on Philippine soil. The hour of your redemption is here. . . . Rally to me. Let the indomitable spirit of Bataan and Corregidor lead on. As the lines of battle roll forward to bring you within the zone of operations, rise and strike. Strike at every favorable opportunity. For your homes and hearths, strike! For future generations of your sons and daughters, strike! In the name of your sacred dead, strike! Let no heart be faint. Let every arm be steeled. The guidance of Divine God points the way. Follow in His name to the Holy Grail of righteous victory."[25]

Next Osmena and then Romulo spoke briefly into the hand-held mike. That ended the little ceremony, and a small cluster of Filipinos, who had been trapped here since the beginning of Kinkaid's bombardment, cheered.

Later Kenney wanted to inspect an old Japanese airfield nearby. MacArthur decided to join him. Kenney recalled that "my enthusiasm cooled when I found that the west end of the field was being used as a firing range by the Japs on one side and our troops on the other . . . We had to halt a couple of times on the way, once until a Jap sniper had been knocked out of a tree about 75 yards off the road and again when we had to wait for about twenty minutes until a Jap tank headed in our direction had been hit and the crew disposed of. We passed the burning tank on the way to the airdrome."

Once there, MacArthur paced around the strip, asking Kenney how quickly it could be made operational. Ricochets of enemy bullets were whining around them. The airman afterward remembered, "I told him I'd like to look at it under more favorable conditions, when I could inspect all of it at the same time. I added that I would feel much better at that moment if I were inspecting the place from an airplane. MacArthur laughed and said it was good for me to find out 'how the other half of the world lives.' "[26]

SURIGAO STRAITS

Now that MacArthur had committed himself to Leyte, now that over 200,000 troops of Krueger's Sixth Army were pouring ashore, the Japanese navy made its great move. Admiral Toyoda, flying his flag on Formosa, had hatched a brilliant plan. His main fleet, led by seven battleships, thirteen heavy cruisers, and three light cruisers, was racing up from Singapore under Vice Admiral Takeo Kurita. Kurita was instructed to divide this force in two, with the smaller detachment, under Vice Admiral Teji Nishamura, entering Leyte Gulf through Surigao Strait while the main body commanded by Kurita himself knifed through San Bernardino Strait. Both jaws would then converge on MacArthur's troop transports and Kinkaid's obsolescent warships. Banzai.

Halsey's Task Force 34, the backbone of his Third Fleet, was guarding San Bernardino Strait. To divert him, a third Nipponese flotilla of four overage carriers and two battleships converted into carriers was steaming down from the Japanese homeland. The mission of its commander, Vice Admiral Jisaburo Ozawa, was to entice Task Force 34 away from Leyte Gulf.

On the night of Monday, October 23, 1944, two U.S. submarines, the *Darter* and the *Dace*, sighted Kurita's main force off the coast of Borneo. At first light Tuesday morning, they torpedoed three of his cruisers, sinking two of them, and warned Halsey and Kinkaid that trouble was on its way. . . . Ozawa, the decoy commander, learned of this

development and tried to draw Halsey toward him by sending out uncoded messages. Halsey didn't pick up the signals, however, and his reconnaissance planes missed Ozawa because they were all flying westward, looking for Kurita's vanguard. Finding it, U.S. planes hit the massive *Musashi* thirty-six times, thereby sending to the bottom a vessel that the Japanese thought unsinkable. . . . Kurita turned his fleet away from Leyte Gulf, intending to sail beyond reach of U.S. naval planes until dark, when he could return. Halsey concluded that he was retreating and could now be ignored. But the American admiral noted that no enemy carriers had been sighted. Believing that there must be some in the vicinity, he sent up reconnaissance planes on broader searches. At 5:00 P.M. they finally discovered Ozawa's bait. Halsey went for it leaving San Bernardino Strait wide open.[27]

Tuesday night, under a roving moon, Admiral Nishimura, commanding Kurita's southern unit, entered the narrow waters of Surigao Strait. Rear Admiral Jesse Oldendorf, USN, had the strait corked. As the enemy vessels came through one by one, Oldendorf "crossed their T"—raked them viciously with broadsides from all his ships. Nishimura drowned and his force was wiped out; at dawn there would be nothing left of it but wreckage and streaks of oil. . . . Now, to his horror, [Kinkaid, who was guarding the San Bernardino Strait learned that the returning] Kurita was almost upon him, and that the Japanese force was intact except for the sunken *Musashi*. Kurita had passed through San Bernardino Strait and was already training his mammoth guns on part of Kinkaid's fleet, six escort carriers and a group of destroyers covering MacArthur's beachheads. The fox was among the chickens.

At 8:30 A.M. Kinkaid radioed Halsey: "Urgently need fast battleships Leyte Gulf at once." There was no response. . . . At this point there occurred one of the most remarkable episodes in the history of naval warfare. Kurita was less than thirty miles from his objective. All that stood between his guns and Kinkaid's carriers was a screen of destroyers and [antisubmarine] escorts . . . The destroyers counterattacked Kurita's battleships, and then their gallant little escorts sprang toward the huge Japanese armada, firing their small-bore guns and launching torpedoes. Kurita's Goliaths milled around in confusion as the persistent Davids, some of them sinking, made dense smoke. Kinkaid's carriers sent up everything that could fly, and Kurita with the mightiest Nipponese fleet since Midway, hesitated.[28]

"WHERE IS TASK FORCE 34?"

[Halsey] had gone so far in chasing the decoy that [his fleet] could not arrive until the next morning. By all the precedents of naval warfare but one, Kurita had won the battle. The exception was confusion. . . . He intercepted and misread two of Kinkaid's messages to Halsey. Believing that Halsey was approaching rapidly, and that he would soon bolt the door of San Bernardino Strait, Kurita turned tail. He passed through the strait a few minutes before 10:00 P.M.—unaware that Halsey's leading ships would not reach it for another three hours.

Thus ended the Battle of Leyte Gulf. It had involved 282 warships, compared with 250 at Jutland in 1916, until then the greatest naval engagement in history. And unlike Jutland, which neither side had won, this action had been decisive. The Americans had lost one light carrier, two escort carriers, and three destroyers. They had sunk four carriers, three battleships, six heavy cruisers, three light cruisers and eight destroyers. Except for sacrificial kamikaze fliers, who made their debut in this battle, Japanese air and naval strength would never again be serious instruments in the war.

"LEAVE THE BULL ALONE"

Thursday evening MacArthur was sitting down to dinner in the restored Price house when he heard staff officers at the other end of the table making recriminatory remarks about Halsey's action "in abandoning us" while he went after the Jap northern "decoy" fleet. The General slammed his bunched fist on the table. "That's enough!" he roared. "Leave the Bull alone! He's still a fighting admiral in my book."

[On the land] MacArthur had achieved strategic surprise. The troops of Shiro Makino's 16th Division were being slowly pushed back on Leyte's Highway 2, toward an eminence which American GIs had christened Breakneck Ridge . . . At the time MacArthur seemed to be just inching along. Unlike commanders of marines and Australians, the two other infantry forces in the Pacific, the General preferred to pause at enemy strongpoints, waiting until his artillery had leveled the enemy's defenses. When American newspapers fretted over this . . . MacArthur said, "If I like I can finish Leyte in two weeks, but I won't! I have too great a responsibility to the mothers and wives in America to do that to their men. I will not take by sacrifice what I can achieve by strategy."[29]

His greatest problem . . . was the weather, which erased the margin that superior naval and air power should have given him. He had called Leyte a springboard, but he was discovering that it could be a very soggy one. In forty days, thirty-four inches of rain fell, turning the island into one vast bog. The steady, drenching tropical monsoon made runway grading impossible . . . Finally a new strip was built on relatively solid ground at Tanauan, nine miles south of Tacloban, and P-38s began flying in and out, but Leyte never became the air base the General needed.[30]

THE COMMAND STYLE

[MacArthur's] staff continued to seethe and churn with plots, counterplots, and intrigues which would have been more appropriate in Medician Florence. Dr. Egeberg and Laurence E. "Larry" Bunker, like most survivors of it, blame Sutherland; "he divided the Gs—[G-1, administration; G-2, intelligence; G-3, operations; G-4, quartermaster]—against each other." But the chief of staff could hardly have pitted officers against one another without the knowledge, and even the encouragement, of the ironhanded commander in chief. What is extraordinary is the degree to which MacArthur convinced them that he knew nothing of the turmoil. . . .

MacArthur, like Roosevelt, was exploiting his position at the center of the staff. Kenney noted how "in a big staff meeting, or in conversation with a single individual, MacArthur has a wonderful knack of leading a discussion up to the point of a decision that each member present believes he himself originated. I have heard officers say many times, 'The Old Man bought my idea,' when it was something that weeks before I had heard MacArthur decide to do. . . . As a salesman, MacArthur had no superior and few equals." In other conferences, the General would identify a military target and invite suggestions on how it might be seized. Each officer would reply, he would ask broad questions, say "Thank you very much, gentlemen," and go off to ponder the problem himself.

Often an aide recalls "he would ask me questions and then answer them. For some of these interchanges I got a clear picture of the connection between chess and war. He might say, 'Now if we do this, which Steve suggested, they might do this, or if they were clever, they might do that. Now if they do this, we should answer them in one of three ways,' and he would outline the other alternatives, and then he would go to the Japanese answer to the six or seven possibilities. By the time he had done this for a day or a week, he would call his staff, establish the strategy which was amazingly frequently the opposite from the feeling of the majority, and which would seem always to have been right."[31]

He never lost an opportunity to remind his staff that while they were talking, other, younger men were dying. Before leaving Hollandia, each of the headquarters officers had chipped in twenty dollars apiece to buy liquor. The shipment arrived after they had left for Leyte, and it could not be forwarded without the General's permission. They chose Dick Marshall as their spokesman. After mess that evening, he cleared his throat and explained the problem. MacArthur asked, "What about the men? Have they got anything?" Marshall explained that they had beer. The General thought awhile and then said: "If beer is good enough for the enlisted men, it's good enough for the officers."[32]

THE LAST STEPPINGSTONE

Altogether [at Luzon] MacArthur would command nearly a thousand ships, accompanied by three thousand landing craft, many of them new arrivals from Normandy, and 280,000 men—more than Eisenhower's U.S. strength in the campaigns of North Africa, Italy, or southern France; more than the total Allied force in the conquest of Sicily. But Yamashita was lying in wait for him with 275,000 men, the largest enemy to be encountered in the Pacific campaigns. . . .

Although [Yamashita] had thirty-six thousand men on the Lingayen beaches, he withdrew them, having concluded that American firepower made resistance at the shoreline pointless, that with Halsey roaming the seas the best he could do was to prolong the struggle for the island, tying up MacArthur to buy time for the Japanese now furiously digging in on the home islands of Dai Nippon.

WALK ON WATER

Before dawn on Wednesday, January 10, the Americans lay off the landing beaches, and a thousand anchors plummeted into the gulf. It was a calm sea; there was less surf than anyone could remember. A typhoon had darted away at the last moment, and the different reactions of Americans and Filipinos to that lucky circumstance says much about their views of the General. U.S. war correspondents wondered whimsically whether he would walk on the water. To the Filipinos it was no laughing matter; many of them believed then, and believe to this day, that the gentle waves lapping the white sands were a consequence of divine intervention. MacArthur was the last man to disillusion them. He knew the power of myth in the minds of the islands' people. If they thought him capable of miracles, their conviction added a powerful weapon to his arsenal, one which his showmanship would polish.

After Krueger's first four divisions had splashed ashore, the commander in chief followed in his Higgins boat. In his memoirs he writes: "As was getting to be a habit with me, I picked a boat that took too much draft to reach the beach, and I had to wade in. . . . " It should be added that a group of peasants watching on the shore cheered lustily and hurried inland to spread the word of his second coming. That, of course, was precisely what he wanted them to do.[33]

"GET TO MANILA"

The General had told Eichelberger that he wanted him to "undertake a daring expedition against Manila with a small mobile force," using tactics which "would have delighted Jeb Stuart." The implication was that such a maneuver was too difficult for Kreuger, and while MacArthur was doubtless playing his two fighting generals against one another—as Napoleon did with his marshals, and as Stalin would soon do in encouraging Zhukov and Konev to race each other to Berlin—the General clearly regarded his senior field commander as unenterprising, and even timid.[34]

The ampitheater in which they were maneuvering, the island's central plain, is about 40 miles wide and 110 miles deep. . . . Though MacArthur had shown the defensive potential of Bataan and Corregidor, south of Manila, Yamashita preferred to withdraw the main body of his troops into the mountains to the east. And MacArthur somehow knew this. He was so sure of it that he saw no need to guard his left flank. "Get to Manila!" he told his field commanders. "Go around the Japs, bounce off the Japs, save your men, but get to Manila! Free the internees at Santo Tomas! Take Lalacanan and the legislative buildings!" But Krueger was haunted by the nightmare of a quarter-million Japanese driving in his flank pickets, cutting him off from the gulf, and "slicing him up like a pie." He wanted to spend two or three weeks consolidating his gains before advancing behind heavy artillery barrages toward the capital, which he assumed would be strongly defended.[35]

The General vehemently disagreed. Those, he said, were the tactics which had destroyed the flower of a generation in the trenches of World War I. Moreover, he pointed out, in his words . . . "I knew every wrinkle of the terrain, every foot of the topography." He saw no reason why flying columns shouldn't move swiftly down the fine roads leading southward between the rice paddies and neat little towns to Manila, which he believed would be undefended. MacArthur and Krueger [often] had words over this. . . . Yet MacArthur never pulled rank on him. Sutherland had frequently urged that Kreuger be "sent home"—Sutherland wanted to lead the Sixth Army himself—and others wondered why he wasn't. The likeliest explanation was that the General knew his plodding subordinate was a useful counterweight to his own bravura.[36]

CONTROL THE STRATEGY

[George Marshall wrote in an official report to the secretary of war] "Yamashita's inability to cope with MacArthur's swift moves" and "his desired reaction to the deception measures" combined "to place the Japanese in an impossible situation." The enemy "was forced into a piecemeal commitment of his troops." . . . "They were unable to conduct an orderly retreat, in classic fashion, to fall back on inner perimeters with forces intact for a last defense. . . . It was a situation unique in modern war. Never had such large numbers of troops been so outmaneuvered, . . . and left tactically impotent to take an active part in the final battle for their homeland."[37]

While Kreuger was investing Clark Field, his commander in chief was dazzling Yamashita with a series of lightning thrusts elsewhere. . . . Without losing a man, an expedition captured the invaluable port of Olangapo. Then he put a regiment ashore at Mariveles, on the peninsula's lower tip. Trapped in a double envelopment, Yamashita's Bataan garrison was isolated and impotent; the peninsula was taken in just seven days.[38]

The only remaining stronghold in the bay itself was Corregidor. In 1942 the Japanese had lost twice their landing force—several thousand men—to the gallant marines on the Rock's beaches. Now, with 5,200 enemy defenders in superb condition and provided with enormous stocks of ammunition, the fortress seemed far more formidable. MacArthur landed a regiment of airborne troops on Topside while an infantry battalion, with exquisite timing, leaped from Higgins boats to storm the Bottomside shore. After losing 1,500 men in a ten-day battle, the enemy commander holed up with the rest in Malinta Tunnel, where they committed suicide spectacularly by igniting a huge mass of explosives and blowing themselves up. The Americans' losses had been 210 men, 50 of them killed in that final blowup.

IN PERSONAL COMMAND

What makes [these events] all the more remarkable is that [MacArthur] was leaving his staff every morning to race around in his five-star jeep like a man forty years younger. "The Chief wanted to be in *personal* command," Eichelberger wrote, "and apparently he has done so." Willoughby wrote afterward: "Constantly on the front line—at times well ahead of it—his sheer physical endurance and his reckless exposure of himself excited the native population and even his own forces to a pitch of effort that became the dismay of the enemy." . . . He was everywhere, doing everything but digging the foxholes and loading the machine-gun belts. He watched the airborne drops from a B-17 overhead. On the central plain, he climbed on tanks to observe enemy patrols through field glasses. On Bataan he ventured five miles beyond American lines, hoping for a glimpse of Corregidor, and was almost strafed by a squadron of Kenny's fighters. He stood erect at an enemy roadblock, and when a nearby Nambu opened

up and an American lieutenant said, "We're going after those fellows, but please get down sir; we're under fire," MacArthur replied crisply, without moving, "I'm not under fire. Those bullets are not intended for me."[39]

In late January he was inspecting the 161st Infantry when the regiment was struck by a tank led counterattack. The American lines buckled, and MacArthur personally rallied the men. When Stimson heard about it, the General was awarded his third Distinguished Service Cross.

On another occasion, just north of Manila, his jeep halted at a blown bridge. . . . Shortly thereafter, he made what he called a "personal reconnaissance" inside the enemy-held city itself, touring the Malacanan Palace grounds and returning to report, like a scout, that he believed GIs "could cross the river and clear all southern Manila with a platoon." . . . As MacArthur had predicted, Yamashita had withdrawn his troops from the city, declaring that "the capital of the republic and its law-abiding inhabitants should not suffer from the ravages of war." MacArthur's headquarters informed senior U.S. officers that plans were being made "for a great victory parade à la Champs Elysees."

"DESTRUCTION IS IMMINENT"

At 6:00 P.M. on Saturday, February 3, patrols of the 1st Cavalry entered the city limits. Three days later, on Tuesday, MacArthur's communique announced: "Our forces are rapidly clearing the enemy from Manila. Our converging columns . . . entered the city and surrounded the Jap defenders. Their complete destruction is imminent."

Although the American public was unaware of the fact—the General's censors told correspondents they couldn't expose his victory communique as a lie—the fall of the capital was a month away . . . Eichelberger wrote on February 21, "the big parade has been called off." That was a shattering understatement. . . . The devastation of Manila was one of the great tragedies of World War II. Of Allied cities in those war years, only Warsaw suffered more. Seventy percent of the utilities, 75 percent of the factories, 80 percent of the southern residential district, and 100 percent of the business district were razed. Nearly 100,000 Filipinos were murdered by the Japanese. Hospitals were set afire after their patients had been strapped to their beds. The corpses of males were mutilated, females of all ages were raped before they were slain, and babies' eyeballs were gouged out and smeared on walls like jelly.

MacArthur blamed the holocaust on [Yamashita] but the guilt lay elsewhere. Yamashita's orderly evacuation into the hills had left about thirty thousand Japanese soldiers and marines under Rear Admiral Sanji Iwabuchi . . . Either Iwabuchi had not received the order from Yamashita declaring the capital an open city, or he chose to ignore it. Once he had decided to defend Manila, the atrocities began, and the longer the battle raged, the more the Japanese command structure deteriorated, until the uniforms of Nipponese sailors and marines were saturated with Filipino blood.

"THE ISLANDS ARE LIBERATED"

[Yet] the contrast between [MacArthur's] casualties and those of the enemy is, in fact, extraordinary. In his Philippine operations after Luzon he lost 820 GIs, while over 21,000 Japanese were slain. On July 5 he could announce: "The entire Philippine Islands are now liberated. . . . The Japanese during the operations employed twenty-three divisions, all of which were practically annihilated. Our forces comprised seventeen divisions. This was one of the rare instances when in a long campaign a ground force superior in numbers was entirely destroyed by a numerically inferior opponent."

In these battles he continued to expose himself to danger at the front. At Brunei Bay and Balikpapan, he insisted on going in with the assault waves. . . . Ashore at Brunei Bay he walked along a road paralleling the beach, about a quarter of a mile inland, with the sound of snipers' shots and machine guns on both sides. Kenney remembers beginning "to feel all over again as I had when we landed in the Philippines at Leyte. A tank lumbered by, and fifty yards ahead, atop a small rise, a rifleman and a machine gunner exchanged bursts of fire. MacArthur walked there to see what was happening. Two dead Japanese lay in a ditch. . . . An Australian army photographer appeared, hoping to take a picture of the General and the bodies. MacArthur refused, and the cameraman squared away to snap the two corpses. Just as his bulb flashed, the photographer fell with a sniper's bullet in his shoulder."[40]

ON TO JAPAN

[MacArthur] looked forward to Soviet entry into the Pacific war. By engaging a million Japanese and taking the sting out of their air force, he reckoned, Stalin would distract the enemy and save thousands of lives.

Meanwhile Hirohito's generals, grimly preparing for the invasion [of Japan] had not abandoned hope of saving their homeland. Although a few strategic islands had been lost, they told each other, most of their conquests, including the Chinese heartland, were firmly in their hands, and the bulk of their army was undefeated. Even now they could scarcely believe that any foe would have the audacity to attempt landings in Japan itself. Allied troops, they

boasted, would face the fiercest resistance in history. Over ten thousand kamikaze planes were readied for "Ketsu-Go," Operation Decision. Behind the beaches, enormous connecting underground caves had been stocked with caches of food and thousands of tons of ammunition. Manning the nation's ground defenses were 2,350,000 regular soldiers, 250,000 garrison troops, and 32,000,000 civilian militiamen—a total of 34,600,000, more than the combined armies of the United States, Great Britain, and Nazi Germany. All males aged fifteen to sixty, and all females aged seventeen to forty-five, had been conscripted. Their weapons included ancient bronze cannon, muzzle-loading muskets, bamboo spears, and bows and arrows. Even little children had been trained to strap explosives around their waists, roll under tank treads, and blow themselves up. They were called "Sherman carpets."

FANATICS OR DOVES?

This was the enemy the Pentagon had learned to fear and hate—a country of fanatics dedicated to harakiri, determined to slay as many invaders as possible as they went down fighting. But there was another Japan, and MacArthur was one of the few Americans who suspected its existence. He kept urging the Pentagon and the State Department to be alert for conciliatory gestures. Kenney notes that the General predicted that "the break would come from Tokyo, not from the Japanese army." . . . A dovish coalition was forming in the Japanese capital, and it was headed by Hirohito himself, who had concluded in the spring of 1945 that a negotiated peace was the only way to end his nation's agony. Beginning in early May a six-man council of Japanese diplomats explored ways to accommodate the Allies.

Had Roosevelt been alive, his fine political antennae might have sensed the possibilities here. But Truman, new in office and less flexible in diplomacy, was swayed by such advisers as Dean Acheson, Archibald MacLeish, and Hopkins who believed that negotiations were pointless; that unless Hirohito was unthroned, the war would have been in vain. The upshot was the Potsdam declaration in July, demanding that Japan surrender unconditionally or face "prompt and utter destruction." MacArthur was appalled. He knew that the Japanese would never renounce their emperor, and that without him an orderly transition to peace would be impossible anyhow, because his people would never submit to Allied occupation unless he ordered it. Ironically, when the surrender did come, it was conditional, and the condition was a continuation of the imperial reign. Had the General's advice been followed, the resort to atomic weapons at Hiroshima and Nagasaki might have been unnecessary.[41]

In an implacable mood then, successive versions of "Downfall," the code word for the invasion of Dai Nippon, were drafted in Washington and revised in Manila. . . . "Downfall" would begin with "Operation Olympic," a frontal assault on Kyushu by 766,700 Allied troops under Kreuger on November 1, 1945, whose purpose would be to secure, in the General's words "airfields to cover the main assault on Honshu." The second phase "Operation Coronet," the landing on Honshu, would follow on March 1, 1946. He himself probably with Eichelberger as his chief of staff would lead that.[42]

He had no illusions about the savagery that lay ahead—he told Stimson that Downfall would "cost over a million casualties to American forces alone"—but he was confident that with the tanks from Europe he could outmaneuver the defenders on the great Kanto Plain before Tokyo.

THE ATOMIC BOMB

With each passing day the General felt surer that peace was very near. Two weeks before Hiroshima he told Kenney that he believed the enemy would surrender "by September 1 at the latest and perhaps even sooner." On Sunday, August 5, a courier arrived from Washington with word that an atomic bomb would be dropped "on an industrial area south of Tokyo the following day." . . . Three days later President Truman suspended B-29 raids on Japan; three days after that, on Wednesday, August 15, Hirohito ordered an end to all hostilities at 4:00 P.M. Tokyo time, telling his people that they must "endure the unendurable and suffer the insufferable." Truman, with the approval of Clement Attlee, Stalin, and Chiang Kai-shek, appointed MacArthur Supreme Commander for the Allied Powers (SCAP).

THE OCCUPATION

One of his first acts, he told Bonner Fellers, would be to give women the vote. "The Japanese men won't like it," said Fellers, and indeed, as events would prove, many of them regarded it as worse than sexual assault. The General said, "I don't care. I want to discredit the military. Women don't like war." It was part of his enigmatic temperament that although he could be ungenerous toward American admirals and uncivil toward his superiors in Washington, he was an imaginative, magnanimous conqueror. He intended, he said, to "use the instrumentality of the Japanese government to implement the occupation." Sitting in front of a Quonset hut and puffing on his pipe, he told an aide that woman suffrage was only one point in his seven-point plan for Japan. The others were disarming Japanese soldiers, sending them home, dismantling war industry, holding free elections, encouraging the formation of labor unions, and opening all schools with no check on instruction except the elimination of military indoctrination and the addition of courses in civics.[43]

"OF ALL THE AMAZING DEEDS"

Later Winston Churchill said: "Of all the amazing deeds in the war, I regard General MacArthur's personal landing at Atsugi [Japan] as the bravest of the lot." John Gunther wrote: "Professors who studied Japan all their lives, military experts who knew every nook and cranny of the Japanese character, thought that 'MacArthur was taking a frightful risk.'" In Manila Sutherland remonstrated: "My God General, the emperor is worshipped as a real god, yet they still tried to assassinate him. What kind of target does that make you?" MacArthur replied that he believed the reported attempt on Hirohito's life was spurious—he was right, although there was no way of knowing it then—and when his C-54, with "Bataan" emblazoned on its nose, touched down for a brief stop on Okinawa, and he noticed that Kenney and the others were strapping on pistols in shoulder holsters, he said, " Take them off. If they intend to kill us, sidearms will be useless. And nothing will impress them like a show of absolute fearlessness. If they don't know they're licked, this will convince them."[44]

The General knew that word of everything he said and did would quickly spread throughout the country. He was determined that the occupation be benign from the outset. Moreover, remembering his tour of duty in Germany after the 1918 Armistice, he realized that in a war-torn, defeated country, food would be at a premium. . . . When the commander of the 11th Airborne ruefully reported that his division had searched all night and found exactly one egg for the Supreme Commander's breakfast, MacArthur immediately issued an order at odds with the whole history of conquering armies in Asia. Occupation troops were forbidden to consume local victuals; they would eat only their own rations. An hour later, he canceled the martial law and curfew decrees Eichelberger had imposed on the city. The first step in the reformation of Japan, he said, would be an exhibition of generosity and compassion of the occupying power.[45]

That evening he was sitting down to dinner in the hotel when an aide reported that he had a visitor outside: Lieutenant General Jonathan M. Wainwright. Liberated from his Manchurian prisoner-of-war camp by the Russians four days earlier . . . was the man the General had left in command [at Corregidor] in 1942 . . . [Wainwright] was haggard and aged. . . . He walked with difficulty and with the help of a cane. His eyes were sunken and there were pits in his cheeks. His hair was snow white and his skin looked like old shoe leather. . . . For three years he had imagined himself in disgrace for having surrendered Corregidor. He believed he would never again be given an active command. This shocked MacArthur. "Why, Jim," he said, "Your old corps is yours when you want it."[46] Wainwright said, "General . . . " Then his voice wavered and he burst into tears.

THE FINAL CEREMONY

Early Sunday morning, two days later, a destroyer took Wainwright out to the slate-gray, forty-five thousand ton battleship *Missouri*, on Tokyo Bay. . . .

[At the ceremony, MacArthur's] stance was a portrait of soldierly poise. Only his hand trembled slightly as he held a single sheet of paper before him and said: "We are gathered here, representatives of the major warring powers, to conclude a solemn agreement whereby peace may be restored. . . . Both the conquerors and the conquered must rise to that higher dignity which alone befits the sacred purposes we are about to serve. . . . To the Pacific basin has come the vista of a new emancipated world. Today, freedom is on the offensive, democracy is on the march. Today, in Asia, as well as in Europe, unshackled peoples are tasting the full sweetness of liberty, the relief from fear." He concluded: "And so, my fellow countrymen, today I report to you that your sons and daughters have served you well and faithfully with the calm, deliberate, determined fighting spirit of the American soldier and sailor. . . . Their spiritual strength and power has brought us through to victory. They are homeward bound—take care of them."[47]

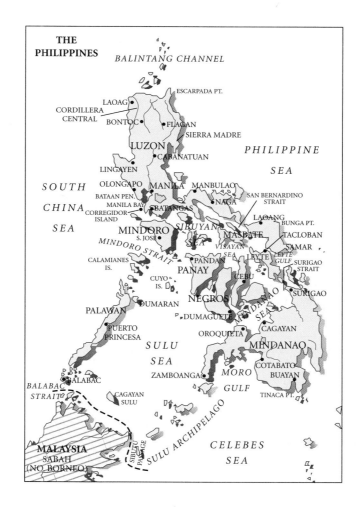

Rudi Gassner and the Executive Committee of BMG International (A)

Rudi Gassner, CEO of BMG International, paused and glanced around the hotel suite at the members of his executive committee. They were not coming to any consensus on the issue at hand. It was May 1993 and the BMG International executive committee was gathered for one of its quarterly meetings, this time in Boca Raton, Florida, during the annual Managing Directors Convention.

Gassner had just congratulated Arnold Bahlmann, a regional director and executive committee member, on his recent negotiation of a reduced manufacturing transfer price for the upcoming year's production of CDs, records, and cassettes. Because business plans for the year had been established in March based on the assumption of a higher manufacturing cost, the new price would realize an unanticipated savings of roughly $20 million.

As a result of these savings, the executive committee now faced some tough decisions. First, they had to decide whether or not to change business targets for each country to reflect the new manufacturing price. If they chose to alter the targets, they had to address the even more delicate matter of whether managing directors' bonuses, which were based principally on the achievement of these targets, should be based on the old or new figures.

Gassner had already discussed this issue with Bahlmann and CFO Joe Gorman, who had run calculations on the impact of the new price for each operating company. These had been distributed to the executive committee before the meeting. Through previous discussions and evaluation of the financial impact, Gassner had formulated his opinion about what should be done.

In his mind, the issues were clear. BMG International had achieved tremendous success and growth in its short lifetime of six years, and the regional directors (RDs) and managing directors (MDs)[1] had every right to feel good about their exceptional performance. (See Exhibits 1 and 2 for company organization charts.) But now Gassner wanted to guard against the company becoming a victim of its own success. He knew that they would have to carefully monitor the economics of the business and maintain their agility in order to meet the challenges of the future. In light of these concerns, Gassner felt that the MDs should be held accountable for the savings from the reduced manufacturing price. The executive committee needed seriously to consider not only adjusting the targets, but also the bonus basis. As he explained, "It seemed fair to me. These were windfall profits coming to the managing directors, and they didn't even have to lift a finger to get them. I didn't want them to become complacent during the year."

The executive committee, however, seemed unwilling even to entertain this possibility. Gassner suspected that some of the RDs were taking the "path of least resistance" because they did not want to return to their MDs and announce that the bonus targets had been changed. His

Research Associate Katherine Seger Weber prepared this case under the supervision of Professor Linda A. Hill.

EXHIBIT 1 BERTELSMANN MUSIC GROUP ORGANIZATION CHART

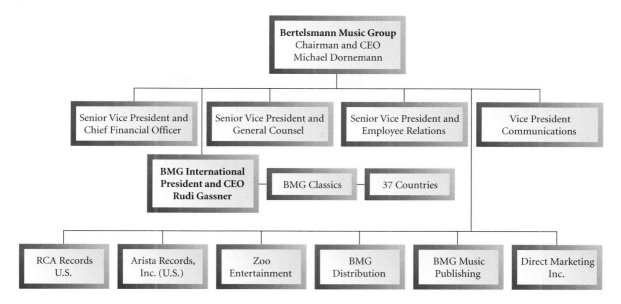

frustration mounting, Gassner wondered if he should drop the issue for now or provoke them by saying what was on his mind: "Listen guys, you're thinking too much like MDs. You should be thinking about what is good for the whole company."

COMPANY BACKGROUND

BMG International was a subsidiary of Bertelsmann AG, a German media conglomerate with over 200 companies and 50,000 employees operating in 37 countries. Founded in 1835 as a lithographic printing company in Guetersloh, Germany, Bertelsmann's interests had grown to include businesses in music, film, television, radio, book, magazine, and newspaper publishing and distribution, as well as printing and manufacturing operations. Still headquartered in the small rural town, Bertelsmann had become the second-largest media enterprise in the world, with 1992 sales of $9.7 billion.

Bertelsmann's corporate charter mandated autonomous business divisions and entrepreneurial operating management, and emphasized respect for the cultural traditions of each country in which it operated. Each business unit had its own, usually local, entrepreneurial management with operating control over its business plan, the development of its assets, its human resources, and its contribution to overall profitability. Delegation of responsibility and authority was supported by perfor-

mance-linked compensation for managers and profit-sharing by all employees.

In 1986, Bertelsmann entered the U.S. market with its purchase of Doubleday and Dell, two large publishing houses, and RCA Records, which had made music history with Elvis Presley in the 1950s. On acquiring RCA, Bertelsmann organized its worldwide music holdings—which also included the American record label Arista, the German label Ariola, and various smaller labels and music publishing and marketing operations—into the Bertelsmann Music Group (BMG). With RCA, BMG entered the ranks of the "Big Six" record companies—CBS, Warner, BMG, Capitol-EMI, PolyGram, and MCA—which supplied 80% of worldwide music sales.[2]

BMG was headquartered in New York under German Chairman and CEO Michael Dornemann, who split the company's operations into two divisions: the United States and the rest of the world. In the United States, BMG's priority was to stem the losses from RCA (which posted a $35 million deficit in 1987) and build market share for the flagging U.S. labels.[3]

With BMG's overseas holdings, Dornemann formed an international division and hired German-born Rudi Gassner, then executive vice president of PolyGram International, as president and CEO (see Exhibit 3). According to Dornemann, Gassner "had the right background in the music business and the right international experience. He best fit the leadership qualities we were looking for."[4] At its inception in 1987, the international

EXHIBIT 2 BMG INTERNATIONAL ORGANIZATION CHART, 1993

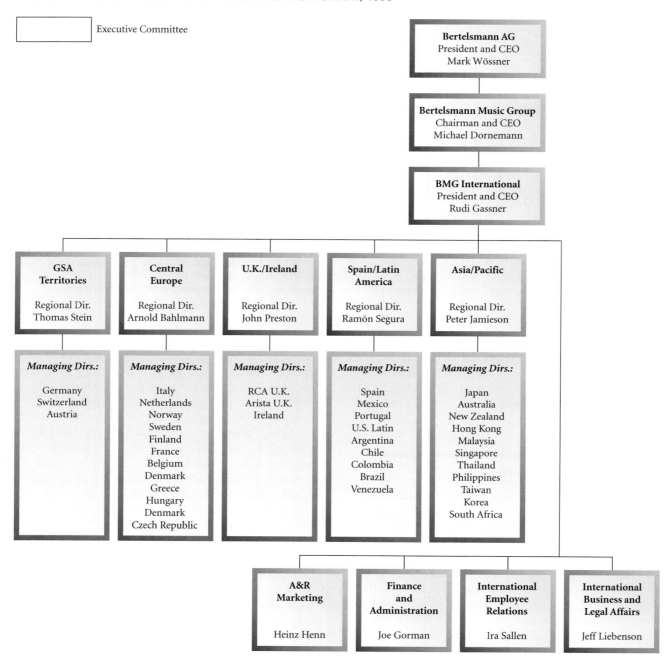

Executive Committee

Bertelsmann AG
President and CEO
Mark Wössner

Bertelsmann Music Group
Chairman and CEO
Michael Dornemann

BMG International
President and CEO
Rudi Gassner

GSA Territories	**Central Europe**	**U.K./Ireland**	**Spain/Latin America**	**Asia/Pacific**
Regional Dir. Thomas Stein	Regional Dir. Arnold Bahlmann	Regional Dir. John Preston	Regional Dir. Ramón Segura	Regional Dir. Peter Jamieson

Managing Dirs.:	*Managing Dirs.:*	*Managing Dirs.:*	*Managing Dirs.:*	*Managing Dirs.:*
Germany Switzerland Austria	Italy Netherlands Norway Sweden Finland France Belgium Denmark Greece Hungary Denmark Czech Republic	RCA U.K. Arista U.K. Ireland	Spain Mexico Portugal U.S. Latin Argentina Chile Colombia Brazil Venezuela	Japan Australia New Zealand Hong Kong Malaysia Singapore Thailand Philippines Taiwan Korea South Africa

A&R Marketing	**Finance and Administration**	**International Employee Relations**	**International Business and Legal Affairs**
Heinz Henn	Joe Gorman	Ira Sallen	Jeff Liebenson

division, also headquartered in New York, comprised operations in 17 countries across the globe. Gassner described the fledgling organization as "a patchwork of companies around the world. It had no mission, no goals, and in total, it didn't make any money. . . . The only way from there was up.[5]

In his first six years, Gassner led the company, which he named BMG International, through a tremendous period of growth. By launching new satellite companies, purchasing small labels, and forming joint ventures, BMG International's presence had expanded by 1993 to include 37 countries. Sales had increased an average of 20% annu-

EXHIBIT 3
RUDI GASSNER
CAREER HIGHLIGHTS

Rudi Gassner
President and CEO, BMG International German, 51 years old
- 1984–1987: Executive VP, PolyGram International, London
- 1983–1984: President, Polydor International (PolyGram), Hamburg
- 1980–1983: President, Deutsche Grammophon (PolyGram), Hamburg
- Fall 1979: Harvard Business School Program for Management Development (PMD)
- 1977–1980: Managing Director, Metronome (PolyGram), Hamburg
- 1969–1977: Sales Manager, Deutsche Grammophon (PolyGram), Munich
- 1964–1969: Music Wholesaling, Munich

ally, reaching $2 billion in 1993 (two-thirds of BMG's overall revenue that year). International market share, which was near 11% in 1987, was a healthy 17%, and as high as 25% in some territories.[6]

BMG International was responsible for marketing and distributing top-selling U.S. artists such as Whitney Houston and Kenny G across the globe.[7] In addition, the company developed such artists as Annie Lennox and Lisa Stansfield (Britain) and Eros Ramazzotti (Italy) in their local territories to be marketed worldwide. On a local level, groups such as B'z (Japan) and Bronco (Mexico) were extremely successful, selling in excess of 1 million units in their respective countries. The company also had extensive classics and jazz catalogues, with artists such as James Galway and Antonio Hart. (See Exhibit 4) for roster of top-selling artists.)[8]

RUDI GASSNER AND BMG INTERNATIONAL

In 1987, at the age of 45, Gassner became the CEO of the newly formed BMG International. "It was a once-in-a-lifetime opportunity," he reflected, "to build what I think a global company should look like." When he arrived at BMG, Gassner adapted quickly to the Bertelsmann culture. "My 17 years at PolyGram gave me the experience to run a global business; that was my know-how," he explained. "But on the other hand, I very much liked the Bertelsmann style. It was very close to my personal style." One of his colleagues at BMG described Gassner's transition:

> Rudi came from PolyGram, which had a very different culture. The Philips PolyGram culture is highly politically charged; it is much more "stand by your beds when the senior management

EXHIBIT 4
SELECTED BMG
INTERNATIONAL
TOP-SELLING
ARTISTS, 1993

ARTIST	COUNTRY OF ORIGIN	UNITS SOLD 1992/1993 (IN THOUSANDS)
Global Superstars:		
Whitney Houston	United States	11,800
Kenny G	United States	2,200
Annie Lennox	United Kingdom	1,200
David Bowie	United Kingdom	700
SNAP	Germany	700
Dr. Alban	Germany	600
Regional Superstars:		
Vaya Con Dios	Belgium	1,300
Juan Luis Guerra	Spain	1,100
Eros Ramazzotti	Italy	1,100
Die Prinzen	Germany	900
Take That	United Kingdom	700
Bonnie Tyler	Germany	500
Local Superstars:		
B'z	Japan	5,700
Bronco	Mexico	1,300
Joaquin Sabina	Spain	500
Jose Jose	Mexico	400
Lucio Dalla	Italy	250

comes in." Rudi changed a lot when he came to BMG. He saw the value in the Bertelsmann managing style; he saw the freedom to do things, and he took it. He passed it on as well.

BUILDING BMG INTERNATIONAL

One of Gassner's first priorities was to instill this culture in the newly acquired companies. He reflected on what he inherited when he joined BMG:

> My first step was basically to get to know the companies and the problems hands-on myself. RCA had been centrally managed out of New York, and the managers in the companies had the attitude that "I'm not doing anything unless somebody tells me what to do." I would find them hiding under tables. I spent the first two years preaching my gospel and saying to the managers, "You are responsible. I can give you advice, but don't send me a memo asking me to sign off here. You are in charge: you are Mr. Italy; you are Mr. France; you are Mr. Belgium."

At the same time, Gassner also began to communicate his vision for BMG International. "There were basically two strategic targets in my mind," he explained:

> One was globalization. Globalization allows you to serve a bigger would market. Every time we added a new country, we would increase our revenue accordingly. The other strategic target was domestic repertoire. I had a great fear of being too dependent on English-speaking repertoire. I made it clear to the managers that their foremost responsibility was developing domestic talent. Joint ventures and acquisitions were another way to add local repertoire.

Gassner also instituted yearly business plans with each of his managing directors. He described the process:

> We [Gassner and each MD] do a budget once a year. The budget is between you and me. I want to know where you are going and how much investment you will need. We talk about revenues and profits. I make a very aggressive bonus plan for them to be able to make a lot of money; if they exceed their targets significantly, they can make up to half their salary as a bonus. In America, this might not have been so sensational, but for those countries who were not used to that, it was pretty new.

According to Gassner, "the majority of the guys came through with flying colors." For those who did not fit with the new program, Gassner held "career counseling sessions," as one colleague referred to them: "When Rudi conducts a career counseling session, it's pretty much over. But he's so smooth and so good at it, that it takes them about a week to figure out that they may have just been fired."

Gassner also turned his attention inward, focusing on his corporate management structure. "One advantage, obviously, was that nothing existed. I could do it any way I wanted. That was fantastic." He made Joe Gorman, who had been the senior finance executive for RCA's international arm, the chief financial officer of BMG International. During Gassner's first two years, Gorman accompanied him as he traveled around the world assessing each operating company.

Gassner's next corporate hire was Heinz Henn to coordinate global A&R marketing.[9] Henn had spent 17 years at EMI in international positions. He described his job interview with Gassner:

> Rudi and I met for the first time on February 17, 1987, at the Park Lane Hotel and had breakfast together. What got me the job was that I ate two breakfasts—I was really hungry that day. He was impressed that somebody could eat two full breakfasts on a job interview.
>
> Seriously, Rudi asked me what I would do if he gave me the job, and I told him that I would do things differently than they had done so far in the industry, particularly [the companies] where we had both come from. I wanted to cultivate local talent in individual markets to build hot acts which we could launch globally. He totally agreed with me. Ever since, he's let me do what I wanted to do.

Gassner described the need for Henn's role:

> Heinz has a dual role: he not only has to break local artists worldwide, he also has to sell Whitney Houston to all the local companies. We need Heinz because the interests of the countries and the regions stop at the borders, and we need a global view on artists. This will give us the competitive advantage; there's more money to be made outside the borders if you do it right.

Henn added:

> You have to have coordination between the regions as far as marketing and promotion activities are concerned because recording and marketing expenses are far too great these days for any one [local] company to be able to earn back its investment in one country only. It requires coordination between regions and also globally.

To round out his corporate staff, Gassner added a human resource executive, Ira Sallen, and legal counsel, Jeff Liebenson. Sallen would be responsible for negotiating and maintaining the managing director's contracts, as well as for worldwide personnel and organizational policies. Liebenson would serve as in-house counsel, assisting in the intricate contracts that were part of operating a complex global enterprise.

Gassner also instituted an annual Managing Directors' Convention in which Dornemann, Gassner, the corporate staff, and all of the MDs and joint-venture partners (JVs) would converge from around the world. A major objective of the annual MD Convention was to provide a forum for the MDs and JVs to give repertoire presentations to each other in an attempt to sell their local repertoire to the other countries.

CREATING A REGIONAL STRUCTURE

As BMG International's number of operating companies continued to grow, it became impossible for Gassner directly to oversee them all. By 1989, he concluded it was time to aggregate the countries into five regions and hire a regional director for each, a plan he had had in mind from the beginning. (See Exhibit 2 for organization chart and Exhibit 5 for revenue and profit distribution by region.) The role of the RD would be "to provide leadership for the region; to oversee the strategic development of the region,

in conjunction with the whole company; and to manage the managing directors." He explained:

I divided Europe into three different categories: the United Kingdom, German-speaking territories, and the rest of Europe. At that time, the German-speaking territories contributed about 50% of our profit, so they were a very important group unto themselves. I promoted Thomas Stein, who was the managing director of the German company, to regional director.

The United Kingdom, despite its relatively small profits, was our largest source of repertoire, a major supplier. I promoted John Preston, who was the MD of RCA Records U.K., to be the regional director of that region.

The MD for Ariola Spain, Ramon Segura, was an outstanding executive who also had, at that time, regional respon-

EXHIBIT 5
BMG INTERNATIONAL REVENUE AND OPERATING RESULT DISTRIBUTION BY REGION

Net Revenue by Region:

1988/1989

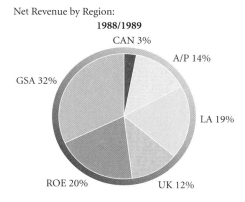

1992/1993

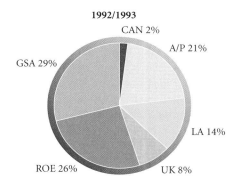

Operating Result (Betriebsergebnis) by Region:

1988/1989

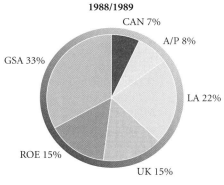

1992/1993

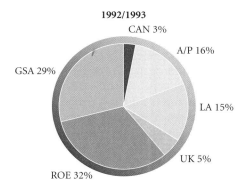

Legend
A/P = Asia/Pacific;
CAN = Canada;
LA = Latin America;
GSA = Germany/Switzerland/Austria;
ROE = Rest of Europe;
UK = United Kingdom.

sibilities for Ariola's Latin American companies. So I kept Spain/Latin America together as a region and made Segura the RD.

Now I needed someone for the rest of Europe. I hired Arnold Bahlmann, who was working in strategic analysis for Michael Dornemann. He was not one of the music managers coming through the ranks. He had never had a line job in his life. Still, I thought, you don't necessarily need the detailed day-to-day experience of running a company to manage a regional territory. It was an organizational task, and I thought Arnold had very good people skills. I thought he was ideal, though it was a hell of a risk to put him in.

At the same time as I promoted John Preston to RD in the United Kingdom, I asked the chairman of the RCA U.K. label, Peter Jamieson, to go out and establish our Asia/Pacific market. I remember a British competitor in the industry joking with me that "wasn't I worried about sending one of my best men out to the colonies?" I thought Jamieson was just the right person for the job. He accepted, and he's done a brilliant job building companies and repertoire in that region.

Gassner maintained the annual business planning system he had established with the MDs, but he now worked through the RDs. As Segura described it, "We are involved throughout the process, but Rudi has final approval." BMG International's fiscal year started July 1 and ran through June 30. In January, the MDs began to prepare their business plans, developing targets for critical measures such as revenue, *betriebsergebnis*,[10] return on sales, market share, revenue per employee, days inventory, and days sales outstanding. Gassner was as much interested in the assumptions used to arrive at the targets as the figures themselves; MDs were expected to include an in-depth analysis of the risks and opportunities they faced based on the current economic climate and market, new A&R releases, and their priority artists.

In February, the MDs met with the RDs to review their plans; the RDs then met with Gassner to discuss regional as well as local goals. Gorman described Gassner's stance in these meetings: "Rudi has a reputation for being tough—fair, but tough. One of the reasons he has that reputation is that he makes you do things which you know you should do, but which you don't want to do." One RD described these sessions as "the famous February meetings. Rudi and I dislike each other a lot in February. But by March we usually agree."

In March, the RDs returned to the MDs with a final plan and targets; Gassner and Gorman joined many of these sessions (see Exhibit 6). At this point, the MDs would have a final opportunity to discuss their plans and the targets would be agreed upon. Gorman described these meetings:

> March is the critical planning month for us. We tell everybody, look, when the meeting is over, we all walk out of here with the

same goals. Period. We can sit in the room an hour, or we can sit there for two days, but in the end nobody is going to leave this room disagreeing on what the goals are. In these meetings, MD bonus criteria are also defined, since *betriebsergebnis* is the primary criterion for bonuses.

One RD described Gassner's approach:

> Rudi plays a different role with each MD, depending on their personality and where he wants the country to go. Sometimes he plays the good cop, and other times he plays the bad cop. He's very versatile, and very results-oriented. When necessary, he knows how to hit people's hot buttons and make them squirm.

According to one MD:

> Rudi knows the business inside and out, and he has an amazing grasp of the details. When he is going through these plans, he will go into particular line items if he wants to. These business plans are like contracts between Rudi and me. Face-to-face with him, I am committing to try to make this target. It's like a moral imperative to get it done.

According to Bahlmann, "The business plans serve their purpose well. If you ask me if I enjoy them—no. It's not enjoyable. I hate the process. But it works." Stein concurred: "The business plans help me explain what I think should be done in my region. It's a fair process because it's based on an objective financial measure." Another RD, however, commented on the danger inherent in the system:

> The business plan process is a necessary and effective tool. But the danger is that it becomes too inflexible. Instead of a jacket which guides, a sort of loose piece of clothing which shapes the way we operate, it becomes a straightjacket and restricts the way we operate.

Even with the addition of the regional directors, Gassner maintained close contact with the local companies around the world. "I emphasize what I call a very flat hierarchical structure," he explained. "I'm never too far removed from what's really happening." While he was primarily in contact with the RDs, Gassner always reserved the right to call the MDs directly, and they "feel absolutely free to call me about anything," according to Gassner. "But they all know that it is a two-way information system. Whatever they tell me, they know I will pass on to their regional director. And whatever they tell the RD, they know he passes on to me." When possible, Gassner made it a point to reach further into the organization by talking informally with local employees "just to double-check that my messages come through."

Gassner's style of running a global business was extremely demanding. Travel was a way of life: he and his corporate staff spent 50% or more of their time away from New York headquarters, and the regional directors traveled constantly throughout their regions. According to Gorman,

EXHIBIT 6
MARCH 1992
BUSINESS PLANNING
MEETINGS ATTENDED
BY RUDI GASSNER
AND JOE GORMAN

LOCATION:	DATE:	REVIEW:	
Munich	March 1	10:00AM	Belgium
		11:30AM	Netherlands
		2:00PM	Italy
	March 2	10:00AM	UK–RCA
		2:00PM	UK–Arista
		4:00PM	UK–Distrib.
	March 3	10:00AM	GSA Overview
		11:30AM	Munich Ariola
		2:00PM	Germany Ariola
		3:45PM	Hamburg Ariola
	March 4	10:00AM	Germany Ariola
		11:30AM	Austria
		2:00PM	Switzerland
	March 5	10:00AM	France Ariola
		11:30AM	France Vogue
		1:30PM	France RCA
		4:00PM	European Regional Overview
New York	March 10	10:00AM	Canada
		2:00PM	Home Office
Hong Kong	March 16	10:00AM	Australia
		3:00PM	Hong Kong
	March 17	10:00AM	Japan
		3:00PM	Taiwan
	March 18	10:00AM	South Africa
		3:00PM	Malaysia
	March 19	10:00AM	Asia/Pacific Regional Overview
New York	March 24	10:00AM	Mexico
		2:00PM	U.S. Latin
		4:00PM	Portugal
	March 25	10:00AM	Brazil
		2:00PM	Spain
	March 26	10:00AM	Latin America Regional Overview

Rudi believes that you are not managing an international company unless you travel extensively, because it's all about people. The financial statements are fine, the statistics are fine. But in the end, you have to sit down with somebody in a room and talk to them to get a real sense for the people and for what's going on. There are things that always come out "by the way. . . . " When you go out to dinner or you're at a concert until 4:00 in the morning, a lot of this comes out.

THE EXECUTIVE COMMITTEE AND THE ECMS

In 1989, after he had established his corporate staff and the regional structure, Gassner formally created an Executive Committee consisting of the five regional directors, the four senior staff members, and himself as the leader (see Exhibit 7). He recalled:

I had always intended to have an executive committee. I always wanted to run a business on the basis of a European board system, like a *vorstand*:[11] although it is chaired by one person and

members have their own portfolios [regions], the committee decides business issues jointly.

The way I see it, the board should decide about important issues strategically or from an investment point of view. And I wanted everybody to be involved in the process, despite the fact that some issues may not have a direct consequence for their region.

You cannot run a global organization without breaking it down into regions—it just becomes impossible. On the other hand, you have to have a global strategy. In our business, the regions are interlinked by artist agreements and by the exchange of repertoire. So it needs both a regional organization and a global vision.

Bahlmann recalled Gassner introducing the concept of an executive committee by describing it as "the group which will lead BMG International." Gassner decided that the committee would meet four times per year at the New York headquarters to discuss current operating issues, and once a year outside of New York to examine long-term

EXHIBIT 7
BMG INTERNATIONAL
EXECUTIVE
COMMITTEE

REGIONAL DIRECTORS

Arnold Bahlmann
Senior VP, Central Europe
• German, 41 years old.
• Promoted from: Senior VP Operations, BMG.
• 3 years strategic planning, Bertelsmann.
• Doctorate in Political Science.
• Master of Business Administration

Thomas Stein
President, GSA Territories
• German, 44 years old.
• Promoted from: Managing Director, BMG Ariola, Munich.
• 14 years sales, marketing, and management in record business.

John Preston
Chairman, BMG Records (U.K.) Ltd.
• Scottish, 43 years old.
• Promoted from: Managing Director, RCA Records, U.K.
• 19 years retail, marketing, and management in record business.

Ramon Segura
President, Spain and Sr. VP, Latin America
• Spanish, 52 years old.
• Promoted from: MD, Spain, and VP Latin American Region, Ariola Eurodisc.
• 31 years sales, A&R, marketing, and management in record business.

Peter Jamieson
Senior VP, Asia/Pacific
• English, 48 years old.
• Promoted from: Chairman, BMG Records U.K.
• 26 years marketing, sales, and management in record business.

NEW YORK CORPORATE STAFF

Heinz Henn
Senior VP, A&R/Marketing
• German, 38 years old.
• Promoted from: Director of International Division, Capitol/EMI America Records.
• 17 years A&R/marketing, promotion, and management in record business.

Joe Gorman
Senior VP, Finance and Administration
• American, 50 years old.
• Promoted from: Director, Operations Planning, RCA Records (U.S.).
• 10 years finance at RCA Records.
• 5 years Arthur Young & Company.
• Master of Business Administration.
• Military service, Captain, U.S. Army.

Ira Sallen
VP, International Human Resources, BMG
• American, 39 years old.
• Promoted from: VP, Human Resources, Clean Harbors, Inc.
• 4 years corporate human resources.
• 2 years Consultant, Arthur Young & Company.
• 5 years research and clinical psychology.
• Master of Business Administration.

Jeff Liebenson
VP, Int'l. Legal and Business Affairs, BMG
• American, 40 years old.
• Promoted from: Director, Legal and Business Affairs, Sports Channel America.
• 15 years legal experience, including 12 in entertainment industry.
• J.D and LL.M. law degrees.

---

strategy. Before each executive committee meeting (ECM), members were polled for agenda items; Gassner then, as he described it, "edited" the suggestions to create the agenda, which was circulated to the group.

Gassner described the first ECM:

> We needed to define the limitations and boundaries of authority among ourselves and the MDs. What should we allow our MDs to do without our approval? What should they have to bring to your level? What should you then bring to my level? We needed certain regulations; it makes our lives easier. It was interesting because of the history of the group coming together—they had not been organized before in a way that had these limitations, and they didn't like it.
>
> I also had to explain the role of the New York staff. There was a lot of theoretical discussion about, for example, Heinz's

responsibility. What can Heinz say about my repertoire and my country? How can Heinz say I have to spend a certain amount of money on an artist that is not valid for my region? My answer to that was always that Heinz cannot say. He can only sit down with you and try to convince you that this is the right thing for you. You've got to see the staff as somebody helping you; it is not some governing body who tells you what to do. They have a dotted-line relationship with your people.

Preston described his perspective on the early meetings:

> At first, there was no role for the RDs. Rudi had things he wanted to do; the agenda was laid out, and we would discuss ways of implementing the agenda. The staff people went into meetings very well prepared and tried to establish a couple of policies with the help of Rudi in order to structure the business. It took us a certain amount of time to find a way of really working together.

Bahlman echoed the same point:

> Rudi needed to establish himself and the regional structure; it was like him telling us, via the agenda, what we're going to do. It was as our "educational process." Although I think we sometimes found it frustrating, we were so busy with our own companies [regions], there was not a lot of resistance.

Gassner found this lack of "resistance" somewhat disconcerting. According to Gorman,

> I remember after the first two ECMs, Rudi saying to me, "Everybody's too nice." He expects strong dissenting opinions. He doesn't want a bunch of people just sitting there mildly accepting anything. To him, a heated argument over an opinion is part of the fun of the job, I suppose. But if you're not used to this, and when I first started with him I wasn't, it jars you a little.

In time, however, the RDs became more vocal. According to Henn," It took quite some time until the group felt comfortable enough with each other that they dared to say what they really wanted to say." According to the RDs, the shift in the ECMs was due to their growing confidence and success in running their regions. As Bahlmann noted:

> About two years ago it turned around. The regional directors and the managing directors make the decisions about the operating businesses and acquisitions. Today in the ECMs, we go more into other issues. More and more, we are finally making decisions together and running the business as a team.

Preston also commented on this shift in emphasis: "In the beginning, the staff and Rudi were more dominant. But now, it's more balanced between Rudi and the RDs, and then the staff."

WORKING TOGETHER

By 1993, the executive committee and the ECMs had been in place for four years, and the meetings had fallen into a fairly regular pattern. Each agenda would include a presentation by Gorman on current financial results relative to targets; a discussion by Henn about A&R developments, new releases, and priority artists; a briefing by Sallen on significant worldwide human resource issues; and an update on each region by the RDs. Gassner described the importance of these regional reviews: "I want to give them room to explain to their colleagues what they're up to. Even though it's not relevant to somebody running South America, for example, he should listen, in my opinion, to what happened in Korea and how do we do business in Korea. Here is where I try to get them involved in the global strategy."

Outside the ECMs there was frequent contact between Gassner and each RD. Contact among the RDs varied, and was most frequent among three of the European directors: Bahlmann, Stein, and Preston. Because they shared so many of the same circumstances and concerns, Gassner established a European subcommittee in 1991. As he explained,

> I created a European board because I didn't want to be in the middle of those discussions all the time. It seemed natural to make Arnold the chairman, since he is also the head of European-wide manufacturing and distribution. I told them: "You guys deal with European issues. Europe is your baby. If you cannot agree, I get the minutes and then I will make a ruling."

Since its inception, the European board had been very effective in achieving the purpose he had intended, according to Gassner:

> They deal with issues that are really not relevant to anybody else before they get to the ECM. They even discuss the ECM agenda before the meetings, and they sometimes come over with what I call a "prefabricated opinion." So now sometimes I have to work to break this group up a little bit.

Depending on their regional circumstances, the roles of the RDs varied significantly. Bahlmann, Preston, and Stein, for example, focused on continuing to carve out market share and bring costs down in their increasingly mature markets. Because of his region's importance as a repertoire supplier, Preston was seen as the "repertoire expert"; Bahlmann, on the other hand, was the "strategy expert." Segura and Jamieson were most concerned with establishing new companies and developing talent in the relatively undeveloped markets of Asia and Latin America. Jamieson commented on the satisfaction of being a "pioneer," as he called it: "Asia/Pacific is a huge, multicultural, diverse, economically varied region which is on exactly the opposite side of the world from America. It has the most growth potential and the most musical excitement, really. It's a very, very exciting place to be." Segura described the unique challenges in his region: "I am constantly battling against the terrible political and economic instability that affects some the countries in my region. These situations cannot be solved with easy solutions or off-the-shelf business recipes."

Over time, the executive committee members developed a strong sense of mutual respect for one another. According to Henn:

> Everybody in that room is the *best* at what he does. The absolute best, and we all know it. It's pretty amazing. We're also total egomaniacs, the whole group of us. But in this company we still work as a team because we give each other the space to be the fool that everyone can be sometimes. Nobody's perfect.

Another RD commented, "I wouldn't necessarily choose these guys as my friends, but when we get together it's pretty awesome."

The group maintained a balanced mix of camaraderie and competition. Gassner, who himself used to play professional soccer, described the committee as "more like a soccer team than [an American] football team"; they frequently played heated games of golf or soccer when they were together. Stein remarked with a laugh, "It's all healthy competition—it's very healthy as long as I'm on top of the others. But seriously, it's a good sort of competitiveness. We are all ambitious people, but we respect each other; there is no jealousy."

Another executive committee member mentioned a different aspect of competition: "Rudi is only 51 [years old], far from the required retirement age of 60; but chances are good that he could move on to other things at Bertelsmann. As a result, there is a certain amount of jockeying for position within the executive committee, and people wonder if a non-German could ever be tapped to run this company."

As for Gassner's role in the ECMs, committee members had varying perspectives. Stein commented that "Rudi has a good relationship with the team. He knows when to be part of the team, and when to say yes or no. But he's always open-minded, and you can discuss things with him; it's like a partnership with him." According to Sallen, "Rudi does a lot of consensus-taking. He floats ideas by people, testing them on the group. He does impose his will, but not often. While he does not hand down many edicts, it is generally clear to all what his feelings are on most issues."

Jamieson, however, observed: "Debates in the ECMs are very rare. Rudi's not a man who needs or wants too many debates. I have never had an informal brainstorming session with him, a relaxed, almost agenda-less discussion. Rudi's management style is essentially autocratic. Henn commented:

> Rudi's brilliant. He's a tyrant; no, not a tyrant, a dictator. He has to be. You don't have a leader if you don't have a dictator. If you don't have a dictator, you won't be successful. Show me a company run by democracy, and I'll show you a loser. There's always got to be one chief and plenty of Indians.
>
> He's very smooth. If he thinks we're coming to a conclusion that is not what his opinion is, he will make sure the whole thing will turn his way. He has the ability to make you feel it was your idea, and if that doesn't work, he'll tell you to go and do it anyway.

Many committee members agreed that it could be difficult to change Gassner's mind. According to Stein, "To influence Rudi, you have to convince him. You have to be prepared properly with logical arguments." Preston added: "You have to be prepared to stand up for your argument. A lot of what he is testing is how much you really believe in what you are saying."

One RD noted that "Rudi usually does not allow himself in any way to be influenced by people who are not speaking directly about the areas for which they are responsible. In other words, he'll be very receptive to me for everything within my area, but when I stray into areas of the general good, I find him very unreceptive. I also find that I can influence him more one-on-one than I can in the ECMs."

Stein commented that he used the ECMs "as a tool to influence things in a way that I think they should go and to make the other RDs aware of things. Whether or not the committee agrees with me is another question." Preston agreed, explaining that he viewed participation in the ECMs as an important responsibility, even if it was sometimes hard to have much influence: "I believe that I have a job in the context of the group to say the things that I believe in order to get the group to behave in ways that I think are the right ones."

Bahlman described the ECM as "an opinion-building exercise," explaining that:

> Real decisions about who gets money for what acquisitions occur outside of the meetings. The other thing is that there has always been money there to do what we wanted. So for me, the group has never been tested to see whether we can really work as a team under pressure when it comes to a fight over who will get funds for what investment.

Jamieson commented:

> Sometimes I feel that the main benefit of my coming all the way from Hong Kong to New York for the ECM is the ability (a) to meet my colleagues and chat with them from time to time, and (b) to have my separate meeting with Rudi, which is my best opportunity to influence him.
>
> We have had some good meetings, and we have had some terrible meetings. Rudi occasionally runs them in an open way in which debate is invited and variations to policy are considered. In reality, there is not a team "working together" at the top; there are executives implementing predetermined policies in different areas. The enormous geography makes it difficult to manage by consensus. With Rudi, you know what you have to do, and you have the freedom to execute the policies in your own region with your own style. Nevertheless, you have to realize that Rudi's style works for him; the proof is his incredible success over the past six years.

Gassner suspected these feelings and opinions in the group. "Many of them probably think I am influencing them more than I should," he commented.

> Sometimes I hear grumblings and they say that they can't always express long-term ideas at the meetings because the meetings are so focused. I think they feel a lot of things are a bit too prepared or precooked. It's true—they have a difficult time convincing me. I am a person who likes to win an argument.
>
> But my opinions are not just invented on the spot. I usually discuss issues one-to-one with certain people beforehand. If I

have a subject on the agenda, I almost always have an opinion of what I think the outcome should be. And then in the ECM, I see if my belief is confirmed. Occasionally, I may not go ahead with my original idea because I see that the entire group is going in another direction. In that case, I will take a step back and try to analyze it one more time, and I may change my mind. But if I see that they agree, or if it's just very important to me, then I obviously try to push it along.

Reflecting on his original hopes for the role of the executive committee, Gassner commented:

It turned out to be a little bit different than I thought. I thought there would be more interface on strategic issues. I had hoped that they would contribute to problems which went beyond their ultimate responsibility.

In part, I guess it's because it's such a diverse group of people. Segura, for example, is an outstanding executive, but because he thinks his English is limited, he would rather discuss issues separately with me than in an open meeting. Bahlmann, on the other hand, is very interested in global strategy though sometimes he doesn't have as much impact as he would like to have. Stein and Jamieson are somewhere in the middle, and they are driven primarily by the success of their own regions. Preston is highly intellectual; he is also the biggest repertoire supplier, and sometimes he thinks we're not paying enough attention to his repertoire. It's a combination of very diverse people. That's probably why the results are still so much influenced by me.

And it may very well have to do with me and the way I run things. I think I know what is good for us. Therefore, when I'm convinced that that's the right way to go, it takes a great effort to get me off that route. However, because it has been successful, it has been hard to say that I should change my style.

THE MAY 1993 ECM

Gassner opened the 1993 Managing Director's Convention in Boca Raton with a speech in which he stressed that the company's key success factor for the future was creating repertoire. "It's local artist development, it's joint ventures, it's acquisitions. That is the way we are going to grow. That is how we will reach our goal of becoming Number 1," he told the audience. He also congratulated them on another year of success in surpassing their business targets, but joked that "I am so naive; you must be lowballing your plans every time, because you have never missed them."

The week-long convention also included a session by Henn on developing A&R; a financial presentation from Gorman in which he emphasized the need to reduce costs and improve efficiency as markets matured and growth in the record business leveled off; a presentation about new recording and media technologies; and a speech by Dornemann about the future of the emerging

Entertainment Group at BMG.[12] While the RDs attended, they played no formal role in the convention.

Whereas the focus in past conventions had been primarily on growth, the topics which formed the agenda for the 1993 MD Convention—global artist development, new technologies, BMG's expansion into new entertainment arenas, and cost control—emphasized disciplined management to position BMG International for the next phase. The MDs were excited about the important new role that BMG International could take on in the future. As Gassner told them, "We're the only company in Bertelsmann that is really global; we're the only ones in Japan, and we have over 300 people there. If Bertelsmann wants to sell film or video games globally, we are there. We have something Bertelsmann can build on."

On the other hand, many of the MDs expressed skepticism about Gassner's "conflicting messages." As one stated, "You can't grow market share unless you're willing to spend money, and you can't cut back on investing in new acts, because you never know who might be the next Rolling Stones." Gassner, however, did not see his goals in conflict: "Yes—it's inconvenient on the one hand to grow and on the other hand to control your costs. It's a difficult task, but I expect both. I cannot allow anyone to just charge ahead regardless of cost. I expect a balance; and I know they can do it."

These issues also figured heavily into Gassner's agenda at the May ECM, which took place during the convention. He knew that the future challenges would demand more cooperation and global strategic thinking on the part of the executive committee. They had all been extremely successful so far in their own regions, but a regional focus alone would no longer be enough to guide BMG International through the uncertain and ever-changing terrain of the next five years.

THE REDUCED MANUFACTURING PRICE

The reduced manufacturing price was a result of negotiations undertaken by Bahlmann with Sonopress, Bertelsmann's central manufacturing operation in Europe, which supplied product to the European countries. These countries were required to purchase a certain percentage of their CDs, records, and cassettes from Sonopress, and as part of his responsibilities as the head of central manufacturing, Bahlmann negotiated the transfer prices annually by comparing Sonopress's bid to those of outside vendors. Because the non-European countries did not source through Sonopress, they would not be affected by the new price.

As Gassner might have predicted, when he brought up the issue at ECM by congratulating Bahlmann, Preston shot

Stein a knowing glance. Preston was required to source his manufacturing through Sonopress even though he could get a better price by using a U.K. vendor. As he explained:

> Because the United Kingdom is such a large repertoire supplier, I have volume benefits which I offer Arnold. He takes my volume, combines it with the other European countries, and negotiates a manufacturing rate with Sonopress in Munich, and then I buy the product back with the exchange rate working against me. Austria pays the same price as I do, getting the benefit of my volume scale.

Gassner then raised the question of what to do in response to the new prices. There was a long pause at the table. Bahlmann responded first by suggesting that the "extra" profit from the regions be placed in investment funds for each territory. Stein argued that this was not necessary "since the money's always there if the investment is good anyway." The group agreed that the money did not need to be placed in a separate fund, but be left to each company to decide how to use.

"OK, so what about the targets?" Gassner asked. Looking down at his copy of the calculations that Gorman had distributed before the meeting, he continued, "There are significant variances here. An MDs *betriebsergebnis* in some cases could be increased by as much as 50% due solely to the price reduction."

Segura then spoke up: "This doesn't affect me in my region, so I can be objective.[13] We have never before changed targets once they have been set. Not for any reason. So I don't see why we should change them this time." Preston added: "I agree. Some years, I'm hurt by the transfer pricing and exchange rate, but our targets have never been eased to reflect this. So why would we change them now that it's working the other way? It doesn't seem fair."

Indeed, many of the executive committee members found the issue an unusual one for the ECM agenda. As Gorman explained,

> To tell you the truth, I was a little surprised when Rudi asked me to calculate the adjusted business targets to reflect the new manufacturing price. I know I'm the one who has been pushing reexamination of our cost structure. But we've never changed the targets. Whether you acquired a company, lost a company, lost a customer, had a major bankruptcy, an artist didn't release—we've had everything you can imagine happen, and I do not remember ever adjusting targets for anybody, for any reason.

Gassner said, however, that he was concerned that some of the MDs might become "complacent" because their *betriebsergebnis* target would be substantially easier to meet if it were not adjusted. "I want to maintain the challenge of an aggressive bonus target, I want the MDs to be held accountable for the savings. I want them to realize that it isn't just a Christmas gift," he explained to the group.

No one at the table responded or looked in Gassner's direction. Gassner then wondered how he could get them to address the question of changing the targets, a possibility they seemed unwilling even to consider.

Arista Records

Ending months of tense behind-the-scenes wrangling, Bertelsmann Music Group announced on May 2, 2000 that Antonio "L.A." Reid would take over as president of its Arista Records division from its founder and longtime leader, Clive Davis on July 1.Reid's long-rumored ascension had been overshadowed by controversy ever since Davis had stormed out of a meeting in the previous fall at BMG headquarters after being notified about the succession plan by global music chief Strauss Zelnick.

Davis, who has a long-standing reputation for being a notoriously obstinate executive, had perceived the succession plan as a move to push him out of the label he had founded 25 years ago. A Harvard-trained lawyer, Davis had made a long and storied career of nurturing and guiding artists from Janis Joplin and Barry Manilow to Whitney Houston and Carlos Santana. Earlier this year, he won a lifetime Grammy award and was inducted into the Rock and Roll Hall of Fame as its only non-performer.

At the age of 66, Davis has remained one of the industry's most hands-on label chiefs, often selecting songs for his artists and producing recordings. Six years ago, BMG had rewarded Davis with an unusually rich $50 million contract for transforming his label into a diverse powerhouse that dominated the sales charts with a string of pop, rap, R&B (Rhythm & Blues), light jazz and country hits. But executives at BMG were becoming increasingly concerned about the future of Arista after Davis left the label. Zelnick explained: "As CEO I have a responsibility to make decisions on what's right for the company, and that includes making sure that we have an appropriate succession plan in place at Arista."

The plan to replace Davis did cause a considerable amount of stir within the music industry. Many artists, among them those who had been groomed by Davis at Arista, expressed their concern about his departure. "It seems that corporations are taking over a lot of the decisions that were once being made by individuals," said Barry Manilow, one of the first artists that had been signed by Davis. "It may make sense to them as a corporation, but when you have talent like Clive Davis, those rules should not apply. When you have someone as brilliant as Clive, you push those corporate rules away and you just let him do his thing."

SUCCESS WITH NEW TALENT

Arista has been remarkable in the growth that it has shown on a consistent basis even during years in which the recorded music industry has shown lackluster sales. This growth has largely resulted from the appeal of the small and highly selective roster of homegrown talent which Davis has managed to develop into top acts. At last count, Arista had only about 35 artists on their roster compared to over 200 that can be found at most other major labels.

Case prepared by Jamal Shamsie, UCLA, to be used for class discussion. Material drawn from published sources. Copyright © 2002 Jamal Shamsie.

According to Davis, "Our artist roster is a fraction of any competitor that has market share. We pride ourselves in our leanness. We have the highest success ratio."

Indeed, a higher percentage of albums released by Davis's label have turned gold and even platinum than at any other major recording label. Davis feels that a large part of the label's success has been due to its practice of building its acts from the ground up, as opposed to picking them up through acquisitions and mergers. Mr. Davis emphasized: "Historically, we have made every release count. The success ratio of our company has been the highest in history, and we don't do it by buying market share or buying other labels; it's all been homegrown."

The reliance on homegrown talent was made possible due to Arista's remarkable success in breaking new acts. These generally also tend to be more profitable than established stars, who can negotiate bigger advances and more lucrative deals for themselves. In fact, a key aspect of the firm's strategies has been to steadfastly refuse to enter the bidding wars for established talent that have cost other labels millions. Mr. Davis stated: "We're not in the banking business. All of Arista's growth has come from internal development. We have not tried to increase profit by buying labels, and the big artist deals often don't pan out."

But Arista has been relatively successful in grooming new talent because of Davis. He is known as a music man who usually plays it by ear, sensing hits and nurturing artists, whether it is a Janis Joplin or a Sarah McLachlan. "I can usually tell a hit in 20 seconds," he says of his envied instinct. "I know by then whether the artist has something or whether I should turn off the tape. A song has to evolve through one or two choruses, of course, but you know straightaway. It has to move you. The lyric has to touch the heart."

BMG's Zelnick clearly understood the role that Davis has played in the growth of Arista into a top music label. "The key to Arista's strategy is focusing on a few artists on which Davis and his team really believe, making great records and persevering until they deliver a hit," he stated recently. "We at BMG follow his lead: We believe in a more limited roster than our competitors, more focus and innovative approaches to marketing the records."

Some of these innovative marketing methods were described by Mr. Ari Martin, Arista's senior director of artist development: "When you're launching an album, you have to alert the public, and a lot of analysis goes into finding the most cost-effective ways of getting the word out. We really got to target it." For that, Arista uses an outside market research company to determine the buying habits of music fans, their familiarity with specific artists, and their buying influences. But this data forms just one of the inputs into the development of the eventual marketing plan. Adds Mr. Martin: "We realize we're not selling tooth-

paste. It's not an exact science. So we rely on our instincts more than any numbers we see."

Arista's strategy of building up talent has not gone unnoticed. Mr. Doug Smith, a buyer at Carnegie, Pa.-based National Record Mart, said that Arista has been excellent at setting up albums with singles. "They always have singles on the radio, getting a buzz out there on the street before they release a record," he elaborated. Similarly, Mr. Al Wilson, senior VP of merchandising at Milford, Mass.-based Strawberries, said that when analyzing Arista, "you could take a sarcastic stance and say that they spend enough money to prefab the hits. But how many labels fail at that strategy? The bottom line is that Arista has the ability to spot talent and then do what it takes to roll that talent into hits."

Although most of Arista's success has been in the area of pop music, Mr. Davis claims that he has pursued promising talent in all areas. According to him: "I don't believe in emphasizing areas. When artists excite you, you sign them if you feel that they could be significant." He emphasized that Arista has taken the slow, steady route, not the glitzy route of buying major superstars and creating a staff of hundreds of people. In the words of Davis: "What we stand for is internal growth, all developed from scratch, with a careful, selective approach to signing artists."

SUCCESS THROUGH GREATER DIVERSITY

Davis also asserts that he laid the bedrock for the success of Arista a few years ago when it began to diversify its portfolio in terms of the kinds of music that it offered and the A&R (Artists and Repertoire) sources that generated the music. Much of this diversification was achieved through the establishment of joint ventures with other producers. The firm formed these joint ventures with others who may have the skills to develop talent within a much broader variety of music. In these ventures, Arista has typically relied on their partner to cover A&R, artist development and artist publicity. For its part, Arista's staff has concentrated mostly on promoting, marketing and distributing the releases from these joint ventures.

In fact, it was Davis who brought Antonio "L.A." Reid into the Arista fold. He anticipated the changing face of R&B and entered into a joint venture with Reid and Babyface, who formed LaFace. He stated: "They had a vision of starting their own company, and I shared the vision that they could be the Motown of the 90s." The association has resulted in the development of successes such as TLC and Toni Braxton. Both of these artists are expected to stay at the top of the box office charts for many years.

Around the same time, the company started Bad Boy Records with Sean "Puffy" Combs. That label has been responsible for the success of many new acts such as Puff Daddy & the Family and the Notorious B.I.G., both of whom released recent best-selling albums. The Notorious B.I.G.'s latest release managed to pass the 1.5 million-unit mark in sales, based on available records.

Arista's next two joint ventures have further expanded its range of acts. Its venture with Dallas Austin resulted in the formation of Rowdy Records. The new label has enjoyed considerable success with hot-selling albums from Illegal and Monica. Their partnership with Time Bomb Records has focused on rock music. Under the leadership of Jim Guerinot, this venture has already released albums by new artists such as Elevator Drops and No Knife.

Where it did not seek out strategic ventures, Arista chose to assemble its own repertoire departments from the ground up. For instance, when Arista perceived a need to get into the country music business in the early 90s, it opened the Arista/Nashville division, headed by Tim DuBois. Since then, Arista/Nashville has become a country powerhouse, boasting a roster that includes Alan Jackson, Brooks & Dunn, Pam Tillis, Diamond Rio, Radney Foster, and BR5-49. Within a few years of its creation, the Nashville division has already grown to account for about 20% of Arista's sales volume.

In general, Mr. Davis attributes much of Arista's success to its adventurous spirit. He claims that other record companies have typically bought other labels in order to increase their market share. In contrast to this approach, Davis states: "We have financed ours from scratch and picked out entrepreneurs, whether they were Puffy Combs with Bad Boy, or Tim DuBois with the Nashville division, or Dallas Austin with Rowdy."

Arista's Vice President and General Manager Roy Lott echoed this sentiment: "I would attribute our success to a decision at the very beginning of the 90s to diversify and expand the repertoire supplying entities that are part of Arista, whether it be our Nashville operation or the current LaFace or Bad Boy ventures, rather than be limited to self-generated A&R, which has continued to grow and be successful."

In order to demonstrate the degree of success that the label has had with its diversification, Mr. Lott referred to Arista's recent hold on the top three spots on the Hot 100 Singles chart. "None of the three records are pop records, and each is from a different product source," he said. "The diversification of A&R and genres of music is contributing to our ability to have success."

SUCCESS AFTER DAVIS?

The appointment of Reid was tied to the decision by Zelnick to buy out the rest of LaFace, bringing it entirely into BMG's Arista division. These moves were regarded as necessary by BMG in order to ensure the survival and growth of Arista beyond Clive Davis. Arista has accounted for about a third of BMG's market share and is considered to be the strongest asset in its U.S. repertoire. "Arista is clearly the jewel in BMG's crown," one industry observer recently remarked.

BMG is clearly confident that Reid has plenty of experience to run Arista. He is also a Grammy-winning producer who started out making hits for such dance acts as Bobby Brown and Paula Abdul. Before being accepted for the position at Arista, Zelnick had Reid complete a six-week executive course at Harvard Business School. Reid stated that he believes that he can keep Arista on top of the charts by adding to its diversity. "We intend to make Arista the home for many Latin artists, record producers and Latin superstars," he explained.

But the continued success of Arista without Clive Davis will not be an easy task. Industry observers believe Reid will face significant challenges in taking over the reins. The departure of Davis is expected to be followed by an exodus of top executives at the label, including the heads of marketing and promotion as well as its general manager. Some of the artists may also choose to leave for another label, especially if Davis decides to launch his own new label.

Reid did acknowledge that he was stepping into a difficult position. "I'm coming into this job behind one of the most important men ever in the record business—and that's a tall order," he stated. "I think it's fair for people to speculate about it." But he added: "Anybody who knows me knows my passion for music—and hopefully that passion will speak loudly in the success we achieve at Arista in the future."

BMG music chief Zelnick emphasized that he believed Reid would build on the foundations that Davis had laid for Arista. "This was never about an ouster," he stated recently. "I have the greatest respect for Clive Davis. BMG has always said that we have to deal with succession planning and contracts as they come up. Our goal has always been the same: Build upon the company creatively. Build upon Clive's great legacy."

EXHIBIT 1
CAREER HIGHLIGHTS

1960	Graduates from Harvard Law School and gets a job at Columbia Records, a division of CBS.
1967	After signing several major artists, like Janis Joplin, Davis becomes president of Columbia Records.
1973	Davis is fired by CBS, allegedly for misuse of funds.
1974	Davis starts Arista record label with backing from Columbia Pictures, a company unrelated to CBS. Within five years, Davis builds the record label into a major success with artists like Patti Smith and Barry Manilow.
1980	Bertelsmann buys Arista for $50 million.
1990s	Davis has continued to be a trendsetter by reviving the careers of Carlos Santana and Aretha Franklin and cultivating stars like Whitney Houston and Sean "Puffy" Combs.

EXHIBIT 2
ARISTA'S ESTIMATED SALES

FOR YEAR ENDING JUNE

1996	$325 million
1997	$395 million
1998	$405 million
1999	$425 million
2000	$440 million

EXHIBIT 3
MUSIC INDUSTRY SALES BREAKDOWN

	1999	**1998**
Universal	27%*	11%
BMG	19%	12%
Sony	16%	17%
WEA	14%	18%
EMI	9%	13%
Polygram		14%

*Includes Polygram

EXHIBIT 4
TOP-SELLING ARISTA ALBUMS

1999		**1997**	
Santana	Supernatural	Tony Braxton	Secrets
TLC	Fan Mail	Usher	My Way
Sarah McLachlan	Mirrorball	Mace	Harlem World
Puff Daddy	Forever	Soundtrack	Soul Food

1998		**1996**	
Usher	My Way	Puff Daddy	No Way Out
The Notorious B.I.G.	Life After Death	Soundtrack	Waiting to Exhale
Brooks & Dunn	If You See Her	Brooks & Dunn	Borderline
The Lox	Money, Power & Respect	Kenny G	The Moment

CASE 6

Algodonera del Plata

As he drove back home by the AU-2 route toward Buenos Aires, José Sánchez reviewed the past months of hard work, since he had been appointed marketing manager of Algodonera del Plata. The challenge had turned out to be an excellent opportunity to put in practice all his knowledge, and the plans already implemented promised encouraging results. However, the dialogue he had just held with Eduardo Gennaro, president of the company, had left him deeply worried. Would it be necessary to advance slower? Or was Eduardo backing down on the promises he had made earlier? In that case, where did he stand? Had it been a good decision to leave his former job in Davor to come to this company at last, or would he be better off searching for a more serious and professional company?

THE COMPANY

Algodonera del Plata was founded in 1940, in Buenos Aires, by Dante Gennaro, an Italian immigrant who had worked in the textile industry in Italy. From the beginning, his major concern was to give the market a product of the best possible quality. This desire gradually pushed his second obsession: the manufacturing technology.

With this philosophy, Dante managed to promote his brand of sports products, under the name Cottone. The line mainly included cotton sweatsuits used by sportsmen and by children and young people for their gym classes at school.

THE SWEATSUIT

Around 1984, fashion development made the sweatsuit a favorite garment, compared with wool sweaters which had been used until that time. The closed collar Scottish Shetland sweaters, or those softer V-necked sweaters, were replaced by the sweatshirt. Young people adopted this garment quickly, because the cotton fabric was soft but still warm and also less expensive. Children preferred the fabric because it didn't "itch," and mothers liked the fabric because their children left the sweatshirts on and thus stayed warm. Besides, it was easy to wash and required no special care, as opposed to wool clothes which stretched if they were mishandled. Sweatsuits presented other advantages in the fashion field: They could be cut in many different shapes, creating clothes of diverse looks, and easily allow a wide range of printing and embroidery, so they could be printed with drawings and inscriptions.

American universities had adopted sweatsuits years ago, printing on them the colors, names, and emblems of each school. These were sold to students and visitors as souvenirs. Soon young people were wearing sweatsuits with

This case has been prepared by Professor Guillermo D'Andrea of the Instituto de Altos Estudios Empresariales, as a basis for class discussion rather than to illustrate effective or ineffective handling of a specific situation.

inscriptions of universities, cartoon characters, tourist places, and other varieties of printings.

The cotton sweatsuit consists of two parts: the sweatshirt and the sweatpant. It is generally a thick, comfortable, and warm garment, even though thinner sweatsuits are made for mild climates. The quantity of cotton in the garment determines its weight and, to a good extent, the final quality of its fabric, garment texture, and durability. Manufacturing and dying are two other stages of the process which determine the final quality.

The quality, shown by the thickness of the garment, the firmness of its colors, and its durability, made Cottone sweatsuits the favorites for being warm and longer lasting. For years, blue and white sweatsuits were the most worn and almost the only ones offered in the best sports shops. Dante supervised not only production, but also all marketing aspects of the company, as it grew in size and market prestige.

THE NEW MANAGEMENT

In 1960, Eduardo Gennaro, 20 years old, the only son of Dante's four children, also became interested in continuing the family business. His training took place within the company, where he worked all positions, starting with simpler ones and ending as head of production. Although Eduardo had not attended university, the years in his father's business made him a specialist on the subject. In 1980, Eduardo began to participate in the management of the company. Five years later, when Dante died at the age of 83, Eduardo took over full responsibilities as manager of the business, leaving Luis Corral in charge of operations. Luis Corral was a Spanish national who had been trained at Dante's side. The commercial issues were assigned to Susana Rios, a 20-year veteran in sales management for the company. Eduardo also named Ramiro Fonseca, then accountant of the company, to the board of directors with profit sharing.

Since 1980, Eduardo and Ramiro Fonseca had developed nine wholly owned exclusive shops under the Raffael brand. These stores accounted for 25% of gross sales. They were located in popular areas of the Capital City and Greater Buenos Aires: one in a neighborhood with discounted clothing stores (Palermo Viejo, Nuñez, Quilmes, Castelar, San Antonio de Padua, Munro and Morón), and one in the Harrod's stores on the traditional Florida street (see Exhibit 1).

One problematic store location was Harrod's. Over time, its operations in Buenos Aires were declining. It had closed all the floors except the ground level, where it rented spaces to several companies. Harrod's had become a "shopping mall" with small independent stores.

The factory outlet sold another 20%, which included second-quality products at discounted prices, and the remaining sales were in clothing and other types of stores.

Eight salespeople in Capital City and 10 salespeople in areas outside Buenos Aires served 500 retailers. Half of the production volume was sold in the area of Buenos Aires, and the rest in the main cities such as Rosario, Santa Fe, Paraná, Córdoba, Mendoza, and Río Negro, thus covering most of the large Argentine territory.

Part of the spinning production was done at the Buenos Aires plant, while other operations such as sewing, cutting, dying, and manufacturing were performed in San Juan to take advantage of tax discounts due to the industrial promotion of that province.

The product line consisted of the classics—blue or white—and fashionable designs. The classics were used in gym classes at schools. Fashionable items had premium prices. They were targeted for women and children, based on the idea that the mother would buy it for the child and then would be tempted to buy another one for herself. Sweatsuits had brighter colors, inscriptions, and small embroidered drawings, and were promoted as daily-wear clothing.

Algodonera sold the sweatsuits for $16. Retail prices averaged $35, ranging from $22 to $50, depending on the location. The summer shirts sold at a manufacturer's price of $8.

THE SITUATION IN MARCH 1993

During the ending summer season, 300,000 garments were manufactured. Inventories amounted to 315,000 units at the end of that period, valued conservatively at $2,900,000. Of these, 100,000 garments belonged to the previous winter season. Annual sales were estimated at $6,000,000, and the company employed 200 people. The monthly overheads amounted to $400,000 (Exhibit 2 shows evolution of sales since 1983).

Historically, Aldogonera had always kept high inventories—about 200,000 garments—following an accounting policy that had proved to be beneficial for the company at times of high inflation. A depreciating stock and an updated sale value generated huge margins that were invested in the financial market. Until 1985, the company had shown a profit for many years. However, the tax policy change in 1985, with the launching of the Plan Austral, called for reappraisals of inventories according to the inflation.

The inventories consisted of four different types of articles:

EXHIBIT 1
MAP OF ARGENTINA
(PROVINCES AND
CAPITAL CITY)

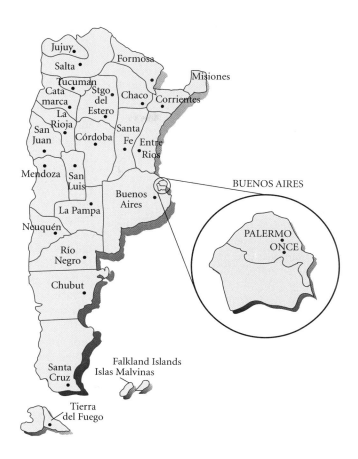

1. Classics, which were produced in advance for the winter season (63,000 garments)
2. Classics production excess from prior years
3. Fashions of the past year received late for delivery, or collections that had not run well

4. Remaining pieces of incomplete collections, by size and color

The remainders were sold at a discounted price at the factory store. Customers were mainly local people. Garments of the third group were sold to Raffael exclusive stores at discounted prices.

A major concern of the two partners was that the cash deficit rose to $800,000 at the end of the season, and therefore they had to request a second credit line to support the upcoming months. The financing of tax payment delays was still expensive, due to the accounting inflationary adjustment and economic stability which caused no currency devaluation and therefore yielded no benefits per inflation.

Eduardo Gennaro summarized the main conclusions of the managers' meeting held in late March 1993. "We need a really aggressive sales manager. We could increase our sales up to 50% without increasing expenses, except direct costs of raw material. We are in a position to become leaders in sweatsuits for schools and leisure time, selling at convenient prices." Immediately the managers began a job search for the right candidate.

EXHIBIT 2   VOLUME OF SALES 1983–93

YEAR	VOLUME (IN THOUSANDS)
1983	470
1984	479
1985	489
1986	519
1987	419
1988	552
1989	398
1990	460
1991	370
1992	430
1993	400 Estimated

THE ARRIVAL OF JOSÉ SÁNCHEZ

Algodonera hired José Sánchez through an executive search firm. Formerly, José held the position as head of product development at Davor, a company that manufactured informal clothes for young people and teenagers, and showed a consistent growth pattern during the past 10 years. With a bachelor degree in business administration, 30-year-old José started to work in May 1993.

By early June, Sánchez presented his plan to the management of Algodonera. Even though some points were arguable, the management team congratulated him for his quick response and encouraged him to continue with the same energy. His diagnosis overlooked various issues.

Some of the newly manufactured garments would later be rejected by clients for several reasons, late in the season or incomplete orders being the most usual. Nevertheless, the sales department approved the entry of a production order, assuming this risk. Some of the clients expressed that Algodonera was a factory of leftovers.

The variety of items was meant to broaden the product line. Apart from differences in size and color, 21 classic style items and 34 fashion garments were manufactured. The latter, in volumes of 2,000 units, made up the main collection. Sánchez's analysis indicated that 80% of sales accounted for 12% of the items, mainly the classic ones.

Sales were developed by 17 salespeople to 600 clients throughout the country. They were compensated through commissions, ranging from 2% to 4%. Sales performance was quite irregular, as were the field assignments (see Exhibit 3).

Sánchez hired a designer to develop new and more fashionable styles. One of the management proposals was to include some older logos on the garments. They turned out to be too old and unknown, so Algodonera decided to search for new ones and create a Cottone Campus collection. This product line would replace the previous one designed by Susana Rios and reduce the number of models.

Another proposal was to close several Raffael stores and open new ones in areas of better socioeconomic levels, once the collection had been improved. This proposal was later postponed by management. The closing of Harrod's store generated long discussions. Even though managers accepted that Harrod's had lost most of its former attractiveness, it was the only shop in downtown Buenos Aires, and they thought it gave prestige to the brand.

To improve sales in the existing stores, Sánchez proposed various ideas. (Due to the scarcity of resources, promotions would be used to stimulate sales at the retail outlets.) Plans included using photographs, stickers for shop windows, posters, and a changeable marquee. Store selection would be important, because of customer diversity. In Buenos Aires, garments were sold in the best sports stores and middle-level stores.

To increase new sales levels, Sánchez proposed to target new clients in selected areas, so as not to affect those better supplied.

Another alternative considered by the management was to accept the proposal made by the owner of the Raffael store in the discount district at Munro. He proposed to become a partner for the opening of a new store, dedicated to selling only second-quality garments. After deliberations and discussions, management went ahead with this alternative.

A third suggestion of selling to franchised chains in the interior of the country was rejected, because management feared that this could harm the brand image.

Lastly, the management would study the alternative of exporting, although Algodonera had no experience in that activity.

To solve the inventory problem, Sánchez proposed to order stock by class criteria. Classic articles would be eliminated from the winter production program, and the rest would be offered to important clients at the provinces, with a 25% discount. Outdated items would be sold to hypermarkets at low prices, either unbranded or under a different brand.

Sánchez started to tour the country, meeting salespeople and clients. He observed big discrepancies: Some stores faired well in retail and customer service, but brand representation was behind his expectations.

At the end of September, after returning from a trip, Sánchez met with Eduardo Gennaro in Gennaro's office. They greeted and then Eduardo posed his concerns.

Eduardo: I'm worried about how we will incorporate new designs into the traditional collection. Our customers are not familiar with this image of the Cottone line, and there may be a possible sales failure. How shall we make this image change? I think the changes you have proposed are generally well directed, but we also have to take into account our people. We have worked with them for a long time and I will not fire them just because we have a couple of bad years. There has to be a less bloody way of improving this situation. What happened with the shops chain we were going to franchise? Inventories are not reduced as it was expected! Our shops are receiving very little attention! Besides, there is still the issue with Susana Rios, and this has to stop right away.

Lately, frictions with Susana Rios were more frequent. The last episode arose when Sánchez proposed to fire some salespeople, beginning with a 69-year-old saleswoman from Tucuman who had 1.5% of total sales and charged a commission of 2%. They had not been in contact with her for months, but this was not unusual.

EXHIBIT 3 SALES FORCE BREAKDOWN

SALESPERSON	WAGE OR COMMISSION (%)	SALES (1000 GARMENTS)		$'000	AREA
		1988	1992	1992	
S. Varela	10	29	17	200	Capital City
M. Loza	2,5	32	11,1	55	Capital City
L. Soprani	4+ travel allowance	9	6	45	Capital City
V. Vinueza	5	32	17	110	North Greater Buenos Aires
M. Duhalde	5	32	14	190	Greater Buenos Aires
N. Freire	4	11	28	170	Greater Buenos Aires
A. Moyano	5	17	17	145	Greater Buenos Aires
Factory Store		87	56		
Raffael Stores		61	40		
I. Srur	4	1	1	12	Tucumán-Santiago Catamarca
D. Becker	5	4	2	26	Northwest
A. Levin	5	11	9	110	Entre Rios
S. Aldrey	4,5	0,7	4	60	Northeast, Santa Fe
D. Nader	4	9	7	43	Cuyo
E. Caretto	5+ tour	35	14	180	Atlantic
C. Nebbia	5	14	12	87	North Buenos Aires
C. Valdeman	6	26	9	190	Córdoba
L. Caubet	7	28	21	270	Rio Negro-Bahia Blanca
S. López	7	24	13	285	Patagonia

Commissions were calculated as a percentage of sales. Salespeople paid their own expenses unless otherwise noted.

José: But, Eduardo, when we evaluated the situation together three months ago, you agreed that these changes were essential to ensure the company's continuity. I'm only implementing them. Besides, we haven't been able to make important promotions to stimulate sales due to the lack of cash.

Eduardo: Of course, I remember those meetings very well, and I still think the same way, but I think you are stepping into issues that are not of your concern. You seem to be playing general manager, instead of marketing manager! There is no area in which you do not intend to make changes! I think you must concentrate on specific marketing aspects and leave the rest to me. Let's see if things calm down a little.

With these words, Eduardo ended the meeting.

HBO

During the winter of 2001, HBO programming chief Chris Albrecht was trying to figure out how he could continue to build upon the no-strings-attached buzz that his cable channel had begun to generate. The buzz started with *The Larry Sanders Show*, in which Gary Shandling played the fictional host of a late-night talk show. The show's ratings paled in comparison with *Friends*, but it drew the kind of unabashed critical praise that HBO has begun to treasure. It attracted writers to HBO who were willing to trade huge up-front payments and back-end profits for the cachet of appearing alongside a smart, self-referential show. With more recent shows such as the *The Sopranos*, a great family drama about crime; *Sex and the City*, a hit comedy of manners with titillating bedroom capers and a fixation on women's shoes; and *Oz*, an innovative, brutal look at prison life, HBO has continued to build itself as the literary magazine of series television.

The cable channel had developed a slogan to highlight the distinctiveness of the original programming that it has been putting on the air. The network's ad campaign has been pounding out a clear and consistent message: "It's not TV, it's HBO." In delivering this message, HBO has been trying hard to distinguish itself from the broadcast networks, which could be accused of having sacrificed quality programming for quick-fix schemes that will deliver large enough audiences. Indeed, the growing level of critical acclaim for original HBO shows led to a recent spoof on an episode of *Saturday Night Live*, with a commercial intoning mock blurbs for *The Sopranos*. The message: "If I had a

choice between having all the mysteries of the universe revealed to me in a glorious flash of light or watching one episode of *The Sopranos*, I'd hesitate, then I'd watch *The Sopranos*."

Meanwhile, network rivals gnash their teeth when *The Sopranos* or *Sex and the City* claims an Emmy or Golden Globe. HBO may be hitting home runs, the argument goes, but how come nobody points out it's playing with aluminum bats? "If NBC only had to schedule *The West Wing*, *Law & Order*, *ER* and *Friends*, you'd say, 'Wow, they're the boutique network,'" says a veteran TV writer who declined to be named, echoing a commonly held view. Indeed, with uncut movies filling up the lion's share of HBO's broadcast day, the channel is at liberty to be thoughtful and exclusive, ordering 10 or 13 episodes of a series and calling it a season. All the while, its commercial network counterparts scramble each year to fill out schedules, ordering series they only half-believe in and deficit-financing star vehicles that end up being expensive embarrassments.

But executives at HBO also realize that they need to build on their original programming. They believe they are more likely to survive on the basis of shows that people cannot find anywhere else than on the basis of movies that can just as easily be viewed elsewhere. This is not an easy task to accomplish, given that the type of innovative shows

Case prepared by Jamal Shamsie, UCLA, to be used for class discussion. Material drawn from published sources. Copyright © 2002 Jamal Shamsie.

that HBO relies upon are hard to come by. Even when Albrecht does come across such shows, it is hard to convince the creators to turn away from the greater revenues that they might be able to get from a more commercial network. But developing the HBO brand has always implied that the channel must struggle to maintain that it is different from ordinary television.

DEVELOPING AN UNCONVENTIONAL SLATE

The typical HBO show comes from a highly respected creative source and deals with a subject that the broadcast networks wouldn't touch. One such show, *Six Feet Under*, which is slated to premiere in June, comes from Alan Ball, the Oscar-winning screenwriter of *American Beauty*, and deals with the business of burying people, seen through a family-run funeral service. The darkly comic pedigree of the series matches Ball's pedigree, which in turn fits the HBO brand: jaded former playwright who grew frustrated with his high-paying, joke-to-joke-to-joke jobs in network TV and wrote what became a mainstream literary hit at the box office.

Six Feet Under is one of two new original shows that HBO intends to roll out in the summer. The other show, *The Mind of the Married Man*, is a half-hour comedy that has been created by stand-up comic-turned-filmmaker Mike Binder. Though it was in development before *Sex and the City* became a hit, the Binder series is bound to be perceived as a male response, given that its three main characters are married men in various stages of thought about love and infidelity. "*Sex and the City* isn't real—it's a fairy-tale release for women," argued Binder. "This show is the naked truth."

Apart from these, HBO claims that it has about 40 scripts in development—everything from a series about hip-hop culture by novelist John Ridley to a comedy about an upscale Los Angeles realtor. Both hip-hop and high-stakes real estate epitomize the HBO milieu. Marry such a subculture and a flawed, dynamic main character and you evidently approximate the HBO brand. One writer who had been working with HBO on the development of a pilot was told to make the main character less likable and not to worry as much about the premise. He recalls that he was told "Just plop us in the world and we'll find our way."

Such notes run decidedly counter to the broadcast networks, where executives usually want likable characters or premises that are apparent early on. They want to ensure that the show will have the elements that are required to make it a commercial hit above everything else. In other words, most of the commercial networks can be accused of slanting their development process to deliver substantial riches down the road. At HBO, the riches can be sacrificed in the interests of getting a show that will receive critical recognition. There is simply the mandate to be "good and different," rather than to do what the other networks do.

As HBO tends to characterize its series development, none of the scripts is more than the germ of an inspiration. Larry David, the writer of *Seinfeld*, was eventually asked to turn his special on HBO into a regular series called *Curb Your Enthusiasm*. Star power is certainly important, but it doesn't carry the day. HBO has passed on a western miniseries from director Sydney Pollack, for example, and a series about an actor called *Kilroy* from George Clooney. Even Christopher Guest and Eugene Levy, who collaborated on the cult movie comedies *Waiting for Guffman* and *Best in Show*, had their pilot about two B-list theaterical agents turned down.

But that's not to say the HBO development process isn't above the same politics and marketeering that plague broadcast network programming. HBO, for instance, puts its pilots through audience testing, though arguably not as slavishly as the broadcast networks do. And sources say the channel has spent a considerable amount of time and money trying to develop a companion series to *Sex and the City*, an indication that target audiences have crept into HBO's thinking.

"My biggest fear is that they'll develop [a brand]," says Bob Odenkirk, a writer and performer with a development deal at HBO and the star for four seasons with David Cross of the HBO sketch comedy series *Mr. Show*. To Odenkirk, the channel's growing mainstream popularity is both blessing and curse. "If you attract this whole big crowd of people, you're going to want to keep them. And to keep them you have to give them what brought them there," he explained.

MANAGING BY IMPROVISATION

During the early years of its existence, HBO was largely billed as a movie channel. Its original programming, under Michael Fuchs, was largely confined to one-hour specials with stand-up comedians. The channel was noted for its frugality with spending money on the development of original series. That began to change when Chris Albrecht and Carolyn Strauss took charge of the channel's original programming. Both of them came to HBO after gaining considerable experience scouting talent for comedy clubs. Albrecht even ran the Improv in New York before taking a job at the cable channel. Both of these programming chiefs rose through the ranks, having been at HBO for nearly fifteen years.

Together, Albrecht and Strauss have been making key decisions regarding the original programming that viewers get to see on HBO. These decisions are made on the basis of their years of experience with scouting talent and managing the live entertainment business. The shows have to push the boundaries of what gets defined as conventional entertainment at most of the other television channels. "I say this in a lot of meetings," said Strauss. "The shows have to become a bit bigger than themselves . . . something that resonates in a larger way. I think our best shows do that."

Binder's *The Mind of the Married Man*, for instance, was in and out of development for years. Strauss, for one, was not a supporter, particularly when the project, then called *My Dirty Little Mind*, dwelt on men's sexual fantasies. There were concerns that Binder wasn't the right person to appear in the show and that the material was not likely to grab enough attention. But Albrecht believed in the basic premise of the show and continued to work with Binder to get it into its final form.

Six Feet Under began in-house, with Strauss thinking HBO should explore death in a series. She had been reading Jessica Mitford's *The American Way of Death Revisited*, and she had watched *The Loved One*, the 1965 black comedy based on the novel by Evelyn Waugh. "I started to think, 'Is there a way to do something about death that could be darkly comic?' This is interesting for us, because other places wouldn't do it." Strauss took her idea around town and mentioned it to Ball, who was not only hot off of *American Beauty*, but also coming from a lousy network experience, with his ABC sitcom, *Oh, Grow Up*. Ball wrote a script, gave it to Strauss and was told to make it darker. "He was still coming out of his ABC experience, so it still had some more conventional sensibilities in there," Strauss explained.

Ball says development at HBO was everything his experience at ABC wasn't. "It seems like there's less levels of bureaucracy to dig through," he stated. "Many times, the lower-level people I would deal with at the networks, I felt like they were second-guessing what their higher-ups would say or think." Writer-producer Thompson added: "To make a good show on HBO is almost easier work. You're living and dying by what you believe in, and you're not being nibbled to death by ducks."

But that doesn't mean that HBO is only likely to stick with those shows that Albrecht or Strauss think highly of. Albrecht described how he had come out of a budget meeting in New York two years ago resolved to cancel *Arli$$*, which premiered in 1996 and stars Wuhl as a sports agent. The show had failed to deliver strong ratings or deliver the kind of critical accolades that might make ratings a moot issue. In fact, it came as close to a ridiculed show as HBO has ever had.

Asked what prevented him from dropping the show, Albrecht stated that he left the budget meeting and headed to Westchester County to look at a pony for his daughter. On the way, he was on the phone with business affairs, discussing the *Arli$$* cancellation, and when they reached the stables, the driver couldn't help himself. He was begging Albrecht not to cancel the series. "Believe me," Albrecht elaborated, "there are people that are paying for HBO every month that don't watch *The Sopranos* and don't watch *Sex*

and the City and don't watch *Curb Your Enthusiasm* that think that *Arli$$* is the best comedy on television."

Everyone agrees that Albrecht thinks differently than most other programming executives. "I look at Tony Soprano, and to me it's Chris Albrecht, in so many ways," said an executive familiar with Albrecht who declined to be named. "His toughness, but also the humanity. He's not your typical network development schmuck. He has a much deeper understanding of the world. . . . He's a textured, somewhat complicated individual. On the other hand, there's a real animal there."

COMPETING FOR IDEAS AND TALENT

Under CEO Jeffrey Bewkes, HBO has raised its budget for original programming to close to $400 million. This 2001 fall, HBO will premiere *Band of Brothers*, a $120 million, 10-part World War II miniseries from Tom Hanks and Steven Spielberg that is based on the book by historian Stephen Ambrose. But while miniseries, original movies, documentaries and specials fall under the original programming rubric, it is the scripted series that have increasingly come to define the HBO brand. Cable outlets such as Showtime, TNT and A&E have shown an ability to compete with HBO's original movies and documentaries. But no other channels have been able to match HBO's branded identity in series.

Albrecht and Strauss are trying to develop more series for the HBO channel. Their goal is to schedule original series and miniseries on Sunday nights year-round. They want to be able to segue from a new season of *Oz* to *The Sopranos* to *Sex and the City*. With *Six Feet Under*, Albrecht is also considering building up Wednesdays as an additional night for new series. But shows that HBO wants are hard to come by and harder to grab. Shows that air on HBO do not generate the kind of revenues that other more conventional programming can generate on network television. Often, HBO has to make substantial financial investments into a show in order to obtain it.

In spite of all their efforts, Albrecht and Strauss do still lose some shows to the more commercial networks. Three years ago, HBO appeared to be in business on a comedy pilot called *Action*, about a movie studio chief modeled after hard-driving producer Joel Silver. Albrecht stated that he came up with the germ of the idea and went to Silver, who brought in Chris Thompson, creator of the network sitcom *The Naked Truth* and a writer for *The Larry Sanders Show*. But Thompson and Silver ended up taking the series to Fox, where it died halfway into its first season. Thompson says that the show would have been ideal for HBO, but that there were too many heavy-hitter profit participants in it to make a deal. But it's also true that Silver and Thompson—and by extension, Columbia TriStar, where they were under contract—saw a far bigger pot at the end of the rainbow if *Action* landed at a broadcast network.

Even Brad Grey, who was involved with the development of *The Sopranos*, tried to sell the show to all the major networks before turning to HBO. He had been an executive producer on the highly acclaimed *Larry Sanders Show*. What he wanted, this time, was to develop a critically successful show that would also be a financial hit. "Well, I'll just say it again, that was a mistake, because I shouldn't have taken it to those other companies," Grey said afterward. "I thought at that point, after *Sanders* and after some of the success of HBO, that the networks would embrace a show like *The Sopranos* and give us more leeway creatively."

This leads critics of HBO to charge that it relies heavily on the kind of shows that are not likely to be acceptable on most other networks. They claim that one of the easiest ways to demonstrate that you're "not TV" is to employ nudity, violence and profanity, something that nearly all HBO original series employ. This is particularly true of reality shows like *G-string Divas*, a behind-the-scenes look at stripper life, and *Real Sex*, a home-movies peek into all manner of sexual appetites. Albrecht definitely agrees that there's violence on *The Sopranos* and *Oz*, and frontal nudity on *Sex and the City*, but he insists that it's only used in the service of the scripts, not for adult males on their couches at night, surfing the cable channels for skin.

"We don't look for things that are taboo," Albrecht adds. "One of the reasons we've held off doing a cop show is I'm not sure that we could do something better than *NYPD Blue* or *Law & Order*. . . . Because there've been so many things done on broadcast networks over the years, it's hard to find subjects." Albrecht claims that *Arli$$* has been a successful show for HBO, because the major networks have been reluctant to do real stories about what happens in sports because of all of their contracts with the major leagues. In referring to a recently cancelled ABC show, Albrecht stated: "*Sports Night* had nothing to do with sports."

By picking topics that other networks choose to avoid and giving more creative freedom to proven talent, HBO has been using its original programming to enhance its brand identity. "There's no amount of money spared to do that," said a source familiar with how the network operates. They go to great lengths to unveil new and returning series with proper aplomb. For example, HBO turned the third-season premiere of the Mafia drama *The Sopranos* into a media-hyped event at New York's Radio City Music Hall. But on a more general level, the channel has sold itself to the public not simply as a content provider, but as a lifestyle choice, really, like making time for yoga.

IT'S NOT TV, IT'S HBO

No one denies that HBO's economic model has contributed mightily to its success. Unlike the broadcast networks, HBO derives its revenue from subscribers paying monthly fees of about $12 over their basic-cable bills. This means HBO's writer-producers do not have to fear the long arm of a standards and practices department. Nor are the network's executives in the "eyeballs business," a term that is used in the industry for trying to attract the most viewers. Instead, HBO continues to search for innovative new shows to keep the percentage of "churn" in the single digits—those viewers who buy the service and then cancel when a particular show that they wanted to view ends its run.

For the final episode of its second season, *The Sopranos* drew an estimated 9 million viewers, unprecedented for an HBO series. Most of its other shows attract around 2 million viewers per airing. This represents a significant achievement, given that HBO is only available in about a quarter of the households. Last year alone, HBO added 1.2 million subscribers, bringing its total base to about 26 million viewers. The increase has helped make HBO a key part of the nearly $7 billion in TV revenue its corporate parent, AOL-Time Warner, reported last year.

But Albrecht and Strauss must find more money to fund the development of more original programming. They are wrestling with raising more revenues by offering some of their original shows for syndication. To begin with, they are not sure what they will be able to get for their programs on the syndication market. Recently, HBO Enterprises, HBO's syndication arm, began offering an edited version of *Sex and the City* to basic cable stations, reportedly at $750,000 an episode, which approaches the astronomical fees garnered in syndication by *Seinfeld*. But the offer was taken off the table amid sentiment that the asking price was exorbitant.

With the huge success of *The Sopranos*, HBO is looking again at the revenues that might be obtained from syndication. The show is the most expensive that the channel has ever put on the air. But this is not an easy issue to address. Beyond the task of making the series palatable to a wider audience, there is another question: Wouldn't letting *The Sopranos* go to a basic cable outlet like TBS diminish the distinction of the HBO brand? Keeping it in the family can only become more crucial for a network having to live up to its boutique image with each new series. In the words of Albrecht: "As the world gets more competitive, and as these series are the things that define us, why would we give them to someone else unless we really needed the money?"

IMPSAT

National frontiers will be lines drawn on the maps meanwhile the business and trade flow will run freely in a global digitalized economy.

—John Naisbitt

Electronic networks form the key framework of XXI century and are critical for the business success and national economic development as the railways were in the Morse's age.

"We are generating a company in a hi-tech new business. I believe that we can achieve leadership in Argentina and that is why we should discuss the expansion plans next week. What kind of company should we develop?" asked Enrique Pescarmona, president of Pescarmona Group of Companies, of Ricardo Verdaguer and Roberto Vivo, president and vice president of IMPSAT. This company had been recently established to enter the satellite communication business. The three men were leaving the main central station, which monitored all IMPSAT services, at the South Dock of Buenos Aires port, a zone that was being recycled. The last rays of the afternoon sun colored the 84-meter tower and white screens of 11 m diameter faced the sky, each one toward one satellite.

"The possibilities offered at present by the satellite technology combine the economy of information transmission with the safety of using a reliable network, and the reduction of communication costs," said Ricardo Verdaguer. "This is a powerful strategic tool to achieve business goals, such as increasing productivity and an accurate response to the market development. The bene-

fits can reach not only our clients, but also their suppliers and even their own customers."

Roberto Vivo repeated the idea that had excited him years ago. "We are in the middle of a transcendental change. Many activities will become virtual, transforming physical activities into electronic ones and this, in turn, will also change the industries. Supplier-client relationships will be direct and continuous, bringing together both parts in the precise necessary moment. Products will become more and more personalized and provided at higher speed. Some governments are perceiving the enormous economical potential of modern communication infrastructures and promoting their development."

"We are going toward a global economy, so we should have a global system," said Enrique Pescarmona. The existence of commercial offices and operations of Pescarmona Group of Companies in different countries of Latin America, Southeast Asia, and the rest of the world provided the opportunity to study the feasibility of starting new businesses in those regions, similar to that in Argentina. Enrique Pescarmona was interested in repeating the experience of Argentina in other markets, as he wanted to export the technological and marketing know-how already developed.

This case has been prepared by Professor Guillermo D'Andrea of the Instituto de Altos Estudios Empresariales, with the collaboration of Engineer Daniel Hourquescus, as a basis for class discussion rather than to illustrate effective or ineffective handling of any specific situation.

At that moment, the company had 20 employees, most of them coming from a satellite project of the Argentine Air Force, the computer data transmission area or the radio-frequency sector. The country was leaving behind a hyperinflation period, during which it had reached a monthly rate of 200%, resulting in a deep social trace.

INDUSTRIAS METALÚRGICAS PESCARMONA (IMPSA)

Enrique Epaminondas Pescarmona arrived in Buenos Aires in 1906, from his native Torino, Italy. Since the age of 13 he had worked there with his father in his family casting shop, manufacturing parts for textile machinery, while studying at night at the technical high school. He went to Mendoza, a province located in midwest Argentine over Los Andes mountains, an area famous for its wine and fruit production. In 1907, he had established his own business and later built the first grape mechanical milling machine and a miniturbine which used the hydraulic energy of the defrost channels. From there, he continued manufacturing equipment for the regional wine industry. Later, the 1930s crisis severely affected business development.

After the 1930s crisis, his son Luis Menotti Pescarmona graduated as master constructor at the Universidad Popular de Mendoza, and joined his father in their business recovery.

In 1946, he founded Construcciones Metalúrgicas Pescarmona S.R.L., later Industrias Metalúrgicas Pescarmona S.A.I.C.&F. (IMPSA), which in 1970 made a major jump when it started to build big hydroelectrical centrals. In 1991, it earned $10.2 million from $198 million in sales, now under the direction of Enrique Menotti Pescarmona (the founder's grandson), an engineer with an MBA from IESE at Barcelona, Spain.

IMPSA was one of a handful of companies in the world that manufactured high-technology turbines, turnkey hydroelectrical centrals, and crane bridges for the U.S. Navy or the Malaysian port. Another $300 million in products were sold by different services companies engaged in activities related to loading transportation, waste collection, satellite transmissions, or wine production. Exhibit 1 shows the group's organization.

THE DEREGULATION OF COMMUNICATIONS

In 1990, interregional meetings of commercial blocks took place to discuss the rules which would give an equalitarian treatment to the different telecommunications carriers, and convince them to satisfy the growing demand for intelligent networks. In the United Kingdom and United States,

commercial clients used their influence to meet their own needs and therefore have the choice among different carriers. The elimination of voice service monopolies had been announced in Europe for 1988. Some of the formerly European closed markets, now liberalized, were the cable and air TV, the satellite data transmission services and those specialized for VSAT systems, and the intercompany or closed groups of clients and networks. Such countries as the UK, the Netherlands, France, and Germany were creating structures to grant licenses for upward link satellite operators, with the risk of provoking a differentiated growth among the European Union members.

Increasing competition and smaller margins for the operating companies were expected due to the deregulation of the telecommunication markets through the elimination of monopolies and tariffs liberalization, especially for long-distance communications. Attracted by the possibility of expanding their operations internationally, domestic operators began to work on strategic alliances, showing an increasing interest in emerging markets. This was one of the most attractive areas of the business, with an annual growth of 17% in the last 10 years and more open to competition than the domestic markets of each country. Tariffs in the United States and Japan had decreased 50% in the last years.

Cable TV companies intended to enter the telephone market, and there was a growing use of cellular systems for personal communications. At the same time, national offices were formed to regulate domestic competition and the scope of company activities industry-wide.

By the end of the 1990s, low orbit satellite systems (LEO) were announced, such as Motorola's Iridium or Bill Gates and Craig MacCaw's Teledisc. Iridium was a project based in 66 satellites in 6 polar orbits at a height of 765 kilometers. It was intended to offer bidirectional voice and data services among movable terminals in any place worldwide, as well as radiodetermination of position, search of personnel, facsimile, and local nets interconnection. The investment was estimated at $4 billion. Teledisc anticipated the installation of 840 satellites in 21 orbits, at a cost of $9 billion, offering voice, data, video, and multimedia services at the beginning of the twenty-first century.

This also reflected the increasing invasion of computers, which were expected to replace telephones and TV sets, as technology succeeded in placing more transistor circuits in smaller space, and the optic fiber offered an unlimited bandwidth capacity for communication transmission. In 1992, a fingernail-size chip held 20 million circuits, and it was expected that number would increase to 1 billion circuits by the year 2000, thus making their use more common and turning the focus of competition to additional services.

Anticipating a growing demand for connections and services, and aiming to attain an optimal and homogeneous

EXHIBIT 1   CORPORACIÓN IMPSA ORGANIZATION CHART AS OF JANUARY 31, 1995

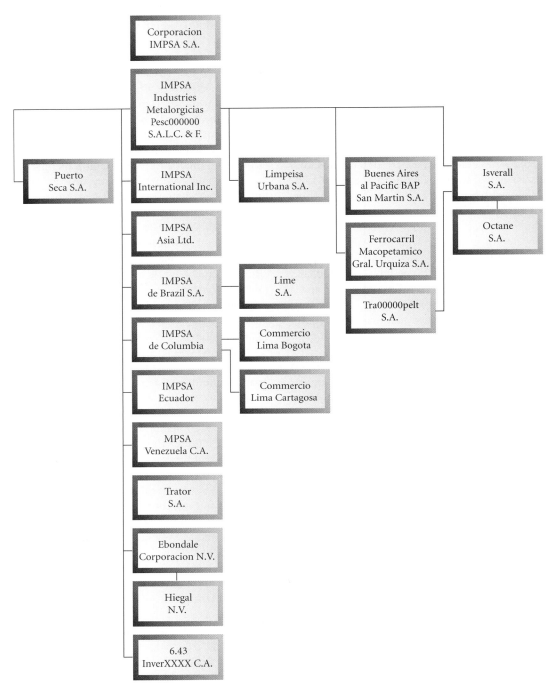

quality of globally standardized services, the alliances between companies started to spring up. ATT formed World Partners with KDD and Singapore Telecom. France Telecom and Germany's DBP Telekom merged into Eunetcom at equal parts, to offer business and international services and information networks, and they were negotiating agreements with AT&T. British Telecom PLC joined MCI to form Concert, focusing on multinational corporations as clients. Telefónica de España formed Unisource, with its partners KPN, Telia, and PTT of Switzerland. The Spanish company entered into Chile, Venezuela, and Puerto Rico, setting up a company in

Argentina with one of the big domestic economic groups, while France-Telecom joined Italy's STET with the same purpose.

Client evolution had a similar rhythm, led by main companies that avoided local suppliers, changed carrier or built their own networks, demanded better services and at a smaller cost, all conscious that alternatives were quickly evolving. Residential and small company markets were still being slightly exploited for interactive services, although cable TV and cellular telephones attained access to that market sector, offering not only entertainment and information, but also bank and shopping services, research, and access to libraries. Books, music, video, and movies were loaded into personal computers through communications, instead of being acquired in stores.

COMMUNICATIONS IN LATIN AMERICA

Meanwhile, in Latin America, the privatization and liberalization of the telecommunication markets were taking place at a much higher speed. During the 1980s, telephone companies in Chile, Mexico, and Venezuela were sold, producing a growth which in some cases duplicated the market size. The Chilean network was one of the first worldwide to adopt digital technology.

In Argentina, the Empresa Nacional de Telecomunicaciones (ENTEL) was privatized in 1990. At that moment, the number of lines was 8 per 100 inhabitants, and the buyers—Telefónica de España and the French Telecom consortium (STET)—announced a density of 20 lines per inhabitant scheduled for 1995.

Brazil, Bolivia, Ecuador, Colombia, Nicaragua, and Peru joined the process of liberalizing their telecommunications with different emphasis, preparing the political ground, studying proposals, or awarding companies. Turnkey contracts for building networks made those processes easier. Competition in long-distance private services was already implemented in Chile, Venezuela, and Colombia, including public services in the case of Chile.

Competitive networks of integrated services did not exist in Latin America. International carriers invested in basic telephone technology, with partial nonintegrated services, mostly in large urban centers. Moreover, the complexity of the Latin American market, with regulations, competition, and different development levels in each country, diminished their interest for assuming greater commitments.

In 1990, the perspective of regional blocks integration appeared more frequently. Meanwhile, the European Community turned into the European Union in 1992, and the NAFTA agreement was outlined in North America. In South America, the presidents of Brazil, Argentina, Uruguay, and Paraguay stated the bases for the organization of a free trade area: the Mercosur. Chile watched the evolution of its neighbors, from a path of progress on which it was a decade ahead.

The markets globalization was finally reaching Latin America, where domestic markets accelerated their evolution, generating interesting opportunity niches. The countries adopted development policies which allow them greater stability, with larger access to markets, and medium- and long-term international credit.

At that time, a worldwide increase of liquidity was observed entering into ventures, and making possible broader availability of medium- and long-term credits. International agencies showed greater interest in financing private businesses, those related to high technology with adequate profitability being the most attractive.

THE VSAT TECHNOLOGY AND ITS APPLICATION TO COMMUNICATIONS

In 1987, Mr. Roberto Vivo, born in Uruguay, had already spent many years managing his building company, specialized in public works. Due to the country's economic difficulties and looking for the diversification into new businesses, he had been studying telecommunications possibilities. He also made contacts with a group of Argentine scientists from the Comision Nacional de Investigaciones Espaciales (National Commission of Space Investigations), who had developed the projects for Argentina's domestic satellite together with the United States, France, and Germany. At that time, telephone communications were administered by a government monopoly, and data transmission was poorly supplied by the Arpac network, according to what Vivo personally verified through some interviews with client companies.

In turn, taking advantage of the fact that his father was the Uruguayan ambassador in Brazil, he decided to visit that country which had set in orbit its first two domestic satellites in 1986. He met Pedro Castello Branco, president of Embratel, who connected him with the two consulting companies that had developed the Brasilsat project. This relationship led him to read his first article about the VSAT technology, recently released from military to commercial use.

Through his relation as IMPSA supplier, he became acquainted with Ricardo Verdaguer, marketing manager, visiting him in 1987. He proposed to him to enter into the communications business, using the (VSAT) satellite technology with a "Shared Hub" concept. This was a new concept, as the initial success of this technology in the United States had been almost exclusively for large private networks.

During the meetings, where technological aspects were detailed and business possibilities were evaluated, Ricardo

Verdaguer immediately understood the implications and potential of the project. Considering IMPSA's experience in the handling of huge projects and technology transfer agreements—both nuclear and capital goods—he decided to present and back up Vivo's project in the company.

Perceiving a decrease of public works, Enrique Pescarmona had already begun a process of diversification, and he decided to enter into the new business. On behalf of IMPSA Corporation, he appointed Verdaguer as responsible for the project.

During 1988, the initial group basically formed by Vivo and Verdaguer was applied to study technological, legal, and commercial aspects of the project. The two options were single channel per carrier (SCPC) or very small aperture terminal (VSAT) technologies.

The greatest possibilities of satellite communications appeared in the early 1980s, when technology allowed the building of smaller satellites but of greater power, which also permitted the utilization of smaller antennas. The launchings also were safer, reducing the failures of one in three, to only 5% of launchings and at a smaller cost.

European and American companies that wished to go abroad with their national networks were applying the VSAT technology. The Holiday Inn chain had hired MCI Communication Corp. for the installation and operation of 300 VSAT in Europe, anticipating its expansion to another 300 in Latin America by the end of the century. Three of the most advanced projects in Europe belonged to the automotive industry: Mercedes-Benz and Volkswagen of Germany, and Renault of France. These companies would connect their central inventory databases with their terminals, to organize their sendings and deliveries where their car models were required. However, the high cost of replacing current installations by hundreds of interactive terminals was one of the most important obstacles. The other one involved regulations, which restrained the possibilities of application to one-way communications in Europe. Regardless of ECC existence, the regulatory context reflected unequal rhythms in the different countries. Then, Spain and Italy kept stricter control over communications than northern countries of the continent.

The access to space was still being controlled, thus maintaining artificially high prices for satellite communications. Previously, satellite capacity in Europe could only be leased to Post, Telephones and Telegraphs (PTT) national companies, and users had to access the services of the state-owned corporation of the country where the upward linking was located. This prevented competition among suppliers of the space segments, as communications were from 3 to 10 times more expensive than in the United States. The market also grew at a 12% annual rate, which was less than half of American or Japanese evolution.

Xerox Ltd. spent three times more in Europe than in the United States for a similar volume of communications. The users of DBP Telekom of Germany could not refute overinvoicings, as the company could not issue a detailed call registry. Belgium has a 20-day waiting period for the installation of a new service, and in Italy regular communications were often cut off.

France, Germany, the Netherlands, and Great Britain were signing an agreement that would allow users of those countries to utilize Eutelsat's capacity from any of the other three signers. It would also grant VSAT licensees the rights to offer two-way services. The licensees could not be international carriers, although if French users could get connections between their own networks and the public ones, they would be able to use the hubs of American operators such as Panamasat and MCI.

The creation of a VSAT network required high investment to achieve a good cost-benefit ratio, but it also could yield cost savings. A study of Hughes Network System Inc., one of the two suppliers of VSAT technology, estimated that a 830 VSAT network covering several European countries would cost 25% less than the equivalent land network of packages commutation. Another users survey performed by the Utisat French Group indicated that a system of 5000 VSAT throughout Europe would cost one-third of the equivalent land network. AT&T had announced plans to invest $350 million in a pan-European network for commercial calls, threatening 20% of the $3000 million in sales of PTT in this segment.

The competition was oriented to the SCPC system, offering exclusive satellite links per client. After a deep analysis, they decided in favor of VSAT technology, which allowed share links between different clients without affecting the service rendered, that is, creating "exclusive virtual links." Then the problem was that only VSAT systems were operating in the "KU" band frequencies, and not in the "C" band, which was the unique satellite band available in Argentina at that time. The next step was to find a supplier of VSAT technology interested in developing the product to operate in "C" band. This certainly demanded meetings and negotiations with different suppliers and finally, after some months, Hughes Network Systems company agreed to develop the first VSAT system in "C" band for IMPSAT.

THE COMMUNICATION MARKET IN ARGENTINA

In 1987, the Argentine government issued a public service demonopolization decree which included telecommunications, making possible the granting of licenses for the rendering of data transmission services to private companies. The following year, IMPSAT achieved that authorization from the Secretaria de Telecomunicaciones, but in order to start operations it was necessary to modify what was established by the Telecommunication Law. By May 1989, through the decree 580 of the National Executive Branch, IMPSAT and the remainder of competing companies were in legal condition to grant services (Exhibit 2).

Within this framework, ENTEL's satellite capacity was contracted to offer satellite communications. In fact, the Argentine communications market was monopolized by the Empresa Nacional de Telecomunicaciones (ENTEL) until 1990. This company operated the public telephone network and the Arpac national network of data transmission, available in main cities of the country. The system was essentially analogical, consisting of copper cables. The saturation and deterioration of the lines added to its scarcity and provided low reliability and service quality.

During that year, Argentine government faced an intensive plan for deregulation and economic openness, seeking to increase general industry competitiveness and to reduce the highly deficit fiscal cost in the telecommunication area. This would mean more efficient, inexpensive, and quality services and at the same time would generate competition, which ought to pull up the sector from the undevelopment in which it had been immersed by 40 years of state-controlled and deficitarian policies. Large investments would be required.

The Argentine market was becoming more and more demanding, although it did not know satellite technology and had little information about telecommunications in general. There was little development in communications matters, as they were based on an old centralized framework which had a highly inefficient image. Clients could wait years to get a telephone line or make illegal payments to officials in order to speed their negotiations, but with uncertain results. There was a relative data processing development, barely prepared for long-distance data transmissions, and surviving segments with statist tendencies. Companies had difficulties setting up in proximity to their resources which were far away from their main markets. ENTEL rented satellite capacity to Intelsat, which practically went unused.

Given the deficit of traditional land systems and vast Argentine geography, with great distances between cities,

satellite use appeared to be an excellent option for the land system. Its advantage was a better cost ration, and its higher quality increased the value of communications performed through this means. The available satellite capacity would be limited in the next two years.

The privatization of ENTEL took place in 1990, dividing it into two areas: north and south. Argentine southern networks were awarded to Telefónica de España (Spanish telephone company), while the Italian-French consortium, Telecom, had won the northern networks. Both companies had seven-year exclusivity in their respective areas until the later deregulation would permit the entrance of other competitors. That period could extend to 10 years, in case certain investment and service goals stated in the bidding conditions were fulfilled.

Three companies had obtained licenses for data transmission: Impsat, Satelnet, and Satelital. Satelnet had been set up by Dynamic Systems, a company engaged in communication equipments supply, then sold to the Argentine branch recently opened by the Banca Nazionale del Lavoro. Satelital, initially created by ALCATEL's Argentine branch, was then acquired by Comsat, a U.S. signatory monopolist company of Intelsat, until its deregulation.

THE BEGINNING OF THE OPERATIONS

The IMPSAT concept was to apply VSAT technology, which until then was only implemented in company networks individually, to many companies that could share the same infrastructure and satellite capacity—a concept called "Shared Hub." That way clients would be permanently connected, but use the channels in a much more efficient way than if it were exclusive. A master station would act as a controller, receiving and redirectioning communications.

Until then, the configurations that were used connected factories and branches with the computer center at the head office, through point by point lines of the public network, that is, by means of copper cables.

The proposed satellite scheme entailed connecting client's central data processing equipment with the Teleport or main central station, through radiolink or optical fiber.

EXHIBIT 2
SALES (%)

	1989	1990	1991	1992 (E)	1993 (E)	1994 (E)
Argentina	5.88	0.2	8.9	21	37.1	63.3
Exports					3.1	14.3
Total	5.88	0.2	8.4	21	40.2	77.6

The information from the client head office would be transmitted to the satellite from the Teleport, then retransmitted by satellite and would be received by little remote satellite stations (denominated VSAT) installed in the client's branches. This VSAT equipment was easily connected to the branch's computers; therefore, the communications would be established in real time and in both directions between clients' branches and the head office.

To connect clients with the main station, a network of optical fiber was installed, covering the center of Buenos Aires, 52 km in a 150-block area. This digitalized network provided reliability to the land communications of important information volumes in real time. The remote installations were rapidly made with small stations (1.8-m-diameter screens), or superior stations for high-capacity links.

An essential advantage, beyond the high reliability, availability, and confidentiality of the information, was the possibility of configuring point-multipoint networks, also called star, and the easiness of doing it through software. A simple software command installed in the master central station would allow the configuration of networks, increase their capacity, or interconnect clients among themselves.

A point to solve was the VSAT technology, which up to that moment had not been tested in shared networks, but it was used in corporative, non-shared nets. In addition, there was no experience on VSAT networks operating with satellites in "C" band all over the world.

A strong investment in equipment would be necessary, plus the need for highly specialized technicians who could continuously update changing technologies. Today's solution could be obsolete tomorrow. Moreover, the changing rhythm of technology affected the supplier companies, which merged or disappeared at great speed.

After months of visits to suppliers, an agreement with Hughes would supply equipment at more suitable values as the volume increased. The initial investment had been forecasted by Vivo at $4 million, for a project of 100 remote entrances or down lines, but it was quickly increased to 500 remote entrances, to make the project more attractive. In spite of this, the estimates for the following years indicated the market would require investments of about $100 million. To raise these funds, it would be necessary to go to the capital market or associate with an important company. The project financing was then a critical aspect that had to be deeply analyzed.

PLANNING COMMERCIAL OPERATIONS

The entrance into the market showed two main alternatives: Attack the market aggressively, winning clients of all possible segments; or face a gradual growth, entering selectively and going along with it and competitor strategies, thus limiting the risks.

Part of the actions should be directed to attract investors who could finance the heavy investments. Fruit of the economic policies of the administration in course, which was controlling inflation and facing an aggressive program of economic modernization, the Argentine capital market was receiving a strong flow of international capitals, estimated at $20 trillion to that moment. Would it be enough to present the ambitious programs of Impsat, or would it be necessary to offer some other types of guarantees to investors who had abandoned the market early in the 1980s, due to the volatility of said period? Would it be necessary to establish some type of alliances, and in that case, with whom?

It was necessary to define the service level to be offered. There were possibilities to render a broad range of additional services, since fax, transmission of images, and data at an international level could be added to the data. Data transmission could be offered initially, and other services could be added gradually, which would allow additional charges for new future services, including 24-hour service.

When setting prices, the company must decide if they would be fixed to take into account distance or installation, and if the tariff level would be competitive with the other telephone companies or differential in relation to them. The base price could be set according to the utilization, similar to traditional telephone services, or a recurrent installment.

There was certain difficulty in the case of clients who managed great volumes of information, because they could saturate the channels. In these cases, the SCPC individual technology per client, with various channels of data, voice and fax, used by the competition, was more advantageous. It was also possible to offer the simultaneous diffusion of information, from a data center to a network of multiple recipients. Regional teleports would be necessary to offer better service in the whole territory, at the same time as clients and information volume increased. For that reason, the clients selection was carefully analyzed, along with the market coverage level.

The service was useful not only for companies who wanted to receive information about their stocks and link their local networks with its central computers, but it also allowed banks to connect with their cashiers networks, credit card companies could verify the purchases and enlarge their coverage, or hotel chains could check room availability in real time.

Conversely, implementing new technologies into daily tasks used to be a critical moment for organizations, especially in the case of great communication networks. Moreover, Argentine companies were quite backward in communications matters and its application possibilities.

Satelnet and Atelital had already begun their operations, selling equipment to industrial clients under SCPC technology. In their interviews with customers, they vaguely let them see disadvantages of the Impsat VSAT system. An alternative was to offer the equipment installation for Impsat's account and a service contract, instead of the sale or leasing.

These decisions would have consequences in Impsat positioning within the market. In order to enlarge the information in this sense and evaluate the situation, they undertook a market research (Exhibit 3).

Four main groups were identified. Of the respondents, 23% had more experience for managing long-distance data communications. Generally, they were banks and big companies with widespread activities around the country. Another 17%, also large companies and medium-size banks, held some culture and specialized advisers tried to find any solution to their problems. A third group mainly included subsidiaries of multinational companies. Although their knowledge level was smaller than that of the first group, they had their own technicians, accounting for 28% of the respondents. The fourth group included pessimists—industries with low telecommunication culture, without personnel or advisers. There were doubts in the managing group about whether to attack all segments from the beginning and open the market aggressively, or address any segment in particular and gradually cover the market.

"They are generally very unsatisfied with the services offered," said Rafael Bustamante, from the research agency.

EXHIBIT 3   IMPSAT MARKET RESEARCH

Market Research Source: CIMAS
Methodology: Multivariable analysis
Sample: 200 first level companies

OBJECTIVES:
Telecommunication needs
Attitudinal framework toward new technologies
New services
Decision-making process
Sensitiveness to tariffs
Data processing equipment
Branches/activities layout

CONCLUSIONS:
High unsatisfaction with services
Inefficiencies impede companies' growth
Telecommunications are not value appreciated
Increasing privatization consciousness
Backwardness in telecommunications countrywide
Good willingness to high-quality services

"They considered them backward and their inefficiency impedes their own company's growth." In this framework, telecommunications are depreciated, claiming technical advice for the implementation of only high-quality new services. Companies were conditioned with regard to investments, plus they did not have their own qualified personnel.

THE SITUATION IN 1990

At the end of that year, Impsat management met to discuss some aspects of the growth strategy and define the guidelines for the next years. Operations in Argentina seemed to be well aimed, as companies showed interest in Impsat services.

The trend toward deregulation and privatization seemed to progress quickly in Latin America. Impsat could make use of its advantage as a regional company, but it was necessary to advance fast. Operation organization in other countries implied investments—obtaining licenses and generating structures of technicians and managers (commercial and those related to the specific operation). See Exhibit 4.

Enrique Pescarmona: We must not forget that bases for the consolidation of Mercosur (common market among Argentina, Brazil, Uruguay, and Paraguay) are being signed. Many of our

EXHIBIT 4   VENEZUELA MARKET CONDITIONS

SUMMARY
Venezuela is experiencing a new crisis, perhaps the deepest of its economic-financial history. Companies' fight to survive implies a strong need of technological updating; meanwhile it is estimated that the financial crash left 25% of circulating assets at the hands of clients who are uncertain about investment alternatives. The new Banking Law will allow the entrance of foreign banks, which has forced local banks to attract funds through aggressive commercial campaigns; however, some experts believe they are not prepared to absorb the foreseeable inflow of new clients, who will not be considered loyal. Therefore, they will have to face simultaneously strong investments in technology and communications.

If Venezuela succeeds in recovering itself after the crisis, it is possible the country will be able to face its entrance to a global economy. The telecommunication network is a key element to connect it with its more advanced neighbors of that area.

In the middle of this crisis, the investments required to install a Teleport with an antenna of 10 m diameter and a master central station would be about $50 million. The geographical position of this facility would allow communications access to the North Hemisphere.

clients will extend their businesses to neighboring countries. In that case, we can also expand our operations abroad, taking advantage of the international structure of IMPSA. We have a contract for waste collection in Colombia, in addition to the metallurgical plant we operate in that country. It would be a good base to set up IMPSAT there.

Ricardo Verdaguer: Keep in mind that we have recently started operations in Argentina. Should we have to grow up internationally at the same time? If it is complex to have technical resources for first-operation growth, how are we going to generate others abroad? There is a risk of affecting negatively the growth in Argentina if we distract resources to other countries.

Although trends indicate we are moving toward a scenario of greater world liberalization in the telecommunications field, we do not forget Brazil is strongly regulated and Uruguay has a solid opposition to privatize its national telephone company, Antel. All of us have read the report about the difficult economic and political situation of Venezuela. The scenario is extremely complex. In addition to regulatory frameworks of each country, we must carefully choose the way and opportunity of expanding abroad.

Roberto Vivo: The best available alternative of almost two or three years ago can be transformed today into a bad option. We should know this, and be current. Without research and change capacity, we would not be useful or we would even disappear. We must not forget that we only have developed experience in a very specific technology, but we cannot show background in data transmission, unlike our competitors. The doubt is if it would be necessary to get associated, and in that case, which kind of partner and which conditions: a local partner in each country or an international one for the whole region, or eventually both alternatives. In any case, it would be necessary to define the partner's capital participation.

Enrique: Don't you think we should think about far away markets? Like Europe, Asia, United States? Soon we could become one of the great world operators in shared networks.

All glances fixed on him and, for a moment, silence invaded the meeting room.

CASE 9

Canon: Competing on Capabilities

In 1961, following the runaway success of the company's model 914 office copier, Joseph C. Wilson, President of Xerox Corporation, was reported to have said, "I keep asking myself, when am I going to wake up? Things just aren't this good in life." Indeed, the following decade turned out to be better than anything Wilson could have dreamed. Between 1960 and 1970, Xerox increased its sales 40 percent per year from $40 million to $1.7 billion and raised its after-tax profits from $2.6 million to $187.7 million. In 1970, with 93 percent market share world-wide and a brand name that was synonymous with copying, Xerox appeared as invincible in its industry as any company ever could.

When Canon, "the camera company from Japan," jumped into the business in the late 1960s, most observers were skeptical. Less than a tenth the size of Xerox, Canon had no direct sales or service organization to reach the corporate market for copiers, nor did it have a process technology to by-pass the 500 patents that guarded Xerox's Plain Paper Copier (PPC) process. Reacting to the spate of recent entries in the business including Canon, Arthur D. Little predicted in 1969 that no company would be able to challenge Xerox's monopoly in PPCs in the 1970s because its patents presented an insurmountable barrier.

Yet, over the next two decades, Canon rewrote the rule book on how copiers were supposed to be produced and sold as it built up $5 billion in revenues in the business, emerging as the second largest global player in terms of sales and surpassing Xerox in the number of units sold.

According the Canon Handbook, the company's formula for success as displayed initially in the copier business is "synergistic management of the total technological capabilities of the company, combining the full measure of Canon's know how in fine optics, precision mechanics, electronics and fine chemicals." Canon continues to grow and diversify using this strategy. Its vision, as described in 1991 by Ryuzaburo Kaku, President of the company, is "to become a premier global company of the size of IBM combined with Matsushita."

INDUSTRY BACKGROUND

The photocopying machine has often been compared with the typewriter as one of the few triggers that have fundamentally changed the ways of office work. But, while a mechanical Memograph machine for copying had been introduced by the AB Dick company of Chicago as far back as 1887, it was only in the second half of this century that the copier market exploded with Xerox's commercialization of the "electrophotography" process invented by Chester Carlson.

This case was written by Mary Ackenhusen, Research Associate, under the supervision of Sumantra Ghoshal, Associate Professor at INSEAD. It is intended to be used as a basis of class discussion rather than to illustrate either effective or ineffective handling of an administrative situation. Reprinted with the permission of INSEAD. Copyright © 1992 INSEAD, Fontainebleau, France.

XEROX

Carlson's invention used an electrostatic process to transfer images from one sheet of paper to another. Licensed to Xerox in 1948, this invention led to two different photocopying technologies. The Coated Paper Copying (CPC) technology transferred the reflection of an image from the original directly to specialized zinc-oxide coated paper, while the Plain Paper Copying (PPC) technology transferred the image indirectly to ordinary paper through a rotating drum coated with charged particles. While dry or liquid toner could be used to develop the image, the dry toner was generally preferable in both technologies. A large number of companies entered the CPC market in the 1950s and 1960s based on technology licensed from Xerox or RCA (to whom Xerox had earlier licensed this technology). However, PPC remained a Xerox monopoly since the company had refused to license any technology remotely connected to the PPC process and had protected the technology with over 500 patents.

Because of the need for specialized coated paper, the cost per copy was higher for CPC. Also, this process could produce only one copy at a time, and the copies tended to fade when exposed to heat or light. PPC, on the other hand, produced copies at a lower operating cost that were also indistinguishable from the original. The PPC machines were much more expensive, however, and were much larger in size. Therefore, they required a central location in the user's office. The smaller and less expensive CPC machines, in contrast, could be placed on individual desks. Over time, the cost and quality advantages of PPC, together with its ability to make multiple copies at high speed, made it the dominant technology and, with it, Xerox's model of centralized copying, the industry norm.

This business concept of centralized copying required a set of capabilities that Xerox developed and which, in turn, served as its major strengths and as key barriers to entry to the business. Given the advantages of volume and speed, all large companies found centralized copying highly attractive and they became the key customers for photocopying machines. In order to support this corporate customer base, Xerox's product designs and upgrades emphasized economies of higher volume copying. To market the product effectively to these customers, Xerox also built up an extensive direct sales and service organization of over 12,000 sales representatives and 15,000 service people. Forty percent of the sales reps' time was spent "hand holding" to prevent even minor dissatisfaction. Service reps, dressed in suits and carrying their tools in briefcases, performed preventative maintenance and prided themselves on reducing the average time between breakdowns and repair to a few hours.

Further, with the high cost of each machine and the fast rate of model introductions, Xerox developed a strategy of leasing rather than selling machines to customers. Various options were available, but typically the customers paid a monthly charge on the number of copies made. The charge covered not only machine costs but also those of the paper and toner that Xerox supplied and the service visits. This lease strategy, together with the carefully cultivated service image, served as key safeguards from competition, as they tied the customers into Xerox and significantly raised their switching costs.

Unlike some other American corporations, Xerox had an international orientation right from the beginning. Even before it had a successful commercial copier, Xerox built up an international presence through joint ventures which allowed the company to minimize its capital investment abroad. In 1956, it ventured with the Rank Organisation Ltd. in the UK to form Rank Xerox. In 1962, Rank Xerox became a 50 percent partner with Fuji Photo to form Fuji Xerox which sold copiers in Japan. Through these joint ventures, Xerox built up sales and service capabilities in these key markets similar to those it had in the United States. There were some 5000 sales people in Europe, 3000 in Japan and over 7000 and 3000 service reps, respectively. Xerox also built limited design capabilities in both the joint ventures for local market customization, which developed into significant research establishments in their own rights in later years.

Simultaneously, Xerox maintained high levels of investment in both technology and manufacturing to support its growing market. It continued to spend over $100 million a year in R&D, exceeding the total revenues from the copier business that any of its competitors were earning in the early 70s, and also invested heavily in large-size plants not only in the US but also in the UK and Japan.

COMPETITION IN THE 1970s

Xerox's PPC patents began to expire in the 1970s, heralding a storm of new entrants. In 1970, IBM offered the first PPC copier not sold by Xerox, which resulted in Xerox suing IBM for patent infringement and violation of trade secrets. Canon marketed a PPC copier the same year through the development of an independent PPC technology which they licensed selectively to others. By 1973, competition had expanded to include players from the office equipment industry (IBM, SCM, Litton, Pitney Bowes), the electronics industry (Toshiba, Sharp), the reprographics industry (Ricoh, Mita, Copyer, 3M, AB Dick, Addressograph/Multigraph), the photographic equipment industry (Canon, Kodak, Minolta, Konishiroku) and the suppliers of copy paper (Nashua, Dennison, Saxon).

By the 1980s many of these new entrants, including IBM, had lost large amounts of money and exited the business. A few of the newcomers managed to achieve a high level of success, however, and copiers became a major business for them. Specifically, copiers were generating 40 percent of Canon's revenues by 1990.

CANON

Canon was founded in 1933 with the ambition to produce a sophisticated 35mm camera to rival that of Germany's world-class Leica model. In only two years' time, it had emerged as Japan's leading producer of high-class cameras. During the war, Canon utilized its optics expertise to produce an X-ray machine which was adopted by the Japanese military. After the war, Canon was able to successfully market its high-end camera, and by the mid-1950s it was the largest camera manufacturer in Japan. Building from its optics technology, Canon then expanded its product line to include a mid-range camera, an 8mm video camera, television lenses and micrographic equipment. It also began developing markets for its products outside of Japan, mainly in the US and Canada.

Diversification was always very important to Canon in order to further its growth, and a new products R&D section was established in 1962 to explore the fields of copy machines, auto-focusing cameras, strobe-integrated cameras, home VCRs and electronic calculators. A separate, special operating unit was also established to introduce new non-camera products resulting from the diversification effort.

The first product to be targeted was the electronic calculator. This product was challenging because it required Canon engineers to develop new expertise in microelectronics in order to incorporate thousands of transistors and diodes in a compact, desk model machine. Tekeshi Mitarai, President of Canon at that time, was against developing the product because it was seen to be too difficult and risky. Nevertheless, a dedicated group of engineers believed in the challenge and developed the calculator in secrecy. Over a year later, top management gave their support to the project. In 1964, the result of the development effort was introduced as the Canola 130, the world's first 10-key numeric pad calculator. With this product line, Canon dominated the Japanese electronic calculator market in the 1960s.

Not every diversification effort was a success, however. In 1956, Canon began development of the synchroreader, a device for writing and reading with a sheet of paper coated with magnetic material. When introduced in 1959, the product received high praise for its technology. But, because the design was not patented, another firm introduced a similar product at half the price. There was no market for the high priced and incredibly heavy Canon product. Ultimately, the firm was forced to disassemble the finished inventories and sell off the usable parts in the 'once-used' components market.

MOVE INTO COPIERS

Canon began research into copier technology in 1959, and, in 1962, it formed a research group dedicated to developing a plain paper copier (PPC) technology. The only known PPC process was protected by hundreds of Xerox patents, but Canon felt that only this technology promised sufficient quality, speed, economy and ease of maintenance to successfully capture a large portion of the market. Therefore, corporate management challenged the researchers to develop a new PPC process which would not violate the Xerox patents.

In the meantime, the company entered the copier business by licensing the "inferior" CPC technology in 1965 from RCA. Canon decided not to put the name of the company on this product and marketed it under the brand name Confax 1000 in Japan only. Three years later, Canon licensed a liquid toner technology from an Australian company and combined this with the RCA technology to introduce the CanAll Series. To sell the copier in Japan, Canon formed a separate company, International Image Industry. The copier was sold as an OEM to Scott Paper in the US who sold it under its own brand name.

Canon's research aiming at developing a PPC technical alternative to xerography paid off with the announcement of the "New Process" (NP) in 1968. This successful research effort not only produced an alternative process but also taught Canon the importance of patent law: how not to violate patents and how to protect new technology. The NP process was soon protected by close to 500 patents.

The first machine with the NP technology, the NP1100, was introduced in Japan in 1970. It was the first copier sold by Canon to carry the Canon brand name. It produced 10 copies per minute and utilized dry toner. As was the standard in the Japanese market, the copier line was sold outright to customers from the beginning. After two years of experience in the domestic market, Canon entered the overseas market, except North America, with this machine.

The second generation of the NP system was introduced in Japan in 1972 as the NPL7. It was a marked improvement because it eliminated a complex fusing technology, simplified developing and cleaning, and made toner supply easier through a new system developed to use liquid toner. Compared with the Xerox equivalent, it was more economical, more compact, more reliable and still had the same or better quality of copies.

With the NP system, Canon began a sideline which was to become quite profitable: licensing. The first generation

EXHIBIT 1 CANON, INC.: TEN-YEAR FINANCIAL SUMMARY (IN ¥ MILLIONS)

	1990	1989	1988	1987	1986	1985	1984	1983	1982	1981
Net sales:										
Domestic	508,747	413,854	348,462	290,382	274,174	272,966	240,656	198,577	168,178	144,898
Overseas	1,219,201	937,063	757,548	686,329	615,043	682,814	589,732	458,748	412,322	326,364
Total Sales	1,727,948	1,350,917	1,106,010	976,711	889,217	955,780	830,383	657,325	580,500	471,262
Percentage to previous year	127.9	122.1	113.2	109.8	93.0	115.1	126.3	113.2	123.2	112.5
Net income	61,408	38,293	37,100	13,244	10,728	37,056	35,029	28,420	22,358	16,216
Percentage to sales	3.6	2.8	3.4	1.4	1.2	3.9	4.2	4.3	3.9	3.4
Advertising expense	72,234	54,394	41,509	38,280	37,362	50,080	1,318	41,902	37,532	23,555
Research and development	86,008	75,566	65,522	57,085	55,330	49,461	38,256	28,526	23,554	14,491
Depreciation	78,351	64,861	57,627	57,153	55,391	47,440	39,995	30,744	27,865	22,732
Capital expenditure	137,298	107,290	83,069	63,497	81,273	917,863	7,594	53,411	46,208	54,532
Long-term debt	262,886	277,556	206,083	222,784	166,722	134,366	99,490	60,636	53,210	39,301
Stockholders' equity	617,566	550,841	416,465	371,198	336,456	333,148	304,310	264,629	235,026	168,735
Total assets	1,827,945	1,636,380	1,299,843	1,133,881	1,009,504	1,001,044	916,651	731,642	606,101	505,169
Per share data:										
Net income										
Common and common equivalent share	78.29	50.16	51.27	19.65	16.67	53.38	53.63	46.31	41.17	34.04
Assuming full dilution	78.12	49.31	51.26	19.64	16.67	53.25	53.37	45.02	38.89	33.35
Cash dividends declared	12.50	11.93	11.36	9.09	11.36	11.36	9.88	9.43	8.23	7.84
Stock price:										
High	1,940	2,040	1,536	1,282	1,109	1,364	1,336	1,294	934	1,248
Low	1,220	1,236	823	620	791	800	830	755	417	513
Average number of common and common equivalent shares in thousands	788,765	780,546	747,059	747,053	746,108	727,257	675,153	645,473	564,349	515,593
Number of employees	54,381	44,401	40,740	37,521	35,498	34,129	30,302	27,266	25,607	24,300
Average exchange rate ($1 =)	143	129	127	143	167	235	239	238	248	222

EXHIBIT 2
SALES BY PRODUCT
(IN ¥ MILLIONS)

YEAR	CAMERAS	COPIERS	OTHER BUSINESS MACHINES	OPTICAL & OTHER PRODUCTS	TOTAL
1981	201,635	175,389	52,798	40,222	470,044
1982	224,619	242,161	67,815	45,905	580,500
1983	219,443	291,805	97,412	48,665	657,325
1984	226,645	349,986	180,661	73,096	830,388
1985	197,284	410,840	271,190	76,466	955,780
1986	159,106	368,558	290,630	70,923	889,217
1987	177,729	393,581	342,895	62,506	976,711
1988	159,151	436,924	434,634	75,301	1,106,010
1989	177,597	533,115	547,170	93,035	1,350,917
1990	250,494	686,077	676,095	115,282	1,727,948

NP system was licensed to AM, and Canon also provided it with machines on an OEM basis. The second generation was again licensed to AM as well as to Saxon, Ricoh, and Copyer. Canon accumulated an estimated $32 million in license fees between 1975 and 1982.

Canon continued its product introductions with a stream of state-of-the-art technological innovations throughout the seventies. In 1973 it added color to the NP system; in 1975, it added laser beam printing technology. Its first entry into high volume copiers took place in 1978 with a model which was targeted at the Xerox 9200. The NP200 was introduced in 1979 and went on to win a gold medal at the Leipzig Fair for being the most economical and productive copier available. By 1982, copiers had surpassed cameras as the company's largest revenue generate (see Exhibits 1 and 2 for Canon's financials and sales by product line).

THE PERSONAL COPIER

In the late 1970s, top management began searching for a new market for the PPC copier. They had recently experienced a huge success with the introduction of the AE-1 camera in 1976 and wanted a similar success in copiers. The AE-1 was a very compact single-lens reflex camera, the first camera that used a microprocessor to control electronically functions of exposure, film rewind, and strobe. The product had been developed through a focused, cross-functional project team effort which had resulted in a substantial reduction in the number of components, as well as in automated assembly and the use of unitized parts. Because of these improvements, the AE-1 enjoyed a 20 percent cost advantage over competitive models in the same class.

After studying the distribution of offices in Japan by size (see Exhibit 3), Canon decided to focus on a latent segment that Xerox had ignored. This was the segment comprising small offices (segment E) who could benefit from the functionality offered by photocopiers but did not require the high speed machines available in the market. Canon management believed that a low volume "value for money" machine could generate a large demand in this segment. From this analysis emerged the business concept of a "personal side desk" machine which could not only create a new market in small offices but potentially also induce decentralization of the copy function in large offices. Over time, the machine might even create demand for a personal copier for home use. This would be a copier that up to now

EXHIBIT 3
OFFICE SIZE
DISTRIBUTION,
JAPAN 1979

COPIER MARKET SEGMENT	NUMBER OF OFFICE WORKERS	NUMBER OF OFFICES	WORKING POPULATION
A	300+	200,000	9,300,000
B	100–299	30,000	4,800,000
C	30–99	170,000	8,300,000
D	5–29	1,820,000	15,400,000
E	1–4	4,110,000	8,700,000

Source: Yamanouchi, Teruo, Breakthrough: The Development of the Canon Personal Copier, *Long Range Planning*, Vol. 22, October 1989, p. 4.

no one had thought possible. Canon felt that, to be successful in this market, the product had to cost half the price of a conventional copier (target price $1,000), be maintenance free, and provide 10 times more reliability.

Top management took their "dream" to the engineers, who, after careful consideration, took on the challenge. The machine would build off their previous expertise in microelectronics but would go much further in terms of material, functional component, design and production engineering technologies. The team's slogan was "Let's make the AE-1 of copiers!" expressing the necessity of know-how transfer between the camera and copier divisions as well as their desire for a similar type of success. The effort was led by the director of the Reprographic Production Development Center. His cross-functional team of 200 was the second largest ever assembled at Canon (the largest had been that of the AE-1 camera).

During the development effort, a major issue arose concerning the paper size that the new copier would accept. Canon Sales (the sales organization for Japan) wanted the machine to use a larger-than-letter-size paper which accounted for 60 percent of the Japanese market. This size was not necessary for sales outside of Japan and would add 20–30 percent to the machine's cost as well as make the copier more difficult to service. After much debate worldwide, the decision was made to forgo the ability to utilize the larger paper size in the interest of better serving the global market.

Three years later the concept was a reality. The new PC (personal copier) employed a new-cartridge based technology which allowed the user to replace the photoreceptive drum, charging device toner assembly and cleaner with a cartridge every 2000 copies, thus eliminating the need to maintain the copier regularly. This enabled Canon engineers to meet the cost and reliability targets. The revolutionary product was the smallest, lightest copier ever sold, and created a large market which had previously not existed. Large offices adjusted their copying strategies to include decentralized copying, and many small offices and even homes could now afford a personal copier. Again, Canon's patent knowledge was utilized to protect this research, and the cartridge technology was not licensed to other manufacturers. Canon has maintained its leadership in personal copiers into the 1990s.

BUILDING CAPABILITIES

Canon is admired for its technical innovations, marketing expertise, and low-cost quality manufacturing. These are the result of a long-term strategy to becoming a premier company. Canon has frequently acquired outside expertise so that it could better focus internal investments on skills of strategic importance. This approach of extensive outsourcing and focused internal development has required consistent direction from top management and the patience to allow the company to become well grounded in one skill area before tasking the organization with the next objective.

TECHNOLOGY

Canon's many innovative products, which enabled the company to grow quickly in the seventies and eighties are in large part the result of a carefully orchestrated use of technology and the capacity for managing rapid technological change. Attesting to its prolific output of original research is the fact that Canon has been among the leaders in number of patents issued worldwide throughout the eighties.

These successes have been achieved in an organization that has firmly pursued a strategy of decentralized R&D. Most of Canon's R&D personnel are employed by the product divisions where 80–90 percent of the company's patentable inventions originate. Each product division has its own development center which is tasked with short- to medium-term product design and improvement of production systems. Most product development is performed by cross-functional teams. The work of the development groups is coordinated by an R&D headquarters group.

The Corporate Technical Planning and Operation center is responsible for long-term strategic R&D planning. Canon also has a main research center which supports state-of-the-art research in optics, electronics, new materials and information technology. There are three other corporate research centers which apply this state-of-the-art research to product development.

Canon acknowledges that it has neither the resources nor the time to develop all necessary technologies and has therefore often traded or bought specific technologies from a variety of external partners. Furthermore, it has used joint ventures and technology transfers as a strategic tool for mitigating foreign trade tensions in Europe and the United States. For example, Canon had two purposes in mind when it made an equity participation in CPF Deutsch, an office equipment marketing firm in Germany. Primarily, it believed that this move would help develop the German market for its copiers; but it did not go unnoticed among top management that CPF owned Tetras, a copier maker who at that time was pressing dumping charges against Japanese copier makers. Canon also used Burroughs as an OEM for office automation equipment in order to acquire Burroughs software and know-how and participate in joint development agreements with Eastman Kodak and Texas Instruments. Exhibit 4 provides a list of the company's major joint ventures.

EXHIBIT 4
CANON'S MAJOR
INTERNATIONAL
JOINT VENTURES

CATEGORY	PARTNER	DESCRIPTION
Office Equipment	Eastman Kodak (US)	Distributes Kodak medical equipment in Japan; exports copiers to Kodak
	CPF Germany	Equity participation in CPF which markets Canon copiers
	Olivetti (Italy) Lotte (Korea)	Joint venture for manufacture of copier
Computers	Hewlett-Packard (US)	Receives OEM mini-computers from HP; supplies laser printer to HP
	Apple Computer (US)	Distributes Apple computers in Japan; supplies laser printer to Apple
	Next, Inc. (US)	Equity participation; Canon has marketing rights for Asia
Semiconductors	National Semiconductor (US)	Joint development of MPU & software for Canon office equipment
	Intel (US)	Joint development of LSI for Canon copier, manufactured by Intel
Telecommunications	Siemens (Germany)	Development of ISDN interface for Canon facsimile; Siemens supplies Canon with digital PBX
	DHL (US)	Equity participation; Canon supplies terminals to DHL
Camera	Kinsei Seimitsu (Korea)	Canon licenses technology on 35mm camera
Other	ECD (US)	Equity participation because Canon values its research on amorphous materials

Canon also recognizes that its continued market success depends on its ability to exploit new research into marketable products quickly. It has worked hard to reduce the new product introduction cycle through a cross-functional programme called TS 1/2 whose purpose is to cut development time by 50 percent on a continuous basis. The main thrust of this programme is the classification of development projects by total time required and the critical human resources needed so that these two parameters can be optimized for each product depending on its importance for Canon's corporate strategy. This allows product teams to be formed around several classifications of product development priorities of which "best sellers" will receive the most emphasis. These are the products aimed at new markets or segments with large potential demands. Other classifications include products necessary to catch up with competitive offerings, product refinements intended to enhance customer satisfaction, and long-run marathon products which will take considerable time to develop. In all development classifications, Canon emphasizes three factors to reduce time to market: the fostering of engineering ability, efficient technical support systems, and careful reviews of product development at all stages.

Canon is also working to divert its traditional product focus into more of a market focus. To this end, Canon R&D personnel participate in international product strategy meetings, carry out consumer research, join in marketing activities, and attend meetings in the field at both domestic and foreign sales subsidiaries.

MARKETING

Canon's effective marketing is the result of step-by-step, calculated introduction strategies. Normally, the product is first introduced and perfected in the home market before being sold internationally. Canon has learned how to capture learning from the Japanese market quickly so that the time span between introduction in Japan and abroad is as short as a few months. Furthermore, the company will not simultaneously launch a new product through a new distribution channel—its strategy is to minimize risk by introducing a new product through known channels first. New channels will only be created, if necessary, after the product has proven to be successful.

The launch of the NP copier exemplifies this strategy. Canon initially sold these copiers in Japan by direct sales through its Business Machines Sales organization, which had been set up in 1968 to sell the calculator product line. This sales organization was merged with the camera sales organization in 1971 to form Canon Sales. By 1972, after three years of experience in producing the NP product line, the company entered into a new distribution channel, that of dealers, to supplement direct selling.

The NP copier line was not marketed in the US until 1974, after production and distribution were running smoothly in Japan. The US distribution system was similar to that used in Japan, with seven sales subsidiaries for direct selling and a network of independent dealers.

By the late 1970s, Canon had built up a strong dealer network in the US which supported both sales and service of the copiers. The dealer channel was responsible for rapid growth in copier sales, and, by the early 1980s, Canon copiers were sold almost exclusively through this channel. Canon enthusiastically supported the dealers with attractive sales incentive programs, management training and social outings. Dealers were certified to sell copiers only after completing a course in service training. The company felt that a close relationship with its dealers was a vital asset that allowed it to understand and react to customer's needs and problems in a timely manner. At the same time, Canon also maintained a direct selling mechanism through wholly owned sales subsidiaries in Japan, the US and Europe in order to target large customers and government accounts.

The introduction of its low-end personal copier in 1983 was similarly planned to minimize risk. Initially, Canon's NP dealers in Japan were not interested in the product due to its low maintenance needs and inability to utilize large paper sizes. Thus, PCs were distributed through the firm's office supply stores who were already selling its personal calculators. After seeing the success of the PC, the NP dealers began to carry the copier.

In the US, the PC was initially sold only through existing dealers and direct sales channels due to limited availability of the product. Later, it was sold through competitors' dealers and office supply stores, and, eventually, the distribution channels were extended to include mass merchandisers. Canon already had considerable experience in mass merchandising from its camera business.

Advertising has always been an integral part of Canon's marketing strategy. President Kaku believes that Canon must have a corporate brand name which is outstanding to succeed in its diversification effort. "Customers must prefer products because they bear the name Canon," he says. As described by the company's finance director, "If a brand name is unknown, and there is no advertising, you have to sell it cheap. It's not our policy to buy share with a low price. We establish our brand with advertising at a reasonably high price."

Therefore, when the NP-200 was introduced in 1980, 10 percent of the selling price was spent on advertising; for the launch of the personal copier, advertising expenditure was estimated to be 20 percent of the selling price. Canon has also sponsored various sporting events including World Cup football, the Williams motor racing team, and the ice dancers Torvill and Dean. The company expects its current expansion into the home automation market to be greatly enhanced by the brand image it has built in office equipment (see Exhibit 1 for Canon's advertising expenditures through 1990).

MANUFACTURING

Canon's goal in manufacturing is to produce the best quality at the lowest cost with the best delivery. To drive down costs, a key philosophy of the production system is to organize the manufacture of each product so that the minimum amount of time, energy and resources are required. Canon therefore places strong emphasis on tight inventory management through a stable production planning process, careful material planning, close supplier relationships, and adherence to the kanban system of inventory movement. Additionally, a formal waste elimination program saved Canon 177 billion yen between 1976 and 1985. Overall, Canon accomplished a 30 percent increase in productivity per year from 1976 to 1982 and over 10 percent thereafter through automation and innovative process improvements.

The workforce is held in high regard at Canon. A philosophy of "stop and fix it" empowers any worker to stop the production line if he or she is not able to perform a task properly or observes a quality problem. Workers are responsible for their own machine maintenance governed by rules which stress prevention. Targets for quality and production and other critical data are presented to the workers with on-line feedback. Most workers also participate in voluntary "small group activity" for problems solving. The result of these systems is a workforce that feels individually responsible for the success of the products it manufactures.

Canon sponsors a highly regarded suggestion program for its workers in order to directly involve those most familiar with the work processes in improving the business. The program was originally initiated in 1952 with only limited success, but in the early 1980s participation soared with more than seventy suggestions per employee per year. All suggestions are reviewed by a hierarchy of committees with monetary prizes awarded monthly and yearly depending on the importance of the suggestion. The quality and effectiveness of the process are demonstrated by a 90 percent implementation rate of the suggestions offered and corporate savings of $202 million in 1985 (against a total expenditure of $2 million in running the program, over 90 percent of it in prize money).

Canon chooses to backward integrate only on parts with unique technologies. For other components, the company prefers to develop long-term relationships with its suppliers and it retains two sources for most parts. In 1990, over 80 percent of Canon's copiers were assembled from purchased parts, with only the drums and toner being manufactured in-house. The company also maintains its own in-house capability for doing pilot production of all parts so as to understand better the technology and the vendors' costs.

Another key to Canon's high quality and low cost is the attention given to parts commonality between models. Between some adjacent copier models, the commonality is as high as 60 percent.

Copier manufacture was primarily located in Toride, Japan, in the early years but then spread to Germany, California and Virginia in the US, France, Italy and Korea. In order to mitigate trade and investment friction, Canon is working to increase the local content of parts as it expands globally. In Europe it exceeds the EC standard by five percent. It is also adding R&D capability to some of its overseas operations. Mr. Kaku emphasizes the importance of friendly trading partners:

> Friction cannot be erased by merely transferring our manufacturing facilities overseas. The earnings after tax must be reinvested in the country; we must transfer our technology to the country. This is the only way our overseas expansion will be welcomed.

LEVERAGING EXPERTISE

Canon places critical importance on continued growth through diversification into new product fields. Mr. Kaku observed,

> Whenever Canon introduced a new product, profits surged forward. Whenever innovation lagged, on the other hand, so did the earnings . . . In order to survive in the coming era of extreme competition, Canon must possess at least a dozen proprietary state-of-the-art technologies that will enable it to develop unique products.

While an avid supporter of diversification, Mr. Kaku was cautious.

> In order to ensure the enduring survival of Canon, we have to continue diversifying in order to adapt to environmental changes. However, we must be wise in choosing ways toward diversification. In other words, we must minimize the risks. Entering a new business which requires either a technology unrelated to Canon's current expertise or a different marketing channel than Canon currently uses incurs a 50 percent risk. If Canon attempts to enter a new business which requires both a new technology and a new marketing channel which are unfamiliar to Canon, the risk entailed in such ventures

would be 100 percent. There are two prerequisites that have to be satisfied before launching such new ventures. First, our operation must be debt-free; second, we will have to secure the personnel capable of competently undertaking such ventures. I feel we shall have to wait until the twenty-first century before we are ready.

COMBINING CAPABILITIES

Through its R&D strategy, Canon has worked to build up specialized expertise in several areas and then link them to offer innovative, state-of-the-art products. Through the fifties and sixties, Canon focused on products related to its main business and expertise, cameras. This prompted the introduction of the 8mm movie camera and the Canon range of mid-market cameras. There was minimal risk because the optics technology was the same and the marketing outlet, camera shops, remained the same.

Entrance into the calculator market pushed Canon into developing expertise in the field of microelectronics, which it later innovatively combined with its optics capability to introduce one of its most successful products, the personal copier. From copiers, Canon utilized the replaceable cartridge system to introduce a successful desktop laser printer.

In the early seventies, Canon entered the business of marketing micro-chip semiconductor production equipment. In 1980, the company entered into the development and manufacture of unique proprietary ICs in order to strengthen further its expertise in electronics technology. This development effort was expanded in the late eighties to focus on opto-electronic ICs. According to Mr. Kaku:

> We are no seriously committed to R&D in ICs because our vision for the future foresees the arrival of the opto-electronic era. When the time arrives for the opto-electronic IC to replace the current ultra-LSI, we intend to go into making large-scale computers. Presently we cannot compete with the IBMs and NECs using the ultra-LSIs. When the era of the opto-electronic IC arrives, the technology of designing the computer will be radically transformed; that will be our chance for making entry into the field of the large-scale computer.

CREATIVE DESTRUCTION

In 1975 Canon produced the first laser printer. Over the next 15 years, laser printers evolved as a highly successful product line under the Canon Brand name. The company also provides the "engine" as an OEM to Hewlett Packard and other laser printer manufacturers which when added to its own brand sales supports a total of 84 percent of world-wide demand.

The biggest threat to the laser printer industry is substitution by the newly developed bubble jet printer. With a new technology which squirts out thin streams of ink under heat, a high-quality silent printer can be produced at half the price of the laser printer. The technology was invented accidentally in the Canon research labs. It keys on a print head which has up to 400 fine nozzles per inch, each with its own heater to warm the ink until it shoots out tiny ink droplets. This invention utilizes Canon's competencies in fine chemicals for producing the ink and its expertise in semiconductors, materials, and electronics for manufacturing the print heads. Canon is moving full steam forward to develop the bubble jet technology, even though it might destroy a business that the company dominates. The new product is even more closely tied to the company's core capabilities, and management believes that successful development of this business will help broaden further its expertise in semiconductors.

CHALLENGE OF THE 1990s

Canon sees the office automation business as its key growth opportunity for the nineties. It already has a well-established brand name in home and office automation products through its offerings of copiers, facsimiles, electronic typewriters, laser printers, word processing equipment and personal computers. The next challenge for the company is to link these discrete products into a multi-functional system which will perform the tasks of a copier, facsimile, printer, and scanner and interface with a computer so that all the functions can be performed from one keyboard. In 1988, with this target, Canon introduced a personal computer which incorporated a PC, a fax, a telephone and a word processor. Canon has also introduced a color laser copier which hooks up to a computer to serve as a color printer. A series of additional integrated OA offerings are scheduled for introduction in 1992, and the company expects these products to serve as its growth engine in the first half of the 1990s.

MANAGING THE PROCESS

Undergirding this impressive history of continuously building new corporate capabilities and of exploiting those capabilities to create a fountain of innovative new products lies a rather unique management process. Canon has institutionalized corporate entrepreneurship through its highly autonomous and market focused business unit structure. A set of powerful functional committees provides the bridge between the entrepreneurial business units and

the company's core capabilities in technology, manufacturing and marketing. Finally, an extraordinarily high level of corporate ambition drives this innovation engine, which is fuelled by the creativity of its people and by top management's continuous striving for ever higher levels of performance.

DRIVING ENTREPRENEURSHIP: THE BUSINESS UNITS

Mr. Kaku had promoted the concept of the entrepreneurial business unit from his earliest days with Canon, but it was not until the company had suffered significant losses in 1975 that his voice was heard. His plan was implemented shortly before he became president of the company.

Mr. Kaku believed that Canon's diversification strategy could only succeed if the business units were empowered to act on their own, free of central controls. Therefore, two independent operating units were formed in 1978, one for cameras and one for office equipment, to be managed as business units. Optical Instruments, the third business unit, had always been separate. Since that time, an additional three business units have been spun off. The original three business units were then given clear profitability targets, as well as highly ambitious growth objectives, and were allowed the freedom to devise their own ways to achieve these goals. One immediate result of this decentralization was the recognition that Canon's past practice of mixing production of different products in the same manufacturing facility would no longer work. Manufacturing was reorganized so that no plant produced more than one type of product.

Mr. Kaku describes the head of each unit as a surrogate of the CEO empowered to make quick decisions. This allows him, as president of Canon, to devote himself exclusively to his main task of creating and implementing the long-term corporate strategy. In explaining the benefits of the system, he said:

> Previously, the president was in exclusive charge of all decision making; his subordinates had to form a queue to await their turn in presenting their problems to him. This kind of system hinders the development of the young managers' potential for decision-making.
>
> Furthermore, take the case of the desktop calculator. Whereas, I can devote only about two hours each day on problems concerning the calculator, the CEO of Casio Calculator could devote 24 hours to the calculator . . . In the fiercely competitive market, we lost out because our then CEO was slow in coping with the problem.

In contrast to the Western philosophy of stand-alone SBUs encompassing all functions including engineering, sales, marketing and production, Canon has chosen to separate its product divisions from its sales and marketing arm. This separation allows for a clear focus on the challenges that Canon faces in selling products on a global scale. Through a five-year plan initiated in 1977, Seiichi Takigawa, the president of Canon Sales (the sales organization for Japan), stressed the need to "make sales a science." After proving the profitability of this approach, Canon Sales took on the responsibility for world-wide marketing, sales and service. In 1981, Canon Sales was listed on the Tokyo stock exchange, reaffirming its independence.

Canon also allows its overseas subsidiaries free rein, though it holds the majority of stock. The philosophy is to create the maximum operational leeway for each subsidiary to act on its own initiative. Kaku describes the philosophy through an analogy:

> Canon's system of managing subsidiaries is similar to the policy of the Tokugawa government, which established secure hegemony over the warlords, who were granted autonomy in their territory. I am "shogun" [head of the Tokugawa regime] and the subsidiaries' presidents are the "daimyo" [warlords]. The difference between Canon and the Tokugawa government is that the latter was a zero-sum society; its policy was repressive. On the other hand, Canon's objective is to enhance the prosperity of all subsidiaries through efficient mutual collaboration.

Canon has also promoted the growth of intrapreneurial ventures within the company by spinning these ventures off as wholly owned subsidiaries. The first venture to be spun off was Canon Components, which produced electronic components and devices, in 1984.

BUILDING INTEGRATION: FUNCTIONAL COMMITTEES

As Canon continues to grow and diversify, it becomes increasingly difficult but also ever more important to link its product divisions in order to realize the benefits possible only in a large multiproduct corporation. The basis of Canon's integration is a three dimensional management approach in which the first dimension is the independent business unit, the second a network of functional committees, and the third the regional companies focused on geographic markets (see Exhibit 5).

Kaku feels there are four basic requirements for the success of a diversified business.

1. a level of competence in research and development;
2. quality, low-cost manufacturing technology;
3. superior marketing strength;
4. an outstanding corporate identity, culture and brand name.

Therefore, he has established separate functional committees to address the first three requirements of development, production and marketing, while the fourth task has been kept as a direct responsibility of corporate management. The three functional committees, in turn, have been made responsible for company-wide administration of three key management systems:

- The Canon Development System (CDS) whose objectives are to foster the research and creation of new products and technologies by studying and continuously improving the development process.
- The Canon Production System (CPS) whose goal is to achieve optimum quality by minimizing waste in all areas of manufacturing.
- The Canon Marketing System (CMS), later renamed the Canon International Marketing System (CIMS), which is tasked to expand and strengthen Canon's independent domestic and overseas sales networks by building a high quality service and sales force.

Separate offices have been created at headquarters for each of these critical committees, and over time their role has broadened to encompass general improvement of the processes used to support their functions. The chairpersons of the committee are members of Canon's management committee, which gives them the ability to ensure consistency and communicate process improvements throughout the multiproduct, multinational corporation.

Using information technology to integrate its world-wide operations, Canon began development of the Global Information system for Harmonious Growth Administration (GINGA) in 1987. The system will consist of a high-speed digital communications network to interconnect all parts of Canon into a global database and allow for the timely flow of information among managers in any location of the company's world-wide organization. GINGA is planned to include separate but integrated systems for computer integrated manufacturing, global marketing and distribution, R&D and product design, financial reporting, and personnel database tracking, as well as some advances in intelligent office automation. As described by Mr. Kaku, the main objective of this system is to supplement Canon's efficient vertical communications structure with a lateral one that will facilitate direct information exchange among managers across businesses, countries, and functions on all operational matters concerning the company. The system is being developed at a total cost of 20 billion yen and it is targeted for completion in 1992.

EXHIBIT 5
CANON
ORGANIZATION
CHART

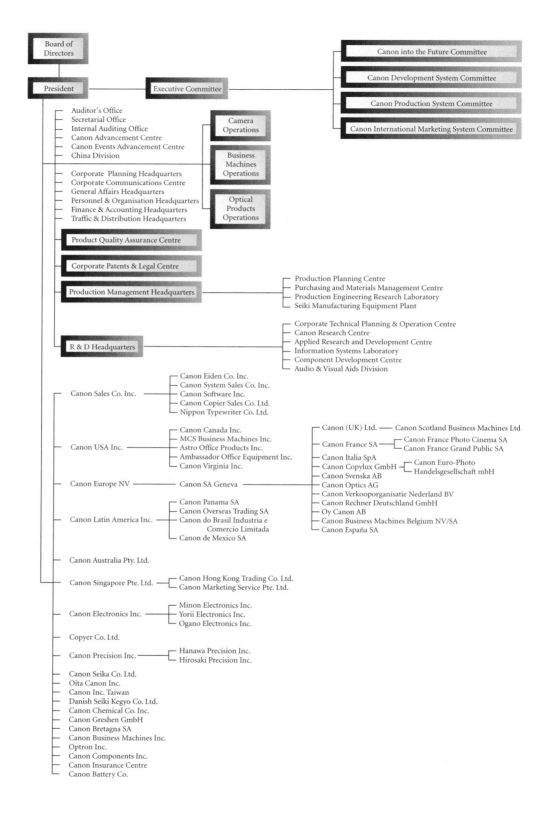

MANAGING RENEWAL: CHALLENGES AND CHANGE

Mr. Kaku was very forthright about some of the management weaknesses of Canon prior to 1975:

> In short, our skill in management—the software of our enterprise—was weak. Management policy must be guided by a soundly created software on management; if the software is weak, the firm will lack clearly defined ideals and objectives. In the beginning we had a clearly defined objective, to overtake West Germany's Leica. Since then our management policy has been changing like the colors of a chameleon.
>
> In the past our management would order employees to reach the peak of Mount Fuji, and then before the vanguard of climbers had barely started climbing, they would be ordered to climb Mount Tsukuba far to the north. Then the order would again be suddenly changed to climb Mount Yatsugatake to the west. After experiencing these kind of shifts in policy, the smarter employees would opt to take things easy by taking naps on the bank of the river Tamagawa. As a result, vitality would be sapped from our work force—a situation that should have been forestalled by all means.

Mr. Kaku's first action as President of Canon was to start the firm on the path to global leadership through establishing the first "premier company plan," a six-year plan designed to make Canon a top company in Japan. The plan outlined a policy for diversification and required consistently recurring profits exceeding 10 percent on sales.

> The aim of any Japanese corporation is ensuring its perpetual survival. Unlike the venture businesses and US corporations, our greatest objective is not to maximize short-term profits. Our vital objective is to continually earn profits on a stable basis for ensuring survival. To implement this goal, we must diversify.

By the time the original six-year plan expired in 1981, Canon had become a highly respected company in Japan. The plan was then renewed through 1986 and then again into the 1990s. The challenge was to become a premier global company, defined as having recurring profits exceeding 15 percent of sales. R&D spending was gradually increased from 6 percent of sales in 1980 to 9 percent in 1985 as a prerequisite for global excellence. As described by Mr. Kaku:

> By implementing our first plan for becoming a premier company we have succeeded in attaining the allegorical top of Mount Fuji. Our next objective is the Everest. With a firm determination, we could have climbed Fuji wearing sandals. However, sandals are highly inappropriate for climbing Everest; it may cause our death.

According to Mr. Kaku, such ambitions also require a company to build up the ability to absorb temporary reversals without panic; ambition without stability makes the corporate ship lose its way. To illustrate, he described the situation at Canon during the time the yen depreciated from 236 to the dollar in 1985 to 168 to the dollar in 1986. With 74 percent of Canon's Japanese production going to export markets, this sudden change caused earnings to fall to 4.6 billion yen, one tenth of the previous year. Some board members at Canon sought drastic action such as a major restructuring of the company and cutting the R&D budget. Mr. Kaku had successfully argued the opposite:

> What I did was calm them down. If a person gets lost in climbing a high mountain, he must avoid excessive use of his energy, otherwise his predicament will deepen . . . Our ongoing strategy for becoming the premier company remains the best, even under this crisis; there is no need to panic. Even if we have to forgo dividends for two or three times, we shall surely overcome this crisis.

While celebrating the company's past successes, Mr. Kaku also constantly reminds his colleagues that no organizational form or process holds the eternal truth. The need to change with a changing world is inevitable. For example, despite being the creator of the product division-marketing company split, he was considering rejoining these two in the nineties:

> In the future, our major efforts in marketing must be concentrated on clearly defining and differentiating the markets of the respective products and creating appropriate marketing systems for them. In order to make this feasible, we may have to recombine our sales subsidiaries with the parent company and restructure their functions to fully meet the market's needs.

While constantly aware of the need to change, Kaku also recognizes the difficulties managers face in changing the very approaches and strategies that have led to past successes:

> In order for a company to survive forever, the company must have the courage to be able to deny at one point what it has been doing in the past; the biological concept of "ecdysis"—casting off the skin to emerge to new form. But it is difficult for human beings to deny and destruct what they have been building up. But if they cannot do that, it is certain that the firm can not survive forever. Speaking about myself, it is difficult to deny what I've done in the past. So when such time comes that I have to deny the past, I inevitably would have to step down.

MP3.com

When Michael Robertson emerged in September 2000 from a Manhattan court, pale beneath his California tan, the chief executive of the MP3.com online music service told reporters that consumers want to be able to listen to their music from wherever they are. That the technology that went into his MP3.com has allowed them to do that. And that the law shouldn't get in the way. Unfortunately, for Robertson, a federal judge had just ruled that his San Diego-based start-up must pay Universal Music Group up to $250 million for infringing on its copyrights. The target of the lawsuit had been a new service called My.MP3.com that was found to be in violation of copyright law because it had compiled a vast online music database for commercial use.

It has only been a little over two years since Robertson, a 32-year-old entrepreneur with blond surfer looks, had started his business, which distributes music over the Internet with a digital compression technology known as MP3. Before he launched his MP3.com site, he was a computer geek who knew nothing about the music business. Even after Robertson had introduced his service, which enables musicians to distribute their music cheaply over the Internet, he was virtually ignored by top labels. But with more and more music being made available, his site has been attracting a great deal of attention. Operating out of a tiny, nondescript office in a San Diego aerospace complex far from the glitzy music capitals of Hollywood and New York, the former software programmer was being feared and loathed by some of the most powerful forces in the $40-billion record industry.

As the world's top record conglomerates struggle to retain their lock on global music distribution, Robertson has emerged as a new kind of rock 'n' roll rebel: a cyber-space capitalist itching for a showdown with the corporate entertainment establishment. His business also illustrates how quickly new technologies and the Internet can shake the foundations of entrenched businesses. "The rules of commerce are changing fast, and the record industry needs to wake up and deal with it," Robertson said. "Fans are tired of paying $15 for a CD to get one good song. Artists are sick of signing their lives away and ending up in debt. That tired, old business model that the companies have exploited for decades is not going to work in cyber-space. If the sleeping giants don't open their eyes pretty soon to the way things work on the Web, they are going to lose a huge, multibillion-dollar opportunity to upstarts like me."

AN INDUSTRY UNDER SIEGE

For most of this century, the big record companies have managed to develop and maintain their power over artists and their audiences. The clout of the major companies came from their advantages in the recording,

Case prepared by Jamal Shamsie, UCLA, to be used for class discussion. Material drawn from published sources. Copyright © 2002 Jamal Shamsie.

manufacturing, distribution and marketing of music. They were able to offer up-to-date studio facilities, press their own records, tapes, and CDs, and dominate retail outlets. Because of their strong position, these big companies have never had to worry about the small independents, who did not have much clout. They would either collapse or get bought out by one of the majors.

These advantages also made it possible for the majors to make the investments on promoting many new acts, by getting their music to the largest possible audience. They pushed these artists through obtaining playtime on top radio stations, broadcasting promotion videos on MTV and developing promotions at the retail outlets. Although most artists do not develop a viable market, the few successes—such as Madonna and Michael Jackson—have been able to pay for the rest. In any case, the big labels were generally able to exert considerable influence on the music that made it to the top of the charts.

But the position of the big record companies was being tested by the advent of new digital technologies. New or existing acts could now record their own music on digital audio tapes and promote and distribute their own music on the Internet. These possibilities are likely to pose the greatest challenge to the system that the major firms have developed to maintain their hold over the industry. In particular, established firms face the threat of MP3, a new format for storing music on the Internet. Digital compression can allow Internet users access to recordings that can be played, in full stereo, on PCs with speakers, in regular CD players and on Walkman-like devices designed for the MP3.

And Robertson's site could best be regarded as just the tip of the MP3 iceberg. The technology has already spawned a new breed of music fans who gather daily in chat rooms and fly-by-night pirate sites on the Internet to swap pilfered hits by artists such as Brandy, Celine Dion and Eric Clapton. These Web-savvy bandits—that is just beginning to expand beyond college students with access to high-bandwidth Internet connections—apparently feel no guilt about ripping off copyrighted recordings to build customized digital jukeboxes on their personal computers.

Even if the music conglomerates could figure out how to curb electronic theft, the industry must confront a more sweeping prospect: a generation of music fans weaned on MP3 that cares only about compiling collections of hit songs with little inclination to purchase music in the album format. This attitude would undermine the economic foundation of the music business, whose profits are generated by manufacturing and distributing albums that contain twelve or more songs and sell them wholesale for about $10.

FROM SOFTWARE TO MUSIC

Robertson is the first to say that he is a music industry novice. Before starting MP3.com, his main music credential was playing clarinet in his high school band in Huntington Beach, a small town in southern California. He grew up in a working-class, fundamentalist household where listening to popular music was discouraged. He graduated from the University of California at San Diego in 1990 with a degree in cognitive science.

After college, Robertson started a computer consulting firm and later sold software tools he had developed. Looking to expand, he started Media Minds, which sold digital-camera software—a business that ultimately failed. The origins of MP3.com can be traced back to 1996, when Robertson founded the Z Company, a Yahoo!-style search engine.

The following year, he and his business partner, Greg Flores, noticed that the term "MP3" was being searched for more and more often on sites like Yahoo! and Infoseek by people looking for digital music. Mr. Flores, now MP3.com's director of sales, tracked down the man who had already been working on an MP3 site. Robertson was impressed enough to buy the rights to the MP3.com domain name and to rename his company.

The new endeavor met with almost immediate success. Robertson and Flores recalled the fateful day when they launched their site. "We set the site up at 10 a.m., and before the day was over we had 10,000 people visit and advertisers calling us cold," Robertson said. "We looked at each other and said, 'This is amazing. What have we stumbled onto here?'"

From there on, Robertson says he started learning about the music business and claims that he was shocked by what he found. In particular he discovered that musicians often get less than 10% of the price of a CD; that despite giving up so little of the sale, labels lose money on about 85% of their artists, depending for profits on hits like Hootie & the Blowfish's *Cracked Rear View*, which has sold 16 million CDs for Atlantic. Robertson also couldn't believe artists lock themselves into long-term contracts, like actors used to do with the Hollywood studios, and give up ownership of their recordings. "The system is broken," he said, "and we can fix it."

Nevertheless, Robertson said he is stunned at how a company as small as his can make so large an impact in so short a time in an industry with as much potential as the record business. He says the site is already turning a profit from the advertising it carries and the CDs it sells. In a little over two years, MP3.com has become one of the leading music sites on the Web—frequented by an estimated 3 million visitors each month, about half of whom Robertson says download a free song during each visit.

A HAVEN FOR ARTISTS

Above all, Robertson believes that artists will use his site to break free from the clutches of the top record conglomerates. He has been working hard to get his MP3.com site to be regarded as a marketing vehicle and record label that's more artist friendly. "We're working for a higher purpose," said Robertson. "We're providing artists with an option besides the traditional industry route—an avenue in which they have control of their destiny and keep ownership of their work."

Although it would seem that artists with a stake in copyright protection would resist aligning themselves with the MP3 movement, several top counterculture acts, including the Beastie Boys, have begun releasing exclusive tracks in the MP3 format. Other mainstream artists, such as Tom Petty and Alanis Morissette, are also beginning to use Robertson's site to try to promote their music independently of the labels. At last count, MP3.com had over 10,000 acts signed up, with another 150 or so being added on each day.

Robertson's site has been especially successful in attracting less-known acts. While a group called Ugly Beauty had been signed with Atlantic, lead singer Christy Schnabel claims that the label did little to promote their CD, which sold just a couple of thousand copies in 1997. The band was dropped by the label at the end of 1998. A few months later, the group changed their name to Lotusland and signed on with MP3.com. In its first couple of weeks on the site, the band got a few dozen downloads a day. Then it was featured on the site's "artist spotlight," and downloads shot up to 1,300 a day. "Our mouths hit the floor," said Schnabel. She insisted that the ability to get its music out there despite the big labels has reinvigorated the band, even if sales have not been soaring.

Robertson believes his site will continue to be a key outlet for many such artists who will come from the major labels as they continue to consolidate. Recently, the merger of Universal with Polygram led to the dismissal of a relatively large number of artists, some of whom were drawn to MP3.com. Claims Robertson: "You can take an artist that never made any money for themselves or the record label, and that same artist can move to the Net and sell one-tenth and make a lot more money."

When they sign up with MP3.com, artists agree to give away one song, which visitors can download free. If the visitor decides to order a full CD of that artist's music, Robertson presses the CD and ships it to the buyer. The artist sets the price, gets 50% of the price on every sale, and keeps full control of the master recording. In order to be able to press CDs on request, MP3.com owns a bunch of company servers which hold the digitized versions of tens of thousands of tunes from a growing number of artists that have signed up with the site. The servers are directly connected to CD burners, each of which can create a disk in just under twenty minutes.

A VIABLE SYSTEM?

Skeptics have argued that Robertson has not built a viable business model that is likely to allow his site or his artists to make much money. They claim that his MP3.com site will have to attract artists that either already have or can quickly achieve high visibility to boost its sales. This can either result from securing acts from the established labels which are already selling well or, alternatively, from artists who achieve hit status through the MP3.com digital label. So far, no new artist signed up with the site has sold more than 10,000 CDs. Val Azzoli, the co-chairman and co-CEO of Atlantic group remarked: "Blah-blah-blah Net, blah-blah-blah dot com. It's all about the artist. The rest means nothing. Unless you have a great artist and great music, it's all bull."

Robertson also has to obtain sales from its visitors who appear to be happy just to download whatever music is offered for free. Many industry observers believe that the free download policy of sites such as MP3.com will only serve to facilitate piracy. "If he sells music, more power to him," said Hilary Rosen, chief executive and president of the Recording Industry Association of America. "I think it's the notion that music can be given away for free forever and there not be a return that is the economic joke."

But the chief executive of MP3.com does not see himself as part of the music establishment. He claims that he is going to be part of the new order in the music business. Robertson, whose site has turned into a pulpit for the MP3 movement, predicts that the established retail, manufacturing and distribution systems will crumble as electronic transmission of music through interactive computer services becomes readily accessible to fans and independent artists. The way he sees it, the record industry has failed to keep up with the rapid pace of technological change represented by the Internet.

Robertson says the industry wastes too much time trying to stop fans from stealing music and not enough energy trying to induce the 100 million consumers who frequent the Internet to purchase their products. He predicts that MP3 will have as big an impact on the record industry as the Xerox copying machine did on the publishing business. Because it will be difficult to prevent fans from creating and transmitting digital copies of a song, music companies will have to revise their business models, perhaps learning to be content with selling the initial release of a new recording to a bigger universe of buyers on the Internet.

"Theft is a cost of doing business on the Internet," Robertson said. "I know the giant companies have spent more than a year trying to develop a universal encryption and watermark security system, but I guarantee you the minute they unveil the thing, some hacker will figure out a way to get around it. It is impossible to secure digital music. The thing these giant corporations need to realize is that finding an illegal music file is like playing a game: You look here. You look there. The search is part of the thrill . . . "

Instead, Robertson believes that firms should be looking for profitable ways to deliver to customers what they are looking for. "The industry needs to focus on how to make it easy for consumers to give them money in one quick, instantaneous transaction," he explained. "The company that solves how to get a consumer from hearing a song on the Net to clicking the mouse and owning it is the company that will thrive. They will crush us like a bug. But if they don't figure out a way soon to make it easier for fans to get music legally than illegally, their days are numbered."

STAYING ALIVE

The legal battle that had embroiled Robertson's site had ensued over the decision to allow consumers to listen to their own CD collection through a My.MP3.com service that had been introduced in March 2000. To make this service easier to use, MP3.com did not require users to load their own music onto a virtual storage locker. Instead, a user had to merely insert a CD into the CD-ROM drive of a computer and log onto MP3.com's Web site, at which point MP3.com would automatically put a copy of the music into the person's virtual locker. A user could also purchase a CD from an online retailer and listen to it immediately once MP3.com had confirmed this transaction.

Robertson was clearly shaken by the judgment against his site, although legal experts agreed that MP3.com had technically violated copyright laws. But there is a growing feeling that the verdict seems to underscore a mismatch between the intentions of traditional copyright law—to strike a balance between the rights of owners and the interests of users—and its effect in the Internet era. "As these cases and others like them get sorted out we will learn to what extent copyright law is being interpreted to give the owners of content an indirect monopoly over the development of useful consumer information technologies," said Peter Jaszi, a law professor at American University.

The judgment represents a serious financial blow to the fledgling Web site. The firm has about $300 million in cash, some of which has been earmarked to settle with the four other major record companies originally involved in the lawsuit. An MP3.com lawyer had already argued before the court that any substantive award of damages would amount to a virtual "death sentence" for the company. Analysts stated that MP3.com should still be able to stay afloat if it managed to keep the damage payment in the $100 million range.

Even if Robertson is able to cope with the financial burdens that have been imposed by legal challenges, questions still remain about the ability of MP3.com to generate substantial revenue solely from new and developing artists. The My.MP3.com service was clearly designed to try and generate more revenue from music from established artists that have released their music through major labels. Marc Schiller, CEO of Electric Artists—a Web music marketer in New York—believes that Robertson will find it tough to make money on unknown talent. "A year from now it will be interesting to see what MP3.com looks like," he stated. "How many people rise above the noise?"

In other words, it is not clear that MP3.com can achieve significant success without moving away from its current business model. In the long run, the site will be forced to adopt more of the practices of the music conglomerates that Robertson presently criticizes. As more and more acts sign on to its digital label, Robertson will also be forced to make decisions about which artists to sign on and push. His site has some tools, such as its list of top picks and its artist highlight sections, that can be used to promote some artists over others.

If this turns out to be the case, Robertson will have just replaced one way of distributing music by another more cheaper way, which allows him to charge less and give back more to the artists. For his part, Robertson shrugs off such suggestions, insisting that it is not yet possible to predict where his site is headed. He summed up: "You have to look at the whole digital music thing as a baby. It's a baby that can't walk and talk yet, but it's just starting to learn."

EXHIBIT 1
INCOME STATEMENTS
IN MILLIONS OF
U.S. DOLLARS

	12 MONTHS ENDING DEC 1999	10 MONTHS ENDING DEC 1998
Revenue	21.9	1.2
Other Revenue	—	—
Total Revenue	**21.9**	**1.2**
Cost of Revenue	9.2	0.2
Gross Profit	**12.7**	**0.9**
Selling / General / Administrative Expenses	33.3	0.2
Research & Development	9.4	0.4
Depreciation / Amortization	22.3	0.6
Interest Expense (Income), Net Operating	—	—
Unusual Expense (Income)	—	—
Total Operating Expense	**74.2**	**1.4**
Operating Income	**(52.3)**	**(0.2)**
Interest Income (Expense), Net Non-Operating	10.9	0.0
Gain (Loss) on Sale of Assets	—	—
Income Before Tax	**(41.5)**	**(0.2)**
Income Tax	(0.1)	0.1
Income After Tax	**(41.4)**	**(0.4)**
Minority Interest	(1.1)	0.0
Equity in Affiliates	—	—
Net Income Before Extra. Items	**(42.5)**	**(0.4)**
Accounting Change	—	—
Discontinued Operations	—	—
Extraordinary Item	—	—
Net Income	**(42.5)**	**(0.4)**
Preferred Dividends	—	—

WFNX-101.7 FM
and Boston's Radio Wars

THE RISK OF SUCCESS

Kurt St. Thomas, the program director of WFNX radio, looked out at a raucous crowd of over 100,000 people on Boston's Esplanade as he waited for the band Green Day to take the stage on Sept. 9, 1994. This show was part of the station's "Disorientation: Welcome Back To School" weekend. At that moment, the show seemed to be the station's crowning achievement.

> "We were putting on the biggest concert in Boston. We had really done something. We'd impacted in some kind of way we hadn't before," said St. Thomas, looking back on the show. "We upstaged every other radio station in Boston. I didn't want the rest of the world to know about this [music]. I didn't want everyone jumping on the bandwagon. But I knew it was too late. We were in big (expletive) trouble."

St. Thomas's feeling turned out to be prophetic. This little 3,000-watt station from Lynn, Massachusetts, *was* about to make a difference. The Green Day concert exploded that day into what the newspapers would later call a "melee." Some of the fans erupted in hysteria as the state police stopped the concert halfway through Green Day's sixth song. In a call to rebel against authority, lead singer Billy Joe had urged the crowd to destroy the surrounding property on the Esplanade. "Pull up the (expletive) flowers," he screamed from the stage. The police fought for hours in the rain to restore order and regain control.

Media attention focused on the event for weeks. CNN and MTV carried the story for days, and local newspapers and television questioned the need for free rock concerts on the Esplanade. But whether or not there would be free concerts, nothing would ever be the same for WFNX.

THE BIRTH OF A STATION

WFNX-101.7 FM was started in 1983 by The Phoenix Media/Communications Group, a local media conglomerate. Founded in 1966, the company was known for its flagship newspaper, *The Boston Phoenix*, which became the largest alternative weekly in New England and the second largest in the country.

The initial mission of WFNX was to serve as a link to the newspaper, appealing to the same audience: educated, affluent, single professionals and students seeking different opinions from those offered by mainstream media. That counterculture role spurred WFNX to choose the emerging

This case was written with the cooperation of WFNX by Brad Mindich (MBA '98) and Associate Professor Robb Kopp, both of Babson College. It was edited by Michael Lelyveld. This is intended for classroom discussion and is not intended to illustrate effective or ineffective handling of an administrative situation. Some financial data have been disguised.

sound known as "new wave" or "alternative" music as its format. No other station in the area was playing similar music. Only one other station in the country, KROQ in Los Angeles, featured "new wave" at the time. The first song to hit the airwaves when WFNX went on the air was "Video Killed the Radio Star" by the Buggles. WFNX focused on bands like Sex Pistols, Missing Persons, Talking Heads and Devo, while mixing in local music, jazz and reggae.

Over the years, WFNX gained a following as the "cool" radio station. It offered something different from the hard-rock music heard on other stations. It also maintained a firm commitment to the local music scene and supported bands like the Mighty Mighty Bosstones, when no other station would.

The WFNX staff had an ear for discovering new national music. The station started throwing parties at local clubs, brining in new, relatively unknown bands like Nirvana and Smashing Pumpkins, which went on to become hugely popular. WFNX established itself as the leader in new music. It became the station to listen to, for those who wanted to hear "the next big thing" before anyone else.

But while the station wanted to stay outside the mainstream, it was also driven to succeed in an industry where competition could be brutal. WFNX was discovering that it was one thing to establish an identity. It was another to defend it in the commercial world of ratio. (see Appendices A–D for background data on WFNX ratings, demographics and revenue trends.)

THE ROLE OF RADIO

Since the 1930s, radio played an important part in the value chain of the music industry and in the media mixes of advertisers. Radio was the music industry's "sampling vehicle." While it was possible to promote an unknown talent via clubs and word of mouth, it was virtually impossible for an "underground" artist to become a major act without the support of radio airplay. Stardom came to depend on radio.

> People did not buy pop music they had never heard. But it was axiomatic that for each single in the top ten, you could sell a million albums. So promotion, the art and science of getting songs on the air, drove the record business. Not marketing, because no amount of advertising or even good reviews and publicity were enough to sell millions of albums. Not sales, because record stores only reacted to demand and did not create it. Even the best A&R (artist and repertoire) staff in the world couldn't save you if radio gave you the cold shoulder.[1]

Record companies grew to include marketing, sales and promotion staff. In the 1970s, independent promoters also became a powerful force. Radio program directors were bombarded with offerings from both established and new artists. There was more new product than there were airplay slots to fill. In this competitive environment, it became a struggle to land a place on a station's playlist. Competition gave rise to abuses like bribery. The "payola" scandals of the early 1960s brought the "pay-for-play" practice to light, and prompted a law enforcement crackdown.

For the advertiser aiming to create awareness and a brand image, radio was an important element in an overall media mix. Radio's strength was that individual stations could target specific demographic groups. Airtime was relatively cheap, allowing advertisers to add higher levels of frequency, or repeated ads, to their media plans. Radio was considered more intimate, personal and imaginative than other media were, but it was useless whenever displays or product demonstrations were required.[2]

Radio was also an excellent medium for local and regional advertisers, because of broadcast range and cost. It was useful for national advertisers, but it required stations in enough markets to conduct a truly national campaign. Consolidation of the radio industry, described later in this case, reduced the administrative burden on the media buyer, making radio potentially even stronger as a media vehicle.

RADIO ECONOMICS: WFNX VERSUS OTHERS

Radio stations had much in common with other businesses when it came to financial statements (see Exhibit 1). But they also had to contend with special expenses, while benefiting from unique revenue opportunities. Primary revenue generation came from selling time slots or advertising "spots." The cost of spots varied with each radio station, primarily based on ratings and signal strength. For example, a one-minute spot in prime time (Monday–Friday, 6 a.m.–10 a.m.) cost approximately $650–$700 at Boston radio station WBCN, which was WFNX's biggest competitor. A comparable spot on WFNX cost $100–$250.

Radio was considered more effective than magazines, newspapers or television as a media buy, with a cost per thousand (CPM) in audience exposure of $40–$50. An average radio station had approximately 500,000 listeners per week. Advertisers could run an ad 40 times on a radio station, compared with buying a one-quarter page ad in *The Boston Sunday Globe*, for example, at the same cost. Since audiences responded to repeated messages, radio was the perfect medium for capitalizing on advertisers' frequency needs. People listened to radio in their cars, at work or at home throughout the day.

Generally, staffing was the biggest expense for radio stations due to high talent costs. Howard Stern, the syndicated

EXHIBIT 1 WFNX FINANCIALS 1997–1993

1997 COMPARED TO 1996 ACTUAL

	TOTAL YEAR ACTUAL 1997 $	TOTAL YEAR ACTUAL 1996 $	+(−) $	+/− %	TOTAL YEAR ACTUAL 1995 $	AS A % OF REVENUE %	TOTAL YEAR ACTUAL 1994 $
REVENUE							
ADVERTISING REVENUE	5,267,625	5,871,308	(603,683)	−10.28%	6,770,715	99.50%	6,506,700
OTHER	18,000	21,226	(3,226)	−15.20%	13,500	0.20%	14,500
TOTAL REVENUE	5,285,625	5,892,534	(606,909)	−10.30%	6,784,215	100.00%	6,521,200
OPERATING EXPENSES							
PROGRAMMING	753,188	707,996	45,192	6.38%	697,852	10.29%	653,056
ENGINEERING	89,526	87,738	1,788	2.04%	84,725	1.25%	72,330
SALES	1,004,628	1,018,771	(14,143)	−1.39%	1,016,950	14.99%	962,879
PROMOTIONS	312,873	324,344	(11,471)	−3.54%	275,695	4.06%	239,550
FINANCE	81,256	79,063	2,193	2.77%	75,565	1.11%	72,510
HUMAN RESOURCES	35,612	13,635	21,977	161.18%	10,900	0.16%	16,100
INFORMATION SERVICES	22,008	16,075	5,933	36.91%	12,500	0.18%	67,500
INTERNET	18,011	0	18,011	N/A	0	0.00%	0
ADMINISTRATION	388,737	339,445	49,292	14.52%	339,440	5.00%	322,149
CORPORATE	421,327	398,565	22,762	5.71%	357,500	5.27%	361,825
TOTAL OPERATING EXPENSES	3,127,166	2,985,632	141,534	4.74%	2,871,127	42.31%	2,767,901
OPERATING INCOME	2,158,459	2,906,902	(748,443)	−25.75%	3,913,088	57.69%	3,753,299
NON OPERATING (INCOME) EXPENSES							
INTEREST (INCOME) EXPENSE	(11,525)	(14,500)	2,975	−20.52%	(45,500)	−0.67%	0
INTERCOMPANY-MANAGEMENT FEES	800,000	803,500	(3,500)	−0.44%	806,250	11.88%	958,445
INTERCOMPANY-ADVERTISING	0	395,000	(395,000)	−100.00%	2,850	0.04%	182,900
TOTAL NON OPERATING ITEMS	788,475	1,184,000	(395,525)	−33.41%	763,600	11.25%	1,141,345
NET EARNINGS (LOSS)	1,369,984	1,722,902	(352,918)	−20.48%	3,149,488	46.44%	2,611,954

"shock jock," was WBCN's morning drive-time personality. Stern cost the station about $500,000 in annual syndication fees. By contrast, WFNX spent relatively modest sums on talent and was able to hire DJs at nearly half the market rate, because the station was seen as the "hip" place to work.[3]

"Money is tight for us, but not an obstacle. We're still profitable, so if we felt that spending $200,000 on high-priced talent would give us X% increase in ratings, then we would do it," said WFNX station manager Andy Kingston. "Because Tai (a former WFNX DJ) was in the mornings for so long, we never thought about it. Also in the early days, WFNX was the only station playing alternative music, so there was no need to pay a lot. Now that the format has become popular, major companies are throwing a ton of money at talent. So, the economics has started to change."

Radio stations also faced the expense of annual licensing fees from companies and publishers' associations such as BMI, ASCAP and SESAC, which represented the rights of musical artists. These groups assigned a percentage of copyright fees to be paid by all stations, based on their gross revenues. WFNX's annual percentage was 1.62% for ASCAP and BMI and 0.75% for SESAC.

Marketing also represented a major cost for typical radio stations. WMJX-Magic 106.7, for example, spent roughly $2 million annually on television, print and billboard advertising. Other Boston stations like JAMN 94.5, WBMX-MIX 98.5 and WXKS-KISS 108 also spent a significant amount on marketing. But neither WFNX nor WBCN advertised on television or billboards, so their marketing expenses were substantially lower than those of competitors.

THE RATINGS GAME

By the time of the Green Day concert, WFNX had established itself as the young, cool station. But it still had to contend with a ratings system in order to achieve financial success.

The system devised by a company called Arbitron was based on diaries, which were randomly mailed to listeners in a local market four times a year. The "diary keepers" were asked to write down when, where and what station they listened to during a one-week period. The diaries were then compiled, so that Arbitron could calculate numbers for each radio station, charting each hour of the day by age group. In the Boston market, the numbers ranged from 0.0 to 9.9.[4] Station managers and advertisers used the data to evaluate the audience for each station. The Arbitron ratings were indicators of a station's market share. It was estimated that a one-point increase in ratings represented about $1 million in profit.[5]

The Arbitron ratings had long been a sore spot for WFNX. Until the Green Day concert, the station had never gone above an average yearly share of 2.0, even though thousands of people attended its concerts and heard its broadcasts in Boston-area stores. One of the main reasons for the low ratings was the station's signal, which was limited to 3,000 watts in an area dominated by 50,000-watt stations like WBCN, KISS and JAMN. The station made several modifications to improve the signal, within the bounds of the Federal Communications Commission (FCC) rules. WFNX turned its antenna to reach more of the greater Boston area and then moved to a tower nearer Boston. Both of these changes made an impact, but there were still many areas that could not receive WFNX clearly. Other possible explanations for low ratings were inadequate marketing or music that was just "too weird" for the general population. WFNX management dismissed both of these ideas.

THE GREEN DAY AFTERMATH— THE WAR BEGINS

WFNX's main competitor was WBCN 104.1 FM, a station with a traditional rock format, playing bands like Aerosmith, Van Halen and Metallica. WBCN was owned by Infinity, a national radio group. Although there had been some rivalry between the two stations over the years, it had been minimal before the Green Day concert and did not greatly concern WFNX. But after the concert, the situation changed. WBCN began introducing more "alternative" music into its format. WBCN had previously played one or two alternative songs per hour. But soon after the show, it began playing three and then four per hour. Other stations also started picking up on alternative. "The Monday after the Green Day show, KISS 108 added Green Day's 'Dookie' to their playlist," said Kurt St. Thomas. "It was mind-blowing."

Boston's radio battle over alternative music reached its peak in the late spring of 1995, when *The Boston Globe* featured two extensive articles on the topic, written by rock critic Jim Sullivan.[6] The stories documented the growth of a younger, more edgy, less commercial "alternative" or "modern rock" sound that was growing in popularity. WFNX was cited as an avatar of this trend. In 1994, it had been named "Alternative Station of the Year" by two trade magazines, *The Gavin Report* and *CMJ*. At the time of these articles, large-share Boston stations such as WBCN and WAAF were already mixing alternative artists into their playlists (see Table 1).

WBCN admitted that its current format, known as album-oriented rock (AOR), was "dead." Although it had actually moved slowly to adopt "modern," WBCN's pro-

TABLE 1

WBCN PARTIAL SONG LIST: Before/After Format Switch

BEFORE JUNE 21–27, 1993		AFTER APRIL 17–23, 1995	
Artist	*Song*	*Artist*	*Song*
Stone Temple Pilots	Plush	Mad Season	River of Deceit
Soul Asylum	Runaway Train	Better Than Ezra	Good
Screaming Trees	Dollar Bill	Bush	Little Things
Porno for Pyros	Pets	Matthew Sweet	Sick of Myself
Aerosmith	Cryin'	Juliana Hatfield	Universal Heartbeat
Steve Miller Band	Wide River	Green Day	She
Lenny Kravitz	Believe	Jeff Buckley	Last Goodbye
Pat Benair	Everybody Lay Down	White Zombie	More Human Than Human
AC/DC	Big Gun	Live	All Over You
Queensryche	Real World	Stone Temple Pilots	Dancing Days
The Odds	Heterosexual Man	The Dave Matthews Band	What Would You Say
Robert Plant	Palms	Offspring	Kick Him When He's Down
Pete Townshend	English Boy	General Public	Rainy Days
Ozzy Osbourne	Changes	RadioHead	Fake Plastic Trees
Donald Fagen	Tomorrow's Girls	Grant Lee Buffalo	Honey Don't Think
Peter Gabriel	Secret World	Nine Inch Nails	Hurt
Brother Cane	Got No Shame	Our Lady Peace	Starseed
Neil Young	Long May You Run	Pearl Jam	Not for You
Sting	Fields of Gold	Stone Temple Pilots	Pretty Penny
Anthrax	Only	Oasis	Live Forever

Source: Jim Sullivan, "Reinventing the Rock of Boston," *The Boston Globe,* May 5, 1995, 57.

gram director, Oedipus, was portraying the station's move in the press as being current with the trends. Some industry pundits like music trade magazine editor Mike Boyle agreed that WBCN was "ahead of the curve." But most observers recognized that WBCN had arrived late to the party and was taking its programming lead from the much smaller WFNX. "WBCN has waddled into alternative with rock mentality," said Dave Mac, an editor at *Hard Report.* "There's more shared music between these types of stations; 'BCN is playing some of the same stuff as 'FNX."[7]

The critics clearly credited WFNX with leading the trend.

"WFNX has not attracted big ratings but it has made a lot of noise, arranging for mega-concerts of leading alternative bands such as the one last Wednesday on Lansdowne Street, and getting known as the commercial station closest to the mythical 'street,' " the *Globe's* Jim Sullivan said. Patrick Lyons, owner of several Lansdowne Street clubs, agreed. "You can't buy 'street.' They [WBCN] have to regain their credibility," he said. Speaking to the press, Oedipus was dismissive of WFNX, saying that it appealed only to a cult audience. "Aside from a lack of power, we're broadcasters and they're primarily a newspaper station. They're an audio magazine. I don't respond to somebody with a 2.0 share," said the WBCN program director.[8]

WFNX also saw the issue as one of identity, bit it stressed commitment. "I'm skeptical of their credibility in this area," said Kurt St. Thomas, speaking of WBCN. "They can sleep

for ten years and suddenly wake up and realize what's going on?"[9] What about the two-share? "There's a point where we'll peak. It's not the mission of the station to be a six-share like KISS-108. We're a niche marketed radio station."[10]

The crossfire between the WFNX and WBCN program directors was more than just one of mutual put-downs. Each had put his finger on the critical issues that shaped the identities of the two stations and would drive their competition. While WBCN pretended it was too big to care about a smaller station, it was worried that WFNX would capture the growth of a new audience. The two stations were actually more alike than either acknowledged. The big difference was time.

As a station that started in the mid-1960s, WBCN had also risen through the decades from a small station that played the counterculture music of its era to become an established success. Much of its music, like its listeners, had grown older. Just as WBCN had once threatened the other, more traditional stations, it was now being threatened by WFNX.

WFNX identified with its smaller share, taking it as a sign that it was in touch with its progressive audience. If St. Thomas was to be believed, the station did not want to be as big as KISS-108. That kind of mass appeal could only adulterate its identification with its real audience. Was the problem one of contradiction? Or could the station succeed by staying small? The message of its music also implied a conflict. Groups like Green Day were hostile toward traditional commercial values and even destructive of property. Could the station promote music with an anti-establishment message and still be a commercial success? Long commercial breaks might pump up the station's revenues, but would they also turn off the station's core audience? Gaining revenues might mean losing identity, and vice versa. Where was the balance? Was there one? Or was it a strategic trap?

WBCN's attempt to label WFNX as a "newspaper station" or an "audio magazine" also hurt, but it raised significant issues. If WFNX was a link to *The Phoenix*, the station may have played a similar role to the weekly newspaper. But it was in a different media context. *The Phoenix* made its own mark in the 1960s by covering issues that were largely neglected by the *Globe*. The market niche existed thanks to the *Globe*'s market dominance. But the radio dial was far more diverse, with a host of commercial rock stations, as well as college stations that appealed to some of the same new-music audiences. Differentiation in radio might mean filling a smaller niche than the one that was available to *The Phoenix*. WFNX seemed to be driving the music scene when it was small and when it was defining itself. Once other stations like WBCN began to respond to the threat, they also started to define WFNX.

DEFENDING THE TURF

The alternative sound was clearly growing. The larger-share stations like WAAF and WBCN faced the task of making the transition to "modern," while still not turning off a mass market audience. WAAF claimed that it had been "blending" formats for years. "As rock has moved in certain directions, we've moved in those directions," said WAAF's general manager, Bruce Mittman. "We have solid, good, guitar-driven alternative songs." Mittman said that music was difficult to categorize, but he conceded that WAAF's playlist was probably 35–40% alternative. WBCN, whose sound had clearly aged along with its listeners, was also engineering a blend. The changeover would pose a problem for WBCN which, along with many other stations, relied on demographics between the wage-earnings ages of 25 and 54. A more "modern" sound would be taking their demographics down into the 18–34 range. For 'BCN the decision was made much easier by parent Infinity's purchase of WZLX, a "classic rock" station. The move allowed the parent company to split its formats and cover the entire rock age range.

While other stations were discovering alternative music, rumors were rampant that a 50,000-watt station in the market was going to "flip" to playing alternative music

exclusively, just like WFNX. The possibilities included WCGY, another traditional rock station. As the rumors became stronger, WFNX learned that WCGY had done a full analysis of an alternative music format and had determined it was not economically viable. The management at WFNX took comfort in the decision.

"I was pushing senior management to buy more vans and to do a heavy street push to make sure we maintained our position, but they were just cocky," said St. Thomas. "The president of the company would announce at every Monday radio meeting that 'no one can afford to duplicate our format.'"

By May 1995, WBCN had completely switched to an alternative music format. But WFNX management continued to see the right side. "I guess I was a little relieved that it was WBCN who switched, as opposed to someone else. I knew that in order to support a station of that size, they couldn't undercut our prices with advertisers," said Andy Kingston, station manager at WFNX. "If someone was going to come at us, this was the best of the possibilities."

Stephen Mindich, chairman of The Phoenix Media/ Communications Group, was also confident that WFNX would hold its ground, despite WBCN's switch.

"I don't think it would be damaging to us," he said. "WFNX didn't skyrocket after the Green Day concert, and I didn't think alternative would be a strong enough format for them [WBCN]. They had a traditional, winning format so why switch? I felt that it would not sustain their long-term audience, but would increase the appeal of the music so we would get some benefit and recognition as the station who played this music first."

THE COMPETITION INTENSIFIES

But WBCN's switch to an alternative station included more than simply playing the music WFNX was playing. WBCN registered with *Monitor*, which was *Billboard* magazine's industry report on radio stations and their formats. There were several damaging aspects for WFNX.

"When a station changes their reporting status in *Monitor*, it's a big deal," said St. Thomas. "The problem for WFNX was that *Monitor* only reports the top 15 stations in a market based on Arbitron ratings, so WBCN was now listed as the alternative station in Boston, even though they had just switched formats."

"WFNX, the heritage alternative station in Boston, wasn't even listed anymore. I knew this was going to hurt us in the industry down the line," he said.

As larger stations began to switch formats, WFNX found it harder to get the bands for its free shows. Record companies that had previously supported WFNX and provided it with the hottest bands now felt an obligation to stations like WBCN, which were far more powerful in signal and influence.

Some record companies also started packaging non-alternative bands like Alanis Morissette and Bush as "alternative," hoping to capture a larger share of the market. Even though these bands were not part of WFNX's "sound," it became a question of playing these groups or losing the chance to get the artists that the station really wanted. WFNX wouldn't compromise. To make matters worse, record companies would sometime signore WFNX altogether in providing bands for concerts. The station's retaliation was to stop playing groups from those labels. Relationships between WFNX and some labels became strained.

RADIO ANARCHY: THE RISE AND FALL

In July 1995, after eight years with WFNX, St. Thomas left to work for Arista Records in New York. WFNX promoted one program director (PD) after another from within the station's ranks, but the moves were not successful. Some DJs also left for other Boston stations. Particularly troubling were the losses of afternoon DJ Neal Robert, who moved to WBCN, and the morning show host, Tai, who left to pursue a talk radio career on WRKO-AM. It was a time of drift.

Unable to find a suitable leader inside the station, WFNX management brought in a new PD in July 1996. In September, the station launched a promotion called "Radio Anarchy" in an effort to stop its slide in the ratings. (See Exhibit 2 for a ratings comparison.) The Radio Anarchy push was meant to raise awareness and distinguish WFNX from other stations. The concept and the name were tested in a few focus groups of both WFNX and WBCN "core" listeners (those who listen to a station virtually exclusively). Occasional (or "cume") listeners were also tested. The name and the concept both registered well.

But within a month of the rollout, the station started getting negative feedback. People were not responding, and many seemed to feel that WFNX did not deliver on its promise of what Radio Anarchy was supposed to be.

"There were no focus groups, no real discussion, no testing of it in print sizes. This was not thought through enough," said Kelly Graml, the station's marketing director. "The PD came in and wanted to make a big splash and had a lot of experience in promotions. So, everyone at the station got behind him on this. Also, we had nothing as far as a promotional message going into the fall, and people were uptight. The problem is that we tried to launch this in a month with a brand new PD who had not assimilated to the station with an understanding of its resources. This kind of process should be done over four to six months . . . "

"Even if Radio Anarchy was a good idea, the process was so flawed that we didn't have time to know. My biggest concern was that we could run the risk of hurting the station," said Graml.

Stephen Mindich, the group's chairman, had decided to go ahead with Radio Anarchy, in spite of misgivings. When the idea failed, he was left searching for answers.

"I never liked the word, but a lot of people felt it had merit, and we had hired a PD who created this concept, which we thought could be done. I think one of the problems was that the music was not at the center of the promotion," Mindich said.

> Also, after watching the ratings slip consistently despite the fact that we had always been viewed as the "real" alternative station and WBCN was the "phony" in all the earlier focus groups we did, I decided to defer my judgment to others who should know more about this than myself and go with Anarchy, which was far different from anything we had done before.

By April 1997, management decided that Radio Anarchy was not living up to expectations. But the new PD was having trouble letting go of the concept, and it was later suspected that the PD was not following some of the music test results.[11] "Radio Anarchy died a slow, painful death.

EXHIBIT 2   COMPETITOR'S SHARE TRENDS • AGES 12+ (MONDAY–SUNDAY 6AM–12MID)

	FALL '94	WIN '95	SPR '95	SUM '95	FALL '95	WIN '96	SPR '96	SUM '96	FALL '96	WIN '97	SPR '97	SUM '97	FALL '97	WIN '98
WFNX 101.7	2.5	2.0	1.8	1.7	1.5	1.5	1.3	1.3	1.2	1.7	1.5	1.3	1.2	1.2
WBCN 104.1	5.4	5.1	4.5	5.7	4.7	5.7	5.0	5.2	4.9	4.8	5.8	5.2	5.2	5.5
WBOS 92.9	2.8	2.4	3.3	2.5	2.2	2.9	2.9	3.0	2.9	3.2	2.7	2.9	2.1	2.5
WAAF 107.3	2.9	2.8	2.8	2.6	2.5	2.7	2.6	2.4	2.8	2.9	2.9	2.9	3.0	2.7
WXKS 107.9	6.0	5.6	5.8	6.1	5.3	5.7	6.9	6.4	5.7	6.0	6.2	6.6	5.9	6.3
WBMX 98.5	4.6	4.8	4.8	3.8	4.2	4.0	3.8	4.0	3.8	3.9	4.2	3.8	3.6	3.9

EXHIBIT 3
RADIO OWNERSHIP
AUGUST 1994
*MCC Broadcasting is the com-
pany name that owns WFNX.*

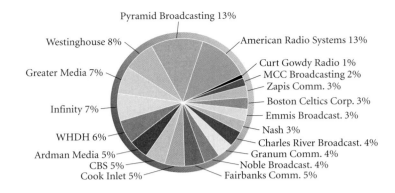

Pyramid Broadcasting 13%
American Radio Systems 13%
Westinghouse 8%
Curt Gowdy Radio 1%
MCC Broadcasting 2%
Greater Media 7%
Zapis Comm. 3%
Boston Celtics Corp. 3%
Infinity 7%
Emmis Broadcast. 3%
Nash 3%
WHDH 6%
Charles River Broadcast. 4%
Granum Comm. 4%
Ardman Media 5%
Noble Broadcast. 4%
CBS 5%
Cook Inlet 5%
Fairbanks Comm. 5%

And because the PD still liked it, we had trouble getting a consensus on what to do next." Graml said. WFNX finally pulled the plug on Radio Anarchy on June 26, 1997. The PD resigned in August.

WFNX had now gone through three program directors in two years. The frequent changes were demoralizing. The station lacked direction, and it was still suffering from a steady drop in ratings. Staff turnover increased as many sales reps left to join WBCN. WFNX suffered a 100% turnover in sales staff in 1996, and a 75% turnover in 1997. The remaining staff worried that they were losing everything good about the station.

THE INDUSTRY CONSOLIDATES

While WFNX was facing both internal and external troubles, consolidation was reshaping the entire radio industry. (Exhibits 3 and 4 summarize the changes in radio station ownership between August 1994 and August 1997. Exhibit 5 shows the evolution of the Boston radio market over 10 years.)

In September 1997, CBS bought American Radio Systems, increasing its number of Boston stations to six.[12] CBS had already acquired Infinity, WBCN's parent company. The new deal would take effect by early to mid-1998.

But under FCC rules, CBS could only own five FM stations and four AM stations in a major market. The Federal Trade Commission only allowed a maximum 40% market share by one company. CBS would have to drop two or more stations to stay below the 40% line in Boston.

It was unclear how CBS would meet these requirements, because the merger would make WBCN and WAAF part of the same group. The outcome was important because WBCN had recently focused more of its competitive attention on WAAF and less on WFNX. WBCN was concerned bout WAAF because it was classified as an "active rock" station, a format that was becoming a significant force across the country.[13] In a recent Boston Arbitron ratings book, WAAF had beaten WBCN in all "dayparts" except for morning drive time. There were three rumors on what CBS would do, if and when the merger was approved. It could sell WAAF outright; it could keep WAAF but try to convince the FCC and FTC that it was purely a Worcester station; or CBS could donate WAAF to Nash Broadcasting, a minority-owned radio group, which would convert the station to an urban format. This last move would have reflected positively on CBS, because the FCC was encouraging more minority-run radio stations.

Regardless of how CBS chose to handle the merger, the fallout from industry-wide consolidation would be significant for independent radio stations like WFNX. Aside from concerns that mergers could create a "Big Brother" that

EXHIBIT 4
RADIO OWNERSHIP
AUGUST 1997

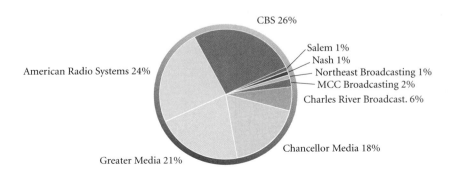

CBS 26%
Salem 1%
Nash 1%
American Radio Systems 24%
Northeast Broadcasting 1%
MCC Broadcasting 2%
Charles River Broadcast. 6%
Chancellor Media 18%
Greater Media 21%

EXHIBIT 5
BOSTON RADIO
FORMAT EVOLUTION:
Format Breakdown

FORMAT	YEARS	STATIONS
Classic Rock	1987–1993	WBCN, WZLX, WCGY
	1994	WBCN, WZLX, WEGQ
	1995–1997	WZLX, WEGQ
Soft Rock	1987–1994	WBOS, WLYT
Alternative	1987–1994	WFNX
	1994	WFNX, WAAF
	1995–1996	WFNX, WAAF, WBCN
	1997	WFNX
Hard Rock	1987–1993	WAAF
Contemporary Hit Radio	1987–1990	WXKS, WZOU
	1991	WXKS, WZOU, WBMX
	1992–1994	WXKS, WJMN, WBMX
	1995–1997	WXKS
Adult Contemporary	1987–1990	WMJX, WROR, WSSH, WVBF
	1991	WMJX, WSSH, WVBF
	1992–1994	WMJX, WSSH
	1995	WMJX
	1996–1997	WMJX, WROR
Modern/Active Rock	1997	WBCN, WAAF
Urban	1987–1994	WILD
	1995–1997	WILD, WJMN
Jazz	1991	WCDJ
	1995–1997	WSJZ
Country	1992–1995	WKLB, WBCS
	1996–1997	WKLB

EXHIBIT 5 BOSTON RADIO FORMAT EVOLUTION: Format Breakdown (continued)

FORMAT	YEAR										
	1987	1988	1989	1990	1991	1992	1993	1994	1995	1996	1997
Classic Rock	12.6	11.1	10.3	9.7	9.1	10.1	10.2	11.8	6.6	6.4	6.0
Soft Rock	2.6	2.4	1.6	3.2	2.5	4.4	4.4	3.4			
Alternative	1.5	1.4	1.9	1.5	1.7	1.9	2.1	5.4	8.7	8.9	1.2
Hard Rock	2.0	2.1	1.8	2.0	3.1	2.3	1.3				
Contemporary Hit Radio	12.2	10.9	11.7	12.9	17.9	15.0	16.1	16.1	5.3	5.7	5.9
Adult Contemporary	13.2	12.9	12.6	13.9	12.8	9.5	10.7	7.6	5.0	8.3	8.9
Modern AC (Soft Alternative)									4.2	3.8	3.6
Adult Alternative									3.1	3.9	3.0
Modern/Active Rock											8.2
Urban	3.0	2.5	2.5	2.0	1.5	1.8	1.7	1.2	9.1	7.8	8.0
Jazz					2.4				3.0	1.6	1.8
Country						4.9	4.7	3.4	4.6	2.8	3.2

Numbers represent cumulative Arbitron Boston: Fall ratings books.

EXHIBIT 5 BOSTON RADIO FORMAT EVOLUTION: Format Breakdown (continued)

STATION	YEAR										
	1987	1988	1989	1990	1991	1992	1993	1994	1995	1996	1997
WBCN	7.4	4.8	5.3	5.2	3.7	5.3	4.7	5.4	4.7	4.9	5.2
WZLX	4.5	4.8	3.1	3.1	2.9	3.6	4.4	4.2	4.1	3.9	3.3
WCGY	0.7	1.5	1.9	1.4	2.5	1.2	1.1				
WBOS	2.2	2.4	1.6	1.7	2.2	3.8	3.7	2.8	2.2	2.9	2.1
WLYT	0.4			0.5	0.3	0.6	0.7	0.6			
WFNX	1.5	1.4	1.9	1.5	1.7	1.9	2.1	2.5	1.5	1.2	1.2
WAAF	2.0	2.1	1.8	2.0	3.1	2.3	1.3	2.9	2.5	2.8	3.0
WXKS	7.0	5.9	6.2	5.7	5.1	7.0	6.5	6.0	5.3	5.7	5.9
WZOU	5.2	5.0	5.5	7.2	9.1						
WILD	3.0	2.5	2.0	2.0	1.5	1.8	1.7	1.2	2.2	1.1	1.8
WMJX	2.9	3.6	4.6	4.9	6.9	5.3	6.6	2.4	5.0	5.3	6.0
WROR	3.2	3.2	2.2	2.5							
WSSH	4.4	3.6	3.5	4.1	2.8	4.2	4.1	3.4			
WVBF	2.7	2.5	2.3	2.4	3.1						
WBMX					3.7	3.5	4.3	4.6	4.2	3.8	3.6
WCDJ					2.4						
WKLB						2.4	2.1	1.6	2.7	2.8	3.2
WBCS						2.5	2.6	1.8	1.9		
WJMN						4.5	5.3	5.5	6.9	6.7	6.2
WEGQ								2.2	2.5	2.5	2.7
WSJZ									3.0	1.6	1.8
WXRV									0.9	1.0	0.9
WROR										3.0	2.9

Numbers represent Arbitron Boston: Fall ratings books. Numbers that do not continue past, or exist before, a particular year indicate the station was either not broadcasting or changed call letters. For example, in 1992 WZOU became WJMN.

would control what the public heard, they also brought together huge sales forces with the ability to offer radio time buys on all of a group's stations at a discount. The advantage was that national advertisers could reach a wider audience in the same market at a low cost. The disadvantage was that the buyer might ignore the benefits of other radio stations and potentially miss a target market.

CHALLENGE FOR THE FUTURE

WFNX was struggling with the question of what to do next.

"We have to focus on who we are," said Kelly Graml. "We need another vehicle to hit the streets, more grass-roots marketing to get the station to reach the people and to market what we have to offer."

"There is no question that the consolidation is a huge concern. But I think everyone at the station is realizing that there needs to be a complete strategy. This past year showed us what happens when there's no strategy," she said. "There are so many things we should be looking at." (See Exhibit 6 for strategic options.)

The station was changing tactics. In addition to putting more effort into marketing, it began playing more hits and fewer new artists. When it did play new sounds, it played them more often in an effort to "own" the group. But Stephen Mindich disputed the idea that WFNX was turning into a hit station.

"We are not shifting to playing just hits," he said. "We are maintaining the tradition of 'FNX's music. I believe, as does the research company we consult, that the newer music we were playing was not as good as the older music. And since people want to hear what they know, we have to make some accommodations. In comparison to other stations, we play the hits far less frequently."

In order to maintain its image as a showcase for new sounds, the station launched a campaign called "What the Future Sounds Like." It also created " 'FNX Interactive," which gave listeners a link to the station through the Internet.

In November 1997, a new program director, Cruze, was hired to bring WFNX back on track with a clear direction and purpose. Cruze planned to capitalize on the traditional position of the station while continuing to play a mix of both new and recognizable alternative music.

EXHIBIT 6 STRATEGIC OPTIONS

WFNX management identified several approaches to preserve and grow its market share in the coming years. The following are excerpts from some key recommendations contained in an internal company memo.

1. **MCC Broadcasting should acquire another station or enter into a local marketing agreement with radio stations serving the areas where our signal is weak**.
   The Boston radio market is being redefined so that the market does not drop out as one of the top 10 markets in the country. Worcester, Mass. and part of southern New Hampshire are being added to increase the size of the market. This redefinition brings the Boston market back to number seven. Because the market is bigger, it is now even more important to consider either buying stations or doing deals with stations that are struggling with their programming and combining the sales efforts. The better option is finding a station willing to simulcast WFNX and share the revenues. The ideal station either to buy or simulcast with would be a station in Worcester since The Phoenix Media/Communications Group owns a newspaper in Worcester. The cost of purchasing a class A station in Worcester is estimated to be around $2 million. (A 50,000-watt station in Boston would cost roughly $80M).

2. **Protect the artistic, political and social values that have been the hallmark of WFNX programming**.
   We believe that if the music can no longer completely define WFNX, then the image that the station projects must do so. WFNX must continue to cater to intelligent listeners and not be misogynistic like other stations. WFNX must also stay "left of center," and by remaining independent, WFNX is able to take more chances. One recent example was our broadcasting Allen Ginsberg's poem "Howl" which contains language not approved by the FCC. WFNX chose to broadcast this because we believe in maintaining freedom of speech. This type of programming, as well as WFNX's commitment to pushing the boundaries of artistic freedom, are ways for WFNX to differentiate itself from its competition.

3. **Attract and retain nine well-trained sales representatives. A full review of our compensation structure may be advisable**.
   It is difficult to keep good sales reps. There has not been a period of more than three weeks over the past three years when we have had a full staff. We are more vulnerable here than in other areas and we need a constant recruitment effort. Recently we have changed our new retail business commission form 15% to 20%. (New retail business is defined as any business that has not been on the station in at least 13 months and is not gained through an ad agency.) Changing this commission structure has helped the recruiting effort, but some other stations have also made this change.

4. **Develop new categories of advertising revenue to lessen the impact of a possible ban on alcohol advertisers using radio**.
   Because of the threat of regulations on alcohol advertising, and because when ratings drop beer advertisers cut their buys with us, we have begun to focus on other areas like recruitment advertising. Companies are spending lots of money in newspapers and not getting the kinds of results they used to get so recruiters are turning to radio; we are planning for $40,000–$50,000 a month in recruitment advertising. Despite the potential bans on alcohol advertising, we are still trying to develop our liquor advertising business. Only a few stations in the market accept liquor ads due to stations' self-regulating. WFNX has always accepted liquor ads and will continue to do so until it is no longer allowed.

5. **Invest in "call out" research. Our competitors use research more than we do. Their success may be attributable to added research**.
   Call out research would test the current music being played and would be helpful for us to know what our listeners like. (Call out research is done by telemarketers who call people, play songs and then ask them questions about the music.) The downside is that this research is very expensive. WBCN does this practically every week and spends approximately $2,200 per week.

6. **Try to get a translator in downtown Boston**.
   A translator allows a station to broadcast on two dial positions at the same time. For example, WFNX would broadcast on 101.7 FM and 101.3 FM. WFNX has approval to use the translator and we are currently broadcasting at three watts in downtown Boston. This allows people who may lose the signal at 101.7 to turn to 101.3 in order to hear the station. Our goal is to have it boosted to 10 watts so that we can have a grater reach, but this will require some time, since the FCC does not allow an immediate switch to 10 watts. We anticipate broadcasting at six watts by the fall.

7. **Develop and/or hire a unique, attention-getting talent for the morning show**.
   This is one of the greatest challenges we have due to the fact that we are in a market competing with Howard Stern, and there is a shortage of talent. Our best hope is trying to develop a show from within the station. Syndication is not an option, because there is no one to syndicate. Our newest concept is to create a morning show of three or four people all on the station at the same time, as a team. This would allow us to develop some synergies and new ideas among the participants.

8. **Develop a more aggressive and cooperative joint sales and marketing strategy between The Phoenix and WFNX**.
   This is an area where we can have a significant impact on our competitors. We have put together a list of our total reach as a company versus our competitors' total reach which shows that, as a whole, The Phoenix Media/Communications Group reaches more people than any of the national radio groups in Boston (see Exhibit 7). Using this knowledge we should craft a sales and marketing strategy that works synergistically between all of our companies and capitalizes on this strength.

"When I got here, I was pleased that the station and the public had not lost the sense that we are the real alternative station in the market," Cruze said. "The good thing is that if you ask 100 people in a room what music WFNX plays, everyone will say alternative. The bad thing we're facing is that if you ask those same people what station they should listen to, most will say WBCN. We have to convince, or re-convince them, that this is the best place to find alternative music; that's why we decided to add the slogan, 'Boston's Real Alternative.' "

Cruze also turned his attention to the DJ line up and match-ups against WBCN. The toughest problem was the morning show.

"Unfortunately, there is no template for a successful, alternative music, morning show. We can't compete with Howard Stern head-on. We need something totally different, but the talent pool is small," he said "Trying to get something to work is an excruciating process." The strategy for other time slots seemed clearer.

"In the afternoon, Nik Carter (on WBCN) plays half the records we do, since WBCN is trying to maintain a hip, funny, wordy show. We counter that by playing more music

and making sure that when WBCN is playing commercials we are playing music. This way, if people are punching back and forth between stations, when they land on us they'll usually hear music. Since playing the best music around is what we're about, it just makes sense."

DECISION TIME ARRIVES

In 1995, the *Globe*'s Jim Sullivan had called WFNX "the Boston area's long-term commercial alternative-music out-let."[14] He cited five straight Arbitron rating periods of improving numbers, from a 2.1 to a 2.5 share. Four years later, the format pioneered by WFNX had become dominant, but the station in 1998 found its historical 2.0 market share in jeopardy. The company had done serious thinking, which had produced some promising alternatives to rebuild its share-of-audience. Now it was up to the management at The Phoenix Media/Communications Group and WFNX to sift through the options, determine whether these covered the entire range of possibilities and move quickly before the station lost more ground to competitors.

EXHIBIT 7
PHOENIX MEDIA/
COMMUNICATIONS
GROUP REACH
VS. OTHERS

PHOENIX MEDIA/COMMUNICATIONS GROUP READERSHIP/LISTENERSHIP			
PUBLICATION	**CIRCULATION**	**PASS ALONG**	**READERS/LISTENERS**
The Boston Phoenix	118,000	2.5	295,000
The Providence Phoenix	60,000	2.5	150,000
The Worcester Phoenix	40,000	2.5	100,000
SUB TOTAL	**218,000**	**2.5**	**545,000**
Stuff Magazine	20,000	3.5	70,000
Stuff@Night	80,000	3.5	280,000
SUB TOTAL	**100,000**	**2.5**	**350,000**
Celtics' Yearbook	75,000	2.5	187,500
Bruins' Yearbook	75,000	2.5	187,500
Boston Marathon Program	75,000	2.5	187,500
SUB TOTAL	**225,000**	**2.5**	**562,500**
Great Woods' Program	500,000	1	500,000
Harborlights' Program	100,000	1	100,000
SUB TOTAL	**600,000**	**1**	**600,000**
WFNX	206,000		206,000
TOTAL PHOENIX MEDIA/COMMUNICATIONS GROUP REACH			**2,263,500**

EXHIBIT 7
PHOENIX MEDIA/
COMMUNICATIONS
GROUP REACH
VS. OTHERS
(continued)

PHOENIX MEDIA/COMMUNICATIONS GROUP VS. BOSTON RADIO

STATION/COMBO	TOTAL CUME	
Phoenix Media/Communications Group	2,263,500	(WFNX with print media group)
CBS Radio	2,063,000	(WBCN, WBZ, WODS, WZLX)
American Radio Systems	1,787,000	(WAAF, WBMX, WEEI, WEGQ, WRKO)
Greater Media	1,609,000	(WBOS, WKLB, WMJX, WSJZ, WRKO)
Chancellor/Evergreen Media	1,424,000	(WXKS-FM, WXKS-AM, WJMN)
WNFX/Concert Programs	806,000	
WFNX/Sports Yearbooks	768,500	
WFNX/Phoenix Newspapers	751,000	
WXKS-FM (Kiss)	729,000	
WBZ-AM	702,000	
WBCN-FM	575,000	
WFNX/Stuff Magazine Group	556,000	
WJMN-FM	543,000	
WMJX-FM	516,000	
WODS-FM	454,000	
WBMX-FM (Mix)	438,000	
WBOS-FM	381,000	
WRKO-AM	367,000	
WCRB-FM	367,000	
WEEI-AM	348,000	
WEGQ-FM	342,000	
WZLX-FM	332,000	
WROR-FM	310,000	
WAAF-FM	292,000	
WKLB-FM	248,000	
WFNX-FM	206,000	
WSJZ-FM	154,000	
WXKS-AM	152,000	
WXRV-FM	104,000	
WILD-AM	82,000	

Arbitron Boston/Summer 1997, Adults 12+ weekly cume.
Information gathered from an internal company memo.

Arbitron–Boston
Demo: Persons 18–34
Day part; M– F 6:00 am–10:00 am

STATION	WI97	SP97	SU97	FA97
WFNX-FM				
AQH Share	4.5	3.5	2.5	2.9
Cume Pers (00)	783	549	566	550
WBCN-FM				
AQH Share	14.1	20	16.4	16.6
Cume Pers (00)	1680	2214	1844	1917
WXKS-FM				
AQH Share	10.6	12.7	11.8	11.6
Cume Pers (00)	1904	2027	1983	1863
WJMN-FM				
AQH Share	7.5	7.3	7.1	8.3
Cume Pers (00)	1399	1449	1340	1522
WBZ-AM				
AQH Share	3.4	3	2.7	4.1
Cume Pers (00)	644	622	542	704
WEGQ-FM				
AQH Share	2.7	3.5	3.9	3.8
Cume Pers (00)	581	764	779	688
WZLX-FM				
AQH Share	4.1	3.5	3.6	3.4
Cume Pers (00)	763	662	676	554
WBOS-FM				
AQH Share	4.8	4.6	4.5	2.6
Cume Pers (00)	1066	1011	1082	901
WROR-FM				
AQH Share	2.9	1.8	1.5	2.3
Cume Pers (00)	424	359	272	353
WAAF-FM				
AQH Share	5	5.7	6.1	5.6
Cume Pers (00)	771	866	901	791
WEEI-AM				
AQH Share	3.1	1.9	1.6	1.4
Cume Pers (00)	492	270	283	256
WCRB-FM				
AQH Share	1.7	0.8	0.8	1
Cume Pers (00)	333	228	218	253

AQH = Average Quarter Hour

AGE	AUDIENCE COMPOSITION
18–44	98%
18–34	82%
21–34	68%
25–34	52%

GENDER	WFNX	MARKET	MARITAL STATUS	WFNX	MARKET
Male	53%	48%	Single	60%	29%
Female	47%	52%	Married/ Divorced	40%	71%

	WFNX	MARKET	COMP. RANK
OCCUPATION			
White Collar	63%	46%	2
Professional/Managerial	33%	24%	3
Exec./Admin./Managerial	16%	11%	3
ANNUAL HOUSEHOLD INCOME			
Median	$53,000	$44,000	2
$50,000 and over	54%	40%	2
$100,000 and over	13%	9%	4
EDUCATION			
College grad or more	43%	28%	3
Postgraduate	14%	12%	5
HOME OWNERSHIP STATUS			
Own home	49%	66%	15
Median value of owned home	$181,000	$159,000	3
Rent	51%	32%	1
PERSONAL COMPUTING			
Household owns a computer	57%	45%	2
Subscribes to an on-line service	14%	8%	3
ENTERTAINMENT & RECREATION			
Bicycling	48%	34%	1
In-line skating	15%	6%	1
Jogging/running	32%	17%	1
Hiking/back packing	33%	17%	1
Snow skiing	28%	16%	1
Aerobic workouts	33%	22%	1
Live theatre	44%	38%	3
Dance or ballet performances	19%	13%	1
Boston Red Sox	32%	20%	2
Boston Bruins	17%	8%	1
Boston Celtics	12%	8%	1
Rock concerts	53%	22%	1
Art gallery/museum	52%	33%	1
Nightclub	58%	30%	1
Attend movies (1 +/past 3 months)	78%	58%	1
Belong to health/exercise club	29%	16%	1

Report based on adults 18+ in Boston Metro, Monday–Sunday 6 a.m.–Midnight (1995 Scarborough).

APPENDIX C
YEAR OVER YEAR
PERCENTAGE
REVENUE GROWTH

APPENDIX D
COMPETITIVE CUME
DUPLICATION:
Percentage of Listeners
Shared with WFNX

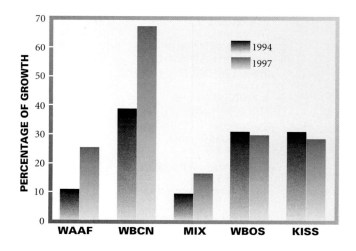

Beijing Mirror Corp.

In January 1996, Mr. Ming Tian, Manager of the Strategic Management Department of Beijing Rearview Mirror HighTech Corporation (Beijing Mirror Corp.), was pondering a development strategy for the corporation. Beijing Mirror Corporation owned the patent for a newly invented type of rearview mirror. This mirror could effectively increase view width and eliminate the blind spot. Its invention and development had the potential to make a tremendous contribution to the transportation industry, by radically reducing traffic accidents. Small-scale production had already started and the goal of Beijing Mirror Corp. was a swift entry into domestic and international markets, as well as a high market share. However, at present it was nearly impossible for the Corporation to achieve its goal solely on its own. Many domestic and overseas companies had submitted offers concerning possible joint ventures or investments. These strategic decisions involved financial, marketing, R&D and production problems, and were now occupying Mr. Tian's thoughts.

PRODUCT BACKGROUND

The importance of a rearview mirror to driving safety was well-known to every driver and members of the auto and transportation industries. Existing external rearview mirrors suffered universal defects such as narrow view width, a large blind spot and serious image distortion. The common remedies were to install more mirrors on both sides in different directions, or to glue a small convex mirror onto the original. The result was a broken image and difficulty for the driver in determining the distance between the object and the vehicle. Furthermore, it was even harder for the driver to glance over two or more mirrors simultaneously. Consequently, traffic accidents could not be effectively avoided. According to some statistics, traffic accidents relating to rearview mirror defects amounted to some 30 per cent of the total traffic accidents in China and 20 per cent in the United States. Such problems were especially severe on expressways.

Mr. Zhang Lixin, an ordinary worker at Tsinghua University, found a solution by combining his personal experience with insight and research. The mirror was designed with different curvature radii both in vertical and horizontal sections. In other words, the reflective surface had a composite curved surface with smooth transition.

Professor Chen Xiao Yue prepared this case with assistance from Zhao Xin and Professor Paul Beamish solely to provide material for class discussion. The authors do not intend to illustrate either effective or ineffective handling of a managerial situation. The authors may have disguised certain names and other identifying information to protect confidentiality.

Such rearview mirrors successfully solved the narrow view width and blind spot problems that were common to mirrors with a single-curved convex or a flat reflective surface. Moreover, because the mirror provided the driver with a satisfactory object image with little distortion, it was a further enhancement to driving safety. High product quality was guaranteed through the use of well-selected raw materials and imported manufacturing equipment. Formal tests by the Research Institute of Automobiles and Research Division of Optical Instruments, Tsinghua University, showed that this mirror thoroughly fulfilled drivers' requirements. This was followed by the praise of experts and drivers after installation and try-out.

PATENT

The increased view-width and non-blind spot rearview mirror invented by Mr. Zhang Lixin was patented at the Chinese Patent Office. The patent would expire in ten years. To overcome its shortage of funds as well as its unfamiliarity with the foreign patent act and the patent application procedure, Beijing Mirror Corp. signed an agency agreement with the C&S Technology Company of the United States to apply for an overseas patent for the product. By January 1996, patents had been granted to Beijing Mirror in 19 different countries and regions. Mr. Zhang Lixin possessed 30 per cent of the total ownership of the patent held by Beijing Mirror Corp. S Department of Tsinghua University, and consequently, Tsinghua University owned the remaining 70 per cent. The patent value was assessed at 200 to 400 million RMB after technical appraisal of the mirror and a rough estimation of its market by domestic experts. (In January 1996, there were 8.31 RMB per US dollar.)

BEIJING MIRROR CORP

In April 1990, the domestic patent was granted for the rearview mirror. Since then, Mr. Zhang Lixin had devoted his life to bringing his achievement into production. During the following years, he contacted numerous factories to seek a manufacturer. However, his approaches were turned down because of the risk and complications associated with the transition process, or because the company was unwilling to compensate Mr. Zhang Lixin for previous research. At a crucial juncture, Mr. Wang Yan, vice-dean of S Department, who had just returned from an overseas training course, suggested that his department cooperate with Mr. Zhang Lixin to support and finance the transla-

tion of the high-technology proposal into real products. Thus, the Beijing Mirror Corp. came into existence as a subsidiary of Tsinghua Enterprise Group.

However, difficulties and challenges continued. One year passed. Hundreds of thousands of RMB appeared to have achieved very little in controlling the distortion created during the production process of the mirror. Opposition to further investment was getting stronger. During this period, Mr. Wang Yan and Mr. Zhang Lixin sold off their personal properties to pursue their goal. S Department decided to make a final investment of 80,000 RMB. Not long afterwards, the first successful mirror was produced. Under the warrant of Tsinghua Enterprise Group, a further low-interest loan of 20 million RMB was obtained from Bank J, a state-owned commercial bank of China, which contributed a great deal toward enlarging the production scale of Beijing Mirror Corp. The current total book value of Beijing Mirror Corp.'s assets amounted to some 30 million RMB. Trial orders from various parts of the country were encouraging. Beijing Mirror Corp. had also acquired a certificate from the Beijing High and New Technological Industrial Development Zone. In addition, the Government provided favorable terms for hi-tech enterprises with respect to finance and taxation to accelerate the development of such an industry. All these conditions worked to Beijing Mirror Corp.'s advantage.

INDUSTRY AND MARKET

MARKET CAPACITY

The annual production of vehicles in China was approximately 1.4 million. Auto production had been soaring recently, with an annual growth rate of 15 to 20 per cent. However, this rate was predicted to decline. The Chinese auto market now accommodated some 20 million vehicles. In both existing vehicles and in yearly production, roughly 50 per cent were large- or medium-sized; that is, the current number of large- and medium-sized vehicles in China was about 10 million, with an annual increase of 700,000. In the world auto market, the yearly production was 50 million or so. Its growth rate was more stable, but lower, than that of the domestic market. Moreover, the proportion of large- and medium-sized vehicles in the international market was far less than in that of the domestic market. The medium- and short-term target market of the Beijing rearview mirror was chiefly external use in large- and medium-sized vehicles because the blind spot problem was most serious in large- and medium-sized vehicles.

MARKET FOR ORDINARY REARVIEW MIRRORS

Ordinary rearview mirrors in the domestic market were divided into three categories: foreign-made; made by joint venture; and domestic-made. Domestic-made rearview mirrors were usually priced around 50 RMB each, while foreign-made mirrors or those made by joint ventures were priced from 150 RMB to 1200 RMB. Although entry into this industry did not require much input of capital and technology, it did demand an obvious technological or price advantage over existing products to earn a desirable market share, because it was a common practice for the mirror manufacturers to have long-term contracts with auto factories, or to conduct their sales through agents. The domestic price of the Beijing rearview mirror was around 250 RMB per piece. The tentative overseas price was $30 to $35 per piece. The final price would be determined according to the ordered quantity.

TECHNOLOGY ENVIRONMENT

Research to eliminate the blind spot of rearview mirrors was being conducted in various countries. There were three types of non-blind spot rearview mirrors. The first was the navigation security system, which provided a clear and stable rearview, while eliminating the blind spot, visual error, and time error. However, owing to the exorbitant cost, it could not be widely applied. The second type was the camera system, which required a lot of maintenance and lacked durability. The third involved a fibre optical system. It shared the same defects as the first type, with a unit price of $200. All these types of rearview mirrors necessitated modification of the auto design. Furthermore, if the mirror broke down, it could cause enormous risk to safe driving. The Beijing Mirror seemed to be quite the opposite. It had already passed numerous tests.

In preparing a development strategy for the company, Mr. Tian prepared the analysis which follows, including the calculations contained in the exhibits.

BEIJING MIRROR CORP.

STRENGTHS

1. The patent eased entry into the market to a large extent.
2. In the foreseeable future, no substitute or other competitive products were anticipated to match both the price and function of the patented product.
3. The quality and function of the product were guaranteed.
4. The Corporation enjoyed a monopoly on the manufacturing technology.

5. The patented product had been tested and certified by the China Motor Vehicle Safety Appraisal and Inspection Centre. A national standard requirement would be established based upon the patent. The Appraisal and Inspection Centre was going to be the sole domestic agent for the product.
6. Since it was a high technology enterprise, most favorable tax treatment had been granted to Beijing Mirror Corp. by the Government. Income tax was exempted in the initial three years and levied only on a reduced rate (50 per cent of the normal rate) for the following three years.
7. A loan with a favorable interest rate was available from Bank J, a state-owned commercial bank of China. The domestic interest rate had been as much as 20 per cent, while the rate required by Bank J from Beijing Mirror Corp. was only 12 per cent.
8. Research and development capability as well as high quality personnel were available with the support of Tsinghua University.

WEAKNESSES

1. The bottleneck in the manufacturing process resulted in a high spoilage rate. This was a considerable obstacle for general efficiency and large-scale production.
2. The product could be easily imitated, and thus the technology could be stolen.
3. Since Beijing Mirror Corp. was a newly established company, the management still needed strengthening. The production and marketing capabilities also required improvement.
4. The degree to which the market would accept this new product remained unknown. Drivers were accustomed to the ordinary rearview mirror and were able to correctly judge the distorted image. Though no serious accidents happened during the try-out, drivers had to adjust to the undistorted image. This adjustment would certainly take time. During the probation period, more problems and accidents would emerge, possibly involving complex regulations and litigation. All this could block the successful entry of the Beijing rearview mirror into the market.
5. The rearview mirror was directly linked with safe driving, as well as life and property security. Consequently, stringent control over quality and function standards was imposed by all the involved countries. Although the Beijing rearview mirror had qualified under the national standard of China, it still could be incompatible with international standards and corresponding regulations. In such a case, Beijing Mirror Corp. would miss the optimal time to enter the world market unless

it could promptly comply with foreign regulations and standards.

MARKETING

The present Marketing Department of Beijing Mirror Corp. had only a few staff members, and had not conducted any vigorous marketing activity. Most of the orders that the company currently had were the result of articles in the press or of public interest aroused by domestic and overseas product exhibitions. Moreover, they were chiefly trial orders for small quantities. In addition to the contract with the C&S Technology Company of the United States, Beijing Mirror Corp. had signed a domestic-exclusive agency agreement with the Appraisal and Inspection Center of China. It was the American company's obligation to enlarge the overseas market and promote the sales of the product vigorously for Beijing Mirror Corp. Apart from these, Beijing Mirror Corp. had no long-term contracts with any other enterprises. The overseas business had not yet started.

FINANCE

The Corporation had very high financial leverage. Production had not reached the optimum scale, with an annual output of only 100,000 pieces. Since the majority of costs were fixed, there was a net loss in the current year, resulting in a negative Owner's Equity. The total amount of the liabilities exceeded the total book value of the Corporation's assets. The Corporation's current ratio did not look good. Receivables tied up a great deal of funds. These were all common problems for domestic enterprises. Advances on sales constituted the greatest proportion of the Corporation's current liability; thus, the Corporation's liquidity could be better than the current ratio indicated.

RESEARCH AND DEVELOPMENT

Experts in various fields, such as optics, the chemical industry, electric-vacuum technology, the auto industry and thermal technology, etc., employed by Beijing Mirror Corp. had made a major theoretical breakthrough and were engaged in perfecting the manufacturing process. Small-scale production was now underway. The current problem was in the heat-forming process. Since the mirror had a composite curved surface, it was very difficult to heat it and cool it evenly; uneven heating or cooling resulted in distortion of the mirror. The spoilage rate of the entire manufacturing process was as high as 40 per cent. Consequently, production efficiency was relatively low,

while the cost was fairly high. Research was being conducted by the Corporation to perfect the manufacturing technology and process, and the spoilage rate would ultimately be expected to decline. The Corporation was also considering the adaptation of the rearview mirror to small-sized vehicles, in order to form a complete product series.

PRODUCTION

The existing production line of the Corporation was imported from Taiwan. Many of the most advanced technologies in the world had been applied to the manufacturing process. Furthermore, Tsinghua University could serve the Corporation with solid technology support. The Corporation also had adopted Computer Assisted Design. No matter what the vehicle model, once the required data (such as the size of the vehicle, the driver's position, and the position of the mirror) were input, a final optimized design of the mirror could be obtained immediately. The mould of the mirror was processed by the CIMS, one of the key experimental projects of the Government, which appeared to be highly efficient and precise.

MANAGEMENT

The Corporation currently had a small staff. It was in urgent need of supportive intermediate management. The Sales Department and Financial Department were especially weak, merely performing the most basic functions, and leaving unfulfilled their proper contribution to the Corporation's development. Some essential functions for manufacturing enterprises such as costing and cost control had not yet been set up in the Financial Department (not to mention the decision-assistance function such as financing the Corporation's development). These defects were mainly due to the short history of the Corporation. Before the business was operating normally, it could hardly be expected to attract high-quality management personnel.

JOINT VENTURE PROPOSAL

The Beijing rearview mirror aroused a great deal of public interest after winning the Gold Prize in the National Patent Exhibition and through its presentation in the Selected Quality Exhibition held in Singapore in April 1995. Many trial orders followed. Several other companies submitted requests to be Beijing Mirror Corp.'s agent, or to cooperate with Beijing Mirror Corp. in developing the product. Among the joint venture proposals, only two came to the negotiation stage.

1. NEGOTIATION WITH THE DOMESTIC PAC COMPANY

PAC Company accepted almost all the terms asked by Beijing Mirror Corp. in the negotiation. Under their proposal, a new firm (Firm X) would be established. The sole asset of the firm would be the ownership of the patent. The original stockholders of The Beijing Mirror Corp. would own 100 per cent of Firm X. The present Beijing Mirror Corp. (without the patent ownership) plus a 20 million RMB input from PAC Company would then become the joint venture (PAC Company insisted on acquiring 30 per cent ownership of Beijing Mirror Corp.). The joint venture would be the exclusive licensee of the rearview mirror. It would also be responsible for the production and sales of the mirror. Five percent of the sales would be paid to the patent owner (Firm X) as the royalty. The negotiation did not refer to the influence that the 30 per cent stock ownership would exert upon the manufacturing and managing decisions. Since PAC Company did not demand the right to take part in the management, the original stockholders would still have control over Beijing Mirror Corp. However, the technology secret would be shared by both sides, although PAC Company's business scope had never been in the high technology area. Its entry was presumed to be motivated by a desire to increase its own profitability, and to find an appropriate investment opportunity for its huge cash surplus.

2. NEGOTIATION WITH CANTISE CO. OF THE UNITED STATES

Cantise Co. Ltd. was an American company with branches in Canada, China and various other Asian countries. Mr. Huang Wei, the president of the company, was born in Mainland China and received his bachelor's degree there before he went to the United States. Cantise Co. Ltd. was founded immediately after he acquired his MBA degree in the United States. The negotiating delegation of Cantise Co. consisted of Chinese, with masters or higher degrees granted overseas before they entered Cantise Co. Cantise Co. did not reveal its overall business information to Beijing Mirror Corp., but the business performance report of the company's brochure showed that the company acted as the overseas agent for Chinese mainland enterprises or as the mainland agent for foreign companies. Cantise Co. could ease Beijing Mirror Corp.'s entry into the North American market, and help to establish a relationship with American manufacturers of vehicle components. Cantise Co. also promised that, once agreement was reached, it would arrange visits to the United States and Canada for the CEOs of Beijing Mirror Corp., and organize meetings for them with the American and Canadian manufacturers to discuss the production and selling of the rearview mirror in North America.

The proposal submitted by Cantise Co. was similar to that of the PAC Company. A new firm (Firm Y) would be planned. The sole asset of the new firm would be the ownership of the patent. The original stockholders of Beijing Mirror Corp. would own 100 per cent of Firm Y. The present Beijing Mirror Corp. (without the patent ownership) plus the 20 million RMB fund input from Cantise Co. would then become the joint venture (Cantise Co. agreed to take no more than 30 per cent of the total ownership of the joint venture). The joint venture would have the exclusive license of the rearview mirror, and could conduct its business worldwide. However, Cantise Co. would require a say in the management and decision-making of the new Beijing Mirror Corp. and access to the license of the rearview mirror as well. It would not, however, engage in any domestic manufacturing or sales activities, but only carry out such activities overseas. When overseas sales of Cantise Co. reached two million pieces per year, the original stockholders of Beijing Mirror Corp. would get 10 per cent of the ownership of the Cantise Co.'s overseas division specializing in the rearview mirror business. As soon as the annual sales of Cantise Co.'s overseas business exceeded four million pieces, the original stockholders of Beijing Mirror Corp. could then increase their equity in that division to 20 per cent, which was the upper limit of its ownership of the division. Before the specified annual sales volume of four million pieces was reached, Beijing Mirror Corp. was authorized to sell the product directly overseas. As soon as Cantise's sales surpassed four million pieces overseas, Beijing Mirror Corp. would have to limit its sales within the country. No other business organization or individual would be granted the license except Beijing Mirror Corp. and Cantise Co.

As mentioned above, capital and human resources were the two most crucial factors for Beijing Mirror Corp.'s successful entry into the world market. The reasons were as follows:

1. The existing rearview mirror market was served by all types of products with various functions. Therefore, interest in the new product had to be aroused by systematic advertising and sales promotion activities. Consequently, a huge amount of sales promotion expense was the first consideration for entry into the target market.

2. The current manufacturing capacity of the Corporation was still quite limited. More long-term assets would have to be purchased to increase the scale of production; this also created demand for more capital. However, the Corporation was currently experiencing a net loss. Although there might be greater cash inflows when sales increased, it was unrealistic to expect that advertising and expansion would be financed solely by operating cash inflow. The Corporation already had a

high proportion of debts, which made further borrowing difficult.

3. The staff of the Corporation was still weak, especially in the Sales Department. It lacked the personnel not only for international marketing, but also for domestic sales promotion.

Therefore, one of the most practical approaches to encourage faster development of Beijing Mirror Corp. was to cooperate with other enterprises. The companies intending to cooperate with Beijing Mirror Corp. had long operating histories as well as considerable knowledge and experience in marketing and management. In addition, they were generally more familiar with the market, each having its own sales network. Cooperation with such companies would not only provide Beijing Mirror Corp. with adequate funds for development, but could also solve the problem of insufficient qualified personnel. However, to get such support, Beijing Mirror Corp. would have to give up part of the ownership, and possibly part of the management authority as well.

THE DECISIONS

Beijing Mirror Corp. was aiming at a relatively high market share both in domestic and in overseas markets. To realize such a goal, the following issues were those Mr. Tian would have to consider in order to draft a strategy for the Corporation's development.

1. *Whether Beijing Mirror Corp. should develop independently, or enter a joint venture with other companies?* A joint venture would support Beijing Mirror Corp. with urgently needed funds and other kinds of resources, at the price of losing partial control over the corporation.

2. *Whether Beijing Mirror Corp. should join with a domestic enterprise or with an overseas enterprise?* Since Beijing Mirror Corp. had already been recognized as a high technology enterprise, most favorable tax treatment was granted by the Government. This eliminated one of the most important motivations for joint venture with foreign companies, since no more favorable tax treatment could be obtained. However, there were other advantages to joint venture, such as a smoother entry into the international market, the easier adoption of foreign advanced equipment, technology, and management as well as foreign capital and staff. The joint venture would also have to obey the laws and regulations of the two countries, and different countries had different taxation and regulatory policies toward the international remittance of royalties and profits. At the same time, problems such as accounting treatment and information disclosure might also exist. A joint venture with Cantise Co. would involve conflicts with

the C&S contract as well, which might lead to arduous litigation. Nonetheless, Cantise Co. believed this was a minor problem.

Since Beijing Mirror Corp. was completely ignorant of the overseas market, it was difficult to find an appropriate way to assess whether the 4 per cent royalty and the 20 per cent upper limit of the division's equity were reasonable.

3. *Which kind of pricing strategy should be adopted?* Cost was temporarily irrelevant in the pricing of the mirror, since there would be no competitors in the market in the near future. Therefore, a demand-oriented pricing method could be applied. The key here was to determine the sensitivity of demand to price, as well as the influence of price upon the goal of quick market entry.

4. *What distribution pattern should be used?* Beijing Mirror Corp. had signed an exclusive agency agreement with the China Motor Vehicle Safety Appraisal and Inspection Centre. It would effectively prevent counterfeit and imitation, thus safeguarding the Corporation's reputation. However, the Corporation would be overly dependent on its sole agent, whose efforts to sell the consigned products would directly affect the Corporation's profit. To ensure consistent revenue, the Corporation would have to provide continuous incentives for the agent. Such incentives were usually not only costly but also highly risky. These concerns could be partially reduced by using a competitive distribution pattern, whether it involved an agency agreement or a goods delivery contract, long-term or short-term, with fixed price or floating price. This would increase both the distribution channels to the markets and the speed of market penetration. The new task of evaluating and controlling the performance of the numerous agents would then emerge.

5. *Which promotion method should be applied?* Products like the rearview mirror were directly related to people's life and property security. Therefore, rigorous standards and regulatory controls concerning the quality and function were imposed by all governments. Although sales promotion through mass media might produce a wide coverage and a fast reaction, regulatory limits might restrict growth. If all required regulations were precisely followed, low efficiency might then result, and optimal timing might be missed.

These were the major aspects under consideration. Mr. Tian was well aware that he had to submit his proposals for Beijing Mirror Corp.'s development strategy as soon as possible. A detailed and well-documented explanation was also expected.

EXHIBIT 1
ORGANIZATION
CHART OF BEIJING
MIRROR CORP.

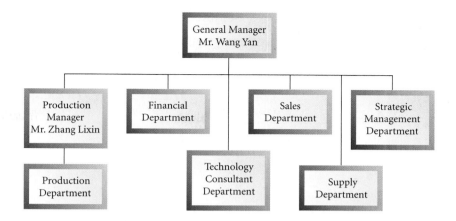

EXHIBIT 2
BALANCE SHEET
BEIJING MIRROR
CORP. DECEMBER 31,
1995 (10,000 RMB)

Current assets	
Cash	180
Accounts receivable	230
Inventory	328
Other receivables and prepaid items	42
Subtotal	780
Fixed assets	2,400
Less: depreciation	353
Net fixed assets	2,047
Other assets	20
Total assets	2,847
Current liabilities	
Bank loans	300
Sales advances	553
Other payables	17
Long-term liabilities	2,000
Owner's equity	
Paid-in capital	400
Capital surplus	200
Retained earnings	(623)
Total of owner's equity	(23)
Total of liabilities and owner's equity	2,847

EXHIBIT 3
PARTIAL INCOME
STATEMENT
BEIJING MIRROR
CORP. FOR THE YEAR
ENDED DECEMBER 31,
1995 (10,000 RMB)

Sales revenue	2,500
Less: operating cost	2,883
Operating income	(383)
Less: Financial expense	240
Earnings before tax	(623)
Less income tax	0
Net income	(623)

EXHIBIT 4 FIXED ASSETS OF BEIJING MIRROR CORP.

	COST (10,000 RMB)	LIFE EXPECTANCY (YEAR)	PRODUCTION CAPACITY (10,000 Ps/YEAR)	DEPRECIATION METHOD
Imported manufacturing line	380	5	50	S/L
Complementary equipment	150	5	50	S/L
Multi-layer coating machine	400	5	50	S/L
Testing machine	100	5	50	S/L
Interim-test machine	150	3		S/L
Moulding machine for mirror case	370	2.5 million pieces		Units of production
Moulding machine for mirror glass	150	2.5 million pieces		Units of production
Factory buildings	440	10	100	S/L
Office facilities	200	10	100	S/L
Set-up of factory building	60	5	100	S/L
Total	2,400			

EXHIBIT 5 SALES FORECAST AND SCHEDULE OF LONG-TERM ASSET INVESTMENT AND DEPRECIATION (FOR 10 YEARS)

SALES FORECAST

The production volume of Beijing Mirror Corp. reached 100,000 pieces in 1995. The predicted volume for 1996 was 300,000 pieces. The target production volume for 1997 was around 700,000 units, roughly 50 per cent of the rearview mirror market for large and medium-sized vehicles. In 1998, with the further penetration of the domestic market, the Corporation would aim for the international market. A total production of 1.5 million was predicted with 1.2 million for the domestic market (80 per cent of the total market share) and 0.3 million for the overseas market. With the domestic market share secured, 1998 would be devoted to the campaign for the international market. The forecasted production volume was two million pieces, which would then remain constant afterwards. Therefore, the sales forecast within the valid period of patent was as follows:

Year	1995	1996	1997	1998	1999	2000	2001	2002	2003	2004
Production (10,000 Ps)	10	30	70	150	200	200	200	200	200	200

SCHEDULE OF LONG-TERM ASSET INVESTMENT AND DEPRECIATION (10,000 RMB)

Year	1994	1995	1996	1997	1998	1999	2000	2001	2002	2003	2004
Investment	2,400		1,030	2,250	1,030	1,610	520	1,550	1,610		
Depreciation		(353)	(394)	(684)	(1,082)	(1,392)	(1,392)	(1,392)	(1,392)	(1,392)	(1,392)
Net Investment	2,400	(353)	636	1,566	(52)	218	(872)	158	(362)	(158)	(1,392)

EXHIBIT 6
COST BEHAVIOR ANALYSIS

1. Variable Costs (RMB/piece)

Raw materials	74.3
Package	12.0
Instruction booklet	2.0
Utilities	5.6
Direct labor	4.0
Depreciation of moulding machines	2.1
Total	100.00

2. Semi-Variable Costs (10,000 RMB)

VOLUME (10,000 PIECES)	BELOW 50	50–100	100–150	150–200	200–250
Promotion expenditure	200	600	1,000	1,000	1,000
Depreciation of the manufacturing line and testing equipment	206	412	618	824	1,030
Maintenance expense	50	100	150	200	250
Fixed part of raw material	50	100	150	200	250
Depreciation of factory building and office facilities	76	76	152	152	228
Indirect labor and salary of non-manufacturing staff	110	110	220	220	330

3. Fixed Costs

Land rent:	400,000 RMB/year
Consultant fee:	1,000,000 RMB/year
R&D:	10,000,000 RMB/year (for the initial three years)
	5,000,000 RMB/year (for the following seven years)
Depreciation of interim-test equipment:	500,000 RMB/year (for the initial three years)

EXHIBIT 7 PRO-FORMA INCOME STATEMENT (10,000 RMB)

Ignore the influence of capital structure and assume the business to be entirely equity-financed.

Year	1995	1996E	1997E	1998E	1999E	2000E	2001E	2002E	2003E	2004E
Sales revenue	2,500	7,500	17,500	37,500	50,000	50,000	50,000	50,000	50,000	50,000
Variable cost	1,001	3,002	7,004	15,008	20,010	20,010	20,010	20,010	20,010	20,010
Contribution margin	1,499	4,498	10,496	22,492	29,990	29,990	29,990	29,990	29,990	29,990
Fixed cost	1,882	1,882	2,588	2,930	3,236	3,236	3,236	3,236	3,236	3,236
EBIT	(383)	2,616	7,908	19,562	26,754	26,754	26,754	26,754	26,754	26,754
Income tax	0	0	0	0	4,013	4,013	4,013	8,829	8,829	8,829
Net income	(383)	2,616	7,908	19,562	22,741	22,741	22,741	17,925	17,925	17,925

EXHIBIT 8 FORECASTED STATEMENT OF CASHFLOW (10,000 RMB)

Year	1994	1995	1996E	1997E	1998E	1999E	2000E	2001E	2002E	2003E	2004E
Net income		(383)	2,616	7,908	19,562	22,741	22,741	22,741	17,925	17,925	17,925
Less: net investment of long-term asset	2,400	(353)	636	1,566	(52)	218	(872)	158	(362)	(158)	(1,392)
Less: working capital input (1)	500	1,000	2,000	4,000	2,500						
Residual value (2)											28,000
Net cashflow	(2,900)	(1,030)	(20)	2,342	17,114	22,523	23,613	22,583	17,707	17,767	47,317

(1) The turnovers of work-in-process, raw material inventory and accounts receivable were all assumed to be 12. Therefore, the net working capital need was 20 per cent of the marginal sales revenue.

(2) The validity of the patent would expire in 10 years. By then, the competition would be accelerated and Beijing Mirror Corp. would have to keep its market share by reducing the price. In that fully competitive market, no enterprise could earn more than the average profit, which was around 25 per cent with a unit price of 185 RMB or so. Also assume that the Beijing Mirror Corp. would maintain annual sales of two million pieces in 10 years. If the scale of production were kept constant, the annual depreciation would roughly equal the annual investment of a long-term asset. Therefore, the net cashflow would approximately equal the net income, about 70 million RMB per year. Using a discount rate of 25 per cent, we get a residual value of cashflow would approximately equal the net income, about 70 million RMB per year. Using a discount rate of 25 per cent, we get a residual value of 280 million RMB.

EXHIBIT 9
VALUATION OF THE PATENT

When estimating the cashflows, inflation factors were deliberately left out of the consideration of sales price and out-of-pocket expense. The replacement cost was also assumed constant when estimating the investment of a long-term asset. As a result, inflation should not be taken into account in determining the discount rate, where the intrinsic risk of the project ought to be the major concern. In the case of the rearview mirror, a discount rate of 20 to 30 per cent was used.

DISCOUNT RATE	NPV (10,000 RMB)
20%	44,307
30%	25,190
50%	8,810
90%	107
100%	−659

IRR = 92 per cent.
The patent was valued between 250–440 million RMB.

EXHIBIT 10
JOINT VENTURE
SCHEME OF BEIJING
MIRROR CORP. WITH
THE DOMESTIC
PAC CO.

ORIGINAL STATE

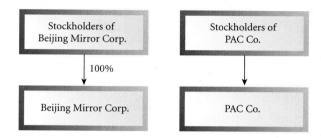

JOINT VENTURE

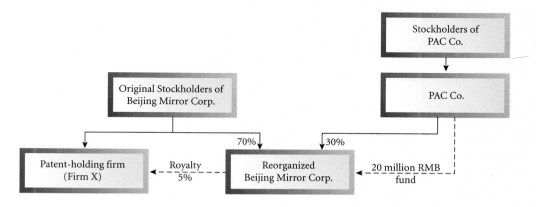

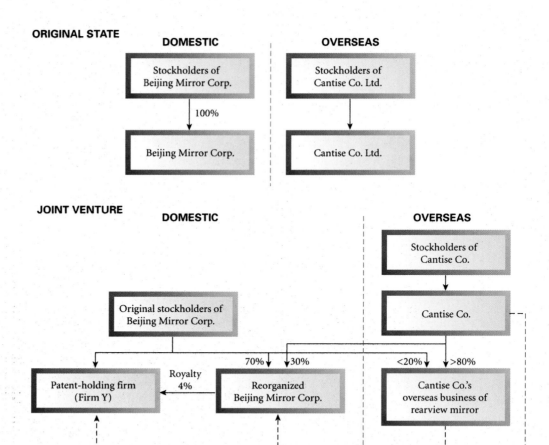

EXHIBIT 12   VALUE OF BEIJING MIRROR CORP. AFTER JOINT VENTURE

Ignore the influence of capital structure and assume the business to be entirely equity-financed.

1. **Joint venture with the domestic company**
    a. *Value of the reorganized Beijing Mirror Corp.*
        Assume the formal start of the joint venture was to be in 1997. Due to the 20 million fund input, the production volume and the market penetration pace of Beijing Mirror Corp. would be greatly increased. The predicted sales for 1997 were 1.5 million pieces. It could be further improved to two million in 1998. Since the domestic market was the target basis for Beijing Mirror Corp. only 30 to 35 per cent of the total sales would be made overseas. The domestic market could be considered well-captured with total annual sales of two million pieces. Therefore, sales of two million pieces could be assumed to remain afterwards.

        The pro-forma income statement is as follows: (10,000 RMB)

Year	1997E	1998E	1999E	2000E	2001E	2002E	2003E	2004E
Sales revenue	37,500	50,000	50,000	50,000	50,000	50,000	50,000	50,000
Variable cost	16,883	22,510	22,510	22,510	22,510	22,510	22,510	22,510
Contribution margin	20,617	27,490	27,490	27,490	27,490	27,490	27,490	27,490
Fixed Cost	2,930	3,236	3,236	3,236	3,236	3,236	3,236	3,236
EBIT	17,687	24,254	24,254	24,254	24,254	24,254	24,254	24,254
Income tax	0	0	3,638	3,638	3,638	8,004	8,004	8,004
New income	17,687	24,254	20,616	20,616	20,616	16,250	16,250	16,250

Since the scale of production was relatively stable, the annual depreciation could be assumed to equal the annual investment in long-term assets. Similarly, the cashflow could be assumed to equal the net income. When the validity of the patent expires, the profitability of the business would decline. The residual value of the reorganized Beijing Mirror Corp. was the same as in Exhibit 8.

The forecasted statement of cashflow is as follows:

Year	1997E	1998E	1999E	2000E	2001E	2002E	2003E	2004E
Residual value								28,000
Net cashflow	17,687	24,254	20,616	20,616	20,616	16,250	16,250	16,250

Discounting the cashflows at the beginning of 1996 with a rate of 30 per cent, we get: NPV = 484 million RMB.

    b. *Value of the patent-holding firm (the applicable tax rate is 33 per cent)*

Year	1997E	1998E	1999E	2000E	2001E	2002E	2003E	2004E
Royalty	1,256	1,675	1,675	1,675	1,675	1,675	1,675	1,675

These cashflows were much safer than the operating cashflows of Beijing Mirror Corp. Therefore, a lower discount rate should be applied. Discounting them back to the beginning of 1996 with a rate of 20 per cent, we would get: NPV = 50.65 million RMB.

    c. *Value held by original stockholders of Beijing Mirror Corp.*

	VALUE (10,000 RMB)	SHARE HELD BY ORIGINAL STOCKHOLDERS OF BEIJING MIRROR CORP.	VALUE HELD BY ORIGINAL STOCKHOLDERS OF BEIJING MIRROR CORP. (10,000 RMB)
Reorganized Beijing Mirror Corp.	48,440	70%	33,908
Patent-holding firm	5,056	100%	5,056
Total			38,964

EXHIBIT 12   VALUE OF BEIJING MIRROR CORP. AFTER JOINT VENTURE (continued)

2. **Joint venture with Cantise Co. Ltd.**
   a. *Value of reorganized Beijing Mirror Corp.*
      The value of the reorganized Beijing Mirror Corp. when forming a joint venture with Cantise Co. was the same as when forming a joint venture with the domestic company.

   b. *Overseas business of Cantise Co.*
      Assume that Cantise Co. started its overseas business of rearview mirrors from 1998. Due to its powerful support of capital and technology, as well as its global distribution network, sales could grow rapidly to a volume of 4,000,000 pieces annually. Also assume that the manufacturing cost and sales price were the same for both the Cantise Co.'s overseas business and the reorganized Beijing Mirror Corp. The Pro-forma Income Statement would appear as follows: (10,000 RMB)

Sales revenue	100,000
Less: variable cost	44,020
fixed cost	7,000
Income before tax	48,980
Less: income tax (T = 30 per cent)	14,694
Net income	34,286

Since the scale of production was relatively stable, the annual depreciation could be assumed to equal the annual investment of long-term assets. Therefore, the net cash flow would equal the net income. Estimation of the residual value of the reorganized Beijing Mirror Corp. was also as before.

The forecasted statement of cashflow is as follows: (1,000 RMB)

Year	1998E	1999E	2000E	2001E	2002E	2003E	2004E
Residual value							56,000
Net cashflow	34,286	34,286	34,286	34,286	34,286	34,286	34,286

Discounting the cashflows to the beginning of 1996 with a rate of 30 per cent, we get: NPV = 62129.

   c. *Value of the patent-holding firm (the applicable tax rate is 33 per cent): (10,000 RMB)*

Year	1997E	1998E	1999E	2000E	2001E	2002E	2003E	2004E
Royalty	1,005	1,340	4,020	4,020	4,020	4,020	4,020	4,020

These cashflows were much safer than the operating cashflows of Beijing Mirror Corp. Therefore, a lower discount rate could be applied. Discounting them back to the beginning of 1996 with a rate of 20 per cent, we would get: NPV = 92.10 million RMB.

   d. *Value held by original stockholders of Beijing Mirror Corp.*

	VALUE (10,000 RMB)	SHARE HELD BY ORIGINAL STOCKHOLDERS OF BEIJING MIRROR CORP.	VALUE HELD BY ORIGINAL STOCKHOLDERS OF BEIJING MIRROR CORP. (10,000 RMB)
Reorganized Beijing Mirror Corp.	48,440	70%	33,908
Overseas business of Cantise Co.	62,129	20%	12,426
Patent-holding firm	9,210	100%	9,210
Total			55,544

EXHIBIT 13
AGENCY AGREEMENT

In order to develop international business, the two parties, on the basis of equality and mutual benefit, came to a formal agreement as follows:

I. Party A (Licensor): Beijing Mirror Corp.

Party B (General Agency): C & S Technology Corp.

Party A agrees to designate Party B as its exclusive general agent outside China for the increased view width and non-blind spot rearview mirror. Party B agrees to bear the expense of applying for the patent and to undertake to develop the market.

II. Rights and Obligations of the General Agent (Party B)

Based on the initial market analysis, Party B agrees to take the following responsibilities:

1. Bearing the necessary disbursements when applying for the patent in relevant foreign countries.
2. Vigorously advancing the overseas market, product promotion, after-sale service, information feedback, etc., in order to form a complete set of services.
3. Keeping commercial secrets and promoting Party A's overseas interests.
4. Enjoying the exclusive right of selling the above-mentioned product outside China.
5. Operating independently and setting up its own distribution network.

III. Rights and Obligations of the Licensor (Party A)

Party A is willing to cooperate with Party B to develop the overseas market jointly and herein promises:

1. To defend the overseas market developed by Party B and to hold Party B blameless.
2. To maintain a regular goods supply of fair quality and adequate quantity.
3. To negotiate with party B on a price suitable to the market.
4. To keep commercial secrets and to defend Party B's overseas interests.
5. To check and keep aware of Party's B's performance from time to time.
6. Without the approval of Party B, not to sell in any form, by any means, the above-mentioned product anywhere outside China.

IV. Patent

The patent belongs to the original inventor regardless of the country or region where an application is sought.

V. Commission

Party B requests 30 per cent of the sales price, with 15 per cent as the market development fee; 10 per cent for the coverage of expenses; and the rest, 5 per cent, as its own profit. The percentage shall be renegotiated if Party A is trapped in a net loss.

VI. Other Items

This agreement becomes effective as soon as it is signed by the two parties, with a validity of two years. When the validity expires, the agreement would automatically roll over with the agreement of the two sides. If the agreement is violated by either party, that party would be held responsible for any loss and damage.

This agreement is expressed both in Chinese and in English, with two copies for each party. However, only the Chinese version could be legally referred to, or be used for litigation purposes.

PARTY A:	PARTY B:
BEIJING MIRROR CORP.	**C&S TECHNOLOGY CO., USA**
Date: November 6, 1994	Date: November 6, 1994
Signature:	Signature:

Lufthansa 2000: Maintaining the Change Momentum

ABSTRACT

In 1991 Lufthansa was almost bankrupt. Eight years later, at the general business meeting on the 16th of June 1999 Jürgen Weber (CEO) announced record results in Lufthansa's more than 70-year history. In eight years, the company had gone from the brink of bankruptcy to becoming one of the world's leading airline companies, a founding member of the STAR ALLIANCE—the airline industry's most comprehensive network—aspiring to become the leading aviation group in the world.

Lufthansa had undergone some radical changes that reversed a record loss of DM 730 million in 1992 to a record pre-tax profit of DM 2.5 billion in 1998 (an increase of 42% compared to 1997 when the pre-tax profit was DM 1.75 billion). Revenues increased by 4.8%, from DM 21.6 billion in 1997, to DM 22.7 billion in 1998. The Seat Load Factor (SLF—proportion of seats filled) reached 73%, a record performance in Lufthansa's history (1.5 percentage points increase compared to 1997 and 9 percentage points increase compared to 1991).

After the first step of the turnaround it was apparent that transformation had just begun and that a much more fundamental change had to follow to assure the company's future. The Lufthansa Executive Board (Vorstand) and the Supervisory Board (Aufsichtsrat) decided to follow a concept of sustaining renewal (rede-velopment) at 3 levels, operational, structural, and strategic. In 1999, none of these processes were fully completed. In fact, sustaining the change process was seen as the key management challenge.

In 1991 Lufthansa was almost bankrupt. It was *the* national airline carrier of the Federal Republic of Germany, state owned, monolithic, and unprofitable.

Eight years later, in 1999, it was a privately owned, profitable company, a core element of the strongest world-wide alliance in the airline industry, aspiring to become the leading aviation group in the world. During the years of 1992–1999, Lufthansa went from a record loss of DM 730 million to a record profit of DM 2.5 billion (Appendix 1). The number of passengers increased from 33.7 million in 1992 to 40.5 million in 1998, while the number of employees decreased from about 64,000 in 1992 to about 55,000 in 1998.

This case was written in co-operation between LBS and Lufthansa School of Business by Dr. Heike Bruch, Visiting Scholar at LBS from the University of St. Gallen (Switzerland), under the supervision of Prof. Sumantra Ghoshal. It is intended to be used as a basis of discussion rather than to illustrate either effective or ineffective handling of a business solution.

RECENT HISTORY

ERA BEFORE WEBER

Founded in 1926, liquidated in 1945 and reborn in 1953, Lufthansa historically represented the characteristic strengths of German industry: a strong focus on reliability, order and technical excellence. Majority owned by the German state, its strategy, organization and culture represented an amalgam of a strong technical orientation, dominated by engineers, together with the bureaucratic values of public administration. Its role as an organ of the state was reflected in its values and beliefs: formal, rule-driven and inflexible, the yellow badges of Lufthansa symbolized independence, permanence and sovereign dignity.

In the second half of the 1980s, under the leadership of Heinz Ruhnau, Lufthansa pursued a policy of "growth through own strength." Based on the belief that only the largest airlines will survive in an era of global competition, Ruhnau had committed the airline to a rapid fleet expansion in order to capture market share. When Jürgen Weber was appointed as CEO in 1991, Lufthansa had enlarged its fleet by some 120 aircrafts to 275.

GULF WAR AND THE BREAKDOWN OF THE AVIATION MARKET

In the late 80s, deregulation triggered intensive price competition. This process, coupled with the steep fall in air traffic during the Gulf War and the subsequent recession, led to a serious over-capacity for the airline industry on a global basis, and severe market slump in Europe. In 1991, the Seat Load Factor (SLF—proportion of available seats filled) went down to about 57% in Europe, compared to a worldwide average of about 65%.

The problem was aggravated because of a remarkable inflexibility concerning capacities and services offered. Deregulation of the airline industry started in 1978 in the US. In Europe, in contrast, while there was some relaxation in regulations, over the 1980s most airlines continued to be owned by their respective national governments who continued to maintain strict control over both routes and landing slots at airports.

REUNIFICATION AND PLANS FOR GROWTH

Lufthansa noticed the crisis later than other companies. Because of the German reunification, Lufthansa enjoyed a boom at a time when the rest of the industry faced this severe market downturn.

In 1991, while overall traffic dropped by 9% in Europe, Lufthansa had an increase of passenger numbers by 11% because of the German reunification. But despite this growth, Lufthansa reported an after-tax loss of DM 444 million in 1991. This result was largely attributed to unique non-influenceable factors like the Gulf War. But results in the second half of 1991 and in the beginning of 1992 also fell below expectations. Although an awareness of a serious crisis began to spread in early 1992, Lufthansa was so programmed on growth and success that employment continued to rise during the first six months. Being a state-owned company, immortality was taken for granted.

> "Even when the crisis became very obvious people still thought: 'We are the German Airline Company, state owned and a prestige organisation. They will never let us die.'"
>
> — *Jochen Hoffmann, Senior Vice President & Executive Vice President Personnel and Labour Relations, Deutsche Lufthansa AG*

THE TURNAROUND

BANKRUPTCY

Outsiders were not so sure about the survival of Lufthansa. In 1992, with only 14 days of operating cash requirements in hand, Jürgen Weber went to all the major German banks asking them for money to pay employee salaries. No private bank believed in the survival of Lufthansa: only a single state-owned institution—the Kreditanstalt für Wiederaufbau—agreed to give Lufthansa the money it needed to pay its people.

REDEVELOPMENT WORKSHOPS

The starting point of the redevelopment concept was a four-week management program about change management, which at the same time was also the birthplace of a group called the "Samurai of Change." The members of this group discussed the results of the program with Jürgen Weber and convinced him of the urgency of a redevelopment process.

On a weekend in June 1992, as a result, Weber invited about 20 senior managers to the training centre at Seeheim[1] for a meeting that was originally entitled "Mental Change." It was aimed at building a network of change-minded managers who would drive the redevelopment process within the company. Shortly before the workshop Jürgen Weber got a deeper insight into the acuteness of the crisis and changed the title from "mental change" to "crisis management meeting." The turnaround began.

The process of this meeting was as important as the outcome. For some managers this Seeheim crisis management meeting was one of their first experiences with interdepartmental co-operation and non-bureaucratic problem solving. The opinions concerning the necessity of drastic actions and the directions of change did not differ much. Facts were too obvious.

"No one had an idea of the gravity and the brutality of the crisis. After a long phase of denial or 'not wanting to believe,' there was a next phase of 'searching for the guilty people' which was followed by an awareness that there was a massive pressure to act. After this, everything went very fast. The goals we committed ourselves to at Seeheim were very ambitious and nobody believed that we could ever meet them, but after this process we committed ourselves to them. The critical question was how to win over other managers and employees for these 'stretching' goals and activities."

— **Wolfgang Mayrhuber, CEO Lufthansa**
Technik AG and former member
of the Operations Team

One way to involve a larger group of managers was to repeat the Seeheim workshop three times with different groups of 50 people. This was done in order to let them live through the same process, let them feel the threat and the urgency and not just inform them of the facts and the appropriate strategy which they had to implement. After the meetings the majority of senior managers within the company were convinced of the necessity for drastic change and committed to a set of extremely ambitious goals.

"In the turnaround we have consciously tried to win the commitment of people through workshops, Town Meetings, etc. With everything I do, I try to demonstrate that at first we have to reach the emotional mobilisation before a rational mobilisation becomes possible at all. Briefly one could say: Hard success through soft processes."

— **Dr. Heiko Lange, Chief Executive**
Personnel, Deutsche Lufthansa AG

"The most important decision was downsizing the fleet, which meant putting aeroplanes into the desert. This was a completely unconventional step. It was necessary for the second important decision: the reduction of staff which also demanded a complete change in mentality because it was simply the opposite of what we had planned."

— **Dr. Peter Hach, Senior Vice President**
Corporate Controlling

The output of the Seeheim meetings was a set of 131 projects or key actions concerning drastic cuts in staff numbers (8000 positions), lower non-personnel costs including downsizing of the fleet (savings of DM 400 million), and increasing revenues (DM 700 million) in order

to reduce the losses of DM 1.3 billion. To implement these actions, Lufthansa adopted the idea of Town Meetings and Jürgen Weber decided to hold as many such meetings himself as possible when visiting different Lufthansa units. By the summer of 1999 he had personally participated in over 200 Town Meetings.

Other senior managers also held Town Meetings in their departments and, in 1999, this practice still remained very prevalent all over the Lufthansa organisation.

Town Meetings

Lufthansa Town Meetings follow a certain structure: When they take place in a foreign country, Jürgen Weber first gets together with key contacts (e.g., transport ministers) and then meets key customers. After this he talks to the local Lufthansa management about their situation, problems, plans, etc. Finally the main item of the agenda is a long and intensive dialogue with the employees. Jürgen Weber explains to them the latest plans and the staff ask questions and present their perspectives on problems and potential improvements.

"It was decisive for the turnaround that we told the employees openly what the situation was. It allowed us to develop common goals between employees, management, work councils, and unions. We could even discuss issues such as staff reduction and productivity increase openly and personally."

— **Jürgen Weber, Chairman and CEO,**
Deutsche Lufthansa AG

"Jürgen Weber wins people personally by his open and authentic communication. He tells them the unvarnished figures and explains how he feels about them. During the turnaround phase, he told them that every morning when looking into the mirror he had an overwhelming feeling of responsibility knowing that Lufthansa would again 'produce' DM 4 million of losses that day. There was a staff of 60,000 and an average of 2 or 3 other people with them depending on Lufthansa, so that he was responsible for 200,000 people. That gave him the enormous urge to change the situation. . . . People are taken by his leadership emotionally and willing to go the way Jürgen Weber points them because they simply understand what he says. It is ingenious because it is so simple. However, it works!"

— **Ursel Reininger, Staff Manager,**
Chairman's Office

"With an almost superhuman involvement Jürgen Weber was getting in contact with people in order to make clear that we were in a serious crisis. The explicit articulation of the crisis was one of the central 'events' in the turnaround. Another important aspect was the direct dialogue with the

employees. There was a saying in those days: 'Schlede[2] is collecting the money, Weber is collecting the people'."

— Dr. Hans Schmitz, Chief Executive of the Lufthansa Technik Logistik GmbH

A second implementation measure was the installation of a special "redevelopment controlling" under the direction of the corporate controller Dr. Peter Hach. This program aimed at monitoring progress and results concerning personnel and non-personnel cost-cutting and the enhancement of revenues.

Last but not least, the Executive Board appointed a group of 12 senior managers representing the main departments of the company — called the San Team (Sanierungsteam = Redevelopment team). This San Team had the task of implementing the 131 projects of "Programm 93." But the team turned out to be too large and not effective enough. Therefore, Jürgen Weber decided to form a smaller and more forceful group. The so-called OPS Team (Operations Team) became an important motor in the implementation process. It consisted at first of Angelika Jakob, head of Cabin Services, Wolfgang Mayrhuber, Technical Director of Lufthansa Maintenance, Matthias Mölleney, Senior Manager Personnel, and an external consultant. Later the OPS Team was joined by Dieter Heinen, Chief of Sales in Germany, and Dr. Christoph Frank, an internal consultant with experience in various change projects. The OPS Team put in enormous effort and succeeded in driving the Programm 93 initiatives into action by defining concrete activities and by constantly monitoring, advising, and supporting the line managers who had the ultimate responsibility for implementation.

Principles of OPS procedures were:

"We made clear that we would not accept excuses. We were pitiless, persistent and unconditional concerning the implementation of the measures. Compared to consultants and the Executive Board we had an important advantage: We knew the company and therefore we had not only personal networks but we also knew what was realistic. We were credible for the people. But the most important factor was that we were sitting in the same boat as them. It was obvious that we did not want to harm them but that we were serious because we had the same personal interest to survive. We did not have a formal hierarchical empowerment—only the power to convince people of the vital necessity of fundamental change."

— Wolfgang Mayrhuber, CEO Lufthansa Technik AG and former member of the OPS Team

Jürgen Weber showed his unconditional commitment to the OPS Team and personally supported all their needs. His demonstrated involvement with the change process was accompanied by various visible actions such as the Executive Board's waiver of 10% of their annual salaries in 1992.

In total, about 70% of the 131 projects of Programme 93 were successfully implemented during the turnaround. The remaining 30% were put into action later and implementation was still going on in 1999. Jürgen Weber intentionally did not insist on immediate implementation of the remaining 30% in order not to risk the consensus with the unions. The absence of strikes and a high level of consensus between management and other stakeholders, in particular the labour unions, was a remarkable feature of the Lufthansa crisis management. And the same philosophy continued to influence all the subsequent decisions and actions as the change process continued into the 1990s.

Consensus as a phenomenon of Lufthansa's soul

"Implementation usually doesn't come easy at Lufthansa. Before you implement anything you need a consensus. More often than not our Executive Board would refuse to decide on an issue because it had not been sufficiently reconciled. 'Open cards' was the outspoken policy of Jürgen Weber. Following that policy we not only achieved a zero pay rise in 1993, but also the privatisation of Lufthansa, the restructuring of our pension scheme, the modernisation of our company structure, and—last but not least—a drastic decrease of workforce resulting in a badly needed increase in productivity. These were dramatic changes. They would never have occurred without the consent of all constituents."[3]

Implementation of staff cuts was the responsibility of line management. For the implementation of Programm 93 it was important that line managers take responsibility for the process in order to realise the unavoidable cuts, on the one hand, and to motivate the remaining employees, on the other hand.

"The most important factor during this hard phase was credibility. This is communication during the crisis. The flying personnel are not only the producing staff but also have direct customer contact. So they should be well informed and must be loyal—even in hard times. This took a lot of energy but was worthwhile."

— Jürgen Raps, Senior Vice President Flight Operations and Chief Pilot

Certainly the cuts of staff caused problems and some very talented "high potentials" left the company because of the perceived threat to their prospects and career aspirations. But, there were also many who concluded exactly the opposite; they were attracted by the challenge to widen the existing scope of thinking and action in order to redevelop Lufthansa in spite of all the difficulties and personal sacrifices needed.

"During the crisis it was a very important experience that working under pressure was also exciting. Nobody complained. On the contrary, people accepted the challenge and really gave their best."

— Dr. Peter Jansen, General Manager Costmanagement, Programm 15

In 1993 the first effects of the effort were noticeable. Numbers of passengers increased, revenues increased, and costs decreased. In November 1993, 18 months after the crisis management meeting, the first success was reported in press and television: "The crane has upwind again."

But Lufthansa was quite aware that the superficial recovery could not guarantee a sustaining success and that a more fundamental change had to follow. To secure its future, the company had to deal with some broader issues including strategic cost savings, privatisation, and the organisational structure. Said Weber:

"We have learned our lesson: don't invest in growth counting on 'automatic' economies of scale. Instead, get your costs down first, then hit the market ready and able to fight a price war. We have to achieve cost leadership and are not yet there. That's why we need a second phase in this turnaround: we can't reduce personnel or salaries further or else the good people will leave. So, we have to restructure Lufthansa, to create cost consciousness, to create transparency, and to push responsibility and entrepreneurship to the lowest possible level."

At the outset of the turnaround, Lufthansa had embarked on negotiations with the German government to privatise the airline. One important stumbling block for privatisation was replacing the pension fund "VBL" (VBL—Versorgungsanstalt des Bundes und der Länder) binding Lufthansa to the German state. It was extremely difficult to untie these "golden chains."

"There were many discussions about VBL and it was quite obvious that it was almost impossible to get out of these obligations. If someone had asked, 80% would have said 'You will never achieve this!' But we made it."

— Jochen Hoffmann, Senior Vice President & Executive Vice President Personnel and Labour Relations, Deutsche Lufthansa AG

In May 1994, the problem of the pension fund was resolved. The German government diluted its holdings to 36% and agreed to a payment of DM 1 billion into the VBL to cover disbursements to present retirees as well as to offer an allowance and guarantee for constituting a separate Lufthansa pension fund. In 1997, Lufthansa became fully privatised.

STRATEGIC COST SAVINGS — PROGRAMM 15

As a private company, Lufthansa experienced increased pressure to be competitive and strategically cost effective. This pressure became even more acute because of the continuing decline of yields (average proceeds per ticket sold), driven by strengthening price competition within the airline industry and a threat of substitution by other transport alternatives (primarily high speed trains). As a strategic answer to these developments Lufthansa continued its transformation process and started "Programm 15."

Programm 15

Programm 15 was a wide-ranging strategic cost management program, designed to make Lufthansa more competitive through cost management and cultural change. The program's goals included:

- Improving the competitive position through cost reduction
- Internationalisation of cost structure and
- Making staff at every level highly cost-conscious and cost-effective in their daily work.

The number 15 stood for 15 pfennig per SKO ("seat kilometers offered"; the cost target for transporting one aircraft seat one kilometer). Lufthansa intended to reduce its costs from 17.7 pfennig in 1996 to 15 pfennig in 2001. This implied an overall cost reduction of 20% within five years (4% annual reduction all over the Lufthansa Group). All Lufthansa departments and companies were affected.

Like the OPS team that monitored and maintained progress on Programm 93, a Programm 15 team was put in place and it worked with certain principles that were distinctively applied making use of the experiences of the turnaround:

The rules of the game for the Programm 15 team

- We confront contentious issues.
- We do what we say.
- We prefer facts, not prejudices.
- We let ourselves be monitored whenever required.
- We inform continuously and currently—together with the responsible departments.
- We inform managers, employees and their representatives before the external public.
- We utilise informal networks to ensure interdepartmental and hierarchy-overlapping communication.
- We try to avoid catchphrases and self-overestimation.

Programm 15 was based on integrated responsibility: The line managers had the responsibility for cost reductions which meant that the achievement of Programm 15 was integrated within their "normal" management objectives and was part of their performance expectations. Programm 15 consciously set stretching goals which were challenging but achievable. Concerning the goals, no compromises were made, but the Programm 15 team consulted line management about the means of cost savings and tried to solve problems through open and honest discussion with those who were responsible for implementation. A tight monitoring and public sharing of results (actual performance data for each individual manager were published regularly) ensured accountability and continuous feedback.

> *"Programm 15 had to take into account some issues that could be called 'typically Lufthansa.' One of the characteristic features of the 'Lufthansa style' is the specific combination of consensus orientation and persistence. Nobody tries to force certain solutions and people are willing to compromise but only in terms of the way of goal achievement, not concerning the goal itself."*

— **Dr. Peter Jansen, General Manager Costmanagement, Programm 15**

To preserve discipline and attention to strategic cost goals, Programm 15 initiated a number of both symbolic and substantive measures. Those included, for example, the location of its office next to the office of Jürgen Weber, discussions of cost reduction measures in Town Meetings, weekly reports in the "Lufthanseat" (the staff journal), and widespread publicity for a few well-selected impressive "success stories."

CORPORATE RESTRUCTURING

At the beginning of the 90s, Lufthansa was functionally organised with six departments (finance, personnel, maintenance, sales, marketing, and flight operations) each led by a member of the Executive Board (Appendix 2).

This structural solution turned out to be inefficient showing symptoms such as high involvement of top management in operational problems, slow decision processes, lack of accountability, low transparency and, finally, an insufficient market proximity. These problems were enhanced by developments in the external environment—airlines were more and more confronted with time-based competition, price competition, and a need for transparency of products and services.

Lufthansa realised that it could not effectively respond to the emerging competitive challenges with its existing functional structure. The goals of Lufthansa's restructuring process therefore were to increase both market proximity and transparency of costs and proceeds, and to reduce the fragmentation of decision processes. The guiding idea behind the restructuring was that Lufthansa would be more successful as a federative group of independent small units than as a monolithic functional block.

Lufthansa considered various organisational alternatives, both in terms of how to break up the integrated operations into smaller, self-contained units and the specific legal and administrative structures for governance of these units. The key criteria for choosing among these alternatives included detailed assessments of the strategic scope of each business, their needs for entrepreneurial freedom, responsibility and accountability, the role of third party business, and the nature of the resulting internal customer-supplier relationships. Finally three business areas were formally separated as legally autonomous and strategically independent subsidiaries: LH Cargo AG (airfreight), LH Technik AG (technical maintenance service) and LH Systems GmbH (IT Services). These joined the existing subsidiaries CityLine (domestic flights), Condor (charter flights), and LSG Sky Chefs (catering). At the same time the tasks and responsibilities of the Executive Board were redefined by strengthening their strategic focus and giving the core business "Passenger Service" (so-called "Passage") a stronger weight.

Persistence with the idea of decentralisation led Lufthansa in 1997 to further operational independence of Lufthansa Passenger Service—the original core of the former airline company "Lufthansa." With 26,000 employees, including 12,500 flight personnel in the cockpit and cabin, Lufthansa Passenger Service was restructured as a Profit Centre, to be led and directed by a six member Management Board. While tax and landing slot considerations prevented the Passenger Service business area from becoming a separate legal entity, this restructuring clearly separated the business from day-to-day influence of corporate top management.

In 1999 the Lufthansa Group Management Board directed the activities of the entire Group through three central functions: the Chairman's Office and the Finance and Human Resource Management functions (Appendix 3).

BUILDING A STRATEGIC NETWORK—STAR ALLIANCE

Apart from the focus on internal costs and structural redevelopment, Lufthansa constantly worked on its external relationships. Having experienced extreme overcapacities by following the philosophy of "growth through own strength," it decided to choose an alternative strategy: "growth through partnerships."

Lufthansa was one of the central founding members of the most comprehensive and probably the most competitive airline network in the world. Since April 1999, when Air New Zealand and Ansett Australian joined the STAR ALLIANCE, the network included 8 members operating in 720 destinations in 110 countries (Appendix 4). In October 1999, ANA (All Nippon Airways) joined the STAR ALLIANCE. This was an important step for the Asian expansion strategy of the alliance (Appendix 5).

CHANGING PATTERN OF COMPETITION IN THE AIRLINE INDUSTRY

The STAR ALLIANCE started functioning in May 1997. By 1999, three other global alliances had emerged: Oneworld, Wings and Qualiflyer (Appendix 6). With the launch of Oneworld in February 1999 competition in the airline industry had taken on a new dimension. This new alliance had five founding members, a common logo and shared the STAR ALLIANCE vision of seamlessly linking the partner airlines' route networks. Lufthansa believed that the Anglo-Saxon culture binding the Oneworld partner airlines could facilitate mutual understanding and shared decision making, making the alliance a potentially cohesive and dynamic force.

Strategically, these developments were of vital importance. At the end of the 20th century, the economic structure of the airline industry was changing from competition between airlines to competition between networks. In consequence, airline networks were striving to intensify integration and common alliance strategies. In 1999, the biggest challenge for STAR ALLIANCE lay in defending its leading position and in expanding its market leadership through integrated network management in a new phase of intensifying competition among the rival networks.

TRADITIONAL ADVANTAGES OF AIRLINE ALLIANCES

Traditionally the core of airline alliances was code-sharing, i.e., using the same flight numbers. In 1999, Lufthansa and United Airlines, for example, served not less than 130 code-share flight destinations. Lufthansa reported that in 1998 a supplement of DM 450 million of revenues was due to the alliance.

Important synergies were also realised through joint sales activities (joint advertising, common frequent flyer programs, joint travel agency contracts, etc.), collective market research, shared facilities such as lounges, and staff exchange. The Landlord Concept introduced within the STAR ALLIANCE in 1997 illustrates the nature and extent of these potential benefits. Aimed at developing a common ground service (ticketing and check-in), 27 key hubs were identified worldwide to start this integration process of sharing airport facilities and services under one roof. At each station one carrier was appointed "landlord" and given the responsibility for airport services like check-in and ticketing for all the other STAR ALLIANCE members. Since the other airlines did not retain any activity in these hubs, the program implied a take over of the entire staff of all the other partner airlines by the "landlord"-airline. For example, in November 1997 all the former Lufthansa employees at Copenhagen were transferred to SAS while Lufthansa took all the SAS employees in Frankfurt.

EMERGENT CHALLENGES—STAR ALLIANCE MANAGEMENT AND STRATEGY

Beyond these traditionally important operational synergies, in 1999 the STAR ALLIANCE was beginning to approach the much more demanding challenges of co-ordinating and integrating strategic activities such as establishing a common global brand, developing a shared technology platform, joint training, and personnel development. While the operating synergies could be managed through ad-hoc teams and task forces, effective co-ordination of these strategic issues required an integrated management structure for the overall alliance as well as a systematic process for co-ordinating the internal strategic activities of all the partners.

In December 1998 the STAR ALLIANCE airlines formed a focused management team to lead the alliance on a day-to-day basis. Until then the alliance activities were co-ordinated by a set of committees and project teams. The presidents of the airlines decided to bundle responsibilities for strategic issues. Jürgen Weber personally championed the need for a permanent management structure in order to give further force and dynamism to the Alliance. The newly appointed Alliance Management Board consisted of six executives who were made responsible for dealing with all the strategic issues of the network and to implement the five-year business plan approved by the airlines' presidents at their meeting in October 1998 in Rio de Janeiro.

There were four key issues of major strategic importance:

- The global network
- Marketing and sales
- Service and product development and
- Information technology

The Management Board was chaired by Lufthansa's Friedel Rödig with Bruce Harris of United Airlines serving as his deputy. The other core members of the Management Board were responsible for specific areas of activity. Ross

McCormack of Air Canada was in charge of the global network development, Per Stendenbakken of SAS was responsible for seamless service and product development, Dieter Grotepass of Lufthansa looked after sales strategy, marketing communications and co-ordination of frequent flyer programs, while all issues related to Information Technology and Automation were the responsibility of United's Bruce Parker.

With the new structure in place, the alliance progressed beyond the stage of a committee-based collaboration, but it was not considered sufficient for a true strategic integration. The central question was whether the success of the alliance demanded a fusion of the partners' different corporate cultures:

> "The key issues for the STAR ALLIANCE will be a common training and development of staff in order to support inter-organisational learning of partner companies, to build a strong alliance glue and network culture but most of all to create a shared customer obsessed alliance spirit."

> — *Thomas Sattelberger, Corporate Senior Vice President Executive Personnel and Human Resource Development*

Another vital question was how such closer integration within the alliance would affect the other Lufthansa companies. A common network strategy and cultural integration were inevitably connected to critical issues concerning branding and identity within the Lufthansa Group. The specialisation within the STAR ALLIANCE and particularly the planned extension of joint procurement could cause serious economic problems for some of Lufthansa's subsidiaries.

For example, the search for synergies within the STAR ALLIANCE included the joint development of IT-solutions. In April 1999 the Management Board of the STAR ALLIANCE signed a Memorandum of Intent concerning the formation of a central STAR ALLIANCE IT Organisation. The main task of this organisation would be to develop a common information system for all the STAR ALLIANCE partners. As a first step, a small team of about 20 people would work on this solution. They would be located in one place, thus eliminating the problems of working across different geographies and time-zones. For LH IT Services this development represented a vital threat for their main market.

> "Within the STAR ALLIANCE Management, United Airlines took responsibility for the EDP. Being a monolithic bloc, United Airline embodies its own IT department which is supposed to take charge of the entire STAR ALLIANCE IT-solution. The market is neglected in this case and Lufthansa IT Services is treated as an external provider, 'standing outside the door' together with 'real externals' such as IBM and Debis.[4] The policy of improving synergy within the STAR ALLIANCE can cost us our main client, Lufthansa. Then we will be completely out of business because other Alliances will not let us in either."

> — *Dr. Peter Franke, Chief Executive Lufthansa IT Services and Lufthansa Systems GmbH*

LUFTHANSA IN 2000

Simultaneous to the STAR ALLIANCE integration process, Lufthansa aimed to evolve from an airline company into an aviation group: the explicit goal was to become the leading provider of air transport services in the world. Lufthansa was trying to achieve this change through

- Growth through partnerships, not by dominance (STAR ALLIANCE),
- Tight cost management (Programm 15),
- Strengthening the company's revenue base, i.e., by expanding direct sales activities.

Lufthansa had identified seven major business areas in the Group and centrally co-ordinated their strategy development process.

STRATEGY PLANNING PROCESS

Strategic aims of the subsidiaries and their implementation priorities were established in a systematic, ongoing planning process, in which all the companies were involved. It rested on two pillars: the shaping of business area strategies, and the region oriented planning process (Appendix 7).

Business Area Strategies

In an annual strategy process the Lufthansa Group Executive Board and the Management Board of each Group company developed a strategic plan for the next five years. At the heart of this process was a structured, intensive dialog rather than detailed financial analysis. Results of this strategy meeting were the methodical guidelines and strategies for each *business area* (starting with "Passenger Service") for the next five years. This applied particularly to global expansion, the approach to customer requirements, market and competitive changes, and relations with other companies in the Group.

Regional Workshops

When the strategies of each Lufthansa company were defined, *regional workshops* followed. These focused on major regions such as Asia, Europe, etc. in order to take into account synergies between different business areas and to develop solutions for internal co-operation. As all Group companies provided either air transport services or services for airline companies, there was a lot of potential for co-ordinating activities of all the companies operating in certain markets. During these workshops core markets were identified, region specific aims were set and possible means were evaluated. The importance of regional strategies was expected to increase over time with the growing global presence of the Lufthansa Group.

THE SEVEN LH BUSINESS UNITS—STRATEGIC POSITIONS AND GROWTH

Lufthansa Passage (Passenger Service) was committed to the strategy of "growth through partnerships" and in 1999 already operated in a strong global network with its STAR ALLIANCE partners. Any of the other companies in the Lufthansa Group considering business ties with a competitor of Lufthansa Passage had to obtain prior approval from the Executive Board. However, alliances were not considered the appropriate growth strategy for all LH subsidiaries.

Each of the seven main companies was supposed to aim at achieving profitable, sustainable growth and a leading position in its world market segment (Appendix 8). In terms of their competitive positions, most of the business areas were already in leadership roles (Appendix 9). Nevertheless their strategies for growth and globalisation varied significantly.

Passenger Service—Lufthansa's Airline, Lufthansa CityLine and Team Lufthansa

In 1999 Lufthansa Passenger Service was by far the strongest business area within the Lufthansa Group. Consisting of *Lufthansa German Airlines* (DM 16.5 billion in revenues in 1998) and *Lufthansa CityLine* (DM 1.5 billion in 1998), "Passenger Service" contributed about 60% of the revenues of the Lufthansa Group (DM 18 billion in 1998).

While Lufthansa German Airlines was an operationally independent unit within the Group, Lufthansa CityLine was an autonomous fully-owned company. CityLine complemented the German and European route networks with scheduled passenger flights on aircraft of up to 80 seats. Coupled with its separate wage agreements, its cost structure allowed Lufthansa CityLine to serve routes that were not profitable for the actual airline unit (in Europe). In 1998 the number of passengers served by the overall business area increased by 14.5% from 3.8 million in 1997 to 4.4 million.

In addition to this, since 1996 new cooperative arrangements with selected regional carriers (Contact Air, Augsburg Airways, Cimber Air and Air Littoral) had led to

all of them flying under the brand name "*Team Lufthansa*" on a franchise basis. These carriers brought passengers to the main hubs of Frankfurt and Munich so that they could use connecting flights within the STAR ALLIANCE route net.

The overall strategic focus of the business area "Passenger Service" was long-term growth linked to strategic partner firms (Appendix 10).

Lufthansa Cargo AG

Since 1995 Lufthansa Cargo AG (the freight company) has been an autonomous 100% Lufthansa owned subsidiary with revenues of DM 3.9 billion in 1998 (1% decrease from 1997 revenues). In 1999 the strategic intent of LH Cargo AG was to become the leading logistic provider in the global market (Appendix 10). It was trying to realise this intent by following a mixed growth strategy. This included international alliances with some STAR ALLIANCE members, vertical integration through networking with forwarders in order to offer customers a complete door-to-door logistic chain, and finally, acquisitions. These strategies were linked to a fundamental change within the cargo business from a traditionally unintegrated transport provider (as a low involvement standard service) to an individualised complex solution supplier. Beyond pure freight transport, Lufthansa Cargo intended to offer solutions for complex global logistics requirements. This was an answer to the increasing demand for full service (door-to-door logistics) and the fast growth of the supply chain management market.

Therefore, future requirements in the Cargo business included a strong customer focus, branch orientation and the competence to build partnerships and alliances over the whole transport chain. These developments were linked to completely new needs concerning competencies and self-understanding: Cargo had never been (with the exception of a smaller cargo charter unit) an autonomous organisational unit before, but a "dependent child" of the passenger business ("Passage"). It was never used to direct customer contact and had never been a provider of complex logistics services.

"There is a need for a mental change. We have not done this sufficiently. Still there is this traditional Lufthansa 'Passage-driven' mentality while an innovative, creative and actively involved organisation is demanded. In 1996 we had a change campaign with different initiatives including an activity tent and numerous workshops that showed an effect but only for a short period. We need a sustaining change of the role and self-image of people. Cargo can not achieve this from its own resources. We need this human capital from outside through acquisitions or recruitment."

— **Michael Kraus, Vice President Global Account and Logistics Lufthansa Cargo AG**

C&N—Tourism

In 1999 Lufthansa's tourist activities were co-ordinated by a holding company named C&N Condor Neckermann Touristik AG. C&N was one of the top three providers of tourist services in Europe. C&N was the result of Condor's vertical integration strategy which led to its merger with NUR (NUR Touristic GmbH, Oberursel) in 1999. The strategic aim of C&N was to establish a high-performance travel group with a leading position in the European tourism market (Appendix 10).

Technical Services

LH Technik AG was a 100% owned Lufthansa subsidiary, which generated revenues of about DM 3.2 billion in 1998. With a market share of 8% in 1999, LH Technik was the global market leader in full-service aircraft maintenance and VIP cabin outfitting. Since its foundation in 1995, Lufthansa Technik AG had succeeded in strengthening its position in the global market. For Lufthansa Technik AG, external non-Lufthansa customers had traditionally played an important role and this importance continued to increase in the late 90s. In 1998, 47% of its revenues were derived from the external market.

In 1999 the strategic focus of Lufthansa Technik was on growth through co-operations with STAR ALLIANCE partners, entry into new markets (through product or service innovations and new facilities) and acquisitions (Appendix 10). For Lufthansa Technik it was difficult to build alliances because it could not develop a network independent from the STAR ALLIANCE. On the other hand it was almost impossible to build an alliance with STAR ALLIANCE partners because United still had a monolithic structure and did not consider "technical maintenance" as a business. For three years (1996–1999) several teams of the STAR ALLIANCE partners worked on potential options for co-operation, the executives of the technical department met on a regular basis (once every three months). The only outcome was the foundation of AirLiance Materials. In 1998, Lufthansa Technik, together with United Airlines and Air Canada, founded this company, which became a trade and service centre for spare parts in Chicago. It aimed at setting a counterweight against the increasing market presence of aircraft manufacturing corporations, which were trying to tie customers closer to themselves by providing maintenance and reconditioning services. They were not only becoming serious competitors for Lufthansa Technik but were also gaining an increasingly monopolistic position.

Catering

Lufthansa LSG Sky Chefs was the catering company of the Group. It generated revenues of DM 2.5 billion in 1998. Its vision was to make the leap from a catering company to a catering group. Other strategic goals included increasing its market share, developing a non-airline catering business such as services for petrol stations and service areas, and going public (Appendix 10).

Ground Services (GlobeGround)

With revenues of DM 0.9 billion in 1998 and a market share of 10% derived from its activities in 80 locations in 23 countries, GlobeGround was the Number One world-wide on the free accessible market for ground services. In 1999 this business was focused primarily on global expansion and strengthening of its market leadership (Appendix 10). GlobeGround had started by focusing on global branding and expanding its global presence through regional partnerships and acquisitions primarily in the US. In March 1999 GlobeGround acquired Hudson General Corp. With 5000 employees, Hudson was the leading provider of airport services in North America which accounted for 44% share of the ground services market world-wide.

Information Technology

Lufthansa Systems GmbH offered IT-based products and services for airlines and companies in transport, travel and tourism industries. In 1998 it generated revenues of DM 0.7 billion. Only 20% of its revenues came from business with external non-Lufthansa customers. In 1999 all IT-related Lufthansa companies formed the business area "Lufthansa IT Services" with Lufthansa Systems as its core. The world-wide market position of Lufthansa IT Services was considered to be expandable. The strategic focus of Lufthansa IT Services was the development of integrated IT activities in the business unit and international expansion through partnerships (Appendix 10).

INTERNATIONALISATION AND BRANDING OF THE LUFTHANSA SUBSIDIARIES

In 1999 not only the growth strategies of the Lufthansa companies varied. Differences could also be seen in their degrees of internationalisation and in their relationships to the brand "Lufthansa": the patterns of the Passenger Service—the airline and traditional core of Lufthansa—and the new emerging decentralised cores of the aviation group varied immensely. Being a member of the STAR ALLIANCE meant that for Lufthansa Passage (Passenger Service), the development could be seen as a "renationalisation" process, especially when taking the Landlord concept into account. In contrast to this, GlobeGround and LSG Sky Chefs had a business linked to local needs and local infrastructures of the respective regions. This not only implied the need for an international orientation and for local integration in each market, but also created a potential tension with regard to the use of the Lufthansa brand. Therefore the name "GlobeGround" was deliberately chosen as a "Lufthansa-neutral" name.

The business characteristics of Lufthansa Technik AG and Lufthansa IT Services were very different. These technically dominated services were less local and demanded a global strategy that was closely associated to the brand Lufthansa, which was meant to indicate competence, high quality and experience in the airline industry.

> *"Lufthansa stands for German values such as preciseness, technical reliability, high quality or expertise which are important positive indicators of our business. The 'Germanness' of Lufthansa is of direct use for our image while this can be the other way round for customer services, which demand more 'non-German' traits such as friendliness or modesty. The name 'Lufthansa' opens doors. We will always be 'Lufthanseats.'"*
>
> *— Dr. Peter Franke, Chief Executive*
> *Lufthansa IT Services and Lufthansa*
> *Systems GmbH*

WHAT DID LUFTHANSA LEARN FROM THE CHANGE?

INVOLVEMENT OF PEOPLE

During the turnaround Lufthansa had developed a certain style of involving people in strategic business processes and networks that was maintained and later supported by the Lufthansa School of Business (founded in 1998). Furthermore, Town Meetings had become a fixed element of the Lufthansa dialogue culture.

> *"We learned to count on people and we got to know that the same people can behave very differently in different situations."*
>
> *— Wolfgang Mayrhuber, CEO Lufthansa*
> *Technik AG and former member*
> *of the OPS Team*

> *"A crisis can split people into losers and winners. It challenges people and leads some to personal excellence because they are pushed to their limits and in that process they learn to overcome themselves."*
>
> *— Ralf Teckentrup, Executive Vice*
> *President Network and Controlling,*
> *Lufthansa German Airlines*

> *"Since the crisis, employees are much more concerned about what happens in the company, they are more informed and they feel more responsible for general business processes."*
>
> *— Jürgen Raps, Senior Vice President*
> *Flight Operations and Chief Pilot*

WEAK SIGNALS, FUNDAMENTAL PROBLEM SOLVING AND STRATEGY PROCESS

Through the experience of being "surprised" by a crisis that the company almost did not survive, Lufthansa developed a sense for weak signals and a specific way for "deeper" problem solving:

> *"Today we handle problems in a different way. We are practising active management. This means that we go deeper, we approach problems and try to solve them instead of being satisfied with superficial façade-solutions."*
>
> *— Dr. Peter Franke, Chief Executive*
> *Lufthansa IT Services and Lufthansa*
> *Systems GmbH*

> *"We have learned in this process that there is nothing that you cannot change."*
>
> *— Dr. Peter Hach, Senior Vice President*
> *Corporate Controlling*

Moreover Lufthansa had gained the competence of systematic strategy thinking and planning.

> *"Before the change process, people were just doing their jobs. Since the crisis there has been a strategic consciousness and a systematic planning of future actions on a high level."*
>
> *— Dr. Peter Hach, Senior Vice President*
> *Corporate Controlling*

LUFTHANSA'S "CHANGED SOUL"

> *"Through this process we have improved customer orientation, service orientation, cost consciousness, and thinking in business terms. Before the restructuring you were almost not allowed to use the word 'profit.' Now there is a pronounced market-oriented thinking and acting."*
>
> *— Jürgen Weber, Chairman and CEO,*
> *Deutsche Lufthansa AG*

> *"Lufthansa has come a long way. We try no longer to treat our customers as petitioners, with the proverbial arrogance we were once famous for. (. . .) We no longer consider the selling of tickets as an act of state but as a skill that we will do better than our competition. (. . .) And last but not least, we have learned to set ourselves ambitious goals and to achieve them. But old habits die hard."[5]*

PRESENT AND FUTURE CHALLENGES (IN 2000)

OPERATIONAL EXCELLENCE

In 1999 one of Lufthansa's most serious challenges was to achieve radical improvements in operational areas such as punctuality, luggage safety, waiting periods, technical reliability and telephone availability. In order to improve the situation for Lufthansa's customers, Jürgen Weber announced a quality offensive at the annual general meeting in June 1999. "Operational Excellence," a project with ambitious goals and significant resources was targeted to establish a basis for drastic improvements in punctuality and quality. The three-year program was expected to work with similar methods and persistence as its predecessor Programm 15.

MANAGEMENT OF THE ALLIANCE

With the arrival of network-versus-network competition rather than the historical airline versus airline battles, the key challenge was to manage the STAR ALLIANCE as a whole. This raised questions such as how to establish the network in the market, how to form a "STAR ALLIANCE" brand, how to create a network identity, and how to handle network borders. A problem linked to this was the inner structure of STAR ALLIANCE which had to cope with the challenges of managing the mental change, getting used to the mechanism of "competition," and shaping the different relationships within the ALLIANCE.

> "STAR ALLIANCE is an organisational innovation. A global network of such flexibility and fluidity coupled with a good balance between integration and differentiation, but also between profit-sharing and trust, did not exist in that large scale dimension before. One optional scenario of the inner structure of the STAR ALLIANCE is a further exploitation of the various relationship intensities between different partner companies. For example it is possible that Lufthansa, SAS and Singapore Airlines use their very intense relation for developing a global cargo integrator. The emergence of specialised sub-networks and corresponding services within the STAR ALLIANCE and a potential differentiation between core members and associates would imply productive tension as well as a lot of business opportunities."

— ***Thomas Sattelberger, Corporate Senior Vice President Executive Personnel and Human Resource Development***

PRESERVING IDENTITY

One vital issue connected to the alliance strategy on the one hand and to the development to an aviation group on the other hand was the preservation of the "Lufthansa" identity. The question was how Lufthansa could become an integrated part of a strong global airline network and at the same time form an integrated aviation group in which the Passenger Service was only one part among others.

> "It is important to preserve the Lufthansa brand under the roof of the STAR ALLIANCE."

— ***Jürgen Weber, Chairman and CEO, Deutsche Lufthansa AG***

> "We have to define what the label 'Lufthansa' means—to us and to others."

— ***Dr. Michael Heuser, Head Lufthansa School of Business***

> "There often is a misunderstanding that Lufthansa Group equals Lufthansa which equals Passage (Passenger Service). Everybody learned this for years and this is the old shared identity."

— ***Dr. Hans Schmitz, Chief Executive of the Lufthansa Technik Logistik GmbH***

Developing a "new" identity demanded defining or developing internal relationships. A core element of the aviation group strategy was a system of clear customer-supplier-relationships between the companies within the Group. These agreements were supposed to be based on market conditions with the stipulation that the Group companies be conceded a "last call."

> "One of the problems of increasing importance throughout the Lufthansa Group is the lack of relations management. We have not yet developed the customer-provider relationships that are necessary for a market-based internal coordination. Internal customers do not behave like normal customers yet. They demand conditions they would never dare to ask for in the external market."

— ***Dr. Peter Franke, Chief Executive Lufthansa IT Services and Lufthansa Systems GmbH***

PRESERVING CONSCIOUSNESS OF THE CRISIS AND OPENNESS FOR CHANGE

Lufthansa's sharpened consciousness for weak signals, costs, etc. and the openness for change caused by the crisis were clearly very important for the record performance in 1998 and 1999. One challenge was how to preserve these attitudes in good times.

> "Lufthansa has to continue in its success path and not become arrogant or practice cost cutting indiscriminately. The most difficult part is to keep people motivated now when the pressure has eased off."

— ***Jürgen Weber, Chairman and CEO, Deutsche Lufthansa AG***

SHAPING THE FUTURE — LUFTHANSA SCHOOL OF BUSINESS

To keep the "sense of urgency" for change and transformation alive, to form a cultural and knowledge platform for the Lufthansa Group and to drive learning and experience along the strategic core processes, Lufthansa established the Lufthansa School of Business at a corporate level in April 1998.

The school's philosophy and activities extended far beyond traditional approaches of training and development. Its task was to tighten the links between strategy, organisational and individual development in order to support the company's key priorities for transformation and future performance.

Thomas Sattelberger, since July 1999 Executive Vice President Product and Service, who was credited as the conceptual architect of the Lufthansa School of Business, explains the particular advantage for Lufthansa as follows:

"In flexible organisations like Lufthansa and even more in a fluid alliance and network organisation like the STAR ALLIANCE, a mental cultural core is necessary. When there is almost no formal system of procedures and regulations there is a need for a mental integration. Like the rock in the river shaping the water, this is one of the central tasks of the Lufthansa School of Business."

LUFTHANSA SCHOOL OF BUSINESS EXPLICITLY FOLLOWS FIVE GOALS:

- Effectively and efficiently supporting key strategic issues of the Lufthansa Group
- Building and tying intellectual capital to the company
- Linking academic expertise and experiences of partner companies to Lufthansa business practice and its needs
- Fostering and developing a corporate leadership and performance culture
- Creating options for personal development and challenges

Within a demanding range of programs the Lufthansa School of Business entered into close world-wide "learning partnerships." Almost all programs—from Master's degree programs to non-degree top management programs—were designed, run and evaluated with global companies to learn with and from the best ("Benchlearning"). By building close relationships with some well-selected academic institutions, the Lufthansa School of Business deliberately avoided concentrating its academic relationships, preferring instead to build a network of leading business schools and universities (among them the London Business School, INSEAD, McGill in Montreal, Indian Institute of Management in Bangalore and Hitotshubashi University in Tokyo).

Initiatives launched by the Lufthansa School of Business included shaping of the so-called "transformation and change networks" of several hundred young potentials or experienced managers. These programs usually lasted 12 months in total. What was characteristic and remarkable about them was their specific composition and setting: Processes of individual learning were directly linked to strategic development and changes in business practices.

"Lufthansa School of Business creates value by the change it initiates for both the individual and the organisation 'Lufthansa.' Our action learning networks contribute not only to the required mental change, they also show visible innovation results."

— **Dr. Michael Heuser, Head Lufthansa School of Business**

Networks "Explorer 21" and the "Climb Program"

"*Explorers 21*" challenges well-selected young professionals to become change leaders early in their careers. Each session consists of 210 Explorers. The "*Climb Program*" is an action learning network of 160 managers world-wide.

The overall goals of these programs include:

- Initiating and fostering mental change
- Creating transformation platforms in critical scale and range
- Delivering significant contribution for putting leadership into action
- Producing visible results and transfers
- Offering self-assessment and benchmarks and
- Forming knowledge and change networks across and within Lufthansa businesses.

Both programs start with a self-assessment based on Lufthansa's leadership tools such as the Lufthansa Leadership Compass (Appendix 11) and the Lufthansa Leadership Feedback (Lufthansa's 360° feedback). During the programs, participants visit excellent companies all over the world to analyse their areas of excellence and to work out business recommendations for Lufthansa. At various times, all network members come together in congresses to discuss findings and recommendations with the Lufthansa management and to make concrete goal agreements.

Sponsors at management levels and peer support are considered vital components of the learning processes. The participants are encouraged to negotiate changes in their job assignments so that they can follow through with implementing the changes they propose.

> "Making recommendations and agreements reality becomes part of the line responsibility again. The participants are supposed to become the change agents for the initiatives including the implementation of their recommendations in their divisions. The specific advantage of these projects is that there is not just a single person in charge of the change process but also a large action network of supportive individuals with the same experience, desire, involvement and commitment to innovation."
>
> — *Dr. Michael Heuser, Head*
> *Lufthansa School of Business*

Jürgen Weber put the value of the Lufthansa School of Business for the entire Lufthansa Group in these words:

> "Our business requires a global mindset and networking capabilities across borders. These capabilities can't be developed with quick-fix solutions. Our Lufthansa School of Business supports our business and strategic objectives. It creates value by building intellectual capital that is difficult to imitate by others."
>
> — **Jürgen Weber, Chairman and CEO,**
> **Deutsche Lufthansa AG**

APPENDIX 1 TEN-YEAR STATISTICS 1989–1998

OPERATIONAL RATIOS[1]		1998	1997	1996	1995	1994	1993	1992	1991	1990	1989
Profit-revenue ratio (profit from ordinary activities[3] revenue)	percent	11.0	8.1	3.3	3.8	3.9	0.4	−4.3	3.5	0.2	4.3
Total return on investment (profit from ordinary activities[3] plus interest on debt/total assets)	percent	13.0	10.9	4.9	5.7	6.3	3.4	−1.1	−0.7	2.2	5.9
Return on equity (net profit/loss for the period[4]/ capital and reserves[5])	[8]percent	22.1	20.5	10.4	21.1[12]	7.4	−3.1	−13.0	−11.7	0.4	2.5
Return on equity (profit from ordinary activities[3]/ capital and reserves[5])		38.4	33.2	12.8	15.3	17.9	2.6	−24.3	−15.4	0.9	12.8
Equity ratio (capital and reserves[5] total assets)	[8]percent	26.9	23.1	28.6	26.8	22.5	16.7	17.9	22.8	29.0	35.8
Net indebtedness—total assets ratio	percent	6.0	10.2	7.7	10.8	19.8	33.6	36.2	33.5	27.5	17.4
Internal financing ratio	[8]percent										
(cash flow[7]/capital expenditure)	[8]percent	91.2	165.2	122.8	181.8	121.3	110.9	59.8	58.1	43.1	80.2
Net indebtedness—cash flow[7] ratio	percent	39.6	59.3	58.7	79.6	141.9	303.1	383.2	302.1	253.5	116.2
Revenue efficiency (cash flow[7]/revenue)	percent	16.1	18.1	11.7	2.5	13.4	10.9	9.3	11.0	0.9	14.1
Net working capital (current assets less short-term debt)	DM billion	−0.3	0.3	3.3	2.4	2.5	2.6	1.5	1.7	1.6	1.6
PERSONNEL RATIOS											
Annualised average employee total		54,867	55,520	57,999	57,586	58,044	60,514	63,645	61,791	57,567	51,942
Revenue/employee	DM	412,886	389,226	359,708	345,577	324,507	293,002	270,862	260,565	250,960	251,344
Staff costs/revenue	percent	24.8	25.6	27.6	27.1	27.9	30.6	33.8	32.4	33.0	33.1

OUTPUT DATA LUFTHANSA GROUP[3]

		1998	1997	1996	1995	1994	1993	1992	1991	1990	1989
Total available tonne-kilometres	millions	20.133,6	19,324.6	20,697.5	19,983.2	18,209.8	17,123.4	16,369.8	14,292.2	13,679.6	12,462.3
Total revenue tonne-kilometres	millions	14,170.4	13,620.9	14,532.8	14,063.1	12,890.0	11,768.4	10,724.8	9,376.2	9,118.5	8,580.8
Overall load factor	percent	70.4	70.5	70.2	70.4	70.8	68.7	65.5	65.6	66.7	68.9
Available seat-kilometres	millions	102,354.4	98,750.0	116,183.1	112,147.2	103,876.9	98,295.3	94,138.1	81,661.8	75,504.6	65,058.5
Revenue passenger-kilometres	millions	74,668.4	70,581.4	81,716.3	79,085.3	72,750.9	67,017.5	61,273.8	52,344.2	50,685.1	44,669.4
Passenger load factor	percent	73.0	71.5	70.3	70.5	70.0	68.2	65.1	64.1	67.1	68.7
Passengers carried	percent	40.5	37.2	41.4	40.7	37.7	35.6	33.7	29.5	26.6	23.4
Paid passenger tonne-kilometres	millions	7,474.1	7,071.1	8,084.8	7,828.4	7,202.4	6,636.6	5,882.3	5,026.6	4,874.8	4,296.3
Freight/mail	t	1,702,733	1,703,657	1,684,729	1,576,210	1,435,636	1,263,698	1,197,870	1,125,168	1,056,526	1,004,600
Freight/mail tonne-kilometres	millions	6,696.3	6,548.0	6,448.0	6,234.7	5,687.6	5,131.8	4,842.5	4,349.6	4,243.7	4,284.3
Number of flights		618,615	596,456	595,120	580,108	536,687	501,139	492,606	431,102	358,522	310,882
Flight kilometres	millions	636.4	614.6	720.5	659.0	620.9	561.1	598.7	516.0	470.0	412.7
Aircraft utilisation		1,010,897	963,675	1,000,723	1,070,238	992,425[14]	973,504	964,776	835,000	817,604	660,431
Aircraft in service		302	286	314	314	308	301	302	275	220	197

[1] As from the 1997 financial year, the financial statements are prepared according to the International Accounting Standards. Thus, previous years' figures are not comparable
[2] Up to 1996 profit from operating activities
[3] Up to 1995 before net changes in special items with an equity portion
[4] Up to 1996 before withdrawal from/transfer to retained earnings and before minority interest
[5] Up to 1995 including the equity portion of special items and up to 1996 including minority interest
[6] Up to 1995 including the debt portion of special items
[7] Calculated as net cash from operating activites as per cash flow statement, up to 1996 financial cash flow
[8] As from the 1995 financial year, the special items with an equity portion set up in individual company financial statements for tax purposes are not included in the consolidated financial statements according to the HGB. The special items brought forward from the 1994 financial year were released in 1995 as extraordinary income amounting to DM 879 million. This additional income was allocated to retained earnings. As a result of this reclassification, earnings before taxes, the net profit for the year, retained earnings and equity (including the equity portion of special items) were all shown with correspondingly higher totals
[9] In 1996 the face value of the shares was diluted to DM 5; previous years' figures were adjusted
[10] DM 1.15 on preference shares
[11] Only guaranteed dividend on preference shares
[12] Net profit less extraordinary result
[13] As from the 1997 financial year, Condor is no longer included
[14] Method of calculation changed

APPENDIX 2
LUFTHANSA'S
ORGANISATIONAL
STRUCTURE IN 1991

Chief Executive Officer

- Chief Executive Finance
- Chief Executive Personnel
- Chief Executive Marketing and Sales
- Chief Executive Technical
- Chief Executive Flight Operations

APPENDIX 3
THE LUFTHANSA
GROUP IN 1999

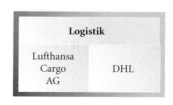

CEO Chief Executive Finance
Chief Executive Personnel

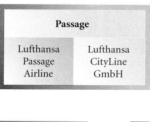

Passage

| Lufthansa Passage Airline | Lufthansa CityLine GmbH |

Logistik

| Lufthansa Cargo AG | DHL |

Technik

Lufthansa Technik AG

AMECO

Catering

LSG Sky Chefs

IT

Lufthansa Systems GmbH
Amadeus
Start

Ground Services

GlobeGround GmbH

Touristik

C&N Touristic AG (50%)

AIRLINE	REVENUES IN BILLION DM	EMPLOYEES	AIRCRAFT	DESTINATIONS	PASSENGERS IN MILLIONS
United Airlines	29.2	92,000	576	257	84
Lufthansa	22.8	58,000	326	271	44.5
All Nippon Airways	14.3	15,000	143	64	40
SAS	8.6	22,000	178	100	21
Varig	5.7	18,000	87	122	10
Thai Airways	5.2	25,000	74	73	15
Air Canada	4.3	24,000	243	124	17.5
Ansett Australia	3.5	17,000	72	95	13.5
Air New Zealand	2.8	10,000	73	69	3

APPENDIX 5
HISTORY OF THE
STAR ALLIANCE

HISTORY OF THE STAR ALLIANCE

1959	SAS and Thai Airways found Thai Airways International
October 1992	Air Canada and United Airlines sign a co-operation letter of intent
October 1993	Lufthansa and United Airlines build a strategic alliance including code-share-flights
June 1994	Lufthansa and United Airlines operate first code-share-flights
May 1995	Lufthansa and SAS agree upon an extensive strategic alliance, including code-share-flights. In the same time United Airlines and Air Canada extend their offer
June 1995	Lufthansa and Thai sign a code-share-agreement
September 1995	United Airlines and SAS sign a co-operation letter of intent starting in April 1996
October 1995	Lufthansa and Thai offer first code-share-flights
February 1996	Lufthansa and SAS start joint flights between Germany and Scandinavia
March 1996	Lufthansa and Air Canada become strategic partners
May 1996	The US Department of Transportation (DOT) frees Lufthansa and United Airlines from the American competition law (Antitrust-Immunity)
June 1996	Lufthansa and Air Canada start joint flights between Germany and Canada
October 1996	SAS and Air Canada announce the signature of a strategic alliance
November 1996	Lufthansa, SAS and United Airlines receive the trilateral Antitrust-Immunity from the DOT
May 1997	Foundation of the STAR ALLIANCE in Frankfurt with the members, Air Canada, Lufthansa, SAS, United Airlines and Thai Airways
October 1997	Varig becomes sixth member of the STAR ALLIANCE
April 1999	Air New Zealand and Ansett Australia join the STAR ALLIANCE
September 1999	All Nippon Airways becomes member of the STAR ALLIANCE

APPENDIX 6 THE BIG FOUR

Dates and figures of the major airline alliances 1998 or 1997, Wirtschaftswoche, No. 14, 1.4.1999, pp. 122ff.

ALLIANCE	MEMBERS	TYPE OF CO-OPERATION	MANAGEMENT	REVENUES IN BILLION US$	DESTINATIONS/ COUNTRIES	AIRCRAFTS	EMPLOYEES IN 1000	PASSENGERS IN MIO
Star Alliance	Lufthansa, Air Canada, Air New Zealand, Ansett Australia, SAS, Thai Airways, United Airlines, Varig, All Nippon Airways, * Singapore Airlines*	Mostly joint-sale, LH/SAS joint ventures	Management Development Board (MDB) and working committees Determination of the Alliance strategy by 6 members of the MDB elected by airline presidents and responsible for specific areas of strategic importance	49.9****	720 destinations in 118 countries****	1629****	266****	212****
Oneworld	British Airways, American Airlines, Canadian Airlines, Cathay Pacific, Iberia, Qantas, Finnair, Japan Airlines,* Deutsche BA**	Planned: AA/BA revenue sharing on North Atlantic routes	1 Managing Director as Direct Report for AA/BA chairmen, plus integrated full-time well resourced management teams	44.5***	680 destinations in 143 countries	1783***	255	206***
Qualiflyer	Swissair, Austrian Airlines, Air Littoral, AOM, Crossair, Lauda Air, Sabena, Tap Air Portugal, Turkish Airlines, Tyrolean, Delta Air Lines**			27.1***	338 destinations in 100 countries	1029***	118***	153***
Wings	KLM, Alitalia, Northwest Airlines, Kenya Airways, Braathens, S.A.F.E., Eurowings, Transavia, Martinair			35.0	680 destinations in 100 countries	1200	101	182

* Membership planned/data not taken into account, ** Associated society, *** 1997, **** including new members Air New Zealand and Ansett Australia

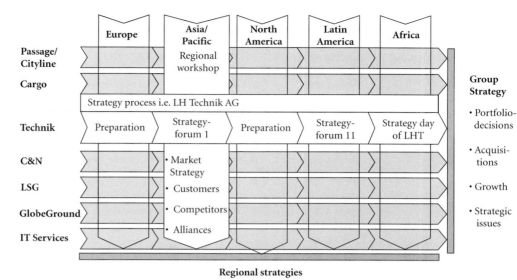

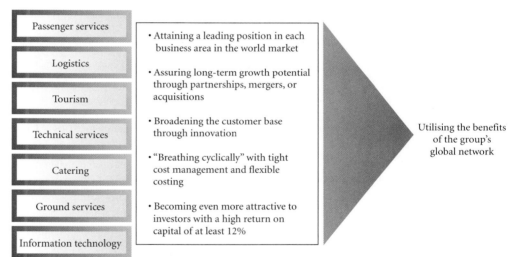

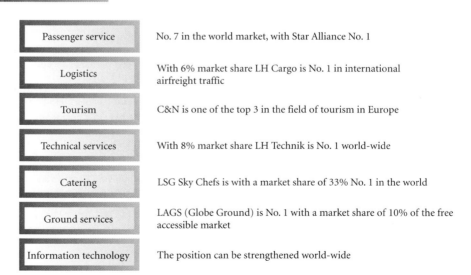

BUSINESS AREA	STRATEGIC FOCUS AND AIMS
Passenger services	**Long-term growth linked to strategic partner firms** ■ Completion of the STAR ALLIANCE and the development of a European competence with regional partner companies ■ Extension of target customer management ■ Reduplication of direct sales until 2003 ■ Simplification of ground and customer processes ■ Ensuring capacity expansions at German airports through strategic partnerships ■ Strengthening quality leadership
Lufthansa Cargo AG	**Becoming the leading logistic service provider on a global market** ■ Completion of the global Cargo alliance ■ Building and expanding the business partnership program with freight forwarders ■ Time-definite services ■ Providing customer oriented integrated solutions for transport and logistics ■ Development of new sales channels (e.g., Internet/virtual malls) ■ Building a global network with partners
C&N— Tourism	**A leading position in the European tourist market** ■ Becoming a powerful, vertically integrated tourism company ■ Concentrating on the most important European markets and becoming No. 1 or 2 in these markets ■ Market leadership in all important segments—disproportionate growth in the premium segment ■ Developing an integrated capacity and yield management ■ Entering new sales channels (e.g., Internet)
Technical services	**Growth** ■ Extension of co-operations with STAR ALLIANCE partners as a counterweight to an increased market presence of aircraft technique manufacturers (such as GE) ■ Entering new markets through global presence and extension of array of products ■ Development of new production platforms (facilities) primarily in Asia and North America ■ Ensuring growth through acquisition and investment
Catering	**Becoming a large catering group and strengthening the global market leadership** ■ Increasing market share until 2003 ■ Development of non-airline catering such as services for petrol stations and service areas ■ 10% revenue share with non-airline catering ■ Going public
Ground services	**Strengthening the market leadership combined with a global expansion strategy** ■ International market presence through global branding as GlobeGround and global Key Account Management ■ Global expansion through regional partnerships with strong local partners ■ Implementing a strategic partnership with Frankfurt airport company
Information technology	**Integration of IT activities in a business unit and international expansion through partnerships** ■ LH becomes a global and integrated provider of IT with a focal point in travel and transport ■ Global expansion through co-operations and acquisitions ■ Bundling and organising IT activities in five business units (reservation systems, infrastructure, airline services, customer services and channel services) ■ Development of the brand "LH IT Services"

Lufthansa's Leadership Compass
"Passion for Business"

Entrepreneurial Leadership
- Vision and Strategy
- Competitiveness and Focus on Customers
- Striving for Profits
- Accountability
- Decisiveness and Risk Taking
- Management of Innovation and Change

Breakthrough Problem Solving
- Management of Complexity
- Interdisciplinary and Conceptual Thinking
- Systematic and Goal Driven Approach
- Intuition and Creativity

Winning Others
- Building Relationships
- Straight Talk
- Influencing and Networking across Borders
- Persuasiveness and Impact
- Assertiveness and Action
- Managing Conflicts

Leading People
- Concern for People
- Leading by Goals
- Developing People and Talents
- Leading in Virtual Teams and Structures

Attitude and Drive
- Striving for Success
- Self-Confidence and Courage
- Ethical Values and Integrity
- Stress Resistance
- Self-Reflection

International Business Competencies
- Professional Know-How
- Conceptual Skills
- Intercultural Competence

The London Free Press (A)—Strategic Change

Phil McLeod had been appointed as the new editor of the London Free Press (LFP) in November, 1987, with a mandate to make changes. Like most other North American daily newspapers, the LFP had been gradually losing readership, and its share of advertising revenues in the community was shrinking. Despite its ability to remain profitable, McLeod thought that it was not living up to its potential, especially since it was the only daily newspaper in London. He feared that there were ominous signs of a continuing decline in market share, which could only mean still lower profits in the future.

McLeod had been hired from the Toronto Star and put in charge of LFP's newsroom and editorial department to do whatever was necessary to reverse this trend. Now, in 1991, he wondered if it would be possible to stop the slow decline of the newspaper or if its shrinkage was an inevitable consequence of broader trends in the information industry and Canadian society.

THE NEWSPAPER INDUSTRY

Newspapers obtained revenues from two sources: from readers, who paid for papers through regular subscriptions or on single-copy basis, and from advertising clients, who hoped to expose their messages to as many members of a community as possible. Conceptually newspapers could be seen as a medium that attracted readers with its editorial content, and in turn delivered those readers to advertisers as potential purchasers.

Advertising sales accounted for about three-quarters of a typical paper's total revenues, but these amounts were closely linked to the paid circulation of the paper. Advertisers' willingness to pay a given rate depended on the size of the audience they could expect to reach with their messages. The price advertisers paid for space in a newspaper was usually based on a combination of 1) total circulation, and 2) penetration, expressed in terms of the percentage of total households reached.

McLeod saw newspapers as having two basic functions: gathering information, and packaging it for resale. Information came in two varieties: public "news"; and private, or advertising information. The news information-gathering function could be further broken down by source:

1. A paper's own reporters gathering local news.
2. Staff reporters responsible for news from distant locales. Many larger newspapers had "bureaux" staffed by their

Detlev Nitsch prepared this case under the supervision of Professor Mary Crossan solely to provide material for class discussion. The authors do not intend to illustrate either effective or ineffective handling of a managerial situation. The authors may have disguised certain names and other identifying information to protect confidentiality.

own people in important cities around Canada and the rest of the world, so they could have proprietary access to any information these reporters uncovered.

3. Exchange arrangements through the corporate umbrella—for example, LFP had a contractual link with Southam News that enabled it, for a fee, to tap into this large organization's worldwide network of news sources. This also allowed papers access to news developed initially for other media.

4. Wire services. Canadian Press (CP), American Press (AP), and Reuters were examples of news agencies that existed solely to provide news on a fee basis to anyone who was willing to pay for it. In some cases (CP for example), the agency was a co-operative owned by newspapers.

The LFP was fairly typical of daily newspapers in that approximately 60 per cent of its space was allocated to advertising (paid messages), with the "newshole," or editorial content, occupying the rest. Of the 40 per cent of the available space dedicated to the newshole, 60 per cent was purchased from wire services or other sources. McLeod estimated that approximately 30 per cent of his $10-million editorial budget was spent on purchased news; one-third of the balance was devoted to re-working or repackaging these stories for publication, and the rest was spent on maintaining the LFP's in-house news-gathering apparatus.

As advertisers became more sophisticated, they were no longer merely interested in a newspaper's raw circulation figures, but rather in its ability to reach those most likely to purchase their products. Electronic media in particular were often able to target very narrow market segments with a high degree of precision. Television programming was being geared to ever-smaller segments of the population, as cable and satellite proliferation expanded the choices available to consumers. With sophisticated demographic market research data, programmers could produce and schedule shows designed to appeal to specific groups, and have relatively high confidence that their target would be reached. This was attractive to advertisers because they could spend their advertising budgets more efficiently, avoiding messages sent to members of the community who were not potential customers. In contrast, daily newspapers were seen as a rather blunt instrument, with potentially broad mass-market coverage but little ability to ensure that a given message had reached its target segment.

PAST PERFORMANCE, FUTURE OUTLOOK

Newspaper companies had enjoyed a very profitable history in North America: at the beginning of the 1980s they boasted a median 9.6 per cent profit margin, compared to a median of less than five per cent for Fortune 500

EXHIBIT 1 YEAR-END NEWSPAPER RESULTS
1991 Stock Market Performance

	GAIN (**)
A.H. Belo (NYSE–BLC)	30.4%
Dow Jones (NYSE–DJ)	23.7%
Gannett (NYSE–GCI)	11.4%
Knight Ridder (NYSE–KRI)	17.7%
McClatchy (NYSE–MNI)	21.9%
Media General (ASE–MEGA)	17.2%
Multmedia (NASDAQ–MMEDC)	9.8%
New York Times (ASE–NYTA)	68.8%
Times Mirror (NYSE–TMC)	47.5%
Tribune (NYSE–TRB)	37.7%
Washington Post (NYSE–WPO)	23.5%
Average Gain	28.6%
Standard & Poors	
– 400 Industrials	6.2%
– 500 Composite	10.3%

Source: Company Reports, Alex Brown & Sons estimates

Industrials. Even though, depending on commodity prices, newsprint accounted for anywhere from 20 to 25 per cent of total costs, newspapers' return on sales ranged from 14 to 18 per cent, while industrials averaged 6 per cent. In 1991, U.S. newspaper companies enjoyed a resurgence in the stock market, outperforming index averages by a large margin (Exhibit 1). This followed several years of sluggish performance during which consolidation and downsizing were the norm in the industry.

Despite this evidence of good performance potential, there were several signs that indicated a long-run trend to declining circulation, reduced revenues and smaller profit margins. Exhibit 2 shows the decline in profitability of a typical North American newspaper company.

Newspapers' level of penetration, or market share as a percentage of households reached, was dropping for news-

EXHIBIT 2 THOMSON—NORTH AMERICAN NEWSPAPERS ($ million)

	1988	1989	1990	1991
Revenues	981	1081	1158	1142
Operating Profit	306	317	282	228
Operating Margin	31.2%	29.3%	24.4%	20.0%

Source: Company Reports, Alex Brown & Sons estimates

papers all across North America. In the U.S., 124 copies of daily newspapers were sold for every 100 households during the 1950s. By the 1970s, the comparable figure was 77, with the drop attributable in part to a decline in the number of two-newspaper households. The Canada-wide circulation growth rate, at 1.7 per cent, was also well below the growth rates of the adult population (2.1 per cent) and of households (3.0 per cent) during the 1970s, even though it still outpaced the growth of total population (1.0 per cent). Similar trends seemed to apply to London, where McLeod had noted that the LFP was losing about a percentage point per year in penetration, down to below 60 per cent in the early 1990s.

While the total circulation of daily newspapers was still increasing, other indicators such as average daily circulation and penetration levels suggested that newspapers were losing readers, and were thus becoming less attractive as an advertising medium. As recently as 1973, daily newspapers had attracted 30.5 per cent of total Canadian advertising expenditures, compared to television in that year with 13.4 per cent. In fact, until 1977, daily newspapers held a larger share of ad revenues than radio, television, and weekly newspapers combined. But the long-run trend since 1972 showed a gradual decline in the newspapers' share, while television and other media continued to gather strength. Daily newspapers still had the largest share of total advertising revenues, but this share was gradually shrinking (Table 1).

Breaking total advertising revenues down into national and local categories yielded further insights into the differing strengths of the competing media. For example, in 1973/74 daily newspapers received 19.8 per cent of their advertising revenues from national accounts. The corresponding figure for television was 73.9 per cent, which shifted upward to 75.3 per cent by 1980, while the dailies'

proportion fell to 18.7 per cent. This suggested that newspapers' heavy reliance on local retail and classified advertising was, if anything, increasing.

DEMOGRAPHICS OF READERSHIP: LONG-RUN IMPLICATIONS

A 1986 study of newspaper readers showed that most readers were in the over-35 age category, and that 75 per cent of people in their 20s did not regularly read the paper. In the past, there had been some support for the notion that newspaper reading habits grew as individuals aged. Cross-sectional studies had turned up much the same data decade after decade, as young non-readers in an early study evolved into 50-year-old newspaper aficionados 30 years later.

But McLeod feared that times had changed, and that these non-readers would be difficult to turn into loyal newspaper customers in the future. The current crop of young adults were the first who had been raised in an age in which television was accepted as a legitimate news source. Unlike previous generations, these people believed and trusted what they saw on the small screen, and did not feel the need to see it in print. The public's familiarity and comfort level with television had grown over time, aided by the medium's presence on the scene of historic events such as the 1963 assassination of U.S. President Kennedy, and the first moon landing in 1969. Also, McLeod admitted that television had proved competent in areas where newspapers were once thought to have a competitive advantage: background and analysis. Network news and news-only cable TV channels were increasingly supplying high-quality, in-depth coverage of important events, with a timeliness and sense of immediacy that newspapers could not match.

Television's new-found strengths might make it impossible for newspapers to attract the current group of younger people. This meant that the expected shift in preference, from television to newspapers as people aged, might not take place this time. Thus the old assumption that readership would stay more or less constant over time appeared to rely on a 'no-change' scenario which did not fit reality.

Some evidence suggested that, by 1991, newspaper readership was recovering from its precipitous decline. Gross circulation was actually up by 32 per cent from 15 years before, while population had only risen 16 per cent. Also, the proportion of Canadian adults reading newspapers had increased from 63 per cent to 68.5 per cent. However, McLeod thought that these numbers were misleading because they focused on overall total circulation instead of daily averages, and they ignored the fact that new newspaper formats had begun to penetrate the market. The gross circulation statistic compared present total readership with comparable figures before the "tabloid era" in many major

TABLE 1 CANADIAN ADVERTISING EXPENDITURES PER CENT SHARE OF TOTAL, BY MEDIUM

MEDIUM	1973	1989
		(Estimates)
Daily Newspapers	30.5	22.8
Catalogues, Direct Mail	20.6	21.9
Television	13.4	15.6
Radio	10.8	8.3
Weekly Newspapers	5.1	6.9
Magazines	2.4	3.1
Other	17.2	21.4

Source: Maclean Hunter Research Bureau

TABLE 2 DAILY CIRCULATION AVERAGES
(1990 TO 1991)

Vancouver Sun	Down 5.5%
Montreal Gazette	Down 5.2%
Ottawa Citizen	Down 4.0%
Kitchener Record	Down 3.7%
Kingston Whig-Standard	Down 3.7%
London Free Press	Down 3.6%
Calgary Herald	Down 3.4%
Calgary Sun	Down 2.5%
Toronto Sun	Down 2.4%
Hamilton Spectator	Down 2.4%
Toronto Star	Down 2.2%
Edmonton Sun	Down 1.3%
Edmonton Journal	Down 0.6%
Windsor Star	Even
Vancouver Province	Up 2.6%

Source: LFP internal documents

Canadian centres. Tabloids were new and very different newspapers, adding 700,000 new readers who were, arguably, in a different category than traditional ones. Also, 14 new Sunday editions had been started in the past seven years, contributing another 1.5 million new readers to the circulation total, but not raising the daily average circulation. Thus, while total circulation was up, daily average circulation per newspaper was still in decline across the country (Table 2).

On this basis, circulation was being outpaced by population growth in virtually every market in Canada. Among other things, this had also placed increasing pressure on the sales function. The London Free Press in 1990 had to sell 81,364 new subscription orders to maintain its average daily home delivery at 85,646 in the city of London. In the previous year, the home delivery average had been slightly higher but only 63,000 new orders had to be sold.

A recent study conducted in the United States and Canada had suggested three main reasons why readers were abandoning newspapers:

1. No time:

   - your paper is hard to read
   - I really don't have any time
   - you don't make it clear why I should make time

2. No news:

   - I saw it all on TV; you gave me nothing new
   - insufficient insight, understanding, depth

3. No interest:

   - nothing for me in the paper
   - I don't share your idea of what is new or important
   - you don't care about what I care about—in fact you often belittle the things my friends and I enjoy

The same study had reconfirmed that one of the causes of newspapers' decline in importance to readers was the fact that other media, principally television, had made news more easily consumable by the public. Comparing statistics over time exposed a trend away from newspapers on virtually every dimension (Table 3).

INDUSTRY CONSOLIDATION TREND

The competitive dynamic among newspapers in Canada had changed gradually over the years. In the past, newspapers had competed as a collection of geographically-dispersed individual markets. While there had been virtually no competition between cities, there had often been intense rivalry among papers within cities. But by the late 1980s, cities with two or more dailies had become a rarity (Table 4). Even in the few locations that still had more than one daily, the papers tended to be positioned in fairly well-

TABLE 3 COMPARISON OF TELEVISION AND NEWSPAPERS
(Percentage of respondents who responded positively to each question)

	1986	1991
MAIN SOURCE OF INTERNATIONAL NEWS:		
Television	63%	73%
Newspapers	21%	16%
MAIN SOURCE OF NATIONAL NEWS:		
Television	69%	75%
Newspapers	19%	16%
MAIN SOURCE OF LOCAL NEWS:		
Television	41%	43%
Newspapers	34%	35%
MOST BELIEVABLE:		
Television	no data	30%
Newspapers	no data	24%
MOST ACCURATE:		
Television	no data	33%
Newspapers	no data	19%
MOST LIKELY TO BE FAIR:		
Television	no data	33%
Newspapers	no data	19%

Source: Environics, reproduced in LFP internal documents

TABLE 4 MAJOR NEWSPAPERS WITH CIRCULATIONS (1991)

CITY	NEWSPAPER	DAILY AVERAGE CIRCULATION
Calgary	Herald	125,000
	Sun	76,000
Winnipeg	Free Press	154,000
Regina	Leader-Post	68,000
Hamilton	Spectator	135,000
Edmonton	Journal	137,000
	Sun	69,000
Vancouver	Province	185,000
	Sun	221,000
Victoria	Times-Colonist	77,000
Winnipeg	Free Press	154,000
Halifax	Chronicle Herald	97,000
Waterloo	K-W Record	75,000
London	Free Press	115,000
Ottawa	Citizen	178,000
Toronto	Star	544,000
	Globe and Mail	311,000
	Sun	272,000
Windsor	Star	86,000
Montreal	Gazette	163,000
	Journal de Montreal	293,000
	La Presse	205,000
Quebec City	Journal de Quebec	102,000
	Le Soleil	99,000

Source: Canadian Advertising Rates and Data, March 1994

defined niches, such as Toronto's Globe and Mail, Sun, and Star. Through consolidation and attrition, the industry had evolved into a series of local newspaper monopolies.

Consolidation had also led to domination of the Canadian industry by a few national or regional chains. Advantages to group ownership were: 1) shared resources, including pooled information services from abroad; and 2) the owner's deep pockets, which enabled a chain newspaper to weather temporary downturns in its financial performance, and gave it access to capital for major investments in technology.

The two largest chains, Southam and Thomson, together controlled 58 per cent of the English-language circulation in Canada. Southam, with 17 of the total 95 Canadian English dailies, had 33.5 per cent of overall circulation, while Thomson, with 36 papers, had 24.5 per cent. These percentages did not, in themselves, suggest that the newspaper market had taken on the characteristics of a monopoly. But by avoiding head-to-head competition among papers in individual cities, the chains' newspapers had managed to enjoy local monopolies and high profits.

THREAT TO THE PUBLIC INTEREST?

Critics of industry consolidation favoured some from of government intervention to help support financially troubled newspapers and to preserve competitive rivalry. Arguing out of concern for the public interest, they cautioned that in single-paper monopolies, readers' opinions would be manipulated by selective reporting and by opinion masquerading as objective journalism. Further, since advertisers would have no alternative outlets for their print messages, they would be at the mercy of greedy newspaper owners, and would become the victims of price-gouging and other undesirable tactics.

Those who saw no problem with the demise of direct competition maintained that newspapers in monopoly markets were able and willing to sustain a high level of journalistic quality, because their resources were not eroded through needless duplication and price competition with rivals. A section of the 19981 Royal Commission on Newspapers suggested that there was no evidence of declining quality or journalistic integrity as a result of industry consolidation. Publishers in single-newspaper towns were characterized as being able to "afford excellence," while still having to compete with other media for advertisers' dollars.

Neither was the trend to group ownership of newspapers seen, by these observers, as a threat to editorial independence. Publishers of chain newspapers frequently made mention of their freedom from interference by their corporate bosses. In support of this contention they cited the fact that some of Canada's most respected papers were being run at a loss by large chains (for example, Thomson's Globe and Mail), implying that high quality standards were not being eroded in pursuit of corporate profitability.

Even the Supreme Court of Canada had indirectly supported the position that the public interest was not threatened by industry consolidation. In ruling on a 1977 case brought under anti-combines legislation, the court held that "the Crown was unable to prove, as the law requires, that a single owner of the [only] five dailies in New Brunswick would be detrimental to the public." In reaching this conclusion, the Court noted the Irving chain's success in increasing the circulation of all five papers, the fact that capital investment had been made in them, and that money-losing papers had been subsidized to enable them to continue operating.

SOCIAL ROLE OF NEWSPAPERS

In Western society, the press had long been viewed as an expression of the right of free speech, and as one of the pillars of democracy. Independence from government and other interference was held to be absolutely essential if editorial quality and integrity were to be preserved. The press was seen as the "watchdog" charged with informing the public about the activities of the state.

There was a sense that the press had a larger role in society than that of other commercial enterprises. Some observers and industry insiders had concluded that newspapers have higher ideals than just making money, and responsibilities beyond simply keeping shareholders happy. While admitting that, at some level at least, financial viability was important, many people nevertheless felt that newspapers had an altruistic mission to present the complete truth, and that the naked pursuit of larger profits would put their editorial objectivity at risk. Newspapers were thus seen to be driven by both a service ethic and a market ethic.

Partly as a result of this extra-commercial role, a mystique had arisen about journalism which led to the belief, among many reporters, that journalists alone were competent to judge what stories the public should see in print, and in what form they should be presented. Among many traditionalists, journalistic quality (as defined by them) should be emphasized over the pursuit of mere profit. Papers which "sold out" in order to target a larger audience were seen to be pandering to the whims of an unsophisticated public whose members often did not know what was good for them.

McLeod saw the notion of newspapers' "altruistic mission" as a self-serving rationalization. He felt it was invoked to support the idea that maintaining the existing editorial process was more important than the consumption of the product, thus providing a rationale for preservation of the status quo. The result, he thought, was that newspapers had lost touch with their communities. By refusing to respond to readers' needs, under the pretext of preserving journalistic integrity, papers were becoming increasingly irrelevant to many potential readers. Print journalism's insular mentality, bred of a grandiose view of its role in society, its professional arrogance, and its past success, had isolated it from those on whom it depended for its survival.

Evidence about the relative profitability of different editorial approaches was equivocal, in any event. Observers could point to successful and unsuccessful examples at both ends of the "quality" continuum. For example, the Globe and Mail, widely perceived as a high-quality paper, was operating at a loss, while other quality papers such as the Washington Post and the New York Times were earning money. At the tabloid end of the spectrum, the Toronto Sun was a financial success, while USA Today was still struggling to break even. It seemed that, for all the criticism levelled at papers which tried to boost circulation by appealing to a larger and, arguably, less discriminating mass market, this "sell-out" tactic was no guarantee of profits. There seemed to be profitable market niches for newspapers following either strategy.

THE LONDON FREE PRESS

The London Free Press was the only daily newspaper in London, Ontario, a southwestern Ontario city of approximately 300,000. It was part of the Blackburn Group Inc. (BGI), which was made up of businesses in the communication and information fields. Begun in 1849, The Free Press had been owned and operated for five generations by the Blackburn family of London, and maintained a strong tradition of community service.

As communications technology evolved, so did the organization's activities in various media. An AM radio station was started in 1922, and in 1953 television was added to the Blackburn empire.[1] An FM radio station completed the growing conglomerate's coverage of the available "instant media."

In addition to these holdings, BGI had also launched Netmar Inc. in 1974, and purchased Compusearch in 1984. Netmar published and distributed weekly newspapers, shopping guides, and advertising flyers in Ontario and Alberta. Compusearch, based in Toronto, was a North American leader in market information and analysis.

In 1991, BGI established Blackburn Marketing Services Inc. (BMSI), an investment and management company formed to develop a portfolio of businesses in the direct marketing area. BSMI had made inroads into the U.S. market through acquisitions and mergers with American market research organizations.

BGI and its operating subsidiaries were private companies, and had been run under Blackburn family control since their founding. The LFP had the longest history, and was the most "legitimate" in terms of traditional journalistic values. Blackburn's senior management were proud that they had been able to maintain both the financial health of the paper and its high journalistic quality while creating a work environment that was described as caring and paternalistic.

The LFP had up-to-date production facilities, and its distribution system was described by McLeod as leading-edge, given the current state of technological development. Minimizing printing and distribution costs was an ongoing effort at the LFP, but any gains made in this area would be incremental. For true strategic impact, McLeod thought he had to focus on the revenue-generating side of the profit equation. This placed the onus for change on the editorial department.

ORGANIZATION

The LFP, like most newspapers, was organized along functional lines. The principal departments were advertising, production, administrative, and editorial. The editorial department of approximately 130 employees was headed by McLeod, and divided into sections that corresponded to the principal sections of the newspaper. Staff were assigned to sports, entertainment, business, political, or local/regional sections on a more or less permanent basis, under the leadership of a senior editor who was in charge of that part of the paper.

Exhibit 3 presents a chart showing the organization of editorial staff within sections of the paper. In operation, it worked as follows: For a typical local news event, a reporter was sent into the field by a senior editor to gather the facts, and to write the story. The piece was then turned over to a copy editor, who would check spelling and grammar, alter its length, or make other changes. After this step, the graphics people took over, adding pictures, diagrams, or maps as required, and physically re-working the story to fit into the page layout that was being planned for that edition. Again, the original story could be changed to meet space restrictions.

McLeod saw several weaknesses in this system. For example, a typical reporter might be assigned to cover local news, and be routinely sent to cover regular meetings of some special-interest group. This reporter might return with a story about a particularly colourful and lively meeting, at which members expressed various forms of outrage and stated their political positions for the record. The story would run in the newspaper, suitably headlined with attention-getting phrases, and the responsible section editor would feel that the job of covering local news had been accomplished. However, the only "outrage" felt might be on the part of the 20 people attending the meeting, and the significance of the event for the greater community could be nonexistent. Without probing more deeply into the reasons behind the meeting, and investigating the possible consequences on a level that went beyond the narrow interests of a particular group, the LFP might not be reporting anything meaningful to readers. Many reporters' roles had been created in response to a specific need in the past, but were maintained today, McLeod had decided, more out of habit than for the intrinsic "newsworthiness" of the material that was ultimately written. When making decisions about how to deploy limited reporting resources to the best possible effect, the test of community relevance was often not applied.

Another problem was that, throughout the traditional process, there was little or no communication between the various production stages. Because the printing schedule of the LFP dictated that the presses start rolling at midnight, the latter steps in the process were often not done until evening, while the original story may have been written that morning. By the time the editors and graphics people first saw the story, its original author could be home in bed,

with no opportunity for input or influence over how it would finally appear in the paper.

The lack of a perceived connection with the community was symbolized by the LFP's physical premises as well. With only one access door, the building itself was not easy for the public to enter. Once inside, they faced a forbidding security checkpoint, a symbolic barrier between the public and the reporters who chronicled their lives. At the same time, McLeod remarked on the fact that none of the editorial staff had a view of the outside from their work area. The lack of a visual link to the city of London reinforced the inward-directed focus of those who purported to be writing about issues and events that were important to the community.

The organization structure also isolated departments within the newspaper from one another. Each section was conceptually and editorially an independent entity, and there was little communication or sharing of information among them. McLeod thought that this arrangement had led, on occasion, to stories falling through the cracks because they did not fit neatly into one of the pre-defined categories. An example of this occurred when a major World Wrestling Federation (WWF) event was scheduled to be held in London. The match was to be held at the London Gardens, which was the biggest arena in the city, and frequently the venue for major music concerts and sports events. The London Free Press often reported on these activities in the next day's edition, and it had been informed by the WWF's sophisticated publicity department about the major wrestling stars who would be making a rare appearance in London. The most popular and biggest money-making wrestlers were more accustomed to appearing in places such as New York's Madison Square Garden or the Fabulous Western Forum in Los Angeles than in a relative backwater such as the 8,000-seat London Gardens.

As it happened however, the sports section of the LFP declined to cover the WWF event because they felt that professional wrestling was not a true "sport," but more a form of staged entertainment. The entertainment editor meanwhile assumed that, since wrestling billed itself as a sport, and its participants were "athletes," the sports section would be reporting on it. The lack of communication between sections, and the fact that professional wrestling could not be neatly pigeonholed as either "sport" or "entertainment," led to neither section covering what was, for many London residents, a major news item.

STRATEGIC RESPONSE

To halt further declines in readership, a major makeover of the LFP was undertaken in 1989, to give it a different look and make it more contemporary, "breezy," and attractive to

EXHIBIT 3 PARTIAL ORGANIZATION CHART circa 1987

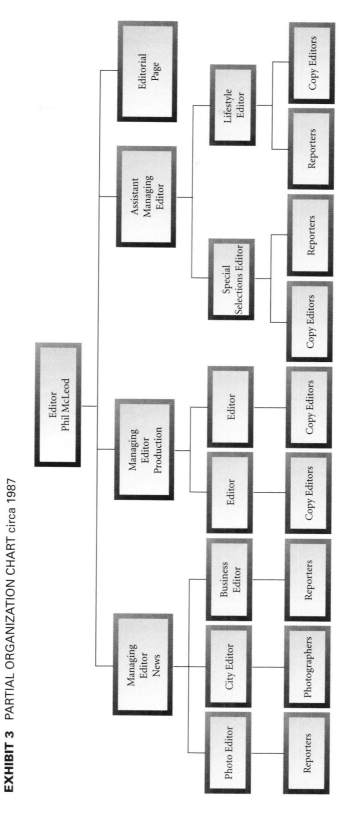

Source: Philip McLeod interview

readers. In what was seen in the trade as a major departure from tradition, the front page was redesigned. The number of stories it contained was reduced in favour of making it more of a road map for the contents of the inside pages. More colour was used, in conjunction with other cosmetic changes designed to make the paper look more user-friendly and less boring.

These changes, while hardly revolutionary to the eye of an average reader, were perceived by some members of the editorial staff as an abandonment of its tradition of editorial excellence. They interpreted the emphasis on readability and graphic attractiveness as an effort to lure readers with pretty pictures and colourful presentation. In the detractors' opinions, an emphasis on the quality of writing was being supplanted by less meaningful priorities.

The increased use of graphics meant that, for the first time, charts, maps, and graphs were incorporated into stories right from the outset, as opposed to being added as a afterthought on a "space available" basis. One group which felt threatened as a result was the staff photographers, who saw their work competing for space with that of the graphics designers. Another unhappy group was the reporters. They felt their preeminent position in the LFP newsroom being eroded, since now much of what they wrote might be captured in a chart or graph. While this had always been the case to a certain extent, graphics and pictorial summaries of key story points were now intended to be an integral part of the creation of an article, to be included in the process right from the start. Reporters thought that their influence over how a story would be presented would now have to be shared with others, who often might have little training in journalism.

RESULTS

Reader response to the changes was mixed. Evidence favouring and criticizing the changes was gathered from focus groups, and was revealed in letters to the editor. From these sources, it became clear that some readers were upset with the new look of the paper and found it disconcerting that items they were interested in were relocated to unfamiliar sections. On the other hand, some reported that they liked the new format, and saw it as a step towards making the paper more readable. While it was difficult to draw quantitative conclusions from this, McLeod estimated that the split "for" and "against" the redesign was about 50-50.

Circulation for 1990, the first full year of operation with the new format, was down three per cent from the year before. However, London was just beginning to feel the effects of a recession at that time, and this made it difficult to disentangle the effect of the change from broader economic trends. The question of how much circulation would have dropped without a change remained impossible to answer.

At the same time as changes in the appearance of the LFP were being implemented, a drive to unionize the newsroom was successfully completed. Though professing considerable philosophical discomfort with their decision, supporters of the unionization effort had decided that this was the only way they could combat what they saw as unilateral and wrong-headed action by the paper's management. In what many saw as a result of the unhappiness of editorial staff about the new direction the LFP appeared to be taking, they voted to go on strike in early 1990. The strike was settled after a few weeks, during which the paper was put together by managerial staff, but unresolved ill feelings remained.

PACKAGE VERSUS CONTENT

McLeod had come to believe that, while a newspaper's packaging was closely linked to its content, the two "must become disentangled in our minds" in order for progress to be made. He had changed the package, following the tradition of consumer goods marketers. Now perhaps something a little more substantive was in order.

In order for readers to see the LFP as an important source of information, the content of the paper would need to reflect their wishes more closely. But changing the content would not be easy. As McLeod put it, a newspaper is like a sausage factory:

> You can put as many good ideas as you want into the front end of the machine, but unless that machine has been retooled to think and act in new ways, it will always turn out more or less the same thing. In other words, whatever goes in, sausages come out. Perhaps sausages with better texture or taste, less fat and fewer calories, but sausages nevertheless.

McLeod felt that the changes would require a substantial "rewiring of our heads," and would be risky because they conflicted with traditional attitudes about journalism. More stories needed to be written about topics that readers were actually interested in, and they needed to be covered in greater depth. At the same time, McLeod no longer believed that each piece in the paper had to be written, edited, and laid out in the final few minutes before the press deadline. "While I wouldn't know the details of the stories, I can tell you two days in advance what 80 per cent of our paper is going to look like," he said. "If we know, broadly, what the subject matter is going to be, why can't we do a better job of background and analysis on those stories we already know are going to be in the paper?"

POTENTIAL RESISTANCE

Opposition to any proposed changes could be high. McLeod was risking criticism for tampering with the natural order of the way newspapers were run, because of the strong entrenched culture that existed in the profession. According to one view, he might be allowing the process of producing a newspaper to be unduly tainted by customer influence.

On a more personal level, the changes might shake many staffers' strongly-held beliefs about how newspapers should produced, and about the role of journalism in a society. Some reporters thought that the atmosphere in the newsroom was already poisoned because of a strong polarization between those in favour of and those opposed to change. Some, who were suspicious of any attempts to solicit their opinion, were guarded about their comments regarding the organizational changes. While these individuals expressed deep concern over the future of the newspaper, they felt alienated, disenfranchised, and devalued because of the changes that had been implemented or proposed. Some had gone for stress counselling to help them deal with the effects.

Opponents also felt that a sacred trust established by the late Walter Blackburn was being violated. The LFP had, until recently, been regarded as a writer's paper because of the consistently high quality of its journalism, as judged by other journalists. There was a strong tradition of editorial freedom, and the reporters had become accustomed to being treated as highly trained and valued professionals. Some feared that, with change, their skills would be devalued in favour of "People" magazine-style writing, which could be executed by relatively unskilled individuals.

One reporter commented:

> Management should be trying to involve people, rather than alienating them. Many of us are deeply concerned about what's going on, but management isn't paying any attention. We've been left behind in this whole thing; nothing coming from us has been listened to. Many people feel disenfranchised, devalued. There's a high level of distrust here, and an adversarial climate. In fact, the environment is so poisoned, I'm worried that what I say to you [that is, the case writer] might be used against me.

There was also resistance to what some saw as the "scourge of MBAs." Market research reports which suggested declining profits and an unsustainable future for the newspaper had been shared with the staff, but they were dismissed by dissidents as mere spreadsheet manipulation. The report authors were characterized as pinstriped automatons bent on forcing higher short-term profits out of a venerable institution by squeezing out its lifeblood. Opponents of change pointed out that none of the blue-suit crowd's forecasts ever came true anyway, and saw the doom and gloom scenarios, with their accompanying recommendations, as a stratagem that allowed MBAs to increase their own consulting revenue.

Scepticism and mistrust was further fuelled by the fact that McLeod's own managerial style was sometimes less than tactful, especially when he was challenging some of journalism's sacred cows. A typical comment about a proposed story might be: "Who cares?", which was intended to mean: "Do our readers feel strongly about this story, or does the way we've presented it give them a reason to care?" However, some reporters, not accustomed to thinking this way, might misinterpret the remark as a personal criticism or as a lack of confidence in their writing ability.

McLEOD'S POSITION

Although he felt strongly that change was needed, McLeod was in a quandary about what form it should take, the urgency with which it should be implemented, and what support or resistance the changes might encounter. BGI management had hired McLeod from the Toronto Star with the expectation that he would be a change agent. The culture of the Star, of which McLeod was a product, was perceived as much less family-like and paternalistic than the LFP. This was partly because it operated in a much more competitive market, but also because of the long tradition of Blackburn family influence on the way the London paper was run. The Blackburn legacy implied that employees would be cared for during difficult periods in their personal and professional lives, and would not be treated as interchangeable chattels or disposable factors of production. McLeod's arrival on the scene, with his outsider's background and perspective, was a signal to some that these traditions might be consigned to history, to be replaced by a much more impersonal bottom-line focus.

Previous editors had also tended to put high-quality journalism at the top of their agenda. As a result, the LFP was widely perceived, both internally and by outsiders, as a "writer's paper." Any change which threatened these priorities would meet with stiff opposition. BGI executives were willing to support any reasonable initiative—Phil McLeod's challenge lay in choosing the right one and avoiding the most serious pitfalls.

CASE 15

NBC

Since its takeover by GE in 1986, NBC had retained a leadership position for more years than any of its television broadcast competitors. Its prime-time success had allowed it to obtain record-setting profits year after year by charging the highest rates for advertising, particularly for its most watched programs. In fact, the top management at NBC had become so confident of their accomplishments that they were occasionally suggesting that they did not merely want to be the leading television network; they wanted to be the only successful network. This goal appeared to be within reach, because NBC executives were convinced that they had put into place a sound strategy for maintaining the network's elevated position in the Neilson television ratings.

However, over the 1998–1999 television season, it became clear that NBC's strategy for dominance was no longer working. The network was forced to relinquish its crown as prime time's most-watched network after a three-year reign. By the end of the 1999–2000 season, NBC had slipped to third place in terms of total viewers, trailing both ABC and CBS. Furthermore, the network had lost its long-standing leadership position among viewers between the ages of 18 and 49 that are most sought after by advertisers. ABC, largely on the strength of the game show *Who Wants to Be a Millionaire*, had pushed NBC out of the lead among this important category of viewers.

These developments had prompted some industry observers to suggest that NBC's once-proud peacock logo was beginning to look like buzzards circling overhead. It was clear that the network was struggling to counteract a combination of familiar factors that tend to drag down a successful network. NBC had failed to come up with a sound strategy to deal with a growing number of its programming problems. The network executives were acutely aware that their development pipeline had failed to produce enough new hits, making it difficult for them to replace popular shows that were being taken off the air. They were also failing to get new hit shows from producers who had provided them with previous winners.

Concerns about the growing threat to its position had already led the network to bring in Scott Sassa during the fall of 1999. Taking over as the new West Coast entertainment executive, he had been expected to help stem the downward turn of NBC's television programming. But in his recent public address, Sassa had to defend the tardiness on the part of his network in offering the so-called reality programming that has been largely responsible for the recent successes of the other major networks. NBC's crop of new shows for the fall of 2000 had met with cool reception from the media buyers, with several shows being retooled before they were launched. "Our shows were pretty horrible," a senior executive from the network admitted. These failures fueled speculation that the network would not be able to do much better in the upcoming season.

Case prepared by Jamal Shamsie, UCLA, to be used for class discussion. Material drawn from published sources. Copyright © 2002 Jamal Shamsie.

THREATENED WITH EXTINCTION?

Long dominant in the television industry, network broadcasters have seen a significant drop in their viewership levels. The three original networks, CBS, NBC and ABC, which commanded almost 90 percent of all television viewers twenty years ago, have seen their share decline to below 50 percent. Even with the addition of three new networks—Fox, WB and UPN— the total share of broadcast networks has not managed to rise much above 65 percent of the television audience.

The steady loss of viewership from year to year has been attributed to several technological developments. Foremost among these is the increase in the numbers of homes that are wired to cable or linked to satellites. Indeed, cable channels have proliferated and the combined share of cable channel viewership has shown a steady increase over the last ten years. For the most part, cable channels have tended to offer more specialized programming that allows them to focus on specific niches among television viewers.

More recently, competition for television audiences has also come from the rise in popularity of the Internet. There are growing indications that the broadcast networks will face a significant loss of viewership from the growing use of the Internet. In households that are presently wired to the Net, people have cut back by a third the time that they spend watching television programs.

Faced with a continuing loss in audience through an explosion of alternate forms of entertainment, the major television networks such as NBC, CBS, ABC and Fox have been fighting back. They have begun to search for new ways to use the television shows that they air and to add new, interactive dimensions to the relationships that they establish with both their viewers and their advertisers. And they are preparing for the day when the functions of a TV set converge with those of a computer.

At the center of the networks' repositioning is the ability to build and market hit entertainment shows. The popularity of a television show is beginning to take on even more importance—"an outright necessity" in the words of NBC's president, Robert C. Wright. For the networks, the hit show is the hub in a growing wheel of interests: promotion platforms for related businesses, sales of replays on cable television or even Internet sites, and the creation of direct links between advertisers and viewers.

The networks expect to capitalize by replaying—or in their term "repurposing"—shows on digital channels or cable channels that they own. They are also exploring the possibility, through the technology of video streaming, of showing programs on the Internet. The networks also expect to sell products related to their shows, though Mr.

Wright of NBC said that is so far a very small part of the business plan. "Today it isn't much of a business, but it may be quite attractive in two to three years."

Networks have already moved into marketing and selling compact discs based on the music offered in a television film. NBC did very well with sales of the soundtrack from its movie *The 60's*. But even as the network industry tries to mutate from a model that relies exclusively on commercials for its income to one that also relies on electronic commerce, executives acknowledge that they must not lose their focus on their core business—show business. "In the end it's still all about the content," said Robert A. Iger, the chairman of the ABC Group, a unit of the Walt Disney Company.

Given the need for content which can be used for multiple purposes, the broadcast networks are redoubling their efforts to find new shows that are likely to become hits. Furthermore, they are trying to have greater control over the shows that they broadcast. One result of that strategy is a move toward even more vertical integration, with networks trying to have ownership of as much of their programming as they can. Mr. Iger stated that without some form of ownership rights, the fees escalate prohibitively after four years if the show turns out to be a hit. For networks now, he said, it becomes untenable if another party controls the economics of a program. "We need to be able to gain some share of the upside that the new technology allows," Mr. Iger said.

It is possible, however, that the chances of finding and developing hit shows may have been hurt by the pressure on network executives to own part of every show they put on. Critics of television programming charged that the networks had begun to put shows on their prime-time schedule largely on the basis of their ability to obtain part ownership. This meant that shows were getting on the air because they represented good network investments, not because they were built around good ideas.

Broadcast network executives insisted that they were still looking for shows that are likely to become successful, without much concern over the availability of an equity stake. They suggested that it is unrealistic to expect new shows to become overnight hits. It may be taking viewers much longer to discover new shows with the explosion of channels on television. "You can still make hits," Mr. Moonves of CBS said. "But more and more you have to show patience." Indeed, many shows in recent years have broken through after some careful nurturing. These include NBC's *Law and Order*, Fox's *Party of Five*, ABC's *Drew Carey*, and CBS's *Everybody Loves Raymond*.

But the relative lack of success in finding new shows has already led to the replacement of executives in charge of programming at two networks, NBC and Fox. The falling ax this time had special meaning for network watchers. In this case, longtime broadcast veterans, Warren Littlefield at

NBC and Peter Roth at Fox, were replaced by executives who built their careers at cable channels: Scott Sassa from the Turner channels and Doug Herzog from MTV and Comedy Central. Mr. Herzog, the executive who brought the outrageous cartoon *South Park* to Comedy Central, said his and Mr. Sassa's arrivals at broadcast networks signaled a "sea change" in the business. Even one holdover top network programmer, Leslie Moonves at CBS, claimed that the networks had to re-invent themselves in order to deal with a growing threat of extinction.

A LEGACY OF SUCCESS

Since the 1985–1986 season, NBC had claimed leadership for total viewers among the broadcast networks, only losing it to CBS and ABC for a four-year period in the early 1990s. Such a level of success had been remarkable for a company that had just been bought up by GE as part of its $6.3 billion purchase of RCA. It had been assumed that these new corporate owners would know little about network broadcasting, being for the most part unable to distinguish between turbines and televisions.

In an address to his employees made a few years ago, a senior executive at ABC felt it necessary to demand: "How can you let those engineers beat us? Those guys make M.R.I. [Magnetic Resonance Imaging] machines." Indeed, ratings and profits at NBC did collapse with the start of the 1991–1992 season, leading to rumors that GE was about to bail out, selling NBC to Disney or to Paramount or to Time Warner. But no such sale took place and NBC managed to climb back to the top four seasons later.

NBC had worked hard to reclaim the top spot, learning from the numerous mistakes that it had made in the late 1980s and early 1990s. Most of its reclaimed success was attributed to astute programming moves that were made by a new team of division managers who had gained considerable experience with television production. Robert C. Wright, who had been placed in charge of NBC after the takeover by GE, brought in experienced producers such as Don Ohlmeyer for the entertainment division, Andrew Lack for the news division and Dick Ebersol for the sports division. In making these appointments, Mr. Wright believed that executives with expertise in how to put a show on television could make superior programmers and division managers.

In terms of entertainment, Mr. Ohlmeyer helped NBC obtain a host of original shows that included *Seinfeld, Friends* and *E.R.* These shows replaced earlier hits such as *The Cosby Show* and *Cheers* and allowed the network to maintain its dominance on Thursday nights. The powerful lineup of hits was heavily promoted as "Must See Television." As a result, NBC would end up getting higher ratings for the night than the other three major networks combined. A few of these shows were also moved to draw viewers to other evenings once it was believed that they had developed a sizable following by having been part of the Thursday evening lineup.

But as the network executives approached the start of the 1998–1999 television season, they were aware that they would have a difficult time holding on to their customary leadership position. "On close analysis one could question NBC's broadcast plan over the last three years," said one longtime packager of television programs. This plan called for establishing NBC, in the words of one NBC executive, as a "premium brand," one with an audience of young, wealthy city dwellers. It believed that the strategy paid off because the network was the only one making real profits, up to $500 million a year.

But NBC's focus on maximizing profits also led to what several executives within the division said were some questionable strategic moves, such as attempting in the fall of 1997 to flood the NBC schedule with a record-breaking 18 comedies. Comedies typically cost less to produce than dramas, draw higher advertising rates and perform better in reruns. Looking to capitalize on its comedy shows, NBC also dropped its Monday night movie, which had been reasonably successful. But few of those comedies worked. Most of these shows, such as *Caroline in the City, Suddenly Susan, Fired Up, Naked Truth* and *Veronica's Closet* dealt with a single women in a media surrounding, usually in New York. Reflecting a widely held view, one former top program executive from a competing network suggested a couple of reasons for this. "It was a combination of so many shows with the same upscale urban premise and simple lack of execution," the executive said.

This left the network without a new hit to replace *Seinfeld* at the start of the 1998–1999 television season. The show had been the network's top comedy show for five years and had been a key anchor in NBC's Thursday night lineup. "*Seinfeld* is so much more important than anybody understood," said Peter Tortorici, a former head programmer at CBS. "How do you replace a show that's popular in Alabama and Boston, even though it was about Jewish characters from New York? That just doesn't come along every day."

Even NBC's own executives concede that their greatest failure was in not being able to find a show remotely close to *Seinfeld* in appeal, despite four years of golden chances on Thursday nights in the spots adjacent to *Seinfeld*. In fact, the network's critics claim that it primarily failed because of a strategy that insisted on appealing to the same audience with every show. "We went with this cookie-cutter approach," one senior NBC executive said. "It just didn't work. And it meant we wasted that 9:30 slot behind *Seinfeld* instead of finding the hit that could help replace it."

Because no hit emerged from all those attempts, NBC was forced to move its next best comedy, *Frasier*, to Thursday at 9, where *Seinfeld* lived. That did help shore up Thursday evening, which had been NBC's stronghold for almost two decades. But in so doing NBC drastically weakened Tuesday. By airing *Frasier* on Tuesdays, NBC had erased ABC's former dominance on this evening. With *Frasier* moved to a different evening and another longtime comedy hit, *Mad About You*, fading in its last season, NBC was in a much weaker position to compete with ABC's stronger comedy lineup.

Moreover, NBC grappled with problems with finding potential new hit shows to replace those that are in decline. From its entire crop of shows that was introduced two season ago, only *Will and Grace*, a comedy about a gay man living with a straight woman, has shown some signs of promise. The lack of replacements has also made the network hostage to the suppliers of its current hit shows. It had to pay the astronomical amount of $13 million an episode to renew the contract for *E.R.*, its top rated show. The enormous cost of that deal hardened NBC's position about insisting on an ownership stake in all its new shows in order to minimize the financial burden that has become associated with the renewal of successful shows.

POSITIONING FOR THE FUTURE

NBC's recent lack of success in developing new hit shows has attracted more attention because it remains the only major network that is not attached to a big Hollywood studio. But executives at the network claim that links to a film studio have not necessarily benefited their rivals. In fact, NBC programming executives have relatively few concerns about a steady supply of new television shows. As long as the network continues to reach enough viewers, they believe that they will continue to have new shows pitched at them.

Furthermore, most of the management at NBC feel that their network is well positioned for the future with its portfolio of networks, stations and Internet holdings. It has had considerable success in drawing new viewers with its CNBC and MSNBC channels. The recent deal with Paxson has also provided the network with a second television station in six of the biggest domestic markets. These new channels have supplied NBC with additional outlets for several of the programs that it produces such as *Dateline*, *The Tonight Show* and *Saturday Night Live.*

But Sassa insists that the network must continue to search for and help to develop new hits to feed all of its growing channels. He stated that NBC still has some of the strongest network shows such as *E.R.*, *Friends*, *Frasier*, *Law & Order* and *Providence*. It has also been able to get strong results from some of its recent news shows such as *The West Wing*, *Law & Order: Special Victims Unit* and *Third Watch*.

NBC executives were especially encouraged by some gains that their network appeared to be making. Their network trailed only ABC during the May 2000 sweeps and was tied with it for most viewers in the crucial 18–49 category. Sassa is also keen to point out that, unlike ABC, they managed to obtain these results on the strength of their regular dramas and comedies. He feels that ABC's leadership is based almost entirely on multiple airings of a highly successful game show whose popularity is certain to decline.

In recent interviews, Mr. Sassa has indicated that he will continue to try and cultivate a more diverse portfolio of shows that can appeal to a much broader audience. In part, this will be accomplished by a stronger emphasis on family programming. Beyond this, however, Mr. Sassa refused to elaborate on the steps that he will take to find and develop new hit shows for NBC. When pushed for further details, Mr. Sassa simply responded: "I can't give you the secrets to the nuclear code."

LVMH: Taking the Western Art de Vivre to the World

Under the heading "A different kind of package holiday," *The Economist* published the following story on 14th July, 2001.

> Nine Hong Kong Chinese recently spent a fortnight travelling through Europe. They started in Frankfurt and ended in Rome, passing through one city a day. Early every morning, a van picked them up from their hotel and drove them to the first Louis Vuitton store on the day's agenda. It parked around the corner, and the Chinese entered the store in pairs. They each bought as many Louis Vuitton handbags as they could carry and then returned to the van, in order to be transferred to the next store.

It was gruelling work, but the women in the van went on the trip because it was an all-expenses-paid way to see Europe. For the organizers of the trip, it was all business, because the handbags the women bought could be sold at 40% premium in Japan, Hong Kong, Shanghai, and other cities in Asia, where the demand for them appeared to be insatiable.

This story is a telling illustration of the "power" of a Louis Vuitton bag on a certain kind of clientele. But what was behind the particular attraction that a simple bag exercised on women all over the world?

The answer: LVMH—Moët Hennessey Louis Vuitton to the uninitiated—the leader with 15% share of the $68 billion global luxury market, with a turnover of 8.5 billion Euro and 46,000 employees worldwide. For rivals, like Francois Pinault, the creator of the aspiring luxury group PPR and LVMH's toughest competitor, LVMH was something of a nightmare. For the hundreds of new graduates of France's top business schools every year, LVMH represented another dream: their employer of choice, bound to put them on the path of quick success. The mention "I work for LVMH" evoked in France and in many other countries an immediate recognition, mostly coupled with respect for having succeeded in becoming part of such an "elite" organization. The brand names people associated with LVMH—Louis Vuitton, Christian Dior, Givenchy, Celine, Guerlain, Tag Heuer, Moet et Chandon, or Pommery—were inextricably linked to the world of luxury and wealth, and the possession of things many desired but few could afford.

To understand better the success of the company, one has to start with story of the man behind it, Bernard Arnault.

EARLY DAYS

The austere young man from Roubaix, a dreary mining town in the North of France, had always been an entrepreneurial spirit. After attending the elite French military and engineering institute, the Ecole Polytechnique, Arnault, unlike most of his classmates who went into big French

This case was written by Katherine Balazs, Ph.D. student at HEC, under the supervision and guidance of Sumantra Ghoshal, Professor at the London Business School.
© London Business School.

companies or government jobs, returned to Roubaix to take over the reigns of the family construction business. When François Mitterrand was elected as president in 1981, Arnault went to the U.S. to settle down there and expand his family's business away from the greedy hands of France's socialists.

When he realized that, against all expectations, Mitterrand would not go on a nationalization binge, Arnault returned to France in 1983, and, at the age of 33, already a successful builder and real estate developer, asked his family lawyer Pierre Godé to scout out some new business opportunities for him. After exploring different options, Godé came up with an unlikely prospect: the bankrupt Boussac Saint-Frères textile conglomerate. Apart from textiles, the group's activities included disposable diapers, a furniture chain, the prestigious but old-fashioned Paris department store Le Bon Marché, a children's park in Paris and—the main attraction to Arnault—the fashion house of Christian Dior. While explaining his decision to acquire Boussac, Arnault recalled an experience he had a few years previously: "I asked a taxi driver in New York, what he knew of France. He could not name the president, but he knew Dior." Arnault bought Boussac in 1984, with an investment of $15 million of his family's money and substantial loans from the bank Lazard Frères.

When he immediately started out with the radical but necessary restructuring of the bankrupt company, ordering layoffs and closing plants, violent reactions from the French press erupted. He created another furor by engaging an Italian, Gianfranco Ferré, as the main designer of Dior, transforming one of France's "holy" cultural institutions into a profitable marketing venture.

He did not take a soft approach when acquiring LVMH either. In 1988 Henry Racamier, senior member of the Vuitton family, asked Arnault to help him fend off some hostile raiders of his LVMH leather goods, champagne, cognac and perfume group. The group at the time was publicly traded but controlled by different factions of warring families. Arnault at first took a minority stake in the company, but when Racamier decided to change the terms of their deal, Arnault himself took the role of those he was supposed to keep at bay. He initiated what became one of the most controversial and confrontational hostile-takeover bids in French business. The skirmishes went so far that François Mitterrand himself decided to get involved publicly and prompted the COB, the French stock market regulator, to start an investigation. When finally Arnault won the battle, it further strengthened his reputation as a ruthless financier, earning him sobriquets such as "wolf in cashmere clothing" and "terminator."

ASSEMBLING LVMH

One of the main characteristics of the LVMH Group was that it pursued from the very beginning an active external growth strategy oriented towards luxury product companies with high development potential. What distinguished the Group from other luxury goods companies was the fact that they were covering a large spectrum of businesses, such as champagne, jewelry, and fashion. Arnault described his growth strategy for the Group in the following way:

> We have two ways to grow LVMH: One is to increase the [sales of our] existing portfolio of brands, as we are doing with Vuitton and with Dior. And the second way is to buy creative companies. I think it's important in a group like ours to build the existing properties with products, but also to add things that can look smaller but which offer a high growth potential. The brands that have creativity, interesting products and the right image, extremely successful and very fast-growing, are limited in numbers. We know how to develop them—it's what we know the best. It's what we have done with Vuitton.

As opposed to other conglomerates that operated in the luxury business, LVMH was the only one whose acquisition strategy was narrowly focused on its field of expertise, luxury brands. They were considered to be, as one person said, "in the genetics of the company." The way these companies were viewed at LVMH could be best expressed by the French term "maisons" (houses) which descibed a concept that went beyond the simple notion of "brand." The brand itself was considered as the emanation of the culture of the "maison," which was a small universe by itself. It included tradition, *savoir faire* (craftsmanship), and *savoir vivre* (the art of living well). In this sense, the brand was the expression of the house, of a creator mastering and transforming exceptional raw material while being inspired by the past, by history, and by the consumers, to produce a product which, on the shelves, was seducing, and was pulled out rather than pushed on the customers.

Arnault's aggressive growth strategy has often been criticized. People have pointed out that LVMH could not grow forever, that it was bound to become too heavy one day. Arnault dismissed this sort of pessimism, referring to the structure of the Group that, according to him, would enable continuous growth for a long time to come. Concetta Lanciaux, Head of Human Resources for the group and a long-term Arnault confidant, confirmed the business logic with which LVMH acquired new companies: some new businesses were immediately profitable, others were invested into with a more medium or long-term view. Or, a Arnault put it, the brands that were the "stars" of the group with the strongest cash flow permitted LVMH to finance those which were in a stage of development.

> While the group remained focused on the luxury goods business, it had developed not only diversity but also a balanced portfolio in terms of risks. Some of the divisions, such as fashion and cosmetics, grew quickly but were also more risky, while those in the champagne and cognac trade were more stable. Those who are stronger today help those which will be strong tomorrow.

While his methods were regarded as controversial, nobody denied that Arnault's way of running the business was hugely successful. In 11 years, the value of LVMH had multiplied 15-fold and its profit had grown by 500%. In addition to Dior, which was held separately from LVMH, Arnault—as this was being written—controlled, among others, Louis Vuitton, Givenchy, Christian Lacroix, Kenzo, Celine and Loewe fashion and leather goods; Dior, Givenchy and Guerlain fragrances; champagne brands Moet & Chandon, Krug and Dom Perignon; Tag Heuer, Fred, Ebel and Chaumet watches and fine jewelry; the two Paris department stores Le Bon Marche and La Samaritaine; the DFS duty-free chain and the Sephora perfumery chain. New additions were being made at a breathtaking pace. Pierre Letzelter, one of the five branch presidents, expressed his appreciation for Arnault the following way:

> The size of the company depends on the size of the boss. If the boss is small, the company is small. And I am not talking about physical size. LVMH has a big boss.

The first big failure in Arnault's career was the highly publicized stock market raid that LVMH launched on the Florentine leather goods and fashion house Gucci. After having acquired 34.4 percent of the company, Arnault felt safely in control of the company and said so. A mistake. Gucci secretly teamed up with Arnault's until then friend, French billionaire François Pinault, and, through a legal twist of issuing new shares, Pinault quickly snapped up 40 percent of Gucci, diluting Arnault's stake to 20 percent in the process.

To add insult to injury, Pinault announced the same day the acquisition of Yves Saint Laurent, one of the great bastions of French fashion that Arnault also coveted. This started off a war among luxury giants like France had never witnessed before. LVMH went to court over Gucci, lost the first round, launched another in a separate Dutch court. Hostilities continued when Arnault, in an effort to outdo Pinault who owned Christie's—and to outdo him well—acquired in rapid succession the Phillips auction house in London, and the biggest and most prestigious French auction house, Etude Tajan.

Revenge on Gucci itself came fast: Arnault teamed up with Prada's Patrizio Bertelli, and outbid Gucci for the con-

trol of Fendi. The main reason for this investment of $950 million was one little bag: the appropriately named Baguette, since it sold like hotcakes, or, to remain in the French context, like hot baguettes. In the year after LVMH had taken its stake, the number of Fendi boutiques in the world went from four to eighty.

Arnault's other shopping sprees brought home Bliss, Hard Candy, Benefit, and Make Up Forever, smaller investments with what he considered to be great potential, consistent with Arnault's professed strategy to "invest in companies with growth potential, rather than those where the company is more mature and growth more difficult." Concetta Lanciaux described Arnault's pivotal role in the luxury industry as follows:

> Basically Bernard Arnault and LVMH established the modern luxury business. Today when you say luxury, you have the tendency to think about something modern, beautiful, but accessible. Luxury was something not generally acceptable when we came, and certainly not accessible. There were a few, extremely elitist families in charge. BA made luxury more accessible to the everyday customer. LVMH formalized the laws of luxury and modernized it. The characteristics of luxury goods are: selective distribution, direct production and marketing, adding value rather than volume, and communication. In the past luxury companies did this but in a very intuitive way, based on previous experience. When LVMH went from family management to professional management, they formalized it.

LVMH GROUP STRUCTURE: THE KEY TO GROWTH AND SUCCESS

I believe that centralized organizations quickly lose their power, effectiveness and competitiveness. This is especially true in the luxury products market. So we kept companies at their human size and grouped them in separate Business Groups or Branches. The goal was to allow the brands in each business to co-ordinate their strategies and develop synergies in fields of common interests such as purchasing, research, logistics, and international distribution networks. This structure was seen as a revolutionary new one in the luxury industry.

—Bernard Arnault

The organizational structure of LVMH developed through a kind of intuitive, iterative process in the heads of Arnault and his top management team. In the beginning the Group consisted of a smattering of individual brands, such as Dior, Celine, Louis Vuitton, and others. In time, these brands were grouped into five different clusters—Branches, in LVMH terminology: Wines and Spirits; Fashion and Leather Goods; Perfumes and Cosmetics; Watches and Jewelry; and Selective Distribution. The next level, the Group level, consisted of Arnault and a few top executives.

THE FUNDAMENTAL PRINCIPLE: AUTONOMY OF BRAND COMPANIES

Respect for brand autonomy and a distinctive identity for each brand company was a fundamental tenet of LVMH's management philosophy. According to Bernard Arnault, the uniqueness of LVMH was found in the fact that it was the only group that federated a great number of prestigious brands. Though LVMH was a large group, it had succeeded in preserving the identity and the autonomy of each brand company, or—in LVMH language—house. Each house was free to adopt the marketing and retailing strategies best suited to its needs, to capitalize on its distinctive positioning. All Group houses shared certain basic values such as creativity, product and service excellence, absolute respect for brand image, and entrepreneurial spirit. This organizational philosophy was clearly articulated by the company:

> The autonomy of each company is indissolubly linked to the entrepreneurial spirit, which constitutes a key value of LVMH management. Our companies will carry on with adapting and evolving by maintaining this entrepreneurial spirit among managers and by encouraging designers to create. This entrepreneurial autonomy allows managers and designers to meet the expectations of consumers and to enhance their creative excellence year after year. The size of the companies must be kept small. Small entrepreneurial companies are able to react quickly to the changing demands of their customers, to the quick evolutions of their specific business and environment. Human size facilitates creativity and innovation and allows a direct contact with the designers and talent. It's the only way to maintain the brand identity and distinctive culture of each company.

This entrepreneurial structure had, according to Arnault, resulted in a particular organizational culture that permeated LVMH and its different companies:

> When we buy a company, the people must not feel that they are joining a big group, but they need to feel that they remain independent, that they work for Mr. Dior, Mr. Vuitton. These companies still employ many members of the founding families, and they are the guardians of tradition. The philosophy of the group is to protect the autonomy and independence of each business unit as if it was still a family owned company. People who work here know this and behave accordingly.

BENEFITING FROM BIGNESS: ROLE OF THE BRANCH PRESIDENTS

While possessing a great amount of autonomy, each company benefited from the strength of the Group. The synergies created within the different branches were one of these strengths; another one was the capacity of LVMH to attract and retain the best talent worldwide by offering them multiple possibilities of career development. Myron Ullman, till recently the Managing Director of the Group, stressed the importance of entrepreneurial autonomy on the one hand and the use of existing synergies on the other hand.

> The group is only now becoming reasonably well structured. Headquarters is very small, Bernard Arnault, myself and a few other people. There is not a lot of daily interaction between us and the brand companies. We expect the companies to be fairly entrepreneurial and autonomous. The synergies are at the branch level. Branches share the control department, the audit department, the information systems department, and the legal department provided by HQ. For example, in the cosmetics branch we have a research laboratory for all the brands in that sector. We have 150 scientists, so given the fact that they work on different lines and products, we get better scientists and we don't get overlapping products. In the branch, the stronger help the weak to become better. The synergies that we derive from the branch structure can also be seen in department stores, where we can get the best place at a favorable price because we have so many brands. When you come in there with Louis Vuitton, Celine, Loewe, Dior Perfumes, practically taking up the whole ground floor of the store, you can negotiate space in a way single brands could never do.

Within the branches, information systems and support were shared. Companies benefited from Group resources and synergies: financial resources, administration (shared service centers), advertising negotiation, purchasing, R&D, production, retail networks, etc. Nothing was duplicated, HR support was common; each of the companies had its own HR people but looked to the branch for consistency. It was the branch that represented the company structure for them, while LVMH as a group played more the role of a bank. Companies did not go to Headquarters for specific support, other than for buying media, which was done at Group level, tax planning, and recruitment of senior management level positions.

While brand company presidents were concerned with one brand's strategy and marketing, branch presidents were concerned with the whole strategic map on which the position of the different brands within the branch had to be balanced. For example, the president of Moët and Chandon looked at the competitive position of Moët, vis-à-vis key competitors. The branch president of Wines and Spirits, to which Moët et Chandon belonged, had to consider the whole market. This did not only mean paying attention to outside competitors, but also to the possibility that certain products within the branch such as Veuve Cliquot and Pommery could compete against each other. This balance between protecting brand autonomy while deriving synergies within branches was a delicate operation.

We have to have a fine balance in the company, we cannot establish "knowledge-databases." Think of it this way: Parfums Christian Dior and Parfums Givenchy, they are both part of the group, but also competitors. So are Pommery and Moët et Chandon. There is a very fine line between making use of the synergies and sharing trade secrets.

Pierre Letzelter described how branch presidents tried to solve this delicate problem:

One of the major problems I was facing was, when we developed "la Grande Dame" (Cliquot), it took business from Dom Perignon. I had to create another, completely different positioning for the different brands and get new, completely different consumers so that the brands would not fight each other. The best way to do this is to find a common enemy. I used to tell the people at the Grande Dame and at Pommery: your enemy is not Dom Perignon, it is Cristal of Roederer!

Apart from determining the market positioning of each brand, branch presidents played a coordinating role, concentrating on the economies that could be achieved by centralizing purchasing among the companies of the branch based on the buying power of the whole group. They worked with a small team of controllers, human resource managers, and "commercial managers," together developing the sales strategy.

TOP LEVEL LEADERSHIP: ARNAULT AND HIS TEAM

At the age of fifty-one, Bernard Arnault was undisputedly the best-known businessman in France, with a personal fortune accumulated over the years that had put him into the top rank of France's wealthiest. Hardly a day went by without the newspapers in France carrying his name. One day he fought for Gucci, the next day he bought Tag Heuer and the day after he concluded a deal about including de Beers in his empire. These acts established Arnault's public image as that of a cold businessman with icy disregard for the human toll of his ambition on centuries-old family companies. In French business circles where, especially in the realm of luxury goods, a more *artisanal* spirit used to prevail, Arnault's Anglo-Saxon way of doing business was considered the height of bad manners.

Friends of his confirmed his competitive spirit, while categorically denying the coldness that was associated with his public image. The Belgian financier Albert Frère, with whom he bought the Chateau Cheval Blanc vineyard and the English fashion house Joseph, described him as fiercely competitive on the tennis courts. Others reproached him for being a nitpicker, obsessively interested in every detail of his business. His answer to this was, "retail is

detail." He stressed the fact that, instead of spending his time in his office pondering papers, he preferred to visit his shops all over the world. When in Paris, Saturdays were spent passing by Louis Vuitton, observing the usually mad rush with which clients threw themselves on the goods, and making small remarks about improvements.

For Myron Ullman, it was Bernard Arnault who was at the heart of the Group's culture. His personal values left an indelible imprint on the activities of LVMH:

I think that the success of the group is attached to the personality of the founder. This company is very much about the personality of Mr. Arnault, and people's understanding of what his expectations are. He has high expectations, he wants the best there is, he does not want to go second class. He has enormous taste, but at the same time he is not just a guy who likes pretty things. The company is a meritocracy. This is what creates the basic values of the business: to be different from others. This philosophy is unspoken, but always present.

Arnault's leadership style was expressed by Ullman in the following way:

He has a very keen sense of mergers and acquisitions, he knows how to negotiate, when to say yes, when to be tough, He is very very smart, very intelligent, he is extraordinarily tenacious. He is prepared to take risks—OK, it's his money, but if he says yes it means yes. He also has a very interesting sense of style, he can look at an ad and in 15 seconds tell you what is good about it and how to make it better. He has good taste. I think he is very charming—when he wants to be. He is a good salesman—when he wants to be. He is regarded as fairly aloof, basically a fairly shy, private person. He is not the gregarious salesman type.

Concetta Lanciaux, President for Human Resource management, described Arnault as an intuitive leader:

Bernard Arnault is not aware of running the company according to any "management practices." What he has done he has built on intuition and then he surrounded himself by people who helped him do it, but it was not any conscious, premeditated way of "strategy making."

In 1999, when Arnault felt that things were becoming too big to handle everything himself, he persuaded Mike Ullman, an American with an eclectic career (from IBM marketing executive to university professor to White House fellow) who had been in charge of the duty-free company DFS, to become Managing Director of LVMH, in charge of running the group.

Ullman's memories of Arnault's way of hiring him, first for the top of DFS, which he drastically restructured at the time of the Asian crisis, and then to run the group were quite unusual:

When I met him, he [Arnault] didn't know who I was, I didn't know who he was. His philosophy was, there is no management, there is no hierarchy, there is no structure, there is nobody responsible to question me. I do my thing, and do it right.

Pierre Letzelter, President of the Selective Distribution branch, described the different leadership roles within the Group:

> The role of Mr. Arnault in the company is to take care of the image of the brands. When I make operational decisions, I never ask Mr. Arnault what to do. But when I touch the image of the brand, I always consult him before. If you present him a project for an advertising campaign, he will tell you immediately if it will work or not, and why, and how to change it. He has a great sense of style, of flair. He is like a hunting dog, he can sniff out the animal way before the hunter can feel it. He is very cultured, more so than anyone I know, and he is very well informed. He has a real added value in terms of product and image. Mr. Ullman is very different from Mr. Arnault. He is a clock, an engineer. Mr. Arnault is an artist, a world by himself, at the same time very rational and very good at the irrational. He has developed me enormously, he taught me not to go and get his approval. He can tell you, I don't like it, but maybe you are right.

Apart from Bernard Arnault and Myron Ullman, LVMH's corporate leadership team includes Concetta Lanciaux, Executive Vice President and Human Resources Director of the Group. As one of the branch presidents put it:

> The success of Mr. Arnault is based on his talent of delegation, his strength is his ability to choose the right people and then give them free hand to do their things. And Concetta Lanciaux has a major talent for recruiting people. She is very good at anticipating the changes of the business. Not in terms of marketing, or organization, but she feels the new trends of the future and recruits and promotes those people who can make LVMH keep up with the trend. She is very courageous, much more so than Bernard Arnault. When someone does not do well, she is the one to fire the person, Arnault would never do it. She is the *èminence grise* behind Arnault.

SPREADING THE "WESTERN ART DE VIVRE"

The central mission of LVMH—its founding philosophy—was, in Arnault's words, to transmit to its clients what he called a "Western Art de Vivre." The concept of "Art de Vivre"—the art of living well—while very well known by the French, is hard to put into words. It is a sense of style, a vivid connection with the past and its traditions, transferred into the present. It is the cult of beauty and creativity at every level, combining ancestral know-how and craftmanship with modern method and a passion for quality.

According to Arnault, the "Western Art de Vivre" was rooted in history; it was full of memory: it perpetuated the tradition of the most ancient and refined craftmanship. For instance, Moët et Chandon was created in 1743, Guerlain in 1828. LVMH's purpose was to spread this "art of living well," through a combination of the tradition, the history, the elegance and the refinement of the old and venerable brands the Group owned with the energy, creativity, innovation, dynamism and modernity that they tried to bring into these brands. To achieve this marriage of opposites had always been Arnault's passion:

> What interests me more then anything is the combination between ideas; between creativity and commercial success. What I am trying to do with the brands is to project modernity into tradition. The history of the brands is very powerful, but in order for them to be a commercial success they need modernity. I think my strength is to combine new ideas with the tradition of the brand and make it a commercial success. I used the idea of "Western Art de Vivre" as something that could be projected into everything we do. It is present throughout the company and constitutes a way of communicating with our customer and our employees. It explains the general mission we have, which is more than just selling products and making profits.
>
> I think that for people who are not European it is interesting to learn and be in touch with this culture, this lifestyle which is different from theirs. Beyond selling products, we bring a part of European history to the world. When I travel in the Far East and am asked about the story of Dom Perignon, it's more than selling champagne. When I speak about Yquem in the world, it's more then wine, it is embedded into the atmosphere of the seventeenth century Bordeaux, the story of the invention of sweet wine. Art de vivre means to live surrounded by the best you can find. And the best, in this case, is supreme products with a history, tradition, roots.

Arnault chose this expression as the central mission for LVMH, in order to express that the Group intended to remain faithful to two values: high quality and creativity. According to him, it was a matter of constantly reviving a tradition and of innovating without breaking with the memory of the brands.

A demonstration of his interest in keeping the "Art de Vivre" alive was the generosity with which Arnault contributed to culture and the arts. Under his auspices, LVMH had pursued an ambitious corporate sponsorship strategy, supporting a wide array of public interest initiatives. One effort was aimed at the revitalization and promotion of France's artistic heritage: LVMH contributed to the restoration of seven rooms in the Chateau of Versailles' North Wing. The Group had sponsored a host of exhibitions and retrospectives including two major exhibitions on Chardin and Fauvism in Paris.

LVMH was also involved in fostering the cultural instinct of younger generations, particularly in fine arts and music. In this vein, the "LVMH Young Artist Award" provided financial aid to art students around the world.

The "1000 seats for young people" project had awarded 14,000 concert seats to young musicians training in Paris conservatories. LVMH also supported young virtuosos by lending them Stradivariuses from its collection and by organizing concerts to promote young talent. Arnault himself possessed a strong artistic streak, a fact that had probably had a strong influence on his professional choices. As a young man, he studied piano seriously, but abandoned it when he realized he would never become one of the world's greats. He had the reputation of having an eye for the visual arts, singling out at exhibitions the most important piece in the room. He also owned the prestigious journal *Connaissance des Arts*, which was held in high esteem by amateurs and professionals alike.

As a showcase for his "Art de Vivre" Arnault unveiled in 1999, with a dinner in New York to the benefit of the Municipal Arts Society, what constituted the most tangible monument of his ambitions: the LVMH "Tower," a 23-story office building on East 57th Street and Madison Avenue. The unusual, cubist façade of the building, the work of French architect Christian de Portzamparc, the youngest winner of the Pritzker Architecture Prize, was cited as being one of the most outstanding architectural statements in New York.

A PHILOSOPHY OF CREATIVITY

According to Gianluca Brozzetti, the President of Louis Vuitton, success in the luxury business had little in common with the marketing mechanisms that applied in other businesses. It required an understanding and the ability to handle something additional and intangible that could not be found in other businesses; the management of something that could not be codified in the production or financial processes—the dream that was built in the head of the customer, who came to buy the products to a great extent for this intangible value added. The key to success was to understand that the product was a receptacle of people's desires and dreams. Customers did not only want to acquire functionality when buying a Louis Vuitton bag, they bought an image, a lifestyle. In order to be able to meet the unspoken expectations of the customers, people working at luxury goods companies had to have a certain sensitivity for understanding this intangible part. Most of the luxury brands that LVMH possessed had been created many years earlier by entrepreneurs who had this certain intuition and feeling for their products. LVMH tried to keep up this creative spirit and the talent to provide meaning for their clients. In Brozzetti's words:

> You have to understand your clients, and once you have understood them, you have to give them something that is not described how to do in books. It is not a detergent that simply has to wash white. What color do you make a bag, what shape?

There are no rules, this is all a decision of judgment, based on what we think we know of the client and his or her expectations. The value is created not only by technology and innovation, but to a great extent by beauty and the emotions the products elicit. Louis Vuitton has written in its chromosomes the spirit of travel, of wealthy people traveling in a sumptuous and innovative way. Add to this an understanding of the expectations that the client has of the product, and mix in some fantasy, the unexpected.

The amazing success of Louis Vuitton since its acquisition by LVMH in 1995 provides an illustration of this combination. Prior to the acquisition, customers bought Louis Vuitton products because they were made very well and they were associated with high quality, but not necessarily with fashion or elegance. Then, in 1997, Arnault hired a new designer, Marc Jacobs, who created new lines of products which were much more modern, identifying the brand with the desirable fashion world.

The step to put Louis Vuitton, the conservatively run but profitable "star" brand of the group, into the hands of such an unconventional designer as Marc Jacobs was a risk not many would have taken. The prestigious bag company founded by trunk-maker Louis Vuitton already held the place of the most profitable luxury brand in the world. Jacobs was an "enfant terrible," who lost his job with American designer label Perry Ellis for turning high fashion into lowly grunge. Arnault took the gamble and won. Louis Vuitton launched Jacobs's first collection with a groundbreaking show in Paris that earned him the place of the designer of the new millennium.

Jacobs did not go about things incrementally. He took the 146-year-old LV logo and put it everywhere, starting off the trend of "logomania." He re-edited the conservative and plain monogram canvas bags in shiny, patent-leather versions in futuristic colors like lilac and steel, attracting a whole new segment of young and hip customers. In the meanwhile, the traditional, best-selling monogram bags were given every imaginable new form and shape, drawing a horde of Asian customers who paraded them at home as status symbols. The collection Marc Jacobs designed for Louis Vuitton was enlarged by a ready-to-wear clothes line. Traditional women's pumps acquired the identifiable pattern of another, more recent creation, the checkerboard. From car blankets to dog collars to hairbands, the LV logo found its place everywhere. Limited editions made the objects even more sought after. Creative details such as luggage strapping for elegant dresses and coarse saddlery topstitching on fine, strappy sandals brought a fresh and original touch to traditional items. As a result of Jacobs's work, Louis Vuitton was able to retain the connotation of providing high quality products, but also acquired one of being extremely hip. This doubled profitability in record time.

Indeed much of LVMH's success came from Bernard Arnault's talent for spotting creative talent and then in shaping a culture in which that creative talent could flourish. He had given a new generation of designers the chance of their lifetime at LVMH: John Galliano at Dior, Alexander McQueen at Givenchy (who later deserted Arnault to join—of all places—Gucci), Marc Jacobs at Vuitton, Michael Kors at Celine and Narciso Rodriguez at Loewe. Designers within the group were also pampered by the investment that LVMH made in their own name labels. This concerned money, but also management support and advice. Designer Michael Kors was not only the artistic director of Celine but also obtained the capital investment from LVMH necessary to open his first Kors store on Madison Avenue. The question why LVMH was such a popular employer with designers was answered by Bernard Arnault as follows:

Designers here know that they have the freedom to create, they are not controlled by others. But their ideas have to be a commercial success. Designers are artists, but artists who have to make sales. The *haute couture* is the showcase, not the money-maker. Galliano's *haute couture* collection for Christian Dior, for example, is not sellable. But it brings a lot of ideas for related products, it attracts the people. Last year we drew an enormous amount of people with the accessories, the bags, scarves that were a declination of the *haute couture* ideas, it was a fantastic success. It is much more interesting to go to a show and see ideas. The dresses you can see in the shop. For the media also it was much more exciting, much closer to a real art presentation.

The results of this commitment to creativity were there for all to see. In 1999, sales of newly launched leather goods increased by 30%. The new Monogram Vernis line accounted for over 10% of Louis Vuitton's sales one year after its launch. In the same year, sales of new champagne *cuvées* jumped 69%. And in the three years, Hennessy had launched a dozen new products.

When asked to describe LVMH's corporate culture, Bernard Arnault provided a clear conception of his vision of the Group.

The general philosophy of the group can be described by the following factors: product quality, creativity, image, entrepreneurial spirit and the willingness of its people to always question their achievements and the striving to be the best. The "cultural assets" of our group are the heritage of creativity, savoir-faire and innovation, *art de vivre* and estheticism, French and European taste, quality and the search for excellence, as well as the transmission of knowledge and an entrepreneurial spirit.

The origins of LVMH's corporate culture were laid down at the very beginning of the existence of the Group. When Arnault took over Dior, the goal he set for his employees was nothing less than to become number one in the world in what they were doing. By setting an objective that seemed almost too ambitious to be attainable, he wanted to mobilize their energy to do their best to get there. This was not always easy. Ambition and thought at this scale did not come automatically to everyone working in the company. Some of the key employees had to considerably adapt themselves to the grand outlook Bernard Arnault had on things, as witnessed by one of the branch presidents:

Mr. Arnault taught me to look for quality above all, disregarding cost. The best things are hardly good enough. When he acquired the auction house Phillips, whose activities are in a business that is not very profitable, he decided to rent the nicest building in New York. When I saw what the rent cost I felt sick. But Mr. Arnault was convinced that it was the right thing to do for the prestige of Phillips. And he made me take an architect that cost a hundred times more than one I planned to use. But, I must admit, in the end he was right. Quality always pays.

According to Philippe Pascal, the President of the Wines and Spirits branch, the common characteristics of LVMH brands were the craftsmanship of dedicated people who were passionate about doing something of outstanding quality. The majority of people working at LVMH professed to love the products they worked with and wanted to make sure that others loved their products, too. One of the things one often heard at the company was, "I want to be the best. I want my wine/bag/dress to be written about as being the best." People in the Group tended to have a very strong feeling of ownership of "their" brands.

COMPETING ON TALENT

The art of making and selling a $3000 dress differed considerably from selling a $3 soap. To run the world's largest and most successful luxury goods group required people of a very special caliber. It was not enough to be a good salesman or -woman. The intangible nature of the products required the person who was in contract with them to possess an additional dimension that could perhaps be expressed by the word culture.

The people responsible for recruiting at LVMH were very particular about what kind of people they were looking for. To be hired by the Group one had to show a great deal of autonomy and entrepreneurship. As described by Bernard Arnault, "at LVMH every manager needs a good dose of entrepreneurship, and people who have a more bureaucratic outlook will not thrive here."

An entrepreneurial outlook was a necessary, but not sufficient condition for a career at LVMH. In addition, it was indispensable for people who wanted to work at the company to be sensitive to the luxury goods business. This sensitivity could manifest itself in different ways, by liking theater, cinema, the arts, beauty. People who travelled a lot and visited the different museums and works of art in other countries would fall into this category. Individuals who had a hard time identifying the difference between renaissance, baroque, and romanticism would not. Recruiters at LVMH paid attention to the way a person dressed, the tie or accessories he or she wore, and the way the person carried him- or herself. People who wanted to be hired had to possess a certain elegance, a perception of beauty. As Bernard Arnault expressed it:

> When we hire executives they have to have the ability to work with designers and they have to like the product so they can talk about it with designers. Obviously it's not possible to come here if you do not like the products. It's like a having a musical ear, you either have it or you don't. Every single person who works at LVMH needs this inclination to a certain degree. They all have to show an understanding and a liking for the products they work with. So we try to hire these kinds of people. Then they are plunged into this kind of atmosphere immediately.

These kinds of people, however, who combined a certain sensitivity for elegance and beauty with a knowledge of the luxury goods business were not easy to come by. In 1990, LVMH had grown to such an extent that Concetta Lanciaux and her recruiting team started to have serious problems finding suitable people for the new companies. After some reflection, LVMH decided to give a chair in marketing to one of the top French business schools, ESSEC, in order to create a place where future recruits would be prepared for the specific marketing rules that governed the luxury goods business. The next step was to sponsor a complete MBA Program in luxury goods management at the same school. Since that time ESSEC has sent out every year about 20 top students who were very well versed in luxury goods management and were hired LVMH. The next step in luxury goods management education was taken by LVMH by replicating the MBA concept in Shanghai, with the reasoning that Asia was one of the most important and rapidly growing markets for LVMH.

Other recruitment programs followed. Launched in 1999 to support Group expansion and the development of new subsidiaries around the world, the Futura program targeted the hiring of high potential managers with four to eight years of international professional experience and a solid educational background such as an MBA. The young managers who came out of this program were confronted immediately by organizational challenges, such as running a profit center or a corporate level department in an international subsidiary. Another program, the "Jeunes Diplômés International" (Young International Graduates) had, in the course of five years, supplied LVMH with a pool of 550 young managers from different countries, with degrees in business and engineering. The recruiting of these young managers with international backgrounds was done in cooperation with top academic institutions in Europe, North America and Asia. In 1999, this network of multi-cultural partnerships was strengthened by the addition of partnerships with the best MBA programs in Latin America. The target for LVMH was to find 50 new graduates per year from the best business schools.

As LVMH's reputation grew, the greatest hindrance to finding the right people became the quality of the candidates, not the lack of applicants. In France, the Group had reached a status where it figured at position two on the list of most popular companies to work for after an education in business. When asked why LVMH seemed to have such a strong attraction for graduates from the best business schools, Bernard Arnault explained:

> If you want to attract top talent it is advantageous to be a diversified group that includes the best-known luxury brands on earth! People at LVMH have unparalleled career prospects, they can choose among start-ups, very big companies, medium-sized firms, they can learn the métier in an outstanding company like Louis Vuitton and then go on to become the CEO of a start-up with huge development perspectives that he or she can run like an entrepreneur. When a person starts at LVMH in a management position he or she can very quickly become an entrepreneur and make a lot of money in the process.

According to Concetta Lanciaux, one of the major arguments that convinced people to work for LVMH was that they could quickly assume positions of responsibility and leadership which would have taken much longer to reach in other companies. The profiles of the people who held responsibility in the company showed that they were often very young. In her words:

> The new graduates who come into the company on management level are immediately given real jobs, we do not send them on a lengthy training program first. This way they learn immediately by doing. Their responsibility is not enormous at first, but they are positioned in real management jobs. We knew that we had no chance to attract top talent if we did like L'Oreal or GE, because our training programs would never be as good as theirs. So we had to differentiate ourselves from them and find a new way to get the best people. It has become one of the main attractions for people who come to LVMH that they start off in a real job. It also helps us to quickly find out if someone is not suitable for the way things work at

LVMH: people who find the initial responsibility too overwhelming leave soon, and this way we get a natural selection of people who like to take on immediate responsibility.

Once hired, LVMH tried to take care of its people as much as possible. One young graduate who encountered personal problems shortly after she was hired by the Group described her experience:

People need to be recognized as individuals, not just cogs in a wheel, and LVMH is good at that. I had some family trouble and the company gave me time off to fix it. One of my colleagues went the hospital and was sent flowers. When a company does things like this, you feel that you want to give back what you received in the form of loyalty and hard work.

In order to offer its employees high-caliber training and development the Group instituted a comprehensive training program. In addition to the seminars offered in each Group company, the LVMH Training Center in Paris and the regional centers in New York, Hong Kong and Tokyo provided inter-company training focused on key areas: development of personnel management, and integration within LVMH. In 1999, 1,550 upper-level managers participated in Group training programs.

The Global Leadership Program launched in 1999 was aimed at stepping up the professional development of the most promising future executives through discussions on risk-taking and innovation moderated by business group leaders and the CEOs of Group companies. To complete this training offer, LVMH House opened its doors in London at the end of 1999. This development and innovation center received executives and high-potential young managers of the Group from all countries. LVMH House made it possible to multiply exchanges of "best practices" on such global issues as leadership and innovation. LVMH House's aim was to promote learning by action through project groups designed by consultants and recognized professionals as well as the Group senior managers.

One of the well-known attractions of the Group to new graduates was the fact that they could offer its people the possibility of internal mobility within the company. The global presence of LVMH, the constant pace of acquisitions with more and more companies joining the ranks of the group created career opportunities at LVMH which were unmatched by any comparable company in the world. Four hundred and twenty management-level employees were transferred to new positions within the Group in 1999, a number that had tripled in three years. To facilitate broadening of experience and perspective, special assignments were developed which enabled employees to work for a defined period in a company other than their own. In 1999, more than 100 managers completed such assignments. People could have an international career by moving between the large number of countries where the group was present. Also, moves between the divisions were encouraged, enabling people to have a varied and changing work environment and tasks.

One of the things that characterized LVMH was the fact that people who worked at the company tended to express repeatedly how proud they were to be part of the "Christian Dior family" of the "Louis Vuitton family." They felt that there was a lot of prestige involved with LVMH companies. This elitism was clearly one of the attractions of the Group. Employees also cherished the fact that they could contribute to the development of the company without having to put up with a lot of bureaucratic procedures and constraints. To quote Thibaut Ponroy, president of LVMH's Guerlain perfumes division:

Mr. Arnault sets people free. When I was working fro the Guerlain family, there were so many cash constraints and they called me up every Monday morning, arguing about what was happening in the shop. There were only five family members in the company, and about 60 of them just waiting for cash. Under LVMH, there is no cash crisis and we are at last free to be creative.

Branch presidents played a major role in developing their people. Pierre Letzelter described his view on the topic.

For many years, capital was hard to find. Now capital is everywhere, but what is hard to find it good people. Good people are never interested just by the money. They are interested by being part of something, of being able to say that they were part of something worthwhile. People need to dream, but the dream has to be achievable. One has to gradually give them more and more challenge, get them to become used to the challenge. We have to create small success stories, that encourages them to go on to bigger success stories. Show them their progress.

Very good people are always under tension. My role is to reduce that tension. The key thing to do in my position is to recruit, to keep, to promote, to develop, to reward. My role is to keep specialists working together, to have them follow a common objective.

Remuneration of management level people at LVMH was based on a fixed base salary, a bonus, and (Group) stock options. Bonuses could reach up to 50 percent of the base salary. Stock options were merit based, reaching up to 1000, or 2000 percent of one's base salary or more. They were given exclusively to the people who LVMH considered "high potentials," those that the Group wanted to keep. The amount of stock options granted to any individual was kept confidential.

FUTURE FOCUS

The luxury business was for many years more a craft industry serving a small, elite group of wealthy customers, but had undergone a change in consumer patterns towards stronger industrialization, "democratization" and internationalization.

LVMH had clearly positioned itself on the forefront in this young industry by transforming itself radically in the years between 1997 and 2001. Formerly a conglomerate of essentially French and independent brands managed exclusively by French executives, LVMH had become an integrated group active in every segment of the luxury business, with a portfolio of international brands and international teams of managers and creators. It had become the benchmark and leader in innovation for the luxury goods industry. Louis Vuitton's strategy of achieving perfect control over distribution had become a model for all the companies in the sector. Also, the strategy of building up a multi-brand group had been copied by numerous players. LVMH also occupied the first place in e-commerce in luxury goods, and its distribution network allowed it to constantly monitor changes in consumer patterns and preferences.

Ongoing changes had made the luxury industry more competitive and professional. Competition between brands had become increasingly fierce in terms of creation, advertising and distribution. In a way, LVMH was a victim of its own success. After a number of record years in terms of profits and growth, expectations had risen to such an extent that the 27 percent increase in operating profits for the year 2000 was met with disappointment and falling share prices.

The company realized that their biggest challenge for the future was to retain the people who had shaped the company's development and success. When asked about what gave him sleepless nights in connection with the LVMH Group, Bernard Arnault talked about the difficulties of finding the right kind of people for his ever-expanding emporium:

> Our biggest challenge now is to be able to attract this very special type of high-level executives and also the right kinds of creative talents for the future. The market is going to continue to grow, but we will only be commercially successful if we can find the right kind of talent and continue in the same spirit as we have done until now. Our success is really based on having the people of the highest caliber, and of this special talent, which is difficult to find. Our structure allows us to further expand, but we need the right people for this. I am very involved in hiring creative talents, this I will also continue to do. And I have to be more and more the spokesman towards the outside. This is a necessity in today's climate to explain what the group is doing and to attract the best people.

Economic slowdown, coupled with LVMH's high exposure to the yen and the US dollar, incorrect loss forecasts, various Internet initiatives, as well as questions about the group's investment in the auction business, made the Group vulnerable in spite of strong demands for its leather goods and fragrances. While the Group had its definite strengths that helped it master the problems it had been confronted with, the future was certain to present challenges exceeding those that LVMH had to face when it was growing to become the most powerful player on the battlefield of the luxury goods business.

CASE 17

Kami Corporation

As Mr. Olano, the new general manager of Kami Corporation, walked through the plant at the Clark Special Economic Zone, Pampanga, Philippines, in early December 1994, he shook his head and wondered how he could improve operations in general and production operations in particular, to make Kami a world-class operation. The problems were many, but the solutions . . . well, they were engineering and production problems and Mr. Olano was not an engineer himself. To make matters worse, the problems were not just on the plant floor, they were in the output from Kami's two lines of Aiwa TV assembly operations. Whereas there should have been three production lines with output of 1,000 units per day per line, there were only two lines as yet installed and they had only managed to reach an output of 500 units per day each.

Aiwa's orders had been running at about 30,000 per month against output of 25,000 per month. Worse yet, Aiwa had indicated that within three months, its orders would be in the 50,000 to 60,000 range and higher thereafter. Mrs. Lee, the owner of Kami corporation through Mega Corporation, had committed to Aiwa to have production capacity of 80,000 units per month—and after three months of operations it was less than a third of that.

MEGA CORPORATION

Mega had been founded by and was owned by the Lee family. By 1994, it had forty subsidiary operations in many industries, such as consumer electronics, automobiles (assembly and distribution of Mazda, Kia, Diahatsu, and BMW), automotive components (Columbian Motors), real estate (such as its industrial park south of Manila in partnership with Samsung), agriculture (a mango plantation and alcohol production from cane sugar), and aquaculture (shrimp and prawn production and processing for export to Japan). Mrs. Lee was in charge of the family's operations in the Philippines. Mr. Lee operated out of Hong Kong and had extensive investments and operations in China.

In consumer electronics, Mega had had a relationship with Sony since the early 1970s, first as the distributor in the Philippines of Sony products and later as an assembler for Sony of its audio and video products. Mega also was the distributor and assembler of Samsung TVs, audio equipment, white goods (refrigerators, microwaves, and so on), Sumida coils, and Murata TV tuners, plus it produced

Professor Don Lecraw prepared this case solely to provide material for class discussion. The author does not intend to illustrate either effective or ineffective handling of a managerial situation. The author may have disguised certain names and other identifying information to protect confidentiality.

Ivey Management Services prohibits any form of reproduction, storage or transmittal without its written permission. This material is not covered under authorization from CanCopy or any reproduction rights organization. To order copies or request permission to reproduce materials, contact Ivey Publishing, Ivey Management Services, c/o Richard Ivey School of Business, The University of Western Ontario, London, Ontario, Canada, N6A 3K7; phone (519) 661-3208, fax (519) 661-3882, e-mail cases@ivey.uwo.ca.

Copyright © 1997, Ivey Management Services.

CASE 17 KAMI CORPORATION **171**

plastic and wooden cabinets. As well, it distributed Aiwa audio products.

This type of relationship was a typical one for many companies in developing countries that had followed an import-substituting development strategy. Under this strategy, the government protected finished goods industries behind high tariff and/or non-tariff barriers to trade. They also imposed lower tariffs on components, semi-finished, and raw materials imports. Although trade protection did foster the development of import substituting industrialization and led to investment in assembly operations, often these ventures were scale inefficient, and produced high-cost products which could neither compete on export markets nor, without continued protection, against imports on a price and quality basis.

As one facet of this protection, often government also restricted foreign investment and had regulations requiring foreign investors form joint ventures with domestic companies, particularly for ventures whose output was oriented toward domestic markets. As well, foreign investment was also often prohibited in the distribution, wholesale and retail trade sectors. This was the situation in the Philippines.

In all these cases, the relationship between the domestic company and its foreign partner had gone from distribution, to assembly from semi-knocked down (SKD) kits supplied by the foreign partner, to assembly from completely knocked down (CKD) kits again supplied by its partner, to assembly using some components made in the Philippines by Mega. Except in this last stage, however, the OEM producer for whom Mega was assembling the final products was the one to order the components, gather them into kits and transfer them to the Mega assembly operation. The OEM producer estimated demand for finished products and insured that sufficient kits were available for production to meet this demand. Even when Mega produced some of the components, production was based on orders placed by the OEM producer according to its forecast of components needs given its demand projections.

Over the past decade, however, many developing countries, including the Philippines, had begun gradually to liberalize both their trade regimes and their FDI systems. The objective was to reorient the manufacturing sector toward being competitive on both export markets and against imports. Over the years, Mega had earned a reputation for the quality of its assembly operations and, as Mega had gained production expertise, it was able to add more and more domestic value added to its assembly operations. Nonetheless, its operations were still largely assembly ones with little in-house manufacturing achieved.

Mega's exports were a very small percentage of sales since production was almost entirely for the domestic Philippine market. At one time, some of the products Mega produced for Samsung had been exported to the U.S., but these exports had ceased when Samsung began production in Mexico. Small volumes of Mega's Sony products were exported to South America.

AIWA

Aiwa was a subsidiary of Sony with a strong presence in the audio market. Although the perception of Aiwa was rather "down market," Aiwa was a technology leader in certain types of audio equipment and components. In fact, in some cases, Sony used components designed and produced by Aiwa and even placed its brand name on Aiwa produced audio equipment. All in all, Aiwa's production share was estimated to be almost 30 per cent of the world market for audio products. In TVs, however, Aiwa was in a much weaker position with substantially less than 5 per cent of the world market.

Aiwa's goal was to supply 50 per cent of the world market for audio products. At the same time, it had decided to make a major push into TVs. It planned to introduce two lines of TVs into the Japanese market in September 1994. To accomplish these goals simultaneously would strain Aiwa's capital and managerial resources if it were to make investments in production facilities. Instead Aiwa's new strategy was to concentrate its resources on product development and marketing and have other firms invest in the plant and equipment and retain 100 per cent equity ownership in their production facilities.

Under these relationships, Aiwa provided the designs and component specifications, a "master components list" which specified not only the components needed but the maximum prices for them. Some of the components on the master list would come from Aiwa, but others could be from other suppliers either identified by Aiwa or by its production partner. If the assembler could identify a components supplier whose product met Aiwa's quality standards, but whose price was lower than the price on the master list, then Aiwa would permit the assembler to source from the new supplier and split the savings with the assembler—even if previously the component had been sourced from Aiwa.

Aiwa paid its assemblers on the basis of the cost of components (up to a maximum of the prices on the master list) plus labor plus a margin per unit produced. Under this system, Aiwa's assemblers did much more than simply assemble from SKD or CKD kits supplied by Aiwa. They had to have or develop expertise in international sourcing, purchasing management, logistics, and inventory control.

Mega Corporation, in partnership with Samsung, owned and operated an industrial park south of Manila on which a TV assembly plant could be located. Just as Mrs. Lee was about to make a firm decision to go ahead with the project with Aiwa at this plant site, however, Mr. Tito Hensen, President and CEO of the Clark Development Corporation, called her with a strong plea to consider the Clark Special Economic Zone (CSEZ) as a site.

Clark Field had had a checkered history as a U.S. air force base. Near the beginning of the Japanese entry into World War II, Japanese planes had caught the U.S. air force planes based at Clark by surprise and had destroyed most of the planes on the ground. During the Vietnam war, B52 bombers stationed at Clark had played a major role in the high level bombing in Vietnam. After the Vietnam war, there was a dramatic decrease in activity at Clark. Nevertheless, by the time of the termination of the bases agreement in 1991, employment of Filipinos at Clark made it the largest employer in the Philippines outside the government. Beyond direct employment, there were extensive spillover effects into the adjacent city due to the spending of U.S. military and civilian personnel and their dependents. As well, despite extensive fencing, there was substantial smuggling and pilferage from Clark with the goods sold in nearby Dau. The U.S. government estimated that together Clark and its navy base at Subic comprised about 4 per cent of the Philippine economy.

Although Clark Field had been less affected by the Mt. Pinatubo explosion than had Subic, redevelopment at Clark had lagged behind that of Subic for several reasons: the U.S. military had not attempted to clean up Clark after the explosion; there had been extensive looting; Subic's port made it ideal for export-oriented manufacturers; and Subic's Richard Gordon had aggressively promoted Subic as an investment site. In addition, Clark was much closer to Mt. Pinatubo than Subic.[1] By 1994, both Subic and Clark had attracted investment in huge duty-free stores, hotels, and other service facilities, but Clark had not been nearly as successful as Subic in attracting manufacturing investment.[2]

When Mrs. Lee visited Clark, she was greeted with devastation. By 1991, Mt. Pinatubo, thirty kilometers away from Clark, had erupted in the largest volcanic explosion the world had seen in more than a century. Five inches of "ash fall," sand, dust and rocks, had fallen on Clark destroying buildings, covering roads, and clogging pipes and sewers. The proposed facility site looked like a desert. The warehouse at the site had crumpled under the weight of the ash fall. Although there were plans to install electrical generating capacity and water supply, at the time any facility would have to install its own generator and truck in its own water supplies.

As Mrs. Lee beheld this site, something in her said, "Let us lease this place." In part, this decision was to help the people of the province of Pampanga who had been devastated first by the explosion of Mt. Pinatubo and later by the "lahar" flows which had buried rice fields and towns under thirty feet of sand. Although many of the professional engineers and technicians had left the area for jobs in Manila

and abroad, there was a large pool of educated, trainable workers in Pampanga who lingered on without jobs. Mrs. Lee felt that she could make a contribution to the shattered lives of the people of Pampanga and that they would repay her with hard work, discipline, and company loyalty.

Before signing a lease agreement at Clark, however, after many meetings with Aiwa managers, she had been able to persuade them that if they reached a production arrangement, Aiwa would accept production from a facility located at Clark. With this agreement in hand, Mrs. Lee had signed the lease agreement for ten hectares of land and began construction of her plant.

KAMI CORPORATION

In May 1994, Mrs. Lee had entered into the agreement with Aiwa to assemble Aiwa TVs in a facility to be constructed at CSEZ.

1. A new company would be formed, the Kami Corporation, with a total capacity of 80,000 units per month and an investment cost of $10,000,000.
2. Aiwa would buy all Kami's production and Kami would produce only for Aiwa.
3. Initially, orders would be in the 20,000 to 30,000 range for the first six months with firm orders placed one month in advance and projections given three months in advance.
4. If Aiwa's launch in the TV market went according to plan, within six months orders would be in the 50,000 to 60,000 range. In subsequent years the orders would rise further, so that eventually demand would be in the 70,000 to 80,000 range.
5. Kami would produce Aiwa's first two models: 14 and 18-inch TVs for sale in Japan (40 per cent), the Middle East (20 to 25 per cent), and the balance to Europe and South America. The U.S. market would be supplied from Aiwa's facility in the U.K.
6. Initially, no sales would be for the Philippine market, which operated on a different reception standard than did Kami's proposed markets.
7. After two years, Kami would also be able to sell in the Philippine market with an estimated volume of 2,000 to 3,000 units per month.
8. Aiwa would initially ship key components in SKD kits, but after three years (by June 1997) they would be in CKD kits.
9. As with its other producers, Kami could source components from whichever suppliers could produce them to Aiwa's quality standards, if their costs were below those on its master components list. Cost savings would be shared between Aiwa and Kami.

10. Kami would receive $140 and $180 for the two models—about $2.00 over direct costs (standard costs for components on the master list plus labor and other estimated direct costs).

11. Kami would be responsible for supplier identification, development, and management.

In addition, Mrs. Lee decided to build a plastic moulding plant at a cost of $10,000,000 to supply both Kami and the other assembly operations within the Mega Corporation with moulded plastic TV casings.

Time was of the essence. In fact, Mrs. Lee had already begun constructing operations at Clark and had ordered the core production equipment before the agreement with Aiwa was finalized. Even with this head start, meeting the deadline for the first shipment set by Aiwa for September 28, 1994, had proven to be impossible to achieve at the Clark facility. Even before the plant was finished, production workers were hired in the areas surrounding the CSEZ and trained in Mega's plants in Manila. By this means, the finished products could have been shipped on time, except for the obstructive behaviour of one customs agent. This agent refused to clear components inputs for assembly in Manila (outside the CSEZ) and re-export. He even refused to cooperate after receiving a direct order from the Director of Customs. Instead he released to the media a statement that Mrs. Lee and the Director of Customs were conspiring to produce TVs for the Philippine market assembled from smuggled components—even though Kami's TVs were produced for Japanese NTSC standards and would be inoperative in the Philippines.

Eventually, the first units were shipped on October 5, the last day that they could have been shipped to meet Aiwa's extended deadline. If they had not left on that day, Kami would have had to ship them by air freight at a considerable loss.

After this scramble to produce and ship the first units, Kami soon moved production to the CSEZ and its 200 production workers began assembly operations in the new, not yet completely finished, facility.

MR. OLANO

Mr. Olano had been closely involved as this project had taken shape. Mr. Olano had an undergraduate degree in accounting. After graduation in 1979, he had worked for three years for SGV, the largest and most prestigious accounting and consulting company in the Philippines. He had resigned from SGV to take a job with the government in the Commission on Audit, the government watchdog accounting department. After three years with the government, in 1983 he had joined Pryce Development Corporation for two years. Then, in 1987, Mr. Olano had joined Mega as an advisor, trouble shooter, and in-house consultant. As of early 1994, Mr. Olano's major job was finance manager at Mega's subsidiary joint venture with Samsung, Samsung Mabuhay. His boss at Samsung Mabuhay had also been his boss when he worked for the government. His boss still retained extensive ties and responsibilities within government, so that much of the day-to-day management of Samsung Mabuhay had rested with Mr. Olano.

Mr. Olano had been surprised by his appointment as general manager of Kami. He had been called in by Mrs. Lee and simply informed of the appointment and his move from Manila, where his family lived, to be general manager at Kami at the CSEZ, sixty miles away. His response had been, "Yes, of course, right away." Mr. Olano learned that he had been selected from a short list of three, the other two on the list being family members. Mega had a long history of appointing either family members or engineers as general managers of their production operations. Mr. Olano was told the reason for his selection was his education, expertise, and experience as an accountant, a "paper shuffler" and technocrat. As Mrs. Lee remarked, "Mr. Kee, the production manager, says that the problem is in the order process. Straighten it out."

Mr. Uy, the acting general manager at Kami, had been in charge of production at Mega's Sony assembly operations where production was about 5,000 units per month. In addition to his position at Kami, he had retained his position as production manager at the Sony operation and two other assignments within the Mega Corporation. His position at Kami had been seen as a temporary one given his other assignments. His assignment had been simply to get Kami going and run it until a permanent general manager was chosen.

Mr. Uy had brought seven production managers with him from Sony operations: the production operations manager, the quality assurance manager, the main production engineer, the automation engineer, and three assistants. Mr. Kee,[3] the production operations manager, had been the senior engineer and the senior production manager under Mr. Uy. This man had expected to receive the position of general manager when Mr. Uy returned to his other assignments with other units of the Mega Corporation.

Mr. Kee resented Mr. Olano's position as general manager on several counts: Mr. Olano was not an engineer; he had no experience in production; except for his experience as a financial manager at Samsung Mabuhay, he had no general management experience; he was younger than Mr. Kee and he had worked for the Mega Corporation for fewer years than had Mr. Kee (seven compared to twelve).

Mr. Kee's fellow production managers generally supported Mr. Kee.

The seven key production managers lived together, socialized together and worked together as a group. They saw Kami's operations as an extension of production. They felt that the other components of Kami—warehousing, inventory control of components and finished products, purchasing and ordering and so on—were satellite operations in support of Kami's main function: production.

In fact, the actual ordering of components was done through Mega's major assembly subsidiary rather than by Kami itself. When inventories of components ran low, the production department would notify the order department (actually one clerk) to place an order. This order was then transmitted to Mega in Manila. The actual order was placed by Mega with the supplier. In addition, Mega had the responsibility of making follow up inquiries and arranging the paperwork for customs clearance. When the components arrived, Mega would be notified, it would then notify Kami and send Kami the necessary documentation and a representative from Kami would go to the pier or airport to clear the goods through customs. This process had caused delays, lack of follow up, and mix ups in ordering. This problem had been identified as the root cause of Kami's production problems—and this was the problem that Mrs. Lee had told Mr. Olano to fix.

THE DECISION

Kami was in trouble. There were substantial order backlogs from Aiwa—and Aiwa's orders were increasing month on month. Whenever Mr. Olano questioned Mr. Kee about the delays in shipping, there was always an excuse: there had been a mistake in ordering, the components had not arrived or they were stuck in customs; they could not be found in the warehouse; finished products were ready, but they could not be located in the warehouse; the necessary export permits had not been obtained. So on and so forth.

Mr. Olano's inspection of the various units of Kami's operations had led him to several conclusions. Since Kami had no in-house expertise in sourcing, orders for components from Philippine suppliers and from abroad were handled from Mega's operations in Manila. This procedure led to delays and to incorrect orders. When delays occurred, messages had to go from Kami to Manila and then to the suppliers. Many rush, expedited, and small orders had to be given to correct mistakes and to address delays—this meant many trips for small orders to the customs warehouse rather than scheduled trips for larger orders. Mr. Olano had considerable expertise with export and import documentation and ordering procedures himself. In the warehouse, components sourced in the Philippines and imported from around Asia were mixed in with finished goods inventory and with rejected components (to be returned) and wastage from the production process. Often components could not be located and finished goods shipments were delayed, even when they were finished, because all of the shipment could not be located quickly. All the floor space in the warehouse was being utilized with boxes stacked as high as could be reached and boxes and parts spilled out into the aisles. There was plenty of airspace, however, above the stacks.

There seemed to be little coordination between the monthly orders received from Aiwa for the next three months, production planning, components needs, orders being placed to ensure delivery in time for production, and the shipment dates specified by Aiwa. This was perplexing, since Aiwa only had two models in production at Kami: the 14-inch and the 18-inch TV sets. Within a year, however, Aiwa planned to introduce five additional models. Unless something changed, the situation could only get worse.

As Mr. Olano remarked:

I was in an uncomfortable situation. The production managers resented the fact that I had the job I had. At most, they wanted me to confine my job to accounting and finance—and leave the rest to them. But when there were delays and backlogs, they always blamed some other unit within Kami—and absolved themselves of responsibility. Yet, if I suggested that I would address the problem that they had identified, with the warehouse, for example, they viewed this with suspicion as encroaching on their authority. I felt like a guest, and an unwelcome one at that, whenever I ventured onto the production floor. Yet I was the general manager who was nominally in charge of the operations. I saw many procedures on the production line that were not according to best practice—and I was sure that the Japanese technicians who were monitoring the installation of the circuit boards saw many more. But what could I do? Even my suggestions that I straighten out the warehouse had been met with disapproval. If I tried to intervene on the production line . . . well, you can imagine.

I knew that Aiwa was complaining to Mrs. Lee about the delays in our deliveries. I also suspected that the Japanese technicians were dissatisfied with the situation and had probably communicated their findings to Aiwa.

I knew that I had to do something, but the question was what—and how? I was having a difficult Christmas season, but I resolved to get going and make things happen so that my New Years's would be better.

*The Richard Ivey School of Business gratefully acknowledges the generous support of John Adamson (MBA '72) in the development of this case.

Strategic Planning at the New York Botanical Garden (A)

Start a major job of institutional planning and change, and you will find there are all of these different stakeholders. My experience in institutional life has been that you might as well find ways to make them happy at the outset. You might as well just take it on up-front and get consensus because otherwise you are going to do it in a piecemeal way. This way you don't dissipate all of your time and energy trying to make everyone happy later on. Because basically you have to make them happy, especially in a troubled institution. You've got to get everyone smoothed out and on-line. If you don't do it up-front, you're doing constantly—and I find that very draining. You can't get anything done—every day you wait for the phone calls from all of the unhappy people. That is the way a lot of people run an institution—they let it come up everyday, they wait, they get exhausted spending so much time and energy dealing with people who aren't on board.

—*Gregory Long*

Gregory Long, president of the New York Botanical Garden, walked slowly to the podium at Sotheby's Auction House.[1] The date was April 21, 1993, and assembled before him were 400 of the Garden's most influential stakeholders—the board, current and potential donors, heads of government agencies and other nonprofit organizations, Garden members, and business executives. All of these listeners had an important potential role in the plan for the Garden's future that Long was about to unveil.

The Sotheby location, like the guest list, had been selected with care. Here in Manhattan, Long reasoned, even marginally interested individuals could easily drop by for the one-hour presentation, with cocktails to follow—unlikely if the presentation had been held in the north central Bronx, the Garden's home. He thought of tonight as the kind of theatrical event for which New York was well-known. Carefully written, orchestrated, and rehearsed, the presentation shared with the public, for the first time, the view of the Garden's future that had emerged during its extensive and inclusive planning process. It presented the "collated results of collective thinking" that had been going on for two years, as Long described it.

He felt that he had been working towards this presentation since his arrival at the Garden as President in 1989. The wording on the Sotheby invitation (contained in Exhibit 1) reflected his conviction: "This is not just a beloved New York City institution getting a facelift; rather the transformation of an institution."

As he prepared to outline the strategic plan and the master plan for the facility that had been two years in the

---

This case was written by Jeanne M. Liedtka, Associate Professor of Business Administration. This case was written as a basis for class discussion rather than to illustrate effective or ineffective handling of an administrative situation. Copyright © 1997 by the J. Paul Getty Trust and the University of Virginia Darden School Foundation, Charlottesville, VA. All rights reserved. *To order copies, send an e-mail to dardencases@virginia.edu. No part of this publication may be reproduced, stored in a retrieval system, used in a spreadsheet, or transmitted in any form or by any means—electronic, mechanical, photocopying, recording, or otherwise—without the permission of the Darden Foundation.*

The New York Botanical Garden recently completed an intensive planning process which has resulted in consensus on commitments and priorities through the end of the decade. You are cordially invited to attend, on Wednesday evening, April 21, 1993, a special presentation announcing plans for the future of this venerable New York City institution as it strives to move forward toward the new century with vitality and meaningful work from the neighborhoods of the Bronx to the rainforests of Brazil. We hope you will join us.

The Host Committee

YOU ARE CORDIALLY INVITED TO ATTEND

A SPECIAL PRESENTATION

HERALDING THE RENAISSANCE

OF

THE NEW YORK BOTANICAL GARDEN

WEDNESDAY, APRIL 21, 1993

FROM 6:00 TO 8:00 P.M.

AT

SOTHEBY'S

1334 YORK AVENUE AT 72ND STREET

NEW YORK CITY

PROGRAM BEGINS AT 6:30 P.M.

THE GARDEN PLAN FOR
THE NEW YORK BOTANICAL GARDEN

GREGORY LONG
President

MRS. DONALD B. STRAUS
Senior Vice Chairman

LYNDEN B. MILLER
Landscape and Garden Designer

SHEILA GRINELL
Author, *A New Place for Learning Science*

THOMAS J. HUBBARD
Chairman

RECEPTION IN THE GALLERY

ON DISPLAY, FINE ENGLISH AND CONTINENTAL SILVER
AND WORKS OF BOTANICAL INTEREST

THE HOST COMMITTEE

NORMA KETAY ASNES

MR. & MRS. MORTIMER BERKOWITZ III

DIANA D. BROOKS

JOAN K. DAVIDSON

MR. & MRS. MARQUETTE DEBARY

BETH RUDIN DEWOODY

MR. & MRS. EUGENE P. GRISANTI

MRS. ANDREW HEISKELL

MR. & MRS. THOMAS J. HUBBARD

PEGGY ROCKEFELLER

SHELBY WHITE & LEON LEVY

The New York Botanical Garden gratefully
acknowledges Sotheby's generosity in hosting this event.

making, Long was concerned—could he create the level of excitement in this community necessary to accomplish the ambitious aims for institutional change that the plan set out? Would these important constituents see the plan as unattainable, given the Garden's current circumstances?

AN OVERVIEW OF THE NEW YORK BOTANICAL GARDEN[2]

The story of the creation of the New York Botanical Garden began with a belated honeymoon visit to England in 1888, taken by a New York City couple, Elizabeth and Nathaniel Lord Britton, both dedicated botanists. Upon visiting the Royal Botanic Gardens at Kew, the couple resolved that New York should have a garden "just like that" at Kew, and embarked on an ambitious, and ultimately successful, campaign to convince politicians and wealthy New Yorkers of the desirability of establishing such a botanical garden.

The New York Botanical Garden was incorporated by a special act of the New York State Legislature in 1891 for the purpose of establishing and maintaining a botanical garden, museum and arboretum "for the collection and culture of plants, flowers, shrubs and trees; the advancement of botanical science and knowledge and the prosecution of original researches therein and in kindred subjects; for affording instruction in the same; for the prosecution and exhibition of ornamental and decorative horticulture and gardening; and for the entertainment, recreation, and instruction of the people."

The 1891 Act directed the Board of Commissioners of the New York City Department of Parks to set aside up to 250 acres of the Bronx Park for the Garden, once the Garden had raised $250,000. The $250,000 was successfully raised; the 250 acres were set aside in the northern half of the Bronx Park; and the City agreed to underwrite a bond issue of $500,000 for buildings and improvements. The Garden opened to the public in 1895.

The 1891 Act remained the Garden's corporate charter. The Garden had pursued its tripartite mission—science, education and horticulture—for over 100 years and still operated on the basis of a partnership between the private and public sectors. The Garden was a museum accredited by the American Association of Museums and was widely recognized as one of the world's leading research and educational institutions in the plant sciences, with extensive programs in plant exploration and systematics, economic botany and scientific publishing. The Garden's Herbarium, a collection of 6,000,000 preserved plant specimens, was the largest in the Western Hemisphere. The Garden's Library housed one of the world's largest botanical and horticultural research collections.

The Garden's grounds in the Bronx also constituted one of America's most famous public gardens. Designated a National Historic Landmark in 1967, the Garden contained an unusual variety of natural topography, a 40-acre tract of virgin forest, historic specialty gardens and living plant collections, and several architecturally significant structures, including the Enid A. Haupt Conservatory.

The Garden was a private not-for-profit corporation under New York law and a tax-exempt organization under section 501(c)(3) of the Internal Revenue Code. The Garden owned the contents of its facilities and collections, and managed and operated its premises and buildings, title to which remained with the City. In this corporate structure, the Garden was similar to other City cultural institutions that occupy City land and structures, including The Metropolitan Museum of Art, The American Museum of National History and Lincoln Center for the Performing Arts. Like those institutions, the Garden came within the jurisdiction of the New York City Department of Cultural Affairs.

THE GARDEN'S SCIENTIFIC PROGRAMS

The Garden was one of the world's leading centers for research in plant systematics and economic botany. The main purposes of the Garden's research were to discover and document plant diversity; to provide the taxonomic system for plants (the nomenclature by which all knowledge about plants is organized and transmitted); and to elucidate the evolutionary biology of plants through modern analysis techniques.

The Garden's Institute of Economic Botany researched the use of plants by human cultures. The Institute's work has been to identify little-known or underutilized plants with medicinal, nutritional, or economic value. Scientists working within the Institute investigated tropical deforestation, medicinal plants, nutrition, disease, sustainable development, and the importance of indigenous knowledge.

The Garden published nine scientific journals and monographic series of approximately 30 nonserial titles each year. Garden scientists taught courses at The City University of New York, Cornell University, Yale University, Fordham University, Lehman College, and other colleges and universities.

THE GARDEN'S EDUCATIONAL PROGRAMS

The Garden's educational programs, both formal and informal, focused on plants and the environment and were designed to meet the educational needs of various constituencies ranging from preschool children to graduate students. The Garden was the only nonacademic institution in the New York City area to offer formal training in botany. The Garden offered over 400 adult education courses each year. Bronx Green-Up was an outreach program that helped communities create gardens in vacant lots in the Bronx. Plant Information and Reference Library Services provided information to the public, staff and students at the Garden.

SIGNIFICANT STRUCTURES AT THE GARDEN

The focal point of the Garden's physical premises was the late-Victorian glass building known today as the Enid A. Haupt Conservatory. Completed in May 1902, it was one of the earliest greenhouses built in America. It was also considered by many architects and historians to be the nation's greatest glass house, and was the largest conservatory for public display in the United States.

Another major edifice at the Garden was the museum building, designed by Robert W. Gibson and completed in 1905. The museum building housed the Herbarium, the Library (in the contiguous Pratt Library Building), other science facilities, an exhibition of living orchids, a retail shop, public reception, and visitor information, restrooms and an auditorium.

A NEW TEAM ARRIVES

Despite its proud history, assets, and significance in its field, the Garden was an institution much in need of rejuvenation—both physically and financially, when Gregory Long arrived to assume the presidency in 1989.

Thomas Hubbard, previously a board member, elected chairman of the Garden's 45-member Board of Managers in June 1991, recalled the circumstances surrounding Gregory Long's selection:

I was on the Committee that selected Gregory. When he interviewed, he already knew more about the Garden then anyone—more than we did. When that meeting was over, we looked at each other and said "he's it.". . . He recognized, from day one, that we needed to get the Garden into the mainstream of New York cultural institutions—and he knew where every dollar in New York was.

The organization, at that time, was "adrift" as one senior manager described it. The Garden had received no major capital spending from the City in years; even maintenance needs had been inadequately met. Because of its parklike landscape and because it charged no admission, the Garden had become, in the perception of many of its users, a public park—a place to bicycle, picnic, walk the dog, throw a Frisbee, or take a leisurely (or less than leisurely) drive through. Long had different ideas:

There was a perception, because this institution was headed by scientists, that this was a campus for those scientists, and the public came and used the campus for passive recreation. We wanted to end the perception of the Garden as a public park. What we wanted users to see in the future was a botanical garden, a museum of plants, and not a public park.

The living plants, so vital to the Garden's mission, could not be properly displayed or cared for in a park-usage environment. Thus, one of Long's early actions, as president, was to fence the Garden, and to ban dogs and cars, a move that was met with dismay on the part of some of the Garden's neighbors:

They were a core group of customers, and we didn't want to lose them. This has been a very difficult issue for us throughout. There was a core group of users who used the Garden in ways that didn't relate to our primary function as a museum, ways that weren't really appropriate, but we needed them anyway.

Resources at the Garden were also severely limited. Richard Schnall, vice president for horticulture, explained: "Staff didn't have the resources to do what they needed to—staff had to fight for a telephone, there was not enough propagation space, and there were too few visitor amenities, like restrooms—it was pretty fundamental stuff."

Several of the Garden's historic structures, the Conservatory, in particular, were known to be in dire need of costly renovations.

The Garden's operating finances were another major cause for concern. Exhibit 2 contains financial statements for the New York Botanical Garden for fiscal years 1991 and 1992. Sources of funds included gifts and grants from individuals, foundations, corporations; appropriations from New York City, New York State and federal government agencies; membership revenues; tuition and publication income; income from retail operations; and income earned on its endowment. In 1991, for instance, the Garden earned just over $500,000 from parking, food, and admissions. Across the street, the Bronx Zoo earned more than $11 million from these operations during the same period. Market value of the endowment at June 30, 1992, was approximately $22 million, with the annual draw on the endowment averaging approximately 6.5 percent. This endowment was seen as inadequate, relative to the size of the Garden's annual operating budget. The Garden's financial dependence on annual appropriations from the City of New York, in particular, left it vulnerable, Long felt, to the vagaries of the City's finances and politics.

This set of serious concerns prompted Long and his executive vice president and chief financial officer, John Rorer, to pursue the idea of embarking on a comprehensive planning process. In explaining their rationale, Long elaborated:

Although the Garden's work was of a high caliber, and demands for its services locally, nationally, and internationally

EXHIBIT 2
STATEMENT OF
CHANGES IN FUND
BALANCES
(fiscal years ending
June 30)

	1991	1992
Fund balance, beginning of year	$408,702	$458,820
Revenues and other additions		
Appropriations—City of New York	5,170,899	4,096,232
Grants and contracts:		
Federal	93,505	127,900
State	1,126,087	1,131,065
Private contracts	42,123	108,078
Private gifts and grants	3,041,993	2,355,407
Special events	1,662,379	2,037,085
Investment income and realized gains	232,298	200,308
Other earned income	2,581,929	2,654,464
Auxiliary enterprises	1,313,925	1,430,952
Total revenues and other additions	$15,265,138	$14,141,491
Expenses and other deductions		
Program Services	$4,816,772	$4,034,805
Support Services	8,251,231	9,015,242
Auxiliary Enterprises	1,260,618	1,340,718
Total expenditures and other deductions	14,328,621	14,390,765
Transfers among funds—additions (deductions)		
Land, buildings, and equipment	(311,160)	N/A
Other transfers	(575,239)	N/A
Total transfers among funds	(886,399)	277,102
Net change to the fund balance	50,118	27,828
Fund balance, end of year	$458,820	$486,648

Source: Morgan Stanley prospectus.

had never been greater, the Garden had a serious and potentially deeply damaging problem. It had grown to be an institution with an operating budget of nearly $21 million and only a precarious, underendowed revenue base in place to support its major commitments. In fiscal-year 1992, income from endowment funded only 9 percent of the operating costs. The Garden itself and its public programs and activities funded only another 33 percent of operating costs. The remaining 67 percent of operating income was derived from contributions by the private sector to the Garden's Annual Fund and from government grants. These two sources are the two least dependable of all not-for-profit revenue sources, especially in today's era of governmental financial crisis and economic recession.

Throughout this period, the Garden was committed to achieving a balanced budget. This had been accomplished only through a combination of aggressive new fundraising efforts and significant reductions in staff and operating expenses. At the same time, it was the strong opinion of the Garden's leadership that further cuts or additional staff reductions would signal a downward spiral in reputation from which it would be impossible to recover. Exhibits 3, 4, and 5 contain a more detailed look at sources of operating support, trends in city and state funding, and changes in full-time positions, over a multiyear period.

Paula Kascel, a professional planner, joined the New York Botanical Garden as director of Long-Range Planning in January 1990, and explained what she saw as Long and Rorer's motivation:

Both saw the significance and value of an institutional exercise that brought sort of new understanding to the organization in terms of where it was headed. Both understood the value of unearthing a large organization and examining it and its old ways and then making decisions based on that familiarity. There was a lot of vestigial behavior, lots of balkanization at the Garden. Gregory and John informed one another in terms of their own experiences and decided together that to really move the Garden forward in terms of its financial stability but also programmatically, it really needed to be examined and then a whole new funding base had to be developed for the institution.

A seven-year time frame was selected for the plan. In explaining his rationale for the choice of such a long time horizon, Long noted: "We had so much to do—there was more than could be done in the usual five-year time frame."

EXHIBIT 3

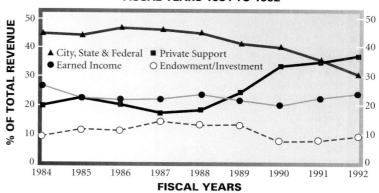

**SOURCES OF OPERATING SUPPORT,
FISCAL YEARS 1984 TO 1992**

Note: Increases in endowment income for FY 87, 88 and 89 resulted
from the extensive use of realized capital gains.

EXHIBIT 4 TRENDS
IN CITY AND STATE
FUNDING,
FY1987–FY1992

	TOTAL CITY AND STATE SUPPORT	% OF TOTAL REVENUE
1987	$6,321,000	40.4%
1988	6,474,000	39.4
1989	6,681,000	36.0
1990	6,964,000	35.0
1991	6,335,000	32.0
1992	5,251,000	25.3

EXHIBIT 5 SUMMARY OF NET CHANGE IN FULL-TIME (FT) POSITIONS FROM FY1989 TO FY1992

	TOTAL FT POSITIONS, FY1989	FT POSITIONS REDUCED, FY1989–92	FT POSITIONS ADDED FY1989–92	NET CHANGE	% CHANGE
Security	43	13.0	0.0	−13.0	−30.2
Operations	48	9.0	0.0	−9.0	−18.8
Horticulture	55	7.0	2.0	−5.0	−9.1
Finance & Administration	35	7.0	5.5	−1.5	4.3
Education	21	4.5	0.0	−4.5	−21.4
Science	51	5.0	0.0	−5.0	−9.8
Retail Sales	10	4.0	0.0	−4.0	−40.0
External Relations/Visitor Services	9	3.0	5.0	2.0	22.2
Garden Magazine	3	3.0	0.0	−3.0	−100.0
Library	16	2.5	0.0	−2.5	−15.6
Development	10	2.0	4.0	2.0	20.0
Rental Marketing	3	0.0	0.0	0.0	—
Total	304	60.0	16.5	−43.5	−14.3

THE PLANNING PROCESS

The planning process that Long and Rorer set in motion consisted of three overlapping phases: (1) the preparation of an early "protoplan," a kind of miniplan written by their senior staff that allowed them to begin the process of fundraising; (2) the program plan, created in a widely inclusive process that involved managers at every level, that set out the Garden's strategy for the future in the key programmatic areas, and incorporated a financial plan of their implications; and (3) the master plan, which detailed the capital projects necessary to achieve the program plan. Exhibit 6 details the components of each of these stages.

The planning process that Long and Rorer devised and implemented was an ambitious one in terms of who it involved, how they worked together, and what they produced.

WHO WAS INVOLVED

Long and Rorer decided that the planning process should involve everyone at the Garden with responsibility for program implementation. In the Botanical Science Research Division, this included all of the individual scientists; in horticulture, it included all curators and head gardeners. Also included were custodial and physical plant managers, as well as those in the finance area. In total, the expanded planning group included about 85 participants, including 12 invited members of the board. In selecting board members, Long and Rorer looked for level of interest, time availability, and people with potentially challenging views. "You don't want to avoid those kinds of ideas until the end of the process; you need to get them integrated early on," Long believed.

Planning-group members participated at four levels. At Level One, front-line program managers offered their input. At Level Two, the directors to whom those managers reported synthesized their managers' input and used it to formulate their own recommendations. At Level Three, the vice presidents—Long's direct reports—synthesized the inputs from Level Two and made their recommendations to Long himself. At each level, presenters reported their recommendations to the entire planning group of 85, for comment and questions. Long them synthesized these recommendations into a final plan that he brought to the board for their approval. It was this plan that he would present tonight at Sotheby's.

HOW THEY WORKED TOGETHER

The emphasis on creating an open forum of discussion prevailed at each level in the planning process. The expanded planning group met once every three weeks in the Snuff Mill, for several hours, for two years. Over this time period, the entire group was invited to listen to presentations from all other managers involved. Each presentation was followed by a question-and-answer session. Attendance at the meetings was high—averaging no less than 60 participants throughout.

The presentations began at Level One with the scientists—the science mission was seen as central and the scientists, as a group, were generally comfortable presenting their work to large audiences. Each scientists was asked to speak about his or her work, its contribution to the Garden, and his or her hopes for their ideal future. Each was asked to describe the kind of resources that would be needed to help him or her achieve their professional vision. Brian Boom, vice president for Science, offered a typical example. The scientists would say things like, "I'm 50 years old, I have another 15 years of active career, this is what I think I can accomplish, given these resources." In horticulture, for example, the curator of the Rock Garden presented his view of what the Rock Garden could be. The emphasis, throughout, was on "blue-sky thinking." All planning members listened to all presentations—security and operations managers listened and presented to the scientists and gardeners and vice versa.

EXHIBIT 6 THE NEW YORK BOTANICAL GARDEN MASTER PLANNING PROCESS:
Making a New Garden, 1989–99

A. THE PROTO PLAN: 1989–91
1. cars and dogs out
2. the museum concept
3. a garden not a park
4. outdoor cafe
5. Rock Garden restoration
6. Forest restoration
7. Beth's Maze and Children's Corner
8. Family Garden upgrade
9. perimeter fence and Metro North Station upgrade
10. interpretation and maps

B. THE PROGRAM PLAN: 1990–92
1. strategic plan for institution
2. Science Plan
3. Horticulture Plan
4. Education Plan
5. Financial Plan

C. MASTER PLANNING: 1991–92
1. visitor experience
2. restoration of buildings and landscapes
3. exhibition facilities
4. education facilities
5. infrastructure survey
6. topographic maps
7. circulation and transportation

The director of Planning, Paula Kascel, played a significant role in the articulation and presentation of each individual's ideas. She worked individually with each presenter beforehand. As she described her role in the "public-performance component": "I didn't guide—I had no agenda. I was there to hear what they did and help them articulate it as best they could, so that their work was presented in the best possible light."

Paula found that her background in theater was often as helpful as her planning expertise in these discussions. "We really worked to make the presentations entertaining," she noted. "Performance values mattered."

The open dialogue after the presentations was sometimes lively, especially as the process progressed and managers at the next level, having listened to their people's presentations, began the process of prioritizing and making decisions as to what would or would not go into the next planning level. Throughout the process, budgeting staff worked with each presenter to develop pending estimates. Exhibit 7 contains a memo outlining the questions to be answered at Level Two.

Level Three began the most difficult phase of prioritization and sequencing. The price tag for the blue-sky thinking was totaled and estimated to be about $235 million. Fundraising consultants estimated that the maximum fundraising capacity of the Garden was no more than $165 million. And so the senior staff took on the challenging role of bringing the "pie-in-the-sky thinking back down to earth," as one described it. Each area was allocated a portion of the $165 million and asked to adhere to this figure in making their choices about what would remain in the plan moving forward. They were then asked to sequence these initiatives and spending across the seven-year planning horizon.

NEW YORK'S FISCAL CRISIS

Approximately nine months into the Garden's planning process, the City of New York began to experience severe financial trouble. This situation had a significant impact on the planning process itself. As CFO John Rorer described the situation:

New York's financial crisis got translated into financial trouble for the New York Botanical Garden as well as other similarly situated institutions around New York City. So we started looking at our financials, saying "What does this mean?" Indeed, if the shape of our funding is changing, how do we ensure survival? So we shifted a bit in our focal point in the planning process and said, "Let's talk about how we structure what we do so that not only can we realize our dreams and visions of the organization, but also so that we can survive financially, because we're going to lose some of our government support and that's clear." We had a small endowment, we didn't generate much money from

visitors, and we knew there was a limit to increased private fundraising. So that was a bit of a shift midstream. We did projections and presented them to the whole planning group and everybody saw the disaster coming, the big deficits, if we didn't change the funding trends that were emerging.

As a result of these discussions, the focus became a blended plan that combined a baseline operational plan for current operations with the more future-focused set of new aspirations for the Garden. The newly configured plan would not be an "add-on wish list," in Long's terms, but a comprehensive blueprint that would "run the Garden" on a day-to-day basis.

This also led to a focus on revenue generation as an important component of the early phases of the plan. Earned-income goals were established for the restaurant and catering facilities, retail operations, and membership. By early 1993, with the strategic plan completed, detailed business plans were being written in each of these areas. These included business-development activities, marketing plans, and pro-forma financial projections, all of which fed into the overall financial plan.

Long and Rorer chose not to wait until the completion of the planning process before acting on several of the issues that arose during planning discussions. One of the initiatives that they undertook immediately was to begin the process of amending the Garden's charter to permit the charging of admission fees. This required an act of the New York State Legislature in Albany, which was successfully passed in July 1991.

Another area where they chose to act immediately was in the realm of computerization. Paula Kascel describes the evolution of this issue:

Everyone was really struggling with technology and doing it at their own pace. This ranged from legal pads and number-two pencils to people who were fairly sophisticated on the Internet (in 1990!). We heard concerns from the Library, from Administration, from Education—we saw that this was strategic issue, an institutional issue. Gregory and John chose to lift it out, put the resources toward it, put it on fast forward. They created information-service programs and started to deal with the issue of information management on an institutional basis. That, to me, is an example of how planning is not a linear process—you can't stop reacting or moving forward just because planning is under way.

BOARD INVOLVEMENT

In addition to including board members as part of the planning team, the board was briefed at each meeting on the progress of the planning process. The board's confidence in Hubbard and Long facilitated the entire board's support for

EXHIBIT 7 THE NEW YORK BOTANICAL GARDEN MEMORANDUM

TO: Level II Planning Participants

FR: Paula Kascel

RE: Revised Level II Planning Summary

DT: September 20, 1990
==================================
Attached is a revised edition of Planning Our Own Future, Level II.

A draft of the narrative questions designed to facilitate your thinking about the future of your department was circulated to you on June 18, 1990. The narrative questions in this revised version remain the same, with two minor changes which are underlined in the following samples:

Page 2 E. How would increased inter-departmental interaction and collaboration better serve the Garden institutionally?

Page 3 A. In ideal terms, how would you like to see your department develop over the next five-year period beginning 7/1/92? (Cancel; reorganize/redirect; develop further.) Please describe in detail.

As you know, in addition to completing all of the information in this summary, Level II presenters are asked to summarize their thinking on a departmental basis for Fiscal Years 1993–1997 in a ten-minute presentation to the members of the Expanded Planning Group.

In these planning presentations, Department Heads are asked to give a clear and concise overview of the goals of their departments, and the actions and resources which will be required to achieve those goals for Fiscal Years 1993–1997. The questions on Pages 3 and 4 of the written summary should serve, in part, as a guide for your planning presentations, although specific questions on Pages 1 and 2 may also be incorporated, based on your individual approach.

II. PROGRAM DIRECTIONS/NEW INITIATIVES OVER FIVE-YEAR PERIOD

A. In ideal terms, how would you like to see your department develop over the five-year period beginning 7/1/92? (Cancel; reorganize/redirect; develop further.) Please describe in detail.

B. Please describe, in order of priority, what specific actions could be taken to more fully develop your department over this five-year period.

C. In order of priority, what new initiative(s) would you like the Garden to undertake in your department in the future? What are the arguments in support of these new initiatives (e.g., benefits to the Garden, etc.)?

D. Describe and estimate what current department expenses could be saved to help fund these new initiatives.

E. Describe and estimate what new or expanded sources of revenue could be identified to support these initiatives.

F. Please highlight any collaborative professional efforts which would be integral to new program initiatives.

G. What are the significant trends which you feel will influence the future direction of your department (both negatively and positively) and which should be considered by the Garden as it plans for the future?

H. Please relate these trends to the specific recommendations and new program initiatives identified by you and by members of your staff.

THE NEW YORK BOTANICAL GARDEN

SEPT. 1990

| PLANNING OUR OWN FUTURE LEVEL II |

Name_____ Title _____ Date _____

I. ASSESSMENT OF CURRENT PROGRAM(S)

A. Please give a general description of your department as it currently exists.

B. The programs and activities of your department are designed to reach/serve whom?

C. How does the work of your department relate to, and support the overall purposes of the Garden?

D. Please describe how your department supports and reinforces activities of other departments.

E. How would increased inter-departmental interaction and collaboration better serve the Garden institutionally?

F. What are the criteria used to evaluate your department?

G. What are the strengths and weaknesses of your department as it is currently designed?

H. How has your department changed since inception?

I. Please name and describe programs, activities or attitudes by other organizations which have influenced your thinking about the future of your department and which could serve as models for NYBG.

the process. "Besides," Hubbard commented, "we had tried a standard boiler-plate approach to strategic planning several years before, with outside help, and nothing ever came of it," so the board was open to trying a different approach. In addition, the New York Public Library, under Long and Vartan Gregorian's leadership, had previously used a process very similar to the one that Long and Rorer now proposed to accomplish a major institutional turnaround that had received international attention.

Paula Kascel, who worked extensively with the board in her role as director of Long-Range Planning, recalled two important points in the planning process when the board raised concerns that required addressing. The first related to the state of the economy.

As Gregory described the situation in the 1990–91 time frame:

> The economy was very bad—the country's, the City's, in general, and we were not a strong enough competitor for the private funding that we would need. There were times when looking at our needs just got overwhelming. We were having tremendous problems just balancing our current budget—we had reduced staff by almost 15 percent between 1989 and 1992—yet everybody seemed to want so much. How would we ever satisfy them? These were the dark days.

Long responded by inviting an economist to speak at a board retreat on the topic of cycles in the economy in relation to philanthropic giving. This talk demonstrated to the board that, at no point since the 1950s, had the bottom fallen out of philanthropic giving. The economist also suggested that the economy would likely be coming out of recession by the time the fundraising campaign would be ready to launch. This reassured the board of the financial feasibility of implementing the plan.

The second issue of concern to the board related to what Paula Kascel described as "talking in details":

> We kept talking to the board in detail. I need computers, I need secretaries, I need more vehicles. Now, going into this level of detail was absolutely necessary, but the board was starting to drown in the details—the minutiae was starting to drown us all—especially the board. In November 1991, Gregory began to talk about how all of these little pieces of individual staff-member needs, at every level of detail, actually advanced a small set of major mission components. Everything fit into one of these three categories that emerged: (1) giving new vigor to Botanical Science research, (2) the public aspect of the museum, and (3) financial stability. If you took all of these individual visions to their natural conclusion, this is the story they told.

The board came to understand how each new vehicle or computer supported a large vision. In the process, they became more comfortable with the plan's detailed focus, having seen its connection with an emerging view of the Garden's future.

COMMUNITY RELATIONS

Throughout the planning process, the opinions and feedback of community members were solicited as input to the plan. As Long described his view of the role of the community: "Seeking the community's opinion and acting on it are essential elements in maintaining good relations, in generating enthusiasm for new developments, and in obtaining community support when it is needed."

An important job of the Garden's Community Relations Committee had been to work with the small group of neighbors in the Bronx who did not want to bring more people into the Garden, to help them to understand that the institution's survival depended upon making the changes contained in the plan.

THE OUTCOMES OF THE PLANNING PROCESS

By April 1993, when Long took the podium at Sotheby's, the strategic-planning process had produced a comprehensive set of program, master, and financial plans.

The program plan outlined three objectives:

Part I: Give new vigor and focus to botanical research.
Part II: Bring more visitors to the Garden and enrich their experience.
Part III: Achieve financial and managerial stability.

All new initiatives were placed within the context of the larger vision outlined by these objectives. The elements of the master plan for the development of the grounds and facilities were incorporated within each of these program areas.

PART I: GIVE NEW VIGOR AND FOCUS TO BOTANICAL RESEARCH

The scientific mission of the Garden would remain central to its purpose of moving forward. In fact, the ongoing habitat destruction, and attendant erosion of plant-genetic diversity, that accompanied tropical-forest destruction made the Garden's historical focus on botanical research even more prominent and vital, the plan argued. In rededicating and escalating the Garden's commitment to collect, verify, and disseminate information on the plant species of the world, the plan made the construction of a new library/herbarium building and the upgrading of laboratory facilities top priorities. It created a new Institute of Systematic Botany, to complement the existing Institute of Economic Botany, formed in 1981. Staffing and endowing the new Institute was a plan priority, as was endowing two additional positions in economic botany. Upgrading the library resource base, through computerization, acquisitions, and conversions, was also included.

PART II: BRING MORE VISITORS TO THE GARDEN AND ENRICH THEIR EXPERIENCE

This part of the plan focused on the public aspect of the Garden and centered on the restoration of the Garden as a living museum. Because, the plan argued, the Garden's distinguished scientific-research programs could never be made to be fully self-supporting, nor could initiatives around environmental education, programs for children, or urban revitalization initiatives like Bronx Green-Up, it was essential that the Garden increase visitor volume and attendant revenues. Accomplishing this required the renovation of the Enid A. Haupt Conservatory as a top priority, establishing a horticulture endowment, and completing a plant inventory. The restoration would require the closing of the Conservatory, the Garden's most popular visitor attraction, for a period of four years. Priorities also included broadening opportunities for learning through the creation of additional programming and a Children's Adventure Garden, and improving the visitor's experience by the addition of more parking, restrooms, and public programming, along with the renovation of the Garden's auditorium, and the construction of a visitor orientation center, and the creation of a new main entrance.

PART III: ACHIEVE FINANCIAL AND MANAGERIAL STABILITY

This portion of the plan focused on ensuring the Garden's future financial health by increasing revenue on three fronts—annual giving, endowment, and earned income. Exhibit 8 details the revenue growth required, by area, in the plan. The construction of a new restaurant and catering facility was an important priority, as was expanding marketing. Advancing institutional management, especially in the area of computers, along with restoring security staff positions, and upgrading maintenance and operations, were also important initiatives.

THE MASTER PLAN

To implement these programmatic priorities, the master plan for the grounds and facilities described the concept of the "Garden within the Garden." The Garden identified the location, in the western portion of the grounds, where institutional investment would be focused and where public activities and horticultural programming would be concentrated. This concept called for restoring existing structures, investing in new buildings and gardens, and providing new amenities to enhance the visitor's experience. Exhibit 9 contains the details of the master plan.

EXHIBIT 8 REVENUE GROWTH REQUIRED
FY1992–99

REVENUE SOURCE	PERCENTAGE GROWTH, FY1992–FY1999
Conservatory admissions/parking/ voluntary contributions	213.0
Indirect costs recovered	200.8
Tour income	193.8
Tuition and fees	109.0
Gross membership income	96.8
Scientific publications	93.9
Auxiliary enterprises	82.6
Miscellaneous income	76.0
Endowment income	51.5
Grants and contracts	43.5
Appropriation—City of New York	43.2
Annual fund	40.4
State appropriation	37.2
Total operating revenues	58.5

THE CAMPAIGN FOR THE GARDEN, 1993–99

Taken together, the comprehensive set of plans created in the strategic-planning process set the stage for the launch of the most ambitious fundraising campaign in the Garden's history, and one of the most ambitious ever undertaken by any New York City cultural institution. Its goal was $165 million, more than twice the Garden's previous fundraising goal of $63 million. Exhibit 10 details the operating, capital, and endowment needs outlined for the campaign.

The $165 million campaign had been broken down into goals for the different sources of support, both government and private. Private sources include corporations, foundations, board members, and other individuals. Present in the Sotheby's audience that night were many of the people who could be most influential in helping the Garden meet these goals.

As Long reached the podium at Sotheby's, the audience became quiet, waiting for the presentation to begin. Some of them, Long conjectured, might be thinking that they had already waited too long for the unveiling of the Garden's hoped-for-future—that two years was too long for a planning process to take. Long disagreed:

> I suppose that you could think of it as a two-year planning process followed by a seven-year implementation period, but that is not how I look at it. We gave ourselves nine years, in total, to get a lot done. I think of our first two years as an investment in reaching consensus among a lot of people about what this institution would become—without which, we could not go on to accomplish significant things. I consider it time well spent.

EXHIBIT 9 THE MASTER PLAN

Spring at the Garden

N

Legend

- **$** ATM
- **?** Information
- **⋔** Restrooms
- **Water fountain**
- **☎** Phone
- **♿** Special needs
- **⛱** Picnic area
- **○** Tram Stop
- **●** Forest entrance
- **✚** First Aid

Additional support for the spring season is provided by **⟵ conEdison** and **Scotts**.

Metro-North Railroad Station

Mosholu Gate

Ornamental Conifer Collection closed for renovation

The buildings and grounds of The New York Botanical Garden are owned by the City of New York. A portion of the Garden's general operating funds is provided by the New York City Department of Cultural Affairs, the New York City Council, and The New York State Office of Parks, Recreation, and Historic Preservation. The Bronx Borough President and Bronx elected representatives in the City Council and State Legislature provide leadership funding.

The New York Botanical Garden is an advocate for the plant kingdom. The Garden pursues its mission through its role as a museum of living plant collections arranged in gardens and landscapes across its National Historic Landmark site; through its comprehensive education programs in horticulture and plant science; and through the wide-ranging research programs of The International Plant Science Center.

1	Enid A. Haupt Conservatory
11	Jane Watson Irwin Perennial Garden
12	Nancy Bryan Luce Herb Garden
13	Irises
15	Conifer Arboretum
16	Peonies
17	Seasonal Walk
18	Demonstration Gardens
26	Daffodil Walk
27	Murray Liasson Narcissus Collection
28	Rock Garden
29	Native Plant Garden
31	Library Building
33	Watson Education Building
34	Arthur and Janet Ross Gallery and Lecture Hall
35	The LuEsther T. Mertz Library
36	The Steere Herbarium (open to researchers)
37	Peggy Rockefeller Rose Garden
37A	Dolores DeFina Hope Tree Peony Collection
38	Lilacs
39	Cherry Valley
40	Magnolias
43	Maple Collection
45	Crabapples
46	Daffodil Hill
47	Conifer Plantations
49	Azaleas and Rhododendrons
50	Forest
51	Forest Edge Trail
52	Snuff Mill (picnic area and trail)
56	Waterfall Overlook
59	Everett Children's Adventure Garden
72	Mitsubishi Wild Wetland Trail
73	Ruth Rea Howell Family Garden
106	Great Garden Clock Visitor Information Plaza

EXHIBIT 10   SUMMARY OF CAMPAIGN NEEDS: Operating, Endowment, and Capital

OPERATING NEEDS

Supporting the Growth of the Annual Fund, 1993–99

1993	$6,300,000
1994	6,800,000
1995	7,200,000
1996	7,500,000
1997	8,000,000
1998	8,400,000
1999	9,000,000

New Vigor and Focus for Botanical Science, 1993–99

Herbarium Computerization	$1,761,000
Staffing the Institutes of Systematic and Economic Botany	1,120,000
Library Catalog Computerization	1,025,000
Forest Research	842,000
Improving Access to Herbarium Collections	675,000
Building Library Staff	479,000
Conserving Library Collections	376,000
Marketing Scientific Publications	240,000
Library Acquisitions	126,000

An American Horticultural Showcase, 1993–99

Building Horticulture Staff	$749,000
Stewardship of the Forest	683,000
Horticulture Computerization	467,000
Turfgrass Improvements	226,000
Completing the Plant Inventory	160,000
Restoring the Montgomery Conifer Collection	100,000
Demonstration Gardens	82,000

Environmental Education, 1993–99

Children's Adventure Project	$3,285,000
Environmental Education in the Forest	651,000
Graduate Program Coordinator	437,000
Marketing for Continuing Education	210,000
Continuing Education Facilities	55,000
Recertifying the Continuing Education Program	45,000

The Visitor's Experience, 1993–99

New Public Programs	$895,000
New Signage and Interpretation	425,000
Audience Research	115,000

Financial and Managerial Stability 1993–99

Conducting a Capital Campaign	$3,300,000
Advertising and Marketing	1,025,000
New Institutional Computer Initiative	872,000
Expanding Maintenance and Operations Staff	680,000
Membership Promotion	593,000
Restoring Security Staff	471,000
Financial Analysis and Planning	360,000
Capital Projects Management	354,000

Retail Operations	300,000
Volunteer Program	296,000
Community Relations Program	280,000
Inventory Controls	145,000
Marketing of Rental Events	105,000

ENDOWMENT NEEDS

Botanical Science Endowments

Science Fund	$9,525,000
Vice Presidency for Botanical Science	1,250,000
Chair in Institute of Economic Botany	1,250,000
Chair in Institute of Economic Botany	1,250,000
Chair in Institute of Systematic Botany	1,250,000
Chair in Institute of Systematic Botany	1,250,000
Chair in Institute of Systematic Botany	1,250,000

Horticulture Endowments

Horticulture Fund	$5,000,000
Rock and Native Plant Garden Curator or Rose Garden Curator	800,000
Horticulture Taxonomist	800,000
Demonstration Gardens	400,000

Endowment to Support New Facilities

Plant Studies Center for the Library and Herbarium	$4,975,000
Children's Adventure Garden	2,000,000

CAPITAL NEEDS

Plant Studies Center for the Library and Herbarium	$28,590,000
Enid A. Haupt Conservatory Restoration and Exhibits	24,860,000
Garden Cafe and Terrace Room	7,500,000
Main Building Facade Restoration	6,200,000
Children's Adventure Garden	4,847,000
Parking and Rest Rooms at the West Gate Entry	2,900,000
The Arthur and Janet Ross Lecture Hall	1,080,000
Snuff Mill Redevelopment and Related Site Improvements	923,000
Satelite Horticulture Facility and Propagation Range Upgrades	800,000
Master Planning	668,000
Miscellaneous Capital Projects	558,000
Replacing Equipment: Horticulture/Operations/Security	475,000
Visitor Center/Entry Plaza at the West Gate	350,000
Relocating the Shop	300,000
Renovating the Laboratories	300,000
Demonstration Gardens Complex	118,000
Woody Plant Nursery	72,000
New Irrigation Systems	60,000

N.B. The total cost of restoring the Enid A. Haupt Conservatory and installing new exhibits includes more than $11,000,000 provided by the City of New York prior to the initiation of The Campaign for the Garden.

EXHIBIT 11
NEW YORK BOTANICAL
GARDEN SENIOR
MANAGEMENT

The following are summaries of the professional and educational backgrounds of the President and the Vice Presidents.

Gregory R. Long, President and Chief Executive Officer. Mr. Long has worked in the management of cultural institutions in New York City for 25 years. Born and raised in Kansas City, Missouri, Mr. Long moved to New York City in 1965, where he attended New York University and received a Bachelor of Arts degree in Art History in 1969. He began his career at The Metropolitan Museum of Art in 1969. He worked in development and public affairs at The American Museum of Natural History from 1972 to 1975 and the New York Zoological Society from 1975 to 1982. From 1982 to 1989 Mr. Long served as Vice President for Public Affairs of The New York Public Library, where he played a leading role in a long-range planning process for the Library's 86 constituent libraries and directed private fundraising in the $307,000,000 Campaign for the Library. Mr. Long was appointed President of the Garden in 1989.

John E. Rorer, Executive Vice President and Chief Financial Officer. Mr. Rorer came to the Garden as Chief Financial Officer in 1989. Before joining the Garden, from 1976 to 1989, Mr. Rorer served in several management positions at Polytechnic University in Brooklyn, New York. His last position there was as Vice President for Finance and Administration and Chief Financial Officer. At Polytechnic, Mr. Rorer also participated in the creation, planning, and development of Metrotech, a $1-billion, 16-acre commercial/academic complex in downtown Brooklyn, adjacent to the University's campus. He held a series of increasingly responsible positions in New York City government from 1969 to 1976. Mr. Rorer is a graduate of Harvard College and holds a Master's Degree in Public Administration from New York University.

Dr. Brian M. Boom, Vice President for Botanical Science. Dr. Boom is the Vice President for Botanical Science and the Pfizer Curator of Botany. Dr. Boom, who came to the Garden in 1983 as a Research Associate, is responsible for setting policy and guiding research efforts for the Garden's programs in basic and applied botany. Prior to his appointment as Vice President for Botanical Science, Dr. Boom served as the Garden's Director of Science Development. Dr. Boom received his Ph.D. in Biology from the City University of New York in 1983. He is also an Adjunct Assistant Professor of Biology at the City University of New York, Adjunct Associate Professor of Tropical Dendrology at the School of Forestry and Environment Studies of Yale University, a Visiting Research Professor at New York University, and an Adjunct Professor at Columbia University.

Rosemarie Garipoli, Vice President for Development. Ms. Garipoli joined the Garden in August 1989. As Vice President for Development she had primary responsibility for the Garden's fundraising. Her previous employment included teaching art history as well as several positions of increasing responsibility in the not-for-profit sector. Prior to joining the Garden she worked for the Bank Street College of Education as Director of Development and Public Affairs and the Jewish Museum as Assistant Director. She holds a BA and an MFA from New York University.

John F. Reed, Vice President for Education. Mr. Reed first came to the Garden in 1965 as an Assistant Librarian. He took on increasing responsibilities including the combined position of Vice President for Education and Director of the Library. During his tenure at the Library he completed many important tasks, notably the 25-year effort to recatalogue the entire collection and make it available on computer. He is a graduate of the University of New Hampshire and has an AMLS from the University of Michigan.

Richard A. Schnall, Vice President for Horticulture. As the Vice President for Horticulture, Mr. Schnall is responsible for planning and budgeting the Garden's horticulture program. Mr. Schnall came to the Garden in 1986. He has also served as the Garden's Arboretum and Grounds Manager and Director of Horticulture. Before joining the Garden, Mr. Schnall was a horticulturist at Haywood Technical College in North Carolina and at the Donald M. Kendall Sculpture Gardens in Purchase, New York.

Marie Sexton, Vice President for External Relations. Ms. Sexton joined the Garden in October 1989. As Vice President for External Relations she oversaw the departments of Public Relations, Special Events, Membership, and Retail Operations. Her previous employment included 10 years with the New York Zoological Society and six years with the New York Public Library as Manager of Public Affairs. She is a graduate of Brown University.

CASE 19

Napoleon Bonaparte: Victim of an Inferior Strategy?

ON THE ROAD TO PARIS, JUNE 19, 1815[1]

Incomprehensible coincidence of fatalities! Grouchy, why did he not immediately return to the battlefield when I summoned him? And how can it be that my Chief-of-Staff Soult only sends a single messenger to recall him? Berthier surely would have sent 12! My other marshal, Ney, did not fare better. He did not execute my orders; in fact he failed me twice, in as many days. Just like d'Erlon, who, at Ligny, hesitated between following Ney's orders and mine. It was his wavering which allowed Blücher and his Prussians to escape. And that I had to leave my brave Davout behind to secure Paris in my absence may yet have been my greatest misfortune. Masséna, Murat, Desaix, Berthier, Lannes, Bessiéres, or Duroc: you too were sorrowfully missed! How different the outcome would have been, if only I could have counted on some of you!

Following his disastrous defeat at Waterloo, Napoleon's head must have been filled with such thoughts. ". . . The victory was so close, yet kept escaping me . . . " He had done everything possible to bring France to glory, leading his people through more battles and victories than Alexander the Great, Hannibal and Julius Caesar combined. Undoubtedly, some of his field marshals and generals grew weary and reluctant to follow his aims of continental annexation, yet they largely stood behind him. Despite his practically infallible personal leadership skills and strategic vision, he had still lost. Questions like "Why did it go so wrong at the end? Why did chance escape me in the end?" are likely to have haunted him on the road back to Paris.

FROM CORSICAN TO EMPEROR OF FRANCE 1769–1821

Born in Ajaccio, Corsica, on August 15, 1769, Napoleon, who was of Italian descent, received a French education, at the Royal Military College in Brienne. On July 14, 1789, the French Revolution broke out when the Bastille was attacked, leading to the downfall of the *Ancien Régime* and King Louis XVI. The Revolution promised *Liberté, Egalité, Fraternité* (Liberty, Equality, Fraternity) for all.

Napoleon first distinguished himself at the Siege of Toulon in 1793, then later in putting down a royalist uprising. This latter success led to his nomination at the head of the "Army of Italy" where his talents as a gifted military commander were fully recognised. Following his invasion of Egypt in 1798, Napoleon successfully led a coup and installed himself as the First Consul of France.

An energetic leader and administrator, he restored civil order, balanced the budget, and established modern-day French administration, overseeing the establishment of the *Code Napoléon*. This code represented a wide-sweeping reform and codification of France's laws in areas such as

This case was written by Atul Sinha, INSEAD MBA, July 1999, under the supervision of Professors W. Chan Kim, Renée Mauborgne, and Ludo Van der Heyden of INSEAD. It is intended to be used as a basis for class discussion rather than to illustrate either effective or ineffective handling of an administrative situation.

commerce, civil and legal procedure, and penal and rural law. The country, worn out after ten years of internal and external strife, was grateful to Bonaparte (as he then was called) for consolidating the rights won by the people during the French Revolution. To permanently mark the transition of France to a new era, Napoleon convinced the Senate to crown him *Empereur des Français* (Emperor of the French) in 1804.

Napoleon fought and won many glorious battles of which Austerlitz was perhaps the most significant. It established his credibility. At the height of his power, Napoleon ruled, directly or indirectly, half of Europe. Though he imposed French practices such as the *Code Napoléon* to integrate countries within the French Empire and sometimes even went so far as to appoint family members as new heirs, he was careful to leave conquered countries otherwise intact. He created the Kingdoms of Bavaria and Wurtemberg, both of which joined the Confederation of the Rhine in 1806, the precursor of today's Germany.

However, Napoleon's use of military might as the principal instrument of policy proved insufficient. Prompted by military difficulties in Spain, his advisors increasingly supported a more balanced implementation of political, diplomatic and economic policies, in addition to the military ones, to ensure a more integrated Europe. Napoleon, annoyed by such apparent dissension, began to isolate himself from his advisors. This inherent lack of balance in Napoleon's actions, however, would eventually erode his influence. Power and success had started to corrupt Napoleon.

The fateful invasion and disastrous retreat from Russia in 1812 united all of Europe against him, thereby hastening his downfall. Although he fought a brilliant last campaign in France against a much superior enemy, the odds proved impossible to uphold. In April 1814, his marshals refused to follow his orders, forcing Napoleon to abdicate his throne. He was sent into exile to the Island of Elba in the Mediterranean, not far from his native Corsica.

Napoleon's first exile was short-lived. Strongly encouraged by the ineptitude of the new monarch Louis XVIII, the younger brother of Louis XVI, he escaped from Elba in March 1815. He bravely faced the troops sent to capture him and they soon followed him, all the way to Paris, where he was welcomed as a liberator. Back in power, he advocated a new and more democratic constitution, and veterans of his old campaigns flocked to his support. Once restored to the throne, Napoleon sought peace with his allies. They rejected his offer, so he resorted to war. The result was the *Campagne des Cent Jours* (the Hundred Days Campaign) into Belgium, which ended in his definitive defeat at the Battle of Waterloo on June 18, 1815. He was sent into his second and final exile at Saint Helena, a remote island in the South Atlantic Ocean, where he died on May 5, 1821. (See Appendix 1.)

NAPOLEON AS A STRATEGIC INNOVATOR IN MILITARY WARFARE

"The Emperor has discovered a new way of waging war; he makes use of our legs instead of our bayonets."

—Anonymous soldier

Napoleon injected a radical new way of thinking into prevailing war strategies of the time. Apart from structural and organisational changes, he conceived two fundamentally new tactics:

CORPS UNITS

Napoleon formed a *"corps d'armée"* system, which led to increased mobility and flexible formations. These corps units operated like self-sustained armies and were capable of fighting independently for a limited period of time. The units were assigned different roles and equipped in consequence. Mobility was of the essence. The exception was the Emperor's personal Guard, composed of elite soldiers who had distinguished themselves in prior battles. The Guard was typically held in reserve, but its presence instilled confidence in the soldiers who knew they could count on these elite troops to change the outcome should the battle take a negative turn.

The corps units were coordinated and controlled via "a communication backbone of marshals," providing the primary and direct link with Napoleon. Each corps had its own general or marshal, acting on a clear mission defined by Napoleon, though this mission could change according to battle conditions. Due to the enormous flexibility of this system, Napoleon was able to implement a more dynamic and evolutionary battle strategy. He had an uncanny ability to determine the enemy's weak spot, probe it, and if confirmed, direct all available forces to that spot. He could mix and match the corps as required by battle conditions. The marshals were critical, as they were the primary link of communication with Napoleon.

TIME AS A STRATEGIC WEAPON

By considering time—and not simply force—as one of the variables, Napoleon introduced enormous flexibility in his strategic approach to every battle. Dynamic configurations offered multiple possibilities as the battle progressed. Strong communication structures allowed him to modify his orders and battle tactics effectively in nearly an on-line basis.

The timely use of flexible corps afforded Napoleon huge advantages in battle. His devastating *"assembly (of troops) and concentration (of force)"* approach to battles was a direct result. It was more than a simple matter of collecting a vast number of units at a given point. On the eve of the battle, it was imperative that the troops be "assembled" rather than "concentrated." By "assembly" Napoleon meant placing major units within marching distance of the intended battlefield, though not necessarily in physical contact with the enemy or one another. It was important that the forces were not only placed at marching distance from the possible battle site, but also that they were sufficiently dispersed on the eve of the battle to permit alternative movements without a major realignment of the formations. The initial dispersion then gave way to a more carefully phased concentration as the battle approached, but also to a larger number of options. After lulling the opponent into a false sense of security (by holding back most of his corps at a two-day march from the planned striking point), the Emperor used to "steal a march" by ordering a rapid movement of his corps under the cover of darkness, thereby gaining a full day of preparations over his enemy. For example, certain of his troops marched an amazing 140 km in 48 hr during the battle of Austerlitz.

Speed, surprise, flexibility, and continual adjustment were some of the key advantages derived from these two innovations. They transformed his army into a single integrated unit, capable of executing an ever-evolving strategy dictated by battle conditions.

LODI: THE PURSUIT OF HIGH AMBITIONS, MAY 10, 1796

> I will lead you into the most fertile plains on earth. Rich provinces, opulent towns, all shall be at your disposal; there you will find honour, glory and riches. [2]

With such statements Napoleon enticed his soldiers and his officers, with the expectation of rewards in return for bravery and obedience on the battlefield. The promise of victory and the opportunity to fight for *"their own country and not for the whims of the King"* strongly appealed to the French soldiers, who furthermore were commanded by people who, even of aristocratic descent, had risen through the ranks and proven themselves on the battlefield. Everyone worked tirelessly to prepare this campaign against the Austrians. The objective was to force them to the other side of the Po River and out of Lombardy altogether. Chief-of-Staff Berthier, an engineer/geographer, planned the strategic moves in the Alps, while other brilliant young officers such as Augereau, Masséna and Murat—all of whom would later be given the rank of marshal—trained the soldiers in the new corps system.

As part of a plan to occupy Milan, Napoleon had accomplished the preliminary task of pushing the Austrians back to the Adda River. This was achieved through repeated concentration of forces at critical places and the brilliant execution of his strategy by the generals and their soldiers. All of his commanders acted in exemplary fashion. As this was Napoleon's first major campaign, he regularly met with his officers to explain his ideas and strategies, as well as to receive and integrate their feedback and their knowledge of the terrain and of enemy formations. Highly confident in his soldiers and in himself, Napoleon resolved to defeat the Austrians quickly. A letter to his superiors in Paris demonstrates this:

> My intention is to catch up with the Austrians and beat them before you have time to reply to this letter. [3]

Napoleon now faced the Austrian Army across the Adda River. Capturing the Lodi Bridge was essential to continue his advance toward Milan. Yet the Austrians had drawn a dozen guns on each side of the bridge. After a stirring speech to his troops, he ordered a column of grenadiers onto the bridge. The first French charge, under a hail of Austrian fire, reached the centre of the bridge before falling back. A second charge was quickly organised. This time many senior officers placed themselves at the column's head. Letting loose a cry of *"Vive la République!"* they charged into the maelstrom and forced the Austrians to abandon the bridge. This battle earned Napoleon the loyalty of his men, who nicknamed him *"Le Petit Caporal"* in recognition of his personal courage and determination. Napoleon urged them on:

> In two weeks' time you have won six victories, taken 21 flags . . . several forts, and conquered the richest part of Piedmont . . . but soldiers, do not deceive yourselves. You have achieved nothing, for everything remains to be done. Neither Turin nor Milan is in our hands. . . There remain battles to fight, cities to take, rivers to cross . . . and friends, I promise, you will achieve all! [4]

MARENGO, JUNE 14, 1800: SAVED BY HIS GENERALS

During his early days as First Consul, Napoleon continued to ensure that his generals were involved in the early stages of campaign planning. On one occasion, he had worked out a brilliant plan to move his army into the Rhine. However, one general disagreed with the plan, suggesting another strategy. Though the suggestion directly contradicted his own plans, Napoleon took the general's advice instead of treating it as an act of insubordination. He understood the advantages of engaging his officers and liked to discuss strategic plans with them, seeking their reactions and advice. These exchanges were also an opportunity for

Napoleon to train and coach his corps commanders in his strategic way of thinking. The increasing complexity of his strategies reinforced his desire to keep them completely aware of the roles and responsibilities of each of the divisions. Napoleon even believed in making the simplest soldier party to his plan and spelling out what was demanded of him. On the eve of a battle, he would typically sleep on the battleground with the soldiers. He believed that the soldier was not a machine to be put into motion, but a reasonable being that must be directed.

His officers' willingness and ability to carry out battle plans autonomously were never more evident than at the Battle of Marengo. For once, Napoleon was facing a situation that he would typically inflict upon his enemies: the Austrians had concentrated their troops in the fields of Marengo. Since his whole strategy rested on the attack, he was caught totally unprepared by the Austrian attack. He needed reinforcements badly and sent an urgent message for help: "I had thought to attack Melas. He has attacked me first. For God's sake, come up if you still can" read Napoleon's hurried note to Officer Desaix. [5] Fortunately, Desaix upon hearing the canon fire in the valley, had already decided to return to the battlefield, which he reached by 3 p.m., much to Napoleon's and his soldiers' relief.

Upon Napoleon's arrival he is reported to have asked his dear Desaix what he thought of it. Napoleon responded that this battle was certainly lost, but that it was only two o'clock [in fact, it was three o'clock], and there was still time, therefore, to win yet another battle. And with that reply, Desaix charged upon the unsuspecting Austrians who already imagined the battle won. The Austrians were paralysed by the ferociousness of the French counterattack. In that brief moment of confusion, another French commander, Kellermann, spontaneously ordered his 400 horsemen to charge, leaving the Austrians even more stunned.

The timing proved to be perfect, and Northern Italy was then recovered for the French Republic.

The victory was acquired without Napoleon ever intervening or giving direct orders. Such was the level of understanding of his strategies and the confidence of his generals. Shortly after 9 p.m., Napoleon had won the Battle of Marengo—at a heavy price. Thousands lay wounded or dead, Desaix among them.

'LE BEAU SOLEIL D'AUSTERLITZ': NAPOLEON'S DOMINATION OF BATTLE AT AUSTERLITZ IN 1805

On the eve of the Battle of Austerlitz, most of the 75,000 French soldiers were in their designated positions for their fight against 90,000 Allied Austrian and Russian forces. As cited previously, Marshal Davout and his army corps were completing a long march of 140 km in only 48 hr to provide Napoleon with reinforcements.

A few days before the famous battle, Napoleon had issued orders for the French troops to retreat whenever they came in contact with the enemy. He willingly let the Allies occupy the heights of Pratzen and deployed his own troops in front of this plateau, Davout on the right, Soult at centre, and Murat and Lannes on the left. He even negotiated only to further suggest French weakness and fear against a superior enemy.

Napoleon's plan was to present to the enemy an intentionally weakened right wing, hoping that this would induce the Allies to attempt to overtake him on that side. In this manoeuver the marching allied forces would expose their own flank to the French centre, which could then charge upon them. The allied manoeuver would also result in weakening their own centre, which Napoleon could then attack by sending the troops under his direct command in a march upon the Pratzen plateau. This movement would cut the enemy army in two and would be continued against its weaker half. Simultaneously, the French cavalry would take on the allied right guard. Heavy fog on the morning of the battle would further help the French by hiding their positions from the enemy and adding greater surprise to their movements.

To keep his men updated and informed, a surprisingly open order of the day was issued:

> The positions we occupy are strong, and as they (the Russians) advance to my right they will expose their flank to me. Soldiers I shall direct your battalions myself. I will hold myself far from the firing line, if with your accustomed bravery, you carry disorder and confusion into the ranks of the enemy. But, if victory should for one moment be uncertain you will see your Emperor exposed to the first blows. [6]

Jomini, [7] the famous Austrian author, later said that never in the history of the world had a leader of an army revealed his plan in this way to the whole of his forces. Wherever Napoleon went for inspection that night, he was greeted with the traditional *Vive l'Empereur!* Taking his men into his confidence he would explain the next day's battle plan. This invariably helped raise the army's morale. Though only a few shared his words, all divisions soon knew that such exchanges were taking place. With his formations in place, with strong morale and a very clear plan, with an unsuspecting enemy who furthermore had been lulled into believing that the French were weak, Napoleon had literally won half the battle before it even began.

The ensuing battle was bloody and brutal. And as expected, the allied army fell into Napoleon's trap, was cut in two, and finally pushed back in three different directions. Nearly 27,000 Russians and Austrians died.

The battle of Austerlitz demonstrated both the capability of Napoleon's marshals to execute complex tactical manoeuvers and the effectiveness of the corps system. Since a corps was divided into smaller units, Napoleon could tailor his attack using combinations of different units to trick the Russians. The battle of Austerlitz was the clearest demonstration of the effectiveness of his deadly war strategies: massive "assembly-and-concentration" principles were applied during his move through Europe, and attacking the central position was effectively exploited in the battle. Napoleon was well aware of his men's needs and motivation and how critical their commitment was to the victory at Austerlitz. As a reward for victory, gold was distributed among the officers. Provisions were made for generous pensions to the widows of the fallen. Napoleon formally adopted orphaned children, permitting them to add "Napoleon" to their baptismal names. *Solidest, je suis content de vous!* The victory bulletin praised his generals and soldiers.

TORN BETWEEN THE DEMANDS OF A PRIME MINISTER AND THE AMBITIONS OF AN EMPEROR, 1807–11

I have done enough soldiering. I must now play Prime Minister for a bit,

Napoleon explained as he convened a cabinet meeting in St.-Cloud. He had subdued the young Russian Czar, Alexander I, and forced the signing of the "Treaty of Tilsit"[8] to isolate Britain from the Continent. Poland had been invaded and was now occupied. Napoleon ruled an empire that stretched from the Pyrenees to the Niemen and controlled a multinational army of 800,000—an unprecedented number in Europe. Napoleon was at his pinnacle, but not without some pressing problems, like the resignation of Talleyrand, his invaluable Foreign Minister.

Talleyrand was one of the few critical voices Napoleon would listen to. Following his Foreign Minister's departure, Napoleon underwent a worrying and very visible transformation. He shut down the vociferous and critical Tribunat, the French legislative assembly, in August 1807. Thin-skinned to attacks by the press, he threatened to close the newspapers. He enforced strict court etiquette, keeping everyone physically at arm's length. He could only be approached with the approval of Duroc, Grand Marshal of the Palace. A letter, dated April 4 to his brother Louis in Holland, clearly displayed a changed Napoleon: "You govern your nation like a docile, timorous monk. . . . A king issues orders and does not beg."[9]

Napoleon's self-imposed isolation manifested itself in his distance from the regular guests he used to invite for parties. Public functions were reduced to a minimum. Apart from daily contact with his secretary, Méneval, Napoleon's only close confidant was Duroc. Even some of his closest soldier-friends were no longer permitted to address him with the French familiar form of you, "*tu.*" Though his official business schedule was as frantic as ever, receiving delegations, etc., his daily chats with his older generals were a thing of the past. Some of his marshals and generals were not on speaking terms with one another. A few of them were upset at not being named marshal or prince, despite their contributions to Napoleon's victories. [10] Apparently, Napoleon's process for promoting generals or assigning titles left a few of them demanding explanations. And the fact that orders to all senior officers came from the desk of the Chief-of-Staff of the Imperial Army, the increasingly loathed Major General Berthier, did little to help matters.

THE FATEFUL ROAD TO MOSCOW AND TO ABDICATION, 1812

When Russia broke the "Treaty of Tilsit," Napoleon recalled his ambassador and declared war on Russia in 1812. For his second campaign on the Russian front, Napoleon's force was the largest Europe had ever seen.

The multilingual army fell under three levels of command, with a first line of 450,000 soldiers reporting to Napoleon. Apart from the main army, Napoleon also disposed of an enormous reserve army of more than 200,000 soldiers. With such a large mass on the move, marching men in formation became extremely difficult. Consequently, many of the corps and reserves were behind schedule. Three great allies of Russia—time, distance and weather—started to work against the French. From the moment the French army crossed the French-Russian border, enormous bottlenecks took place. Lack of proper food and fatigue were soon demoralising the army. Soldiers began throwing away their heavy supplies, even including cartridges.

It seemed that Napoleon had overestimated his soldiers' commitment, their limits, as well as the logistical challenges the armies would face. Almost all the marshals, including his Chief-of-Staff, Berthier, argued vehemently against this campaign, saying that invading Russia was madness. They continued their protest during the campaign. Alone in his single-mindedness and supremely confident in his superior intellect and vision, Napoleon kept overruling them. As Caulaincourt, Ambassador to Russia, recalled:

> Time and again, the Emperor repeated that the Russians, whom everyone had claimed to be so numerous, had in fact no more than 150,000 men. . . [He] added that he was sure that we [Caulaincourt and the other French generals opposing the campaign] had deceived him personally about everything down to the problems of the Russian climate, insisting that winter here was like in France, except that it just lasted longer. These accusations against us were repeated on many occasions. I reiterated to the Emperor, quite in vain as it turned out, that I had not exaggerated in the least, and that as his most faithful servant, I had revealed the full truth about everything. But I failed to make him change his mind. [11]

Nor was Chief-of-Staff Berthier spared from Napoleon's wrath. "Wild abuse was heaped on him for his frank advice, as a reward for his constant work and devotion."[12] Napoleon continually complained that Berthier's staff was incompetent, ". . . no one planned ahead." He refused to trust anyone, even Berthier, to make the smallest decision or give the simplest order, without his stamp of approval.

Even his marshals were becoming uncooperative. Napoleon expressed his distrust of Murat. Murat, who disliked fellow marshal Ney, could not agree on battle plans, and even fought with Davout. Their dislike for Berthier grew stronger.

Despite all this, Napoleon was able to keep his men marching toward Moscow. Finally after chasing the Russians for a long time, Napoleon faced them at Borodino Field, about 70 km from Moscow. It proved a Pyrrhic victory: one in every three soldiers died. The next day the French army invaded Moscow, and Napoleon took the Kremlin. After waiting a month for the Czar of Russia to surrender, Napoleon ordered the retreat of his troops on October 19. With nearly two-thirds of the men dead, the survivors started the long march back home through the harsh and wintry Russian landscape, continuously attacked by Russian cavalry. Ney and his cavalry fought bravely and considerably helped the French retreat.

Napoleon now had most of Europe united against him. He faced the Allies at the Battle of Nations in Leipzig in October 1813, but withdrew on the third day against a much superior enemy. The Allies finally entered France and notwithstanding brilliant military leadership during the Campaign of France, where with 70,000 men he was able to contain 350,000 Allied troops. The Emperor finally was forced into exile on the Island of Elba. Napoleon bid a dramatic farewell to his troops in the *Cour des Adieux* at the *Château de Fontainbleau*[13] on April 20, 1814. His last words to his loyal Guard were *Bring me my eagle*. He kissed the French flag, while many soldiers wept.

THE LAST CAMPAIGN: 100 DAYS TO WATERLOO

A mere nine months later, Napoleon escaped from Elba with the help of some generals and 1,200 soldiers from his personal guard. His arrival in France took the authorities by surprise. The French people, on the other hand, reacted with surprising calmness. Well aware of inflation, steep prices and King Louis XVIII's incompetence, Napoleon played to the peasants, who were on the verge of losing all the freedoms that had been won during the Revolution. He assured them that they would not lose their lands to the "*émigrés*"—the aristocrats who were about to return to reclaim their titles and their lands. He seduced the town's people with promises of fiscal reforms. Everywhere he went, he promised peace and prosperity with popular statements such as the following:

> I am coming back to protect and defend the interests that our Revolution has given us. I want to give an inviolable constitution, one prepared by the people and myself together.[14]

French authorities sought out occasions to challenge him. On one such occasion, the French army was ordered to use all means to stop him. Napoleon stepped forward and faced the muskets, baring his chest. With a remarkable mixture of bravado and charisma, he called on the regiment to join him:

> I heard you calling me in my exile and have overcome every obstacle and peril to be here. . . Take up those colours that the nation has proscribed, those colours around which we have rallied for 25 years, in fending off enemies of France. Put on the same tricolour cocarde that you wore during your finest days . . . [and] take up the eagles that presided over you at Ulm, Austerlitz, Jena, Eylau, and Friedland.[15] . . . Soldiers, come rally around the banner of your leader![16]

Sending up the cry "*Vive l'Empereur*," the Fifth Regiment changed sides. In the meantime, the king had issued a warrant for Napoleon, sending Marshal Ney to arrest him. Once confronted with his former commander, Ney changed his mind, pressured by many of his troops to do so, and defected along with 6,000 men. Napoleon made a grand entrance at the Tuileries Palace in Paris on March 20, 1815 and was restored to the throne.[17]

Britain, Austria, Prussia and Russia met in Vienna on March 25 to sign the Treaty of Vienna and form the Seventh Coalition. To ensure that Napoleon would "*be absolutely beyond the possibility of causing trouble*," a massive attack on each of France's borders was planned.

Thus began the Campaign of Belgium. Napoleon's plan was to strike first, targeting the combined forces of Wellington and Blucher in the North. But he found it difficult to select his marshals—many were dead, others were unwilling to join him. In the end, he named Marshal Soult as his Chief-of-Staff and Marshals Ney and Grouchy as commanders of the army's wings.

French preparations for the offensive lasted from June 6 to 14. The Imperial Guard and the reserve cavalry were placed within a 30-km area more than 200 km away from the Franco-Belgian border. Executed in complete secrecy, the speed and surprise of his advance into Belgium gave Napoleon a tremendous advantage even before the first bullet was fired.

On the morning of June 15, Napoleon's army converged on the allied armies of his opponents. Since Wellington and Blücher's armies were dispersed over a large area, the key strategy was to occupy a "central position" between them, dividing them so they could be defeated one at a time. By occupying a vital lateral road, the French army would also be able to break the Anglo-Dutch armies' line of communication. Ney would be responsible for containing the Anglo-Dutch forces, while Napoleon and Grouchy would destroy Blücher and his Prussians. They would then join and take on Wellington. If successful, the strategy would culminate in one of Napoleon's finest military victories.

From the very start, however, imperfections started to show the cracks of the French command structure. General Vandamme's corps received their movement orders after a considerable delay from Soult, which created a subsequent delay in crossing the Sambre river. Uncharacteristic chaos reigned in communication orders on June 16 at Ligny. Ney was to contain the Anglo-Dutch forces at a place called Quatre-Bras, while Napoleon and Grouchy would march against the Prussians in Ligny. Ney waited the whole morning for his orders before acting on his own initiative. This proved to be a decisive mistake. Even when Ney finally received Napoleon's orders to return to Ligny to complete the victory against Blücher, one suspects that he had difficulty in understanding the Emperor's "central position" tactic, which created further confusion. After all, Napoleon had planned everything by himself, neglecting to transmit the information to his marshals, and Berthier was no longer there to carefully translate Napoleon's thoughts into clear orders for the marshals. This was the single biggest factor working against Napoleon. "In three hours' time, the campaign will be decided," remarked a then optimistic Napoleon. "If Ney follows his orders through, not a gun of the Prussian army will get away; they will be taken in the very act."[18] But Ney arrived too late, while d'Erlon and his corps spent the day walking back and forth between the two battles. The Prussians escaped, including Blücher who was left wounded on the battlefield, but finally recovered thanks to French delays in pursuing the retreating Prussians into the night.

More misunderstandings compounded the French army's confusion two days later at Waterloo. On the morning of the battle, Napoleon had rejected most of his fellow commanders' advice. Chief-of-Staff Soult's cautious remark that Grouchy should be recalled was discarded; Prince Jerôme's report that Wellington and Blücher were planning to join forces was dismissed as "trivial." Mistakes were made. During one attack, for example, a strange and outdated formation was used, contrary to Napoleon's instructions, resulting in heavy losses for the French. To recover his position, Ney overreacted in a cavalry attack, angering Napoleon. "This is a premature movement which may lead to fatal results," thundered Napoleon, "he [Ney] is compromising us."[19]

Everything that could possibly go wrong had, from the very beginning. Though Napoleon had crafted a brilliant strategy, his marshals were failing him. But there was still a chance to defeat Wellington and win the battle. Napoleon's only worry was that Blücher would reinforce Wellington's forces. Napoleon knew that his army would not be able to sustain the onslaught of their combined forces and hoped that Grouchy's corps would prevent Blücher from reaching Wellington. Then the opportunity vanished: Blücher met up with Wellington late in the evening, as he had promised him, and the Battle of Waterloo was over—exactly 100 days after Napoleon's return to France.

Aug. 15, 1769	Birth in Ajaccio (Corsica)
May 15, 1779	Entrance in the Military School of Brienne
Oct. 17, 1784	Admission to the *Ecole Militaire* (Military College) in Paris, which he graduates from a year later 42nd out of 58
June 1788	Joins his regiment in Auxonne
Sept. 1789–Feb. 1791	Third stay in Corsica, participates in the island's political turmoil
May 1792	Arrives in Paris
Aug. 10	Assists at the assault on the *Tuileries* Palace
June 11, 1793	Has to leave Corsica with his family and goes to Toulon
Dec. 18	British withdraw from Toulon and he is appointed *Général de Brigade*
Aug. 9, 1794	Arrested, but soon released
Oct. 5, 1795	Participates in defeating a royalist uprising in Paris
Oct. 26	Appointed General of the Army of the Interior
March 2, 1796	Appointed Commander in Chief of the Army of Italy
May 10	*Victory at the Battle of Lodi*
Oct. 17, 1797	Peace with Austria at Campo-Formio
May 19, 1798	Departs for Egypt
July 21	Victory at the Battle of the Pyramids
Aug. 1	Nelson destroys the French fleet at Aboukir
May 10, 1799	Withdraws from Acco after an 8th unsuccessful assault
July 25	Victory at Aboukir
Aug. 23	Leaves the Army to Kléber and returns to France
Nov. 9	Following a coup, Bonaparte is appointed Consul, with Sieyēs and Ducos
Dec. 15	Declaration of a new Constitution
Feb. 17, 1800	Appointment of *Préfets*
May 20	*Crosses the Alps with his Army at the Saint Bernard pass*
June 14	*Victory at the Battle of Marengo*
Nov. 1	Publication of the *Parallèle entre César, Cromwell, Monk et Bonaparte*
Dec. 24	Attempt on his life at Rue Saint-Nicaise
July 15, 1801	Signature of the *Concordat,* which re-establishes the Catholic Church
March 25, 1802	Peace of Amiens with England
May 19, 1802	Introduces the *Légion d'Honneur*
May 6, 1803	Break with England
May 18, 1804	*Napoléon Bonaparte* is appointed *Empereur des Français*
May 19	Eighteen amongst his senior officers are named *Maréchaux d'Empire*
Dec. 2	Crowned Emperor in the presence of Pope Pius VII
Oct. 21, 1805	Franco-Spanish fleet defeated at Trafalgar, where Nelson dies
Dec. 2	*Victory at Austerlitz*
July 12, 1806	Creation of the Confederation of the Rhine
Oct. 14	Victories at Iena (Napoleon) and Auerstadt (Davout) against Prussia
Nov. 21	Decrees the *Blocus Continental* against commerce with England
June 14, 1807	Victory at Friedland against Russia
July 7 and 9	Signature of Peace Treaties at Tilsit with Russia and Prussia
March 1, 1808	Creation of the *Noblesse d'Empire* (Imperial Nobility)
May 2	Uprising in Madrid against the French presence in Spain
April 8, 1809	Austria attacks Bavaria
July 6	Victory against Austria at Wagram, Pius VII is arrested

April 2, 1810	*Napoléon* marries Marie-Louise, daughter of the Austrian Emperor
July 10	Holland is integrated into France
Aug. 21	Bernadotte, a former general, is appointed Hereditary Prince of Sweden
June 24, 1812	*La Grande Armée crosses the river Niemen into Russia*
Sept. 7, 1812	*Victory at the Moskova (Borodino)*
Sept. 14	*French enter Moscow*
Oct. 18	*Decision to leave Moscow and return to France*
Nov. 27	*Disastrous crossing at the Berezina river*
Dec. 5	*Leaves his retreating army for Paris*
March 13, 1813	Prussia declares war on France, but is defeated at Lützen and Bautzen
June 21	Victory of Wellington at Vittoria, Spain is lost
Aug. 12	Austria declares war
Oct. 16–19	*Battle of Nations at Leipzig, Napoleon retreats, and Germany is lost*
Nov. 16	So is Holland
Jan 17, 1814	Murat defects and the French domination of Italy is in jeopardy
Jan. and Feb.	*Campaign of France: victories at Brienne, Champaubert, Montmirail, Montereau, and Reims*
March 31	Marmont capitulates in front of Paris
April 6	*Abdicates without conditions in Fontainebleau*
May 4	*Arrival on the Island of Elba for his first exile*
March 1, 1815	*Return on French soil at Golfe-Juan*
March 7	*First French troops rally to Napoleon*
June 16	*Victory against the Prussians at Ligny*
June 18	*Disaster at Waterloo*
Oct. 16	*Beginning of his second and final exile on the Island of Saint Helena*
May 5, 1821	Death of *Napoléon Bonaparte*

*Events in italics are described in more detail in the case.

Napoleon, Emperor of the French, by a Decree of May 19, 1804, appointed eighteen officers of the French Army to be *Marshals of the Empire* (*"Maréchaux d'Empire"*). Four of them were honorary marshals from the Senate. The other fourteen were on the active list.

The four honorary Marshals were:

KELLERMANN, aged sixty-nine, son of a merchant.
LEFEBRE, aged forty-nine, son of a miller.
PERIGNON, aged fifty, son of a landowner.
SERURIER, aged sixty-two, son of an officer of the Household Troops.

The fourteen Marshals on the active list were:

BERTHIER, aged fifty-one, son of a surveying engineer.
MURAT, aged thirty-seven, son of an innkeeper.
MONCEY, aged fifty, son of a lawyer.
JOURDAN, aged forty-two, son of a doctor.
MASSENA, aged forty-eight, son of a tanner and soap-manufacturer.
AUGEREAU, aged forty-seven, son of a working mason.
BERNADOTTE, aged forty-one, son of a lawyer.
SOULT, aged thirty-five, son of a lawyer.
BRUNE, aged forty-one, son of a lawyer.
LANNES, aged thirty-five, son of a peasant farmer.
MORTIER, aged thirty-six, son of a farmer.
NEY, aged thirty-five, son of a barrel-cooper.
DAVOUT, aged thirty-four, son of an officer.
BESSIERES, aged thirty-six, son of a surgeon.

Eight were subsequently added:

In 1807 VICTOR, aged forty-three, son of a soldier.
In 1809 MacDONALD, aged forty-four, son of a soldier.
MARMONT, aged thirty-five, son of an officer.
OUDINOT, aged forty-two, son of a brewer.
In 1811 SUCHET, aged forty-one, son of a silk-manufacturer.
In 1812 SAINT CYR, aged forty-eight, son of a tanner.
In 1813 PONIATOWSKI, aged fifty, son of a prince.
In 1815 GROUCHY, aged forty-nine, son of a marquis.

*This Appendix is taken from A. G. MacDonnell's excellent book on Napoleon, entitled: "Napoleon and His Marshals." It was originally published by Macmillan and Co., 1934, and re-edited in the "Prion Lost Treasures," London, 1996.

Honda Motor Company 1994

Starting from scratch in industries dominated by giants, Honda Motor Company, Ltd., had been a major force in revolutionizing the motorcycle and small car industries of the world. What were the keys to success for this unique Japanese company? After moving into third position in Japan's auto industry and developing the largest single selling auto in the U.S., the Accord, in the early 1990s, where could Honda look for future successes?

A JAPANESE ENTREPRENEUR

Mr. Soichiro Honda began his career at Arto Shokai, an auto repair shop in Tokyo. At age 16, during the Great Kanto earthquake in 1923, the young apprentice who had never driven a car leapt to the wheel of a customer's vehicle and in a bit of daring-do maneuvered it to safety. Soon the owner-"master" set up Mr. Honda as head of a branch of Arto Shokai in Hamamatsu, Honda's home town. There Honda patented cast-metal spokes to replace the wooden ones—like those that burned out, almost wrecking his car, during the earthquake episode—and gathered the first of over 100 personal patents in his lifetime. The Japanese trading companies soon began exporting his spokes all over the Far East.

By age 25, Honda was one of the youngest Japanese entrepreneurs around. He became *the* Hamamatsu playboy, not only plying from one geisha house to the next, but piling geishas into his own car for wild drives and drunken revels around the town. In one such escapade his car full of geishas went off a bridge, but landed safely in the mud—no injuries. In another, he tossed a geisha from a second story window. She landed on some electric wires below—from which a suddenly sobered Honda carefully extracted her—again fortunately no injuries. These are only some of the many colorful stories about the young Mr. Honda.

Honda also loved motors and engines. When the head of Arto Shokai suggested Honda might build a racer (on his own time), Honda spent months of midnight hours to build a car from spare parts and war surplus aircraft engines. He soon began to drive his products himself, to win races, to make basic changes in racing car designs, and soon to set new speed records. But in the All Japan Speed Rally of 1936, traveling at 120 kph—a record not exceeded for years—another car jumped in front of Honda, demolishing Honda's car and leaving him with lifetime injuries, which redirected his energies from racing toward engineering. Seeing more opportunities in manufacturing than repairs, Honda formed Tokai Heavy Industries in 1937 to make piston rings for cars.

Case Copyright © 1995 by James Brian Quinn. Research associates: Allie J. Quinn and Penny C. Paquette. Primary references include: T. Sakiya, *Honda Motor: The Men, The Management, The Machines,* Kodansha International, Ltd. Tokyo, 1982; S. Sanders, *Honda: The Man and His Machines,* Little Brown, Boston, 1975; R. Guest, "The Quality of Work Life in Japan. . . ," *Hokudai Economic Papers,* Tokyo, Vol. XII, 1982–83; R. Shook, *Honda: An American Success Story,* Prentice Hall, 1988. Numbers in parentheses indicate the reference and page number for material from a previously footnoted source.

PISTON RINGS AND WAR

But Honda knew nothing about the complex casting processes involved. For months he and his assistant lived in their factory, day-and-night. Honda became a working hermit, complete with uncut hair and bristling chin. His limited savings wasted away. He sold his wife's jewelry to keep on, but he persisted, knowing his family would starve if he failed. After many frustrating failures, Honda sought the specialized technical knowledge he lacked because he had dropped out of school. After painfully gaining entry to the Hamamatsu High School of Technology—ten years older than his classmates, an unprecedented act in age-and-class-conscious Japan—Honda promptly upset the authorities by only attending classes of interest to him, listening carefully to what mattered to him, and not even taking notes on the rest. He refused to take examinations, saying that a diploma was worth less than a movie ticket; at least the ticket guaranteed you got into the theater.[1]

As Honda began to understand the technicalities of his product, he sold rings to the low end of the market, but soon developed special automated equipment that let him meet the major manufacturers' quality standards for rings and later for aircraft propellers. During the war American bombings and an earthquake destroyed much of his operation. Honda sold off the rest of his assets as the war ended. With the proceeds he bought a huge drum of medical alcohol, made his own sake, and spent an inebriated year visiting with friends and trying to decide what to do next.

HONDA MOTORS BEGINS

The postwar era was terrible. Japan's cities were destroyed. City dwellers had to sortie into the country to buy their daily food. Trains were overcrowded and gasoline was in short supply. Honda later said, "I happened on the idea of fitting an engine to a bicycle simply because I didn't want to ride the incredibly crowded trains and buses myself, and it became impossible for me to drive my car because of the gasoline shortage."[2] Using small, war-surplus gasoline powered motors which had provided electricity for military radios, Honda made motor bikes that were an instant hit.

Honda realized that his simple motorbikes would not last long once Japan began its postwar recovery. In 1949 he raised some $3,800 from friends and designed a longer range two stroke, 3 hp (98cc) machine—the Type D with a superior stamped metal frame, christened the "Dream." Soon Honda was selling 1,000 bikes and motorcycles a month to black marketeers and small bicycle shops. But Honda's bill collectors often found their customers had disappeared or gone bankrupt before they paid the com-

pany. Honda was more interested in the product and its engineering than in profits. Production and sales were doing well, but the company was facing imminent bankruptcy. Honda welcomed the recommendation of an acquaintance that he take on Takeo Fujisawa as his head of finance and marketing. Fujisawa's heavy and ponderous style contrasted sharply with Honda's waspish, impatient, even rude directness, but the two became friends for life.

They moved the company from sleepy, gossipy, Hamamatsu—where the neighbors objected to Honda's flamboyant, noisy, sake-filled 3 a.m. returns on his motorcycle—to Tokyo and promptly applied for government support to produce 300 motorcycles per month. MITI—Japan's coordinating agency for industrial, technology, and trade affairs—thought no one could sell that many motorcycles, and denied its support. Ignoring MITI's skepticism, Fujisawa wrote an impassioned letter to all of the 18,000 bicycle shops in Japan, presenting Honda's product as their wave of the future and promising to train them in its sale and repair. While Japan's largest producers typically had only regional distribution, Honda soon had a national network of 5,000 dedicated dealers.

Next, instead of emulating the 4 stroke, side-valve machine competitors had, Honda created a 146cc 4 stroke, overhead valve (OHV) engine which doubled the available horsepower with no added weight, and became the basis for Honda's appeal to the high performance marketplace. Honda integrated the production of the key components, engines, frames, chains, and drives essential to top performance. But it out-sourced non-critical parts as much as possible, and purchased a relatively small old sewing machine plant for assembly operations. Lacking large scale production facilities, Honda and his people designed special small scale assembly equipment—and simply stayed at work each day as long as it took to meet orders.

"MR. THUNDER"

While other manufacturers milked a single winning design in the domestic marketplace, Honda thought Type E did not hit a wide enough market. "I concluded I must make a motorcycle that would substitute for the bicycle."[2] Honda developed a new 50cc engine from the ground up, and coupled this with a small friendly looking frame for informal users. Sensing an untapped market niche for local delivery vehicles for small businesses, he designed in a step-through frame, an automatic transmission, and one hand controls that allowed riders to carry a package in the other hand. The market for the "Cub" boomed, and Honda moved into large volume manufacturing for the first time.

In 1951, top officials of the larger Japanese manufacturers invited Honda and Fujisawa to attend a private meeting to determine incentive policies for Japanese exporters. Honda refused to attend, thus beginning a long pattern of nonparticipation with the central political and business forces directing Japan's economic recovery. He felt that high quality goods needed no such supports and knew no national boundaries.

Honda was talkative, energetic, gregarious—always excited by the technology and his products, never (according to Mr. Fujisawa) "by the profits we would make next year." But Honda earned the nickname Kaminari-san—"Mr. Thunder"—because of his instantaneous temper and sometimes erratic behavior. He spent most of his time in the factory or development shop working side-by-side with his workers. Employees from his early years remember his shouting at engineers or pounding himself on the head when they made a mistake. On one occasion, after finding some bolts improperly tightened, he grabbed a wrench from a technician, did the job right, and then popped the technician with the wrench while shouting, "You damned fool. This is how you are supposed to tighten bolts."[1] People later avoided close contact when Honda was carrying a wrench.

EXPANDING INVESTMENTS

Honda's financial problems were solved in a unique way. Once they saw the Honda Cub, dealers were so impressed that they came to the company to buy whatever inventory they could. This was in sharp contrast to their usual practice of selling whatever models the big manufacturers had been able to force on them. Fujisawa cleverly used this demand to his advantage. He allocated production to those who could pay in advance and began weeding out slow paying distributors and dealers. Soon Honda had not only the widest, but the strongest, motorcycle dealer network in Japan. Unable and unwilling to obtain government financing and lacking access to Japan's closely controlled equity markets Mr. Fujisawa used creative—high risk—trade financings to see the company through its major plant and distribution expansions.

EXPANSION TO WORLD MARKETS

About this time Honda decided that motorcycle racing could assert to the world his company's true expertise in motorcycle design. After some disappointing initial entries in international races, Honda realized that the key to success was lighter, more efficient engines, getting more power from more thorough combustion. Honda engineers ultimately designed an engine with the cam shaft at the top—the then unique overhead cam (OHC) engine—and made crucial discoveries about mixing gases in the combustion chamber that led to the CVCC engines of its later automobiles.

Honda's motorcycles won the Manufacturer's Team Prize for the company in 1959 and the first five places (in both 125 and 250cc sizes) at the Isle of Man races in 1961. These were considered the "Olympics of racing" at the time.

TIME FOR STRATEGY

While Mr. Honda was mesmerized by the sheer technological questions of these "racing years," Mr. Fujisawa was concerned with the company's longer term strategy. He thought there was a large untapped market for smaller, safer "bikes," geared to customers who resisted larger motorcycles as expensive, dangerous, and associated with the black leather jacket crowd. He wanted a small 50cc bike for novices, youthful executives, or young couples. At first Mr. Honda ignored his colleague's unusual vision. Then around 1958, Honda designed and built a full-sized example of a "scooter" that would do the trick. Fujisawa was immediately excited by the product and soon predicted sales of 30,000 units per month—a bit ambitious in a Japanese market that then constituted only 20,000 per month for all two-wheelers.

Now considered to be the Model T of two-wheeled vehicles and probably Honda's masterpiece, the new motorbike was called the Super Cub. Revolutionary in design, the Super Cub had a light, carefree image, a step-through configuration which made it easier for women to ride, and a graceful, stylish appearance. The company's best selling earlier model had sold only 3,000 units per month. Yet Honda invested 10 billion yen in a single factory to build 30,000 Super Cubs a month, with no guarantee of maintaining that level of sales. Fujisawa intuitively pushed ahead. He described the Super Cub to retailers as "more like a bicycle than a motorcycle," and began to sell the vehicles directly to retailers, mostly bicycle shops. By 1959 Honda was the largest motorcycle producer in the world.

AMERICAN HONDA

Honda and Fujisawa thought the time now had come to pursue the world market actively. Honda executives regarded Europe and Southeast Asia as the best markets to target, since Americans were so tied to the automobile and held an unattractive image of motorcycles and their riders. After several unsuccessful years of trying to pry open the underdeveloped country markets of Asia, Mr. Fujisawa—thinking that American preferences might set the trends for the rest of the world—targeted the U.S. as crucial. Despite onerous exchange restrictions by the Japanese

FIGURE 1
THE FIRST SUPER-CUB
("STEP-THROUGH")
INAUGURATED IN 1958
Source: Honda Motor
Corporation.

government, American Honda Motor Co. was formed in June 1959 with a Los Angeles headquarters, and its own executive vice president, Mr. Kihachiro Kawashima.

The company had gone to MITI for a currency allocation, but was rebuffed. MITI reasoned that if the giant Toyota had earlier failed at the same venture, how could Honda succeed? Its meager $110,000 currency allocation meant Honda had to start its U.S. operations with only $250,000 of paid in capital. Initially, Honda's cycles did not sell well in the U.S. But Kawashima and his two associates dug in, shared an apartment for $80 a month, rented a warehouse in a run-down area of Los Angeles, and personally stacked motorcycle crates, swept the floors, and built and maintained the parts bin. Early 1960 became disastrous when customers reported Honda's larger motorcycles frequently leaked oil or experienced serious clutch failures on the longer, harder, and faster roads and tracks of the U.S. In a move that presaged later policies, Kawashima air-freighted the motorcycles to Japan where engineering teams, working night and day, found a way to fix the problem in one short month.

Then events took a surprising turn. Up to this point, executives of America Honda had promoted sales of the larger, more luxurious motorcycles because they seemed more suited to the U.S. market. Although they had not attempted to sell the 50cc Super Cubs—priced at $250 vs. $1500 for bigger European and American bikes—through U.S. dealers, the executives rode them around Los Angeles themselves and noticed the bikes attracted considerable attention. With the larger bikes facing engineering problems, American Honda decided to increase emphasis on its 50cc line, just to generate cash flows.

American Honda was extremely concerned that it not lose the "black leather jacket" customers which comprised the high margin portion of the business. But Honda's retail-ers continually reported that Super Cub customers were normal everyday Americans. Because of Japanese government restrictions, however, American Honda had to operate on a cash basis, building its inventory, advertising, and distribution systems without using Japanese generated yen. The Pascale article (Reading 5-3) details Honda's unique entry strategy to the U.S. By 1962–63 Honda's export earnings (from motorcycles) surpassed those of Nissan or Toyota. And by 1965, Honda America's motorcycle sales had jumped to $77 million and a whopping 63% market share.

FOUR WHEELS FOR HONDA

In the 1950s Japan had intensified its now famous programs for coordinating the development of selected high priority industries. MITI announced in 1960 that it planned to divide the existing passenger car manufacturers into three groups (a mass-production car group, a mini-car group, and a special-purpose vehicle group) and that no other manufacturers would be permitted to enter. The government reasoned that the move would reduce destructive domestic competition and allow the industry to achieve scale economies for world penetration. But Honda, which would have been foreclosed from the market, was outraged. Fortunately, the proposal was never officially enacted. But it did stimulate Mr. Honda, who had dreamed since childhood of building automobiles, to move rapidly.

RACERS AND NEW TECHNOLOGY

Although MITI actively opposed Honda's entry into automobiles, at the 1962 Tokyo Motor Show, Honda revealed a light-duty (T-360) truck and a (S-500) sports car prototype. The T-360 performed like a sports car and was the first truck of its class to permit high speeds. Soon Honda introduced the N-360 mini car, with an air-cooled, two-cylinder engine, and a front wheel drive (FWD) system unprecedented in automobile design. The N-360 was an instant success and captured 31.2% of Japan's total sales in its class, a mere two months after is 1967 introduction.

As he moved to automobile engines, Mr. Honda adapted the technology he had created for his previous motorcycle designs. Honda's basic approach had always been to develop a special engine to solve each specific problem. Since he was strapped for cash, he had designed efficient small engines which were compact but powerful. Replicating their motorcycle strategy, Honda engineers by 1964 had developed a Formula I racer. The company's 1965 Formula I entry won Honda's first Grand Prix victory in Mexico City. In 1966 Britisher Jack Brabham drove to eleven straight victories in a Honda Formula II equipped with a 4 cylinder 1,000cc (160 HP) water-cooled engine. But within a few years Honda withdrew his cars (and later his motorcycles) from racing, saying the company had gained all the technology and publicity it could from that source.

THE CVCC

In 1970 the U.S. Congress amended the Clean Air Act, requiring a 90 percent reduction in the emission of hydrocarbons, carbon monoxide, and nitrogen oxides by 1976. From the beginning Honda engineers had sought an engine that Mr. Honda demanded offer both the highest internal efficiency and greatest "external merit" in terms of its cleanliness and safety. Recognizing that any system which used an after-treatment device inherently wasted the potential energy of fuel, the company had developed its surprisingly effective CVCC (compound vortex controlled combustion) engine.

Each cylinder ignited a much richer fuel mixture (about 4.5:1) in an auxiliary chamber and let the explosion expand into a main chamber, which had the desired lean (18:1 or 20:1) mixture to keep operating temperatures low within the engine, while minimizing exhausts. Detroit executives vociferously maintained that such "stratified charge" engines could only be put on small cars. But Honda proved its principle by modifying two 8-cylinder Chevy Impala engines to its design and improving their engine efficiency, gasoline mileage, and emission characteristics sufficiently to meet promulgated 1975 air quality standards. At that time, CVCC was the only engine in the world which, operating in its normal mode, could meet the proposed U.S. Air Quality Standards. Despite Detroit's continued opposition, Honda used the CVCC and its superbly engineered small

cars in three basic models (red, white, and brown) to invade the U.S. marketplace. Lacking distribution, Hondas were at first sold as "second cars" through established U.S. dealerships.

HONDA IN THE 1980s

By the late 1980s Honda had become the fourth largest maker of American cars. Honda had decided in 1979 to build a 150,000 unit U.S. auto assembly plant alongside its Marysville, Ohio motorcycle plant. Accords began rolling off in December, 1982. When that plant's capacity became seriously strained in 1985, Honda moved quickly to double it. The new space was used to produce Honda's popular Civic, the smallest and least expensive car Honda sold in the U.S. Honda's investments in plant were substantially below competitors'. The $250 million Honda had invested in its Marysville plant compared favorably with the $660 million Nissan had spent for a similar capacity plant in the U.S.[3] or the $500 million Toyota was preparing to spend on its new 200,000 unit Camry facility.[4] About 1/2 the value of a Honda's parts was imported from Japan. Some were made to order by the parent company (especially for the Accord) but others were cheaper than U.S. parts or of higher quality. Honda said it had planned to use a higher proportion of U.S. made parts, "but the attitude of some suppliers was that their job was only to give us the parts, and that we must check the quality ourselves. . . . We told them that wasn't enough, we expected 100% good parts." Some suppliers responded, others did not. Honda could build a fully equipped 1985 Accord for about $8,000, some $1,000–$1,500 less than it cost General Motors to build a comparably equipped version of its Buick or Olds line. And by 1988 it could ship the cars to Japan from the U.S. at a profit.

Honda aggressively built its image in the U.S. through a quietly sophisticated advertising program. According to professional analysts, American consumers perceived the Honda name as being synonymous with quality, just as they perceived the Sony brand. Engineering and automotive magazine ratings of the world's best cars almost always included the Honda Accord. In the mid-1980s, testers for Road and Track had paired the Mercedes-Benz 190E with the Accord SE-i; the Mercedes at $23,000 scored 166 points, the Accord at $13,000 scored 163.[5]

In 1983 Honda eased past Mazda to take over the number three sales position with 8% of the Japanese market, following Toyota's 41% share and Nissan's 26%. Honda's partly plastic bodied, CRX two-seater car won the Car of the Year Award in Japan, leading all contenders by a big margin. And in America, EPA gave the CRX its highest rating for fuel economy—51 miles per gallon.

THE TECHNOLOGY ORGANIZATION

Honda Motor Company had long operated under an "expert system" which Mr. Fujisawa initiated, where creative people—experts—could fully utilize their skills and be rewarded appropriately. Fujisawa sought a flat or "paperweight" organization in which a promising person was not dependent upon or restrained by his immediate superior. He envisioned the organization as a kind of web "with engineers lined up sideways instead of top to bottom." According to Dr. Kowomoto of Honda R&D, any number of people could have top engineering positions based solely on their technical "expert" qualifications, even with no one reporting to them.

Fujisawa's organization recognized that fundamental research was unique. It needed to concentrate on scientific understanding, faced many non-commercializable failures, and rarely worked well in a structured environment. By contrast production/development had to be carefully controlled, financially driven, and make no mistakes. Honda's researchers could define their own research themes and pursue their projects to conclusion. However, research was focused on product-oriented activities in small teams, typically 2 to 10 people. Engineering was independent of Research and concentrated on process development.

INTEGRATED DESIGNS

Once development began, projects were managed across research, design, product engineering, and early production stages. Each person in a project group both maintained his own specialty and worked directly with other team members. Dr. Kowomoto emphasized that few risks were taken once a product or process was prototyped. Using its special coordination techniques, Honda operated on a 2–3 year cycle from development to production, as compared to a worldwide average of over 4 years for the auto industry.

Honda's development process centered on its SED (Sales, Production Engineering, and Development) system. Through constant reviews and their own training, engineers were encouraged to "think like customers." Each group on a team advanced its arguments based on its own analysis of the potentials, requirements, constraints, it saw for the new product. Interactions among the groups was based on a principle that the company characterized as "mutual aggression." Each was strongly encouraged to pursue its individual position all the way until a final decision was reached. Within R&D different subgroups pursued competing technical solutions until the most appropriate one was selected by the team. The R&D organization developing new products had "no pyramidal or hierarchical organization, just

engineers and chief engineers." On a project team, titles did not influence decisions; even the newest engineers—in a manner antithetical to most Japanese companies—were to "argue frankly" with senior people, including vice presidents who might be on or visit their team. One person—like a metallurgy specialist—might be on many different teams simultaneously, developing completely different new products in parallel for each.

A very specific schedule was set for each project early on, and no deviations from the schedule were allowed despite problems which might develop. People were expected to work as hard as necessary to maintain planned progress, which was reviewed every 3 months by an SED oversight group, where each function presented its views as vigorously as possible. Development people argued for the best technological solution, Engineering for the best quality-cost solution, and Sales to see that the design fitted market trends. Since Honda first introduced its cars in Japan, they had to be successful in the Japanese market. But the same car—modified only for local safety, right hand driving, or environmental standards—had to meet other countries' market demands as well. Although Honda, as a smaller manufacturer, outsourced many of its raw materials, sheet metal, and fabricated parts (other than key engine parts), it had been reluctant to share its design information with outside suppliers until final specifications were set.

Because its cars had often featured new technology Honda noted that its process was often one of "trial and error." For example, in 1970 Honda's 1300cc model introduced with considerable confidence by Marketing had suffered a terrible market failure. In contrast, the Civic had an unstylish look which many feared would not sell well. Instead it became a popular product and Honda's staple-volume production model with a potential for long product life. The first marketed model of the Honda Prelude had so little power that it was sometimes the "Quaalude." But the company quickly restyled it, increased the power of its engine, gave it a much more "macho" appeal, and made it a success.

A unique aspect of Honda's design process was the fact that workers could suggest and implement process changes themselves right on the production line. A visitor would see small areas (20′ x 20′) out on the factory floor where workers were building their own new prototype processes. When asked if they were supervised by engineers, the answer would be, "No! If they need engineers they will find them." Changes were not limited to single work stations. Workers had automated whole body-panel and body-assembly sections this way. Each year Honda sponsored an "idea contest" and gave awards for its employees' most ingenious ideas, both for company use and for sheer inventiveness. One winner was a three-wheeled "all terrain" powered bike that became a major product line.

PRODUCTION ORGANIZATION

Honda also enjoyed some unique policies in the production area. In its foreign operations, it encouraged employees to wear uniforms, like its Japanese employees. Most did. Each individual was called an "associate," a term which described how each person related to other members of the organization and conveyed a feeling of respect for the individual. Overseas, Honda preferred to develop its own people in order to reduce the chances of employees bringing bad work habits with them. Newly hired associates were often rotated to other tasks and dispatched to Honda plants in Japan where they learned Honda's methodologies of producing to exact specifications.

Once trained, Honda promoted the best qualified person to do a job. Unlike other companies in Japan, seniority never had a high priority in determining advancement. Even in its U.S. operations, where other companies stressed seniority, young Honda managers often occupied high positions that would take 5 to 10 years more to achieve in other companies.

Everyone was treated as an equal. Even the ubiquitous, identical uniforms of Honda employees emphasized equality, rather than rank. Everyone ate in the same cafeteria. No one had a private office. Managers and engineers routinely handled parts and equipment on the shop floor. Soichiro Honda believed that good leaders should perform even the most undesirable jobs willingly, and at least once. Accordingly, he was known to sweep factory floors, empty ash trays, and pick up paper towels from restroom floors wherever he went.

Dr. Robert Guest, a world authority on automotive organizations, described Honda's organization practices this way. "Almost all members of Honda's operating management started in the shop itself, as did 65% of its Japanese sales personnel. Mr. Honda by skill and temperament was a 'shop man' who was always concerned about the product, production details, and more importantly about the role played by people on the shop floor and their creative potentials. There is frequent movement of workers laterally and through promotions. Everyone understands that automation will be targeted first at the most onerous tasks. Much of the machinery at Honda is built by a Honda engineering subsidiary, which was set up because of the many new ideas that were originated by the workforce themselves.

"No one fears problems of technological unemployment, as growth continues. Work standards are written up by the employees themselves, in conjunction with their foremen. Honda threw out American style scientific management systems when they found that their workers slowed down while being timed and objected to the process."[6]

ORGANIZATION STRUCTURE

True to their stated policy of "proceed always with ambition and youthfulness," Soichiro Honda (68) and Takeo Fujisawa (62) retired from active management of the company on its 25th anniversary in 1973, becoming "advisers" to the firm. During the 1980s, the top management group was assembled on the 3rd floor of Honda's Tokyo headquarters office—using an open-plan executive suite where 32 directors worked together in a single open room. Just as in Honda's factories, senior executives including Honda's president occupied desks in an open office with chairs scattered around. While decisions at this level were widely discussed in the room, Honda's president Tadashi Kume, an engineer who had earlier opposed and defeated Honda in a showdown over the development of air-cooled engines, was clearly the first among equals. He was "a passionate man in the Honda tradition, a man who, like the founder, sometimes shouted to make himself heard. . . . He listed as his hobby drinking sake, but cars, and more particularly the engines in them were still his passion."

Through the 1980s the company's unique management structure had three levels. At the top was a board of directors, consisting of 24 company officers, including its 2 "supreme advisors." Within the board was a senior managing director's group, a decision making body consisting of the president, two executive vice presidents, and four senior management directors. The president's expertise was in technology; one vice president's was in sales; and the other, responsible for the company's financial policies, was an engineer by training and a generalist by experience at Honda.

At the corporate level, this group controlled three specialist groups, each made up of managing directors and ordinary directors and joined as needed by the heads of semi-independent affiliated companies. The three specialist groups were responsible for matters relating to "people, things, and money." The individual sections and divisions responsible for day to day operations and for specific areas of profit-making reported to the "president's office." They were under the general oversight of the specialist groups, which did not represent any specific section with daily responsibilities for profit. Among other things, these specialist groups were responsible for overseeing major new projects of the company. Examples were the task forces to select production sites for Honda's U.S. motorcycle (and later, automobile) assembly operations.

At the operational level, Honda had utilized basically a worldwide functional organization for its line activities.

For example, a North American Sales Division reported directly to the headquarters Sales group; overseas Production divisions to the headquarters Manufacturing group; and small overseas R&D units to corporate R&D. However, engine R&D, engine manufacture, and manufacture of some key subassemblies were kept in Japan. Some products were designed and built in Japan directly for export; some were built in Japan and modified for export; others were built entirely in overseas operations.

THE EUROPEAN MARKET

In contrast to its U.S. strategy, Honda had been reluctant in the 1980s to invest heavily in Europe, apart from its motorcycle plants. It had undertaken a joint production arrangement with British Leland for a new 2 liter car, bigger than any Honda had ever built. Total Japanese penetration of European markets was also not nearly as great as in the U.S. Quotas had long restricted imports of Japanese cars into individual European countries. But Spain and some of the "Mediterranean countries" with lower labor costs were pressing to break these quotas in 1992. Building sales in Europe would be difficult against the well-known, high quality, and accepted European brands. However, many European producers had not updated their plants as dramatically as either the Japanese or the Americans, and some of the great European brands had not won a "Car of the Year" award in over a decade.

The European market had been highly fragmented by national boundaries, language differences, and special taste preferences. The Common Market in 1992 was supposed to mitigate this. However, like the Japanese and American markets, over-capacity (of about 20%) plagued the European marketplace in the late 1980s. This was largely offset by exports of the upper-line European cars, like BMW, Daimler-Benz, Jaguar, Saab, and Volvo, mostly to the U.S. Few of the "lower-end" European cars enjoyed a substantial export market. But because of such considerations, France, Italy, and Spain (which together accounted for about 40% of total European sales) had been virtually closed to Japanese producers, and other countries had applied ceilings to Japanese imports.

Cost structures in the automobile industry began changing rapidly in the late 1980s. Components and materials comprised about 50%–60% and labor about 20% of an auto's factory cost. Plants for sophisticated components like engines, gear trains, or trans-axles might cost $500–$800 million, while assembly plants were decreasing in size, but increasing in the complexity of their flexible automation. About 30% of the pre-tax price of a car was accounted for by marketing and distribution. While U.S.-owned companies had a strong presence in Europe, Japanese companies had been much later to enter. Japanese car companies' investment problems were compounded by rapidly increasing price cutting and retail competition in Japan. Toyota and Nissan seemed strong enough to withstand any onslaught, but both Mitsubishi and Mazda were plagued with scale and distribution problems, despite some fine individual products.

MID-1990s ISSUES

Although still drawing heavy fire from politicians and the American press, the Japanese auto presence in North American had shifted significantly. Many more Japanese cars were being produced in the U.S.—736,000 cars in 1987 and 1,687,000 in 1992. At the same time Japanese motor vehicle exports to the U.S. had dropped from 3.4 million to 1.7 million cars per year. Japanese automakers had invested over $9.6 billion in U.S. plants through 1992. Honda led the field, with total investments of $2.6 billion and production capacity for 458,000 units in the U.S. The comparative investments, employment, and units for other Japanese companies are shown in Exhibit 1. Japanese automakers purchased $13.6 billion worth of U.S.-made parts and materials annually and 158,000 cars built in Japanese-owned or joint-ownership plants were exported from the U.S. to other countries. In 1992, their exports of 114,600 cars exceeded the big three automakers' exports of 105,600. Honda was the second largest exporter of passenger cars (after General Motors) with 55,850 cars exported to countries other than Canada. American companies enjoyed numerous alliances with Japanese companies as shown in Exhibit 2. Honda had major facilities in Marysville, Ohio; Torrance, California; Denver, Colorado; and Mojave Desert, California.

A MAJOR REORGANIZATION

In 1990, when Mr. Nobuhiko Kawamoto became CEO of Honda he radically reorganized the company. He took line responsibility for the company's global automobile operations and for Honda R&D. He then reorganized the business into three product lines—automobiles, motorcycles, and power equipment. A year later, in a second stage of this reorganization, he divided the automobile operation into four regional components: (1) the Americas, (2) Europe, the Middle East, and Africa, (3) Asia and Oceania, and (4) Japan. Chief operating officers in each region then had the authority for development, production and sales, and marketing. The executive committee at world headquarters, of which Mr. Kawamoto was a member, was free of line

EXHIBIT 1 JAPANESE AUTOMAKERS' INVESTMENTS IN THE U.S., 1992

	TOTAL INVESTMENT (MILLIONS OF DOLLARS)	MODELS	UNITS PRODUCED	EMPLOYEES
Honda	$2,600	Accord, Civic	458,251	10,200
Nissan	$1,300	Altima, Sentra	300,328	5,860
Mazda	$ 550	Mazda MX-6 and 626 Ford Probe	169,566	3,700
Mitsubishi	$1,400	Mitsubishi Eclipse Chrysler Laser and Talon	140,156	3,100
Toyota	$1,150	Toyota Corolla Geo Prism	256,799	4,200
Subaru-Isuzu	$ 620	Fuji Legacy Isuzu Pickup and Rodeo	124,020	1,900

Source: "How Japanese Automakers Contribute to the U.S. Economy," Japan Automobile Manufacturers Association, Inc., 1993.

responsibilities, focusing on long-term global strategies. A group of coordinating staff operations remained at headquarters. There were four support groups responsible for motorcycles, automobiles, power products, and service parts, respectively. Mr. Kawamoto noted, "This new blueprint will give Honda greater agility."

Some keys to Mr. Kawamoto's strategy for the Americas were: increasing automobile capacity in the U.S. and Canada to 720,000 units by 1997 and starting up auto production in Mexico in 1995; expanding Honda's U.S. engine plant from 500,000 to 750,000 engines per year in 1998, including production of Honda's first U.S. made V-6

EXHIBIT 2 PARTNERSHIPS BETWEEN JAPANESE AND U.S. AUTOMAKERS, 1992

	JAPANESE	U.S.	RELATIONSHIP
Capital Ties	Isuzu Motors	GM	GM owns 37.5% of Isuzu
	Suzuki	GM	GM owns 3.5% of Suzuki
	Mazda	Ford	Ford owns 24.5% of Mazda
	Mitsubishi Motors	Chrysler	Chrysler owns 5.9% of Mitsubishi
Joint Production	Toyota Motor	GM	NUMMI
	Nissan Motor	Ford	Joint production of minivans
	Mazda	Ford	AutoAlliance International, Inc.
	Suzuki	GM	CAMI (Canada)
Joint Development	Nissan Motor	Ford	Joint development of minivans
Supply of Vehicles	Mazda	Ford	Mutual supply of completed cars
	Mitsubishi Motors	Chrysler	Supply of completed cars to U.S.
	Isuzu Motors	GM	Supply of completed cars to U.S.
	Suzuki	GM	Supply of completed cars to U.S.
Supply of Parts	Toyota Motor	GM	Supply of parts to Japan
	Toyota Motor	Chrysler	Supply of parts to Japan
	Nissan Motor	GM	Supply of parts to Japan
	Mazda	Ford	Mutual supply of parts
	Mitsubishi Motors	Chrysler	Mutual supply of parts
	Isuzu Motors	GM	Supply of parts to U.S.
	Suzuki	GM	Supply of parts to U.S.
Sales in Japan	Honda Motor	Chrysler	Sales of Chrysler cars in Japan
	Mazda	Ford	Sales of Ford cars in Japan
	Isuzu Motors	GM	Sales of GM European cars in Japan

Source: "How Japanese Automakers Contribute to the U.S. Economy," Japan Automobile Manufacturers Association, Inc.

engines in 1996. All of this would expand Honda's total North American investment to more than $3.8 billion. The company's stated goal was "to establish in the United States a self-reliant motor vehicle company, which will be an important part of Honda's international operation with the resources to compete in the world market."

Mr. Kawamoto noted, "We have been able to raise the local content of our U.S.-made automobiles to over 80%. . . . More than 60% of the cars we sell in America are made there. Several models have been developed in America as well. . . . We are expanding engine production in the U.S. and auto production in the U.S. and Canada—without building new plants. We are doubling our North American R&D capabilities, lowering the cost of development and manufacturing, increasing our use of local parts and materials. We will begin auto production in Mexico with the support of our U.S. manufacturing operations. . . . By the end of the decade we will double exports of automobiles and component sets from the U.S. and Canada."

Mr. Kawamoto also looked elsewhere, "Honda's unique experience in marketing and manufacturing motorcycles [in the Asia/Oceania] will be invaluable as the Asian automobile market grows. Through our own factories and joint ventures, we produce almost 3 million motorcycles in Asia outside of Japan. . . . In the future we believe the auto industry will experience modest growth in mature markets. But the potential for growing demand in emerging markets could have a major impact. Such growth will place new demands on the world's energy supply. It will also increase CO_2 levels, raising environmental concerns."

NEW CAR: NEW CULTURE

To support these changes Mr. Kawamoto launched the most wrenching cultural realignment in Honda's history. After he took office in June 1990, the Japanese auto market began a three year slide. By December 1992 Ford's Taurus had broken Accord's run as the top selling car in America, and early 1993 Accord sales plunged as Honda removed the dealer rebates it had introduced to battle Ford. Profits slumped 62% in the first quarter of 1993. To offset this, Kawamoto pushed development of replacements for its great—but 1980s styled—Accords and Civics. Fortunately, design of the new Accord (for entry in 1994) had started in 1989. But Mr. Kawamoto thought that Honda's earlier design practices had "lacked discipline"—a 10% cost overrun on the just completed 1990 Accord. He was determined to change that culture, although he was a product of it and a protégé of Soichiro Honda.

Despite the great market success of the 1990 Accord, Kawamoto's design team set new objectives for the '94 design: (1) hold total spending level with the 1990 Accord, (2) cut new investment in half, (3) carryover 50% of the parts from the 1990 Accord, and (4) anchor the price at the 1990 Accord's level. Although he let four "studios" compete actively on styling the '94 Honda for its markets, Kawamoto sought strongly to avoid the production glitches which occurred when the 1990 "Japanese-designed" Accord was produced internationally. As a portion of the new car's technical design, its engineers borrowed the Variable Valve Timing and Lift System from Honda's $60,000 NSX sports car. Research for the engine had begun in 1984 and was introduced as the VTEC in Japan's Civic in 1991. This lean-burn engine got 55–60 miles to the gallon on the highway. Honda then managed the startling feat of introducing manufacture of the new Civic with a new engine on two continents simultaneously. It also began experimentation with Orbital Engine's advanced two stroke engines which offered over 75 mpg, but had been spurned by U.S. companies.

CURING "BIG COMPANY DISEASE"

Before introducing these changes, Mr. Kawamoto had personally toured the facilities employing 70% of Honda workers and interviewed suppliers and dealers to see what they thought of Honda. He concluded that in its rapid growth, Honda had contracted "big company disease" and had lost touch with its customers. Its policy had been not to sell cars on price, but to consistently promote them on value. This view, and the complexity of Honda's organization, convinced him that there were "too many walls within our organization." To remedy this, he changed the open-space, sharing style in Honda's central office to a new style where each person had a specific responsibility. Decisions would be made by that executive alone. Once a plan was approved, each member of the board assumed responsibility for implementation in his area.

In its largest international operation, Honda began gradually transferring management from Japanese to Americans. Overall, one-third of its employees were foreign. Honda's American operations were becoming larger than those in Japan, and there was much press discussion of Honda possibly moving its headquarters to the U.S. Through 1993, however, Honda had not sold its shares on international markets or consciously tried to diversity its ownership base. The issue of local control was compounded by questions of whether Honda cars made in the U.S. were considered "Japanese imports" in the EEC or whether Canadian-produced Hondas or parts sent to the U.S. were "Japanese" or covered under NAFTA. In 1991, 38% of a Honda's value was in parts imported by Honda—26% from U.S.-based Japanese suppliers and 16% from U.S. suppliers—while 20% of costs were in depreciation and overhead. For the Honda's engine, 58% of its value was in parts imported by Honda. U.S.-based Japanese suppliers provided another 37%, and U.S. suppliers produced only 5% (or $58) of its value. With auto vehicles and parts making up approximately $30 billion of the U.S.-Japanese trade deficit of $35 billion in 1991, these statistics presented tender political issues.

WINNERS AGAIN

Capping off these changes, in 1992 the Honda Civic won the Japanese Car of the Year Award and the 1994 Accord won *Motor Trend's* Import Car of the Year Award. Since the U.S. accounted for over three-quarters of total Accord volume, a majority of the development effort for the new fifth generation model went into devising a package with maximum appeal to U.S. customers. After Ford's Taurus-Sable slipped past the Accord for top sales honors in 1992, Honda had vowed to retake the number one position. Consequently, despite its improved features, Honda held the '94 Accord DX prices to 1993 levels. The new Accord was specially designed to make a stronger visual statement than its predecessors, yet maintain its family appeal. Styling for the

new car was locked in by December 1990, twelve months earlier in the design process than for preceding cars. To ensure its transition to the U.S., 57 production engineers and their families from Honda America were transported to Japan.

Improving customer satisfaction beyond the legendry Accords of the late 1980s was difficult. However, features like 38% more torsional rigidity and 25% increased bending stiffness along with strengthening the central tunnel, firewall, and pillar constructions—as well as redesigned crumple zones to provide a quantum increase in occupant protection—vastly improved functional quality. Along with this came a world class passenger environment with many of Honda's uniquely engineered "extras" for passenger comfort and convenience. Despite featuring an 8.1 second 0–60 MPH capability, the new Honda VTEC (Variable Valve Timing and Lift Electronic Control) engine gave substantially improved mileage. All these features boomed export sales of the new Accords as well as redesigned Civics. Data on Honda's U.S. sales are shown in Exhibits 3 and Exhibit 4.

By 1993 the Japanese market for automobiles was quite mature and competitive. The nation's economy was

EXHIBIT 3
U.S. MARKET SHARES BY MANUFACTURER, 1981–1993

	SHARE OF TOTAL CAR MARKET						
	1981	1983	1985	1987	1989	1991	1993
General Motors	44.6	44.3	42.7	36.6	35.2	35.6	34.1
Ford	16.6	17.2	18.9	20.2	22.3	20.0	22.0
Chrysler	9.9	10.4	11.3	10.8	10.4	8.6	9.8
Honda	4.4	4.4	5.0	7.2	8.0	9.8	8.4
Toyota	6.7	5.9	5.3	6.0	6.9	9.1	8.7
Nissan	5.5	5.7	5.2	5.2	5.2	5.1	5.7
Mazda	2.0	1.9	1.9	2.0	2.3	2.7	3.1
Mitsubishi	NA	NA	0.5	0.6	1.1	2.0	2.0
Others	10.4	10.2	9.1	11.4	8.5	7.2	6.2

	SHARE OF SALES OF DOMESTIC CARS			
	1987	1989	1991	1993
General Motors	50.2	46.3	45.4	42.3
Ford	28.5	29.3	25.6	27.3
Chrysler	13.6	14.1	10.4	11.4
Honda	4.5	5.0	7.9	6.2
Toyota	0.6	1.0	5.4	5.5
Nissan	1.7	1.4	1.8	3.7
Mazda	0.0	0.4	1.3	1.5

Source: Ward's *Automotive Yearbook*, various years.

EXHIBIT 4   HONDA'S POSITION IN U.S. CAR MARKET—1994

	TOTAL UNITS SOLD IN SEGMENT	PERCENTAGE OF TOTAL UNITS SOLD	AMERICAN SHARE	JAPANESE SHARE	OTHER SHARE	HONDA SHARE
Budget	779,468	8.7%	51.7%	40.0%	8.3%	0.0%
Small	1,740,847	19.4	60.7	35.6	3.7	15.3
Lower mid-range	1,196,142	13.3	74.2	19.7	6.1	5.6
Mid-range	2,602,198	28.9	64.4	34.7	0.9	14.1
Upper mid-range	870,833	9.7	83.2	16.7	0.1	0.0
Near Luxury	431,200	4.8	39.2	24.6	36.2	2.0
Luxury	655,401	7.3	62.7	18.2	19.1	5.5
Sporty	642,280	7.1	69.7	29.4	0.9	0.0
Specialty	72,148	0.8	44.1	38.3	17.6	0.7
Total	8,990,517	100.0				

Note: The five top-selling cars in each segment are shown below:

Budget	Nissan Sentra, Dodge Neon, Toyota Tercel, Plymouth Neon, Chevrolet/Geo Metro
Small	Ford Escort, Saturn, Honda Civic, Toyota Corolla, Chevrolet Cavalier
Lower mid-range	Pontiac Grand Am, Chevrolet Corsica-Beretta, Nissan Altima, Ford Tempo, Acura Integra
Mid-range	Ford Taurus, Honda Accord, Toyota Camry, Oldsmobile Ciera, Buick Century
Upper mid-range	Buick LeSabre, Nissan Maxima, Ford Crown Victoria, Chevrolet Caprice, Mercury Grand Marquis
Near luxury	Chrysler New Yorker, Buick Park Avenue, Volvo 800 Series, BMW 3 Series, Lexus ES300
Luxury	Cadillac DeVille, Lincoln Town Car, Cadillac Seville, Acura Legend, Lincoln Continental
Sporty	Ford Mustang, Chevrolet Camaro, Ford Probe, Mitsubishi Eclipse, Pontiac Firebird
Specialty	Chevrolet Corvette, Mistubishi 3000GT, Dodge Stealth, Nissan 300ZX, Mercedes-Benz SL

Source: "1995 Market Data Book," *Automotive News.*

EXHIBIT 5
DOMESTIC SALES OF VEHICLES BY JAPANESE AUTOMAKERS, 1992–1993 (thousands of units)

	1992			1993		
	FULL SIZE CARS	MINIS	TRUCKS & BUSES	FULL SIZE CARS	MINIS	TRUCKS & BUSES
Toyota	1,574	—	655	1,465	—	593
Nissan	886	—	314	821	—	277
Honda	402	65	129	340	81	131
Mazda	275	49	159	228	44	133
Mitsubishi	222	113	409	228	129	360
Fuji	78	94	136	97	92	122
Suzuki	26	227	283	24	225	280
Daihatsu	20	225	189	23	202	173
Isuzu	17	—	148	5	—	124
Total	3,498	774	2,505	3,232	772	2,268

Source: 1994 Ward's *Automotive Yearbook.*

undergoing a serious stagnation with auto production forecast to drop 5–6% in 1994 and 1995. Honda's 1993 passenger car sales in Japan stayed about one-fourth of Toyota's and 40% of Nissan's in Japan. (See Exhibit 5.) Its imports of Accords and Civics made Honda the leading automobile importer in Japan. In keeping with this trend, Honda was reducing its capacity in Japan from 1.22 million units to 1 million units in the mid-1990s. In North America, on the other hand, its U.S. plants produced 417,000 automobiles, and Honda Canada added another 102,000 units. Honda's Acura maintained its leadership among all luxury import plates in North America, while its motorcycles accounted for nearly 30% of all U.S. motorcycle sales. In Europe, Honda produced approximately 35,000 Accords in its Swindon (U.K.) facility. Trends in the European marketplace are indicated in Exhibit 6, 7. Company and comparative financial data for Honda in the early 1990s appear in Exhibits 8, 9, 10.

1993 AND BEYOND

Given the massive capital requirements of the automobile industry, few would have thought a new entrant like Honda could have survived, much less prospered, in the capital intensive world of automobiles. (See Exhibits 11 and 12 for data on world auto demand by region and the largest automakers.) But as *Fortune* concluded, "A few years ago when Japanese cars flooded the American market, Detroit appeared frozen in indecision. The established Japanese companies, by comparison, seemed invincible. Now relative newcomer Honda is making all the other Japanese car makers look ponderous and timid . . . against a company willing to take risks and move fast."[3] While the markets of the mid-1990s posed formidable new challenges for Japan's number 3 auto producer, Mr. Kawamoto was determined to position his company for continued growth in its complex markets.

EXHIBIT 6 EUROPEAN NEW CAR REGISTRATIONS BY MANUFACTURER (thousands of units)

	1985		1988		1992		1993	
	UNITS	PERCENT	UNITS	PERCENT	UNITS	PERCENT	UNITS	PERCENT
VW Group	1,529	14.4	1,930	14.9	2,358	17.5	1,879	16.45
GM Total[b]	1,212	11.4	1,375	10.6	1,679	12.4	1,480	12.96
Peugeot Group	1,226	11.5	1,672	12.9	1,645	12.2	1,401	12.27
Fiat Group	1,304	12.3	1,916	14.8	1,604	11.9	1,271	11.12
Ford Total[a]	1,268	11.9	1,466	11.3	1,521	11.3	1,311	11.48
Renault	1,139	10.7	1,326	10.2	1,433	10.6	1,196	10.47
BMW	290	2.7	355	2.7	441	3.3	369	3.23
Nissan	307	2.9	378	2.9	438	3.2	402	3.52
Mercedes	394	3.7	445	3.4	410	3.0	355	3.11
Austin Rover	420	3.9	448	3.5	331	2.5	363	3.18
Toyota	248	2.6	349	2.7	338	2.5	314	2.75
Mazda	203	1.9	245	1.9	269	2.0	193	1.69
Volvo	255	2.4	265	2.0	201	1.5	172	1.51
Honda	n/a	n/a	140	1.1	175	1.3	162	1.42
Mitsubishi	116	1.1	156	1.2	161	1.2	138	1.21

(a) of which more than 99% is sold by Ford Europe
(b) of which more than 98% is sold by Opel/Vauxhall
Source: 1989, 1993, and 1994, Ward's *Automotive Yearbook.*

EXHIBIT 7
EUROPEAN CAR
MARKETS

	PERCENTAGE OF EUROPEAN MARKET	NEW CAR REGISTRATIONS (000)			JAPANESE IMPORT PENETRATION (%)		
		1988	1991	1993	1988	1991	1993
France	15.0	2,217	2,031	1,721	2.9	4.3	4.5
Germany	30.8	2,808	4,159	3,194	14.8	14.7	13.7
Italy	17.3	2,184	2,341	1,890	0.0	2.9	4.6
Spain	6.6	1,046	887	742	0.7	3.2	4.6
UK	11.8	2,216	1,593	1,778	11.4	11.6	12.7
Total Europe	100.00	12,978	13,504	11,424	11.3	13.4	12.4

EUROPEAN MARKET SHARES FOR JAPANESE AUTOMAKERS

	MARKET SHARE (%)		
	1988	1991	1993
Nissan	2.9	3.2	3.5
Toyota	2.7	2.7	2.8
Mazda	1.9	2.1	1.7
Mitsubishi	1.2	1.4	1.2
Honda	1.1	1.2	1.4

Source: Ward's *Automotive Yearbook,* various years.

EXHIBIT 8
HONDA MOTOR CO.,
LTD., SEGMENT DATA

	1990	1992	1993	1994
MOTORCYCLE BUSINESS				
Net sales (billions of yen)				
Japan	134	164	167	154
North America	34	57	55	59
Europe	81	123	138	107
Other	99	175	210	227
Total	348	519	570	547
Unit sales (thousands)				
Japan	802	804	733	671
North America	98	124	102	114
Europe	343	316	347	292
Other	1,744	2,370	2,769	3,092
Total	2,987	3,614	3,951	4,169
Operating income (loss)	na	21	45	49
AUTOMOBILE BUSINESS				
Net sales (billions of yen)				
Japan	856	1,185	1,118	1,034
North America	1,627	1,875	1,542	1,465
Europe	237	373	378	298
Other	114	177	242	236
Total	2,838	3,610	3,280	3,033
Units sales (thousands)				
Japan	679	669	616	566
North America	946	953	794	828
Europe	191	196	181	156
Other	120	143	202	203
Total	1,936	1,961	1,793	1,753
Operating income (loss)	na	128	49	4
POWER PRODUCTS/OTHER BUSINESSES				
Net sales (billions of yen)				
Japan	na	97	95	94
North America	na	109	124	126
Europe	na	37	39	34
Other	na	21	25	28
Total	115	263	283	282
Unit sales (thousands)				
Japan	106	99	89	92
North America	537	436	531	607
Europe	437	382	399	425
Other	441	499	515	590
Total	1,521	1,416	1,534	1,714
Operating income (loss)	na	4	14	26

EXHIBIT 9
HONDA MOTOR CO.,
LTD., FINANCIAL
AND OPERATING
STATISTICS
(billions of yen;
thousands of units)

	1986	1989	1990	1992	1994
Net sales and other operating revenue	¥3,009	¥3,489	¥3,853	¥4,392	¥3,863
Cost of sales	1,917	2,544	2,764	3,199	2,820
Selling, general, and administrative	555	584	702	847	775
Operating income	319	177	201	153	78
Net income	147	97	82	60	24
Cash dividends paid	11	11	13	14	14
Research and development	136	184	186	192	189
Interest paid	33	25	36	43	35
Total assets	1,817	2,284	2,842	3,154	2,921
Stockholders' equity	761	901	1,085	1,098	967
Depreciation	110	131	165	191	143
Capital expenditures	281	279	333	238	122
Unit sales					
Motorcycles	3,093	3,032	2,987	3,614	4,169
Automobiles	1,365	1,903	1,936	1,961	1,753
Power products	1,816	1,543	1,521	1,416	1,714
Number of employees	59,000	71,200	79,200	90,500	91,300
Average exchange rate (yen amounts per U.S. dollar)	239	128	143	133	108

Source: Honda Motor Company, Ltd., Annual Report, various years.

EXHIBIT 10
COMPARATIVE
FINANCIALS—FY 1992
(millions of dollars)

	HONDA[1]	NISSAN[2]	MAZDA[3]	TOYOTA[4]
Sales	33,059	48,255	20,470	81,307
Other Income	118	576	6	330
Total Revenues	33,177	48,831	20,476	81,637
Cost of Sales	24,083	37,764	17,870	70,172
S, G & A Expense	6,373	9,331	2,272	9,387
Interest Expense	321	1,227	323	395
Other Expenses	80	—	—	—
Income Before Taxes	984	1,251	136	3,423
Income Taxes	505	510	75	1,700
Other Special Items*	—	—	—	—
Net Income	488	762	70	1,903
Cash Dividends	102	264	61	538
Inventories	3,600	5,762	1,080	3,375
Total Assets	23,757	53,177	12,129	76,662
Long-Term Debt and Other Oblig.	4,541	13,795	2,451	12,603
Shareholders' Equity	8,301	13,645	3,151	37,751

*Honda—Equity Earnings; Nissan—Minority Interests and Extraord. Items; Mazda—Net of Equity in Net Income of Unconsolid. & Affil. Cos. and Minority Interest; Toyota—Special Items; Ford—Minority Interest (Equity in Net Income of Unconsolid. subs. is included under Other Income).
(1) Honda Motor Co., Ltd. manufactures and sells motorcycles, autos, pumps, lawn mowers, power tillers, etc.
(2) Nissan Motor Co., Ltd. manufactures and sells autos, rockets, forklifts, textile machinery, boats, etc.
(3) Mazda Motor Corp. manufactures passenger cars, trucks, buses, machine tools, etc.
(4) Toyota Motor Co., Ltd. manufactures passenger cars, commerical vehicles, prefabricated housing units, etc. Merged with Toyota Motor Sales Co., Ltd. July 1982.
Source: Compiled from Moody's Industrial Manual and Moody's International, 1989 edition.

EXHIBIT 11 WORLD VEHICLE PRODUCTION (in thousands)

| | 1987 | | 1991 | | | |
| | | | CARS | | TOTAL | |
COMPANY	CARS	TOTAL	UNITS	OVERSEAS %	UNITS	OVERSEAS %
1. General Motors (USA)	5,605	7,497	4,969	49.8	6,635	43.9
2. Ford (USA)	4,000	5,892	3,452	66.1	5,138	52.7
3. Toyota (Japan)	2,796	3,730	3,597	11.6	4,511	9.4
4. VW Group (Germ.)	2,338	2,475	2,921	49.9	3,088	49.0
5. Nissan (Japan)	2,017	2,658	2,333	16.6	3,026	23.0
6. Peugeot Group (France)	2,301	2,512	2,257	50.1	2,467	51.5
7. Renault (France)	1,742	2,053	1,706	20.8	2,004	18.7
8. Honda (Japan)	1,362	1,581	1,765	31.2	1,909	28.9
9. Fiat Group (Italy)	1,675	1,880	1,637	27.7	1,899	37.3
10. Chrysler (USA)	1,186	2,188	660	22.7	1,674	35.8
11. Mitsubishi (Japan)	595	1,231	1,104	17.2	1,595	11.9
12. Mazda (Japan)	858	1,202	1,251	13.3	1,551	10.6
13. Suzuki (Japan)	297	868	542	2.0	913	6.0
14. Daimler-Benz (Germ.)	596	823	576	0.0	861	12.5
15. Hyundai (Korea)	545	607	670	4.3	795	3.5
16. VAZ (USSR)	725	1,605	675	0.0	687	0.0
17. Daihatsu (Japan)	142	598	420	0.0	670	0.0
18. Fuji-Subaru (Japan)	267	605	388	15.0	644	18.1
19. BMW (Germ.)			536	0.0	536	0.0
20. Isuzu (Japan)	204	542	130	0.0	471	0.0
21. Kia (Korea)			260	0.0	425	0.0
22. Rover Group (UK)	472	537	396	0.0	420	0.0
23. Volvo (Sweden)			281	32.7	343	32.4
TOP 40 MANUFACTURERS	**32,727**	**44,609**	**33,957**		**44,335**	
Japanese Cos.	8,536	13,080	11,531		15,381	
North American Cos.	10,792	15,663	9,081		13,517	
Western European Cos.	10,371	11,759	10,565		11,912	
Eastern European Cos.	2,086	2,975	1,502		1,730	
Korean Cos.	790	966	1,121		1,424	
TOTAL WORLD PRODUCTION	**33,007**	**45,914**	**34,656**		**46,496**	

Source: Compiled by the Motor Vehicle Manufacturers Association of the U.S., Inc. from reports of various overseas motor vehicle associations. Published in *Facts and Figures, 1989* and *1993.*

EXHIBIT 12
FREE WORLD PASSENGER CAR DEMAND BY REGION (millions of units)

	1985	1987	1992	1997
U.S.	11.0	10.3	10.5	11.1
Canada	1.1	1.1	1.1	1.2
Europe	10.6	12.4	12.9	13.7
Latin America	1.2	1.1	1.6	2.0
Mid-East	0.4	0.3	0.6	0.7
Africa	0.3	0.3	0.5	0.7
Asia-Pacific	4.2	4.4	5.3	6.1
Total	28.8	29.9	32.5	35.5

Source: 1989 Ward's *Automotive Yearbook,* page 77.

The Acer Group: Building an Asian Multinational

The Taipei-based Acer Group had just celebrated its 20th anniversary: from small beginnings, by the late 1990s Acer was producing personal computers, motherboards, peripherals, fax machines, dynamic random access memory (DRAM) microchips, application specific integrated circuits (ASICs), hybrid microelectronics and software. It was also seeking to develop new products for the consumer electronics and communications fields. Under the dynamic and inspired leadership of its chairman and CEO Stan Shih, Acer had grown to be the number five computer company in the world, Taiwan's leading brand-name exporter and the largest PC-compatible manufacturer in South East Asia. Acer was a leading brand name in more than 30 countries, holding top position in 13 markets including Indonesia, Malaysia, Philippines, and Thailand, as well as in Latin American countries such as Chile, Mexico, Panama and Uruguay. Standing at 8th position in the overall US market, it was the third largest supplier to US retail channels. Acer also ranked among the top three companies globally in the monitor business and in the top five world-wide in mid- and high-end PC servers and CD-ROM drive production.

Over the last three years, Acer had set industry records, with over 50% growth in 1993, more than 70% in 1994 and more than 80% in 1995. By 1995, PC shipments had reached 4 million units, plus an additional 1.7 million CD drives, 3.5 million monitors and 52 million memory chips. Net income in 1995 was US$413 million on sales of US$5.83 billion (see Exhibit 1). Pre-audit results showed Acer Group revenues for 1996 would exceed last year's sales figure with PC shipments projected to hit 5.5 million. By 1996 the group was operating 80 offices in 38 countries around the world, employing more than 16,700 staff from 50 different nations. As well as establishing overseas branches, Acer's practice was to form joint ventures with local partners and promote local shareholder investment to increase its share in strategic markets, thus aiming to develop into a publicly traded local company in various different countries while maintaining a global brand.

As the year 2000 approached, Acer planned aggressive action to consolidate a position as a leading provider of world class products and components for a new information technology age. Its strategy of encouraging local investment and expanding overseas joint ventures, based on current rates of expansion, aimed at reaching its "21 in 21" goal of 21 publicly listed companies by the beginning of the 21st century, to become a consortium of borderless networked companies, a US$10 billion "company of companies."

This case was written by Deborah Clyde-Smith under the supervision of Professor Peter J. Williamson. It is intended to be used as a basis for class discussion rather than to illustrate either effective or ineffective handling of an administrative situation.

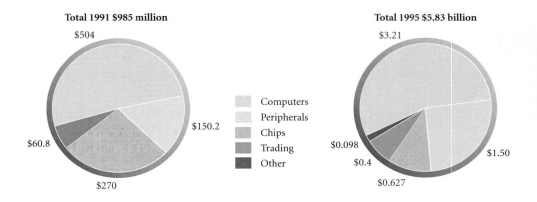

EXHIBIT 1
ACER GROUP'S
PERFORMANCE
Source: Acer Group.

Total 1991 $985 million

$504

$150.2

$60.8

$270

Computers
Peripherals
Chips
Trading
Other

Total 1995 $5.83 billion

$3.21

$0.098

$0.4

$1.50

$0.627

ACER'S HISTORY: 20 YEARS YOUNG

Stan Shih, realising the market potential of the microprocessor and microcomputer industries, teamed up with four partners to found Multitech International in June 1976 (the name was not changed to Acer until 1988). The partners dropped out, but Shih in the following years built the company from a US$25,000, eleven employee beginning into a world player. The firm began by importing electronic components, publishing trade journals and consulting on high-tech issues. Up to 1980, Multitech trained engineers for Taiwan's information industry, and designed products for local manufacturers (including the Dragon Chinese language CRT terminal, winner of Taiwan's most prestigious design award) plus CRT terminals for export.

GROWTH THROUGH THE 1980s

In 1981, the Multitech Industrial Corporation, precursor to Acer, was established. Since the company first began building micro-based equipment in its early years, constant emphasis on R&D had led to the introduction of many innovative products, and 1981–1990 were growth years. In 1981, the firm launched MPF–1 and MPF–2, respectively, an 8 bit learning kit and 8 bit home computer successful in Taiwan and exported to the UK, Germany, Hong Kong and Singapore. In 1983, Acer was a pioneering developer of PC-compatibles with its XT/PC, and in 1984 switched to production of IBM compatible PCs which used the same microprocessors and ran the same software as the original IBM machines, and were very successful. On this basis, net profits grew by 43% per annum from 1984–88. In 1988, the company name was changed to Acer and it went public, coinciding with an all time high on the Taipei stock market.

The firm had achieved a reputation for innovation. Leveraging its close co-operation with the dominant American microprocessor Intel, Acer was repeatedly among the first companies world-wide to market computers on the basis of newly developed chips. In 1986 it beat IBM and was second only to Compaq to announce a 32 bit 386 PC based on Intel's 386 microprocessor, leading to considerable media attention and fanfare in the computer press. Acer was one of the first Taiwanese firms to develop its own brand for international markets, and subsequently moved more of its business away from supplying established computer companies (original equipment manufacturing or OEM) to sales of its own brands. In 1991, Acer set an industry standard by designing the world's first chip CPU upgrade technology, "ChipUp."

STORM CLOUDS

All was not smooth sailing, however. Shortly after becoming a publicly listed company in 1988, Acer had suffered a significant "brain drain," with many employees selling their stock and leaving. After 1988, profitability began to decline and Shih became concerned about the company's heavy dependence on the PC business. In response, the decision was taken to broaden the product range by moving into more sophisticated segments of the computer industry, a move which ultimately contributed to the company's first loss-making year in 1990. In 1987, Acer had acquired Counterpoint, an American producer of multi-user systems, for US$6m; by 1989, however, poor performance meant that most of Counterpoint's factories had to be closed and its products discontinued. In 1990 came the acquisition of Altos, another American multi-user system producer, for US$94m; in 1992, Altos was still unprofitable.

Alliances and joint ventures had been formed with a number of western companies, the most significant being with the American firm Texas Instruments in 1989 for production of 4 megabit DRAM chips. Acer put in 58% of the capital, US$71.9m, while Texas Instruments provided the technology. TI-Acer began production in March 1992, coinciding with a price drop for DRAM chips to about a quarter of the 1989 level. This was a risky venture which was nearly disastrous: the market for DRAM chips traditionally suffers huge swings of over and under supply, and for two years Acer poured millions into the scheme. The venture did eventually prove successful, generating 80% of Acer's profits in 1993, and a third in 1994, whilst also guaranteeing Acer a steady supply of competitively priced DRAMs for its PC manufacturing operations.

In addition to problems with its American operations, Acer was trying to survive intense price cutting in the highly competitive PC market—PC prices slumped by 25– 40% in 1991, and continued to fall at much the same rate in 1992. These factors combined to give Acer in 1992 its third annual loss in three years. It posted a US$2.8m loss after tax on sales of US$1.26 billion, and the following year the Taipei stock exchange downgraded its stock, since its earnings-to-revenue ratio was not sufficient to maintain blue-chip standing. Despite the problems, however, Shih succeeded in keeping his team of experienced Acer executives, and in retaining his reputation as one of Taiwan's entrepreneurial visionaries. The challenge now was to transform Acer into one of the industry's leaders despite its slim resources.

RE-ENGINEERING THE COMPANY

To succeed Acer had to enhance efficiency, cut costs and scale down the organisation to strengthen competitiveness. This was achieved through setting up independent business units, planning a new global business model, downsizing, diluting shareholdings, and the development of the "fast food" style logistics and assembly structure. The company shed about 8% of its work force (400 employees) including several layers of management at head office. Other overhead reductions included cutting inventory from a 90 to a 45 day supply—the difference between current and obsolete technology. Conventional wisdom might have dictated that Acer should close the North American operations that were proving a drain on the whole company, but senior management wanted to hold on to the dream of becoming "a leading global high-tech company." Dependent upon outsiders to run his North American operation, Shih had hired Leonard Liu (formerly chairman of IBM's software development laboratories in California) as president. It was Liu who organised the acquisition of Altos, which rather than giving Acer the hoped for firm foundation in America, drained the company of US$100m. Liu resigned in early 1992, and was replaced with Ronald Chwang, who had moved to Acer in 1986 from Intel. At this

time, Shih began his re-engineering of Acer, and his willingness to try the introduction of new and innovative management strategies and to take risks succeeded in turning the company around, with rapid growth between 1992 and 1996 propelling it into the top ranks of the global computer industry and positioning the company for continued expansion in the years ahead.

GLOBALISATION: OVERCOMING THE INITIAL HURDLES

THE IMAGE PROBLEM

In many respects, Acer had been typical of Taiwanese high-tech companies: it had benefited from Taiwan's aggressive technology programmes, such as cheap government loans, and had a factory in Hsinchu science based Industrial Park, created by the government in the early 80s and where companies enjoyed tax advantages and government funding for innovative R&D. Yet Taiwan retained an image problem, and for this reason Shih often tried to disassociate the company from its origins in the public mind. "Taiwan's reputation is for low-end products," he commented once, "even bankrupt companies in Silicon Valley have a better image than companies from Taiwan." Even within Asia, Taiwan suffered from a poor reputation, with many consumers not believing a Taiwanese company capable of sophisticated technology.

Shih admitted problems did exist: "Our (Asia's) quality is not consistent, and we have not known how to communicate our brand names effectively to the market. At Acer, we are aggressive in trying to change this image." His contention was that the best Asian companies had lower cost structures and were better prepared than the big US companies to deal with rapid change. The IT industry in Taiwan was dynamic and cost effective, with much US educated and local Chinese talent, and tremendous production capability to support new technologies. (About 60% of Taiwan's university population consisted of science and engineering students, compared with 44% in Korea and 32% in Japan, but Taiwanese engineers earned about half their US counterparts.) Yet the perception of low quality, low price that the "Made in Taiwan" label carried continued to affect Acer's efforts to penetrate world markets, despite the fact that its plants around the world were certified compliant with ISO 9000, the world's foremost quality assurance standard.

Acer pursued a two-pronged strategy to create a global brand image. On one level, the company contributed to government-supported campaigns to improve the perception of Taiwanese products, and to joint efforts with private enterprises: Acer co-founded the Brand International

Promotional Association, and joined such government promotion efforts as Taiwan's Image Enhancement Programme (of which Shih was chairman) and brand name advertising campaigns which did enjoy some success.

The second prong of Acer's strategy was to promote its own brand image. When Acer's name was changed from Multitech in 1987, this was partly due to the company's desire to adopt a name suitable for expansion into a worldwide marketplace. Multitech was considered too long and not original enough. "Acer" comes from the Latin for "active, sharp, incisive," qualities on which the company's corporate culture was built. It also carries the connotation of winner or ace, and the name was intended to pave the way to a new corporate identity. It is short and easy to remember: it needed to be registered in over 100 different countries and have no negative implications in any of them.

Without the resources of its big rivals, Acer needed to keep the cash coming in, and Shih concentrated on the company's strengths as a small, flexible and aggressive local manufacturer while it progressively invested to build its brand. It looked for the most cost-effective routes to brand building. The foundation for Acer's brand-building strategy was a consistent commitment to supplying high-quality, innovative merchandise. Acer deployed its R&D capability toward being first on the market with technological breakthroughs which, in turn, helped the company win media attention. It used its strategic alliances with overseas companies to raise awareness of the Acer name. Contrary to the low profile adopted by many of its Asian competitors, Acer continually used PR channels to promote its goals and achievements. As more financial resources became available, high-profile advertising (such as the displays on the luggage trolleys in international airports around the world) was stepped up. In Europe in 1991, for example, Acer's average brand name recognition rate was only 5%, so a massive advertising campaign was launched in 1992, with a shift from computer to more general publications. By 1995, Acer budgetted $150–$170 million on advertising worldwide, the total being split 25% for Central and South America, 25% for Asia, 33% for North America and 17% for Europe. In late 1995, still suffering from low brand awareness in the US despite its top ten position, Acer had determined to double its media budget, and begin broadcast advertising in addition to print campaigns.

SCARCITY OF INTERNATIONAL MANAGEMENT EXPERIENCE

A further hurdle to globalisation of the company came in the shape of lack of managers with international experience: Shih conceded that Acer's top management remained too technically oriented, and needed to learn more about the market. "This is the weak point of Taiwanese companies—they are not able to exploit their technical capability to the level where it reaches their market potential . . . global expansion and decentralisation demand many qualities from mangers—business sense, understanding of corporate mission, the ability to control operations and adjust to change. It is very difficult to develop such people, especially foreign managers in overseas operations," Shih noted.

Localising management abroad proved a big challenge, while cultural differences also posed communication problems. Outsiders sometimes found it difficult dealing with the intricacies of Acer's organisation, where the spreading of responsibility among several people at headquarters made decision making slow. Also, the Taiwanese practice of job rotation, in which personnel moved around frequently in order to gain experience, hindered the formation of relationships with overseas colleagues. Acer therefore began to concentrate on sending more Chinese managers overseas to train the local executives gradually in preparation for greater autonomy at a later stage: while it was not difficult to motivate Chinese managers (or those in developing countries) it was found that people from the advanced countries tended to feel they knew better than headquarters, thus hindering the development of team spirit and mutual trust.

INADEQUATE ACCESS TO DISTRIBUTION AND MARKET INTELLIGENCE

In the early days, by Shih's own admission, Acer lacked presence in foreign markets and had little understanding of what was needed to establish a sound presence overseas, as well as a lack of knowledge of legal systems in various countries. Following his early successes, Shih recruited managers from outside the company to oversee Acer's rapid growth in the late 80s, thus precipitating an excessively rapid expansion which he later admitted had been "beyond our capacity" and which took the company into the red between 1990–1992. These people—in particular Leonard Liu, from IBM, chairman of Acer America—operated in a different fashion from Acer traditional culture, causing internal warfare and the loss of many good employees. Shih came to understand that Liu's appointment was a mistake, and that he had delegated too much too early. Moving back into control (after offering his own resignation, which the Board refused) Shih stopped trying to emulate IBM and instead began to shape Acer in his own distinctive fashion.

Outside the USA, Acer's infrastructure was built more gradually. In Europe, for example, Acer began selling its products to distributors in 1984, after making contact through trade fairs and advertising. It was then decided to establish a European office to improve distribution and its understanding of the rapidly expanding market. This office was set up in 1985 in Dusseldorf by Teddy Lu, previously in charge of managing relations with European customers in Taiwan, with three local employees. In the early years, the team concentrated on establishing relationships with the most efficient European distributors, and developing OEM sales. Acer Europe grew rapidly, and after three years contributed almost a third to group sales, though market share varied considerably from country to country. By 1988, it was decided that Acer should set up its own subsidiaries in markets where the potential size could justify them, thus hoping to better understand local particularities, and establish direct links to dealers and corporate accounts. By 1992, Acer had subsidiaries in Denmark, France, Italy, Germany, Holland and the UK. Direct sales to dealers meant higher margins and brought Acer's management closer to the market.

Problems in the US at this time were forcing most Taiwanese manufacturers to re-think distribution techniques: hence in 1991 Acer introduced the "Acros" micro-computer range to be sold through mass distribution channels including computer supermarkets. "Acros" rapidly accounted for almost half Acer America's sales, and was subsequently introduced in Germany to be sold via a big consumer electronics chain.

REASSESSING PROFIT POTENTIAL IN THE CHANGING COMPUTER INDUSTRY

By 1995, Stan Shih believed the personal computer was at the centre of the computer, communications and consumer electronics products mainstream, and the industry was much different to that of the 80s, having become an open environment, an industry based on the use of standard components to create various types of systems. This Shih referred to as the "disintegrated" mode, being the opposite of the vertical integration mode used by companies such as IBM or Digital Equipment Corporation in the early days. At that time, there were no accepted industry standards for components: under the disintegrated business mode, each standard component represented an industry segment. As a result, customers benefited from a much better performance-to-cost ratio, as open systems led to greater competition in the industry. Competition had also provided opportunities for new players to find a niche in the market. Systems were relying more and more on modular open standard components, and the industry becoming increasingly disintegrated.

In the new IT age, a change had also occurred in the infrastructure: rather than being defined by industry giants, the infrastructure was created by third parties including hardware, software and component suppliers, the

media and end users. A further development was in the way businesses competed: technology and manufacturing leaders were now spread around the world, making technological competition increasingly global. With markets divided into segments along regional or national lines, a new environment of global cooperation and competition had emerged, with competitors forming alliances aimed at strengthening each other's business models. The large investment required to develop new products meant many companies could not survive without cooperating with rival manufacturers. As their overseas operations matured, many multinational corporations were becoming increasingly "borderless" in the way they operated their businesses.

STRATEGIC INNOVATION AT ACER: REWRITING THE RULES OF THE GAME

THE SMILING CURVE

According to Shih's philosophy, the key to success in the new age was providing value: by succeeding in value added business segments, companies could do well in the disintegrated mode. To explain the trend, he created a chart he called his "smiling curve" (see Exhibit 2).

Value is added, Shih argues, in component production on the left side, and marketing distribution on the right. The dotted line represents the traditional computer industry value added curve. In the early days, companies such as Acer started from the centre, sourcing the components, assembling the system and then marketing the product. By the mid-1990s, there was no longer any value added in assembling computers, which could be done by anyone, and to succeed in the new IT age, it was necessary to gain a top position in component segments such as software, CPUs, DRAM, ASICs, etc. as a distribution leader in a country or region.

Since universal standards meant global competition, to succeed on the left side, a company needed technology and a strong manufacturing capability, and in some areas a lot of capital. On the distribution side, success required a good image, brand name awareness, well-managed channels and effective logistics. For both sides, however, it was essential to be a leader of the segment, and Shih believed the chief factors for success in the disintegrated mode to be speed, cost, volume and value. Speed meant fast response to changes, and fast time to market with new products; cost comprised overhead management, inventory reduction and minimising risks. Companies with access to strong R&D, engineering and manufacturing resources were best equipped to enter volume production quickly. Effective channels for distributing high value products were also necessary for building a strong brand name image and generating more

EXHIBIT 2
THE "SMILING CURVE"
Source: Acer Group.

STAN SHIH'S SMILING CURVE

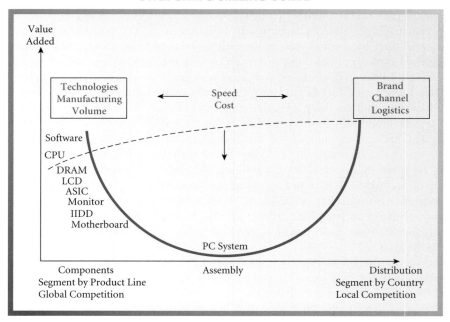

NOTES TO THE SMILING CURVE

- The dotted line indicates the growth path of traditional IT industries
- Computer system manufacturers used to provide nearly all "value added"
- In the new IT Age, there is no "value added" in assembling a computer—anyone can make a PC today out of standard off-the-shelf components
- "Value-added" is manufacturing key components & marketing brand name products

value. On the component side, Acer was in the top five world-wide for all the segments currently pursued, and in distribution was the leader in developing countries and targeting a top five position in the US and top ten in Europe.

THE FAST FOOD BUSINESS MODEL

One of the keys to Shih's re-engineering of Acer was his concept of the "fast food" model of computer supply, based on the example of the uniform quality with which McDonald's produces hamburgers world-wide: the approach being to assemble Acer products locally while still maintaining consistency. The assembly process was consequently spread to 35 sites around the world, while tight controls were prescribed to ensure workers everywhere followed the same testing procedures. Components were prepared in large mass manufacturing facilities, then shipped to assembly sites close to local customers. Retail buyers of Acer computers were guaranteed the "freshest" ingredients—the latest technology—because Acer made them itself and sped them from Taiwan and Malaysia to its

assembly sites: motherboards were flown in directly, while CPUs, hard drives and memory were purchased locally to fill individual user requirements (Exhibit 3). This provided for economies of scale, plus the ability to tailor individual products to suit the needs of individual customers, the result being standardised quality, customisable products and lower inventory costs. "We serve fresh PCs everywhere, not stale models." Rather than marketing computers based on six-month-old ideas and specifications, the turnaround time from idea to market dropped to only one or two months. Acer was turning over its inventory more than seven times per year, making it one of the most efficient PC manufacturers selling through retail channels. The high turnover aided Acer in achieving a 34% return on equity, as against an industry average of 15–20%. Without this decentralisation of operations, many analysts believed Acer could not have met the price cutting challenge of industry leaders such as IBM and Compaq. By 1995, Compaq had realised the advantages of local production, and had opened a few offshore sites, but Shih was dismissive: "Acer is the only company doing the fast food business right now."

EXHIBIT 3
THE "FAST FOOD"
MODEL
Source: Acer Group.

FAST FOOD BUSINESS MODEL

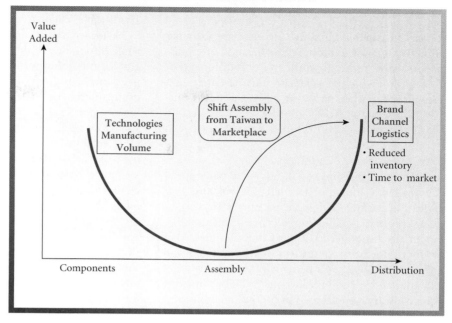

KEY WORDS IN THE NEW IT AGE

- Speed: time to market; time to volume; time to phase out; inventory turnover times; no idle time
- Cost: low overhead; low material cost; low manufacturing cost; high productivity; no idle assets
- Volume: economies of scale; purchasing power; marketing efficiency
- Value: new technology; lower prices; better quality; easy to purchase/use/get support for

LOCAL TOUCH, GLOBAL BRAND: A NETWORK OF JOINT VENTURES

The use of joint ventures to build international capability, conserve capital and help raise awareness of the Acer brand name was a further important element of Shih's strategy: the most successful joint ventures were with Texas Instruments on the TI-Acer semiconductor plant, and with MBB, a subsidiary of the German Daimler Benz group, on a hybrid electronics firm. In 1995, Acer also had joint ventures with partners in Thailand, Indonesia, India, Mexico, Brazil, Chile, Argentina and South Africa.

Shih regarded his "local touch, global brand" philosophy—the formation of joint ventures with local partners and encouragement of local shareholder investment—as a "key to corporate good citizenship." Since competition on the distribution side was local, alliances with strong local partners were needed to achieve eventual leadership. Acer consequently formed alliances with local partners to leverage its competitive edge in components with its partners' leading position in local markets. The philosophy

also served as a means to integrate global talent and capital reserves to compete with the big names for market share.

Local touch empowered the management team in each market to decide on product configurations, pricing strategies and promotional programmes that were right for its particular territory. These managers were mainly local to the area or country, with in most cases a single Taiwanese joining them to aid communications with headquarters in Taipei. Thus Shih's re-engineering of Acer sought to overcome its competitive weaknesses by rendering them irrelevant: "Taiwan doesn't have enough people who are really skilled in foreign languages and familiar with foreign cultures to enable us to direct a global marketing effort from Taipei . . . I turned this weak point into a great strength, a core competence." "Local touch" meant more for Shih than just local assembly—through local management and shareholder majorities, Acer aimed to become a true local identity in markets around the world, while maintaining its world-class global identity.

PIONEERING FRONTIER MARKETS: ACER IN MEXICO AND SOUTH AFRICA

Another way in which Acer sought to re-write the rules of the global game was to pioneer frontier, and often distant, markets early, rather than the more traditional pattern of expansion which emphasised starting either with large, established markets or successively expanding outward from home base. Acer's approach in Mexico and South Africa provide good examples of this strategy at work.

In 1996, one in three PCs sold in Mexico was an Acer, giving it a 32% market share, way ahead of that of competitors such as IBM, Compaq or Hewlett Packard, and Acer and its Mexican partner Computec Co. operated to establish a new venture to handle assembly, marketing and distribution for all Latin America. When Computec formed in 1989 to distribute Acer computers, it discovered a gap between the high priced PCs being sold to the corporate market by IBM and HP, and the low quality clones aimed at the private consumer, and zeroed in on the small business and home PC market. The joint venture, formed in 1992, invested heavily in marketing, and by 1993 when the price wars hit Mexico, the company had begun assembling its products in a suburb of Mexico City.

This gave Acer a crucial edge: local assembly enabled Acer to keep prices down and keep pace with rapidly developing technology—the local plant substituted components which became obsolete quickly, rather than waiting to import finished computers with up-to-date components. The Mexican management continually revised tactics (with considerable latitude from Taipei) to deal with problems such as the peso crisis of December 1994. Acer broke with the custom of quoting dollar prices and listed in pesos; while the computer market shrank by 40% it launched a new model, continued to buy TV time and targeted new customers, winning contracts to supply the state-owned power company and the main public university. "We had great flexibility to make decisions and respond quickly to the market" to quote the company's general director. The next step was set to be the manufacture of components and subassemblies such as motherboards and monitors, probably on the US border, for the North American market.

Cooperation with local markets also paid off for Acer in South Africa, where many multinationals shied away from a potentially unstable market during the transition from apartheid to majority rule. Acer's manager/investors took the risk of moving forward in their coverage of the country, which in late 1995 consisted of five branches, 16 distributors and a network of 1,800 dealers, giving the brand tied second place in the market.

THE CLIENT SERVER ORGANISATION

The flexible "client server" business model—which sought to harness basic human motivation for mutual support while responding to the trend toward increased dispersion and local autonomy—stressed the need to achieve independence simultaneously with cooperation among Acer group members. Following its re-engineering, strategic business units (SBUs) were formed to take primary responsibility for R&D, manufacturing, product management and OEM sales, while regional business units (RBUs) took the lead on distribution, service and marketing. This new structure allowed for faster decision making based on changing conditions in each region, while independent ownership and responsibility provided added motivation and incentive. Yet the objective was not to recreate a "multi-domestic" structure comprising largely independent, national businesses linked to headquarters primarily through a system of financial control (the model traditionally adopted by many European multinationals). Instead, drawing the analogy from a PC network, Acer sought for each business unit to act as both a "client" and a "server" within the global network (see Exhibits 4 and Exhibit 5). Thus, in addition to acting as clients for the SBUs' products, the RBUs also act as "servers," providing local market intelligence and "best practice" to SBUs and other RBUs. The quasi-independent SBUs, meanwhile, also act as both

EXHIBIT 4 CLIENT-SERVER RELATIONSHIPS

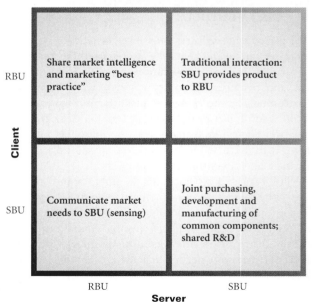

INTERACTION IN ACER'S CLIENT-SERVER ORGANISATION

	Server	
	RBU	**SBU**
RBU (Client)	Share market intelligence and marketing "best practice"	Traditional interaction: SBU provides product to RBU
SBU (Client)	Communicate market needs to SBU (sensing)	Joint purchasing, development and manufacturing of common components; shared R&D

EXHIBIT 5
THE CLIENT-SERVER
ORGANISATION
Source: Acer Group.

ACER REGIONAL BUSINESS UNITS (RBUs)

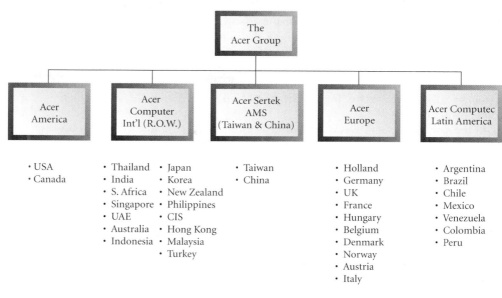

| Acer America | Acer Computer Int'l (R.O.W.) | Acer Sertek AMS (Taiwan & China) | Acer Europe | Acer Computec Latin America |

- USA
- Canada

- Thailand
- India
- S. Africa
- Singapore
- UAE
- Australia
- Indonesia

- Japan
- Korea
- New Zealand
- Philippines
- CIS
- Hong Kong
- Malaysia
- Turkey

- Taiwan
- China

- Holland
- Germany
- UK
- France
- Hungary
- Belgium
- Denmark
- Norway
- Austria
- Italy

- Argentina
- Brazil
- Chile
- Mexico
- Venezuela
- Colombia
- Peru

Global Brand, Local Touch

ACER STRATEGIC BUSINESS UNITS (SBUs)

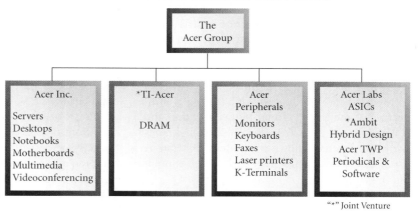

Acer Inc.	*TI-Acer	Acer Peripherals	Acer Labs ASICs
Servers Desktops Notebooks Motherboards Multimedia Videoconferencing	DRAM	Monitors Keyboards Faxes Laser printers K-Terminals	*Ambit Hybrid Design Acer TWP Periodicals & Software

"*" Joint Venture

clients and servers to each other through joint purchasing, design and manufacturing of common components and shared R&D.

BUILDING THE CULTURE OF AN ASIAN MULTINATIONAL

LEADERSHIP AND VISION

In any discussion of Acer's development, the force of character of Stan Shih as leader and motivator comes over as a powerful driver behind the company's success. Yet Shih, a modest man of humble origins, unlike many of the prosperous busi-

nessmen from Taiwan, did not inherit a successful business or a fortune to start one, nor did he have the political connections which facilitate such an enterprise. He always stressed his modest beginnings, but his dream was the creation of a Chinese multinational firm. In the words of Ronald Chwang, president of Acer America, "Stan is one of the few leaders in the industry with a vision. He believes in the role he wants Acer to play. He sees opportunities ahead of others."

Acer's dream in the 70s was to popularise microprocessor technology in Taiwan, in the 80s to move into the top ten players in the world PC industry, in the 90s to be in the "top 5 in '95, 21 in '21 and 2000 in 2000." As a talented engineer, Shih always maintained his involvement with technical product development, but at the same time possessed the ability to steer his growing high-tech company through some very turbulent years in the PC market. "Technically he is very much in touch with the industry, even though he delegates a lot" (Chwang) and it was Shih's own attitudes which were largely the inspiration behind the tirelessness of his engineers, always willing to rise to the challenge of any new technology which might take the company to the front.

At the same time, Shih was deeply rooted in tradition, deriving inspiration from the ancient Chinese board game "Go," or wei chi, in which players have to follow certain strategies and consider the long-term effects of every move. "In Go, you always play from the corner, then the side, the main reason being that you need less resources to occupy the corner. As we don't have the kind of resources that Japanese or American companies have, Acer started its business in smaller markets. That gives us the advantage, because these smaller markets are becoming bigger and bigger, and the combination of many small markets is not small," said Shih. The "Go" strategy was set to become ever more as growth in smaller emerging markets took off.

Shih won considerable acclaim over the years for his success with Acer, with many media and other citations and awards for his individual and corporate contributions to the computer industry and to world trade and commerce. These included being named an International CEO of the year by *Financial World* magazine in 1995, the same year in which he received the Emerging Markets CEO of the Year, presented in Washington, DC, during a joint annual meeting of the International Monetary Fund and the World Bank, for being a CEO whose "vision and company performance has best shown the pattern that can be offered as a model to other emerging markets and companies around the world."

VALUES AND CORPORATE CULTURE

Up to the mid-1980s, Acer's management motivated employees with the theme of the "Dragon Dream": Chinese children are repeatedly told of the country's former glory, and Shih's dream was to resurrect some of this greatness. (While successful and well received, it was later felt that perhaps too much patriotism was not a good thing for an aspiring multinational.) Shih introduced a flat hierarchy, with middle management involved in decision making, although this hierarchy was in fact still fairly rigid. The philosophy behind the culture was one of equality and frugality (with Shih himself setting the example). He believed "human nature is essentially good" and the firm invested more than was usual on employee training, while exercising less control than normal over its workers. While wages were fairly modest, Acer did offer other benefits, including a potentially lucrative stock purchase plan.

Shih was not a typical all powerful Chinese chief executive: "We don't believe in control in the normal sense. We feel there is another way to succeed. We rely on people, and build our business around them." He always listened carefully to others' views, and did not object to his top executives having a high public profile. His employees called him by his English first name, and he professed to treat every employee as his boss, as they were his shareholders and thus all equal. (Employee ownership in the company in 1995 accounted for about 30%.)

Corporate slogans were considered by Shih an integral part of Acer's corporate identity system for their ability to convey a company's business philosophy: Acer began with the slogan "The Microprocessor Gardeners," progressing to "Bridge the Gap for a Better Tomorrow," "Global Vision through Technology," "Technology for Everyone," and then "Fresh Technology Enjoyed by Everyone, Everywhere."

Shih felt that in general Chinese companies were infused with too much family influence, and strongly disagreed with the traditional philosophy that businesses should be handed down to sons rather than capable managers. Acer offered opportunities for committed talent from anywhere, regardless of background. Talented people, he believed, would not necessarily be happy working for a foreign company without real participation—hence the Acer vision of a progressive global partnership, with local management and local shareholder majority. "We are demonstrating a new way to run a business. It is not just new for Taiwan, it is new for the world. It is truly a 21st century approach." People in the local operations of Acer companies could be proud to contribute to their society and be a local company, and there was a common goal to become part of a world class IT company.

There is an old Chinese saying that it is better to be the head of the chicken than the tail of the ox—it is better to run your own shop than be an employee in a large enterprise (and better to be a leader in a small segment than an also-ran in the mainstream). Hence the plan to make a lot of Acer employees heads of chickens—Taiwanese people like to be their own boss, and have a strong entrepreneurial spirit. Acer had always pursued a decentralised management model, upon which the client server structure was built, and a management philosophy stressing that fast decision making, direct communication and a reliable organisation were the keys to success. At the heart of the client server organisation lay a closely linked team of mature and experienced managers committed to the success of their own "piece of the Acer group" as well as to ensuring Acer's overall long-term growth. Acer's top managers were loyal and had worked together closely for a long time: through regular summits, strategies were continually outlined and new possibilities explored for contributing to overall group success.

Mutual understanding and trust, communication and consensus were the cornerstones of Acer's management strategy: thinking and dealing in a human way, cultivating an easy working environment, providing the right motivation, setting competitive but achievable goals. "Acer's success depends on team work between managers with business sense. Corporate performance is based on people," observed Shih.

LEVERAGING THE MULTINATIONAL NETWORK

In June 1995, Acer unveiled its new mission statement: "Provide Fresh Technology to Be Enjoyed by Everyone, Everywhere." Fresh, for Shih, meant more than just "new," which could carry connotations of unproven, expensive and risky—it meant the best high value, low risk, user friendly and affordable technology. Moreover, the "fresh" concept applied not just to technology; fresh ideas were equally important for business strategy, and the key to survival in a rapidly changing industry. Shih foresaw a shift in focus, as consumer electronics and related markets became the target for Acer brand products, his policy being to rely on the core PC technologies that Acer had always specialised in, using them in products for the home that were "digital, interactive and smart."

In September 1995, Acer launched the Aspire line of stylish multimedia home PCs. Acer America, working closely with the California design company Frog Design, created the revolutionary Aspire look and crafted the overall design concept, while Acer Inc.'s powerful PC product expertise developed the tooling and internal PC technology. Acer Peripherals Inc. added innovative monitor and keyboard technological assistance, and much of the creative work behind the global promotion campaign was supported by Acer operations in the US, Singapore and South Africa—a good example of the group's combination of a deep resource base plus flexible strategic design and organisational structure. The sleek grey Aspire, a radical departure from the bland look of the PC for the last 15 years, was an immediate huge hit in America, the key selling point being the innovative award-winning design, which attracted rave reviews and caused the then troubled Acer America's sales to nearly double in the fourth quarter of 1995. Having previously had an uninspiring image in the US and with nothing to lose, Acer was able to take a gamble on something radical which the market leaders were perhaps too risk-averse and complacent to attempt.

At the same time, Acer was also designing a computer aimed at markets in the developing world, the Acer Basic, a "monitorless" budget computer "for the masses" to be launched in summer 1996, on which construction costs were slashed by the use of a 100 megabyte "zip" drive instead of an expensive hard disk, and by incorporating less expensive chips and software. In 1996, Acer also planned the launch of the AcerKids and AcerEden computers aimed at families with children, "monitorless" boxes able to play a host of IBM compatible games and education programmes on audio and video disks. From these, Shih hoped to spawn a host of future information appliances to carry Acer higher up the industry's ranks. By the turn of the century, he hoped to see Acer offering everything from Internet services and software to manufacturing cellular telephones, wide screen TVs and digital video disc players as well as PCs and microchips, a leader in a new market of intelligent consumer products.

Some saw this as over-ambitious: shipment growth in the US cooled from 75% in the fourth quarter of 1995 to 25% in the first quarter of 1996, despite cutting the price of the Aspire in the autumn, and earnings from its chief profit maker, chips, had fallen—Shih admitted the company would fall short of its forecast of US$217m net profit due to the fall in memory chip prices. Acer planned to boost its name recognition with a new ad campaign—despite the Aspire's success, Acer was still outflanked in brand awareness in the West by the industry giants such as Sony, Compaq, IBM and NEC—to expand its distribution by the end of 1997 from mass market chains to office supply and computer stores, and to renew its assault on the corporate market. At the same time, Acer was continuing its push into markets everywhere—number one in Asia, Africa and the Middle East, number two in Latin America, number three in India. In Russia, Acer was delivering computers from a new plant in Finland, 20 km from the border, in five days (instead of five weeks) with sales rising from $3.4m to $42m in 1995. Thanks to intensive advertising, Acer had higher name recognition in Russia than Compaq or Toshiba.

While US companies were turning increasingly to Taiwan's cheap, highly skilled labour, Acer was already moving to even lower cost manufacturing bases, opening plants in the Philippines and Malaysia, and with plans eventually to move into China. In March 1996, an IDC report released in Boston predicted that by the year 2000, the top three players in the PC market would be Hewlett Packard, Compaq and Acer.

However, there was also the possibility that Acer might confuse consumers with too wide a range of products, that the new products required high investment but had low margins, and might not sell. Moreover, a simple design like the AcerBasic was easily copied, and Acer might itself end up competing with low-cost imitators. But Shih believed that by steadily building a low cost manufacturing base and accumulating skill in all digital technologies, Acer always retained the option, if necessary, of returning to being a behind the scenes supplier of components and systems sold by the big brand names. (At this time, half the PCs Acer manufactured were still under OEM agreements for other brand names, and a good deal of its global clout had been gained through strong OEM relationships with the big American and Japanese manufacturers.) One way or another, he was determined to be a major player in the digital age.

LOOKING TO THE FUTURE

"21 IN 21"

The initial public offering in August 1995 of Acer Computer International (ACI), the regional business unit responsible for marketing and services in the Asia Pacific, Africa, the Commonwealth of Independent States and the Middle East, and 75% owned by Acer Inc., met with overwhelming response and was 19 times subscribed at its close, with the 9.43 million shares available for public subscription and the 3.17 million reserved for ACI management, employees and associates all snapped up, confounding the popular belief that US dollar offerings on the Singapore stock market tended to elicit a lukewarm response. In September, Acer announced that Acer Peripherals had applied to the Taiwan stock exchange to offer 32.3 million shares, intending to launch its IPO in March the following year, and Acer Sertek successfully followed suit in late 1996.

Shih's plan to break Acer into 21 public companies listed around the world would open investment in the company to foreigners, as Taiwan enforced strict protectionist barriers against outside capital, with no foreign institution permitted to own more than 7.5% of a listed company in Taiwan. Under his grand design, Acer's Latin American marketing company went public in Mexico in late 1996, and Acer America and TI Acer were to be floated within two years. These being core subsidiaries, Acer kept a 40% stake, but in less crucial subsidiaries, Acer's ownership might be as little as 19%. "Eventually Acer will have a majority of local ownership in each country, and no one will be able to say that we are a Taiwanese company." Ultimately the spinoffs would halve Shih's own stake in the group to about 5%.

Shih stood to gain new sources of financing and new opportunities to motivate managers with stock ownership: without majority control, however, some questioned whether he could maintain his hold over the group. "Some people talk about control with 51% ownership. But I control through an intangible approach, common interest." Naturally independent units would face investor pressure to protect their own interests: "To meet their requirements, we will have to provide value added." It was unheard of for the founder of a Taiwanese company to relinquish so much control, as he acknowledged: "US and Japanese companies would never do this. To them, risk is losing control. My answer is that I am willing to lose control, but make money." Once Acer was broken up, however, the group would no longer be able to use profits from units such TI Acer and Peripherals—which together accounted for 60% of the group's 1995 earnings—to subsidise losses overseas, which might affect the marketability of the companies.

NEW FRONTIERS

Shih believed that Acer's strong foundation making PCs put it in an excellent position for capitalising on the anticipated convergence of the computer and consumer electronics markets in the late 90s. "We believe the industry is on the verge of a transition to new usage platforms." By the turn of the century, he wanted 15% of Acer's revenues to come from a line of "information appliances." Acer planned the launch of a wide screen TV able to double as a computer monitor, with DVD players, high speed CD ROM drives, set-top boxes for cable and satellite TV and a combined fax, scanner and colour printer to follow the next year. Acer Peripherals was to begin work on a plant to make plasma displays for flat screen monitors and TVs, and Acer was investing heavily in telecommunications to develop wireless and integrated services digital network (ISDN) modems and video phones.

Reflecting on these developments and their future implications, Shih noted: "Revenues may be limited in the warm-up stage, but the potential lies in the future. Even so, our resources will not be defocused by these efforts, as we will commit even more to the server, notebook and many other software and peripherals technologies. We believe these are long-term investments today for securing our position in emerging markets." With the boost from these products, Acer expected to reach $10 billion in sales by 1999, and to become a "household brand name" around the globe. "Because we are from Taiwan, people do not appreciate our strengths yet. But we have patience. We have a very long-term plan: affordable fresh technology to be enjoyed by everyone, everywhere. That is our mission statement," Shih reiterated.

CASE 22

AmBev: The Making of a Brazilian Giant

After a year of intense uncertainty, on March 30, 2000 the heads of two of Brazil's greatest corporate rivals had cause to celebrate. They were about to give birth. The pair were Marcel Hermann Telles, Chairman of Cervejaria Brahma, and Victório De Marchi, Managing Director of Antarctica Paulista, and with the news that CADE (the Brazilian antitrust authority) had given its blessing to their merger plans, they were about to create a corporate giant in the Brazilian beverage industry. The subject of great public debate, this largest merger in Brazilian corporate history was to result in the creation of American Beverage Company (*AmBev* for short). With combined sales of US$8.4 Billion, AmBev was to dwarf its domestic competitors, claiming 70% of the Brazilian beer market and almost 40% of the nation's entire beverage market. The combined workforce comprised of 17,000 employees and 50 factories produced an annual 8.9 billion liters of beer. The product line was no less impressive, consisting of 37 brands of beers, 40 brands of soft drinks, 7 brands of mineral water, 7 varieties of natural juices, 8 isotonic sport drinks and 10 different iced teas.

The merger between Brahma and Antarctica was to be the final chapter in what had been an historic rivalry. For over a hundred years the competition between the two for the leadership of the Brazilian beer market had been fierce. However, personal relationships between the two companies were not necessarily unfriendly. Telles and De Marchi often met informally to discuss various economic and political issues. It is rumoured that it was during one of these "get-togethers" in May 1999 that the merger idea was conceived. While discussing the generalised challenges globalisation posed for Brazilian firms, and in particular their own, Telles, who was known for his informal and forthright style, asked De Marchi:

"Victorio, if we were to do business in another country, do you think Brahma and Antarctica would work together?"

This thinly disguised proposal was received with a surprising response:

"Yes, I do." De Marchi paused for effect, "But why not here, in our own country?"

And so it started. In complete secrecy, both Telles and De Marchi each elected two executives to a team tasked with sketching out a blueprint of what, behind closed doors, came to be known as the "Dream Project," the creation of a Brazilian multinational from the merger of Brahma and Antarctica. Both of the companies chose a young, aggressive manager, and an older, more seasoned and conservative executive to represent them in the team. The intent was to balance daring and experience, and after 40 days, the joint team arrived at an agreement and the merger plan was made public.

Case prepared by Thomaz Wood Jr., Flávio Vasconcelos, and Miguel P. Caldas, FGV-EAESP, Brazil. Revised and edited by Daniel Ronen, Portman Business Consultancy, under the supervision of Joseph Lampel, City University Business School. Copyright © 2002 Thomaz Wood Jr., Flávio Vasconcelos, and Miguel P. Caldas, FGV-EAESP.

Not unexpectedly, the proposed merger generated intense public and political debate, fanned by the media and press editorials. Many questioned the wisdom of creating a firm with so much market power. The companies, however, brought in a specialist media communications firm to develop strategies to promote the plan and attempt to shift the debated issue away from domestic local market dominance, to one of survivability in a global marketplace. The timing was important as the media was aware of an idea, promoted by the once socialist Brazilian President Fernando Henrique Cardoso, for "more Brazilian multinationals." This was in response to the wave of U.S. and European corporate titans, including BellSouth Corp. and Carrefour, having descended on the country in recent years, totalling $56B in foreign direct investment between 1998–2000 alone, snapping up scores of local companies and relegating others to the status of also-rans.

The government, however, still mindful of the strong opposition to the merger, moved with care. CADE, the Brazilian anti-trust regulator, scrutinized the proposed merger closely over a period that lasted for almost ten months. During this time, Brahma and Antarctica had to put their merger plans on hold. Any action anticipating the merger approval, such as plant rationalization, was forbidden. Telles and De Marchi had to continue to manage their two companies separately, while defending their case to CADE officials together. Conditional to the eventual CADE approval was the disposal of one of the firms' key brands, although this was subsequently overridden and switched to a lesser brand upon legal appeal.

When the approval finally came through, Telles and De Marchi could celebrate, but only briefly. As they toasted their victory, they also knew that many difficult decisions about the future of AmBev lay ahead of them.

THE BACKGROUND

THE GLOBAL CONTEXT

The end of the 1990s was characterized by a steep rise in merger and acquisition activity. The union of major companies such as Exxon and Mobil, Citicorp and Travelers, Boeing and McDonnell Douglas, and Daimler-Benz and Chrysler had set the mood for a new corporate game. Throughout the 1990s, and particularly toward the latter half, mergers and acquisitions became the strategy of choice for firms bent on rapid growth.

The global beer industry did not escape this trend. Historically, most brewers tended to focus, almost exclusively, on their own domestic markets. During the 1990s, however, large domestic beer companies were increasingly expanding their international operations, and in the process, were becoming large multinational corporations. The Dutch brewery Heineken (the second largest brewery in the world) bought the Spanish brewery Cruzcampo, while firms such as the Belgian Interbrew group and the South African Breweries were closely examining strategic alliances, mergers and acquisitions as means of reducing operating costs and fostering rapid growth. See Table 1.

THE BRAZILIAN CONTEXT

The creation of AmBev took place during a unique juncture in the political and economic life of Brazil. After four decades of import restrictions, the Brazilian economy went through a process of rapid liberalization in the beginning of the 1990s. Import barriers were largely lifted, and the world's largest privatization process initiated. As a result, Brazilian companies were suddenly confronted

TABLE 1
WORLD'S LARGEST
BREWERIES IN 1998

COMPANY	COUNTRY	REVENUES (US$ BILLION)
Anheuser-Busch	USA	11,2
Heineken	The Netherlands	7,3
AmBev (Antarctica + Brahma)	Brazil	6,6
South African Breweries	South Africa	6,4
Carlsberg	Denmark	4,6
Kirin	Japan	4,5
Interbrew	Belgium	4,2
Miller	USA	4,1
Foster's Brewing Group	Australia	3,0
Modelo	Mexico	2,0

Source: Exame (July 14, 1999)

with international competitors that had superior technology, greater economies of scale, access to inexpensive capital, and more advanced management methods. Not surprisingly, many Brazilian companies had been unable to cope and were either closed down or sold to multinational corporations.

Some Brazilian companies, however, fought back, investing heavily to improve their technological and managerial resources. These included Pão de Açúcar, a leading Brazilian retailer (US$ 4,2 Billion in revenues in 1998), Bradesco Bank (US$ 15,5 Billion in revenues and US$ 57,7 Billion in assets in 1998), and the industrial conglomerate Votorantin (US$ 3,6 Billion in revenues in 1998). However, they still remained significantly smaller than their main multinational competitors.

Increasing economies of scale through merger and acquisitions was perceived as the obvious solution, but many Brazilian companies took this route with mixed results. The merger between Brahma and Antarctica, however, went beyond what had been attempted previously. It was a milestone and was heralded as an example for other domestic companies, endorsed by the government. Brazilian President Fernando Henrique Cardoso declared, following a meeting with Telles, "It is either internationalize or be internationalized." The message was clear: Go forth and conquer.

AN HISTORIC RIVALRY

For decades, Brazilians wishing to drink a beer had to answer the question: "Antarctica or Brahma?" In more recent times, the choices had increased but both brands had overwhelmingly remained the favourites. Brahma and Antarctica had been engaged in an ad war since the beginning of the century. That fight got louder in the 50s and nastier in recent years. It was common for celebrities to be used to sing the virtues of both sides.

When Brahma launched its Malzbier in 1914 the beverage was presented as "especially recommended to nursing moms." Antarctica started to sell its Guaraná soft drink in 1921, something which Brahma copied only six years later.

During the 1990s the dispute between Washington Olivetto's *W/Brasil* ad agency, which had the Antarctica account, and *Justus* serving Brahma, boiled over. The war was never so heated as during the 1994 soccer World Cup Finals in the United States when stadiums were invaded by fans of both beers. Brahma was presented as "Number 1" while Antarctica was "The National Preference." The rivalry had also spread to the famed Brazilian "Carnaval," with each firm heavily sponsoring competing events—Brahma in Rio de Janeiro, and Antarctica in Salvador.

THE KEY PLAYERS

BRAHMA—THE DOMINANT PARTNER

Founded in 1888 in Rio de Janeiro by the Swiss Joseph Villiger, Cervejaria Brahma had enjoyed strong growth in the Brazilian market for almost a century. A major turning point in the history of the company took place in 1989, when this traditional brewery was acquired by a group of investors led by Jorge Paulo Lehmann. Even though Lehmann did not take direct charge of Brahma's operations, he was instrumental in transforming the organization. Under his guidance, the company adopted a new set of values based on competitive meritocracy, and on an almost obsessive focus on performance.

In the years that followed the acquisition, Brahma became an aggressive and entrepreneurial company, marked internally by its informal culture. Productivity levels rose from 1,200 to 8,700 hectoliters per employee, beating all records in the industry.

The external expansion of the business began in 1994, when Brahma acquired a brewery in Venezuela and built a plant in Argentina. But despite the success of these first steps, Brahma's executives knew that competing in a global scale would require even more daring moves.

An example of Brahma's aggressive style was the proposal it made to buy the American brewery Anheuser-Busch, the largest beer company in the world (US$ 11,2 Billion in revenues in 1998). The offer fell below the price that Anheuser-Busch was willing to accept, but it signaled Brahma's arrival on the international stage as a force to be reckoned with.

In 1999, the international expansion strategy was halted. With the sharp devaluation of the Brazilian currency, and high interest rates in the domestic capital market, the acquisition of foreign companies was no longer feasible. Ultimately, Brahma turned to its domestic competitors to find a partner that would make it strong enough to confront the challenge of international competition.

ANTARCTICA—THE IDEAL PARTNER

Founded three years before Brahma, in 1885 by a group of friends from São Paulo, Companhia Antarctica Paulista had remained a highly conservative company, a cultural antithesis of what Brahma had come to represent in the 1990s.

In fact, from the early 1990s the firm had been losing market share. Its response to the opening of the Brazilian economy was to seek an alliance with Anheuser-Busch. The plan foresaw increasing the equity position by the American partner in the Brazilian business, ultimately reaching 30% of voting capital in 2002. However, the severe economic turbulence that rocked Brazil during the beginning of 1999, and in particular the drastic currency devaluation, forced the American partner to terminate the relationship. It was the failure of this alliance with Anheuser-Busch which opened the way for the alliance with Brahma. One of the key motivations for the alliance with Anheuser-Busch had been the acquisition of knowledge from this global firm. During the years that the two companies had worked together, Antarctica had adopted a number of its partner's management practices, although without an appreciable impact on performance.

The basic economics of the industry pointed to a merger that should deliver increasing economies of scale and stronger cash flow for financing business expansion, and the merger with Brahma promised to deliver these benefits. It also held out the prospect of creating a company that would not only protect its domestic base against foreign incursion, but would also make possible a regional expansion.

KAISER—THE YOUNG UPSTART

Launched in 1982 as a collaborative venture by several Coca-Cola franchisees, Kaiser Beer had grown to become AmBev's main competitor in the Brazilian market. The founders had created Cervejarias Kaiser to capitalize on a perceived opportunity to leverage their existing soft-drinks distribution network to sell, develop and market a new brand of beer.

In 1990, Kaiser teamed up with Heineken, bringing into Brazil the technology that had earned the Dutch company second place in the global list of brewers. This enabled Kaiser to serve a beer with the same *premium* flavor as its prominent and popular European relatives.

Kaiser's product rapidly became one of the most famous market phenomena in the history of Brazil's low-alcoholic beverage industry. So successful was the growth that Coca-Cola itself decided to directly join the Brazilian brewer as a shareholder. Not surprisingly, when Telles and De Marchi announced the project to create AmBev, Kaiser reacted promptly, starting a broad and aggressive advertising campaign opposing the merger. Unsurprisingly, Coca-Cola was reported to be one of the fiercest opponents of the AmBev merger.

AMBEV—THE FUTURE

For Telles and De Marchi, the merger between their two companies was seen as essential and publicly declared that "Without the merger, we will not have enough scale to face the international market." Despite this and following the successful outcome of the CADE decision, Telles and De Marchi saw three major challenges to AmBev's future success.

Integrating the Two Companies

Brahma was twice the size of Antarctica and accordingly Brahma shareholders gained control of 46% of the new company, while the not-for-profit foundation that controlled Antarctica gained a 23% share. The merger's architects clearly intended to create the more dynamic Brahma management style and culture in the new company, but this was not going to be a simple task. Following the merger, industrial operations were to be integrated, realizing synergies and economies of scale that could generate savings estimated at $250M per annum. However, sales, marketing, and distribution activities were to be kept separate, generating a degree of internal competition among the several *rival* brands owned by the new company. De Marchi proclaimed that "these are independent businesses that will fight each other for market share." This internal competition-driven model had been previously adopted at Brahma and was regarded as a highly successful mechanism for preventing complacency and encouraging continuous improvement, but it directly clashed with the traditional Antarctica style. This cultural shift demanded significant investments of management's time and energy. It clearly was not going to be easy.

AmBev's Consolidating in the Brazilian Market

AmBev needed to fully develop and exploit Brazil's huge market potential, and in so doing, consolidate its position as national market leader. For this to take place, AmBev needed to overcome two main difficulties. First, it had to raise consumption levels. Although the Brazilian market consists of 170 million consumers and 1 million points of sale, *per capita* beer consumption has traditionally remained relatively low at about 50 liters, and this consumption was heavily concentrated into few regions (see Table 2). A need existed to understand the rationale for this

TABLE 2 COST STRUCTURE OF THE BEER INDUSTRY IN BRAZIL AND MEXICO (%)

	BRAZIL	MEXICO
Producers + Distributors	36	52
Taxes	30	26
Retailers	34	22

Source: Cervejaria Brahma

market behavior and identify and implement appropriate strategies. Second, AmBev needed to resolve an unfavorable cost structure in its local value chain. Compared to other Latin American countries, Brazilian beer producers received a relatively low share of the consumer "point of sale" price, in part because of high taxes but also because of retailers' margins. This was obviously a major barrier to profit increases.

AmBev's Latin American Push

Publicly, AmBev's stated strategic intent was to internationalize: to create a Brazilian multinational as important in Latin America as Brahma and Antarctica were within Brazil. The Latin American beverage market is highly attractive. Beer consumption in Central and South American markets is growing at about 4% annually, and was expected to exceed that of the USA by 2002 (see Table 3). Outside of Brazil, the largest players included Modelo and Femsa in Mexico, and Bavaria in Colombia. However, international firms were becoming more active with Modelo being 37% owned by Anheuser-Busch, and South Africa's Interbrew holding 22% of Femsa. It was also reported that European breweries were interested in entering the Latin American market.

An article in the UK's *Financial Times* summed it up as follows: "With all but 3.4% of AmBev's 76.4m hectolitre sales for 1999 originating in Brazil, in the long run, the combined company will have to expand internationally to create additional value and diversify its risk, analysts say." For a concerted internationalization effort, AmBev would need to tackle the issues of scale, geographic coverage, profitability and growth potential, in an industry that was in the midst of rapid globalization.

DECISIONS, THIRSTY DECISIONS

The decisions facing Telles and De Marchi were clearly going to be tough ones. Their first and perhaps most immediate is deciding AmBev's strategic focus in the period following the merger. Should the new company postpone international expansion strategies and focus on

TABLE 3 BEER CONSUMPTION ACROSS THE WORLD IN 1999

ORDER	COUNTRY	BEER CONSUMPTION (*10,000 KL)
1	USA	2300.4
2	China	2073.7
3	Germany	1046.3
4	**Brazil**	788.0
5	Japan	715.1
6	U.K.	589.2
7	Mexico	494.2
8	Russia	381.5
9	Spain	271.2
10	South Africa	260.6
11	France	228.3
12	Poland	226.0
13	Canada	207.6
14	Czech Rep.	180.3
15	Australia	176.2
16	Venezuela	170.0
17	Colombia	160.0
18	Italy	155.6
19	R. Korea	148.0
20	Netherlands	133.8
21	Argentina	130.5
22	Philippines	124.0
23	Rumania	112.8
24	Thailand	105.0
25	Belgium	100.0

Source: Kirin Brewery Company, Limited

reducing costs, creating synergies, and reconciling their different organizational cultures? Or should AmBev use the Brazilian market as a springboard, pursuing an expansion strategy by acquiring other regional players in order to establish itself as a major Latin American multinational?

In mid-August 2000 Marcel Herrmann Telles, co-chairman and director of AmBev (NYSE-Listed ABV), rang the Wall Street Stock Exchange closing bell in New York, celebrating the successful merger. The future, however, was an open book.

Wipro Corporation: Balancing the Future

Azim H. Premji returned from Stanford University in 1967, abandoning his engineering studies, to take charge of the family business that was left rudderless due to the sudden demise of his father. Over the next 27 years, Premji transformed the Rs 7 crore[1] cooking and baking fats company—Western India Vegetable Products Limited—into the Rs 724 crore diversified Wipro Corporation that, in 1994, was one of the top 100 publicly held companies in India. Apart from being the market leader (#1) in the traditional cooking fats business, the company held the #2 position in India both in information technology and in medical systems businesses and held the #3 slot in the precision engineered hydraulic products business (see Exhibit 1). Over the preceding ten years, the company's sales and profit after tax had grown at an annual compounded rate of 26% and 25% respectively and its net worth had recorded compounded annual growth rate of 22%. Over the same period, capital appreciation and dividends had yielded an average 62% compounded annual return to the company's shareholders who also had the satisfaction of seeing their company being widely cited as a model of the "ethical corporation."

In 1994, however, the company was in the midst of what Premji described as a "paradigm shift" in its environment. Radical changes in the Government's economic policies and the resulting large scale entry of multinational companies (MNCs) in India had led to competition that was not only much more fierce but also qualitatively different from the past. As a result Wipro was confronting a situation where it had to make some hard choices or else risk hitting the dividers on the road.

Perhaps the most fundamental choice was about the very basic identity of the company. Even though Premji disliked the label of a conglomerate, Wipro was essentially a combination of a number of very different businesses. Unrelated diversification had proved to be an effective means to growth in a regulated environment. However, the regulatory and other barriers that had prevented large global companies from operating directly in India, and had partly facilitated Wipro's successes, were being rapidly dismantled. As a consequence, Wipro, to stay competitive, needed to support each of its businesses with significant financial and managerial investments against competitors with the world's best technologies and brands as well as deep pockets and commitments. Should Wipro sustain all the businesses through such investments? Or should it focus on a relatively few businesses and build a more homogeneous portfolio? Should it, through such a process, aim to become a very different company than it was in 1994?

This case was written by Professors J. Ramachandran of the Indian Institute of Management, Bangalore, and S. Ghoshal of the London Business School. It is intended to be used as a basis for class discussion rather than to illustrate either effective or ineffective handling of a business situation.

Copyright © Indian Institute of Management, Bangalore, and the London Business School.

EXHIBIT 1
ESTIMATED MARKET
SIZE AND SHARES

	ESTIMATED MARKET SIZE (Rs MILLION) 1993	WIPRO SALES (Rs MILLION) 1993
INFORMATION TECHNOLOGY		
Wipro Infotech	33,228	2,238
Wipro Systems	8,848	257
Total	42,076	2,495
WIPRO CONSUMER PRODUCTS		
Vanaspati	33,300	1,091
Toilet Soaps	19,433	875
Toiletries	2,132	135
Leather Products	7,500	72
Total	62,365	2,193
HEALTH CARE		
Wipro-GE	3,269	589
Wipro BioMed	3,158	121
Total	6,427	710
WIPRO FLUID POWER	1,768	262
WIPRO LIGHTING	9,585	37
Grand Total	122,213	5,697

Wipro Financial Services is excluded from above.
Source: Company documents.

A similar review was necessary of the company's basic management approach. What should be the roles and responsibilities of the teams managing each of the businesses? How should the corporate management, including Premji himself, add value? Historically, the corporate–division relationship in Wipro followed neither a holding company philosophy, nor that of a typical integrated industrial company. Should the somewhat ambiguous but highly flexible relationship that had been so effective in the past be continued in the future? Or did it need adaptation—perhaps some more clarity and formalisation—given the increasing size and complexity of the company and of the businesses themselves?

WIPRO IN 1994

In 1994, Wipro Corporation's activities spanned vanaspati, toilet soaps, toiletries, hydraulic cylinders, computer hardware and software, lighting financial services, medical systems, diagnostic systems and leather exports. While the various activities were structured into 5 distinct legal entities, Wipro Corporation, for the purposes of management

control, was split into 8 separate "mini companies" each with its own separate "equity" (see Exhibit 2). These were Wipro Consumer Products, Wipro Lighting, Wipro Fluid Power, Wipro Financial Services, the two businesses in the field of information technology—Wipro Infotech and Wipro Systems—and finally the two health care related businesses Wipro GE and Wipro Biomed. While Wipro had international tie-ups in many of its activities, only Wipro GE, its medical systems business, was a financial joint venture between Wipro and the US giant General Electric (GE).

WIPRO CONSUMER PRODUCTS

The Rs 200 crore Wipro Consumer Products (WCP) was, for long, the largest "company" in Wipro Corporation's portfolio. However, following three flat years in turnover, it yielded this position to Wipro Infotech in 1993 (see Exhibit 3). It manufactured and marketed the traditional vanaspati products, fatty acid and glycerine, toilet soaps, toiletries and leather products for the export market.

In 1994, WCP produced vanaspati at three plants spread over the western and southern parts of India, the markets it

EXHIBIT 2 WIPRO CORPORATION

CHAIRMAN	Azim Hazam Premji
	Rs 724 1 crores

Group Companies

Wipro Consumer Products 1947	Wipro Fluid Power 1975	Wipro Infotech 1981	Wipro Systems 1983	Wipro Biomed 1989	Wipro GE 1990	Wipro Lighting 1991	Wipro Financial Services 1992
			Ashok Soota Vice Chairman				
P.S. Pai President	M.S. Rao President	Ashok Soota President	V Chanrasekaran Chief Executive	Vinod Wahi Chief Executive	Vivek Paul President	Varun Nijhawan President	S.R. Gopalan Chief Executive

Products

Edible Oils Soaps & Toiletries	Hydraulic Systems	Computers, Communication & IT Solutions	Software Development & Services	Medical Analytical Instruments	GE Medical Systems	Lamps & Luminaires	Corporate Financial Services
Rs 199.8 cr	Rs 19.7 cr	Rs 320 cr	Rs 43.7 cr	Rs 12.5 cr	Rs 60 cr	Rs 22 cr	Rs 46 cr

EXHIBIT 3   WIPRO CORPORATION PORTFOLIO: Turnover and Profits

	1993–94			1992–93			1991–92			1990–91		
	Sales	PBT	PAT	Sales	PBT	PAT	Sales	PBT	PAT	Sales	PBT	PAT
WCP	2193.84	71.95	39.61	2042.30	59.50	32.20	2148.00	103.00	75.00
WIL	2237.60	97.40	68.90	1818.80	75.00	45.50	1550.00	53.30	28.60
WSL	257.50	9.84	9.84	169.40	35.30	31.90	60.00	19.20	18.90
HEALTH CARE								
Wipro GE	589.46	23.73	17.73	356.40	13.90	8.90	228.40	2.90	0.90
Wipro BioMed	121.86	8.92	4.87	51.30	4.40	1.80	32.10	(3.60)	(3.60)
Wipro Engineering	261.50	23.90	13.90	168.40	15.80	7.60	98.00	9.60	3.10
Wipro Financial Services	20.96	10.10	10.10	—	—	—	—	—	—
Wipro Lighting	36.98	(16.15)	(16.15)	—	—	—	—	—	—
Total	5715.00	205.83	157.62	4624.90	187.70	125.30	4178.80	157.70	105.00

operated in. The industry was segmented along geographical lines due to high transportation costs. All the players operated in specific geographic pockets (see Exhibit 4). The company's "Camel" and "Black Bird" brands, which served the needs of commercial users like biscuit manufacturers and bakeries, were the market leaders in the institutional segment; and its flagship brand "Sunflower" had recorded gains in market share, despite increased competition, in the consumer segment.

The market for vanaspati, which constituted 15% of the edible cooking medium market in India, was fiercely competitive and margins were wafer thin. P. S. Pai, President, WCP, said:

> On the one hand we confront fierce competition from small unorganised players among whom tax evasion is rampant and on the other we are faced with a government policy which provides 9% advantage to a new entrant in a 4% margin business!

The favourable government policy had led to large scale entry and in 1994 the industry was riddled with excess capacity. Further, prices of the major raw material—edible oil—fluctuated on a daily basis. As a consequence the vanaspati business had become what Pai described as a "commodity trade" business:

> Today even the consumer segment has become price dependent. Vanaspati is a low margin–low value addition business. Material cost control is the key. Both input prices and output prices fluctuate on a daily basis. Every Monday morning I sit along with my Vice Presidents in charge of buying and sales—all of us have been with Wipro for over fifteen years now—and

take positions for the week. Our practice for over two decades, when Premji first introduced it, has been to take weekly positions and not daily positions. That it works is reflected in our bottom line.

Vanaspati operations contributed to over half of the WCP turnover in 1993–94. However, its share in the WCP turnover has been coming down over the years due to growth in the other WCP activities, especially its toilet soap business. In 1993–94 the toilet soap business contributed Rs 64.4 crore to WCP's turnover.

While WCP had earlier entered the toilet soap market through Bubbles, a special soap for children, and had also established a distinct niche through Wipro Shikakai, a special hair care soap containing soap nut extract, long cherished for hair care and cleansing properties in India, its real success in that business had followed the 1985 launch of Santoor, a soap based on a turmeric–sandalwood combination, a traditional Indian recipe for beauty and skin care. Pai explained:

> Swastik, which had been the leader in hair care soaps, was dying due to internal troubles. We seized the opportunity and entered that segment with Wipro Shikakai. Similarly when Mysore Sales International—whose Mysore Sandal brand was the market leader in the sandalwood segment—was experiencing management trouble, we sensed an opportunity and launched Santoor.

In 1994, despite the dominance of the Indian toilet soap market by Hindustan Lever, the Indian subsidiary of the Anglo-Dutch giant, Unilever, and P&G–Godrej, the local joint venture of the US giant Procter and Gamble, Wipro's "ethnic" brands held their own. Their success was both due

EXHIBIT 4 VANASPATI INDUSTRY PRODUCTION (1992–93) (in tons)

WEST ZONE

Wipro	36,293	
Other leading producers		
MP Oil Federation	21,137	
Madhusudhan Industries	20,071	
Aswin Vans.	16,025	
IVP Limited	10,631	
Dipak Veg.	10,252	
Godrej Foods	9,362	
West Zone Total		199,692

SOUTH ZONE

Wipro	4,427	
Other leading producers		
Lipton	7,409	
A.P Agrawal Industries	14,115	
South Zone Total		42,170

EAST ZONE

Wipro	—	
Other leading producers		
Kusum Products	18,199	
HLL (associate of Lipton)	9,499	
Ipinit Vans.	7,418	
East Zone Total		47,261

NORTH ZONE

Wipro	—	
Other leading producers		
Lipton	24,623	
United Vanaspati	15,683	
North Zone Total		104,349
All India		393,472

Source: Vanaspati Manufacturers' Association of India.

to their sharp focus on distinct niches and the absence of competition from the toilet majors in these niches. Pai said "our strategy in the toilet soaps business is to operate below the radar zones of the giants. They know about it and respect us for it."

While scanning for "below the radar zone" opportunities, the WCP team, in 1990, identified an opportunity in the baby care products market, long dominated by the local subsidiary of the US multinational Johnson and Johnson (J&J). The Wipro team not only found the J&J products to be high priced, but also found the retail channels to be extremely dissatisfied with the service they received from J&J. They sought to leverage both—Wipro's reputation for quality and the strong links they had built up with the retail channel—and launched the Wipro Baby Soft range of products, with price as the principal benefit to the con-

sumer. With substantial advertising support in the launch year, the Baby Soft range quickly garnered an 18% share of the market.

The Baby Soft range, however, could not gain any further share as J&J reacted strongly. J&J stepped up its ad spends significantly and launched a number of strong promotion schemes for the channel. WCP went on the defensive as the Baby Soft range was not contributing to the bottom line. It streamlined and reoriented its advertising budget and in 1994, the company planned to use direct marketing in a major way for generating volumes and to use mass media to primarily create reassurance about the product.

The launch of Baby Soft also signaled WCP's entry into the toiletries market with talcum powder, a segment dominated by another Unilever subsidiary in India, Ponds. In 1993–94 Wipro Baby Soft talcum powder and Santoor beauty talc together had 2.6% share of the talc market and contributed Rs 3.75 crore to WCP's turnover.

"High fashion" shoe uppers was another product in WCP's portfolio. This export market oriented business generated a turnover of over Rs 7 crore, bulk of which stemmed from sales to a single customer viz., Clarks of UK. The returns from this business had improved following devaluation and partial convertibility of the Indian rupee.

In 1994, Pai and his team were in the middle of preparing a ten-year perspective plan for WCP. Not only were they targeting to regain their lost leadership position in the Wipro Corporation's portfolio, they were seeking to increase their market share in all the product categories, significantly. Pai said:

> We are aiming for 10% of both the Edible Fats[2] market and the Indian toilet soap market by the end of 10 years. It is a 10 year investment now. The days of three year pay back period are over. We need to invest in building brands. The competition, especially from the MNCs, is severe, and returns not easy to come by despite our strong distribution strength.

WIPRO FLUID POWER

Wipro Fluid Power (WFP), in 1994, was a Rs 20 crore operation. The company was the market leader in hydraulic cylinders and its customers included all the major earth moving and construction equipment manufacturers in India viz., TELCO, Escorts JCB and Bharat Earth Movers Limited. WFP's product range included hydraulic truck tipping systems, pumps, valves, and custom built hydraulic systems. It manufactured hydraulic tipping systems with technical know-how from Nencki, Ag Switzerland. It also had a strategic alliance with Eaton Corporation, USA for marketing their steering systems, hydrostatic transmissions and other hydraulic elements in the Indian market.

Wipro entered the hydraulics market in 1973. M. S. Rao, President, WFP, who has been with WFP right from inception said, "Hydraulics seemed a good niche market to get into, requiring just the kind of investments we could afford with out size of business at that time." Premji added: "It was a high growth market and the competition was weak. We were confident that by focusing on the right segments we could generate significant returns."

At the time of its entry, Wipro did not have any in house capability for the manufacture of hydraulic cylinders. Nevertheless, it decided not to take on any foreign collaborator for the manufacture of cylinders as it wanted to avoid getting locked into rigid foreign specifications. A small research and development team was set up to design and develop the cylinders. Market acceptance of the product developed in-house was difficult to come by. The resistance was high, not the least of which was due to Wipro's then image of a vanaspati company. However, due to the good quality, good design and superior performance of its products, WFP improved its market position and in 1994 was the fastest growing and best known manufacturer of hydraulic cylinders. Between 1990 and 1994, the company's turnover, despite recessionary trends in some of the end user market segments like machine tools and hydraulic cranes, had nearly trebled with an even better performance on the profitability front. Premji attributes the sustained improvement in WFP's market position to Wipro's strong belief in R&D and customer service.

> We have invested considerably in R&D facilities and have established expertise in offering design solutions to meet customers' specific requirements and are able to absorb and adopt proven and recognised designs. As a consequence our relations with our major customers are very strong. Some time back when we had a strike in our manufacturing facility, our customers were willing to wait for our product.

In 1994, WFP was being positioned to act as one of the spearheads to Wipro's plans to become a global operation. Premji said, "We are targeting to be global players in the hydraulic cylinders business as we are highly cost and design competitive." WFP had begun its export thrust in 1991 with the export of 500 cylinders to Sweden. Since then it has been exporting this product to other countries in Europe and Japan. The company was investing Rs 15 crore over the next three years to widen its product range and improve its presence in the international markets.

WIPRO INFOTECH

In 1994, the Rs 320 crore Wipro Infotech (WIL) was the second largest information technology company in India. Its product offerings included PCs, minis, superminis, engineering workstations, mini super computers, on-line transaction processing mainframes, laser and dot matrix printers, etc., and software products and services addressed to specific customer needs. In 1994, WIL received for the fourth consecutive year the Government of India Department of Electronics Award for Excellence in Electronics. The company had been a recipient of a number of other awards including the National R & D Award for Electronics. The Wipro PC was the only PC in India to have been awarded the Department of Electronics Certificate of Quality. Independent computer and business journals routinely rated WIL as best on various parameters including professional management and customer trust.

Wipro's entry into the computing industry was spurred by the exit of IBM from India in 1977. At that time Premji was seeking to further diversify Wipro's product portfolio and the Indian computer industry, in the absence of a global major like IBM, seemed to offer a good opportunity for Wipro to pursue. Premji expected the demand for computers for commercial applications to grow rapidly and zeroed in on the minicomputer as the appropriate product as it provided the benefits of a mainframe computer (viz., a multi user environment) without being as expensive.

While identification of minicomputers as the appropriate product was relatively easy, it was not easy to access the technology. This was the era of proprietary technology and minicomputer pioneer—Digital Equipment Corporation (DEC)—controlled the technology. WIL ruled out the option of approaching DEC for technology as it did not expect the American company to be interested in a partner with no lineage in computing (or electronics) and located in "far away" India. Further, the company assessed that even if DEC were interested, it would be merely interested in providing Wipro with "kits" for assembly and would not part with the technology. It, therefore, decided to develop its own minicomputer using Intel's 8086 chip. The choice was largely dictated by the non-proprietary nature of the Intel chip, the availability of other support chips (for Input–Output operations and Memory) for the 8086 and by Intel's plans to develop advanced and faster microprocessors (the subsequent 80286/386/486, etc.). To save time and cost, WIL opted to source the operating software and internal circuitry from a small firm in the US called Sentinel, and a yet to be fully developed database management software from Tominy, another small firm located near Sentinel's office in California.

It took WIL about a year to sort out all the design and software related issues and develop a marketable product. In 1981 WIL unveiled the WIPRO Series 86 at the annual computing fair of the Computer Society of India.

The WIPRO Series 86 was an instantaneous hit and WIL quickly emerged as the market leader (#1) in mini-computers, a position it held in 1994. The company kept pace with the technological changes in the global computing industry largely on the strength of its close relationship with Intel, supported by its own in house R&D. It had access to Intel's newest offerings six months before their commercial release by Intel. This enabled WIL to offer products in the Indian markets which incorporated the latest Intel technology almost at the same time when products incorporating this technology were available in the global markets.

WIL also exploited the other changes in the global industry to enhance its product range in the Indian market. The opening up of the PC market, following IBM's radical decision to throw open the technology for PCs to other manufacturers, provided WIL with an opportunity to enter the PC segment of the computing industry. WIL's entry, however, was delayed (HCL, the market leader, launched its PC much ahead of WIL) as it did not have the license to manufacture PCs. It had to wait for a change in the government's policy in this regard.

The company, with a view to absorb the new technology, opted to manufacture PCs by importing components instead of opting for the then popular "kit" approach, which essentially involved importing PCs in completely knocked down form and assembling them and marketing them. Within a year of the launch of the WIPRO Genius range of PCs, WIL became the second largest (after HCL) PC vendor in India.

In 1988, WIL entered into an alliance with Sun Microsystems, USA for the manufacture and marketing of Sun workstations and quickly became the leader in the workstation market in India. Ashok Soota, President WIL said:

It was the first relationship we actively sought. The workstation market was growing rapidly and we decided to enter it. Sun was the obvious choice as it was the leader.[3] Sun, however, was reluctant to allow us to manufacture, as they did not want to invest their time. I told them we did not want any Sun personnel in India, we just needed the documentation and training for 3–4 of our people. They finally agreed. Within three weeks of receipt of the first shipment from Sun we were rolling out Sun products from our manufacturing facility. They visited us one year later for auditing our facilities. After that visit, they agreed to our exporting to the Russian market from here.

Following its success in the workstation market, WIL wanted to grow faster than the rest of the industry. Soota explained, "The only way to do so was to expand the existing segments we were operating in and to enter new segments and become a broad line player."

To become a broad line player WIL embarked on a strategy of entering into technological and/or marketing tie-ups with international companies. It entered into a technology tie-up with Seiko-Epson of Japan, for the manufacture of dot matrix printers and emerged as one of the leading players in the market for printers (#2 in 1994). In addition it also marketed Epson's laser printers. It entered the mainframe market segment through an alliance with the Tandem Computers USA for marketing their on-line transaction processing systems for mission critical applications, and with Convex Computers for marketing their superminis in India. And in 1993, the company entered into a strategic alliance with Apple to market the Macintosh range of computers in the Indian market.

WIL also entered the export market for both hardware and software. It exported its own PCs and the products it manufactured on the Sun platform and undertook software development projects for its partners, Tandem and Sun.

The first part of the 1990s saw a sea change in the computing industry in India. Virtually all the global majors entered the market, either directly or through joint ventures. Digital Equipment, which had a joint venture with its erstwhile distributor, Hinditron, and Fujitsu, which had a presence through the ICL subsidiary in India, ICIM, were joined by Hewlett Packard which acquired a 26% stake in HCL, the market leader in India, and IBM which re-entered by setting up a joint venture with Tata, the largest industrial house in India, as its partner (see Exhibit 5). WIL, however, stayed away from any overall alliance with a single company. Soota explained:

Last thing I want to do is surrender my independence. Because of our demonstrated capabilities, we are the first choice for most new entrants. We have the largest and the best dealer and after sales service network in the country. Our Wipro brand equity is high. It is synonymous with quality and integrity. We are also known and respected for the way in which we manage our relationships with foreign partners. In fact, IBM, as we discovered later, had been looking at us as potential joint venture partners. When they had come to meet us they did not tell us they were exploring a joint venture. Instead they told us they were exploring sourcing opportunities from India. We were cool and full of macho feeling then. We don't regret it. I believe we can be competitive without a joint venture. We are in a position to offer the best technology solution to the customers in India and not be tied down to a single technology solution because of our wide ranging alliances.

In 1993, WIL won the largest single order in Indian computing industry history from the Bombay Stock Exchange (BSE), the leading stock exchange in India. The order, for the second phase of the computerisation of the BSE, was for Rs 38 crore. Umesh Bajaj, Vice President, Transactions Solutions Division, said "We won the order as we offered the Tandem product. Tandem was ideally suited for the solution they were seeking in that phase." WIL had won the order for the first phase of the computerisation as

EXHIBIT 5 FOREIGN PARTNERS OF MAJOR PLAYERS IN THE COMPUTER INDUSTRY IN 1993

COMPANY	SALES (Rs MILLION)	PROFITS/(LOSS) (Rs MILLION)	FOREIGN PARTNER	SALES ($ BILLION)	PROFITS/(LOSS) ($ BILLION)
HCL–HP	2490	(30)	Hewlett-Packard	16.4	0.55
Wipro Infotech	2230	689	Sun Microsystems	3.62	0.17
ICIM	1220	135	Fujitsu	27.9	(0.26)
Digital Equipment	1110	(50)	DEC	14.03	(2.79)
Tata Unisys Ltd	910	10.36	Unisys	8.42	0.36
Modi Olivetti Limited	520	(30)	Olivetti	6.5	(0.53)
PSI	180	(958)	Bull	5.7	(0.89)

Source: *Business Today*, August 7–21, 1993, p. 68.
Notes:
1. Except Wipro Infotech, all other foreign players had a direct or an indirect equity stake in the Indian Operations.
2. In addition to the above, IBM entered in 1992 with an equal 50:50 joint venture with the Tata Group.

well. It had, for that phase, offered a Sun machine based solution. Soota said, "We won both the orders because we could offer the product most suited for the solution the customer was seeking."

However, WIL's strategy of offering the "best technology solution" was increasingly being rendered difficult by the technological and other developments in the global computing industry. The accelerated shift towards open systems, the emergence of networking environments and the rapid growth in client server computing were blurring the lines differentiating the various product market segments globally and in India. As a consequence companies who were once in distinct market niches had begun to compete with one another. Sun, for example, sought to grow beyond the workstation market and pursued the market for commercial applications aggressively. As a part of this effort it targeted the financial services industry, a niche occupied by Tandem. Both now competed in this market segment world-wide. This had a direct impact on WIL. Sun, following the loss of the BSE order, and with a view to increase its share of the Indian financial services market, appointed[4] ICIM as a value added reseller of its products in this market segment in India. ICIM was fairly strong in this segment in India. Additionally, Fujitsu, which had a stake in ICIM (through ICL UK), was the largest world-wide OEM vendor for Sun.

The rapid technological changes had also resulted in most computer firms entering into a complex web of alliances, including alliances with their competitors. In some cases this involved acquisition of an equity stake. For example, HP, which had a joint venture with HCL, WIL's major competitor in the Indian market, acquired an equity stake in Convex with whom WIL had a tie-up for its super-minis range of computers.

WIL, thus, was increasingly being forced to cope with the conflict arising out of its multiple alliances and interests. Not only was there an overlap between its representation of Tandem and Sun in the Indian market, it also faced an overlap between its own indigenously developed line of products which were addressing the commercial applications market in India, and the Sun line of products, as Sun increasingly sought a greater share of the commercial applications market. In response, WIL restructured its organisation. It carved itself into nine business divisions (see Exhibit 6), each with its own marketing and sales staff, distribution channels, and finance and human resources departments. Each division was set up around its distinct product lines. For example, the Network Systems division was created around the Sun Platform and Sun solutions, the Business Solutions Division was responsible for WIL's indigenously developed line and the Transactions Solutions Division was responsible for the Tandem and Convex lines. Each of these divisions were allowed, and, indeed, expected to compete with each other freely in the market place.

A. V. Sridhar, Chief Executive, Network Systems Division, said:

> We work as a company within the company. Earlier on, our field sales force was not clear whether to quote a client with out WIL's Synergy Line or with the Sun line. Now, we compete independently. This year we increased our sales of Sun line substantially by addressing the commercial applications market. In a number of cases we competed head-on with the Business Solutions Division. For example, for the second phase of the BSE order we competed with the Transactions Solution Division.

Soota added, "Our greatest challenge today is to manage the multiple interests. It is quite demanding. So far it has

EXHIBIT 6 WIPRO INFOTECH LIMITED

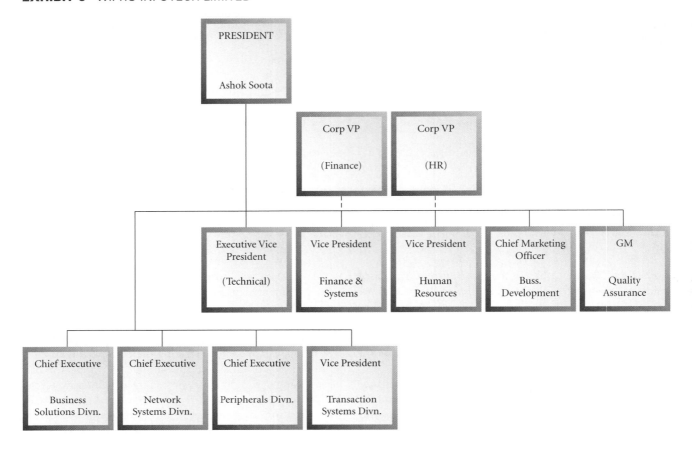

worked well. Though I must add that Sun was not too happy about losing the BSE order to Wipro–Tandem. But that is part of the game. Ultimately, it is a function of how we grow each of the lines."

In addition to growing the existing product lines, WIL was seeking to further leverage its strong R&D capabilities. In 1994, the company renamed its R&D as Global R&D and was in the process of expanding the number of its "India Development Centres." Conceived in 1993, these centres provided high level support in developing advanced products for a few select clients. It had already set up three such centres in association with Tandem, Sun and NCR respectively and was planning to set up two more such centres in association with Chorus of France and Ungermann Bass of Germany. Dr. Sridhar Mitta, Executive Vice President (Technical) said:

> In 1990, we had to make a choice: we either closed down our R&D, as most other competitors had done, or go global. I felt if we created an international environment here, we could be global providers of technology, services and products. We identified our core competencies as hardware design, operating systems and networking technology. We decided to stick to

them and work with a few select customers whom we chose with great care. We also made sure that we do not add more than two customers per year. Our strategy paid off. In 1994, we earned a revenue of Rs 21 crore.

Soota was also pursuing opportunities for growing WIL beyond the computer industry. The increasing integration between computers and telecommunication was opening up new horizons for WIL. Soota was targeting the emerging market—estimated to be in excess of Rs 400 crore by 1996–97—for value added telecom services. The company had already entered into tie-ups with Nokia, the Finland-based global leader in cellular phones for installation, service and maintenance of cellular networks[5] and with the UK-based British Telecom for other value added telecom services.

WIPRO SYSTEMS

In 1994, Wipro Systems was one of the star performers in the Wipro Corporation's portfolio having achieved a growth of over 70% in it revenues. The 44 crore business was the fifth largest software operation in India and was primarily in the business of exporting software including both provision of professional on site services to the overseas clients, and undertaking off shore (in India) software development projects for its international clientele (see Exhibit 7). In addition, it operated in the domestic market, where, apart from developing customised and standard software packages, it marketed imported software products.

Wipro Systems commenced operations in the early eighties to tap the growing demand for software. In the initial years, it focused on developed packaged products on the PC platform for both the domestic and international markets. While its Instaplan, a project management software package, was successful (selling over 40,000 copies in the US market) all others failed. Most of the other products, which were essentially look alikes of international products such as Lotus 1-2-3, performed poorly even in the domestic market where pirated versions of the international products were available at rock bottom prices.

Up to 1988–89, the business was in the red. In 1989–90, following a change in the CEO, it turned the corner by making a profit of Rs 0.3 crore on a turnover of Rs 2.9 crore. The turnaround was achieved largely by selling imported software products, principally products of Ashton Tate, in the domestic market.

In 1990, following yet another change in the CEO, Wipro Systems changed its focus once again. This time it focused on providing on site professional services—disparagingly referred to as "body shopping"—to overseas clients. Until this time, it had steadfastly refused to enter the market for these services, though most software houses in India earned a bulk of their revenues by providing these services. Wipro Systems' entry into this market had a substantial impact on its performance. Turnover increased by over Rs 8 crore in 1991–92 and profits nearly doubled. And for the first time since its operations began, its cumulative profit performance was positive.

Following the turnaround, the then CEO set about expanding the company's hardware facilities and invested Rs 8 crore in acquiring an IBM ES/9000 mainframe. The company also sought to re-enter in the domestic packaged software products market and started developing a new accounting software package called Compact.

EXHIBIT 7
SOFTWARE INDUSTRY
IN 1993 (Rs million)

	SIZE			
	DOMESTIC SOFTWARE		EXPORT SOFTWARE	
	Rs	%	Rs	%
Turnkey	2156	44	—	—
Professional Services	—	—	3510	52
Products and Packages	1764	36	675	10
Consultancy	245	5	1620	24
Training	392	8	—	—
Data Processing	196	4	405	6
Others	147	3	540	8
Total	4900	100	6750	100
(Industry Size in 1986–87)	900		500	
Cumulative Average Growth Rate	32.6%		54.31%	
Forecast for 1994–95	14,000		16,000	

	MAJOR PLAYERS IN 1993	
	EXPORT SOFTWARE Rs MILLION	DOMESTIC SOFTWARE Rs MILLION
1. Tata Consultancy Services	1754.80	410.00
2. Tata Unisys Ltd.	560.00	134.00
3. Digital Equipment (India) Ltd	317.80	—
4. CitiCorp	209.40	77.70
5. Wipro Systems Ltd	172.00	80.80
6. CMC Ltd	—	269.90
7. Onward Computer Technologies		94.40
Top 15 players share	63.5%	37.3%

Source: National Association of Software and Service Companies.

In 1992, the business experienced yet another change in the CEO. While the earlier CEOs had been recruited from outside, V. Chandrasekharan, the new CEO, was an "insider." Prior to assuming this position, he was the vice president in charge of customer services at Wipro Infotech. Chandrasekharan said:

> While I was an insider in the sense that I was from the Wipro group, I was still an outsider here, because over the years an iron curtain had been erected between Wipro Systems and Wipro Infotech. Ironically Wipro Systems at that time considered Wipro Infotech as its major competitor and not the market leader, Tata Consultancy Services.

Soota, who took over as Vice Chairman of Wipro Systems at the same time, added:

> To break down the walls, we did contemplate merging the two as Wipro Infotech also had strong presence in software development. We, however, decided against it as we felt that the merger could result in Wipro Systems losing IBM and HP as its customers. Wipro Infotech competed against these two in the hardware market.

Following the changes in the leadership, Wipro Systems reviewed its focus. Chandrasekharan said:

> We looked at the market opportunity differently. We were essentially a "services" company. Our strength was our highly talented pool of engineers. We wanted to leverage this strength fully so we targeted the market for off shore software development projects. We decided to focus on a few large accounts and penetrate these accounts deeply and increase our share of the software projects from these companies. We then set about looking for customers, who would be interested in building a long-term relationship and who would over time consider us an extension of themselves. At that time GE was looking for outsourcing software from India. We bid for GE's business. They evaluated us, along with others, before awarding any business to us. Here we leveraged Wipro Infotech's standing in the marketplace.

This strategy to focusing on a few large accounts paid off handsomely. In 1994 over half its software exports revenues came from a few clients like GE, USA, Bell Northern Research, Canada, Sequent Computer Systems, USA, etc. By 1994, it had established three software development centres (SDCs) in Bangalore—a fourth was on the anvil—dedicated to servicing the software needs of individual clients. The largest of them, the GS-SDC,[6] had a core group of 140 software engineers who exclusively handled software development, conversion and maintenance assignments for major GE businesses in the US and Far East. In addition it had a person positioned in GE, USA as an account manager, whose cost was borne by GE as it felt that having such a person improved the service significantly. Chandrasekharan said:

> We intend to replicate this strategy by taking on a few more major clients and becoming their extension to achieve software exports of a $100 million by year 2000. We will continue to operate in the on-site services market but would increasingly move towards off shore projects.[7] This is rendered even more essential with the new visa restrictions imposed by the US government, which makes obtaining visas for on-site service providers a cumbersome and difficult process.

In 1993–94, Wipro Systems achieved a turnover of Rs 43.7 crore. Software exports accounted for Rs 30 crore (previous year Rs 17.1 crore) or 69% of the total revenue. Of the Rs 13 crore revenue from the domestic market, Rs 4 crore came from consultancy service and the rest from sale of imported software products in the domestic market. The business had agency/distribution tie-ups with Borland, SPSS, WordPerfect, Novell, etc. Besides distributing Borland products within the country, it was authorised to duplicate, market and service Borland products in India, Sri Lanka and Nepal. Its own products, however, continued to fare poorly. It withdrew Compact, the accounting package targeted at large business, from the market as it realised that the large corporate customers preferred customised accounting software over packages software.

In 1994, Wipro Systems' profits were at an all time high of Rs 4.38 crore. This was in spite of the company having to bear the heavy interest and depreciation charges arising from its Rs 8 crore investment in the IBM ES/9000 mainframe, which had failed to pull in adequate revenue. Software projects on the IBM mainframe were hard to come by, as the market had shifted to client-server computing, following explosive growth in the computer networks. Chandrasekharan said, "We should have foreseen this. But the dominating personality of the earlier CEO caused a breakdown in our otherwise rigorous planning process." Premji, however, did not agree. "We had no reason to doubt his judgment. After all he had delivered results."

Wipro Systems had, in 1993, reorganised its staff around technology and marketing functions. The technology function, headed by a former vice president (R&D) at Wipro Infotech, was split into groups around hardware platforms like VAX, IBM, Tandem, etc., and around market segments like telecom, systems software, etc. The overseas marketing function was reorganised along territorial lines. Eight overseas offices were opened in the US (which accounted for over 90% of the export revenues). Additionally, an office was opened in the UK, and a consultant appointed for France.

It had also entered into arrangement with Epson Malaysia, an 80% Epson owned joint venture there, for achieving entry into the South East Asian markets. Chandrasekharan said:

> We have moved away from being a "personality" led organisation, to a more decentralised and systems driven organisation. A "personality" led organisation cannot tap the huge market

opportunity lying out there. While one can feel happy at growing at rates better than Indian industry, we need to realise that even the largest software company in India has only a micro cent share.

In 1994, Wipro Systems was aiming to be one of the top three software operations in India by the year 2000. Soota said:

> The key issue of course is holding on to talented people. The burgeoning growth of software exports industry has attracted the attention of every major industrial house and almost all of them are planning to enter this industry. Further, all the major computer companies (IBM, etc.), who were earlier customers, are setting up or expanding their operations in India. We are one of the prime targets for their recruitment managers.

WIPRO GE

In 1994, with a turnover of nearly Rs 60 crore, Wipro GE (WGE) was the second largest player in the medical systems market in India (see Exhibit 8). The Rs 500 crore Indian medical equipment market comprised both imaging systems and therapy instruments, with the former constituting 60% of the market. WGE's product offerings were mainly in this segment. Apart from marketing the products it manufactured—CT Scanners, ultrasound systems and Image Intensifiers for X-Ray systems—at its Bangalore facilities, the company marketed and supported the whole range of GE's value added medical systems in India. The company also marketed X-ray equipment manufactured by another local GE joint venture: Elpro International Limited.

In the late eighties, Wipro had identified, as part of its regular opportunity scanning exercise, medical electronics as an area to diversify. Despite its relatively low potential for growth in terms of turnover, the medical equipment market seemed to offer a good opportunity because of its very high profit potential. Wipro entered this market in 1988 by representing Beckman Instruments, USA. It, however, was keen to go beyond being a distributor of medical equipment of overseas companies and set up local manufacturing facilities.

At the time Wipro was seeking to expand its presence, GE was looking for tie-ups to shore up its presence in India. It had an agency tie up with IGE, which marketed its medical equipment, including the low end X-ray systems manufactured by its local joint venture, Elpro. After considering over 40 prospective partners, GE narrowed its choice down to two: Wipro and its arch rival in the computer industry, HCL. Vivek Paul, President, Wipro GE, who was part of the original GE negotiating team for the joint venture, said:

EXHIBIT 8 MEDICAL SYSTEMS

MARKET SHARE (1992–93) (%)

Siemens	32
Wipro GE	28
Phillips	10
Hitachi	4
Picker/Network	4
Toshiba	1
Shimadzu	1
Others	15
Refurbished	5

Source: Company estimates.

> We looked at Wipro because it was a trusted name. But it was not Wipro's manufacturing or service capability which swung the deal, though they were of great importance, especially Wipro's capability to manage and importantly grow businesses with high technology content. It was the compatibility between our values and Wipro's values that critically influenced the choice. Both demand very high standards of performance and integrity and importantly both believe in being competitive without compromising on integrity.

Prasanna, who was then corporate vice president at Wipro Corporation, took over as President of the joint venture with Vivek Paul[8] as the marketing director. The company started its operations by taking over the marketing activities of IGE. Local manufacture began in early 1992. Girish Gaur, formerly vice president operations at WGE, and currently corporate vice president, human resources at Wipro Corporation, said:

> We laid down for ourselves three milestones when we acquired the land for manufacturing facility in April 1991. One was that the plant would be operational in a year's time. We commenced assembly operations in February 1992. The second milestone was to reverse, at least partially, the flow of components by becoming a world class plant by March 1993. Within the first full year of operation we achieved 60% indigenisation on the ultrasound scanners. What's more we received orders for Rs 20 million worth of components from GE Japan. We also shipped locally manufactured ultrasound scanners to Samsung Medical Systems, South Korea. The third milestone was to develop a new product for the global market by March 1994. We have already developed the prototype of a compact portable ultrasound scanner, designed by our product development team, for the global markets, which would be marketed world wide as a GE product.

The local manufacturer enabled it to offer superior support to customers—a key advantage in the highly competitive medical equipment market. All the global players were operating in India either through their own subsidiaries, as was the case with Siemens, Germany (the world leader) and Phillips, Holland, or through Indian representatives as was the case with Toshiba (Indchem), Hitachi (Blue Star), Picker (HCL subsidiary, Network) and Shimadzu (Toshniwal). Vivek Paul said:

> We are successful, despite the tariff benefit afforded to imported systems,[9] because we are committed to offer the Indian medical fraternity something more than just the world's best technology. We offer them total solutions. This includes project feasibility analysis, site planning, marketing support, applications training and the luminary[10] programme. We are keen to build a strong domestic market base. This is crucial for our plan of becoming an important regional sourcing centre for GE to fructify. The larger we become in the domestic market, greater the chances of becoming a global sourcing centre.

WGE's pans to become a global sourcing centre received a fillip in 1993 when, following changes in the government policy, GE increased its equity stake in the company to a majority 51%. Wipro agreed to GE raising its stake on the understanding that it would use WGE as a global sourcing point for ultrasound equipment, subject to the local joint venture meeting GE's quality standards. The two partners also made an agreement that GE's medical software development will be done at Wipro GE. In 1993, WGE had exported medical and information services software worth US$1.1 million to GE.

WIPRO BIOMED

Wipro Biomed was formed in 1988 to lead Wipro Corporation's foray into health care. It began by marketing and servicing bio research and diagnostic systems from Beckman Instruments, USA. The company started expanding its activities in 1992–93 with a view to becoming a "single comprehensive source" for bio research and diagnostic instruments. According to Vinod Wahi, Chief Executive of Wipro Biomed:

> We were anyway meeting the same customer, in the research institutes, in the universities and in the R&D establishments of the pharmaceutical companies with our Beckman products. We thought why not leverage this and become a single comprehensive source to these customers.

In 1994, the company was representing, beyond Beckman, Becton Dickinson, Bio-Rad Labs, and Serono Diagnostics. It also had an Application Laboratory at Delhi which provided on-line tailor made solutions to specific customer application needs.

Following Wipro GE's successful entry into hospitals with their Radiology and Imaging systems, Wipro Biomed targeted the hospital segment. The company tied up with PPG Hellige of Germany, a pioneer in the field of cardiol-

ogy equipment having launched the world's first portable electrocardiograph in 1929, to market their cardiology and patient monitoring systems in India. "We realised that we would be able to leverage our corporate reputation for quality and service—apart from Wipro GE, Wipro Infotech had a presence as it was selling computers to hospitals—and build a strong presence in this segment," Wahi explained.

Wipro Biomed, however, had its own sales team and operated independently of Wipro GE. "We do participate in their bid for turnkey projects. We, however, do not differentiate between Wipro GE and Siemens or others. We are keen on increasing our market share. Wipro GE is not obliged to buy the products of the companies we represent," Wahi said.

In 1993, Wipro Biomed entered the analytical instruments market by representing Hewlett Packard (HP), USA, a world leader in test and analytical instruments, for a select range of their products. "HP was keen on our representing their entire range; we, however, could not as some of them clashed with Beckman. We now represent them in products which are complimentary," explained Wahi.

In 1994, the Rs 13.5 crore Wipro Biomed was making a foray into manufacturing. It extended its Beckman collaboration into a manufacturing one and was setting up a plant to manufacture diagnostic reagent kits with know-how from the American company.

WIPRO FINANCIAL SERVICES

In 1994, Wipro Financial Services (WFS) recorded the best performance in Wipro Corporation's portfolio. It had generated revenues totalling Rs 46.1 crore (up from Rs 2.1 crore in the previous year) and a post tax profit of Rs 3.62 crore (previous year Rs 1 crore). According to S. R. Gopalan, President WFS, the spectacular performance was due to the clear focus the company had since its inception in 1992.

> We focused on asset and trade financing for "high tech" products like computers, medical systems, telecom systems, energy systems and one or two other specialised areas. We did not aim to be everything to everyone. We leveraged our expertise and intimate knowledge of these areas: both of the technology, especially the obsolescence factor, and the needs and profiles of the customers for these hitech products. We put this expertise to use in tailoring products and services to meet the individual needs of the customers. For example, we have a scheme under which we extend financing facilities to customers for the purchase of Solar Photovoltaic Water Pumping System manufactured by Tata BP Solar India Limited. In terms of customers we targeted the midrange companies, who often do

not have a smooth access to the banking system like the large companies do.

The activities of WFS included leasing, equipment finance and advisory services. It extended medium to long term finance to companies for the purchase of capital equipment. The advisory services included advice on ways to raise funds in the debt market, assessment of companies for take-over and on working capital facilities. Contrary to the prevailing practice amongst most financial services companies in India (see Exhibit 9), the company did not operate in the consumer finance segment. Asked why WFS did not participate in this segment, Gopalan said:

> This activity is manpower intensive and people are the scarcest resource today. Prompt customer service is the key to success in financial services. Otherwise why would a customer opt for a relatively high cost source like us and not go to a bank which is cheaper. We are a lean outfit. All our employees are what we call "generalised specialists." The executive in charge of resource mobilisation, for example, is trained to, in the absence of the marketing executive, put together a financial package for a customer. Entering consumer finance would imply expanding our manpower base. We do not want to do that. We want to remain a lean outfit. For example, I do not have a personal secretary. I use the pool support. We also do not have a switch board operator. The phone when it rings shrills like a fire engine. Anyone of us would pick it up. I usually wait for it to ring a couple of times. If nobody picks it up, I do. This is not because we can't afford a switch board operator. We don't feel the need for one.

Wipro had contemplated diversifying into financial services in the mid-eighties, when the industry experienced a boom. Most industrial houses in India had entered this industry at that time as did a number of "fly by night" operators. However, following the advice of consultants it had employed, the company had decided against this proposal. Gopalan said:

> We finally entered it in 1992, largely due to the impetus provided by the reforms in the financial sector. On hindsight we should have entered the industry much earlier.

In 1994, the business was intensely competitive. The industry had undergone massive transformation following the government's decision to throw the financial sector open for participation by both domestic and international companies. Almost all the leading global players, Goldman Sachs, Jardine Fleming, Alliance Capital, Merrill Lynch, Peregrine, GE Capital, James Capel, had set up base in India either directly or through joint ventures or tie-ups ("association" arrangements) with Indian finance companies. The erstwhile development financial institutions too were rapidly evolving into full fledged financial "services" companies. ICICI, a leading financial institution, for example, had tied up with JP Morgan and had started a separate investment banking joint venture.

Access to funds, especially low cost funds, was critical to success in the industry. Financial services companies were allowed to raise debt funds of the order of 10 times the shareholders' funds. In order to leverage this facility, Wipro Corporation, after the initial success of WFS, hiked its investment in WFS equity to Rs 5 crore, up from the initial Rs 0.75 crore. WFS was in the process of mobilising additional debt funds. Gopalan said, "Securing additional credit lines from the banks and financial institutions is not very difficult for us because of our corporate reputation."

In 1994, WFS was planning to grow aggressively. It was not averse to a tie-up with an international player, including setting up of a joint venture. Gopalan said, "We expect the partner to provide not only expertise in some areas in financial services like operating in the foreign exchange

EXHIBIT 9 MAJOR PRIVATE SECTOR PLAYERS IN FINANCIAL SERVICES

	GROSS INCOME	PROFIT AFTER TAX	NET WORTH	(Rs MILLION) BUSINESS FOCUS
1. Kotak Mahindra	775	260	670	Trade Financing Capital Markets Operation; Lease Vehicle Finance (Cars)
2. Sundaram Finance	1500	200	910	Vehicle Finance (Trucks); Lease
3. Apple Industries	500	165	700	Lease; Trade Finance; Vehicle Finance (Cars)
4. Lloyds Finance	320	145	700	Trade Finance Lease
5. 20th Century Finance	725	135	560	Asset Finance Merchant Banking
6. Ashok Leyland Finance	510	93	250	Vehicle Finance (Trucks)
7. ITC Classic	570	75	575	Lease; Trade Finance; Merchant Banking
8. Tata Finance	490	70	525	Lease; Trade Finance

Source: Company estimates.

WIPRO LIGHTING

Lighting was a major new diversification for Wipro. Premji explained:

> We enter businesses where competition is either weak or indifferent and where we can leverage our "management" capability. Lighting business offered good margins, provided the business was well managed. We found that despite the presence of major players like Phillips India (the Indian subsidiary of the Dutch multinational) and Crompton Greaves, who have over the years invested in building their brands, the lighting market was a semi-commodity market and that distribution held the key. We had access to the retail channel through Wipro Consumer Products and importantly a distinctive competence in dealer management.

In the first phase of diversification, Wipro Lighting (WL) invested Rs 40 crore in setting up its manufacturing facilities. WL's product range consisted of incandescent and fluorescent lamps and a full range of luminaires for industrial and office lighting, street lighting, flood lighting and special lighting systems for varied applications. In addition, WL sourced products from other lighting companies—a practice common to the lighting business in India.

WL launched its Wipro brand of lighting products in the southern and western markets of India in 1992–93. In its first full year of operation, 1993–1994, WL achieved a turnover of Rs 22 crore. It, however, failed to generate profits. WL's expectations that it would be able to leverage access to the retail channel through Wipro Consumer Products and achieve a strong presence in the market place was only partially realised. Over 60% of lighting products were purchased from electrical outlets—a channel not accessed by WCP. Further, WL confronted strong competition in the marketplace especially from MNCs. The economic reform programme had not only attracted new MNC entry—GE, Wipro's joint venture partner in Wipro GE, acquired an equity stake in the local company Apar and had put in a bid to acquire a stake in the ailing Mysore Lamps[11]—it had also resulted in Phillips Holland, the parent company of the market leader Phillips India—evincing greater interest in the operations of its local subsidiary. The MNC parent had raised its equity stake in the subsidiary to a controlling 51% and had started transferring state of the art technology to the local subsidiary.

These developments had led to Wipro Lighting rolling back its plans to go national. "We will do that next year. It took us some time to understand this business. I think we set ourselves rather unrealistic targets," Premji said.

HOLDING THE CORPORATION TOGETHER

Premji described Wipro as a diversified *integrated* corporation. The integration was achieved through a set of shared beliefs and leadership values, through people and through management processes.

INTEGRATION THROUGH SHARED BELIEFS AND LEADERSHIP VALUES

Premji had, in 1973, "much before it became fashionable to do so," articulated a set of beliefs (see Exhibit 10), which since then have governed the management of Wipro. Premji said, "The Wipro Beliefs give a common cause and a sense of purpose across the businesses making Wipro in essence *one company*. Our Beliefs define our basic philosophy of managing business and will remain the spirit and essence of Wipro."

> Our beliefs are mutually compatible and supportive of one another. All of them have equal priority and need for constant practice. Our goals, objectives, policies and actions flow from our Beliefs. Conceptually, our Beliefs are at the top of the pyramid (see Figure 1). From them flow our five year goals, three year/annual objectives for the corporation and business units, departmental objectives and individual objectives. To meet the challenges of the future we are prepared to change everything about ourselves except our Beliefs, as they along guide, govern and bind us together as an organisation. It is essential that we consciously internalise our Beliefs and be fanatical about consistently practising them. If we fail to honour our Beliefs, we will lose credibility, not only as individuals, but also as an organisation. (pp. 1–2, Wipro Beliefs)

According to Premji:

> At Wipro we walk the talk. For example, we are not flexible about boosting our sales by securing orders the non Wipro way. If any deal requires practices that compromise our integrity, we will not do it. We have blacklisted a number of customers who seek paying or accepting favours while entering into business deals. I do not think by adopting this stance we are losing market share. The business heads are expected to achieve their targets—despite lack of flexibility over issues of integrity. I expect them to factor this inflexibility in while setting targets. Ultimately I believe any customer seeks good technology, good after sales service and a competitive price. We offer all of them. We will not compromise on these three critical factors. We can therefore afford to be inflexible on the integrity issue.

EXHIBIT 10

WIPRO BELIEFS

1. Respect for the individual. People are our greatest asset.
2. Achieve and maintain a position of leadership in each of the businesses we are in.
3. Pursue all tasks to accomplish them in a superior manner.
4. Govern individual and company relationships with the highest standards of conduct and integrity.
5. Be close to the customer in action, example and spirit, and ensure superior quality products and services.
6. Measure our effectiveness by the long term profits we achieve for our enterprise.

WIPRO LEADERSHIP QUALITIES

1. Wipro Leaders make and meet aggressive commitments always with accountability, decisiveness, and uncompromising integrity.
2. Wipro Leaders have a clear and customer focused vision. They create the vision, live and breathe it, and communicate it effectively to motivate others.
3. Wipro Leaders are able to energise and invigorate others and have a high-energy approach themselves.
4. Wipro Leaders are self-confident.
5. Wipro Leaders exhibit ownership in thought and action—and value this in other members of the team.
6. Wipro Leaders are committed to excellence through quality, speed, simplicity and elimination of unnecessary bureaucracy.
7. Wipro Leaders develop star performers yet build teams: they consider their people as cherished assets, whose individual and team commitment is crucial for organisational success.

Source: Company documents.

Almost every year Wipro issued 30 to 40 notices to the employees who were suspected to be short on the integrity front. And if any inappropriate behaviour is proved, the employee is sacked—regardless of his or her position. "Recently, in 1993, we dismissed the employee union leader at Wipro Fluid Power, when we discovered that he had falsified his travelling expenses. Following the dismissal we had a strike at Wipro Fluid Power. We preferred taking a strike,

FIGURE 1

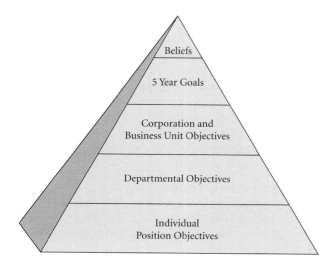

even though the market was just coming out of recession and the customers were wanting delivery. We preferred to explain to the customers the principled stand we took," Premji added.

The Wipro Beliefs had not undergone any change since they were first articulated, save for the addition, in 1982, of a sixth Belief, "Being Close to the Customer." In 1992, a proposal for dropping the Belief "Measure our Effectiveness by the Long Term Profits We Achieve for Our Enterprise" was once again made (it had earlier been contemplated in 1989). It was argued that enough emphasis had been built into the organisation on profits and that it did not merit inclusion in Wipro Beliefs and that it would be appropriate to incorporate it as part of the five year goals. However the Belief was retained.

Wipro believed that leadership played a critical role in embedding a value-based culture that was in consonance with Wipro Beliefs. Pai said, "I lead by example. My staff see me operating without a personal secretary and yet, they know, I have all the information at my fingertips. Therefore, when I exhort my team to save on costs, I am credible." Girish Gauer added, "At Wipro the prerogative of and the responsibility for providing leadership is not that of the top management alone. All the employees, whether in the field, or on the shop floor or at the top of the business are Wipro leaders." The company had articulated a set of Wipro Leadership Qualities (see Exhibit 10). All the employees were expected to possess/acquire these qualities.

INTEGRATION THROUGH PEOPLE

Though closely held—Premji's family held over 75% of the equity—Wipro had a strong and powerful top management team of professionals. "One of Premji's outstanding abilities has been to repeatedly recognise, develop and support highly talented executives," said Soota. Almost every one of Wipro's businesses had been built around and in turn built by the people who were heading them. The turnover at the top had been negligible and the long tenure of the people with the corporation was a strong integrating force.

Wipro believed in employing the best people and investing in them. It recruited from leading educational institutions in India by participating in their campus placement programmes and built its management from within, save for specialised or strategic requirements. According to Gopalan, President of WFS, and formerly chief financial officer at WIL, "For every new business we enter, the internal person is given a shot at it, and only if someone internal is not available or suitable, someone from outside is taken." However, Wipro did not have a strong record of rotating people across the businesses. Often the business unit heads were reluctant to release talented people, as each business was considered fairly specialised and distinctive. "We have not felt the need for it so far, the growth in each of our businesses has provided exciting career growth opportunities for the employees. This however is changing to some extent now with the movement of people from Infotech to Systems, etc.," said Girish Gaur.

The culture at Wipro was an open and sharing one. Gopalan said, "I am psychologically incapable of coping with intrigue. I am very uncomfortable operating in environments which are full of politics and where decisions are not taken on grounds of merit. At Wipro, we have independence of work. I do what is essential for the business and not worry about it. If I am fired, I am very sure that if I were sitting in the decision maker's chair—Premji in this case—I too would arrive at the same decision. I can get fired only for unethical behaviour or nonperformance. Not for any other reason." Soota added, "We discuss even our 'dirty linen' in the open. Sometimes I think we are much too open."

Discussion on managerial values, business plans, strategies and policies was encouraged. Every year, after the annual planning exercise was completed in March, Premji travelled across the country to the offices of the various businesses and addressed the employees to communicate and share the plan with them and invite their suggestions. While Premji shared the plans for the corporation as a whole, the respective business unit head shared the plans for the business to which the employees belonged. "This reduces dependence on control mechanisms, improves individual commitment to goals and adoption of sound methods." Premji said.

Wipro was the first company in India to introduce an employee stock ownership programme. The Wipro Equity Linked Reward Programme (WELRP) was a novel one. Each Wipro business, regardless of its legal status, had its own separate internal "equity" and "net worth." Part of the compensation of the employees entitled to participate in the WELRP programme was linked to the growth in the "net worth" of that particular business. In 1994, the eligibility to participate in WELRP had been pushed down to the middle levels of the management hierarchy.

INTEGRATION THROUGH MANAGEMENT PROCESSES

Each of Wipro's businesses enjoyed a wide latitude and operated quite independently. However, approved corporate wide policies were inviolable, regardless of the circumstances the individual businesses might find themselves in. Premji said, "Each business exists for the enhancement and betterment of the whole corporation." Asked whether it would be right to describe him as a hands-off manager, Premji said: "Yes and no. I spend a lot of time with my people, asking the right kind of questions to find out what is happening in our various businesses. I may not be an operations man. But then, neither am I merely an investor-chairman." Chandrasekharan added, "He is a details man. Although he allows us tremendous freedom, he knows exactly what is happening where."

The Wipro corporate office played an important role in ensuring the "betterment of the corporation as a whole." Certain powers and responsibilities were reserved for the Wipro Corporate Office. These were:

a: *Setting:*
Beliefs, goals and basic policies
Certain plan drivers and other standards of measurements

b: *Approving:*
Plans and budgets
Appointments at middle management and above
Employee salary structures, benefits and incentive plans
Appointment of advertising agencies
Interaction with the government on key policy issues
Charity and other contributions

c: *Responsibility for:*
Selecting statutory auditors and counsel
Corporate audit across the corporation

The corporate office held the overall responsibility for the corporation's finance, human resource, corporate planning and business development, and government and legal affairs functions. While each of the businesses independently carried out these functions, the heads of these functions at the individual businesses had a dotted line relationship with corporate functional heads.

The annual planning exercise was the key operational management process by which the integration was sought to be achieved. Each business prepared its own business plans for the year. Wahi said, "In addition to our open culture, one of our strengths is our very strong planning and review culture. We document not only our plans but also have a rigorous system of preparing minutes of our review meetings. We have monthly reviews with the Chairman and quarterly reviews with the CEC (Corporate Executive Council)." According to Chandrasekharan, however, the documentation often exceeded what was necessary or desirable: "We generate too much paper. We need to reduce it. We need to appreciate that there is no perfect plan. We need to change it as we go along. Excessive details kill the spirit. Increasingly I find ourselves moving away from being a presentation-discussion oriented company to a paper document oriented company."

Each business was required to define its key result objectives for the year. The number of variables for which the objectives were required to be defined was restricted to six. In 1994, the corporate office defined four of the variables, with the definition of the other two being left to the discretion of the individual businesses with only a stipulation that the variables defined by them be measurable. Two of the variables defined by the corporate office were Speed and Customer Satisfaction and were to be valid for the next five years. Each business was expected to reduce all current cycle times by 20% each year and increase by 5 points each year the percentage of customers who rated Wipro "over all" a 5 and 4 in a 1 to 5 point scale. The other two variables stipulated by the corporate office for which the individual businesses had to define their objectives were Financial and Employee Morale. The measurement criteria for the Employee Morale objective was through an annual Employee Perception Survey, attrition rates and internal growth. The individual business financial objectives were to necessarily cover objectives on: (a) Sales, Sales Growth and Market Share; (b) Profit Before Tax; (c) Profit After Tax; (d) Cash Flow; (e) Return on Average Equity; and (f) Return on Capital Employed.

The corporate office also informed the individual businesses of the norms for approval of investments. In 1994, these were 29% return on average equity and a minimum 22% return on capital employed. All investment proposals had to meet these criteria for approval. Only in exceptional cases, where the proposal came from the newer businesses and the considerations were strategic, proposals which did not meet these criteria got approved. Additionally a debt equity norm was specified. Gowrishankar said, "We specify the debt equity norm as each business unit organises its own debt funds. We believe in adhering to strick self-imposed norms. At WFS, for instance, we maintain debt to equity ratio at 6:1 even though the company is entitled to go up to 10:1."

Pai said, "We are in many ways a strongly decentralised operation. I am not dependent on the corporate office. In fact I keep them at arms' length. However, I must admit we are much too finance dominated." Endorsing this view, Gopalan said, "The plan, once approved, gives me the target and the authority but it also freezes my opportunity."

The annual plans were approved by the CEC comprising of Premji, the presidents of the various businesses, and the corporate heads of finance and human resources. CEC was the apex policy-making body at Wipro. Apart from articulating the vision for Wipro Corporation as a whole, it was the final arbiter of policies in Wipro. While the corporate office monitored the performance of the individual businesses on a monthly basis, the CEC met every quarter to assess, comprehensively, the performance of the individual businesses and the corporation as a whole. The CEC also approved of extra plan corporate initiatives (strategic thrusts) and other corporate wide programs. "CEC enables the Chairman to manage the diversity," Gopalan said.

In 1994, apart from the CEC, there were two other councils which were for discussing common issues across the various businesses and to initiate and implement corporation-wide strategic thrusts. These were the Wipro Finance Council (FC) and the Wipro Human Resource Council (HRC). The formation of two other councils, the Materials Council—which would focus on supplier management—and the Marketing Council—which would focus on the marketing dimension—was being debated by the CEC.

The FC was headed by the Corporate Vice President (Finance) and had the chief financial officers of all the businesses as members. In 1994, the FC had embarked on an extra plan initiative of achieving a corporate-wide savings/earnings to the tune of Rs 2.5 crore through adoption of superior financial practices in the corporation. The HRC was headed by the Corporate Vice President (Human Resources) and had the chiefs of the human resource function in all the businesses as members. In 1994, the HRC was the prime driver of the PRIDE programme, which aimed to bring about a mind-set change within the various businesses. Girish Gaur, the chief of the HR council explained, "PRIDE—which stands for **P**roductivity improvements, a **R**esponsive organisation, and **I**nvolved People, by **D**riving Change and **E**mpowering them—is a method of problem resolution. It involved setting up of cross functional teams, each comprising 5 to 7 members, who are then given the mandate to find solutions to specific problems." In 1994, 29 cross functional teams were functioning at Wipro, and the number was expected to go up to 130. Premji said, "We need to shake people up to rethink the business. A business-as-usual attitude will not succeed in the drastically changing environment."

BALANCING THE FUTURE: CHALLENGES IN 1994

The fundamental challenge confronting Wipro was *how* to sustain its growth in the changed environment. The competition it confronted was severe. And the competitors in most of its businesses were multinationals, who not only had immense financial power but could also leverage their global product and marketing technologies.

BALANCING THE PORTFOLIO

In the past, Wipro, as a part of its growth strategy, had sought international tie-ups in businesses where partners brought technology, access to global markets and process know-how while Wipro brought access to local markets, management capability and in most cases an existing presence. In the changed policy environment, the MNCs sought a greater involvement in the businesses, in the form of both greater equity stakes and greater say in the management. The challenge Wipro faced was twofold: (a) *how* to achieve the right balance in its portfolio between financial joint ventures and those which were independent of such financial partnerships and (b) *how* to ensure that Wipro continued to bring value to the table on an ongoing basis to be an equal partner.

Premji said:

> When GE sought to increase its stake in Wipro GE, we debated their acquisition of the majority stake over an eight month period. It was a tough emotional decision. GE is a 51% mindset company. I had to go beyond myself as a majority owner of Wipro and put the employees ahead. We did drive a hard bargain. We got an equal representation on the Board and also finalised the norms for transfer pricing—always a thorny issue in joint venture. We also made an agreement that while GE's medical software development will be done at Wipro GE, the information services software projects will be carried out by Wipro Systems. I am, however, aware that they would increasingly want to be in the driving seat. In future, our focus would be on setting financial targets for Wipro GE and leveraging the learning the association with GE provides us in our other businesses, including transferring their best practices.

Vivek Paul, who continued to be a member of the CEC even after the change, said:

> Some things have definitely changed. We are in transition. We have started using the Delhi Office of GE for our government liaison work. Further, the GE planning exercise is carried out two months before the Wipro planning exercise. So, today we are juggling two sets of numbers as the definition of the financial year varies. Additionally, there are three different sets of

demands being made on me. While Wipro wants to maximise contribution, the GE Medical Systems Division headquarters wants to maximise top line and the GE international division wants Wipro GE to become a low cost base of operation.

Following the GE acquisition of a majority stake in Wipro GE, the CEC decided that it would derive 75% of its profit after tax, as a corporation, from businesses in which Wipro controlled the destiny and was not subordinate to financial joint venture partners. "This has been a difficult decision, particularly when as a Corporation, we are uniquely positioned to attract and have joint ventures with leading companies in each of the six businesses we are in," said Premji.

The CEC took two more policy decisions:

1. It would take on joint venture partners *only* in products where product success was critically dependent on having a technological edge and it could not access the required technology otherwise. For example, in the health care business it planned to operate in the joint venture mode and/or represent world leaders in the specific product market segments. Similarly, the relationship with Nokia was expected to evolve into a 50:50 joint venture.

2. It would not enter into financial partnerships where the company had a strong brand franchise, and/or where it was on top of world class technology and/or where it had a cost edge. Further, in businesses where it could develop technology on its own or *cafeteria shop* technologies from medium size European, American and Asian companies, it would not take on joint venture partners and would retain its independence. Soota said, "As we search more in this area, we are amazed how much high quality technology is available today with medium size companies."

The adoption of these policies implied that the company would continue to operate independently or through technology licensing arrangements in its information technology business. However, in a sudden turnabout in late 1994, the company signed a memorandum of understanding with ACER, Taiwan, the tenth largest PC company in the world, to set up a joint venture to manufacture and market jointly branded PCs. The tie-up also envisaged setting up of a design centre for software and hardware services. Asked about the turnabout, Soota said, "Currently the market is dominated by local brands, but one must acknowledge the strengths and pull of MNC brands. One has seen it in other industries and one cannot take it lightly. At the same time there is no need to be overawed." Premji added, "The trick is to know when to take partners and when not to take partners and generate enough self-confidence and not be naive or macho. We need to balance our control and growth needs."

BALANCING GROWTH

Wipro aspired to be among the top 10 most admired corporations in India. The key attributes identified for this reputation were quality of management; quality of products and/or services; innovations; growth in net worth; financial soundness; ability to attract, develop, and retain talented people; and use of its assets and exports. Wipro planned to periodically commission independent polls to evaluate its performance on these criteria.

Additionally it aspired to be among the top 10 industrial groups in India in terms of profits after tax by the year 2002–2003. The financial targets articulated in the Wipro 10 year vision was a sales of Rs 10,000 crore, profits before tax of Rs 500 crore and profits after tax of Rs 300 crore. The vision also envisaged 20% of the sales coming from exports and overseas presence, with marketing presence in 50 countries.

Wipro was seeking to realise this vision without adding more industries to its portfolio. Premji said, "I am not looking to add greater diversity. We are essentially looking at related businesses." While admitting the need to contain the diversity, Gopalan said, "We also need to re-examine our portfolio and our growth strategy. We have a large number of relatively small sized businesses operating in relatively small sized markets. We today cut off the option of contemplating a Rs 500 crore project."

The vision identified resource mobilisation as the critical factor which would impact the achievement of the objectives. Premji said, "Our current shareholding pattern allows more than enough latitude to dilute ownership, if necessary, without losing operational and management control. But we need to maximise internal resource generation. Consequently profit after tax and cash flow were adopted as the two key plan drivers. We need to make sure that we are getting the maximum bang for our buck," Premji said.

As a part of its efforts to realise the vision, the planning process was modified to build in a "commitment to commitments" mind-set. In the past, actual performance invariably fell short of the plan targets. From 1994, commitments made in the plan were treated as sacrosanct. Actual performance was required to be within 5% of the plan target. "At GE this is strictly followed. The business units **had** to achieve their plans. We need this kind of American toughness built into our management processes," said Girish Gaur. "The plan commitments have to be taken seriously. Without it resource planning becomes very difficult," said Gowrishankar. Not all the business unit heads were in full agreement with the adoption of the Commitment to Commitment policy. According to Vivek Paul, "GE itself is rethinking its policy." Pai said, "I believe

in setting ourselves high targets and attempting to achieve them. It does not matter if we end up achieving only 80% of it. What is more important is to aim high. Why not let each business unit head decide what is more appropriate?" Premji, however, did not agree. "It is a question of mindset. I do not think stretched targets cannot be specified under the new dispensation."

BALANCING MANAGEMENT

The issue of balance between integration and independence was being debated within Wipro. As described by Soota, "Today, only our values are common. Otherwise we are almost six different companies, with every business unit head focusing only on their respective businesses. We need to achieve greater integration." However, this sharp focus on one's "own" business had its advantages, as Soota admitted. "Most of us are heavily involved in managing our own business. That has been our model so far and has worked well. We run our businesses as proprietors. I do not go beyond into the Wipro Corporation level issues. That is largely the domain of Premji and the corporate office. They do get heavily involved at a start-up business like lighting, which requires financial support and nurturing. For established businesses like WIL, they would get involved only if I need help. Otherwise we operate quite independently except for participating in the CEC. Apart from Premji, who is our strongest integrating force, it is our shared values which integrate us."

However, according to Gopalan, "We value common threads too much today. We seek too much order. We must increasingly learn to live with unintegrated diversity and with ambiguity. I would prefer CEC to be a driver of growth rather than being a policy-making body. I do not think we are today tapping fully the capability of the Wipro top management." Another senior manager echoed this view. "Take the issue of employee remuneration. We try to balance the compensation of our employees across the various businesses. We need to appreciate the fact that the competition we confront is very different in different businesses."

Retention of talented people was a common problem confronted by all the Wipro businesses. The strategy of most new entrants, especially MNCs, was to raid well-managed Indian companies for talent. Wipro was one of the prime targets. Premji said, "Beyond competition in the product markets, retention of talented people is the biggest challenge confronting us at Wipro. I personally believe that the new environment provides much more opportunities to grow and prosper. The key, however, lies in holding on to talented people. Our biggest strength has been our people; our management capability. We need to sustain it."

TV Asahi Theatrical Productions, Inc.

In April 1996, Kenji Sudo, Vice President of TV Asahi's Theatrical Productions, Inc., was in a pensive mood. He had just heard that one of their musicals had been nominated for a variety of Tony Awards.[1] This was tremendous news. It was the 50th anniversary of the Tony Awards and this year's televised show was expected to be a spectacular event. Even in a run-of-the-mill year, getting a Tony nomination almost guaranteed that the musical would be profitable, and possibly very profitable because of the TV exposure.

Yet, there was also some unsettling news. During the past week he had been talking to several top managers in TV Asahi (pronounced *ah-saw-hee*), the Japanese parent company of the Theatrical Productions unit. All of the managers had voiced some doubt about the role of the Theatrical Productions subsidiary in TV Asahi. Through these conversations, Kenji realized that they didn't understand the business, and inevitably they didn't know what to do with it.

This lack of commitment was clearly a concern for Kenji. He had spent 14 years of his life building the subsidiary into a profitable musical theatre production company and the number one Asian company in the U.S. live theatre business. Last year the subsidiary had been very profitable and Kenji thought these results would go a long way toward improving the attitude of top management toward the subsidiary, but this appeared not to be the case. He wondered what Asahi would do about the Theatrical Productions unit, and of course the ultimate question for him was, what should he do about it?

TV ASAHI AND THE NEWSPAPER AND BROADCASTING INDUSTRY IN JAPAN

TV Asahi Theatrical Productions, Inc., was part of TV Asahi's Special Events Division whose parent company was Asahi National Broadcasting Co., Ltd. (TV Asahi) of Japan (see Figure 1 for an organizational chart). TV Asahi was part of a small keiretsu[2] involving interlocking ownership of three other companies: Asahi Shimbun (newspapers), Toei (movies and TV production) and Obunsha (publishing). The Asahi group of companies was privately owned by the employees and three Japanese families. The largest company in this group was the Asahi Shimbun, the largest newspaper company in Japan. This newspaper company dominated the other two companies in a variety of ways including having the largest revenues, profits, and ownership

Professors Patrick Woodcock and Paul Beamish prepared this case solely to provide material for class discussion. The authors do not intend to illustrate either effective or ineffective handling of a managerial situation. The authors may have disguised certain names and other identifying information to protect confidentiality.

Ivey Management Services prohibits any form of reproduction, storage or transmittal without written permission. This material is not covered under authorization from CanCopy or any reproduction rights organization. To order copies or request permission to reproduce materials, contact Ivey Publishing, Ivey Management Services, c/o Richard Ivey School of Business, The University of Western Ontario, London, Ontario, Canada, N6A 3K7; phone (519) 661-3208; fax (519) 661-3882; e-mail cases@ivey.uwo.ca.

Copyright © 1996, Ivey Management Services.

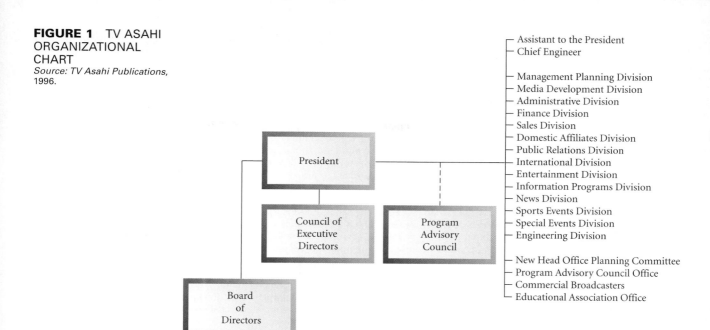

Assistant to the President
Chief Engineer

Management Planning Division
Media Development Division
Administrative Division
Finance Division
Sales Division
Domestic Affiliates Division
Public Relations Division
International Division
Entertainment Division
Information Programs Division
News Division
Sports Events Division
Special Events Division
Engineering Division

New Head Office Planning Committee
Program Advisory Council Office
Commercial Broadcasters
Educational Association Office

President

Council of
Executive
Directors

Program
Advisory
Council

Board
of
Directors

Auditor

in them. The presidents of the smaller companies were appointed by the Asahi Shimbun and had always been former Asahi Shimbun managers.

THE JAPANESE NEWSPAPER INDUSTRY

The Japanese newspaper industry was tightly controlled and dominated by a few privately owned firms. There were five major players in the industry, with Asahi being the largest. Most of these companies had some degree of regional focus, while others differentiated themselves by focusing on specialized news such as business or sports. None of these companies faced any direct international competition since foreign firms faced enormous entry barriers related to the Japanese language, culture and distribution, all which were very critical to the business. None of these companies had newspaper interests outside of Japan.

In general, the industry had been slow to respond to the technological changes and related shifts in economies of scale and scope which had been the rage of English language-based newspapers around the world. The retiring competitive environment had produced organizations that were quite conservative and bureaucratic. Historically, the industry had been very profitable, but the recession of the early '90s had affected all sectors including this one.

THE JAPANESE TELEVISION INDUSTRY

The television broadcasting industry was also relatively concentrated. Yet, it was clearly more competitive and dynamic than the newspaper industry. This was due to a variety of factors including the continual demand for creativity in programming, and technological developments, as well as both national and international competition. National competition was significant in comparison to the newspaper industry because the incremental costs of broadcasting nationally versus regionally were relatively small. Therefore, a company tended to broadcast in as many regions as its license allowed. International competition was moderate, but some English TV programming was broadcast in the populated regions (e.g., CNN news), and very popular international programs were dubbed into Japanese (e.g., "Dallas"). The larger broadcasting companies all had international divisions which were largely unprofitable.

There were four large national TV broadcasting companies in Japan. They were, in order of size, Nippon Hoso Kyokai (NHK), Fuji Television Network, Inc. (Fuji TV), Tokyo Broadcasting System (TBS) and TV Asahi. In addition, there was a variety of smaller regional companies (e.g., TV Tokyo, and Kansai TV) and some pay television

TABLE 1
SUMMARY
DESCRIPTION OF TOP
THREE COMPETITORS

NHK is the largest national broadcasting company and because of its size and dominance in the industry, it is often referred to as the Japanese Broadcasting Corporation. NHK is focused entirely on television and radio broadcasting in Japan, although NHK does license some of its news, cultural, and business programs to broadcasters in other countries who desire some Japanese content for their local audiences. This company is very research and development oriented. It was the major force behind Japan's development of the high definition television standards and broadcasting equipment. Now it is the only company in the world that broadcasts high definition digital signals. From a programming perspective, NHK is known for its sports programming. In conclusion, this company has considerable technical and programming skills compared with the other competitors. The large market share and historical government support allowed it to develop these skills and consequently build market share that could support the skills.

FUJI TV is owned by a company called Jujisankei Communications Group. It is the second largest television broadcaster in Japan and it is particularly well known for its animation, children's programming and variety shows. This company is a largely diversified mass media company. It has taken an aggressive approach to international development through acquisitions and joint ventures with companies such as US Today. It acquired a number of companies in Europe relating to creative software production and licensing rights. It also produced Japanese musical productions. It owns its own theatre hall for live theatre as well as an art gallery with many of Picasso's sculptures. The company is into publishing computer software and multimedia (the best Internet site), computer magazines, Internet shopping, and it owns a few regional newspapers, and a film business. Its core competence is its creative programming capabilities.

TBS is a national television and radio broadcasting company. TBS is a relatively aggressive company that tends to produce racy shows, at least for Japanese standards. It is in all types of production from drama, to news broadcasting. Recently, it got itself into trouble with investigative reporting of a "Tokyo bombing cult." TBS is the third largest broadcaster, just slightly larger in revenues than Asahi.

Source: Company Internet sites and Time Warner documents on the Japanese media industry.

channels (e.g., Japan Satellite Broadcasting). A summary description of the top three firms is provided in Table 1.

TV ASAHI

TV Asahi was the smallest of the four national broadcasting companies in Japan. Despite its ranking, it was a sizable organization. Its revenues for 1995 were in excess of $1 billion U.S. and it had over 1,300 employees worldwide.

TV Asahi started in 1959 as a small news and information educational channel. It had quite naturally evolved into its present niche which was news and information programming, although it carried some variety drama, animation and sports programming. In addition, the company produced or promoted concerts, musical theatre, art exhibits, and other international cultural events. Yet, over 50 per cent of TV Asahi's programming was live broadcasting reflecting its news and information content. It was the first station to introduce prime time evening news.

Internationally, TV Asahi had 21 international news bureaus, the two most important being Paris and New York. These 21 international offices were used to establish a balanced global coverage of international news events, to establish ties with other broadcasters around the world, to

develop international co-productions, and to sell Asahi's programming to non-Japanese broadcasters.

TV Asahi had been involved in cooperative international programming and news reporting for over a decade. In 1982 it signed an exclusive agreement with CNN (U.S.) centered around joint news and information programming. It had also worked collaboratively with a number of other foreign news broadcasters including TF1 (France), RTL (Germany), BBTV (Thailand), CTV (Taiwan), CCTV (China), RTRC (Russia), and RTM (Malaysia). In addition, Asahi offered Japanese news, culture, and entertainment to television stations that broadcast to a Japanese audience in New York, San Francisco, Los Angeles, and Hawaii, although this was a very small part of its broadcasting business.

However, Asahi was in the process of trying to broaden its scope of broadcasting skills and products into the non-news sectors of the industry. For example, it was currently trying to build a reputation in children's animation shows; it had developed a very popular children's animation show in Japan and it was selling this show, with some success, to foreign broadcasters. The managers believed that the only way Asahi would grow and challenge some of its rivals was to add non-news related shows. In their opinion, they had as much of the news market as they were going to capture in Japan, and moving into non-Japanese news broadcasting in a foreign country would be very difficult, if not impossible. So their one avenue for growth was in the more popular TV shows such as variety, drama, etc. Thus, they were slowly exploring ways of developing some of the skills that their rivals had in this aspect of broadcasting.

ORGANIZATIONAL CHARACTERISTICS

TV Asahi's organizational chart is shown in Figure 1. The Chairman was a former newspaper executive appointed from Asahi Shimbun, as were all previous Chairmen. In addition, a few other top managers were from Asahi Shimbun. This gave the company a distinctive "news culture."

Organizationally, the company was relatively conservative and bureaucratic in both its systems and structures. None of the employees, including Kenji, was paid based on performance. The reporting systems tended to be quite formal and seniority was clearly an important issue in career advancement. In fact, Asahi had all of the classical Japanese organizational attributes. Life-time employment was the norm and personnel got to know each other through socializing during work and the frequent (often biweekly) after work "get togethers" for drinks. Socializing was important because it made the cooperative Japanese decision making and working environment function smoothly. It also provided workers with mentors and management contacts which could later prove valuable when the person moved into a management position. This system also inculcated the organizational culture (e.g., group decision making approach, etc.) into the employees.

TV Asahi's conservative organizational style was due, in part, to its heritage in the news industry and ownership roots in Asahi Shimbun. The news programming format provided the least amount of motivation for innovation and change, simply because a news report was a news report in any language and station. News stations tended to differentiate themselves based on the operational aspects of gathering and reporting news. In essence, the depth and speed of coverage differentiated a good station from an "also ran." In this respect, TV Asahi was clearly an extension of Asahi Shimbun. Yet, such a culture had clearly gotten in the way of the move toward a more creative broadcasting format and content.

Such a classical Japanese organizational approach had proven to be very effective in producing organizational efficiency, decision making leading to very effective implementation, and a focused organizational strategy. Yet, it had also created some concerns. The most prominent was the lack of creativity and specialization leading to a lack of

fundamental research and development in the organization. A cooperative and generalist approach tended to attenuate the ability of the organization to take risks in decision making and to try creative ideas. In some Japanese industries, this had clearly been a problem.

NEW FORCES ACTING ON THE TV INDUSTRY

Governmental controls on the industry had also contributed to the tempered competitive environment. The Japanese government had historically controlled the industry through regulatory policies that restricted channel ownership. Channels were awarded on the basis of availability and the owners perceived honor, reverence, and trustworthiness in Japanese society. Historically, it had been very important for the owners to be standard bearers of cultural honor, probity, and respect because they were reporting the news. Unlike North Americans, the Japanese were very concerned about what was televised. In particular, they did not condone programming that brings shame to them or their society. To a large extent the government had used ownership as a method of self-monitoring. This had resulted in an industry that had historically been concentrated in a few hands. Such a restrictive industry structure was wonderful for the companies. They enjoyed a stable competitive environment and commensurate levels of profitability.

However, a number of forces were changing the nature of the business. The recession, which began in 1992 and still continued, had reduced profitability dramatically in the broadcasting business, due to the "shrinkage" in advertising volume and rates. TV Asahi and Fuji TV had both delayed the development of their new headquarters office buildings. TV Asahi's was to be a 50-floor office building with a large theatre and retail shopping mall at the ground level. All of the broadcasters were searching for ways to save money and reorganize to improve efficiency. Some companies had even laid off workers for the first time since their inception some 40 years ago. Bankruptcies were at an all-time high and this was expected to continue for the near term. The financial crisis had forced two banks into bankruptcy and more were expected to follow.

The government was also looking at ways to deregulate the broadcasting industry in the next two years. The change in policy was being driven by the availability of many more channels and the merging of a variety of technologies including telecommunications, satellite dishes, computers, digital broadcasting, and international competition. If Japan did not implement this deregulation, there was the potential that a wide variety of competitors would circumvent the present regulations, thus creating chaos. Furthermore, the government had come to view competition as essential to the development of new technologies and innovations in this fast-changing industry.

The four national broadcasters were, however, not pleased with this movement toward deregulation. They had been fighting the deregulation movement in a number of ways, but the predominant approach was to use political suasion. Having come from such a non-competitive environment, it was about the only response that they knew and had practised over the years. It now appeared that some sort of deregulation was going to occur within the next several years, and ultimately full deregulation was viewed as a distinct possibility in the long term.

THE SPECIAL EVENTS DIVISION

The Special Events Division of TV Asahi, which the Theatrical Productions unit was part of, employed approximately 50 people. The mandate for this Division was to enhance the image of TV Asahi through the sponsoring of various special events. A few of these events had been turned into TV specials and/or publications. The division had become involved in a wide and eclectic number of activities including the following:

- It published a number of different magazines and educational videos.
- It had created a campaign, called The Sakura Campaign, to further world peace in which cherry trees had been planted annually for the last five years at the former site of the Berlin wall.
- It had funded and produced several art exhibitions; the latest one was an exhibition of Vincent van Gogh. A variety of publications had resulted from this show.
- It had brought a variety of musical talent, both classical and popular, to Japan. Some of the recent performers included Prince, New Kids on the Block, and Van Halen. It brought the Vienna Boys Choir to Japan annually for a series of concerts.
- In addition, it had brought Broadway musical productions to Japan through the Theatrical Productions sub-unit.

The Special Events Division was not perceived as one of the more dynamic divisions in TV Asahi. Its objective was primarily to "give back" to the community and Japanese society, and secondarily, to create unusual and different TV programming material. The primary objective, although unusual by Western standards, was considered an important aspect of Japanese business and represented the cooperative interface between business and Japanese society. Most Japanese companies accomplished this in some manner.

Despite this honorable objective, the Special Events Division was not considered one of the more exciting places to work in Asahi. In fact, a transfer to the division was jokingly referred to as early retirement. A number of managers in the division were "burnt out" TV Asahi managers who had transferred to the division to get out of the hustle and bustle of the demanding TV business. An indication of the instability in this division was the turnover of the President. As long as Kenji could remember, the President of the Special Events Division had been replaced on a yearly basis either due to retirement or a transfer.

TV ASAHI THEATRICAL PRODUCTIONS, INC.

Asahi Theatrical Productions was founded because of a fondness for music by TV Asahi's second highest manager, Mr. Hidedata Nishimura. In particular, Hidedata loved western-style musicals and he felt that the Japanese public would also enjoy this form of entertainment if they were exposed to it. His idea was to bring these musicals to Japan using Asahi's Special Events Division. However, the division did not have the staff or skills to do this. Therefore, in 1982 he recruited Mr. Kenji Sudo and Mr. Yasu Kata Nishimura, his younger brother, to manage the selection and licensing of the musicals in New York, and to manage the operational aspects in Japan respectively.

Kenji Sudo was well suited to the position. He had been employed at Fuji TV in New York for the previous 20 years. During this time he had developed strong Western management skills including an entrepreneurial bent, something that would become quite useful in his new position.

Kenji immediately went to work and was able to license the Japanese rights to the musical "Sophisticated Ladies." This musical toured Japan during 1983. After that Asahi licensed "My One and Only" in 1984 and "Dreamgirls" in 1986 (see Table 2). The first two musicals were not financial successes, but they provided Asahi with some notoriety, particularly with young Japanese girls who loved this form of entertainment. The third production, "Dreamgirls," was a major hit. It ran almost double the length of the previous two productions in Japan and it more than paid for itself. From it, Asahi received considerable publicity and recognition, and the top managers in TV Asahi received a tremendous amount of adulation because they were often asked by top managers in other large companies and institutions if they could get some tickets for them because every show was sold out.

At this point, both Kenji and Hidedata knew they had developed an interesting business opportunity. Furthermore,

TABLE 2
ASAHI'S THEATRICAL
HISTORY

YEAR	TITLE	INVOLVEMENT	JAPANESE ACTIVITIES
1983	Sophisticated Ladies	Japanese tour	32 performances
1984	My One and Only	Japanese tour	32 performances
1986	Dreamgirls	Japanese tour	53 performances
1988	Blues in the Night	Producer	
	Westside Story	Japanese tour	43 performances
1989	Can-Can	Japanese tour	35 performances
	Blues in the Night	Japanese tour	48 performances
1990	South Pacific	Japanese tour	32 performances
1991	The Secret Garden	Producer	
1991	Grand Hotel	Japanese tour	48 performances
1992	Jelly's Last Jam	Producer	
	Guys and Dolls	Producer	
1993	The Secret Garden	Japanese tour	60 performances
	Guys and Dolls	Japanese tour	61 performances
	The Who's Tommy	Producer	
	Blues in the Night	Japanese tour	46 performances

Kenji was starting to develop some important contacts and musical theatre specific knowledge. Based on this and the success of "Dreamgirls," Asahi formalized the Theatrical Productions Unit into TV Asahi Theatrical Productions, Inc., in 1988. Mr. Hidedata assumed the role of President, a role that was little more than a Japanese figurehead of the corporation. He left all operational details to the two Vice-Presidents, Kenji and Yasu Kata, who ran their separate operations in the U.S. and Japan, respectively.

Additionally, in 1988 Asahi began investing in musical productions rather than just buying the Japanese rights to them. As a producer,[3] Asahi would now have more favorable access to the licensing rights of top musicals, although it would have to select its investments during the inception stages of the project, prior to the knowledge of whether the musical would be a hit or not. Its first investment was in an off-broadway production called "Blues in the Night." It was not a financial success, and from this Kenji realized that he must concentrate on major investments and top Broadway musicals, not off-Broadway productions.

In 1991, Kenji's associate and sponsor in Japan, Hidedata set up a company, called International Musical, Inc. (IMI), to handle secondary and amateur performance rights and licensing in Japan. Hidedata was retiring in 1994, and IMI would allow him to continue to work in a business that had been his hobby for more than 10 years. IMI complemented Asahi Theatrical Production's work by focusing on secondary musical rights and licenses, and it would work with Asahi whenever possible. Furthermore, IMI would leave the Broadway and West End[4] musical rights and licenses to Asahi.

In 1991, Kenji managed to convince Asahi to make another investment in a musical production. This time it was a Broadway musical entitled "The Secret Garden." This was a considerable breakthrough for Asahi Theatrical Productions. Investing in Broadway or West End theatre production was a risky business for anyone. Only two of ten investments made money, another one of ten would break-even, and the other seven would lose money. These were very poor odds and some top managers in Asahi were not terribly comfortable making such an investment. To become an investor, or a producer as they were called in the business, a company had to invest $250,000 to $500,000. The producers then had no real rights to the musical other than to the profits derived from the show. In other words, this did not give the investor the right to take the show to Japan. These rights had to be negotiated separately, and a producer had no more legal claim to the rights than a non-producer, although investing in a musical obviously gave the investor an inside track on getting the rights.

On average, about five Broadway and West End musicals were shown annually. There were almost 100 theatres on Broadway and in the West End (split about half and half, and only a half dozen in each location focused on musicals). Most of these theatres searched out directors who had creative ideas, or less often, were presented with creative ideas. Directors having successful track records, such as Andrew Lloyd Webber, were widely sought after because they could attract talent, money, and ultimately, a paying audience. While the directors looked after the creative and artistic side of the production, the theatres managed the business aspects of the show including financing, advertising, selling of tickets, etc.

Broadway theatre management was a difficult business and many of the theatres were jointly owned because of the rarity of skills and assets necessary. A successful theatre owner was a rare commodity because the position required a unique mix of skills, including excellent communication skills, good contacts in the business, adroit intuition as to the wishes and desires of the audience, and hard-core business acumen. Needless to say there were few people who had developed such a complex mix of skills. Thus, the few successful theatre companies tended to buy up those that failed. On Broadway there were only about three to four owners that had been successful at developing musicals with any sort of consistency. Ultimately the directors could take their talent anywhere and Andrew Lloyd Webber, the most successful musical director in the world, often selected a theatre not based on its past record but based on its willingness to pay royalties and provide financial support for the production.

Unfortunately, musicals tended to be either big hits or big busts. A show that received poor reviews by the critics on opening night might not even last a week. A big hit that had garnered a variety of Tony Awards might play for over a year on Broadway and, subsequently, in different international location. The Tony Awards were important to a show because getting a Tony nomination provided four minutes of television air-time for the show during prime-time viewing. Such television coverage would be unaffordable to all but the largest and most successful shows, yet it contributed enormously to the awareness and image of the musical.

BRINGING A MUSICAL TO JAPAN

Getting the rights to a musical and bringing it to Japan was a very involved process. First the rights to the music and/or story had to be purchased. Then the talent (performers) had to be "acquired." The easiest way to do this was to wait until the show ended its Broadway run and then bring the actors to Japan. Signing the performers involved dealing with their managers and unions. Star performers often required separate negotiations, while regulars had more standard contracts. Then the unions had to be satisfied that the theatre was up to standard and that the appropriate care (e.g., flight, travel, hotel, food, rest, etc.) was provided to its members. The union negotiations often represented the most frustrating part of the negotiation process because of their restrictive rules, and at times their perceived confrontational approach. In addition to all of this, theatres had to be secured (they had to be rented two years in advance of the actual show in Japan because of the lack of appropriate venues), sets had to be transported and/or built, back stage personnel had to be acquired and/or trained. Thus, getting a show to Japan was not only time consuming, but expensive. To bring a Broadway production to Japan cost U.S.$7 to $8 million.

Asahi had developed some skill in putting on these musical productions in Japan. Mr. Yasu Kata Nishimura, the manager of the Japanese operations, had developed excellent liaisons, and where necessary, contacts in the Japanese theatre industry. Finding an appropriate theatre was one of the most difficult obstacles to overcome in putting on live theatre in Japan. Large Broadway-type theatres were very rare in Japan, and often another type of venue had to be adapted for the situation. Yasu Kata had become quite proficient at managing the Japanese tours. He had developed relationships with the large theatre owners. He understood the needs and desires of the various western directors, actors, and workers. He also had developed considerable knowledge in the business aspects of the production such as advertising, promotion, ticket sales, etc. In addition, Yasu had developed a subtitling system that allowed the Japanese audience to follow the story in Japanese, and some of the stories were published using Asahi's publishing subsidiary. Clearly, Kenji and Yasu had become a very effective team.

To aid with the financing of the Japanese tours, Asahi got sponsors. These sponsors would usually contribute about one million U.S. dollars, a sum that would help defray some initial costs. Then, the remaining costs would be covered, if possible, by ticket sales. In general, because of the enormous costs of most productions that Asahi brought to Japan, it was lucky to break-even, although the odd one had been profitable. It should also be noted that although Asahi had purchased the rights for a Japanese musical theatre tour, that did not give it the right to broadcast the show on television. The TV rights involved further negotiations of licensing agreements which were even more complex and costly than those of the Japanese tour rights. Usually, after a musical had been televised, the potential for live theatre runs to that audience was limited. Therefore, any royalty payments for television rights had to consider the opportunity costs of losing any subsequent live theatre royalties.

The success of the investment in "The Secret Garden" motivated Kenji and Asahi into becoming more involved in the investment side of the business. One of Kenji's more important associations was with Mr. Landesman, President of Jujamcyn Theatres, who was one of the top Broadway theatre owners that tended to specialize in musicals. Through Kenji's close association with Mr. Landesman, he actively sought new musical productions in which he could invest. This relationship developed into a formal agreement in the early 1990s by which Asahi agreed to invest $1 million annually in Jujamcyn Theatre productions over the next three years. This non-exclusive agreement was due to expire in the next year. Based on this agreement, Asahi, through Kenji, was offered investments in every Broadway musical that Jujamcyn Theatres developed. Kenji would make a decision whether to invest or not, based on Landesman's recommendations. Then Kenji would submit a formal investment proposal to TV Asahi and Asahi would usually take about three to four months to officially give the okay for the investments. So far head office had never said no to a show that Kenji had committed to, and in fact, Kenji often wondered on what basis they would turn down a project that he recommended.

From 1992 to 1996, Kenji had committed Asahi, as producer, to seven musicals. Most of them were profitable and some of them were very successful. During that time, only three musicals were brought to Japan and a fourth was scheduled to begin a Japanese Tour this year (1996). All of the musicals that toured Japan were ones in which Asahi had initially been a producer. Furthermore, during this time, all of the musicals that they had invested in had received some sort of Tony Award whether it be for a singer, song or for the musical itself. The 1992 musical "Guys and Dolls" received the coveted Tony's Best Revival Musical. Clearly, the investment aspect of the business was going very well.

Asahi's success was also due to Kenji's induction as a voting member for the Tonys in 1993, the only Asian to be given such an honor. This provided Kenji with considerable notoriety which allowed him to establish a broad network of relationships in this rather cliquish and exclusive business.

Asahi's managers clearly did not understand the business, but some of them were enjoying the successes of the Theatre division. Presidents of other major Japanese corporations had asked them for tickets to performances. Kenji had also been able to introduce TV Asahi's top executives to several top U.S. executives. For example, the Kennedy Center had been a Jujamycn investor, and when the President of the Kennedy Center, a very well known figure in U.S. business circles, came to Japan, Kenji arranged a dinner with him and the President of TV Asahi. All of this brought considerable honor to TV Asahi top managers. However, Kenji wondered whether this was enough to keep them interested in the business.

Kenji was the principal person behind the success of Asahi's Theatrical Productions investing. He had the contacts and the understanding of the business skills and entrepreneurial attitudes that were necessary in the business. He even had a good sense of humor which stood him in good stead when he had to mix with his business peers in New York. Other than Kenji, the only other employee in Asahi Theatrical Productions was Kenji's assistant, a Japanese woman who looked after office details while Kenji developed business opportunities. Kenji negotiated which musicals they would invest in and usually committed Asahi to a dollar figure for each production. Other legal and financial aspects were handled by either outside help or by TV Asahi in its head office.

THE QUESTION OF THE FUTURE

TV Asahi Theatrical Productions, Inc., had been very profitable in 1995, making a profit of approximately $1.5 million on revenues of about $15 million U.S. Needless to say, such revenues and profits were small when compared to TV Asahi's annual revenues (i.e., the sales were less than one per cent of TV Asahi's revenues). However, in Kenji's eyes there was considerable opportunity for further growth. This included additional investment in musicals, investments in other types of live entertainment, and attempts to move more into the theatre management and creative side of the business. There was also the considerable, yet untapped, opportunity of musicals in the West End Theatres in London. Demand for Broadway musicals had exploded, particularly outside of Broadway and the West End. If Asahi could tap into this growth, it could become a significant player in the business. There was also the potential of trying to integrate the creative and artistic talent represented in this business into the TV business.

The problem was that Kenji and Yasu Kata, his Japanese counterpart, didn't actively support any growth opportunities since Hidedata had retired from TV Asahi, although it had not actively dissuaded growth in the past. Neither Kenji nor Yasu Kata had actively trained others in TV Asahi, so their specialized skills were quite unique. Now, Yasu Kata was scheduled to retire in less than two years and Kenji had inquired about a replacement for Yasu Kata. He found out that TV Asahi had no plans in place for replacing Yasu Kata—in fact they really had not thought about it. Kenji was in his mid-50s and, as a U.S. resident, did not have to, and did not want to, retire at the mandatory Japanese retirement age of 60. He felt that he had considerable energy left to devote to this business over the next decade. Kenji was also involving some young Japanese located in New York, largely university musical and theatre students, in his business dealings and associations. He saw his role as an informal mentor and friend to these Japanese associates, none of whom were formally employed by Asahi.

Unfortunately, Kenji realized that part of the problem was that since Nishimura's retirement neither he nor Yasu Kata had developed a strong set of new relationships with TV Asahi's top managers. Prior to Nishimura's retirement, Kenji had been in constant contact with Nishimura. They both understood the business and the other's desires and attitudes about a decision. However, Kenji had not been a life time employee of TV Asahi, and in fact, had not even been employed with TV Asahi in Japan. This was a disadvantage because he now had few contacts with whom he could develop a relationship in TV Asahi. Not only was he not a TV Asahi person, but he had lived outside of Japan for over three decades.

While Kenji pondered his fate, he wondered what must be going through the minds of the top TV Asahi Executives in Tokyo. They appeared not to understand the business. It represented a relatively small amount of their deployed assets, yet he felt strongly that it could contribute more to TV Asahi's future. Disney Corporation had just invested in a Broadway theatre and some of the other Japanese broadcasting corporations had been actively getting involved in theatre during the last several years.

Two recent musical successes in Japan were motivating other broadcasters to consider this type of unusual and highly desirable source of entertainment as an investment and potential broadcasting opportunity. Asahi had a tremendously successful run of the show "The Secret Garden," which had won a Tony Award prior to its Japanese tour. Then Japan Broadcasting (JBS) invested nearly $2 million in the Broadway show, "The Will Rogers Follies," winner of the 1991 Tony Award for best musical. JBS had negotiated the rights to broadcast the show to its TV audience in late 1995, and it was expected that the show would complete a Japanese tour after its five year stint on Broadway. JBS had accomplished this feat by hiring a New York-based media consultant and paying a lot of money. NTV, a subsidiary of NHK, had also become involved in televising Broadway musicals. They had produced and televised the musical show, "Annie," in Japan solely for the purpose of a television production, and they were continuing to try to work with top directors to find new shows to be televised. Suntory, Inc., Japan's largest liquor company, had also invested in musicals during the past four years. They had developed an agreement with another Broadway and off-Broadway theatre owner, Shubert Theatres. This relationship had produced eight shows including "The Grapes of Wrath," "The Heidi Chronicles," and "City of Angels." Suntory was expected to sign another long-term agreement with Shubert in the upcoming months. The message was quite simple that Japanese money was willing to invest in top Western musicals. It also indicated to Kenji that considerable opportunity existed for this business and his talents within a variety of Japanese companies.

Televising the shows in Japan was viewed as a tremendously risky business. But the financial risks were moderated in some decision maker's eyes by the realization that it would provide recognition and very high advertising ratings to the channel. Financially, some felt that a musical broadcast might break-even if it was combined with an Asian tour followed by an Asian-only broadcast of the show, as long as the show was a hit. However, this was a difficult thing to manage and it clearly posed a variety of risks. The key to any musical was getting the right one. Clearly, the Japanese were most interested in top Broadway and West End musicals. In this regard, the audiences were quite discerning and they knew the difference between a first and second-rate show. In addition, the musicals best suited to Asian audiences were those that had little conversation and lots of music because much of the audience did not understand English.

FUTURE

Every year Asahi had renewed the contract that employed Kenji. However, Kenji was now wondering what the company would do when this year's or possibly next year's contract renewal came up. Furthermore, what should he do? Kenji realized that the key to figuring out what he should do really lay in figuring out what TV Asahi would do, given its options.

Kenji realized that TV Asahi had a variety of options available to it. It could withdraw financial support now; it could do nothing; or it could get actively involved in further developing the Theatrical Production's activities. Ultimately, Asahi's decisions would affect his decision. Yet, there was also the broader question of whether he should be proactive or reactive. These were complex questions with many cultural ambiguities. He knew that he had become partially Western and partially Japanese in his management attitudes, something that made his decision even more complex. Should he manage this situation as a Westerner or as a Japanese manager? He had worked, and he thought he always would work, for a Japanese company, yet he also realized that he would have to continue to work in this business in the U.S. In this regard, his brain was telling him one thing, but his heart was telling him something quite different.

The Richard Ivey School of Business gratefully acknowledges the generous support of the Richard and Jean Ivey Fund in the development of this case.

CASE 25

Selkirk Group in Asia

From their modern brick building in Victoria, Australia, it seemed a long way from the economic crisis that had engulfed Asia in the past 18 months. At one side of the board table sat Bernie Segrave, the Managing Director of the Selkirk Group of Companies and the person who had taken direct charge of the group's export marketing strategy across Asia. On the other side, and with a view of the large brick chimney that announced Selkirk Brick's presence in the local community, sat Peter Blackburn, Export Manager and the person being groomed to progressively take over the exporting responsibilities. Both were looking at the export performance graphs of the group over the past five years as background preparation for their forthcoming trip.

Ahead of them (in late October 1998) was an overseas tour to meet their existing network of agents and potential customers in Singapore, Thailand, Hong Kong and Taiwan. Their largest market, Japan, was not included in this tour. The reasons for the tour were quite straightforward in Segrave's mind:

> We have made a strategic decision to continue developing and building relationships in Asia in these bad times. We went to Japan earlier this year. In this downturn, we are very lucky we have good agents in Japan. If Japan goes, we don't want to think about it—but I guess the rest of the world goes as well.
>
> Asia is very important in the long term because we continue to develop products of excellent technical quality which are appreciated by Asians. It's very important to us in terms of sales and output. Within five years we expect to have either a subsidiary or a selling arm in an Asian destination.

At issue was how to continue developing their business in Asia. Both Segrave and Blackburn were wondering about the business opportunities they would uncover and whether it was time to review their export strategy and organisation for the region.

SELKIRK BRICK—A FAMILY BUSINESS FOR OVER 100 YEARS

Selkirk Brick was established in 1883 when the gold rush in colonial Victoria brought together fortune seekers and entrepreneurs from across the world. Chinese, Scots, Irish and even Californians were among the immigrants who saw the opportunity to prosper in the colony. Among them was Robert Selkirk, a Scottish stonemason, who sought to capitalise on the building boom accompanying the wealth

---

Lambros Karavis prepared this case under the supervision of Professor Paul Beamish solely to provide material for class discussion. The authors do not intend to illustrate either effective or ineffective handling of a managerial situation. The authors may have disguised certain names and other identifying information to protect confidentiality.

Ivey Management Services prohibits any form of reproduction, storage or transmittal without its written permission. This material is not covered under authorization from CanCopy or any reproduction rights organization. To order copies or request permission to reproduce materials, contact Ivey Publishing, Ivey Management Services, c/o Richard Ivey School of Business, The University of Western Ontario, London, Ontario, Canada, N6A 3K7; phone (519) 661-3208; fax (519) 661-3882; e-mail cases@ivey.uwo.ca.

Copyright © 1999, Ivey Management Services.

generated from gold and wool. He started making bricks using a local clay deposit in Allendale but moved to nearby Ballarat in 1900 where suitable clay deposits had been identified on ten hectares of land in Howitt Street, the present-day site of the works and head office.

Though clay bricks and pavers were often seen as a low-tech product, there was, in fact, considerable technical expertise required to produce a high quality product. Apart from selecting the right clays as the raw material for firing into bricks and pavers, a number of other factors needed to be managed carefully. The moisture content in the clay was critical to both moulding and firing outcomes achieved. Various oxides and other additives were used to achieve specific colors and finishes. Kiln temperature, length of time in the kiln and airflows also needed to be carefully controlled to achieve consistency in strength and color characteristics.

The high quality of Australian clay bricks and pavers has led to their extensive use as a building material for external cladding. Many houses had been traditionally built with double brick walls, particularly in the more temperate climate zones in Australia ranging from New South Wales, through Victoria, South Australia and Tasmania (refer to Exhibit 1 for geographic locations in Australia). In recent years, the use of brick had declined as brick veneer, steel frames, timber, concrete and even mud-brick homes gained popularity with the home buyer. Increasingly, clay bricks and pavers were being used as architectural features rather than simply as a construction material.

From a study of the company's history (see Appendix 1), Selkirk Brick could be characterised as a company which was managed in a financially conservative manner but which embraced (world-class at the time) technological innovation to maintain technical superiority and cost efficiency in the marketplace. It was a company which had resisted buyouts and generational fragmentation in the process.

The shareholders were well aware that by the time a family company reached the fifth generation, it was unlikely to accommodate the needs of all who might expect to work there. Robert Selkirk, who became Chairman in 1985 and was in charge of marketing, commented on the roles of the working shareholders:

> It's something that you have to work at every day of your life. There are conflicts; we all see things differently. The challenge is to try to put personal and family disagreements to one side when in the office.

Jim Selkirk, Finance Director since 1986, suggested a few basic requirements for a family company: no gamblers, squanderers or alcoholics; no tendency to over-borrow or be over-acquisitive; be prepared to spend most of your

EXHIBIT 1 GEOGRAPHIC LOCATIONS

time with the company; and no expensive or messy divorces.

Overall, the Selkirk family believed their success stemmed from a number of features: a mix of family and non-family directors, conservative finance, market leadership through technology, maintaining a good reputation in the market and a belief that nothing happens until you make a sale. They saw themselves as adaptable, able to make decisions quickly, having a close rapport with repeat customers, and constantly examining their strategies to produce long-term success.

THE SELKIRK GROUP—DIVERSIFICATION IN THE 1980s AND 1990s

Between 1982 and 1992, the company made three major acquisitions, none of which were cheap but all of which were easily absorbed into the balance sheet:

- Phillips Bricks and Pottery Pty Ltd was acquired in 1982. This Bendigo-based company had a strong market-presence in north-western Victoria and was converted from the traditional extruded to the higher-priced pressed brick production in 1986. (Segrave became Managing Director of Phillips in 1983.)
- In 1987, Selkirk purchased Hick Timbers in Altona (a suburb of Melbourne) in a move that took it outside bricks

but still serving the needs of the building industry. Hick was a specialised supplier of structural timber importing softwoods from the USA, Canada, New Zealand and Finland and supplying engineered timber beams.

■ Shepparton Bricks and Pavers, one of Victoria's largest concrete building and landscaping products manufacturers was acquired in 1992. While Selkirk had been supplying clay pavers since 1983, this acquisition took the company into the less expensive concrete paver business in a booming market for pavers.

At a time when Australian entrepreneurs like (the subsequently convicted) Alan Bond and (the fugitive) Christopher Skase had created conglomerates through leveraged acquisitions, Selkirk Brick had been tempted to the brink of over-expansion, according to Jim Selkirk, but was saved at the eleventh hour by a bidder with deeper pockets. To date, its diversification had been within the confines of its perceived area of expertise, the building industry. Each of the acquisitions was valuable for adding manufacturing capacity and for providing additional sales outlets. Each office and outlet sold the complete range of Selkirk products.

Hick Timbers was closed down in 1997 though the company name was retained. Margins in the timber business were falling for players and the company was being outmuscled in the marketplace by large integrated timber and hardware groups such as Bunnings (which had established a series of home/trade superstores across the Melbourne metropolitan area). The Board of Selkirk had taken a common-sense but courageous strategic decision to quit while they were ahead.

While diversifying through acquisition, Selkirk Brick also embarked on a three-stage, A $5 million program of modernisation between 1982 and 1986 which resulted in world-class product quality outcomes. This investment program involved modernising the processes for extrusion and material preparation in the first stage, improving the productivity and energy efficiency of the drying tunnel in the second stage, and replacing the 25-year-old tunnel kiln with an energy-efficient one in the final stage.

By 1988, pavers had come to represent 20 per cent of the company's production volume and Selkirk Brick was recognised as the only brick company supplying products compliant with Australian Products Standard AS1225. While most of the product sales were in Victoria, the sales region was progressively being extended into the South Australian and New South Wales marketplace where product quality and service were being used to overcome price and transport barriers to competition. Selkirk was reputed to have a 15 per cent share in the Victorian clay building products market and was the largest privately owned brick company in Australia.

Selkirk Brick survived the severe economic recession that hit Victoria in the early 1990s by halving production at one stage and closing one plant for ten months in 1991. By late 1993, utilisation had recovered to 75 per cent and by 1998 the plants were operating again at full capacity. Selkirk Brick acquired Stratblox, a manufacturer of quality concrete building products located in the Gippsland region of Victoria in 1998. This acquisition meant that Selkirk had geographically encircled the Melbourne metropolitan area through a series of country acquisitions and had established itself as the dominant player in rural Victoria.

The capacity of the Selkirk Group of Companies exceeded 70 million bricks and pavers prior to that acquisition. Production capacity at Bendigo was 10 million units (bricks and pavers) per annum while Shepparton capacity was 23,000 tonnes per annum. The Gippsland acquisition added 27,000 tonnes per annum of capacity. Total Victorian sales were in the range of A$25 and A$30 million per annum (refer to Exhibit 2 for external estimates of group revenue). The company employed 170 people, 100 people at the Ballarat head-office and operations alone. With the acquisition of Stratblox, Selkirk Brick could no longer be seen as a specialist clay brick and paver company (refer to Appendix 2 for additional information on the Australian Brick and Paver Industry) but as a more broadly diversified company in the clay and concrete brick and paver business.

Company documents indicate that each of the acquisitions was a wholly owned subsidiary of Selkirk Brick Pty Ltd but they were managed autonomously, each with its own Board of Management and Board of Directors. In 1998, Robert Selkirk was Non-Executive Chairman of the Board, Bernie Segrave was the Managing Director, Jim Selkirk was the Finance Director, and Iain Selkirk was the

EXHIBIT 2   GROUP SALES ESTIMATES

YEAR	SALES REVENUE ($A MILLIONS)
1987/88	$19.9
1988/89	$24.8
1989/90	$25.5
1990/91	$20.7
1991/92	$19.0
1992/93	$23.5
1993/94	$24.9
1994/95	$25.8
1995/96	$23.2
1996/97	$22.2
1997/98	$27.8

Note: Estimates derived from industry data.

Works Director. In 1994, Jamie Selkirk (son of the Chairman) became the first of the fifth-generation to join the family company.

ASIA—A SELKIRK SUCCESS STORY OF THE 1990s

The export trading activities of Selkirk Brick began in earnest in 1992 when Robert Selkirk attended a Global Business Opportunities Convention in Osaka, Japan. A Japanese company had been looking at securing a supply of sandstone from Australia and had seen Selkirk pavers extensively used at Bond University in Queensland. (A major Japanese construction and development company was a joint-venture partner in the university at the time). Selkirk pavers had been selected for their ability to withstand the high traffic and high humidity requirements of Australia's first private university in 1988. Following a visit of Japanese personnel to the plant in Ballarat, a trading alliance was formed and Selkirk began to export to Japan. As Robert Selkirk reminded people within the company, not everybody had approved of the move at the time:

> Six years ago, we wouldn't have believed where we are now. It was all done on an exploratory "try it and see" basis. We had (Prime Minister) Paul Keating telling us that Australian companies had to be in Asia. There was considerable criticism at the time on the expense and management attention being directed to the export efforts. We were advised that we had to be patient. Then we got the first order within twelve months and it was done on a handshake.

Total exports had grown strongly from the first export order to Japan of 49,000 paving units (approximately six containers) in 1992. Exports to all destinations increased by 735 per cent in 1993, followed by a 69 per cent increase in 1994 and a 150 per cent increase in 1995. Flat sales in 1996 and 1997 were followed by a massive increase in 1998 to approximately four million units. While initial sales were to Japan, by 1998 Selkirk Brick was exporting pavers and some bricks across Asia to countries such as Hong Kong ('94) and Taiwan ('96) as well as Singapore, Indonesia, New Zealand and Malaysia. Japan was the largest export destination but healthy sales were beginning to be experienced in Taiwan where product quality and service were considered to be key selling features.

By 1998, Asian exports had become a small but increasingly important part of Selkirk Brick's business. Exports accounted for just under 10 per cent of total sales volume (slightly higher in terms of sales value) in the 1997/98 financial year and that figure was expected to increase. Well over 25 per cent of paver manufacturing volume was now being exported. The clay paver market had been facing low growth and market share losses in the highly competitive Australian market to cheaper pavers made from concrete and other composite materials. Exports were an important sales outlet for the company.

Selkirk had a policy of appointing non-exclusive distributor agents in the marketplace and currently had 18 distributors across Asia: five in Japan, four in Hong Kong, three in Taiwan, two in Singapore, and one each in Malaysia, Indonesia, Thailand and New Zealand. Letters from overseas parties interested in purchasing directly and offering their local services were inevitably referred back to the nearest agent. Product was usually sold C.I.F. (Cost, Insurance and Freight to Destination Port). Prices ex-factory and loaded into containers were generally 70 per cent of the C.I.F. price. Anecdotal data suggested that a unit price of A$0.47 F.O.B. (Free on Board at Shipping Port) for shipped products could be sold for as high as A$2.00 per unit in Japan to end-users (refer to Exhibit 3 for Export Pricing Nomenclature and Value-Added). The use of agents did mean, however, that there was a lack of information on who was the ultimate user of products and what margins were being charged locally.

EXHIBIT 3
EXPORT PRICING NOMENCLATURE AND VALUE-ADDED

Ex-factory gate Goods in vehicle at factory gate.	A$3500/container
Free alongside ship (F.A.S.) Goods unloaded off vehicle on wharf at port of origin.	A$3800/container
Free on-board (F.O.B.) Goods loaded on vessel at port of origin.	A$4000/container
Cost, insurance and freight (C.I.F.) Goods on vessel at port of destination with insurance premiums included.	A$5000/container
Market price Price of goods at final consumer market.	A$12000 to $17500/container

Information on the clay brick and paver market across Asia was otherwise limited and generally anecdotal in nature. Housing construction materials varied considerably across the region and clay bricks were not traditionally used. Local brick manufacturers in countries such as Malaysia ran "cottage-industry" facilities using kilns with inadequate temperature controls and with a poor understanding of quality control mechanisms. Brick walls were often rendered and thus considered a "filler" material which did not require high quality standards. Clay brick and pavers were being increasingly seen in large "upper middle class" housing estates across the region where developers were taking the lead in developing suburban housing and shopping communities.

Exports to the region came from a number of countries, with Canada, the United States, the United Kingdom, South Africa and Australia mentioned frequently. Export data often lumped clay bricks and pavers with other construction materials such as timber and composite materials. The Australian data on exports were derived from shipping data collected at ports of origin but some ports used different classification methods, making accurate information difficult to ascertain. Australian brick and paver products were reputed to have more durability, better water repelling capability and more vibrant color attributes than the cheaper product sourced from local or imported Asian producers.

SALES DISTRIBUTION AGREEMENT IN JAPAN

Exports to Japan had grown steadily from 900,000 units in 1995/96 to 1.8 million units in 1996/97 and 3.5 million units in 1997/98. One reason for the growth was a five-year distribution agreement that had been signed in 1997 with a leading Japanese building products company and that agreement was expected to triple current export figures within two years. Segrave commented on his experiences in doing business with their Japanese agents:

We find the Japanese are very tough negotiators—but also very fair. We are thrilled they fully appreciate the technical qualities of our products. So often here in Australia, aesthetic requirements dominate a specifier's consideration. Mind you, we have been developing a clay brick with smaller width dimensions and new colors to suit the Japanese market (in conjunction with the Stonehenge Group, a major builder in urban Victoria). Our wide variety of pavers and special shapes also meets their needs.

Understand that the Japanese do not tolerate mediocrity which means you must send your most senior people to negotiate with them. In 1992 we had employed a retired General Manager of a large clay brick and paver company in Western Australia who had the requisite seniority, technical

knowledge and excellent sales skills to become our first Export Manager.

One must also be courteous, pleasant and respectful with the Japanese and become practised in Nemawashi: the art of building relationships and personal trust over time. Our success can be measured by the fact that the 1997 distributor agreement had everybody from the Managing Director down to the most senior functional managers attending the Agreement Signing ceremony. What may look like a simple commercial arrangement to us was a symbol of strategic intent and business partnering in their eyes.

While exact details of the 1997 Sales License Agreement were confidential, certain aspects of the Agreement have been disclosed (refer to Appendix 3).

Selkirk retained the brand and trademark for its range of products in Japan, prohibited the transfer of distribution rights to other companies without its approval, had the ability to terminate the agreement with 90 days' notice and ensured any arbitration was done through "officially approved" channels. The term of the agreement was for five years and required 90 days' written notice on either side to terminate. Advertising and sales promotions in Japan were at the expense of the agent.

The Japanese agent had secured a number of conditions in the agreement as well. No new agents were to be appointed without their prior agreement. The primary language of the agreement was English but it was to be interpreted under Japanese commercial law. The bricks and pavers were to carry a Japanese logo and meet the requirements of the Japanese Industrial Standard but to be labelled as "Made in Australia." All products were to be inspected and certified by Selkirk Brick as meeting the product and shipping standards specified in the agreement, with the agent being able to reject shipments in Japan if these conditions were not met.

THE EXPORT FUNCTION IN SELKIRK BRICK

The Group Managing Director, Bernie Segrave, was directly responsible for overseeing all export matters including communication with the main agents, creating new relationships across Asia and being one-half of the trade show that travelled to Asia every four to five months. He spent approximately 15 per cent of his time on export-related matters across a year but this time allocation varied between 100 per cent and zero per cent on a weekly basis. Having started in sales and marketing with Selkirk Brick in 1968, Segrave brought significant experience and credibility to the role. He reported directly to the Board of Directors (see Exhibit 4: Organisation Chart).

EXHIBIT 4 ORGANISATIONAL CHART

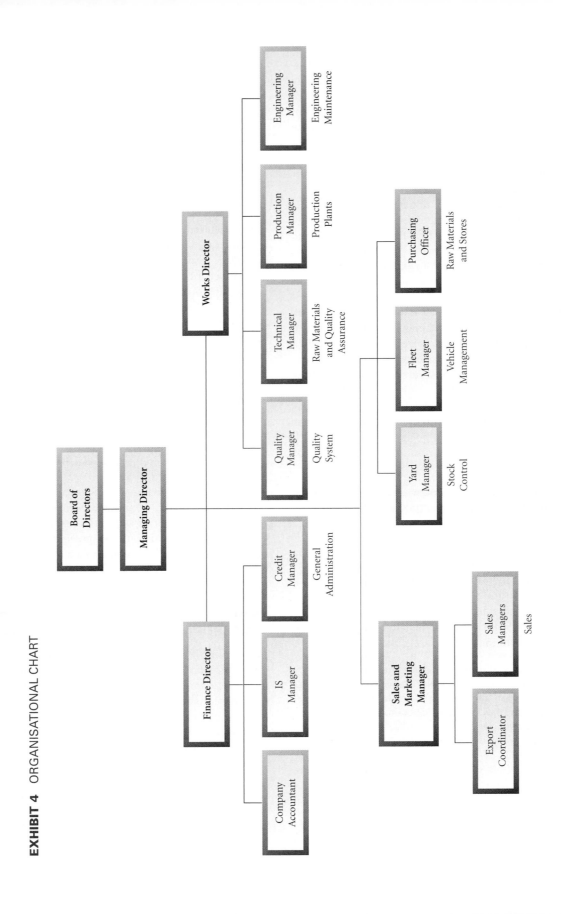

The Export Manager, Peter Blackburn, spent between five and 20 per cent of his time on export matters during the course of a week. He reported directly to the Group Managing Director on these export matters. The rest of the time, Blackburn was officially the Regional Sales Manager for Western Victoria. In addition to maintaining relationships with agents across Asia, Blackburn was involved in developing products for export markets and ensuring that products exported met the highest technical standards. One of his current projects was working with an Australian residential building group to develop smaller, thinner bricks for the Japanese market.

Blackburn had joined Selkirk Brick four years ago though he had extensive industry experience with NuBrik. He was in the process of gradually assuming responsibility for all export business matters and had accompanied Segrave on all the recent overseas export development tours. In his view, Selkirk had been successful in Asia because it spent time building relationships with its agents, delivered products required in the marketplace on the basis of technical excellence and service rather than price alone, was committed to helping agents secure orders and maintained face-to-face relationships in order to avoid "long-distance communications and language" barriers.

Assisting the senior export marketing duo was Clare McGuinness, Export and Agency Sales Coordinator, who spent some 80 per cent of her time specifically on export matters. Among her responsibilities were receiving export orders, arranging all aspects of an export order (stock, shipping, letters of credit and export documents) and preparing all correspondence for Segrave on export related matters. All product for export markets was palletised and containerised at the brick yard adjacent to the head office in Ballarat. Selecting the appropriate bricks and pavers to ensure that they met required quality and aesthetic standards was considered to be critical in meeting customer needs. The Yard Stock Controller, Steve Banks, played an important role in this.

Overseas trips to visit agents and develop new business opportunities were generally scheduled every four to five months with Segrave and Blackburn travelling together to visit two to three countries over a two- or three-week period. Accompanying them on these trips was a technical reference manual, "The Selkirk Technical Advantage," that contained over 400 pages of technical specifications, photos of significant building projects where Selkirk bricks and pavers had been used across Asia, and a whole range of information on Frequently Asked Questions. This manual was provided for the exclusive use of agents in each country as a selling tool but was not to be distributed further.

The cost of these overseas trips was substantial for a small family-owned company, each in the range of A$15,000 to $25,000 depending upon the countries visited and the length of the trip. Typically, these trips involved more than meeting with existing agents. They included talking to customers, meeting with architects and providing technical information on products and services offered. Often these visits coincided with local trade fairs and with Austrade government missions to specific countries. The company tried to see each overseas agent at least once per annum. Most of the agents had visited Selkirk Brick's operations at head-office at least once and some of the Japanese agents had visited three or four times each.

LOOKING TO THE FUTURE OF ASIA

The future of the Australian export business to Asia was in some doubt in early October 1998. According to the internationally respected newsmagazine *Business Week*, Asia was experiencing a widespread social backlash to the collapsing economic situation and stringent conditions imposed by the IMF (International Monetary Fund). The headlines of one issue (August 17, 1998) were quite pointed:

- Joblessness is soaring in Japan.
- Bitterness is growing in Korea.
- Political opposition is rallying in Thailand.
- Will the repercussions of recession scuttle Asia's economic reforms?

The Asian crisis had, in fact, spread to create global financial risk from collapsing economies and the flight of capital needed to underpin economic growth. Malaysia had already imposed currency controls on the Ringgit and in China there was strong evidence that Beijing was resorting to import controls and other measures to keep the Asian crisis at bay. Indonesia was still an open currency economy (despite moves earlier that year to establish a Currency Board) but the value of the Rupiah (R12,000 to the US$1.00) meant that imports were effectively priced out of the market.

During the months of August and September, the Australian dollar had suffered a significant decline against the U.S. dollar, dropping to a low of US$0.56 per A$1.00 before recovering to US$0.63. In 1997 the Australian dollar had traded at US$0.73. Though not suffering as high a devaluation as the Thai Baht or the Indonesian Rupiah, the Australian dollar had devalued in line with the decline in the Japanese Yen and Korean Won against the U.S. dollar because Japan and South Korea were the major export market destinations for Australian products. The Australian balance-of-trade data suggested that a falling Australian dollar rate and an aggressive shift to European and North American markets had reduced the (potentially negative) impact of the Asian crisis on the Australian economy.

In this global economic context, the prospects for future export business were difficult to predict. Segrave was expecting a large export order from the Greater China triangle (China, Hong Kong and Taiwan) but the strength of home startups in the local building industry in Victoria meant that export orders would be competing with local orders in the short term. The forthcoming trip would be useful in providing first-hand evidence on the future prospects for their export business across Asia. This would be another factor to consider in developing a strategy and organisational structure for their Asian export business.

At this stage, Selkirk did not have any licensing agreements, joint-venture operations or subsidiaries overseas. Segrave thought it was an interesting question:

> These types of strategic alliances are all useful. In fact, we have a new product right now which we are considering licensing to Asian companies.
>
> We would consider a licensing agreement (for bricks and pavers) if someone wanted to do it on their own in Asia. We would joint-venture if that was more appropriate (and it was commercially viable). These both have great benefits as we don't really know much about the Asian marketplace. Establishing an Asian subsidiary would depend upon the state of our core business in Australia.

It also depends upon the state of Asia and the business opportunities that arise. We have thought of dedicating one plant here in Ballarat to meeting (the higher standard) needs of the Asian marketplace. This would allow us to ensure product quality and still take advantage of our unique clay deposits.

Thus far Selkirk Brick had concentrated on exporting product to Asia and using existing production capacity to meet market needs. The current strategy of appointing export agents made sense in that context.

Nevertheless, there was some concern that increasing exports to the region and a future recovery of the Asian marketplace would change the economics of competing locally as brick and paver utilisation increased. In that case, product and brand licensing would become attractive alternatives and technical support agreements would become viable. Segrave was also concerned that new technologies could make "mini-kilns" economically viable and change the economic attractiveness of local production. This would require a change not only in their international export strategy but also to their whole way of doing business in Asia.

The Richard Ivey School of Business gratefully acknowledges the generous support of The Richard and Jean Ivey Fund in the development of this case.

APPENDIX 1   HISTORICAL HIGHLIGHTS OF SELKIRK BRICK

Extracted from a profile of Selkirk Brick, one of eight companies examined by Edna Carew and published in *Family Business: The Story of Successful Family Companies in Australia*.

- In 1883, Robert Selkirk began making bricks using a clay deposit in Allendale, Victoria. Bricks were hand-made using moulds. A brick press and engine purchased in 1892 signalled the beginning of mechanised production.
- In 1905, Selkirk was using coal-fired kilns to produce five brick types in batches. During that year, they began continuous firing of bricks on a three-shift, 24-hour, seven-day a week basis.
- In 1921, James Selkirk assumed control of Selkirk Brick (upon the death of his father) and was assisted by Bill Gillman, his brother-in-law, as company secretary.
- In 1935, James Selkirk suffered a heart attack and was ultimately succeeded by his two sons, Bill and Ron Selkirk. They managed the business until they enlisted and handed over control to Bill Gillman (Uncle Willy) during the war years.
- The post-WWII years saw Bill and Ron return to the family business, with Bill managing operations and staffing while Ron handled management and accounting.
- The late '40s and '50s were years of a great (re)building boom for Australia and Selkirk often needed to resort to a lottery to allocate bricks to customers. Innovation was central to its continued success; mechanised claypit in 1952, forklifts in 1953, its own transport company in 1954, "packaged" bricks in 1955 and the appointment of its first Sales Rep in 1959.
- By 1962, the brick works was completely redeveloped and a tunnel-kiln was built that allowed a clean-burning butane gas and an automated plant, both of which substantially enhanced the quality of bricks produced but also left the company with debt that stretched it financially for the next decade.
- During the '60s, the boom market evaporated and Selkirk Brick began to market its bricks across state boundaries into New South Wales and Canberra (the national capital). In 1969, Bill and Ron Selkirk became joint chairmen of the company.
- In 1974, production capacity was doubled to 50 million bricks a year with Plant No. 2 commissioned in Ballarat and in 1978 the fourth generation of Selkirks (Robert, Iain and Jim) was appointed to the Board.
- Bill and Ron Selkirk retired from day-to-day management in 1981; Ian McCoy (who had joined the company in 1951) became Chairman and several other long-term employees, who had joined the Board in 1969, were also promoted.

The Australian clay brick industry was small, accounting for 0.09 per cent of GDP in 1997/98. Products included clay bricks and pavers used in new housing construction (70 per cent), housing renovations (15 per cent) and commercial construction (15 per cent). The state of New South Wales had the largest market share (36.3 per cent) followed by Queensland (18.9 per cent), Western Australia (17 per cent) and Victoria (16.9 per cent). Exports were low at 2.3 per cent of turnover in 1997/98 and imports were negligible.

MARKET DEMAND AND PRICES

Industry turnover reached $906 million in 1992/93 but then declined to $728 million in 1996/97 before climbing to $780 million in 1997/98. Clay brick production was estimated to be 1,532 million bricks in 1997/98. Approximately 87 per cent of housing was constructed using clay brick (typically as brick veneer, with the external walls using brick and interior walls using plaster or fibre board). Premium bricks (used in exterior walls) cost approximately $500 per 1,000 bricks while seconds (used as fill-in) cost in the order of $300 per 1,000. Pavers represented 15 per cent of production but less than 10 per cent of sales revenue.

The outlook for 1998/99 was for a solid increase in sales to $880 million due to a strong residential housing construction demand fuelled by low mortgage interest rates, a strong domestic economy (despite the Asian crisis) and widespread concerns that the proposed 10 per cent value-added tax in July 2000 would increase housing costs. (Clay bricks and pavers were currently exempt from wholesale sales tax.) The long-term market demand was expected to decline as new materials (concrete bricks, steel panels, and prestressed concrete) and new construction techniques (steel frames in particular) acted as substitutes. Steel-framed buildings using steel or corrugated iron cladding were reputed to cost about two-thirds the cost of brick-veneer.

Prices across markets were believed to be stable with competition based on product differentiation and distribution networks. High transportation costs and fear of price wars in a concentrated marketplace led to careful geographic competition. The industry cost structure had been estimated as follows:

- Material purchases   9%
- Electricity and fuel   12%
- Freight and cartage   8%
- Repairs and maintenance   7%
- Wages and salaries   22%
- Other (overheads/profits)   42%

INDUSTRY COMPETITION

Industry concentration was considered to be relatively high with the top five competitors accounting for 85 per cent of sales: the top four competitors also accounted for 35 of the 75 enterprise units in the Australian market.

COMPANY	MARKET SHARE	INDUSTRY REVENUE
Boral Limited	33%	$235 million
CSR Limited	21%	$150 million
Pioneer International	13%	$95 million
Futuris Limited	10%	$72 million
Brickworks Limited	8%	$56 million

The industry could be divided into three strategic groups:

National Competitors   Boral, Pioneer and CSR were competitors nationally with operations in a number of states. They were all diversified building products companies with manufacturing interests in related markets and with significant overseas manufacturing interests. Boral and CSR were each reported to have brick manufacturing capacity of 500 to 550 million bricks across Australia. Boral, Pioneer and CSR had recently been penalised by the Australian Consumer and Competition Commission for collusive pricing in the Queensland cement market.

Regional Competitors   Futuris (Western Australia), Brickworks (NSW/Queensland) and Selkirk (Victoria) were considered to be regional players. They were specialist clay brick and paver companies, with a number of plants and brands under their umbrella. Futuris had a manufacturing capacity of 200 million bricks.

Local Competitors   A number of small companies with local distribution and very small production capacities. Pioneer was the dominant player in Victoria with a 50 per cent market share followed by Boral with 25 per cent. Victoria's share of national production had fallen from 21 per cent in 1990/91 to less than 17 per cent in 1993/94. Overcapacity was considered to be high. Production in 1997/98 had reached 2177 million bricks.

INTERNATIONAL BUSINESS

Australian bricks were gaining export markets across Asia due to their natural colors and strength. Boral was successfully exporting through its Western Australian subsidiary, Midland Bricks. Exports had risen to $14.9 million in 1993/94 but had fallen subsequently to $14.0 million in 1994/95 and remained at that level in the two years that followed. The three largest companies all had overseas brick-making operations though the scale and importance of these varied considerably.

APPENDIX 3
OUTLINE OF
DISTRIBUTOR
SALES AGREEMENT

1.1	Definitions
1.2	Appointment period
1.3	Terms and conditions of sale
1.4	Trademarks
1.5	Advertising and sales promotions
1.6	Management reports
1.7	Product specifications
1.8	Acceptance test and inspections
1.9	Termination, extensions and revisions
1.10	Transfer of rights
1.11	Business secrecy
1.12	Force majeure
1.13	Arbitration
1.14	Notice addresses
1.15	Governing laws

Sportsmake: A Crisis of Succession

For almost a year following Jim Claymore's death in the crash of his private plane outside Las Vegas, Sportsmake, the sport equipment company he founded and ran, remained rudderless. Claymore was a legend in the industry. A champion pentathlon athlete, he believed that high quality sports equipment at affordable prices should be made available to what he called the "serious non-athlete": the person who pursued athletic activities intensively but non-competitively.

Out of this vision emerged a range of products, some proprietary and other licensed, which gained a reputation for performance and durability. The company outsourced all its manufacturing, but kept rigorous controls over its designs and quality. As Claymore was fond of telling his staff: "I am comfortable with letting others take the manufacturing margins. Our advantage is in the loop we create between the serious non-athlete and the retailer. So keep your eye on potential equipment for the serious non-athlete and spend your energies convincing the retailer that the equipment we are developing will be a best seller."

The company grew rapidly from sales of $200,000 in 1974, to $20 million in 1984, to current sales of $120 million. In 1996 the company went public. Claymore used the injection of capital to acquire Sportsmake's first retail operation: Hike and Bike—a chain of stores specialising in the newly emerging area of leisure camping and biking. The success of this acquisition led to other acquisitions, not all of them successful. Perhaps the biggest gamble was the acquisition in 1997 of the giant Winter Sportsworld for

$400 million. The acquisition put considerable strain on Sportsmake's resources, and proved to be a harder operation to integrate into Sportsmake's ethos and methods of doing business than originally anticipated.

Claymore was known to be a demanding but generous boss. Alternately tyrannical and charming, he frequently popped into people's offices for an informal chat. His subordinates dreaded these chats, but also admitted that they felt strangely elated and energised by the visits. Joe Murphy, a marketing manager in the outdoor sports division, described these chats as ". . . a mixture of third-degree questioning by the police and an encounter with a bible thumping evangelist." "You feared what he will find out, but you also felt enthused by his approval. It was quite an experience. . . ".

Immediately after the funeral, the board turned to Roy Claymore, the founder's son, as a possible successor. He took over as interim CEO and did his best to ensure continuity. However, it quickly became clear that his heart was not in it. He notified the board that he intended to step down by the end of the year to resume his former career as medical researcher at the University of South Carolina. With Roy out of the picture, the board began to consider other candidates to head the company. A number of names were brought forward, but after a brief discussion only two remained: Tony Petroski, vice president in charge

Case written by Joseph Lampel, City University Business School, London. Copyright © Joseph Lampel, 2002.

of marketing, and Marcia Davenport, vice president in charge of finance.

The contrast between the two candidates could hardly be greater. Petroski had spent all his career in Sportsmake; starting as a sales clerk at the age of 17, and ending as vice president of corporate marketing thirty-two years later at the age of 49. Davenport, on the other hand, had only recently arrived at Sportsmake. She began as assistant to Stanley Cramer, Sportsmake's vice president of finance in 1993, and had upon his retirement four years later been given the top finance job in the company.

Petroski's ethos if not his entire personality had been shaped by his years in the company. He first came to the notice of Jim Claymore when, while taking his annual holidays in the Swiss Alps, he managed to obtain a contract for Sportsmake's new high performance skis from one of Switzerland's most exclusive ski resorts. He was subsequently promoted to head the winter sports division, and within five years of his appointment he doubled the sales of the division from 20 million to 40 million.

Petroski's greatest coup as head of winter sports was masterminding the company's entry into the snowboarding market. Petroski was among the first in the United States to detect the potential of snowboarding as a mass sport. After a trip to a ski resort in Vermont he came back to Denver full of enthusiasm for the new sport. He instructed his development team to drop their work on special composite skis and instead concentrate their efforts on designing a snowboard. His staff was accustomed to Toni's "wild ideas," but this time they thought he had truly gone over the edge. As Jack Rorty, chief equipment designer, recollected many years later: "some of us were willing to concede that it was possible to downhill on one ski without breaking your neck, but even these people felt that the demand for such equipment was limited. We were dealing with a fad—a winter sport version of the hula hoop. Making high performance skis was our real business, and any distraction was going to cost us dearly."

Petroski had the last laugh on the sceptics. Sportsmake's "Quickboard" became one of the division's most profitable products. It set new industry standards, and was the preferred equipment in many snowboarding competitions.

The episode cemented Petroski's reputation as a man with an uncanny talent for spotting new products. When Jack Lindsay, who ran corporate marketing since 1967 died suddenly in 1987, he was the natural choice for the job. Jim Claymore delivered the news in person. Shaking Petroski's hand he remarked: "Well Toni, the fun is over. Now all you have to do is learn to stomach the bad coffee at head office with the rest of us."

If Petroski was the quintessential company man, Davenport embodied the spirit of the professional man-

ager. Born in California to an affluent real estate developer father and a paediatrician mother, Davenport earned an undergraduate degree in Economics in Berkley before joining one of the leading retail banks in the San Francisco area. After five years during which she rose to the position of manager of small business loans, she headed east to pursue MBA studies at the Wharton Business School.

Later she often reflected with some nostalgia on her time at the Wharton school. She stood out as one of the brightest and most energetic students, and in spite of the heavy load she found time to extracurricular activities. Every afternoon she took two hours off to jog and swim, and on weekends she often went on long hikes with her boyfriend (later her husband), John Mercner.

Mercner was in the midst of his law studies at the University of Pennsylvania law school when the couple met. They decided to look for a job in the New York area. He accepted a position in one of New York's most prestigious law firms, and she accepted a position in the finance department of one of the largest department stores in the city. Their careers, however, did not prosper equally. He found the pressure stifling, and it was increasingly clear that he was not going to make partner. She, on the other hand, rose rapidly to become assistant to the vice president in charge of finance. After five years of enjoying life in New York, they both accepted that the time had come to move on. Although Mercner had a number of offers, the best one came from Smith, Prizker, and Cohen, a Denver law firm specialising in energy and transportation. Davenport had a number of offers—none compared with her New York position. After considering the offers, she settled for a position as assistant to the Vice President in charge of finance in Sportsmake.

Davenport knew that accepting Sportsmake's offer was a gamble. Traditionally Sportsmake promoted from within. It was well known that Claymore scrutinised each candidate personally, and that he gave disproportionate weight to such things as a person's competitive spirit and commitment to sports. Rumour even had it that managers had been denied promotion because Claymore thought they were mediocre skiers or handled their tennis racquet poorly. In her interview with Claymore, Davenport noticed little emphasis on her athletic activities. They chatted briefly in passing about Davenport's addiction to jogging, but in general the conversation revolved around Davenport's New York experience. Like many people before her, Davenport found the interview exhausting yet exhilarating. Ultimately, Claymore's persuasive powers overcame her hesitations and she accepted the offer.

Davenport did not regret her decision. Almost immediately after being hired she was put in charge of what is arguably the most important financial decision in the history of Sportsmake: the decision to go public. Working closely with Claymore, she planned and executed the public offering of Sportsmake's shares. The share began trading at 7 1/4 and within seven months it had moved up to 9 1/2. Following this success, Davenport became deeply involved in the company's acquisition strategy. She spent much time investigating acquisition targets. Her reports and presentations were highly prized by Claymore who came to rely on her observations and advice. When Stanley Cramer retired in 1997, no one was surprised when she was promoted as his successor. From her new position she not only supervised routine financial matters, but also became deeply involved in corporate strategy, in particular the integration of Winter Sportsworld, and much discussed and considerably delayed reorganisation of Sportsmake.

If a company can be said to hold its collective breath, then Sportsmake was certainly doing just that on the morning of Friday the 26th of November when the board of directors met to discuss and render their decision. For some the choice was clear. Petroski was the embodiment of Sportsmake, and the natural successor in both spirit and talents to the legendary Claymore. For others, however, Petroski was an embodiment of what Sportsmake was rather than what it should become. The future, these people felt, lay with Sportsmake under Davenport—a diversified sports equipment firm which is in the process of transforming itself into a modern and professionally managed corporation.

S.A. Chupa Chups

ACHIEVING DOMESTIC MARKET LEADERSHIP

What is the key to such sweet success? Chupa Chups are just better.

—*Enrique Bernat*

The company's success story begins with the vision and drive of Chupa Chups founder and president, Enrique Bernat Fontlladosa. He was born in Barcelona in 1924 into a family with a confectionery tradition. His grandfather had one of the first sweet manufacturing plants in Spain, and his father and uncles had confectionery shops in Barcelona.

During the tough post–Civil War period in Spain, Bernat combined his studies with an apprenticeship in a retail store. In 1955 he travelled to Asturias (central-north Spain) to work as general manager for a sweets manufacturer. The company, S.A. Granja Asturias, was founded in 1940 but was experiencing financial difficulties. About 18 months after his appointment the company started to flourish and the first profits were reported. Bernat chose this moment to propose a radical change in strategy: instead of producing hundreds of different sweets for one market, would the company consider producing just one product for several markets? It was necessary to find an innovative product for the Spanish market. It would have to add something new to the end-customer (the child) and, principally, to the buyer (the mother). Bernat remembered how children were admonished because they had stained their hands, faces and clothes with their sweets. He pro-posed the idea of a sweet on a stick—what is now known around the world as a lollipop.

The board took a sceptical view of this plan, judging it to be the madness of an ambitious youngster. But Bernat had faith in his idea, so progressively he bought the shares of the company. In 1957, he took over as the sole share-holder. The first lollipop, under the Chups brand, was introduced in 1958. Triggered by the success of the first radio commercial where the musical slogan prompted "Chupa un Chups" ("suck a sucker"), the product name was changed three years later to Chupa Chups.

THE PRODUCT

An early technical difficulty in developing the product was the quality of the stick. It had to be strong enough to resist manipulation but soft enough not to hurt the child's mouth. In a period when Spain was still largely closed to foreign trade, Bernat found the quality of wood required in Central Europe. Later, in 1960, when plastics technology was developed, the company was one of the first in the

This case was written by Regina S. Kilfoyle, Sloan Fellow of the London Business School, under the supervision and guidance of Professor Sumantra Ghoshal. The research support of Norma Enright, Juan F. Iturri and Wolf Waschkuhn—all students in the LBS Sloan Fellowship Programme—is gratefully acknowledged, as is the advice of Mr. Dominic Houlder and the co-operation of the management and staff of S.A. Chupa Chups.

© London Business School, 1996.

world to develop a plastic stick that was safer and more resistant to splintering than wood. In another innovation in 1962, the first whistling lollipop in the market was introduced. A version of this lollipop, "Melody Pop," was still being sold around the world in the mid-1990s.

Product adaptation has been kept to the minimum, but some local tastes have prevailed over the decades. For example, sugar-free lollipops sell well in Scandinavia, while Finnish consumers snap up the salted liquorice pops developed specifically for them. Japanese buyers enjoy the original flavours, but a recently developed green tea flavour is now popular, while in China lighter colours are considered lucky. For the Saharan Desert region, the company adjusts its formulas of natural ingredients to prolong product shelf-life. Wrappers and presentation materials also are adapted by printing in the languages of the many local markets.

There have been very few complaints about the company's products. Indeed, it is only when Chupa Chups is completely confident about its quality that a new product is introduced under the Chupa Chups brandname. One of the very few complaints they have received was from a New York woman who claimed to have fallen because she slipped on a Chupa Chups stick. She requested $500 as compensation and without further investigation, the company paid up.

PROCESS TECHNOLOGY

The popularity of Chupa Chups quickly grew in the company's early years, with production averaging circa 3,000 kg per day, and a corresponding increase in the number of points of sale. Having developed the product, Bernat decided that the company had to develop its own process technology. In order to do this Chupa Chups bought a company in the metal-mechanic sector called Construcciones Mecánicas Seuba. The name was subsequently changed to Confipack.

Within a few years Confipack developed the machinery, first, to produce spherical sweets, later, a "hole puncher" to introduce the stick, and, lastly, the paper wrapping machine which enabled production capacity to expand from 500 to 4,800 units per hour. This technology enabled production to reach 4,500 kg/day in the early 1960s, the equivalent to 80 million Chupa Chups per year, and a turnover of 28 million ptas (nearly US $500,000).

MARKETING AND DISTRIBUTION

The company started advertising its product very early in its life through radio and later TV campaigns, as well as through intensive use of point-of-sale publicity. In 1969

Chupa Chups commissioned the renowned Catalán artist Salvador Dalí with the design of its brilliant red and yellow wrapper, an identifying mark that has been adapted to local markets and continues to be used today.

In an unusual move, the company developed its own distribution system. During this period an innovative system of "cash on delivery" was instituted. The sales representative travelled with supplies of the product, executing the sale, delivery and cash settlement simultaneously. Following a careful adaptation of inexpensive SEAT cars, salesmen were able to carry sufficient volume to visit between 40 to 50 customers a day. To facilitate the cash settlement, the product was packaged in envelopes of 140 units with a price of 100 ptas, thus eliminating the need to give change to the retailer. This sales and distribution system proved to be vital in enabling the rapid expansion of the company in Spain. In 1962, the company instituted a parallel distribution system for the whistling pop which mirrored this format. The director of Coca Cola in Spain was recruited to manage these successful distribution operations.

MOVING BEYOND HOME SHORES

In 1968 we made our first visit to Japan, making contacts with Japanese manufacturers/distributors who were very surprised to meet a Spaniard selling sweets on a chop stick. It took a long time for the Japanese to overcome their initial revulsion to sucking in public to become one of Chupa Chups' biggest customers.

—Enrique Bernat

With a dominant presence in the Spanish market, the company faced a dilemma concerning further growth. The options were either to leverage the existing national distribution network to diversify into other confectionery and food products, or to develop new geographic markets which would enable the sale of a narrow product range such as Chupa Chups.

Chupa Chups elected the latter course. The company began exporting to France, replicating its successful distribution system which it built in partnership with a French manufacturer. The partner was reimbursed by Chupa Chups via combined payments for products sold plus shipping costs according to weight. Two hundred French salesmen in small cars quickly gained Chupa Chups a strong share of the French lollipop market. Its distribution partner was soon exposed as a cheat, however. The French company was weighting the Chupa Chups containers with stones to inflate its reimbursement.

Chupa Chups management bided its time, establishing alternative systems before responding with legal action.

This situation, in combination with the 20 per cent export fees imposed by the Franco government in Spain, had persuaded Chupa Chups management to begin some manufacturing abroad. In 1970, the company offered to purchase the facilities and brandname of a renowned but bankrupt French confectionery company. But the French courts blocked the sale, citing the potential for a lollipop monopoly! Nevertheless, Chupa Chups eventually bought a large share in this company while acquiring another suitable plant in Bayonne for production of Chupa Chups branded products intended for EC countries.

GROWING PAINS

During the years 1960–67, Chupa Chups followed an expansion plan in Spain, France, Germany and the United States, replicating the formula of a single appealing, top-quality product distributed by its own salesforce. In 1966, the first foreign commercial office was opened in the Champs Elysées in Paris, followed by an office in New York one year later. By 1968, the first foreign wholly-owned subsidiary, Société Bernat et Cie, was established in France.

During this period, Chupa Chups also was looking eastwards. It entered the Japanese market in 1968. The company contemplated entering the Chinese market, but the Cultural Revolution of 1967 put a hold on this move.

These ambitious expansion plans met more than one setback along the way, however. While experiencing success in France, despite the vagaries of its partnership, the company's first entry into the German market was a failure. The company exited after one year, although it re-entered in 1970 and Germany has since emerged as one of Chupa Chups' largest markets, served through its subsidiary Uniconfis GmbH.

After some trial and error, the Chupa Chups formula also met great success in the United States. New York was to be the test case, and it provided a salutary lesson. Perhaps naively, the company saw the United States and New York as culturally similar to Spain. A Cuba-born distributor was chosen, and soon he was managing a large group of salesmen who were in touch with the vast numbers of corner shops in the city. The salesmen were remunerated with a small base salary and a sales-based commission. The direct sales system took hold just as in Europe. But soon after, although sales flattened, the salesmen continued working without complaint. Puzzled by this behaviour, Enrique Bernat made an unscheduled midnight trip to New York. He found a distribution system which had been adapted to the sale of marijuana! Chupa Chups selected another distributor.

1968–87: SOME STRUCTURAL CHANGES

By the late 1970s, the Spanish lollipop market was becoming saturated and rising labour costs were putting pressure on the dedicated distribution network. In 1970, the sales and distribution network had grown to more than 500 people representing nearly two-thirds of the company payroll. Following the difficult recognition that this self-distribution structure was incompatible with rapid foreign expansion, Chupa Chups reduced its distribution staff to eight people, spinning the rest of the group off as another wholly-owned subsidiary, Chupa Chups Diversificación, which managed independent salesmen in Spain for both Chupa Chups confections and imported products, including Trebor (part of Cadbury) and Mon Cheri chocolates, Wrigley's and Lamy-Tutti chewing gums, and mints from Vivil, a German producer.

The "downsizing" was well managed, with many of the company's former sales representatives becoming very successful distributors/businessmen. And Chupa Chups Diversificación has been highly successful. In the late 1989s, Chupa Chups joined forces with McLane USA (part of the WalMart Group) and Repsol (Spain's largest industrial group) to establish a sophisticated distribution company to convenience stores, petrol stations, mini-markets and fast food franchises, including Burger King and Pizza Hut. In 1982, an additional subsidiary called Uniconfis Corporation, USA, was established in Atlanta dedicated to product distribution.

"But the 1970s were hard years," recounted Executive Vice-President Xavier Bernat, eldest son of company founder Enrique Bernat.

> "Struggling" is the word to describe us during that period. We were dismantling our own distribution business and building an external system. In addition, our sales had flattened. We couldn't grow any more in our home market. We were working to increase foreign sales, but there were strong trade barriers in many markets. How did we get through this time? Sales in Japan began climbing and we had great success in the USA. We certainly were helped by the popularity of "Kojak," the television series about the detective with a lollipop perpetually in his mouth. Plus some luck, perhaps.

Or perhaps persistence. During these years, the company was learning, sometimes the hard way, exactly how best to market and distribute its product. In the 1980s, commercial subsidiaries were established in Bonn, London and Atlanta. Worldwide sales began to climb again in the mid-1980s. A significant change at headquarters underpinning this expansion was the beginning of a more formal planning process. By the mid-1980s, the company had reached an annual production level of 1000 million units, with the USA (200 m units), France (120 m units), Japan

(120 m units), Spain (80 m units) and Italy (40 m units) emerging as its principal markets.

Up to the late 1980s all production took place in the Spanish and French plants, namely:

- Villamayor in Asturias, northern Spain—6,500 sq. m with a capacity for 20 metric tons per day.
- San Esteve de Sesrovires near Barcelona—9,000 sq. m with a capacity for 60 metric tons per day.
- Bayonne in south-east France—7,000 sq. m producing 1 million sweets per day.

This was complemented by a factory in Elche in Spain owned by S.A. Regalin (82 per cent owned by S.A. Chupa Chups) manufacturing liquorice products. This factory was later relocated to Slovenia for more cost-effective production.

TAKING ON THE WORLD

Commenting on reported Mafia problems in the Russian market:

> *Problems are everywhere, and the Mafia may be everywhere. But consumers are everywhere, also, and they eat every day.*

> *—Enrique Bernat*

Following its success in developed countries, Chupa Chups began to target less developed countries during the late 1980s. "In this period," Xavier Bernat stated, "we began to attack the world."

As mentioned previously, the Chinese market seemed the most attractive. The liberalization of foreign investment which began in 1979 under Mr Deng's rule was likely to continue. The market had the potential to be extraordinarily large, and it was mostly untapped territory for foreign confectionery makers. However, finding the right Chinese partner proved difficult and research went on for several years. Ironically, China was not the site for Chupa Chups' first joint venture. While Chupa Chups was continuing its opportunity search in China, the Soviet market began to open.

ENTERING RUSSIA

The Soviet Union allowed foreign investment from 1987. The new law stipulated that foreign ventures work with a Soviet partner. In 1990, Chupa Chups' long-standing Soviet shipping associate put them in touch with the Soviet Foods Minister. He recommended contacting a confectioner in Leningrad with a factory, a strong brand and an interest in partnership. While the Soviet producer, Azart,

would continue manufacturing its own line of products, Chupa Chups financed 60 per cent of a new Chupa Chups production line at Azart's plant. A two-tiered deal was struck. With financing from its Dutch Antilles finance subsidiary, Chupa Chups bought into the partnership. A second deal was arranged for the partner to rent production equipment from Chupa Chups. Chupa Chups retained title to the equipment because Soviet property rights were unclear.

The financial risks to providing the equipment were minimal: Chupa Chups shipped slower, older machinery obsolete for the Spanish plants but suitable for Soviet workers unused to working with or maintaining high-tech, computerized equipment. (The factory workers were subcontracted from Azart to Neva Chupa Chups.) It was planned that twenty-five Soviet employees would be trained in Spain in the operation of the older equipment. Locally produced items would be limited to the "Chupa Chups Classic," with other products shipped in from Spain. Supplies of sugar and glucose would be sourced locally, adhering to centrally established, stringent quality specifications. All other production supplies, from flavouring to packaging, would be sourced from Barcelona.

Chupa Chups staff were installing the last pieces of the production line in Leningrad on the day of the Russian coup. All communications with the staff were cut off. Reports of a potential revolution filled the news. Was the Leningrad location secure? Back in headquarters, a worried Enrique Bernat waited for some news. Three long days later, the staff reported in safe. Six months later, the Russian economy was wide open. Neva Chupa Chups was in production, and opportunities were rife in the new Russia. So were the problems.

Russian Accounting Systems

"We entered at the right time," said Miguel Otero, General Manager, International Investments, for S.A. Chupa Chups. "But the situation was a shock to us because developments there were so unexpected as so fast." Learning as they went, Chupa Chups and their Russian partner weathered a series of economic crises including hyperinflation and losses due to currency devaluation and non-existent banking systems. For example, payments wired from outlying regions took weeks to reach St Petersburg (Leningrad had readopted its original name following the collapse of the USSR), by which time inflation had greatly diminished the transaction value. Checking accounts did not exist, so many local payments were made in cash; customers would arrive at the plant with sacks of roubles slung over their shoulders. Reacting to needs, Neva Chupa Chups quickly developed contracts allowing payment terms in roubles but which were valued at the US dollar rate on the date of payment. The situation improved in 1993 when the raw materials and dollar markets were liberalized and inflation dropped to a mere 1,000 per cent.

The economy was cooling, relatively, but change at Neva Chupa Chups seemed endemic: that year their Russian partner, Nikolai Azarov, had to raise capital to privatize the state-owned Azart. He sold 15 per cent of Azart's share of Neva Chupa Chups to S.A. Chupa Chups, and a further 10 per cent to a St Petersburg bank (of which Neva Chupa Chups owned 5 per cent). His company retained only 15 per cent ownership, but Azarov still had an influential voice at Board meetings. For instance, despite his lamentations that after four years Azart had no money to show for its work with Neva Chupa Chups, Azarov had been an outspoken proponent of reinvesting Neva Chupa Chups profits into a new factory with greatly increased capacity. And it was he who arranged discussions in 1995 between Neva Chupa Chups' general manager and the owner of Russia's largest bread baker and distributor. As a result, by 1996 a new line of cakes baked on the Russian's premises was ready for marketing in Russia under the Chupa Chups brand. In typical Bernat fashion, this newest joint venture involved family: Enrique Bernat's brother, representing the maternal, bakers branch of the family, visited Russia regularly to advise on the start-up.

Neva Chupa Chups Takes the Market

A Spanish general manager was sent to Leningrad for the start-up in 1991, along with a finance director and a Russian speaking logistics manager. However, while great strides were made in organizing production, other problems continued to dog Russian operations. For instance, the Russian press galloped with a negative publicity campaign concerning the "Painted Chupa Chups." This temporarily tongue-dying lollipop was labelled carcinogenic by the Russian media and had to be withdrawn.

The growing power of the Russian "Red Mafia" also posed a potential threat to the venture's success. Three other major Spanish manufacturers operating in Russia—sausage maker Campofrio and cava (Catalán sparkling wine) producers Codorniu and Freixenet—were likewise dealing with security threats and demands for "security payments." In fact, Freixenet had to reach agreement with the hard-core of the Mafia which controls the distribution of alcohol and tobacco, and Codorniu withdrew from the market after thieves murdered four of the company's security guards and pilfered 230,000 cases of cava. Market conditions were, as they say, difficult.

The Spanish general manager established an efficient production line and was effective in dealing with the slow moving Soviet bureaucracy (as, for example, when Confipack technicians required full investigation and a permit from the KGB before entering the Soviet Union).

But the accelerating new Russian economy was making it difficult to plan company development or to make profits.

Neva Chupa Chups' situation improved suddenly following the September 1993 "Sweet Expo" in Moscow. Xavier Bernat attended this meeting. Encountering representatives from every major Western confectioner from Cadbury to Wrigley, he fully realized the potential of the Russian market and wasted no time in allocating resources to shore up the money-losing subsidiary. A new general manager, Walter Borio Almo, was sent from headquarters in 1993 along with a new Spanish financial director. A Mexican of Italian-Spanish heritage, Borio spoke five languages fluently and quickly gained a working knowledge of Russian. But with years of commercial experience throughout Europe with S.A. Chupa Chups and other multinationals, even he was challenged by the situation at Neva Chupa Chups. He related with animation:

> Our "offices" contained one desk, one chair, and eight salesmen in a queue for our one telephone. Our production line was completely ready but was functioning at 50 per cent of capacity due to lack of demand. Customers would arrive, purchase one $25 box of lollipops, then drive 10 kilometres down the road and sell our products from the back of their cars. Our own fledgling sales system relied on the efforts of eight independent salesmen paid $185 per month to walk from kiosk to kiosk in all weather conditions promoting our goods. They were wearing out their shoes selling one box of lollipops a day to each kiosk. And without a car, Russia is a big country! . . .

> Our warehouse consisted of only 200 square metres located on the 5th floor and equipped with shelves too narrow for our boxes. The lift couldn't hold more than one box of lollipops, so it took two hours to load a truck, box by box—when the lift was working, that is. But we had faith in our product, so we quickly made some changes.

Organizational Systems

Borio and his team began planning their expansion in the Russian market. As a priority, relations with Azarov were improved and more Azart space was freed for the joint venture. ("After the first time Nikolai and I got drunk together, the ice began to melt," confided Borio.) Equally critically, the team established commercial systems, such as setting prices and minimum sales orders, targeting customers and distributors, and planning promotions.

Direct sales to kiosks were stopped in January 1994. Minimum orders were raised from $25 to $1,000 and later, in 1995, to $5,000. Partial credit for the enlarged order size was given to customers meeting three criteria, viz, (i) they had been Neva Chupa Chups customers for more than six months; (ii) they had established corporate structures which allowed them to move the product, such as warehouses and computers; and (iii) they already distributed for other quality companies such as Mars, etc.

Concerning distribution, the usual Chupa Chups approach of distributing through top manufacturers was modified for Russia: since Western companies were not manufacturing at that time in Russia, Neva Chupa Chups selected Russian third party distributors with a track record of distribution for the best confectioners. Borio aimed to have a distributor in each of the 65 Russian cities with a population of 300,000 or more. By 1995, he had appointed distributors in 43 cities, and these provided hubs to penetrate all parts of Russia until such time as the total goal was achieved.

Advertising adapted to the Russian media was held back until distribution was assured, but a television campaign released to run through April, May and June led to spiralling demand. A popular feature of the Russian television ads was the genuine footage of Russian cosmonauts sucking on Chupa Chups while on duty in the Mir space station. The cosmonauts had requested supplies of their favourite candy—Chupa Chups—as a substitute for cigarettes which were forbidden in the space station. (Xavier Bernat knew the Director of the Mir Programme who facilitated videotaping in space of Chupa Chups—truly a universal product.) With the growth in sales, larger warehouses had been acquired which allowed sufficient stocks to meet demand. By April 1994, the production line was working at full capacity for two shifts. That June, a third shift was added.

Similarly, corporate structures had to be built from the ground up. A 25-year-old Russian, formerly a lieutenant in the Soviet army, was hired immediately as sales manager to build the commercial team. The new territory was divided into five regions, each headed by a young Russian product market manager, most with international experience or experience in other multinational corporations within Russia, and most formerly with the Soviet military. A new marketing director, an American, arrived from Barcelona in November 1995, but the remainder of the 100 member staff were Russian, including managers, secretaries, line foremen, the quality control scientist, and mechanical engineers.

The Situation in November 1995

Neva Chupa Chups bought a satelite dish in 1994 to improve telephone access. Although still Spartan, the offices had been modernized using $50,000 from the parent company. Separate desks were made available for everyone and a computer was placed on each desk. Multiple telephone lines rang constantly, and the interaction of sales staff, secretaries, uniformed factory staff and managers was carried on in the open plan office in a mixture of Russian, Spanish and English. (In fact, the environment had become exactly like headquarters in Barcelona which likewise had

an open floor plan, a multinational staff and an energetic atmosphere.) In the centre of this humming activity sat Walter Borio with a large bust of Vladimir Lenin holding a Chupa Chups Classic lollipop on the corner of his desk.

By 1995, the venture had emerged as a roaring success. Dividends to the partner were related to production, so the facility ran at 100 per cent capacity. However, sales exceeded even this capacity, so Chupa Chups' new Chinese plant was required to ship products to Russia to meet demand. Sales had climbed steadily: $6 million in 1992; $13 million in 1993; $25 million in 1994; and $35 million in 1995. Operations achieved break-even in 1994, with the first profits coming in 1995. The Russian staff worked hard, according to Chupa Chups management, and they had been fully trained in Chupa Chups production techniques. A new factory was under construction, and plans were in hand to install new, more sophisticated equipment by the summer of 1996. The locally manufactured product line was planned for expansion beyond the "Chupa Chups Classic" to include "Melody Pops" and other more complex lollipops, inaugurating production of these outside the Spanish and French plants.

Even the Mafia had been dealt with in a creative fashion: low margin confectionery products were not so attractive to the Mafia as alcohol, tobacco or banknotes, anyway, but Neva Chupa Chups counter-offered the Mafia's overtures with a 5 per cent reduction off the wholesale price of lollipops.

CHINA OPENS UP

On Chupa Chups' persistence:

> *Looked at China—the cultural revolution. More negotiations!*
> *Looked at China—Mao dies. More negotiations!*
> *Looked at China—Mao's widow came to power. More negotiations!*
> *Looked at China—Mao's widow 'resigns.' More negotiations!*
> *Looked at China—Tiananmen Square. More negotiations!*
>
> **—Enrique Bernat**

While pleased with developments in the Russian market, Chupa Chups management continued looking for opportunities to enter the Chinese market. Following the fruitless negotiations with Bei Jing First Confectionery Company, another delegation from the Chinese government arrived in Barcelona in 1994 seeking Spanish business partners for Chinese enterprises. One such enterprise was Tian Shan, a subsidiary of Guan Sheng Yuan of Shanghai, the largest Chinese confectionery producer. Following up on this contact, Chupa Chups' managers visited Shanghai and a joint venture agreement was quickly developed between the two companies.

In opening its Chinese venture, Chupa Chups adhered to its expansion model: it entered into a partnership with a local organization in a country with an underdeveloped distribution network; took the majority share of the partnership (67 per cent); and provided the equipment. "It's possible to have a 100 per cent foreign-owned company in China, but it's the work of a crazy person," commented Xavier Bernat. "You must pay to get clearance from fourteen commissions at least—for the real estate, the buildings, the firemen's health insurance, and so on. We've found a good partner, a serious company that had the only lollipop production line in the market. We work together on everything."

Organizational Systems

In November 1994, the Shanghai Chupa Chups Guan Sheng Yuan Food Co., Ltd, opened its doors. Building on their Russian experiences, Chupa Chups established a production and management structure similar to that of Neva Chupa Chups. The local plant focused on the producing the "Chupa Chups Classic" only, using proven Chupa Chups technology. Their partner continued to maintain its own successful confectionery line. Raw materials such as glucose and sugar were sourced locally while other materials, packaging and complex lollipops were shipped from Spain. Management consisted of a mixture of expatriots and national staff. The general manager was the former head of Chupa Chups' highly successful German subsidiary, the finance director was Spanish, while the deputy general manager was recruited locally in China and dealt principally with Chinese finances and managed the accounting systems.

Marketing and Sales

Like the Russian operation, marketing and distribution also was developed with national staff, although in a slightly more complex fashion: Chinese law forbade wholesale distribution by foreign firms of any goods not produced within China. But Chupa Chups intended to export to China its more complex products and some supplies. Management was on the point of signing a contract with a Chinese distributor. But Enrique Bernat strongly advised the Executive Group not to rely on the efforts of a single distributor, but to develop its own direct distribution system in this market with its vast potential. So Chupa Chups set up a commercial sales company based in Singapore and Hong Kong with mainland Chinese who had previously worked for Mars and Pepsi Cola in China. This group provided inward distribution of Chupa Chups products and also some supporting marketing services in exchange for a commission. While acknowledging that developing distribution in a country the size of China has been challenging, Xavier Bernat and the Executive Committee believed that the decision to maintain direct control of distribution in China was correct.

EXPANDING INTO INDIA AND BEYOND

In 1996, Chupa Chups continued to eye new markets, especially those with exploding populations. Many of these developing markets, however, present trade barriers to foreign companies, leading Chupa Chups to develop local partnerships instead of relying on imports. Chupa Chups signed a joint venture agreement in 1994 with a company based in Madras, India, to begin production of the " Chupa Chups Classic." As with the previous joint ventures, Chupa Chups contributes the technology and marketing expertise to the venture and the partner provides the site. The new plant was expected to be operational by late 1996. In addition, Chupa Chups has plans to enter Mexico with a local partner who will hold 10 per cent of the joint venture. The facility will capitalize on low labour costs and the recently unified, duty-free North American market. Plans for constructing a facility in Brazil were announced at the end of 1995. The company fully intends to continue all of its joint venture partnerships, even after operations are well established, according to Xavier Bernat.

In comparing the three established joint ventures, International Investment General Manager Miguel Otero contrasted the bureaucracy and the banking systems. In Russia, he said, dealing with the government is no problem. Permission for entry and expansion is easily obtained. The Chinese government also will facilitate foreign ventures. The Indian government, apparently, is quite another matter. "The British left behind many wonderful systems," he said, "including a very large bureaucracy."

On the other hand, banking systems range from sophisticated (India) to bureaucratic (China) to chaotic (Russia). The company even had provisions for 'bad bank transactions' in Russia. At one point the currency situation became so bad in the former USSR that Neva Chupa Chups staved off a cash crisis by distributing sunflower seeds from the Ukraine to Spain and the United States to earn the hard currency required by the Soviets of all foreign companies. This system was functional until the former USSR was broken up, the Ukraine gained independence, and the deal had to be abandoned.

FINANCING THE INTERNATIONAL EXPANSION

Prior to Spain's entry to the European Union (EU), Chupa Chups' international expansion was financed by preferential bank lines of credit and, after Franco's death, tax incentives offered by Spain to foster the development of export activities. In addition, the Chupa Chups Group and in particular, the Bernat family, could provide start-up support. More recently, Chupa Chups continues to fund its expansion through a shrewd combination of company funds and grants/low interest loans offered by the EU and other government agencies, as well as through its partnership arrangements. These activities, combined with a successful track record of negotiating with Russian, Chinese and Indian governments reveal Chupa Chups' strengths in managing government relations.

Financing arrangements are somewhat different for each situation. Flexibility and adaptation to local conditions are crucial. Chupa Chups' philosophy has been to share financial responsibility. With joint ventures, its intention is to seek partnerships but retain majority share.

Russia

Early funding for Neva Chupa Chups was provided by the Chupa Chups Group. In 1996, however, given the established track record of the Russian subsidiary, external financing for this subsidiary was being sought from the European Bank of Reconstruction and Development (EBRD) for the new 10,000 sq. m factory plus warehouse on the outskirts of St Petersburg. Construction and working capital costs were estimated at $25 m. If EBRD funding was not forthcoming, Neva Chupa Chups would finance the project through profit reinvestment and slowed payments to S.A. Chupa Chups for supplies.

China

The Chinese subsidiary also was financed using relatively risk-free capital. The China State Bank provided long-term financing at market rates directly to the partner in Shanghai with no backing required from Chupa Chups. The China State Bank also financed working capital requirements and could authorise up to $30 m of financing without central government approval.

India

The Indian venture partner had agreed to invest its share, with the backing of an Indian bank, primarily to construct the factory. Chupa Chups would contribute the dedicated equipment to the venture, but due to order backlogs at Confipack, these could not be delivered until mid-1996 at the earliest.

MANAGEMENT OF INTERNATIONAL OPERATIONS

Once a subsidiary had been established, Chupa Chups management approach focused on putting financial control systems in place. Any new manufacturing subsidiary was also embedded into the global procurement system and in Chupa Chups' system of plant specialization. All subsidiaries were involved in developing marketing, advertising and distribution. (See Exhibit 2 for Chupa Chups Group sales for 1994.)

THE FINANCIAL SYSTEM

In addition to information circulated by frequent telephone conversations and faxes, financial reports from subsidiaries included daily updates faxed to Barcelona with information on production, sales, cash/financial situation, stocks and debtors. These were brief, one-page reports which Walter Borio, GM of Neva Chupa Chups, contrasted a bit smugly with the onerous paperwork required of the GMs of other multinationals' subsidiaries. "It's incredible the reports they have to send to headquarters. The other GMs have no time to do anything but prepare reports, while I am able to work," he stated.

Monthly reports provided deeper sales information as well as P&L and balance-sheet information. Frequent meetings took place between subsidiary management and headquarters staff. Finally, annual sales, financials and monthly milestones were established via annual budget forecasts. It was expected that the entire financial system, including all the daily and monthly reports would be integrated in the future via a new linked global IT system.

THE PROCUREMENT SYSTEM

The central procurement system provided the global operations with all raw material (aside from sugar and glucose) necessary to ensure the production of Chupa Chups in a standard format. This was particularly true for the packaging materials such as the wrappers, tins and cartons in which the lollipops were presented. All these items were produced in Spain, labelled in multiple languages where appropriate, and shipped to subsidiaries.

PLANT SPECIALIZATION AND TRANSFER OF TECHNOLOGY

All the Spanish plants and the plant in Bayonne in southern France produced the sophisticated lollipops (i.e., Melody Pops, Fantasy Balls, Tattoo Pops, etc.) and shipped them to other markets. The new Neva Chupa Chups plant was the first outside of Spain and France that was scheduled to produce some of the sophisticated products beginning in 1996. However, the 'Chupa Chups Classic' was produced in all plants.

The proprietary process technology, one of the competitive advantages of Chupa Chups, was transferred only gradually from the centre to subsidiary plants. The level of sophistication of the equipment shipped was increased over time: at the beginning very robust, used machinery was shipped to new plants, followed later by the high technology equipment developed more recently by Confipack.

A procedure of prudence, risk-minimization and acknowledgement of local skills could be discerned on the part of Chupa Chups in this approach. First, Chupa Chups' entire capability of process technology was revealed only after a certain period of a mutual trust and co-operation. Second, workers could gain experience with, for them, new process technology before operating and maintaining more sophisticated machinery. In turn, Chupa Chups could easily develop potential local sales of "Classic" products through older, fully amortized equipment, while sophisticated machines could be employed only when their output could be maximally exploited.

MARKETING

In 1996, worldwide marketing efforts of Chupa Chups were directed by Willem van Brakel, a Dutchman. At least a dozen other nationalities were represented on the marketing team. All spoke multiple languages although marketing meetings were conducted in English as a courtesy to the UK manager who spoke no other language. The team consisted of 12 area marketing managers each responsible for 5–10 countries. They were all based in Barcelona but travelled about 40 per cent of the time. In this way they stayed in touch with country distributors and salespeople, and could make customer calls with the salespeople. They were intentionally not called sales managers. If an area market manager returned from an exploratory trip to a new territory with a full order book, the trip was considered a failure. The staff aimed to agree on marketing plans with an exclusive distributor, not to make direct sales.

In addition, there were nine product managers who worked directly with areas where there was either a subsidiary or a joint venture. All marketing staff participated in an unofficial and constant flow of information facilitated by the office's open floor plan. The company also had an open-door policy which facilitated decision-making, and Executive Vice-President Xavier Bernaut was in daily touch with area marketing managers. The decision process was therefore short and direct, typically involving the area manager and Xavier Bernat, with input sometimes from two to three other marketing staff.

The second arm of the marketing department was responsible for product and packaging development, advertising/promotions and consumer research. Children remained the primary customers, so product and packaging innovation was seen as a critical success factor in maintaining the customers' interest, especially since the product range was limited to one item. Recent new products have included the Fantasy Ball (bubblegum and rub-on tattoos) and Wind Ball (a game with candy). Until recently, Enrique Bernat himself participated directly in product introductions: he would sit behind the counters of small shops, observing customer reactions to the new product and listening to their comments. Staff also served constantly as test marketers. They dipped into open dishes of new products placed throughout the offices and gave feedback on them.

DISTRIBUTION

Given the nature of the product and the vision of Enrique Bernat, to have the brand name Chupa Chups etched in people's minds, the product had to be displayed on as many shelves as possible. From its early days, Chupa Chups planned to internationalize. It had preferred to do so through exclusive distributors wherever possible, rather than creating new subsidiaries. But apart from nationalistic trade barriers, another barrier to entering markets was access to the right distribution channels. According to Xavier Bernat, the "right" distributors were those with excellent local market knowledge, and with wide sales networks (wholesale and retail level) at the appropriate locations and not too many products in their portfolio. Chupa Chups' early lessons were reflected in its clarity of action in distribution through its three-fold approach:

- Chupa Chups operated through its own distribution company only in key markets.
- Exclusivity was sought after in any contracts with foreign distributors.
- The foreign distributors were carefully selected.

Chupa Chups undertook an in-depth analysis of the existing distribution structure in a country and its competitive forces. It focused on that country's top distributors (e.g., Cadbury, Unilever, Nabisco, etc.). Once this research was complete, area managers then would approach the top national distributors with a detailed marketing plan. It was reported that their high level of knowledge about the local market conditions regularly flabbergasted local partners during negotiations.

There was a clear preference to select distributors who had their own manufacturing facilities, usually other confectioners. Thus these manufacturers could spread their fixed distribution costs over a bigger volume. Chupa

Chups' rationale was to have a dedicated distributor who was not distracted by thousands of others' product lines. Chupa Chups also believed that a distributor who was also a manufacturer had a better fit to the culture of Chupa Chups, itself a manufacturer with strong distribution skills.

ADVERTISING

As part of the distribution agreement, Chupa Chups sought the physical and psychological involvement of the distributors. This was particularly true of the advertising and promotion process. The distributors' participation in advertising and promotions not only resulted in more opinions, but also in more potential solutions to issues. With distributors all over the world, creative ideas abounded, although Chupa Chups screened them carefully to ensure all promotions protected its brand.

Chupa Chups contracted with an advertising agency in Spain but also worked with many different agencies abroad, in particular linking with the distributors' agencies. Chupa Chups typically selected medium or even small advertising agencies. The Chupa Chups account was therefore significant to the agencies. The advertising and promotion brief was many times directed by headquarters but creative ideas often were initiated elsewhere.

THE CHANGING FOCUS OF MARKETING

Chupa Chups' advertising acknowledged the fact that within their traditional markets birth rates were falling. Consequently, there were fewer children eating lollipops. Chupa Chups recognized a long time ago that if there was a Chupa Chups at home, an adult would eat it, but they would not go out and buy it. Therefore, the company was changing its advertising focus towards teenagers and adult customers. Late teens were important targets since their activities often were mimicked by younger, pre-teens who otherwise might stop eating lollipops at around age 10. In Australia, for example, the company launched a successful campaign to college and university students with the slogan Smoke a Chupa Chups, and they sponsor Light Fridays in discos with sweets as opposed to cigarettes. Chupa Chups also has launched a new mouth freshening product, Smints, aimed at adults.

FLOW OF PROMOTIONAL IDEAS

Chupa Chups' marketing philosophy was to develop goals and advertise campaigns centrally and then allow subsidiaries to adopt portions selectively as appropriate to their markets. Promotional ideas were initiated anywhere within the company and discussed with headquarters, subsidiaries and distributors before a campaign was developed further at headquarters. The campaigns across most countries tended to follow the main theme of displaying a Chupa Chups to the viewer, though within Spain, where knowledge of the product was high, Chupa Chups had developed advertising which did not show the product to the viewer.

THE CHUPA CHUPS PHILOSOPHY

We don't have to tell the General Managers what to do. They know the company strategy.

—*Xavier Bernat*

DECISIONS

All strategic moves and investments were decided by consensus by the Executive Committee, which included three family members—Xavier, Marcos and Ramon—and two other senior general managers. Enrique Bernat, while withdrawing himself from most daily operations of S.A. Chupa Chups, still spent about 10 per cent of his time on Chupa Chups activities, and he retained a strong influence on the Committee, illustrated by his advice to establish direct distribution in China.

The Executive Committee reported to the Board, which was comprised entirely of family members. Therefore all Board members shared common objectives and points of view. Actually, there were no formal Board meetings. This speeded decision-making which could be reduced to 24 hours, as opposed to a month or more with other corporate boards. Chupa Chups' speed and decisiveness were demonstrated when senior staff returned the Chinese delegation's visit within a month of their initial meeting in Barcelona to explore real joint venture possibilities.

Once subsidiaries or joint ventures were established, the placement of appropriate staff was a major mechanism by which headquarters helped the subsidiaries. Once installed, the subsidiaries' managers were encouraged to make decisions on the ground. In return, they were expected to achieve financial self-sufficiency for the subsidiary within 2–3 years. The threshold of a 15 per cent profit margin was a means by which the performance of the subsidiary management was measured.

Formal reports were demanded (see Finance section), but the lines of communication between management and staff and between headquarters and subsidiaries remained open and informal. For example, the family was highly accessible. Enrique Bernat was nearly always available for discussion, although the best time to catch him informally, according to a junior staff member, was on Saturdays between 10:00 and 2:00 when he was always in his office. Executive Vice-President Xavier Bernat was a lot more involved and accessible. Product market managers rang him directly from field visits to discuss ideas and problems, as did subsidiary managers.

"We are not like some other multinationals with a formal top group and seven reporting divisions," exclaimed Xavier Bernat. "We have a structure, yes, but we really are a conglomeration of companies developing products. We have sold 30 billion lollipops and believe we will sell 30 billion more, maybe in more sophisticated ways, but with the same focus as always."

STAFF DEVELOPMENT

I have always taken care that people feel good about working with us. It is vitally important that they feel happy at work; that they like the job.

—Enrique Bernat

"I am a Chupa Chups boy," explained one production engineer. He described the characteristics of a true Chupa Chups staff member: "First, they're crazy because they work very long hours, buy they like it. Second, it's a happy company. Third, they live the philosophy of a Basque saying, 'We always do the impossible and a miracle a day.'" Finally, a family-owned business, it retained the feel of family. After about three years with the company, staff gained the full confidence of the top—the Bernats—and of the other managers. They then were authorized to take decisions, and failure was accepted so long as the decisions were taken based on defensible logic.

The Bernat family had consciously developed an enthusiastic environment within the company. "The consumer market is very competitive, so we must maintain a super-motivation among the staff," explained Xavier Bernat. "In some sectors you must be conservative, but not in this one. We don't sell a product. We sell a world, a philosophy, an attitude." Indeed, the atmosphere in offices and factories was palpably energetic and friendly. And many staff members walked around the office or factory floor with a Chupa Chups in their mouths.

Enrique Bernat attributed the company's success to its ability to recruit talented staff and admitted to paying above-average salaries. There were many nationalities represented with the company, yet typically after three years they all shared the Chupa Chups mentality. The exchange of staff between headquarters and subsidiaries, as well as between subsidiaries, facilitated the transfer of the Chupa Chups culture. For example, following on the great success in Germany, the German manager was transferred into the GM role in Shanghai. The management team at Neva Chupa Chups likewise consisted of experienced Chupa Chups staff members.

Although not actually Chupa Chups employees, factory staff at the joint ventures were involved in problem-solving, such as machine installation or repairs, as well as quality control programmes. All staff also shared in celebrations, such as the annual lunches hosted by the general managers of Neva Chupa Chups and Azart to celebrate their birthdays.

Chupa Chups staff, however, attributed the company's success to the role that the Bernat family played in the day-to-day operations of the company. Company legends were frequently repeated concerning the vision and drive of founder Enrique as well as the acumen of son, Xavier. "Their involvement is fundamental to the company's success," explained a staff member. Why? "Because the Bernats like this company!"

EXHIBIT 1
THE CHUPA CHUPS
GROUP

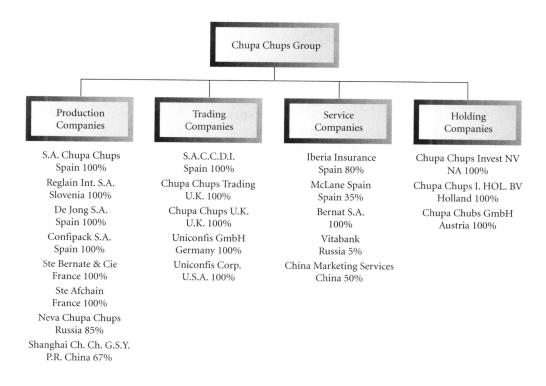

Chupa Chups Group

Production Companies

S.A. Chupa Chups
Spain 100%

Reglain Int. S.A.
Slovenia 100%

De Jong S.A.
Spain 100%

Confipack S.A.
Spain 100%

Ste Bernate & Cie
France 100%

Ste Afchain
France 100%

Neva Chupa Chups
Russia 85%

Shanghai Ch. Ch. G.S.Y.
P.R. China 67%

Trading Companies

S.A.C.C.D.I.
Spain 100%

Chupa Chups Trading
U.K. 100%

Chupa Chups U.K.
U.K. 100%

Uniconfis GmbH
Germany 100%

Uniconfis Corp.
U.S.A. 100%

Service Companies

Iberia Insurance
Spain 80%

McLane Spain
Spain 35%

Bernat S.A.
100%

Vitabank
Russia 5%

China Marketing Services
China 50%

Holding Companies

Chupa Chups Invest NV
NA 100%

Chupa Chups I. HOL. BV
Holland 100%

Chupa Chubs GmbH
Austria 100%

EXHIBIT 2 CHUPA CHUPS GROUP (ESTIMATED) CONSOLIDATED SALES, END-1994

COMPANY	% OWNERSHIP	CURRENCY	TOTAL SALES*	EXCHANGE RATE	INTERCOMPANY SALES (%)	TOTAL SALES IN PTAS**	INTERCOMPANY SALES (PTAS)**	CONSOLIDATED SALES (PTAS)**
S.A. Chupa Chups	100%	Ptas	13,588,900	1.0	40%	13,588,900	5,435,560	8,153,340
Regalin Int. S.A.	100%	Ptas	356,000	1.0		356,000		356,000
Ste. Bernat et Cie	100%	F.F.	70,000	24.5		1,715,000		1,715,000
Conf Afchain S.A.	100%	F.F.	9,837	24.5		241,007		241,007
Neva Ch Ch A/O	85%	$US	25,681	130.0		2,837,751		2,837,751
De Jong S.A.	90%	Ptas	331,000	1.0		297,900		297,900
Confipack S.A.	100%	Ptas	522,000	1.0		522,000		522,000
S.A. Ch Ch Distribution	100%	Ptas	2,731,000	1.0		2,731,000		2,731,000
Uniconfis GmbH	100%	D.M.	38,363	85.0		3,260,855		3,260,855
Uniconfis Corp	100%	$US	18,200	130.0		2,366,000		2,366,000
Ch Ch Trading	100%	$US	27,032	130.0	40%	3,514,160	1,405,664	2,108,496
Total confectionery						**31,430,572**	**6,841,224**	**24,589,348**
McLane—Spain	35%	Ptas	5,321,000	1.0		1,862,350		1,862,350
Iberia Insurance	80%	Ptas	8,233,000	1.0		6,586,400		6,586,400
Total other						**8,448,750**		**8,448,750**
Total						**39,879,322**	**6,841,224**	**33,038,098**

* All figures in 000s.
** In 000s Ptas.

EXHIBIT 3
CHUPA CHUPS GROUP
PROJECTED SALES,
1994–2000

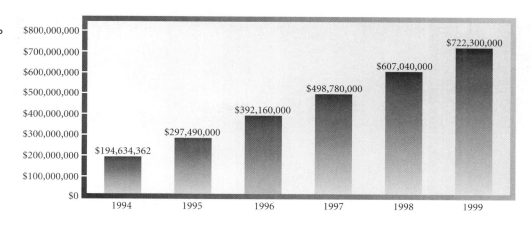

EXHIBIT 4 OPENING
LETTER TO A
COMPANY BROCHURE

A message from the President

Everything started almost 40 years ago when I undertook the thrilling objective of specializing in lollipops, in order to obtain a unique product of better quality than any other lollipop known in the world. The achievement of this objective has been extremely rewarding not only in terms of the benefits to my company but also because it has brought enormous satisfaction and enjoyment to many millions of consumers.

The Chupa Chups history is acknowledged as a classic example of creative intuition and state of the art technology. With the expansion of the Group such essential elements for success are no longer limited only to S.A. Chupa Chups.

As this booklet shows, many new companies have joined the group. All of them, be it manufacturing, commercial or service companies, share one main characteristic: Faith.

The absolute faith in a product, in inexhaustible creativity, in professional honesty, the unshakeable faith in the consumer, and faith that the body and soul of a product must be an object loved by the consumer.

And nobody knows better than the staff of our Company, that there is nothing more exigent than faith.

Enrique Bernat Fontlladosa
President

Mountbatten and India

Louis Francis Albert Victor Nicholas Mountbatten, Viscount of Burma, was, at forty-six, one of the most famous men in England. He was a big man, over six feet tall, but not a trace of flab hung from his zealously exercised waistline. . . . Mountbatten knew perfectly well why he had been summoned to London. Since his return from his post as Supreme Allied Commander Southeast Asia, he had been a frequent visitor to Downing Street as a consultant on the affairs of the Asian nations that had fallen under S.E.A.C.'s command. On his last visit, however, the Prime Minister's questions had quickly focused on India, a nation that had not been a part of [Mountbatten's] theater of operations. The young admiral had suddenly had "a very nasty, very uneasy feeling." His premonition had been justified. Attlee intended to name him Viceroy of India. The viceroy's was the most important post in the Empire, the office from which a long succession of Englishmen had held domain over the destinies of a fifth of mankind. Mountbatten's task, however, would not be to rule India from that office. His assignment would be one of the most painful an Englishman could be asked to undertake—to give it up.

A HISTORIC TRAP

Mountbatten wanted no part of the job. He entirely endorsed the idea that the time had come for Britian to leave India, but his heart rebelled at the thought that he would be called on to sever the ancient links binding England and the bulwark of her empire. To discourage Attlee, he had produced a whole series of demands, major and minor, from the number of secretaries he must be allowed to take with him, to the make of the aircraft, the York MW-102 which had carried him around the world as Supreme Commander Southeast Asia, which would be placed at his disposal. The admiral still hoped somehow to resist Attlee's efforts to force the Indian assignment on him. . . .

There was much more to Mountbatten than his [impeccable] public image reflected; the decorations on his naval uniform were proof of that. The public might consider him a pillar of the Establishment, but the Establishment's members themselves tended to regard Mountbatten and his wife as dangerous radicals. His command in Southeast Asia had given him a vast knowledge of Asian nationalist movements, and there were few Englishmen who could match it. He had dealt with the supporters of Ho Chi Minh in Indochina, Sukharno in Indonesia, Aung San in Burma, Chinese Communists in Malaya, unruly trade unionists in Singapore. Realizing that they represented Asia's future, he had sought

Case compilation copyright © 1990 by James Brian Quinn. All sections reproduced by permission from Larry Collins and Dominique Lapierre *Freedom at Midnight* (Simon & Schuster, Inc. 1975). Copyright © 1975 by Larry Collins and Dominique Lapierre. All rights to original copyright holders. Page references [] are at the end of each quoted section. Deleted sections (. . .) and minor clarifications [] made by Professor Quinn as noted.

accommodations with them rather than try to suppress them as his staff and the Allies had urged. The nationalist movement with which he would have to deal if he went to India was the oldest and most unusual of them all. In a quarter of a century of inspired agitation and protest, its leadership had forced history's greatest empire to the decision that Attlee's party had taken to quit India in good time rather than to be driven out by forces of history and rebellion.

THE SUBLIME PARADOX

The Indian situation, the Prime Minister began, was deteriorating with every passing day, and the time for an urgent decision was at hand. It was one of the sublime paradoxes of history that at this critical juncture, when Britain was at last ready to give India her freedom—she could not find a way to do so. What should have been Britain's finest hour in India seemed destined to become a nightmare of unsurpassed horror. She had conquered and ruled India with what was, by the colonial standard, relatively little bloodshed. Her leaving threatened to produce an explosion of violence that would dwarf in scale and magnitude anything she had experienced in three and a half centuries there.

The root of the Indian problem was the age-old antagonism between India's 300 million Hindus and 100 million Moslems. Sustained by tradition, by antipathetic religions, by economic differences subtly exacerbated through the years by Britain's own policy of divide and rule, their conflict had reached a boiling point. The leaders of India's 100 million Moslems now demanded that Britain destroy the unity she had so painstakingly created and give them an Islamic state of their own. The cost of denying them their state, they warned, would be the bloodiest civil war in Asian history. Just as determined to resist their demands were the leaders of the Congress Party, representing most of India's 300 million Hindus. To them, the division of the subcontinent would be a mutilation of their historic homeland, an act almost sacrilegious in its nature.

Britain was trapped between those two apparently irreconcilable demands. Time and again British efforts to resolve the problem had failed. So desperate had the situation become that the present viceroy, an honest, forthright soldier, Field Marshal Sir Archibald Wavell, had just submitted to the Attlee government a final, and drastic, recommendation [called Operation Madhouse]. Should all else fail, he proposed, the British should "withdraw from India in our own method and in our own time and with due regard to our own interests; we will regard any attempt to interfere with our program as an act of war which we will meet with all the resources at our command. . . ."

Each morning brought a batch of cables to the India Office announcing an outburst of wanton savagery in some new comer of the subcontinent. It was, Attlee indicated, Mountbatten's solemn duty to take the post he had been offered. . . . Wavell had all the right ideas, Mountbatten thought. "If he couldn't do it, what's the point of my trying to take it on?" Yet he was beginning to understand that there was no escape. He was going to be forced to accept a job in which the risk of failure was enormous and in which he would easily shatter the brilliant reputation he'd brought out of the war.

POLITICAL CONDITIONS

If Attlee was going to drive him into a corner, Mountbatten was determined to impose on the Prime Minister the political conditions that would give him some hope of success. His talks with Wavell had given him an idea what they must be. He would not accept, he told the Prime Minister, unless the government agreed to make an unequivocal public announcement of a precise date on which British rule in India would terminate. Only that, Mountbatten felt, would convince India's skeptical intelligentsia that Britain was really leaving and infuse her leaders with the sense of urgency needed to get them into realistic negotiations.

Second, he demanded something no other viceroy had ever dreamed of asking: full powers to carry out his assignment without reference to London, and above all, without constant interference from London. The Attlee government could give the young admiral his final destination, but he alone was going to set his course and run the ship along the way.

"Surely," Attlee said, "you're not asking for plenipotentiary powers above His Majesty's Government, are you?"

"I am afraid, sir," answered Mountbatten, "that that is exactly what I am asking. How can I possibly negotiate with the Cabinet constantly breathing down my neck?"

A stunned silence followed his words. Mountbatten watched with satisfaction as the nature of his breathtaking demand registered on the Prime Minister's face, and he hoped that it would prompt Attlee to withdraw his offer. Instead, the Prime Minister indicated with a sigh his willingness to accept even that. . . . As he got back into his Austin Princess, a strange thought struck Mountbatten. It was exactly seventy years to the day, almost to the hour, from the moment when his own great-grandmother had been proclaimed Empress of India on a plain outside Delhi. [16–20]

LAST TATTOO FOR A DYING RAJ

George VI [Lord Mountbatten's cousin] comprehended perfectly well that the great imperial dream had faded and that the grandiose structure fashioned by his great-grandmother's ministers was condemned. But if the empire had to disappear, how sad it would be if some of its achievements and glories could not survive, if what it had represented could not find an expression in some new form more compatible with a modern age. "It would be a pity," he observed, "if an independent India were to turn its back on the Commonwealth."

The Commonwealth could indeed provide a framework in which George VI's hopes might be realized. It could become a multiracial assembly of independent nations, with Britain *prima inter pares* at its core. Bound by common traditions, a common past, by common symbolic ties to his crown, the Commonwealth could exercise great influence in world affairs. If that ideal was to be it was essential that India remain within the Commonwealth when she got her independence. If India refused to join, the Afro-Asian nations, which in their turn would accede to independence in the years to come, would almost certainly follow her example. That would condemn the Commonwealth to becoming just a grouping of the Empire's white dominions instead of the body the King longed to see emerge from the remains of his empire. . . .

Sitting there in their Buckingham Palace sitting room, Victoria's two great-grandsons reached a private decision that January day. Louis Mountbatten would become the agent of their common aspiration for the Commonwealth's future. In a few days Mountbatten would insist that Attlee include in his terms of reference a specific injunction to maintain an independent India, united or divided, inside the Commonwealth if at all possible. In the weeks ahead, there could be no task to which India's new viceroy would devote more thought, more persuasiveness, more cunning than the one conceived that afternoon in George VI's sitting room, that of maintaining a link between India and his cousin's crown. [45–46]

THE CORONATION

The closing chapter in a great story was about to begin. In a few minutes, on this morning of March 24, 1947, the last Englishman to govern India would mount his gold-and-crimson viceregal throne. Installed upon that throne, Louis Mountbatten would become the twentieth and final representative of a prestigious dynasty, his the last hands to clasp the scepter that had passed from Hastings to Wellesley, to Cornwallis and Curzon. The site of his official consecration was the ceremonial Durbar Hall of a palace whose awesome dimensions were rivaled only by those of Versailles and of the Peterhof of the Tsars. . . .

In Poona, Peshawar and Simla—wherever there was a military garrison in India—troops on parade presented arms as the first gun exploded in Delhi. Frontier Force Rifles, the Guides Cavalry, Hodsons and Skinners Horse, Sikhs and Dogras, Jats and Pathans, Gurkhas and Madrassis

poised while the cannon thundered out their last tattoo for the British raj. As the sound of the last report faded through the dome of Durbar Hall, the new viceroy stepped to the microphone. The situation he faced was so serious that, against the advice of his staff, Mountbatten had decided to break with tradition by addressing the gathering before him.

"I am under no illusion about the difficulty of my task, " he said. "I shall need the greatest good will of the greatest possible number, and I am asking India today for that good will." As he finished, the guards threw open the massive Assam teak doors of the Hall. Before Mountbatten was the breathtaking vista of Kingsway and its glistening pools, plunging down the heart of New Delhi. Overhead the trumpets sent out another strident call. . . . That brief ceremony, he realized, had turned him into one of the most powerful men on earth. He now held in his hand an almost life-and-death power over four hundred million people, one-fifth of mankind. [90–91]

OPERATION SEDUCTION

India's last viceroy might, as he had glumly predicted at Northolt Airport, come home with a bullet in his back, but he would be a viceroy unlike any other that India had seen. Mountbatten firmly believed "it was impossible to be viceroy without putting up a great, brilliant show." He had been sent to New Delhi to get the British out of India, but he was determined that they would go in a shimmer of scarlet and gold, all the old glories of the raj honed to the highest pitch one last time.

He ordered all the ceremonial trappings that had been suppressed during the war restored—A.D.C.s in dazzling full dress, guard-mounting ceremonies, bands playing, sabers flashing—"the lot." . . . He intended to replace Wavell's "Operation Madhouse" with a kind of "Operation Seduction" of his own, a minirevolution in style directed as much toward India's masses as toward their leaders, with whom he would have to negotiate. It would be a shrewd blend of contrasting values, of patrician pomp and a common touch, of the old spectacles of the dying raj and new initiatives prefiguring the India of tomorrow.

Strangely, Mountbatten began his revolution with the stroke of a paint brush. To his aides' horror, he ordered the gloomy wooden panels of the viceregal study, in which so many negotiations had failed, covered with a light, cheerful coat of paint more apt to relax the Indian leaders with whom he would be dealing. He shook Viceroy's House out of the leisurely routine it had developed, turning it into a humming, quasi-military headquarters. He instituted staff meetings, soon known as "morning prayers," as the first official activity of each day.

Mountbatten astonished his new I.C.S. subordinates with the agility of his mind, his capacity to get at the root of a problem and, above all, his almost obsessive capacity for work. He put an end to the parade of *chaprassis*, who traditionally bore the viceroy his papers for his private contemplation in green leather dispatch boxes. He preferred taut, verbal briefings.

"When you wrote 'May I speak?' on a paper he was to read," one of his staff recalled, "you could be sure you'd speak, and you'd better be ready to say what was on your mind at any time, because the call to speak could come at two o'clock in the morning."

But it was, above all, the public image Mountbatten was trying to create for himself and his office that represented a radical change. For over a century, the viceroy of India, locked in the ceremonial splendors of his office, had rivaled the Dalai Lama as the most remote god in Asia's pantheon of ruling gods. Two unsuccessful assassination attempts had left him enrobed in a kind of security cocoon isolating him from all contact with the brown masses that he ruled. . . . Hundreds of bodyguards, police, and security men followed each of his moves. If he played golf, the fairways of his course were cleared and police were posted along them behind almost every tree. If he went riding, a squadron of the viceroy's bodyguard and security police jogged along after him.

Mountbatten's first announcement, that he and his wife or daughter would take their morning horseback rides unescorted, sent a shock wave of horror through the house. It took him some time to get his way, but suddenly the Indian villagers along the route of their morning rides began to witness a spectacle so wholly unbelievable as to seem a mirage: the Viceroy and Vicereine of India trotting past them, waving graciously, alone and unprotected.

Then he and his wife made an even more revolutionary gesture. He did something that no viceroy had deigned to do in two hundred years; he visited the home of an Indian who was not one of a handful of privileged princes. To the astonishment of all India, the viceregal couple walked into a garden party at the simple New Delhi residence of Jawaharlal Nehru. While Nehru's aides looked on dumb with disbelief, Mountbatten took Nehru by the elbow and strolled off among the guests casually chatting and shaking hands. The gesture had a stunning impact. "Thank God," an awed Nehru told his sister that evening, "we've finally got a human being for a viceroy and not a stuffed shirt."

Anxious to demonstrate that a new esteem for the Indian people now reigned in Viceroy's House, Mountbatten accorded the Indian military, two million of whom had served under him in Southeast Asia, a long-overdue honor. He had three Indian officers attached to his staff as A.D.C.s. Next, he ordered the doors of Viceroy's House opened to Indians. Only a handful of Indians had been invited into its precincts before his arrival. He instructed his staff that there were to be no dinner parties in the Viceroy's House without Indian guests. And not just a few token Indians. Henceforth, he ordered, at least half the faces around his table were to be Indian. . . .

Not long after their arrival, *The New York Times* noted that "no viceroy in history has so completely won the confidence, respect and liking of the Indian people." Indeed, within a few weeks, the success of "Operation Seduction" would be so remarkable that Nehru himself would tell the new viceroy only halfjokingly that he was becoming a very difficult man to negotiate with, because he was "drawing larger crowds than anybody in India." [93–95]

STRAIGHT FOR CIVIL WAR

[But time was short. George Abell, whose reputation for brilliance and understanding of India was unsurpassed] told Mountbatten with stark simplicity that India was heading straight for a civil war. Only by finding the quickest of resolutions to her problems was he going to save her. The great administrative machine governing India was collapsing. The shortage of British officers, which was caused by the decision to stop recruiting during the war, and the rising antagonism between its Hindu and Moslem members meant that the rule of that vaunted institution, the Indian Civil Service, could not survive the year. The time for discussion and debate was past. Speed, not deliberation, was needed to avoid a catastrophe.

Coming from a man of Abell's stature, those words gave the new viceroy a dismal shock. Yet, they were only the first in a stream of reports and actions which engulfed him during his first fortnight in India. He received an equally grim analysis from the man he had handpicked to come with him as his chief of staff, General Lord Ismay, Winston Churchill's chief of staff from 1940 to 1945. A veteran of years on the subcontinent as an officer in the Indian Army and military secretary to an earlier viceroy, Ismay had concluded that "India was a ship on fire in mid-ocean with ammunition in her hold." The question, he told Mountbatten, was could they get the fire out before it reached the ammunition?

The first report that Mountbatten received from the Bristish governor of the Punjab warned him that "there is a civil-war atmosphere throughout the province." It mentioned [in passing] a recent tragedy in a rural district near Rawalpindi. A Moslem's water buffalo had wandered onto the property of his Sikh neighbor. When its owner sought to reclaim it, a fight, then a riot erupted. Two hours later, a hundred human beings lay in the surrounding fields, hacked to death with scythes and knives because of the vagrant humors of a water buffalo. Five days after the new viceroy's arrival, incidents between Hindus and Moslems took ninety-nine lives in Calcutta. Two days later, a similar conflict broke out in Bombay, leaving forty-one mutilated bodies on its pavements.

Confronted by those outbursts of violence, Mountbatten called India's senior police officer to his study and asked if the police were capable of maintaining law and order in India. "No, Your Excellency," was the reply, "we cannot." . . .

Mountbatten quickly discovered that the government with which he was supposed to govern India, a coalition of the Congress Party and the Moslem League put together with enormous effort by his predecessor, was in fact an assembly of enemies so bitterly divided that its members barely spoke to one another. It was clearly going to fall apart, and when it did, Mountbatten would have to assume the appalling responsibility of exercising direct rule over one-fifth of humanity himself, with the administrative machine required for the task collapsing underneath him.

Confronted by that grim prospect, assailed on every side by reports of violence and the warnings of his most seasoned advisers, Mountbatten reached what was perhaps the most important decision he would make in India in his first ten days in the country; it was to condition every other decision of his viceroyalty. The date of June 1948 established in London for the transfer of power, the date that he himself had urged on Attlee, had been wildly optimistic. Whatever solution he was to reach for India's future, he was going to have to reach it in weeks, not months.

"The scene here," he wrote in his first report to the Attlee government on April 2, 1947, "is one of unrelieved gloom. . . . I can see little ground on which to build any agreed solution for the future of India." After describing the country's unsettled state, the young admiral issued an anguished warning to the man who had sent him to India. "The only conclusion I have been able to come to," he wrote, "is that unless I act quickly, I will find the beginnings of a civil war on my hands." [95–96]

THE FOUR INDIANS

Because of the urgency of the situation facing him, Mountbatten had decided to employ a revolutionary tactic in his negotiation with India's leaders. For the first time in its modern history, India's destiny was not being decided around a conference table, but in the intimacy of private conversations. . . . Five men would participate in them: Louis Mountbatten and four Indian leaders. The four Indians had spent the better part of their lives agitating against the British and arguing with one another. All were past middle age. All were lawyers who had learned their forensic skills in London's Inns of Court. . . .

In Mountbatten's mind, there was no question what the outcome of that debate should be. Like many Englishmen, he looked on India's unity as the greatest legacy Britain could leave behind. He had a deep, almost evangelical desire to maintain it. To respond to the Moslem appeal to divide the country was, he believed, to sow the seeds of tragedy. Every effort to persuade India's leaders to agree on a solution to their country's problems in a formal meeting had led to a deadlock. [But here in the privacy of his study] he was going to try to achieve in weeks what his predecessors had been unable to achieve in years—get India's leaders to agree on some form of unity. . . .

THE KASHMIRI BRAHMAN

Nehru was the only Indian leader whom Mountbatten already knew. [At the end of World War II] to the horror of his staff Mountbatten rode through Singapore's streets in his open car with Nehru at his side. His action, his advisers had warned, would only dignify an anti-British rebel. "Dignify him?" Mountbatten had retorted, "It is he who will dignify *me*. Some day this man will be Prime Minister of India." [97–98]

There was a great deal to bind the scion of a three-thousand-year-old line of Kashmiri Brahmans and the man who claimed descent from the oldest ruling family in Protestantism. They both loved to talk, and they expanded in each other's company. Nehru, the abstract thinker, admired Mountbatten's practical dynamism, the capacity for decisive action that wartime command had given him. Mountbatten was stimulated by the subtlety of Nehru's thought. He quickly understood that the only Indian politician who would share and understand his desire to maintain a link between Britain and a new India was Jawaharlal Nehru.

With his usual candor, the Viceroy told Nehru that he had been given an appalling responsibility and he intended to approach the Indian problem in a mood of stark realism. As they talked, the two men rapidly agreed on two major points: a quick decision was essential to avoid a bloodbath and the division of India would be a tragedy. Then Nehru turned to the actions of the next Indian leader who would enter Mountbatten's study, the penitent Mohandas Gandhi marching his lonely path through Noakhali and Bihar. The man to whom he had been so long devoted was, Nehru said, "going around with ointment trying to heal one sore spot after another on the body of India instead of diagnosing the cause of the eruption of the sores and participating in the treatment of the body as a whole."

In offering a glimpse into the growing gulf separating the Liberator of India and his closest companions, Nehru's words provided Mountbatten with a vital insight into the form that his actions in Delhi should take. If he could not persuade India's leaders to keep their country united, he was going to have to persuade them to divide it. Gandhi's unremitting hostility to partition could place an insurmountable barrier in his path and confront him with a catastrophe. His only hope, then, would be to divorce the leaders of Congress from their aging leader. Nehru would be the key if that happened. He was the only ally Mountbatten must have; only he might have the authority to stand up against the Mahatma.

Now that words had revealed the discord between Gandhi and his party chief, Mountbatten might be forced to widen and exploit that gap to succeed. He needed Nehru, and he spared no effort to win his support. On none of India's leaders would Operation Seduction have more impact than on the realistic Kashmiri Brahman. . . . Taking Nehru to the door, Mountbatten told him, "Mr. Nehru, I want you to regard me not as the last British viceroy winding up the raj, but as the first to lead the way to a new India." Nehru turned and looked at the man he had wanted to see on the viceregal throne. "Ah," he said, a faint smile creasing his face, "now I know what they mean when they speak of your charm as being so dangerous." [101–102]

THE MOST FAMOUS ASIAN ALIVE

[The next man to see Mountbatten was unique, a saint in his own time. He was Mohandas Gandhi—called Mahatma, meaning "Great Soul."] At every village, his routine was the same. As soon as he arrived, the most famous Asian alive would go up to a hut, preferably a Moslem's hut, and beg for shelter. If he was turned away, and sometimes he was, Gandhi would go to another door. "If there is no one to receive me," he had said, "I shall be happy to rest under the hospitable shade of a tree." Once installed, he lived on whatever food his hosts would offer—mangoes, vegetables, goat's curds, green coconut milk. Every hour of his day in each village was rigorously programmed. Time was one of Gandhi's obsessions. Each minute, he held, was a gift of God to be used in the service of man. . . . He got up at two o'clock in the morning to read his Gita and say his morning prayers. From then until dawn he squatted in his hut, patiently answering his correspondence himself with a pencil, in longhand. He used each pencil right down to an ungrippable stub, because he held that it represented the work of a fellow human being and to waste it would indicate indifference to his labors. . . .

The aging leader did not stop with words. Gandhi had a tenacious belief in the value of one concrete act. To the despair of many of his followers who thought a different set of priorities should order his time, Gandhi would devote the same meticulous care and attention to making a mudpack for a leper as preparing for an interview with a viceroy. So, in each village he would go with its inhabitants to their wells. Frequently he would help them find a better location for them. He would inspect their communal latrines, or if, as was most often the case, they didn't have any, he would teach them how to build one, often joining in the digging himself. [52]

Determined to convert [the Congress Party] into a mass movement attuned to his nonviolent creed, Gandhi presented the party a plan of action in Calcutta in 1920. It was adopted by an overwhelming majority. From that moment until his death, whether he held rank in the party or not, Gandhi was Congress's conscience and its guide, the unquestioned leader of the independence struggle. . . . Gandhi's tactic was electrifyingly simple, a one-word program for political revolution: noncooperation. Indians, he decreed, would boycott whatever was British; students would boycott British schools; lawyers, British courts; employees, British jobs; soldiers, British honors. . . .

Above all, his aim was to weaken the edifice of British power in India by attacking the economic pillar upon which it reposed. Britain purchased raw Indian cotton for derisory prices, shipped it to the mills of Lancashire to be woven into textiles, then shipped the finished products back to India to be sold at a substantial profit in a market that virtually excluded non-British textiles. It was the classic cycle of imperialist exploitation, and the arm with which Gandhi proposed to fight it was the very antithesis of the great mills of the Industrial Revolution that had sired that exploitation. It was a primitive wooden spinning wheel. For the next quarter of a century Gandhi struggled with tenacious energy to force all India to forsake foreign textiles for the rough cotton khadi cloth spun by millions of spinning wheels. Convinced that the misery of India's half million villages was due above all to the decline in village crafts, he saw in a renaissance of cottage industry, heralded by the spinning wheel, the key to the revival of India's impoverished countryside. For the urban masses, spinning would be a kind of spiritual redemption by manual labor, a constant, daily reminder of their link to the real India, the India of half a million villages. [61–62]

"The British want us to put the struggle on the plane of machine guns where they have the weapons and we do not," he warned. "Our only assurance of beating them is putting the struggle on a plane where we have the weapons and they have not." Thousands of Indians followed his call, and thousands more went off to jail. The beleaguered governor of Bombay called it "the most colossal experiment in world history and one which came within an inch of succeeding."

It failed because of an outburst of bloody violence in a little village northeast of Delhi. Against the wishes of almost his entire Congress hierarchy, Gandhi called off the movement because he felt that his followers did not yet fully understand nonviolence. Sensing that his change of attitude had rendered him less dangerous, the British arrested him. Gandhi pleaded guilty to the charge of sedition, and in a moving appeal to his judge, asked for the maximum penalty. He was sentenced to six years in Yeravda prison near Poona. He had no regrets. "Freedom," he wrote, "is often to be found inside a prison's walls, even on a gallows; never in council chambers, courts and classrooms." [64]

"A leader," Gandhi replied, "is only a reflection of the people he leads." The people had first to be led to make peace among themselves. Then, he said, "their desire to live together in peaceful neighborliness will be reflected by their leaders." [53]

[Once Winston Churchill had called Mohandas Gandhi "a half-naked fakir."] Now that half-naked fakir was sitting in the viceregal study, "to negotiate and parley on equal terms with the representative of the King-Emperor." He's rather like a little bird, Louis Mountbatten thought, as he contemplated that famous figure at his side, a kind of "sweet, sad sparrow perched on my armchair." . . .

So important had Mountbatten considered this first meeting with Gandhi, that he had written the Mahatma inviting him to Delhi before the ceremony enthroning him as viceroy. Gandhi had drafted his reply immediately, then, with a chuckle, told an aide, "Wait a couple of days before putting it in the mail. I don't want that young man to think I'm dying for his invitation." That "young man" had accompanied his invitation with one of those gestures for which he was becoming noted and which sometimes infuriated his fellow Englishmen. He had offered to send his personal aircraft to Bihar to fly Gandhi to Delhi. Gandhi had declined the offer. He had insisted on traveling, as he always did, in a third-class railway car.

To give their meeting a special cordiality, Mountbatten had asked his wife to be present. Now, with the famous figure opposite them, worry and concern swept over the viceregal couple. The Mahatma, they both immediately sensed, was profoundly unhappy, trapped in the grip of some mysterious remorse. Had they done something wrong? Neglected some arcane law of protocol? . . .

[Finally] a slow, sorrowful sigh escaped the Indian leader. "You know," he replied, "all my life, since I was in South Africa, I've renounced physical possessions." He owned virtually nothing, he explained—his Gita, the tin utensils from which he ate, mementos of his stay in Yeravda prison, his three "gurus." And his watch, the old eight-shilling Ingersoll that he hung from a string around his waist because, if he was going to devote every minute of his day to God's work, he had to know what time it was.

"Do you know what?" he asked sadly. "They stole it. Someone in my railway compartment coming down to Delhi stole the watch." As the frail figure lost in his arm-chair spoke those words, Mountbatten saw tears shining in Gandhi's eyes. It was not an eight-shilling watch an unknown hand had plucked from him in that congested railway car, but a particle of his faith. After a long silence, Gandhi began to talk of India's current dilemma. Mountbatten interrupted with a friendly wave of his hand.

"Mr. Gandhi," he said, "first, I want to know who you are." He was determined to get to know these Indian leaders before allowing them to begin assailing him with their minimum demands and final conditions. By putting them at ease, by getting them to confide in him, he hoped to create an atmosphere of mutual confidence and sympathy in which his own dynamic personality could have greater impact. The Mahatma was delighted. He loved to talk about himself, and in the Mountbattens he had found a charming pair of people genuinely interested in what he had to say. He rambled on about South Africa, his days as a stretcher-bearer in the Boer War, civil disobedience, the Salt March. Once, he said, the West had received its inspiration from the East in the messages of Zoroaster, Buddha, Moses, Jesus, Mohammed, Rama. For centuries, however, the East had been conquered culturally by the West. Now the West, haunted by specters like the atomic bomb, had need to look eastward once again. There, he hoped, it might find the message of love and fraternal understanding that he sought to preach. [103–104] [Much later] India's new viceroy moved into a serious exchange with Gandhi with trepidation. He was not persuaded that the little figure "chirping like a sparrow" at his side could help him elaborate a solution to the Indian crisis, but he knew that he could defeat all efforts to find one. The hopes of many another English mediator had foundered on the turns of his unpredictable personality. It was Gandhi who had sent Cripps back to London empty-handed in 1942. His refusal to budge on a principle had helped thwart Wevell's efforts to untie the Indian knot. His tactics had done much to frustrate the most recent British attempt to solve the problem of liberation. Only the evening before, Gandhi had reiterated to his prayer meeting that India would be divided "over my dead body. So long as I am alive, I will never agree to the partition of India." . . .

It had always been British policy not to yield to force, he told Gandhi, by way of opening their talks on the right note, but his nonviolent crusade had won, and come what may, Britain was going to leave India. Only one thing mattered in that coming departure, Gandhi replied. "Don't partition India," be begged. "Don't divide India," the prophet of nonviolence pleaded, "even if refusing to do so means shedding rivers of blood."

Dividing India, a shocked Mountbatten assured Gandhi, was the last solution he wished to adopt. But what alternatives were open to him? Gandhi had one. So desperate was he to avoid partition that he was prepared to give the Moslems the baby instead of cutting it in half. Place three hundred million Hindus under Moslem rule, he told Mountbatten, by asking his rival Jinnah and his Moslem League to form a government. Then hand over power to that government. Give Jinnah all of India instead of just the part he wants, was his nonviolent proposal.

"Whatever makes you think your own Congress Party will accept?" Mountbatten asked.

"Congress," Gandhi replied, "wants above all else to avoid partition. They will do anything to prevent it."

"What," Mountbatten asked, "would Jinnah's reaction be?"

"If you tell him I am its author his reply will be, 'Wily Gandhi,'" The Mahatma said, laughing. [106–109]

THE BULLY

Why, this man is trying to bully me, an unbelieving Louis Mountbatten thought. His Operation Seduction had come to a sudden, wholly unexpected halt at the rocklike figure planted in the chair opposite his. With his Khadi dhoti flung about his shoulders like a toga, his bald head glowing, his scowling demeanor, his visitor looked to the Viceroy more like a Roman senator than an Indian politician.

Patel was Indian from the uppermost lump of his bald head to the calluses on the soles of his feet. His Delhi home was filled with books, but every one of them was written by an Indian author about India. He was the only Indian leader who sprang from the soil of India. Emotion, one of his associates once observed, formed no part of Patel's character. The remark was not wholly exact. Patel was an emotional man, but he never let those emotions break through the composed facade he turned to the world. If he gave off one salient impression, it was that of a man wholly in control of himself. In a land in which men talked constantly, threw their words around like sailors flinging away their money after three months at sea, Patel hoarded his phrases the way a miser hoarded coins. His daughter, who had been his constant companion since his wife's death, rarely exchanged ten sentences with him a day. When Patel did talk, however, people listened.

Vallabhbhai Patel was India's quintessential politician. He was an Oriental Tammany Hall boss who ran the machinery of the Congress Party with a firm and ruthless hand. He should have been the easiest member of the Indian quartet for Mountbatten to deal with. Like the Viceroy, he was a practical pragmatic man, a hard but realistic bargainer. Yet the tension between them was so real, so palpable, that it seemed to Mountbatten he could reach out and touch it. Its cause was in no way related to the great issues facing India. It was a slip of paper, a routine government minute issued by Patel's Home Ministry dealing with

an appointment. But Mountbatten had read it as a calculated challenge to his authority.

Patel had a well-earned reputation for toughness. He had an almost instinctive need to take the measure of a new interlocutor, to see how far he could push him. The piece of paper on his desk, Mountbatten was convinced, was a test, a little examination that he had to go through with Patel before he could get down to serious matters. The Viceroy looked at the note which had offended him, then passed it across his desk to Patel. Quietly he asked him to withdraw it. Patel brusquely refused. Mountbatten studied the Indian leader. He was going to need the support of this man and the machinery he represented. But he was sure he would never get it if he did not face him down now.

"Very well," said Mountbatten. "I'll tell you what I'm going to do. I'm going to order my plane."

"Oh," said Patel, "why?"

"Because I'm leaving," Mountbatten replied. "I didn't want this job in the first place. I've just been looking for someone like you to give me an excuse to throw it up and get out of an impossible situation."

"You don't mean it," exclaimed Patel.

"Mean it?" replied Mountbatten. "You don't think I am going to stay here and be bullied around by a chap like you, do you? If you think you can be rude to me and push me around, you're wrong. You'll either withdraw that minute, or one of us is going to resign. And let me tell you that if I go, I shall first explain to your prime minister, to Mr. Jinnah, to His Majesty's Government, why I am leaving. The breakdown in India which will follow, the blood that will be shed, will be on your shoulders and no one else's." Patel stared at Mountbatten in disbelief. A long silence followed, "You know," Patel finally sighed, "the awful part is I think you mean it." "You're damned right I do," answered Mountbatten. Patel reached out, took the offending minute off Mountbatten's desk and slowly tore it up. [109–111]

THE FATHER OF PAKISTAN

The man who would ultimately hold the key to the subcontinent's dilemma in his hands was the last of the Indian leaders to enter the Viceroy's study. A quarter of a century later, an echo of his distant anguish still haunting his voice, Louis Mountbatten would recall, "I did not realize how utterly impossible my task in India was going to be until I met Mohammed Ali Jinnah for the first time."

Inside the study, Jinnah began by informing Mountbatten that he had come to tell him exactly what he was prepared to accept. As he had done with Gandhi, Mountbatten interrupted with a wave of his hand. "Mr. Jinnah," he said, "I am not prepared to discuss conditions at this stage. First, let's make each other's acquaintance." Then with his legendary charm and verve, Mountbatten turned the focus of Operation Seduction on the Moslem leader. Jinnah froze. To that aloof and reserved man who never unbent, even with his closest associates, the very idea of revealing the details of his life and personality to a perfect stranger must have seemed appalling. Gamely Mountbatten struggled on, summoning up all the reserves of his gregarious, engaging personality. For what seemed to him like hours, his only reward was a series of monosyllabic grunts from the man beside him.

The man who would one day be hailed as the Father of Pakistan had first been exposed to the idea at the black-tie dinner at London's Waldorf Hotel in the spring of 1933. His host was Rahmat Ali, the graduate student who had set the idea to paper. Rahmat Ali had arranged the banquet with its oysters on the half shell and un-Islamic Chablis at his own expense, hoping to persuade Jinnah, India's leading Moslem politician, to take over his movement. He received a chilly rebuff. Pakistan, Jinnah told him, was "an impossible dream." The man whom the unfortunate graduate student had sought to lead a Moslem separatist movement had, in fact, begun his political career by preaching Hindu-Moslem unity.... [115]

Like Gandhi, Jinnah had gone to London to dine in the Inns of Court and had been called to the bar. Unlike Gandhi, however, he had come back from London an Englishman. He wore a monocle, superbly cut linen suits, which he changed three or four times a day to remain cool and unruffled in the soggy Bombay climate. He loved oysters and caviar, champagne, brandy and good Bordeaux. A man of unassailable personal honesty and financial integrity, his canons were sound law and sound procedure. He was, according to one intimate, "the last of the Victorians, a parliamentarian in the mode of Gladstone or Disraeli."

A more improbable leader of India's Moslem masses could hardly be imagined. The only thing Moslem about Mohammed Ali Jinnah was the fact his parents happened to be Moslem. He drank, ate pork, religiously shaved his beard each morning, and just as religiously avoided the mosque each Friday. God and the Koran had no place in Jinnah's vision of the world. His political foe Gandhi knew more verses of the Moslem holy book than he did. He had been able to achieve the remarkable feat of securing the allegience of the vast majority of India's ninety million Moslems without being able to articulate more than a few sentences in their traditional tongue, Urdu.

Jinnah despised India's masses. He detested the dirt, the heat, the crowds of India. Gandhi traveled India in filthy third-class railway cars to be with the people. Jinnah rode first-class to avoid them. Jinnah had only scorn for his Hindu rivals. He labeled Nehru "a Peter Pan"; a "literary figure" who "should have been an English professor, not a politician"; "an arrogant Brahman who covers his Hindu trickiness under a veneer of Western education." Gandhi, to Jinnah, was "a cunning fox," "a Hindu revivalist." The sight of Mahatma, during an interval in a conversation in Jinnah's mansion, stretched out on one of his priceless Persian carpets, his mudpack on his belly, was something Jinnah had never forgotten or forgiven....

His disenchantment with the Congress Party dated from Gandhi's ascension to power. It was not the impeccably dressed Jinnah who was going to be bundled off to some squalid British jail half naked in a dhoti and wearing a silly little white cap. Civil disobedience, he told Gandhi, was for "the ignorant and the illiterate." The turning point in Jinnah's career came after the 1937 elections, when the Congress Party refused to share with him and his Moslem League the spoils of office in those Indian provinces where there was a substantial Moslem minority. Jinnah, a man of towering vanity, took Congress's action as a personal insult. It convinced him that he and the Moslem League would never get a fair deal from a Congress-run India. The former apostle of Hindu-Moslem unity became the unyielding advocate of Pakistan, the project that he had labeled an "impossible dream" barely four years earlier. [116–117]

Mountbatten and Jinnah held six critical meetings during the first fortnight of April 1947. They were the vital conversations—not quite ten hours in length—that ultimately determined the resolution of the Indian dilemma. Mountbatten went into them armed with "the most enormous conceit in my ability to persuade people to do the right thing, not because I am persuasive so much as because I have the knack of being able to present the facts in their most favorable light." As he would later recall, he "tried every trick I could play, used every appeal I could imagine," to shake Jinnah's determination to have partition. Nothing would. There was no trick, no argument that could move him from his consuming determination to realize the impossible dream of Pakistan.... He had made himself the absolute dictator of the Moslem League. There were men below who might have been willing to negotiate a compromise, but as long as Mohammed Ali Jinnah was alive, they would hold their silence....

Mountbatten and Jinnah did agree on one point at the outset—the need for speed. India, Jinnah declared, had gone beyond the stage at which a compromise solution was possible. There was only one solution, a speedy "surgical operation" on India. Otherwise, he warned, India would perish. When Mountbatten expressed concern that partition might produce bloodshed and violence, Jinnah reassured him. Once his "surgical operation" had taken place, all troubles would cease and India's two halves would live in harmony and happiness. It was, Jinnah told Mountbatten, like a court case that he had handled, a dispute between two brothers embittered by the shares assigned them by their father's will. Yet two years after the court had adjudicated their dispute, they were the greatest friends. That, he promised the Viceroy, would be the case in India. . . .

. . . "India has never been a true nation," Jinnah asserted. "It only looks that way on the map. . . . The cows I want to eat, the Hindu stops me from killing. Every time a Hindu shakes hands with me he has to go wash his hands. The only thing the Moslem has in common with the Hindu is his slavery to the British." . . . [118]

For Jinnah, the division that he proposed was the natural course. However, it would have to produce a viable state, which meant that two of India's great provinces, the Punjab and Bengal, would have to be included in Pakistan, despite the fact that each contained enormous Hindu populations. Mountbatten could not agree. The very basis of Jinnah's argument for Pakistan was that India's Moslem minority should not be ruled by its Hindu majority. How then to justify taking the Hindu minorities of Bengal and the Punjab into a Moslem state? If Jinnah insisted on dividing India to get his Islamic state, then the very logic he had used to get it would compel Mountbatten to divide the Punjab and Bengal.

Jinnah protested—that would give him an economically unviable, "motheaten Pakistan." Mountbatten, who didn't want to give him any Pakistan at all, told the Moslem leader that if he felt the nation he was to receive was as "moth-eaten" as all that, he would do well to abandon his plan.

"Ah," Jinnah would counter, "Your Excellency doesn't understand. A man is a Punjabi or a Bengali before he is Hindu or Moslem. They share a common history, language, culture and economy. You must not divide them. You will cause endless bloodshed and trouble." "Mr. Jinnah I entirely agree." "You do?" "Of course," Mountbatten would continue. "A man is not only a Punjabi or Bengali before he is a Hindu or a Moslem, he is an Indian before all else. You have presented the unanswerable argument for Indian unity." "But you don't understand at all," Jinnah countered—and the discussion would start again.

Mountbatten was stunned by the rigidity of Jinnah's position. "I never would have believed," he later recalled, "that an intelligent man, well educated, trained in the Inns of Court, was capable of simply closing his mind as Jinnah did. It wasn't that he didn't see the point. He did, but a kind of shutter came down. He was the evil genius in the whole thing. The others could be persuaded, but not Jinnah. While he was alive nothing could be done." [191]

If Louis Mountbatten, Jawaharlal Nehru, or Mahatma Gandhi had been aware in April 1947 of one extraordinary secret, the division threatening India might have been avoided. That secret was sealed onto the gray surface of a piece of film, a film that could have upset the Indian political equation and would almost certainly have changed the

course of Asian history. Yet so precious was the secret which the film harbored that even the British C.I.D., one of the most effective investigative agencies in the world, was ignorant of its existence. The heart of the film was two dark circles no bigger than a pair of Ping-Pong balls. Each was surrounded by an irregular white border like the corona of the sun eclipsed by the moon. Above them, a galaxy of little white spots stretched up the film's gray surface toward the top of the thoracic cage. That film was an x-ray, the x-ray of a pair of human lungs.

The damage was so extensive that the man whose lungs were on that film had barely two or three years to live. . . . The lungs depicted on them belonged to the rigid and inflexible man who had frustrated Louis Mountbatten's efforts to preserve India's unity. Mohammed Ali Jinnah, the one unmovable obstacle between the Viceroy and Indian unity, was living under a sentence of death. . . . [124]

Mediating along in his study after Jinnah's departure, Mountbatten realized that he was probably going to have to give him Pakistan. His first obligation in New Delhi was to the nation that had sent him there, England. He longed to preserve India's unity, but not at the expense of his country's becoming hopelessly entrapped in an India collapsing in chaos and violence. . . .

Military command had given Mountbatten a penchant for rapid, decisive actions, such as the one he now took. In future years, his critics would assail him for having reached it too quickly, for acting like an impetuous sailor and not a statesman, but Mountbatten was not going to waste any more time on what he was certain would be futile arguments with Jinnah. . . . Neither logic nor Mountbatten's power to charm and persuade had made any impact on him. The partition of India seemed the only solution. It now remained to Mountbatten to get Nehru and Patel to accept the principle and to find for it a plan that could get their support.

THE INDIAN RAJAHS

Yadavindra Singh presided over the most remarkable body in the world, an assembly unlike any other that man had ever devised. He was the Chancellor of the Chamber of Indian Princes (the fabled Rajahs). His state of Patiala in the Punjab was one of the richest in India. He had an army the size of an infantry division, equipped with Centurion tanks to defend it if necessary.

The princes' anachronistic situation dated to Britain's haphazard conquest of India, when rulers who received the English with open arms or proved worthy foes on the battlefield were allowed to remain on their thrones provided that they acknowledged Britain as the paramount power in India. The system was formalized in a series of treaties between the individual rulers and the British Crown. The Princes had recognized the "Paramountcy" of the King-Emperor as represented in New Delhi by the viceroy, and they ceded to him control of their foreign affairs and defense. They received in return Britain's guarantee of their continuing autonomy inside their states. [See map page 308.] . . .

Certain princes like the Nizam of Hyderabad or the Maharaja of Kashmir ruled over states which rivaled in size or population the nations of Western Europe. Others like those in the Kathiawar peninsula near Bombay lived in stables and governed domains no larger than New York City's Central Park. Their fraternity embraced the richest man in the world and princes so poor that their entire kingdom was a cow pasture. Over four hundred princes ruled states smaller than twenty square miles. A good number of them offered their subjects an administration far better than that the British provided. A few were petty despots more concerned with squandering their states' revenues to slake their own extravagant desires than with improving the lot of their peoples. Whatever their political proclivities, however, the future of India's 565 ruling princes, with their average of eleven titles, 5.8 wives, 12.6 children, 9.2 elephants, 2.8 private railway cars, 3.4 Roll-Royces, and 22.9 tigers killed, posed a grave problem in the spring of 1947. No solution to the Indian equation would work if it failed to deal with their peculiar situation. [165, 166]

A SUBTLE MOSAIC

Inevitably, Mountbatten's decision would lead to one of the great dramas of modern history. Whatever the manner in which it was executed, it was bound to end in the mutilation of a great nation. . . . To satisfy the exigent demands of Mohammed Ali Jinnah, two of India's most distinctive entities, the Punjab and Bengal, would have to be carved up. The result would make Pakistan a geographic aberration, a nation of two heads separated by 1,500 kilometers (900 miles) of Himalayan mountain peaks, all purely Indian territory. Twenty days, more time than was required to sail from Karachi to Marseilles, would be needed to make the sea trip around the subcontinent from one half of Pakistan to the other. [120] . . .

The Punjab was a blend as subtle and complex as the mosaics decorating the monuments of its glorious Royal past. To divide it was unthinkable. Fifteen million Hindus, sixteen million Moslems, and five million Sikhs shared the neighborhoods and alleyways of its 17,932 towns and villages. Although divided by religion, they shared a common language, joint traditions, and a great pride in this distinctive Punjabi personality. Wherever the boundary line went, the result was certain to be a nightmare for millions of human beings. Only an interchange of populations on a

scale never effected before in history could sort out the havoc that it would create. From the Indus to the bridges of Delhi, for over 500 miles, there was not a single town, not a single village, cotton grove or wheat field that would not somehow be threatened if the partition plan were to be carried out.

The division of Bengal at the other end of the subcontinent held out the possibilities of another tragedy. Harboring more people than Great Britain and Ireland combined, Bengal contained thirty-five million Moslems and thirty million Hindus spread over an expanse of land running from the jungles at the foot of the Himalayas to the streaming marshes through which the thousand tributaries of the Ganges and Brahmaputra rivers drained into the Bay of Bengal. Despite its division into two religious communities, Bengal, even more than the Punjab, was a distinct entity of its own. Whether Hindu or Moslem, Bengalis sprang from the same racial stock, spoke the same language, shared the same culture. They sat on the floor in a certain Bengali manner, ordered the sentences they spoke in a peculiar Bengali cadence, each rising to a final crescendo, celebrated their own Bengali New Year on April 15. Their poets like Tabore were regarded with pride by all Bengalis. [122]

A land seared by droughts that alternated with frightening typhoon-whipped floods, Bengal was an immense, steaming swamp, in whose humid atmosphere flourished the two crops to which it owed a precarious prosperity, rice and jute. The cultivation of those two crops followed the province's religious frontier rice to the Hindu west, jute to the Moslem east. But the key to Bengal's existence did not lie in its crops. It was a city, the city that had been the springboard for Britain's conquest of India, the second city, after London, of the Empire, and the first port of Asia—Calcutta, site of the terrible Hindu-Moslem killings of August 1946.

Everything in Bengal—roads, railroads, communications, industry—funneled into Calcutta. If Bengal was split into its eastern and western halves, Calcutta, because of its physical location, seemed certain to be in the Hindu west, thus condemning the Moslem east to a slow but inexorable asphyxiation. If almost all of the world's jute grew in eastern Bengal, all the factories that transformed it into rope, sacks and cloths were clustered around Calcutta, in western Bengal. The Moslem east, which produced the jute, grew almost no food at all, and its millions survived on the rice grown in the Hindu west. . . .

Yet, no aspect of partition was more illogical than the fact that Jinnah's Pakistan would deliver barely half of India's Moslems from the alleged inequities of Hindu majority rule which had justified the state in the first place. The remaining Moslems were scattered throughout the rest of India so widely that it was impossible to separate them. Islands in a Hindu sea, even after the amputation, India would still harbor almost fifty million Moslems, a figure that would make her the third-largest Moslem nation in the world, after Indonesia and the new state drawn from her own womb. [123]

THE GOVERNORS

The eleven men seated around the oval table in the conference chamber solemnly waited for Lord Mountbatten to begin the proceedings. They were, in a sense, the descendants of the twenty-four founding fathers of the East India Company, the men whose mercantile appetites had sent Britain along the sea lanes to India three and a half centuries earlier. . . . Their meeting was an awkward confrontation for Mountbatten. At forty-six, he was the youngest man at the table. . . . He was a comparative stranger in the India to which most of the eleven governors had devoted an entire career, mastering its complex history, learning its dialects, becoming, as some of them had, world-renowned experts on the phases of its existence. They were proud men, certain to be skeptical of any plan put before them by the neophyte in their midst. . . . [126]

Mountbatten began by asking each governor to describe the situation in his province. Eight of them painted a picture of dangerous, troubled areas, but provinces in which the situation still remained under control. It was the portrait offered by the governors of the three critical provinces, the Punjab, Bengal, and the Northwest Frontier Province, that sobered the gathering.

His features drawn, his eyes heavy with fatigue, Sir Olaf Caroe spoke first. He had been kept awake all night by a stream of cables detailing fresh outbursts of trouble in his Northwest Frontier Province. The labyrinth grottoes of his mountainous province sheltered scores of secret arms factories, from which flowed a profusion of ornate and deadly weapons to arm Mahsuds, Afridis, Wazirs, the legendary warrior tribes of the Pathans. The situation in the N.W.F.P. was close to disintegrating, he warned, and if that happened, the old British nightmare of invading hordes from the northwest forcing the gates of the Empire might be realized. The Pathan tribes of Afghanistan were poised to come pouring down the Khyber Pass to Peshawar and the banks of the Indus in pursuit of land they had claimed as theirs for a century. "If we're not jolly careful," he said, "we are going to have an international crisis on our hands."

The portrait drawn by Sir Evan Jenkins, the taciturn governor of the Punjab, was even grimmer than Caroe's. . . . Whatever solution was chosen for India's problems, he declared, it was certain to bring violence to the Punjab. At least four divisions would be needed to keep order if partition was decided upon. Even if it was not, they would still face a demand by the Sikhs for an area of their own. "It's

absurd to predict the Punjab will go up in flames if it's partitioned," he said; "it's already in flames." [127]

The third governor, Sir Frederick Burrows of Bengal, was ill in Calcutta, but the briefing of the province's situation as offered by his deputy was every bit as disquieting as the reports from the N.W.F.P. and the Punjab. When those reporters were finally finished, Mountbatten's staff passed out a set of papers to each governor. They carried the details, Mountbatten announced, "of one of the possible plans under examination." It was called, "for easy reference," Plan Balkan, and it was the first draft of a partition plan that Mountbatten had ordered his chief of staff, Lord Ismay, to prepare a week earlier. . . . The plan, aptly named for the Balkanization of the states of Central Europe after World War I, would allow each of India's eleven provinces to choose whether it wished to join Pakistan or remain in India; or, if a majority of both its Hindus and Moslems agreed, become independent. Mountbatten told his assembled governors that he was not going to "lightly abandon hope for a united India." He wanted the world to know that the British had made every effort possible to keep India united. If Britain failed it was of the utmost importance that the world know it was "Indian opinion rather than a British decision that had made partition the choice." He himself thought a future Pakistan was so inherently unviable that it should "be given a chance to fail on its own demerits," so that later "the Moslem League could revert to a unified India with honor."

Those eleven men who represented the collective wisdom of the service that had run India for a century displayed no enthusiasm for the idea that partition might have to be the answer to India's dilemma. Nor did they have any other solution to propose.[128]

VISIT TO PESHAWAR

Louis Mountbatten had decided to suspend temporarily the conversations in his air-conditioned office while he, personally, took the political temperature of his two most troubled provinces, the Punjab and the N.W.F.P. The news that he was coming had swept over the Frontier. For twenty-four hours, summoned by the leaders of Jinnah's Moslem League, tens of thousands of men from every corner of the province had been converging on Peshawar. Overflowing their trucks, in buses, in cars, on special trains, chanting and waving their arms, they had spilled into the capital for the greatest popular demonstration in its history.

Now those tall, pale-skinned Pathans prepared to offer the Viceroy a welcome of an unexpected sort to Peshawar. . . . The police had confined them in an enormous low-walled enclosure running between a railroad embankment and the sloping walls of Peshawar's old Mogul fortress. Irritated and unruly, they threatened to drown the conciliatory tones of Operation Seduction with the discordant rattle of gunfire.

They were there because of the anomalous political situation of a province whose population was 93 percent Moslem, but was governed by allies of the Congress Party. . . . Stiffed by Jinnah's agents, the population had turned against the Congress leader Ghaffar Khan who supported Gandhi and the government that he had installed in Peshawar. The huge, howling crowd greeting Mountbatten, his wife and seventeen-year-old daughter Pamela was meant to give final proof that it was the Moslem League and not the "Frontier Gandhi" that now commanded the province's support. [129] The crowd, growing more unruly by the hour, threatened to burst out of the area in which the police had herded them and start a headlong rush on the governor's residence. If they did, the vastly outnumbered military guarding the house would have no choice but to open fire. The resulting slaughter would be appalling. It would destroy Mountbatten, his hopes of finding a solution, and his viceroyalty in a sickening blood bath.

There was one way out, an idea condemned by the police and army commander as sheer madness. Mountbatten might present himself to the crowds, hoping that somehow a glimpse of him would mollify them. Mountbatten pondered a few moments. "All right, I'll take a chance and see them." To the despair of Caroe and his security officers, Edwina, his wife, insisted on coming with him. . . . A few minutes later, a jeep deposited the viceregal couple and the governor at the foot of the railway embankment. On the other side of that precarious dike, 100,000 hot, dirty, angry people were shouting their frustration in an indecipherable din. Mountbatten took his wife by the hand and clambered up the embankment. As they reached the top, they discovered themselves only fifteen feet away from the surging waves of the sea of turbans. The ground under their feet shook with the impact of the gigantic crowd stampeding forward in front of them. That terrifying ocean of human beings incarnated in their shrieks and gesticulations the enormity and the passions of the masses of India. Whirling spirals of dust stirred by thousands of rushing feet clotted the air. The noise of the crowd was an almost tangible layer of air crushing down on them. It was a decisive instant in Operation Seduction, an instant when anything was possible. . . . In that crowd were twenty, thirty, forty thousand rifles. Any madman, any bloodthirsty fool could shoot the Mountbattens "like ducks on a pond."

For the first few seconds Mountbatten did not know what to do. He couldn't articulate a syllable of Pushtu, the crowd's language. As he pondered, a totally unexpected phenomenon began to still the mob, stopping perhaps with its strange vibrations an assassin's hand. For this entirely unplanned meeting with the Empire's most renowned warriors, Mountbatten happened to be wearing the short-sleeved, loose-fitting bush jacket that he had worn as Supreme Allied Commander in Burma. Its color, green, galvanized the crowd. Green was the color of Islam, the blessed green of the hadjis, the holy men who had made the pilgrimage to Mecca. Instinctively, those tens of thousands of men read in that green uniform a gesture of solidarity with them, a subtle compliment to their great religion.

His hand still clutching hers, but his eyes straight ahead, Mountbatten whispered to his wife, "Wave to them." Slowly, graciously, the frail Edwina raised her arm with his to the crowd. India's fate seemed for an instant suspended in those hands climbing from the crowd's head. A questioning silence had drifted briefly over the unruly crowd. Suddenly, Edwina's pale arm began to stroke the sky; a cry, then a roaring ocean of noise burst from the crowd. From tens of thousands of throats came an interminable, constantly repeated shout, a triumphant litany marking the successful passing of the most dangerous seconds of Operation Seduction.

"Mountbatten Zindabad!" those embittered Pathan warriors screamed, "Mountbatten Zindabad!" ("Long live Mountbatten!") [130–131]

SLAUGHTER AT KAHUTA

[Soon, however,] a shocked Mountbatten was to get his first direct contact with the horrors sweeping India in the cruel springtime of 1947. The naval officer who had seen most of his shipmates die in the wreck of his destroyer off Crete, the leader who had led millions through the savage jungle war in Burma, was overwhelmed by the spectacle he discovered in that village of 3,500 people, which had once been typical of India's half million villages.

For centuries, Kahuta's dirt alleys had been shared in peace by 2,000 Hindus and Sikhs and 1,500 Moslems. That day, side by side in the village center, the stone minaret of its mosque and the rounded dome of the Sikhs' gurudwara were the only identifiable remnants of Kahuta left on the skyline of the Punjab. Just before Mountbatten's visit, a patrol of the British Norfolk Regiment on a routine reconnaissance mission passed through the village. Kahuta's citizens, as they had been doing for generations, were sleeping side by side in mutual confidence and tranquility. By dawn, Kahuta had for all practical purposes ceased to exist, and its Sikhs and Hindus were all dead or had fled in terror into the night.

A Moslem horde had descended on Kahuta like a wolf pack, setting fire to the houses in its Sikh and Hindu quarters with buckets of gasoline. In minutes, the area was engulfed in fire and entire families, screaming pitifully for help, were consumed by the flames. Those who escaped were caught, tied together, soaked with gasoline and burned alive like torches. Totally out of control, the fire swept into the Moslem quarter and completed the destruction of Kahuta. A few Hindu women, yanked from their beds to be raped and converted to Islam, survived; others had broken away from their captors and hurled themselves back into the fire to perish with their families.

"Until I went to Kahuta," Mountbatten reported back to London, "I had not appreciated the magnitude of the horrors that were going on." This confrontation with the crowd in Peshawar and the atrocious spectacle of one devastated Punjabi village was the last proof Mountbatten needed. Speed was the one absolute, overwhelming imperative if India was to be saved. . . . And if speed was essential, then there was only one way out of the impasse, the solution from which he personally recoiled, but which India's political situation dictated—partition. [131–132]

THE SHATTERED DREAM

The last, painful phase in the lifelong pilgrimage of Mahatma Gandhi began on the evening of May 1, 1947, in the same spare hut in New Delhi's sweepers' colony in which a fortnight before he had unsuccessfully urged his colleagues to accept his plan to hold India together. Crosslegged on the floor, a water-soaked towel plastered once again to his bald head, Gandhi followed with sorrow the debate of the men around him, the high command of the Congress Party. The final parting of the ways between Gandhi and those men, foreshadowed in their earlier meeting, had been reached. All Gandhi's long years in jail, his painful fasts, his hartals and his boycotts had been paving stones on the road to this meeting. He had changed the face of India and enunciated one of the original philosophies of his century to bring his countrymen to independence through nonviolence; and now his sublime triumph threatened to become a terrible personal tragedy. His followers, their tempers worn, their patience exhausted, were ready to accept the division of India as the last, inescapable step to independence. . . .

Gandhi's tragedy was that he had that evening no real alternative to propose beyond his instincts, the instincts those men had so often followed before. This night, however, he was no longer a prophet. "They call me a Mahatma," he bitterly told a friend later, "but I tell you I am not even treated by them as a sweeper." Jinnah, he told his followers, will never get Pakistan unless the British give it to him. The British would never do that in the face of the Congress majority's unyielding opposition. They had a veto over any action Mountbatten proposed. Tell the British to go, he begged, no matter what the consequences of their departure might be. Tell them to leave India "to God, to chaos, to anarchy if you wish, but leave." . . .

Nehru was a torn and anguished man, caught between his deep love for Gandhi and his new admiration and friendship for the Mountbattens. Gandhi spoke to his heart, Mountbatten to his mind. Instinctively, Nehru detested partition; yet his rationalist spirit told him it was the only answer. Since reaching his own conclusion that there was no other choice, Mountbatten and his wife had been employing all the charm and persuasiveness of Operation Seduction to bring Nehru to their viewpoint. One argument was vital. With Jinnah gone, Hindu India could have the strong central government that Nehru would need if he was going to build the socialist state of his dreams. Ultimately, he too stood out against the man he had followed so long. With his and Patel's voices in favor, the rest of the high command quickly fell in line. Nehru was authorized to inform the Viceroy that while Congress remained "passionately attached to the idea of a united India," it would accept partition, provided that the two great provinces of Punjab and Bengal were divided. The man who had led them to their triumph was alone with his tarnished victory and his broken dream. [132–134]

"SHEER MADNESS"

All Mountbatten's hopes had foundered, finally, on the rock of Jinnah's determined, intransigent person. . . . For the rest of his life, Mountbatten would look back on that failure to move Jinnah as the single greatest disappointment of his career. His personal anguish at the prospect of going down in history as the man who had divided India could be measured by a document flown back to London with Ismay in Mountbatten's viceregal York, his fifth personal report to the Attlee government.

Partition, Mountbatten wrote, "is sheer madness," and "no one would ever induce me to agree to it were it not for this fantastic communal madness that has seized everybody and leaves no other course open. . . . The responsibility for this mad decision," he wrote, must be placed "squarely on Indian shoulders in the eyes of the world, for one day they will bitterly regret the decision they are about to make." [134]

More serious, however, was the real concern which underlay his growing apprehension. If the implications in the plan that he had sent to London were fully realized, the great Indian subcontinent would be divided into three independent nations, not two. Mountbatten had inserted in his plan a clause that would allow the sixty-five million Hindus and Moslems of Bengal to join into one viable country, with the great seaport of Calcutta as their capital.

Contrasted to Jinnah's aberrant, two-headed state, that seemed an entity likely to endure, and Mountbatten had quietly encouraged Bengal's politicians, Hindu and Moslem alike, to support it. He had even discovered that Jinnah would not oppose the idea. He had not, however, exposed it to Nehru and Patel, and it was this oversight that disturbed him now. Would they accept a plan that might cost them the great port of Calcutta with its belt of textile mills owned by the Indian industrialists who were their party's principal financial support? If they didn't, Mountbatten, after all the assurances he had given London, was going to look a bloody fool in the eyes of India, Britain, and the world.

A sudden inspiration struck Mountbatten. He would reassure himself privately, informally, with the Indian leader, whom, to the distress of his staff, he had invited to vacation with him in Simla, [Jawaharlal Nehru]. [159] To show the plan to Nehru without exposing it to Jinnah would be a complete breach of faith with the Moslem leader, they pointed out. If he discovered it, Mountbatten's whole position would be destroyed. For a long time, Mountbatten sat silently drumming the tabletop with his fingertips.

"I am sorry," he finally announced, "your arguments are absolutely sound. But I have a hunch that I must show it to Nehru, and I'm going to follow my hunch." That night, Mountbatten invited Nehru to his study for a glass of port. Casually, he passed the Congress leader a copy of the plan as it had been amended by London, asking him to take it to his bedroom and read it. Then perhaps he might let him know informally what reception it was likely to get from Congress. Flattered and happy, Nehru agreed.

[After a few hours], Nehru began to scrutinize the text designed to chart his country's future. He was horrified by what he read. The vision of the India that emerged from the plan's pages was a nightmare . . . an India divided, not into two parts but fragmented into a dozen pieces. Bengal would become, Nehru foresaw, a wound through which the best blood of India would pour. He saw India deprived of the port of Calcutta along with its mills, factories, steelworks; Kashmir, his beloved Kashmir, an independent state ruled by a despot he despised; Hyderabad become an enormous, indigestible Moslem body planted in the belly of India, half a dozen other princely states clamoring to go off on their own. The plan, he believed, would exacerbate all India's fissiparous tendencies of dialect, culture, and race to the point at which the subcontinent would risk exploding into a mosaic of weak, hostile states. White-faced, shaking with rage, Nehru stalked into the bedroom of his confidant V. P. Menon, who had accompanied him to Simla. With a furious gesture, he hurled the plan onto his bed. "It's all over!" he shouted. . . .

Mountbatten got his first intimation of his friend's violent reaction in a letter early the following morning. For the confident Viceroy, it was "a bombshell." As he read it, the whole structure he had so carefully erected during the past six weeks came tumbling down like a house of cards. The impression that his plan left, Nehru wrote, was one of "fragmentation and conflict and disorder." It frightened him and was certain to be "resented and bitterly disliked by the Congress Party." Reading Nehru's words, the poised, self-assured Viceroy, who had proudly announced to England that he was going to present a solution to India's

dilemma in ten days' time, suddenly realized that he had no solution at all. The plan that the British Cabinet was discussing that very day, the plan that he had just assured Attlee would win Indian acceptance, would never get past the one element in India that had to accept it, the Congress Party.

Mountbatten's critics might accuse him of overconfidence, but he was not a man to brood at setbacks. Instead of descending into a fit of despondency at Nehru's reaction, Mountbatten congratulated himself on his hunch in showing him the plan, and set out to repair the damage. [161] To redraft his plan, Mountbatten called into his study the highest-ranking Indian in his viceregal establishment. It was a supreme irony that at that critical juncture the Indian to whom Mountbatten turned had not even entered that vaunted administrative elite, the Indian Civil Service. No degree from Oxford or Cambridge graced his office walls. No family ties had hastened his rise. V. P. Menon was an incongruous oddity in the rarefied air of Viceroy's House, a self-made man.

Mountbatten informed Menon that before nightfall he would have to redraft the charter that would give India her independence. Its essential element, partition, had to remain, and it must continue to place the burden of choice on the Indians themselves. Menon finished his task in accordance with Mountbatten's instructions by sunset. Between lunch and dinner, he had performed a tour de force. The man who had begun his career as a two-finger typist had culminated it by redrafting, in barely six hours on an office porch looking out on the Himalayas, a plan that was going to encompass the future of one-fifth of humanity, reorder the subcontinent, and alter the map of the world. [162–163]

A DAY CURSED BY THE STARS

[When the day came to approve this plan] the lusterless eyes of Robert Clive gazed down from the great oil painting upon the wall at the seven Indian leaders filing into the Viceroy's study. Representatives of India's 400 million human beings, those millions whom Gandhi called "miserable specimens of humanity with lusterless eyes," they entered Mountbatten's study on this morning of June 2, 1947, to inspect the deeds that would return to their peoples the continent whose conquest the British general had opened two centuries before. The papers, formally approved by the British Cabinet, had been brought from London by the Viceroy just forty-eight hours before. . . .

For the first time since he had arrived in Delhi, Mountbatten was now being forced to abandon his head-to-head diplomacy for a round-table conference. He had decided, however, that he would do the talking. He was not going to run the risk of throwing the meeting open for a general discussion that might degenerate into an acrimonious shouting match that could destroy his elaborately wrought plan. Aware of the poignancy and historic nature of their gathering, he began by noting that during the past five years he had taken part in a number of momentous meeting at which the decisions that had determined the fate of the war had been taken. He could remember no meeting, however, at which decisions had been taken whose impact upon history had been as profound as would be the impact of the decision before them.

Briefly, Mountbatten reviewed his conversations since arriving in Delhi, stressing the terrible sense of urgency they had impressed on him. Then, for the record and for history, he formally asked Jinnah one last time if he was prepared to accept Indian unity as envisaged by the Cabinet Mission Plan. With equal formality, Jinnah replied that he was not, and Mountbatten moved on to the matter at hand. Briefly, he reviewed the details of his plan. The dominion-status clause that had ultimately won Winston Churchill's support was not, he stressed, a reflection of a British desire to keep a foot in the door beyond her time, but to assure that British assistance would not be summarily withdrawn if it was still needed. He dwelt on Calcutta, on the coming agony of the Sikhs.

He would not, he said, ask them to give their full agreement to a plan, parts of which went against their principles. He asked only that they accept it in a peaceful spirit and vow to make it work without bloodshed. His intention, he said, was to meet with them again the following morning. He hoped that before that, before midnight, all three parties, the Moslem League, Congress, and the Sikhs, would have indicated their willingness to accept the plan as a basis for a final Indian settlement. If this was the case, then he proposed that he, Nehru, Jinnah, and Baldev Singh announce their agreement jointly to the world the following evening on All India Radio. Clement Attlee would make a confirming announcement from London.

"Gentlemen," he concluded, "I should like your reaction to the plan by midnight." [191–192]

A NOD OF THE HEAD

[That night] in Louis Mountbatten's study the lights still burned, illuminating the last meeting of his harrowing day. He stared at his visitor with uncomprehending disbelief. Congress had indicated in time their willingness to accept his plan. So, too, had the Sikhs. Now the man it was designed to satisfy, the man whose obdurate, unyielding will had forced partition on India, was temporizing. Everything Jinnah had been striving for for years was there, waiting only his acknowledgment. For some mysterious reason, Jinnah simply could not bring himself this night to utter the word that he had made a career refusing to pronounce— "yes."

Inhaling deeply one of the Craven A's that he chainsmoked in his jade holder Jinnah kept insisting that he could not give an indication of the Moslem League's reaction to Mountbatten's plan until he had put it before the League's Council, and he needed at least a week to bring its members to Delhi. All the frustrations generated by his dealings with Jinnah welled up in Mountbatten. Jinnah had gotten his damn Pakistan. Even the Sikhs had swallowed the plan. Everything he had been working for he had finally gotten, and here, at the absolute eleventh hour, Jinnah was preparing to destroy it all, to bring the whole thing crashing down with his unfathomable inability to articulate just one word, "yes."

Mountbatten simply had to have his agreement. Attlee was standing by in London waiting to make his historic announcement to the Commons in less than twenty-four hours. He had gone on the line personally to Attlee, to his government with firm assurances that this plan would work; that there would be no more abrupt twists like that prompted by Nehru in Simla; that this time, they could be certain they had approved a plan that the Indian leaders would all accept. He had, with enormous difficulty, coaxed a reluctant Congress up to this point, and, finally, they were prepared to accept partition. Even Gandhi, temporarily at least, had allowed himself to be bypassed. A final hesitation, just the faintest hint that Jinnah was maneuvering to secure one last concession, and the whole carefully wrought package would blow apart.

"Mr. Jinnah," Mountbatten said, "if you think I can hold this position for a week while you summon your followers to Delhi, you must be crazy. You know this has been drawn up to the boiling point. . . . The Congress has made their acceptance dependent on your agreement. If they suspect you're holding out on them, they will immediately withdraw their agreement and we will be in the most terrible mess."

No, No, Jinnah protested, everything had to be done in the legally constituted way, "I am not the Moslem League," he said. . . .

"Now, now, come on, Mr. Jinnah," said Mountbatten, icy calm, "don't try to tell me that. You can try to tell the world that. But don't kid yourself that I don't know what's what in the Moslem League. . . . Mr. Jinnah, I'm going to tell you something. I don't intend to let you wreck your own plan. I can't allow you to throw away the solution you've worked so hard to get. I propose to accept on your behalf.

"Tomorrow at the meeting," Mountbatten continued, "I shall say I have received the reply of the Congress, with a few reservations that I am sure I can satisfy, and they have accepted. The Sikhs have accepted. . . . Then I shall say that I had a very long, very friendly conversation with Mr.

Jinnah last night, that we went through the plan in detail, and Mr. Jinnah has given me his personal assurance that he is in agreement with this plan.

"Now at that point, Mr. Jinnah," Mountbatten continued, "I shall turn to you. I don't want you to speak. I don't want Congress to force you into the open. I want you to do only one thing. I want you to nod your head to show that you are in agreement with me. . . . If you don't nod your head, Mr. Jinnah," Mountbatten concluded, "then you're through, and there'll be nothing more I can do for you. Everything will collapse. This is not a threat. It's a prophecy. If you don't nod your head at that moment, my usefulness here will be ended, you will have lost your Pakistan, and as far as I am concerned, you can go to hell." [196]

The meeting that would formally record the Indian leaders' acceptance of the Mountbatten plan to divide India began exactly as Mountbatten had said it would. Once again, on the morning of June 3, the Viceroy condemned the leaders to an unfamiliar silence by dominating the conversation himself. As he had expected, he said, all three parties had had grave reservations about his plan and he was grateful that they had aired them to him. Nonetheless Congress had signified its acceptance. So, too, had the Sikhs. He had had, he said, a long and friendly conversation the previous evening with Mr. Jinnah, who had assured him the plan was acceptable.

As he spoke those words, Mountbatten turned to Jinnah, seated at his right. At that instant Mountbatten had absolutely no idea what the Moslem leader was going to do. The captain of the *Kelly*, the supreme commander who had had an entire army corps encircled and cut off by the Japanese on the Imphal Plain, would always look back on that instant as "the most hair-raising moment of my entire life." For an endless second, he stared into Jinnah's impassive, expressionless face. Then slowly, reluctance crying from every pore, Jinnah indicated his agreement with the faintest, most begrudging nod he could make. His chin moved barely half an inch downward, the shortest distance it could have traveled consonant with accepting Mountbatten's plan. With that brief, almost imperceptible gesture, a nation of forty-five million human beings had received its final sanction.

A SHARP CRACK

However abortive its form, however difficult the circumstances that would attend its birth, the "impossible dream" of Pakistan would at last be realized. Mountbatten had enough agreement to go ahead. Before any of the seven men could have a chance to formulate a last reservation or doubt, he announced that his plan would henceforth constitute the basis for an Indian settlement.

While the enormity of the decision they had just taken began to penetrate, Mountbatten had a thirty-four-page,

single-spaced document set before each man. Clasping the last copy himself with both hands, the Viceroy lifted it over his head and whipped it back down onto the table. At the sharp crack that followed the slap of paper on wood, Mountbatten read out the imposing title on his equally imposing document—"The Administrative Consequences of Partition."

It was a carefully elaborated christening present from Mountbatten and his staff to the Indian leaders, a guide to the awesome task that now lay before them. Page after page, it summarized in its dull bureaucratic jargon the appalling implications of their decision. None of the seven was in even the remotest way prepared for the shock they encountered as they began to turn the pages of the document. Ahead of them lay a problem of a scope and on a scale no people had ever encountered before, a problem vast enough to beggar the most vivid imagination. They were now going to be called upon to settle the contested estate of 400 million human beings, to unravel the possessions left behind by thirty centuries of common inhabitation of the subcontinent, to pick apart the fruits of three centuries of technology. The cash in the banks, stamps in the post office, books in the libraries, debts, assets, the world's third-largest railway, jails, prisoners, inkpots, brooms, research centers, hospitals, universities, institutions and articles staggering in number and variety would be theirs to divide.

A stunned silence filled the study as the seven men measured for the first time what lay ahead of them. Mountbatten . . . had forced these seven men to come to grips with a problem so imposing that it would leave them neither the time nor the energy for recrimination in the few weeks of coexistence left to them.

"NO JOY IN MY HEART"

Shortly after seven o'clock on that evening of June 3, 1947, in the New Delhi studio of All India Radio, the four key leaders formally announced their agreement to divide the subcontinent into two separate sovereign nations. As befitting his office, Mountbatten spoke first. His words were confident, his speech brief, his tones understated. Nehru followed, speaking in Hindi. Sadness grasped the Indian leader's face as he told his listeners that "the great destiny of India" was taking shape, "with travail and suffering." Baring his own emotions, he urged acceptance of the plan that had caused him such deep personal anguish, by concluding that "it is with no joy in my heart that I commend these proposals to you."

Jinnah was next. Nothing would ever be more illustrative of the enormous, yet wholly incongruous nature of his achievement than that speech. Mohammed Ali Jinnah was incapable of announcing to his followers the news that he had won them a state in a language that they could understand. He had to tell India's ninety million Moslems of the "momentous decision" to create an Islamic state on the subcontinent in English. An announcer then read his words in Urdu. . . . [197–199]

Gandhi walked into Mountbatten's study at 6 p. m. His prayer meeting was at seven. That left Mountbatten less than an hour in which to ward off a potential disaster. His first glance at the Mahatma told Mountbatten how deeply upset he was. Crumpled up in his armchair "like a bird with a broken wing," Gandhi kept raising and dropping one hand lamenting in an almost inaudible voice: "It's so awful, it's so awful."

In that state Gandhi, Mountbatten knew, was capable of anything. A public denunciation of his plan would be disastrous. Nehru, Patel, and the other leaders the Viceroy had so patiently coaxed into accepting it would be forced to break publicly with Gandhi or break their agreement with him. Vowing to use every argument his fertile imagination could produce, Mountbatten began by telling Gandhi how he understood and shared his feelings at seeing the united India he had worked for all his life destroyed by this plan. Suddenly as he spoke, a burst of inspiration struck him. The newspapers had christened the plan the "Mountbatten Plan," he said, but they should have called it the "Gandhi Plan." It was Gandhi, Mountbatten declared, who had suggested to him all its major ingredients. The Mahatma looked at him perplexed.

Yes, Mountbatten continued, Gandhi had told him to leave the choice to the Indian people, and this plan did. It was the provincial, popularly elected assemblies which would decide India's future. Each province's assembly would vote on whether it wished to join India or Pakistan. Gandhi had urged the British to quit India as soon as possible, and that was what they were going to do. "If by some miracle the assemblies vote for unity," Mountbatten told Gandhi, "you have what you want. If they don't agree, I'm sure you don't want us to oppose their decision by force of arms."

Approaching seventy-eight, Gandhi was, for the first time in thirty years, uncertain of his grip on India's masses, at odds with the leaders of his party. In his despair and uncertainty, he was still searching in his soul for an answer, still waiting for an illuminating whisper of the inner voice that had guided him in so many of the grave crises of his career. That June evening, however, the voice was silent, and Gandhi was assailed by doubt. Should he remain faithful to his instincts, denounce partition, even (as he had earlier urged) at the price of plunging India into violence and chaos? Or should he listen to the Viceroy's desperate plea for reason? . . .

Less than an hour later, cross-legged on a raised platform in a dirt square in the midst of his Untouchables colony, Gandhi delivered his verdict. Many in the crowd before him had come, not to pray, but to hear from the lips of the prophet of nonviolence a call to arms, a fiery assault

on Mountbatten's plan. No such cry would come this evening from the mouth of the man who had so often promised to offer his own body for vivisection, rather than accept his country's division. It was no use blaming the Viceroy for partition, he said. Look to yourselves and in your own hearts for an explanation of what has happened, he challenged. Louis Mountbatten's persuasiveness had won the ultimate and most difficult triumph of his viceroyalty.

As for Gandhi, many an Indian would never forgive him his silence, and the frail old man whose heart still ached for India's coming division would one day pay the price of their rancor. [200]

THE ANNOUNCED DATE

For Mountbatten the public announcement was the apotheosis, the consecration of a remarkable *tour de force*. In barely two months, virtually a one-man band, he had achieved the impossible, established a dialogue with India's leaders, set the basis of an agreement, persuaded his Indian interlocutors to accept it, extracted the whole hearted support of both the government and the opposition in London. He had skirted with dexterity and a little luck the pitfalls marring his route. And as his final gesture he had entered the cage of the old lion himself, convinced Churchill to draw in his claws and left him too, murmuring his approbation.

[As] Mountbatten concluded his talk to the assembled world press [there was] a burst of applause. He opened the floor to questions. He had no apprehension in doing so. "I had been there," he would recall later. "I was the only one who had been through it all, who'd lived every moment of it. For the first time the press were meeting the one and only man who had the whole thing at his fingertips." Suddenly, when the long barrage of questions began to trickle out, the anonymous voice of an Indian newsman cut across the chamber. His final question was the last square left to Mountbatten to fill in the puzzle he had been assigned six months before.

"Sir," the voice said, "If all agree that there is most urgent need for speed between today and the transfer of power, surely you should have a date in mind?"

"Yes, indeed," replied Mountbatten.

"And if you have chosen a date, sir, what is that date?" the questioner asked.

A number of rapid calculations went whirring through the Viceroy's mind as he listened to those questions. He had not, in fact, selected a date. But he was convinced it had to be very soon.

"I had to force the pace," he recalled later. "I knew I had to force Parliament to get the bill through before their summer recess to hold the thing together. We were sitting on the edge of a volcano, on a fused bomb and we didn't know when the bomb would go off." Like the blurred images of a horror film, the charred corpses of Kahuta flashed across Louis Mountbatten's mind. If an outburst of similar tragedies was not to drag all India into an apocalypse, he had to move fast. After three thousand years of history and two hundred years of *Pax Britannica*, only a few weeks remained, the Viceroy believed, between India and chaos. He stared at the packed assembly hall. Every face in the room was turned to his. A hushed, expectant silence broken only by the whir of the wooden blades of the fans revolving overhead stilled the room. "I was determined to show I was the master of the whole event," he would remember.

"Yes," he said, "I have selected a date for the transfer of power."

As he was uttering those words, the possible dates were still spinning through his mind like the numbers on a revolving roulette wheel. Early September? Middle of September, middle of August? Suddenly the wheel stopped with a jar and the little ball popped into a slot so overwhelmingly appropriate that Mountbatten's decision was instantaneous. It was a date linked in his memory to the most triumphant hours of his own existence, the day in which his long crusade through the jungles of Burma had ended with the unconditional surrender of the Japanese empire. A period in Asian history had ended with the col-

lapse of that feudal Asia of the Samurai. What more appropriate date for the birth of the new democratic Asia arising to take its place than the second anniversary of Japan's surrender? His voice constricted with sudden emotion; the victor of the jungles of Burma, about to become the liberator of India, announced:

"The final transfer of power to Indian hands will take place on August 15, 1947." [201–202]

As soon as the radio announced Mountbatten's date, astrologers all over India began to consult their charts. Those in the holy city of Benares and several others in the South immediately proclaimed August 15 a date so inauspicious that India "would be better advised to tolerate the British one day longer rather than risk eternal damnation." . . .

"What have they done? What have they done?" one famous astrologer shouted to the heavens whose machinations he interpreted for man. Despite the discipline of his physical and spiritual forces acquired in years of yoga, meditation, and tantric studies in a temple in the hills of Assam, the astrologer lost control of himself. Seizing a piece of paper he sat down and wrote an urgent appeal to the man inadvertently responsible for this celestial catastrophe. "For the love of God," he wrote to Mountbatten, "do not give India her independence on August 15. If floods, drought, famine and massacres follow, it will be because free India was born on the day cursed by the stars."

FIGURE 1
INDIA UNDER THE
BRITISH RAJ

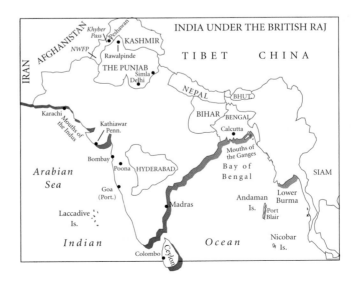

CASE 29

Saatchi & Saatchi Worldwide: Globalization and Diversification

Robert Louis-Dreyfus, chief executive of Saatchi & Saatchi Worldwide (Saatchi), was faced with what business journalists would euphemistically call a challenge. His company had run up considerable losses in 1989 and 1990, largely due to preferred dividends and extraordinary items, but had been able to remain marginally profitable on regular (pretax) operations. In the first six months of 1991, however, even this turned into a £4 million loss, and the outlook for the near future was dim. According to the *Wall Street Journal* there appeared to be no signs of recovery in the key advertising markets for the rest of 1991, or even through 1992 (*Wall Street Journal* 1991). Furthermore, while Louis-Dreyfus had done much to improve the company's equity position, mostly be selling off peripheral businesses, Saatchi was still burdened by a heavy debt load. It was clear that Louis-Dreyfus had to act quickly to ensure the short-term survival of his financially troubled company. However, he also had to set out a clear strategy to improve the firm's long-term prospects.

Louis-Dreyfus had been hired as chief executive officer (CEO) in January of 1990 at the moment that Saatchi had been balancing on the brink of financial insolvency, due to its empire-building acquisition spree. He undertook a full financial and strategic review that concluded that the board's decision to concentrate on the communication business (advertising, direct marketing, public relations, media services, and so on) and to turn away from the concept of a full-range services company was correct. The case for selling a broad package of services to multinationals, from advertising to computer expertise and management consulting, could make sense, but the bottom-line results indicated that the company had overpaid when buying these businesses. By mid-1991, Louis-Dreyfus had disposed of 10 out of 12 of the consulting businesses (for a total net extraordinary costs in 1989 and 1990 of £99 million) and had pushed through a recapitalization plan, which provided some short-term breathing space.

Long-term survival, however, would have to come from turning around the company's core advertising business. In the past many philosophical and heated debates about "globalization" had occurred in the office of Maurice Saatchi, one of the two founding brothers. Now Louis-Dreyfus had to decide whether the company's vision to offer

This case was written by Ron J.H. Meyer, with the assistance of Nancy Peterson and Kathleen Pinnette, as a basis for class discussion rather than to illustrate effective or ineffective handling of an administrative situation. This case was compiled from publicly available sources and supplemented by information kindly provided by Saatchi & Saatchi. Copyright © 1994 by Ron Meyer, Rotterdam School of Management, Erasmus University.

"global" advertising services was to remain the company's central strategy for the future or whether there were other alternatives open.

THE TRIUMPHANT EARLY YEARS (1970–1986)

The Saatchi brothers founded their company in the Soho district, London's ad agency heartland, in 1970. Charles Saatchi, described as one of the most eccentric and reclusive businessmen since Howard Hughes, was barely 27 years old at the time, and brother Maurice was 24.

The agency soon built up a reputation for simple, provocative ads. The 1971 print ad promoting contraception, for example, showed a pregnant man and asked, "Would you be more careful if it was you who got pregnant?" The agency came to prominence in 1979 with the advertising campaign that helped the Conservatives oust the Labour Party in Britain and put Margaret Thatcher in office. "Labour Isn't Working," said one poster depicting a long line of unemployed people.

They were an unlikely pair to conquer Madison Avenue, but in the 1980s, the Iraqi brothers focused their attention on just that. Maurice and Charles were ignored or laughed at when they announced that they someday would rule over the world's largest advertising agency. By 1988, after a long spree of acquisitions, their concern employed 16,600 people in 58 countries, and had client billings of $13.5 billion, giving it control of five percent of the worldwide advertising market, according to *Advertising Age*. The company's biggest international accounts included British Airways, Procter & Gamble, Sara Lee, Johnson & Johnson, and Toyota. Saatchi's competitors were no longer laughing.

The brothers had set themselves on their spectacular growth course by acquiring other advertising companies. The largest coup was the $400 million buyout in 1986 of Ted Bates agency, based in New York. This triumph allowed Saatchi to take the title of the world's biggest ad business. In the meantime the Saatchis had also set their sights on the consulting business, announcing that Saatchi would become the largest consultancy too. The purchase of 12 consultancy firms, including big companies like Hay Management, proved they were serious.

The Saatchis were eminently successful, or so it would seem when looking at the numbers. *Money Observer* reported (January 1989) only 37 UK companies had succeeded in raising their dividends by more than 10 percent a year over the previous decade. Saatchi was the leader of the pack, achieving a compound average of over 20 percent, due to record-breaking new business gains of four percent of the UK advertising market. Exhibit 1 outlines Saatchi's growth and major acquisitions between 1970 and 1988.

THE SEEDS OF DESTRUCTION (1986–1988)

While the financial highlights up to 1988 looked quite impressive (see also Exhibits 2 and 3), Saatchi's appetite for acquisitions was accompanied by some symptoms of indigestion. Following the purchase of Bates in 1986, a string of client account losses and staff departures plagued the company. Especially in the United States, Saatchi lost several accounts due to the fact that client companies did not want to deal with the same ad agency as their competitors had. Large consumer product companies, such as Procter & Gamble and Colgate-Palmolive, were concerned about confidentiality and conflicts of interest because their merged ad agency now also carried a competitor's account, so they withdrew hundreds of millions of dollars worth of business.

One of the important staff departures was that of Marten Sorrell, Saatchi's top financial executive.[1] His expertise was sorely missed, when, soon after his departure, Saatchi bought out Ted Bates for what many view as an exorbitant price. Besides his financial expertise Sorrell had also played cheerleader to investors at Saatchi. After his departure, no one replaced him as an intermediary between management and the shareholders. This reinforced the perception that the brothers were interested in other things besides Saatchi and shareholder value.

Another problem was that some of Saatchi's acquisitions, like Hay, had completed their earn-out periods. Some executives feared that those companies no longer had the incentive to keep the profit increases going as strongly. Poorly handled earn-out deals encouraged the selling shareholders to milk the business, because that's the way they get the maximum earn-out.

Then in 1987 the brothers undauntedly attempted to bid for two British banks, Midland and Hill Samuel. This backfired on them miserably and signalled shareholders to their apparent lack of focus. For the first time shareholders of the publicly owned company and others openly began to question the brothers' strategy for the business. Had the company's vast growth, by means of aggressive acquisitions, truly added value to the companies purchased? Or was Saatchi, as some critics claimed, an example of "dyssynergy?"

As problems started to mount, Saatchi's share price showed a significant drop (see Exhibit 4), which presented the company with further difficulties. The key to Saatchi's growth in the 1980s was its high stock price, a weak dollar, and a policy of buying companies on an installment plan. Saatchi's strong price-earnings ratio, which topped 27

EXHIBIT 1
EIGHTEEN YEARS OF
UNINTERRUPTED
GROWTH

DATE	PRETAX PROFITS (£ MILLIONS)	NOTEWORTHY EVENTS
1970		Saatchi & Saatchi formed.
1975	0.4	Merger with Compton Partners to construct publicly quoted company.
1979	2.4	Saatchi & Saatchi becomes largest UK agency.
1981	3.6	Second agency network started by acquisition of Dorland Advg. Saatchi becomes largest European agency group.
1982	5.5	Saatchi becomes a worldwide agency network by the acquisition of Compton Communications in the United States.
1983	11.2	US stock exchange listing obtained.
1984	20.0	Enters consulting market with acquisition of Hay Group.
1985	40.4	Forms marketing services by acquisition of Rowland (PR), Siegel & Gale (design), and Howard Marlboro (sales promotion).
1986	70.1	Major expansion in advertising with acquisition of Dancer Fitzgerald Sample, Backer & Spielvogel, and Ted Bates Worldwide. Saatchi becomes world's largest agency group.
1987	124.1	Paris listing obtained. Acquisition of Litigation Sciences and Peterson & Company. Merged nineteen units into two global networks: Saatchi & Saatchi Advertising Worldwide, ranking No. 2, and Backer Spielvogel Bates Worldwide, ranking No. 3.
1988	138.0	Formation of Zenith centralized media buying. Acquisition of Gartner information systems consultancy. Becomes world's tenth largest consulting firm. Tokyo listing obtained.

EXHIBIT 2
SAATCHI'S REVENUE
AND PRETAX PROFITS,
1978–1988

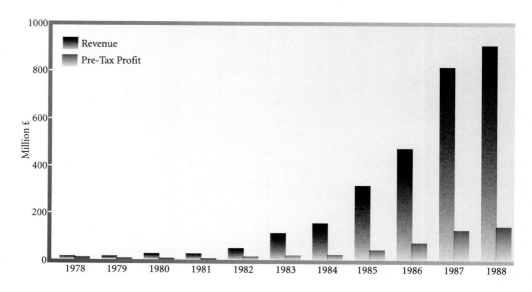

EXHIBIT 3
SAATCHI'S EARNINGS
AND DIVIDENDS PER
SHARE, 1978–1988

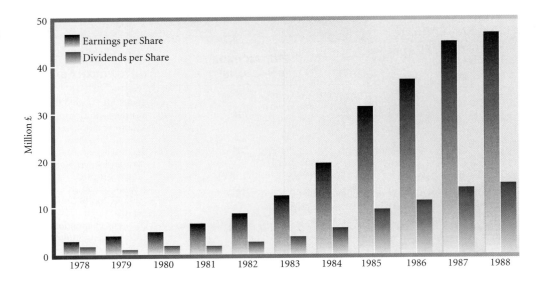

times, allowed it to raise capital in London for a downpayment on acquisitions followed by performance-based payments typically over three to five years. The declining dollar helped to make the American acquisitions relatively cheap. However, when the share price fell, the company could no longer raise money.

THE UNRAVELLING GIANT (1989–1991)

By early 1989 it had become clear to Saatchi's directors that the company's financial results would take a turn for the worse. After 18 years of nonstop growth, Saatchi's operating profit in the first half of 1989 was set to decline by approximately 40 percent compared with the first half of 1988. Publicly Saatchi bravely stated that "we see this as a pause for breath in our growth," and claimed that there was no deep or secret reason for the weak financial results. It was merely a case of advertising suffering because some US clients were worried about the "new" Bush administration and the budget deficit. Ad spending postponed from the first half to the second half that year had caused the damage. However, by mid-June of 1989 Saatchi had seen itself forced to put its consultancy division up for sale.

Saatchi had collected a mishmash of 12 consulting companies offering advice ranging from employee compensa-

EXHIBIT 4
SAATCHI'S LONG-
TERM SHARE PRICE,
1973–1990

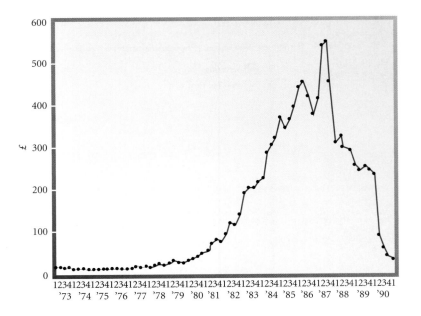

tion and jury selection to real estate strategies and computer systems. Victor E. Millar, head of Saatchi Consulting, was given the assignment to dispose of all of these companies as quickly as possible.

The pressure to sell was high, as the company was strapped for cash. All the profits for the year would be used for dividends; therefore a sale would provide breathing space. Selling proved more difficult though as buyers were interested in bits and pieces, due to the wide variety of services Saatchi owned. Also, the urgency of the sale, from Saatchi's perspective, encouraged lower bids. The company was at first wary to sell these businesses at such a tremendous loss. Hesitation only worked against Saatchi, and when it finally completed its divestments, it sold the businesses for about £100 million after initially expecting between £250 and £350 million.

The company that had been unable to pay preferred dividends in October 1990 confirmed that it would be unable to pay dividends on its ordinary shares in early 1991. Huge fiscal year net losses were triggered by massive writedowns on its disposal of the consulting businesses for 1990. The company said the write-downs, amounting to £76.9 million, reflected a hardnosed decision by Saatchi to take its lumps in 1990 (see Exhibit 5).

In January 1991 Saatchi unveiled a major recapitalization plan to save itself from insolvency. At the time analysts believed it was unlikely the troubled company would be able to redeem the original shares in 1993. The plan was revised in February to allow the troubled advertising company to survive intact but proposed handing over control to its preferred shareholders.

The plan, which was approved in March 1991, gave Saatchi's Europreference holders 65 percent of the company, and handed the two largest holders, ESL and London-based St. James's Place Capital, a seat apiece on the board. Both also provided additional capital to the company by underwriting a sizable chunk of a new £55 million rights offering. With the consultancy businesses divested and the balance sheet strengthened, Saatchi was now prepared to move forward in its strategy of focusing on its communications businesses.

SAATCHI'S "TOTAL COMMUNICATION SERVICES" STRATEGY

The Saatchi brothers relinquished responsibility as joint chief executives on January 1, 1990, handing the position over to the French-born advertising executive, Robert Louis-Dreyfus. Maurice and Charles remained on the board, and Maurice also stayed on as chairman. The new chairman's role was to focus on client relationships and broader strategy, while that of the chief executive was to concentrate on operational management and to assume profit responsibility toward the board. The choice of Louis-Dreyfus fell in line with Saatchi's announced plan to sell consulting and concentrate on communication services (see Exhibit 6).

Louis-Dreyfus announced his strategy to expand Saatchi's share of the advertising pie, primarily through internal growth as opposed to Saatchi's traditional method of acquisitions. When he took over at Saatchi, the major

EXHIBIT 5
CONSOLIDATED PROFIT AND LOSS ACCOUNT
(in £ millions)

	1990	1989	1988
Turnover	4,353.6	4,364.1	3,796.1
Revenue (gross profit)	808.1	973.5	862.2
Profit ordinary activities before exceptional items and tax	35.8	61.3	116.4
Exceptional items	(0.2)	(39.5)	21.6
Profit ordinary activities before tax	35.6	21.8	138.0
Taxation on profit on ordinary activities	(23.1)	(37.2)	(50.4)
Profit (Loss) on ordinary activities	12.5	(15.4)	87.6
Minority interests	(5.3)	(2.9)	(3.7)
Preference dividends	(28.5)	(18.2)	(8.8)
Extraordinary items	(76.9)	(22.0)	
Profit attributable to ordinary shareholders	(98.2)	(58.5)	75.1
Ordinary dividends	(14.2)	(25.1)	
Retained profit (loss)	(98.2)	(72.7)	50.0
Profit (Loss) per ordinary share (in pence)	(15.3)	(23.1)	48.1

EXHIBIT 6
SAATCHI'S DIRECTORS
IN 1990

Saatchi, Maurice, BSc Econ, 44, chairman. Worked on new business development at Haymarket Publishing from 1968 to 1970, when he formed Saatchi & Saatchi. Chairman of Saatchi since 1985. Trustee of the Victoria and Albert Museum and governor of the London School of Economics.

Louis-Dreyfus, Robert, MBA, 44, chief executive. In 1982 appointed COO of IMS, the leading pharmaceutical market research company; in 1984 CEO. Negotiated sale of IMS to Dun & Bradstreet in 1988. Joined Saatchi as chief executive in January 1990.

Levitt, Theodore, PhD, 66, Non-executive director. Currently emeritus professor of business administration at Harvard. Appointed in March 1991.

Mellor, Simon, BSc, 36, director. Joined Saatchi in 1976. Director of corporate communications since November 1990.

Russell, Thomas, PhD, 59, Non-executive director. Elected director of IMS in 1984 and chairman in 1987.

Saatchi, Charles, 47, director. Co-founder.

Scott, Charles, FCA, finance director, CFO of IMS from 1986 until he joined Saatchi in January of 1990.

Sinclair, Jeremy, 44, deputy chairman. Founding member of Saatchi.

EXHIBIT 7
TOP TEN ADVERTISING
ORGANIZATIONS
IN 1990

RANK	ORGANIZATION	GROSS INCOME ($ MILLIONS)	% GROWTH (OVER 1989–90)
1.	WPP Group	2,712.0	12.9
2.	Saatchi & Saatchi	1,729.3	9.7
3.	Interpublic Group	1,649.8	10.4
4.	Omnicom Group	1,335.5	13.4
5.	Dentsu	1,254.8	(0.6)
6.	Young & Rubicam	1,073.6	16.0
7.	Eurocom Group	748.5	58.5
8.	Hakuhodo	586.3	0.1
9.	Grey Advertising	583.3	19.1
10.	Foote, Cone & Belding Communications	563.2	5.9

EXHIBIT 8
TOP TEN US-BASED
CONSOLIDATED
AGENCIES IN 1990

RANK	AGENCY	GROSS INCOME ($ MILLIONS)	% GROWTH (OVER 1989–90)
1.	Young & Rubicam	1,001.4	15.7
2.	Saatchi & Saatchi Advertising Worldwide	825.7	11.5
3.	Ogilvy & Mather Worldwide	775.3	10.8
4.	McCann-Erikson Worldwide	744.7	11.3
5.	BBDO Worldwide	723.8	10.2
6.	Backer Spielvogel Bates Worldwide	715.6	8.0
7.	J. Walter Thompson	690.7	10.3
8.	Lintas Worldwide	676.5	10.4
9.	DDB Needam Worldwide	625.2	16.2
10.	Grey Advertising	583.3	19.1

international agencies controlled about 18 percent of total ad revenue worldwide, with Saatchi's share about 25 percent of that (see Exhibit 7 and 8). In the next 10 years, Louis-Dreyfus predicted, the major agencies' share of total ad revenue would double, and "I would like to increase our share of the sector to a third from 25 percent (*Business Week* 1990)." Louis-Dreyfus intended to achieve such spectacular internal growth by implementing a two-pronged strategy, namely, by offering "one-stop shopping" and "global communications services."

Saatchi had learned from its past experience in consulting that cross-reference of clients between service companies has its limits, but believed that this was not a problem for the closely related communications activities. Saatchi's managers believed that a client buying Saatchi's advertising services would also be willing to let the Saatchi Group take care of its other communication needs such as direct marketing, public relations, and market research. Having the total range of communications services, it was felt, would maximize the opportunities for cross-reference and might attract new clients preferring "one-stop shopping." Louis-Dreyfus therefore agreed that Saatchi should keep all its communication service companies (see Exhibit 9) and should hold regular meetings at the national level to determine cross-referral opportunities.

While there were opportunities for synergy, there was also the threat of conflicting client accounts among the company's add agencies. Saatchi therefore decided to create two distinct and separate advertising agency networks, which were seen to be in direct competition with one another, thus ensuring client confidentiality.

SAATCHI'S GLOBAL MARKETING APPROACH

The second, long-standing aspect of Saatchi's strategy, besides being a total communications services company, was to build up the company's capability for launching "global" advertising campaigns. Maurice and Charles had been early converts to the idea of global marketing, championed by Theodore Levitt of Harvard Business School. The idea basically holds that cultures are becoming so similar that products can be marketed the same way everywhere. Louis-Dreyfus supported the global advertising notion, but with more caution than the Saatchi brothers. He agreed that Saatchi was right to expand into different markets to serve multinational clients, but added, "Creativity isn't the same everywhere. You can't apply the same principles in England, France and America."[2]

While warning against excessive "globalization," Louis-Dreyfus by no means abandoned his belief in the basic

premises. He and Maurice recruited Theodore Levitt to the company board in March in 1990 and reiterated that global marketing is an evolutionary process. Thus, Saatchi will be at the forefront of implementing this strategy for clients who compete transnationally, but will also rededicate itself to those clients currently operating only in local environments. A listing of Saatchi's Western European clients, multinational versus local, is set forth in Exhibit 11. Multinational clients are those operating in more than one country, but needn't necessarily be pursuing transnational standardization, although they could potentially in the future.

To be able to offer multinational clients global advertising campaigns, Saatchi has arranged its advertising business within a regional and worldwide matrix (see Exhibit 12). On the one hand the company is organized geographically, with agencies in each country of operation and coordination between neighboring countries achieved by means of regional management boards. On the other hand Saatchi is also organized by client, whereby worldwide account directors (WADs) and regional account directors (RADs) are responsible for representing multinational client needs across all agencies. WADs and RADs are currently running the 12 biggest international accounts.

SAATCHI'S FUTURE

In May 1990 Saatchi's shares rose slightly following the news that Louis-Dreyfus had dismissed Roy Warman and Terry Bannister, two senior managers at Saatchi. The dismissals were interpreted by the markets as a sign that Louis-Dreyfus had won strategic control of the company from the Saatchi brothers, and that he now had the authority to get to grips with its financial problems.

A year later, as the share price continued to drop, Louis-Dreyfus had implemented the recapitalization plan that strengthened the Saatchi balance sheet and divested its consulting business for a loss. The company had its strategy of total communications service and global advertising on track. However, the operating margins were still under great pressure and would continue to fall during 1991. Furthermore, world advertising expenditure was expected to decline in 1991 (see Exhibit 13).

Meanwhile, Maurice Saatchi, chairman, rededicated the company to the principles of creativity that had built it in the first place and offered a new definition of great advertising. "It means creative work that is so simple and direct that it strikes a chord in humans everywhere," he said. But the question on Louis-Dreyfus's mind was whether this was enough to get Saatchi out of the red.

EXHIBIT 9
SAATCHI'S
COMMUNICATION
ACTIVITIES

ACTIVITY	COMPANY	CLIENTS
Advertising	**Saatchi & Saatchi Advertising Worldwide** No. 2 International Advertising Agency 135 offices in 32 countries	General Mills, Sara Lee, Procter & Gamble, J&J, Hewlett Packard, Toyota
	Backer Spielvogel Bates Worldwide No. 6 International Advertising Agency 159 offices in 46 countries	Philip Morris, Hyundai, King Fisher, Rover, BAT Industries, Mars
	Independent Agencies Campbell, Mithun, Esty No. 16 Advertising Agency in US 7 offices in US and Canada	Chrysler, Kroger, ConAgra, Texaco, 3M
	KHBB: No. 17 Advertising Agency in UK **AC&R:** No. 38 Advertising Agency in US **Hall Harrison Cowley:** UK regional network	
Direct Marketing	**Kobs & Draft Worldwide** No. 6 International Direct Marketing Agency 21 offices in 18 countries	Chase Manhattan, IBM, Mars, Rover
Public Relations	**Roland Worldwide** No. 6 International Public Relations Company 29 offices in 19 countries	Du Pont, J&J, Mars, P&G, Sandoz
Media Services	**Zenith Media Worldwide** Established 1988, offices in London, Paris, Madrid, Barcelona, and Milan	Allied Lyons, Amstrad, Phillip Morris
Other	**Howard Marlboro Group** — In-store marketing **HP:ICM** — Face-to-face communications **Siegal & Gale** — Corporate identity and design **National Research Group** — Market research **Yankelovich Clancy Shulman** — Market research	

EXHIBIT 10
AN EXAMPLE OF
TRANSNATIONAL
ADVERTISING

PAN-EUROPEAN ADVERTISING FOR PROCTER & GAMBLE

Procter & Gamble (P&G) is Saatchi's number one client, with operations in 130 countries. About 70 percent of P&G's business is done in world brands, of which Pampers is one of the most famous. It was introduced to the US market in 1968 as the first disposable diaper in the world. Expansion followed in the mid-1970s, first in Europe and followed by the Middle East and Asia. Today it is brand leader in 14 European markets and has recently been launched in Poland and Yugoslavia, with Hungary to follow soon. But today's success was not always the case.

In the early eighties Pampers had not kept up with technical developments, and by the mid-eighties had found itself squeezed by low-cost competitors moving up-market, leading to lower prices and sagging profitability. In 1985 the company relaunched with an upgraded product in all European markets. Millions of dollars were invested in new production lines. All countries shared the same objectives: rebuild share and maintain profitability in the face of higher product costs.

However, while the objectives were the same, the marketing executions differed in each country. Since there was no agreed learning on 'what really worked,' each country did what it judged best for its market. Advertising, media, promotional activity were done on an individual market basis. There were 10 different TV campaigns produced across Europe. The results of the launches were disappointing across Europe, as the exceptional product performance did not match the higher prices and unexpected product issues surfaced. The problem became worse when each country tried to fix it their own way. R&D, agencies, and the plant had several requests from each country to address.

As Pampers reached its lowest point at the end of 1985, the company realized it needed to fundamentally reorganize in order to survive. The right balance needed to be found between global, European, and local marketing. The most significant issues identified were lowering manufacturing costs by striving for economies of scale, searching for innovative product initiatives with pan-European application, and sharing worldwide and European ideas in areas such as product, packaging, advertising, and direct marketing. In 1986 the European diaper business was reorganized into a pan-European operation to reap transnational synergies. Two new senior positions were created at P&G, namely, a divisional manager with volume and profit responsibility for the total diaper business across Europe, and a European marketing manager.

Saatchi decided to reorganize its team to mirror the P&G structure. Together the companies worked on "keeping it simple and back to basics." The basics for the advertising development came out of the previous experience gleaned from 10 different pieces of advertising. The pan-European approach meant that Saatchi has given P&G much less advertising (through standardization), but of much higher quality (by transferring learning effects across borders). Since 1987 the formula has been an undeniable success, as the following Euro volume growth figures show:

Index vs. previous year

1986	100
1987	110
1988	132
1989	127
1990	127

EXHIBIT 11
PRIMARY WEST
EUROPEAN CLIENTS

COUNTRY	MNC CLIENTS	LOCAL CLIENTS	TOTAL 1990 ($ M)
Austria	15	20	65
Belgium	24	11	15
France	53	30	275
Germany	42	35	238
Ireland	17	15	23
Italy	26	20	286
Netherlands	37	20	73
Spain	25	31	131
United Kingdom	60	41	745

EXHIBIT 12
ORGANIZATIONAL
DIAGRAM OF
SAATCHI'S
ADVERTISING
BUSINESS

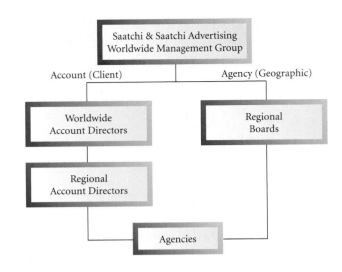

EXHIBIT 13 ESTIMATED WORLD ADVERTISING EXPENDITURE (annual % change)

	1991 VS. 1990		1992 VS. 1991		1993 VS. 1992		1994 VS. 1993	
	Current Prices	Constant Prices	Current Prices	Constant Prices	Current Prices	Constant Prices	Current Prices	Constant Prices
Major Media*								
North America	−1.8	−5.9	1.4	−2.2	3.2	−0.8	3.3	−0.7
Europe	3.4	−2.0	8.0	2.4	8.3	2.2	8.8	2.1
Asia/Pacific	6.0	1.7	8.1	3.9	8.3	3.6	8.5	3.8
Latin America	11.8	n/a	14.6	n/a	18.0	n/a	18.6	n/a
ROW	9.6	n/a	9.9	n/a	11.4	n/a	12.3	n/a
Subtotal**	2.0	−2.9	5.5	0.7	6.6	1.3	7.0	1.4
Direct Mail								
North America	4.7	0.6	5.1	1.2	5.1	1.0	5.0	0.9
Europe	4.0	−1.4	5.0	−0.6	7.0	0.8	8.0	1.4
Other Media***								
US	5.0	0.7	5.0	1.3	5.0	1.0	5.0	1.0
Japan	4.3	1.1	5.6	2.7	5.7	2.2	5.7	2.2
Total	2.7	−2.0	5.4	0.9	6.3	1.3	6.7	1.4

*TV, print, radio, cinema and outdoor.
**Constant prices exclude Latin America and the rest of the world.
***Includes point-of-sale, sales promotion expenditure.

CASE 30

McKinsey & Company: Managing Knowledge and Learning

In April 1996, halfway through his first three-year term as managing director of McKinsey & Company, Rajat Gupta was feeling quite proud as he flew out of Bermuda, site of the firm's second annual Practice Olympics. He had just listened to twenty teams outlining innovative new ideas they had developed out of recent project work, and, like his fellow senior partner judges, Gupta had come away impressed by the intelligence and creativity of the firm's next generation of consultants.

But there was another thought that kept coming back to the 47-year-old leader of this highly successful $1.8 billion consulting firm (see Exhibit 1 for a twenty-year growth history). If this represented the tip of McKinsey's knowledge and expertise iceberg, how well was the firm doing in developing, capturing, and leveraging this asset in service of its clients worldwide? In his mind, the task of knowledge development had become much more complex over the past decade or so due to three intersecting forces. First, in an increasingly information and knowledge-driven age, the sheer volume and rate of change of new knowledge made the task much more complex; second, clients' expectations of and need for leading-edge expertise were constantly increasing; and third, the firm's own success had made it much more difficult to link and leverage the knowledge and expertise represented by 3,800 consultants in 69 offices worldwide. Although the Practice Olympics was only one of several initiatives he had championed, Gupta wondered if it was enough, particularly in light of his often stated belief that "knowledge is the lifeblood of McKinsey."

THE FOUNDERS' LEGACY[1]

Founded in 1926 by University of Chicago professor, James ("Mac") McKinsey, the firm of "accounting and engineering advisors" that bore his name grew rapidly. Soon Mac began recruiting experienced executives and training them in the integrated approach he called his General Survey outline. In Saturday morning sessions he would lead consultants through an "undeviating sequence" of analysis—goals, strategy, policies, organization, facilities, procedures, and personnel—while still encouraging them to synthesize data and think for themselves.

In 1932, Mac recruited Marvin Bower, a bright young lawyer with a Harvard MBA, and within two years asked him to become manager of the recently opened New York office. Convinced that he had to upgrade the firm's image in an industry typically regarded as "efficiency experts" or "business doctors," Bower undertook to imbue in his associates the sense of professionalism he had experienced in his time in a law partnership. In a 1937 memo, he outlined his vision for the firm as one focused on issues of importance to top-level management, adhering to the highest standards of integrity, professional ethics, and technical excellence, able to attract and develop young men of outstanding qualifications, and committed to continually raising its stature

This case was prepared by Prof. Christopher A. Bartlett. Copyright © 1996 by the President and Fellows of Harvard College. Harvard Business School case 396-357.

YEAR	NUMBER OFFICE LOCATIONS	NUMBER ACTIVE ENGAGEMENTS	NUMBER OF CSS*	NUMBER OF MGMs†
1975	24	661	529	NA
1980	31	771	744	NA
1985	36	1823	1248	NA
1990	47	2789	2465	348
1991	51	2875	2653	395
1992	55	2917	2875	399
1993	60	3142	3122	422
1994	64	3398	3334	440
1995	69	3559	3817	472

*CSS = Client Service Staff (All professional consulting staff)
†MGM = Management Group Members (Partners and directors)
Source: Internal McKinsey & Company documents.

and influence. Above all, it was to be a firm dedicated to the mission of serving its clients superbly well.

Over the next decade, Bower worked tirelessly to influence his partners and associates to share his vision. As new offices opened, he became a strong advocate of the One Firm policy that required all consultants to be recruited and advanced on a firm-wide basis, clients to be treated as McKinsey & Company responsibilities, and profits to be shared from a firm pool, not an office pool. And through dinner seminars, he began upgrading the size and quality of McKinsey's clients. In the 1945 New Engagement Guide, he articulated a policy that every assignment should bring the firm something more than revenue—experience or prestige, for example.

Elected Managing Partner in 1950, Bower led his ten partners and 74 associates to initiate a series of major changes that turned McKinsey into an elite consulting firm unable to meet the demand for its services. Each client's problems were seen as unique, but Bower and his colleagues firmly believed that well-trained, highly intelligent generalists could quickly grasp the issue, and through disciplined analysis find its solution. The firm's extraordinary domestic growth through the 1950s provided a basis for international expansion that accelerated the rate of growth in the 1960s. Following the opening of the London Office in 1959, offices in Geneva, Amsterdam, Düsseldorf, and Paris followed quickly. By the time Bower stepped down as Managing Director in 1967, McKinsey was a well-established and highly respected presence in Europe and North America.

A DECADE OF DOUBT

Although leadership succession was well planned and executed, within a few years, the McKinsey growth engine seemed to stall. The economic turmoil of the oil crisis, the slowing of the divisionalization process that had fueled the European expansion, the growing sophistication of client management, and the appearance of new focused competitors like Boston Consulting Group (BCG) all contributed to the problem. Almost overnight, McKinsey's enormous reservoir of internal self-confidence and even self-satisfaction began to turn to self-doubt and self-criticism.

COMMISSION ON FIRM AIMS AND GOALS

Concerned that the slowing growth in Europe and the U.S. was more than just a cyclical market downturn, the firm's partners assigned a committee of their most respected peers to study the problem and make recommendations. In April 1971, the Commission on Firm Aims and Goals concluded that the firm has been growing too fast. The authors bluntly reported, "Our preoccupation with the geographic expansion and new practice possibilities has caused us to neglect the development of our technical and professional skills." The report concluded that McKinsey had been too willing to accept routine assignments from marginal clients, that the quality of work done was uneven, and that while its consultants were excellent generalist problem solvers, they often lacked the deep industry knowledge or the substantive specialized expertise that clients were demanding.

One of the Commission's central proposals was that the firm had to recommit itself to the continuous development of its members. This meant that growth would have to be slowed and that the MGM-to-associate ratio be reduced from 7 to 1 back to 5 or 6 to 1. It further proposed that emphasis be placed on the development of what it termed "T-Shaped" consultants—those who supplemented a broad generalist perspective with an in-depth industry or functional specialty.

PRACTICE DEVELOPMENT INITIATIVE

When Ron Daniel was elected Managing Director in 1976—the fourth to hold the position since Bower had stepped down nine years earlier—McKinsey was still struggling to meet the challenges laid out in the Commission's report. As the head of the New York office since 1970, Daniel had experienced first hand the rising expectations of increasingly sophisticated clients and the aggressive challenges of new competitors like BCG. In contrast to McKinsey's local office-based model of "client relationship" consulting, BCG began competing on the basis of "thought leadership" from a highly concentrated resource base in Boston. Using some simple but powerful tools, such as the experience curve and the growth-share matrix, BCG began to make strong in-roads into the strategy-consulting market. As McKinsey began losing both clients and recruits to BCG, Daniel became convinced that his firm could no longer succeed pursuing its generalist model.

One of his first moves was to appoint one of the firm's most respected and productive senior partners as McKinsey's first full-time director of training. As an expanded commitment to developing consultants' skills and expertise became the norm, the executive committee began debating the need to formally update the firm's long-standing mission to reflect the firm's core commitment not only to serving its clients but also to developing its consultants (see Exhibit 2).

But Daniel also believed some structural changes were necessary. Building on an initiative he and his colleagues had already implemented in the New York office, he created industry-based Clientele Sectors in consumer products, banking, industrial goods, insurance, and so on, cutting across the geographic offices that remained the primary organizational entity. He also encouraged more formal development of the firm's functional expertise in areas like strategy, organization and operations where knowledge and experience were widely diffused and minimally codified. However, many—including Marvin Bower—expressed concern that any move towards a product-driven approach could damage McKinsey's distinctive advantage of local presence which gave partners strong connections with the business community, allowed teams to work on site with clients and facilitated implementation. It was an approach that they felt contrasted sharply with the "fly in, fly out" model of expert-based consulting.

Nonetheless, Daniel pressed ahead, and the industry sectors quickly found a natural client base. Feeling that functional expertise needed more attention, he assembled working groups to develop knowledge in two areas that were at the heart of McKinsey's practice—strategy and organization. To head up the first group, he named Fred Gluck, a director in the New York office who had been out-spoken in urging the firm to modify its traditional generalist approach. In June 1977, Gluck invited a "Super Group" of younger partners with strategy expertise to a three-day meeting to share ideas and develop an agenda for the strategy practice. One described the meeting:

> We had three days of unmitigated chaos. Someone from New York would stand up and present a four-box matrix. A partner from London would present a nine-box matrix. A German would present a 47-box matrix. It was chaos . . . but at the end of the third day some strands of thought were coming together.

At the same time, Daniel asked Bob Waterman who had been working on a Siemens-sponsored study of "excellent companies" and Jim Bennett, a respected senior partner to assemble a group that could articulate the firm's existing knowledge in the organization arena. One of their first recruits was an innovative young Ph.D. in organizational theory named Tom Peters.

EXHIBIT 2 McKINSEY'S MISSION AND GUIDING PRINCIPLES (1996)

McKINSEY MISSION

To help our clients make positive, lasting, and substantial improvements in their performance and to build a great Firm that is able to attract, develop, excite, and retain exceptional people.

GUIDING PRINCIPLES

SERVING CLIENTS

Adhere to professional standards
Follow the top management approach
Assist the client in implementation and capability building
Perform consulting in a cost-effective manner

BUILDING THE FIRM

Operate as one Firm
Maintain a meritocracy
Show a genuine concern for our people
Foster an open and nonhierarchical working atmosphere
Manage the Firm's resources responsibly

BEING A MEMBER OF THE PROFESSIONAL STAFF

Demonstrate commitment to client service
Strive continuously for superior quality
Advance the state-of-the-art management
Contribute a spirit of partnership through teamwork and collaboration
Profit from the freedom and assume the responsibility associated with self-governance
Uphold the obligation to dissent

REVIVAL AND RENEWAL

By the early 1980s, with growth resuming, a cautious optimism returned to McKinsey for the first time in almost a decade.

CENTERS OF COMPETENCE

Recognizing that the activities of the two practice development projects could not just be a one-time effort, in 1980 Daniel asked Gluck to join the central small group that comprised the Firm Office and focus on the knowledge-building agenda that had become his passion. Ever since his arrival at the firm from Bell Labs in 1967, Gluck had wanted to bring an equally stimulating intellectual environment to McKinsey. Against some strong internal resistance, he set out to convert his partners to his strongly held beliefs—that knowledge development had to be a central, not a peripheral firm activity; that it needed to be ongoing and institutionalized, not temporary and project based; and that it had to be the responsibility of everyone, not just a few.

As one key means of bringing this about, he created 15 Centers of Competence (virtual centers, not locations) built around existing areas of functional expertise like marketing, change management, and systems. In a 1982 memo to all partners, he described the role of these centers as twofold: to help develop consultants and to ensure the continued renewal of the firm's intellectual resources. For each Center, Gluck identified one or two highly motivated, recognized experts in the particular field and named them practice leaders. The expectation was that these leaders would assemble from around the firm, a core group of partners who were active in the practice area and interested in contributing to its development. (See Exhibit 3 for the 15 Centers and 11 Sectors in 1983.)

To help build a shared body of knowledge, the leadership of each of the 15 centers began to initiate a series of activities primarily involving the core group and less frequently, the members of the practice network. A colleague commented on his commitment to establishing the centers:

> Unlike industry sectors, the centers of competence did not have a natural, stable client base, and Fred had to work hard to get them going. . . . He basically told the practice leaders, "Spend whatever you can—the cost is almost irrelevant compared to the payoff." There was no attempt to filter or manage the process, and the effect was "to let a thousand flowers bloom."

Gluck also spent a huge amount of time trying to change an internal status hierarchy based largely on the size and importance of one's client base. Arguing that practice development ("snowball making" as it became known internally) was not less "macho" than client development ("snowball throwing"), he tried to convince his colleagues that everyone had to become snowball makers *and* snowball throwers. In endless discussions, he would provoke his colleagues with barbed pronouncements and personal challenges: "Knowing what you're talking about is not necessarily a client service handicap" or "Would you want your brain surgery done by a general practitioner?"

BUILDING A KNOWLEDGE INFRASTRUCTURE

As the firm's new emphasis on individual consultant training took hold and the Clientele Sectors and Centers of Competence began to generate new insights, many began

---

EXHIBIT 3
McKINSEY'S EMERGING PRACTICE AREAS: Centers of Competence and Industry Sectors, 1983

CENTERS OF COMPETENCE	CLIENTELE SECTORS
Building institutional skills	Automotive
Business management unit	Banking
Change management	Chemicals
Corporate leadership	Communications and information
Corporate finance	Consumer products
Diagnostic scan	Electronics
International management	Energy
Integrated logistics	Health care
Manufacturing	Industrial goods
Marketing	Insurance
Microeconomics	Steel
Sourcing	
Strategic management	
Systems	
Technology	

---

to feel the need to capture and leverage the learning. Although big ideas had occasionally been written up as articles for publication in newspapers, magazines, or journals like *Harvard Business Review*, there was still a deep-seated suspicion of anything that smacked of packaging ideas or creating proprietary concepts.

This reluctance to document concepts had long constrained the internal transfer of ideas and the vast majority of internally developed knowledge was never captured.

This began to change with the launching of the McKinsey Staff Paper series in 1978, and by the early 1980s the firm was actively encouraging its consultants to publish their key findings. The initiative got a major boost with the publication in 1982 of two major best-sellers, Peters and Waterman's *In Search of Excellence* and Kenichi Ohmae's *The Mind of the Strategist*. But books, articles, and staff papers required major time investments, and only a small minority of consultants made the effort to write them. Believing that the firm had to lower the barrier to internal knowledge communication, Gluck introduced the idea of Practice Bulletins, two-page summaries of important new ideas that identified the experts who could provide more detail. A partner elaborated:

> The Bulletins were essentially internal advertisements for ideas and the people who had developed them. We tried to convince people that they would help build their personal networks and internal reputations. . . . Fred was not at all concerned that the quality was mixed, and had a strong philosophy of letting the internal market sort out what were the really big ideas.

Believing that the firm's organizational infrastructure needed major overhaul, in 1987 Gluck launched a Knowledge Management Project. After five months of study, the team made three recommendations. First, the firm had to make a major commitment to build a common database of knowledge accumulated from client work and developed in the practice areas. Second, to ensure that the databases were maintained and used, they proposed that each practice are (Clientele Sector and Competence Center) hire a full-time practice coordinator who could act as an "intelligent switch" responsible for monitoring the quality of the data and for helping consultants access the relevant information. And finally, they suggested that the firm expand its hiring practices and promotion policies to create a career path for deep functional specialists whose narrow expertise would not fit the normal profile of a T-shaped consultant.

The task of implementing these recommendations fell to a team led by Bill Matassoni, the firm's director of communications and Brook Manville, a newly recruited Yale Ph.D. with experience with electronic publishing. Focusing first on the Firm Practice Information System (FPIS), a computerized database of client engagements, they installed new systems and procedures to make the data more complete, accurate, and timely so that it could be accessed as a reliable information resource, not just an archival record. More difficult was the task of capturing the knowledge that had accumulated in the practice areas since much of it had not been formalized and none of it had been prioritized or integrated. To create a computer-based Practice Development Network (PDNet), Matassoni and Manville put huge energy into begging, cajoling, and challenging each practice to develop and submit documents that represented their core knowledge. After months of work, they had collected the 2,000 documents that they believed provided the critical mass to launch PDNet.

Matassoni and his team also developed another information resource that had not been part of the study team's recommendations. They assembled a listing of all firm experts and key document titles by practice area and published it in a small book, compact enough to fit in any consultant's briefcase. The Knowledge Resource Directory (KRD) became the McKinsey Yellow Pages and found immediate and widespread use firm-wide. Although the computerized databases were slow to be widely adopted, the KRD found almost immediate enthusiastic acceptance.

Making the new practice coordinator's position effective proved more challenging. Initially, these roles were seen as little more than glorified librarians. It took several years before the new roles were filled by individuals (often ex-consultants) who were sufficiently respected that they could not only act as consultants to those seeking information about their area of expertise, but also were able to impose the discipline necessary to maintain and build the practice's databases.

Perhaps the most difficult task was to legitimize the role of a new class of consultants—the sepcialist. The basic concept was that a professional could make a career in McKinsey by emphasizing specialized knowledge development rather than the broad-based problem-solving skills and client development orientation that were deeply embedded in the firm's value system. While several consultants with deep technical expertise in specialties like market research, finance, or steel making were recruited, most found it hard to assimilate into the mainstream. The firm seemed uncomfortable about how to evaluate, compensate, or promote these individuals, and many either became isolated or disaffected. Nonetheless, the partnership continued to support the notion of a specialist promotion track and continued to struggle with how to make it work.

Matassoni reflected on the changes:

> The objective of the infrastructure changes was not so much to create a new McKinsey as to keep the old "one firm" concept functioning as we grew . . . Despite all the talk of computerized databases, the knowledge management process still relied heavily on personal networks, old practices like cross-office

transfers, and strong "One Firm" norms like helping other consultants when they called. And at promotion time, nobody reviewed your PD documents. They looked at how you used your internal networks to have your ideas make an impact on clients.

MANAGING SUCCESS

By the late 1980s, the firm was expanding rapidly again. In 1988, the same year Fred Gluck was elected managing director, new offices were opened in Rome, Helsinki, São Paulo, and Minneapolis bringing the total to 41. From the partners' perspective, however, enhancing McKinsey's reputation as a thought leader was at least as important as attracting new business.

REFINING KNOWLEDGE MANAGEMENT

After being elected MD, Gluck delegated the practice development role he had played since 1980 to a newly constituted Clientele and Professional Development Committee (CPDC). When Ted Hall took over leadership of this committee in late 1991, he felt there was a need to adjust the firm's knowledge development focus. He commented:

> By the early 1990s, too many people were seeing practice development as the creation of experts and the generation of documents in order to build our reputation. But knowledge is only valuable when it is between the ears of consultants and applied to clients' problems. Because it is less effectively developed through the disciplined work of a few than through the spontaneous interaction of many, we had to change the more structured "discover-codify-disseminate" model to a looser and more inclusive "engage-explore-apply-share" approach. In other words, we shifted our focus from developing knowledge to building individual and team capability.

Over the years, Gluck's philosophy "to let 1,000 flowers bloom" had resulted in the original group of 11 sectors and 15 centers expanding to become what Hall called "72 islands of activity," (Sectors, Centers, Working Groups, and Special Projects) many of which were perceived as fiefdoms dominated by one or two established experts. In Hall's view, the garden of 1,000 flowers needed weeding, a task requiring a larger group of mostly different gardeners. The CPDC began integrating the diverse groups into seven sectors and seven functional capability groups (see Exhibit 4). These sectors and groups were led by teams of five to seven partners (typically younger directors and principals) with the objective of replacing the leader-driven knowledge cre-

ation and dissemination process with a "stewardship model" of self-governing practices focused on competence building.

CLIENT IMPACT

With responsibility for knowledge management delegated to the CPDC, Gluck began to focus on a new theme—client impact. On being elected managing director, he made this a central theme in his early speeches, memos, and his first All Partners Conference. He also created a Client Impact Committee, and asked it to explore the ways in which the firm could ensure that the expertise it was developing created positive measurable results in each client engagement.

One of the most important initiatives of the new committee was to persuade the partners to redefine the firm's key consulting unit from the engagement team (ET) to the client service team (CST). The traditional ET, assembled to deliver a three- or four-month assignment for a client was a highly efficient and flexible unit, but it tended to focus on the immediate task rather than on the client's long-term need. The CST concept was that the firm could add long-term value and increase the effectiveness of individual engagements if it could unite a core of individuals (particularly at the partner level) who were linked across multiple ETs, and commit them to working with the client over an extended period. The impact was to broaden the classic model of a single partner "owning" a client to a group of partners with shared commitment to each client.

Although client impact studies indicated the new structure led to a longer-term focus and deeper understanding of issues, it also raised some concerns. Some felt that the new approach biased resource allocation to the largest clients with the biggest CSTs. Others felt that CSTs tended to be more insular, guarding proprietary concepts and reaching out less often for firm-wide knowledge.

The latter concern in part reflected changes in the locus of knowledge development being advocated by CPDC. In response to concerns within the partnership about a gradual decline in associates' involvement in intellectual capital development, the CPDC began to emphasize the need for CSTs to play a central role in the intellectual life of McKinsey. (See Exhibit 5 for a CPDC conceptualization.) Believing that the CSTs (by 1993 about 200 firm-wide) represented the real learning laboratories, the CPDC sent memos to the new industry sector and capability group leaders advising them that their practices would be evaluated by their coverage of the firm's CSTs. They also wrote to all consultants emphasizing the importance of the firm's intellectual development and their own professional devel-

EXHIBIT 4 GROUP FRAMEWORK FOR SECTORS AND CENTERS

FUNCTIONAL CAPABILITY GROUPS	CLIENTELE INDUSTRY SECTORS
Corporate Governance and Leadership	**Financial Institutions**
Corporate organization	Banking
Corporate management processes	Insurance
Corporate strategy development	Health care payor/provider
Corporate relationship design and management	**Consumer**
Corporate finance	Retailing
Post-merger management	Consumer industries
Organization (OPP/MOVE)	Media
Corporate transformation design and leadership	Pharmaceuticals
Energizing approaches	**Energy**
Organization design and development	Electrical utilities
Leadership and teams	Petroleum
Engaging teams	Natural gas
Information Technology/Systems	Other energy
To be determined	**Basic Materials**
Marketing	Steel
Market research	Pulp and paper
Sales force management	Chemicals
Channel management	Other basic materials
Global management	**Aerospace, Electronics, and Telecom**
Pricing	Telecom
Process and sector support	Electronics
Operations Effectiveness	Aerospace
Integrated logistics	**Transportation**
Manufacturing	**Automotive, Assembly, and Machinery**
Purchasing and supply management	Automotive
Strategy	Assembly
Strategy	
Microeconomics	
Business dynamics	
Business planning processes	
Cross-Functional Management	
Innovation	
Customer satisfaction	
Product/technology development and commercialization	
Core process redesign	

Source: Internal McKinsey & Company document.

opment, for which they had primary responsibility. Finally, they assembled data on the amount of time consultants were spending on practice and professional development by office, distributing the widely divergent results to partners in offices worldwide.

DEVELOPING MULTIPLE CAREER PATHS

Despite (or perhaps because of) all these changes, the specialist consultant model continued to struggle. Over the years, the evaluation criteria for the specialist career path had gradually converged with the mainstream generalist promotion criteria. For example, the specialist's old promotion standard of "world-class expertise" in a particular field had given way to a more pragmatic emphasis on client impact; the notion of a legitimate role as a consultant to teams had evolved to a need for specialists to be "engagement director capable"; and the less pressured evaluation standard of "grow or go" was replaced by the normal associate's more demanding "up or out" requirement, albeit within a slightly more flexible timeframe.

EXHIBIT 5
CPDC PROPOSED
ORGANIZATIONAL
RELATIONSHIPS
Source: Internal CPDC
presentation.

NETWORKS FOR INVOLVEMENT

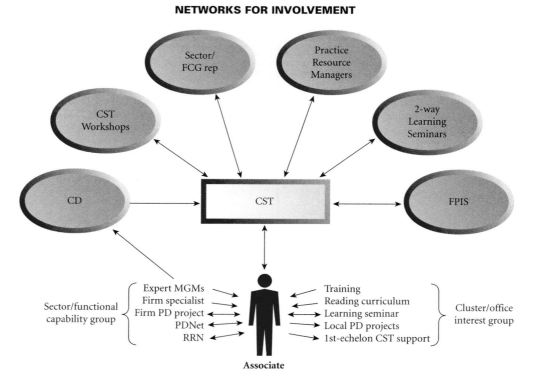

Associate

Although these changes had reduced the earlier role dissonance—specialists become more T shaped—it also diluted the original objective, and in late 1992 the Professional Personnel Committee decided to create two new career paths for client service support and administrative (CSSA) staff:

- The first reaffirmed a path to partnership for practice-dedicated specialists who built credibility with clients and CSTs through their specialized knowledge and its expert application. Their skills would have them in high demand as consultants to teams (CDs) rather than as engagement directors (EDs).
- The second new option was the practice management track designed to provide a career progression for practice coordinators, who had a key role in transferring knowledge and in helping practice leaders manage increasingly complex networks. Valuable administrators could also be promoted on this track.

Despite the announcement of the new criteria and promotion processes, amongst associates and specialists alike there was still a good deal of skepticism and confusion about the viability of the specialist track to partnership. (See Exhibit 6 for an overview comparison.)

Throughout the period of change, Gluck kept returning to his long-term theme that, "it's all about people." He said:

There are two ways to look at McKinsey. The most common way is that we are a client service firm whose primary purpose is to serve the companies seeking our help. That is legitimate. But I believe there is an even more powerful way for us to see ourselves. We should begin to view our primary purpose as building a great institution that becomes an engine for producing highly motivated world-class people who in turn will serve our clients extraordinarily well.

KNOWLEDGE MANAGEMENT ON THE FRONT

To see how McKinsey's evolving knowledge management processes were being felt by those on the firm's front lines, we will follow the activities of three consultants working in three diverse locations and focused on three different agendas.

JEFF PETERS AND THE SYDNEY OFFICE ASSIGNMENT

John Stuckey, a director in McKinsey's Sydney office, felt great satisfaction at being invited to bid for a financial services growth strategy study for one of Australia's most respected companies. Yet the opportunity also created some challenges. As in most small or medium sized offices, most consultants in Sydney were generalists. Almost all

EXHIBIT 6
ALTERNATIVE CAREER
PATH FOCUS AND
CRITERIA

CAREER PATHS/ROLES

CSS PATHS		CSSA PATHS	
General Consulting	Specialized Consulting	Practice Expertise	Practice Management Administration

FOCUS

Perform general problem solving and lead implementation	Apply in-depth practice knowledge to studies	Leverage practice knowledge across studies	Codify and transfer knowledge
Develop client relationships	Develop client relationships	Create new knowledge	Help administer practice
	Build external reputation		

Source: Internal McKinsey & Company presentation.

with financial industry expertise had been "conflicted out" of the project due to work they had done for competing financial institutions in Australia.

Stuckey immediately began using his personal network to find how he might tap into McKinsey's worldwide resources for someone who could lead this first engagement for an important new client. After numerous phone calls and some lobbying at a directors' conference he identified Jeff Peters, a Boston-based senior engagement manager and veteran of more than 20 studies for financial institutions. The only problem was that Peters had two ongoing commitments that would make him unavailable for at least the first six weeks of the Australian assignment.

Meanwhile, Stuckey and Ken Gibson, his engagement director on the project, were working with the Sydney office staffing coordinator to identify qualified, available, and nonconflicted associates to complete the team. Balancing assignments of over 80 consultants to 25 ongoing teams was a complex process that involved matching the needs of the engagement and the individual consultants' development requirements. A constant flow of consultants across offices helped buffer constraints, and also contributed to the transfer of knowledge. At any one time 15 to 25 Australian consultants were on short- or long-term assignments abroad, while another 10 to 15 consultants from other offices were working in Australia. (Firm-wide, nearly 20% of work was performed by consultants on inter-office loans.)

They identified a three-person team to work with Peters. John Peacocke was a New Zealand army engineer with an MBA in finance from Wharton and two years of experience in McKinsey. Although he had served on a four-month study for a retail bank client in Cleveland, since returning to Australia he had worked mostly for oil and gas clients. Patty Akopianz was a one-year associate who had worked in investment banking before earning an MBA at Harvard. Her primary interest and her developing expertise was in consumer marketing. The business analyst was Jonathan Liew, previously an actuary who was embarking on his first McKinsey assignment.

With Peters' help, Stuckey and Gibson also began assembling a group of internal specialists and experts who could act as consulting directors (CDs) to the team. James Gorman, a personal financial services expert in New York agreed to visit Sydney for a week and to be available for weekly conference calls; Majid Arab, an insurance industry specialist committed to a two-week visit and a similar "on-call" availability; Andrew Doman, a London-based financial industry expert also signed on as a CD. Within the Sydney office, Charles Conn, a leader in the firm's growth strategies practice, agreed to lend his expertise, as did Clem Doherty, a firm leader in the impact of technology.

With Gibson acting more as an engagement manager than an engagement director, the team began scanning the Knowledge Resource Directory, the FPIS and the PDNet for leads. (Firm-wide, the use of PDNet documents had boomed in the eight years since its introduction. By early 1996, there were almost 12,000 documents on PDNet, with over 2,000 being requested each month.) In all, they tracked down 179 relevant PD documents and tapped into the advice and experience of over 60 firm members worldwide. A team member explained:

Ken was acting as EM, but he was not really an expert in financial services, so we were even more reliant than usual on the internal network. Some of the ideas we got off PDNet were helpful, but the trail of contacts was much more valuable . . . Being on a completely different time zone had great advantages. If you hit a wall at the end of the day, you could drop messages in a dozen voicemail boxes in Europe and the United States. Because the firm norm is that you respond to requests by colleagues, by morning you would have seven or eight new suggestions, data sources, or leads.

At the end of the first phase, the team convened an internal workshop designed to keep client management informed, involved, and committed to the emerging conclusions. Out of this meeting, the team was focused on seven core beliefs and four viable options that provided its agenda for the next phase of the project. It was at this point that Peters was able to join the team:

> By the time I arrived, most of the hard analysis had been done and they had been able to narrow the focus from the universe to four core options in just over a month. It was very impressive how they had been able to do that with limited team-based expertise and a demanding client. . . . With things going so well, my main priority was to focus the team on the end product. Once we got a clear logical outline, I assigned tasks and got out of the way. Most of my time I spent working on the client relationship . . . It was great learning for John and Patty, and both of them were ready to take on a management role in their next engagements.

In November, the team presented its conclusions to the board, and after some tough questioning and challenging, they accepted the recommendations and began an implementation process. The client's managing director reflected on the outcome:

> We're a tough client, but I would rate their work as very good. Their value added was in their access to knowledge, the intellectual rigor they bring, and their ability to build understanding and consensus among a diverse management group . . . If things don't go ahead now, it's our own fault.

John Stuckey had a little different post-engagement view of the result:

> Overall, I think we did pretty good work, but I was a bit disappointed we didn't come up with a radical breakthrough. . . . We leveraged the firm's knowledge base effectively, but I worry that we rely so much on our internal expertise. We have to beware of the trap that many large successful companies have fallen into by becoming too introverted, too satisfied with their own view of the world.

WARWICK BRAY AND EUROPEAN TELECOMS

After earning his MBA at Melbourne University, Warwick Bray joined McKinsey's Melbourne office in 1989. A computer science major, he had worked as a systems engineer at Hewlett Packard and wanted to leverage his technological experience. For two of his first three years, he worked on engagements related to the impact of deregulation on the Asia-Pacific telecommunications industry. In early 1992, Bray advised his group development leader (his assigned mentor and adviser) that he would be interested in spending a year in London. After several phone discussions the transfer was arranged, and in March the young Australian found himself on his first European team.

From his experiences on the Australian telecom projects, Bray had written a PD document, "Negotiating Interconnect," which he presented at the firm's annual worldwide telecom conference. Recognizing this developing "knowledge spike," Michael Patsalos-Fox, telecom practice leader in London, invited Bray to work with him on a study. Soon he was being called in as a deregulation expert to make presentations to various client executives. "In McKinsey you have to earn that right," said Bray. "For me it was immensely satisfying to be recognized as an expert."

Under the leadership of Patsalos-Fox, the telecom practice had grown rapidly in the United Kingdom. With deregulation spreading across the continent in the 1990s, however, he was becoming overwhelmed by the demands for his help. Beginning in the late 1980s, Patsalos-Fox decided to stop acting as the sole repository for and exporter of European telecom information and expertise, and start developing a more interdependent network. To help in this task, he appointed Sulu Soderstrom, a Stanford MBA with a strong technology background, as full-time practice coordinator. Over the next few years she played a key role in creating the administrative glue that bonded together telecom practice groups in offices throughout Europe. Said Patsalos-Fox:

> She wrote proposals, became the expert on information sources, organized European conferences, helped with cross-office staffing, located expertise and supported and participated in our practice development work. Gradually she helped us move from an "export"-based hub and spokes model of information sharing to a true federalist-based network.

In this growth environment and supported by the stronger infrastructure, the practice exploded during the 1990s. To move the knowledge creation beyond what he described as "incremental synthesis of past experience," Patsalos-Fox launched a series of practice-sponsored studies. Staffed by some of the practice's best consultants, they focused on big topics like "The Industry Structure in 2005," or "The Telephone Company of the Future." But most of the practice's knowledge base was built by the informal initiatives of individual associates who would step back after several engagements and write a paper on their new insights. For example, Bray wrote several well-received PD documents and was enhancing his internal reputation as an expert in deregulation and multimedia. Increasingly he was invited to consult to or even join teams in other parts of Europe. Said Patsalos-Fox:

> He was flying around making presentations and helping teams. Although the internal audience is the toughest, he was getting invited back. When it came time for him to come up for election, the London office nominated him but the strength of his support came from his colleagues in the European telecom network.

In 1996, Patsalos-Fox felt it was time for a new generation of practice leadership. He asked his young Australian prótegé and two other partners—one in Brussels, one in Paris—if they would take on a co-leadership role. Bray reflected on two challenges he and his co-leaders faced. The first was to make telecom a really exciting and interesting practice so it could attract the best associates. That meant taking on the most interesting work, and running our engagements so that people felt they were developing and having fun.

The second key challenge was how to develop the largely informal links among the fast-growing European telecom practices. Despite the excellent job that Soderstrom had done as the practice's repository of knowledge and channel of communication, it was clear that there were limits to her ability to act as the sole "intelligent switch." As a result, the group had initiated a practice-specific intranet link designed to allow members direct access to the practice's knowledge base (PD documents, conference proceedings, CVs, etc.), its members' capabilities (via home pages for each practice member), client base (CST home pages, links to client web sites), and external knowledge resources (MIT's Multimedia Lab, Theseus Institute, etc.). More open yet more focused than existing firm-wide systems like PDNet, the Telecom Intranet was expected to accelerate the "engage-explore-apply-share" knowledge cycle.

There were some, however, who worried that this would be another step away from "one firm" towards compartmentalization, and from focus on building idea-driven personal networks towards creating data-based electronic transactions. In particular, the concern was that functional capability groups would be less able to transfer their knowledge into increasingly strong and self-contained industry-based practices. Warwick Bray recognized the problem, acknowledging that linkages between European telecom and most functional practices "could be better":

> The problem is we rarely feel the need to draw on those groups. For example, I know the firm's pricing practice has world-class expertise in industrial pricing, but we haven't yet learned how to apply it to telecom. We mostly call on the pric-

ing experts within our practice. We probably should reach out more.

STEPHEN DULL AND THE BUSINESS MARKETING COMPETENCE CENTER

After completing his MBA at the University of Michigan in 1983, Stephen Dull spent the next five years in various consumer marketing jobs at Pillsbury. In 1988, he was contacted by an executive search firm that had been retained by McKinsey to recruit potential consultants in consumer marketing. Joining the Atlanta office, Dull soon discovered that there was no structured development program. Like the eight experienced consumer marketing recruits in other offices, he was expected to create his own agenda.

Working on various studies, Dull found his interests shifting from consumer to industrial marketing issues. As he focused on building his own expertise, however, Dull acknowledged that he did not pay enough attention to developing strong client relations. "And around here, serving clients is what really counts," he said. So, in late 1994—a time when he might be discussing his election to principal—he had a long counseling session with his group development leader about his career. The GDL confirmed that he was not well positioned for election, but proposed another option. He suggested that Dull talk to Rob Rosiello, a principal in the New York office who had just launched a business-to-business marketing initiative within the marketing practice. Said Dull:

> Like most new initiatives, "B to B" was struggling to get established without full-time resources, so Rob was pleased to see me. I was enjoying my business marketing work, so the initiative sounded like a great opportunity. . . . Together, we wrote a proposal to make me the firm's business marketing specialist.

The decision to pursue this strategy was not an easy one for Dull. Like most of his colleagues, he felt that specialists were regarded as second-class citizens—"overhead being supported by real consultants who serve clients," Dull suggested. But his GDL told him that recent directors meetings had reaffirmed the importance of building functional expertise, and some had even suggested that 15%–20% of the firm's partners should be functional experts within the next five to seven years. (As of 1995, over 300 associates were specialists, but only 15 of the 500 partners.) In April 1995, Dull and Rosiello took their proposal to Andrew Parsons and David Court, two leaders of the Marketing practice. The directors suggested a mutual trial of the concept until the end of the year and offered to provide Dull the support to commit full time to developing the B to B initiative.

Dull's first priority was to collect the various concepts, frameworks, and case studies that existed within the firm, consolidating and synthesizing them in Several PD documents. In the process, he and Rosiello began assembling a core team of interested contributors. Together, they developed an agenda of half a dozen cutting-edge issues in business marketing—segmentation, multi-buyer decision making and marketing partnerships, for example—and launched a number of study initiatives around them. Beyond an expanded series of PD documents, the outcome was an emerging set of core beliefs, and a new framework for business marketing.

The activity also attracted the interest of Mark Leiter, a specialist in the Marketing Science Center of Competence. This center, which had developed largely around a group of a dozen or so specialists, was in many ways a model of what Dull hoped the B to B initiative could become, and having a second committed specialist certainly helped.

In November, another major step to that goal occurred when the B to B initiative was declared a Center of Competence. At that time, the core group decided they would test their colleagues' interest and their own credibility by arranging an internal conference at which they would present their ideas. When over 50 people showed up including partners and directors from four continents, Dull felt that prospects for the center looked good.

Through the cumulative impact of the PD documents, the conference and word of mouth recommendations, by early 1996 Dull and his colleagues were getting more calls than the small center could handle. They were proud when the March listing of PDNet "Best Sellers" listed B to B documents at numbers 2, 4, and 9 (see Exhibit 7). For Dull, the resulting process was enlightening:

> We decided that when we got calls we would swarm all over them and show our colleagues we could really add value for their clients. . . . This may sound strange—even corny—but I now really understand why this is a profession and not a business. If I help a partner serve his client better, he will call me back. It's all about relationships, forming personal bonds, helping each other.

While Dull was pleased with the way the new center was gaining credibility and having impact, he was still very uncertain about his promotion prospects. As he considered his future, he began to give serious thought to writing a book on business to business marketing to enhance his internal credibility and external visibility.

A NEW MD, A NEW FOCUS

In 1994, after six years of leadership in which firm revenue had doubled to an estimated $1.5 billion annually, Fred Gluck stepped down as MD. His successor was 45-year-old Rajat Gupta, a 20-year McKinsey veteran committed to continuing the emphasis knowledge development. After listening to the continuing debates about which knowledge development approach was most effective, Gupta came to the conclusion that the discussions were consuming energy that should have been directed towards the activity itself. "The firm did not have to make a choice," he said. "We had to pursue *all* the options." With that conclusion, Gupta launched a four-pronged attack.

He wanted to capitalize on the firm's long-term investment practice development driven by Clientele Industry Sectors and Functional Capability Groups and supported by the knowledge infrastructure of PDNet and FPIS. But he also wanted to create some new channels, forums, and mechanisms for knowledge development and organizational learning.

Building on an experiment begun by the German office, Gupta embraced a grass-roots knowledge-development approach called Practice Olympics. Two- to six-person teams from offices around the world were encouraged to develop ideas that grew out of recent client engagements and formalize them for presentation at a regional competition with senior partners and clients as judges. The 20 best regional teams then competed at a firm-wide event. Gupta was proud that in its second year, the event had attracted over 150 teams and involved 15% of the associate body.

At a different level, in late 1995 the new MD initiated six special initiatives—multi-year internal assignments led by senior partners that focused on emerging issues that were of importance to CEOs. The initiative tapped both internal and external expertise to develop "state-of-the-art" formulations of each key issue. For example, one focused on the shape and function of the corporation of the future, another on creating and managing strategic growth, and a third on capturing global opportunities. Gupta saw these initiatives as reasserting the importance of the firm's functional knowledge yet providing a means to do longer term, bigger commitment, cross-functional development.

Finally, he planned to expand on the model of the McKinsey Global Institute, a firm-sponsored research center established in 1991 to study implications of changes in the global economy on business. The proposal was to create other pools of dedicated resources protected from daily pressures and client demands, and focused on long term research agendas. A Change Center was established in 1995 and an Operations Center was being planned. Gupta saw these institutes as a way in which McKinsey could recruit more research-oriented people and link more effectively into the academic arena.

Most of these initiatives were new and their impact had not yet been felt within the firm. Yet Gupta was convinced the direction was right:

> We have easily doubled our investment in knowledge over these past couple of years. There are lots more people involved in many more initiatives. If that means we do 5–10% less client work today, we are willing to pay that price to invest in the future. Since Marvin Bower, every leadership group has had a commitment to leave the firm stronger than it found it. It's a fundamental value of McKinsey to invest for the future of the firm.

FUTURE DIRECTIONS

Against this background, the McKinsey partnership was engaged in spirited debate about the firm's future directions and priorities. The following is a sampling of their opinions:

> I am concerned that our growth may stretch the fabric of the place. We can't keep on disaggregating our units to create niches for everyone because we have exhausted the capability of our integrating mechanisms. I believe our future is in developing around CSTs and integrating across them around common knowledge agendas.

> *Historically, I was a supporter of slower growth, but now I'm convinced we must grow faster. That is the key to creating opportunity and excitement for people, and that generates innovation and drives knowledge development. . . . Technology is vital not only in supporting knowledge transfer, but also in allowing partners to mentor more young associates. We have to be much more aggressive in using it.*

> There is a dark side to technology—what I call technopoly. It can drive out communication and people start believing that e-mailing someone is the same thing as talking to them. If teams stop meeting as often or if practice conferences evolve into discussion forums on Lotus Notes, the technology that has supported our growth may begin to erode our culture based on personal networks.

> *I worry that we are losing our sense of village as we compartmentalize our activities and divide into specialties. And the power of IT has sometimes led to information overload. The risk is that the more we spend searching out the right PD document, the ideal framework, or the best expert, the less time we spend thinking creatively about the problem. I worry that as we increase the science, we might lose the craft of what we do.*

These were among the scores of opinions that Rajat Gupta heard since becoming MD. His job was to sort through them and set a direction that would "leave the firm stronger than he found it."

EXHIBIT 7 PDNet "BEST-SELLERS": March and Year-to-Date, 1996

	NUMBER REQUESTED	TITLE, AUTHOR(S), DATE, PDNet #	FUNCTIONAL CAPABILITY GROUP/SECTOR
March 1996	21	**Developing a Distinctive Consumer Marketing Organization** *Nora Aufreiter, Theresa Austerberry, Steve Carlotti, Mike George, Liz Lempres (1/96, #13240)*	Consumer Industries/ Packaged Goods; Marketing
	19	**VIP: Value Improvement Program to Enhance Customer Value in Business to Business Marketing** *Dirk Berensmann, Marc Fischer, Heiner Frankemölle, Lutz-Peter Pape, Wolf-Dieter Voss (10/95, #13340)*	Marketing; Steel
	16	**Handbook for Sales Force Effectiveness—1991 Edition** *(5/91, #6670)*	Marketing
	15	**Understanding and Influencing Customer Purchase Decisions in Business to Business Markets** *Mark Leiter (3/95, #12525)*	Marketing
	15	**Channel Management Handbook** *Christine Bucklin, Stephen DeFalco, John DeVincentis, John Levis (1/95, #11876)*	Marketing
	15	**Platforms for Growth in Personal Financial Services (PFS201)** *Christopher Leech, Ronald O'Hanley, Eric Lambrecht, Kristin Morse (11/95, #12995)*	Personal Financial Services
	14	**Developing Successful Acquisition Programs to Support Long-Term Growth Strategies** *Steve Coley, Dan Goodwin (11/92, #9150)*	Corporate Finance
	14	**Understanding Value-Based Segmentation** *John Forsyth, Linda Middleton (11/95, #11730)*	Consumer Industries/ Packaged Goods; Marketing
	14	**The Dual Perspective Customer Map for Business to Business Marketing** *(3/95, #12526)*	Marketing
	13	**Growth Strategy—Platforms, Staircases and Franchises** *Charles Conn, Rob McLean, David White (8/94, #11400)*	Strategy
Cumulative Index (January–March)	54	**Introduction to CRM (Continous Relationship Marketing)—Leveraging CRM to Build PFS Franchise Value (PFS221)** *Margo Geogiadis, Milt Gillespie, Tim Gokey, Mike Sherman, Marc Singer (11/95, #12999)*	Personal Financial Services
	45	**Platforms for Growth in Personal Financial Services (PFS201)** *Christopher Leech, Ronald O'Hanley, Eric Lambrecht, Kristin Morse (11/95, #12995)*	Personal Financial Services
	40	**Launching a CRM Effort (PFS222)** *Nick Brown, Margo Georgiadis (10/95, #12940)*	Marketing
	38	**Building Value Through Continuous Relationship Marketing (CRM)** *Nick Brown, Mike Wright (10/95, #13126)*	Banking and Securities
	36	**Combining Art and Science to Optimize Brand Portfolios** *Richard Benson-Armer, David Court, John Forsyth (10/95, #12916)*	Marketing; Consumer Industries/Packaged Goods
	35	**Consumer Payments and the Future of Retail Banks (PA202)** *John Stephenson, Peter Sands (11/95, #13008)*	Payments and Operating Products
	34	**CRM (Continuous Relationship Marketing) Case Examples Overview** *Howie Hayes, David Putts (9/95, #12931)*	Marketing
	32	**Straightforward Approaches to Building Management Talent** *Parke Boneysteele, Bill Meehan, Kristin Morse, Pete Sidebottom (9/95, #12843)*	Organization
	32	**Reconfiguring and Reenergizing Personal Selling Channels (PFS213)** *Patrick Wetzel, Amy Zinsser (11/95, #12997)*	Personal Financial Services
	31	**From Traditional Home Banking to On-Line PFS (PFS211)** *Gaurang Desai, Brian Johnson, Kai Lahmann, Gottfried Leibbrandt, Paal Weberg (11/95, #12998)*	Personal Financial Services

Source: Month by Month (McKinsey's internal staff magazine).

Sony: Regeneration (A)

SONY: REGENERATION (A)

"Are you sure?" Nobuyuki Idei had asked in complete astonishment. He had just been informed by Norio Ohga, his boss and the President of Sony, that he, Idei, had been selected to take over the leadership of perhaps Japan's best known global company. The choice of Idei, passing over the heads of 14 executives with higher seniority, was an unprecedented move for a Japanese company. It was March, 1995 and Idei had been a board member of Sony for less than one year.

Over the preceding 49 years, Sony had quickly grown from a small factory to the second-largest global consumer electronics company with one of the most respected brand names in the world, developing a series of epoch-making products including the transistor radio, the "Walkman," and the compact disc player. But, according to some observers, the "Sony myth" had begun to fade after executives of the generation that founded the company such as former presidents Masaru Ibuka and Akio Morita retired from hands-on leadership roles.

One evident problem for Sony—and for most of the Japanese consumer electronics companies—was how to cope with declining profit margins, caused by intense competition and the cripplingly high exchange rate. Another problem, more specific to Sony, was its much-publicised foray into the movie business. Sony Pictures Entertainment had proved to be a huge financial drain for the company

and Sony's management had lost its direct control over this US-based subsidiary.

In addition to these problems, Idei was acutely aware of the growing importance of computers and communications equipment in the consumer electronics market and the increasing convergence of computing, telecommunications and electronic entertainment in new multimedia products. He, therefore, concluded that his first priority was to articulate a new corporate vision, which would ensure that the company would evolve from the analog to the digital era. In his first speech as the president of Sony, Idei called on all Sony employees to see the company's 50th anniversary as both the end of an era and the beginning of another:

> To ensure that Sony remains an excellent company over its next fifty years, I have set forth "regeneration" as a new management theme. This is a concept that preserves the original founding spirit by renewing ourselves and aiming for even greater heights. . . .

SONY CORPORATION[1]

> We started our journey fifty years ago—in 1946 when Japan was reborn with a completely different set of values. People had to spend dark and restless nights under the extreme circumstances

This case on Sony was prepared by Tomohiro Kida and Hidehiko Yamaguchi, MBA students at the London Business School, under the supervision and guidance of Professor Sumantra Ghoshal.
© London Business School, 2001.

of chaos and shortages immediately after the war. However, despite the desperate mood in those days, people were ready to rise up against the damage of the war with dreams and hopes in their hearts. Sony was born among the people's dreams and hopes of those days.

— Excerpt from corporate brochure
"Sony's Journey"

FOUNDATION

On May 7 1946, Masaru Ibuka, Akio Morita and a small group of engineers founded Tokyo Tsushin Kogyo (the predecessor of Sony Corporation) in a corner of a bombed-out department store. The new company, capitalised at only ¥190,000, had no machinery and few scientific equipments. Its only resources were the creativity, technical knowledge and enthusiasm of the founding members.

Ibuka recalled his objective of establishing the company— "The first and primary motive for setting up this company was to create a stable work environment where engineers who had a deep and profound appreciation for technology could realize their societal mission and work to their heart's content. . . . The reconstruction of Japan depended on the development of dynamic technologies" (see Exhibit 1 for the founding prospectus).

In 1958, the company name was changed to Sony, a combination of the two words: "sonus," the origin of "sonic" and "sound," and "sonny" which meant "my dear." When Ibuka and Morita initially proposed the new name, almost everyone including the company's own staff took immediate exception to the idea, because in those days it was unusual for a Japanese company to spell its name in Roman letters. "It's taken ten years since the company's foundation to make

EXHIBIT 1
EXCERPT FROM THE FOUNDING PROSPECTUS OF TOKYO TSUSHIN KOGYO

PURPOSE OF INCORPORATION

a. To establish an ideal factory that stresses a spirit of freedom and open-mindedness, and where engineers with sincere motivation can exercise their technological skills to the highest level;

b. To reconstruct Japan and to elevate the nation's culture through dynamic technological and manufacturing activities;

c. To promptly apply highly advanced technologies which were developed in various sectors during the war to common households;

d. To rapidly commercialise superior technological findings in universities and research institutions that are worthy of application in common households;

e. To bring radio communications and similar devices into common households and to promote the use of home electric appliances;

f. To actively participate in the reconstruction of war-damaged communications network by providing needed technology;

g. To produce high-quality radios and to provide radio services that are appropriate for the coming new era;

h. To promote the education of science among the general public.

MANAGEMENT POLICIES

a. We shall eliminate any unfair profit-seeking practices, constantly emphasize activities of real substance and seek expansion not only for the sake of size;

b. We shall maintain our business operations small, advance technologically and grow in areas where large enterprises cannot enter due to their size;

c. We shall be as selective as possible in our products and will even welcome technological challenges. We shall focus on highly sophisticated technical products that have great usefulness in society, regardless of the quantity involved. Moreover, we shall avoid any formal demarcation between electronics and mechanics, and shall create our own unique products uniting the two fields, with a determination that other companies cannot overtake;

d. We shall fully utilize our firm's unique characteristics, which are well known and relied upon among acquaintances in both business and technical worlds, and we shall develop production and sales channels and acquire supplies through mutual cooperation;

e. We shall guide and foster sub-contracting factories in ways that will help them become independent, and we shall strive to expand and strengthen mutual cooperation with such factories;

f. We shall carefully select employees, and our firm shall be comprised of minimal number of employees. We shall avoid having formal positions for the mere sake of having them, and shall place emphasis on a person's ability, performance and character, so that each individual can fully exercise his or her abilities and skills;

g. We shall distribute the company's surplus earnings to all employees in an appropriate manner, and we shall assist them in a practical manner to secure a stable life. In return, all employees shall exert their utmost effort into their job.

Source: Company's Web site.

the name Tokyo Tsushin Kogyo widely known in the trade. After all this time, what do you mean by proposing such a nonsensical change?" However, Ibuka and Morita argued that the domestic purchasing power in the Japanese market was still weak, so the Western markets were to be pursued for sales. Their wish was to have a company name, which was easy to read and remember in any country around the world.

PRODUCT MILESTONES

Sony's product development was often characterised by its unique engineering orientation. The company was not motivated to meet consumers' explicit needs, using available technologies. Rather, its engineers were strongly interested in applying newly developed technologies to create completely new products that people would long for, once they had seen them. "We aim to provide products that make people say, 'This is it!' the moment they hold it in their hands, 'I like this' when they use it, and 'I like this so much that I can't let it go' after they have used it over the years," explained Ohga. "Sony has always created something different while doing things others did not. That is why Sony's products are innovative and provide answers to people's underlying needs."

The transistor radio was one of the early successes in Sony's history. Although the transistor had been invented by the Bell Labs in the US in 1947, everybody thought that it was useful for only simple devices such as hearing aids. But Ibuka thought differently and believed in its potential. "A transistor can be a substitute for a big, hot and short-lived vacuum tube, which will result in products that are smaller, consume less electricity, and are resistant to damage." Vacuum tube radios were already popular for entertainment and information, but the size of a radio back then was almost as big as a small refrigerator. Ibuka wanted to develop a portable radio that could go anywhere.

Even the engineers at Western Electric, the parent company of Bell Labs who owned the transistor technology licenses, strongly recommended that Sony should make hearing aids. However, "Let's make radios," was Ibuka's answer. "Let's use transistors for a consumer product which anyone can afford to buy. Otherwise we'll be wasting our time. Let's work on a transistor radio from the scratch, whatever difficulties we may face," stressed Ibuka. Encouraged by Ibuka's enthusiasm, Sony's engineering staff rose to the challenge. After much trial and error over almost two years, the company finally launched one of the first transistor radios in 1955. The first pocket-sized radio, the TR-63, soon followed, in 1957.

Building on its success in transistor radios, Sony aggressively continued to introduce revolutionary products into the consumer electronics market. Using the transistor tech-

nology it had learned, Sony beat the competition to the emerging markets for transistor TVs (the TV8-301 in 1960) and transistor videotape recorders (the PV-100 in 1963), both of which were the world's first products in their categories. It further launched the first home-use open-reel VTR, the CV-2000 and solid-state condenser microphone, the C-38 in 1965. Sony's 1968 introduction of the Trinitron colour TV tube, which provided brighter, sharper TV images with less distortion than the conventional picture tubes, began another decade of its explosive growth. The most successful products in its history, the "Walkman" personal stereo and the Compact Disc Player emerged in 1979 and in 1982 respectively (see Exhibit 2 for the history of product launches).

There were failures too, along the way. Between 1976 and 1988, Sony's Betamax camp lost the fight with the VHS camp of Matsushita and JVC for home-use VCR market share. Although the Betamax format was launched earlier and its image quality was clearly superior to the VHS format, the VHS camp worked more actively to supply its products to other consumer electronics manufacturers on an OEM basis and made advances in the software business. One Sony employee recalled, "Sony learned a lot. We learned the hard way that quality and originality aren't always the deciding factors in creating a standard consumer electronics format."

Sony also stumbled in its efforts to enter the computer devices market. Traditionally, the majority of Sony people had stood by the belief that the core of Sony's electronics business would always be audio visual equipment for the masses and therefore its R&D efforts in the computer field had been minimal. But Kazuo Iwama, who became president in 1976, believed that Sony could not survive the 1990s without computer-related technologies, and began product development in the office automation (OA) and microcomputer fields. His effort led to the introduction in the early 1980s of the "Series 35" word processor, the portable "Typecorder" typewriter, the "SMC-70 series" microcomputer, and the "HB-55" MSX-standard personal computer. Unfortunately, these computer-related products did not interest consumers very much and the company could not establish a presence in the market. This failure in the 1980s confirmed the traditional view that "Sony is an AV manufacturer."

THE EXPANDING DREAM

From the very inception, Sony people, particularly Morita, were confident that their company and its products would be recognised around the world in the near future. One day in 1955, Sony received an order of 100,000 radios from Bulova, a major US watch manufacturer. "Your price is

EXHIBIT 2
HISTORY OF PRODUCT
LAUNCHES

1950	"G-Type," Japan's first tape recorder
1955	"TR-55," Japan's first transistor radio
	"TV8-301," world's first transistor television
1963	"PV-100," world's first compact transistor VCR
1968	"Trinitron" colour TV
1971	3/4 inch, U-matic VCR
1975	"Betamax" VCR for home use
1979	"Walkman," the headphone stereo
1982	CD player
	"Betacam," a single-unit, 1/2 inch, broadcast use camera
1985	Single-unit, 8mm video camera
1987	Digital Audio Tape (DAT) deck
1988	"Mavica," electronic, still-image camera
1989	High-resolution, High-Band system, 8mm video series, "CCD-TR55," lightweight, compact-size, single-unit 8mm video
1990	"HD Trinitron," 36-inch, colour HDTV for home-use
1991	"Kirara Basso" Series with "Super Trinitron" picture tube
1992	MiniDisc (MD) system
1993	"Digital Betacam" system, broadcast-use, component digital VCR
1994	World's first high-brightness, green light-emitting diode
1995	Technology Plasmatron, flat panel display
	Digital video camcorder for home-use, Digital Handycam
	Basic specifications of new format for high-density optical disc finalized, including new format name, DVD
1996 (expected)	Personal head-mounted LCD monitor "Glasstron"
	Cyber-Shot Digital Still Camera
	"VAIO" PC by SONY
	FD (flat display) Trinitron
1997 (expected)	DVD video player

okay with us," said Bulova, "but we won't sell them under the Sony name. We'll have to market them under our own brand name. Nobody in this country has ever heard of Sony." Although his colleagues asked Morita to accept the largest and most attractive order that Sony had ever got, Morita decisively refused it. "On no account should we permit the use of their brand name. We've got our own, Sony, and we should stand by it." Bulova's president was scornful of Morita's lack of business sense, saying "Our brand has a world reputation with 50 years of history behind it." But Morita countered, "Fifty years ago, how many people knew your name? We're in the same position as you were then, and this is the first of our 50 years. In 50 years' time we'll have made the name Sony as famous as yours."

As Morita had expected, the "Sony" brand obtained global recognition at a good pace. The pocket-sized radio (TR-63) priced at $39.95 became the first hit in the US and Europe in 1957. Its successor model, the TR-610, was brought out the following year and sold half a million sets worldwide between 1958 and 1960. More importantly, while the label "made in Japan" was still regarded as synonymous with low quality in those days, the Sony name was looked on as top quality even in the US. Leading department stores and quality specialty stores in the US, Europe and Japan vied to create TR-610 displays and traded the product at a premium.

Morita's initial goal was to build up overseas markets that would yield 50% of the company's gross sales. Thanks to the transistor radio, its overseas market accounted for 42% of total sales in 1960 and the 50% goal became almost achievable. Next came step two. Morita asserted, "We must go to the heart of the matter. . . . Sony can become stronger by setting up overseas offices." Regional operation centres and local sales companies were set up in the US and Europe over the 1960s and 70s. Morita then put forward his plans to construct production facilities near the markets that Sony served, such as Shannon (Ireland, 1960), San Diego (1972) and Bridgend (Wales, 1974).

Over the 1980s, as the yen–dollar exchange rate shifted from 200 Yen/US$ to the 100 Yen/US$ range, Sony responded by expanding overseas production. In addition to Europe and the US, it built its fourth regional centre of operations and nine plants between 1985 and 1990 in Asia where its operations were relatively protected from the immediate effect of the strong yen and also constituted a promising market. Each regional centre in the US, Europe, and Asia was raised to the status of regional headquarters and given the authority to make decisions regarding production, sales, logistics, technology, and financing to maximise operational efficiency and meet regional needs. As a result, Morita introduced a new principle "global localisation" in 1988. "This is a new way of life for Sony, whereby we meet local needs with local operations while following common global concepts and technologies."

Morita not only expanded the company geographically but also steered it into new areas of businesses. The first diversification step involved electronics-related products which connected to Sony's main line of business. Sony/Tektronix Corporation was established in 1965 to manufacture and market instrumentation and measuring equipment in Japan. The next step came in 1975, when Sony and Union Carbide Corp. established a battery manufacturing and marketing joint venture called Sony-Eveready Inc. While the initial successes achieved in measuring instruments and batteries were the results of joint efforts with other companies, Sony utilised the experience gained through these ventures to eventually develop proprietary technologies and products that made substantial contribution to the company's overall growth.

Looking back on the Betamax debacle, Morita had often reflected that Sony would not have lost the battle if it had controlled a software library at the time. Understanding that hardware and software were no longer distinct businesses, Sony set up a joint venture, CBS/Sony Records Inc., in 1968 to enter the music business and it eventually acquired the partner, CBS Records, in 1988. Sony also purchased Columbia Pictures Entertainment Inc. for $3.4 billion in 1989. It was, at that time, the biggest M&A transaction involving a Japanese company and intensified the growing uneasiness in the US that the Japanese would take over "American Culture," contrary to Sony management's intention. CBS Records and Columbia Pictures were later renamed Sony Music Entertainment Inc. and Sony Pictures Entertainment Inc. respectively.

Sony's plan was to use its intimate knowledge of Hollywood to come up with breakthrough products, support them with its music and movies and increasingly make money on the branded software it sold rather than just the platforms. This strategy worked on the music side. Ohga guided Sony's music division into the top position in the Japanese record industry in just ten years. Endorsements from Sony stars like Mariah Carey, Billy Joel and Pink Floyd undoubtedly contributed to sales of CD and Mini-Disc players. However, no such synergy surfaced from Sony's ownership of film libraries, and that division averaged losses of $200 million a year.

After the second half of the 1970s, Sony started establishing a number of joint ventures in a diverse range of fields, many of which seemed to have no relation to electronics products. In 1979, Sony announced that Sony Creative Products Inc., an affiliate company of CBS/Sony, would produce and market cosmetics as a new line of business. In the same year, Sony established a joint venture agreement with US life insurance giant The Prudential Insurance Co. and called this company Sony Prudential Life Insurance Co., Ltd. Sony also began importing and selling sports goods in Japan, teaming up with a Pepsico Inc. subsidiary to establish Sony Wilson Inc. However, as Sony continued to diversify its operations in publishing, luxury goods, cosmetics, insurance and restaurants, many people both inside the company and outside expressed concern that Sony was spreading its resources too thinly, which could be detrimental to its core electronics business.

Even though Sony had expanded its operations into new industry segments, electronics business still represented the company's core activity in 2001. In terms of geographic region, Japan, US, and Europe were almost equally important segments for the company (see Exhibit 3 for business segment information).

THE SPIRIT OF SONY

It was widely believed that all Sony employees shared a unique "DNA" which dated back to the founding prospectus that Ibuka penned for the company in 1946. He wrote of his wish to build a company whose employees gained satisfaction and pleasure from their work and to create a joyful, dynamic workplace. Rather than establishing a system of control, Ibuka wanted to create a pleasant working atmosphere and an open-minded corporate culture. Sony had always used these fundamental principles when developing its HR policies. Despite the enormous changes over the years both inside and outside Sony, the company's dedication to realizing these objectives remained the same.

RECRUITING EFFORTS

In the early years, it was relatively difficult for Sony to recruit new graduates, due to the dual handicaps of a short history and low name recognition. The majority of new university graduates were hired by Japanese big businesses rather than small ventures like Sony and they were willing to work for only one company for their entire career in

EXHIBIT 3
SEGMENT
INFORMATION

SALES AND OPERATING REVENUE

INDUSTRY SEGMENTS:

	1991	1992	(Yen in millions) 1993	1994	1995
Electronics	2,961,909	3,149,847	3,161,878	2,944,221	3,206,830
Video Equipment	908,399	896,379	828,366	668,537	691,116
Audio Equipment	881,777	947,770	928,010	840,723	898,507
Televisions	552,464	592,616	633,723	617,901	708,574
Others	619,269	713,082	771,779	817,060	908,633
Entertainment	733,599	778,820	831,040	789,500	776,608
Music Group	476,057	449,601	446,506	461,752	494,931
Picutures Group	257,542	329,219	384,534	327,748	281,677
Consolidated	3,695,508	3,928,667	3,992,918	3,733,721	3,983,438

GEOGRAPHIC AREAS:

	1991	1992	(Yen in millions) 1993	1994	1995
Japan	1,024,484	1,057,648	1,028,207	1,023,692	1,098,394
USA	1,055,448	1,119,174	1,215,954	1,154,454	1,152,081
Europe	1,017,804	1,080,005	1,039,802	832,751	905,416
Other	597,772	671,840	708,955	722,824	827,547
Consolidated	3,695,508	3,928,667	3,992,918	3,733,721	3,983,438

Source: Company report.

those days. To overcome these handicaps, Sony made a significant effort to develop a relaxed culture and working environment, which could attract candidates from other companies even under the lifetime employment system in Japan. In addition, the company avoided rigid corporate rules so as to create an environment in which new recruits could contribute to the company from their first day. Most of these experienced personnel were outstanding engineers with strong belief in "Ibuka-ism" and a clear and unique self-direction in electronics product development.

Even after Sony became large and well-known enough in the 1970s to regularly recruit university graduates, it continued to hire experienced people, rather than relying solely on fresh graduates. Ibuka believed that this "mixed blood" policy had contributed to making Sony a much stronger company. Tsunao Hashimoto, who played a major role in personnel development then, said, "Today, Sony should not be the same as it was yesterday. Sony must evolve and develop from the knowledge and experiences brought by its employees who come from outside the company."

One of Sony's distinctive policies in recruiting new staff lay in deliberately underemphasizing the candidates' academic background. In 1966, Morita wrote a book called *Never Mind School Records* arguing that companies should place emphasis on the capabilities of individuals rather than on their academic backgrounds. Following his argument, Sony introduced its open-entry system for university graduates, whereby applicants were asked not to name their respective schools. This was a sharp departure from the well-entrenched Japanese corporate norm of respecting a clear hierarchy of academic institutions, with Todai (Tokyo University) clearly at the top, and giving significant weight to a candidate's university and academic records in both recruitment and promotion decisions.

In 2001, Sony was clearly one of the most admired companies that Japanese university graduates wished to join. Though it had become much easier for Sony to attract the most talented students, the company was worried about a possible side effect. As described by a senior HR manager, "We conduct in-depth interviews with all prospective candidates and carefully read their essays prior to an employment decision. They do not necessarily have to be the so-called 'best talents.' We would rather hire those who have something really different from others and own a driving force to achieve their unique dreams. But I suspect the very recognition of our name may attract not those who we really want to hire, but the less entrepreneurial people who expect Sony to give them directions or just feed them."

PERSONNEL MANAGEMENT

Ibuka and Morita believed that jobs should be done by people who not only had the ability, but also had a personal passion in doing them. Since its founding, Sony's top management had been keen on building an open, meritocratic approach to personnel management. "Internal recruiting system" was introduced in the 1960s to make it clear that talented, enthusiastic employees would be given the chance to progress within Sony and to provide a mechanism for the movement of staff. The system allowed every employee to apply for any position in which he or she was interested, with or without permission from the immediate boss. Once an employee received an "offer" from the desired division, the current boss essentially could not reject the move. Every year, more than 300 employees moved to their preferred positions using this unique system. This system ensured not only employee mobility within the company, but also managers' effort to motivate their subordinates. In order to retain talented people within their groups or divisions, managers always had to set challenging tasks that could excite their staff or allow them to work on projects they particularly wanted to tackle.

Historically, Sony had not been a leading company in terms of formal employee training. Instead of providing organised educational programmes for its employees, Sony relied more on OJT (on the job training) to improve the skills of both its engineers and non-engineers. This was partly because the company aggressively hired experienced people who already possessed the requisite skills, and also because its corporate culture valued self-starters in acquiring skills and knowledge to achieve their own goals above those who waited to be trained by the company. Of course, as the size and complexity of the organisation increased, a more structured training programme was gradually developed. However, at Sony, such training was considered an opportunity to discuss issues with the top management rather than as a place just to listen to lectures quietly. Sony's top executives regularly joined discussions at the training programmes, hoping that they could find a new talent who might be assigned an important project in the future.

Leadership development programmes were run on an ad-hoc basis rather than as an integrated part of a holistic HR system. The most famous initiative in this area was the "Idei juku," a task-force style action learning opportunity. It was initiated by Idei when he was a director in an attempt to identify, grow and evaluate future senior officers. In the task force, 6–8 middle managers, typically in their mid 30s, were selected across the organisation and given a chance to closely work with Idei. Unlike usual task forces, no specific mission was given to the participants but instead, they were expected to identify possible problems in the company and draw up an organisational response to those problems over a half year period. At the end of the period, the team made a presentation to the top management of the company including Idei himself. After Idei took the helm of the organisation, this initiative was scaled up and the Sony University was created as an institutional effort to develop the company's future leaders.

In sync with many other Japanese corporations, Sony avoided highly leveraged incentive systems, and relied on ability-based or even seniority-based reward, which gave it flexibility in job assignment without defining detailed job descriptions. Good performance of an employee was acknowledged, not so much by sharply differentiated financial rewards, but through the opportunity to work on more interesting assignments, often aligned to the employee's personal dreams and aspirations. Both management and employees generally supported this "undeveloped" personnel policy, which they believed had kept Sony people entrepreneurial for a long time. A young employee described how his performance was judged at Sony, "Even if a new project I initiated fails, I am not blamed for it, as long as the project is seen to have been challenging, with the potential for creating something new for the company. But my assessment may be downgraded if I work on the same project in the same way as yesterday."

Sony employees were not reluctant to leave the company if they found more challenging and interesting job opportunities outside the company. In fact, Sony people were highly appreciated by executive search firms and were frequently offered attractive senior positions in entrepreneurial ventures or subsidiaries of non-Japanese businesses. Interestingly, Sony's top management encouraged such people to do the best in their next career stages. Then, several years later, Sony would often re-hire them as long as they wanted to work for Sony again and still possessed the requisite skills. These practices were highly unusual for established Japanese businesses, where both management and employees believed they should be loyal to a single company for life and changing employers was a synonym for "going over to the enemy."

R&D ENVIRONMENT

The bulk of Sony's R&D efforts were divided into three different research layers. The Sony Research Centre, which had a long history since 1961, handled the more basic research-oriented activities. On the other hand, the

Advanced Development Laboratory that had been established in 1994 focused on more product-oriented R&D fields. Technical developments that were closely associated with existing products had been transferred to each business group or divisional company.

A director of an in-house research centre once introduced five questions as guidelines for engineers: 1) Will the current research project lead to the development of new business fields? 2) When and to what business field will the project contribute? 3) What sets the project apart from other projects? 4) Is the research being pursued of the same high quality as that at the top level in the world? and 5) Is the project attractive enough to interest business groups within the company? In addition, Sony engineers tended to ask themselves, "Is this Sony-like?" The criterion for "Sony-like" varied from one engineer to another. One argued, "Sony products should be designed small and cool," but another believed, "The question is whether we can go beyond what consumers have expected."

Although each engineer had a different view of "Sony-like" from others, "challenge to new" had always been an indispensable component of Sony's R&D approach. In the 1960s, the *Asahi Weekly* carried an article on the consumer electronics industry which called Sony "a corporate guinea pig." "Toshiba has now outpaced Sony in the field of transistors, with close to 2.5 times greater output than the former leader. Toshiba's strength is certainly drawn from its corporate strategy of investing whatever capital is necessary to profit on the products it sees as lucrative. Sony, the pioneer in transistor production, has played the guinea pig for Toshiba admirably." Initially Sony engineers greatly resented the metaphor. In later years, though, they willingly accepted it as reflecting Sony's spiritual ways of challenging the status quo to create completely new products. Indeed, when Masaru Ibuka, a co-founder and later Chief Advisor of Sony was awarded a medal of honour by the Japanese Government, he was presented a figure of a guinea pig by the employees of the company. As one of them described, "One of our most important jobs is determining how to apply the latest developments in electronics to new consumer products. . . . Today, those who simply do the same work over and over in the same way will gradually fall behind the times. . . . By taking this guinea pig approach to products, there is always something new to challenge."

Sony's dynamic R&D environment was partly attributable to its management's deep understanding of and keen interest in technology. Not only Ibuka but also all of his successors were familiar with the latest technologies and aware of each engineer's strengths and the particular product that he or she was working on at the moment. They also knew what could motivate Sony engineers to work

hard. Ibuka said when he was shown the first prototype U-matic VTR machine, "So you've managed to build this marvellous machine. Just think, the next one will be even better!" This response was typical of his attitude. Even while earnestly congratulating someone for successfully completing a project, he would be looking ahead to the next step. "I love seeing Ibuka with a smile on his face, so I always do my best," said an engineer, referring to the obvious delight with which Sony management greeted any new product or technology.

However, it was often the case that Sony engineers continued their product development efforts that truly interested them, even if their bosses were not on board. Nobody would be surprised to find a colleague working on a project behind the boss's back. In fact, "Walkman" was initially developed by an engineer who manufactured an experimental model for his hobby rather than for his job. Playstation, a major source of Sony's profits since its introduction, was also initially rejected by management as a gambling toy in the late 1980s. Ken Kutaragi, who initiated the plan for Playstation, always had to wander around in the company to secure R&D budgets from his supporters, averting top management's intervention. Indeed, while Sony engineers typically worked very hard to develop "approved" products, many also simultaneously pursued projects, based on personal interest. Looking back on his days at Sony, Leona Esaki, who invented the Esaki diode and won a Nobel Prize in physics later, described the company's unique R&D environment as "organised chaos."

TOLERANCE FOR FAILURE

One of the enduring characteristics of Sony, deeply embedded in the company by Ibuka and Morita, was a culture in which people were allowed to make mistakes: "We believe we can get the best out of each and every employee by having such a culture. It makes individuals committed to whatever work they do," said Ohga. "They are committed to any job they do because they know they can do whatever they want without being afraid of being criticised for failure."

One of the ways in which Ibuka and Morita built this culture was by making it a habit to tell stories about their own mistakes. For example, Sony's first mass-production G-Type videocassette recorder, failed to sell initially and almost pushed the company into bankruptcy. It was the first product of its kind in Japan and a good illustration of Sony's technological prowess. The company went through many trials and tribulations to develop the product but none of them sold. With hindsight, the reason was obvious—no one had ever seen such a product before and as a result had no idea how to use it. At that time, it had occurred neither to Ibuka nor to Morita that such a technologically advanced product might not sell. Morita later reviewed this experience and his learning from it: "It was the moment that I determined what I was going to do: I had to become a salesman for the company. I had to get the products' value proposition across to possible customers." Morita of course was an engineer by education. Without this setback he might have continued to pursue a career in technology—and Sony would not have grown to the multi-billion dollar company that it became.

Management of Sony's overseas subsidiaries, Sony of America (SONAM) among others, provides another good example of a history full of trial and error. Appointing Harvey Schein, an aggressive salesperson and cost-cutter, as the CEO and President of SONAM was arguably one of Morita's greatest mistakes. While SONAM's sales grew under Schein, his strong ego created conflict not only within the American operation but also between the American operation and the company's headquarters in Japan. This destroyed rather than created value, and Schein was asked to leave the company after five and a half years. "However," according to Ohga, "the important thing is, those failures had a pay-off later because our co-founders learned from them." Indeed, it would be fair to say that as a result of its mistakes, Sony had developed a capacity for running its overseas operations that was head and shoulders above that of most other Japanese companies.

MANAGEMENT TEAM

Sony founders had always worked as a team like "two people running in a three-legged race." From the foundation through the 1970s, Ibuka and Morita drove the rapidly growing company with their charismatic leadership. Though both had engineering backgrounds, Morita focused on non-engineering activities such as marketing, sales, and finance, while Ibuka focused on product development. Collectively, however, they established a tradition in Sony in which the role of the top management was seen primarily as that of the "Chief Innovation Officer," whose primary job was to shake up the status quo and set an environment for innovation.

In the 1980s, as Ibuka withdrew from the forefront of management, a new management team needed to be formed. However, Sony had not developed any formal procedures for planning management succession, such as a succession committee run by external directors. Therefore, the company had to rely on one individual's decision and, consequently, the process of selecting a successor was not very transparent.

Morita initially appointed Kazuo Iwama, who combined an excellent understanding of technology with outstanding people skills, but was also his brother-in-law, as the next president in 1976. Although Morita did not mean to be partial to his relative at all, his decision was harshly criticised.

Following the untimely death of Iwama, Ohga took the presidential position in 1982. Despite the fact that Ohga was not an engineer but a professional baritone before joining Sony, he had worked closely with Sony's founding members for developing radios and tape recorders since 1950 and thus understood Sony's electronics equipment technology very well. Working alongside chairman Morita and other key managers, Ohga's new management team pressed ahead with the development of a new management strategy and organisational structure in order to change the founder-driven Sony into a truly top-ranking company with a more formal way of decision-making. Ohga set forth his new business strategy of diversification and aimed to place sales of consumer electronics products on an equal footing with sales of other businesses by 1990.

Ohga was also instrumental in establishing Sony's corporate structure. Sony had been able to grow without rigorous control systems thanks to the combination of founders Ibuka and Morita, who fused great technological ideas with inspiring and charismatic leadership. Ohga believed that Sony could no longer rely on such a leadership-dependent management approach, and had to develop proper planning, budgeting and control systems to maintain its growth record. He introduced a business group system, under which a number of "mini companies" or business groups were created and he gave the head of each group the responsibility and authority for all its operation from product development to sales. The new business groups were also expected to maintain their own profit and loss statements and balance sheets. He reorganised 19 business groups into 8 divisional companies in April 1994, to further develop a more self-contained and efficient operation within the company (see Exhibit 4 for the company's organisation structure).

Although Morita was seen as the backbone of the company, he had not been involved in day-to-day operations since the late 1980s. Sony sustained its most painful blow in 1993, when Morita suffered a stroke and was not expected to return to management. Now Ohga had to make the big decisions about what to do at Sony without the support from Morita. Reflecting on his long period as president, Ohga reached a conclusion that it was time for him to hand over the helm to the next generation of management. However, as was the case with Morita, Ohga had no succession plan at that time and agonised over the choice of a successor for a full year.

EXHIBIT 4
ORGANISATION
STRUCTURE
(introduced
in April 1994)

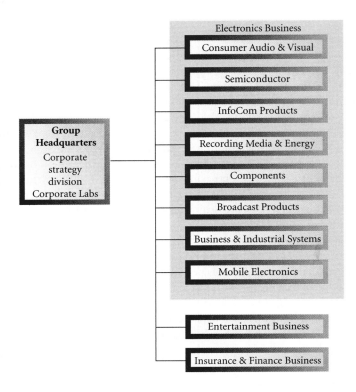

Electronics Business
Consumer Audio & Visual
Semiconductor
InfoCom Products
Recording Media & Energy
Components
Broadcast Products
Business & Industrial Systems
Mobile Electronics

Group Headquarters
Corporate strategy division
Corporate Labs

Entertainment Business
Insurance & Finance Business

SONY IN THE 1990s

The early 1990s were often characterised as years of darkness and tumult in Sony's history (see Exhibit 5 for stock price chart).

First of all, in Hollywood, Morita's vision of "global localisation" had produced a result opposite to what he had intended. Partly to calm the anti-Japanese and anti-Sony sentiment in America, Morita and Ohga had to give Michael Schulhof, the chairman of the Sony Corporation of America, and other American managers a largely free hand in the US operation. Schulhof spent some $800 million to recruit two producers, Jon Peters and Peter Guber, who had never headed a major film company, to run the studio. But the two producers soon proved unqualified for the roles. Columbia and its sister Tri-star studios produced big-budget bomb after bomb, including "The Last Action Hero," "Mary Shelley's Frankenstein" and "I'll Do Anything." Peters was forced out in 1991, and Guber followed three years later. The $40 billion-in-sales company eventually announced $3.2 billion in write-offs and losses in its movie business in November 1994.

Moreover, Sony's innovation engine started creaking at that time. Particularly in the late 80s and early 90s, the company seemed to be losing some of the flair that had made it the industry's leading innovator for much of its history.

EXHIBIT 5
STOCK PRICE CHART

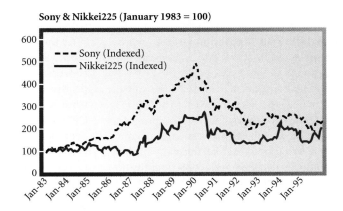

Sony & Nikkei225 (January 1983 = 100)

- - - Sony (Indexed)
—— Nikkei225 (Indexed)

Sony went for years without an original hit product, except that the $300 Playstation video game machine, introduced in 1994, turned out to be a big success. At the company New Year's party in January 1995, at which management often highlighted big new products, Ohga had to dwell at length on lithium-ion batteries. "Right now, we're kind of in the defensive mode," said Minoru Morio, executive deputy president. "We have to predict change and be on the offensive."

Some observers suggested that the strict budgetary control, which was introduced in the 1980s, was at least in part to blame for the diminishing entrepreneurial spirit and growing bureaucracy at Sony. Under the new system, Sony's divisional managers were responsible for efficient R&D and production and tended to emphasize relatively safe products that were likely to sell well, rather than truly innovative ideas which needed a significant amount of development costs and also carried higher risks. What was worse, in order to maintain sales under pressure, they tended to adopt an aggressive pricing strategy that earned Sony considerable notoriety among competitors. One analyst said, "Sony drives prices so low. . . that any sense of quality premium that the company enjoyed before has been all but extinguished."

These were the more conspicuous signs of the difficulties facing Sony, but at their root were the significant changes occurring in its main consumer electronics business. The industry was very profitable in the 1970s and 1980s, given the rapid introduction and penetration of new products such as colour TVs and VCRs. Over this period, Sony, Philips, and Matsushita emerged as the leading players on the global field. However, the 1990s saw the emergence of competition from newly industrialised countries such as South Korea and prices of audio/visual equipment declined rapidly. Unlike the personal computer industry, increases in volume did not compensate the price declines. And unlike other mature industries such as automobiles, the consumer electronics business could not necessarily rely on rising demand in the developing world for its future growth. In fact, most Asian countries had already built homegrown consumer electronics companies.

At the same time, the industry had failed to create any new "killer" product. The Mini Disc, the digital compact cassette, and the digital audio tape had all petered out, unable to secure broad market acceptance. As digital videodisks (DVD), which could hold an entire movie or offer PC users a gargantuan medium for multimedia programmes, were expected to be the next "killer" consumer electronics product, Sony was making a stubborn bid to establish an industry standard for it. Sony and its partner Philips announced their original format in 1994, but it lost ground to a competing format from a consortium led by Toshiba and Time Warner. The battle threatened to become a replay of the Betamax–VHS fiasco.

Sony's slump was evident from the fact that its sales and profits remained flat or declining for the entire first-half of the 1990s. Earnings, 120 billion yen ($903 million at the time) as recently as 1992, were just 15 billion yen ($149 million) in 1994. For the fiscal year ended March 1995, Sony was expected to be about $2.8 billion in the red because of the write-off in the movie business. Debt, once a scant 18% of capitalisation, had reached nearly 50% (see Exhibit 6 for the income statement).

Beyond these operational difficulties, the company was also facing a potentially more disruptive strategic challenge. The emerging digital technology indicated that in addition to its traditional consumer electronics rivals such as Matsushita, Toshiba and Philips, Sony would soon face new competition from computer and telecommunication companies as well. Traditionally, consumer electronics and computers were distinct fields. However, at the beginning of the 1990s, microprocessors and OS technologies were rapidly improving and the leading companies in these fields had begun to yield a considerable amount of influence over the entire electronics industry. The telecommunications industry had also come to influence Sony's traditional businesses.

NEW LEADER: NOBUYUKI IDEI

IDEI'S BACKGROUND

Idei was the first president of Sony to have risen from the bottom. The son of an economics professor, Idei studied international politics and economics at Tokyo's Waseda University, where his father taught. A month after graduation in 1960, he joined Sony, aspiring to work for a company that he thought would succeed in the European market where he was interested in working. Over the 1960s and 1970s, Idei spent close to a decade in Europe. He then moved back home and consistently landed assignments in important product groups at critical moments. He was head of the audio division in the early 1980s when the compact disk player was successfully introduced. In 1983 he jumped to Sony's nascent computer business, which did not perform very well but stirred his interest in the symbiosis of hardware and software. When he was a general manager in the video group, Sony dropped its Beta videocassette format in favour of the dominant VHS. In the 1990s, as a director in charge of advertising, product design and public relations, Idei concentrated his efforts on promoting the Sony brand image.

On March 22, 1995, following an extraordinary board of directors meeting, Ohga announced Sony's new president and top management. He chose Idei as his successor, although he would retain his influence over the company

EXHIBIT 6 INCOME STATEMENT

	03/1995	03/1994	03/1993	03/1992	03/1991	03/1990	03/1989
				(YEN MILLION)			
Net sales	3,826,693	3,609,873	3,879,427	3,821,582	3,616,517	2,879,856	2,145,329
Insurance revenue	138,747						
Other operating revenue	25,143	123,848	113,491	107,085	74,259	65,386	56,143
Total sales & operating revenue	**3,990,583**	**3,733,721**	**3,992,918**	**3,928,667**	**3,690,776**	**2,945,242**	**2,201,472**
Cost of sales	2,916,475	2,755,840	2,928,912	2,838,344	2,505,554	1,938,016	1,475,352
SG&A expenses	842,783	878,213	937,546	910,774	887,773	712,035	565,621
Insurance expenses	132,798						
Loss on write-off of goodwill	265,167						
Operating income (loss)	**(166,640)**	**99,668**	**126,460**	**179,549**	**297,449**	**295,191**	**160,499**
Interest & dividend income	22,362	38,395	46,086	62,646	64,892	44,190	22,609
Foreign exchange gain, net	22,789	35,435	22,432	36,474	37,209		4,818
Other income	32,417	46,318	43,660	44,887	40,475	47,363	32,591
Total other income	77,568	120,148	112,178	144,007	142,576	91,553	60,018
Interest expense	65,354	69,217	91,361	104,504	102,681	70,883	32,550
Foreign exchange loss, net						48,708	22,451
Other expenses	66,522	48,437	54,716	64,457	72,753	39,724	
Total other expenses	131,876	117,654	146,077	168,961	175,434	159,315	55,001
Ordinary income (loss)	**(220,948)**	**102,162**	**92,561**	**154,595**	**270,697**	**227,429**	**165,516**
Gain on subsidiary stock sale				61,544			
Income before income taxes	(220,948)	102,162	92,561	216,139	264,591	227,429	165,516
Current income taxes	84,108	59,869	83,322	73,201	146,184	128,017	91,129
Deferred income taxes (benefits)	(18,935)	18,743	(33,528)	17,126	6,214	(1,041)	4,047
Total income taxes	65,173	78,612	49,794	90,327	152,398	126,976	95,176
Income (loss) before minority interest	(286,121)	23,550	42,767	125,812	118,299	100,453	70,340
Minority int in consolidated subsids	7,235	8,252	6,507	5,691	112,193		
Equity earnings					4,732	2,355	2,129
Net income (loss)	**(293,356)**	**15,298**	**36,260**	**120,121**	**116,925**	**102,808**	**72,469**

in his new role as chairman. This announcement came as a great surprise to the business community. Idei had just become managing director in charge of advertising, public relations and product design the previous year.

Ohga explained that Sony's president had to be a person who understood technology and could communicate with engineers. "Although not an engineer, Idei can talk with and challenge engineers." Idei also fulfilled the requirement of understanding Hollywood and Silicon Valley better than other directors, and had the proper balance of hardware and software abilities. "I really feel that Mr. Idei has that software spirit," Ohga said at a news conference. "There are a number of people who can operate a hardware business. But someone who can operate a software business and raise the morale there, that is something that not everyone can do."

IDEI'S BELIEFS

As the head of the microcomputer and office automation business divisions in the 1980s, Idei had experienced the difficulties of promoting Sony's computer business. Though his efforts had turned out to be unsuccessful, Idei had since then been an enthusiastic supporter of Sony's move into the PC and software industries. He insisted that the transition from analog to digital technology would drastically change both the AV industry and people's lifestyles in the 1990s.

Between 1993 and 1994, when he had no idea that he would soon be the company's president, Idei had presented his draft on Sony's comprehensive strategy to Ohga. His report included three goals for the company,

1. Maintain the top position in the audio/visual industry
2. Develop a standard architecture in the home/personal computer devices, defending its consumer electronics business against the emerging computer makers
3. Create an electronic distribution business of software, developing network infrastructure and "intelligent" audio/visual equipment

Not much had come out of that report. People at Sony had always thought of themselves as being in the audio-visual business. The earlier failure in the computer business was still fresh in their minds. And, while the overall performance was not spectacular, there was no sense of a crisis in the company. So, there was no stimulus to pick up on Idei's proposal for re-entering the PC business.

Taking over the president's position in 1995, Idei argued intensely that information technology and a company-wide computer culture be developed in Sony. Said he: "Even though markets for our boxes will continue to grow for the next five years, our brand image and production power aren't enough to compete into the next century. We have to shift our thinking toward developing, along with the PC and software industries, what in effect are audio/visual-oriented computers and components and the software to play on them. If we can do this, I believe Sony can become the master of the digital universe." Idei concluded that his main role as president should be to "regenerate" Sony's entrepreneurial founding sprit so that the company could survive and thrive in the era of digital innovation.

Idei further contemplated how he would like to change Sony and what types of products he wanted Sony to develop in the future. He coined the phrase "Digital Dream Kids" to reflect Sony's commitment to realising the dreams which could be attained through new digital technologies. "Living in a digital age is very exciting for people of all ages. Young and old alike are truly mesmerised by digital technology. These people, or digital dream kids, are our future customers. And we must also become dream kids at all levels of Sony to continue to create something new, something that will meet our future customers' expectations," he added.

MOVES TO REGENERATION

Immediately following his inauguration as Sony's fifth president, Idei initiated several bold moves, parting ways with the deliberate, rule-by-consensus approach of conventional Japanese management. The initial scepticism about his leadership disappeared very quickly as he successfully exhibited his authority and his willingness to break from the past.

First, Idei succeeded in settling the DVD format war with Toshiba and its allies in September 1995, announcing that the companies involved in developing different formats had agreed on a unified single standard, incorporating the best of both.

His next move was to clean up the mess in the movie business. Idei persuaded Ohga, who had always been in favour of Schulhof, the chairman of Sony Corporation of America (SONAM), that it was time for his protégé to go. Soon after Schulhof finally resigned under pressure in December 1995, Idei announced that SONAM's executive committee would be broadened to include the heads of film and record businesses in addition to the head of the electronics business, and he would directly oversee the committee during his regular trips to the US.

Furthermore, a revision of corporate structure came only two years after Ohga had designed the structure in 1994 with a corporate headquarters and eight independent business units. The previous eight business groups would be reorganised into ten new autonomous "companies." Marketing and R&D were consolidated as separate departments, and an executive board was created to provide overall direction and integration. While the previous structure required each business unit to be responsible for the whole process from product development to sales, Idei thought that co-ordination among business groups was not sufficient to make the company responsive to the rapid external changes. Therefore, he decided that some company functions such as R&D and marketing needed to be integrated to facilitate Sony's overall ability to enter into new business areas. Two of the new companies—the Information Technology Company and the Personal & Mobile Communication Company—clearly reflected Sony's greater emphasis on the new business areas which had become increasingly important with the development of multimedia. The executive board was given a clear mandate to help co-ordinate the efforts of the 10 business units that would comprise the core of Sony (see Exhibit 7 for the new corporate structure).

Most importantly, Idei announced an alliance with Intel, named as "The G.I. Project" representing G for Andy Grove and I for Nobuyuki Idei. The initiative was targeted at using technology from both companies to introduce a new device into the home computer market in the autumn of 1996. Idei saw the personal computer as the vehicle that would bring his digital vision to life. "The move of PCs into the home, combined with the digitisation of the consumer audio/video industry, is leading to the birth of a new consumer electronics market."

Some industry veterans contended that Sony's launching of a PC was a risky strategy at an uncertain time in the market. "Profit margins in the PC business are razor thin, and Sony will enter the market just as growth in the U.S. PC market starts slowing and competitors start initiating new price cuts." An executive in a PC manufacturer also

EXHIBIT 7
NEW ORGANISATION
STRUCTURE
(introduced in
April 1996)

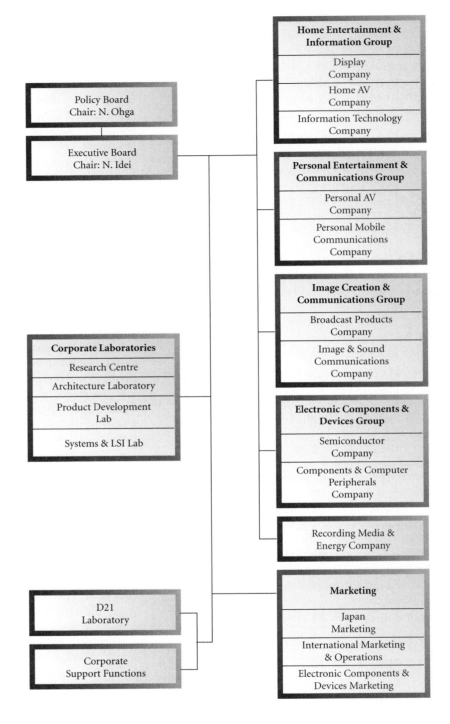

warned, "PC is a hard business in which to make money. The value added is in the components today. Besides, it has faster product development cycles than the audio/video industry, technology becomes obsolete faster, and there is a different logistics structure because inventory changes so rapidly."

Even within the company, the majority of engineers were doubtful about its success in this new business area. One of the major reasons was Sony's past failures in this area. The company had entered the PC business with an MSX machine in 1983. The MSX had been launched by Microsoft as a fun-oriented computer focusing on games and sound. When a Microsoft agent in Japan approached Sony, he had already successfully persuaded other consumer electronics companies, including Matsushita and Toshiba, to support the standard. Sony, afraid of missing the MSX boat, had decided to jump into the business—indeed, Idei was the sub-head of the business unit in charge of the initiative. However, the MSX market failed to take off as expected because the IBM PC/AT machine and Microsoft's MS-DOS were becoming the de facto global standard. Sony withdrew from the PC market in 1991. Sony had also failed to make progress in the engineering workstation business. It launched its first UNIX-based product, NEWS, in 1987 but was unable to gain traction in the marketplace even though the product had a good reputation technologically.

Because of these setbacks, apathy toward the PC was widespread throughout the organisation. Ohga, Idei's predecessor, was unenthusiastic on the grounds that the PC was a bad fit with Sony's values. "Sony's raison d'être is to produce products that no one has ever seen or even imagined. The PC business does not fit with this value set because it is essentially a mishmash of components whose standards are pretty much determined by industry giants like Intel or Microsoft. There is little space to produce Sony-type products, so the PC business is of little interest to us." Others questioned whether the PC business fit Sony's traditional strategic approach. "Sony's key success

factor is to develop a product earlier than anybody else and dominate the market by leveraging first-mover advantage. In fact, some of our products have been sold at below production cost to gain early market share. This strategy has worked well since we could recoup lost profit at a later stage when production costs fell thanks to economies of scale and the learning-curve effect. The problem is, this no longer works in the PC business because the structure of the industry is firmly established and there seems to be no niche into which we can fit."

However, Idei was firmly convinced that entering the PC business would be an indispensable step in the "regeneration" strategy. "It will allow Sony to break its pattern of customer relations. Our traditional market force is selling the box to the big dealer. If you have to start handling the computer, communication with the user is a very important part," said Idei. "We should introduce the computer in the market in order to prepare for the future kind of digital implements, which would also require the same kind of communication with the user." In addition, Idei seemed pretty confident of Sony's success in the home PC market. "We are going into the PC market from the viewpoint of consumer electronics. The home market is still growing rapidly, but today's architecture of the personal computer is difficult to use. I expect Sony to be a pioneer in developing a 'more simplified' computer, as simple to use as the TV."

Reorganization at Axion Consulting (A)

Matt Walsh turned off his computer and was getting ready to leave for home when Marvin Curtis stuck his head into the office and said, "Say Matt, can I see you for a couple of minutes? It is about next week's board meeting."

Despite being in a hurry to catch the late evening train, Walsh was loath to refuse Curtis's request. They had recently clashed over a decision to hire additional staff and putting him off, regardless of the excuse, could aggravate an already uneasy relationship.

Walsh therefore put down his briefcase, sat back in his chair, and motioned Curtis to sit in the chair opposite him.

"Sorry to barge in so late in the day," said Curtis, "but I thought it important to find out what you think about Howard Fisk's plans for reorganizing Axion."

Walsh was entirely surprised by Curtis's question. He also had his doubts about the planned reorganisation, but he was uncertain whether he could honestly share them with Curtis. "What is the problem?" he asked cautiously, thinking it best to find out where Curtis stood before he revealed his own thoughts on the matter.

Curtis needed no encouragement. He had clearly been mulling over the issues for quite a while, and now it all came tumbling out. "I do not wish to be patronising," he said, "but as a newcomer, you may not be entirely familiar with the history of Axion. I am sure you know that we began our existence as a small group of economists specialising in policy analysis for the public sector. This was back at the end of the 1980s when the privatization of public services was the rage. Subcontractors were cheaper, but often they did not deliver quality. What governments wanted, and what we delivered, was an evaluation of these services. We were in an excellent position to advise as to which company should get the bid, which bid should be renewed, and which should be refused."

"Eventually, however, governments began to do this for themselves, and do it quite effectively. As the market for our basic products matured, we diversified into the more lucrative but also much more competitive area of management consulting. We started hiring MBAs, many with previous consulting experience: a marked departure from our traditional recruitment in departments of economics. The influx of people with different backgrounds was bound to change things. We always had our disagreements—which group of people does not? But we also had enough in common to resolve these differences and get on with the job. But over time, we found that our disagreements were escalating out of hand. Our arguments were not only about issues, they were about values and identity as well. The economists dismissed the consultants as snake oil salesmen, and the consultants dismissed the economists as woolly-brained ivory tower dwellers. We kept trying to patch things up by setting up a balanced executive committee and rotating the presidency, but nothing worked. In the end, we turned to an outsider for salvation, and to

Prepared by Joseph Lampel, City University Business School, London, with the assistance of Daniel Ronen. Not to be used or reproduced without author's permission. Copyright © Joseph Lampel, 2002.

transcend the divisions we chose Howard Fisk, a scientist who had spent much of his career in industry. I have to confess that I was not in favour of this appointment, but my voice did not carry the day."

Matt Walsh knew that Curtis was not entirely candid on this point. His opposition was not based on principle alone; it was driven as much, if not more, by personal ambition. Marvin Curtis had wanted the job of president for himself. He was one of Axion's founding partners and an influential member of the executive board. But he also had the sort of acerbic personality that made enemies. It was no secret that he believed a behind-the-scenes deal to look for an outside candidate had denied him his turn at the presidency.

"I may not have been enthusiastic about Howard," continued Curtis, "but I agree with his central contention: We have to change if we are to survive. My main concern is with the changes he is proposing. I believe that his idea of splitting Axion into business units, each specialising in different areas, will increase our differences, aggravate competition for resources and reduce our incentives for cross unit co-operation. Why should the Quality Evaluation business unit help E-Commerce if they know that when all is said and done, resources are divided according to how many clients you bring in? And if there is no co-operation between the different units, where is our innovation going to come from? Specialising is good for focus and this produces quick results in the marketplace, but in the long run we will be suppressing the creative flows which made us so successful in the first place."

Walsh had been listening intently, but said little. He shared Curtis's concerns, but his views were tempered by the knowledge that he stood to gain from the reorganization. Matt expected to head one of the business units that Howard Fisk proposed to set up. Or at least, that was what he had thought until recently.

For years Matt Walsh had been trying to set up a group that specialises in R&D management consulting, but he was frustrated by the lack of support. He believed that Axion was ignoring an important area in the emerging knowledge economy. The plan that Fisk unveiled during the last general meeting proposed the setting up of such a group, and Matt Walsh was of course delighted and grateful that Fisk had endorsed his idea. It was also inevitable that he, in turn, reciprocated by giving Fisk his support and endorsement.

However, in the weeks that followed, things began to change. Fisk indicated that perhaps it was not the right time to create an R&D Management consulting unit. Setting up the other business units was consuming more resources than initially anticipated. Fisk had, however, reiterated his commitment to Walsh's proposed unit, and had suggested that Walsh needed to prepare the grounds for it more carefully, by enlisting the support of others in the organization. Walsh followed his advice faithfully by discretely lobbying for his project whenever possible. He encountered little overt opposition, but he also formed the impression that without a strong ally on the board, his project would remain in limbo. Now that Marvin Curtis was making a clear pitch for his support, he was beginning to wonder if Curtis was that person.

Reorganization at Axion Consulting (B)

Howard Fisk pushed aside the papers in front of him, and looked around the table. "There is one other item of business I would like to raise before you dig into the delicious sandwiches Jenny so kindly ordered from the deli across the street. As some of you may know, Robert Leonardi, the managing director of Perkins & Evans, has announced his intention to step down at the end of the year. What you probably do not know is that key members of the executive committee of Perkins & Evans have recently approached me with the view towards exploring the possibility of a merger between Axion and Perkins & Evans." He paused for a moment, letting the news sink in, and then continued. "Of course, this is strictly informal at this point, and will go no further if I do not have your support. However, I do not mind telling you that I am excited by the prospects. I think you would all agree that Perkins & Evans is a young and dynamic management consulting company. Their expertise in turning around financially troubled high-technology firms has attracted much press attention. They are slightly smaller than we are, and their client base is more diverse, but to my mind the potential synergy is there, if we are willing to work towards it."

There was nervous murmur around the table. Most of the committee had been caught off guard, and they were venting their surprise in no uncertain terms. Howard Fisk held up his hand, "I know, I know," he said, "more information is clearly in order. I have prepared a dossier with a complete analysis which you can pick up on the way out.

Time, however, is of the essence. I must let Perkins & Evans know if we intend to explore the idea further, or whether it is a non-starter. So let me have your views, and do not be afraid to be honest with me. I can certainly take it."

Matt Walsh looked around the table. The executive committee was made up of six people, excluding Howard Fisk. Of the six, two would almost certainly be against any such move, and two would strongly support it. Marvin Curtis had made no secret of his unhappiness about where Axion was going under Fisk, and would therefore oppose the initiative. Bruno Neri, who Curtis had recruited and trained, was likely to echo his mentor's opinion. On the other side, Salma Porter was likely to support the initiative. She was open in her admiration for Fisk's leadership qualities. Joe Wolberg owed his position on the committee to Howard Fisk. In principle, one would expect him to give Fisk his support, but lately he had showed an independent streak, clashing with Fisk over the new Knowledge Management initiative.

That left Jeremy Gold and Matt Walsh. As far as Walsh was concerned Gold was an enigma. A highly respected economist, he had left academia to join the fledgling Axion for reasons that were not entirely clear. He had supported Fisk's appointment, but had not prospered under the new

Prepared by Joseph Lampel, City University Business School, London, with the assistance of Daniel Ronen. Not to be used or reproduced without author's permission. Copyright © Joseph Lampel, 2002.

regime. His vote could go either way. The same could be said of Matt Walsh himself. He was torn between supporting and opposing Howard Fisk. He appreciated Fisk's dynamism and talent for spotting opportunities, but at the same time he was becoming increasingly alarmed at Fisk's unpredictability and his tendency to embrace initiatives before they were fully explored. He leaned back in his chair and tried to concentrate. Even if his vote did not carry the day, his decision could affect his position and future prospects at Axion.

Empire Plastics

A PROJECT TO REMEMBER

In June 1991, **Ian Jones** a production manager with **Empire Plastics Northern (EPN)** was pondering the latest project to increase the production rate of oleic acid. This was the third project in six years targeting the oleic acid plant for improvement and arose from the policy followed by the group's directors. This was to identify profitable plants and invest in improving their productivity and profitability, thus avoiding the need for investment in brand new facilities.

The installation of the "wet end"[1] went well and no problems were experienced. However, the "dry end" was a different story. It wasn't working a year on from practical completion, except in short bursts. They were still making changes to it. Jones had known all along that the technology on the dry end was relatively new and might prove troublesome, but the procurement department at **Empire Consultants** in their wisdom recommended its use. Granted, they did send a couple of guys over to Italy to see some similar plants first.

Jones constructed an organisational chart and set about examining the key issues raised by this project (see Fig. 1).

Jones had been appointed as commissioning manager at the commencement of the project. He remembered some of the nightmares experienced by colleagues during two earlier oleic acid projects and firmly resolved to make this one dif-ferent; it was going to be "his" to manage on completion, and he was going to make his presence felt from the outset.

The execution of the project had been overseen by the group's engineering arm, **Empire Consultants (EC)**, headed up by **Henry Holdsworth** as site project manager and **John Marshall** as construction engineer. It was a good team. The project was ambitious, but there were several signs of progress in the beginning. What did perplex him though was Marshall's apparent lack of enthusiasm.

Holdsworth described the project as a double management contract and in this respect it was an unusual project. Empire Consultants traditionally assumed the role of management contractor and directly organised the trade contractors and discipline consultants. Times were changing though and both Holdsworth and Marshall had commented on the increasing frequency with which projects were now being tendered as complete packages to outside management contractors. This was their first project that involved two management contractors simultaneously, and neither Marshall nor Holdsworth was happy. Their own involvement had not been clearly defined. **Western Construction** had a £3.1 million contract for the "wet end"

This case was prepared by Dr. Paul D. Gardiner, Department of Business Organisation, Heriot-Watt University, Edinburgh. It is intended to be used as the basis for class discussion rather than to illustrate either effective or ineffective handling of a management situation.

The case was made possible by the cooperation of an organisation which wishes to remain anonymous.

© 1994 P. D. Gardiner, Heriot-Watt University, Edinburgh.

FIGURE 1 ORGANISATIONAL AND CONTRACTUAL RELATIONSHIPS

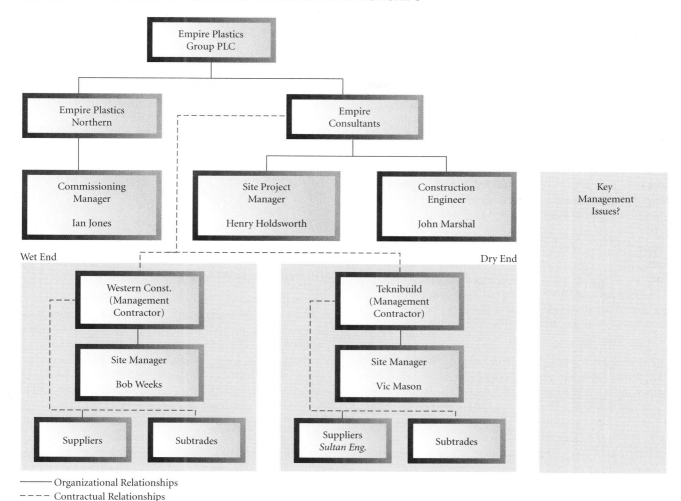

——— Organizational Relationships
- - - - Contractual Relationships

and **Teknibuild** a £6.0 million contract for the "dry end." These two contractors provided all the design and management effort during the project. EC's role was effectively reduced to acting as construction policemen; checking that design and construction were being carried out in accordance with the original process diagram and that EPN's demanding process control and safety requirements were being maintained.

Selecting the management contractors turned out to be extremely protracted and Holdsworth, encouraged by Jones, went ahead and ordered reactors for the wet end and a fluidised bed dryer for the dry end. Over 50% of the total material requirements were on order before either contractor had been formally appointed. Jones was confident that by doing this they could cut the project duration by several months. Nobody had asked Marshall for his opinion.

CONFLICT AHEAD

The first line breaks were in October 1988. Site operations were supervised by Marshall and the two contractor site managers: **Bob Weald** from Western and **Vic Mason** from Teknibuild.

As a construction engineer, Marshall was familiar with the antics of clients and client representatives, especially regarding their tendency to try and make changes. He commented:

Clients always try and change things! When they see the job in the flesh as it were they go "Oh, we need some extra paving round here, or extra railings there!" But if they didn't ask for that at the start, they won't get it. If they want an extra 100 metres of paving they have to pay for it. In this project we had about £500k set aside for contingency purposes, that is unforeseen eventualities over and above the price fixed with the management contractors. If that is not used up by the end of the contract, as in this case, then we can give the clients some extras.

Jones recalled that by June 1989 relationships were not going at all well at the dry end. Empire Consultants had procured a fluidised bed dryer, a cooler and over 300 associated parts, and as the purchasers of this equipment they were the ones responsible for chasing up design drawings from the supplier, **Sultan Engineering**.

Unfortunately, Teknibuild, who as management contractors were supposed to design and build the plant, had problems getting the necessary information from Sultan to design the steelwork and foundations. As Marshall had noted earlier:

They [Teknibuild] were constantly at our doors and throats looking for more information to get on. They didn't seem to have enough data to design properly, which led to conflict very early on. We got off to a bad start and that feeling carried on right to the end of the job. I think in every discipline we had problems with Teknibuild. Our discipline engineer against their discipline engineer.

The only exception to this was with the electrical and instrumentation work. Marshall had put that down to the E & I subcontractor coming in at the back end of this log jam of information; giving them more time to get it right.

While this was going on, Jones got more and more frustrated. In his opinion a lot of time was wasted between Teknibuild and Empire Consultants for no good reason. He was sure that Teknibuild had more than enough design information to do their job.

When confronted by Jones, Marshall remarked that the truth probably lay somewhere in-between, but added that he was "*particularly dismayed at Teknibuild's unwillingness to spend man-hours on the design until they had 100% definition from Sultan Engineering,*" almost to the point where they knew where every nut and bolt was. It was a real mess . . . and Marshall was accepting none of the blame.

On the other hand, things went fine with Western Construction. Their approach was much more relaxed; they had a design office on site with low overheads, whereas Teknibuild worked from head office in a large design office with high overheads.

On one occasion Marshall had asked for Teknibuild's planner to come down and take some site measurements. The reply he received was not very constructive: "*I don't know if I can do that, it's at least a couple of hours to get down*

there." Holdsworth agreed that Teknibuild were constantly watching their man-hours:

You felt all the time that they were looking for profit rather than trying to get the job done. Even Teknibuild's construction man, Vic Mason, had internal conflict with his own designers. But with Western it was the other way round, you really felt they were seeking to set a good impression.

Jones thought that perhaps communication with Western had been good because their design and construction people operated side by side, communication was just across the corridor; whereas Teknibuild's site men had difficulty getting answers out of Head Office. Marshall had always maintained that the best run jobs are the ones in which you get a good design-construction liaison, particularly by having the designers on-site with you.

FAILING . . . FORWARDS

Jones considered that in future it might be a good idea to insist that management contractors set up a local design team on site. Current practice was to leave it up to the contractor, but these days EC had few designers of their own to help.

The trouble with management contractors, he surmised, is that you create an extra link in the communications chain—a large link that can easily break down, and in his experience did break down.

Relationships had been better at the wet end, he felt, because Marshall and Weald had worked together before. Marshall knew Weald, knew how he worked, where he was coming from. They could trust each other.

At the Teknibuild end, Vic Mason, their site manager, caused no end of conflict. He was a bit belligerent; thought he knew best, had done it all before, and couldn't be told anything. It never really got out of hand . . . just a bit heated at times. At the end of the day, Marshall maintained that Mason's intentions were ultimately to get the job built. But Jones remained unimpressed, even if Mason's main trouble was his own designers and suppliers.

Driving home, Jones wondered what the effect of the company's new policy on managing projects would be on people like Harry Holdsworth and John Marshall. He couldn't help remembering what Marshall had said about Teknibuild and Western independently setting up their own enquiries and going out for bids separately; there did seem to be a lot of repetition—maybe Marshall was right in viewing the new system as "*a very inefficient way of doing projects.*"

Kao Corporation

Dr Yoshio Maruta introduced himself as a Buddhist scholar first, and as president of the Kao Corporation second. The order was significant, for it revealed the philosophy behind Kao and its success in Japan. Kao was a company that not only learned, but "learned how to learn." It was, in Dr Maruta's words, "an educational institution in which everyone is a potential teacher."

Under Dr Maruta's direction, the scholar's dedication to learning had metamorphosed into a competitive weapon which, in 1990, had led to Kao being ranked ninth by *Nikkei Business* in its list of top companies in Japan, and third in terms of corporate originality (Exhibit 1). As described by Fumio Kuroyanagi, Director of Kao's overseas planning department, the company's success was due not merely to its mastery of technologies nor its efficient marketing and information systems, but to its ability to integrate and enhance these capabilities through learning. As a result, Kao had come up with a stream of new products ahead of its Japanese and foreign competitors and, by 1990, had emerged as the largest branded and packaged goods company in Japan and the country's second largest cosmetics company.

Since the mid-1960s, Kao had also successfully used its formidable array of technological, manufacturing and marketing assets to expand into the neighbouring markets of Southeast Asia. Pitting itself against long-established multinationals like Procter & Gamble and Unilever, Kao had made inroads into the detergent, soap and shampoo markets in the region. However, success in these small markets would not make Kao a global player, and since the mid-1980s, Kao had been giving its attention to the problem of how to break into the international markets beyond the region. There, Kao's innovations were being copied and sold by its competitors, not by Kao itself, a situation the company was keen to remedy. But would Kao be able to repeat its domestic success in the United States and Europe? As Dr Maruta knew, the company's ability to compete on a world-wide basis would be measured by its progress in these markets. This, then, was the new challenge to which Kao was dedicated: how to transfer its learning capability, so all-conquering in Japan, to the rest of the world.

THE LEARNING ORGANIZATION

Kao was founded in 1890 as Kao Soap Company with the prescient motto, "Cleanliness is the foundation of a prosperous society." Its objective then was to produce a high quality soap that was as good as any imported brand, but at a more affordable price for the Japanese consumer, and this principle had guided the development of all Kao's products

This case was prepared by Charlotte Butler, Research Assistant, and Sumantra Ghoshal, Associate Professor at INSEAD. It is intended to be used as the basis for class discussion, rather than to illustrate either effective or ineffective handling of an administrative situation.

Copyright © 1991, by INSEAD, Fontainebleau, France.

EXHIBIT 1
THE RANKING OF
JAPANESE TOP
COMPANIES, 1990

1. Honda Motors	79.8
2. IBM-Japan	79.4
3. SONY	78.4
4. Matsushita Electrics	74.5
5. Toshiba	69.9
6. NEC	69.8
7. Nissan Motors	69.8
8. Asahi Beer	67.4
9. KAO	66.6
10. Yamato Transportation	66.4
11. Fuju-Xerox	66.3
12. Seibu Department Store	66.2
13. Suntory	65.8
14. Nomura Security	65.4
15. NTT (Nippon Telegraph & Telephone)	65.3
16. Omron	65.1
17. Ajinomoto	64.3
18. Canon	64.3
19. Toyota Motors	63.9
20. Ohtsuka Medicines	63.8

Notes: Points are calculated on the basis of the following criteria:
　　1. The assessment by Nikkei Business Committee's member corporate originality, corporate vision,
　　　 flexibility, goodness.
　　2. The result of the researches among consumers.
Source: Nikkei Business, 9 April 1990.

ever since. In the 1940s Kao had launched the first Japanese laundry detergent, followed in the 1950s by the launch of dishwashing and household detergents. The 1960s had seen an expansion into industrial products to which Kao could apply its technologies in fat and oil science, surface and polymer science. The 1970s and 1980s, coinciding with the presidency of Dr Maruta, had seen the company grow more rapidly than ever in terms of size, sales and profit, with the launching of innovative products and the start of new businesses. Between 1982 and 1985 it had successfully diversified into cosmetics, hygiene and floppy disks.

A vertically integrated company, Kao owned many of its raw material sources and had, since the 1960s, built its own sales organization of wholesalers who had exclusive distribution of its products throughout Japan. The 1980s had seen a consistent rise in profits, with sales increasing at roughly 10 per cent a year throughout the decade, even in its mature markets (Exhibit 2). In 1990, sales of Kao products had reached ¥620.4 billion ($3,926.8 million), an 8.4 per cent increase on 1989. This total consisted of laundry and cleaning products (40 per cent), personal care products (34 per cent), hygiene products (13 per cent), specialty chemicals and floppy disks (9 per cent) and fatty chemicals (4 per cent) (Exhibit 3). Net income had increased by 1.7 per cent, from ¥17.5 billion ($110 million) in 1989 to ¥17.8 billion ($112.7 million) in 1990.

Kao dominated most of its markets in Japan. It was the market leader in detergents and shampoo, and was vying for first place in disposable nappies and cosmetics. It had decisively beaten off both foreign and domestic competitors, most famously in two particular instances: the 1983 launch of its disposable nappy brand Merries which, within 12 months, had overtaken the leading brand, Procter & Gamble's Pampers and the 1987 launch of its innovative condensed laundry detergent, the aptly named Attack; as a result of which the market share of Kao's rival, Lion, had declined from 30.9 per cent (1986) to 22.8 per cent (1988), while in the same period Kao's share had gone from 33.4 per cent to 47.5 per cent.

The remarkable success of these two products had been largely responsible for Kao's reputation as a creative company. However, while the ability to introduce a continuous stream of innovative, high quality products clearly rested on Kao's repertoire of core competences, the wellspring behind these was less obvious: Kao's integrated learning capability.

This learning motif had been evident from the beginning. The Nagase family, founders of Kao, had modelled some of Kao's operations, management and production facilities on those of US corporations and in the 1940s, following his inspection of US and European soap and chemical plants, Tomiro Nagase II had reorganized Kao's pro-

EXHIBIT 2 THE TREND OF KAO'S PERFORMANCE

			BILLIONS OF YEN				MILLIONS OF US$
Years Ended 31 March	1985	1986	1987	1988	1989	1990	1990
Net Sales	398.1	433.7	464.1	514.4	572.2	620.4	3,926.8
(increase)		+8.9%	+7.0%	+10.9%	+11.2%	+8.4%	
Operating Income	16.5*	19.853*	31.7	36.5	41.4	43.5	275.5
(increase)				+15.2%	+13.5%	+5.1%	
Net Income	9.4	10.5	12.9	13.4	17.5	17.8	112.7
(increase)		+12.3%	+22.5%	+4.2%	+30.4%	+1.7%	
Total Assets	328.3	374.4	381.0	450.4	532.3	572.8	3,625.5
Total Shareholders' Equity	114.4	150.9	180.2	210.7	233.8	256.6	1,624.1

Note: The US dollar amounts are translated, for convenience only, at the rate of ¥156 = $1, the approximate exchange rate prevailing on 30 March 1990.
*Non-consolidated.

duction facilities, advertising and planning departments on the basis of what he had learned. As the company built up its capabilities, this process of imitation and adaptation had evolved into one of innovation until, under Dr Maruta, a research chemist who joined Kao in the 1930s and became president in 1971, "Distinct creativity became a policy objective in all our areas of research, production and sales, supporting our determination to explore and develop our own fields of activity."

THE PAPERWEIGHT ORGANIZATION

The organizational structure within which Kao managers and personnel worked embodied the philosophy of Dr Maruta's mentor, the seventh century statesman Prince Shotoku, whose constitution was designed to foster the spirit of harmony, based on the principal of absolute equality; "Human beings can live only by the Universal Truth, and in their dignity of living, all are absolutely equal." Article 1 of his constitution stated that "If everyone discusses on an equal footing, there is nothing that cannot be resolved."

Accordingly, Kao was committed to the principles of equality, individual initiative and the rejection of authoritarianism. Work was viewed as "something fluid and flexible like the functions of the human body," therefore the organization was designed to "run as a flowing system" which would stimulate interaction and the spread of ideas in every direction and at every level (Exhibit 4). To allow creativity and initiative full rein, and to demonstrate that hierarchy was merely an expedient that should not become a constraint, organizational boundaries and titles were abolished.

Dr Maruta likened this flat structure to an old-fashioned brass paperweight, in contrast to the pyramid structure of Western organizations: "In the pyramid, only the person at the top has all the information. Only he can see the full picture, others cannot. . . . The Kao organization is like the paperweight on my desk. It is flat. There is a small handle in the middle, just as we have a few senior people. But all information is shared horizontally, not filtered vertically. Only then can you have equality. And equality is the basis for trust and commitment."

This organization practised what Kao referred to as "biological self-control." As the body reacted to pain by sending help from all quarters, "If anything goes wrong in one department, the other departments should know automatically and help without having to be asked." Small group activities were encouraged in order to link ideas or discuss issues of immediate concern. In 1987, for example, to resolve the problem of why Kao's Toyohashi factory could achieve only 50 per cent of the projected production of Nivea cream, workers there voluntarily formed a small team consisting of the people in charge of production, quality, electricity, process and machinery. By the following year, production had been raised to 95 per cent of the target.

In pursuit of greater efficiency and creativity, Kao's organization has continued to evolve. A 1987 programme introduced a system of working from home for sales people, while another will eventually reduce everyone's working time to 1,800 hours a year from the traditional level of 2,100 hours. Other programmes have aimed at either introducing information technology or revitalizing certain areas. 1971 saw the "CCR movement," aimed at reducing

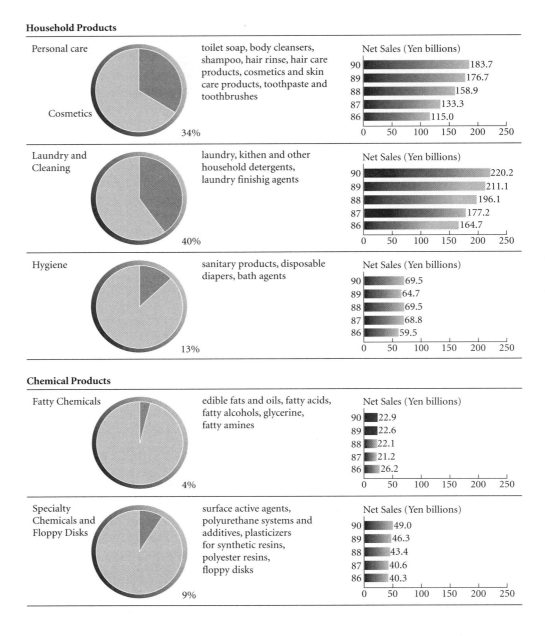

Household Products

Personal care

Cosmetics

34%

toilet soap, body cleansers, shampoo, hair rinse, hair care products, cosmetics and skin care products, toothpaste and toothbrushes

Net Sales (Yen billions)
90 183.7
89 176.7
88 158.9
87 133.3
86 115.0
0 50 100 150 200 250

Laundry and Cleaning

40%

laundry, kithen and other household detergents, laundry finishig agents

Net Sales (Yen billions)
90 220.2
89 211.1
88 196.1
87 177.2
86 164.7
0 50 100 150 200 250

Hygiene

13%

sanitary products, disposable diapers, bath agents

Net Sales (Yen billions)
90 69.5
89 64.7
88 69.5
87 68.8
86 59.5
0 50 100 150 200 250

Chemical Products

Fatty Chemicals

4%

edible fats and oils, fatty acids, fatty alcohols, glycerine, fatty amines

Net Sales (Yen billions)
90 22.9
89 22.6
88 22.1
87 21.2
86 26.2
0 50 100 150 200 250

Specialty Chemicals and Floppy Disks

9%

surface active agents, polyurethane systems and additives, plasticizers for synthetic resins, polyester resins, floppy disks

Net Sales (Yen billions)
90 49.0
89 46.3
88 43.4
87 40.6
86 40.3
0 50 100 150 200 250

the workforce through computerization. "Total Quality Control" came in 1974, followed in 1981 by Office Automation. The 1986 "Total Cost Reduction" programme to restructure management resources evolved into the "Total Creative Revolution," designed to encourage a more innovative approach. For example, five people who were made redundant following the installation of new equipment, formed, on their own initiative, a special task force team, and visited a US factory which had imported machinery from Japan. They stayed there for three months until local engineers felt confident enough to take charge.

Over time, this group became a flying squad of specialists, available to help foreign production plants get over their teething troubles.

MANAGING INFORMATION

Just as Dr Maruta's Buddha was the enlightened teacher, so Kao employees were the "priests" who learned and practiced the truth. Learning was "a frame of mind, a daily matter," and truth was sought through discussions, by testing and investigating concrete business ideas until something

EXHIBIT 4
ORGANIZATIONAL
STRUCTURE
Source: Company profile
brochure.

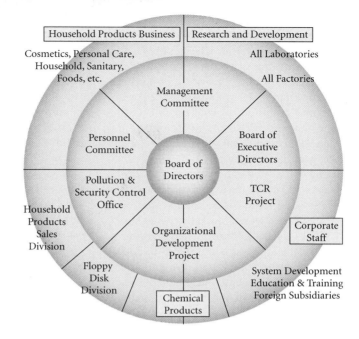

was learned, often without the manager realizing it. This was "the quintessence of information . . . something we actually see with our own eyes and feel with our bodies." This internalized intuition, which coincides with the Zen Buddhist phrase *kangyo ichijo*, was the goal Dr Maruta set for all Kao managers. In reaching it, every individual was expected to be coach; both to himself and to everyone else, whether above or below him in the organization.

Their training material was information. And information was regarded not as something lifeless to be stored, but as knowledge to be shared and exploited to the utmost. Every manager repeated Dr Maruta's fundamental assumption: "In today's business world, information is the only source of competitive advantage. The company that develops a monopoly on information, and has the ability to learn it continuously, is the company that will win, irrespective of its business." Every piece of information from the environment was treated as a potential key to a new positioning, a new product. What can we learn from it? How can we use it? These were the questions all managers were expected to ask themselves at all times.

Access to information was another facet of Kao's commitment to egalitarianism: as described by Kuroyanagi, "In Kao, the 'classified' stamp does not exist." Through the development of computer communication technologies, the same level of information was available to all: "In order to make it effective to discuss subjects freely, it is necessary to share all information. If someone has special and crucial information that the others don't have, that is against

human equality, and will deprive us and the organization of real creativity."

Every director and most salesmen had a fax in their home to receive results and news, and a bi-weekly Kao newspaper kept the entire company informed about competitors' moves, new product launches, overseas development or key meetings. Terminals installed throughout the company ensured that any employee could, if they wished, retrieve data on sales records of any product for any of Kao's numerous outlets, or product development at their own or other branches. The latest findings from each of Kao's research laboratories were available for all to see, as were the details of the previous day's production and inventory at every Kao plant. "They can even," said Dr Maruta, "check up on the president's expense account." He believed that the increase in creativity resulting from this pooling of data outweighed the risk of leaks. In any case, the prevailing environment of *omnes flux* meant that things moved so quickly "leaked information instantly becomes obsolete."

The task of Kao managers, therefore, was to take information directly from the competitive environment, process it and, by adding value, transform it into knowledge or wisdom. Digesting information from the marketplace in this way enabled the organization to maintain empathy with this fast moving environment. The emphasis was always on learning and on the future, not on following an advance plan based on previous experience. "Past wisdom must not be a constraint, but something to be challenged," Dr Maruta constantly urged. Kao managers were discouraged from making any historical comparisons. "We cannot talk about history," said Mr Takayama, Overseas Planning Director. "If we talk about the past, they [the top management] immediately become unpleasant." The emphasis was rather, what had they learnt today that would be useful tomorrow? "Yesterday's success formula is often today's obsolete dogma. We must continuously challenge the past so that we can renew ourselves each day," said Dr Maruta.

"Learning through cooperation" was the slogan of Kao's R & D; the emphasis was on information exchange, both within and outside the department, and sharing "to motivate and activate." Glycerine Ether, for example, an emulsifier important for the production of Sofina's screening cream, was the product of joint work among three Kao laboratories. Research results were communicated to everyone in the company through the IT system, in order to build a close networking organization. Top management and researchers met at regular R & D conferences, where presentations were made by the researchers themselves, not their section managers. "Open Space" meetings were offered every week by the R & D division, and people from any part of the organization could participate in discussions on current research projects.

A number of formal and informal systems were created to promote communication among the research scientists working in different laboratories. For example, results from Paris were fed daily into the computer in Tokyo. The most important of these communication mechanisms, however, were the monthly R & D working conferences for junior researchers which took place at each laboratory in turn. When it was their own laboratory's turn to act as host, researchers could nominate anyone they wished to meet, from any laboratory in the company, to attend that meeting. In addition, any researcher could nominate him or herself to attend meetings if they felt that the discussions could help their own work, or if they wanted to talk separately with someone from the host laboratory. At the meetings, which Dr Maruta often attended to argue and discuss issues in detail, researchers reported on studies in progress, and those present offered advice from commercial and academic perspectives.

THE DECISION PROCESS

"In Kao, we try collectively to direct the accumulation of individual wisdom at serving the customer." This was how Dr Maruta explained the company's approach to the decision process. At Kao, no one owned an idea. Ideas were to be shared in order to enhance their value and achieve enlightenment in order to make the right decision. The prevailing principle was *tataki-dai*; present your ides to others at 80 per cent completion so that they could criticize or contribute before the idea became a proposal. Takayama

likened this approach to heating an iron and testing it on one's arm to see if it was hot enough. "By inviting all the relevant actors to join in with forging the task," he said, "we achieve *zo-awase*; a common perspective or view." The individual was thus a strategic factor, to be linked with others in a union of individual wisdom and group strategy.

Fumio Kuroyanagi provided an illustration. Here is the process by which a problem involving a joint venture partner, in which he was the key person, was resolved:

> I put up a preliminary note summarizing the key issues, but not making any proposals. I wanted to share the data and obtain other views before developing a proposal fully. . . . This note was distributed to legal, international controllers to read . . . then in the meeting we talked about the facts and came up with some ideas on how to proceed. Then members of this meeting requested some top management time. All the key people attended this meeting, together with one member of the top management. No written document was circulated in advance. Instead, we described the situation, our analysis and action plans. He gave us his comments. We came to a revised plan. I then wrote up this revised plan and circulated it to all the people, and we had a second meeting at which everyone agreed with the plan. Then the two of us attended the actual meeting with the partner. After the meeting I debriefed other members, discussed and circulated a draft of the letter to the partner which, after everyone else had seen it and given their comments, was signed by my boss.

The cross-fertilization of ideas to aid the decision process was encouraged by the physical layout of the Kao building. On the 10th floor, known as the top management floor, sat the chairman, the president, four executive vice-presidents and a pool of secretaries (Exhibit 5). A large part of the floor was open space, with one large conference table and two smaller ones, and chairs, blackboards and overhead projectors strewn around: this was known as the decision space, where all discussions with and among the top management took place. Anyone passing, including the president, could sit down and join in any discussion on any topic, however briefly. This layout was duplicated on the other floors, in the laboratories and in the workshop. Workplaces looked like large rooms; there were no partitions, but again tables and chairs for spontaneous or planned discussions at which everyone contributed as equals. Access was free to all, and any manager could thus find himself sitting round the table next to the president, who was often seen waiting in line in Kao's Tokyo cafeteria.

The management process, thus, was transparent and open, and leadership was practised in daily behaviour rather than by memos and formal meetings. According to Takayama, top management "emphasizes that 80 per cent of its time must be spent on communication, and the remaining 20 per cent on decision-making." While top management regularly visited other floors to join in dis-

EXHIBIT 5
LAYOUT OF KAO
OFFICES

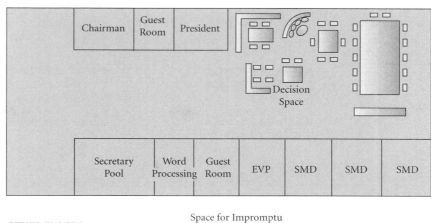

OTHER FLOORS

Space for Impromptu
Meetings and Discussions

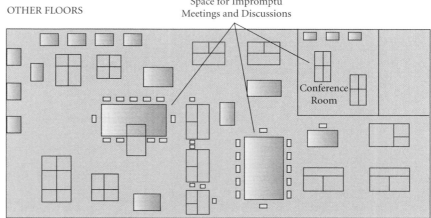

cussions, anyone attending a meeting on the 10th floor then had to pass on what had happened to the rest of his colleagues.

INFORMATION TECHNOLOGY

Information technology (IT) was one of Kao's most effective competitive weapons, and an integral part of its organizational systems and management processes. In 1982, Kao made an agreement to use Japan Information Service Co.'s VAN (Value-Added Networks) for communication between Kao's head office, its sales companies and its large wholesalers. Over time, Kao built its own VAN, through which it connected upstream and downstream via information linkages. In 1986 the company added DRESS, a new network linking Kao and the retail stores receiving its support.

The objective of this networking capability was to achieve the complete fusion and interaction of Kao's marketing, production and R & D departments. Fully integrated information systems controlled the flow of materials and products; from the production planning of raw materials to the distribution of the final products to local

stores: no small task in a company dealing with over 1,500 types of raw materials from 500 different suppliers, and producing over 550 types of final products for up to 300,000 retail stores.

Kao's networks enabled it to maintain a symbiotic relationship with its distributors, the *hansha*. Developed since 1966, the Kao *hansha* (numbering 30 by 1990) were independent wholesalers who handled only Kao products. They dealt directly with 100,000 retail stores out of 300,000, and about 60 per cent of Kao's products passed through them. The data terminals installed in the *hansha* offices provided Kao with up-to-date product movement and market information, which was easily accessible for analysis.

Kao's Logistics Information System (LIS) consisted of a sales planning system, an inventory control system and an on-line supply system. It linked Kao headquarters, factories, the *hansha* and logistics centres by networks, and dealt with ordering, inventory, production and sales data (Exhibit 6). Using the LIS, each *hansha* sales person projected sales plans on the basis of a head office campaign plan, an advertising plan and past market trends. These were corrected and adjusted at corporate level, and a final

CASE 35 KAO CORPORATION

EXHIBIT 6
KAO'S INFORMATION
NETWORK
Source: Nikkei Computer,
9 October, 1989 (Nippon Keizai
shinbunsha).

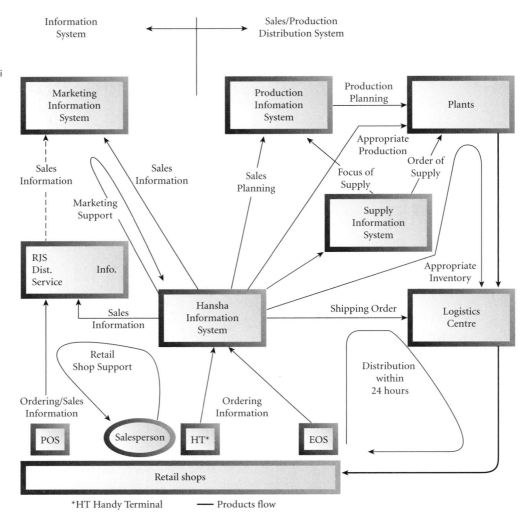

Information System ← → Sales/Production Distribution System

*HT Handy Terminal ——— Products flow

sales plan was produced each month. From this plan, daily production schedules were then drawn up for each factory and product. The system would also calculate the optimal machine load, and the number of people required. An on-line supply system calculated the appropriate amount of factory stocks and checked the *hansha* inventory. The next day's supply was then computed and automatically ordered from the factory.

A computerized ordering system enabled stores to receive and deliver products within 24 hours of placing an order. Through a POS (point of sale) terminal, installed in the retail store as a cash register and connected to the Kao VAN, information on sales and orders was transmitted to the *hansha*'s computer. Via this, orders from local stores, adjusted according to the amount of their inventory, were transmitted to Kao's logistics centre, which then supplied the product.

Two other major support systems, KAP and RSS, respectively helped the wholesale houses in ordering,

stocking and accounting, and worked with Kao's nine distribution information service companies: the Ryutsu Joho Service Companies (RJSs). Each RJS had about 500 customers, mainly small and medium-sized supermarkets who were too small to access real-time information by themselves. The RJSs were essentially consulting outfits, whose mandate was to bring the benefits of information available in Kao VAN to those stores that could not access the information directly. They guided store owners by offering analysis of customer buying trends, shelf space planning and ways of improving the store's sales, profitability and customer service. The owner of one such store commented: "A Kao sales person comes to see us two or three times a week, and we chat about many topics. To me, he is both a good friend and a good consultant . . . I can see Kao's philosophy, the market trend and the progress of R & D holistically through this person." According to Dr Maruta, the RJSs embodied Kao's principle of the information advantage: their purpose was to provide this advantage to store owners, and the success of the RJSs in building up the volume and profitability of the stores was ample evidence of the correctness of the principle.

Kao's Marketing Intelligence System (MIS) tracked sales by product, region and market segment, and provided raw market research data. All this information was first sifted for clues to customer needs, then linked with R & D "seeds" to create new products. New approaches to marketing were sought by applying artificial intelligence to various topics, including advertising and media planning, sales promotion, new product development, market research and statistical analysis.

Additional information was provided by the Consumer Life Research Laboratory which operated ECHO, a sophisticated system for responding to telephone queries about Kao products. In order to understand and respond immediately to a customer's question, each phone operator could instantly access a video display of each of Kao's 500 plus products. Enquiries were also coded and entered into the computer system on-line, and the resulting database provided one of the richest sources for product development or enhancement ideas. By providing Kao with "a direct window on the consumer's mind," ECHO enabled the company "to predict the performance of new products and fine tune formulations, labelling and packaging." Kao also used a panel of monitor households to track how products fitted into consumers' lives.

In 1989, Kao separated its information systems organization and established a distinct entity called Kao Software Development. The aim was to penetrate the information service industry which, according to Japan Information, was projected to reach a business volume of ¥12,000 billion ($80 billion) by the year 2000. In 1989, the market was ¥3,000 billion ($20 billion). One IBM sales engineer forecast, 'by 2000, Kao will have become one of our major competitors, because they know how to develop information technology, and how to combine it with real organization systems.'

In 1989 Kao's competitors, including Lion and Procter & Gamble, united to set up Planet Logistics, a system comparable to Kao's VAN. Through it, they aimed to achieve the same information richness as Kao. But Dr Maruta was not worried by this development. Irrespective of whatever information they collected, he believed that the competitors would not be able to add the value and use it in the same way as Kao did:

> As a company we do not spend our time chasing after what our rivals do. Rather, by mustering our knowledge, wisdom and ingenuity to study how to supply the consumer with superior products, we free ourselves of the need to care about the moves of our competitors. Imitation is the sincerest form of flattery, but unless they can add value to all that information, it will be of little use.

SOFINA

The development of Sofina was a microcosm of Kao's *modus operandi*. It illustrated the learning organization in action since it sought to create a product that satisfied the five principles guiding the development of any new offering: "Each product must be useful to society. It must use innovative technology. It must offer consumers value. We must be confident we really understand the market and the consumers. And, finally, each new product must be compatible with the trade." Until a new product satisfied all these criteria, it would not be launched on the market. At every stage during Sofina's creation, ideas were developed, criticized, discussed and refined or altered in the light of new information and learning by everyone involved, from Dr Maruta down.

The Sofina story began in 1965 with a "vision." The high quality, innovative product that finally emerged in 1982 allowed Kao to enter a new market and overtake well-established competitors. By 1990, Sofina had become the highest selling brand of cosmetics in Japan for most items except lipsticks.

THE VISION

The vision, according to Mr Daimaru (the first director of Sofina marketing), was simple: to help customers avoid the appearances of wrinkles on their skin for as long as possible. From this vision an equally simple question arose: "What makes wrinkles appear?" Finding the answer was the spring that set the Kao organization into motion.

Kao's competence until then had been in household and toiletry personal care products. However, Kao had long supplied raw materials for the leading cosmetics manufacturers in Japan, and had a technological competence in fats and soap that could, by cross-pollination, be adapted to research on the human skin. Accordingly, the efforts of Kao's R & D laboratories were directed towards skin research, and the results used in the company's existing businesses such as Nivea or Azea, then sold in joint venture with Beiersdorf. From these successes came the idea for growth that steered the development of Sofina.

THE GROWTH IDEA

The idea was to produce a new, high quality cosmetic that gave real value at a reasonable price. During the 1960s, there was a strong perception in the Japanese cosmetics industry that the more expensive the product, the better it was. This view was challenged by Dr Maruta, whose travels had taught him that good skin care products sold in the United States or Europe were not as outrageously expensive. Yet in Japan, even with companies like Kao supplying high quality raw materials at a low price, the end-product was still beyond the reach of ordinary women at ¥10–20,000.

As a supplier of raw materials, Dr Maruta was aware of how well these products performed. He also knew that though cosmetics' prices were rising sharply, little was being spent on improving the products themselves, and that customers were paying for an expensive image. Was this fair, or good for the customer? Kao, he knew, had the capacity to supply high quality raw materials at low cost, and a basic research capability. Intensive research to develop new toiletry goods had led to the discovery of a technology for modifying the surface of powders, which could be applied to the development of cosmetics. Why not use these assets to develop a new, high quality, reasonably priced product, in keeping with Kao's principles?

To enter the new market would mean a heavy investment in research and marketing, with no guarantee that their product would be accepted. However, it was decided to go ahead; the product would be innovative and, against the emotional appeal of the existing competition in terms of packaging and image, its positioning would embody Kao's scientific approach.

This concept guided the learning process as Sofina was developed. It was found that integration of Kao's unique liquid crystal emulsification technology and other newly developed materials proved effective in maintaining a "healthy and beautiful skin." This led Kao to emphasize skin care, as opposed to the industry's previous focus on make-up only. All the research results from Kao's skin diagnosis and dermatological testing were poured into the new product and, as Dr Tsutsumi of the Tokyo Research Laboratory recalled, in pursuing problems connected with the product, new solutions emerged. For example, skin irritation caused by the new chemical was solved by developing MAP, a low irritant, and PSL, a moisturiser. By 1980, most of the basic research work had been done. Six cosmetics suitable for the six basic skin types had been developed, though all under the Sofina name.

During this stage, Kao's intelligence collectors were sent out to explore and map the new market environment. Information on products, pricing, positioning, the competition and above all, the customers, was analyzed and digested by the Sofina marketing and R & D teams, and by Kao's top management. Again and again Dr Maruta asked the same two questions: How would the new product be received? Was it what customers wanted?

THE GROWTH PROCESS

Test marketing began in September 1980, in the Shizuoka prefecture, and was scheduled to last for a year. Shizuoka was chosen because it represented 3 per cent of the national market and an average social mix; neither too rich nor too poor, too rural nor too urban. Its media isolation meant that television advertisements could be targeted to the local population, and no one outside would question why the product was not available elsewhere. The local paper also gave good coverage. In keeping with Kao's rule that "the concept of a new product is that of its advertising," the Sofina advertisements were reasoned and scientific, selling a function rather than an image.

Sofina was distributed directly to the retail stores through the Sofina Cosmetics Company, established to distinguish Sofina from Kao's conventional detergent business and avoid image blurring. No mention was made of Kao. Sofina's managers found, however, that retailers did not accept Sofina immediately, but put it on the waiting list for display along with other new cosmetics. The result was that by October 1980, Kao had only succeeded in finding 200 points of sale, against an objective of 600. Then, as the real parentage of Sofina leaked out, the attitude among retailers changed, and the Sofina stand was given the best position in the store. This evidence of Kao's credibility, together with the company's growing confidence in the quality and price of the product, led to a change of strategy. The 30-strong sales force was instructed to put the Kao name first and, by November, 600 outlets had been found.

Sofina's subsequent development was guided by feedback from the market. Direct distribution enabled Kao to retain control of the business and catch customer responses to the product at first hand. To Mr Masashi Kuga, Director of Kao's Marketing Research Department, such information "has clear added value, and helps in critical decision-making." During the repeated test marketing of Sofina, Kao's own market research service, formed in 1973 to ensure a high quality response from the market with the least possible distortion, measured the efficacy of sampling and helped decide on the final marketing mix. This activity was usually supported by "concept testing, focus group discussions, plus product acceptance research." Mr Daimaru visited the test market twice or three times each month and talked to consumers directly. Dr Maruta did the same.

Every piece of information and all results were shared by the Sofina team, R & D, Kao's top management, corporate marketing and sales managers. Discussions on Sofina's progress were attended by all of these managers, everyone contributing ideas about headline copy or other issues on an equal basis. Wives and friends were given samples and their reactions were fed back to the team.

From the reactions of customers and stores, Kao learnt that carrying real information in the advertisements about the quality of the product had been well received, despite differing from the normal emphasis on fancy packaging. This they could never have known from their detergent business. Another finding was the importance of giving a full explanation of the product with samples, and of a skin analysis before recommending the most suitable product rather than trying to push the brand indiscriminately. They also learned the value of listening to the opinion of the store manager's wife who, they discovered, often had the real managing power, particularly for cosmetics products.

Decisions were implemented immediately. For example, the decision to improve the design for the sample package was taken at 3.30 p.m., and by 6.30 p.m. the same day the engineer in the factory had begun redesigning the shape of the bottle.

The results of this test marketing, available to the whole company, confirmed the decision to go ahead with Sofina. Kao was satisfied that the product would be accepted nationally, though it might take some time. A national launch was planned for the next year. Even at this stage, however, Dr Maruta was still asking whether consumers and retail store owners really liked Sofina.

THE LEARNING EXTENDED

Sofina finally went on nationwide sale in October 1982. However, the flow of learning and intelligence gathering continued via the *hansha* and MIS. Kao, the *hansha*, the retailers and Sofina's customers formed a chain, along which there was a free, two-way flow of information. The learning was then extended to develop other products, resulting in production of the complete Sofina range of beauty care. In 1990, the range covered the whole market, from basic skin care to make-up cosmetics and perfumes.

In fact, the product did not achieve real success until after 1983. Dr Tsutsumi dated it from the introduction of the foundation cream which, he recalled, also faced teething problems. The test result from the panel was not good; it was too different from existing products and was sticky on application. Kao, however, knowing it was a superior product that lasted longer, persevered and used their previous experience to convert the stickiness into a strength: the product was repositioned as "the longest lasting foundation that does not disappear with sweat."

In the early 1980s, while market growth was only 2–3 per cent, sales of Sofina products increased at the rate of 30 per cent every year. In 1990, sales amounted to ¥55 billion, and Kao held 15.6 per cent of the cosmetics market behind Shiseido and Kanebo, though taken individually, Sofina brands topped every product category except lipsticks.

Within Japan, Sofina was sold through 12,700 outlets. According to Mr Nakanishi, director of the Cosmetics Division, the marketing emphasis was by that time being redirected from heavy advertising of the product to counselling at the point of sale. Kao was building up a force of

beauty counsellors to educate the public of the benefits of Sofina products. A Sofina store in Tokyo was also helping to develop hair care and cosmetics products. A Sofina newspaper had been created which salesmen received by fax, along with the previous month's sales and inventory figures.

Knowledge gathered by the beauty advisers working in the Sofina shops was exploited for the development of the next set of products. Thus, Sofina "ultra-violet" care, which incorporated skin lotion, UV care and foundation in one, was positioned to appeal to busy women and advertised as "one step less." The Sofina cosmetics beauty care consultation system offered advice by phone, at retail shops or by other means to consumers who made enquiries. From their questions, clues were sought to guide new product development.

A staff of Field Companions visited the retail stores to get direct feedback on sales. Every outlet was visited once a month, when the monitors discussed Kao products with store staff, advised on design displays and even helped clean up. Dr Maruta himself maintained an active interest. Mr Kuroyanagi described how Dr Maruta recently "came down to our floor" to report that while visiting a certain town, he had "found a store selling Sofina products, and a certain shade sample was missing from the stand." He asked that the store be checked and the missing samples supplied as soon as possible.

Depite Sofina's success, Kao was still not satisfied. "To be really successful, developing the right image is important. We've lagged behind on this, and we must improve."

As the Sofina example showed, in its domestic base Kao was an effective and confident company, renowned for its ability to produce high quality, technologically advanced products at relatively low cost. Not surprising, then, that since the 1960s it had turned its thoughts to becoming an important player on the larger world stage. But could the learning organization operate effectively outside Japan? Could Kao transfer its learning capability into a very different environment such as the United States or Europe, where it would lack the twin foundations of infrastructure and human resource? Or would internationalization demand major adjustments to its way of operating?

KAO INTERNATIONAL

When the first cake of soap was produced in 1890, the name "Kao" was stamped in both Chinese characters and Roman letters in preparation for the international market. A century later, the company was active in 50 countries but, except for the small neighbouring markets of Southeast Asia, had not achieved a real breakthrough. Despite all its investments, commitment and efforts over

25 years, Kao remained only "potentially" a significant global competitor. In 1988, only 10 per cent of its total sales was derived from overseas business, and 70 per cent of this international volume was earned in Southeast Asia. As a result, internationalization was viewed by the company as its next key strategic challenge. Dr Maruta made his ambitions clear; "Procter and Gamble, Unilever and L'Oréal are our competitors. We cannot avoid fighting in the 1990s." The challenge was to make those words a reality.

THE STRATEGIC INFRASTRUCTURE

Kao's globalization was based not on a company-wide strategy, but on the product division system. Each product division developed its own strategy for international expansion and remained responsible for its worldwide results. Consequently, the company's business portfolio and strategic infrastructure varied widely from market to market.

SOUTHEAST ASIA

As Exhibit 7 illustrates, Kao had been building a platform for production and marketing throughout Southeast Asia since 1964, when it created its first overseas subsidiary in Thailand. By 1990, this small initial base had been expanded, mainly through joint ventures, and the company had made steady progress in these markets. The joint ventures in Hong Kong and Singapore sold only Kao's consumer products, while the others both manufactured and marketed them.

One of Kao's biggest international battles was for control of the Asian detergent, soap and shampoo markets, against rivals like P&G and Unilever. In the Taiwanese detergent market, where Unilever was the long-established leader with 50 per cent market share, Kao's vanguard product was the biological detergent, Attack. Launched in 1988, Attack increased Kao's market share from 17 per cent to 22 per cent. Subsequently, Kao decided on local production, both to continue serving the local market and for export to Hong Kong and Singapore. Its domestic rival, Lion (stationary at 17 per cent) shortly followed suit. In Hong Kong, Kao was the market leader with 30 per cent share and in Singapore, where Colgate-Palmolive led with 30 per cent, had increased its share from 5 per cent to 10 per cent. Unilever, P&G and Colgate-Palmolive had responded to Kao's moves by putting in more human resources, and consolidating their local bases.

In Indonesia, where Unilever's historic links again made it strong, Kao, Colgate-Palmolive and P&G competed for the second position. In the Philippines, Kao had started local production of shampoo and liquid soap in 1989, while in Thailand it had doubled its local facilities in order to meet increasing demand. To demonstrate its commitment to the Asian market where it was becoming a major player, Kao had established its Asian headquarters in Singapore. In that market, Kao's disposable nappy Merrys had a 20 per cent share, while its Merit shampoo was the market leader.

NORTH AMERICA

Step 1—Joint Venture

In 1976, Kao had embarked on two joint ventures with Colgate-Palmolive Company, first to market hair care products in the United States, and later to develop new oral hygiene products for Japan. The potential for synergy seemed enormous; Colgate-Palmolive was to provide the marketing expertise and distribution infrastructure, Kao would contribute the technical expertise to produce a high quality product for the top end of the US market.

1977 saw a considerable exchange of personnel and technology, and a new shampoo was specially developed by Kao for the US consumer. Despite the fact that tests in three major US cities, using Colgate-Palmolive's state of the art market research methods, showed poor market share potential, the product launch went ahead. The forecasts turned out to be correct, and the product was dropped after 10 months due to Colgate-Palmolive's reluctance to continue. A Kao manager explained the failure thus:

> First, the product was not targeted to the proper consumer group. High price, high end-products were not appropriate for a novice and as yet unsophisticated producer like us. Second, the US side believed in the result of the market research too seriously and did not attempt a second try. . . . Third, it is essentially very difficult to penetrate a market like the shampoo market. Our partner expected too much short term success. Fourth, the way the two firms decided on strategy was totally different. We constantly adjust our strategy flexibly. They never start without a concrete and fixed strategy. We could not wait for them.

The alliance was dissolved in 1985. However, Kao had learnt some valuable lessons: about US marketing methods; about Western lifestyles; and, most of all, about the limitations of using joint ventures as a means of breaking into the US market.

Step 2—Acquisition

In 1988, Kao had made three acquisitions. In May, it bought the Andrew Jergens Company, a Cincinnati soap, body lotion and shampoo maker, for $350 million. To acquire Jergens's extensive marketing know-how and established distribution channels, Kao beat off 70 other bidders, including Beiersdorf and Colgate-Palmolive, and paid 40 per cent more than the expected price. Since then, Kao has invested heavily in the company, building a new multi-

EXHIBIT 7 THE HISTORY OF KAO'S INTERNATIONALIZATION

AREA	COMPANY	YEAR	CAPITAL	MAIN PRODUCTS
Asia				
Taiwan	Taiwan Kao Co. Ltd	1964	90	Detergent, soap
Thailand	Kao Industrial Co. Ltd	1964	70	Hair care products
Singapore	Kao Private Ltd	1965	100	Sales of soap, shampoo, detergents
Hong Kong	Kao Ltd	1970	100	Sales of soap, shampoo, detergents
Malaysia	Kao Pte. Ltd	1973	45	Hair care products
Philippines	Philippinas Kao Inc.	1977	70	Fats and oils
Indonesia	P. T. PoleKao	1977	74	Surfactants
Philippines	Kao Inc.	1979	70	Hair care products
Indonesia	P. T. Dino Indonesia Industrial Ltd	1985	50	Hair care products
Malaysia	Fatty Chemical Sdn. Bdn.	1988	70	Alcohol
Singapore	Kao South-East Asia Headquarters	1988		
Philippines	Kao Co. Philippines Laboratory			
North America				
Mexico	Qumi-Kao S. A. de C. V.	1975	20	Fatty amines
	Bitumex	1979	49	Asphal
Canada	Kao-Didak Ltd	1983	89	Floppy disk
USA	Kao Corporation of America (KCOA)	1986	100	Sales of household goods
	High Point Chemical	1987	100 (KCOA)	Ingredients
	Kao Infosystems Company	1988	100 (KCOA)	Duplication of software
	The Andrew Jergens	1988	100 (KCOA)	Hair care products
USA	KCOA Los Angeles Laboratories			
Europe				
W. Germany	Kao Corporation GmbH	1986	100 (KCG)	Sales of household goods
	Kao Perfekta GmbH	1986	80 (KCG)	Toners for copier
	Guhl Ikebana GmnH	1986	50 (KCG)	Hair care products
Spain	Kao Corporation S. A.	1987	100	Surfactants
W. Germany	Goldwell AG	1989	100	Cosmetics
France	Kao Co. S. A. Paris Laboratories			
Spain	Kao Co. S. A. Barcelona Laboratories			
W. Germany	Kao Co. GmbH Berlin Laboratories			

million dollar research centre and doubling Jergens's research team to over 50. Cincinnati was the home town of P&G, who have since seen Jergens market Kao's bath preparations in the US.

High Point Chemical Corporation of America, an industrial goods producer, was also acquired in 1988. As Kao's US chemical manufacturing arm, it had since begun "an aggressive expansion of its manufacturing facilities and increased its market position." The third acquisition, Info Systems (Sentinel), produced application products in the field of information technology.

In Canada, Kao owned 87 per cent of Kao-Didak, a floppy disk manufacturer it bought out in 1986. A new plant, built in 1987, started producing 3.5 inch and 5.25

inch diskettes, resulting in record sales of $10 million that same year. Kao viewed floppy disks as the spearhead of its thrust into the US market. As Mr Kuroyanagi explained: "This product penetrates the US market easily. Our superior technology makes it possible to meet strict requirements for both quantity and quality. Our experience in producing specific chemicals for the floppy disk gives us a great competitive edge." In what represented a dramatic move for a Japanese company, Kao relocated its worldwide head office for the floppy disk business to the United States, partly because of Kao's comparatively strong position there (second behind Sony) but also because it was by far the biggest market in the world. The US headquarters was given complete strategic freedom to develop the business globally. Under the direction of this office a plant was built in Spain.

EUROPE

Within Europe, Kao had built a limited presence in Germany, Spain and France. In Germany, it had established a research laboratory, and through its 1979 joint venture with Beiersdorf to develop and market hair care products, gained a good knowledge of the German market. The strategic position of this business was strengthened in 1989 by the acquisition of a controlling interest in Goldwell AG, one of Germany's leading suppliers of hair and skin care products to beauty salons. From studying Goldwell's network of beauty salons across Europe, Kao expected to expand its knowledge in order to be able to develop and market new products in Europe.

Kao's French subsidiary, created in January 1990, marketed floppy disks, skin toner and the Sofina range of cosmetics. The research laboratory established in Paris that same year was given the leading role in developing perfumes to meet Kao's worldwide requirements.

Kao's vanguard product in Europe was Sofina, which was positioned as a high quality, medium-priced product. Any Japanese connection had been removed to avoid giving the brand a cheap image. While Sofina was produced and packaged in Japan, extreme care was taken to ensure that it shared a uniform global positioning and image in all the national markets in Europe. It was only advertised in magazines like *Vogue*, and sales points were carefully selected; for example in France, Sofina was sold only in the prestigious Paris department store, Galeries Lafayette.

ORGANIZATIONAL CAPABILITY

Organizationally, Kao's international operations were driven primarily along the product division axis. Each subsidiary had a staff in charge of each product who reported to the product's head office, either directly or through a regional product manager. For example, the manager in charge of Sofina in Spain reported to the French office where the regional manager responsible for Sofina was located, and he in turn reported to the director of the Divisional HQ in Japan. Each subsidiary was managed by Japanese expatriate managers, since Kao's only foreign resource was provided by its acquired companies. Thus, the German companies remained under the management of its original directors. However, some progress was made towards localization; in Kao Spain (250 employees) there were "only six to ten Japanese, not necessarily in management." Kao's nine overseas R & D laboratories were each strongly connected to both the product headquarters and laboratories in Japan through frequent meetings and information exchange.

Mr Takayama saw several areas that needed to be strengthened before Kao could become an effective global competitor. Kao, he believed "was a medium-sized company grown large." It lacked international experience, had fewer human resource assets, especially in top management and, compared with competitors like P&G and Unilever, had far less accumulated international knowledge and experience of Western markets and consumers. "These two companies know how to run a business in the West and have well established market research techniques, whereas the westernization of the Japanese lifestyle has only occurred in the last 20 years," he explained. "There are wide differences between East and West in, for example, bathing habits, that the company has been slow to comprehend."

Kao attempted to redress these problems through stronger involvement by headquarters' managers in supporting the company's foreign operations. Mr Kuroyanagi provided an insight into Kao's approach to managing its overseas units. He described how, after visiting a foreign subsidiary where he felt change was necessary, he asked a senior colleague in Japan to carry out a specific review. The two summarized their findings, and then met with other top management members for further consultation. As a result, his colleague was temporarily located in the foreign company to lead certain projects. A team was formed in Japan to harmonize with locals, and sent to work in the subsidiary. Similarly, when investigating the reason for the company's slow penetration of the shampoo market in Thailand, despite offering a technologically superior product, HQ managers found that the product positioning, pricing and packaging policies developed for the Japanese market were unsuitable for Thailand. Since the subsidiary could not adapt these policies to meet local requirements, a headquarters marketing specialist was brought in, together with a representative from Dentsu—Kao's advertising agent in Japan—to identify the source of the problem and make the necessary changes in the marketing mix.

Part of Mr Kuroyanagi's role was to act as a "liaison officer" between Kao and its subsidiaries. Kao appointed such managers at headquarters to liaise with all the newly acquired companies in Europe and Asia; their task was to interpret corporate strategies to other companies outside Japan and ensure that "We never make the same mistake twice." He described himself as "the eyes and ears of top management, looking round overseas moves, competitors' activities and behaviours and summarizing them." He was also there to "help the local management abroad understand correctly Kao as a corporation, and give hints about how to overcome the cultural gap and linguistic difficulties, how to become open, aggressive an innovative."

Kao's 1990 global strategy was to develop "local operations sensitive to each region's characteristics and needs." As Mr Takayama explained, these would be able "to provide each country with goods tailored to its local climate and customs, products which perfectly meet the needs of its consumers." To this end, the goals of the company's research centres in Los Angeles, Berlin, Paris and Santiago de Compostela in Spain, had been redefined as: "to analyze local market needs and characteristics and integrate them into the product development process," and a small market research unit had been created in Thailand to support local marketing of Sofina. Over time, Kao hoped, HQ functions would be dispersed to Southeast Asia, the Untied States and Europe, leaving to the Tokyo headquarters the role of supporting regionally based, locally managed operations by giving "strategic assistance." There were no plans to turn Jergens or other acquired companies into duplicate Kaos; as described by Dr Maruta "We will work alongside them rather than tell them which way to go."

The lack of overseas experience among Kao's managers was tackled via a new ¥9 billion training facility built at Kasumigaura. The 16-hectare campus, offering golf, tennis and other entertainment opportunities, was expected to enjoy a constant population of 200, with 10 days' training becoming the norm for all managers. To help Kao managers develop a broader and more international outlook, training sessions devoted considerable attention to the cultural and historical heritages of different countries. A number of younger managers were sent to Europe and the United States, spending the first year learning languages and the second either at a business school, or at Kao's local company offices.

"If you look at our recent international activity," said Mr Kuroyanagi, "we have prepared our stage. We have made our acquisitions . . . the basis for globalization in Europe, N. America and SE Asia has been facilitated. . . . We now need some play on that stage." Kao's top management was confident that the company's R & D power, "vitality and open, innovative and aggressive culture" would ultimately prevail. The key constraints, inevitably, were people. "We do not have enough talented people to direct these plays on the stage." Kao could not and did not wish to staff its overseas operations with Japanese nationals, but finding, training and keeping suitable local personnel was a major challenge.

Kao expected the industry to develop like many others until "there were only three or four companies operating on a global scale. We would like to be one of these." Getting there looked like taking some time, but Kao was in no rush. The perspective, Dr Maruta continually stressed, was very long-term, and the company would move at its own pace. "We should not," he said,

> think about the quick and easy way, for that can lead to bad handling of our products. We must take the long term view . . . and spiral our activity towards the goal. . . . We will not, and need not hurry our penetration of foreign markets. We need to avoid having unbalanced growth. The harmony among people, products and world wide operations is the most important philosophy to keep in mind . . . only in 15 years will it be clear how we have succeeded.

CASE 36

Unipart Group of Companies: Uniting Stakeholders to Build a World-Class Enterprise

The course in the Unipart U is about to begin and students are busily writing their names and where they have come from on the name cards found at their seats. As the front of the tent-style cards are turned to face the instructor, the students notice that the back of the cards say "smile" and outline suggestions for class participation.

This course is the first experience at the company "university" for most of the 50 or so class participants. The lecture room, one of 14 in the university complex, is bright, clean and colourfully furnished. Like all others, the room is named after a contributor to the advancement of human knowledge—in this case, Dalgarno, the inventor of sign language. Students gaze curiously at the recent-model laptop computer resting on the podium, the table full of academic books and research studies, and the two impressive wall-sized video screens surrounding the room. The instructor seems very much at ease in this advanced learning environment. He has taught the same course many dozens of times and has attended virtually all of the other courses taught by university faculty members since 1993.

As the last few students take their places, the instructor begins the session with a self-introduction:

> Good Morning, my name is John Neill. I serve as the Group's Chief Executive and as a member of the faculty here at the University. And I am very pleased to welcome each of you to Unipart U.

Over the next two hours, Neill energetically and skillfully outlines the competitive challenge within the global auto-motive industry and builds a foundation for the stakeholder philosophy within the Unipart Group of Companies (UGC)—one of the few manufacturing firms in the United Kingdom to earn world class production honours. Among those in the lecture theatre are UGC employees, suppliers, government officials, directors and employees from companies interested in learning from the UGC approach, and members of the local community.

THE UNIPART EXPERIMENT

In 1997, UGC achieved its fifth consecutive year of record breaking turnover and profits, with turnover in excess of £1 billion for the second year in a row. UGC's revenues were earned primarily in the automotive parts manufacturing, sourcing and distribution businesses in the United Kingdom and with export into Europe. The group of companies also included UniqueAir, one of Britain's top ten independent mobile telephone airtime providers; Complete Communications, a full service creative agency; and TTC, a parts operation specialising in the truck and trailer marketplace.

This case was prepared by Anne Duncan under the guidance of Professor Sumantra Ghoshal. It is intended to be used as a basis for class discussion rather than to illustrate either effective or ineffective handling of an administrative situation. The cooperation and support of the Unipart Group of Companies are gratefully acknowledged.
© Anne Duncan, London Business School (1998)

During a year of rapid expansion and growth in 1996, UGC, together with Honda of the UK Manufacturing and its affiliates in Japan, entered into a joint venture partnership in three manufacturing companies: Unipart Yachiyo Technology, Unipart Yutaka Systems, and Unipart Yanagawa Engineering. UGC also has established Kautex Unipart Ltd, a joint venture with plastics specialist Kautex UK Ltd., and Unipart-TVS Ltd, a joint venture with the TVS Group of India.

UGC also acquired Railpart which supplied and repaired traction and rolling stock parts for passenger and freight trains. The Railpart business operated as a discrete company based in Doncaster. Unipart also backed the successful management buyout team in its bid for National Railway Supplies Ltd (NRS) which specialised in the servicing, repair and distribution of products such as signalling and telecommunications equipment.

By April 1997, the company had nearly doubled its size through carefully planned investment and growth. It was widely considered a great British success story, a company called "the beacon for British industry." Ironically, John Neill, who has been both operational and inspirational leader of the company since he headed the successful management buy-out, was wary of the accolades. A realist, Neill was quickly angered by signs of complacency in the organisation. He was quick to point out that there are no guarantees for future success in the fiercely competitive global marketplace where survival and prosperity hinged on the company's ability to deliver outstanding service to its customers. In a letter to employees, he wrote:

> Our philosophy has always been to take the long term view and try to make the right investment decisions in the best long term interests of the company even if we know that they will reduce profits in the short term. Many of Britain's most successful business leaders tell me that they would gladly swap their publicly quoted status for Unipart's position because that would enable them to do the right things for the future. I am sure many of you will remember our investments in responsive delivery which had a significant impact on our profits at the time. The benefits to all our stakeholders have become quite clear, subsequently, as the development of the industry-leading standard of customer service provided the platform for future growth and expansion in a fiercely competitive market place.
>
> We have achieved a great deal during the last ten years because we have recognised the need to meet ever higher standards of customer service with continuously improving levels of efficiency and competitiveness. This experience should prepare us well for the more demanding challenges of the market place in the years ahead. For example, some forecasters are talking about nearly seven million cars of excess capacity by the year 2000. Consumers have wider choices, they require lower prices and more innovative and attractive products. The pressures that this will bring to bear on Europe's vehicle producers are very serious for everyone in the demand chain. We will have to find new ways of improving our efficiency, customer service and quality, at a rate that is faster than ever before. I believe that the combination of determination, creativity and our special Unipart spirit should enable us to face the future with confidence.

DECADE OF CHANGE

The UGC of 1998 was a very different organisation from the one which Neill and others formed in a 1987 management buy-out of several companies within the transportation group, British Leyland. At the time of the buy-out, consumer demands for "more car for less" and escalating global competition in the automotive industry had rendered UK auto manufacturers uncompetitive. Few in the industry or in the City agreed with Neill that the clearly third-rate factories which were to be transformed into UGC's manufacturing division (Unipart Industries) were worth keeping in a portfolio of companies that included a parts sourcing and marketing division (Unipart International) and a profitable parts management and distribution system (Demand Chain Management).

But Neill, who had management experience with General Motors before assuming the role of Managing Director of BL's parts division, had seen an opportunity to build a world class enterprise by employing a radically different management model based on "shared destiny relationships." His optimism stemmed from his view that 65% of activity in most western manufacturing firms was non-value-added with an additional 30% that was necessary but non-value-adding. Based upon research he had seen, Neill had deduced that only 5% of effort actually added value. He had concluded that progressively eliminating non-value-added activity by employing so called "lean production" methods perfected in Japan, presented a significant opportunity.

Yet, gaining dramatically improved levels of productivity and quality from workers whose hourly and by-the-piece wages provided little incentive for performance levels above the minimum, would not be easy.

THE UK AUTOMOTIVE INDUSTRY: 1970s–1980s

The 1970s and 1980s were crisis years in the UK automotive industry. The oil shortages in the early 70s brought the already struggling industry to the brink of financial ruin such that the British Government was forced to step in and purchase the British Leyland group in 1975. During this time both a heavily unionised workforce and autocratic management contributed to create a confrontational climate. The results were poor product quality, frequent labour strikes, work slow-downs, and an overall lack of innovation. In the mid-80s, Prime Minister Margaret Thatcher finally refused further financial aid to the ailing company, pointing out that government support of BL had already reached £1.4 billion.

While management–employee relations were historically adversarial, company–supplier relations weren't much better. Purchasing managers beat down suppliers to obtain lowest prices, thus encouraging suppliers to continually cut product quality and seek price increases in creative ways. Instead of resulting in cost reductions and quality improvements through innovation, the process created a pattern of poor product quality at escalating prices.

Having joined BL's parts division in a marketing role in 1974, John Neill knew that, "our business was locked into decline." He and colleague Frank Hemsworth developed and carried out a transformation plan to change the climate within the parts dealers' network, an important distribution channel for BL's aftermarket parts products. Parts dealers typically saw themselves as fierce competitors. Neill and Hemsworth initially focused on selling the dealers on the mutual benefits of working together to stretch the potential gains for everyone. The "Partnership '75" program was a great success. As dealers began to understand and realise the potential for improved results, Neill and Hemsworth began to introduce their innovative management approaches to other parts of the company. By 1980, a series of triumphs had so clearly benefited both Unipart and its client parts dealers that Neill was beginning to ask himself, "What kind of company could we create? Can we get people to give their contribution enthusiastically?"

In 1984, BL sold Jaguar through a flotation; but the cash this action generated could not stop the downward spiral. In 1986, Thatcher assigned the task of determining what to do with BL to Graham Day, the man who had re-engineered British Shipbuilders. In 1987, BL was split up with DAF purchasing the BL trucks division, Volvo purchasing buses, and British Aerospace purchasing the car manufacturing division, which was then renamed Rover.

Unipart, the parts division, was sold to a group comprised of management and six investors, including the Rover Group with a 20% stake. Forward thinking in two areas—the configuration of ownership and the securing of a significant long-term customer contract—provided the foundation for Unipart's new start. Leading the privatisation effort, John Neill convinced the investors that 12% of UGC shares should be designated for employees of the firm. He also secured the interest of Unipart's largest customer, Rover Group, in UGC's success by ensuring that

Rover was able to take a 20% ownership stake in the newly privatised Unipart Group of Companies. One outcome was to result in the renewal of its original contract in 1992. This time it was to stretch into the next century with the Chief Executives at both Rover and Unipart publicly saying they were now entering into a lifetime relationship.

1987: A NEW UNIPART

As the Chief Executive of the now independent Unipart Group of Companies, John Neill recognised that the historically confrontational atmosphere was a significant barrier to realising efficiencies and achieving radical improvements in quality and innovation. Increased competition from German and especially Japanese manufacturers had led to a productivity gap of 2–1 between Japanese and UK manufacturers, and an astonishing 100–1 gap in quality, according to studies commissioned by the UK Department of Trade and Industry and conducted by Anderson Consulting and others.

Neill was determined that an independent Unipart could succeed by transforming this context. According to Neill:

> We made a mess of our industry. The short-term power-based relationships have failed us. Many Western companies still believe that is a superior way to secure competitive advantage. I think they're absolutely wrong.
>
> We must create shared destiny relationships with all of our stakeholders; customers, employees, suppliers, governments and the communities in which we operate. It's not altruism, it's commercial self-interest.

Instead of what he termed the "Model A" way of working, characterised by these power-based relationships involving "win-lose" transactions in the drive for short-term financial rewards, Neill's "Model B" firm would be radically different. By operating with a "win-win" corporate philosophy based upon creating and sustaining long-term, mutually beneficial relationships among the various stakeholders in the business, Neill believed that UGC could become world class.

> Our vision is to build the world's best lean enterprise. That means continuously integrating learning into the decision-making systems of the company. People cannot be forced to learn and innovate, but within the right context, they can be encouraged to do so.

This "stakeholder concept" was to become an important cultural anchor and guide to behaviour with UGC. In addition to shareholders, Unipart "stakeholders" included employees, customers and suppliers throughout the chain, and the people in the communities in which the company operated. John Neill and his team began speaking of "shared destinies" with the goal of establishing the stakeholder concept as the core value within UGC and its immediate external environment.

1987–1991: LEARNING FROM JAPAN

From the start, UGC executives knew that making the transformation from an under-performer to a world-class company would require new ways of thinking and managing, new ways of manufacturing, and new ways of working with suppliers to provide outstanding products and services to customers. In 1987, UGC decided to establish a dialogue with Rover's partner, Honda. Honda was a global leader in product quality and one of the world's most productive manufacturers. More importantly, for the purposes of learning, John Neill knew in making the initial approach to Honda that the company would be receptive to working with one of its stakeholders, in this case UGC.

In 1987, at Honda's invitation, Neill and a group of UGC employees went to Japan on a learning mission. Honda introduced the UGC group to its Japanese fuel tanks supplier, Yachiyo Kogyo. The plan was to provide the UGC team with a first-hand look at how Honda and a superior supplier worked together for mutual benefit. The sharing of knowledge and information with a potential competitor, particularly production techniques and management processes, was a concept alien to Western business practice. Yet this type of intra-supply chain relationship was common in the vertically co-ordinated "keirestsu" conglomerates which characterised the Japanese automotive industry.

At Yachiyo Kogyo (YK), the UGC representatives witnessed "whole process thinking" in action, as employees and suppliers worked together in teams that extended across the entire value stream. YK employees assumed significant responsibilities and were continuously learning new "process" skills which they applied to bringing costs down and product quality up. The UGC group was introduced to concepts which many western manufacturers had failed to adopt such as "lean production methods" involving "kanban" systems (just-in-time manufacturing), "kaizen" (continuous improvement), and the use of quality circles and cross-functional teams to solve problems, improve processes and spawn innovations.

The UGC team members were inspired by what they saw. Mark Trevelyan, a shop floor worker in Oxford Automotive Components, a UGC subsidiary, remembered how motivated and proud the Yachiyo Kogyo workers seemed: "I thought, God I wish we could work in a nice place like this." Others reacted similarly and were eager to take home many of the ideas they had seen and try them out in the Oxford Automotive's facility.

The UGC team and the new ideas, however, met significant employee resistance back on the shop floor in Oxford. Union officials found the concepts threatening, and many of the individual employees were sceptical, and resisted the slightest suggestion of changes. John Neill offered the motivated employees a corner of the Oxford plant where they were encouraged to use what they had learned to reconceive the manufacturing process. They used the concept of "u-cells" to reconfigure their workspaces and they organised themselves into teams. Team members were trained and became skilled in handling most or all of a particular production process. The goal was to eliminate non-value-added waste where ever it was found.

The results of this visible experiment included a radical improvement in productivity and a significant reduction in space used. For the workers, the process of direct employee involvement made the production jobs more interesting, and the team oriented approach created a supportive and motivating atmosphere. These successes prompted others in the plant to want to learn. Soon the ideas spawned by the team's learning in Japan and adapted to its UGC/Oxford Automotive Components context were being utilised across the entire facility.

OCC CIRCLES

UGC was beginning to change. New ideas and best practices were being adapted to create Unipart processes and programs. John Neill believed that copying was not the answer. Learning and adapting to suit UGC's unique needs and opportunities were the key. Referring to the adoption of ideas, Neill said:

> If you copy, the best you can ever be is several years behind. We've found our own way. It's a commitment to continually learning and adapting the best ideas to fit the unique context at Unipart.

One of UGC's most important successes in realising the benefits of lean production processes came from the "Our Contributions Count" circles. OCC circles were Unipart's adaptation of Japanese quality circles. Any employee who spotted an opportunity to eliminate waste would "register" and, at his or her choice, lead an OCC circle. Once registered, a team was formed, often by the individual who registered the circle. If solving "the problem" involved developing new skills, employees were encouraged and supported in developing the skills through formal as well as informal training and education, usually in the Unipart U.

The OCC circle had a facilitator—usually a colleague from within the division who has been specially trained for the role—who attended the first circle meetings helping the team to proceed smoothly and use its time to good effect.

The facilitator also provided support and coaching in the techniques of Creative Problem Solving the Unipart Way, a five-stage approach to problem solving in teams that is taught to all employees through the Unipart U.

The OCC circle set specific goals, received management sponsorship, and initially had three months to report its progress. When the goals were reached—usually within six months—the circle was automatically disbanded.

The process of participating in OCC circles and the subsequent recognition of management and peers were highly motivating to UGC employees. Company officials noted a pattern of repeated involvement on the part of employees who participated in an OCC circle. At any given time 30% of all UGC employees were involved in an OCC circle. At the Coventry-based manufacturing site, Premier Exhaust Systems, over 90 percent of employees were registered in active circles. Recognition of circle members included well-attended quarterly ceremonies where the teams and individuals were congratulated and their achievements were presented to an audience of peers and senior managers.

John Neill credited OCC circles with dramatically eliminating waste, improving productivity and positively impacting the UGC culture. He estimated that OCC circles had directly saved the company £5 million in the first few years and kept the organisation focused on the continuous improvement objective.

TEN(D)-TO-ZERO: CREATING SHARED DESTINY RELATIONSHIPS WITH SUPPLIERS

From the Japanese, UGC had learned the value of seeing every part of the value stream as important to the whole. But this historic pattern of buyer–supplier relationships within the automotive industry in the UK had resulted in an adversarial environment that discouraged co-operation and information sharing.

Recognising that the supplier in its own supply chain had to be world class if UGC's product and service offerings were to become world class, the company conceived and initiated a program called Ten(d)-to-Zero to involve suppliers in the business improvement process. Ten(d)-to-Zero underpinned the Unipart–supplier relationship by first teaching lean production concepts to suppliers and partners throughout the value chain, and then creating relationships between UGC and supplier employee teams.

Rather than functioning as the traditional supplier rating system, Ten(d)-to-Zero emphasised joint UGC–supplier performance measurements across ten criteria, five of which were common to all UGC divisions. The ten performance areas were mutually reviewed and scores were mutually agreed between UGC and each supplier. The goal was to continue to bring scores down to zero in each area (zero transaction costs, zero lead time, zero logistics, zero defects and zero delivery errors) with both UGC and each supplier enjoying the benefits of process and quality improvements, and cost reductions.

By 1992, the benefits of lean production processes, the Ten(d)-to-Zero program, OCC circles and other programmes had begun to be realised. In a British Department of Trade and Industry benchmarking study conducted by Anderson Consulting and Cardiff Business School, the Unipart subsidiary, Premier Exhaust Systems, became the only UK supplier to meet world-class standards on quality. PES subsequently won the titles "Best Engineering Factory, Best Midlands Factory and Best Factory in Britain" awarded by *Management Today* magazine and Cranfield Institute. The achievement prompted a visit by the Queen to Premier Exhausts as recognition of the firm's achievement.

The Group's strengths in driving its three goals: continuous improvement in quality, continuous reduction in cost, and continuous increases in customer service, is attributed directly to the employees on the shop floor. Credited with driving improvements through the application of shared learning from the best companies in the world, UGC's employees are often its most public ambassadors.

Such was the case in 1994 when Her Majesty the Queen visited PES to open an extension to the manufacturing site. During the hour long visit, the factory was turned into a showcase of achievement that praised the efforts of Premier's employees, suppliers and customers.

One of Premier's employees, Debbi Clapham, says the day she met the Queen was the most memorable in her whole life. That's not a long life to choose from, she's only 29. She's been working at Premier Exhaust Systems since she was 19.

When Debbi came to Unipart she expected "a job," in at 8 a.m. out at 4.30 p.m., Friday afternoons off. Then she learned a few things. She started taking part in Our Contributions Count circles. Debbi did a few courses and then she looked one day at the process she worked on. In her own words, she saw a problem and she sat down with a few of the lads to sort it out. They did, in an unsupervised project, in company time and when they ran out of time they worked on their own after work and even on a weekend. It was their enthusiasm that motivated them.

Debbi and her team made a simple fix to a simple process. It saved the company considerable money in the long term and on December 8, 1995, Debbi had the opportunity to tell her story to the Queen. She was chosen because what she did was generally the best example of how OCC circles allow ordinary people to do extraordinary things.

1992–1994: REPOSITIONING UGC FOR GROWTH

1992 was a pivotal year for UGC. Many of the early efforts were generating positive results. There was a new constructive attitude and atmosphere of trust that people could feel within the company. The company's vision of a shared destiny was acted upon with across the board elimination of hourly wages in place of salaries for all employees. The concept of working in teams had taken hold. In March, trade unions were de-recognised and in place of union shop foremen representing collective interests of individuals, team leaders co-ordinated with their team members in the collective interest of improving UGC performance.

Record profits were reported for 1992 (up 26% to 24.9 million on an 8% increase in turnover to £714.1 million). By 1993, 42% of Unipart equity was owned by the employee group.

With a view to developing its manufacturing business, UGC acquired Advanced Engineering Systems and its Unipart Information Technology division introduced Lotus Notes to link groups and projects across the company. In 1994, UGC also acquired Ketlon, a transmission parts manufacturer for Jaguar, Ford, GM, Honda and Rover. At the same time, the company entered into a joint venture with Air International Group to design, develop and manufacture air conditioning, heating and ventilation systems for the European automobile market.

The third consecutive year of record profits and record turnover made UGC one of the UK's most watched and applauded companies. Though some still considered John Neill's experiment with building a stakeholder-oriented company not yet fully tested, others believed that the trend in results was promising for the future.

UGC executives considered the news on the company's performance to be good, but continued to emphasise that the achievements to date were not enough. Competition in the automotive parts and components industry continued to intensify. In Japan, industry productivity remained three times that of UK manufacturers, according to the Department of Trade and Industry sponsored study.

John Neill decided that the Unipart Group's goal of becoming a world-class enterprise could not be achieved with what he and his colleagues considered as the weak links in their supply chain, as well as in the internal organi-sation. Teaching and leveraging the benefits of the shared destiny models across UGC's 1200+ suppliers required constant focus and was time consuming.

UGC suppliers had begun to realise the mutual benefits of Ten(d)-to-Zero, and they increasingly sought to bring their sub-suppliers into the process. To accommodate the demand, more time and resources would need to be focused on supplier training and development. Internally, while certain parts of UGC mastered new skills or created innovations, in the opinion of UGC executives, it took far too much time for these ideas and the learning to be shared throughout other areas of the company. John Neill and his management team concluded that Ten(d)-to-Zero and other advanced concepts and skills weren't being developed fast enough and that a greater investment needed to be made in the creation, sharing and transference of knowledge.

UNIPART U

1993 saw the opening of "Unipart U"—the company's in-house university and a £2 million investment in training and education. *A UGC adaptation of successful models such as Motorola University in Illinois, Unipart U was conceived to be far different and to have far more organisational impact than a traditional employee training centre.* Its vision and mission statements were ambitious:

> The Vision of Unipart U: To help create the World's Best Lean Enterprise.
> Mission of Unipart U: Unipart U will develop, train and inspire people to achieve World Class performance within UGC companies and amongst its stakeholders.

Courses were offered to all UGC stakeholders and were focused on developing advanced general skills. They were designed and taught primarily by UGC employees so as to leverage the acquired learning. The theories behind as well as the methods involved in many of the processes were taught, using real-life examples and where appropriate, simulations, games and role playing. Courses were designed to help stakeholders to think creatively and to develop appropriate mental tools.

Noted automotive industry academic, Dan Jones of Cardiff Business School, who co-authored the book, *The Machine That Changed the World*, became the Unipart U principal. Jones met regularly with a "Dean's Group," comprised of John Neill's senior team. Together they developed the curriculum and expanded the thinking about how to use the "U" to leverage internal and external knowledge to build a true learning organisation. Involvement of the operating company heads ensured that the education programs were relevant to current challenges within each division.

Unipart U faculty members were selected from across the company and across areas of expertise. Among the new members of the faculty was John Neill himself who created an introductory, required course on the Ten(d)-to-Zero concept called the Philosophy and Principles of Ten(d) to Zero. Neill would commit six hours per week to running his course.

An impressive information technology centre and library were created adjacent to the University. At Neill's request, glass walls were used, to ensure that the "Leading Edge" and the "Learning Curve," as these two units were called, were highly visible and welcoming. Employees could walk-in, sit in front of a computer and learn a little or a lot, with help from trained and friendly staff. Five laptop computers are available for check-out from the library. The Learning Curve stocked business books, periodicals and other publications, including material recommended by faculty as suggested reading for particular courses. Any UGC employee could borrow Learning Curve materials and could make requests and suggestions for new materials to be acquired.

The results of establishing the University surpassed expectations. Soon, an expansion was planned. Much the same as a community church, synagogue or temple, Unipart U became the centrepiece of individual and organisational development within UGC. It was the place where learning was the priority, where theory met practice, where assumptions were challenged and where mistakes could be made. It was the place where colleagues became teachers and collaborators, where fear of change evolved into confidence and capability. As the company stretched and challenged its members to achieve new goals, Unipart U served as the platform for individuals to acquire new skills and knowledge necessary to meet these goals.

Unipart U's role as a spiritual centre was equally evident in its ability to instil company values and to develop and defuse a common language. As more and more employees and suppliers absorbed concepts such as continuous process improvement, lean production methods, providing outstanding personal customer service, and eliminating waste, cultural norms shifted and there was an observable unity of expectation that allowed people to move quickly from identifying problems or opportunities to developing and implementing solutions.

The potential of Unipart U had only begun to be realised. By institutionalising the learning process, in the dynamic form of the Unipart U, John Neill believed that UGC had created an important and powerful strategic resource. The "U" was creating an important, highly leveragable competency on both the organisational and individual levels: the competency for learning. Unipart U was now the catalyst for closing productivity gaps, and building the kind of stakeholder-oriented organisation that Neill believed could survive competition and become a world-class performer. Neill called it "the platform from which we will see the future."

COMMUNICATIONS, RECOGNITION AND SUPPORT

Throughout the repositioning and growth periods, UGC management used strategic methods of communication to inspire UGC's stakeholders. UGC's Complete Communications division created "News at 10" style regular video programmes called "Grapevine" highlighting achievements, introducing ideas and reinforcing key concepts such as lean production and continuous improvement.

All UGC employees watched the programmes with their peers and supervisors and then completed feedback forms which helped Complete Communications staff to determine the effectiveness of each programme. John Neill was personally involved in decisions about the content of each Grapevine and the high quality of the programmes was a reflection on the British Broadcasting Corporation (BBC) reporters and camera crews who worked on each new programme.

To recognise and reinforce achievements, UGC used special events. The monthly Mark-in-Action Awards programmes recognised employees who had demonstrated outstanding personal customer service. Recipients were nominated by a colleague who had to provide full documented details to an independent panel of judges with convincing reasons as to why the nominee deserved the award. Unlike the vacuous "employee of the month" programmes often found in companies, the Mark-in-Action Awards were highly respected within UGC.

Employees found support in many other forms. One of the most visible was UGC's investment in a £1 million state of the art fitness and well-being centre called "The Lean Machine." Fitness equipment and classes were available to employees for a small fee. Stress reduction, nutrition and alternative therapy treatments, including massage, aromatherapy and acupuncture, were also offered at the employee well-being centre called "The Orchard." The entire facility was located at the Group's Oxford headquarters. It was adjacent to, and soon became linked in many people's minds with Unipart U. The Lean Machine offered the same high quality design and programmatic features which characterised Unipart U. John Neill was often found using the facilities and talking informally with employees.

BENEFITING STAKEHOLDERS

Many UGC employees and company stakeholders became outspoken advocates of the company's experiment in building a shared destiny organisation. It seemed that the more ambitious an associate was, the more he or she could benefit from the many changes and new offerings within the company. The following two examples, picked from a wide variety of such cases, illustrate the new individual attitudes and the resulting business benefits that were created by the company's new management philosophy.

Judith Harris started as a secretary and through a series of promotions had become Unipart International's product manager, for brakes in 1996. Norman Finn was Director of Sales for UGC battery supplier Tungstone. Finn had been toughened by the adversarial buyer–supplier climate of the 1970s and 80s. Each of these individuals experienced the benefits of Unipart's stakeholder philosophy on both the individual and collective levels.

JUDITH HARRIS: FROM PERSONAL ASSISTANT TO PRODUCT MARKETING MANAGER

Having worked as a secretary in two jobs which offered few opportunities for growth, Judith Harris got married and learned shortly after that her husband had multiple sclerosis. This discovery made her face the fact that she would need to develop an independent professional career. In 1988 she sat in an interview with Frank Hemsworth with just this thought in mind.

Over the course of the three hours sitting in Frank's office at Unipart, Judith could not quite believe how well the two seemed to get along, and how encouraging Frank was about her desires to have the company support her plans to pursue further education and career development.

Judith was offered and accepted the position as personal assistant to Frank, the Managing Director of Unipart International, the company's parts marketing division. During the first three months as Frank's personal assistant in the division, it became clear to Judith that there "was something very special about Unipart. It is a very positive company with many young people. There is a certain vibrancy about the place which made me realise they do things differently here."

She was quickly given a wide range of responsibilities as she and Frank began working together. Frank's eagerness for Judith to grow and take on significant challenges was matched by the supportive atmosphere that Judith felt made Unipart, "a safe place to fail." She reflected, "There is always someone you could call on, or a course you could take . . . and, as long as you are up front about things, you are encouraged to try new things. It is okay to make mistakes here."

Frank offered Judith one half-day off from work each week to support her four year educational programme for a Certificate and Diploma in Management studies. The rest of the staff in the group helped to cover for her if emergencies required attention during times that she was away. For three years this situation continued, but Judith became eager to try another role as she entered her fourth and final year of business studies at night school. Frank helped Judith to discover other career options within Unipart by allowing her to spend specific days working in other company departments so that she could get a first-hand look at a variety of options. Following an interview with the Marketing Director, Judith was offered a Marketing Assistant position supporting one of the product teams. However, after a few short months Judith was offered a role in Marketing Services after a divisional restructure.

"Suddenly I had left this safe, secure position and I was thrown into the fast paced area of product promotions. It was a *totally* different level. I had six months to develop a three month product promotion," she recounted with a tone of amazement. "I found out quickly what was meant by a team effort. Everyone worked together to help launch the spring promotion."

In 1996, when an opening for Brake Products Manager in Unipart International came up, two people approached Judith and suggested that she apply. Not thinking that she had the capability or experience to assume the role, Judith resisted. However her colleagues, one of whom was the incumbent being promoted elsewhere, convinced Judith to apply. Armed with her newly acquired Marketing Diploma (acquired at night school during her time in Marketing Services), Judith was selected and offered the Brake Products Manager position ahead of several other candidates.

At the time, the promotion prompted Judith to comment on the incredible personal and professional changes which she had experienced since joining Unipart. "I've actually gone beyond anything I ever dreamed of doing before. I used to be too frightened to actually express my own views. That has changed. Now, I'll try to do anything; I have the confidence. This has even spilled over into my personal life, as I do such things as travelling independently, something I did last year for the first time."

Judith credited such Unipart University courses as the team-building and problem-solving programmes, with helping her and her colleagues to leverage the benefits of working in groups. The courses helped employees to develop a common understanding of how to work in groups as a Unipart team member, and how to solve problems and accomplish tasks in a team. Judith and her colleagues found that as a result, when rotating onto new projects, and thus joining a new team, everyone already had a common basis of understanding and language such that the group could quickly move from formation-related activities to performance-oriented activities. Judith commented at the time, "I've been able to put into practice what I was learning in theory. Unipart has taken a risk by investing in me, and it has taught me a whole different way of working and new ways of thinking."

NORMAN FINN: FROM SUPPLIER TO PARTNER

In 1994, Tungstone, a 100-year-old manufacturer and supplier of batteries, won Unipart's award as Ten(d)-to-Zero programme "Supplier of the Year." But in 1986–1987, when the words "strategic alliance" were first circulating within the buyer–supplier conversations between UGC and Tungstone, the problems between the two firms would not have suggested that any type of positive recognition would be forthcoming.

As Unipart's major battery supplier, Tungstone was supplying 35 types of batteries to Unipart, most of them branded as Unipart products. Tungstone-made batteries such as Unipart's "Samson" were sold by Unipart through more than 2000 designated "Unipart Car Care Centres" throughout the United Kingdom. Tungstone's chronic unreliability in supply peaked in 1989 when the company offered less than 50% product availability to Unipart within the agreed target of 2–3 days. This prompted a meeting between UGC's senior managers, including John Neill, and the CEO of Tungstone, John Richardson. Norman Finn, Director of Sales & Marketing for Tungstone Batteries, characterised the comments and complaints from Unipart as "seriously concerning." Stated Finn, "Unipart was clearly saying, 'this alliance hasn't taken off.'"

At one time, Tungstone held 20–25% of the UK replacement battery market. But with shrinking market share in 1989, the company was considering exiting the automotive battery market to focus instead on the other battery sectors where it competed; the meeting with Unipart could force a decision.

Replacement batteries were a seasonal product, with demand peaking significantly during winter months. The battery manufacturing industry had a history of unreliability in supply due in part to these weather based surges in ordering. For quality reasons, orders were the trigger for subsequent manufacturing. Once produced and charged, batteries in inventory had a shelf life of about 8 months while still retaining their original properties. Though most industry competitors produced similar lines of high quality batteries the entire industry was under-performing in

product availability. This situation presented Tungstone with an opportunity for differentiation if the company could improve the cycle times of the ordering, manufacturing and delivery process.

"We recognised that we're good at making batteries, and Unipart's good at distributing them," stated Finn. "After taking a hard look at the situation, we took the decision to stay in the automotive market. This meant that we needed to have a very open meeting with Unipart; more open than ever before. We needed to understand exactly what we had to do to significantly improve our performance with one of our best customers."

Finn credited the personal involvement of both John Neill and John Richardson with creating the context of mutual commitment. Both organisations "owned" the problem and committed to improving product availability dramatically. Teams from Tungstone and UGC were formed under the UGC Ten(d)-to-Zero programme, with the challenge of bringing performance measurements across ten criteria from the level of "ten" (unacceptable performance) to "zero" (world-class performance).

Using the framework of Ten(d)-to-Zero, the two teams took a systems approach and analysed the entire production and distribution chain, involving everything from ordering and manufacturing through to delivery and end-customer installation. Together, the teams developed innovations in such areas as forecasting, electronic data interchange, and production processes. The results were significant and rapid. From a low point of 48% on time availability in 1989, the teams generated 80% product availability in the winter of 1990–1991.

Such results were not without difficulties, and Finn recounted, "We got a lot closer to Unipart with this new problem-solving project. At times, we were exchanging information which even I was uncomfortable sharing with one of our customers. There were times when we had to break through difficult conversations and barriers, too."

He continued, "We've worked with other companies who talk about strategic alliances, but Unipart is the only one of these companies that really takes these things seriously. Alliances are not easy, and require an incredible amount of hard work every day; it is a process of continuous attention to the very smallest of details and a joint commitment to achieving the outcome. We didn't stop at 80%. Today, for example, we are generating results in the range of 96–97% on-time availability. We are no longer behind the curve."

Benefits of the Ten(d)-to-Zero process extended beyond the scope of the Tungstone/UGC relationship. Finn, whose attitudes had been shaped in the days of automotive industry confrontations in the 1980s, found himself convinced that the shared destiny, stakeholder approach could generate greater benefits for both suppliers and customers. "We began taking many of the things that we learned in the relationship with Unipart and bringing them to some of our other customers," Finn said. "We found that not everyone was ready for it. I think that's why alliances often don't work out: there is not a serious enough commitment to work through the hardest most difficult parts of the process."

As important as the company results were for Tungstone, Finn found that he had also personally gained enormously from the process, particularly in learning to appreciate the value of a stakeholder oriented approach. "You have to go through the trust barrier and you can't get complacent at any time; can't take things for granted. We had to change; I had to change. In the early discussions, I was on the other side of the fence. I found out that you get out of it what you put into it. I had to start off with a more open mind, and now I'm at the point where I believe there are benefits in what Unipart calls a shared-destiny philosophy."

1996 AND BEYOND: NEW CHALLENGES

Unipart's financial and operational performance, and the clear benefits that had been derived by its stakeholders were being threatened again by the intensification of competition in the global sourcing of parts, and more frequently, entire components and sub-assemblies by original equipment auto manufacturers, would result in radical consolidation within the parts supplies industry. As auto manufacturers dramatically cut the total number of suppliers with which they dealt, local and national level parts manufacturers would be marginalised. Possibly 20 or fewer global players, with significant geographic coverage and R & D capabilities, would emerge to dominate the parts and components industry. In such a climate, experts suggested that world-class product quality and price performance would be essential but not enough. Geographic reach, in the form of global operations, networks and/or alliances, would be crucial to surviving competition in the future.

In light of the industry changes, UGC executives reaffirmed the company's relentless commitment to reducing costs and increasing quality. However, with proven processes in place to further these activities, the group's strategic focus was being shifted. The intent was to leverage the company's recognised reputation for quality in its core business areas, so as to generate new business and diversify the customer base.

In 1995–1996, UGC won what executives considered several important new contracts and the company entered into several new ventures. Early in 1996, Unipart DCM, the company's logistics and warehousing division, won its first contract to manage the computer parts business for

Hewlett-Packard. It was an important step for DCM, allowing the division to show its capabilities outside the automotive industry for the first time. Before the end of the year, HP would extend the contract to four other areas of its business.

The venture supported the company's strategy to win new business in areas where it had developed capabilities and resources. DCM, for example, was a leading provider in profitably and seamlessly managing complex customer sourcing and distribution systems. It was the company's largest division with one-third of all employment, and was the division that had made the most progress in exploiting UGC's significant investment in advanced technologies, such as electronic data interchange (EDI).

Within the manufacturing division, there was rapid and dramatic growth. Unipart Industries won a first ever supply contract with Mercedes Benz for original equipment for the new "A" Class vehicle. Mercedes announced its plans to award the contract to Unipart with news stories headlined "Unipart goes to the top of the A Class."

The division also announced a joint venture with Kautex UK, a leading European plastics manufacturer. The new joint venture company called Kautex Unipart Ltd would be based in a new factory in Coventry and would produce plastic fuel systems to meet the growing demand in the automotive industry for plastic fuel tanks.

Also in 1996, Unipart, Honda of the UK Manufacturing and three of Honda's Japanese affiliates entered into a £90 million joint investment to form three new manufacturing companies to be based in UK factories. The new companies, based in Coventry, Kent and Oxford, would design and manufacture original equipment components such as floors and sunroof assemblies for Honda's Swindon-based UK automotive assembly plant. There were also plans in place for the companies to design and manufacture components for other auto manufacturers in Europe. The joint ventures served to reconfirm the multilateral benefits of the shared-destiny philosophy over time. Honda, now a UGC customer, and its Japanese supplier Yachiyo had been instrumental in the early learning and transformation efforts at Unipart. Ten years later, the relationship was continuing to prove fruitful for all these companies.

Perhaps the greatest challenge of all, and the area of highest uncertainty lay in UGC's complex and multidimensional relationship with Rover. While UGC's operations had grown and become more diversified, the fact remained that Rover continued to be a large and important customer. The contract, expiring in 2002, would soon come up for renewal discussions in a very different context following BMW's acquisition of Rover.

In September 1995, the long-term partnership between Rover and Unipart was threatened by rumours of a take-over. Rover, which still had a 20% stake in UGC, was reported in the press to have sought to regain control of UGC so as to control its profitable parts distribution system. Tensions were high. The debate about Rover's intentions, fuelled by press speculation, brought public support from Unipart's other investors.

Unipart's employee group (now owning around half the company) and its institutional investors (owning 30% of stock) voiced their support for Unipart to remain an independent company. The press suggested that Rover's offer price was deemed too low, and because of fears that assets would be sold off and the stakeholder culture would be abandoned. But Unipart's stakeholders were quick to point out that they strongly supported the company's control of its own destiny.

After several weeks of press speculation, BMW scotched the rumours with a public statement issued by BMW chief executive Berndt Pietchestrieder. In a press statement issued early on a Saturday morning, Pietchestrieder said: "Neither Rover nor BMW has any intention of making a bid for UGC. We have enjoyed a long relationship with UGC and together provide a good parts service for our dealers and customers. We are working with UGC to continuously improve that service and to enable UGC and Rover to realise their long-term strategic objectives."

BMW's declared strategy for Rover was to use the brand as the lead in entering new, particularly developing, markets around the globe. But Rover's continued losses, poor history of reinvestment, and widely recognised lack of product innovations were draining BMW's resources. BMW executives recognised that a turnaround required a new strategy, capital investments and leadership. In 1996 the announcement was made that BMW would invest more than £600 million to retool and revitalise Rover. There were also changes in the leadership at the company, with BMW installing a new Rover chief executive, and new heads of the world-wide and UK marketing and sales operations.

For Unipart, the future impact of the changes in strategy and leadership at BMW/Rover, particularly the possibility of extending the long-term contract, remained unclear. Had there been a take-over bid for Unipart, observers thought Rover would have sold many parts of UGC, particularly manufacturing, so as to focus the company on the business of world-wide sourcing and distribution of Rover parts. In this way, Rover would have been following the industry practice whereby the profitable parts distribution businesses are retained and milked for profits by the vehicle manufacturers.

This practice has been especially fruitful for manufacturers in Europe where certain exemptions had allowed them to engage in restrictive practices. Experts predicted that these European Union "block exemptions" would be eliminated in early 2000. This would have the effect of opening up the replacement parts market since original equipment auto dealers, who were currently required by manufacturers to stock only genuine name brand replacement parts, would then be able to stock less expensive off-brand replacement parts. At that time, Unipart would be well-positioned with a foot in each business. It sourced and supplied Rover-branded parts to Rover's official dealers, and it had its own line of Unipart-branded parts distributed through a network of 2500 independent wholesalers and garages called Unipart Car Care Centres.

In April 1996 UGC's 1995 financial results were announced. John Neill credited continued cost cutting and productivity improvements, as well as expanded overseas trading as key factors which contributed to another record setting year. Profits increased 12.8% to £32.6 million on 11.6% higher sales revenues at £864 million. With regard to productivity, improvements of 30% were noted in some Unipart manufacturing facilities.

The stakeholder concept had become integral to UGC's thinking and was the way in which the firm operated. "The spirit is our core competence; it's the product of twenty years!" stated Neill. He continued to emphasise this philosophy in his introductory U course and it was reinforced throughout the firm's activities. But was it sustainable when competitors continued to drive costs down and when the expiration of the long-term Rover contract approached?

Unipart U continued to be the central organising vehicle for Unipart to access and leverage both internal and external knowledge. Unipart U's courses were considered outstanding, intellectually stretching opportunities for most of the company's employees. The professional development of senior managers was a less structured process. Beyond meetings of the Dean's group and short seminars, some managers believed that getting new ways of thinking into the more senior ranks required bringing it in from outside. Some managers wished that company development programmes for senior executives went beyond training to providing deeper, more strategy-oriented educational opportunities geared toward the challenges of leadership in the radically changing industry. In 1995 and 1996 the company did, in fact, hire several prominent "outsiders" to join its senior management team. Yet while the curriculum of Unipart U was under continuous review, there were no current plans for offering the kinds of high level, lens honing programmes that had evolved in such corporate "universities" as that of General Electric and Motorola.

Effective leadership had been a key component of UGC's success. The company had a talented and proven senior management team. Among them were John Neill and several of his senior level colleagues who had been tireless evangelists for change within the company for almost 20 years. In a lean operating company there is very little room for "slack." Growth plans in the company, particularly moves into entirely new business areas, led the management team to consider whether greater attention should be focused on succession planning as the management scope for a relatively small group of senior managers began to stretch.

In early 1997, the acquisition of Railpart, the former division of British Rail which provided parts for rolling stock, and the partnership established with National Railway Supplies, the management buy-out from BR which provided parts for much of the track operations, positioned Unipart well for an entry into the rail sector.

In a statement to the press, John Neill outlined his vision for the future of the newly-privatised rail companies and Unipart.

> The relationship will build on Unipart's values and experience of delivering outstanding customer service, strategic use of new technology, and adding value from the Group to build strong, self-reliant management teams.
>
> As other countries are following Britain's privatisation strategies in areas such telecommunications, we can see the potential for rail privatisation in other countries creating new opportunities. Unipart has consistently taken the long-term view and, in this relationship with NRS, we see the potential to build a truly world-class company in the railways sector.

No one at Unipart or in the respective partner companies underestimated the task of integrating the best elements of Unipart's customer focus to these new rail companies. Both Railpart and NRS would be given the opportunity to learn from UGC's wide range of experience, but it was widely recognised that they would have to find their own way in building a culture—and a reputation—devoted to customer service much in the same way that Unipart had in its earliest days after the management buy-out. There are those who commented that Unipart had a strategic advantage—particularly given what one observer had described as the all important "John Neill" factor.

In 1996, after almost ten years as Unipart Chief Executive, John Neill was still the company's institution builder and greatest motivator. As UGC Director of Group Communications, Frank Nigriello, who joined the company in 1994, stated,

> The pace here is breathless. Clearly this emanates from John. He generates the enthusiasm and gives the recognition that makes people simply do things they didn't think possible. I've never experienced such personal involvement and sense of responsibility in even the lowest levels of an organisation as here at Unipart. The attitude here is contagious.

Neill believed that leadership was "situational" and emphasised that his rise to the role of leading Unipart's turnaround and growth was sparked by the opportunity to "create value for the citizens." The shared destiny concept was the right idea at the right time. It continued to capture the imagination of Unipart's stakeholders. Enabling individual stakeholders such as Judith Harris and Norman Finn to realise their full potential in turn had allowed Unipart to realise its full potential, and the communities in which the firm operated to realise theirs.

Neill was careful to emphasise that his was not a "soggy" or "socialist" management concept. Rather it was a long-term crusade in which everyone benefited through the creation of real value. "We are doing it our own way. We invent what we are doing and then put language around it," stated Neill. "The challenge that we have is to inspire our stakeholders to have a role; to cause people to want to participate."

With John Neill so vital to UGC's past success and to building and sustaining its performance culture, some people were concerned that he might retire soon and that no visible replacement had been identified within the company. Even John Neill recognised that change was the constant at UGC. On a Tuesday in January he completed another session teaching his course to stakeholders at Unipart U by encouraging everyone to consider *learning* as their lifelong mission. He promised that if they did so, and were not afraid to try new things, they would get a lot more out of their lives. He then turned to several of the remaining participants, and said "Did I tell you that I'm developing a new course?" . . .

Workbrain Corporation[1]

It's almost as if I had another eye added to my head. This person would give me insight to see different perspectives, yet at the same time be part of the company. I don't like the term "outsider" but, really, it's like adding a new function to the business that allowed me to think in new directions.

— *David Ossip, President and CEO of Workbrain Corporation*

INTRODUCTION

Eric Green, the newly hired vice-president, Corporate Development at Workbrain Corporation, looked at his offer letter (which was one half page long) and wondered how his role would evolve. There was no job description in the letter, and the president of the firm had given him some far-reaching and abstract goals. The position had been described to him as one that would mainly involve developing external partnerships with some emphasis on the internal development of the firm. However, from Green's perspective, there were many issues that needed to be handled both on the internal and external sides of the business. At the time, the Workbrain sales team was in the process of securing a major client, there were some growth goals that needed to be achieved and there were no organizational protocols for making a sale in place. There was little time to organize his new office.

ERIC GREEN

Eric Green had recently graduated from an MBA program in Fontainebleau, France. Having both practised corporate law and been a management consultant, he had several years of corporate experience behind him, yet when he graduated he had entrepreneurial aspirations. It was through the process of trying to start his own business that he was made aware of Workbrain.

A couple of my friends and I had worked together in cyber-entrepreneurship class and we had put together a business plan that we were quite excited about. After school, we came back thinking we would shop it around to see what we would find.

In the course of doing that I called a friend of mine who had been involved in the Internet for five years in Toronto who

Trevor Hunter prepared this case under the supervision of Professor Mary Crossan solely to provide material for class discussion. The authors do not intend to illustrate either effective or ineffective handling of a managerial situation. The authors may have disguised certain names and other identifying information to protect confidentiality.

I figured would be a good person to run it by. He referred me to David Ossip saying that David was a strong technology guy and could probably shed some light on the industry. He also suggested that David was starting a company and that I might want to look at it.

I went to the (old) Workbrain website and it didn't look that interesting. My friend called me later and said that David wanted me to call him and he felt I would be a good fit with his company. I thought he would want me to be an implementation consultant and that was not what I was looking to do. I was looking for business development, with a more strategic focus. When I finally met with David we didn't talk about my business plan at all because what he told me about the company was a very powerful and compelling story. It was almost too good to be true; he was looking for somebody to do exactly what I wanted to do, and it was in a company at the exact stage of development that I wanted, in the industry I wanted.

Green's role was very loosely defined and there were high expectations of him. He was given a lot of responsibility but also a lot of autonomy to make the decisions he needed to make and David Ossip was completely on his side. Ossip described the role and the type of person he wanted to fill it:

> The individual I was looking for was someone who was very bright, who was a quick thinker, someone who could push the organization and really push me into growing it and who would be able to communicate the vision to the other people in the organization.
>
> I also wanted someone who could function as a recruiter to get other very bright people into the company. I needed a person who would be able to work out how we were going to get the right people we needed into the corporation, and how we were going to come up with an environment to keep them.
>
> Also, we had to define what these people would be doing. Because we were a new company, a lot of the time we would have to hire people before we had active projects and we had to make sure that they would be busy and productive even though they might be (in consultants' terms) on the beach.
>
> I wanted someone who could come in and think in almost textbook terms of how we could scale the business up and build an infrastructure while the rest of us were focused on more operational kinds of functions. It was right up front that I thought about this position.

Ossip did not have to sell Green on the job. Green knew Ossip's track record and was confident in his abilities. Although the job was not well defined, Green felt that the way it was presented to him, this job would offer him the challenges he wanted:

> He described the role as both external development and internal development. I knew coming in that I would be wearing many different hats. On the external side I would be helping with the strategy, the marketing side and forming alliances. Since we knew that we wanted to partner with consulting firms, my background made me a good fit. On the internal side, I would be managing the strategic growth of the company, which was of interest to me since some of my experience was applicable to that as well.
>
> When I first joined the company we were in the middle of an RFP (request for proposal) development for a large client that we were pitching and it was a good opportunity to get involved right away. I was helping to draft documents about a system that I didn't really know. At the time I was the only person in the company who didn't have a technical background.

WORKBRAIN

Workbrain was founded in 1999 by a group of former employees of a leading supplier of client-server labor management systems, headed by president and CEO David Ossip. Years earlier, Ossip had founded this previously very successful company that had specialized in time and attendance management.

Ossip possessed a combination of technical, industry and management experience that he turned into a successful business that was eventually purchased by a larger firm. When he sold the firm and began thinking about starting a new company, he was able to gather together a trusted group of former colleagues to form the management team out of which the concept for Workbrain was born.

The members of the Workbrain management team all had extensive contacts in various industries and were recognized for their firm's expertise. At the time of Green's arrival, Workbrain was not very large. Table 1 presents a list of all the employees and their roles. As can be seen, at the time, every employee was also a senior executive.

The firm had secured US$5.5 million in start-up capital from investors. The main activities in the small offices they rented were either the preparation of the RFP or the development and testing of the system.

TABLE 1

NAME	ROLE
David Ossip	President and CEO
Martin Ossip	Executive Director
Ezra Kiser	VP and GM, US Operations
Scott Morrell	VP Technology
Raymond Nunn	VP Operations
David Stein	VP Sales
Eric Green	VP Corporate Development

From his knowledge of the industry, Ossip recognized that an opportunity existed in the form of the millions of routine employee transactions that took place to track and manage hourly or "blue-collar" workforces (e.g., time-clock entries, employee scheduling, overtime allocation, etc.). Exhibit 1 presents the competitive position of Workbrain in relation to its indirect competitors. Several firms had developed automated systems to manage the activities of so-called "white-collared" or professional workers (e.g., expense reports, travel schedules, etc.); however, there were no firms that focused directly on the "blue-collar" workforce. Considering that in the United States alone, it was estimated that there were 64 million "blue-collar" workers,[2] there was clearly an opportunity. The market was generally broken out on a "per seat" basis, which referred to a per employee calculation. Therefore, the market size calculation was found by taking the number of employees in target companies multiplied by the dollar value per seat. The enterprise software industry generally priced its software between US$100 to US$300 per seat.

Workbrain's main product was an e-business application suite that combined workforce management, workplace administration and workplace community process automation.

The market in which Workbrain operated was highly competitive, yet the other firms all could be described as indirect competitors. There were no other firms that had workforce management products specifically designed for the large "blue-collar" workforce. Those "blue-collar" workforce management systems that were available were either "shrink-wrapped systems" that were "optimized for smaller organizations with less complex hourly labor rules," or were "based on older client-server technologies" that were more difficult and costly to deploy.

A direct comparison with the workforce management industry leader, Kronos Inc. (which had an estimated 50 per cent of the market), revealed that more than 75 per cent of the company's installed base used UNIX and DOS-based applications that meant they had limited Internet functionality.[3] Internet functionality was the basis of Workbrain's product and was in line with industry analysts who predicted that much of the workforce management would soon be web-based. The low implementation cost, flexible architecture and Web-based ease of operation gave Workbrain a strong competitive advantage.

Once the product was installed, managers of Workbrain's clients could more effectively automate hourly employee processes such as time and attendance tracking, activity-based costing and employee scheduling. At the same time their clients' employees could, in turn, request shift changes, vacations, and overtime, administer their benefits claims and carry out a host of other value-added, third-party transactions. In short, the product allowed Workbrain's clients to

EXHIBIT 1
COMPETITIVE
POSITIONING OF
WORKBRAIN
Source: Company reports and Web sites; Workbrain Analysis, 2000.

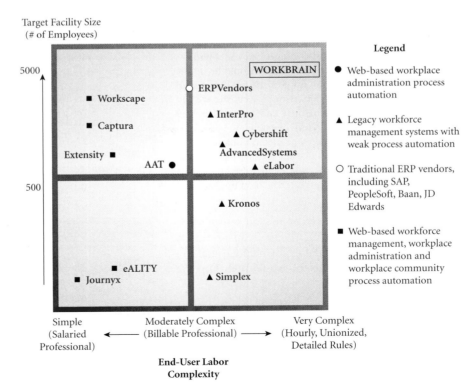

better manage their workforce through real time information transfer and analysis, while also providing the hourly employees more control over their activities and access to information that they needed to better perform their jobs and make their lives away from work easier, all through web-based technology.

There were clear benefits to the clients in that the system would significantly reduce a number of administrative costs and payroll charges. It was estimated that form-processing costs ranged between $36 and $175 per submitted form[4] when one included the time spent filling in, submitting, approving and auditing employee-related forms. For a facility employing 500 or more employees these costs would add up quickly. In addition, automated time and attendance systems reduced input errors and misrepresented working times that, on average, resulted in a loss equivalent to one per cent to six per cent of total payroll costs.[5] Improved labor analytics allowed managers to perform robust scenario analyses to determine impacts of potential labor policy changes and union contract terms on their firm's financials.

Ossip discussed one of the many examples of how a client could decrease costs by using Workbrain's product:

Forms for any type of business process can be created and defined in real-time. This is just one of the many business objects embedded in our system. For example, if a company wanted to create something like a new safety glove requisition form project from scratch, that required access passwords and security for every employee, the cost could easily reach $100,000 to get it started. When our system is installed, it would be a five-minute job. To send out a new type of process form, the new form is created first. Since everyone has a mailbox with complete messaging service built in, the new report is just a business object that is then messaged out to everyone. Our system allows companies to create a data store that can be uploaded (things like procedure manuals, ISO check-lists, etc. can be accessed). We make it more convenient for the employees to access the information they need to do their jobs.

Employees were presented with a number of services and functions designed to enhance their work and personal lives through a web-based interface allowing them to contact their managers through any Internet access portal. Beyond directly work-related functions, a worker would be presented with e-mail, and a business-to-employee "concierge" service through which they could take salary cash advances, make travel arrangements, and take advantage of e-procurement systems. These employee services would be provided through various alliances with partner firms who would gain direct access to many regular users with each additional contract. David Ossip described the product as follows (Exhibit 2 presents a screen shot of one of the Workbrain web pages):

The first level of contact is the employee self-service access, through kiosks onsite or from other Internet portals. Below

EXHIBIT 2
SCREEN SHOT OF THE WORKBRAIN SYSTEM
Source: Workbrain Corporation, 2000.

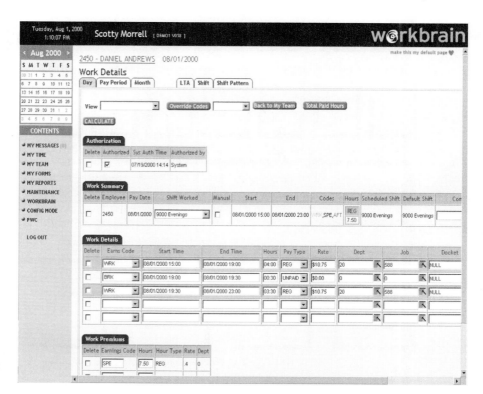

that are the workforce management systems, which are our expertise—time and attendance plus labor analytics, shop floor data capture, attendance control, scheduling, etc. (Exhibit 3 presents a graphic of the concept). We believe that provides the client with an information layer that benefits them. In between the Workbrain transaction servers we can design different types of business objects that can either be provided by us or by other companies.

If an employee wants to see her/his pay, there is a pay stub viewer. The employee can see the pay stub before it's printed. For benefit administration an employee can change the benefit plan to see different scenarios (this could be provided by a partner like Wattson Wyatt or Mercer Consulting in the form of additional modules). Another module might be incentive calculators, where an employee gets points based on things that are accomplished which can then be used to purchase things.

The vision is the end-to-end total solution. We want to own the "blue-collar desktop." It is completely web-based so it can be accessed from any web portal. They can log-on, check their time, do their schedule and at the same time they can use these other business objects that we have provided for them.

Our advantage is that our competitors only do one facet of the solution (i.e., the workflow automation or the workforce management) but they can't do the full end-to-end solution.

We provide a very different view point because all we are tying to do is make it friendlier. We believe that in the long run, in order for companies to retain people, they have to make the workplace more friendly or less frustrating to do things. That is what we are selling. That is the vision. It is not just our time and attendance management expertise that gives us our advantage. Our comprehensive approach (we view ourselves as consultants), the thoroughness of our proposals, and the quality of our work is what sets us apart.

It was clear that Ossip placed a high level of importance on the recruitment of alliance partners. Exhibit 4 presents Workbrain's strategy for alliances. The product was seen as a "win-win-win" situation for the client, their employees and the partners since it bought everyone together in a virtual marketplace where job-shifts, benefits, processes, products and services were exchanged in one arena.

Along with cutting-edge technology, there were two other keys to success that Ossip recognized: alliances and people, both of which fell under Green's responsibility. Exhibit 4 presents the firm's strategies for ensuring that these keys were in place. Distribution and content were the two important components to their strategy that alliances gave Workbrain.

EXHIBIT 3 GRAPHIC OF THE WORKBRAIN CONCEPT
Source: Workbrain Corporation, 2000.

WORKBRAIN ePROCESS AUTOMATION PLATFORM

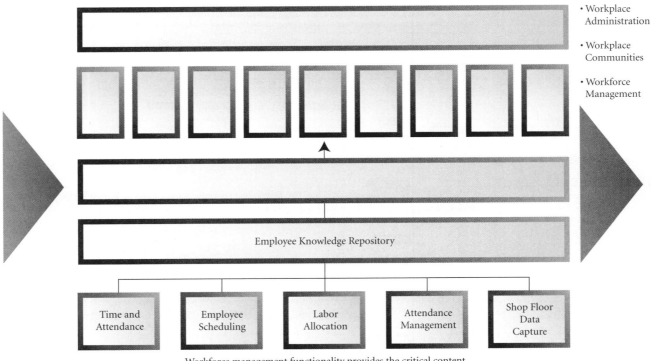

- Workplace Administration
- Workplace Communities
- Workforce Management

Employee Knowledge Repository

| Time and Attendance | Employee Scheduling | Labor Allocation | Attendance Management | Shop Floor Data Capture |

Workforce management functionality provides the critical content for automation of other employee-centric processes

EXHIBIT 4 WORKBRAIN'S ALLIANCE AND RECRUITING STRATEGY

ALLIANCE STRATEGY

Workbrain recognizes that strategic alliances and partnerships are critical to the company's success, enabling the company to scale revenues quickly, leverage its resources and focus on software development. Accordingly, Workbrain will partner with best-in-class companies to establish and enhance its market position.

Partnership opportunities fall into four categories:

■ *Sales and Marketing Partners.* Channel partners who will sell and co-market Workbrain solutions. The value to Workbrain would include expanded distribution and business scalability. As well, the value-added sales approach taken by some of these partners will position Workbrain as part of a broader business process redesign solution, potentially leading to higher prices and faster sales cycles. Value to partners would include a percentage of product sales and the ability to offer a broader set of solutions to clients. Such partners would include:
—Systems consultants and management consultants with strong technology capabilities (e.g., PriceWaterhouseCoopers, Andersen Consulting, A. T. Kearney/EDS, Origin, Cambridge Technology Partners)
—HR consultants with technology practices (e.g., Watson Wyatt, AON)
—Enterprise software vendors (e.g., PeopleSoft, JD Edwards, SAP)
—Application Service Providers (e.g., Corio, US Internetworking)

■ *Implementation Partners.* Systems integrators and consultants who will lead and support the implementation of Workbrain solutions. As in the case of sales and marketing partnerships, implementation partners will help increase the scalability of Workbrain by not limiting the company's execution capacity. These partners will derive value by earning software configuration fees, systems integration fees, software development fees (e.g., designing additional modules to leverage the system's workflow infrastructure), and training fees. It is expected that in most cases, these partners will also have sold the Workbrain solution to the client. This group would, therefore, include the systems integration firms and the ASPs outlined above.

■ *Solution Partners.* Hardware and software vendors whose products will be bundled with Workbrain to offer a more complete solution to clients. The benefits to Workbrain would include an enhanced value proposition and expanded solution portfolio, as well as a co-marketing channel. Solution Partners would derive value through hardware and software sales, as well as new and/or strengthened customer relationships. This group would include:
—OEMs, including makers of PCs and servers (e.g., Dell, Compaq), Internet appliances (e.g., Netpliance), wireless devices (e.g., Palm, Research in Motion), and data capture devices (e.g., Synel Industries)
—Enterprise software vendors (e.g., PeopleSoft, JD Edwards, SAP)
—E-business software vendors and service providers (e.g., Ariba, Icarian, Healtheon/WebMD, RewardsPlus)

■ *Commerce Partners.* Providers of goods and services who will enhance the value of the workplace community aspect of the Workbrain solution. These partnerships are fundamental to Workbrain to execute its vision to be the gateway for hourly employees to the outside world. By providing the 'sticky' content for hourly workers (e.g., payment and schedule information), Workbrain can build a large user base that would be attractive to other companies seeking to acquire customers. Transaction fees would be shared between the client, Workbrain, and the Commerce Partner. This group of partners would include:
—Incentive management administrators (e.g., Maritz)
—B2E aggregators (e.g., Perksatwork.com, employeesavings.com)
—B2C vendors (e.g., Expedia.com, Citibank, E-trade, Paymybills.com, Amazon.com)

Workbrain is currently developing training and alliance programs to ensure that partners work effectively with Workbrain in executing all aspects of its strategy.

Rapid market penetration is key to Workbrain's long-term success. Although it is anticipated that in the longer term, the majority of software sales will be derived from channel partners, Workbrain is committed to building a strong direct sales force that will build market presence and complement our Sales and Marketing Partners.

HUMAN RESOURCES STRATEGY

Workbrain management recognizes that in today's competitive labor market, the ability to attract, develop, retain and inspire exceptional people is the single most important key success factor in building a great company. Workbrain's growth philosophy, therefore, focuses on excellence in recruiting, workplace environment and compensation policies.

■ *Recruiting.* Workbrain is growing rapidly in Toronto and Atlanta by aggressively recruiting both experienced industry professionals and new graduates. Workbrain is looking primarily for results-oriented employees who understand the implementation needs of complex projects. Accordingly, the company's recruiting resources are focused on attracting experienced project managers from the industry segments that Workbrain serves. Workbrain management is leveraging their industry relationships to identify, recruit and train these sales and technology leaders with strong client contacts. Undergraduate, MBA, and IT recruiting is being conducted in conjunction with innovative human resources firms. Incentive compensation for *all* Workbrain employees recognizes their contribution to the firm's recruiting strategy.

■ *Workplace Environment.* Workbrain management is intensely focused on creating an inspiring place to work, where risk-taking, results, creativity, and fun are all valued and rewarded. Responsibility is distributed to allow employees to make a real impact and to create uniquely stretching jobs. Cutting-edge productivity technologies and workplace amenities (including on-site health club memberships), flexible work hours, a relaxed workplace, and a genuine respect for work/life balance are all part of Workbrain's work environment.

■ *Compensation.* All Workbrain employees receive highly competitive cash and equity-based compensation and best-in-class benefits, including health and dental insurance, continuing education, and a broad variety of employee perquisites.

Source: Workbrain Corporation, 2000.

THE CHALLENGE

Workbrain was armed with what seemed like an industry-leading product, and highly skilled people to implement and service the systems and able salespeople to find clients. The key now was to develop an organization that would allow Ossip to bring his vision to reality and that job fell to Eric Green.

One of the first things I did was to put together an organizational chart that described who did what. It only had about five boxes. I tried to get an idea of all the internal activities that went on in the company such as legal, accounting, operations, technology, and who owned what. There seemed to be no real definition of roles. It seemed as though everyone was just working on this RFP and everything was directed towards a client focus at that point.

David didn't necessarily think in terms of organizational structure. I don't think that was really his interest. I think he was very much product-driven. He really loved the technology. He loved playing around with the coding. I guess I was the one who was supposed to be focusing on the internal growth and managing that growth.

One of the major things I did was really push the recruiting forward. More than once I was referred to as the "fluffy" guy; it became a bit of a joke where people would say that if it was not selling or coding, then it was fluffy. For example, on my first day they were interviewing a candidate for the position of Director of Human Relations. I met with him and we really didn't click. At the end of the day we met to discuss whether we should make him an offer. Everyone was very nonchalant about it and David liked him because he saw an immediate need to hire someone for the HR position—which is a credit to David because a lot of entrepreneurs just don't think HR is important. I didn't want to talk out of turn but I really didn't feel he was right for the job for a few reasons. I left that day afraid that I had insulted some people, but we couldn't afford to make hiring mistakes, especially at that stage in the company's life. On the one hand there was a sense of urgency that we needed to fill roles and get people doing things, but if we made mistakes, it would have been a lot harder to correct them.

One of the things that seemed to be like a black hole was the whole selling process because David Stein, VP Sales, was used to doing almost everything. He is technical. He's a great salesman. He's very smart. He can do the documentation. He can do everything. He felt that all he needed to do was hire people like himself, but people like him were impossible to find. He had a very unique skill set. I put together charts and documents to visually communicate what it was that I wanted to get across. It helped David Stein separate some of the issues that he may have been co-mingling. I wanted him to create an organizational structure to allow him to understand the type of people he needed to hire and what skills they needed to possess. It put some clarity around what his organization needed to look like.

I was stressing recruiting, but it was really more strategic thinking. I was getting them (the senior managers) to realize that there were a lot of complimentary skills sets out there. They didn't have to find every skill resident in one person. I think that since these guys worked in small companies where a few people did a lot of different things, especially in an industry where a person's experience is very industry-related, some people had to take a leap of faith that we could hire someone with general skills rather than industry-specific knowledge.

Another thing that was a bit concerning was that compensation seemed to be somewhat ad hoc. Salary levels and difficult compensation packages that included options were not really well thought out. I had to determine how much a VP or an analyst should be paid. I felt that we couldn't hire anyone until we really understood or knew what we were going to offer them in compensation.

Another important task was to develop job descriptions. We had to ask a lot of questions. What would this person be doing? What skills were we looking for and where could we find them? We needed to build processes to answer these questions. To do this we needed to start from the job descriptions and really think about what needed to get done and what each department was responsible for and who was going to do what.

There was one watershed moment where it seemed to me that it all became clear to everyone. I had been under the assumption that everyone had been working with the same vision and the same growth plan, that to me was represented by the business plan that was put together before I was hired. To me, the business plan was the company. What I later learned was that due to time constraints, some of the technical and implementation team had not been as involved in the planning process as they should have. There was some resentment that they had not been a part of it because some of them were founders of the firm. There was a disconnect about where they thought the company was going that had manifested itself in the way they were thinking about hiring.

At a meeting of the senior managers, which David Ossip could not attend, the department heads were discussing projects on the horizon, the expected value, and how many people they felt were needed for each project. I felt that we needed to hire about ten implementation people. They came out with numbers like 2.3 people for a project. I felt this was wrong and that it indicated that there was an assumption that we would grow using internally generated cash—I felt that we needed to get big fast. I suggested that the business would come but we needed to build up the infrastructure, which to me was the people.

There was definitely a lot of cynicism from the guys who came from a different environment who were not in this new economy, dot.com kind of thinking. To them it seemed ridiculous to hire people with nothing to do right now. I thought we had a lot to do. There was a lot of infrastructure to be developed for every group. All the materials and processes had to be developed because we were starting from scratch. We needed to get up to speed before we could take on another project and to me that seemed like a lot of work. People needed to be convinced that there was work to do that was not immediately realizing value or revenue.

At the conclusion of that meeting I think a lot of us were quite frustrated and I realized that a lot of those guys had never even seen the business plan. They weren't really quite sure what the vision was.

When David came back he saw that I was really frustrated. He called everyone into a meeting and walked everyone through the vision as he saw it and how the company should grow. This wasn't going to be a company that would grow using internally generated cash; we needed to build quickly. This is what we were promising investors. We were supposed to be 170 people by September 2001 and we had clear revenue targets. We couldn't do that by building incrementally. When David heard about the 2.3 people thing, he reiterated that we should not be thinking that way. We needed to get everyone on the same page and he said specifically that I was here to do that. Because I came from a big company, I thought like a big company and that's what we needed to be and, although I was pulling people in a different direction, that was the way we had to go.

That stands out in my mind as a real turning point in the company. It's not as if it changed overnight, but that started the sequence of events that started to get everyone on the same page. What was encouraging the whole time was that David had taken the step to hire someone like me in the first place because his last company didn't have anyone like me. To me that meant that as tough as this stuff might be to sell internally to get people thinking a certain way, I had his buy in.

It wasn't my vision. These guys had it before I got here. It disappeared for a little while under the bulk of the work that we had. I think that for the guys that came from the previous company it was a bit of a mind shift on a couple of fronts. On the product front, they had to stop thinking only in terms of time and attendance functionality and think more broadly, remembering that this was just one process within the system, and what we were building was a platform for all sorts of processes. Secondly, they had to stop thinking in terms of incremental growth and think more big bang. We were going to be up to 60 people after only eight months in business; that meant that we needed to think big. We needed big company processes. We needed to hire people dedicated to hiring and we needed to act like a big company. We needed to develop our infrastructure to support what we thought we were *going* to be. The people who came from the last company just had to get their heads around it.

In its first months of existence, Workbrain was on pace to exceed its revenue goals. However, the firm still needed to develop the crucial partnerships and client relationships that were required to secure investors in its next round of funding. With this success came more challenges in maintaining the vision, cementing and creating new processes and mental models within the firm. As divisions grew, the roles of the managers would have to be altered and new divisions would need to be created. As the firm grew, how could the culture Ossip espoused be maintained? The firm was staffed with and pursued highly talented, and thus much sought-after, people. How could they be retained? The task of answering these questions lay on the shoulders of Eric Green.

Warner Brothers

On July 16, 1999, the entertainment world awoke to the sudden news of the resignations of Robert A. Daly and Terry Semel, the co-chairmen of Warner Brothers. Their resignations represented the end of one of the most stable and successful relationships with a studio in Hollywood history. Under Mr. Daly and Mr. Semel's leadership, Warner had dominated the film industry, seemingly unaffected by the problems besetting its rivals, which tend to careen from surprise blockbuster to major write-off, from old management to new.

Blessed with the longest running management team in the movie business, Warner had consistently outperformed its competitors. Their movies were always equipped with the best crews, effects and talents that money could buy. For many years, there had been no reason for Mr. Daly or Mr. Semel to move away from this tried and true strategy of reliance on star-driven high-budget event films. For 16 of the 19 years that they reigned, the firm had ranked among the top three studios in terms of U.S. market share. It placed first eight times and second five times during this period.

But in the last few years, Mr. Daly and Mr. Semel had been subject to increased criticism because of the lackluster performance of their film slate, as reflected by Warner's declining market share. The duo's simple strategy of casting top stars in big event movies did not seem to be working as well. Their most recent expensive flops included big star vehicles as *Father's Day*, *The Postman* and *The Avengers*. The studio's deteriorating track record with big budget star driven vehicles suggested that the elements that a movie needed to have for success in the market were changing. Even New Line Cinema, a recent acquisition of Time Warner, was scoring bigger and bigger successes with low-to-medium budget movies with relatively fresh, not as yet discovered, stars and directors.

Both Mr. Daly and Mr. Semel denied that their decision had been influenced by Warner's declining performance. They emphasized that they were leaving the studio to pursue other possible opportunities. But industry observers believed that the exit of these two Warner executives was prompted by their concerns about the changes that were confronting the film studios. If these changes continue to take hold, they would raise serious questions about the benefits of Mr. Daly and Mr. Semel's free spending approach to making movies. Recent hits such as *Analyze This* and *The Matrix* were championed not by the top duo, but by the newly recruited production chief, Lorenzo di Bonaventura. Warner's expensive big event film for the summer *Wild, Wild West* opened to a weak box office and dismal reviews, making it unlikely to make much money for the studio.

"They did a great job for the last 19 years," said Gordon Crawford, senior vice-president of Los Angeles–based Capital Research and Management Company, one of Time

---

Case prepared by Jamal Shamsie, UCLA, to be used for class discussion. Material has been drawn from published sources. Copyright © 2002 Jamal Shamsie.

Warner's large shareholders. "On the other hand, from a Time Warner perspective, they weren't going to take the company forward for the next 20 years, so it was inevitable that the Bob and Terry show would come to an end at some point. The company can discuss restructuring now, because it was never going to happen with Bob and Terry there."

HERITAGE OF THE MOGULS

Both Mr. Daly and Mr. Semel had been trained at the knee of legendary Time Warner chairman Steven J. Ross, one of the last great movie moguls who died in 1992. Mr. Ross gave his executives independence and a relatively free rein and, perhaps more important, was an extravagant spender whose largess endeared him to stars, directors and producers. He relished the glitz of Hollywood, cultivating top talent with gifts and perks.

The philosophy was well thought out. Mr. Ross believed that his studio would benefit from ongoing relationships with top stars, directors and producers because they were essential for the success of movies. Mr. Daly and Mr. Semel learned the formula well. They courted big name talent and used them to create big movies that they believed the public would flock to see. The lavish gifts and perks were designed to attract and keep such highly regarded talent at the studio as part of its expanded family.

To Mr. Daly and Mr. Semel, the Warner family consisted of a select group of top movie talent with whom they had carefully cultivated a strong relationship. Their films usually resulted from extravagantly high priced deals that they regularly made with the same big-budget and big-star movie producers like Jerry Weintraub, Jon Peters and Joel Silver. For the most part, these films also tended to draw on the same stars and directors that had created hits in the past. "Bob and Terry are the only two guys in our era who achieved a kind of old-Hollywood continuity with movie stars and world-class filmmakers, whether it was Stanley Kubrick, Clint Eastwood, Mel Gibson, Oliver Stone, Barry Levinson, Kevin Costner or Dick Donner," said producer Bill Gerber, a former Warner Bros. co-president of production.

The continuity was based on the loyalty of this top talent which was amply rewarded by the studio. Even by Hollywood standards, Warner's practices under Mr. Daly and Mr. Semel appeared to have set new standards for excessiveness. However, in the flush times of the mid-80s to the early 90s, when the studio produced hits, the extravagances were accepted by the company's hierarchy as the way Hollywood does business. It was Mr. Daly and Mr. Semel, after all, who seemed to possess the magic key that

opened doors to success while all around them studio chieftains lost their heads in corporate upheavals.

Their focus on heavy spending in order to be able to make star studded event films with top directors and producers worked for many years. Warner excelled at making a wide range of such movies. It not only turned out such lucrative movie franchises as *Batman* and *Lethal Weapon*, it created dazzling special-effects films such as *Twister* and *Contact* and mounted thrilling dramas like *The Fugitive*. At the same time, it managed to deliver gritty, thought-provoking films such as Clint Eastwood's Oscar-winning western *Unforgiven* and films with social and political themes such as Spike Lee's *Malcolm X*, Oliver Stone's *JFK* and Roland Joffe's *The Killing Fields*.

But cracks were beginning to appear in this blockbuster strategy, particularly over the last couple of years. Expensive star studded flops like *The Postman* with Kevin Costner, *Father's Day* with Robin Williams and Billy Crystal, *Mad City* with Dustin Hoffman and John Travolta, Clint Eastwood's *Midnight in the Garden of Good and Evil*, *The Avengers* with Uma Thurman and Ralph Fiennes, Barry Levinson's *Sphere* and the animated *Quest for Camelot* had begun to raise questions about the duo's strategy. It appeared as if Mr. Daly and Mr. Semel were backing films that were no longer able to command the revenues that they might have attracted in the past.

A SEISMIC INDUSTRY SHIFT

Over the last couple of years, movie studios have come under tremendous pressure to cut costs to bolster thin profit margins by making fewer, cheaper, lower-risk films. In particular, studios have begun to cut back on the expensive gambles on star-studded vehicles that Mr. Daly and Mr. Semel were known for. Fewer higher budget films are being grabbed by the studios and these movies are being approved only when a partner has been found to share the financial risk. "Everybody has been forced to see the cold realities of the very narrow profit margins of the movie business," said Brian Glazer, producer of films like *Ransom* and *Apollo 13*.

To some degree, the studios were also beginning to question the necessity of star driven big event movies. In recent years, most of the industry profits have come from films like *There's Something About Mary*, *The Wedding Singer*, *Rush Hour* and *Waterboy*. All of these have tended to be more modestly budgeted movies with unknown directors and upcoming stars. The public flocked to see these movies because of their interest in fresh faces that were associated with an easily identifiable concept.

Industry observers claim that the success of these new kinds of films has signaled seismic shifts in the market.

Gradually, the studios were trying to figure out newer ways of catering to the younger audiences, particularly males aged 15 to 25, who are most likely to generate the biggest box office bucks. As other entertainment options have continued to develop, it has become harder to draw this target market to movies. Studios who had some degree of success have attempted to push for fresher approaches that could appeal to this younger audience whose tastes have become harder to define.

Given these changes, Mr. Daly and Mr. Semel were being criticized for their continued reliance on a team of older stars, directors and producers who churned out weak or formulaic movies. Their emphasis on packaging films around top talent has left them with little experience in finding and nurturing difficult or risky scripts into breakout hits. Both Mr. Daly and Mr. Semel have therefore been reluctant to seek out more adventurous material and take chances with unproven talent. As a result, Warner's films have been weighed down with tired concepts, aging stars and over-the-hill producers that have had scant appeal for the young audience that other studios were pursuing.

Mr. Daly and Mr. Semel have also faced an uphill task in producing successes from their existing franchises. The last installments of the studio's most successful franchises, *Batman* and *Lethal Weapon*, seem to have played themselves out, leaving it unclear how successfully they can still be reworked. The duo has been unable to develop any new franchises even though they have tried to dust off the scripts of old hit TV shows. Although *Maverick* worked with Mel Gibson and Jodie Foster, *The Avengers* starring Ralph Fiennes and Uma Thurman was a clear flop and the recent *Wild Wild West*, with the bankable Will Smith and Kevin Kline, does not seem likely to lead to a franchise.

Even as their strategy looked like it was coming apart, Mr. Daly and Mr. Semel seemed unable to make the necessary changes to their filmmaking methods. By sticking with their tried and true methods, the two of them left the cheaper, more adventurous films without stars to other studios like Miramax and New Line Cinema, which is now owned by Time Warner. These firms had mastered a new strategy of creating hits from lower budgeted movies with the likes of Mike Meyers, Adam Sandler, Gwyneth Paltrow and Cameron Diaz. New Line was triumphant with youth-oriented fare such as *Austin Powers: The Spy Who Shagged Me* and *Rush Hour*. Miramax, on the other hand, claimed the market for more adult-oriented films with *Shakespeare in Love* and *The English Patient*.

Referring to the strategy that Mr. Daly and Mr. Semel had stuck with over the years, a top producer who spoke on condition of anonymity stated: "They're relying on old horses that haven't been delivering for years. A studio is like a living organism. You have to keep bringing in new talent, new players, reinventing yourself. And this hasn't happened at Warners."

PLOTTING A NEW COURSE

The decision by Mr. Daly and Mr. Semel to leave immediately cast the normally stable Warner Brothers studios in turmoil. Their departure is expected to represent the end of an era which was characterized by high-octane film franchises, star-producing deals and legendary perks to top producers and directors. Speaking for Time Warner, chairman Gerald M. Levin said he was saddened by the decision. "There is never a good time to lose this kind of talent," he said, "but our film, TV and music businesses, and our company as a whole, are in excellent shape, and there is tremendous depth of management throughout our organization."

Under Daly and Semel, Warner had already started to cut back costs in many areas. The studio had made news when it recently shelved two big-budget action films: a new version of *Superman* which was to star Nicholas Cage and Kevin Spacey and a proposed Arnold Schwarzenegger movie *I Am Legend*. It also terminated expensive production deals with established producers such as Arnon Milchan, Arnold Kopelson and Mel Gibson. This has allowed the studio, with the help of production chief di Bonaventura, to turn to directors and producers who are outside the tight in-group that have managed to dominate the studio's offerings for years.

In order to reduce its risk exposure, Warner has also increased the number of films that it is co-financing with other firms. The studio used some form of co-financing on 12 of the 21 movies that it released in 1999. The most prominent deals were with Village Roadshow Pictures and Bel Air Entertainment. Both of these firms were headed by WB veterans who have already served some years with the studio.

But none of these changes provide any clear signal about the kind of studio that Warner Brothers is moving toward. "Everything we've had with Bob and Terry dates back so long," said veteran filmmaker Dick Donner. "This place was just home. It's strange to think they would be gone. Sure, I'll miss them in the business world. But it's so much more than that. This is the place you chose to be because of them. . . I would say their legacy is this: They continued the history of the great American studios. They never let that down. Whoever comes in will have to follow that."

EXHIBIT 1

With the Cost of Films Going Up ...

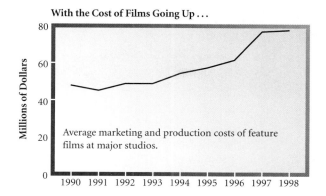

Average marketing and production costs of feature films at major studios.

... And Revenue Growth Slow ...

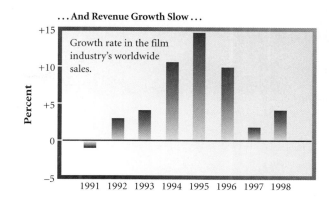

Growth rate in the film industry's worldwide sales.

... Studios Have Begun Making Fewer Movies

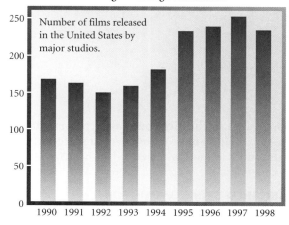

Number of films released in the United States by major studios.

Sources: Motion Picture Association of America: Paul Kagan Associates.

EXHIBIT 2 FILM MARKET SHARE

YEAR	SHARE	RELATIVE POSITION
1992	19.1%	1st
1993	18.9%	1st
1994	16.4%	2nd
1995	16.5%	2nd
1996	15.7%	2nd
1997	10.8%	4th
1998	11.1%	3rd

EXHIBIT 3 FILM & TELEVISION REVENUES

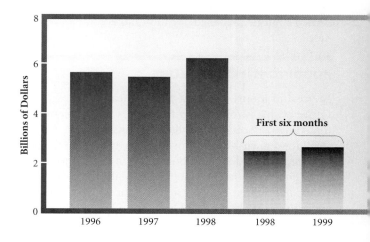

First six months

CASE 39

Intel Corporation

In 1968 Robert N. Noyce (age 40) and Gordon E. Moore (age 39) broke away from Fairchild Semiconductor to form Intel Corporation. They concentrated on semiconductor memory components for the computer industry. When Intel started, no market existed for its principal product. By the late 1970s Intel's trailblazing technologies had irrevocably restructured the electronics, computer, and communications industries. In the 1980s semiconductors were affecting social changes many believed would be as profound as those of the industrial revolution. Not without cause did CEO Moore say, "We're in the business of revolutionizing society."[1] Opportunities seemed boundless. But in the early 1990s continuing technological advances and Japan's massive competitive capabilities presented unprecedented strategic challenges for this unique company.

BUDDING ENTREPRENEURS

Noyce and Moore made an unusual team. Although the future of this revolutionary technology was unknown at that time, Noyce—an inveterate young tinkerer from a small Iowa town—headed for MIT to study about the new field only to find it had no courses on semiconductors. Taking his Ph.D. (in electron physics) at the top of his class, Noyce had joined Philco's semiconductor division. Two and a half years later, he got a call from William Shockley, the inventor of the transistor, who was starting a new semiconductor company in Palo Alto (California). Noyce and Moore, a Ph.D. chemist from Cal Tech, arrived there the same day.[2] Thus began one of the most successful technical partnerships of modern times.

FAIRCHILD SEMICONDUCTOR

The imaginative Shockley had assembled a group of bright young scientists, but the operation fell apart when eight of them left only a year later. Shockley's managerial shortcomings had totally alienated them.[3] Even while with Shockley, the group had looked upon Noyce as a leader. His enthusiam—and his approach to everything with the idea that it was going to work—easily infected people. One of the members of the group wrote to a friend of his family who worked for Hayden Stone, the New York investment firm. Hayden Stone soon arranged to finance the new semiconductor company the young entrepreneurs wanted

Case compilation copyright © 1995 by James Brian Quinn. The first part of the case is based on the Intel Corporation case written in 1985 and revised in 1995 by Professor Quinn. The generous support and cooperation of the Adolf H. Lundin Professorship at the International Management Institute, Geneva, Switzerland and the Intel Corporation in the development of this case is gratefully acknowledged. Numbers in parentheses indicate the reference and page number for material from a previously footnoted source. The second part of the case is based on the Intel Corporation case written in 1989 by George W. Cogan, under the supervision of Associate Professor Robert A. Burgelman, and edited in 1995 by Professor Quinn with permission from the author. Case Copyright © 1989 by The Trustees of Leland Stanford Jr. University. Revised 1991.

to organize. The eight young founders contributed about $500 apiece . . . but most of the start-up money came from Fairchild Camera and Instrument Corporation which also received an option to buy the group's budding company, known as Fairchild Semiconductor. (2,147)

BIG COMPANY BLUES

The company, which started in a rented building in Mountain View, California, grew fast. By 1968 Noyce was supervising nearly 15,000 employees in the United States and abroad. Both he and Moore achieved major technical advances in semiconductor technology at Fairchild (including the first planar integrated circuit and the first stable MOS transistor). But both men had begun to find big-company life less and less satisfying.

When Fairchild Camera had exercised its option to buy out Fairchild Semiconductor in 1959 and make it into an operating division, the originators each got about $250,000 worth of stock in Fairchild Camera. Buy Noyce and Moore began to feel that a company as big as Fairchild could not easily expand into new areas of semiconductor technology. Noyce said, "Fairchild was getting big and clumsy. LSI had been talked about a good deal, but there was no commitment behind it."[4] New ventures in such a complex field initially lose money—sometimes a lot of it—and it is often difficult to justify big losses to directors and stockholders. Moore and Noyce finally left Fairchild Semiconductor (in the summer of 1968). But not before they had built the company into a $150 million enterprise, one of the Big Three in its field along with Texas Instruments and Motorola.

A NEW COMPANY

"We figured LSI (Large Scale Integration) was the kind of business we'd be interested in. We both had started in technology, not in computers or finance. It would be fun for us," said Noyce. Noyce and Moore decided that their new company should try to establish itself as a specialist and leader in the computer memory field, a field where semiconductors had had very little impact and no larger companies were present. As Moore explains, "It's very tempting for a little company to run in all directions. We went the other way. It was our objective to dominate any market in which we participated."

VENTURE CAPITAL

The pair knew they would need quite a bit of money to start up. Fortunately, Noyce had already had considerable personal exposure to the investment community. Among his acquaintances was Arthur Rock, who had helped to arrange the original financing for Fairchild Semiconductor while he was at Hayden Stone.

"It was a very natural thing to go to Art and say, 'Incidentally, Art, do you have an extra $2.5 million you would like to put on the crap table?'" said Noyce. Rock had long before become convinced of Noyce's abilities as a manager. But he also knew that men who run big companies for others don't necessarily make good entrepreneurs. So Rock, a cautious man, grilled Noyce on his goals and his emotional and financial commitment to the idea. "My way with people who want to start companies is to talk to them until they are exhausted—and then talk to them some more," said Rock. "Finally, I get an impression what their real objectives are, whether they have integrity, whether they are interested in running a big company, whether their goals are big enough. One of the things I'm interested in is whether the management puts a limit on the company they want. If they do, I get fearful." (2,149) Noyce wanted to grow to $100 million in 10 years.[4] Rock was pleased with Noyce's responses and by the fact that both Noyce and Moore were willing to invest substantial amounts of their own money, about $250,000 each.

Intel (a contraction of "integrated electronics") started in the enviable position of having so many would-be investors that it could choose those it preferred. "People had known Bob and were kind of lined up to invest in the company," said Rock. Rock purchased $300,000 worth of convertible debentures and brought in other investors who took an additional $2.2 million. Later Intel sold 154,000 shares of common stock in private placements for $2.2 million. The common was immediately oversubscribed.[5] Ultimately, paid-in capital for Intel amounted to about $17.5 million. But after its initial debenture issues, Intel did not find it necessary to borrow or to use its line of bank credit. During this period the company owned almost all its facilities.

Total sales growth of integrated circuits (I/Cs) in the 1970s would exceed 20% per year.[6] I/Cs would have even more impact on electronics than transistors had, although no one knew then precisely when or how. It cost millions to develop initial technologies, to build facilities, and to make the first successful chips. But production bugs make yields a miserable 1–5% of each run. Over 100 steps had to be performed perfectly in sequence. With tolerances of a few microns (millionths of a meter) required, a fleck of dust would cause a faulty device. And reliability testing of the circuits had to be meticulous, a million or more tests for each chip. Nevertheless, this miraculous technology, when mastered, would drive the cost of transistors down 10,000-fold or more. (2,151–152) Older vacuum tube companies couldn't cope with these uncertainties.[7] And customers, so-called "systems houses," were often afraid of trusting their design secrets to outside I/C suppliers.[8] This was the business Intel set its cap for.

A COMPLEX TECHNOLOGY

"The 1103 was a brand-new circuit-design concept, it brought about a brand-new systems approach to computer memories, and its manufacturing required a brand-new technology," added Andy Grove, then V.P. Operations. "Yet it became, over the short period of one year, a high-volume production item—high volume by any standards in this industry." Making the 1103 concept work at the technology level, at the device level, and at the systems level and successfully introducing it into high-volume manufacturing required . . . a fair measure of orchestrated brilliance. Everybody from technologists to designers to reliability experts had to work to the same schedule toward a different aspect of the same goal, interfacing simultaneously at all levels over quite a long period of time . . . Yet I would wake up at night, reliving some of the fights that took place during the day on how to accomplish various goals." (2,155)

"The operating style that evolved at Intel was based on the recognition of our own identity," said Grove. "The semiconductor industry consisted of companies that typically fell into one of two extremes: technology leaders and manufacturing leaders. Neither of these types of leadership would accomplish what we wanted to do. We wanted to capitalize on new technology and we wanted to sell our technology and our engineering over and over again. This meant high volume. We regarded ourselves as essentially a manufacturer of *high-technology jelly beans.*"

EARLY ORGANIZATION

"A manufacturer of high-technology jelly beans needs a different breed of people. The wild-eyed, bushy-haired, boy geniuses that dominate the think tanks and the solely technology-oriented companies will never take their technology to the jelly-bean stage. Similarly, the other stereotype—the straight-laced, crewcut, and moustache-free manufacturing operators of conventional industry—will never generate the technology in the first place." A key question was how to find and mix the two talents. There weren't many experienced engineering or manufacturing people, and top young graduates were sought after by everyone. "In engineering we needed to orient toward market areas and specialized customer needs—such as computer mainframe memories, increasingly sophisticated peripheral capabilities, general purpose I/Cs, and timing circuits." Engineering had to come through *first* with a workable design for what the customer would need most.

But in manufacturing Intel needed to standardize as much as possible. In production, said Grove, "We actually borrowed from a very successful manufacturer of medium technology jelly beans—McDonald's hamburgers. When you thought about their standardized process and standardized module approach, it had much to offer in our technology." But there was also a sociological reason for what became known as the "McIntel" approach. Noyce was convinced that the day of the huge production unit was gone, that modern workers performed better in smaller, more informal production units. And by 1975 Intel had such units in various Santa Clara towns as well as in Oregon, the Philippines, and Malaysia. In each area Grove introduced perhaps the toughest quality control and monitoring systems in the industry and a system of rewards to match Intel's production philosophy.

Finally Intel realized that reliable delivery was perhaps the most important single issue in marketing its chips. Intel quickly evolved its well known motto, "Intel Delivers." But these words had to be backed by careful practices and dramatic policies to be credible to a skeptical marketplace. For example, at one point early in its history, Intel convinced Honeywell to give it a contract for a custom memory device. Honeywell had already placed contracts with six semiconductor manufacturers including Texas Instruments and Fairchild. "We started about six months later than the others," recalls Grove, "and we were the only ones to deliver the device, about a year later." (2,158)

LIVING ON THE BRINK OF DISASTER

"This business lived on the brink of disaster," explained Moore. "As soon as you could make a device with high yield, you calculated that you could decrease costs by trying to make something four times as complex, which brought your yield down again." Overeager technologists could easily miscalculate future yields and pledge deliveries they could not meet or set prices that turned out to be below their costs. Said Noyce, "If you look at our stuff and melt it down for silicon, that's a small fraction of cost—the rest is mistakes. Yet we chose to work on the verge of disaster because that meant doing the job with finesse, not brute strength." Early entry allowed Intel quick recovery of development costs through high prices for unique products. It also meant "experience curve" advantages in costs over those who entered later. Volumes were growing so rapidly that future plant space was a necessity, but the technology was moving so fast that one never knew two years ahead what products would be made in the plants. Still plant construction might easily take more than two years for planning and implementation.

The conflicting strategic requirements of production, engineering, marketing (plus international operations) required some unique policy and organizational solutions for the young Intel. Intel had an insatiable need for skilled personnel and tried some imaginative ways of meeting it. The company hired new employees for its wafer-processing facility at Livermore months before that plant went into operation and bused the employees 35 miles each way daily to Santa Clara to train them. To hang on to skilled people, Grove used a technique that he called "Peter Principle recycling."* Instead of firing foremen and other managers who flopped when promoted to more demanding jobs, he split tasks, giving them smaller responsibilities. Some of these "recycled" people again advanced to higher positions; only a few left.

Middle managers at Intel were monitored carefully but had considerable operational freedom. "Lots of guys starting new companies are interested in keeping their fingers in every part of the pie," said Moore. "I think Bob and I were relatively willing to relinquish day-to-day details. For example, Intel had streamlined purchasing to the point where the engineer in charge of a project could buy a $250,000 tester, or whatever he needed, by simply signing for it—provided it was in his budget. . . . (In a big company) you would need seven different signatures on a piece of paper to spend any money," said Moore. Noyce and Moore also tried to keep operations as informal as they could. Spaces in the huge Intel parking lot were not marked with officials' names. . . . "If Bob gets to work late," said Moore, "he parks way out in the corner of the lot. I think this will continue. Sometimes it's a pain in the neck. But the other problem is, once you start marking parking spaces, where do you stop." (2,189–2,190) The rule still held in the 1980s.

Decision Point

What are the key factors for success in each functional area?

What specific policies should Intel develop to meet the conflicting requirements of manufacturing, engineering, and the market?

What specific organizational form should Intel undertake in its early years?

THE MICROPROCESSOR

Among the more exciting potentials of the mid-1970s was the emerging impact of another Intel invention—the microprocessor. By 1972 a number of LSI chips capable of significant computation had been produced or were in

design for small calculators or intelligent terminals. A Japanese calculator company, Busicom, asked Intel to develop a 12-chip set for a high-performance programmable calculator series. ROM—read-only memory—chips would customize each model for specific uses. As he worked on the problem, Intel's M. E. "Ted" Hoff concluded that Busicom's design was too complex to be cost effective. Hoff had been utilizing a DEC PDP8 and was struck by its lean architecture versus the complexity of the Busicom design. With a relatively primitive instruction set, the PDP8 could perform highly complex control and arithmetic functions because of its large program memory. Hoff proposed to Intel management a program to design a simpler, more general-purpose, more powerful single-chip processor. If successful, such a device might have applications well beyond just calculators.

Intel's management responded quickly and enthusiastically. A small team soon defined a 3-chip design: a 4-bit CPU, a ROM program memory, and a RAM (random access memory) data memory. This design was vastly aided by the concurrent invention of the EPROM (erasable programmable read-only memory) by Dov Frohman at Intel. But it still languished for lack of staffing until Frederico Faggin—later cofounder of Zilog—arrived from Fairchild in early 1970. Faggin worked furiously on the silicon design, and in only nine months produced working samples of the chips that would become the MCS-4 microprocessor, the world's first "micro" computer.

In some complex negotiations with Busicom, Intel won the right to sell the MCS-4 chips to others for non-calculator applications. The marketing department saw microprocessors as possibly a 10% slice of the minicomputer market, then at 20,000 units per year. While Intel management thought it might obtain as much as 90% of this market in its early stages, there was widespread skepticism about the microprocessor in the industry. Many saw it as too slow and small to be of much use. But Intel went ahead.

Even as Intel was working on the MSC-4, a parallel development was underway that would lead to its first 8-bit processor, the 8008. Then in 1974 Intel introduced its much more powerful 8080, which quickly became accepted as the 8-bit standard and was widely second sourced. Faggin, Hoff, and Mazor carefully designed the 8080 to be compatible in software with the earlier 8008. This policy of upward compatibility had been followed for all Intel machines thereafter. The 8080 was the first Intel microprocessor announced before it was actually available, "to give customers lead time to design the part into new products." Now things were moving fast. In only three years, microcomputers had exceeded the population by both

---

*The Peter Principle said that an organization kept on promoting its people until they reached a level beyond their competency, where they were held. Thus managements of all organizations became incompetent.

minis and mainframe computers combined. (2.189–190) The first 8-bit single-chip computer (CPU, I/O, RAM, and ROM) was Intel's 8048, introduced in 1976. With it a whole new era of computers and automation began.

PRACTICES ATTUNED TO THE TIMES

The company had grown larger and more complex in the 1970s and '80s. But it worked hard to keep its management systems attuned to the times. A few key elements in its approach follow.

THE TOP TEAM

By 1982 Intel's "two-headed monster"—Noyce and Moore—had become a three-headed "executive office." Chairman Moore—pensive and more reserved in his habits—was the company's long-range thinker, charting overall product strategies. The more gregarious Noyce, now vice chairman, had become Intel's Mr. Outside and was increasingly recognized as one of the industry's major spokesmen. Andy Grove (then age 45) was president and chief operating officer. Although less visible than Noyce and Moore in the early years, Grove was increasingly recognized as the personality driving Intel's internal affairs. "Grove has to be the world's most organized guy," said an admiring Moore. "He sees problems developing much sooner than other people, and he's interested in the people and people interactions needed to solve them."

The three worked well together, respecting each other's technical abilities, and arguing openly and without rancor when they disagreed. To maintain a close touch with the organization each man was in a separate area of Intel's Santa Clara complex. Their offices were indistinguishable from all the other cubicles that secretaries and junior executives worked in. All office walls in Intel were only shoulder high partitions, there were no doors on any offices (including Moore's), no limousines, and no executive dining rooms. Any of the top three was likely to plop down at a table in their building's cafeteria and join in a lunch chat with whomever was there. Said one group of employees, "It's exciting to know you may see and talk to the very top guy at any time. You feel a real part of things."

COUNCILS AND CONFRONTATION

Intel had tried hard to avoid communications barriers and structural bureaucracies. While the company was decentralized into relatively small operating units, people might still have several bosses, depending on the problems at hand. Virtually all staff functions—purchasing, operating procedures, employee compensation, and so on—were handled by "councils" of line managers. There were usually several dozen—ninety were once counted—of such councils operating at one time. On the councils all people participated as equals, with new members free to openly challenge top managers. "The idea," said Grove, "is to remove authority from an artificial spot at the top and place it where the most knowledgeable people are. . . . I can't pretend to know the shape of the next generation of silicon or computer technology any more. People like me need information from those closest to the technology. We can't afford the hierarchical barriers to the exchange of ideas that so many corporations have. The technology is moving too fast."

This free exchange of ideas was reinforced by a policy of "constructive confrontation." Each member of a team was expected to challenge *ideas* openly and aggressively, but never to attack an individual's motives for presenting an idea. Employees said, "Things can get very rough in a meeting. You'd be surprised at the things people can say. But if you are seeking a solution, it's OK." Grove himself set the tone. "When he walks into the room, things can get electric. . . . I've seen him listen to a carefully prepared report for a while and shatter the room with 'I've never heard so much bullshit in my life.' " The company has courses on "constructive confrontation" for all its rising executives and includes the concept in its early training of people in Intel's philosophy.

THE WORLD OF HIGH ACHIEVERS

Like all other groups and individuals in Intel, the councils were required to set performance objectives and be measured against them. Assignments were set by the council and agreed to by each employee and his supervisor. Grove said, "This takes a lot of time but everyone knows exactly whom they report to on each item—and so do their supervisors. We can't afford to leave anything to chance as we grow larger." Performance measurement pervaded everything. When Noyce had joined Shockley, he had said, "I had to test myself, to know if I could hold my own with the best." In 1982 the attitude persisted: "We are seeking high achievers. And high achievers love to be measured because otherwise they can't prove to themselves that they're achieving. Measuring them says that you care about them. . . . (But it must be an honest review.) Many people have never had an honest review before. They've been passed along by school systems and managements that don't want to tell people when they don't measure up. We tell them, 'Here are the things you did poorly. And here are the things you did well.' "

Intel had MBO (management by objectives) everywhere. Each person had multiple objectives. All employees wrote down what they were going to do, got their bosses' agreements and reviewed how well they performed with both their management *and* peer groups. This made the review a communication device among various groups as well. A key to the system was the "one-on-one" meetings between a supervisor and subordinate. The meeting belonged to the subordinate who went to the boss, provided the agenda, told the boss what he was doing, and saw whether there was any assistance the boss could offer. These meetings were required for everyone on a regular basis. They might occur weekly for newcomers, but they were seldom less than monthly for anyone. In any meeting at Intel problems were put forward first, and everyone dug in to solve them.[9]

FORMAL ORGANIZATION

There was no large corporate staff in the usual sense. Instead the top division managers formed the "executive staff" whose job was to worry about the whole business, not just their individual portions of it. Expectedly, Intel was leery of formal organization charts. Within its structure "flexibility" dominated. Teams were formed for special problems. And planning was performed across all divisions toward a selected set of strategic business segments (SBSs), Intel's version of the strategic business units (SBUs) used in other companies. Noyce said, "Strategic planning is imbedded into the organization. It is one of the primary functions of line managers. They buy into the program. They carry it out. They're determining their own future."[10]

An interesting example of this was the bubble memory group established as a separate entrepreneurial division within Intel. In 1970 Bell Laboratories discovered that in certain materials, it was possible to create small densely packed magnetic bubbles whose location and polarity could be controlled to store enormous quantities of information in a very small space. Although greeted with enthusiasm at first, the technology was difficult to reduce to practice, and most larger companies gave up on it in the late 1970s. A few small entrepreneurial concerns persisted, however; and in 1978 one of these came to Intel with a promising approach ready for scale up and possible introduction. Intel brought the company in as a separate division with a very unusual incentive program to maintain its management's enthusiasm and entrepreneurial flair. In 1982, Intel bubble memories with 1 million bits per chip capacity were commercial and a 4 million-bit chip was announced for release late in the year.

THE INTEL CULTURE

Many observers felt that the "Intel culture" was a major determinant of its success in the wild world of the 1980s. This "culture" was an odd mixture of discipline and flexibility that pervaded the company. So important was this "culture" that all employees were put through a course on it soon after they arrived. This was especially important in a company like Intel where half of the people might have been present only a year or less. The top three executives consistently taught in this course as they did in the complex of other courses set up to maintain Intel's competitiveness. Grove said, "Management must teach to have the courses believed. . . . It takes a lot of time. But nothing could be more important than understanding how we operate and what makes Intel unique. Intel is a complete philosophy not just a job."

At Intel people were expected to be disciplined, to work hard. There are clocks and "sign-in sheets" for all people who arrived after the rigorous 8:00 A.M. starting hour. Even top executives followed this rule. Someone once said, "Intel is the only place I've ever seen where 8 A.M. meetings start at 8." Many people don't like the demands Intel makes and its lack of structure. Some employees said, "Some people can't understand that no one will tell them what to do. They have to define what they are going to do and then live up to it. We've seen lots of people quit in the first month because they can't take the pressure." But those who stay like the atmosphere. "It's great to say you work at Intel. You know you're the best. . . . I guess it's a real pride in being first, in being on the frontier. You know you're really a part of something very big—very important." At Intel employees had put over $60 million of their own money into its stock, which had never paid a dividend.[11] Perhaps this was why Intel was able to meet the mid-1980s downturn with its "20% solution." Under this program many of the professional staff agreed to work an extra day a week—without extra pay—to get out new products and to break production bottlenecks as necessary, allowing Intel to rocket out of the recession with a momentum of new products and processes few enjoyed.

"Quality Circles," Total Quality Control, and Quality Assurance programs had long been present in Intel, along with a monthly cash bonus system for quantity and quality of production output. The latter was announced at a monthly bonus meeting in which performance, suggestions, and solutions were discussed directly with the people doing the job on the production line. But noted Noyce, "In a larger organization there is a frustration. It takes longer to see the results of what you're doing. You push on one thing a year and see some movement. In a small organization you can turn on a dime and change direction. With 10,000 people, you break the organization into small manageable units, so you can change the direction of one unit at a time. . . ."

"But in development you can't afford that. You have to move fast, to be first. But you're in a realm where no one has done before what you're trying to do. You have to measure absolutely everything, so when something goes wrong, you have some idea of what went wrong. You don't change something unless you've proved it on a pilot basis first, so that it won't louse up something else. . . . Yet you have to compete against other people who may not know this—and get lucky. You also have to compete against the massive capacities of the large Japanese companies to change the whole marketplace if they make a right decision and you don't. None of us—no one—has managed a company in this kind of technology and this competition before. We have to write the book for the future. It's quite a challenge."

Moore had stated the ultimate challenge in these terms, "We intend to be the outstandingly successful company in this industry. And we intend to continue to be a leader in the revolutionary technology that is changing the way the world is run."[11] The question was how to do this in an era in which many saw the once almost mystically high technology chip business moving into a commodity era.

INTEL IN THE 1990s

Intel's revenues had fallen during the mid-1980s as its top management discontinued several low-margin product lines and reduced its work force of 25,400 by 7,200. Intel's losses for 1986 exceeded $200 million, as the entire industry suffered while it adjusted to the new Japanese capacity and slackening demand. In 1987, Intel began to emerge from the recession. While the company adopted a sole sourcing strategy for its microprocessor products, demand grew dramatically for its 386 microprocessor* product line. In the middle of 1989, the company's expected sales had nearly tripled to $3.1 billion. By 1989, it had the highest return on sales of any major semiconductor company in the world. (See Exhibits 1–4.)

In 1984 Intel had left the direct random access memory (DRAM) market. Intel's experience in the DRAM marketplace mirrored that of several other U.S. competitors who also exited during the 1985–1986 recession. In 1985, the entire DRAM market shrank by over 50% to $1.4 billion. However, by late 1987, demand once again began to outpace supply, and DRAM suppliers enjoyed market growth and renewed profitability. By 1987, Japanese companies controlled the overwhelming majority of the DRAM market since only two U.S. manufacturers, Texas Instruments and Micron Technology, remained. [Although IBM does not sell DRAMs, it is one of the world's largest producers for its own use.]

By 1990, Japanese companies commanded 87% of the $8 billion DRAM market, U.S. companies held about 8%, and Korean companies held the remaining 5%.[12] Korean market share was likely to increase as Korean firms announced investment plans of over $4 billion by the early 1990s. In order to address marketing concerns that the company have a full product line, Intel, in 1987, had signed a long-term sourcing agreement with Samsung Semiconductor for DRAM chips under which Intel would market the Korean chips under its own name. *Electronic Buyers News* reported that Intel had sold more than 10 million 256K and 1-megabit DRAMs during 1988 through its commodity operation. Prevailing prices suggested that the

---

*386, 486, and 860 are all trademarks of the Intel Corporation.

EXHIBIT 1
MAJOR WORLDWIDE
SEMICONDUCTOR
FORMS
(ranked by annual sales)

	1994	1991	1986	1981
Intel	9,850	3,800	880	500
NEC	8,830	5,335	2,560	9,828
Toshiba	8,250	5,330	2,270	768
Motorola	7,005	3,850	1,960	1,185
Hitachi	6,755	4,250	2,160	824
Texas Instruments	5,560	2,820	1,800	1,295
Samsung	5,005	—	—	—
Mitsubishi	3,805	2,685	—	308
Fujitsu	3,335	3,150	1,145	482
Matsushita	2,925	2,125	1,145	379

Source: Integrated Circuit Engineering Corporation.

EXHIBIT 2 SEMICONDUCTOR MARKETS AND COMPETITORS

	Total Sales	Total Discretes	Total Integrated Circuits	32/64 Bit Micro-Processors	MCUs	Total Micro-components	MOS MEMORIES DRAM	SRAM	EPROM	EEPROM	Flash	ROM	MOS Memories Total	Analog	MOS LOGIC Standard Cell	Gate Arrays
Intel	9,850	0	9,850	8,390	825	9,450					353					
NEC	8,830	975	7,885		900	1,775		330				455	3,440	765	280	610
Toshiba	8,250	1,670	6,580		375	735		370					3,400	925	230	560
Motorola	7,005	1,159	6,580	510	1,500	2,365		330						920		185
Hitachi	6,755	1,025	5,730		600	990		575				255	2,935			250
Texas Instruments	5,560	60	5,500	100		1,005		30						810	445	
Samsung	5,005	640	4,365					225	190			335	3,940			
Mitsubishi	3,805	585	3,220		600	640		220					1,755			
Fujitsu	3,335	360	2,975		225			195				190			180	595
Matsushita	2,925	780	2,145		525	510								920		140
Other 1994	44,060	6,646	36,650	1,315	1,950	6,530	23,050	1,835	1,220	500	507	840	16,535	9,905	2,795	2,200
TOTAL	**105,380**	**13,900**	**91,480**	**10,315**	**7,500**	**24,000**	**23,050**	**4,110**	**1,410**	**500**	**860**	**2,075**	**32,005**	**14,245**	**3,930**	**4,540**

Source: Integrated Circuit Engineering Corporation.

EXHIBIT 3
EXHIBIT 3
INTEL CORPORATION
HISTORICAL FINANCIAL
SUMMARY
(millions of dollars,
unless otherwise noted)

	1994	1989	1984	1979
Sales	11,521	3,127	1,629	663
Cost of goods sold	5,576	1,721	883	313
Gross margin	5,945	1,406	746	350
R & D	1,111	365	180	67
SG & A	1,447	483	315	131
Operating profit	3,387	557	251	152
Profit before tax	3,603	583	298	149
Income tax	1,315	192	100	71
Net Income	2,288	391	198	78
Depreciation	1,028	190	114	40
Capital investment	2,441	351	388	97
Working capital	875	1,242	568	115
Fixed assets	5,367	1,284	778	217
Total assets	13,816	3,994	2,029	500
Long-term debt	392	412	146	0
Equity	9,267	2,549	1,360	303
Employees (thousands)	32,600	22,000	25,400	14,300
Revenue per employee ($)	353,405	142,136	64,134	46,364
Return on sales (%)	19.86%	12.50%	12.20%	11.80%
Return on assets (%)	16.56%	9.80%	11.80%	21.90%
Return on equity (%)	24.69%	15.30%	17.60%	38.00%

Source: Intel Corporation, various Annual Reports.

EXHIBIT 4 FINANCIAL STATISTICS FOR SELECTED COMPETITORS FISCAL 1993 (millions of dollars)

	INTEL	MOTOROLA	TEXAS INSTRUMENTS	NEC	TOSHIBA	HITACHI	MATSUSHITA
Total sales	8,782	16,963	8,523	35,096	44,960	71,847	64,307
Cost of goods sold	2,535	10,351	5,657	24,153	32,477	51,573	44,407
SG & A	2,138	3,776	1,247	10,183	11,823	18,202	18,214
Net income	2,295	1,022	456	65	118	633	238
Capital expenditures	1,933	2,187	730	2,108	2,743	5,762	2,588
Research & development	970	1,521	590	2,565	3,024	4,699	3,706
Depreciation	717	1,170	617	2,092	2,481	4,817	3,080
Total assets	11,344	13,498	5,756	39,606	51,948	86,710	79,540
Shareholders' equity	7,500	6,409	2,315	7,667	10,852	28,730	31,932
Long-term debt	426	1,360	694	9,376	9,810	9,954	12,237
Employees (thousands)	30	120	59	148	175	332	254

Source: Compustat Worldscope database and individual company annual reports.

DRAM reseller business generated well over $100 million in revenue by 1990.

The dramatic decline in U.S. position led some industry observes to predict the eventual downfall of the entire U.S. semiconductor industry. The concern over U.S. competitiveness and dependence on foreign suppliers led several companies to announce plans to form a joint DRAM venture. A group of semiconductor and computer companies (including Hewlett Packard, Intel, IBM Corp., Digital Equipment Corp., LSI Logic Corp., National Semiconductor, and Advanced Micro Devices) agreed in June 1989 to form U.S. Memories, Inc., investing an initial $50,000 each. The venture required $1 billion in capitalization over several years and intended to use IBM's design for a 4-megabit DRAM as its introductory product offering early in 1991. The unusual arrangement between competitors required federal antitrust clearance [13] and faced opposition from some vocal critics.

NEW TECHNOLOGY DRIVERS

Until 1985, Intel managers thought of DRAMs as the company's technology driver. Historically, DRAMs had always been the first products to employ new technology. Even though it never went into production, the 1-megabit DRAM was Intel's first attempt at a 1-micron geometry. Sun Lin Chou, then the leader of the DRAM technology development group, said it was typical for DRAMs to precede logic products in linewidth reduction by at least one year.

In 1990, Sun Lin Chou expressed some skepticism in discussing the cumulative volume model for learning in the semiconductor industry:

The traditional model of a technology driver says that the more you do, the more high-volume products you run, the more productive you get. That means in order to stay on the leading edge, you need a product you can ramp into high-volume production rapidly. There is some truth to the model, but it can be carried to an extreme.

There are certainly ways of learning that can be carried out at much lower volumes. Our recent experience suggests that you can learn without massive volumes. If so, that takes away the requirement or urgency to have a traditional technology driver. We think it is possible to achieve mature yields by processing only about 10,000 wafers versus the old model's predicted requirement of 1,000,000 wafers. But you have to use intelligence.

You don't learn quickly when you increase volume by brute force. You have to learn by examining wafers. Learning is based on the number of wafers looked at, analyzed, and the number of effective corrective actions taken. Even if you have processed 1,000 wafers, the technical learning probably only came from the 10 wafers you analyzed. Technical learning is time and engineering constrained, not number of wafers constrained.

There are also a great number of things you can do in an open loop system. For example, you can see or guess where particles are coming from and remove them without really knowing for sure whether they are a yield limiter. You don't take the time to get the data to justify the fix: you don't do a detailed study; you just fix what seems broken. You have an intuition about what to do. The Japanese have really led the way on this. You don't undertake an ROI analysis to figure out the cost/benefit for every little improvement. You just fix everything you can think of. Everyone can participate.

Craig Barrett, Executive Vice President and General Manager of the Microcomputer Components Group, believed the importance of DRAMs to technology leadership had been overestimated by most industry observers:

At one time DRAMs really were a technology driver for Intel. DRAMs are still the single biggest product in the industry as a whole. They are about $8–10 billion of a $50 billion market. And they are certainly a learning vehicle for some.

When we got out of DRAMs we were concerned that we might suffer from the lack of volume. We tried to address that concern by selectively staying in the EPROM business. Even though the EPROM volume is not as big, it is a volume product. But I would have to conclude that after two generations post-DRAM we do not miss it as a technology driver.

I think that the industry used the notion of technology driver as a crutch. We were late waking up to the fact that we did not need to run volume in order to learn. There are other ways to be intelligent. You don't have to depend on volume if you depend on good engineering.

We have data to show that our learning as represented by lowering defect density has actually accelerated in the past two generations when plotted as a function of time or as a function of cumulative wafers put through the fab. For each generation since 1985, 1.5 micron, 1 micron, and most recently 0.8 micron, each defect density trend line is downward sloping with the most recent generations having the steepest slopes.

While we have some volume from our EPROM line and we make lots of efforts to transfer learning from one facility to another, we focus on basic techniques to accelerate learning: design of experiments, statistical process control, and just plain good engineering.

While we do have a lot of high-margin wafer starts, we still have a significant mixture of products. We have 256K EPROMs, 1 meg, 2 meg, and just recently, 4 meg in addition to our microcontrollers which are all very cost sensitive. We chose to stay in those commodity businesses partly because it does "keep us honest." Of course, it also represents a significant part of our revenue and it helps to amortize R&D expenditures.

Gerry Parker, Vice President of Technology Development, had a slightly different perspective on the issue of technology drivers:

There is no single technology driver at Intel. We focus our technology development on logic and nonvolatile memory products. More than ever before, we watch what the rest of the industry is doing and try to follow trends. The DRAM is the industry's driver, because it is the highest-volume product and DRAM suppliers are the biggest equipment purchasers. There have been some really fascinating developments in the industry. I think that the entire industry paradigm has shifted in the past several years.

A great deal of the know-how is now generated at the equipment suppliers. We try to stay in the mainstream by purchasing the most advanced equipment, but then we optimize it to maximum advantage for our products.

For example, I know that a certain stepper vendor is developing a new tool that will accommodate a certain maximum chip size. It will not be able to process larger chips. The size is driven by the needs of Toshiba's next generation DRAM. They are building the equipment to satisfy the demands of their largest customer.

You can bet that all of Intel's next generation parts will be designed to capitalize on the DRAM tool. We will put that constraint on our designers. The equipment vendor will be ready to produce those steppers in volume and will be happy to supply us with a few machines. We could ask them to design a special tool for us, but it would be inferior because we wouldn't command the same level of attention that Toshiba gets.

Attitude is important and has led to the changes. The Japanese really have taught us something. They expect excellence from equipment vendors and make *them* develop the expertise to provide the best possible equipment. If a piece of equipment has a problem, the vendor is right there in the fab fixing it, and he can make appropriate changes on the next generation.

In Japan, all the technicians set the machines to the exact settings that are specified by Applied Materials. If the process doesn't work, Applied Materials gets blamed. In the United States, we tend to be more inventive: each technician sets the machine to an optimum that he has determined. When you operate like that, it becomes more difficult to blame the vendor when the yields are down.

As a result of this fundamental change in the equipment suppliers' role, learning now resides in the industry not just in the company. That is a complete shift. Just to prove it, look at this example. A Japanese ball bearing company, NMB, with no expertise in the semiconductor industry, had $500 million in excess cash and decided to get into the DRAM business. They got vendors to sell them equipment and set it up, and they contracted with consultants to sell them a process and get it running. In a short time they were the most automated semiconductor factory in the world. That could never have happened even five years ago. . . . The latest equipment is essential to getting the highest yields. Equipment vendors allow Intel and even new start-ups to keep up with the latest industry advances.

EPROM AND FLASH

By the end of 1986, Intel has also exited the static random-access memory (SRAM) businesses, stopped development of electrically erasable programmable read-only memory (EPROM), sold its memory systems division, and sold its bubble memory subsidiary. Intel's only remaining position in memory businesses was in EPROMs. In 1986, Intel commanded a 21% share of the $910 million market versus 17% of an $860 million market two years earlier. In 1989, EPROMs were manufactured in five of Intel's fabrication sites.

Intel's continued dominance in the EPROM business arose partly from a successful legal battle against Hitachi and other Japanese companies accused of selling EPROMs below cost in the United States. Intel successfully fended off the attack through actions taken by the U.S. government.

In September 1986, Intel top management requested a middle-level manager to prepare a study of each memory business and make recommendations for Intel's long-term strategy. The manager recommended that Intel maintain its position in the EPROM business.

Intel top management decided to keep the EPROM operation as a relatively high-volume product to drive learning, but primarily as an enabling technology for the microcontroller business. Intel's microcontrollers integrate EPROM functionality and use an EPROM process technology. In 1989, Intel remained the EPROM market leader, with 21% market share of a billion-dollar market.

FLASH

The middle manager also recommended that the company devote resources to a new memory technology called Flash. He said:

Flash is very similar to EPROM, in functionality, but it is much cheaper to make. Basically, it costs less than EPROM, but you can erase it electrically instead of with light. This is a major cost-functionality discontinuity in EPROM semiconductor technology and has significant implications. One can envision low-end solid-state reprogrammable systems for instance, as well as simpler field service for ROM/EPROM-based systems.

Contrasting Flash to DRAM reveals some interesting perspectives. Flash does not have the flexible write functionality of DRAM, but it is nonvolatile. Additionally, Flash is actually a simpler-to-manufacture read-write technology because it is not constrained by the need for a large capacitor in each memory cell. About 80% of the current DRAM cell is active, whereas only 5% of the Flash cell is. That means that Flash can shrink like mad.

Another paradigm change has resulted in our working on a truly parallel processor, or neural network, that uses a version of Flash technology. By making an analog instead of a digital

EXHIBIT 5

COST PER 2.5-INCH
DRIVE, 1988–1994
(20–200 megabyte
drives, midyear
OEM quantities)
Source: "You Can Take It
With You," *Forum on
Portable Computers and
Communications.* October 2–3,
1990, Bear Stearns & Co.,
New York.

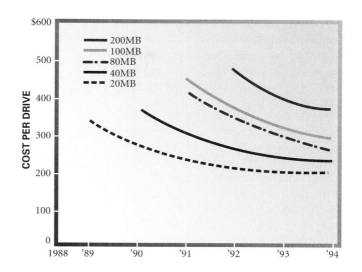

device, we can develop a low precision but very high performance "trainable analog-memory processor." It remains to be seen what applications will evolve from this capacity but it has exciting possibilities.

If Flash leads to miniaturization of computers from portable to hand-held units, neural nets may solve hand-writing recognition. This combined with a notebook computer would result in a very user-friendly tool for a large market.

By 1990, some industry observers began to recognize the potential for Flash as a replacement for conventional magnetic disk drives in laptop and portable computers.* Some industry specialists noted that solid-state disks, when compared to traditional Winchester drives, can consume up to

*Microsoft had decided to support the technology by releasing file management software that lets MS-DOS treat Flash like disk drives.

300 times less power, are 15 times more durable, can withstand much more heat, and are up to 100 times faster. Other industry specialists, however, noted that there has been a 100-fold "shrink" in the size of 20–40 MB drives since the late 1970s (from 2,300 cubic inches for the 14-inch drive to 23 cubic inches for the current 1-inch drive) and that during that time, price has decreased by a factor of ten and access time improved by a factor of two.[14] Exhibit 5 shows projections of prices for various 2.5-inch disk drive capacities.

While the current installed base of portables was fewer than 5 million units, the future potential is estimated in the tens of millions.[14] Although Flash was still more expensive than traditional magnetics, its learning curve was much steeper. Exhibit 6 shows price projections for different storage technologies.

In 1990, Intel announced a credit card size "Flash memory card," available in 1- and 4-megabyte storage units and

EXHIBIT 6

IPC CARD COST
PROJECTION,
1990–1993
Source: "You Can Take It
With You," *Forum on
Portable Computers and
Communications.* October 2–3,
1990, Bear Stearns & Co.,
New York.

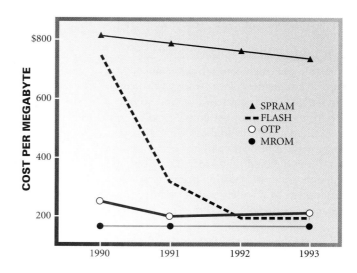

priced at $298 and $1,198, respectively. The new storage system would offer an important alternative to floppy and hard disk drives in portable computers because it used less power and offered improved performance. The reduced power demands, for instance, extended battery life between 10 and 100 times for portable computers.

By 1994, Intel predicted it would have a 16-megabit Flash chip. The chip would enable a cost-competitive alternative to the industry standard 50-megabyte hard drive on a credit card size format.

Western Digital was reportedly developing Flash subsystems that could be managed like magnetic media and could be interfaced into a system like a disk drive.[14] Texas Instruments was also developing its own Flash technology, which reportedly used less power than Intel's during data writing.

NEW MICROPROCESSOR STRATEGY

During the same week in 1985 when Intel made the decision to close Fab 5 in Oregon for DRAM production, it announced shipment of the 32-bit 80386. The electronics industry received the 386 microprocessor with great enthusiasm. Just one year later, in the third quarter of 1986, customers had completed development of new products, and the first products to contain the 386 were shipped. The power of the 386 to leverage previous software led to the most rapid ramp-up of production for any microprocessor in Intel's history. By the end of 1987, just two years after the 386's introduction, Intel had shipped an estimated 800,000 units as compared to 50,000 for the earlier 8086 at two years after its introduction. By 1989, some analysts believed that Intel was too dependent on the 386 and its support chips, estimating that they generated nearly $1 billion, or between 30% and 40% of the company's revenues during fiscal 1988.

A new corporate strategy added to Intel's early success with the 80386. During previous generations, Intel supported a cross-licensing agreement with AMD (Advanced Micro Devices) in which AMD acted as a second source and provided development of support chips. Intel's top management made the decision to make AMD perform under the existing agreement or be prepared to act as a sole source for the 386. [Intel believed that AMD did not earn rights to the 386 design under the existing licensing agreements. Intel's decision led to a widely publicized dispute with AMD that was still unresolved at the time of case development.]

Craig Barrett described some of the factors that figured in the decision:

Basically, Intel got to the point where it could generate enough customer confidence to pull it off. There were at least several forces at work.

Our quality thrust of the early 1980s began to pay off in improved consistency on the manufacturing line and overall better product quality. In addition, customer-vendor partnerships became more prevalent throughout our business. For example, we had recently started selling Ford a microcontroller product, the 8061. They proclaimed that total cost was more important then purchase price alone and decided to work with us closely and exclusively—sort of on the Japanese model. We learned a great deal from that which carried into our other customers and to our vendors.

We had also decided to pursue a "vendor of choice" strategy in 1984 which led to improved customer satisfaction. Finally, the experience with earlier x86 generations led us to believe that we could accurately forecast demand for the 386 and put sufficient manufacturing capacity in place.

With improved manufacturing consistency and better forecast accuracy, we realized that it wasn't always necessary to have a second source to keep the customer satisfied. As our second source deal with AMD came unraveled, we put in the capability to never miss a shipment by adding strategic inventory and redundant capacity. Since then we have never missed an 80386 customer commitment.

The pitfalls of our strategy are obvious. You can fall on your sword. And it only takes once to lose the confidence of your customers. Also, the business is sufficiently profitable that everyone is gunning for you. They try to make clones of your product or substitutes.

Bob Reed, Chief Financial Officer, underlined the importance of intellectual property to Intel and to the semiconductor industry:

Intel has looked around for an edge against competitors. When we look back 10 years from now we may see that intellectual property protection saved the U.S. semiconductor market.* The protection will essentially lead to a segmentation of the semiconductor industry into maybe 10 industries, all with leaders. Intel's sole source strategy for the 386 is a good example of a winning strategy. Now Motorola is also a sole source.

This does not imply much more complicated contractual relationships with customers. For example, Intel has no penalty clauses for nondelivery of parts; however, we never miss a delivery. The stakes have been raised on both sides of the table. At Intel, the legal department has grown from 5 to 20 internal people in the past 5 years. In addition, we retain outside counsel. We vigorously pursue anyone who infringes on our intellectual property rights.

In order to support the sole sourcing strategy, the Portland technology development group began developing a 1-micron

---

*In a landmark decision in 1986, the U.S. courts agreed with Intel that computer code embedded in silicon is covered by U.S. copyright laws, thus affording protection for Intel's chip designs.

version of the 386, a significant reduction in chip size from the original 1.5-micron geometry. Increased functionality and integration depend on the ability to "shrink" the microprocessor, allowing more space to integrate new features. Jack Carsten, formerly an Intel senior vice president, said:

> Lots of people talk about the design team that developed Intel's 386 chip. It's a great product. But, the great unsung heroes at Intel are the people who successfully developed the "shrink" technology for the 386. That reduction in geometry led to higher-performance parts as well as greatly increased yields.

Exhibit 7 shows the evolution as the result of the shrinking CPU technology.

Sun Lin Chou discussed the role of the Portland Technology Development Group:

> In the past 2 years the situation has changed significantly. We don't just do process development in Portland. We have designers in Portland who leverage our ability to make use of leading-edge technology sooner. Some of those designers are old DRAM designers who have been retained.
>
> In the old days, memory was always the first product to use a new process. First, we would get the yields up on memory, then a couple of years later the logic product would use the process. We stabilized the process on memory, then did logic. Since logic takes longer to design, it is easier to do it that way. Now we have no DRAMs; the concept of technology driver has changed.
>
> Our challenge is to get logic products up on new processes sooner than we ever have before. To do that, we have accelerated and integrated the design process. We use the Portland designers to design standard cells which can then be used by chip designer

groups. We also take existing logic parts that have proven designs and use the new standard cells to generate "shrink" designs. Instead of using memory to ramp production, we are now using logic products redesigned with smaller geometrics.

The 80486 was introduced in April 1989. With over 1 million transistors, the 486 microprocessor contained nearly four times the circuit elements in the 386. The 486 had taken a total of 130 person-years in design effort compared to 80 for the 386. It had benefited from a fourfold increase in proprietary specialized design tools created by Intel. The overall investment in the 486 development had been more than $200 million. In keeping with its strategy of upward compatibility, Intel had designed the new offering to run software developed for its predecessors. The 486 was expected to be especially important in the growing market for a new class of "servers," which could store information for an entire corporation and send it out as needed to PCs in response to queries from different types of users.

RISC VERSUS CISC

By the early 1990s, Intel had established a dominant position in the personal computer microprocessor business based on complex instruction set computer (CISC) design. Every manufacturer of advanced IBM-compatible personal computers had to purchase a 386 or 486 microprocessor from Intel. Similarly, those manufacturers or their customers had to purchase operating system software from Microsoft Corporation in order to maintain backward

EXHIBIT 7
SILICON TRENDS AND
PC INTEGRATION
Source: Santa Clara
Microcomputer Division,
Intel Corporation.

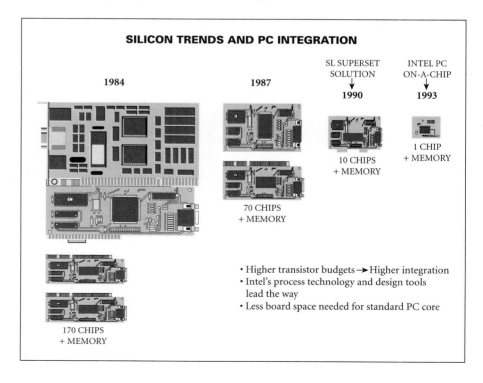

SILICON TRENDS AND PC INTEGRATION

1984   1987   SL SUPERSET SOLUTION ↓ 1990   INTEL PC ON-A-CHIP ↓ 1993

10 CHIPS + MEMORY   1 CHIP + MEMORY

70 CHIPS + MEMORY

170 CHIPS + MEMORY

• Higher transistor budgets → Higher integration
• Intel's process technology and design tools lead the way
• Less board space needed for standard PC core

compatibility with the thousands of programs already developed for the PC market. [Microsoft was the sole source for the IBM PC operating system, MS-DOS. In conjunction with IBM, Microsoft also developed a new operating system, OS/2, which took advantage of the 286 and 386's multitasking features, while maintaining upward compatibility.] (See Exhibit 8 for forecasts.)

The engineering workstation market—characterized by high-performance graphics and computation ability—was pioneered by Sun Microsystems. In some of its earlier systems, Sun used the Intel 386 chip, but instead of MS-DOS chose the UNIX operating system. [Unlike MS-DOS, the UNIX operating system is capable of taking advantage of the multiprocessing feature of the 386. In addition, UNIX is an "open" program and available from multiple sources—although many of the versions are not compatible.]

Sun Microsystems' president, Scott McNealy, believed that Intel was charging too much for its processor, so he initiated the development* of a new processor using a competing architecture called RISC (reduced instruction set computer).** Following a strategy of "open" standards,

McNealy made the Sun RISC chip design (SPARC) available to his competitors. In addition to the SPARC chip, several other RISC chips appeared from MIPS and Motorola, capable of supporting some version of the UNIX operating system environment. While RISC microprocessors were simpler than CISCs, the system logic that surrounds the RISC microprocessor is more complex; all that RISC does is to transfer system complexity from the microprocessor to the system logic. RISC was far behind CISC on the learning curve. In 1990, Intel shipped over 8 million 32-bit CISC microprocessors, while the 10 RISC suppliers combined shipped no more than 200,000 units.[15]

THE i860 STORY

Intel's initial response to RISC architecture was to call it "the technology of the have nots." As several companies announced new RISC chips, Intel developed an internal jargon referring to the competitor chips as YARPs, or "yet another RISC processor."

Yet, within the Intel design organization, a designer named Les Kohn had been trying for several years to initiate a RISC program:

> It was very difficult to see from Intel's perspective on the x86 architecture [that RISC had some definite technical advantages]. Between 1982 and 1986, I made several proposals for RISC projects through the Intel product planning system, but I wasn't successful. RISC was not an existing business, people were not convinced that the market was there, and the design would have been way too big to do in a skunkworks.

---

*While Sun designed the chip, it did not have chip-making expertise and farmed out the actual manufacturing of the chip to several silicon foundries.

**The RISC actually preceded the CISC architecture. Instructions are the lowest-level commands a microprocessor responds to (such as "retrieve from memory" or "compare two numbers"). CISC microprocessors support between 100 and 150 instructions while RISC chips support 70 to 80. As a result of supporting few instructions, RISC chips have superior performance over a narrow range of tasks and can be optimized for a specific purpose. Through combinations of the reduced instruction set, the RISC architecture can be made to duplicate the more complex instructions of a CISC chip, but at a performance penalty.

EXHIBIT 8
INTEL X86-COMPATIBLE COMPUTERS WILL DOMINATE PCs, WORKSTATIONS, MIDRANGE, AND EVENTUALLY ALL COMPUTING
Source: Intel company records.

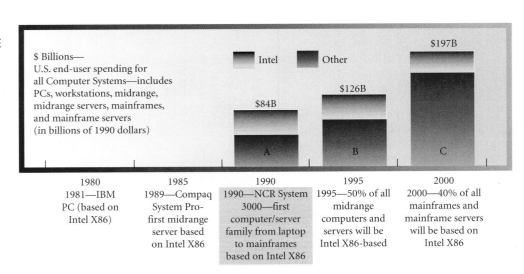

$ Billions— U.S. end-user spending for all Computer Systems—includes PCs, workstations, midrange, midrange servers, mainframes, and mainframe servers (in billions of 1990 dollars)

1980	1985	1990	1995	2000
1981—IBM PC (based on Intel X86)	1989—Compaq System Pro-first midrange server based on Intel X86	1990—NCR System 3000—first computer/server family from laptop to mainframes based on Intel X86	1995—50% of all midrange computers and servers will be Intel X86-based	2000—40% of all mainframes and mainframe servers will be based on Intel X86

A. 41% Intel X86-based
B. 64% Intel X86-based
C. 85% of U.S. end-user spending will be for Intel X86-based computer systems

In 1986, I saw that our next generation processors would have 1 million transistor chips, and I started working on the idea of a RISC-based processor that would take full advantage of that technology. We drafted a product requirement document that outlined market size, pricing, and rough development cost. We positioned it as a coprocessor to the 80486 and made sure that it could be justified on that basis. We designed it as a stand-alone processor, but made it very useful as an accessory to the 486. We made sure it was very different from the x86 family so that there would be no question in the customer's mind of which product to use. The really fortuitous part came when presentations to several large customers generated a lot of positive feedback to senior management. There was also a whole group of customers who did not previously talk to Intel because they were more interested in performance than compatibility. 3D graphics, workstation, and minicomputer accounts all got very interested. In the end, it looked like the 860 would generate a whole new business for Intel.

Kohn's new chip has a 64-bit architecture with floating point and integer processing as well as enhanced graphics capability. The chip utilized design concepts found in supercomputers, and its design team of 50 wore tee shirts with a miniaturized CRAY supercomputer icon resting on a chip. But top management saw it as a coprocessor for the 486. Kohn commented on Intel's unique position to produce a 1 million transistor RISC chip:

Intel has historically led the industry in having the most transistors—at least in terms of widely used, commercial microprocessors. To do it on the schedule we did required a very close working relationship between technology development and the design teams.

In a lot of cases, RISC companies worked with external vendors for the fabrication of parts so they either had to design for the lowest common denominator of those technologies or they wouldn't necessarily get access to the most advanced technology.

Another factor was the design tools. Intel made a strategic decision to invest in advanced CAD tools. Our new database manager allowed us to manage the several thousand files that go into this chip. It made sure that people didn't make changes that got lost or that two different people weren't making changes to the same file at the same time. We also used a new generation of workstation-based circuit design that was very graphic, allowing the engineers to work directly with schematics and display results graphically.

In February 1989, Intel announced the 860 not as a coprocessor, but rather as a stand-alone RISC processor. Top management decided to join the RISC processor race. Grove said:

We had our own marketing story for the chip, but our customers changed it. They said, "Listen, this isn't just a coprocessor chip. This could be the central processor of a supertechnical workstation." Occasional sarcastic jibes aside, we were in

no position now to dump on RISC as a technology. Our chip showed what the real potential of RISC was.[16]

SYSTEMS BUSINESS

In 1985 Les Vadasz became senior vice president and general manager of the Intel Systems Business, which by 1990 was expected to contribute over $1 billion to sales. Originally, the Systems Business provided technology to enable the growth of Intel's semiconductor business. For example, development systems, which allowed customers to design their own systems and to write software for microprocessor applications, provided a significant portion or revenue. Vadasz said:

We were providing customers multiple choices at different levels of integration. If they wanted microprocessors or board-level products, we could provide either. Now we are more like an independent business. We make a range of products: PC-compatibles for OEMs, mainframes through a joint venture, and even parallel supercomputers based on the 386 and 860 processors. We also make PC enhancement boards and sell them through retail channels.

We have organized around segmented strategies for each market. We must recognize that each of our segments requires a different business structure. For example, supercomputers and PCs require entirely different manufacturing disciplines. The PC enhancement business requires a retail understanding, its own sales force, a different kind of documentation, and, of course, its own product engineering. Each new capability can then be deployed into other areas. But you must exercise discipline in how you use your capabilities.

Several of the businesses started as ventures in the Intel Development Organization (IDO), which Vadasz also headed. Vadasz continued:

IDO looks a bit like an internal venture capital fund. It is funded by the corporation and has its own miniboard of Gordon Moore, Bob Reed, and me. It serves to isolate a new idea from the quarterly cycles of Intel's business. We create an isolated investment unit and see how it does. These units are managed with an iron hand, but on their own merits.

The guiding question at Intel is: Where can we add intellectual value? Some semiconductor people used to grow crystal ingots [raw material for semiconductors], but they found they could not add value there. Others, specializing in crystal growth, became more effective suppliers. DRAMs were like that, the lowest value added component in the chain always tends to spread, so you get perfect competition in that area.

Some industry observers believed Intel's Systems Business represented a bold strategy which might alienate its customers. Not only did Intel have a sole source position, it could become a potential competitor to some of its customers—companies like Compaq, Tandy, or Olivetti.

ISSUES FOR THE 1990s

In reviewing the recent history of the company, Mr. Grove wondered how to top the "awesome new $3 billion Intel." Among the U.S. semiconductor companies, Intel was clearly a leading performer in 1990, but what steps would be necessary to continue that performance?

In particular, Grove wondered about the future role of the relatively low-margin EPROMs in what was now "the microprocessor company." Should Intel get out of EPROMs to free resources for microprocessors, or should they be continued? This was particularly important in light of the potential future of Flash. He also questioned the role of RISC and the implications of Intel's endorsement of that technology. Was RISC a distortion of Intel's microprocessor strategy or part of it? What options could Intel pursue? Finally, he wondered what larger environmental forces might help or inhibit Intel in sustaining its current growth and profitability throughout the 1990s.

The National Bicycle Industrial Company: Implementing a Strategy of Mass-Customization

A group of senior managers, including the Managing Director of the National Bicycle Industrial Co. (NBIC), a subsidiary of Japanese industrial giant Matsushita, were reflecting upon the success of their firm over the last few years. NBIC is a leading manufacturer of bicycles. In 1987, the firm introduced the most innovative and revolutionary production system the Japanese bicycle industry had ever seen. The system, named the *Panasonic Order System* (POS), employed state-of-the-art techniques in bicycle production to manufacture 'custom-made' bicycles. Using robots, computers, and skilled workers, the system blends human skills and advanced manufacturing automation to allow potential customers to custom-order bicycles. When ordering a custom-made bicycle, customers can choose from about eight million possible variations based on model type, color, frame sizes, and other features. Using this system the firm delivers a high-quality "crafted" bicycle within two weeks of the customer's order.

With the introduction of POS the firm gained national and international attention and became the envy of the industry. In 1992, General Motors Corporation, the world's largest manufacturing firm, sent a team of executives to study the firm's "mass-customization" strategy and its implementation through the POS.[1]

Despite the firm's growing recognition, the senior management group was considering changes in the firm's mass-customization strategy. To explore what changes were required by senior management, and the questions they might raise, this case looks at the Japanese bicycle industry, NBIC's strategy and position within that industry, and the nature of issues facing the company during mid-1993.

THE JAPANESE BICYCLE INDUSTRY

The Japanese bicycle industry's history dates from the Meiji restoration period, which began around 1868. It was during this period that European-styled bicycles were first introduced into Japan. During the Meiji restoration, Japan's governing body and its government began modeling the Japanese political system after Western governments. The State, to end its isolation from the rest of the world, encouraged foreigners to visit Japan.

As foreigners arrived in Japan, they brought with them their bicycles. When these bicycles needed repairs, they sought the assistance of hunting gun repair shops, established during the earlier Tokugawa period. These small shops, in and around the cities like Tokyo and Osaka,

This case was prepared by Assistant Professor Suresh Kotha of the Stern School of Business, NYU while visiting at IUJ and research assistant Andrew Fried of IUJ, as the basis for class discussion rather than to illustrate either effective or ineffective handling of an administrative situation. Some field research was provided in the early stages of the project by Ken Zekavat. Copyright © 1993 Suresh Kotha.

began to fix bicycles. Skills acquired with pipes and screws to produce guns during the Tokugawa period enabled shop owners to apply their talents to service and repair bicycles. Over time these small repair shops began to produce bicycles modeled after European bicycles. The first domestic bicycle frame was manufactured in 1889, exactly 29 years after the invention of the bicycle by Pierre Michaux in France. Slowly, this gave rise to the Japanese bicycle industry (JETO 1990).

Bicycle demand in Japan grew rapidly in the early 1970s due to the robust growth in the economy and the resulting strong consumer demand. Several environmental changes including the growth of suburban residential areas and the building of large shopping areas in the periphery of cities contributed to an increase in bicycle demand. The bicycles were mainly for commuting to railway stations and shopping areas and back. Additionally, the introduction of the small or "miniwheel" that coincided with the popularity of the "miniskirt trend" vastly improved women's appeal for bicycles.[2] Women became an important market segment and the industry introduced a greater variety of colors and models to appeal to this segment. The growing demand resulted in bicycle standardization and the adoption of mass production systems by Japanese manufacturers.

The 1973 "oil shock" had a chilling effect on Japan, and bicycle production dropped over 18 percent to 7.6 million. The industry hoped that demand for bicycles would develop (in lieu of automobile purchases) under a 1973 energy savings plan, but this trend didn't develop and bicycle demand plateaued around 7 million units. Exhibit 1 shows the production, shipment, exports and imports of bicycles in Japan for a 10-year period starting in 1982. The domestic production and shipment of bicycles has remained somewhat stable throughout the late 1980s and early 1990s. Exports of Japanese bicycles have gradually declined as the Japanese yen has increased in strength and imports into Japan from neighboring Taiwan and China have grown steadily during this period. Exhibit 2 shows bicycle production for the different segments in Japan.

MANUFACTURERS AND ASSEMBLERS

Bicycle producers in Japan are subdivided by the industry into two groups: manufacturers and assemblers. The distinction between these two types lies mainly in (a) the degree of backward vertical integration achieved by the firms that belong to each group, and (b) the level of final product assembly carried out before shipment by firms in each group. For example, the manufacturers produce their own bicycle frames and forks, the two critical structural components of the bicycle, and purchase the remaining components from parts suppliers. Also, the bicycles produced by this group were approximately 70 percent assembled at the time of shipment to wholesalers. The assemblers purchase all their components from outside parts suppliers and only assemble the bicycles as their name denotes. Historically, manufacturers accounted for most bicycles produced. Starting in the 1980s, the shipment of bicycles between the manufacturers and assemblers was evenly split with each accounting for approximately 50 percent of the industry.

In 1992, the Japanese bicycle industry consisted of over 80 bicycle manufacturers and hundreds of parts suppliers. The top five manufacturing firms were Bridgestone, National, Miyata, Maruishi, and Nichibei Fuji. Bridgestone Cycle Co. was the industry leader with 18 percent of the domestic market. Bridgestone was followed by NBIC and Miyata, with nine percent and eight percent of the market respectively. The top five assemblers were Yokota, Deki,

EXHIBIT 1
BICYCLE DEMAND IN JAPAN 1982–1992
(units, 000s)

YEAR	PRODUCTION	SHIPMENT (1)	EXPORT (2)	IMPORT (3)	TOTAL DEMAND (1−2+3)
1982	6,532	6,624	674	13	5,963
1983	7,039	6,996	864	6	6,138
1984	6,810	6,839	856	28	6,011
1985	6,785	6,808	888	40	5,960
1986	6,583	6,638	682	158	6,114
1987	7,379	7,742	416	580	7,636
1988	7,509	7,624	325	900	8,119
1989	7,792	7,881	200	857	8,538
1990	7,969	8,033	226	667	8,474
1991	7,448	7,416	203	940	8,153

Source: Japan Bicycle Manufacturer's Association.

EXHIBIT 2
BICYCLE PRODUCTION
BY TYPE
(000s units)

	1984	1985	1986	1987	1988	1989	1990	1991
Roadsters	57	42	37	38	35	38	35	27
Light cycles	916	1017	1339	2296	2893	3486	3694	3511
Sports cycles	1465	1304	999	883	761	562	501	405
Juvenile cycles	756	795	726	770	772	770	788	747
Children*	566	565	542	546	555	520	527	477
Mini cycles	2871	2753	2687	2570	2192	2065	1822	1426
Others**	181	308	254	275	301	350	602	855

Source: Japan Bicycle Promotion Institute.
*Geared towards preschool children with 12"–16" wheels. The standard size bicycle had wheels which were 26 or 27 inches.
**Includes adults' tricycles, motorcross bikes, mountain bikes, high-risers, heavy weight load-carrying bicycles, track racing bikes, bicycles for acrobatics, etc.

Hodaka, Saimoto and Wani. Yokota led the group of assemblers with nine percent of the market. Deki and Hodaka were next with eight percent and seven percent of the market respectively. Together the top five members of each group accounted for over 75 percent of bicycles produced in Japan (see Exhibit 3).

PARTS SUPPLIERS

In 1992, there were approximately 327 firms that produced individual parts and related items. Compared to bicycle producers, parts supplier firms were in the business of producing standardized parts in large volume and were more automated than complete bicycle producers.

In 1992, Shimano was the largest supplier of bicycle parts commanding a dominant market share. The other major parts suppliers were Araya, Sakae, and Cat Eye. Unlike the Japanese automobile industry, where exclusive suppliers are the norm, bicycle parts suppliers sold components to multiple firms. The growing supply of bicycle parts from Southeast Asian countries made it very difficult for Japanese suppliers to compete in labor-intensive segments of the industry such as bicycle chains, pedals and wheels. To remain competitive some suppliers began moving their production facilities to South East Asian countries where labor costs were lower than in Japan. Others entered into joint ventures with parts suppliers from Taiwan and China.

EXHIBIT 3
MARKET SHARE OF
MAJOR BICYCLE
PRODUCERS

COMPANIES	1992 PRODUCTION (UNITS, 000)	MARKET SHARE	1993 PRODUCTION (EST.)
Top five manufacturers			
Bridgestone	1400	18%	1450
National	700	9%	700
Miyata	640	8%	610
Maruishi	310	4%	310
Nichibei Fuji	200	3%	200
	3250	43%	3270
Top five assemblers			
Yokota	710	9%	750
Deki	630	8%	700
Hodaka	530	7%	570
Saimoto	400	5%	400
Wani	290	4%	290
	2560	34%	2710

Source: Cycle Press, No. 76, February, 1993.

DISTRIBUTION

Bicycles in Japan were distributed through wholesalers, retailers, supermarkets, and department stores.[3] There were approximately 1,600 wholesales and about 38,000 retailers in 1990. While many wholesalers were subsidiaries of the large manufacturers such as Bridgestone, NBIC and others, retail outlets for the most part were small "mom and pop stores." Approximately 60 percent of bicycles sold were transferred from wholesalers to retailers and the remaining were distributed through supermarkets and department stores located throughout Japan. In the past large company owned wholesalers dominated the distribution of bicycles. Recently, large supermarket chains and household superstores or 'home centers' have started to sell bicycles. According to industry experts, the growing number of such outlets was one important reason for the steady rise in imported bicycles (see Exhibit 4).

COMPANY BACKGROUND

NBIC was Japan's second largest manufacturer of bicycles in 1992 with sales reaching about ¥20 billion. The firm marketed bicycles under three different brand names, Panasonic, National and Hikari. NBIC targeted each brand at a unique market segment, and together the three brands covered the wide spectrum of bicycles sold in Japan. They ranged from high quality, high price sports and fashion bicycles (Panasonic) to bicycles that were used primarily for transportation from home to the nearest train station or supermarket and back (Hikari). National and Hikari brands together constituted the bulk of NBIC's production and sales. Panasonic, the company's more expensive line, accounted for a little less than 20 percent of total production in 1992.

NBIC began to manufacture and sell bicycles in 1952. At first growth in sales was slow, but picked up rapidly within a few years after the firm's inception. Between 1952 and 1965, the firm produced almost a million bicycles. In 1965, due to ever increasing demand the firm completed the construction of a new factory in Kashihara city on the outskirts of Osaka, and moved its operations to this factory (see Appendix A for a brief outline of the company history). At Kashihara city the firm had two factories located next to each other. NBIC's management called them the mass production factory and custom-factory. The custom-factory, initially conceptualized as a pilot plant, was built in 1987.

In 1992 according to published estimates, the firm produced a combined total of 700,000 bicycles in these two

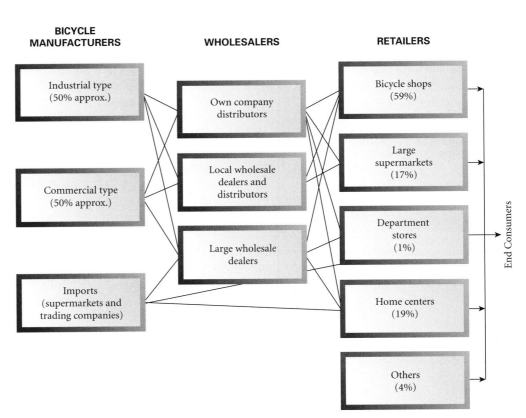

EXHIBIT 4
THE JAPANESE
BICYCLE DISTRIBUTION
SYSTEM—1992

BICYCLE MANUFACTURERS

Industrial type (50% approx.)

Commercial type (50% approx.)

Imports (supermarkets and trading companies)

WHOLESALERS

Own company distributors

Local wholesale dealers and distributors

Large wholesale dealers

RETAILERS

Bicycle shops (59%)

Large supermarkets (17%)

Department stores (1%)

Home centers (19%)

Others (4%)

End Consumers

factories. Over 90 percent of these were produced in the mass production factory and shipped to Matsushita's sales subsidiaries. High-end Panasonic bicycles were produced in the custom-factory and shipped to dealers to be delivered to individual customers. While most line workers worked at the mass production factory, a few of NBIC's best skilled workers produced bicycles at the custom-factory. Operating on a single-shift basis throughout the year, they produced a small fraction of the firm's production at this factory.

In early 1993, the firm employed 470 people with a little over 66 percent classified as direct or line workers, and the rest as indirect workers. A little over 50 percent of indirect workers were in the production engineering and design departments of the firm. The line workers belonged to the company union and actively participated in "quality circle" programs. Workers met once a month, as part of these programs, to discuss quality and safety issues. Additionally, management periodically tested line workers and ranked them according to their skill level. The highest skilled workers were given the opportunity to work at the custom-factory where wages were higher.

NBIC "sold" its bicycles to 10 sales companies. These sales companies distributed bicycles to approximately 9000 retailers located throughout Japan that were part of the Matsushita group. Regular monthly meetings were held between management at NBIC and the sales companies to discuss sales trends and manufacturing concerns.

MASS-CUSTOMIZATION STRATEGY

THE GENESIS

The original idea for making custom-made bicycles came from the firm's President. The firm's Managing Director, who headed the team that implemented the idea, recollected:

> It all started when our President visited a famous department store in Osaka. He noticed that women could custom order dresses that were then delivered by the store in two weeks. He wondered if it was possible for National to produce bicycles in this way. When we were on a trip to the US, he mentioned this idea. At that time we were used to making a few specially designed bicycles for some customers, like Olympic racers, but offering a custom-made bicycle to everyone was a different matter altogether.

Within a few days after their return, the Managing Director began giving serious thought to the idea mentioned by the firm's President. The bicycle industry was in the doldrums, demand was sluggish and the average unit price the customer was willing to pay for a 'standard' bicycle was drop-

ping (see Exhibit 5). According to a report in the *Far East Economic Review* (December 7, 1989):

> Although some Japanese component makers are riding high on the mountain bike boom, the rest of the Japanese bicycle industry is in the doldrums. The stronger yen has hurt exports of Japanese-made bicycles because of their higher cost overseas. Today, bicycle assembly for the US and European markets is centered in Taiwan, dominated by such aggressive new makers as Giant, Merida, and Fairy.

Though the average price of a sporting bicycle was increasing, this segment was not growing as anticipated by many large producers. It was under these conditions that the managing director with other senior managers at NBIC decided to change the firm's strategy by trying something bold. According to one senior manager:

> We were manufacturing bicycles in lot sizes greater than 50 in our factory. Now we were challenged by our President to produce bicycles in lot sizes of one. More importantly, the orders received were to be completed and delivered within two weeks. We not only had to convince ourselves that this was possible, but we had to convince our design people, our manufacturing people and line workers that this was a *good* and *feasible* idea.

Initally, not everyone at NBIC was unanimous in their support for this revolutionary idea. Some senior members at NBIC felt that it would require a large investment and also entailed a tremendous risk for the firm. They asked: What if NBIC failed in this attempt? Some also argued that the market for the sports bicycle in Japan was shrinking, though admittedly at a slower pace when compared to other segments (see Exhibit 2). Further, some industry analysts outside the firm said that such a strategy would be impossible to develop and implement. As one senior manager speaking for his colleagues recollected:

> We also had our own doubts during those early days, though we never mentioned this to our president or workers because we were committed to at least trying to see if this project would work. However, in our mind we gave it a 50 percent chance of success.

According to the Managing Director, the firm had only a few broad objectives when it started on the road to customization. First, the firm wanted to double the amount of high value-added products the firm sold by accommodating the *individual* needs of the customer. Second, NBIC wanted to devise a "system" of production and delivery that clearly differentiated its high-end Panasonic brand from competitor products, and also meet the growing need for variety in the marketplace. During the late 1980s, as the demand for bicycles plateaued, there was increasing competition among the manufacturers. To gain market share,

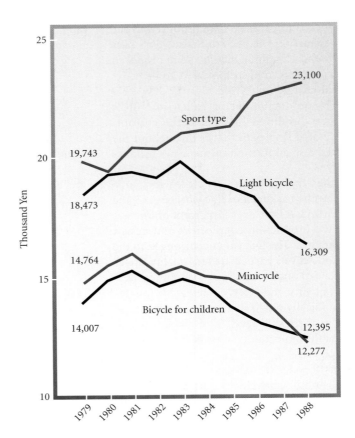

firms introduced many new model types. For example, NBIC offered over 250 different model types during 1987, and within each model type customers had a choice of color and other options. Management changed about 80 percent of models yearly. Similarly, not to be outdone, the industry's largest producer offered over 300 models during the same period.

Within a few weeks of its inception, the Managing Director assembled a project team that consisted of senior members of his management team, a designer, a few process engineers and some highly skilled, experienced line workers. Discussing the implementation of the project he fondly recalls:

> We worked long hours. We proposed and debated many new ideas for days. We started with a few people, but as the project began to progress, more people were added. Within a few weeks we established a pilot plant in a large empty warehouse next to the factory. Still, numerous issues had to be addressed and solved, but as time went on we were convinced that the project was doable. We knew we had the capability, because many of us had spent most of our professional lives making bicycles.

Motivated by the relentless effort of their leader, the team successfully tackled one concern after another to complete the project in a mere four months. By July 1987, the team converted the pilot plant to one that was fully operational and running. It was seven months since the firm's President visited the department store in Osaka.

The firm in June 1987 unveiled its strategy to Japan's bicycle industry to the dismay and surprise of its major competitors. The new system they had devised was aptly named the *Panasonic Ordering System.*

THE PANASONIC ORDERING SYSTEM (POS)

THE ORDER PROCESS

A customer ready to order a high-end bicycle walked into a Panasonic bicycle dealer equipped for POS and the dealer, using a unique measuring and gauging machine, noted the exact physical measurements of the customer including the size of the frame, the length of seat post, the position of the handle bar, and the extension of the handle bar stem. The customer was allowed to select the model type, the color scheme, and other features for their bicycle. Details on the number of models, colors and options that were available are provided in Exhibit 6. When completed, the dealer immediately sent this information to the control room of the custom-made factory via facsimile transmission.

Once the facsimile order form was received in the master control room of the custom-factory, the receiving atten-

EXHIBIT 6 POS SYSTEM SELECTION OF MODELS
AVAILABLE (Japan)

	TYPE	NO. OF MODELS
Bicycles	Road	10
	Triathlon	5
	Time Trial	3
	ATB	2
	Track	1
Frame	Road & Triathlon	4
	Time Trial	—
	ATB	—
	Track	1
	Frame Color	Pattern
	1 Color	15
	2 Colors	40
	3 Colors	15

Source: NBIC Company Records.

dant immediately entered the information into the firm's host computer to register and control the customer's order specifications. The host computer then assigned each order a unique bar code label. This label, which traveled with the evolving bicycle, instructed and controlled each stage of manufacturing operation. At various stages in the process, line workers accessed the customer's unique requirement using the bar code label and a scanner. This information, displayed on a CRT terminal at each station, was fed directly to the computer controlled machines that were part of a local area computer network. Using such information, workers at each station performed the required sequence of operations assisted by machines. Exhibit 7 provides an overview of the entire manufacturing process used by NBIC, and Exhibit 8 provides an illustration of the POS factory layout.

THE MANUFACTURING PROCESS

At the heart of the POS lay the design and manufacturing capabilities of NBIC. Almost all the machines used in the manufacturing process were developed and built exclusively for use in the custom-factory. A significant portion of this development work was carried out by the firm's own design and process engineers with assistance from the parent company's engineering staff. While the computer hardware used in POS was purchased from outside vendors, much of the software employed to control and monitor the system was developed and written internally by NBIC's software engineers.

The production process began when the Computer-Aided Design (CAD) system, located in the control room, scanned the bar code label to access information on the customer's order. A "blue print" of the bicycle's frame and other structural details was produced in about three minutes.[4] Information from the CAD system was automatically sent to the raw material supplies area located next to the control room. Here small lights, placed in front of the raw material bins, were automatically lit based on the customer's specifications. The materials from the bins that were lit were then picked up by a worker and sent to the factory.

Frame and front fork production

The first step on the factory floor involved the cutting of tubes that formed the frame of the bicycle. Customer specifications were transferred to the computer assisted "tube cutting" machine. This machine then automatically sized and held the tubes in place while a worker cut them using a rotary saw. The surfaces where two tubes were to be welded together were then "arch" cut, using a special machine. According to the factory manager, this process improved the rigidity of the frame and precision of the joints during the brazing process. Small parts, such as brake guides, were then carefully brazed to the frame by a skilled worker.

The tubes were then carried to the "front triangle assembly" machine. This machine, using special jigs and other features, automatically aligned and held the tubes together, while they were *tack* welded to form the front triangle of the frame. The joints of the frame were then *brazed* by automatic brazing machines. Following this process, a worker using the "rear fork assembly machine" *tack* welded the chain stay hanger section, the seat stay and the seat lug section. These were then brazed to the frame. These processes brought together the front and rear triangle sections to complete the bicycle frame. According to NBIC's process engineers, the automated machines used in the brazing process incorporated optical sensors capable of detecting temperature differences to +/− one percent. Such precision was required to ensure metal integrity, and to prevent the warping of the tubes during the process.

The final step involved the use of a 'slitting and reaming' machine. In this process the seat lug, attached earlier, was slit and the inside of the seat tube reamed. This process ensured that the seat pillar could be adjusted smoothly and fixed firmly. The time taken to cut, braze and assemble the frame was about 25 minutes.

The tubes that formed the front fork of the bicycle were cut and assembled using processes similar to that of the frame.

Quality check

The completed frame and fork were then placed on a three-dimensional automatic measuring machine, designed by the firm's parent company engineers. This machine checked

EXHIBIT 7 THE PRODUCTION PROCESS AT THE CUSTOM-FACTORY

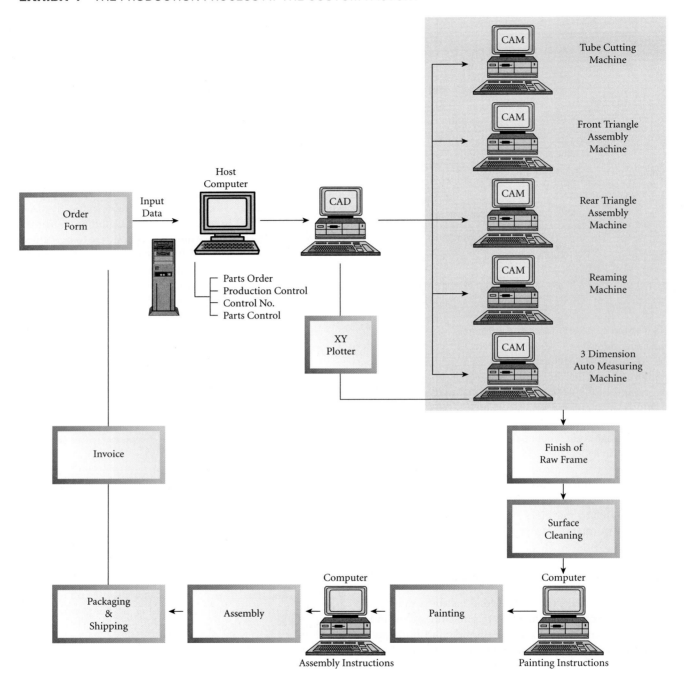

EXHIBIT 8
LAYOUT OF THE POS/PICS FACTORY

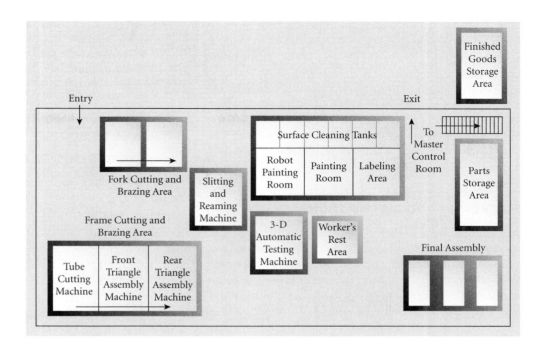

the actual measurements of the assembled frame and fork against the customer's original specification stored in the host computer's memory banks. Small variations, if any, were detected and displayed on a CRT terminal or plotted using the attached plotter. This process was completed in less than 60 seconds.

Painting
Both completed frame and front fork were then moved by overhead conveyors to the surface cleaning area and immersed in special solutions. This process prevented the early rusting of the frame and improved the ability of the subsequent paint to adhere more uniformly to the surfaces. The cleaning process took about 10 to 15 minutes to complete. The bicycle frame and front fork were then transferred to a 'preliminary' painting room to be automatically painted by a robot. Again, the robot received its instructions from the factory's host computer via the bar code label. According to the factory manager, NBIC was the first bicycle manufacturer to introduce a robot in the painting process for bicycles.

Following this, two skilled workers completed the "final" by painting the "hard-to-reach" areas using electrostatic spray guns. Finishing touches and customer's "special" painting instructions were completed by the workers.

Labeling and engraving process
This process involved printing or engraving the customer's name on the bicycle frame or handle bar stem. A skilled worker, using a silk screen process, printed the customer's

name and transferred it on to the frame. Or alternatively, a name engraving machine engraved the name of the customer on the handle stem. With the completion of this process, the frame was ready for the final assembly process.

Final assembly and shipping
The final assembly involved the mating of the completed frame and fork with the appropriate wheels, chain, gears, brakes, tires and other components that constitute a complete bicycle. During this process the "derailleur" adjustment and the "rotation" adjustment of the bearing section were completed. Also, the seat pillar and seat lug section were checked and adjusted according to customer specifications. Each bicycle was fully assembled and tested by a single skilled craftsman. The assembly process was performed in any one of the three main assembly stations and took about 30 minutes. The completed bicycle was then boxed and sent to a holding area, outside the factory, to be picked up for delivery. They were generally shipped the same day.

The entire manufacturing and assembly time required to complete a single customer order was approximately 150 minutes. In 1989, the factory employing 18 workers (15 workers were employed in 1987) had the capability to make about 60 custom-order bicycles daily. It received orders for approximately 12,000 bicycles, an increase of 20 percent over the previous two years. A significant portion of these orders were from customers in Japan.

A year after the introduction of the POS, the company unveiled a new system named Panasonic Individual Customer System (PICS). The purpose of PICS was to offer custom-made bicycles to customers in overseas markets, especially in countries like Australia, the US and Germany. PICS used the same customized manufacturing technology as the POS, but offered customers the choice of much larger frame sizes more suitable to western customers. The time taken from order to delivery was increased from two weeks to three weeks under PICS.

MARKETING AND DISTRIBUTION

According to General Manager of Sales at NBIC, customer service, "appropriate" pricing, and extensive communication were all an integral part in NBIC's mass-customization strategy. Domestic customers were guaranteed a delivery time of two weeks, not a day more but also not a day less. He pointed out that: "We could have made the time shorter, but we want people to feel excited about waiting for something special." According to a manager at the factory, custom-made Panasonic bicycles were priced only about 20 to 30 percent higher (depending on the particular model and features selected) when compared to a "comparable" bicycle produced at the mass production factory.

Under the POS, it was the factory that was given the responsibility to communicate directly with customers. Shortly after the factory received the customer's order, a personalized computer generated drawing of the bicycle was mailed with a note thanking the customer for choosing the POS. This was followed up with a second personal note, three months later, inquiring about the customer's satisfaction with his or her bicycle. Finally, a "bicycle birthday card" was sent commemorating the first anniversary of the bicycle.

According to the General Manager in-charge of sales, dealership selection played an important role in pursuing their strategy. In early 1993, only about 15 percent of 9,000 domestic dealerships were part of the POS (see Exhibit 9). They explained the reasons for this:

We cannot afford to make mistakes. Mistakes can be very costly. It is important that customers don't lose confidence in our system. We have to be very careful in selecting knowledgeable and committed dealers so that they send us the correct information. We can't tolerate mistakes at any stage.

RESPONSE TO POS

COMPETITORS IMITATE NBIC

NBIC's strategy of offering a truly custom-made bicycle surprised all its major competitors. Within months, the two other leading manufacturers of bicycles scrambled to develop and implement their version of mass customization. In a year, both offered their own "unique" versions of mass customization. But, they were unable to duplicate all aspects of NBIC's strategy as noted by a senior manager at Bridgestone in early 1993:

The trouble with this segment is that it is too small, perhaps 10,000 or more. It costs a lot of money to advertise for such a small segment. Since NBIC was the first firm to introduce this idea, they have established a strong image in the customer's mind. When you mention customization, the consumer only thinks of Panasonic. Also, National's parent company Matsushita is famous for its marketing savvy, and it is difficult for us to match them. We as a company have not paid much attention to this segment. I expect we will in the future, because we too want to be known for our innovativeness.

According to a knowledgeable source in the industry, NIBC was the only company to have successfully mastered the art of mass customization, and that competitors were unable to offer the same degree of variety NBIC offered. Unlike NBIC, leading competitors simply increased the inventory of frames types and model sizes they carried to accommodate the variety demanded by its customers. According to the Managing Director:

One of our competitive advantages is that we are located in Osaka close to all the major parts suppliers. Frequency and reliability of parts delivery from our suppliers has helped us

EXHIBIT 9
NBIC'S DISTRIBUTION SYSTEM

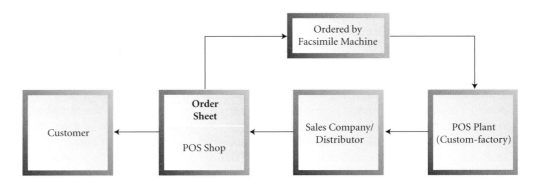

'truly' custom build bicycles. There is little need to hold large inventories of finished frames and other parts unlike others outside the Kansai region.

EXTENSIVE MEDIA COVERAGE

Soon after the announcement of the POS, journalists following this industry began expounding on its revolutionary nature. These Japanese stories were soon picked by foreign journalists who write about Japanese manufacturing practices. Within a span of two years, NBIC was featured in *Fortune*, the *New York Times*, and *Washington Post*. One leading American television network, ABC, featured the firm in its regular prime-time *World News Tonight* program hosted by its chief anchor person Peter Jennings. The German Public Television network produced a documentary for European audiences. Additionally, NBIC receives many requests from other manufacturing firms for information about its new system. Within a few years of the introduction of POS, *Fortune* magazine (Moffat 1990) noted that:

> The concept has so intrigued executives and engineers that they have been flocking from as far away as Italy to this factory in Kokubu, in western Japan, to study it. Big Japanese manufacturers of consumer goods are also taking note, hoping to improve their own production system. . . . [NBIC] built these one-of-a-kind models by replacing mass production with flexible manufacturing. The method is being employed all over Japan to shrink small-lot production jobs to lots of one.

While NBIC's customized bicycles manufactured under the POS system only accounted for two percent of total production, the effect of worldwide attention had a dramatic effect on the company's high-end segment.

COMPANY'S SALES INCREASE

Before the introduction of POS, NBIC's market share was languishing behind its two major competitors in the high end segment. Within a few years of the introduction of POS and PICS, the firm's total high-end (Panasonic) market share position improved dramatically. For the first time in its history, NBIC become the industry's second largest manufacturer of high-end bicycles (see Exhibit 10 and Exhibit 11).

Reflecting on the events of the last few years, members of the senior management at NBIC glowed with pride about the achievements of their firm. Despite the repeated attempts by competitors to offer customized bicycles, the "Panasonic" name was increasingly viewed as the only "truly" mass customized bicycle in Japan. The firm was now viewed as the leader and innovator in the industry. Still, this

EXHIBIT 10   PRODUCTION BY TOP FOUR MANUFACTURERS (units, 000s)

COMPANIES	1987	1992	1993 (ESTIMATE)
Bridgestone	1,330	1,400	1,450
National	754	700	700
Miyata	620	640	610
Maruishi	379	310	310

Source: Estimates published by *Cycle Press*, 1993.

EXHIBIT 11   NBIC "PANASONIC" BRAND GROWTH 1986–1992

	1986	1987	1992	FUTURE TARGET
Units (% of total production)	4%	7%	18%	—
Revenues (% of total sales)	10%	13%0	27%	50%

was not the time to rest on past laurels; there were some major concerns facing NBIC and the industry in 1993.

OUTLOOK FOR THE FUTURE

Total company sales in 1992 grew marginally by 1.2 percent, but exports of NBIC's Panasonic bicycles were down by over 50 percent. This significant decrease in exports was the result of many factors including: the aggressive export strategies of firms in Taiwan, China and other neighboring countries; the continued strengthening of the Japanese yen against the US dollar; the softening of the demand for bicycles in Europe and the United States; and the increased competition in overseas markets. The news on the domestic front was not very encouraging either. The sales of domestic bicycles had been stagnant for some time. Forecasts for 1993 indicated only modest overall growth. According to an industry source, the Japanese industry was steadily undergoing structural change. The assemblers were beginning to exploit the growing supply of less expensive bicycle parts from overseas, to the dismay of major manufacturers. According to early industry predictions for 1993, Yokota's share of the market was expected to grow even larger in 1993. And Deki, the second largest assembler, was expected to match NBIC in the production of bicycles (see Exhibit 3).

ROLE OF CUSTOMIZATION AT NBIC

In early 1993, given the domestic and international situation, senior managers were pondering the future role of mass customization at NBIC. The lessons and the manufacturing skills the firm had acquired in the custom factory were readily transferable to the mass production factory. Skilled workers from the custom factory were regularly used for training line workers in the larger mass production factory. Over the last few years, the mass production factory was undergoing slow, but significant changes. Lot sizes employed in production were steadily decreasing. Over the last few years lot sizes were reduced from 50 to a mere 20 in 1993.

Senior management were now examining the feasibility of turning the mass production factory into a custom-shop. The goal was to increase the revenues contributed by the high-end segment to 50 percent of total sales within the next five years. More importantly, its likely impact on the firm's overall strategy was unclear. Some managers were under the view that the size of this custom segment should not be nurtured to grow beyond the current size. The firm should maintain it as a small high-value niche market to maintain customer interest and high prices. Others argued for a strategy to increase the size of this segment.

APPENDIX A
THE HISTORY OF NATIONAL BICYCLE

1918	■ Matsushita Electric (Parent Company) was founded.
1952	■ Commencement of bicycle manufacturing and sales.
1956	■ Began manufacturing and selling racing bicycles.
1960	■ National Bicycle Factory established in Sakai city.
1965	■ Production of National Bicycle reached 1 million units.
	■ National Bicycle completed new factory in Kashihara city.
1967	■ Japanese National Bicycle racing team adopts bicycles for World Championships.
1971	■ Commencement of export of Panasonic bicycles to the United States.
1972	■ Japanese Olympic bicycle team adopts Panasonic bicycles for the Munich Olympics.
	■ Production total reaches 3 million.
1973	■ National Bicycle installed new automated assembly line.
1974	■ Gojyo National Bicycle Parts Co. was established (wheel assembly factory).
1979	■ Commencement of export to Europe, Canada, and Australia.
	■ Formation of the Panasonic Racing Team in the United States.
1980	■ Seven millionth bicycle produced.
1983	■ Eight millionth bicycle produced.
1985	■ Nine millionth bicycle produced.
1986	■ Adoption of "Panasonic" brand name for top-class racing bicycles in Japan.
1987	■ Unique "Panasonic Order System" initiated starting on June 1st—receives acclaim from both inside and outside the industry.
	■ Ten millionth bicycle produced.
1988	■ First orders received February 1st for "PICS" 3-week delivery order system for United States customers.

Source: NBIC Company Records.

NovaCare, Inc.

NovaCare was one of the largest and most rapidly growing national providers of contract rehabilitation services to health care institutions. Between 1988 and 1991, NovaCare had grown 37.5% per year to $151 million in revenues. It provided speech-language, occupational, and physical therapy to patients with physical disabilities principally resulting from stroke, degenerative neurological disorders, or orthopedic problems. In 1991, NovaCare had over 3,000 contracts to provide rehabilitation services in approximately 1,800 facilities in over 32 states (see Figure 1). Despite its outstanding successes, NovaCare faced several important strategic issues.

Chief among these was how to position itself in the rapidly changing, problem-ridden health care industry of the early 1990s. Second was how to develop and organize its professional staff to provide the most efficient, highest-quality care in the rehabilitation field. Third was how best to develop the information, control, and incentive systems necessary to achieve these goals. An important portion of these efforts would be the development of NovaNet, an information system designed to accelerate the collection of field operations, administrative, and billing data. NovaCare had just completed pilot testing of NovaNet, but the system had not achieved anticipated productivity results. Chief Executive Officer John Foster wondered whether NovaNet should be released to the field, developed further, or designed for other purposes. NovaNet could be a key element in the company's future strategy.

NOVACARE'S EARLY HISTORY

NovaCare began as a company named Inspeech, which coordinated a group of clinicians acting as entrepreneurs; each contracted independently and managed his or her own professional activities. Inspeech provided some common support services, financing, and professional management activities for which the clinicians were not specially trained. By 1985 Inspeech had become the largest speech rehabilitation practice in the country, with about 120 clinicians and $5 million in revenues. But Inspeech was operating in a crisis mode: the company had problems meeting its payroll, and its credit line was running out. Seeking further capital and management support, Inspeech sold out to Foster Management Company, a venture capital firm with about $130 million of capital under management. John Foster was the senior general partner of Foster Management Company (FMC).

After some initial excitement about the new ownership and the security its capital infusion gave, the clinicians' productivity suddenly plummeted. They began to question the motivation of the new management. They saw the FMC group as "businesspeople" concerned about profitability rather than as caregivers concerned about patient wellness. At this point, John Foster decided to take a more

Case Copyright © 1992 by James Brian Quinn.

Research assistants on this case were William Little and Patricia Higgins. The kind generosity and assistance of NovaCare, Inc., are gratefully acknowledged.

FIGURE 1
NOVACARE NETWORK

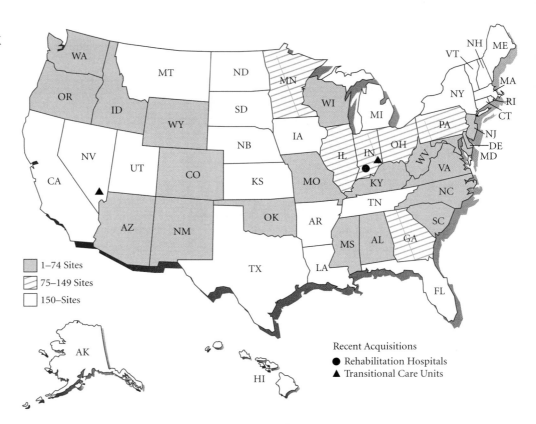

direct role as CEO, and his management team began emphasizing both patient care and the need for productivity. For 18 months, the new management team worked at rationalizing the business and made several complementary acquisitions with FMC funds. In November 1986, Inspeech made a public offering and raised about $40 million of equity.

Foster management had recognized that there was a cluster of rehabilitation therapies in nursing homes which might be offered on a complementary basis. The most closely related of these were speech, physical, and occupational therapy. In 1987, it diversified into the last two. Inspeech then grew quickly through market development and acquisition of other therapists' practices. Unfortunately, the company's rapid growth was accompanied by problems. John Foster said,

> We had very high levels of clinician turnover and a broad level of dissatisfaction throughout the company, partly reflecting indigestion from the 19 acquisitions we had made. Most health care professionals had never worked inside a large successful organization. They were, by tradition, sole practitioners. They were caregivers, and therefore highly sensitive, sensitized people. It was a very subtle thing to bring the concepts of business and productivity to a group of people who have been trained into a special mind-set, who have another lan-

guage, and who were so sensitive to quality of care. Their view generally was that productivity and quality were mutually exclusive.

The company reached a low point in early 1988; customers were confused about how to interface with the company's multiple services. Its stock price was dropping. The clinician staff was quitting, and the company was missing its performance goals. Hal Price, Divisional Vice President, commented about this period,

> It was very confusing. . . . We had different sets of standards, different benefits. . . . It was all a result of trying to bring different businesses into the company and not doing a smooth job of integrating them. Despite the fact that the financial results were not good, we knew that at a local facility level we were delivering good service.

In July 1988, the company reorganized into four geographic divisions each with a staff organization to support its business. Bud Locilento, Vice President of Human Resources, noted,

> We had been working from a highly centralized model of management. As we continued to grow very rapidly, we were losing our efficiency as an organization and made the decision to move to a more decentralized model. We would grow by

penetrating new market areas and then densifying existing markets. We would modify our structure to reflect that approach.

A NEW VISION

In addition to decentralizing significantly, the company undertook a process that was widely referred to as a "healing event," following its many acquisitions and rapid growth. In 1989, the company's name was changed to NovaCare to reflect its broader spectrum of rehabilitation services. It also undertook to develop and document a complete new set of vision and culture statements. These consisted of a Vision Statement, a Statement of Purpose, and a Statement of Beliefs. John Foster said, "These are integral to the culture of the company and the employee/manager relationship. These beliefs are an agreement between the corporation and the employee and create a report card that everyone can use to evaluate the performance of the company." NovaCare's Statement of Purpose begins with the words,

> We are fundamentally a clinical organization. All investment and organizational resources are intended to support the successful interaction of a clinician and the patient.
>
> The Direct Care Provider is the key person in our organization. All the corporate staff and resources exist to support the clinician in providing care to the patient. Line management supports the clinician in direct patient care. Technical experts, in turn, support line managers in providing the highest quality programs. This structure enables each Direct Care Provider to make the best clinical judgments.

The company's Vision Statement makes the following key points:

- "We apply our clinical expertise to benefit our patients through creative and progressive techniques.
- Our people are our most valuable asset. We are committed to the personal, professional, and career development of each individual employee. We are proud of what we do and dedicated to our company. We foster team work and create an environment conducive to productive communications among all disciplines.
- Our customers include national and local health care providers who share our goal of enhancing the patient's quality of life. In each community, our customers consider us a partner in providing the best possible care. Our reputation is based on our responsiveness, high standards, and effective systems of quality assurance. Our relationship is open and proactive.
- NovaCare is people committed to achieving excellence.
- Our ethical and performance standards require us to expend every effort to achieve the best possible results."

The company's Statement of Beliefs documented and detailed four major principles: (1) respect for the individual, (2) service to the customer, (3) pursuit of excellence, and (4) commitment to personal integrity. These were elaborated in a 16-page pamphlet that was widely distributed and constantly reinforced. John Foster said, "I have spent a great deal of time on the road and in the field articulating our purpose and beliefs. In time, the soul of the company will come to be less a matter of 'it feels good to be here' and more a matter of an articulated set of values and highly precise purposes." Larry Lane, Vice President of Regulatory Affairs, echoed the statements and added, "The Purpose and Beliefs Statements provide very strong language about making a difference, empowering clinical behavior, service, advocacy, training, and commitment to professional skills. These concepts are central to our success and the way we operate on a day-to-day basis."

PROFESSIONAL STAFFING ISSUES

Demand for clinical professionals was significantly greater than supply. In late 1991, the company employed approximately 2,300 full-time equivalent (FTE) therapists in the provision of patient care. At that same date, the company had open positions for 800 additional full-time therapists who, if hired, could generate revenues immediately. The company employed 23 recruiters in eight regions, representing the largest recruiting function in the rehabilitation services industry. It differentiated its professional opportunities by offering a career ladder which was typically unavailable in other institutional settings. This allowed a trained professional to progress through clinician, team leader, district clinical coordinator, district manager, area manager, clinical consultant, and possibly divisional vice president. In addition, clinicians might choose to do administrative activities like recruiting, sales, or quality assurance.

The company performed sophisticated national salary surveys to ensure that its compensation programs were competitive. It provided excellent benefits and incentive bonuses for clinical productivity that exceeded industry averages. It awarded incentive stock options—commencing at the district manager level—on the basis of performance. It also invested significantly in clinical and management training programs for its professionals. It offered clinical training at company and independent university seminars, it had developed an interactive self-study video library for clinicians to use at home, and an expanding management training curriculum was mandatory for all district and area managers. As a result of these and other employee relations programs, NovaCare had increased its number of new hires by 130% from fiscal 1988 to fiscal

1990 and had reduced its therapist turnover from 55% in 1988 to 27% in 1991. Its number of FTEs (excluding therapists from acquired companies) had increased at a 33% compound annual growth rate. Nevertheless, the shortage continued. John Foster estimated that each turnover cost the company $5,000 in recruiting costs and about $20,000 in lost revenue.

A THERAPISTS' COMPANY

A unique attribute of the company was that "NovaCare was a therapy company managed by therapists. It was a relatively young organization, hard charging, tending to be athletic, and 90% female," according to John Foster. He noted, "Clinicians tend to be high-caring, highly affiliative people. NovaCare employs many working mothers. This has important implications in terms of training, traveling, continuing education, and promotional opportunities." In 1991, the company was seeking clinicians in all of its fields, including:

- *Speech-language pathology*—the diagnosis and treatment of speech, language, swallowing, and hearing disorders usually arising from stroke, head injury, degenerative neurological disorders, or cancer. The speech-language pathologist is a licensed clinician with a baccalaureate degree and a clinically specific master's degree.
- *Occupational therapy*—improving muscular and neural responses to overcome patients' deficiencies for the basic activities of daily living. Occupational therapists were licensed professionals with a clinically specific baccalaureate degree; certified occupational therapy assistants (COTAS) could provide therapy under the supervision of an occupational therapist. Occupational therapy involved (1) restoring sensory functions, (2) teaching compensatory techniques to improve independence for daily living activities such as feeding, toileting, or bathing; and (3) designing, fabricating, and fitting assistive devices.
- *Physical therapy*—improves muscular and neural responses to enhance patients' physical strength and range of motion. The physical therapist was a licensed clinician with a clinically specific baccalaureate degree. Physical therapy comprised the application of stimuli like heat, cold, water, electricity, massage, or exercise.

NovaCare's revenue breakdown between the therapies is estimated in Table 1.

AN INVERTED ORGANIZATION

NovaCare refers to its organization as "inverted." The entire company exists to support the clinician in the delivery of service to the patient. John Foster considers himself "the lowest man in the inverted organization with everyone between me and the clinician in place solely to support the clinician. . . . This is a very important piece of understanding, not only for our clinical people to have in the field, but also for all of us as staff members to understand what role and relative importance we play in the organization." Vice President of Human Resources Bud Locilento says, "Our goal today is to get each clinician to have a high sense of empowerment, to make decisions for the patient, for the customer, and for their own well-being—instead of having them feel like they are swimming upstream against a pyramidical organization."

Running and maintaining an inverted organization required constant training, empowerment, and reinforcement. It was often confusing to hear executives referring to "my bosses," meaning those people closer to the field contact point, rather than the corporate center. Mr. Foster continued to try to find ways to get feedback or "instructions" from the field. He had established a Chairman's Council consisting of 15 to 20 people from around the entire country who met twice a year. These were representatives, clinical and managerial, from different divisions who represented a cross section of opinion and thought. Before each meeting, the representatives were to canvass their local groups to collect information and feedback for discussions. The company also had a bimonthly newsletter to keep clinicians informed, reinforce positive happenings in the company, pose issues for feedback, and reinforce the vision of

TABLE 1
NOVACARE REVENUE
BREAKDOWN,
1987–1991

	1987	1989	1991 Year	2Q	3Q
Speech-language pathology	79%	51%	39%	39%	38%
Occupational therapy	16%	30%	39%	39%	40%
Physical therapy	5%	19%	22%	22%	22%

Source: Estimates by Alex Brown, Inc.

the company. NovaCare clinicians, as sole practitioners operating in a remote nursing home or health facility, had to be independent decision makers. Yet in their formal training, they were not educated for this, nor were they prepared to make the compromises often required within a health care facility or nursing home environment.

A CLINICIAN FOCUS

Patient screening, or who goes on the caseload and when, is a critical issue for both NovaCare's and the health care facility's profits. Given the limited number of trained clinicians and the desire of all parties to show maximum patient benefit, it was often difficult to make choices among those who needed care, who would not benefit from care, and who could pay for care. Treatments eligible for repayment varied among different insuring groups. Unfortunately, when clinicians were trained, they were taught how to treat a particular condition, not how to identify from a pool of patients those whose conditions could be adequately and economically treated. Larry Lane, Vice President of Regulatory Affairs, said, "Our orientation has been to empower the clinicians to use professional judgment first and then fall back onto the other issues—are there constraints that will inhibit my professional judgment from being fully carried out?"

Within these limits, a clinician would assess and diagnose a patient and determine a strategy of treatment. The clinician had to establish long-term objectives for the treatment and define success on a case-by-case basis. From the fiscal intermediary's perspective, as long as the clinician had selected a legitimate therapy strategy for a disorder that fell under the payor's guidelines—and as long as the patient showed measurable progress—treatment might proceed. However, the clinician's time availability, specific skill capabilities, and psychic energy levels were also important. Certain forms of rehabilitation could be extremely taxing for the clinician. For example, the continuous physical and psychic drain of treating geriatric or seriously impaired individuals could rapidly "burn out" a clinician. Hence, it was essential to allow some significant variation in the types of patients, disorders, and locations that a clinician experienced. It was also important that the clinician not have to travel extensively between facilities. A number of subjective judgments were required to obtain the right balance.

THE SUPPORT ORGANIZATION

The organization supporting the field clinicians (also called direct care providers, or DCPs) was structured regionally. Each clinician belonged to a group called a district. Each district earned annual revenues of approximately $1 million and was home for an average of 15 FTE clinicians. Clinicians were coordinated by a district manager, district managers by an area manager, and area managers by a division vice president. An area had approximately $7–10 million in business. There were three to four area managers per division and four national divisions organized by geography. The four division vice presidents were coordinated by a vice president of field operations. In 1991, the business was managed on a weekly basis; clinicians scheduled their weekly activities in conjunction with their district manager. On Friday, clinicians telephoned their district managers to report their results—both clinical and administrative—for the week. The district manager consolidated these data and reported a summary to corporate headquarters on the following Monday.

An area manager described the weekly work activity as follows:

> Our whole company travels Tuesday through Thursday. On Friday, DCPs call the District Manager and report how many patients they've seen, how many evaluations they've done, how much time they've spent in preparation and documentation, and how many units of therapy service they've delivered. On Monday, I spent 9 hours on the telephone with each one of my District Managers going over each of the clinician reports. By 3:00 p.m. that afternoon I report to my Division Manager, who consolidates the information to be sent to the Corporate Operations Officer by 8:00 a.m. Tuesday morning. We are spending 20–25% of our time relaying information.

The district manager's job was to handle customer relations and develop good relations with each clinician. One of the division vice presidents, Hal Price, commented, "We've worked hard to reduce the number of facilities so the District Manager can spend as much time as possible with customers listening to their issues, addressing their problems, trying to constantly reassure them. You need to be constantly in front of the facility's management and staff. . . . Because employee retention is such a major concern for the company, the District Manager's role is critical to ensuring a happy work force." A key management challenge at the district level was the ratio of facilities covered to the number of clinicians. The converse of this question frequently got posed: "How many patients are going unserved in a given facility?"

Timothy Foster (no relation to John Foster), NovaCare's CFO, described the problem this way:

> Our central operations problem is that our service, as we charge it to the customer, is priced for the amount of time we spend with each patient, specific to that patient. So for every 15 minutes we spend treating a patient, we are reimbursed a given rate. Any individual therapist works in two or three facilities. That's the premise of our business—there isn't enough reimbursable activity to employ a full-time therapist in any one facility. We are a consolidator of the practice in each facility and among several facilities.

Since the therapist is a fixed cost, we are motivated to optimize billable activity, or production, much as lawyers would be motivated to optimize their productivity/billable time. On the other hand, a Director of Nursing in a facility is looking for many other behaviors that have nothing to do with billable time—team work, consulting or advising, in-servicing and so on—that contribute to the long-term good of the facility and its caregiving capacity. But our therapist is not incented to do that by virtue of the way our incentive bonus program is oriented toward personal productivity, which may suggest that they get out of the facility quickly when there aren't any more patients to treat on a direct basis that day and go to the next facility.

COMPLEXITY OF THE CUSTOMER

NovaCare contracted with nursing home chains and independent operators for the provision of rehabilitation services to their patients. Contracts were written for one year, but could be cancelled on 90 days' or less notice by either party. NovaCare was compensated on a fee-for-service basis from the nursing home, which in turn usually collected from a third-party payor, for example, an insurance company. NovaCare usually indemnified its customers against payment denials by third-party payors. For success, NovaCare had to serve many different constituencies. Each constituency had a different set of needs and expectations. Any group of people who had the ability to influence performance or contract termination directly at a customer facility was considered a constituency.

- *The patient* expects to get well by the treatment and expects a good personal relationship with the clinician. As the ultimate recipient of the service, although frequently not the direct payor, the patient could also influence third-party payors like insurance companies or local Medicare administrators. Their insurers—usually the ultimate payors for the service—would tell the nursing home they were unhappy, and the service would be cancelled.
- *The director of nursing* has a strong caregiving orientation and is immediately attendant to the patient's needs. However, the director also has to coordinate the therapist's activities with all of the other patient support activities in the nursing area.
- *The nursing home administrator* is concerned with the quality of care and efficiency of operations as well as having a financial responsibility. The administrator's compensation is usually measured in financial terms. Consequently, administrators look for optimal financial performance, with minimum risk, for the rehabilitation unit which NovaCare was contracting to serve and manage.
- *Owner-managers* were frequently removed from clinical issues, other than as they impacted regulatory compliance. Their primary responsibility was financial performance.
- *Third-party payors* were interested in maximizing therapeutic effects for lowest cost.

Each constituency had its own special array of needs and expectations from tender patient care and improved wellness, through smooth hassle-free service, to efficiency and optimal reimbursement, to defending the institution from any possible negative impacts like lawsuits or loss of reputation.

NovaCare served not just individual nursing facilities, but also many of the major nursing home chains on a national level. For these customers, NovaCare provided an additional level of services. Dr. Arnold Renschler, Chief Operating Officer, said,

> We provide our major customers, for example, a quarterly report that tells them what we're doing in terms of the generation of revenues for them on a therapy-by-therapy basis, and location-by-location basis. That's a capability a smaller operator simply would not have. We have a full-time officer of the company who stays abreast of regulatory changes, changes in reimbursement, and the implications of potential future changes. He is seen as a resource to our major customers on all-regulatory issues.

The corporate staff of NovaCare numbered slightly over 100. The staff's size and functions were carefully tracked as a percentage of revenue, and this percentage had continued to shrink with time. Bud Locilento attributed this to "getting better people, increasing our reliance on technology and systems, and moving many of the staff functions into the field."

INCENTIVE SYSTEMS

An elaborate compensation system supported the highly decentralized, "inverted" organization of NovaCare. Starting in the days of Inspeech, the company had defined productivity in terms of 15-minute "units of billable time." The primary billable activity was direct patient care. But "units" included any time spent documenting what was done with the patient, consulting with other professionals, direct preparation time, patient care meetings, or anything done directly on behalf of the patient. In December 1984, the productivity standard was set at 100 units (or 25 hours) of billable time per week for each clinician. Above this, a bonus system came into effect. The remainder of the clinician's time was to allow them to do practice building, engage in marketing activities, and create a steadier flow of patients. The most productive therapists actively sought out opportunities to develop their practice and worked with doctors and other nursing home staff personnel to get patients needing care into their caseload.

NovaCare had developed state-of-the-art marketing programs to help make the facilities in which its clinicians worked real magnets for referrals from the community. NovaCare wanted potential referral sources (doctors, nurses, patients, nursing home directors, etc.) to recognize both the availability and quality of its service delivery. The therapist was the key link in converting the company's service concept into a reality. Each clinician was paid a bonus based on the number of units of patient care delivered each week over the agreed-upon standard. However, since speech and occupational therapy were the high-margin services offered within a nursing home, the physical therapy bonus system was quite different.

NovaCare earned 100% of its revenues from service activities. These were dependent on the ability of its clinicians to form and cultivate one-to-one relationships with patients, facilities, and key personnel in those facilities. The company's revenues were constrained by the available time per clinician, available billable time per clinician, and the number of clinicians. NovaCare's management went to great lengths to educate its clinician work force that productivity and quality of care were in fact synonymous. It went even further, pointing out to the therapists that "In the process of being productive we are, in fact, enhancing our professions, enhancing the quality of care, and demonstrating the professional qualifications of our clinical staff."

QUALITY AND REVENUE CONTROL

Quality was an assumed ingredient in the delivery of health care services, although it was not precisely defined or measured by institutions, insurance companies, or other payors. NovaCare, through its systems and management practices, had attempted to "set the standard of care for its field" and to take the lead position within its industry. Hal Price said, "I don't think there is anyone in the country that comes close to doing what we do—delivering on a consistent basis, on a similar scale, the quality of care that we now deliver to our customers." NovaCare constantly sought areas for minor improvements leading to perfection in the delivery of its therapies. Quality control was a basic responsibility of therapists.

District managers were measured on the revenue side of the business only. They were not accountable for managing costs. They were rewarded for (1) productivity, (2) gross unit production measured against budget, (3) retention of people, and (4) supplemental goals contained in personally agreed-upon management objectives. Productivity, production, and retention each accounted for 30% of the district manager's measured performance. Ten percent was allocated to the supplemental goals.

Area and division managers had incentives on three components: (1) gross operating profit, (2) retention,

and (3) supplemental goals. Gross operating profit was 50%, retention 30%, and supplemental goals 20% of their performance measurement package. Operating profit incorporated both net revenue and margin performance targets.

NOVACARE'S STRATEGY AND FUTURE MARKETS

NovaCare's basic strategy had been to grow by consolidating practices of rehabilitation services through a program of disciplined internal growth and acquisitions. The strategy was designed to capitalize upon several external structural factors: (1) an unserved and growing demand for rehabilitation services, (2) an increasing concern with health care costs and the needs of the elderly, and (3) a highly fragmented competition made up of smaller regional firms and care centers. By 1991, the U.S. health care industry was in a state of crisis. The United States spent over $2,500 per person on health care and in the aggregate over $700 billion. Medicare alone cost roughly twice what Britain's entire national health service cost. It was estimated that at least 20% of all health care spending in the Untied States was on administration. Deep concerns had been expressed about the quality of health care in the United States. Yet the Congressional Budget Office projected that federal spending on health care programs would increase to almost 20% of its budget in 1996. There was an extensive national debate about (1) how to finance health care in the future, (2) access to the health care system for much of the population, and (3) the problems of delivering quality care to an increasing percentage of an aging or disabled population.

An industry report on the rehabilitation marketplace read:

> We expect the medical rehabilitation market, which had annual revenues of about $11 billion in 1990, to grow at an annual rate of 15–20% through the 1990s.
>
> Operating margins for well-managed, mature operations exceed 20%. We expect to see growth in this market for the following reasons:
>
> ■ The number of people who experience activity limitations is increasing, as is the age and size of the population.
> ■ The availability of rehabilitation is growing, as are consumers' and third-party payors' awareness of its benefits.
> ■ Technological advances are expanding the pool of patients who can benefit from rehabilitation.
> ■ The current focus on physical fitness, independence, and quality of life is expected to continue.

■ The rehabilitation setting is cost effective relative to services in the acute care setting. Increasingly, insurers using a managed care approach are recognizing the economic benefits of rehabilitation. Studies have shown that for every dollar spent on rehab, anywhere from $11 to $38 is saved.[1]

Under the Medicare program, reimbursement for therapy services was cost based in all but the inpatient, acute care hospital setting. Coverage of rehabilitation therapies by Medicare had been expanded to include outpatient care for occupational therapy in 1987 and swallowing disorders in 1989. Regulators and third-party payors viewed rehabilitation services favorably because of the cost effectiveness of these services relative to acute care facilities. The principal settings for rehabilitation therapies were acute care hospitals, dedicated rehab hospitals, comprehensive outpatient rehab facilities, nursing homes, schools, outpatient clinics, psychiatric hospitals, and the patient's home. Among these providers, small (fewer than 350 bed) institutions frequently contracted with third-party suppliers to manage their rehabilitation requirements. The estimated contract therapy market is shown in Table 2.

According to industry data, in 1988 more than 71% of nursing homes outsourced their occupational therapy as did over 90% of those providing speech-language pathologies therapy. The same data indicated that rehab services compromised less than 1% of nursing home expenses. A greater number of homes provided physical therapy services, but 67% contracted for these as well. The Omnibus Budget Reconciliation Act of 1987 mandated that as of October 1, 1990, all nursing homes must be able to provide all three rehabilitation therapies. However, cost and other factors made this difficult to do internally. According to a professional association survey, only 14,400 of the 129,000 therapists certified in 1989 worked in a long-term care setting. There was a ratio of less than one speech-language pathologist for every ten facilities and one occupational therapist for every eight facilities. NovaCare's ratios

were one speech-language pathologist for every three facilities it served and one occupational therapist for every two facilities. The changing mix of its services is shown in Table 3.

NovaCare's competition was made up of some regional companies, sole proprietors, and small-group practices within communities. The largest regional firms were approximately one-third to one-half NovaCare's size. Many of NovaCare's nursing home customers were national companies. In addition to an aggressive acquisition strategy, NovaCare focused its sales strategy on increasing the density of customers in existing markets to reduce the impact of travel on employee morale and productivity. By integrating its therapy programs, the company had realized significant growth through bringing to the attention of the caregiving institution the other therapies that NovaCare offered. As Table 4 indicates, NovaCare's growth had been extremely rapid and its stock market performance spectacular (see Table 5).

NOVANET: AN INFORMATION STRATEGY

In its 1990 IOK Report, the company described its new NovaNet initiative:

> The company has implemented, on a pilot basis, a laptop computer network enabling each clinician to record and transmit billing, payroll, productivity, and clinical documentation information daily. This innovation is designed to (1) eliminate much of the clinician's administrative burden, increasing time available for patient care; (2) reduce selling, general and administration expenses associated with information gathering and data processing; (3) accelerate the billing cycle thereby reducing days sales outstanding in receivables; and (4) improve the company's ability to capture and correlate clinical data in support of quality assurance standards. Management believes that this proprietary system will further distinguish the company as the employer of choice for therapists.

TABLE 2 ESTIMATED CONTRACT THERAPY MARKET, 1988–1993 (in millions of dollars)

	SPEECH			OCCUPATIONAL			PHYSICAL			TOTALS		
	1988	1993E	CGR	1988	1993E	CGR	1988	1993E	CGR	1988	1993E	CGR
Nursing homes	$250	$365	8%	$250	$550	17%	$300	$420	7%	$800	$1,335	11%
Hospitals, other[a]	300	420	7	300	460	9	1,000	1,470	8	1,600	2,350	8
Home health	250	365	8	300	505	11	550	900	10	1,100	1,770	10
Therapy total	**$800**	**$1,150**	**8**	**$850**	**$1,515**	**12**	**$1,850**	**$2,790**	**9**	**$3,500**	**$5,455**	**9**

CGR—Compound growth rate.
[a] "Wholesale" pricing, that is, revenues generated by providers.
Source: Robertson, Stephens & Co. estimates.

TABLE 3 PRODUCT MIX BREAKDOWN BY FACILITY AND TYPE OF CONTRACT, 1990–1991

CONTRACT TYPES	12-31-90	6-30-91	9-30-91	9-MONTH %CHANGE
Total Facilities	**1,813**	**1,724**	**1,804**	**−0.5**
Speech-language pathology contracts only	815	589	574	−29.6
Occupational therapy contracts only	45	49	59	31.1
Physical therapy contracts only	49	51	49	0.0
Speech-language pathology and occupational therapy contracts only	321	348	365	13.7
Speech-language pathology and physical therapy contracts only	44	23	22	−50.0
Occupational therapy and physical therapy contracts only	29	33	34	17.2
Speech-language pathology, occupational therapy, and physical therapy contracts	510	631	694	36.1
Total Contracts	**3,227**	**3,390**	**3,606**	**11.7**
Total speech-language pathology contracts	1,690	1,591	1,655	−2.1
Total occupational therapy contracts	905	1,061	1,152	27.3
Total physical therapy contracts	632	738	799	26.4

Source: Alex Brown, Inc., reports.

NovaNet was projected to be a $7–10 million information systems investment, the largest investment in systems NovaCare had ever made. The system would allow each clinician to report results daily. John Foster stated, "We believe NovaNet will have significantly short-term, positive implications for clinician productivity. Over the long term, as we learn from the data that we collect, it will have a substantial impact on total productivity."

The NovaNet system had two components—an administrative and a clinical component. The administrative component was intended to eliminate duplicate forms, redundant or erroneous data entry, and administrative paperwork. Quality of documentation was important to NovaCare's customers to satisfy state and federal health care standards and to both NovaCare and the customer for reimbursement. Another objective was to free up time for clinicians so they could have more time to spend with patients. The system was intended to replace existing manual systems and telephone call reporting. Part of the design philosophy was to automate the front end of the manual process—the collection of data from the clinicians—without altering back-end processing systems. The latter

TABLE 4
NOVACARE FINANCIAL PERFORMANCE HISTORY, 1988–1991 (in thousands, except earnings per share)

	1991	1990	1989	1988
Net revenues	$151,532	$102,110	$69,975	$56,612
Gross profit	56,403	39,478	25,586	11,505
Gross profit margin	37%	39%	37%	36.5%
Operating profit	29,875	19,534	8,999	3,162
Operating profit margin	20%	19%	13%	5.6%
Loss on marketable securities	—	—	—	(2,468)
Net income (loss)	20,315	12,382	5,107	(1,045)
Net income per share	0.64	0.43	0.19	(0.04)
Working capital	66,721	41,680	33,294	31,515
Total assets	127,489	87,912	73,609	72,386
Total indebtedness	1,037	14,075	15,908	18,915
Total liabilities	13,975	25,107	23,831	27,781
Stockholders' equity	113,514	62,805	49,778	44,605
Return on average equity	23.0%	22.2%	10.9%	(2.4%)
Annual average FTEs	1,929	1,375	na	na
Revenues per FTE	79	74	na	na
Annual average therapist turnover rate	27.0%	32.0%	39.0%	na

Source: Rehabilitation Today, November–December 1991, and company reports.

TABLE 5
NOVACARE
STOCK MARKET
PERFORMANCE,
1989–1992E

SHARE PRICE DATA

	1988	1989	1990	1991
High	7⅝	8¼	11⁵⁄₁₆	29⅞
Low	1¹⁵⁄₁₆	2⁷⁄₁₆	6½	12¾

EARNINGS PER SHARE

	1989		1990		1991		1992E	
	Amount	Y/Y % Change	Amount	Y/Y % Change	Amount	Y/Y % Change	Amount	Y/Y % Change
1Q	$0.04	NM	$0.08	100.0%	$0.14	75.0%	$0.19	35.7%
2Q	0.04	NM	0.09	125.0	0.15	66.7	0.21	40.0
3Q	0.05	NM	0.12	140.0	0.17	41.7	0.23	33.1
4Q	0.07	NM	0.14	100.0	0.18	28.6	0.24	33.3
FY	$0.20	NM	$0.43	115.0	$0.64	48.8	$0.87	35.9

SOURCES OF PROFIT

	1991	1992
Therapy services	91%	87%
Rehabilitation centers	—	11
Interest income	9	2
Total	100%	100%

ANNUAL FINANCIAL DATA (IN MILLIONS OF DOLLARS)

	1989	1990	1991	1992E
Total revenues	$70.0	$102.0	$151.5	$281.8
Cash flow	6.0	13.3	21.2	34.5
Pretax margin	11.2%	18.6%	20.2%	17.0%
Return on average equity	12.8%	22.0%	23.0%	NE
Return on average assets	7.0%	15.3%	19.0%	NE

NE—No estimate. NM—Not meaningful. Y/Y—Year to year.
Source: Alex Brown & Sons, October 2, 1991.

included the billing system—which was provided by Shared Medical Systems—and a number of in-house management systems.

NovaNet was seen as providing several initial advantages. It provided accurate documentation for reports and billings, and it eased the administrative burdens of clinicians. Further, NovaNet would give clinicians a communication vehicle they currently did not have, allowing them to communicate electronically with their supervisors or other clinicians. One feature under consideration that excited many clinicians was potential use of the technology in the treatment of their patients. NovaCare management had initially targeted a 3% gain in productivity, that is, clinicians billing 103 units per week rather than 100 standard units. But much greater potentials were available. On average, clinicians spent 35% of their time in activities unrelated to direct patient care, that is, documentation, meetings, and traveling. Management also expected to be able to extend district managers' "spans of communication" beyond the current average of 15 clinicians, yet provide more time to improve the quality of relations with therapists and customer institutions.

NovaNet had been designed by a multifunctional team, including a project committee made up of the company's controller, vice president of MIS, vice president of professional services, and vice president of operations. Under this committee's supervision, a small design team had defined the parameters of the system and laid out its major design objectives. The team was made up of clinicians and staff people. The project's review and cost-benefit analysis had calculated a 1.7-year direct payback for the initial investment and a 33% return over a 5-year period. But various executives saw other less measurable quality, morale, flexibility, information exchange, and strategic applications as providing even greater long-term benefits. The question was how to implement the system best to achieve these longer-term potentials at the same time as NovaNet achieved desired short-term payback goals.

NovaCare only had a small systems group and made extensive use of outside service bureaus. It also had a strategy to outsource as much of the programming work as would be compatible with its goals. Given the breadth and scope of NovaNet, the company contracted with CompuServe to develop and deliver the system. CompuServe proposed to write the PC software, provide the telecommunications network, and staff an "800 number support desk" for questions. NovaCare's Board gave approval for the project, and system design began in January 1990.

IMPLEMENTATION AND QUESTIONS

Prior to the implementation of the NovaNet pilot, a time study had looked at how clinicians spent their time. This data was compared with similar data from groups participating in the NovaNet pilot after a period of use. It was found that productivity had not increased. Pat Larkins, Vice President of Professional Services, commented, "Our clinicians had to get used to the technology. I don't think you could get the desired increase in productivity by just teaching them how to input information, as opposed to also showing them how to use the information as a means of changing their established behaviors." Nevertheless, with the initial results at the clinician level less than promising, management began to look to other areas of productivity improvement to pay for the system in the short run, while it developed longer-term strategic uses.

Meanwhile, various government agencies were increasing their demands for information from all health care providers. The Health Care Finance Administration (HCFA), which managed the Medicare program, was attempting to define standards for basic data formats and electronic data submissions. The government and insurers had a vital interest in how effective their expenditures were in delivering better health care to patients. The Medicare program in particular was moving to a more outcomes-oriented approach in how it reimbursed for patient care. John Foster noted:

> As the largest service provider in our field, we should have some economies of scale in the collection and use of data that are not available to anyone else. In fact, if we develop the system right, it might provide the ultimate barrier to entry for other competitors. Along with our other strategic initiatives to penetrate existing markets further and to acquire entry into new markets, NovaNet could be among our most important strategic investments.

Dr. Arnold Renschier said,

> One of the issues being debated internally right now is: "Do we go ahead and roll out a successful administrative function (which is already available) before we have a successful clinical component for NovaNet?" Once we resolve that question, the administrative piece could be rolled out almost immediately. The big opportunity, though, in terms of improved productivity, consistency of treatment, and the potential to measure outcomes derives from the clinical piece. . . . If only the administrative piece is rolled out, the clinician will not feel the same degree of affirmation that they would experience if the clinical piece were working.

Yet if NovaCare did not go ahead, there could be significant public and employee relations problems for NovaCare. Internally, many clinicians had knowledge of the pilot and were eager to obtain the help it offered. Externally, NovaCare had announced its plans for NovaNet, and therefore many investment houses, customers, and shareholders might have anticipated benefits from the system.

NovaCare had to proceed cautiously. It operated within a highly regulated environment: 80–90% of its billing were dependent on Medicare reimbursement. Said Tim Foster, "The biggest strategic threat in any health care business is the regulatory environment and the questions of reimbursement from the public or private sector." Regulations or interpretations of existing laws could quickly change to stimulate, redirect, or curtail specific therapies or their reimbursement. Intermediaries also constantly used their ability to interpret or change reimbursement. These and the constant flow of new rehabilitation needs and therapeutic techniques were a continuing challenge.

Other threats included competition for rehabilitation patients from nursing homes themselves. Many nursing homes were trying to move out of the "hotel and beds" portion of the business and into higher-margin activities. Growing nursing homes might obtain a sufficient number of patients to justify employment of internal therapists. If consolidation occurred around these centers, NovaCare could be left primarily with the smaller facilities, with few patients, and highly dispersed from a travel standpoint. In addition, if the government undertook a massive program for training therapists, the labor situation could change from a shortage to a surplus condition, seriously affecting NovaCare's margins. It was in this context that NovaCare's top management had to consider how best to position the total company, its organization, its controls and incentives, and its NovaNet information system for maximum future effectiveness. (See Exhibit 1 for brief profiles of NovaCare's competitors.)

Referring to the company's purposes and beliefs, John Foster noted,

> As we make these decisions and we look around at successful leadership companies, we observe that those companies with the highest integrity also have the highest returns on capital and the highest profit margins on sales. Therefore, we are satisfied that if we are prepared to do whatever we do right, the yield should be outstanding financial performance. Quality, productivity, and integrity are the things that serve our shareholders best in the long run.

EXHIBIT 1
COMPETITOR
SITUATION:
Brief Profiles

In October–November, 1991, *Rehab Management* ran an article profiling the rehab industry's largest providers. The following is summarized from that source.

Baxter Health Care Corp's Physical Therapy Division was purchased by $8 billion Baxter in 1984. Its history was in sports medicine. Baxter established the division as an entrepreneurial company within the parent. In 1991, the division had started a growth campaign to add as many as 150 centers in five years. Its stated intention was to focus on the outpatient market. The division handled roughly 100,000 patient visits a year and was establishing data bases on treatment, outcomes, and quality control.

MedRehab, Inc. had three primary business lines: contractual services in long-term care settings (350 nursing home sites); its own operation in 39 outpatient clinics; and 51 hospitals where it provided physical, occupational, speech, and respiratory therapy services. Founded in May 1987 as a start-up company, MedRehab had acquired a number of existing regional rehab companies. MedRehab saw the switch from inpatient to outpatient professionals at work and claimed to be maintaining a retention rate of better than 80% on an annualized basis. It had affiliations throughout the country with 75 universities which trained physical, occupational, and speech therapists.

HealthSouth Rehabilitation Corp. was an entrepreneurial company formed in 1984 and taken public in 1986. It had attempted to build outpatient rehab centers and hospitals that would be more cost effective than keeping patients in higher cost settings. It had built 40 facilities in its first five years and had continuing growth plans in similar directions. With 3,000 counties in the United States and only 175 comprehensive rehab facilities, HealthSouth saw no barriers to its development. Using careful financial controls, it had maintained a strong balance sheet and was able to move rapidly and price competitively.

Rehab Hospital Services Corp. was founded in 1979 and purchased by National Medical Enterprises in 1985. Since then, it had grown from six facilities to 33 facilities, 18 managed units, and two transitional living centers. It had one rehab outpatient facility of its own and was currently building three more. Its plans stated that it would seek to build five to ten freestanding hospital facilities per year. In 1991, it claimed to be the largest rehabilitation company in the country. It was aggressively managed and would consider all forms of expansion, both internal and through acquisitions. In public statements, it emphasized its "one to two referral marketing" program to generate new business. In each of its areas, it tried to develop "focused administrators," willing to take risks and aggressively pursue opportunities. It claimed its distinctive advantage was its human resources capability.

Continental Medical Systems was founded in 1986. It had a presence in 36 states, with 22 operating rehab hospitals in 11 states, 57 outpatient centers in 18 states, and four contract therapy companies which had a presence in 30 states. With over 7,500 employees, it had opened eight new hospitals in 1991 and was planning another eight in 1992. Its target was to be a billion-dollar company in the mid-1990s. It had purchased three of its 22 operating hospitals and all four of its contract service companies.

Healthfocus, Inc. was started in 1963 as a partnership. It was purchased by Hyatt in 1971 and then acquired by American Medical International (AMI) in 1980. It had started a rehab division in 1985 which officers and employees later purchased in a leverage buyout. Healthfocus had 55 freestanding clinics in 13 states and contracts with 85 hospitals in 31 states. In 1991 it was looking at work-health programs to augment its rehab and hospital activities.

There were also a number of other smaller regional players with specialized services, facilities, or capabilities. However, acquisition prices were increasing rapidly because of the success of these "Big 7" players and NovaCare.

CASE 42

Lechabile: IT as a People Business

On May 12, 1999, Lechabile's management team met in the boardroom for a weekly management meeting. The company was faced with a two-fold strategic issue that had to be resolved: First, how to manage the numerous growth opportunities that presented themselves to the small IT start-up. Secondly, how to manage the increasing numbers of new employees that accompanied growth.

With respect to the second point, one board member expressed concern that a particular employee was failing to add value in his division and proposed his redeployment. Another noted that a different employee was not properly skilled and suggested his prompt, thorough training to rectify the problem. Managing Director Winston Mosiako reflected on the successful interviews he had conducted with eager new staff members over the past two weeks. In view of increasing issues centered on performance, the MD said to his colleagues: "It seems that we need a formal performance management system—one that would be in keeping with our culture of empowerment." He asked them: "What do you propose?"

COMPANY BACKGROUND

We had reached the stage when either we were going to see out our careers at IBM, or we were going to move on and do something for ourselves. The IT industry has a pent-up demand for a company like this and we are moving incredibly fast.[1]

In 1998, Lechabile was founded by seven IBM systems engineers and professionals who had accumulated more than 150 years of IT experience amongst them. Whilst black owned and controlled, Lechabile held the view that both the company shareholders and management should represent the diverse population of South Africa. Within one year, Lechabile had increased ranks from the seven founding members to thirty-eight employees. The company's asset base had also grown from R3,5 million to R50 million in a single year.

EMPOWERMENT PHILOSOPHY

The Lechabile philosophy derived from two objectives: 1. To build a significant sized information technology company whose composition reflected the demographics of South Africa in all respects; 2. To increase the information technology expertise in South Africa by focusing on education and the transfer of skills.

When asked why the seven left IBM and the IT giant's accompanying benefits, culture and reputation, they responded: "We saw a gap for a black IT company in the market and the opportunity to make an impact—to make a difference." Without transferring companies, the original seven could not envisage their own vertical growth as blacks. By the mid-1990s, IBM-South Africa was experiencing a series of major changes in ownership and management. IBM was seemingly characterised by a corporate culture and a fat bureaucracy, lacking the opportunity for individual growth and autonomy sought by the seven. In June 1997, four IBM employees designed a vision for a small IT company—one that would empower other blacks and historically disadvantaged South Africans. They approached IBM's Chief Executive with this vision. At the end of February, when seven months passed and nothing had happened, the seven former IBM employees left to launch Lechabile. The seven spanned the required roles of the start-up. With his experience in senior management, Winston Mosiako was asked to be MD. Iqbal Hassim looked after finances. Simon Ndoro, Andile Mfengwana and Robby Moabi took on the servicing of clients. And Vincent Williams and Zainul Nagdee were assigned to sales (see Exhibit 1 for the six-member Management Team; see Exhibit 2, Organisational Structure).

The vision, together with the mission and values, were the three pillars that laid the foundation for the company's practice. Lechabile's vision centred on being a leading IT player with a competitive edge, offering a range of quality products and solutions, as well as a leading provider of highly skilled IT professionals with partners nationally and internationally.[2] The founding members chose "Lechabile" as the company's name because it illustrated their vision. "Lechabile"—a word derived from the language of the Sotho—meaning "the sun is rising." In the words of the seven company founders, "when the sun rises, it brings joy, hope and light to people."

The mission of the company encompassed the intersecting objectives of growth, competence, ethics, IT customer satisfaction and empowerment:

> To achieve and sustain an above average growth of the business. To maintain the highest level of competency and ethical standards. To supply leading products combined with outstanding service and value for money. To build a competitive, profitable niche-focused IT business. To honour commitments and strive for customer satisfaction. To provide highly skilled IT professionals from the previously disenfranchised communities with recognised qualifications.[3]

Lechabile viewed IT as a "people business" and declared its commitment to forging special relationships with clients, employees and associates; to respecting all individuals; and, to consistent quality service that exceeded customer expectation.

As mentioned, a total of 38 individuals were employed at Lechabile. Racially, Lechabile's staff consisted of 29 blacks, four Asians, three coloureds (South African term for mixed-race descent), and two whites. Of these, nine were women, including chairperson Pearl Mashabela.

As of June 1999, ownership consisted of the following (see Exhibit 3 for Lechabile's Subsidiaries & Associated Companies):

- 15 per cent held by a company entitled "debis IT Services"—a joint venture between the Daimler/Benz company and Denel Informatics.

EXHIBIT 1
THE MANAGEMENT
TEAM

WINSTON MOSIAKO: Managing Director
21 years IT experience in systems engineering, consulting and business management.

ANDILE MFINGWANA: General Manager, Services
11 years system engineering experience, specialising in operating systems and subsystems.

ZAINUL NAGDEE: General Manager, Sales
21 years IT experience in management, consulting, marketing and technical sales. Experience in Project Management.

KEVIN PAUL: General Manager—Lechabile Communications
Over 16 years in the IT and Telecommunications. Strong in business management, project management and consulting.

SIMON NDORO: General Manager, Education and Training
23 years IT experience in systems engineering and consulting, specialising in operating systems, subsystems software and DB/DC.

CHRISTY CHETTY: Manager, Durban Branch
IT career spans 23 years. Experience in database administration and ADABAS Natural environment. Systems Engineering services on OS/390 and VSE/SA operating systems.

EXHIBIT 2 LECHABILE'S ORGANISATIONAL STRUCTURE

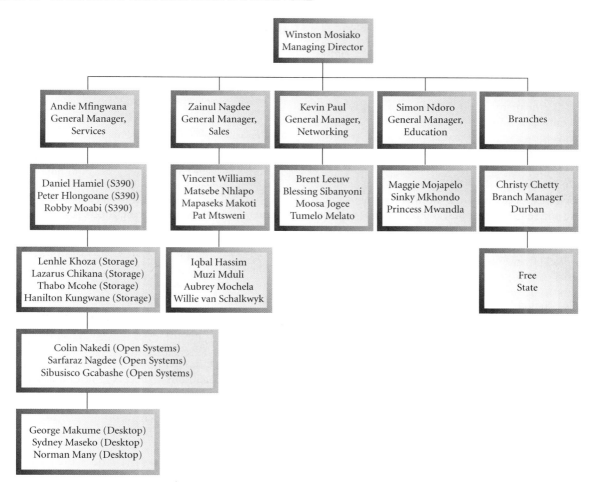

- 3 per cent held by a trust established for previously disadvantaged individuals employed by debis.
- 82 per cent held by the seven founding members who provided the initial seed capital.

IT INDUSTRY PROFILE

The IT industry was one characterized by change. During the late 1990s, the information technology services market achieved exceptional growth. In 1998, IT services repre-

EXHIBIT 3
LECHABILE'S
SUBSIDIARIES
AND ASSOCIATED
COMPANIES

Lechabile Information Technology Services (PTY) Ltd.	100%
Lechabile Technology KZN (Pty) Ltd	100%
Lechabile Technology Free State (Pty) Ltd	100%
Lechabile Communications (Pty) Ltd	50%
Jointly with Nambita Technologies	
Lechabile's AST (Pty) Ltd	50%
LSIT (Pty) Ltd	50%

Lechabile owns 80 per cent of the Durban Company, and local employees retain ownership of the remainder.
Source: Lechabile Company Profile. Courtesy of Lechabile, June 1999.

sented US$350 billion worldwide in the areas of programming, systems integration, consulting, outsourcing, education, training and maintenance services revenues. The market was expected to double over the five year period from 1997 to 2002, to total US$622 billion. The industry's rapid growth had been driven by several factors, including rapid changes in technology, year 2000 (Y2K) computer problems, and the increasing development and implementation of complex enterprise resource planning (ERP) systems. Worldwide growth for the year was forecast at 18 per cent of the industry.[4]

Domestic Market

The graph[5] reveals the historical and forecast growth rates in software and services revenues, and their increasing contribution to overall IT markets in South Africa. In 1998, the software and services sector contributed close to 48 per cent of overall IT revenues.

For 1994, the reported contribution of software to total IT was 40 per cent. By the year 2000, software's contribution to total IT revenues was forecast to rise to 55 per cent.

Strategy

Lechabile employed a four-pronged strategy. First, Lechabile emphasised service and support, viewing both as the key to differentiating the company from competitors. Lechabile's strategy was driven by an apparent commitment to customer satisfaction, ensuring that the client received the highest value for the service. Second, Lechabile operated a relationship-oriented business; they were in the business of forging client relationships and alliances. To this end, knowing the needs of the clients was paramount. The third part of the strategy was an emphasis on target

EXHIBIT 4 BUSINESS UNITS

- Large Systems Solutions
- Storage Systems Solutions
- Networking Solutions
- Systems Management Solutions
- Open Systems Solutions
- Desktop Solutions
- Application Development Solutions

Source: Lechabile Company Brochure. Courtesy of Lechabile, June 1999.

markets. Lechabile identified customers as those with the following attributes:

- They required a high-quality service provider
- They desired to build a long-term relationship
- Information technology was a key part of their business strategy
- Hardware and software products were essential to the total solution.

Fourth (an extension of the first objective), Lechabile aimed to differentiate itself from competitors by fulfilling the promise made to the consumer.

Building Capacity & Transferring Skills

Lechabile employed eight trainees to become IT specialists in their chosen disciplines. The transfer of skills had been occurring internally and externally. Internally, the company focused on programmes to allow employees to develop their skill sets to encompass marketing, technical and business skills. It has developed externally such that

SOFTWARE & SERVICES REVENUES

staff in larger corporations who needed mentoring and skill building from black role models received this from Lechabile. Strategic alliances with international partners such as Hewlett Packard, IBM and EMC (which sold data storage solutions) allowed Lechabile staff to undertake specialised transfer programs. Moreover, Mosiako elaborated, "This has extended to our client companies too. For example, AST (Advanced Software Technologies) in Pretoria asked where they could find good black IT staff. We found them and helped mentor them. Not just on a short-term focus of their skills, but we keep contact with the recruits in a mentoring role. Now they [AST] want six more."[6]

An additional project was launched in conjunction with South Africa's Police Services (SAPS). Lechabile gave three unemployed people with university degrees, jobs in IT operations at the SAPS Pretoria Office. Lechabile paid the salaries for five months, and SAPS gained the IT personnel. The performance of the new recruits was discussed during monthly meetings held jointly by SAPS-Lechabile.

Lechabile also purchased an IMB franchise, an IBM Authorized Center of Education, with the intention of providing a formal training college for students and employees. Students would take formal computer courses, and at the end of the nine-month period, receive an internationally recognised IBM certificate. In line with Lechabile's values and vision, the company offered the following:

LECHABILE'S SOCIAL RESPONSIBILITIES

- A technology institute
- After hours training in a Competency Centre
- Hands-on training and guidance
- IT career counseling
- Community Centre Support in IT training and teaching
- Black professionals as mentors

A training centre to provide entry-level IT skills was also established, with a philanthropic bent. General Manager of Sales, Zainul Nagdee explained: "We commit to train three to four people for free during every course that has a full classroom."[7] Building competence was part of the company's culture.

CULTURE OF EMPOWERMENT

One of the fundamental elements underpinning Lechabile's culture was that of empowerment. Lechabile Sales Consultant, Matsebe Nhlapo defined an empowering organisation as one in which the employee was given the opportunity to reach her full potential: academically, professionally, irrespective of colour or gender. The seven foundling members claimed they had been empowered by leaving IBM to start up their own company. But what of other Lechabile employees? Would a black company be empowering to white staff as well?

Willie Van Schalkwyk, a white employee, noted that yes, Lechabile provided the right environment to encourage professional growth, regardless of colour. When Nhlapo was asked to rate the company as an empowering organisation on a ten-point scale, with 1 being the most empowering environment, she ranked Lechabile as a 3. She said she was delighted with the degree of empowerment in Lechabile, but tempered her score with a 3 because there was still progress to be made integrating women into the company. "My expectations are extremely high and I am impatient for change,"[8] she emphasised. Nhlapo considered Lechabile's culture to be empowering due to several factors: a prevailing environment of openness and a relatively flat structure without the same rigid hierarchy and procedures that were a trademark of the large corporate entities.

Employees were autonomous and independent, taking on their respective job responsibilities at Lechabile whilst aware that they contributed to the company's bottom line. General Manager (GM) of Education and Training, Simon Ndoro said: "Empowerment has created an enabling environment. We've done this by allowing them to grow as they please in the company. But we find we do have to restrain this freedom in respect to dealings with the customer."[9]

The management team claimed that empowerment did not end with the formation of Lechabile. It began there. They stated: "Empowerment is not something we do, but something we are."[10] Their collective notion of empowerment encompassed economic, black and organisational empowerment. In their view, by entering an enabling organisation such as Lechabile, an employee became entrenched in an environment where one could freely approach the MD of the company to discuss a problem. Indeed, Mosiako had recently completed a two-week round of interviews with all members of the company to discuss their questions, perspectives and concerns. The founding members of Lechabile knew firsthand that, given South Africa's apartheid past, young black recruits were often uncomfortable asking questions of their white male supervisors. In response, Lechabile worked to create a climate in which racial and cultural barriers were broken down and new employees had the confidence to pose questions to their managers—and often in their native languages.

One of the founding members added: ". . . [E]mpowerment is not just for ourselves but for everybody that is part of Lechabile . . . We believe you can't be empowered without being reasonably well off or at least being independent."[11]

An outsider visiting the company would quickly take note of the informal yet professional mood of the office. An atmosphere of good humour and friendliness prevailed. Nhlapo added that she was particularly attracted to Lechabile because of this work environment. In addition, the start-up offered her opportunity for growth and increased autonomy. She also appreciated the company's young, fresh approach and their method of channeling grievances within the organisation.

Conflict Resolution

"Being friends, our first policy was to resolve conflicts by closing the door and saying exactly what we feel, in any language, in any way, as equals. We call it soul-cleansing."[12] The original seven created this method of resolving problems by meeting behind closed doors when an issue was identified. They spoke with their counterparts openly and freely, addressing vexing issues and concluding meetings with key action points to be taken. So successful, this manner of managing conflict began to be adopted by the organisation as a whole, contributing to the company's enabling environment.

When the ex-IBM professionals began the venture, they quickly recognised that they could not simply be IT professionals or systems engineers as before. They had to become leaders and managers who assumed greater responsibility, "to reinforce the mission and set the standard."[13] The seven realised, with the introduction of new staff, that they must make a long-term investment in people. While they recognised that attrition would be a natural process over time, they wanted to attract the kind of candidates who would be interested in joining a leading organisation, one that was cutting-edge and highly attractive to job-seekers.

> We are very much a learning type of organisation, we feel we will make a contribution to the broader society . . . We haven't lost anyone yet, and we have to create the environment such that they [employees] will want to stay here . . . although most people know they would grow with this organisation.[14]

Training & Mentorship

It was in this vein that mentorship and training programs were introduced to both develop and channel the talented individuals that later joined the company's ranks. Due to the small size of the company and its recent development, Lechabile could afford to hire new employees without employing hard and fast human resource management policies. Instead, new recruits were assigned to supervisors who would meet and advise them on an adhoc basis.

A "route map" for their training would be drawn up for employees to follow, depending on their skill set, level of experience and prior training. Mosiako remarked:

> The only way to bring new employees up to speed is to take them with you in mentorship. Most of them come from university or technikon without much experience, and need to learn by example.[15] Ndoro noted, "Some of our recruits come from other companies without a disciplined approach. We from IBM have learnt how to plan and execute a project. They still need to learn this.[16]

Vincent Williams, one of the founding members, commented: "In IBM we could not make decisions. Now we do. So in Lechabile, employees should be able to make decisions without us."[17] Ndoro added, "Although the newer, inexperienced staff are not yet ready."[18] By mid-year 1999, members of the management team began to acknowledge that training was simply the starting point to ensure quality employee performance; the ongoing management of performance needed to be addressed and employed as a formal practice within the company.

Prizes and Awards

Management highly valued its employees and provided performance incentives for staff. These were primarily monetary bonuses and dinner awards. While employees enjoyed the empowerment culture and altruistic ideals of the company, they perhaps appreciated the financial gains even more, and found the sales quotas a great motivating mechanism.

IBM VS. LECHABILE

> When you work for a company like IBM you tend to take a lot of things for granted and you expect a lot of things to happen and they do . . . Working for a smaller organisation, you have to set the standards.

> *—Winston Mosiako, MD[19]*

The original seven had amassed much knowledge and experience from their years at IBM. As a result, they sought to retain many effective IBM practices at Lechabile, instituting them within a small company context. For instance, education, training and mentorship were key components of the IBM way that Lechabile was replicating, as noted previously. The seven former IBM employees had also learned to conduct problem-solving analysis while at IBM, identifying and weighing the pros and cons of any situation. This was a skill that all seven continued to utilise beyond their corporate experience. Nevertheless, as IBM members they had faced a rigid hierarchy that often thwarted individual action and the introduction of innovation due to the laborious channels associated with corporate culture. "We were quite senior in IBM," said Mosiako, "but not moving. Each new MD had a new programme for our development—but I found after a while that as a 'high flier' I was in fact flying lower than some others."[20]

In Lechabile's small and enthusiastic environment, all seven would meet periodically to discuss the issues facing the company. After a wide-ranging discussion, they would arrive at a set of resolutions and a plan for implementation. According to Lechabile, the group was able to make decisions collectively at the top level, and execute them rapidly. As decisions became more complex and the growing organisation brought even more issues to the table, decision making itself emerged as an issue, leading the management team to appoint a three-man committee to look into the decision-making process. In this manner, the company was able to introduce and execute change within Lechabile quickly, and stay on top of developments in the industry.

BLACK ECONOMIC EMPOWERMENT

The Black Information Technology Forum defined black economic empowerment as "measurable skills transfer, significant black equity shareholding, operational involvement and blacks involved at senior decision-making levels."

Whether one is on Wall Street or in Johannesburg, few management topics have received the same attention as "empowerment." In January 1999, Harvard Business Review Senior Editor Suzy Wetlaufer reported that nearly 30,000 articles had appeared in the media on the topic. Critics contend that empowerment is simply "lip service." For instance, management guru Chris Argyris claimed that empowerment initiatives arguably failed to penetrate through all layers of the organisation, and that employees were generally not involved in decision making of any real importance to the company as a whole. Argyris concluded that empowerment rings hollow: "the disparity between myth and reality is irreconcilable."[21]

THE CONTEXT

Since the general election in 1994, the issues of affirmative action and black economic empowerment have become increasingly more important in South Africa against the background of racial imbalances and unequal opportunities of the past.[22]

In South Africa, the context leading to localised definitions of "empowerment" was quite unique from other countries, such as American and British notions of empowerment. In the South African post-apartheid era, empowerment was generally accepted to mean the upliftment of the historically disadvantaged population—including blacks, coloureds and Indian peoples—equal access to opportunity.

Affirmative action measures were some of the first legalised methods to seek socio-economic upliftment for the previously disadvantaged. The parallels between affirmative action and black economic empowerment initiatives were distinct. In a survey conducted by FSA-Contact, it was found that the primary rationale for the implementation of affirmative action policies by businesses (of their own volition within the business sector) were as follows:

- Strategic business decision (29 per cent)
- Desire to overcome the inequalities of the past in terms of racial discrimination (25 per cent)
- Social responsibility (20 per cent)
- To obtain a competitive advantage (16 per cent)
- Pressure from trade unions or employees (6 per cent)
- Threat of government imposing a quota system (4 per cent)[23]

The Black Information Technology Forum (BITF) claimed that black economic empowerment manifested as "measurable skills transfer, significant black equity shareholding, operational involvement and blacks involved at senior decision-making levels." While most agreed on the value of achieving the aspects identified above by BITF, the debate revolved around how these were to be achieved. By mid-1999, it became widely known that many empowerment transactions had been of questionable empowerment value and many of these transactions had been reproved for being little more than "get-rich-quick schemes for a small elite, " while failing to create the necessary jobs, skills and a larger middle class for black South Africans on a wider scale[24] (see Exhibit 6—Black Empowerment in South Africa, Franchise Ownership). Indeed, critics claimed that the abuse of the word "black empowerment" by NAIL (New Africa Investments Ltd.) directors in the NAIL fiasco proved that empowerment was simply a euphemism for enrichment.

Gavin Pieterse, the Black Economic Empowerment Commission (BEEC) Deputy Chairman, outlined the biggest obstacles thwarting BEE, as the absence of a nationally understood, accepted and collective definition of BEE—and a coherent and clearly defined set of basic measures and benchmarks.[25]

With regard to the BEE debate, the *Financial Mail* recently noted: "There are signs that the empowerment movement as we know it has had its day . . . Investors are unhappy with the investment trusts and holding companies that are so popular with empowerment companies. Between them, African Partnerships, Hosken Consolidated Investments (HCI) and Brimstone, for instance . . . have . . . given about R2,2 bn back to shareholders in partial unbundling. Weak markets have forced them to concede

EXHIBIT 5
SERVICES & PRODUCTS

Lechabile provides a broad range of products, which include services, education, software and hardware independent of the company from any brand name supplier. This allows freedom to recommend IT solutions comprising of a mix of products that best meet a customer's unique business requirements.

In today's world no one supplier has all the solutions. So when the need arises Lechabile will enter into strategic alliances with any other organisation to address a particular customer's business needs.

IT EDUCATION AND TRAINING:

We provide a variety of courses to help maximise the productivity gained from the use of your systems. Onsite and classroom courses available.

IMPLEMENTATION SERVICES:

Lechabile offers a flexible program where clients decide on the level of involvement required in the installation of solutions.

PERFORMANCE MONITORING AND CAPACITY PLANNING:

We have the skills to analyze the performance and tuning of all aspects of your system including the operating system, network, disk and tape, and to recommend ways to improve performance and capacity.

SOFTWARE AND HARDWARE:

We sell a complete range of servers and software from Personal Computers to Large Systems. In addition we also market peripherals including Storage products, Printing, Tape products and Networking.

NETWORKING SERVICES:

Design, support and supply of Networking products in the Wide Area Networking and Local Area Networking. We provide clients with a choice of individual and packaged Internet and Intranet solutions.

PROJECT MANAGEMENT:

We will provide project management for IT projects. We create a single point of contact for you with a plan for overall project co-ordination and will manage all information systems vendor services for you.

SOFTWARE ADMINISTRATION AND CONSULTANCY SERVICES:

We will manage your entire software portfolio to enable you to yield maximum financial benefits from the provisions of software terms and conditions as well as other offerings that are available. We will also assist with budget planning, contract renewals and software audits across the entire software base.

CONSULTANCY AND PROFESSIONAL SERVICES IN THE FOLLOWING AREAS:

- IT Architecture and Strategy
- Security Audit
- IT Management
- Managed Operations
- Business Transformation

Source: Lechabile Company Brochure. Courtesy of Lechabile, June 1999.

EXHIBIT 6
BLACK
EMPOWERMENT
IN SOUTH AFRICA:
Franchise Ownership
(percent of total)

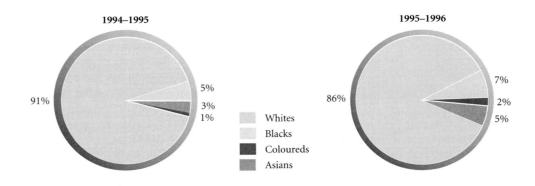

they could not do anything useful with the money."[26] The same article emphasised the growing trend of investors going the private equity route, investing in unlisted companies where they could access cash flows and achieve "broader empowerment objectives such as skills transfer." Some listed companies, frustrated with black empowerment partners who did not show up at board meetings and failed to add value, had begun to set quantitative targets to measure the performance of their partners. Some merchant banks were unwilling to conduct more black empowerment deals. One banker remarked: "I have other things to do; for example, privatisations in the rest of Africa."[27]

In a *Financial Times* cover story on BEE, Gary Kobane Morolo, CEO of Co-ordinated Network Investments, stated that the question of success or failure was simply premature. "We must not forget where we are starting from," said Morolo. In the life of a nation in which six per cent of the population has run the economy for decades—four, five and even ten years was not long enough to create long-lasting change, Morolo argued.

Litha Nyhonyha, CEO of Thebe Financial Services, pointed to the Malaysian example. When Malaysia began its wealth distribution programmes, the indigenous Bumiputra population had been elbowed out of the economy by the Chinese. In 1969, following race riots, the Malaysian government implemented the New Economic Policy, with explicit numerical targets to redistribute wealth in favour of the Bumiputras. Malaysia's programme was continued for two decades before it was considered to have made lasting improvements.

SUCCESSES?

The future of black economic empowerment in South Africa is wired.[28]

If empowerment is such a lofty unreachable goal, how does a truly empowered organisation function? And which companies are examples of effective empowerment? AES, a US-based electricity company, was deemed to be one such success. AES's operations were based on autonomy and trust. Employees at all levels take responsibility for decision making, for their work, and for the success of the organisation as a whole.[29] Both the Chairman and CEO of AES viewed the greatest challenge of empowering an organisation as persuading its leaders to consistently give up the power to make decisions.

Effective empowerment must incorporate risk-sharing partnerships. All parties must have something at stake, so that there is a full commitment to the successful outcome of a venture. The only reason to support empowerment partnerships is that shareholders expect the empowerment group to add significant value to the company.[30]

According to the consultancy BusinessMap, in January 1999 there were 35 black-controlled firms on the Johannesburg Stock Exchange (JSE), with a total market capitalisation of about 5.5 per cent (R58,7 billion) of the JSE's total capitalisation, with IT firms leading the way. Black empowerment deals in the information and telecommunications (infotel) industries were around R4,5 billion for the period 1996 to 1998. *The Mail & Guardian* reported: "Not only do the information, communication and technology sectors offer opportunities for wealth creation . . . these industries have become integral to the economy as a whole."[31]

In contrast to many empowerment groups that offered an investment or equity, Lechabile was a fully formed company, equipped with the right people, skills and ready to go. The founders had all the required capital, intellectual and financial, to fund and launch Lechabile on their own. Moreover, Lechabile claimed that empowerment was not just a slogan or selling point for the company, it was their living philosophy, and, a palpable feature of the company's environment. Iqbal Hassim noted: "We saw that other black empowerment groups were just investment vehicles. We actually do the job."[32] Nevertheless, as the company expanded and satellite offices cropped up in other cities, the implicit culture would become more difficult to maintain and increasingly vulnerable to change. And, Lechabile began to realise, if they expected the "culture of empowerment" to endure, they had to think about ways to capture this culture within the formal systems of the organisation.

Lechabile had formalised the training and mentoring of employees. In Lechabile's view, the company was creating the right type of environment for empowerment to take root. For instance, Zainul Nagdee emphasised the company's practice of giving employees the authority to make important decisions—and to make them on the company's behalf. They also encouraged employees to achieve vertical growth within the company. Lechabile's intent was to create autonomy among individuals, which would lead to efficiency and success within the company—and a challenging, encouraging work climate.

GROWTH

In addition to setting up a formal performance management system, and fostering the empowerment of the organisation as growth occurred, one of the central questions facing Lechabile was: at what pace should we grow? Opportunities abounded. These included gaining an investor to grow the business; selling a 25 per cent stake to a white-owned company who may want to exert some management influence over the business; merging with another black company to create larger, more powerful companies by way of the alliance; securing a loan and investing the capital into growing the business; listing on the stock exchange; or, acquiring other companies (see Exhibit 7 for the Company's Financials). For example, Kevin Paul joined Lechabile when Lechabile acquired his company, which became Lechabile Communications (Pty) Ltd. Lechabile was courted by a number of investors and strategic partners, receiving invitations almost daily from investors, often from white companies keen to take over. This option posed lucrative opportunities for the owners, introducing the dilemma: Should the owners put their own financial interests first, or those of the company, in order to retain Lechabile's character as an empowering organisation. In response to this question, one company member made the point: "What has made Lechabile what it is, is that we are a 'black company.' Investors want to retain the directors—we are the ones who attract the business."[33]

Willie Van Schalkwyk, IT Specialist for Lechabile, who had amassed years of experience in the industry, expressed both confidence in the company's future and a mild concern that the company was growing too rapidly. He projected that Lechabile would go public in two years time, "provided that they [the company] understand growth must be steady but secure."[34]

Another concern emerged as the company grew; the experience of the directors in finance and marketing had been appropriate for a small company, but now called for greater expertise. Members of the management team also expressed an intent to shed "non-core"[35] areas of the business. Yet, they needed to decide what to do with the staff in those areas. Of concern was the absence of a performance measure to determine who among the staff was not being productive, as well as how many new employees they would need to hire in order to meet their growth objectives. In the boardroom on May 12, the Lechabile six-member management team was debating how large they wanted to grow, how quickly, and how to answer the strategic questions they faced along the way.

CONCLUSION

During the board meeting, Mosiako received several proposed plans for implementing a formal performance management system within the company. Two of the strategies appeared most viable. The first involved a detailed performance management review to be performed monthly by Lechabile supervisors who would monitor the employees' daily, weekly, monthly and yearly sales targets, and other aspects of their performance. An elaborate point system would allow employees to earn bonuses. The second plan was less structured. It allowed employees to set their own targets. They would remain unchecked, provided they met the minimum monthly performance quotas. Rather than have the supervisors evaluate their performances, staff members would conduct their evaluations of themselves, submitting these on a monthly basis. The fifth member of the team suggested a third option. He indicated that it might in fact be a mistake to introduce a formalised performance management system. After all, he said, "That's why we left IBM. I don't want to see a return to bureaucracy. Let's rather stay as we are—it's working well." Mosiako had to decide on a single course of action for the company. The MD considered which of the three options was most consistent with Lechabile's vision and culture.

EXHIBIT 7
LECHABILE'S
BALANCE SHEET,
APRIL 30, 1999

LECHABILE INCOME STATEMENT FOR PERIOD ENDING APRIL 30, 1999

	NOTES	1999
		R
Revenue		19 992 345
Cost of sales		15 859 569
Gross profit		4 132 776
Operating costs		4 604 299
Operating loss before interest	1	(471 523)
Interest paid		1 380
Interest received		173 700
Loss before taxation		(299 203)
Taxation	2	133 714
Accumulated loss at end of the year		(432 917)

LECHABILE BALANCE SHEET APRIL 30, 1999

	NOTES	1999
		R
Capital employed		
Share capital	3	98
Accumulated loss		(432 917)
Total shareholder's deficit		432 819
Long-term liabilities	4	253 767
Directors' loan	6	1 256 107
Total capital employed		1 077 055
Employment of capital		
Property, plant and equipment	5	681 437
Loan granted to associated company	7	122 792
Current assets		
Accounts receivable		8 376 553
Bank balances and cash		703 941
Total current assets		9 080 494
Current liabilities		
Accounts payable	4	8 673 954
Taxation		133 714
Total current liabilities		8 807 668
Net current assets		272 826
Total employment of capital		1 077 055

NOTES TO THE ANNUAL FINANCIAL STATEMENTS APRIL 30, 1999

	1999
	R

1. Operating loss before interest
This is arrived at after taking the following items into account:
Auditors' remuneration

Audit fees—current year	38 650
	1 850
	40 500
Depreciation (including capitalised leased assets)	
Computer equipment and computer software	20 735
Office furniture	32 730
	53 465
Directors' emoluments—managerial services	560 000

EXHIBIT 7
(CONTINUED)

	1999
	R

2. Taxation

South African normal tax:

Current taxation current year	133 714

3. Share capital

Authorised

1 000 ordinary shares of R1 each	1 000

Issued

98 ordinary shares of R1 each	98

4. Long-term liabilities

	R
Total finance lease and installment sale liabilities	288 856
Less: Current portion included under accounts payable	(35 089)
Long-term portion	253 767

The finance lease liability is repayable in monthly installments of R7 523 over a period of 60 months. Interest is payable at 19,081% p.a. The liabilities are secured by office furniture having a net book value of R278 976.

5. Property plant and equipment

	COMPUTER EQUIPMENT & COMPUTER SOFTWARE	OFFICE FURNITURE	TOTAL
	R	R	R
1999			
Cost			
Additions	102 696	632 206	734 902
End of the year	102 696	632 206	734 902
Accumulated depreciation			
Depreciation	20 735	32 730	53 465
	20 735	32 730	53 465
Carrying value			
End of the year	81 961	599 476	681 437

Office furniture is encumbered as disclosed in note 4.

	1999
	R

6. Directors' loans

Iqbal Hassim	80 000
Andile Mfingwang	188 357
Lebogang Winston Mosiako	198 750
Robert Moabi	198 750
Zainul Nagbee	198 750
Simon Ndoro	198 750
Teboho Vincent Williams	192 750
	1 256 107

These loans are currently unsecured, interest free and have no fixed terms of repayment.

7. Loan to associated company

Lechabile Communications (Pty) Ltd	122 792

The Lechabile Communications (Pty) Ltd loan has been subordinated in favour of other creditors of the company until such time as the assets of Lechabile Communications (Pty) Ltd, fairly valued, exceed its liabilities.

Source: Lechabile, 1999.

CASE 43

Phil Chan

Saturday, September 26, 1998. "We're getting there!" thought Phil Chan as the Air France flight took off from Paris on its was to Lagos, Nigeria. Phil Chan was the Vice-President Marketing of Basic Software, a middle-sized Hong Kong–based software producer. He was going to Lagos to close a business deal that Allen Lee, the owner of Basic Software, had been negotiating in the preceding weeks. Phil had left his home in Hong Kong 16 hours earlier and he looked forward to reaching his final destination.

Phil decided to review one more time the specifics of the deal, and the strategy that he would follow in the next day's meeting with his Nigerian partners. This was his first trip to Africa and he was somewhat uncertain about local business practices. Since he would be in Lagos for a short stay, he wanted everything to go smoothly.

THE DEAL

The deal required Basic Software to facilitate a financial transaction involving an international transfer of funds and would earn the company over $5 million, their 35 per cent share of the US$14.3 million deal. Allen Lee had been approached a month earlier by Tokunbo Jacobs with the business proposal (see Exhibit 1 for a copy of Mr. Jacobs' initial letter to Mr. Lee). Intrigued by the prospect, he entered into discussions with Mr. Jacobs. Mr. Lee was in the process of negotiating a sale in Bahrain on the Persian Gulf and thought that Africa could offer additional prospects

for his company: "Business is all over the world for us. You have to adapt yourself to the fact that conditions are different in other countries from how they are here. This is just part of living in today's world."

In response to his inquires, he received further details on the deal (see the two faxes in Exhibit 2 and Exhibit 3) and decided to send Phil Chan to Nigeria to complete the negotiations with the Nigerians.

THE NIGERIAN CONTEXT

Nigeria offered significant business opportunities (for a profile on Nigeria, see Exhibit 4). With 115 million people, Nigeria was the giant among Africa's 55 countries. Home to both Christians and Muslims, it possessed great assets. Nigeria's Gross Natural Product was the fifth largest on the

Professor Jean-Louis Schaan prepared this case with Professor Paul Beamish solely to provide material for class discussion. The authors do not intend to illustrate either effective or ineffective handling of a managerial situation. The authors may have disguised certain names and other identifying information to protect confidentiality.

Ivey Management Services prohibits any form of reproduction, storage or transmittal without its written permission. This material is not covered under authorization from CanCopy or any reproduction rights organization. To order copies or request permission to reproduce materials, contact Ivey Publishing, Ivey Management Services, c/o Richard Ivey School of Business, The University of Western Ontario, London, Ontario, Canada, N6A 3K7; phone (519) 661-3208; fax (519) 661-3882; e-mail cases@ivey.uwo.ca.

Copyright © 1998, Ivey Management Services.

African continent (in 1996 it amounted to US$28 billion). The country was endowed with significant resources. For example, Nigeria was among the world's largest producers of peanuts and rubber. It also produced important quantities of cotton, cocoa, yams, cassava, sorghum, corn and rice.

Nigeria was a producer and exporter of petroleum. Oil revenues were channeled towards the creation of an industrial base and the strengthening of the agricultural sector. Other important industries included mining (natural gas, coal) and processing (oil, palm, peanuts, cotton, petroleum).

PHIL'S POSITION

Phil Chan wondered how to approach the negotiations with the Nigerians and resolve a few issues which had not been addressed. He wanted the deal to go through without upsetting his partner. Phil had recently read a business publication which emphasized the need to be "skillful in the art of bargaining" when dealing with Nigerians (see Exhibit 5).

Phil and Allen had agreed on what should be obtained from the Nigerians. They believed that five percent (i.e., $715,000) was more than sufficient to cover the contingencies associated with the completion of this deal. They wanted the contingency fund reduced from 10 per cent to five per cent and their share raised from 35 per cent to 40 per cent.

Phil's plan was to negotiate the financial commitments to be made by both sides prior to the release of funds in order to minimize Basic Software's exposure. To have a clear picture of the expenses to be incurred in the implementation of the deal and of the respective contributions expected from each side, he wanted to examine the proforma financial statements prepared by Mr. Tokunbo. His objective was to modify them to Basic Software's advantage.

In a phone conversation with Mr. Tokunbo, Phil had found that in order to do business with the Nigerian government and its agencies, it was necessary to be registered in the official list of pre-qualified suppliers. Various approvals and stamps were required in the registration process. The US$48,000 requested in the September 21st fax was for that purpose.

Phil also wanted to obtain a written commitment that all expenses and advances incurred by Basic Software would be reimbursed from the contingency fund including his travel and accommodation expenses that amounted to just over $5,000.

Phil brought with him all the documents requested by the Nigerian partners, including a power of attorney signed by Allen Lee which authorized him to conclude the deal on behalf of Basic Software.

As he closed the Nigerian file and put it back in his briefcase, Phil wondered how he should conduct the negotiations in order to achieve his objectives without jeopardizing the relationship.

Initial Letter Sent by Tokunbo Jacobs to Allen Lee

26th August 1998

Tokunbo Jacobs
32 Falkar Street, Lagos, Nigeria
Tel. 234-1-874235, FAX 234-1-442157
TELEX *37854* RT NG

Dear Mr. President,

I am Mr. Tokunbo Jacobs, a staff of Nigerian National Petroleum Corporation (NNPC) and a member of the "Tenders Committee" of same corporation. I got your contact address through a close relation who is the corporate affairs manager of Nigerian Export Promotions Council. The transaction which is detailed below is being presented to you based on mutual trust and confidentiality.

After due consultation with other members of the Tender Committee, I have been specifically mandated to arrange with you the remittance of US$14.3M. being an over estimated sum resulting from contract executed by an expatriate contractor. The original value of this contract was purposely over inflated by us (Tender Committee) with the sum of $14.3M. Now that the firm have received their supposed payments accordingly and the projects commissioned, I want you to nominate an account into which this money will be paid for division between us and you.

Sharing terms are:—35% to you as the owner of the account into which the money will be paid, *55 per cent* to the officials of the three parastatals. 10% is set aside for contingencies. The big bosses of the three parastatals involved in this transaction namely:—Nigerian National Petroleum Corporation (NNPC) Federal Ministry of Finance (FMF) and Central Bank of Nigeria (CBN) are aware and behind the deal.

Meanwhile, you are required to indicate your interest through my FAX LINE or TELEX or by personal call. Please in your reply include your personal telephone, fax, and telex numbers for easy communications.

You can be rest assured that within few weeks of my receipt of your positive reply this amount will be remitted into your nominated account.

May I demand with the highest respect for the code of business morality and secrecy that under no circumstance should you circumvent or share with any uninvolved person the contents of this letter and other vital documents that may arise in the course of this noble transaction until it is accomplished.

I look forward to your pragmatic conformity to this mutual proposition.

Yours faithfully,

TOKUNBO JACOBS

EXHIBIT 2

September 12 Fax from Jacobs to Lee—12 September 1998

FROM: TOKUNBO JACOBS

<u>ATTENTION: ALLEN LEE</u>

Thanks for your fax of 9th September 1998 accepting to do this business with us. As you rightly mentioned there must be some responsibilities from your company to see this deal through. As a matter of fact you will be required to send to us some basic documents regarding your company to enable us process payment to your account.

These requirements are:

Two of your company's letter headed papers
Two of your company's proforma invoices
Bank particulars in which the said money will be transferred to:
the name of the bank, the account number, the telex number of the bank

On receipt of these above requirements the money will be remitted within twenty one working days.

Allen, I will suggest you visit us with the requirements to expedite this deal and to enable the officials involve in this transaction meet with you person to person for more confidence and to enable to meet who we are entrusting our money. Furthermore I want your personal home phone number for easy communications. Remember we will not hesitate to ask for your assistance financially if the need arises which will be duely deducted from the 10% set aside as contingencies during the process of this transaction. All request needed by you will be given proper attention.

Note: There is no risk whatsoever in this transaction putting into consideration our good home work and calibre of people involve in this deal.

Acknowledge receipt of this message through my fax number 442157.

Thanks and God bless.

TOKUNBO JACOBS

EXHIBIT 3

September 21 Fax from Jacobs to Lee

FAX: 21ST SEPTEMBER 1998

FROM: TOKUNBO JACOBS
ATTENTION: ALLEN LEE

Consequent to our telephone discussions, these are the required information. When you despatch those documents via DHL courier service, including your company's catalogues fax the air way bill number to me to enable me pick them up in earnest.

I want you to realize that there are some expenses which we cannot afford to ignore if this transaction must succeed highfreely. We will need US$48,000.00 in order to off-set these expenses. We therefore solicit you to assist us with the already set aside amount. As regards the account:

Beneficiary:	Larry Olunitgo
Bank Name:	National First Bank of Nigeria PLC
	Broad Street, Branch Lagos
	Nigeria
Account Number:	1554

Below is the format for the attorney:

The Governor of Central Bank of Nigeria
Tinubu Square Lagos

Dear Sir,
Letter of Authority

I wish to inform you that I Mr. Allen Lee, the president of Basic Software Company of Hong Kong hereby authorize barrister Eze Bakoto to sign on my behalf for the release of the sum of US$14.3 million U.S. dollars being payment for contract completed in 1996 for N.N.P.C. This is due to my present indisposed condition.

I look forward to your anticipated co-operation.

Yours faithfully,

Allen Lee (President).

N.B.: The about format should be typed on your company's letter-headed paper and should be included with the courier documents.

EXHIBIT 4
NIGERIAN FILE

1963	The establishment of the Republic of Nigeria.
1966	Military coup. The Biafran war begins, lasting two years and causing several million deaths of which approximately two million were Biafran.
1983	Military coup. Benral Buhari overturns President Shagari.
1984	Demonetization operations; bank notes are no longer in circulation and are replaced by a new currency.
1985	State coup. General Ibrahim Babangida replaces General Buhari.
1986	End of the flat exchange rate. Seventy percent devaluation of the Naira and currency fluctuations.
1990	Unsuccessful state coup against President Babangida.
	42 military shot after aborted state coup of April 22nd, 1990.
1991	Riots provoked by Shiite fundamentalists cause two hundred deaths.
1993	Civilian elections held. Results annulled by Babangida, who then steps down and gives power to an interim government.
1994	General Abacha overthrows government.
	Widespread strikes against regime of Abacha, who arrests union leaders.
1995	Dissident writer Sara-Wiwa hanged. International pressure on Abacha builds.
1996	National Election Commission of Nigeria names five political parties allowed to participate in future elections.

GNP per person: US$240/1996,
United Nations Development
Programs, The World Bank

Area: 923,768 sq km

Density: 117 persons/sq km

Capital: Lagos—10,000,000 inhabitants

Educational attainment: 47%

Languages spoken: English and approximately 200 dialects

Agricultural land: 34%

Average annual inflation rate: 1990–1996 - 37.6%

Total external debt: US$31,407 million

EXHIBIT 5
DOING BUSINESS
IN NIGERIA

Greetings: In Nigeria greetings are highly valued among the different ethnic groups. Refusing to greet another is a sign of disrespect. Due to the diversity of customs, cultures, and dialects that exist among the different ethnic groups in Nigeria, English is widely used in exchanging greetings throughout the country. Visitors are advised and encouraged to greet while in Nigeria. "Hello" is the most popular greeting. More formal greetings, such as "Good Morning," "Good Afternoon," and "Good Evening" are also appropriate. Avoid the use of casual of colloquial greetings and phrases such as "Hi" or "What's happening?" In addition, visitors are also encouraged to be courteous and cheerful when exchanging greetings. Do not be arrogant. Nigerians treat visitors with respect and, in return, expect to be treated with respect. Personal space between members of the same sex is much closer than in North America. This may cause discomfort to those not accustomed to conversing at close quarters.

Visiting: Nigerians try very hard to please their guests. Although Nigerians are generally not too concerned with time, they know about the western habit of punctuality and expect their western friends to arrive at the appointed time. Most Nigerians prefer "African time" to western punctuality. Nigerians treat their guests with congenial respect and expect their guests to respond in the same manner. Nigerians possess a rich heritage and hope for a bright future as a modern African nation, and thus can be offended by the "superior" attitude of some visitors.

Tipping: A dash (from the Portuguese word *das*, meaning "give") is a common Nigerian form of compensation in money, goods, or favours for services rendered. With the exception of services performed by waiters or bellhops, a "dash" is normally paid before the service is given. If the service offered is not desired, a firm refusal is usually necessary. The government is officially committed to discouraging certain kinds of "dash" that resembles bribery, such as payments for help in clearing customs, getting visas, or obtaining preferential treatment from government officials. But the custom is widespread and one has to be skillful in the art of "bargaining."

Personal Appearance: Dress varies according to the area and the culture. In the Muslim north, dress is very conservative for both men and women. Dress is more casual in the non-Muslim east and west. Shorts are not considered appropriate attire for Nigerian adults. For men, a shirt and tie are appropriate for formal and most other semi-formal occasions. Visitors will be most comfortable in cotton clothing—polyester is too warm. Traditional Nigerian men's dress is loose and comfortable. Although women in the cities and young girls often wear western dress, most women wear traditional long wraparound skirts, short-sleeved tops and head scarves. The fabric is renowned for its color and patterns.

Gestures: Nigeria is a multicultural nation and gestures differ from one ethnic group to another. Generally, pushing the palm of the hand forward with the fingers spread is a vulgar gesture and should be avoided. One should not point the sole of the foot at a person. Using the left hand in eating (unless left-handed) or in receiving something from someone has a bad connotation. The Yorubas (a large major ethnic group), in addition to the Ibibios and Igbos (two smaller, although major ethnic groups) will wink if they want their children to leave the room.

General Attitudes: Individual Nigerians are proud of the unique cultural heritage of their particular ethnic group. There is some ethnic tension, but continuing efforts are gradually unifying the nation. The Nigerians are striving to create a modern industrial society that is uniquely "African," and not "western." Because of negative connotations attached to the word "tribe," Nigerians avoid its use and "ethnic group" is often used in its place. Life in Nigeria moves at a relaxed pace with the exception of Lagos which can be very frenzied. People are generally not as time-conscious as in the west.

Language: English is the official language in Nigeria. However, because of the Nigerian mother tongue influence, spoken English may be difficult to understand. Pidgin English (broken English) is widely spoken by uneducated Nigerians, although even educated people widely use Pidgin English as a medium of informal conversation among themselves. Each of the over *250* ethnic groups also has its own distinct language. Hausa, Yoruba, and Ibo are widely spoken. Educated Nigerians usually are fluent in several languages.

Religion: In very general terms, Nigeria can be said to be divided between the Muslim North (47%) and the Christian South (34%), with a strong minority of traditional religions throughout the country (18%). However, it is important to note that both the Christians and the Muslims have strong missionary movements all over the whole country making the division of faiths into particular regions not exactly accurate. In addition, Nigerians may claim membership in a particular religion but may also incorporate traditional worship practices and beliefs into their daily life.

EXHIBIT 5
(CONTINUED)

Family: Although the technical details of family structure vary from culture to culture, Nigerian families are generally male-dominated. The practice of polygamy is common throughout the country. The protected status of Muslim women in Nigeria is similar to other Muslim countries; however, most other Nigerian women enjoy a great degree of freedom by influencing family decisions and engaging in open trade at the market place, where the money they make is their own. Large families traditionally help share the workload at home. Nigerians pay deep respect to their elders. Children are trained to be quiet, respective, and unassertive in their relations with adults. Marriage customs vary, but the payment of bridal wealth (money, property, or service traditionally given to the family of the bride by the husband) is common throughout the country.

Social and Economic Levels: Nigerians have the third highest average income in sub-Sahara Africa, but are still very poor by western standards. The average home consists of 1.4 rooms and more than three people per room. About 30% of the people live in absolute poverty. Nigeria once had the ninth lowest crime rate in the world, but without current statistics, it is difficult to determine the country's rank today.

Business Schedules: Most businesses are open from 8:00 AM to 12:30 PM, and then reopen from 2:00 to 4:30 PM. Government officers are open from 7:30 AM to 3:30 PM Monday through Friday. Many establishments and shops are also open on Saturdays with shorter hours. Every fourth Saturday is "Sanitation Day" (where no one is allowed on the street before 10:00 AM) and shops normally are not ready to receive business before noon. Sunday is the normal day of rest. Business appointments must be made in advance. Due to the poor telephone communication, business is often discussed on a person-to-person basis rather than via the telephone. Westerners are expected to be prompt, even though they may have to wait for some time after arriving.

Source: Canadian High Commission, Lagos.

Natura: The Magic Behind Brazil's Most Admired Company

Exame magazine, in charge of a yearly company ranking in Brazil, compared the cosmetics company Natura, winner of the Most Admired Company Award in 1998,[1] to the ideal Brazilian business model,

A school of Samba [Brazilian dance groups who practice all year to perform in Carnival]. Reasons: its capacity to mobilize for each year, in a synchronized movement, spontaneous and informal, a mass of people highly motivated around a common goal

— **Exame,** *July 8, 1998, "Excelência Perfumada"*

Luiz Seabra, Guilherme Leal and Pedro Passos, the three presidents of Natura, got together at their São Paulo headquarters after the recognition ceremony. The publicity had added pressure to come to a decision on Natura's new growth strategy. Natura had perfected its success formula in recent years; a well-trained and motivated door to door direct sales force of 220,000, selling premium, high margin cosmetic and personal care products to middle and upper class customer segments in Brazil (an unusual customer base in the direct sales industry). Natura had built a strong brand with the highest consumer loyalty in the industry by incorporating honesty and ethics into its marketing approach. The Company's turnover had grown at 37% CAGR[2] in the preceding 6 years and in 1997 return on capital reached 22.3%, significantly higher than the 4.8% median reached by the largest 500 companies in Brazil, and most Fortune 500 companies. The three presidents feared

Natura would be tempted to rest comfortably on its laurels with its 9% sales growth in 1998, which although humble compared to its past performance was still way above the industry average of 2%.

The market environment had only become increasingly competitive. Domestic competition had intensified with the opening of the Brazilian market and the stabilization of the economy in 1994, and Natura's second attempt to internationalize had yet to yield gains. The removal of import tariffs and the creation of trading blocks like Mercosur made the region much more attractive for foreign players. Large corporations already established in Brazil like Avon, P&G and Gessy Lever had begun to wake up from their slumber and new players had begun to pour into the region. Imports in the sector rose to US$ 250mm in 1997, more than double the US$ 118mm in 1996. Global consolidation trends put increasing pressure on Natura. With 36 major mergers and acquisitions in the preceding decade the industry was becoming increasingly concentrated in the hands of a few major global players. For Natura, the implications were that it had to benchmark itself against international standards of quality and innovation, and face competitors with deeper pockets and diversified product

This case was prepared by Marcela Escobari, visiting researcher at LBS, under the supervision and guidance of Professor Sumantra Ghoshal and Professor Don Sull. This case is intended to be used as a basis for class discussion rather than to illustrate either effective or ineffective handling of an administrative situation. The cooperation of Natura S.A. and Fundaçao Dom Cabral is gratefully acknowledged.

portfolios. The Brazilian consumer now had a more stable income, but had also become more demanding. As a result, Natura's impressive growth and margins were both under threat.

The options for growth meant diverging from Natura's traditional success formula: to expand Natura's cosmetics and skin care lines with nutritional supplements and healthcare products or to consider channels outside of direct selling such as stores or the Internet. New product segments could leverage Natura's strong brand and sales force, but would demand a new marketing strategy, a new R&D division, and acquiring expertise in a completely different industry. A change in the sales channel would undermine the current sales force, but may be anticipating future market trends.

As was often the case, each of the three presidents looked at the issue from different angles. Seabra, the founder, was worried it would be hard to provide customers with the same quality of innovative concepts as in cosmetics, and thought broadening the sales channel from direct selling would go against the relationship building philosophy they had expounded for the last 30 years. It would be an act of treason toward Natura's faithful Consultants (the name given to direct sellers at Natura). Leal, CEO and president, on the other hand was enthusiastic. Going into Internet sales was a futuristic concept that had not been tried by competitors in Brazil yet, and could represent unlimited growth. Leal thought an expansion into new segments would require Natura to merge or set a joint venture to acquire know-how. Passos, Natura's COO and president, was concerned about whether Natura had the resources for these initiatives now, and needed a quick resolution to plan how the new factory they were building would incorporate production lines for nutritional products.

As with all major decisions, Natura's growth strategy would have to be negotiated until consensus was reached. But this time they could not afford the luxury of dragging the decision for a year, as had happened the last time that they were not able to reach consensus.

GLOBAL INDUSTRY DYNAMICS

GROWTH AND CONSOLIDATION IN THE GLOBAL COSMETICS INDUSTRY

The cosmetics and personal care industry was dominated by large established players with increasingly global operations. The size of the market reached US$ 168.2 billion in 1998, a 3% dip from 1997 due to the recession in Latin America and Asia. This was an exception to the impressive growth throughout the 1990s as consumers in industrialized countries traded up to premium brands and the industry expanded with the constant introduction of new products. The future looked promising with industry experts pointing to the emergence of a global middle class of 2–2.5 billion in the next 10–15 years, which would move to luxury labels faster than any previous middle class ever did.[3] The power to capture this growth as well as the recuperation of emerging markets resided with the increasingly smaller number of global giants who had come to dominate the industry. The global market share of the top 20 players had grown to 72% in 1998, with the 10 top companies holding 54%.[4] Over the 1990's there were 36 acquisitions in the industry valued at US$ 15bn. Some of the largest included J&J buying Neutrogena in 1994 for US$ 1bn, P&G buying Max Factor in 1991 for the same amount, and Estee Lauder buying Aveda in 1998 for US$ 300mm, to add a "natural" brand.

BLURRING BOUNDARIES

The cosmetics industry had been traditionally separated into three main categories based on sales channel and price: the expensive prestige brands sold primarily through department stores or specialized stores; the cheaper mass retail market brands sold through drug stores and supermarkets and the middle-market direct sales brands sold door to door. These divisions were becoming blurred as the larger players tried to reach consumers of all income brackets. Some examples of this included L'Oreal's acquisition of Maybelline, a traditionally prestige company buying a mass market brand, or Avon, the largest direct sales player starting to sell through stores in malls to capture wealthier customers.

The strategic priority for most of the players in the industry was to develop and promote "megabrands" on a global basis (like P&G's "Oil of Olay" or Beiersdorf's "Nivea"), lead the industry in R&D, and expand market share through acquisitions and joint ventures.

THE PRESTIGE SECTOR

The prestige sector included companies with expensive brands such as L'Oreal (sales of US$ 12.4bn in 1998), the largest player, and other global companies like Estee Lauder, Chanel, Christian Dior, Clarins, Guerlain, and Shiseido. These players focused on selling status and technological innovation. They tended to spend heavily on advertising and to promote separate brands for specific niche populations. For example, Estee Lauder's *Prescriptives* was targeted toward the professional woman; *Origins* had a natural or "green" positioning; *M·A·C* appealed to the generation X/glamour crowd, while *Aramis* marketed men's items. Building a prestige brand to compete on its own implied huge investments over long periods of time; hence the preference for expansion through acquisition—both for accessing established brands and to obtain the benefits of synergies in R&D and administrative expenses.

THE MASS-MARKET SECTOR

The traditional mass-market brands sold through drugstores and supermarkets by companies like P&G (Cover Girl, Oil of Olay), Unilever, Gillette, Colgate-Palmolive and Revlon represented the largest segment with 63% of total cosmetics sales. The mass market had become more important with globalization since it was the most accessible channel in foreign countries. Competition had become fierce in this sector with prestige players entering the mass-market through acquisitions (i.e., L'Oreal/Maybelline), and the emergence of an "upper mass-market," offering products with the scientific advances typically available in prestige products, but at lower prices. The pressure had been felt by players like P&G who was undergoing a major restructuring, and Revlon, which appeared to be in the process of selling one or more of its businesses.

DIRECT SALES

Direct sales organisations (DSO) could be categorised as a separate business due to its distinctive strategies in marketing, recruiting and growth. Throughout history, DSOs had been very successful in attracting a population with restricted access to the formal job market by providing a profitable, flexible and nurturing work environment. In the cosmetics business, the major DSO's included Avon (US$ 5.2bn in sales), Mary Kay (approx. US$ 1.1bn) and Amway (US$ 5.7bn). They targeted their products to the middle/ lower class segments, which were usually also the socio-economic levels from which they built their sales force. Natura was a rare exception using direct sales to sell prestige products in Brazil.

Avon, the largest player with presence in 131 countries, had traditionally targeted the lower-middle class market, but was trying to shed its grandmotherly image and attract wealthier and younger customers. Avon had set up stands in malls around the U.S., quite a revolutionary departure from its 113 years of direct selling. Although the experiment had attracted first-time users, it was expected to take business away from its direct sales force.

BRAZILIAN COSMETICS INDUSTRY

When Natura was created in 1969 there was a clear division in the Brazilian cosmetics market; on one side were the cheap mass products found in drugstores and supermar-

kets, and on the other, a few luxury products sold in specialised stores. Outside of Avon who entered Brazil in 1959 with local production facilities, there was almost no foreign competition. Import substitution policies implemented in the seventies, with prohibitively high import tariffs, spurred domestic production for a virtually captive market. These anarchic policies lasted until the early 80s when almost every American bank cut off its credit lines to Brazil due to political instability in the region, bringing about a long-lasting recession. In the mid-eighties, attracted by high margins in the sector, giants like P&G and Unilever entered Brazil—where Unilever was operating since the 60's—investing significant amounts and buying brands and companies. By this time Natura had built a prestige brand and a loyal customer base.

As Brazil opened its market in the 1990s, more foreign competition flooded in, and many of the Brazilian producers either disappeared or were bought out. Most local companies could not keep up with the innovation necessary to compete. For international players, Brazil was a naturally attractive market—the 5th largest market in the world in hygiene and beauty products consumption (measured in dollars), and the 6th largest in cosmetics. It was also 27th in income per capita which, given its large population base (170 million), implied huge potential for increased consumption. With the inflow of foreign players, the cosmetics sector became even more concentrated than the food sector. Natura turned down repeated acquisition attempts, and was able to thrive in the face of strong competitors.

In 1998, sales of cosmetics and toiletries in Latin America amounted to US$ 18.5bn, of which Brazil represented almost half. Consumption in this sector more than doubled in Brazil in the three years after 1994 as inflation came under control, and a new middle class began to emerge. In 1998, the largest player in the industry was Avon, with US$ 840mm in sales, followed by Natura. Other companies with significant presence include Gessy Lever, O'Boticario and L'Oreal. Among more upscale newcomers were Christian Dior, Shiseido and Davidoff.

Avon competed with Natura for the same sales force, but its products were targeted to a lower-income client base, with average prices of one third of Natura's. Avon had over 500,000 resellers in Brazil, with a much lower productivity than that of Natura's Consultants. In 1996, the average sale for an Avon representative was US$ 2,450 while Natura's was US$ 3,432. Product-wise, Natura's closest rival was O'Boticario, a Brazilian company with 1,616 stores, and a strong portfolio in perfumes. O'Boticario positioned its products 10–20% cheaper than Natura's.

BACKGROUND OF NATURA

In 1999, Natura marketed and distributed 300 prestige products across seven main categories: perfume, skin care, hair care, color cosmetics, sun screen, deodorants and children's products, targeted at the middle and upper class segments. Most of Natura's production took place at a factory in Itapecerica, on the outskirts of São Paulo, which produced 300 SKUs (stock keeping units), and operated at 90-95% capacity. A US$ 110mm project to be completed in 1999 would replace this factory with more modern facilities and five-fold capacity increase. In 1998, Natura had sales[5] of US$ 692mm and an EBITDA of US$ 83mm. Only 3% of sales came from international operations, mostly in Argentina, Chile and Peru.

HISTORY

Luiz Seabra, Natura's founder, was first introduced to the cosmetics world when working for a multinational company at the age of 16. One of his most memorable projects was the launch of an electric shaver, quite a pioneering product in Brazil in the early 60's. While helping with an innovative marketing scheme, Seabra first learned about the skin as a "live organ." He continued taking courses in physiology, biochemistry and other topics related to therapeutic cosmetics, quite unusual for an economics student. Following his interests in this subject, he joined Bionat in 1966, a small family laboratory that produced cosmetics. After three years, he decided to quit and start Natura with Berjeaut—son of Bionat's owner.

They founded Natura with US$ 9,000 and the idea of incorporating principles of therapeutic treatments in the production of cosmetics. They set up their first store in a garage, using the selling points that still characterised Natura: a personalised approach and products customised to Brazil's humid climate and local skin types.

THE BIRTH AND FALL OF THE 5-COMPANY STRUCTURE

The business only took off when the direct sales approach was implemented. After some failed attempts, Seabra partnered with Yara Amaral, an executive with extensive experience in direct sales and founded Pró-Estética—to distribute products in São Paulo and manage the sales force. Other channels like drugstores and franchises were considered, but Seabra thought that it would be difficult to pass on Natura's therapeutic concepts to store attendants or investors. With distributors, Natura would have to provide high margins, and allow them to determine the way to sell, or invest heavily in publicity to help sales. Without the

resources to invest in marketing, and wanting to maintain Natura's image, the direct sales method appeared to be the only viable option. They were surprised to find a large pool of capable women eager to embrace the opportunity offered by Natura. The economic recession at the time created pressure for women to find alternative sources of income, and service an existing demand that had not yet been exploited.

In order to have national distribution, Berjeaut brought in Guilherme Leal and created **Meridiana** in 1979, to distribute Natura's products to the whole country except São Paulo (covered by Pró-Estética) and Rio de Janeiro (covered by an independent distributor). Guilherme was trained in business and, following a change of government, had just lost his job at a public railroad company. As Natura continued to grow in the early 80s, new partners were brought in and additional companies were founded. Yara Amaral, Beal and a cosmetics producer founded **YGA** to make colour cosmetics and perfumes, and **Éternelle** was created to replace the independent distributor in Rio de Janeiro. Pedro Passos was brought in by Leal to head the industrial area at the YGA factory in 1983. They had worked together at the railroad company, and had continued to play soccer on the same team every week. When asked what he saw in Passos, a production engineer from the Polytechnic Institute in São Paulo, Leal answered, "he was a player with character and a powerful inner drive."

This growing corporate structure helped Natura experience explosive sales growth in the 80s, aided by Brazil's closed economy, high inflation and unstable currency which made foreign competition unfeasible. The 5-company structure was an effective response to the needs for quick growth and new capital infusion. It also provided an internal competitive dynamic which pushed the company forward.

> Meridiana wanted to surpass Pró-Estética in sales, YGA wanted to surpass Natura in sales. There was a fight to see who had a more important participation in the sales channel. During this time when we were relatively alone in the market, that internal competitive energy forced each [company] to make more innovative products and improve quality, trying to win the attention of the consultants. This internal struggle created energy for growth.
>
> — *Pedro Passos, COO and president,*
> *Natura*

Natura's sales jumped from US$ 5mm in 1979 to US$ 170mm in 1989 (43% CAGR). The number of Consultants grew from 1,000 to 33,000 for the respective years. Natura's growth was quite unusual during what was seen as the "lost decade" for many Brazilian businesses. During this time 9 zeros were removed from the currency, 10 failed currency plans were attempted and 11 finance ministers rotated through office.

Finally, at the height of the economic crisis in 1989, Natura's growth came to a screeching halt. Inflation of 89% per month, costly capital and the opening of the Brazilian economy contributed to Natura's instability. Earnings slumped and Natura was forced to dismiss 15% of its workforce. As new competitors started to pour in, Natura realised it had limited production capacity, an outdated product portfolio, low quality services to its sales force, and a complex decision-taking process due to the 5-company structure. Internal conflicts within the company made it difficult to react to the changing environment.

> The energy created by the 5 companies became negative energy. By 1989 we needed a more long-term plan, to invest in a new factory, technology, professionals—but we couldn't agree on a common strategic plan for the different companies. . . . There were four major partners who owned 80% of the companies, but they weren't the same ones in each company. Decisions became slow, we couldn't agree on new products, new price policies . . . the interests [of the major shareholders] were not homogeneous. We had reached an impasse.

> — *Pedro Passos, COO and president,*
> *Natura*

The shareholders had polarised their positions; one group led by Seabra and Leal wanted to invest significantly in growing the business while the others were content with Natura's performance and wanted to cash out. Finally Seabra and Leal bought out the stakes[6] of the other shareholders and, together with Pedro Passos (a minority shareholder at the time) created the existing triumvirate to lead the company towards growth. Decisions would have to be negotiated and discussed but there was an underlying common goal.

RESTRUCTURING AND PROFESSIONALISATION

A three-year period of transformation followed. The 2 factories and 3 distribution centres were merged into one company under one brand—Natura. The headquarters moved to a new factory, with 50% increased capacity, and the production and distribution centres were centralised. The new owners reinvested all profits to develop new operational, information and planning systems and revamp the product line with new technology. The original values and vision of the company were reinforced and the company became increasingly aware of its social responsibilities. Realising that the company was becoming larger than its owners could handle, a new management team was recruited from multinationals. Nine of the 11 directors in 1999 were brought in from the outside. This move created some tensions with the incumbent middle management

and fears of disruption in Natura's culture, although they helped benchmark best practices and incorporate international management tools into the company. Natura was ready for the new boom that came in 1994 with the Real Plan[7] and subsequent economic stabilisation. In the following 4 years, the company grew by over 500%.

THE ATTEMPT TO GO INTERNATIONAL

Going international seemed like a natural growth progression for a company growing at the pace of Natura in the 1980's, and a necessary hedge to the sporadic economic crisis faced by Brazil. After 3 attempts, Natura realized the difficulties with exporting a brand and an image outside of Brazil. The first attempt to go abroad was not structured; it began through the initiative of a few ex-Natura managers who started distribution in Bolivia and Chile importing the products from Brazil. In a similar manner distribution was opened in Peru, Paraguay, Uruguay on a small scale. In 1994, the effort was revisited with added commitment to Argentina. An ex-manager of Avon was hired to head the office in Argentina, but without much guidance from the headquarters and no background on Natura, it ended a complete failure.

> We didn't have the knowledge where we needed it . . . We created an Avon operation down in Argentina with the Natura brand. It is very different, the concept, the value added, the demonstration [of the product] . . . Our prices in Brazil are normally 3 times higher than Avon, because we have a niche market, quality, and a brand image which support this.

> — *Guilherme Leal, CEO and president,*
> *Natura*

The growth in Brazil at the time was so high, there were no internal human resources to devote to Argentina.

> Natura was growing at a rate of 100% per year, and between growing 100% in Brazil where we had an important critical mass and growing 300% starting from zero, it was better to grow at the headquarters. It was a matter of resources; we did have financial resources, but we lacked primarily human resources. The Brazilian operation consumed 110% of their time.

> — *Breno Lucki, Director of International*
> *Operations, Natura*

The sales structure used in Brazil was not replicated in Argentina. In an effort to grow the sales channel fast, the incorporation of new consultants was not restricted by a minimum ordering amount. More than 50% of the channel was either "ghost" (invented names to earn the incentives offered to Consultants who recruit new Consultants) or final customers who wanted to benefit from the discounts. The turnover of Consultants was high and sales volume was low. The group realized internationalization was much harder than expected.

The strategy was revisited once again in 1998 and efforts were targeted to Argentina. New managers from Brazil were appointed, and all directors at the headquarters were held accountable with ten percent of their bonus linked to the performance of the international operations. In 1999, international sales reached US$ 20 million and profits were still awaited.

THE "MAGIC" BEHIND NATURA

In 1999, Natura was the largest Brazilian-owned cosmetics company, and the most profitable in the sector. It had a very favorable image among Brazilians, recognized and admired for producing quality products and for being a socially conscious company. The combination had earned Natura the title of best company in the hygiene and cosmetic sector in Brazil for three consecutive years, despite not being the largest player in the sector. Many business analysts had sought to pinpoint the formula of Natura's success, and had often resorted to "Natura's magic" in trying to explain its performance and consistent customer loyalty under difficult circumstances.

TRUTH IN COSMETICS

Natura's motto, "Truth in Cosmetics," resonated strongly among employees at all levels. According to Seabra, Natura's founder, "in an industry famed for promises and the pursuit of success at any price, Natura prides itself in offering a truthful approach to consumers." This philosophy translated into products that were clearly labelled and a sales force trained to give informed advice regarding the ingredients and appropriateness of each product. Natura's products must somehow contribute to the "well-being" of its customers, both through its choice of technology and the message behind each product. For example, Natura could not produce hair colouring products, because the process inevitably harms the hair. Same with nail polish; Natura did not include it in their cosmetics line until the R&D department found a formula that did not have formaldehyde and toluene, ingredients that tend to debilitate the nail.

New products and lines were usually launched with a message of how it contributed to customers' well-being, which was incorporated into commercials and the training to Consultants. The Mother/Baby ("Mama/Bebe") creams, for example, were associated with the Shantalla method,

encouraging the touch and caressing which created stronger ties between the child and the mother. Chronos, the "anti-signs" cream, was marketed with the message that beauty was not achieved through the pursuit of youth but through the right attitude toward ageing. Natura believed this approach had contributed to its loyal customer base, and was a key differentiation factor for its products.

> We believe we can help transform people's lives and the society. We do what we believe and make a profit from it. The functionality of the product is just one aspect of the necessities it provides... we deliver in our products much more than functional answers, we deliver emotions, spiritualism, intellectual ideals that can improve people's lives.
>
> — *Guilherme Leal, CEO and president,*
> *Natura*

ADVERTISING

Natura's marketing campaigns highlighted the theme of "Truth in Cosmetics" which sometimes went against the norms of the industry. For example, its commercial for the Chronos line (anti-wrinkle cream) used Natura consumers over 30 years of age instead of young models, with the implicit message according to Leal that "you will not look like Claudia Schiffer with our products, but you're still beautiful." This campaign, called "Real Pretty Women," exalted middle age beauty, "since outside of technology, a woman's beauty depends on her harmonious relationship with time and the different phases of life."

This campaign had made Chronos one of the most profitable lines in Natura even though the product did not seem very different than most anti-wrinkles lines in the industry. Araujo explained how the way Natura launched this line challenged the logic of the industry:

> We had a big discussion about how to label our products for different age groups. All marketing benchmarks advised against putting the ages on the product since women tend to avoid any product that clearly identifies their age. Natura challenged this notion because it went against its concept of truth.
>
> — *Marcelo Araujo, Commercial Director,*
> *Natura*

> The composition of the product is also differentiated. Lancome has 3 different products for wrinkles, one with vitamin A, another with vitamin C and another with vitamin D, which sell based on brand recognition. Our product incorporates the 3 vitamins. Why? Because the 3 vitamins are good for the skin, and how could we answer to a consumer who asked us why we separate the vitamins . . .
>
> — *Philippe Pommez, R&D Director,*
> *Natura*

DIRECT SALES: WIN THROUGH RELATIONSHIPS

Luiz Seabra realised early the power of relationships in people's well being, and decided to make Natura a vehicle for these rewarding relationships. The direct sales method was an integral part of Natura's business identity, and although alternative methods like franchising, or even catalogue sales had been proposed throughout time, they had so far been discarded. Natura believed that it was the only significant company worldwide to successfully use direct sales to access upper and upper-middle demographic segments.

An army of 220,000 Consultants, who received continuous training and the highest commissions in the industry, provided Natura with a significant competitive edge and created a strong barrier to entry to other newcomers. Natura's sales managers believed there were an additional 440,000 informal resellers who sold Natura products. They usually "subcontracted" from active Consultants because they did not qualify themselves or because they wanted to help a family member achieve sales targets. Managers perceived this practice as harmless given Natura's established reputation in the market.

R&D: BUY INSTEAD OF PRODUCE IN-HOUSE

In an industry where constant innovation was the key barrier to entry, Natura knew that it could not compete with its global competitors on creating technology from scratch. Instead, it focused on coming up with innovative concepts and marketing schemes and then tracking patents and buying the technology from universities and research centers around the world. According to Philippe Pommez, Natura's R&D director, this efficient patent tracking system was a sustainable R&D policy because the technology already existed,

> The hard part is not finding the new technology, it is deciding what you are looking for. This is where Seabra's conceptualisation of new products and new lines becomes indispensable.
>
> — *Philippe Pommez, R&D Director, Natura*

The R&D department had close connections with universities in France and the U.S. This strategy allowed Natura to be competitively innovative, producing a new product every 3 working days (an output comparable to companies like 3M). Almost 40% of Natura's revenues were derived from products introduced within the last 2 years. This was achieved with an R&D department of only 150 people and a budget of around 3.0% of net sales. Most of Natura's competitors spent close to 3.5% of *sales* on R&D. L'Oreal, the producers of Lancôme and Maybelline, spent US$ 370mm, equivalent to 3% of sales and 48% of net income in 1998, and Shiseido alone spent US$ 200mm on R&D, four times as much as Natura.

INNOVATION / PRODUCT DEVELOPMENT

Natura's innovation process started with a monthly meeting between the three presidents, the Marketing director and the R&D director, where new ideas and technological advances would be discussed. New product ideas could be quickly tested in the market because Consultants could obtain immediate feedback from the customers. Consultants were encouraged to call clients after the sale of a new product simply to gauge their reactions, and maintain a flowing relationship.

> We can be so quick in putting products in the market because we can get immediate feedback, there's no need to create test groups, etc. The close relationships between customers, consultants and promoters can give us a good notion of the product's acceptance within a week. With one of our perfumes, we realized it would be a failure from the consultant's reactions, even before it was put into the market. It was removed from the catalogs within 3 weeks.
>
> — *Philippe Pommez, R&D Director, Natura*

Natura's faith in the concepts behind its products often challenged industry precedents. One of Natura's daring ideas was the Mother/Baby product line launched in 1993. Although research showed that J&J, with 90% market share, had an unassailable lock in this market, Natura decided to enter anyway and succeeded in capturing a staggering share of the sector. The marketing strategy that associated the product with creating closer ties between the mother and baby, the appealing packaging and the brand's reputation for high quality helped the line's entry to this market. Similarly, Natura ventured into the luxury perfumes segment, which was dominated by established international brands and captured an impressive 30% share, with similar conceptual—rather than technological—innovation.

Natura's presidents believed that it was becoming harder to come up with truly innovative concepts, and they were constantly trying to stop the innovation meetings from becoming a routine.

VALUES

Luiz Seabra wanted to build Natura as a values-based company from its inception, and his commitment to truth and to the value of relationships had impacted every aspect of the company: its products, training programs, relationships among employees, etc. Natura's self-defined purpose was to provide well-being/being well; "to create and market products and services that promote the individual's harmonious, pleasant relationship with himself/herself and his/her own body (well-being), and at the same time with others and the world (being well)." Seabra acknowledged this might seem like "an oxymoron in today's cosmetics industry," but believed that Natura had projected and been consistent with this philosophy in all its dealings with employees and customers.

Seabra was a firm believer in the power of relationships and demonstrated this in the way he treated his employees and the sales force. He personally called every manager and director on their birthdays, he knew the names of the cleaning personnel in his office, and avoided formality in his interactions with people. His personal conduct had become a source of many of the stories and anecdotes that almost defined the soul of the company. Most employees were ready to expound on Natura's values of transparency and respect in its approach toward employees, customers and the world around it. Manoel Luiz, manager in the IT services division, joined Natura in 1996 after heading the IT department at Einstein Hospital, São Paulo's most prestigious hospital, and explained his reasons,

> Why am I working here!? . . . I have never seen a company like this one, never. The treatment of all the people, the truth with which we work throughout the chain: with our suppliers, our employees and our resellers. It is everything, treatment, truth, payment, benefits, the vision, the mission. . . . To give you one example, this year our founder-president is living in London, and the 6th of March was my birthday. I went away for the weekend, and when I arrived there was a message from him from London: "I am very sorry I haven't met you but I'm calling to say happy birthday, happy new year of life." It is very different—in the hospital I had to call people by, Mr, Dr, to have some respect, this is not the way that I show respect. These are not the relationships I want in my life.

> — *Manoel Luiz, Manager in IT, Natura*

The office layout of Natura's headquarters reflected this sense of openness and camaraderie. Everybody except the three presidents sat in opaque pink cubicles in a large open space, from directors to customer service attendants. Everybody ate at the same cafeteria and there were no parking spaces reserved for management. Leal proudly contrasted Natura's culture to that of a bank he worked for earlier, where elevators were blocked every morning so the President of the company could ride alone while the rest of the employees watched as they waited.

COMMITMENT TO SOCIETY

According to Leal, the value of a firm was proportional to the quality relationships it had with the entire community, promoting material, emotional and spiritual enrichment. He was the driving force behind Natura's social endeavours, which centred primarily on community-based educational programs. Some programs were run by Natura employees, while others were managed in conjunction with NGO's to aid public schools. In 1997, Natura Consultants raised US$ 1.5mm selling T-shirts and cards to fund 46 community education projects, and every year 10% of dividends went to a department that promoted social causes. In 1998, Natura donated an additional US$ 2.5mm from company profits.

FLEXIBILITY FOR MIDDLE MANAGEMENT

Middle management enjoyed a very high level of flexibility and autonomy in the organization. Of their annual bonus, half depended on the sales target achieved by the Company, and the other half was based on achieving the targets of their particular division. Managers devised their own yearly targets and then discussed them with their direct bosses. Because of this freedom to set their own targets, people tended to aim very high—much higher than what they would accept if the targets came down from above.

Although managers set their own targets, they needed to be consistent with Natura's overall goals. Every September, all the managers received Natura's yearly strategic plan devised by a council of top management led by Pedro Passos. The plan described the overall goals for the year, including growth targets in the domestic and international area, growth in new businesses, etc. Each manager then prepared the strategic plan of each area (sales, IT, logistics, manufacturing, etc.) that would help Natura achieve these goals.

> I ask myself, what do I have to do to leverage the goals of Natura? I prepare my plan first. For example, I have to have more availability of the system, more facilities for the Consultants, etc. I discuss it with my director who passes it on to Pedro. Pedro tells us it's good here, it's not enough here . . . It is discussed until everyone agrees.

> — *Manoel Luiz, Manager in IT, Natura*

SALES MANAGEMENT

Natura's sales organization had three basic levels: Sales Manager (20), Sales Promoters (550) and Consultants (220,000). Each sales manager was in charge of 20–30 Promoters who covered a specified geographical area. Each Promoter was responsible for training and supervising a group of Consultants in a neighborhood or a whole city in more dispersed areas.

Wooing new Consultants into Natura and keeping them was one of the Promoters' major jobs. Natura fiercely competed with the other major international direct sales companies such as Avon, Amway and Mary Kay for its share of this autonomous and highly mobile workforce. To do this, Natura offered one of the highest average compensation packages in direct sales industry, a 30%[8] profit on any product sold. Natura also tried to differentiate itself through the constant and personalized contact with the Sales Promoter, a complete sales support system, and Natura's positive image in the marketplace. Sales Promoters organized "Natura Meetings" for their Consultants every 21 days (equals one cycle) which provided continual training and reinforcement of Natura's values. These meetings tended to be fun gatherings where Promoters would present promotions of new products, and provide a thorough description of the product, its ingredients, attributes and target customer. For every meeting, the Promoter counted on a video and the newsletter "Natura Consulting" put together by the headquarters for every cycle. Consultants received free courses, free support materials and were part of an elaborate recognition program, which celebrated both performance and seniority. They could order products directly by phone and receive products at home, free of charge with one of the fastest services in the world. Avon's sales force, in contrast, needed to send the orders through the Promoter only during their periodic meetings.

Natura had 2 service hotlines that supported Promoters on the administrative chores. The CAN (Centro de Atendimento Natura) provided pre and post-sales support for the Consultants, 14 hrs a day. With 400 operators receiving 420,000 calls per month, it was one of the largest phone-based support centers in Brazil. They received product orders and provided information on delivery times, bills, promotions, and products. They provided any type of information for Natura's 23 lines, and over 300 products. When a Consultant called to place an order, the attendant inputted the request on the computer which was electronically sent to the warehouse where products were picked automatically and filled in boxes. Natura was able to send a package 24 hrs after the request was made.

Natura's customer service hotline (SNAC), played an important role in collecting feedback from customers. The 40 telephone operators received 50,000 calls a month, regarding all types of customer needs; complaints, feedback, questions about products, etc. To encourage feedback from Brazilian customers unused to these services, these attendants enjoyed a high degree of flexibility and authority in solving customer concerns. Attendants could reimburse or replace a product under any circumstance, they could pay doctor's fees in case of adverse reactions to Natura products, reschedule Consultants' debts if appropriate, etc.

BUILDING RELATIONSHIPS IN THE SALES STRUCTURE

Natura differentiated its direct sales operations by emphasising the development of strong relationships between its Consultants and the ultimate consumer. Consultants were trained to create trusting relationships with their clients, to provide personalised advice and educate their clients on the benefits of Natura's products. Partly due to this personalised treatment, Natura had the highest consumer loyalty within the industry.

Relationship building was encouraged not only toward clients, but also within the organisation's structure. Sales Promoters, each in charge of 250–300 Consultants in a specific region, had more than a sales co-ordination role, they served as counsellors and friends. The Promoter met the Consultants at their homes on a one-to-one basis through the interview process and was thereafter available to discuss non-work related issues. Unlike the competition, most of the Promoter's salary was linked to retention of Consultants rather than sales.

During "Natura Meetings" every 3 weeks, Promoters introduced new products and promotions, and took the opportunity to socialize and share experiences. They usually invited a fraction of their Consultants—50–60 at any given reunion—to maintain a manageable group. The meetings often took place at the Promoter's house, where the whole family participated in the cooking and decoration, creating an intimate and personal atmosphere. The meetings were full of cheering and applauding as almost a quarter of the Consultants present received a gift of some sort; for high performance in sales, bringing new Consultants or random lotteries. Each Promoter was free to incorporate other activities during these reunions. For example, at the beginning of the year a Promoter devoted her session to explaining the reasons behind the recent currency devaluation and its repercussions, and on another occasion she celebrated Mother's Day reading poems and singing. Natura had the lowest turnover ratio among all direct sales companies.

TRAINING AND DEVELOPMENT OF THE WORKFORCE

Natura provided continual training programs for the sales force on topics ranging from product portfolio to lectures on ethics and citizenship. Managers could choose from a variety of training programs: in 1998 there was a choice of 58 courses in the areas of corporate management, production security, computer programs, operations, and quality. All managers and directors received an average of 180 hours of training in 1998. Outside of these voluntary programs, all managers were fully introduced to the mission and values of the company, its products, and sales structure. Managers also had the option of participating in an executive management program in one of the most prestigious Business Administration colleges in Brazil.

The Sales Promoters benefited from an extensive and structured training program; after two formal training sessions in the first 3–4 months of work, Promoters were required to return to the headquarters every two years for a week-long Advanced Formation Program, taught by experienced Promoters, Sales Managers and outside experts. New Promoters were matched with more experienced Promoters in the same region, to build mentoring and support relationships that often lasted throughout his or her career.

RECRUITMENT

The majority of the managers and directors were recruited through word of mouth or personal recommendations. This method had worked best in finding people that fit Natura's culture. There was also an emphasis on hiring from within, so positions were advertised internally first to provide career advancement opportunities to employees.

THE THREE PRESIDENTS

The three president structure at the top had been a unique feature of the company since 1995. Internally, most employees believed that the three personalities complemented each other, in a wonderful symbiosis. As Seabra explained,

> Our management team would not be as vigorous and efficient if it was based on the personality of one sole leader. The market is so complex now that a leader must dominate different languages: act with sensibility on one side, and American pragmatism on the other.

> — *Luiz Seabra, founder and president,*
> *Natura*

The distribution of roles among the three was a natural process and reflected their different training and personalities. Seabra's intuition to gauge customers' needs and his charismatic and sincere approach toward the employees were key to Natura's culture. He had an important role in the product innovation committee and was in charge of leading important ceremonies for the sales force. Leal was the acting CEO, who concentrated on the strategy and the future direction of the Company, while Pedro Passos maintained tight control over operations, making sure that all existing activities were run smoothly and efficiently. The interaction between the three had little formalisms or

manuals, and had been perfected over the years. The three were often described as separate parts of single body.

> If Leal is the head, and Passos is the arms and legs of the company, Seabra would be the soul and memory of the company's vision.

> — Exame, *July 1998*

THREE PERSONALITIES

Many of the concepts behind Natura's product lines and the values that underlie the Company's culture came from Seabra's personal beliefs. Influenced by Jungian and Buddhist philosophy, Seabra was a mystical, soft-spoken character. He built two temples (one Buddhist and the other Shintoist) and a catholic Chapel in his back yard. Probably influenced by the Jungian analyst he visited for over a decade, Seabra tried to look at the world through mythology. When talking to the Consultants, instead of using complex marketing jargon to explain what moves the market, Seabra preferred to tell a story of Ananque, the goddess of necessity. Seabra was relatively the most removed from the day to day running of Natura, but provided the deeper insights on consumer needs and served as an inspiring force during the innovation meetings.

> Luiz [Seabra] is a man with a big passion that is the philosophy behind Natura. He is a very nice person to work with, because he is very calm and his approach is normally conciliatory.

> — *Pedro Passos, COO and president,*
> *Natura*

Seabra was also the key figure in periodic award ceremonies for the Promoters and Consultants. His presence and moving speeches were usually the most awaited events in these gatherings. His motivating role was not limited to the stage; he personally called each of the 150 directors and managers to compliment them on their birthday.

> I do this as reverence to life. Not everybody values birthdays this much. I use the occasion to show that life should be celebrated. Because life is sacred.

> — *Luiz Seabra, founder and president,*
> *Natura*

Leal was in charge of the strategic issues. He joined the company in 1979 on the distribution side. Leal looked out for Natura's strategies at all levels. He led the internationalisation process, and was looking into other growth alternatives like moving into new products, finding potential partners, and modernising the Company. He constantly sought to institutionalise Natura's successful practices, but also looked outside for new ideas.

Guilherme [Leal] is different [than Seabra]. He is looking at the future and new trends at all times. He is very provocative—to make the company change. He is not nervous, but loves to constantly put new challenges to the company.

> — *Pedro Passos, COO and president,*
> *Natura*

Leal was behind Natura's decision to bring in a new management team and devised Natura's variable compensation system. Leal was usually the one bringing new ideas, challenging the group to take risks, and just *do* things. As he said, "the how will be determined on the way." Passos provided an example of Leal's daring ideas,

> Guilherme, 10 years ago proposed we should go sell in Asia. We didn't even know how to sell in Porto Alegre [south of Brazil], but he wanted to sell in Asia. He challenges our routines with new ideas.

> — *Pedro Passos, COO and president,*
> *Natura*

Leal believed that creating positive and respectful working relationships within the company and towards the community was essential for sustainable success. He was the driving force behind Natura's praised social endeavours. When asked about the company's purpose, Leal answered,

> When I was asked about the future of this company twenty years ago, I replied our purpose was to create the largest cosmetics company in the world. This is a small purpose. Now our purpose is even greater, to make the world a better place.

> — *Guilherme Leal, CEO and president,*
> *Natura*

Aside from the income from sale of T-shirts and cards, Leal set a fixed percentage of the Company's dividends toward social programs. Leal's sense of social responsibility extended outside Natura: he had established ETOS, an association to teach corporate ethics to business people, and had decided to donate most of his net worth to a foundation he was expecting to create in the future.

Leal brought Passos into Natura in 1983 to bring technical expertise to one of the factories. Three years later he became a stockholder and in 1995, a co-president at Natura. Passos was described as pragmatic and efficient. He determined the how-tos of achieving the company's goals and ran the company on a day to day basis. In charge of operations, he spent half of his time in the factory in Itapecerica. He reported to the board Natura's strategic plan, capital structure and human resources policies. The 11 Directors reported directly to him.

Passos usually had to put the breaks to Seabra and Leal's running imagination, and looked out for the bottom line. He gave the others a sense of what was too expensive or dangerous. Few in Natura knew the exact day to day numbers as he did. According to him, most did not need to know. They needed to know if Natura achieved its broad targets—knowing the details of the ups and downs would bring people's motivations down.

Each president approached issues from different perspectives. Both Leal and Seabra often joined the rest of the employees in the cafeteria or the coffee bar in a corner of the floor. Leal used this time to discuss pending issues, gauge concerns and had once approved a marketing plan in one of those breaks. Seabra on the other hand went to simply enjoy the company of people, and affirmed, "don't dare to think I do that to capture news about the company."

MEETINGS

The presidents believed in integrating the decision process across business lines. They merged the original 5 companies so that all decisions would have to be negotiated and discussed among the three. The percentage of stock they owned did not influence the decision power held by each. Most issues were resolved in a series of meetings at different levels of the organisation to encourage teamwork and discussions, although most decisions were still reached in an informal manner, "on the corridor" as they put it. In a recent article on Natura, the authors summarised this system,

> Natura's management style can harmonise informality, intuition, cleverness with the necessary accuracy to control and run the company.

> — **Exame,** *business magazine*

Openness and inclusiveness were hard-wired in Natura through a proliferation of committees at all levels of decision making. At the top, the 3 presidents met periodically to discuss major strategic issues like whether they should continue with direct sales, whether they should expand in Latin America or Eastern Europe, etc. These meetings began with Leal articulating the issue at hand and its repercussions. Seabra tended to examine the issue from unexpected angles, and Passos provided a reality check and brought everybody down to earth. They often disagreed openly, but not on a personal level. These meetings were not scheduled on a regular basis, but happened "spontaneously."

> There is no process, it's informal and just requires "lending an ear." When one feels we need a rule, we try to create one, for example with the issue of setting up a Board. Otherwise, in

reality we go to each other when the heart orders, in the corridors, by telephone, in meetings. It's rarely an economic matter; normally it's a question regarding the climate of the company. A rule, "what's above 5 million must be reached by consensus," that's ridiculous. If it's changing the climate of the company then it's required.

— *Guilherme Leal, CEO and president,*
Natura

The Natura Strategy Planning committee brought together the 10 Directors from different business areas with Passos twice a month. They discussed results, followed up on strategies, HR policies (salary, bonus, benefits, etc.) and determined the main strategies that needed to be followed on a 5-year horizon. The strategies were communicated to all employees. Every 3 months the presidents held a meeting first with the 96 senior managers and then with a much broader group of supervisors, to answer any concerns and listen to ideas. Seabra believed that such discussions developed interest and creativity among the workforce. Through these meetings and a monthly publication distributed around the company, all the employees had an opportunity to know about and understand the decisions that were taken and how they were consistent with Natura's values.

There were no set rules for decision making. Certain issues, like those pertaining to the structure of the company, needed consensual agreement. This had sometimes led to impasses. The decision to separate the production and distribution centers dragged for a year, before consensus was reached.

Yet most decisions were made unilaterally. For example, Passos decided to hire services to install SAP, and Leal found out about this decision which involved millions of dollars through the newspapers. On a different occasion, Passos decided to call back a product from the market because of quality problems. It was not a problem the consumer could notably feel; the wax in one of their lipstick products was crystallising, which made it uncomfortable to wear. Passos gave orders to advise all the Consultants of the incident so they could pass it on to customers and reimburse them. According to Passos, this decision was in accordance to Natura's values and thus he did not need to discuss it with the other presidents.

NATURA SURVIVING ITS OWNERS

Having 3 presidents meant that the company could continue running if one decided to take a break, which had resulted in the establishment of "Sabbatical years." In 1997, Leal took off for a year to Boston, to take some business courses at Harvard, examine some alliance possibilities for Natura and just take a break. Seabra was on Sabbatical in 1999 in London, perfecting his English, and as he put it, "taking some distance from the protected walls of Natura and experience life, with its joys and hardships." Aside from a refreshing break, it provided a healthy separation where they could more objectively perceive the opportunities and threats facing Natura.

> The company needs to have its identity independent from the identity of its leaders. This is our challenge today, transcend Leal, Seabra and Passos.

— *Guilherme Leal, CEO and president,*
Natura

Slowly, Leal and Seabra were trying to move away from the day to day operations of the company, and institutionalize their legacy. This was difficult since many managers continued to rely on Seabra's inspiration and Leal's leadership. Given that they explicitly discouraged family members from working for the company, there were no family heirs to the throne, and there was no set career path to the top for other managers. A big question in everybody's mind was whether this leadership structure could be duplicated when the original leaders left, and whether the lack of institutionalized processes would affect Natura's ability to survive in the future. The presidents were attempting to deal with these issues,

> We are trying to build a process to make the company less dependent in the founders. We have some targets, to build the board of the company, develop people to substitute Guilherme, Luiz and me. We have a remuneration system to make all employees stockholders, we have a very aggressive stock option plan for directors. In the future we plan to make Natura public to make it easier to substitute the people and the founders, and to involve our executives in our credo and our values.

— *Pedro Passos, COO and president,*
Natura

AVOIDING THE FAILURE OF SUCCESS: HOW TO SUSTAIN GROWTH

The three Presidents were gathered at the headquarters . . . Leal made the situation clear to the other two: on the growth side, the boom years for Natura were gone, competition was increasing and margins were falling due to the recession. Natura had bet on a new revamped attempt to internationalize, allocating resources to the Argentinean market in an attempt to replicate the Brazilian formula. Results were mixed and the operation was still in the red.

One alternative was to venture into new products in Brazil, which fit the brand's "well-being" theme. It would probably be easier and quicker to build on Natura's brand at home than to export a culture to Argentina. If Natura decided to enter this new market, should it consider a joint venture with an experienced player or acquiring a smaller company that had the technology? In the merger option, would they risk becoming a mere division of a multinational? Could they do it alone? Another option was to use alternative sales channels like stores or the Internet to grow more rapidly. Would that affect the "Natura's way"? Did they have the resources to implement these strategies? They were considering an IPO in the following year, which might bring the necessary capital for these projects, but, at the same time, might restrict the power of action they had historically enjoyed. Could Natura survive?

EXHIBIT 1 NATURA'S FINANCIAL PERFORMANCE 7 YEARS

CONSOLIDATED HISTORICAL INCOME STATEMENTS (US$ MILLION)

Year ending Dec 31,	1993	1994	1995	1996	1997	1998
Gross Sales	145.7	236.8	462.6	583.1	634.9	691.5
Taxes on Sales	−54.9	−88.3	−128.0	−160.5	−172.3	−183.5
Net Sales	90.8	148.5	334.7	422.6	462.6	507.9
Cost of Goods Sold	−35.3	−44.6	−128.7	−150.3	−169.3	−190.3
Gross Profit	55.5	103.9	206.0	272.2	293.3	317.6
Operating Expenses	−31.0	−65.4	−133.5	−184.2	−206.7	−235.2
Operating Income - Brazil	24.5	38.5	72.5	88.0	86.6	82.4
Operating Income - International	−0.4	−2.5	−4.4	−5.8	−6.4	−6.6
Operating Income - Consolidated	24.1	36.0	68.1	82.2	80.2	75.9
Net Interest Income (Expense)	5.0	5.6	3.5	−0.4	−1.1	−1.8
Gain (Loss) on Conversion to Dollars	−9.8	−8.0	−5.7	−2.9	−3.6	−2.6
Others	−3.0	1.6		−4.6	−1.4	−4.7
Extraordinary Items	−10.8	−33.7	−1.9	−26.8	−25.3	−25.3
Income Tax	−3.1	−3.1	−18.4	−15.2	−16.2	−17.4
Net Income	2.4	−1.6	45.6	32.3	32.6	24.0
Items	13.2	32.1	47.5	59.1	57.9	49.3
EBIT	24.1	36.0	68.1	82.2	80.2	75.9
Depreciation and Amortization	1.5	2.9	2.2	4.4	5.7	6.6
EBITDA	25.6	38.9	70.3	86.6	85.9	82.5

EXHIBIT 1   NATURA'S FINANCIAL PERFORMANCE 7 YEARS (CONTINUED)

CONSOLIDATED HISTORICAL INCOME STATEMENTS (US$ MILLION)

Year ending Dec 31,	1992	1993	1994	1995	1996
Assets					
Current Assets					
Cash and Cash Equivalents	10.9	12.7	12.4	32.5	21.1
Accounts Receivables	5.8	7.0	32.1	41.9	57.2
Inventories	6.2	7.6	17.0	25.8	32.0
Other Current Assets	0.2	0.8	2.1	15.5	13.9
Total Current Assets	23.1	28.1	63.6	115.7	124.2
Net Property, Plant & Equipment	20.1	58.9	26.3	35.3	60.3
Other Assets	2.2	0.9	2.7	3.0	4.6
Total Assets	**45.4**	**87.9**	**92.6**	**154.0**	**189.1**
Current Liabilities					
of LT Debt	0.8	2.0	2.1	0.8	16.9
Accounts Payable	2.4	3.8	7.9	13.6	13.4
Taxes Payable (Tributaries)	4.4	3.4	9.2	17.3	14.5
Social Contribution Tax	0.8	0.4	1.2	8.8	5.7
Social Security Tax	1.0	2.4	5.4	4.2	9.1
Other Current Liabilities	2.1	11.0	10.1	11.0	7.5
Total Current Liabilities	11.5	23.0	35.9	55.7	67.1
Non-Current Liabilities					
Long-Term Debt	0.9	0.3	0.2	1.5	1.7
Other Non-Current Liabilities	5.5	16.1	11.3	2.0	7.9
Total Non-Current Liabilities	6.4	16.4	11.5	3.5	9.6
Total Liabilities	**17.9**	**39.4**	**47.4**	**59.2**	**76.7**
Stockholder's Equity					
Common Stock	27.6	48.6	45.1	83.3	72.6
Minority Interest	0.0	0.0	0.0	0.0	0.0
Shareholder Debentures	0.0	0.0	0.0	11.6	39.8
Total Stockholder's Equity	27.6	48.6	45.1	94.9	112.4
Stockholder's Equity	**45.5**	**88.0**	**92.5**	**154.1**	**189.1**

EXHIBIT 2 ORGANIZATIONAL CHART—NATURA

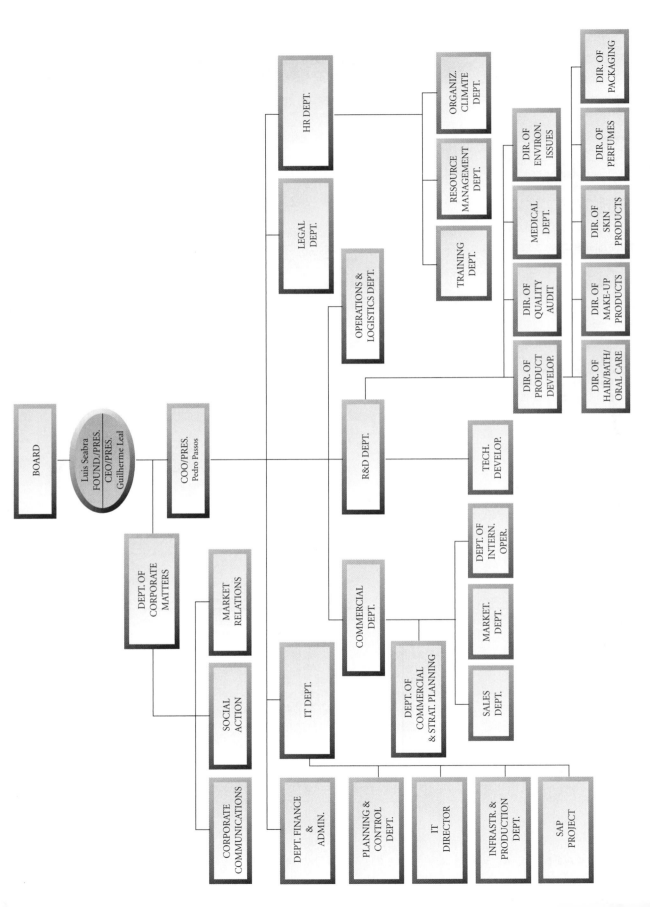

EXHIBIT 3 NATURA'S COMPETITORS

MAJOR COMPETITORS (FOREIGN)

	Head-quarters	Entrance to Brazil	Brands	Products	Method of Sales	Sales Force/# of Distributors in Brazil	US$-Sales Brazil '98	Profit Margin-Brazil '98	US$-Sales Global '98	Profit Margin-Global '98	# of countries present
L'Oreal	France	1972	Lancome, Biotherm, Maybelline, Helena Rubinstein	Cosmetics, Personal Care, Skin Care	Department Stores, Specialized Stores				12.4 bn		
Gessy Lever	U.S.A.	1953	Pond's, Elida Gibbs, Lever	Skin Care, Deodorants, Hair, Soap	Supermarkets, Drugstores						
Proctor & Gamble	U.S.A.	1988	Oil of Olay, Cover Girl	Make-up, Deodorants, Hair	Supermarkets, Drugstores						
Johnson & Johnson	U.S.A.	1953	Johnson & Johnson	Hair, Baby Product Line, Sun Protection	Supermarkets, Drugstores						
Avon	U.S.A.	1959		Cosmetics, Personal Care, Jewellery	Direct Sales	500,000 resellers			5.2bn		131
Shiseido	Japan										
Colgate-Palmolive	U.S.A.			Deodorants, Oral Care	Supermarkets, Drugstores						
Revlon	U.S.A.			Make-up	Supermarkets, Drugstores				(143 mm) loss		
AMWAY		1991		Cosmetics, Personal Care, Nutrition Homecare, Hometech	Direct Sales	70,000 resellers			5.7 bn		49
Estée Lauder	U.S.A.		Clinique, Estée Lauder, Prescriptives, Origins								
Mary Kay Christian Dior Oriflame Davidoff	U.S.A.				Direct Sales						29
Nature's Sunshine		1994		Nutritional Suplements and Natural Cosmetics		150,000 resellers/300 distributors					

MAJOR COMPETITORS (LOCAL)

	Head-quarters	Entrance to Brazil	Brands	Products	Method of Sales	Sales Force/# of Distributors	US$-Sales Brazil '98	Profit Margin-Brazil '98	US$-Sales Global '98	Profit Margin-Global '98	# of countries present
O'Boticario		1978		Cosmetics, Make-up, Perfumes	Franchise	1,616 stores					
Natura	São Paulo	1969	Chronos, Simbios, Essencial, Mama/Bebe	Cosmetics, Skin Care	Direct Sales	230,000 resellers			69.15	3.5%	

EXHIBIT 4 NATURA'S SHARE IN THE BRAZILIAN COSMETICS MARKET

	Year	BRAZILIAN MARKET Volume (tons)	Net Income (US$ 000)	NATURA Volume (tons)	Net Income (US$ 000)	Natura's Share of Its Target Market (vol)
Skin Care	1997	21,522	355,016	1,954	64,419	18.2%
	1998	21,561	332,170	1,976	63,304	19.1%
Sun Protection	1997	1,589	59,869	130	6,791	10.1%
	1998	1,575	68,190	107	5,329	7.8%
Perfumes	1997	15,823	616,318	1,834	172,090	28.8%
	1998	15,856	598,467	2,028	198,542	33.2%
Deodorants	1997	34,951	400,311	1,297	54,374	13.7%
	1998	28,220	393,262	1,608	64,966	16.5%
Hair	1997	242,752	892,810	3,713	45,916	5.1%
	1998	263,632	882,503	3,716	42,544	4.8%
Soap	1997	210,944	521,100	1,339	33,985	6.5%
	1998	224,275	514,305	1,375	33,204	6.5%
Make-up	1997	513	205,433	42	30,500	14.9%
	1998	580	236,916	44	31,629	13.4%
Total CFT Market	1997	636,578	4,245,897			
	1998	669,600	4,256,759			
Total Target Market	1997	530,381	3,086,702	10,393	412,019	13.5%
	1998	571,480	3,063,312	10,958	444,417	14.5%

*CFT Market refers to Cosmetics, Fragrances and Toiletries market

PRODUCTIVITY PER RESELLER (BRAZIL)

	DIRECT SALES OF COSMETICS IN BRAZIL (US$ BILLION)	RESELLERS ('000'S)	SALES/RESELLERS (US$)	NATURA RESELLERS ('000'S)	SALES/NATURA RESELLER (US$)
1993	1.2	570	2,105	65	2,241
1994	2.0	708	2,754	70	3,382
1995	3.1	865	3,584	112	4,131
1996	4.0	1,269	3,152	145	3,432
1997	4.0	1,195	3,350	185	3,340
1998	3.8	1,128	3,348	207	4,343

EXHIBIT 5 EMPLOYEE SURVEY ON ORGANIZATIONAL CLIMATE AT NATURA

FACTORS	NATURA 1995	NATURA 1997	NATURA 1999	MARKET	BENCHMARKS
Number of responses	661	812	990	21,079	4,895
Clarity of objectives	46	59	62	60	74
Adequacy of structure	42	53	60	60	73
Quality of decision process	36	44	53	51	65
Integration and communication	41	50	55	56	65
Management style	41	49	55	54	60
Orientation for personal development	46	54	65	51	58
Organizational vitality	64	69	74	62	71
Salary	45	54	56	50	55
Development of human resources	37	51	54	50	62
Image	84	89	93	80	85
Quality and productivity	67	74	80	75	80
Integration with the community	68	77	85	69	80
Partnerships	52	58	62	57	65
Average	**51**	**59**	**65**	**59**	**68**

A Restaurant
with a Difference

Since they first met, Mark Rapport and Jenny Lindstrom had often toyed with the idea of leaving their current jobs and venturing out on their own. Given their temperament, their experience, and their current situation, this made a lot of sense. He was an award-winning journalist for the *Boston Globe* who had once roamed the world's trouble spots in search of stories, but now was confined to the newspaper's main office on Morrissey Boulevard where he read other people's copies and wished he had never been promoted to Senior Foreign Editor. She began her professional life as a mathematician, moved to software engineering during the 1970s when the field was in its infancy, and eventually became one of the team at Vox Tech which pioneered the first commercial voice recognition programs. The excitement of research and development, however, came to an end when Vox Tech was acquired some years later by Trans Globe Solutions; an information technology company whose one-stop approach to computer procurement ("You come to us, we shop for you") made it one of the largest IT suppliers of computer software and equipment. However, research and development hardly fitted this strategy, so the voice recognition team was disbanded and Jenny was reassigned to customer support—a job she detested but performed with her usual professionalism.

When they discussed their future business they agreed that there was no point in just starting another business. What they wanted was a business that made going to work each morning an adventure. So many evenings after work they would bounce ideas around. Usually, one put forth an idea they had been mulling over, and the other would raise questions and suggest alternatives. The process was taxing—they often had protracted arguments—but they enjoyed the exploration. For while they were different, they also complemented each other well. Mark was an intuitive thinker who relentlessly followed his flashes of insight. By contrast, Jenny was an acute observer who systematically developed ideas she usually got from something she heard or saw.

On this particular evening, it was Mark who came home with an idea that had been buzzing in his head all day. Jenny could sense Mark's excitement. Nevertheless, as was their custom they did not discuss business during supper. As soon as the dishes were cleared Mark leaned forward and began to explain his idea.

"You remember Sam's, the diner across from my office building. You know the one with the neon sign that flashes a soup bowl and a sandwich."

"Yes," said Jenny, "I seem to remember it. It makes a decent chicken sandwich but the coffee is abysmal."

"Well," said Mark, "I took our Middle East correspondent for lunch today, and I have to tell you it was an unmitigated disaster. He looked at the menu and after some thinking ordered a lamb pastrami sandwich. We waited for almost half an hour and still no sandwich. Forty minutes

Prepared by Joseph Lampel, City University Business School, London. Not to be used or reproduced without author's permission. Copyright © Joseph Lampel, 2002.

later with some prodding on my part the sandwich arrives. He bites into the sandwich and the expression on his face says it all. I call the waitress over and tell her: 'You call this a sandwich? How long has this meat been in the freezer?'"

"She apologises and whisks away the sandwich. However, I am not satisfied. I ask for the manager. He comes over and apologises again, and tells us that the lunch is on the house. Now I am satisfied, but I am also curious. 'You know,' I tell the manager, 'I have been coming here for years, but I have never had this problem before.' The manager nods his head, and says: 'Well, we often have this problem with dishes that are on the menu but that are rarely ordered. At the end of each day the cook checks to make sure that we have enough of everything for the next day, but he does not check to make sure that too much has been left from the previous day. Usually things move fast enough so this is not a problem, but once in a while the food stays in the fridge too long and then I have to eat humble pie. If cooks were not so hard to find I would give this one a piece of my mind, but since he is as temperamental as they come, all I can do is simply remind him to check more carefully and hope for the best.'"

"This got me thinking. Why are restaurants so static? Why do places like Sam's have the same menu for years? Clearly, the manager should have dropped this sandwich from the menu long ago, but the menu stays the same and customers that are unhappy or want something different simply go elsewhere."

"What if we were to start a restaurant that was different. A restaurant where the menu changed as demand changed. Think about this Jenny. With today's technology it would not be so difficult. Each waitress would have a palm top computer instead of a paper pad. She would write the order on this pad and then transmit the order directly to the kitchen. At the end of each week the orders would be totalled and the demand analysed. Dishes that fell below a certain volume would be deleted from the menu. And using a laser printer we could print a new menu each week at fairly low cost."

As he spoke Mark could see the doubts on Jenny's face. So before she had a chance to speak he decided to bring out his trump card. "You know how much we both love food. Not just finding new dishes in interesting restaurants, but trying out new recipes in our own kitchen. Well, this restaurant will allow us to combine our passion for food with our wish to build a business where we are constantly experimenting and exploring. Each week we will introduce new dishes. If they work out, fine, if not, we will drop them. Think of all the fun we will have, searching for new recipes, trying them out in the kitchen, and then waiting to see how well they are received."

Jenny could contain herself no longer. "It does not sound like fun to me!" she said with some exasperation. "Have you thought of all the problems? A restaurant where the menu changes all the time! Have you given thought to the kitchen operations? Where will we find a cook that will tolerate a constantly changing menu? What about shopping for provisions and ingredients? It is difficult enough to do this at the lowest cost possible when the menu stays the same, how are you going to do this when it changes all the time?"

Mark was on the defensive, but he was not going to give up that easily. "You must know," he said, "that one of the oldest principles of business is that 20 percent of all products account for 80 percent of all the sales. I am sure that restaurants are no exception. It may well be true that kitchen operations will be more expensive, but we will save much more by removing from the menu dishes that add to our inventory and overhead costs."

"This may well be the case," responded Jenny, "but then people rarely eat alone. They often come with partners or friends who may actually want a dish that is not popular. What are you going to do about them? What if they prefer to go elsewhere, and by default take their partners or friends with them?"

"Of course, there are things that still need to be worked out," retorted Mark, "this is the nature of good strategy. You cannot work everything out in advance. It would be foolish to try, and even more foolish to do it and believe that you have succeeded. It is certain that we will have to explore and solve many problems, but in the meantime think about this from a wider perspective: This will be the first 'learning' restaurant in this city, perhaps the first in the entire country. Think of the publicity this will generate. This alone will attract tremendous attention. People will come from everywhere to try out our concept. Our initial business is guaranteed, and with it the initial period of time we need to iron out our problems. By the time that buzz begins to fade we will have a working restaurant based on a concept that is truly novel, and furthermore, a restaurant with a difference, a place of work that satisfies our craving for exploration and novelty. Come on, Jenny, where is your spirit of adventure?"

"My spirit of adventure is intact," responded Jenny. "I am simply not persuaded that what you propose is either practical or for that matter truly innovative."

CASE NOTES

Case 3
MacArthur and the Philippines

1. Frazier Hunt, *The Untold Story of Douglas MacArthur*. New York: Devin-Adair Co., 1954, p. 318.
2. Charles A. Willoughby and John Chamberlain, *MacArthur, 1941–1951*. New York: McGraw-Hill, 1954; Charles A. Rawlings, "They Paved Their Way with Japs," *Saturday Evening Post*, October 7, 1944.
3. Hunt, *Untold*, p. 318; Douglas MacArthur, *Reminiscences*. New York: McGraw-Hill, 1964, pp. 166–167; Alfred Steinberg, *Douglas MacArthur*. New York: Putnam, 1961, p. 113; Willoughby and Chamberlain, *MacArthur*, p. 206.
4. Richard H. Rovere and Arthur M. Schlesinger, Jr., *The General and the President, and the Future of American Foreign Policy*. New York: Farrar, Straus and Young, 1951, pp. 65–66; Willoughby and Chamberlain, *MacArthur*, p. 206.
5. Jay Luvaas, ed., *Dear Miss Em: General Eichelberger's War in the Pacific, 1942–1945*. Westport, Conn.: Greenwood Press, 1972, p. 75.
6. Gavin M. Long, *MacArthur as Military Commander*. London: 1969, p. 219; Earl Blaik, *The Red Blaik Story*. New York: Arlington House, 1974, p. 501; James M. Burns, *Roosevelt: The Soldier of Freedom, 1940–45*. New York: Harcourt Brace Jovanovich, 1970, p. 488.
7. Daniel E. Barbey, *MacArthur's Amphibious Navy: Seventh Amphibious Force Operations, 1943–1945*. Annapolis: U.S. Naval Institute, 1969, p. 219; Blaik, *Red Blaik Story*, p. 501; Burns, *Roosevelt*, p. 488.
8. Author's interviews with Roger Egeberg, October 18, 1976; MacArthur, *Reminiscences*, p. 199; Dorris Clayton James, *The Years of MacArthur, 1941–1945, Vol. II*. Boston: Houghton Mifflin, 1975, p. 530; Luvaas, *Miss Em*, p. 155; William D. Leahy, *I Was There*. New York: Whittlesey House, 1950, p. 250; Stanley L. Falk, *Decision at Leyte*. New York: W. W. Norton, 1966, p. 28.
9. Leahy, *I Was There*, p. 251; James, *Vol. II*, p. 530; MacArthur, *Reminiscences*, p. 197.
10. David J. Steinberg, *Philippine Collaboration in World War II*. Ann Arbor: University of Michigan Press, 1967, p. 101; George C. Kenney, *The MacArthur I Know*. New York: Duell, Sloan and Pearce, 1951, pp. 155–156; Willoughby and Chamberlain, *MacArthur*, p. 233.
11. MacArthur, *Reminiscences*, p. 198; Leahy, *I Was There*, pp. 250–251.
12. Robert R. Smith, *Triumph in the Philippines*. Washington, D.C.: Office of the Chief of Military History, Department of the Army, 1963, p. 11.
13. John Toland, *The Rising Sun*. New York: Random House, 1970, pp. 533–534; Barbey, *Amphibious*, p. 227; Robert J. Bulkley, *At Close Quarters: PT Boats in the United States Navy*. Washington, D.C.: Naval History Division, 1962, p. 376; William F. Halsey and Joseph Bryan III, *Admiral Halsey's Story*. New York: Whittlesey House, 1947, p. 199.
14. Halsey and Bryan, *Admiral Halsey's Story*, pp. 198–201; Henry H. Arnold, *Global Mission*. New York: Harper, 1949, pp. 527–528; James, *Vol. II*, pp. 537–539; Toland, *Sun*, p. 534; George C. Kenney, *General Kenney Reports: A Personal History of the Pacific War*, Washington, D.C.: Office of Air Force History, U.S. Air Force, 1987, p. 434.
15. Manuel Quezon, *The Good Fight*. New York and London: D. Appleton-Century Co., 1946, p. 295; Robert I. Eichelberger, with Milton McKaye, *Our Jungle Road to Tokyo*. New York: Viking Press, 1950, p. 181; J. Griggin, "Philippines," *Holiday*, July 1967.
16. Carlos P. Romulo, *I Saw the Fall of the Philippines*. Garden City, N.Y.: Doubleday & Co., 1942, p. 54; David Steinberg, *Collaboration*, pp. 104–105.
17. James, *Vol. II*, pp. 542–543.
18. Carlos P. Romulo, *I See the Philippines Rise*. Garden City, N.Y.: Doubleday & Co., 1946, p. 190; Toland, *Sun*, p. 537; David Steinberg, *Collaboration*, p. 101.
19. MacArthur, *Reminiscences*, p. 172; Hunt, *Untold*, p. 314.
20. Toland, *Sun*, p. 534; "Promise Fulfilled," *Time*, October 30, 1944.
21. MacArthur, *Reminiscences*, p. 212; Kenney, *Know*, p. 156; Alfred Steinberg, *Douglas MacArthur*, p. 127.
22. Falk, *Leyte*, p. 29; Hunt, *Untold*, p. 342.
23. Author's interviews with Egeberg, October 18, 1976; MacArthur, *Reminiscences*, p.216; James, *Vol. II*, pp. 554–555; "MacArthur Returns and Returns," *Life*, February 18, 1972; Kenney, *General*, p. 448; Charles A. Lockwood and Hans C. Adamson, *Battle of the Philippine Sea*. New York: 1967, pp. 157–158; "Battle for the Philippines," *Fortune*, June 1945.
24. Author's interviews with Romulo, October 18, 1976; Romulo, *Rise*, pp. 3, 94–95; Falk, *Leyte*, p. 111.
25. Records of General Headquarters, United States Army Forces, Pacific (USAF-PAC), 1942–1945; Carlos P. Romulo, *I Walked with Heroes*. New York: Holt, Rinehart and Winston, 1961, pp. 235–236; James, *Vol. II*, pp. 557–558; MacArthur, *Reminiscences*, pp. 216–217; Long, *Commander*, p. 152; Falk, *Leyte*, p. 103; David Steinberg, *Collaboration*, p. 105; Vorin E. Whan, ed., *A Soldier Speaks: Public Papers and Speeches of General of the Army Douglas MacArthur*. New York: Praeger, 1965, pp. 132–133.
26. Kenney, *General*, p. 452.
27. Romulo, *Rise*, p. 165.
28. Falk, *Leyte*, p. 220.
29. Falk, pp. 71, 273; James, *Vol. II*, p. 580; Toland, *Sun*, pp. 576–577.
30. James, *Vol. II*, p. 585, Eichelberger, *Jungle*, p. 174; Falk, *Leyte*, p. 293.
31. James, *Vol. II*, p. 584; Kenney, *General*, pp. 64–65; author's interviews with Egeberg, October 18, 1976.
32. Edward M. Flanagan, Jr., *The Angels: A History of the 11th Airborne Division, 1943–1946*. Washington, D.C.: Infantry Journal Press, 1948, p. 621.
33. MacArthur, *Reminiscences*, p. 241; James, *Vol. II*, p. 621.
34. *The New York Times*, January 11, 1945; MacArthur, *Reminiscences*, p. 242.
35. Hunt, *Untold*, p. 364; Bertram C. Wright, comp., *The 1st Cavalry Division in World War II*, Tokyo: Toppan Print Co., 1947, pp. 125–128; author's interviews with Romulo, October 18, 1976; Flanagan, *Angels*, pp. 77–80; author's interviews with Egeberg, October 18, 1976; James, *Vol. II*, p. 641; Romulo, *Rise*, p. 191.
36. MacArthur, *Reminiscences*, pp. 245–246; Luvaas, *Miss Em*, p. 225.
37. Luvaas, *Miss Em*, p. 203; Eichelberger, *Jungle*, p. 187; MacArthur, *Reminiscences*, p. 260.
38. Luvaas, *Miss Em*, p. 203.
39. "In Remembrance of MacArthur," *Life*, April 17, 1964; Luvaas, *Miss Em*, p. 260; Willoughby and Chamberlain, *MacArthur*, p. 267.
40. Luvaas, *Miss Em*, pp. 278–279; Kenney, *General*, pp. 552–553; Kenney, *Know*, pp. 132–133.
41. Hanson W. Baldwin, *Great Mistakes of the War*. New York: Harper, 1949, p. 97.

42. Records of General Headquarters, United States Army Forces, Pacific (USAF-PAC), 1942–45; James, *Vol. II*, pp. 765–766; Leahy, *I Was There*, p. 385; Leslie R. Groves, *Now It Can Be Told*. New York: Harper, 1962, pp. 263–264.

43. Hunt, *Untold*, p. 402.

44. James, *Vol. II*, p. 785; Norman Richards, *Douglas MacArthur*. Chicago: Children's Press, 1967, p. 76; Jules Archer, *Front-Line General: Douglas MacArthur*. New York: Messner, 1963, pp. 143–144; John Gunther, *The Riddle of MacArthur: Japan, Korea, and the Far East*. New York: Harper, 1951, p. 2.

45. Courtney Whitney, *MacArthur, His Rendezvous with History*. New York: Alfred A. Knopf, 1955, p. 216; MacArthur, *Reminiscences*, p. 271; "On the Record," *Time*, March 31, 1947; James, *Vol. II*, pp. 786–787.

46. Collection of Messages (radiograms), 1945–1951; Whitney, *Rendezvous*, pp. 216–217; James, *Vol. II*, pp. 787–788; MacArthur, *Reminiscences*, pp. 271–272; William Craig, *The Fall of Japan*. New York: Dial Press, 1967, pp. 297–298.

47. Toshikazu Kase, *Journey to the Missouri*. New Haven: Yale University Press, 1950, p. 13; MacArthur, *Reminiscences*, pp. 276–277.

Case 4
Rudi Gassner and the Executive Committee of BMG International (A)

1. Managing Directors managed local operations in a particular country; each MD reported to one of five Regional Directors.

2. Purkiss, Alan, "Let's Hear It for the Unsung Hero," *Accountancy*, June 1992, pp. 70–73.

3. Dannen, Frederick, *Hit Men: Power Brokers and Fast Money Inside the Music Business* (New York: Vintage Books, 1991), pp. 246–261.

4. "BMG's Five Year Man," *Music Business International*, Vol. 3, No. 1 (January 1993), p. 18.

5. Ibid.

6. According to Gassner, a 1% worldwide market share gain was worth around $250 million in revenue. ("Charting the Future" speech, May 1993, Boca Raton, Florida.)

7. The "prestige market" of the U.S. was the most important supplier of recorded music around the world, and BMG's Arista, led by long-time music executive Clive Davis, had launched two global superstars, Whitney Houston and Kenny G, who reached No. 1 and 2 on the *Billboard* album chart. In 1993, Houston's soundtrack for *The Bodyguard* sold 20 million copies and became one of the top-selling albums of all time, fueling a significant portion of BMG's revenue in the U.S. and abroad. (Lander, Mark, "An Overnight Success—After Six Years," *Business Week*, April 19, 1993, pp. 52–54.)

8. In addition, BMG International had an agreement with MCA/Geffen to market and distribute that company's products outside the U.S. The MCA/Geffen deal gave BMG International access to such stars as Guns 'N' Roses, Nirvana, Aerosmith, Bobby Brown, and Cher.

9. "A&R" was a record industry term that stood for "artist and repertoire," record company products. In record companies, investing in A&R to develop talent was analogous to a manufacturing concern investing in R&D. "A&R marketing" was essentially product marketing.

10. *Betriebsergebnis* was a German accounting term roughly translated to mean profit plus interest costs. The official language at BMG International was English (German was never spoken if a non-speaker was present); *betriebsergebnis* was the only German word the company used.

11. A *vorstand* was a German managing board consisting of full-time executive members who carried out the day-to-day operation of the

company. It was distinguished from the supervisory board (*aufsichsrat*), which consisted of shareholders and employee representatives. (Parkyn, Brian, *Democracy, Accountability, and Participation in Industry*)(Bradford, West Yorkshire, England: MCB General Management Ltd., 1979), p. 105; and Kennedy, Thomas, *European Labor Relations* (Lexington, Massachusetts: Lexington Books, 1980), p. 185.

12. In response to trends toward multimedia entertainment technology, Dornemann had begun to look toward expanding BMG's reach in the entertainment industry to include television and even film. Industry analysts speculated that Dornemann was interested in purchasing an independent film studio, but such a deal had not yet materialized. In September 1993, BMG announced a joint venture with Tele-Communications, Inc., the largest cable system operator in the U.S., to launch a hybrid music video/home shopping cable channel that would rival MTV and VH-1. (Robichaux, Mark and Johnnie L. Roberts, "TCI, Bertelsmann Join to Launch Music, Shopping Cable Channel," *Wall Street Journal*, September, 17, 1993.)

13. Since the Latin American region included Spain and Portugal, Segura was affected minimally by the reduced price.

Case 11
WFNX–101.7FM and Boston's Radio Wars

1. Frederic Dannen, *Hit Men: Power Brokers and Fast Money Inside the Music Business*, New York City: Vintage Books, 1991.

2. Terrence Shimp, *Promotion Management and Marketing Communications*, 3rd Edition (1993), Chapter 13—"Media Strategy"; and *Advertising, Promotion and Supplemental Aspects of Integrated Marketing Communications*, 4th Edition (1997), Chapter 12—"Analysis of Advertising Media;" Dryden Press.

3. Salaries for DJs varied depending on the size and ratings of the radio station. The average salaries for the top 15 markets are as follows: $167,000—morning show DJ, $65–80,000—midday DJ, $45,000—evening DJ. When alternative stations were separated from the average, the salary for an alternative morning show DJ was $67,000 versus $228,000 for contemporary-hit radio (CHR) DJs.

4. These numbers represent a share of a particular radio market, so in a smaller market a station could have numbers as high as a 30 share. In contrast, a station in New York City that had a four share would be considered gigantic since it is a four share of a very large market.

5. This is a general standard. Some jumps in ratings would represent larger percentages in revenue and profit. For example, if a station jumped from a 2.0 to 4.0, it would account for significantly more than $2 million since the station had suddenly captured such a large part of the market.

6. Jim Sullivan, "Alternative to What?" *The Boston Globe*, April 2, 1995; and "Reinventing the Rock of Boston," May 5, 1995.

7. Sullivan, "Reinventing the Rock of Boston," 66.

8. Ibid.

9. Ibid.

10. Sullivan, "Alternative to What?" B27.

11. Music tests are used to determine which songs are still liked by listeners by playing small segments of songs and having the listeners rate the songs according to if they recognize it and if they like or dislike it. If a song like "Roxanne" by The Police was tested and the majority of listeners did not like it or were "burned out" on it, it would be removed from the station's music rotation.

12. WBCN, WBZ, WODS, WZLX, WAAF, WBMX, WEEI, WEGQ, WRKO.

13. "Active rock" mixes alternative artists like Pearl Jam and Nirvana with hard rock bands like Aerosmith and Metallica.

14. Sullivan, "Alternative to What?" B27.

Case 13
Lufthansa 2000: Maintaining the Change Momentum

1. Seeheim later became the home of the Lufthansa School of Business.
2. Dr. Klaus Schlede was the Chief Executive Finance at that time.
3. Dr. Hach, P. Senior Vice President Corporate Controlling, Speech held at the Top 100-Forum at Stockholm, "An Attempt of a Phenomenological Approach to Lufthansa's Soul," 22.2.1996.
4. Debis is an autonomous IT subsidiary of the Daimler Chrysler Group.
5. Dr. Hach, P. Senior Vice President Corporate Controlling, Speech held at the Top 100-Forum at Stockholm, "An Attempt of a Phenomenological Approach to Lufthansa's Soul," 22.2.1996.

Case 14
The London Free Press (A)—Strategic Change

1. The TV station was sold in 1993 because the Blackburn Group felt it no longer fit the news focus of its other holdings, and because it needed substantial new investment to stay competitive in the entertainment field.

Case 17
Kami Corporation

1. Subic had received more ash fall during the explosion due to a tropical depression in the South China Sea which had reversed the usual wind patterns to be toward Subic and away from Clark.
2. As part of the investment incentives, the government allowed each Filipino $200/year (later reduced to $100) in duty free purchases; residents of the areas surrounding Clark and Subic were allowed $200/month; and all visitors and returning Filipinos were allowed $2,000 duty free shopping at the two bases within 48 hours of arrival in the Philippines.
3. This name has been disguised.

Case 18
Strategic Planning at the New York Botanical Garden (A)

1. Sotheby's Auction House made its auditorium available for use, free of charge, to nonprofit institutions in the New York City area.
2. Much of the following history is excerpted from a Morgan Stanley prospectus, dated July 18, 1996, for revenue bonds for the Trust for Cultural Resources of the City of New York.

Case 19
Napoleon Bonaparte: Victim of an Interior Strategy?

1. Marshals Grouchy and Ney commanded, respectively, the right and left wings of the French Army in the battle of Waterloo, which also saw Marshal Soult act for the first time as the Emperor's Chief-of-Staff. Soult had succeeded Berthier, who had been his longtime and favourite chief-of-staff, ever since the first campaign in Italy. He died in 1815, upon hearing of his Emperor's return from exile on the Island of Elba. Masséna, Murat, Desaix, Berthier, Lannes, Bessières and Duroc were some amongst Napoleon's superb field marshals and generals who either had died earlier or did not take part in the events at Waterloo.
"Correspondence," Vol. 1, No. 91, 107: Chandler, David G. "The Campaigns of Napoleon: The Mind and Method of History's Greatest Soldier." Macmillan, 1973.
2. Correspondence, Vol. 1, No. 91, p. 107: Chandler, David G. "The Campaigns of Napoleon: The Mind and Method of History's Greatest Soldier."
3. Chandler, David G. "The Campaigns of Napoleon: The Mind and Method of History's Greatest Soldier." Macmillan, 1973: 53.

4. Alan Schom, "Napoleon Bonaparte," Harperperennial, 1998, p. 47.
5. Melas was the Austrian commander. Desaix was possibly Napoleon's finest commander.
6. Alistair Horne, "How Far from Austerlitz—Napoleon 1805–1815," St. Martin's Press, 1997, p. 146.
7. Jomini was a famous Austrian war historian who also fought against Napoleon.
8. The "Treaty of Tilsit" was signed twice, once with the Russians to maintain an alliance between France and Russia, and the second treaty two days later with Prussia, which lost a substantial part of land. A large portion of Germany thus came under French control.
9. Alistair Horne, "How Far from Austerlitz—Napoleon 1805–1815," St. Martin's Press, 1997, p. 233.
10. Eighteen Marshals of the Empire (Maréchal d'Empire) were named by Napoleon in 1804, the day following his nomination as Emperor of the French (Empereur des Français). He later introduced other imperial titles, such as Duke and Prince, to further recognise exceptional service in battle.
11. Alan Schom, "Napoleon Bonaparte," Harperperennial Press, 1998, p. 602.
12. Alan Schom, "Napoleon Bonaparte," Harperperennial Press, 1998, p. 603.
13. Fontainebleau became the Imperial Court and an important centre for Napoleon.
14. Alan Schom, "Napoleon Bonaparte," Harperperennial Press, 1998, p. 713.
15. Ulm, Austerlitz, Jena, Eylau, and Friedland were famous victories of Napoleon.
16. Alan Schom, "Napoleon Bonaparte," Harperperennial Press, 1998, p. 710.
17. Louis XVIII escaped France and sought exile in Belgium.
18. Chandler, David G. "The Campaigns of Napoleon: The Mind and Method of History's Greatest Soldier." Macmillan, 1973: 1041.
19. Chandler, David G. "The Campaigns of Napoleon: The Mind and Method of History's Greatest Soldier." Macmillan, 1973: 1084.

Case 20
Honda Motor Company 1994

1. T. Sakiya, *Honda Motor: The Men, The Management, The Machines.* Tokyo: Kodansha International, Ltd. 1982.
2. S. Sanders, *Honda: The Man and His Machines.* Boston: Little Brown, 1975.
3. "Honda the Market Guzzler," *Fortune,* February 20, 1984.
4. "Toyota's Fast Lane," *Business Week,* November 4, 1985.
5. "A Car Is Born," *Business Week,* September 13, 1993.
6. R. Guest, "The Quality of Work Life in Japan. . . ," *Hokudai Economic Papers,* Tokyo, Vol. XII (1982–1983).

Case 23
Wipro Corporation: Balancing the Future

1. Crore = 10 million.
2. The edible fats market included, apart from vanaspati, edible refined oils. The edible refined oil market was yet another competitive market, with a multitude of players, including WCP rival in the vanaspati market, Lipton. The other major players were the ITC—a Rs 40 billion diversified company and one of the largest private sector companies in India with presence in cigarettes, hotels, printing and packaging businesses, and the government cooperative National Dairy Development Board, the current market leader in the edible oils market.
3. Apollo (later acquired by HP) was the other major player in workstations and had a tie-up with HCL.

4. Sun's tie-up with WIL did not preclude it from appointing other representatives. It had earlier appointed PCL—one of the fast growing companies in the Indian computing industry—to sell its systems, even though it had a tie-up with WIL at that time. However, the arrangement did not last as PCL failed to make much headway in the market.

5. Nokia had a tie-up with HCL for marketing its pagers.

6. The other two were the Bell Northern Research SDC and the Sequent Computer Systems—SDC.

7. In 1994, 32% of the software export revenues came from off shore software development and the target for 1995 was to increase this share to 55%.

8. Vivek Paul took over as President in the second half of 1993 following Prasanna's appointment to the China team in GE Medical Systems Division in the US.

9. Imports of complete systems were exempt from any customs duty while Wipro GE incurred a 15.5% customs levy on the import of its raw materials and a 5.5% excise levy on its finished product.

10. Under this program the world's leading physicians and researchers come and interact with their Indian counterparts on the latest achievements of medical imaging.

11. Wipro Lighting too had bid for acquiring a stake in Mysore Lamps, one of the oldest manufacturers of lighting products in India.

Case 24
TV Asahi Theatrical Productions, Inc.

1. The Tony Awards are the most prestigious live theatre awards in the world, and are quite literally the Academy Awards of the theatre industry.

2. A keiretsu is a group of Japanese firms that usually has joint ownership and operates to varying degrees as one large firm. The degree of inter-linking ownership can be quite small (e.g., 5%). The operational linkages can include sharing of capital, exchange of technology, and personnel, and joint management decision making.

3. *Note*: Investors are called producers in the musical theatre business.

4. Broadway and West End are the theatres, in New York and London (U.K.), respectively, that produced the best plays and musicals in the world.

Case 29
Saatchi & Saatchi Worldwide

1. Mr. Sorrell, a brilliant empire builder, went on to make the WPP Group the biggest global ad company (see Exhibit 7) by buying J. Walter Thompson and Ogilvy & Mather, thus overtaking Saatchi's lead position.

2. Graham Thomas, vice chairman of Saatchi, in a memorandum to the authors dated April 8, 1993.

Case 30
McKinsey & Company: Managing Knowledge and Learning

1. The Founders' Legacy section draws on Amar V. Bhide, "Building the Professional Firm: McKinsey & Co., 1939–1968," HBS Working Paper 95-010.

Case 31
Sony: Regeneration (A)

1. This section is based on "Genryu" published by Sony Corporation to mark its 50th anniversary.

Case 34
Empire Plastics

1. The "wet end" refers to chemical processing plant, the "dry end" to new product drying equipment.

Case 37
Workbrain Corporation

1. Some of the information in this case is taken from internal Workbrain documents authored by Daniel Debow, Matt Chapman, Eric Green and other members of the Workbrain management team.

2. U.S. Bureau of Statistics.

3. Hambrecht & Quist, 1999.

4. American Express & AMR Research, 1997.

5. American Payroll Association.

Case 39
Intel Corporation

1. "The Five Best Managed Companies," *Dun's Review*, December 1980.

2. Gene Bylinsky, quoted from *The Innovation Millionaires*. Copyright © 1976, 1974, 1973, 1967 by Gene Bylinsky. Reprinted with the permission of Charles Scribner's Sons.

3. *Electronic News*, December 27, 1974.

4. "Meet Bob Noyce," *Computer Decisions*, June 1974.

5. *The Wall Street Journal*, October 4, 1969.

6. "Special Report: Where the Action Is in Electronics," *Business Week*, October 4, 1969.

7. *Electronic News*, August 26, 1968.

8. *Electronics*, March 31, 1969.

9. "Intel Gambles for Continued Rapid Growth," *International Management*, November 1981.

10. "Creativity by the Numbers," *Harvard Business Review*, May–June 1980.

11. "American Industry and What Ails It, *The Atlantic*, May 1980.

12. George Gilder, *Microcosm*. New York: Simon & Schuster, 1989, p. 152. (These figures do not include U.S. captive suppliers—IBM and AT&T. If captive suppliers are included, Japan's share of the U.S. market falls to 65%.)

13. *The Wall Street Journal*, June 21, 1989, p. B5, and *San Francisco Chronicle*, June 22, 1989, p. C1. (Some companies, notably Apple and Sun Microsystems, were reluctant to invest in U.S. Memories, due to relationships with existing DRAM manufacturers, according to the *San Francisco Chronicle*, September 26, 1989.)

14. *Business Week*, November 26, 1990, p. 122.

15. Goldman Sachs, *The Future of Microprocessors*, April 23, 1990.

16. *The Wall Street Journal*, February 28, 1989, p. A1.

Case 40
The National Bicycle Industrial Company: Implementing a Strategy of Mass-Customization

1. The term "mass-customization" was first coined by Stanley M. Davis in *Future Perfect* (Reading, MA: Addison-Wesley, 1987).

2. In the past, Japanese bicycle manufacturers produced bicycles originally designed around European models. The lower average height of Japanese women made it difficult for them to use such bicycles. The miniwheel's small wheel diameter, lower saddle mount and U-type frames made it very appealing to women.

3. According to industry reports, labeling firms as either wholesalers or retailers was problematic, because a majority of them operated jointly as wholesale and retail ventures.

4. According to the factory manager, prior to the introduction of the CAD system this process took the company draftsmen about 180 minutes.

Case 41
NovaCare, Inc.

1. Donaldson, Lufkin, and Jenrett, *Health Care Services and Hospital Management–Industry Report*, February 1, 1991.

Case 42
Lechabile: IT as a People Business

1. Winston Mosiako, quoted in *Computerweek*, March 16, 1999.
2. All company information gained from the following: Lechabile Company Profile, 1999, Lechabile company brochure, Lechabile business plan and Lechabile press clippings, Lechabile company archives, courtesy of Lechabile.
3. Ibid.
4. *US Industry and Trade Outlook* 1998: Information Services, Section 26.
5. Currency is in thousands of rand. IT services graph and domestic market information from Lechabile Business Plan, January 1998. Courtesy of Lechabile.
6. Winston Mosiako, interview with the authors, May 4, 1999.
7. Quote from local newspaper article, press clipping from Lechabile Company archives.
8. Matsebe Nhlapo, interview with the authors, May 12, 1999.
9. Simon Ndoro, interview with the authors, April 22, 1999.
10. Seven founding members, interview with the authors, May 4, 1999.
11. Ibid.
12. Zainul Nagdee and Iqbal Hassim, interview with the authors, April 22, 1999.
13. Interview with the authors, April 22, 1999.
14. Iqbal Hassim and Zainul Nagdee, interview with the authors, April 22, 1999.
15. Mosiako, interview with the authors, May 4, 1999.
16. Simon Ndoro, interview with the authors, May 12, 1999.
17. Vincent Williams, interview with the authors, May 12, 1999.
18. Simon Ndoro, interview with the authors, May 12, 1999.
19. Winston Mosiako, interview with the authors, April 22, 1999.
20. Winston Mosiako, interview with the authors, April 22, 1999.
21. *Harvard Business Review*, January–February 1999.
22. From a report by ABSA Bank at the following Web site: http://www.absa.co.za/econ_structure/affirmative.htm.
23. Ibid.
24. Ibid.
25. From http://www.iii.co.za/vignette/news/businessreport/0,2812,347,00.html.
26. *The Financial Mail*, June 4, 1999.
27. Ibid.
28. From *The Mail & Guardian* Web site, April 30, 1999, at http://www.mg.co.za/mg/za/news.html.
29. Ibid.
30. Ibid.
31. Ibid.
32. Iqbal Hassim, interview with the authors, April 22, 1999.
33. Winston Mosiako, interview with the authors, June 4, 1999.
34. Willie Van Schalkwyk, interview with the authors, June 7, 1999.
35. Sales/business where less than 50 machines were involved, and setting up of information kiosks.

Case 44
Natura: The Magic Behind Brazil's Most Admired Company

1. Natura was chosen best company of the year by *Exame*, Brazil's major business magazine. Natura has also been the number one company in the hygiene and cosmetics sector for the last three years, 1997, 1998 and 1999. *Exame* Maiores e Melhores 98 (*Exame* Largest and Best 98).
2. Growth rate determined based on US$ figures, which account for devaluation (equivalent to inflation during the period). Inflation and devaluation go relatively hand in hand for the period of 1980–1998.
3. Arnold Browth, chairman of Weiner, Edrich , Brown Inc. discussed major industry trends in the Fragrance Foundation's "View from the Top" ceremony on Jan 26, 1999.
4. Euromonitor, 1998.
5. Sales does not include the 30% mark-up which is the margin received by the Consultants.
6. Seabra and Leal bought 26% stake in Natura for US$ 25 million from the other important shareholder. The resulting ownership left Seabra with 37.9%, Leal with 36%, Passos with 9% and the remaining in the hands of minority shareholders.
7. The Real Plan was a currency stabilization program implemented in 1994 by Fernando Henrique Cardoso, the finance minister at the time. The new program of macroeconomic policies was based on a reduction in public expense, increased federal taxes, tighter controls over state-owned banks, and an acceleration of the privatization program. When Cardoso became president in 1995, his administration took further steps in Brazil's economic liberalization process.
8. Of a product's suggested retail price of R$ 100, Consultants need to pay R$ 70 to Natura.

NAME INDEX

Abdul, Paula, 55
Abell, George, 293
Acheson, Dean, 37
Ackenhusen, Mary, 75n
Adamson, Hans C., 32n, 476
Adamson, John, 175n
Aimo, Walter Borio, 280
Akopianz, Patty, 327
Albrecht, Chris, 62–65
Alexander I, 194
Alexander the Great, 190
Ali, Rahmat, 298
Amaral, Yara, 458
Arab, Majid, 327
Araujo, Marcelo, 460
Archer, Jules, 38n, 477
Arnault, Bernard, 160–70
Arnold, Hap, 29, 30
Attlee, Clement, 38, 290, 291, 294, 305
Aung San, 290
Austin, Dallas, 55
Azarov, Nikolai, 280
Azzoli, Val, 90

Bahlmann, Arnold, 40, 46, 47–48, 49, 50, 51–52
Bajaj, Umesh, 240
Balazs, Katherine, 160n
Baldwin, Hanson W., 37n, 476
Ball, Alan, 63, 64
Bannister, Terry, 315
Barbey, Daniel E., 29n, 30n, 476
Barrett, Craig, 403, 406
Bartlett, Christopher A., 319n
Beamish, Paul, 109n, 254n, 263n, 447n
Bennett, Jim, 321
Bernat, Enrique, 276, 278, 280, 281, 282, 284, 286
Bernat, Xavier, 278, 280, 281, 282, 284, 285, 286
Bertelli, Patrizio, 162
Bewkes, Jeffrey, 64
Bhide, Amar V., 319n, 479
Binder, Mike, 63, 64
Blackburn, Peter, 263
Blackburn, Walter, 155
Blaik, Earl, 28n, 29n, 476
Blamey, Sir Thomas, 27
Bonaparte, Louis, 194
Bonaparte, Napoleon, 27, 190–99, 194n, 478
Bonaventura, Lorenzo di, 390
Bond, Alan, 265
Borio, Walter, 281, 283
Bower, Marvin, 319–20, 321
Boyle, Mike, 97
Brabham, Jack, 204
Brakel, Willem van, 284
Branco, Pedro Castello, 69
Brandy, 89
Braxton, Toni, 54
Bray, Warwick, 328–29
Britton, Elizabeth, 178
Britton, Nathaniel Lord, 178
Brown, Bobby, 43n, 55, 477
Browth, Arnold, 456n, 480
Brozzetti, Gianluca, 166
Bruch, Heike, 124n
Bryan, Joseph, 30n, 476
Bulkley, Robert J., 30n, 476
Bunker, Laurence E., 34
Burgelman, Robert A., 394n
Burns, James M., 28n, 476
Burrows, Sir Frederick, 301
Bustamante, Rafael, 73
Butler, Charlotte, 355n
Bylinsky, Gene, 394n, 479

Caesar, Julius, 190
Cage, Nicholas, 392
Caldas, Miguel P., 229n
Capal, James, 247
Cardoso, Fernando Henrique, 230, 231, 459n, 480
Carey, Mariah, 337
Carlson, Chester, 75n

Carmer, Stanley, 274
Caroe, Sir Olaf, 301, 302
Carsten, Jack, 407
Carter, Nik, 104
Celine, 160, 162, 167
Cervejarias Kaiser, 232
Chamberlain, John, 28n, 36n, 476
Chamberlain, Stephen J., 28
Chan, Phil, 447–54
Chandler, David G., 190n, 192n, 196n, 478
Chandrasekharan, V., 244–45, 250, 251
Chapman, Matt, 382n, 479
Chen Xiao Yue, 109n
Cher, 43n, 477
Chiang Kai-shek, 30, 38
Churchill, Winston, 38, 293, 296
Chwang, Ronald, 219, 225–26
Clapham, Debbi, 374–75
Clapton, Eric, 89
Claymore, Jim, 273, 274, 275
Claymore, Roy, 273
Clive, Robert, 304
Clooney, George, 63
Clyde-Smith, Deborah, 217n
Cogan, George W., 394n
Collins, Larry, 290n
Combs, Sean "Puffy," 54–55
Conn, Charles, 327
Conner, Sarah, 5, 8–26
Cook, Jonathan, 435n
Cooke, Sam, 6
Corral, Luis, 58
Costner, Kevin, 391
Court, David, 329
Cramer, Stanley, 275
Crawford, Gordon, 390–91
Cross, David, 63
Crossan, Mary, 146n
Crystal, Billy, 391
Curtis, Marvin, 348–49, 350

Daimaru, Mr., 363
Daly, Robert A., 390
D'Andrea, Guillermo, 57n, 66n
Daniel, Ron, 321, 322
Dannen, Frederick, 41n, 94n, 477
Davenport, Marcia, 274–75
David, Larry, 63
Davis, Clive, 43n, 53–56, 477
Davis, Stanley M., 411n, 479
Day, Graham, 372
Debow, Daniel, 382–89n, 479
DeMarchi, Victório, 229, 230, 232
Desaix, Officer, 193
Diaz, Cameron, 392
Dion, Celine, 89
Doman, Andrew, 327
Donner, Dick, 391, 392
Dornemann, Michael, 41, 44, 46, 51
DuBois, Tim, 55
Dull, Stephen, 329–30
Duncan, Anne, 370n

Eastwood, Clint, 391
Ebersol, Dick, 158
Egeberg, Roger, 29n, 32n, 34, 476
Eichelberger, Robert I., 28, 31n, 35, 36, 38, 476
Eisenhower, Dwight D., 28, 35
Enright, Norma, 276n
Esaki, Leona, 340
Escobari, Marcela, 455n

Faggin, Frederico, 397
Falk, Stanley L., 29n, 32n, 33n, 34n, 476
Fellers, Bonner, 38
Fiennes, Ralph, 391, 392
Finn, Norman, 377, 378–79
Fisk, Howard, 348–49, 350–51
Flanagan, Edward M., Jr., 35n, 476
Flores, Greg, 89
Fonseca, Ramiro, 58

Forbes, Ted, 5n
Foster, Jodie, 392
Foster, John, 423–24, 425, 426, 433
Foster, Radney, 55
Foster, Timothy, 427–28
Frank, Christoph, 127
Franke, Peter, 131, 134, 135
Frère, Albert, 164
Fried, Andrew, 411n
Fuchs, Michael, 63
Fujisawa, Takeo, 201, 202, 205, 206

Galliano, John, 167
Galway, James, 43
Gandhi, Mohandas, 294–98, 299, 303, 304, 307
Gardiner, Paul D., 352n
Gassner, Rudi, 40–52, 477
Gates, Bill, 67
Gaur, Girish, 245, 249
Gennaro, Dante, 57, 58
Gennaro, Eduardo, 57, 58, 60
George VI (King of England), 291–92
Gerber, Bill, 391
Ghoshal, Sumantra, 75n, 124n, 234n, 276n, 355n, 370n, 455n
Gibson, Ken, 327–28
Gibson, Mel, 391, 392
Gibson, Robert W., 179
Gilder, George, 400n, 479
Gluck, Fred, 321, 322, 324, 330
Godé, Pierre, 161
Gold, Jeremy, 350–51
Gopalan, S. R., 246–47, 250, 253
Gordon, Richard, 173
Gorman, Joe, 40, 44, 46, 48, 49
Grami, Kelly, 99, 100, 102
Green, Eric, 382–83, 386, 388, 389, 479
Gregorian, Vartan, 185
Grey, Brad, 65
Griggin, J., 31n, 476
Grossan, Mary, 382n
Grouchy, Marshal, 190, 196, 478
Grove, Andy, 345, 396, 398, 409, 410
Groves, Leslie R., 38n, 477
Guan Sheng Yuan, 281
Guber, Peter, 342
Guerinot, Jim, 55
Guest, Christopher, 63
Guest, Robert, 206, 212n, 478
Gunther, John, 28, 38, 477
Gupta, Rajat, 319

Hach, Peter, 126, 127, 134, 478
Hall, Ted, 324
Halliday, Billie, 6
Halsey, Admiral, 27, 30, 31, 32, 33, 35
Halsey, William F., 30n, 476
Hammer, Maxwell S., 5, 7–8
Hannibal, 190
Harris, Judith, 377
Hart, Antonio, 43
Hassim, Iqbal, 440n, 443n, 480
Heinen, Dieter, 127
Hemsworth, Frank, 372
Henn, Heinz, 44, 48, 49, 51
Hensen, Tito, 172–73
Herzog, Doug, 158
Heuser, Michael, 135, 136, 137
Heyden, Ludo Van der, 190n
Higgins, Patricia, 423n
Hill Samuel Bank, 310
Hitachi, 246, 404
Ho Chi Minh, 290
Hoff, M. E. "Ted," 397
Hoffman, Dustin, 391
Hoffmann, Jochen, 128, 136
Holdsworth, Henry, 352, 353, 354
Honda, Soichiro, 200–202, 204, 206
Horne, Alistair, 193n, 194n, 478
Houston, Whitney, 43, 53, 477
Hubbard, Thomas, 179, 183, 185

Hughes, Howard, 310
Hunt, Frazier, 27n, 28n, 35n, 38n, 476, 477

Ibuka, Masaru, 333, 334, 340, 341
Idei, Nobuyuki, 333, 339, 343–47, 344–45
Iger, Robert A., 157
Isabella, Lynn A., 5n
Ismay, General Lord, 293
Iturri, Juan, 276n
Iwabuchi, Sanji, 36–37
Iwama, Kazuo, 335, 341

Jackson, Alan, 55
Jackson, Michael, 89
Jacobs, Marc, 166, 167
Jacobs, Tokunbo, 447, 448
Jakob, Angelike, 127
James, Dorris Clayton, 29n, 31n, 32n, 34n, 35n, 476, 477
Jamieson, Peter, 46, 48, 49, 50
Jansen, Peter, 127–28
Jenkins, Sir Evan, 301
Jennings, Peter, 421
Jérôme, Prince, 196
Jinnah, 305–6
Joel, Billy, 337
Joffe, Roland, 391
John, Prince, 4
Jomini, 193, 193n, 478
Jones, Dan, 375
Jones, Ian, 352, 353, 354
Joplin, Janis, 53, 54
Juio, Matsuichi, 28

Kaat, Yasu, 261
Kaku, Ryuzaburo, 75, 82, 83, 85, 87
Karavis, Lambros, 263n
Kascel, Paula, 180, 183, 185
Kase, Toshikazu, 39n, 477
Kata, Yasu, 259
Kawamoto, Nobuhiko, 207–8, 209, 212
Kawashima, Kihachiro, 203
Kee, Mr., 174–75
Kennedy, John F., 148
Kennedy, Thomas, 47n, 477
Kenney, George C., 27–28, 29n, 30, 31, 32, 33n, 36, 37, 38, 476
Kenny G., 43, 477
Kida, Tomohiro, 333n
Kilfoyle, Regina S., 276n
Kim, W. Chan, 190n
King (admiral), 28–29
Kingston, Andy, 96, 98
Kinkaid, Tom, 31, 33, 34
Kiser, Ezra, 383
Kline, Kevin, 392
Kohn, Les, 408–9
Kopelson, Arnold, 392
Kopp, Robb, 93n
Kors, Michael, 167
Kotha, Suresh, 411n
Kowomoto, Dr., 205
Kraus, Michael, 132
Krueger, 27, 33, 35, 36, 38
Kubrick, Stanley, 391
Kuga, Masashi, 364
Kume, Tadashi, 206
Kurita, Takeo, 33
Kuroyanagi, Fumio, 355, 360, 368, 369
Kutaragi, Ken, 340

Lack, Andrew, 158
Lambert, T. J., 5
Lampel, Joseph, 3n, 273n, 348n, 474n
Lanciaux, Concetta, 161, 162, 164, 165, 168–69
Lane, Larry, 427
Lange, Heiko, 126
Lapierre, Dominique, 290n
Larkins, Pat, 433
Leahy, William D., 29, 30, 38n, 476, 477
Leal, Guilherme, 455, 456, 458, 459, 460, 465–66, 480
Lecraw, Don, 171n
Lee, Allen, 447, 448
Lee, Mrs., 171, 172, 173, 174
Lee, Robert E., 27
Lee, Spike, 391
Lelyveld, Michael, 93n
Lennox, Annie, 43
Leonardi, Robert, 350

Letter, Mark, 330
Letzelter, Pierre, 162, 164, 165, 169
Levin, Gerald M., 392
Levinson, Barry, 391
Levitt, Theodore, 314, 315
Levy, Eugene, 63
Liebenson, Jeff, 44, 48
Liedtka, Jeanne M., 176n
Lindsay, Jack, 274
Lindstrom, Jenny, 474–75
Little, William, 423n
Littlefield, Warren, 157–58
Liu, Leonard, 219, 220
Locilento, Bud, 424–25, 426, 428
Lockwood, Charles A., 32n, 476
Long, Gavin M., 28n, 476
Long, Gregory, 176, 179, 182, 183, 185
Lott, Roy, 55
Louis-Dreyfus, Robert, 309–10, 313, 315
Louis XVI, 190, 191
Louis XVIII, 191, 195n, 478
Lu, Teddy, 221
Luiz, Manoel, 462
Luvaas, Jay, 28n, 29n, 35n, 36n, 37n, 476
Lyons, Patrick, 97

MacArthur, Douglas, 29n, 31n, 35n, 38n, 476, 477
   in the Philippines, 27–39
MacCaw, Craig, 67
Mackenzie, W. L., 30
MacLeish, Archibald, 37
Madonna, 89
Manilow, Barry, 53
Manville, Brook, 323
Marshall, Dick, 3 4–35
Marshall, George, 28, 30, 31, 35–36
Marshall, John, 352, 354
Martin, Ari, 54
Maruta, Yoshio, 355, 356, 357, 358–60, 363–64, 365–66, 369
Mason, Vic, 353, 354
Matassoni, Bill, 323–24
Mauborgne, Renee, 190n
Mayrhuber, Wolfgang, 126, 127, 134
McGee, Robert, 6
McKaye, Milton, 31n, 476
McKinsey, James "Mac," 319
McLachlan, Sarah, 54
McLeod, Phil, 146, 147, 148, 152, 154, 155
McNealy, Scott, 408
McQueen, Alexander, 167
Mercner, John, 274
Meyer, Ron J. H., 309n
Meyers, Mike, 392
Michaux, Pierre, 412
Milchan, Aaron, 392
Millar, Victor E., 313
Mindich, Brad, 93n
Mindich, Stephen, 98, 99, 102
Mitarai, Tekeshi, 77
Mitford, Jessica, 64
Mitta, Sridhar, 242
Mitterrand, François, 161
Mittman, Bruce, 98
Mohammed Ali Jinnah, 297–99, 300, 301, 303–4, 306–7
Mölleney, Matthias, 127
Moonves, Mr., 157
Moore, Gordon E., 394–410
Morio, Minoru, 343
Morisette, Alanis, 90, 99
Morita, Akio, 333, 334, 336, 338
Morolo, Gary Kobane, 443
Morrell, Scott, 383
Mosiako, Winston, 435n, 439, 440, 441n, 444n, 480
Mountbatten, Louis Francis Albert Victor Nicholas, 290–308
Murphy, Joe, 273

Nagasi, Tomiro, II, 356–57
Nagdee, Zainul, 439, 440n, 443, 480
Ndoro, Simon, 439, 440n, 480
Nehru, Jawaharlal, 293, 294–95, 299, 303, 304, 306, 307
Neill, John, 370, 371, 372, 374, 375, 376, 378, 380, 381
Neti, Bruno, 350
Ney, Marshal, 190, 195, 196, 478
Nhlapo, Matsebe, 439, 440, 480
Nimitz, Chester William, 27, 28, 29, 30, 31
Nishamura, Teji, 33

Nishimura, Yasu Kata, 260
Nitsch, Detlev, 146n
Noyce, Robert N., 394–410
Nunn, Raymond, 383

Odenkirk, Bob, 63
Ohga, Norio, 333, 335, 340–41, 343–45, 347
Ohlmeyer, Don, 158
Ohmae, Kenichi, 323
Olano, Mr., 171, 174–75
Oldendorf, Jesse, 33
Olivetto, Washington, 231
Osmena, Sergio, 32–33
Ossip, David, 382, 383–86, 388–89
Ossip, Martin, 383
Otero, Miguel, 279–81, 282
Ozawa, Jisaburo, 33

Pai, P. S., 237, 251
Palermo Viejo, 58
Paltrow, Gwyneth, 392
Paquette, Penny C., 200n
Parker, Gerry, 404
Parkyn, Brian, 47n, 477
Parsons, Andrew, 329
Pascal, Philippe, 167
Passos, Pedro, 455, 456, 458, 459, 464, 465, 466
Patel, Vallabhbhai, 297, 307
Patsalos-Fox, Michael, 328–29
Paul, Vivek, 245, 246, 252, 253
Peacocke, John, 327
Pescarmona, Enrique, 66, 70, 73–74
Pescarmona, Enrique Epaminondas, 67
Pescarmona, Enrique Menotti, 67
Pescarmona, Luis Menotti, 67
Peters, Jeff, 326–28
Peters, Jon, 342, 391
Peters, Tom, 321, 323
Peterson, Nancy, 309n
Petroski, Tony, 273–74, 275
Petty, Tom, 90
Pietchestieder, Berndt, 380
Pieterse, Gavin, 441
Pinault, Francois, 160, 162
Pinnette, Kathleen, 309n
Pollack, Syndey, 63
Pommez, Philippe, 460, 461
Ponroy, Thibaut, 169
Porter, Salma, 350
Premji, Azim H., 234, 239, 248, 250, 251, 252
Presley, Elvis, 41
Preston, John, 45, 46, 48–49, 51–52, 52
Price, Hal, 424
Purkiss, Alan, 41n, 477

Quezon, Manuel, 31, 32, 476
Quinn, Allie J., 200n
Quinn, James Brian, 27n, 200n, 290n, 394n, 423n

Racamier, Henry, 161
Ramachandran, J., 234n
Ramazzotti, Eros, 43
Rao, M. S., 239
Rapport, Mark, 474–75
Raps, Jügen, 127, 134
Rawlings, Charles A., 28n, 476
Reed, Bob, 406
Reid, Antonio "L.A.", 53, 54, 55
Reininger, Ursel, 126
Renschler, Arnold, 428, 433
Richard, King, 4
Richards, Norman, 38n, 477
Richardson, John, 378
Richardson, Robert C., 29
Ridley, John, 63
Rigby, Eleanor, 6
Rio, Diamond, 55
Rios, Susana, 60
Robert, Neal, 99
Roberts, Johnnie L., 51n, 477
Robertson, Michael, 88–91
Robichaux, Mark, 51n, 477
Robin Hood, 3–4
Rock, Arthur, 395
Rodriguez, Narciso, 167
Romulo, Carlos P., 31, 32–33, 476
Ronen, Daniel, 348n
Roosevelt, Eleanor, 31, 32

Roosevelt, Franklin D., 28–30, 32, 34
Rorer, John, 179–80, 182, 183
Rorty, Jack, 274
Rosen, Hilary, 90
Rosiello, Rob, 329–30
Ross, Steven J., 391
Roth, Peter, 158
Rovere, Richard H., 28n, 476
Ruhnau, Heinz, 125
Russell, Thomas, 314

Saatchi, Charles, 310, 313, 314, 315
Saatchi, Maurice, 309–10, 313, 314, 315
St. Thomas, Kurt, 93, 96, 97, 98, 99
Sakiya, T., 201n, 202n, 478
Sallen, Ira, 44, 48, 49, 50
Sánchez, Josá, 57, 60–61
Sanders, S., 201n, 478
Sandler, Adam, 392
Santana, Carlos, 53
Sassa, Scott, 156, 158, 159
Sattelberger, Thomas, 131, 135, 136
Schaan, Jean-Louis, 447n
Schalkwyk, Willie Van, 439, 444
Schiller, Marc, 91
Schlede, Klaus, 127n, 478
Schlesinger, Arthur M., Jr., 28n, 476
Schmitz, Hans, 126–27, 135
Schnabel, Christy, 90
Schnall, Richard, 179
Schom, Alan, 192n, 195n, 478
Schulhof, Michael, 342
Schwarzenegger, Arnold, 392
Scott, Charles, 314
Seabra, Luiz, 455, 456, 458, 459, 460, 461–62, 464, 466, 480
Segrave, Bernie, 263, 264, 265–66, 267
Segura, Ramon, 45–46, 48, 52
Selkirk, Iain, 265–66
Selkirk, Jim, 264, 265–66
Selkirk, Robert, 263–64, 265–66
Semel, Terry, 390
Shamsie, Jamal, 53n, 62n, 88n, 156n, 390n
Shandling, Gary, 62
Shih, Stan, 217, 218, 219, 220, 221, 223, 225, 226, 227, 228
Shimp, Terrence, 94n, 477
Shockley, William, 394, 398
Shotoku, Prince, 357

Silver, Joel, 391
Simon, Mellor, 314
Sinclair, Jeremy, 314
Singh, Yadavindra, 299
Sinha, Atul, 190n
Skase, Christopher, 265
Smirnov, Francisco, 6–7
Smith, Doug, 54
Smith, Robert R., 30n, 476
Smith, Will, 392
Soderstrom, Sulu, 328–29
Soota, Ashok, 240, 241–42, 244, 253
Sorrell, Marten, 310, 479
Soult, Marshal, 190n, 196, 478
Spacey, Kevin, 392
Sridhar, A. V., 241
Stain, David, 383
Stalin, Joseph, 38
Stansfield, Lisa, 43
Stein, David, 388
Stein, Thomas, 45, 48, 49, 50, 52
Steinberg, Alfred, 28n, 31n, 476
Steinberg, David J., 29n, 31n, 32n, 476
Stern, Howard, 94–95, 104
Stimson, Henry Lewis, 36, 38
Stone, Oliver, 391
Strauss, Carolyn, 63–64
Stuckey, John, 326–28
Sudo, Kenji, 254
Sull, Don, 455n
Sullivan, Jim, 96n, 97, 104n, 477
Sun Lin Chou, 403, 407
Suzuki, Sosaku, 31

Takayama, Mr., 360–61, 368, 369
Takigawa, Seiichi, 85
Teckentrup, Ralf, 134
Telles, Marcel Hermann, 229, 230, 231, 232, 233
Thatcher, Margaret, 310, 372
Thomas, Graham, 315n, 479
Thompson, Chris, 64
Thurman, Uma, 391, 392
Tian Shan, 281
Tillis, Pam, 55
Toit, Sanet du, 435n
Tojo Hideki, 31
Toland, John, 30n, 31n, 34n, 476

Travolta, John, 391
Trevelyan, Mark, 373
Truman, Harry S., 38
Tsutsumi, Dr., 364, 365

Ullman, Myron, 163, 164–65, 165

Vadasz, Les, 409
Vandamme, General, 196
Van Schalkwyk, Willie, 444n, 480
Vasconcelos, Flávio, 229n
Verdaguer, Ricardo, 66, 69–70, 74
Vidal, Gore, 28
Villiger, Joseph, 231
Vivek, Paul, 245n, 479
Vivo, Roberto, 66, 69, 70, 74

Wainwright, Jonathan M., 38
Walsh, Matt, 348–49, 350–51
Warman, Roy, 315
Waschkuhn, Wolf, 276n
Waterman, Bob, 321, 323
Wavell, Sir Archibald, 291, 292
Weald, Bob, 353
Webber, Andrew Lloyd, 260
Weber, Jürgen, 124, 125, 126, 127, 128, 134, 135, 137
Weber, Katherine Seger, 40n
Weintraub, Jerry, 391
Wellington, Duke of, 27, 28, 195–96
Wetlaufer, Suzy, 441
Whitney, Courtney, 38n, 39n, 477
Williams, Robin, 391
Williams, Vincent, 440, 480
Williamson, Peter J., 217n
Willoughby, Charles A., 27, 28n, 476
Wilson, Joseph C., 75
Wolberg, Joe, 350
Wood, Thomaz, Jr., 229n
Woodcock, Patrick, 254n
Wright, Bertram C., 35n, 476
Wright, Robert C., 157, 158
Wyatt, Wattson, 386

Yamaguchi, Hidehiko, 333n
Yamashita, Tomoyuki, 31, 35–37

Zelnick, Strauss, 53, 54, 55

ABC, 156, 157, 158
AB Dick company, 75n, 76
Acer Group, 217–28, 252
    company history, 218–19
    future for, 228
    globalization of, 219–21
    leadership and vision at, 225–26
    leveraging multinational network, 227–28
    reassessing profit potential, 221
    strategic innovation at, 221–25
    values and corporate culture, 226–27
Acer Peripherals Inc., 227, 228
Acquisitions, 230, 366–68, 456
Addressograph/Multigraph, 76
Advanced Micro Devices, 403, 406
Advanced Software Technologies, 439
Advertising, 460
    in domestic market, 277
    in international operations, 285
    in newspapers, 146–47, 148
    Pan-European, 317
    in Russia, 281
Advertising spots, 94
A&E, 64
Aerosmith, 43n, 96, 477
AES, 443
Affirmative action, 441
African Partnerships, 441
Aiwa, 171, 172–73
ALCATEL, 71
Algodonera del Plata, 57–61
    arrival of José Sánchez, 60–61
    company, 57
    in March 1993, 58–59
    new management, 58
    sweatsuit manufacture, 57–58
Alliance Capital, 247
Alliances, 218–19, 387
    in automobile industry, 207, 208–10
    strategic, 378, 439
Altos, 219
AM, 79
AmBev, 229–33
    Brazilian context, 230–31
    decisions in, 233
    future of, 232–33
    global context, 230
    ley platers in, 231–32
American Express, 385n, 479
American Honda Motor Co., 202–3
American Payroll Association, 385n, 479
American Radio Systems, 100
AMR Research, 385n, 479
Amway, 457, 462
Anheuser-Busch, 231–32
Antarctica Paulista, 229, 231–32
Anzio, Battle of, 28
AOL-Time Warner, 65
Apple Computers, 403n, 479
Araya, 413
Arbitron ratings, 96, 98, 100
Area market manager, 284
Argentina, communications in, 70–71
Ariola, 45–46
Arista Records, 41, 53–56, 99
    success in, 53–55
A&R marketing, 44n, 477
Arto Shokai, 200
Asahi National Broadcasting Co., Ltd., 254
Asahi Shimbun, 254–55, 257
ASCAP, 96
Asian multinational corporations
    building, 217–28
Asia-Pacific telecommunications industry, 328
Asiola, 41
Association arrangements, 247
Astral Records, Ltd., North America, 5–26
    CD industry and, 5–6
    history of company, 6–7
    under Sarah Conner, 8–26
Astral Records, Ltd., U.K., 6–7

Atelital, 73
Atlantic records, 90
AT&T, 68
Austerlitz, Battle of, 193–94
Australian clay brick manufacturing industry, 271
Automobile industry. See also specific manufacturers
    alliances in, 207, 208–10
    capital requirements of, 212
    cost structures in, 207
    in the UK, 371–72
Aveda, 456
Avon, 455, 457, 462
Axion Consulting, 348–51
Azart, 280
Azea, 363

Babyface, 54
Backward integration, 82–83
Bad Boy Records, 54–55
Balance-sheet information, 283
Banca Nazionale del Lavoro, 71
Bankruptcy, 125
Basic Software, 447–54
Baxter Health Care Corp's Physical Therapy Division, 434
BBTV, 256
Beastie Boys, 90
Beckman Instruments, 245, 246
Becton Dickinson, 246
Beiersdorf, 363, 366, 368, 456
Bei Jing Confectionary Company, 281
Beijing Mirror Corp., 109–23
    finance, 112
    joint venture proposal, 112–23
    management, 112
    market capacity, 110, 111
    marketing, 112
    patent, 110
    product background, 109–10
    production, 112
    research and development, 112
    strengths, 111
    technology environment, 111
    weaknesses, 111–12
Bel Air Entertainment, 392
Belgian Interbrew group, 230
Beliefs, integration through shared, 248–49
Bell Labs, 322, 335, 399
Bell Northern Research, 244, 479
BellSouth Corp., 230
Bendini, Lambert & Locke (BLL), 5, 7
Benefits, 162
Berjeaut, 458
Bertelsmann AG, 41, 50
Bertelsmann Music Group (BMG), 41, 53. See also BMG
    International
Best technology solution, 241
Betriebsergebnis, 46n, 477
Bharat Earth Movers Limited, 238
Bicycle industry in Japan, 411–12
Bionat, 458
Bio-Rad Labs, 246
Blackburn Group Inc. (BGI), 151, 151n, 478
Blackburn Marketing Services Inc. (BMSI), 151
Black economic empowerment, 441–43
Black Economic Empowerment Commission, 441
Black Information Technology Forum, 441
Bliss, 162
BMG International, 40–52, 53, 55
    building, 44–45
    business plan at, 40, 46
    company background, 41–43
    creating a regional structure, 45–47
    executive committee at, 40–41, 47–51
    globalization and, 44–45, 46–47
BMI, 96
BMW, 171, 207, 380
Body shopping, 243
Boeing, merger with McDonnell Douglas, 230
Bombay Stock Exchange, 240
Bomb Records, 55
Borland, 244

Boston Consulting Group (BCG), 320, 321
The Boston Phoenix, 93, 98
Boussac Saint-Frères textile conglomerate, 161
BR5-49, 55
Bradesco Bank, 231
Brain drain, 218
Brand autonomy, 163
Brand image, creating global, 219–20
Brand International Promotional Association, 219–20
Brazil
    cosmetics industry in, 457
    multinational corporations in, 229–33
    Natura in, 455–73
Bribery, 94
Bridgestone Cycle Co., 412, 414
Brimstone, 441
British Airways, 310
British Broadcasting Corporation (BBC), 376
British Commonwealth, 292
British Leyland, 207, 371–72
British Rail, 381
British Shipbuilders, 372
British Telecom PLC, 68, 242
Broadcasting industry, deregulation of, 257–58
Bronco, 43
Brooks & Dunn, 55
Buggles, 94
Buloba, 335–36
Bunnings, 265
Burger King, 278
Burroughs, 80
Busicom, 397
Business area strategies in strategic planning, 131
Business doctors, 319
BusinessMap, 443
Business marketing competence center, 329–30
Business plans, 40, 46, 87
Business-to-business marketing initiative, 329–30
Business units, 132–33, 349
    in driving entrepreneurship, 84–85
    strategic, 224–25, 399
B'z, 43

Cadbury, 278, 280, 284
CADE, 229, 230
Cafeteria shop technologies, 252
Canon, 75–87
    building capabilities, 80–83
    company background, 75–77
    leveraging expertise, 83–84
    move into copiers, 77–79
    personal copiers, 79–80
    process management, 84–87
Cantise Co., 113
Capabilities
    building, 80–83
    combining, 83
    joint ventures in building international, 223
Capital-EMI records, 41
Capital injection, 273
Capitalism, cyberspace, 88
Capital Research and Management Company, 390–91
Carrefour, 230
Cash on delivery, 277
Cat Eye, 413
CBS, 156, 157, 158
    purchase of American Radio Systems, 100
CBS Records, 41, 337
CCR movement, 357–58
CCTV, 256
CD industry, 5–6
Celestial Records, 6
Centralized copying, 76
Cervejaria Brahma, 229, 231
Change, openness for, 135
Change management, 125
Change momentum, maintaining, 124
China, Chupa Chups in, 281–82, 283
China State Bank, 283
Christian Dior, 160, 161, 162, 164, 167, 456, 457
Christian Lacroix, 162

Christie's, 162
Chrysler, merger with Daimler-Benz, 230
Chupa Chups Diversification, 278
Citicorp, merger with Travelers, 230
Clarins, 456
Clark Development Corporation, 173
Clean Air Act (1970), 204
Client relationship consulting, 321
Client-server business model, 224–25
Client-server labor management, 383
Client service, 319–20
Client service support and administrative staff, 326
Client service team, 324, 326
CNBC, 159
CNN News, 255, 256
Coated Paper Copying (CPC) technology, 76, 77
Coca-Cola, 232, 277
Code Napoléon, 190–91
Colgate-Palmolive, 310, 366, 457
Columbian Motors, 171
Columbia Pictures Entertainment Inc., 337
Columbia TriStar, 64–65
ComDisc, 6
Comedy Central, 158
Commodity trade business, 237
Communications
    application of VSAT technology to, 69–70
    in Argentina, 70–71
    deregulation of, 67–69
    in Latin America, 69
Compact, 244
Companhia Antarctica Paulista, 229, 231–32
Company man, 274
Compaq, 218, 222, 224, 227, 409
Compartmentalization, 329
Competition, for ideas and talent, 64–65
Complete Communications, 370
Compusearch, 151
Computec Co., 224
Computer-Aided Design (CAD) system, 417
Computer Assisted Design, 112
Computer industry, reassessing profit potential in changing, 221
Comsat, 71
Concept testing, 364
Concert, 68
Consciousness, preserving, on the crisis, 135
Consolidation, 456
    in newspaper industry, 149–50
    in radio industry, 94, 102
Construcciones Metalúrgicas Pescarmona S.R. L., 67
Continental Medical Systems, 434
Continuous improvement, 373
Co-ordinated Network Investments, 443
Copyer, 76, 79
Copyright infringement, 88, 91
Corporate culture, values and, 226–27
Corporate restructuring, 129
Cosmetics industry, growth and consolidation in global, 456
Cottone, 57
Counterpoint, 218
CPF Deutsch, 80
Cruzcampo, 230
C&S Technology Company, 112
CTV, 256
Cyberspace capitalism, 88

Daimler-Benz, 207, 223
    merger with Chrysler, 230
Dalgarno, 370
Davor, 57, 60–61
DBP Telekom, 68, 70
de Beers, 164
Decision to go public, 275
Dedicated distribution network, 278
Deki, 412, 413, 421
Dell publishing, 41
Demand chain management, 371–72
Demographics of readership, 148–50
Dennison, 76
Dentsu, 368–69
Deregulation
    of broadcasting industry, 257–58
    of communications, 67–69
    trend towards, 73
Designs, integrated, 205–6
Development strategy, 111

Devo, 94
DFS duty-free chain, 162, 164
Diahatsu, 171
Differentiation strategy, 98
Digital compression technology, 88, 89
Digital Equipment Corporation, 221, 239, 240, 403
Direct sales organization, 76–77, 457, 461, 462
Disney, Walt, Company, 157
Disney Corporation, 262
Distinct creativity, 357
Distribution
    in domestic market, 277
    in international operations, 284–85
Diversification, 77, 82, 83, 84, 85, 309–18
Divisionalization, 320
Domestic market, achieving leadership in, 276–77
Donaldson, Lufkin, and Jenrett, 430n, 479
Doubleday publishing, 41
Double management contract, 352
Downsizing, 278

Eastman Kodak, 80
Eaton Corporation, 238–39
Ecole Polytechnique, 160
Efficiency experts, 319
Egalitarianism, 359
Eipro International Limited, 245
Electric Artists, 91
Electronic data interchange, 379
Electronic theft, 88–92
Elevator Drops, 55
EMC, 439
Empire Consultants, 352
Empire Plastics, 352–54
Empowerment
    black economic, 441–43
    culture of, 439–40
    philosophy, 435–37
Empresa Nacional de Telecommunicaciones (ENTEL), 69, 70
Entrepreneurship, 394–95
    business units in driving, 84–85
    Japanese, 200–201
Epson Malaysia, 244–45
Estee Lauder, 456
Éternelle, 458
Europe, Kao in, 368
European Bank of Reconstruction and Development, 283
European Telecombs, 328–29
European Union, 69
    Spain's entry to, 282–83
Exclusive distributor, 284
Expert system, 205
Export function, in Selkirk Brick, 267, 269
Export pricing nomenclature and value added, 266
Exports, 60, 172
External partnerships, 382
Exxon, merger with Mobil, 230

Fairchild Camera, 395
Fairchild Semiconductor, 394–95
Fast food business model, 222
Federal Communications Commission (FCC), radio rules of, 96, 100
Fendi, 162
Field assignments, 60
Financial system, in international operations, 283–85
Flat hierarchy, 226
Flexibility, for middle management, 462
Fly by night operators, 247
Fly in, fly out model of expert-based consulting, 321
Focus groups, 99, 364
Ford Motor, 210, 375
Foster Management Company, 423–24
Fox, 64, 157
France, Chupa Chups in, 277–78
France Telecom, 68, 69
Franchising, 60
Frog Design, 227
Frontier markets, pioneering, 224
Fuji Television Network (Fuji TV), 255
Fujitsu, 240, 241
Fuji Xerox, 76
Functional committees, in building integration, 85–86

Galaxy Records, 5, 6
Galeries Lafayette, 368
GE Capital, 247

GE Medical Systems, 252
General Electric, 235, 244, 245, 246, 248, 253
    takeover of NBC by, 156, 158
Generalised specialists, 247
General Motors, 204, 207, 375, 411
General Survey outline, 319
Germany, Chupa Chups in, 278
Gessy Lever, 455, 457
Gettysburg, Battle of, 27
Ghaffar Khan, 302
Gillette, 457
Givenchy, 160, 162, 164, 167
Global Information system for Harmonious Growth Administration (GINGA), 85
Globalization, 44, 66, 76, 87, 219–21, 277–83, 309–18
Globe and Mail, 150, 151
Go (Chinese board game), 226
Goldman Sachs, 247, 408n, 479
Goldwell AG, 368
Gowrishankar, 251
Great Britain, India and, 290–308
Green Day (band), 93, 97–98
    concert by, 96–98
Group organization, 3–4
Growth
    balancing, 253
    sustaining, 466–67
Growth strategy, 161–62, 252, 443–44, 456
Gucci, 162, 167
Guerlain, 160, 162, 456
Gulf War, impact of, 125
Guns 'N' Roses, 43n, 477

Hambrecht & Quist, 384n, 479
Hansha, 361–62, 365
Hard Candy, 162
Harrod's, 58, 60
Hashimoto, Tsunao, 338
Hayden Stone, 394, 395
Hay Management, 310
HBO, 62–65
    competing for ideas and talent, 64–65
    developing unconventional slate, 63
    managing by improvisation, 63–64
HBO Enterprises, 65
Health Care Finance Administration, 433
Healthfocus, Inc., 434
HealthSouth Rehabilitation Corp., 434
Heineken, 230
Hewlett Packard, 83, 224, 227, 240, 241, 246, 328, 403, 439
Hick Timbers, 264, 265
Hidedata, 258, 259
High Point Chemical Corporation, 367
Hikari, 414
Hike and Bike, 273
Hinditron, 240
Hindustan Lever, 237
Holiday Inn, 70
Honda Motor Company, 200–216, 371, 373, 375, 379
    automobiles of, 203–4, 204–5, 207–16
    beginnings of, 201–2
    in European market, 207
    global expansion of, 202–3
    motorcycles of, 201–2, 204, 209
    in the 1980s, 204–5
    in the 1990s, 207–16
    organizational structure in, 206–7
    Sales, Production Engineering, and Development system in, 205
    technology and, 205–7
    in U.S., 202–3
Hosken Consolidated Investments, 441
Hughes Network System Inc., 70
Human resources strategy, 387
Hypermarkets, 60

IBM, 75, 76–77, 220, 221, 222, 224, 227, 239, 244, 347, 363, 403, 408, 439, 440–41
ICICI, 247
Ideas, competition for, 64–65
Identity, preserving, 135
Imitation strategy, 420–22
Import barriers, lifting of, 230–31
Import-substituting development strategy, 172
Improvisation, management by, 63–64
IMPSAT (Industrias Metalúrgicas Pescarmona), 66–74
    communication market in Argentina, 70–71
    communications in Latin America, 69

IMPSAT (*cont.*)
  deregulation of communications, 67–69
  operations beginning, 71–72
  planning commercial operations, 72–73
  situation in 1990, 73–74
  VSAT technology and its application to communications, 69–70
Incentive systems, 428–29
Independence, for India, 290–308
India
  Chupa Chups in, 282, 283
  Mountbatten in, 290–308
  multinational corporations in, 234
Industrias Msralúrgicas Pescarmona S.A.I.C. & F., 67
Infinity, 96, 100
Information management, 358–60
Information strategy, 430–34
Information technology, 357, 361–63
  as people business, 435–46
Information Technology Company, 345
InfoSystems, 367
Innovation, 461
Inspeech, 423
Instrument Corporation, 395
Integrated designs, 205–6
Integrated services digital network, 228
Integration
  backward, 82–83
  functional committees in building, 85–86
  through management processes, 250–52
  through people, 250
  through shared beliefs and leadership values, 248–49
  vertical, 157
Intel Corporation, 218, 219, 347, 394–410
  culture, 399–400
  entrepreneurship, 394–95
  issues for the 1990s, 410
  new microprocessor strategy, 406–8
  in the 1990s, 400–403
  organizational structure, 396
  practices attuned to the times, 398–99
  systems business, 409–10
  venture capital, 395–96
Internal recruiting, 339
International Musical, Inc. (IMI), 259
International operations
  advertising in, 285
  distribution in, 284–85
  financial system in, 283
  management of, 283–85
  marketing in, 284, 285
  plant specialization in, 283–84
  procurement system in, 283
  transfer of technology in, 283–84
Internet
  as competition to television, 157
  functionality, 384
  MP3.com as business on, 88–92
Intrapreneurial ventures, 85
Inventory control, 60
  kanban system of, 82
Inverted organization, 426–29
IPOs, 467
  launching of, 228
Iridium, 67

Jacquar, 207
Jaguar, 372, 375
JAMN, 96
Jantus, 231
Japan
  bicycle industry in, 411–12
  entrepreneurship in, 200–201
  newspaper industry in, 255
  sales distribution agreement in, 267, 272
  television industry in, 255–56
Japan Broadcasting, 262
Japan Satellite Broadcasting, 256
Jardine Fleming, 247
JCB, 238
Jergens, Andrew, Company, 366
Job descriptions, 388
Job rotation, 220
Johnson & Johnson, 310, 456
Joint ventures, 80, 112–23, 172, 174, 217, 218–19, 223, 245, 247, 279, 282, 285, 337, 363, 366, 371, 379
JVC, 335

Kaiser Beer, 232
Kaizen, 373
Kami Corporation, 171–75
Kanban system of inventory movement, 82
Kangya ichijo, 359
Kansai TV, 255
Kao Corporation, 355–69
  in Europe, 368
  information technology, 361–63
  as learning organization, 355–57
  managing information, 358–60
  in North America, 366–68
  organizational capacity, 368–69
  organizational structure, 357–58
  Sofina, 363–65
  in Southeast Asia, 366
  strategic infrastructure, 366
Kao-Didak, 367–68
Kao Soap Company, 355–56
Kautex UK Ltd, 371, 379
Kautex Unipart Ltd., 371
KDD, 68
Keiretsu conglomerates, 373
Keiretsu, 254*n*, 479
Kenji, 257, 258, 259, 260–61
Kennedy Center, 261
Kenzo, 162
Kia, 171
KISS, 96, 97
Know-how transfer, 80
Knowledge infrastructure, building, 322–24
Knowledge management, 319–31
  refining, 324
Knowledge Resource Directory, 323
Kodak, 76
Koiso, 31
Konev, 35
Konishiroku, 76
KPN, 68
Kreditanstalt für Wiederaufbau, 125
Kronos, Inc., 384
KROQ, 94
Krug and Dom Perignon, 162

LaFace, 54, 55
Lamy-Tutti, 278
Landesman, 260
La Samaritaine, 162
Latin America
  Acer in, 228
  AmBev in, 233
  communications in, 69
Lazard Frères (bank), 161
Leadership
  development programmes, 339
  in domestic market, 276–77
  situational, 381
  succession in, 273–75, 319–20, 333
  thought, 321
  top level, 164–65
  values in, 248–49
  vision and, 225–26
Leadership values, 248–49
Lean production, 371, 374
Le Bon Marché, 161, 162
Lechabile, 435–46
  company background, 435
  conflict resolution, 440
  empowerment philosophy, 435–37, 439–40, 441–43
  IBM versus, 440–41
  industry profile, 437–39
  prizes and awards, 440
  subsidiaries and associated companies, 437
  training and mentorship, 440
Leica, 77
Leveraging, 83–84
  of multinational network, 227–28
Licensing, 77, 79
Life-time employment, 257
Lion, 356, 363, 366
Litton, 76
Local business practices, 447
Local investment, encouraging, 217
Local touch, global brand philosophy, 223
Loewe, 162, 167
London Free Press, 146–55
  organization of, 151–52
  package versus content, 154

potential resistance, 155
  results, 154
  strategic response, 152, 154
L'Oreal, 456, 457, 461
Lotusland, 90
Lotus Notes, 375
Louis Vuitton, 160, 162, 164, 166, 170
LSI Logic Corp., 403
Lufthansa, 124–45
  building a strategic network, 129–31
  business units, 132–33
  corporate restructuring, 129
  internationalisation and branding of subsidiaries, 133–34
  lessons learned, 134
  maintaining the change momentum, 124
  present and future challenges, 135–36
  recent history, 125
  shaping the future, 136–37
  strategic cost savings, 128–29
  strategy planning process, 131–32
  turnaround, 125–28
LVMH, 160–64
  assembling, 161–62
  autonomy of brand companies in, 163
  competing on talent, 167–69
  early days, 160–61
  future focus, 170
  group structure, 162–65
  role of branch presidents, 163–64
  spreading the "*Western Art de Vivre,*" 165–67
  top level leadership, 164–65

Make Up Forever, 162
Management
  balancing, 253
  flexibility for middle, 462
  by improvisation, 63–64
  integration through, 250–52
  of international operations, 283–85
Manufacturing, in building capabilities, 82–83
Marketing
  in building capabilities, 81–82
  for domestic market, 277
  in international operations, 284, 285
  MP3.com and, 90
  philosophy of, 285
  in Russia, 280
Market niche, 98
Market research reports, 155
Mars, 282
Mary Kay, 457, 462
Mass-customization, 411–22
Matsushita, 75, 335, 343, 411
Max Factor, 456
Maybelline, 456
Mazda, 171, 204, 207
Mazor, 397
MCA records, 41
McDonald's, 222, 396
McDonnell Douglas, merger with Boeing, 230
MCI Communication Corp., 68, 70
McKinsey & Company, 319–32
  Commission on Firm Aims and Goals, 320
  doubts, 320–21
  emerging practice areas, 322
  leadership succession, 319–20
  managing success, 324–30
  mission and guiding principles, 321
  new focus, 330
  revival and renewal, 322–24
McKinsey Global Institute, 330
McKinsey Yellow Pages, 323
McLane USA, 278
Media Minds, 89
MedRehab, Inc., 434
Mega Corporation, 171–72, 172–73, 174
Mentorship, 440
Mercedes-Benz, 70, 379
Mercer Consulting, 386
Mercosur, 69
Mergers, 229, 230
Meridiana, 458
Merrill Lunch, 247
Metallica, 96
Mexico, pioneering frontier markets in, 224
Microsoft, 346–47, 407–8
Midland Bank, 310

Mighty Mighty Bosstones, 94
Military strategy
    of Napoleon Bonaparte, 27, 190–99
    in Philippines, 27–39
Minolta, 76
Miramax, 392
Missing Persons, 94
Mita, 76
MITI, 203
Mitsubishi, 207
Miyata, 412
Mobil, merger with Exxon, 230
Moët et Chandon, 160, 162, 163, 165
Moët Hennessey, 160–61
Mon Cheri, 278
Moslem League, 294, 301
Motorcycles, Honda manufacture of, 201–2
Motorola, 67
Mountbatten, 290–308
    Civil War, 293–94
    Gandhi and, 294–98, 299, 303, 304, 307
    governors, 301
    Indian problem, 291
    Jinnah and, 303–4, 305–6
    Kahuta slaughter, 302–3
    Kashmiri Brahman, 294–95
    Nehru and, 293, 294–95, 299, 303, 304, 306, 307
    Operation Madhouse, 291, 292
    Operation Seduction, 292–93, 295, 297, 298, 302
    parition of India, 300–303
        date of, 307–8
        plan for, 303–4
    Patel and, 297, 307
    Peshawar visit, 301–2
    Singh, 299
MP3.com, 88–92
MSNBC, 159
MTV, 158
Multinational corporations
    Brazilian, 229–33
    building Asian, 217–28
    in India, 234
Multinational network, leveraging, 227–28
Multitech Industrial Corporation, 218, 220
Munro and Morón, 58
Murata TV tuners, 171
Music industry, role of radio in value chain of, 94
Mysore Lamps, 248n, 479
Mysore Sales International, 237

Nabisco, 284
NAFTA, 69, 209
Nakanishi, 365
Nash Broadcasting, 100
Nashua, 76
National Bicycle Industrial Company, 411–22
    company background, 414–15
    distribution, 414
    future outlook, 421–22
    manufacturers and assemblers, 412–13
    mass-customization strategy, 415–16
    panasonic ordering system, 413–20
        response to, 420–21
    parts suppliers, 413
National Commission of Space Investigation, 69
National Railway Supplies Ltd., 371, 381
National Record Mart, 54
National Semiconductor, 403
Natura, 455–73
    advertising, 460
    commitment to society, 462
    direct sales, 457, 461
    globalization, 465–66
    growth and consolidation, 456
    history, 458
    innovation/product development, 461
    magic behind, 460–64
    mass-market sector, 457
    meetings, 465–66
    middle management, 462
    organizational structure, 458
    presidents, 464–65
    prestige sector, 456–57
    professionalisation, 459
    recruitment, 464
    research and development, 452
    restructuring, 459
    sales management, 462–63

sales structure, 463
sustaining growth, 466–67
training and development of workforce, 463–64
truth in cosmetics, 460
values, 461–62
NBC, 156–59
    legacy of success, 158–59
    positioning for the future, 159
    threats to, 157–58
NEC, 227
Neilson television ratings, 156
Netmar Inc., 151
Neva Chupa Chups, 279–81, 283
New Line Cinema, 390, 392
News forces, impact of, on television industry, 257–58
Newspaper industry, 146–48
    consolidation in, 149–50
    demographics of readership in, 148–50
    future outlook for, 147–48
    in Japan, 255
    past performance, 147–48
    social role of newspapers in, 150–51
New York Botanical Garden
    board involvement, 183, 185
    community relations, 185
    educational programs, 178–79
    fiscal crisis, 174
    management team, 179–83
    outcomes of planning process, 185–86
    scientific programs, 178
    strategic campaign for, 186
    strategic planning at, 176–89
New York Times, 151
Nichibei Fuji, 412
Nigeria, doing business in, 447–48, 453–54
Nippon Hoso Kyokai (NHK), 255
Nirvana, 43n, 94, 477
Nissan, 203, 207
Nivea, 363
Nokia, 242
No Knife, 55
Normandy, Battle of, 28
North America, Kao in, 366–68
Notorious B.I.G., 55
NovaCare, Inc., 423–34
    competitors, 434
    early history, 440–42
    future markets, 429–33
    incentive systems, 428–29
    inverted organization, 426–29
    professional staffing, 425–26
    quality and revenue control, 429
    support organization, 427–28
    vision statement, 425
NovaNet, 423, 430–34
Novell, 244
Nuñez, 58
Nyhonyha, Litha, 443

O'Boticario, 457
Obunsha, 254
Oedipus, 97
OEM basis, 79, 80, 83, 172
Olivetti, 409
Omnes flux, 359
One Firm policy, 320
Operation Madhouse, 291, 292
Operation Seduction, 292–93, 295, 297, 298, 302
Organizational capacity, 368–69
Original equipment manufacturing (OEM), 218
Our Contributions Counts circles, 373–74
Outsourcing, 273

PAC Company, 113
Panasonic Order System (POS), 411, 414, 416–20
    response to, 420–22
Pan-European advertising, 317
Pão de Açúcar, 231
Paradigm shift, 234
Parts commonality, 83
Patent tracking system, 461
Pay for play practice, 94
Payola scandals, 94
People
    integration through, 250
    involvement of, in strategic business processes, 134
Pepsi Cola, 282
Peregrine, 247

Perkins & Evans, 350
Peripheral businesses, sell off of, 309
Personal & Mobile Communication Company, 345
Personnel management, 339
Pescarmona Group of Companies, 66
Peter Principle recycling, 397, 397n
Phil Chan, 447–54
    Nigerian context, 447–48, 453–54
Philco, 394
Philippines, MacArthur in, 27–39
Phillips, 343
Phillips Brick and Pottery Pty Ltd, 264
Phillips Holland, 246, 248
Phoenix Media/Communications Group, 93, 98, 104
Pink Floyd, 337
Pitney Bowes, 76
Pizza Hut, 278
Plain Paper Copying (PPC) technology, 76, 77, 79
Plan Austral, 58
Plant specialization, in international operations, 283–84
Policy changes, 3–4
PolyGram records, 41, 43
    merger with Universal, 90
Pommery, 160
Portfolio, balancing, 252
PPG Hellige, 246
Practice development initiative, 321–22
Practice Olympics, 319, 330
Practice-sponsored studies, 328–29
Prada's, 162
Prasanna, 245
Premier Exhaust Systems, 374
Privatization
    of public services, 348
    trend towards, 73
Process technology, 277, 284
Procter & Gamble, 237, 310, 317, 355, 356, 363, 366, 455, 456, 457
Procurement system, in international operations, 283–85
Product adaptation, 277
Product development, 461
Product line, broadening, 60
Pró-Estética, 458
Professional manager, 274
Professional staffing, 425–26
Profit and loss, 283
Profit potential, reassessing, in computer industry, 221
Prudential Insurance Co., 337
Pryce Development Corporation, 174
PTT, 68, 70
Public services, privatization of, 348

Quality, revenue control and, 429
Quilmes, 58

Radio
    album-oriented rock format on, 96–97
    alternative music format on, 98
    consolidation of industry, 94, 102
    differentiation in, 98
    ratings game for, 96, 99
    role of, 94
    switching formats on, 98–99
Radio economics, 94–96
Railpart, 381
Rank Xerox, 76
RCA, 158
RCA Records, 41, 45, 76, 77
Readership, demographics of, 148–50
Reality programming on television, 156
Record companies, threat of the Internet to, 88–92
Recording Industry Association of America, 90
Recruiting, internal, 339
Recruitment strategy, 337–39, 464
Redevelopment workshops, 125–28
Re-engineering, 219
Regeneration, 333–47
Regional business units (RBUs), 224
Regional workshops, in strategic planning, 131–32
Rehab Hospital Services Corp., 434
Renault, 70
Reorganization, 348–51
Repsol, 278
Repurposing, 157
Research and development, 461
    environment for, 339–40
Restaurant, strategy for running, 474–75
Reunification, 125

Revenue control, quality and, 429
Revlon, 457
Ricoh, 76, 79
Risk-sharing partnerships, 443
Rover Group, 372, 375, 379–80
Rowdy Records, 55
RTL, 256
RTM, 256
RTRC, 256
Russia, Chupa Chups in, 279–81, 283
Ryutsu Joho Service Companies, 362

S.A. Chupa Chups, 276–89
    achieving domestic market leadership in, 276–77
    advertising, 285
    distribution, 277, 284–85
    financial system, 283
    globalization in, 277–83
    management of international operations, 283–85
    marketing, 277, 284, 285
    organizational structure, 287
    philosophy of, 285–86
    plant specialization and transfer of technology, 283–84
    process technology, 277
    procurement, 283
    product of, 276–77
    staff development, 286
S.A. Granja Asturias, 276
S.A. Regalín, 279
Saab, 207
Saatchi Consulting, 313
Saatchi & Saatchi Worldwide, 309–18
    early successes, 310
    future of, 315
    global marketing approach, 315
    seeds of destruction, 310, 312
    total communication services strategy, 313–15
    unravelling giant, 312–13
Sagura, 49
Saimoto, 413
Sakae, 413
Sakura Campaign, 258
Sales distribution agreement in Japan, 267, 272
Sales incentives, 82
Sales levels, efforts to increase, 60
Sales management, 462–63
Sales performance, 60
Sales structure, building relationships in, 463
Sam's (diner), 474–75
Samsung, 171, 172, 174
San Antonio de Padua, 58
Sara Lee, 310
Satelital, 71
Satelnet, 73
Saxon, 76, 79
SCM, 76
Search engines, 89
Second-quality sales, 60
Selkirk Brick, 263–64, 265
    export function in, 267, 269
    historical highlights of, 270
Selkirk Group in Asia, 263–71
    diversification in, 264–66
    future for, 269–70
    organization structure, 268
    sales distribution agreement in Japan, 267, 272
    success story in, 266–67
Sephora chain, 162
Sequent Computer Systems, 244, 244n, 479
Sergeant and Pepper Investments, 6
Serono Diagnostics, 246
SESAC, 96
Sex Pistols, 94
SGV, 174
Shanghai Chupa Chups Guan Sheng Yuan Food Co., Ltd., 282
Shared destiny relationships, 371, 374–75
Shared Hub concept, 69–70, 71–72
Sharp, 76
Shepparton Bricks and Pavers, 265
Shimadzu, 246
Shimano, 413
Shiseido, 456, 457
Showtime, 64
Shubert Theatres, 262
Singapore Telecom, 68
Situational leadership, 381

Smashing Pumpkins, 94
Smiling curve, 221–22
Smith, Prizker, and Cohen, 274
Snowball making, 322
Snowball throwing, 322
Social role of newspapers, 150–51
Société Bernat et Cie, 278
Society, commitment to, 462
Sofina, 363–65, 368
Sofina Cosmetics Company, 364
Software development centres, 244
Sonopress, 51
Sony, 171, 172, 174, 227, 333–47
    foundation, 334–37
    under Idei, 343–47
    management policies, 334
    management team, 341
    in the 1990s, 342–43
    personnel management, 339
    product milestones, 335
    purpose of incorporation, 334
    R&D environment, 339–40
    recruiting efforts, 337–39
    tolerance for failure, 340–41
Sony-Eveready Inc., 337
Sony of America (SONAM), 341, 342, 345
Sony Pictures Entertainment, 333
Sony Prudential Life Insurance Co., 337
Sony/Tektronix Corporation, 337
Sotheby's Auction House, 176
South Africa, pioneering frontier markets in, 224
South African Breweries, 230
Southam (newspaper chain), 150
Southeast Asia, Kao in, 366
Spain, entry into European Union, 282–83
Sportsmake, 273–75
Sprague, Courtenay, 435n
SPSS, 244
Staffing, professional, 425–26
Stakeholder concept, 372–73, 380
Stand-alone SBUs, 84–85
STAR ALLIANCE, 124, 129–31
    management of, 135
STET, 69
Stop and fix it philosophy, 82
Stratblox, 265
Strategic alliances, 378, 439
Strategic business processes
    involvement of people in, 134
    problem solving in, 134
Strategic business units (SBUs), 224–25, 399
Strategic change, 146–55
Strategic cost savings, 128–29
Strategic infrastructure, 366
Strategic innovation, 221–25
Strategic network, building, 129–31
Strategic planning, 399
    at New York Botanical Garden, 176–89
Strategic planning process, 131–32
    business area strategies in, 131
    regional workshops in, 131–32
Strategy of open standards, 408
Subic, 173
Subsidiary management, 85, 172, 283, 285
Substitution, 84
Succession in leadership, 273–75, 319–20, 333
Suggestion program, 82
Sultan Engineering, 354
Sumida coils, 171
Sun Microsystems, 240, 403n, 479
Supplier-client relationships, 66
Support organization, 427–28

Tag Heuer, 160, 162, 164
Tai, 96, 99
Talent, competition for, 64–65
Talking Heads, 94
Tandem Computers, 240, 241, 242, 244
Tandy, 409
Task-force style action learning, 339
Tataki-dai, 360
Technological unemployment, 206
Technology, in building capabilities, 80–81
Technology licensing arrangements, 252
Teknibuild, 353, 354
TELCO, 238
Teledisc, 67
Telefónica de España, 68, 69, 71

Television
    demographics for, 157
    impact of news forces on, 257–58
    in Japan, 255–56
    media strengths of, 148
    Neilson ratings in, 156
    reality programming on, 156
    repurposing, 57
Telia, 68
Ten(D)-to zero, 374–75, 378–79
Tetras, 80
Texas Instruments, 80, 218–19, 396
TFI, 256
Thebe Financial Services, 443
Theft, electronic, 88–92
Thomson (newspaper chain), 150
Thought leadership, 321
3M, 76
Time Warner, 343, 390, 391, 392
TLC, 54
TNT, 64
Tokai Heavy Industries, 200
Tokyo Broadcasting System (TBS), 255
Tokyo Research Laboratory, 364
Tokyo Tsushin Kogyo, 334–35
Tolerance for failure, 340–41
Tony Awards, 254, 261
Toronto Star, 146
Toshiba, 76, 246, 340, 343
Total Quality Control, 358
Toyota, 33, 203, 204, 207, 310
Trade barriers, 172, 282
Transfer of technology, in international operations, 283–84
Trans Globe Solutions, 474
Travelers, merger with Citicorp, 230
Trebor, 278
TTC, 370
Turnaround strategy, need for, 309
Turner channels, 158
TV Asahi Theatrical Productions, Inc., 254–62
    bringing a musical, to Japan, 260–61
    future for, 261–62
    newspapers, 254–55
    organizational characteristics, 257
    special events division, 258
    television, 255–57
        news forces acting on, 257–58
TVS Group of India, 371
TV Tokyo, 255

Ugly Beauty, 90
UK automotive industry, 371–72
Unemployment, technological, 206
Uniconfis Corporation, 278
Uniconfis GmbH, 278
Unilever, 237, 284, 355, 366, 457
Union Carbide, 337
Unipart Group of Companies, 370–81
Unipart-TVS Ltd, 371
Unipart Yachiyo Technology, 371
Unipart Yanagawa Engineering, 371
Unipart Yutaka Systems, 371
UniqueAir, 370
Unisource, 68
United States, Honda in, 202–3
U.S. Air Quality Standards, 204
U.S. Memories, 403
Universal Music Group, 88
    merger with PolyGram, 90
Universal standards, 221–22
USA, 244
Utisat French Group, 70

Value-added, third-party transactions, 384–85
Value added business segments, 221, 361
Values, 461–62
    corporate culture and, 226–27
    integration through leadership, 248–49
Van Halen, 96
VAX, 244
Vendor of choice strategy, 406
Venture capital, 395–96
Vertical integration, 157, 356
Veuve Cliquot, 163
Village Roadshow Pictures, 392
Virtual storage locker, 91
Vision, leadership and, 225–26

Vivil, 278
Volkswagen, 70
Volvo, 207
Vorstand, 47*n*, 477
Votorantin, 231
Vox Tech, 474
VSAT technology, 67
    application to communications, 69–70
Vuitton, 167

WAAF, 98, 100
Wahi, 251
WalMart Group, 278
Wani, 413
Warner Brothers, 390–93
Warner Records, 41
Washington Post, 151
Waterloo, Battle of, 190, 191, 195–96
WBCN, 94, 96, 97, 98, 99, 100, 104
W/Brasil ad agency, 231
WCGY, 98
Wei chi (Chinese board game), 226
West End Theatres, 261
Western Construction, 352–53
Western Digital, 406
Western Electric, 335
Western India Vegetable Products Limited, 234

WFNX, 93–108
    birth of, as station, 93–94
    decision time, 104
    defending the turf, 98
    future for, 102–4
    Green Day aftermath, 96–98
    industry consolidation, 100–102
    intense competition at, 98–99
    mission of, 93–94
    radio anarchy, 99–100
    radio economics, 94–96
    ratings game, 96
    risk of success, 93
    role of radio, 94
Wipro Biomed, 235, 246
Wipro Corporation, 234–53
    balancing growth in, 253
    balancing management in, 253
    balancing portfolio in, 252
    integration in
        through management processes, 250–52
        through people, 250
        through shared beliefs and leadership values,
            248–49
    organizational structure, 236
    subsidiaries in, 234–48
Wipro Equity Linked Reward Programme, 250

Wipro Financial Services, 235, 246–48
Wipro Fluid Power, 235, 238–39, 249
Wipro GE, 235, 245–46, 252
Wipro Infotech, 235, 239–42
Wipro Lighting, 235, 248
Wipro Shikakai, 237
Wipro Systems, 235, 242–45
WordPerfect, 244
Workbrain Corporation, 382–89
    competitive positioning, 384
Workforce, training and development of, 463–64
Workforce management, 384
Workplace administration, 384
Workplace community process automation, 384
World Partners, 68
World War II, in the Philippines, 27–39
Wrigley's, 278, 280
WZKX, 98

Xerox Corporation, 75, 76, 79, 90

Yachiyo Kogyo, 373
Yahoo!, 89
Yokota, 412, 413, 421
Yves Saint Laurent, 162

Z company, 89
Zilog, 397